On the Just Punishment of Heretics

by

Alfonso de Castro, O. F. M

Translated by

Rev. Paul M. Kimball

Dolorosa Press
Camillus, New York

Copyright © 2024 Rev. Paul M. Kimball
All rights reserved.
ISBN: 979-8-9865260-1-0

To order additional copies, please contact us.

Dolorosa Press

www.dolorosapress.com
avemaria@dolorosapress.com

Contents

Introductory Texts iii
Preface xix

BOOK ONE

Chapter I 1
What is heresy?

Chapter II 17
On how great is the wickedness of heresy.

Chapter III 25
On the difference between a heretical, erroneous, temerarious, scandalous, and other propositions of a similar character.

Chapter IV 39
On the various ways by which it can be proved that some proposition is heretical.

Chapter V 63
Who can judge about heresy, and pronounce sentence, which all are obliged to obey?

Chapter VI 79
Whether the Pope can delegate to someone the power of judging about the faith, such that those things which would be defined by a legate of the Pope about the faith, ought to be necessarily held by all as the true faith?

Chapter VII **103**
    Who ought to be declared a heretic?

Chapter VIII **127**
    On the solution of certain doubts, which arise from the things said in the previous chapter.

Chapter IX **137**
    What is pertinacity, and who ought to be called pertinacious, such that on these grounds he can be reckoned to be a heretic?

Chapter X **151**
    What kind of admonition ought to be adequate, so that he who has contemned it, would rightly be deemed pertinacious?

Chapter XI **169**
    On the declaration of faith made by someone before an assertion of heresy, whether it avails to free him from the mark of heresy.

Chapter XII **179**
    Concerning blasphemers, whether they ought to be reckoned to be heretics.

Chapter XIII **191**
    Concerning fortune tellers and soothsayers, and other diviners, whether they ought to be called heretics.

Chapter XIV **201**
    Regarding magicians, whether they ought to be deemed heretics, and punished as such.

Chapter XV **219**
    On sorcerers, whether they ought to be called heretics, and punished as such.

Chapter XVI **237**
Whether lamiae and Striges ought to be deemed heretics.

Chapter XVII **257**
Concerning those believing, harboring, supporting, and defending heretics, whether they ought to be deemed heretics, and punished as such.

Chapter XVIII **277**
That the arrested heretic ought not to be punished immediately: but his amendment ought to procured, and how.

Chapter XIX **287**
That one ought not to publicly dispute with a heretic, especially a pertinacious one.

Chapter XX **307**
Although it is not absolutely good to dispute with a heretic, it is still good and holy to write against heretics.

Chapter XXI **323**
That the heretic if he repents, ought to be mercifully received by the Church.

Chapter XXII **329**
That heretics returning to the faith for the first time, ought not to be received all equally, and with equal mercy.

Chapter XXIII **343**
Regarding apostates, whether they ought to be received kindly and with mercy when they return to the Church, just as other heretics.

Chapter XXIV 353
If a heretic recants, what ought to be required of him, before he may be received to the communion of the Church?

BOOK TWO

Preface..363

Chapter I...365
Who deservedly ought to be reckoned an incorrigible heretic?

Chapter II 383
That the relapsed heretic is rightly reckoned incorrigible, and who ought to be called "relapsed."

Chapter III..399
That it is just and necessary to punish heretics.

Chapter IV 415
It is replied to the objections of those who argue in favor of the impunity of heretics.

Chapter V..427
Concerning the punishments of heretics, and firstly regarding the bodies, and then it is treated regarding the spiritual punishments individually, and now firstly about the confiscation of temporal goods.

Chapter VI 443
That a heretic, from the time of the crime committed, loses all ownership of his goods, even before the declaration of the judge: yet the government treasury cannot seize the goods, except after the declaration of the judge.

Chapter VII 463
On the second punishment of heretics, which is the privation of all rule over subjects of whatever kind.

Chapter VIII 485
The punishment of heretics about which was treated in the preceding chapter is proved to be just by manifest reasons.

Chapter IX 497
Concerning another punishment of heretics, which is infamy, and of the others which follow from it.

Chapter X 513
Whether it is just that on account of the father's heresy that the Catholic son be punished?

Chapter XI 529
It is replied to the objections, which in the beginning of the preceding chapter were put forth for the opposite stance.

Chapter XII 551
That heretics ought to be punished with the penalty of death, whether it be that such a death is inflicted upon them by the sword, or fire, or any other way.

Chapter XIII..575
It is replied to the objections of those who say that heretics ought not to be punished with death.

Chapter XIV 593
Whether it is permitted to attack heretics by war, after it is fully established about their pertinacity, and rebellion.

Chapter XV..631
That the books of heretics ought to be burned.

Chapter XVI 653
Some arguments whereby some try to prove that heretics' books ought to be permitted are answered.

Chapter XVII 671
Whether it is permitted for someone who has heretical books to read them.

Chapter XVIII 691
Concerning the spiritual punishments of heretics, and firstly concerning excommunication, from which arise another, which is the deprivation of burial.

Chapter XIX 705
Whether a heretic could be excommunicated after death.

Chapter XX 717
It is replied to the objections which could be adduced in favor of the opinion of Abbas and the Gloss.

Chapter XXI 733
Whether a bishop, or any other priest, having become a heretic loses that ecclesiastical power which is called by theologians the power of Order.

Chapter XXII 749
Whether a bishop having become a heretic, by that very fact, loses the power of episcopal Order.

Chapter XXIII 765
Whether a bishop who has become a heretic is by that very fact deprived of all power of jurisdiction, even if he be the Pope.

Chapter XXIV 793
It is replied to the reasons which are objected by those who maintain the contrary opinion.

Chapter XXV 817
Whether a witness, who knew that someone has fallen into heresy, is held, although he has not been questioned, to report him to a judge, even before his fraternal correction.

Chapter XXVI 835
Whether the son accusing one of his parents of heresy ought to be on account of this freed from those penalties, which on account of the parent's heresy, ought to be inflicted upon him by law.

BOOK THREE

Preface 873

Chapter I 877
It is taught that there are many ways, whereby heresies can be duly impeded, lest they arise, and it is specially discussed about one of them.

Chapter II 899
The first extrinsic cause of heresies, which is the lack of preaching God's word, which if it is taken away, it opens the door for many heresies to arise.

Chapter III 915
Concerning the second cause, from which heresies arise, which is the indiscriminate preaching of God's word by anyone without any distinction, and without any examination.

Chapter IV 937
Concerning the third cause, which is the negligence of the bishops, and of other pastors of the Church.

Chapter V 967
   Concerning the fourth cause of heresies, which is the unworthiness of bishops and other priests.

Chapter VI 989
   Concerning the fifth cause of heresies, which is the translation of Sacred Scripture into the vernacular language.

Chapter VII 1013
   The objections are answered, which are made by those who contend that Sacred Scripture ought to be translated into the vernacular language.

Chapter VIII 1031
   Concerning the last cause of heresies, which is the constant and incautious reading of books of heathens.

Chapter IX 1051
   Concerning the remedy against the aforesaid cause of heresies.

Letters of Approbation 1075

Acknowledgement

Special thanks are hereby given to Boone Larson, who tirelessly edited this work with much dedication. May our Divine Judge reward him for his charity and willingness to aid the publication a book that aims to defend the truths He taught while on earth.

Introductory Texts

Greeting to the Reader

I beseech you, fair-minded reader, that you would not judge this book merely by its cover, assuming that merely secular things, and legal things are treated in it, which things often are accustomed to be treated by others discussing the same subject. For this book has many more things inside, than it indicates on the cover. Because not only lawyers: but also theologians can benefit from it in many places, as the author points out in the book's preface. If you give it a chance, I have no doubt that you will like this book, and praise it more than I.

Imperial Imprimatur

His Royal Majesty permits that the book of Alfonso de Castro, *On the Just Punishment of Heretics*, may be printed without punishment and freely distributed, as appears in the document confirmed and undersigned by the same Majesty.

Letter to the King

To the most invincible and most Christian Emperor Charles V, the ever-Increaser of the Realm, the first Catholic King of the same name, Brother Alfonso de Castro, of Zamora, of the Order of Friars Minor desires your eternal felicity and perpetual victory over your enemies.

While I think within myself, O most Christian Emperor, and turn my mind and soul towards this miserable world,

I cannot but sigh, and groan from the lamentation of my heart, seeing that so many and such heretics have traversed in this world, who cause very much trouble to learned men, and hence to the whole Church, such that the Church has never endured so many, or such fierce enemies. For these men's desire to harm is so great that there is nothing from the highest to lowest that they do not try to pull down. For neither God, nor His Virgin Mother, nor the Apostles, nor the Evangelists, nor the rest of the Saints, nor finally the whole Church militant, which is the only spouse of Christ, do they wish to spare: but they bark at any of them with impudent temerity, and with canine teeth try to bite it. Now they undertake to do this not with a fickle, or negligent, and foolish mind: but as rabid and hungry dogs they attack everything, and no stone do they not move, so that the wickedness that they have conceived in their mind, they perpetrate in deed.

For there is scarcely any teaching so foul, or execrable, or pestiferous and abominable, approved by ancient heretics, that, even though buried by very long oblivion, these heretics do not try to revive, if thence they hoped that they could grab some weapon whereby they could in some way hinder the Catholic Church, or its highest ruler. They deny Peter's primacy; they give the priesthoods to all Christians without distinction. They make all priests equal to bishops. They take away all the ancient ceremonies of the Church handed down from the Apostles, and kept until the present time: and bring in certain new ones thought up by them. They diminish the Church's Sacraments, so that they might retain fewer antidotes of sin. Now so that they might persuade that they have not taken away anything useful from the Church, while denying the strength and power of the Sacraments, they added poison to poison. They take away the celibacy of the whole clergy. They teach to violate all vows made to God. They reject every order of monastic life. They completely banish all praises, by voice, or by musical instruments in churches dedicated to God, which the Church has been accustomed to sing to God at appointed hours. Finally there was this one goal of them all, namely, that they could overthrow the whole order of the Church instituted by Christ our Savior Himself, and kept by His Apostles until the present time, and form for us a new, and very badly instituted and very deformed church, so that you, O most Christian emperor, because of your prudence and goodness, would not be allowed to have any nation whatsoever be subject to you. Now what they have so anxiously desired, God permitting, and the devil their father wickedly inciting, in large part (alas) they have achieved. For their virulent teaching, which Paul bearing witness, "spreadeth like a canker" (II Tim. 2, 17), has very exceedingly, and powerfully advanced, so that there is now scarcely any province of the Christian name, of which some part is not infected by this pestilence.

Now in order to resist these very fierce and bloodthirsty enemies, many Catholic and learned men from the whole Christian world have opposed themselves as a defensive wall of the Church, who by word and writing fought most zealously against their deadly teachings. The first man of them all, the very learned John Eck, wrote many books against them, who also publicly disputed with Luther, the leader himself of this faction. Next Johann Faber, Bishop of Vienna, Caspar Schatzgeyer[1] of the Order of Friars Minor, Johann Cochlaeus, Conrad Köllin,[2] Johann Dietenberger,[3]

---

1 In Latin, Gaspar Sagerus.
2 Conrad Köllin was Dominican apologist and early Thomistic commentator who was born in Ulm, Germany in about 1476, and died in Cologne in 1536.
3 Johann Dietenberger (ca. 1475–1537) was a German Catholic Scholastic theologian.

Introductory texts

Konrad Wimpina,[4] Jerome Emser,[5] Johannes Mensing,[6] and many other Germans, are related to have written, whom I have not known even by name. And not only the Germns, among whom this pestilence arose, wrote against these heretics. But from every nation, which when recognizing Christ received [its] name from Him, many very learned men by troops published many and various books against these very pernicious enemies of the Church, by which they tried with much dexterity to fight for, defend, and enlarge the Catholic Church. In Lower Germania in fact, which is near to Upper Germania, Jacques Masson,[7] Albert Pighius, Jacob van Hoogstraten of the Order of Preachers,[8] and many others wrote, and to compose a list of them all would be wearisome. In England King Henry VIII himself first wrote, as though he had resolved to himself, that he never would desert the right faith which he then knew. After the king John Fisher wrote, then bishop, and afterwards Cardinal priest of the Holy Roman Church: a man very renown for holiness as well as his teaching, who is certainly worthy to be reckoned among the holy martyrs, who when he reached old age we know willingly and gladly laid down his neck to the sword for the Catholic faith. In France, although he is not French himself, Josse van Clichtove of Nieuwpoort wrote

---

4   Konrad Wimpina (Wiminae, Wiminesis; real name Konrad Koch) (1465–1531) was a German Roman Catholic theologian and humanist of the early Reformation period. His family, whose name was Koch, came from Wimpfen on the Neckar, hence he was called Wimpina.
5   Jerome (or Hieronymus) Emser (1477–1527) was a German theologian.
6   Johannes Mensing (Mensingk) (1477–1547) was a German Dominican theologian.
7   Or Jacobus Latomus in Latin.
8   Jacob van Hoogstraten (ca. 1460–1527) was a Flemish Dominican theologian and controversialist. He was born in Hoogstraeten, Belgium.

many books against the recent heretics. After him Jérôme de Hangest, Nicholas Le Grand,[9] of the Order of Friars Minor in the commentaries which he published on the Epistle to the Romans and on the Epistle to the Hebrews, and many others wrote. In Italy the first to write was Sylvester Mazzolini, Master of Sacred Palace.[10] After him was Lancelotto Politi, both of the Order of Preachers.

From Spain, because it was in itself well enough vigilant and guarded, few men until now, yet very learned ones, have written against these heretics. Dominic Soto[11] of the Order of Preachers, who held continually for many years the chair of theology in the distinguished University of Salamanca, in the Council of Trent where he now labors by command of Your Imperial Majesty, he published a distinguished work on nature and grace against these recent heretics. Andreas de Vega of the Order of Friars Minor, a man expert in three languages, also in this Council of Trent to which by command of the His Most Serene Majesty, Philip your Caesar along with me was appointed, published a book on justifying faith filled with much doctrine against Luther. I finally, the least of all, published some years ago a certain large work, in which all heresies, which from the Ascension of Christ our Savior into heaven until the present time assailed the Church, having been collected together, disputing against them all individually, and putting forth the originators and founders of them all: so that even in this way I might make plain to all, that the recent heretics have drawn their heresies from the dregs cast out of the Church long ago.

---

9 He died in A.D. 1560.
10 Sylvester Mazzolini, in Italian Silvestro Mazzolini da Prierio, (or Sylvester Prierias) (1456 or 1457–1527) was a theologian born at Priero, Piedmont; he died at Rome when the imperial troops forced their way into the city, leading to the Sack of Rome.
11 Dominic Soto, or Domingo de Soto, (1494–1560) was a renowned Dominican theologian.

But even though they have been very skillfully fought by all these, and many other very learned men, such that they plainly and clearly triumphed over these enemies of the Church, still these men have never returned to their senses, or ceased to rave. Because their obstinate impudence, and impudent obstinacy is so great, such that although clearly conquered still they have never wanted to yield, nay, rather having been made more hardened therefrom, and every day more pertinacious in their opinion they increased their madness, daily bringing forth such new, and such different teachings, that we may rightly believe that they think of nothing else than of how each of them could harm the Church. For even if often among themselves (as was always wont to be with heretics) there is no agreement about doctrine, to such an extent that any one of them differs from another, more than both of them from the Church: yet concerning this point there is agreement among themselves, and this is the greatest cause of forming friendship among them, and the strongest bond of the acquired friendship, if only they could all together pull down the greatest defense of the Church, they could weaken its power, and resist its commands. These men truly are those serpents, whom God threatened through Jeremias the prophet that He would send among us, "against which there is no charm" (8, 17). For "Their madness is according to the likeness of a serpent: like the deaf asp that stoppeth her ears: which will not hear the voice of the charmers; nor of the wizard that charmeth wisely" (Ps. 57, 5-6).

Since therefore in fact it has already been well ascertained by me that pleasant poultices are of no use for these men, I have deemed it necessary that more bitter remedies be used, so that one would now not deal with them with words, but with clubs, whips, and swords, so that the pain would make them wiser, who abusing the benignity that has been shown to them persist in their foolishness until now, and vexation might give them the understanding, which excessive kindness was not able to give. Yet heretics fearing this vexation, in order that they might deliver themselves from it by serpentine astuteness, have taught that the punishment of heretics is not allowed, and they have called those who punish them "tyrants" instead of "kings," or that they force them to accept the faith by punishments or tortures. For in this way they thought that they would deter, and completely withhold the intention of Christian rulers from punishing these men: so that perhaps gaining their end in this way, or rather having obtained impunity by force, they could more freely teach heresies by words and writings. Therefore moved by this reason I decided to discuss the punishments which are rightly due to heretics with a long treatment in this work, so that Christian rulers, having been rightly persuaded about the punishments of heretics, would let to pass none of those punishments, which laws determine against heretics, but rather that they would command them to be inflicted upon any pertinacious and obstinate heretics: so that by fear of punishments they may be forced to not dare babble similar novelties and insanities, and in this way they might at last recover from their errors. Even if they perhaps (which may God avert for the sake of His clemency) imitating Pharao shall harden like the anvil of the hammerer: still some (as it is reasonable to believe) will be wiser by another's expense.

Now this work, which, God being the author, I have already completed,[12] I rightly thought ought to be dedicated to you alone, very Christian Caesar; you who have such a fervent

---

12 *Ad umbilicum usque perduxi* is the idiom used here for completing a book. "*Ad umbilicum ducere* means to complete or finish complete a book. For navels are, as [Pomponius] Porphyrion interprets, certain bone or wooden or [animal] horn ornaments, imitating our belly button, which were added to books already completed; and this proverbial expression was born" (Erasmus, *Adagiorum chilias*. in *Opera omnia Desiderii Erasmi* (Amsterdam: Elsevier Science Publishers, 1993), vol. 2-1, pp. 247 f.).

zeal for the Catholic faith derived from your ancestors as though it were a hereditary right: that for the sake of defending or propagating the faith, you have never refused to undergo in any way any hard and endless labors. For from that time when for the first time the highness of emperors submitted itself to Christ's humility, and received a name from Him, there never was an emperor (far be, I beseech you, the suspicion of a word of adulation) who for the defense and spread of the Christian religion, exposed himself to so many and such great labors, even if Charles truly the Great, whom you succeed by blood, patrimony, dignity, and name, be reckoned among them. For you entered many more provinces than he for defending religion; many more dangers of sea for the same reason you not only put to the test but underwent. You went out to many stronger enemies of the Christian religion, than he ever did. Through so many different misfortunes, and through so many dangers for the defense of the Christian religion you roamed widely, as the famous Hercules, whom the poets fable as a conqueror of monsters, you seem to surpass by many parasangs[13]: especially since for subduing those monsters, which are accustomed to slaughter souls, you carried out those labors, which the pagans falsely said that Hercules underwent for subduing those which could harm bodies alone. I reckon that this only could be desired regarding you and your merits, that you would have a writer equal to your deeds, who would be able to relate things befitting to your deeds, and might agreeably recite their glory to posterity. Achilles and Ulysses undeservedly had such sort: or such a writer, such as Alexander known as the Great chose to be the painter for portraying the image of his body. It would indeed be just that the image of your so great deeds be depicted by no one but a very eloquent poet or orator. I

---

13 I. e., a Persian measure of distance equal to thirty stadia (Herodotus, *Histories*, bk. 6, c. 42) or some three and a half or four English miles.

Introductory texts

omit here the very powerful Turk, and very ferocious enemy of the Christian name, gloriously put to flight in Vienna, and Tunis, captured by you under the very hot heat of the sun, and delivered from the hands of very powerful barbarous tyranny, and many others from the Turks and Saracens by the victories had through your commanders on land and sea.

Those things alone, which for the bringing back of heretics, so that either you might attract or force them to return to their senses, you have very patiently borne, are so many, and so great, that you have already attained immortal glory by them among your posterity, and may you receive at length a perpetual crown from God. For often having left your wife, the very Christian Empress, who was very dear to you, also having left the very powerful kingdom of Spain, which ought to be much dearer than a wife herself and children, through very dreadful tempests of the sea, and very rough travels through mountains, you went to Germany, so that a great part of it, which had withdrawn itself from the unity of the Church, you might reconcile to the same. In which matter you very well imitated and portrayed that true shepherd, who left the ninety-nine sheep which he had accepted to feed in the desert, so that he might find the hundredth which he had lost. Very often for reconciling religious discords, which were gushing forth in Germany, very many assemblies, which they now call Diets, you celebrated from within the whole of that illustrious nation: two or three times in Worms, twice also in Augsburg, the same number of times in Ratisbon, and I do not know how many times in Speyer. In all these acting as a truly Christian emperor, sometimes you reproved them: often, according to Paul's counsel,[14] you pleaded, sometimes with great moderation you corrected, hoping, that at some time God would give them repentance, and in this way they might escape the snares of the devil, by whom they were being held captive. You gave yourself

---

14 Cf. II Tim. 4, 2.

so modestly to them, that you were seen by many to have taken away some of your high imperial dignity for the sake of recuperating them. But those who were reproaching this to you, Most Christian Caesar, were not attending to how much ought to be tolerated, so that the wandering sheep may be found, and led back to the flock whence unknowingly it had left.

But these men, for whom you, wishing to take care of their welfare, have endured so many and such great things, such that you seem to have omitted nothing which befits a Christian ruler, have not recognized the favor: but abusing your goodness they have daily grown worse. For those who before denied only the Church's authority, and had cast off from themselves only its yoke, which they had carried before for a long time, after a short time broke out to such a rebellion, that against you yourself who deserve much commendation from them, to whom they had bound themselves by a very firm pledge of obedience, so shamelessly in the face many other things, and especially in the face the Christian religion, many of them have rebelled, so that they are not afraid to take up arms against Your Imperial Majesty, and provoke you to public battle. Now this very great rebellion of a very ferocious people, you repressed with very great prudence and strength, so that you twice attained a glorious victory over them all without blood. For that always was more glorious before all, and was held to be a more illustrious victory, which was without blood. Therefore you, O most invincible Caesar, have now attained a very good victory worthy of perpetual praise over the enemies, you who by force have coerced without the shedding of blood the principal leaders of this rebellion, and by arms attack all the rest, so that they would suppliantly ask pardon for their past conspiracy, and would humbly submit to your command.

It remains that they all return to the Lord's flock whence they had departed: and you would force them to come under

Introductory texts

the yoke of ecclesiastical obedience, which they had rejected long before: and you would continually keep by punishments urging them in the faith once received, just as you have kept until now the Spanish people, no less free and wild, in your obedience and the true Catholic faith. Yet I beseech Your Imperial Majesty, that you would not think that these things were said by me so that by my exhortations I would wish to draw you as one unwilling: but so that I may spur on one running willingly. Now so that this, which we wish for, you may be able to do easily, it is incumbent upon us all to solicit God by prayers, so that He may keep you a long time in health, and He may favor all your holy endeavors, as He has hitherto done. Farewell Most Christian Caesar, and I pray that you may be pleased with this work of mine. From your Salamanca, on the eighteenth day of October. In the year of the Lord, 1547.

Proof of Examination and Approbation of this Work made by the Ordinary of Salamanca

Since the Very Reverend Doctor Quodorniga, vicar and official ordinary of this diocese of Salamanca, has consigned to my trust the judgment of this book you wrote entitled, *On the Just Punishment of Heretics*, and wherefore I have seen, read through, and fully examined the same book, I affirm and declare by my testimony that everything propounded in it is pious, confirming the true faith, and extirpating contrary heresies, in addition to teaching sound morals: but also completely pulling out the opposite by the roots. All which things were done to this end with marvelous talent, and worked out with diligent industry. Hence so far from anything in it being either opposing or dissonant to the Catholic faith, the piety of the Christian religion, or holy morals: so that this book may be fully approved and accepted by all: which book indeed upholds those who are constant and firm in their faith, and can make them firmer, but also strengthens the vacillating and the wayward, and leads them back to the right path: nevertheless it is useful, and clearly necessary especially for those to whom the inquisition of the true faith has been entrusted. Namely, it instructs the same men, and also indicates with a singular dexterity, with perspicuity, and shows as by the finger, how their office ought to be executed according to the Divine rules. It also instructs Ecclesiastical prelates, as well as all who care for souls, and moreover it puts before their eyes their both grave and greatest duty; then it clearly teaches the manner whereby they can fully perform their office. Add to these things, that it also gravely and wisely instructs preachers of God's word, how to correspond to the office of preaching committed to them (as they are bound according to the sacred rules) so that they could procure with God's help the salvation of souls, which they ought to especially desire. Which sound testimony, because it is true, I have decided to indeed confirm by my signature below. Dated Salamanca, the third day of the month of June. In the year of the Lord, 1547.

Magister Francis Sancho, the cathedral of Salamanca.

Testimony of Examination and Approval of the Work made by the Minister General of the Friars Minor

To his very dear brother in Christ, the Venerable Father Alfonso de Castro, of the regular Observance, of the Province of Saint James, as most erudite lector, and highly esteemed Father, Friar Giovanni [Matteo de] Calvi, Minister General of the whole same Order, and servant, greetings [*salus*] in the Author of salvation [*salutis*] Himself, Our Lord Jesus Christ.

Introductory texts

So great is the fecundity and sweetness of your genius, that with continual lucubrations, studies, and attending to compositions, you strive to bring to light something of the New Indies. Since therefore a book, containing three parts, which you entitled, *On the Just Punishment of Heretics*, moreover compiled, and the same for the honor of the most exalted and most high God, of all Christendom, and the glory of our Franciscan Order, and the common utility of readers, you desire to bring to light in set type, we, who gave the aforesaid book to venerable Father Friar Andreas de Vega, the very learned lecturer in Salamanca, to be examined, and we have found it (as he himself related to us) in all and through all consonant and conformed to Catholic and the orthodox teaching of the Fathers, not wishing to hide longer such a great treasure hidden until now: so that we may comply with your and our wishes, by the series of these letters, with the merit of salutary obedience, we give permission to you to print the celebrated book. Given in Trent, on the twenty-seventh of July. In the year 1546.

Brother Giovanni, who [signs] above with his own hand.

Friar Francis Menesius to the most revered and highly erudite Father Friar Alfonso de Castro

Many greetings.[15]

Although long ago I have already seen and not rushed negligently through that marvelous work of yours, *Against All Heresies*, already famous throughout the world, and published multiple times, so highly learned Father Alfonso, I have now begun to read this more recent book which you entitled, *On the Just Punishments of Heretics*, and

---

15 *S. P. D.*, i. e., *Salutem Plurimam Dicit*, taken from Cicero.

I am amazed at the persevering constancy of assiduous labor, and the pious resolution of a faithful soul, next, the harmonious agreement of order in it, and finally, as a most delightful seasoning of the rest, the cultivated and polished phrases. For this reason I said that I began to read: because having enjoyed these pleasures from without, I have not ventured to penetrate the inner sanctum[16] and depths. Naturally, those things greatly require, besides an extraordinary knowledge of both theological majesty and law, that one be exercised not slothfully in the other disciplines. To a man of this kind, wherever at length he can be found, I leave all the rest both to be evaluated and disseminated. For, so that I may touch upon something from only one small part, that is, the preface, how shall I say how becomingly you address His Imperial Majesty before his very face? How clear-sightedly do you uncover and reveal the minds of all heretics? How diligently you gather the defenders of the truth from all the different parts of the world, their qualities, and the individual titles published? How honorably and respectfully you call to mind the Imperial deeds? How piously and prudently you either excuse or interpret the preceding course of events of the same Majesty, or what pleases you and Truth Himself more, you gladly praise highly? Finally, how effectively you incite and exhort for future execution? Not undeservedly then we pass over the rest to someone weighing in a balance more wisely. But, so that I do not leave my abilities untried, well done, O most ardent cataphract of the Franciscan army, most outstanding author of remarkable things, invincible propagator of the orthodox faith, universal destroyer of sacrilegious faithlessness, very sagacious confuter of all impiety; I say that you are a most industrious cultivator of the Lord's vineyard, and I will not cease to admonish, to exhort, and entreat that you always apply yourself to outstanding deeds

---

16 *Adytum*, i. e., the innermost sanctuary of an ancient Greek temple.

of this kind: whereby you may happily seek to attain for yourself the heights of heaven, and to always heap not commonplace luster upon our most holy Order. Farewell.

Preface

There are different and diametrically opposed judgments given by some men concerning the punishment of heretics, for whom even though they are extreme and deviate very far from equity, nevertheless there are no lack of patrons, who moreover now receive support of those judgments, and very pertinaciously endeavor to support them. For there are some men having much of the arrogance of the Pharisees, so morose and intractable, that they reckoned that all heretics ought to be persecuted with irreconcilable hatred, and without any leniency of punishment. When they conceive that someone has fallen into heresy, they rejoice in an astounding manner, as victors exult when they divide captured spoils, and stirred up on the spot by an unbridled fury, they hurl upon him a thousand reproaches, they say a thousand insults in his face, and finally they very quickly decide that he ought to be delivered to the fire. For by this hatred of heretics, as though it were by a certain and indubitable sign, they try to show to others that they are very ardent, zealous persons for the Catholic faith, and that they are very constant fighters: as if the Christian faith necessarily has fury conjoined, and they completely reject from themselves all kindness, and leniency in correcting.

Yet in order that I may to some extent console these men, who have not completely strayed from the true rule of justice, I indeed admit that they have zeal for the Catholic faith: but even so they do not moderate and temper it according to knowledge. Because wanting to establish their own justice, they have forgotten the justice of God.[1] For the justice of God, which Paul teaches is, that "with modesty admonishing them that resist the truth: if peradventure God

---

1 Cf. Rom. 10, 3.

may give them repentance to know the truth, and they may recover themselves from the snares of the devil, by whom they are held captive at his will" (II Tim. 2, 25-26). It indeed behooves a good ruler that weighing the weakness of others from his own weakness, through the leniency of humility and kindness he would endeavor to deliver those erring from the snare of error, rather than through harshness drive them away into the pit of perdition.

A surgeon will certainly be deemed savage and deservedly too harsh, who employs completely no leniency of remedies, and having tried no other remedies strives to cure all wounds with burnings. For firstly one ought to apply pleasant medicines, and find out whether the wound can be healed with any gentle remedies, which when he understands from the case itself that it cannot be of any benefit, then it will be good to use harsher medicines, and cut off that infected part, in a desperate case, lest the infection itself spread to other parts of the body, and thus infect the whole body and destroy it. Imitating this example, those, under whose command is the right and power of determining the punishment of heretics, ought firstly to heal the consciences of those who have fallen into heresy, to remove the slowly spreading ulcers, to burn some, not to amputate: finally, what cannot be healed, to cut off with sorrow. He who afflicts heretics with insults at the first meeting, without having tried any other remedies whereby they could be led back to the fold of the Catholic Church, immediately decides that their lives ought to be taken away: desire not to heal, but to kill. For God reproaches these men through the prophet Ezechiel saying: "The weak you have not strengthened, and that which was sick you have not healed, that which was broken you have not bound up, and that which was driven away you have not brought again, neither have you sought that which was lost" (34, 4).

Preface

Again there are others teaching the completely opposite opinion, who can nowise bear that heretics, no matter how pertinacious, be punished with some punishment: and for this reason they mark the Catholic Church with a black coal,[2] and it has decreed various kinds of punishments of this kind against the right of the heretic, and has made those things allowable [*fas*] (as they say) by published decrees. Kings, and other leaders of the Christian world, because they punish heretics, and force them with blows to uphold the faith which they received in Baptism, they call tyrants. Those who think in this way, that one in this regard is permitted room for conjectures or suspicions, seem to me to be not defending the case of others, but their own. For I suspect that they so teach, so that when impunity has been granted to heretics, they can more freely either preach by word or teach by writing the heresies that they wish. Assuredly these men wish to pour out in public those opinions they conceived in their mind which are against the faith of the Catholic Church: but forced by fear of punishment they dare not mutter them. And for this reason the punishment of heretics annoys them, which hold in check their unbridled desire for speaking and writing. Therefore, some men seek that heretics be left unpunished, and so that perhaps in this way they may acquire impunity for themselves, which having been gained they could freely teach whatever they please.

Both of these two views, very different and opposed to each other: one on account of its harsh severity, the other on account of its excessive laxity and pernicious indulgence, it seems to me, ought to be abandoned. In this work I have resolved to teach the middle between these two, which goes very far apart from both, veering neither to the right nor to the left. Nevertheless, the chief goal of this work of ours: to fight for the Catholic Church, as a son for the honor of his mother,

---

2 The Romans marked in their calendars auspicious days with white chalk, the inauspicious days with black coal.

against those who teach the impunity of heretics, and defend it in the way I shall be able to do with my dim wits,[3] so that I may show that she has decreed nothing unjust, and she has decreed nothing which is unbecoming a true mother. No one ever (that I know) has discussed this subject. For even though many Catholic theologians and learned men in our times have written against those men who teach the impunity of heretics, who argue with many and very evident reasons, in favor of the punishment of heretics, that the punishment of heretics is very just, yet none of them, one could hitherto see, proved that all those punishments, which were decreed by canon and civil law against heretics are just: nor about this matter did any of them ever discuss. Which matter certainly ought not to have been passed over, especially since there are many in our times, who pertinaciously contend that they are unjust. And I know many legal experts have discussed more than enough about the punishments of this kind, yet none of them, whom I have known, have directed even any part of their disputation to this goal, that he would prove that all those punishments are justly inflicted upon heretics. I suspect that this disputation was omitted by all by this occasion, that they think that it is wicked to dispute about the goodness of laws and justice, which they all reckon to be holy, and hence ought to be venerated as Divine oracles. Even if they may be very holy, still there are not lacking those who are not afraid to stick a black mark [*theta nigrum*[4]] on them. Therefore, I presently take up the defense abandoned by all of these laws, which decree some punishments for heretics, with this intention, that I maintain not only to the best of my ability that they all are very justly inflicted: but I will also persuade

---

3 *Pinguiori, qua potuero Minerva agere.* Minerva is the goddess of wisdom, and thickness or fatness was classically associated with dullness of mind.

4 The *theta nigrum* ("black theta") or *theta infelix* ("unlucky theta") is a symbol of death in Greek and Latin epigraphy.

Preface

others very forcefully so that (with God's favor) they may come to have the same opinion.

Now so that I may piously and fully perform this task, I have decided to divide this work into three books, wherein I reckoned could be included whatever pertains to it. In the first book I will discuss about heresies themselves, and I will show, who they are, and how they ought to be correctly admonished about their heresies, so that if perhaps having acknowledged their error they would want to return to the path of truth, we may teach, by what benignity and mercy they ought to be received by the Church. Next, I will treat in the second book regarding those heretics, who hold so firmly onto their heresies, that they nowise can be torn away from them: I will both enumerate one by one the punishments, which have been decreed for them by law, which after having been accurately presented, I will prove with God's help that they all are very justly inflicted for many and very evident reasons. Finally in the third book I will show some ways by which in my opinion one can prevent heresies, lest any heretics thereafter arise among Christians, whom the prelates of the Church and rulers of the world cannot leave unpunished without the ignominy of laxity and slothfulness.

Yet before everything I would like that theologians and lawyers, to whom I hope this work will be beneficial, to be exhorted, so that if at any time when reading one or the other thing in this work about very well-known principles of their profession he shall see me to have spoken perhaps longer then he would wish, that he would not on that account be inflamed with anger towards me, or condemn this work: but that he understand that I wrote those things not for himself, but for men of another profession. For there are certain things very well known to lawyers, about which theologians are little versed. There are again other things very clear to theologians, even among those things which pertain to heretics, which are not so clear to lawyers.

Since I am going to dispute about all those things in this work, lest perhaps I fall into that pit which I intend to prepare for others, I first of all testify to the fact that I do not wish to hold anything contrary to the teaching of the Catholic Church: but I completely subject both this work and myself to the judgment of the same Church. But if perhaps, as there are mistakes of human understanding, it happens that I at some time deviate in this work from the opinion, which the Catholic Church teaches and holds, I beseech all that they would think that I spoke not of set purpose, but through ignorance or negligence. And that thing from the outset I beg to be held as something recanted: because I have sworn on the words of the Catholic Church, and I have promised obedience to her Christ, Who always teaches her, to immediately bring my understanding into captivity.[5] For which reason I confess that I am prepared to obey all the definitions of the Catholic Church, just as the Divine oracles.[6]

Brother Alfonso

---

5 Cf. II Cor. 10, 5.
6 I. e., Sacred Scriptures.

BOOK ONE

Chapter I

What is heresy?

Before treating the punishment of heretics, I ought to start with the definition of a heretic, so that it may be plain to all what the thing is about which we have begun the present disputation. But because all who even mediocrely know the etymology of the word, know that the word "heretic" is derived from "heresy": hence I reckoned that the present disputation needs to be longer, such that I would begin it from the definition of "heresy": and from thence I may set out more easily to the definition of "heretic." Even though I amply treated about this matter in the work which I published, *Against All Heresies*, nevertheless I decided to speak at greater length and more precisely. Because those things which we now treat aim at enabling it to be known to those who judge about heretics, and have to punish them, by what kind of mark they ought to brand all those erring about the faith. It is very necessary for judges of this kind to know all things of such sort, for this reason alone, that not all errors, even if they deal with matters of faith, ought to be given equal weight. Firstly, therefore, let us explain the bare meaning of the name, and therefrom we will be able to better investigate the true definition of heresy.

Because heresy is not a Latin, but Greek word, its etymology and meaning ought to be sought from the Greeks, and not from the Latins, as certain learned men do not do enough when discussing about either a Greek or Latin word. These derive "heresy" from "adhering" [*haerendo*], and on account of it they think that any assertion ought to be called "heresy,"

Book 1, Chapter 1

because anyone relying solely upon his own judgment, would pertinaciously adhere to it. Peter Paludanus[1] gives this charming etymology of the word.[2] Hostiensis,[3] in his *Summa*, derives this word of "heresy" from *erciscor*,[4] which by an ancient designation means "to divide." But this etymology is much more ridiculous than the previous one, because he could have easily understood, if he had considered, that the first syllable of this word "heresy" [*haeresis*] is written by a diphthong, *ae*, and with an aspiration [the letter 'h']. But this word, *erciscor*, has neither a diphthong in the beginning, nor an aspiration. Abbas in the chapter, *Firmissime*,[5] assigns a triple derivation of this word, "heresy." For he says that it is derived from this word, *adhaero*, or from this word, *erciscor*, or from this word, *erro*.[6]

I am certainly not surprised that they do not know these things, which did not belong to their profession: but I am surprised that things which they did not know, they were not afraid to teach with authority. It was indeed legitimate that about this matter, with which they were completely unacquainted, they would have consulted learned men,

---

1 Paludanus, or Petrus de Palude, (1277-1342) was a French Dominican theologian and Patriarch of Jerusalem, known by the scholastic title *Doctor fructuosus*.
2 *In quartam Sententiarum* (Salamanca: Andrea de Portonariis, 1552), dist. 13, q. 3, p. 159.
3 Blessed Henry of Segusio (ca. 1200-1271), usually called *Hostiensis*, was the Cardinal-Bishop of Ostia and Velletri and a canonist.
4 *Summa aurea* (Cologne: Lazarus Zetzner, 1612), col. 1359. Perhaps there was a typographical error in the edition viewed by the author, because both the 1517 and 1612 editions have *herciscor* instead of *erciscor*. *Herciscor* is the passive form of *hercisco* which means "to divide an inheritance."
5 *Decretals of Gregory IX*, bk. 5, tit. 7 (*De haereticis*), c. 10, §1 (*Firmissime*).
6 *Erro* in Latin means "I err."

What is heresy?

having been taught by whom they could have afterwards taught others without shame. Wherefore having rejected these and other etymologies of this word of the same ilk, we say that "heresy" in Greek is the same thing which *electio* [choice] means in Latin. For "heresy" is derived from the Greek verb αἱρέομαι, which means the same thing in Latin as *eligo* [I choose]. And for this reason, the views or opinions of philosophers are sometimes called heresies: because everyone chose that opinion which pleased himself the most. For in this way Cicero says in his [*Stoic*] *Paradoxes*, "Cato... belongs to that sect [*haeresi*] which aims at no embellishments."[7]

Therefore, because "heresy" is a choice, it follows that the faith of Christians never can be truly called a heresy. For this faith does not depend upon man's choice, nor is it invented by human genius; but it is by God inspiring and revealing the things shown to men. "My speech and my preaching," says Paul, "was not in the persuasive words of human wisdom, but in shewing of the Spirit and power" (I Cor. 2, 4). And again elsewhere: "For by grace you are saved through faith, and that not of yourselves" (Eph. 2, 8). By which words Paul taught clearly enough that the Catholic faith is not invented by human reason, nor does it depend upon men's choice: but from God's calling and gift. Hence, according to the true meaning of this word, it could nowise be called heresy. We find however that the Catholic faith was at one time called a sect: but this was by wicked and unbelieving men, or by those who even though they are Christians, still they hardly understand the dignity of the Catholic faith. For the Jews living in Rome said to Paul when he came there: "We desire to hear of thee what thou thinkest; for as concerning this sect, we know that it is everywhere contradicted" (Acts 28, 22). It was called a sect by unbelievers: yet faithful Catholics never, except perhaps when too little instructed, permitted

---

7 Preface, n. 2.

this, namely, that the Christian religion inspired by God and not invented by man would be called a heresy or sect.

Hence Theophylactus, when expounding the words of Paul, "Beware lest any man cheat you by philosophy, and vain deceit" (Col. 2, 8), speaks thus: "Do you observe whence is the deception? Namely, that human reasonings intervene. And hence they are called heresies, because they are men's opinions. The faith of Christians however is not the teaching of men: wherefore neither does it obtain such a name [that it would be called heresy]."[8] And Tertullian, in the book, *Prescription against Heretics*, near the beginning, says: "Heresy in Greek means 'a choice,' whereby a man either teaches [false doctrines to others] or adopts them [for himself]. For this reason it is that [Saint Paul] said that a heretic is 'condemned by his own judgment' (Tit. 3, 11), because he has himself chosen that for which he is condemned. But we are permitted to introduce nothing based on our own judgment, nor to choose what someone else has introduced from his own judgment. We have the Lord's Apostles as our models; for even they did not of themselves choose to introduce anything, but faithfully delivered to the nations (of mankind) the doctrine which they had received from Christ."[9]

Thus, every assertion, and the assertion alone which depends upon human choice, can be called either a true or false "heresy," according to the bare etymology of this word. But theologians and other faithful Catholics, when applying the meaning of this word to the teachings of the faith, have said that that only is heresy which is discerned to clearly oppose the Catholic faith, because in the emphatic assertion of these things one prefers one's own opinion to Holy Writ or the Church's definition, even though one ought (according to Paul's counsel) "to bring into captivity every understand-

---

[8] *Commentarius in Epistolam ad Colossenses* (PG 124, 1239A).
[9] C. 6 (PL 2, 18B).

ing unto the obedience of Christ" (II Cor. 10, 5). Therefore the word "heresy" is disreputable: although to heathens it is indiscriminate, befitting a true and false assertion. Accordingly, heathens suppose that they are free, such that anyone may think according to his own judgment. We, however, who have an allegiance to the words of Sacred Scripture and the Catholic Church, deem it a wicked deed, to deviate even a hair's breadth from their stance.

But perhaps here someone will object that heresy is not a choice, because a choice is an act of the will: but heresy is an act of the intellect. Now to this objection we reply thus: that although it is an operation of the intellect, still it proceeds from the election of the will, by command of which the intellect is moved for assent: just as faith also proceeds from one's affection. Hence Augustine says: "A man can come to church unwillingly, can approach the altar unwillingly, partake of the Sacrament unwillingly: but he cannot believe unless he is willing. If we believed with the body, men might be made to believe against their will. But believing is not a thing done with the body. Hear the Apostle: 'With the heart, we believe unto justice.' And what follows? 'But, with the mouth, confession is made unto salvation' (Rom. 10, 10)."[10] And what he said about true faith, whereby one believes that which one ought to believe, one ought to say completely the same about heresy, whereby someone believes not the Catholic truth, but the error contrary to it, such that no one can adhere to error or heresy, unless he is willing. Therefore, heresy is not a choice [of the intellect]: but it proceeds from the choice of the will.

After having explained the etymology of the word, it is necessary that we show the definition of the thing. Heresy is the false assertive declaration or presentation of the Catholic faith so opposing, that it cannot be with it at the same time. There are many things which are put into this definition: but

---

10 *Tractates on the Gospel of John*, tract. 26, n. 2 (PL 35, 1607).

whether this is done with good reason, we will soon discuss. When we said that heresy is a false declaration or presentation, we showed clearly enough that anything done or anything performed is not heresy: because heresy does not regard exterior works, nor does it depend upon them, so that it may be called heresy: but upon the intellect. For heresy is not in deeds: but in the error of the intellect judging this or that. He who steals, unless he thinks that this is permitted to him, is nowise guilty of heresy. He who fornicates, or kills, or commits some other similar crime, never will be said to have fallen into heresy for this reason. And according to this way [of thinking] that opinion comes to be understood, which taught that some deed is heresy, such that the heresy is not referred to the deed, but to the judgment given about the deed. For in this way Gregory of Nazianzen ought to be understood, when he called simony heresy,[11] not in fact

---

11 *Decretum Gratiani* (2, C. 1, q. 1, c. 11 (PL 187, 482C-483B)). "It cannot be doubted that he who attempts to purchase a gift of God for a price, can remain in the Sacred Order by reason of another Order, or be recalled. Such a one ought to be cut off from communion in every way. That a gift of the Holy Ghost be compared a price, what else is this besides a capital crime and the simoniacal heresy? How horribly such is avenged in both Testaments is easily made evident by many examples. Giezi sold the gift of Naaman's health, the Syrian; he lost the same gift of health when Eliseus avenging, he was made a leper. Also Simon Magus, when he wished to buy the same grace of the Holy Ghost, heard his sentence of condemnation from Saint Peter: 'Keep thy money to thyself to perish with thee, because thou hast thought that the gift of God may be purchased with money.' Likewise, the Lord put out of the Temple those who by buying and selling this grace were sinning in regard to grace, rebuking one by one the sellers and buyers, and with scourging casting them out of the Temple; whereby it is clear that the sellers and buyers were devoid and empty of the grace of the Holy Ghost. "In the works of Blessed Gregory Nazianzen, many of which exist in Greek and Latin, no

What is heresy?

because the simoniacal deed itself, for instance the buying or selling of spiritual things, is heresy. For he who buys or sells spiritual things, although he sins very gravely, still he will not be stained with the crime of heresy: unless he would think that it is permitted to him.

But perhaps here someone will object that inquisitors of heresy punish often those as heretics who have been caught in some Jewish ceremony, or in some rite of the Saracens. If a deed done without an error of the intellect ought not to be called heresy: why are these men punished as heretics? If you say that by that very fact arises a just suspicion, so that those doing those things would judge that it ought to be so done: why will not the same suspicion justly also arise from theft, or murder, or adultery, such that one would believe that those executing those things think that those things can be done without sin? To this objection a certain learned man in a *repetitio*, or if you prefer, *relectio*,[12] which he had of a heretical proposition, responds, saying: the suspicion of heresy arises from a deed, when the work itself was praised by some heresy, or at least permitted; for then it is allowed to suspect about the one so doing (as he says) that he favors such a heresy, which that deed proves; for example, if someone is circumcised, or religiously observes the [Jewish] Sabbath, this sort of man rightly falls into the suspicion of Judaic perfidy, or that he believes that the ceremonies of the Old Law also ought to be observed by Christians, because the Ebionite heretics of old so thought. If, however, that work was not ever praised by any heresy, he says that from

---

such passage is found. However similar words are found in the letter of Tarasius to [Pope] Hadrian [I]." (*Corpus Juris Canonici*, edited by Aemilius Friedberg (Graz, Akademische Druck- und Verlagsanstalt, 1959), p. 360).

12 The *relectio* or *repetitio* was the formal address that university chairs had to give once a year in a solemn academic ceremony.

that work, although it be a grave sin, the suspicion of heresy justly ought not to arise.

But that this cannot be defended is very clearly proved by the fact that nearly no crime can be committed from which, according to this opinion, one ought not to suspect that the one so doing thinks wrongly about the faith: because the malice of men has prevailed to such an extent that there is scarcely any sin which did not have some patron. For if you wish to speak about the carnal copulation, there is no species of it so pestilent, or heinous offshoot, which was not praised by someone. The Nicolaites, the Florians, and the Adamites said that the promiscuous use of women is licit. The Greeks defend simple fornication from sin. Finally, every carnal intercourse whatsoever it may be, whether between men, or between women, if carnal lust burns too ardently, was judged by the Waldensians to be licit. All the Christian believers know that the restitution of stolen property is necessary for attaining the salvation of one's soul, yet the Greeks (as Guy the Carmelite[13] relates about them[14]) teach that this is not necessary. The killing of oneself has been so condemned by all the faithful, that they say that it has no place of pardon before God. Yet the Circumcellions praised it to such an extent, that they called it martyrdom. And not only killing: but the cutting off an any limb, unless it would happen for the safeguarding of the good health of the body, was also condemned by all believers. Yet the heretical Valesians (as Blessed Augustine relates[15]) said that the cutting off of the male members is necessary for serving God well. The Beguines and Beghards praised the disobedience of subjects, and Luther subscribed to them on this point saying that the obedience which inferiors render to superi-

---

13 Alias, Guido Terreni.
14 *Summa de haeresibus et earum confutationibus* (Paris: *Prelum Ascensianum*, 1528), fol. 25, c. 17.
15 *On Heresies, to Quodvultdeus*, c. 37 (PL 42, 32).

What is heresy?

ors is miserable servitude. The Lampetians, the Apostolics, the Wycliffites, and the Lutherans teach that the violation of vows is licit. Finally, Eunomius taught that no work ought to be condemned if faith is present.

Therefore, since such is the case: they, who say that from any deed, that consists in what has been approved by some heresy, suspicion of heresy deservedly arises, necessarily have to concede that all such men who have fallen into any of these crimes that were praised by various heretics, which we have just now enumerated, rightly incur the suspicion of heresy, and for that reason can be arrested and punished. Therefore, it would be necessary that every fornicator, one unwilling to restore what was stolen, one castrating himself, everyone violating any vow, every liar, perjurer, finally every wicked man to be suspect of heresy, because long ago there were heresies which said that these particular things are licit. Far be, nevertheless, such great and very unjust severity from a Christian man. For if it ought to be done, it would be necessary to say that there is no crime from pure malice or weakness: but that they all are from ignorance. But there are many sins from pure malice, which men commit knowing that they act wrongly. For instance, it is evident in those about whom Job says that "they on purpose have revolted from him" (34, 27), and in those who sin with the intention of repenting, who, unless they thought that they were acting wrongly, would never intend to repent afterwards. Thus, since there are many such men, it is evident that it is not just that we would suspect about all men, that they, when they commit some crime, think that they ought to act in this way.

Now why one would be allowed to suspect this about one person more than another, I think arises from the nature of the crime itself. For there are some deeds to which all men are prone, and inclined by nature, and regarding them, even when the conscience contradicts, we often fall headlong: as are the pleasures of the flesh, the desire for riches, and the longing for honor. And in these things unless something be added which can deservedly increase the suspicion, from the mere deed I do not think that a just suspicion can arise. So that if someone fornicates, or steals, or lies, or is ambitious for honors, or refuses to obey his superior, or some other similar thing of the same ilk, he commits a crime: although he would sin according to quality of the fault, still he will not be suspected of heresy on account of this alone, as he believes that what he does is permitted for himself. For when we are incited to those sins by our flesh, it happens, that although we know that those things are evil, still we do not fear to commit them.

Still there could be such circumstances in sins of this kind, that on account of which strong suspicion of heresy would justly arise from the deed itself. As for instance, if a priest or a religious who is not a priest, were to publicly contract marriage, even though he could not deservedly be reckoned a heretic from simple intercourse, still on account of the adjoined matrimony he is deservedly presumed a heretic, especially if he has contracted matrimony publicly, or publicly celebrated the wedding, because such a man with just reason ought to be believed to think wrongly about the Sacraments of the Church. Nevertheless, I will not believe that an equally strong suspicion ought to be had of him, if he had done this secretly, because it can be deservedly suspected about him that he acted by an artifice, namely, so that in this way he might enjoy the woman, whom otherwise he could not procure. And I reckon the same thing ought to be said of him who while his wife is alive knowingly marries another.

There are other works very different from these which we have mentioned, which the will naturally shuns, and for desiring them, unless for instance from another strong passion, or strongly impelled from an error of the intellect, that same thing never will be undertaken of itself. For example, man's will naturally shuns the killing of oneself, the cutting off of a limb, on account of the implanted love of his own flesh: because (as the Apostle says) "No man ever hated his own flesh" (Eph. 5, 29). And in these deeds (certainly in my opinion), lest we temerariously suspect anything, it firstly ought to be inquired whether some vehement passion preceded, which impelled to perpetrate such a horrendous crime. For it could happen by an impotent and unbridled hatred of lust, that someone would cut off the virile member, having been conquered by the irksomeness of temptation. For we know that it happens that some men by the irksomeness of anguish, or of some other sorrow, which they cannot endure, inflict death upon themselves, so that at least they may find an end by this way of sorrow and anguish. And certainly those who commit these and similar deeds ought to be believed to have committed such a horrendous crime from weakness or having been conquered by vehement passion.

But if it be due to another cause, not from pusillanimity of spirit, or from vehement passion, that they had fallen into such a crime, it will then be necessary to suspect that they have been infected with such a heresy, such that they believed that this which they did was licit for them. Because when the will of itself was not moved to those things, neither from passion nor from weakness (as we suppose) it necessarily is befitting that we believe that it was moved from an error of the intellect to do it. There are again other works, to which the will is moved not of itself, nor also does it shun them of itself: because they have nothing whereby they could allure or repel the will of themselves: but the will is indifferent and undetermined regarding those things, when they are abstractly shown to it by the intellect. Such are the Jewish ceremonies, or rites of the Saracens: for example, the religious observance of Saturday, abstinence from things strangled and from blood, or from other foods prohibited by the Mosaic law, unless perhaps it would be established that such abstinence is done for the sake of bodily health; fasting on the Lord's day, eating the Pascal lamb according to the Jewish rite, or anything similar; to baptize images, or bodies of the dead, to break in pieces the images of the Saints, to trample upon the Sacrament of the Altar. When a man does these things, it is certain that his will is moved by the intellect to desire them. For it is not moved by objects: because (as we said) the object is not of such sort that it could allure the will. Nor is it moved of itself, or by its own flesh: because neither the will nor the flesh has any inclination to those works. The consequence is therefore that we believe that it was moved by the intellect, such that the will would not have wanted this deed, unless the intellect persuaded it that it is something good. In these men therefore a very strong suspicion of heresy can justly arise from the deed done exteriorly, such that he who does such things may deservedly be presumed to believe that this which he does is something good. For Aristotle says that in accord with the disposition of a man, so does he speak and act.[16]

Next, it ought to be added in the definition of heresy, that it is necessary that such a false proposition is opposed to the Catholic faith, in order that it can be called heresy. For there are many false propositions, which nowise deserve to be called heresy: because they nowise oppose the faith. For just as not every truth pertains to the faith: so neither does every falsity or error deserve to be called heresy. All these things are proved by the testimony of Augustine, who in his *Enchiridion* addressed to Laurentius, after he had said that there is no sin to err in certain matters, he added these words which follow: "In short, a mistake in matters of this kind, whatever its nature and magnitude, does not relate to the way whereby we approach God, which is the faith of Christ 'that worketh

---

16 "Each man's conception of his end is determined by his character, whatever that may be" (*Nicomachean Ethics*, bk. 3, c. 5, n. 17 (1114b24-25)).

by charity' (Gal. 5, 6). For the 'mistake pleasing to parents'[17] in the case of the twin children was no deviation from this way; nor did the Apostle Peter deviate from this way, when, thinking that he saw a vision, he so mistook one thing for another, that, until the Angel who delivered him had departed from him, he did not distinguish the real objects among which he was moving from the visionary objects of a dream; nor did the Patriarch Jacob deviate from this way, when he believed that his son, who was really alive, had been slain by a beast. In the case of these and other false impressions of the same kind, we are indeed deceived, but our faith in God remains secure. We go astray, but we do not leave the way that leads us to Him. But yet these errors, though they are not sinful, are to be reckoned among the evils of this life which is so far made subject to vanity, that we receive what is false as if it were true, reject what is true as if it were false, and cling to what is uncertain as if it were certain. And although they do not trench upon that true and certain faith through which we reach eternal blessedness, yet they have much to do with that misery in which we are now living. And assuredly, if we were now in the enjoyment of the true and perfect happiness that lies before us, we should not be subject to any deception through any sense, whether of body or of mind."[18] From these words it is clearly apparent that not every false assertion ought to be called heresy. If nevertheless those things oppose the Catholic faith, we say that every such thing ought to be labeled as heresy.

Yet I know that some men say that many things are necessary, so that an assertion would deserve to be called heresy. For there are some men teaching that all those things are required for heresy, which are required for a man to be made a heretic. And certainly those who assert these things, "have

---

17 Virgil, *Aeneid*, bk. 10, ln. 392. The parents were delighted at the close resemblance, and the mistakes which it occasioned.
18 C. 21 (PL 40, 243).

missed the road entirely."[19] Because the one is very easily distinguished from the other. For it is possible that someone would assert a heretical proposition, who nevertheless ought not to be called a heretic. That this is so, clearly appears in him who would have asserted such a proposition not with an obstinate mind, and him who asserts what he does not know, especially if he was not obliged to know it. For ignorance excuses this man, so that he may not be called a heretic. The proposition asserted by him, however, I do not see by what way it can be delivered from the mark of heresy if it can be established that it opposes the Catholic faith. For that some men say that no assertion ought to be labeled as heresy, unless it is opposed to a Catholic proposition which all the faithful are bound to know, seems ridiculous, and said with audacious temerity, because by this reason alone they attack all the outstanding Doctors and Saints who have written about heresy, such as Irenaeus, Augustine, and Philastrius. For these men branded many errors, which according to the opinion of these men, by no means deserved to be called heresy, since they were not against Catholic propositions which all are obliged to know.

Furthermore, there are many propositions pertaining to the Catholic faith, which not all are obliged to know. If nevertheless someone knows those are Catholic propositions beyond one's obligation, and he knowingly dissents from them, and asserts contrary or contradictory ones: no one doubts that such contradictory propositions ought to be called heresies, and yet they are not opposed to the Catholic propositions which all are bound to know. And if some knowledgeable and educated Christian were to pertinaciously assert those contradictory propositions, he would rightly be called a heretic. But an uneducated man asserting those things, even though he errs, yet he would not be called a heretic, because

---

19 *Tota errant via,* or "are completely off track," taken from Terrance, *Eunuch,* Act 2, scene 2, ln. 14.

What is heresy?

he errs in those things which he was not bound to know. As for example, if some learned Christian man, knowing the contrary is contained in Holy Writ, were to assert that Esau was not the son of Isaac, or David did not beget Solomon, doubtlessly he would be called a heretic, and for no other reason than because he asserts the heresy with an obstinate mind. But if a simple and uneducated man were to assert any of these things, although he would not be called a heretic on this account, nay, nor will he be reckoned to have sinned, still the proposition asserted by him will always be called heretical. Otherwise it would be necessary to concede that the same proposition asserted by someone ought to be called heresy, which if asserted by another, would not deserve to be called heresy.

Now how erroneous it would be to concede this, will be manifest to a moderately well taught man, if he considers that the proposition does not depend upon the assertor, so that such-and-such would be said. "Nothing is changed in reality" (says Aristotle) "by the fact of an affirmation or denial on the part of anyone."[20] If the proposition is true, by whosoever it be said, even if he is very untruthful, it will always be true. If the proposition is false, by whosoever it be said, even if at other times he was always found to be truthful, it will be false. Wherefore, it is necessary that if the proposition is heretical, if it is asserted by anyone, it also always will be heretical. This proposition: "God is three and one": whether a Jew, or a Saracen, or a pagan, or a Christian, asserts it, a Catholic proposition is always said: hence its contradictory proposition, namely: "God is not three and one," said by anyone, will always be heretical, even though not everyone who asserts it ought necessarily to be called a heretic: because (as we will teach afterwards) it is not enough for someone to deserve to be called a heretic, because he asserts a heretical proposition. Again, the word "heresy" is not

---

20 *Perihermeneias* [or *On Interpretation*], c. 9 (18b39).

originate from "heretic": but vice versa, "heretic" is derived from "heresy": thus it is not necessary that a proposition, which ought to be called heresy, be asserted by a heretic, but quite on the contrary, that he who ought to be called a heretic, would assert a heretical proposition. Therefore, from these things it is established that they err who say regarding this, in order that some proposition may be called heresy, it is highly necessary that it be asserted by a Christian man.

Nevertheless, we rightly admit this is necessary for this, namely, that someone would deserve to be called a heretic, that he shall have received faith in Baptism: because "heretic" (as we said) is derived from "heresy": but not "heresy" from "heretic": and a man from his assertion and confession receives a name: that he be called a "believer" or "heretic." But the proposition nowise depends upon the assertor, that it deservedly can be called "heretical" or "Catholic." And for this reason, many learned men erred on this point: because they neglected to consider this. For they confused into one thing the things which pertain to heresy and the things which go with being a heretic, as though the definition of both were the same, and the same disputation ought to be had about both things. Nevertheless we (as was befitting) examining and investigating more have known that the things are completely different, and so we make different disputations about them. Now we have spoken about "heresy," but afterwards we will treat about the "heretic": so that we may show who ought to be called by such a name. Therefore, so that we may summarize those things which we have said about heresy, we say that heresy is a false proposition opposed to the Catholic faith.

Chapter II

On how great is the wickedness of heresy.

How great the wickedness of heresy is anyone can easily understand from this: if one considers how great is the goodness and power of faith. For as Aristotle says, "By means of the straight line we know both itself and the curved."[1] Now the power of faith is so great, that without it, nothing can be pleasing to God: and without the same something cannot be made truly good. Because it is that which opens the way to the other virtues, shows the end to them towards which they should direct their acts. For just as among the other virtues, which are called by the commonly used and now accepted word, "cardinal," prudence is the first: because it directs the others and shows the way whereby they ought to go: so also among those which are called the theological virtues, faith is the first: because it teaches the rest what they ought to do. No one without faith knows what to hope for, or what he ought to love. A man destitute of faith, will never love God (as he ought): because he will never understand that He is the rewarder or truly good. "He that cometh to God must believe that he is: and is a rewarder to them that seek him" (Heb. 11, 6). Faith is that which shows to us the reward of our labors, and by this administers strength to us for laboring, and makes us constant in the same labors. This faith is that which instructs us to despise all temporal things and to love God more than all created things. For he who has the true faith about God, does not desire to become rich in the miserable things of this world, because when he considers eternal things, temporal things

---

[1] *De anima*, bk. 1, c. 5 (411a5).

are esteemed as worthless to him. And wherefore Paul counted all things as dung, that he might gain Christ.[2]

By this, Moses despised honors, pleasures and riches. Having been made great by faith, he "denied himself to be the son of Pharao's daughter: rather choosing to be afflicted with the people of God than to have the pleasure of sin for a time: esteeming the reproach of Christ greater riches than the treasure of the Egyptians. For he looked unto the reward" (Heb. 11, 24-26). When he denied that he was the son of Pharao's daughter, he despised the royal dignity, and hence he declared that he considers as worthless the honors of this world. Choosing to be afflicted with the people of God, who were serving in mud and bricks, rather than to have the pleasure of temporal sin: he clearly showed us how much he esteemed the pleasures of this world. But since the reproach of Christ, that is, the injuries patiently endured either for Christ or in the likeness of Christ, he esteemed greater riches than the treasures of the Egyptians: he declared clearly enough what he thought about the riches of this world. Now the reason from which this contempt of all temporal things proceeded Paul expressed, saying: "For he looked unto the reward." For the reason why he chose to be poor and despised was because he believed that other, much greater things remain hereafter, which would be acquired though poverty and insults. Faith is that which makes us sons of God. As Paul when writing to the Galatians says: "You are all the children of God, by faith in Christ Jesus" (3, 26). This is the life of the just, because, as Habacuc says, "The just shall live in his faith" (2, 4). This is the basis and foundation of the whole Christian structure, upon which, whatever pertains to true piety and religion, rests. For this is truly that most firm rock upon which the Lord founded His Church,[3] upon which Paul commanded us all that we be grounded and

---

2 Cf. Phil. 3, 8.
3 Cf. Mt. 16, 18.

settled, and immoveable from the hope of the gospel which we have heard.[4]

Hence, we have now clearly proved (as I think) that heresy is a very bad vice because it destroys faith, which is the foundation of all religion, without which nothing else is of any avail. For where the foundation is lacking, nothing else can be built above: and if anything were to have been built above, it is necessary that it would fall down. When faith has been taken away, a very wide gate is opened to every vice, no matter how depraved and great. For as faith prepares and opens the way to the other virtues, so on the contrary heresy prepares the way to all vices. Hence the Catholic faithful are conquered from harassment by heretics, as Job wrote saying: "They have rushed in upon me, as when a wall is broken, and a gate opened" (30, 14). Blessed Gregory, when interpreting these words, says: "But it is as if 'the wall were broken,' when by the promptings of the wicked, faith, which is in our Redeemer, is done away in the hearts of some. And when power is awarded to the perverse in this life, what else but 'a door' of error is opened? And so it is as if the wall being burst asunder and the door opened the wicked rush in upon the good, when power being received temporally, the corrupt set themselves to pull down the very defenses of faith too in the hearts of some."[5] For which reason Solomon, when mystically speaking about the wickedness of heresies in Proverbs, said: "A foolish woman and clamorous, and full of allurements, and knowing nothing at all, sat at the door of her house, upon a seat, in a high place of the city" (9, 13-14). For [Venerable Bede] deems that these words ought to be understood of heresy, when speaking thus: "This woman is heresy, truly the opposite of wisdom, which loftily announced its Divine mysteries: 'foolish' namely, by foolish understanding, and 'clamorous' by babbling, and full of the

---

4 Cf. Col. 1, 23.
5 *Moralia*, bk. 20, n. 53 (PL 76, 169C-D).

enticement of vices: knowing completely nothing, as the Apostle says: 'If any man think himself to be something, whereas he is nothing, he deceiveth himself' (Gal. 6, 3). She sits, however, and 'in the door of her house,' that is, in the teachers of falsity, who lead miserable men into the inner chambers of perfidy by deceiving."[6]

Nevertheless, I have decided to point out to the reader here, lest from these words of mine, he may take an occasion of suspecting that I think that all the works of unbelievers are sins, as Gregory of Rimini[7] teaches: because I shun with might and main[8] his opinion and position. I indeed admit that without faith no work is meritorious, and deserving of eternal life: yet it does not follow from this that every such work is a sin: because these two things, namely, sin and merit, are not so closely divided or separated from each other, such that he who departs from one immediately goes over to the other. For there is some middle ground between them, which is separated from both extremes, so that there are some human deeds, that is, deeds done with consideration of the mind and liberty of the will: which are undeserving of either reward or punishment. But even though all works of unbelievers should not be called sins, still disbelief opens a very wide door for introducing all vices. Whence it happens that he who is an unbeliever is very apt to perpetrate every crime. For just as he who has lost his bodily eyes badly defends himself against his enemies: because their darts, of which one ought to beware of, he cannot see: so he who has abandoned the Catholic faith, which is the eye of our conscience, cannot

---

6 *Allegorica expositio in Parabolas Salomonis*, bk. 1, c. 9 (PL 91, 967C). This quotation is incorrectly attributed to St. Jerome in the text.

7 Gregory of Rimini was an Augustinian theologian, born at Rimini, Italy, in the second half of the thirteenth century, and died at Vienna, 1358. He was one of the chief leaders of the Nominalists.

8 *Manibus et pedibus recedo*.

On how great is the wickedness of heresy

be delivered from the temptations of the demons: because without faith the invisible enemies and their darts are not seen, and hence not guarded against.

For this reason, the demons ardently strive to tear out these eyes from the Catholic faithful: so that the less they would be recognized, the more easily they could harm their souls. After Samson's eyes were torn out, the Philistines led him bound in chains, and shutting him up in prison made him grind:[9] so the demons after they have removed the eyes of the conscience, that is, the faith, from someone, keep him bound, and make him fall. For when faith has been taken away, mutual charity among neighbors vanishes, the bond of peace is dissolved, concord is broken, these worthless and perishable things are esteemed above their worth. God is seen to be worthless and not worshipped (as He ought); finally, all religion is profaned, and all piety perishes. Hence [Pseudo-]Pope and Martyr Felix [I] in his letter to Bishop Paternus speaks thus: "Heresy is truly very wicked, and inimical to the Gospel truth, which does not harm some portion: but uproots the very foundations of the Christian religion. For whosoever it catches and carries away to itself, it makes to fall not only into this crime, but into many other crimes, and by the old enemy himself persuading, they become not merely persecutors of the Church, but also of her priests."[10]

But here someone perhaps will doubt, and deservedly, whether heresy is a more serious sin than schism; now the cause of the doubting is this, that we read that schism was punished by God more severely. But (this notwithstanding) we say that heresy is much worse than schism. Because according to the rule of [Aristotle[11]], something is so much the

---

9 Cf. Jud. 16, 21.
10 *Epistulae dubiae*, letter 1, (PL 5, 145C). Cf. *The False Decretals of Pseudo-Isidore*, letter 14 of Pope St. Leo I (PL 130, 788B).
11 "What is worse is contrary to what is best" (*Nicomachean Ethics*, bk. 8, c. 10 (1160b10)). St. Augustine is incorrectly cited here

worse, the more it is opposed to a greater good. But heresy is opposed to the First Truth, which is God. Schism, however, even though it is said to be against charity, still it is not said to be against that part of charity, which pertains to God: but against that part which regards one's neighbor. For schism is against the good of fraternal charity and unity. Now although charity is greater than faith, still only it is deemed greater by that part, whereby it regards God: and schism is not opposed to this part, but it is opposed to that part, which regards one's neighbor, and this part is less than faith. Hence, we conclude that heresy from its nature is a more serious sin than schism: because heresy opposes Divine Truth upon which faith rests. Schism, however, is opposed to fraternal charity, and breaks the unity of the Church. Nevertheless, we admit that there can be some circumstances on account of which a schismatic is guilty of a more serious fault than a heretic: for example, if greater contempt is present: or because he does more harm through schism than through heresy. But although these, or other similar things, befall schismatics, they do not inhere to them by nature: and hence the nature of schism ought not to be not reckoned from them. For the gravity of sin is determined from its nature, from those things which are inherent and natural to them, not from circumstances which can occur.

Now we indeed admit what is objected, namely, that schism is punished more severely [than heresy]. Because the book of Numbers clearly teaches this when relating that Dathan and Abiron, on account of this crime, were swallowed up alive by the earth:[12] but this does not prevent heresy from being a more serious sin. Because although the final punishments, namely, which are inflicted upon sinners after death, are imposed according to the measure of the offense (as it is

---

instead of Aristotle.
12 Cf. Num. 26, 9-10.

read in Deuteronomy, chapter twenty-five[13]), still those which are inflicted during this life, are not always given according to this measure. For pains and torments in this life are not only given as a punishment, but also as a medicine: namely, so that by them sins may be cured, and sinners themselves afterwards might be on their guard against similar things, and others by the threat of those [punishments] may take heed to themselves from those same [punishments], and take care to abstain from those [sins]. For this reason, a lesser and lighter sin, because nevertheless it has been often committed, or because there is a greater proclivity to it, is sometimes punished more severely: so that through fear of the punishment, those [sinners] or others may be kept from committing those offenses. Now the Jewish people were always inclined towards sedition and schism: as from the perusal of Sacred history one can know easily. And a clear testimony about this matter is also found in the book of Esdras speaking thus: "This city of old time hath rebelled against kings, and seditions and wars have been raised therein" (I Esdras 4, 19). Therefore, it was right to inflict harsh penalties: so that, as by certain very painful singeing, they may be restrained from a very widespread fault.

---

13 "According to the measure of the sin shall the measure also of the stripes be" (v. 2).

Chapter III

On the difference between a heretical, erroneous, temerarious, scandalous, and other propositions of a similar character.

Because I said that there are some propositions, which, even though they cannot be rightly deemed heretical, nevertheless on account of the various disreputable censures of those propositions, as for example: because they are erroneous, scandalous, or temerarious; they can be prevented, by those to whom this belongs, from being preached to the people, or taught in any way: I have considered it to be necessary to treat about the difference between these propositions: so that from thence it may be established by what kind of censure any false proposition ought to be branded. Since I have sufficiently treated about the heretical proposition in the first chapter of this work, it is unnecessary either to repeat or add anything at present. A proposition will be called "erroneous" absolutely (if it be defined without any restriction of the word): because it is a false proposition. And I now say that a false proposition is not only that one, whereby something is stated otherwise than it is: but also that proposition, to which someone assents otherwise than he ought: for example, that he assents more firmly or more surely than he ought. For Blessed Augustine, when defining error in his *Enchiridion*[1] addressed to Laurentius, speaks thus: "To err is just to take the false for the true, and the true for the false, or to hold what is certain as uncertain, and what is uncertain as certain."[2] From which words it is clearly established that every person errs who assents to a doubtful or opinionable proposition with the certitude of faith, and all

---

1 This work is also titled, *On Faith, Hope and Charity*.
2 C. 17 (PL 40, 240).

such assent is erroneous: because even if what one assents to were perhaps true: still he assents otherwise than he ought: since he holds uncertain things as being certain.

Now if we speak in this way about an erroneous proposition, there is absolutely no difficulty to distinguish between heresy and an erroneous proposition: since it is evident that one is a genus, but the other is its species. For the erroneous proposition is the genus, which contains heresy under itself as its species: because every heresy is an erroneous proposition: yet not vice versa ought every erroneous proposition be called heresy. But it is not a small difficulty to know how heresy and an error in faith differ between themselves. Because if there is an erroneous proposition, it follows that it is false: and if it is erroneous in the faith, it is necessary that its falsity be against the truth of faith. But something false, because it opposes the true faith, I know not by what way it can be exempted from being called heresy. Hence it is that there is no difference between those two: and certainly, if there is some difference, it is so hidden that it was hidden from all who wrote about this matter. Because none of those who wrote about the various condemnable propositions taught anything whence this difference could be known. Juan de Torquemada[3] in his *Summa ecclesiastica* defines the erroneous proposition absolutely: but he does not define the erroneous proposition in the faith.[4] A certain [Pedro[5]]

---

3 Juan de Torquemada (1388-1468) was an ecclesiastic and uncle of the Inquisitor, Tomás de Torquemada.

4 "A proposition asserting what is false is called an erroneous proposition" (*Summa de ecclesia* (Michele Tramezzino, 1561), bk. 4, pt. 2, c. 11, fol. 384r).

5 The author was not "Martín García [Puyazuelo (1441-1521)], an inquisitor of old in the kingdom of Aragon, and afterwards bishop of Barcelona," as incorrectly stated here in the text. Rather the author was a Dominican friar, Pedro García (died 1506), who was named a member of the commission by Pope Innocent VIII

On the difference between a heretical, erroneous, and other propositions

García, in a certain small book[6] which he published against some conclusions of [Giovanni] Pico della Mirandola,[7] when treating the diversity of these propositions at the beginning of the book, says with the same words, with nearly no word changed, which are found in Juan de Torquemada. Concerning Guy the Carmelite, one is ashamed to speak: because when discussing the heresies, although he writes nothing absolute and complete, he also does not make any mention at all about the differences of these propositions.

Yet among some censures of the various universities and different councils: it seems that there is some difference between those two: because regarding the various assertions they are defining, they deem some to be heretical, others to be erroneous in the faith. Now that this is really the case can be proved from those things which were defined in the Council of Constance: because when in the eighth session of the same council many assertions of John Wycliffe were condemned, still not all were branded with the same note: but some of those censures were branded as heretical, others erroneous, and others scandalous. If someone desiring to be freed from these difficulties were to say that it is merely a difference of words, and not of things, such that a heretical proposition

---

to deliberate on the conclusions of Giovanni Pico. Pedro García was the chaplain of Cardinal Rodrigo de Borja (the future Pope Alexander VI) and much later the bishop of Ales in Sardinia from 1484 to 1490.

6 This book is entitled, *Determinationes magistrales contra conclusiones apologeticas Joannis Pici Mirandulae* (Rome: Eucharius Silber, 1489). It was written on the instructions of Innocent VIII. The quotation referred to here can be found in the fifth chapter of the section on the first apologetic conclusion of Giovanni Pico. Cf. Martin Biersack, *Juan Rodríguez de Pisa, letrado y humanista granadino, traductor de Pico de la Mirandola* in *Bulletin Hispanique*, 111-1 (2009).

7 Giovanni Pico della Mirandola (1463-1494) was an Italian philosopher and scholar.

is completely the same as an erroneous proposition in the faith, I would most willingly consent to his opinion, saying that those universities in their censures used such a variety of words merely for the ornamentation of speech, such that they called propositions of the same note at one time heretical, and at another time erroneous. And Juan de Torquemada seems to have been of this opinion: because in the book and section cited above, he says these words which follow: "An error about anything [that ought to be believed] contained in Sacred Scripture, or pertaining to history, or to the articles of faith, or to morals, will be called heresy."[8]

Yet if I am forced to admit that there is some difference between an erroneous proposition in the faith, and a heretical proposition, I will say what I think: yet I am prepared to obey someone teaching better things. Now so that what I shall say may be made clearer, it is necessary to firstly point out that there are different kinds of things to be believed. For there are some such things which exceed our power of understanding, such that our mind could not attain to understanding them: unless it firstly believe, concerning which things Isaias according to the Septuagint version says: "If you will not believe, you will not understand" (7, 9). And faith properly deals with these things. Now an assertion which opposes these things which ought to be believed is properly called heresy. There are other things which do not surpass all the power of the intellect, and they are those things which the intellect by its own power (not excluding here God's universal concurrence) can attain: but the intellect having been obscured by sins cannot know, and for this reason God having taken compassion on us willed to make them known to us through Sacred Scripture: so that if by our malice impeding we are unable to know those things by ourselves, we might understand at least by God teaching them. Such are these propositions: "God exists." "God

---

8 *Summa de Ecclesia*, bk. 4, c. 6, fol. 379v.

is one." "God is intelligent." "God is omnipotent." All these propositions can be known by the natural light of reason: but malice which blinded their intellect was the cause why they were unknown to many nations.

For Paul, speaking about these and other similar propositions, when rebuking the foolishness and blindness of the pagan philosophers, said: "…who detain the truth of God in injustice: because that which is known of God is manifest in them" (Rom. 1, 18-19). [Hervé de Bourg-Dieu[9]] when expounding these words, says: "'The truth of God,' that is, that He is the true God, 'they detain in injustice,' because although they truly know that the worship of highest veneration ought to be shown to God the sole Creator, they unjustly show it to the creature… For they knew the truth itself, which they hide from others, because 'that which is known of God,' that is, what could be known of God by natural capability, 'is manifest in them.' For there are many things which they could not know about God through nature, as is the mystery of the Incarnation and Passion, which He hid from the wise men of the world. But it could be naturally known about God, that He is God, because every creature shows that it is not itself God, but, that is, there is something else which made it, the service of Whom it is necessary to render; such that what was known about God, was manifest to them."[10] And such propositions as these are not properly the object of faith: since they can be comprehended by natural reason. For as Blessed Gregory says, "Faith would have no merit if human reason furnishes it with experimental proofs."[11]

---

9 This quotation is incorrectly attributed here to St. Anselm of Canterbury, but instead belongs to Hervé de Bourg-Dieu (1080-1150), a French Benedictine exegete.
10 *Commentaria in epistolas Pauli-In Epistolam ad Romanos* (PL 181, 610A-B).
11 *Homilies on the Gospels*, hom. 26, n. 1 (PL 76, 1197C).

Therefore, such an assertion, which is opposed to those things which ought to be believed, which could be proved by national reason, are said to be erroneous in the faith. As for example, that God is not one: that God is not omnipotent; that Christ was not a man for three days [in the tomb];[12] that man's soul is produced from human seed, as the brute animals; that the charity, whereby we love God, is the Holy Ghost; and the active life is more excellent than the contemplative. All these propositions ought to be called errors in the faith, because they can be confuted by natural reason. I reckon therefore that this is the difference between a heretical proposition and a proposition erroneous in the faith: namely, that heresy properly so called is opposed to those things that ought to be believed, which are above all the power of the intellect. But an error in the faith is against those things that ought to be believed, which can be proved by natural reason. If, however, something to be believed were of this kind, so that besides natural reason it could also be proved by Sacred Scripture, or the decision of the Church, or by other ways whereby those things which we are bound to believe can be proved, the assertion which opposed that which is to be believed, will be called heretical and erroneous in the faith at the same time. Such is this proposition: God is not one. For, because its falsity can be proved by natural reason, it will be called a proposition erroneous in the faith. But because the same thing can be proved by Sacred Scripture, it will

---

12 This error was held by Roger Bacon who wrote: "Because of ignorance in regard to these two problems the multitude holds that dead Caesar is a man, that a dead man is an animal, and that Christ was a man during the three days [in the tomb] and [it holds] another unlimited number of false and very foolish things about restriction and ampliation in propositions and about necessities and contingencies and other things, all of which are to be disputed in an orderly way in their proper places" (*Compendium Studii Theologiae* (Aberdeen: Typis Academicis, 1911), p. 63).

be called a heretical proposition: and the pertinacious assertor of that or another similar proposition will be deemed a heretic: and as such he deservedly should be punished.

Still another difference can be given between these two, by the fact that heresy is always against that which we are bound to believe. For there are many theological propositions which consist merely of an opinion, which we are neither bound to believe or disbelieve. But one is free hold an opinion for or against as he pleases. Of such sort are these propositions: "In the Sacraments of the New Law there is some quality causing grace." "The Blessed, by God so doing, can see one Divine Person without seeing another." "Beatitude consists more in vision, than in love." He who denies any of these propositions, would not be a heretic. Still if anyone were to assert one or another of them as an article of faith, such that he would deem the opposite assertion to be heretical, such a man would err in the faith, and (as we will say below in the eighth chapter) he would be a heretic: because he adheres to that proposition more firmly than he ought. For he errs according to Augustine's opinion: because he holds what is uncertain as certain: just as one would err who holds what is certain as uncertain. If these distinctions between a heretical proposition, and one erroneous in the faith, do not please someone, I do not wish to fight against him: but I ask him to offer a better one, because (as I said) I am prepared to hear someone teaching better things.

I heard from some men that there was a certain very learned man, publicly teaching in the Complutense University, who, so that between these two things he might make some differentiation, distinguishing in this way firstly about error in a public lecture, saying: a proposition can be said to be erroneous in two ways. For it can be erroneous by a logical error, and every false proposition is erroneous by this error. Hence it would be, that every proposition erroneous in faith by a logical error, also ought to be called heretical: because every such proposition says what is false in the faith. A proposition can be called erroneous in the faith in another way, by a theological error: and it is that proposition which is against the common opinion of theologians. Among which there are many which nowise deserve to be called heresy. And it was said to me, when he taught this, he gave as this example: This proposition: "The Virgin Mary was conceived in original sin," is erroneous in faith by a theological error; because it is against the common opinion of present-day theologians, yet it should not be called heretical; because its contradictory proposition does not pertain to the Catholic faith, and the Church has never decreed that it must be held as the Catholic faith. How true this distinction of the erroneous proposition is, I leave to the reader to judge, merely advising that he consider, how it can be called a proposition erroneous in the faith, which does not oppose the faith either on the part of its assertion, or on the part of him who asserts it more firmly than he ought. For even if we were to concede that everyone who asserts something against the common opinion of theologians, errs by a theological error: still it is not necessary to say that every such man errs in the faith. Because it is severe to say that someone be said to error in the faith, when the proposition, which he asserts, is not against the faith, nor the manner of asserting is against the faith: because he does not adhibit greater faith to that proposition than he ought.

A proposition "savoring of heresy," or badly expressing those things which pertain to the faith, is that proposition which in the first meaning, which the words show on their first impression, has a heretical sense: although when piously understood has some true meaning. Jean Gerson[13] in his *De vita spirituali animae* says that a proposition savoring of heresy is the same thing as an error.[14] But I nowise think that

---

13 Jean de Charlier de Gerson (1363-1429) was a French scholar and Chancellor of the University of Paris.
14 Lecture 2, corollary 7, *Opera omnia* (Antwerp: sumptibus So-

On the difference between a heretical, erroneous, and other propositions

this opinion of his is true. Because no proposition can be said to be erroneous, unless firstly it is settled about its meaning. But there are many propositions which can give various and very diverse meanings: one of which is Catholic, the other heretical. Thus, it is undeserved that such a proposition simply, and absolutely without any examination, or distinction would be called an error, which can have a true and Catholic meaning. Therefore, it follows that a proposition of this kind ought to be examined about its meaning, before the note of error be branded upon it. Yet it will always be said to savor of heresy, because from the force of its words it is open to having a heretical as well as a Catholic meaning. As for instance these propositions: "The Father is greater than the Son." "Christ is a creature." "There are three Gods." "To eat meat, or not to eat meat is irrelevant to Christian perfection." "Pagan philosophers in the natural law alone could be saved." This latter proposition savors of heresy: because if it excludes faith, it is heretical; if it does not exclude faith in God, it is true: and thus in this way when uttered alone it seems to savor of heresy, and stands in need of explanation. These propositions, albeit when piously understood have some true meaning, still according to the apparent meaning of the words, they express heresy.

Thus, when these propositions, or others of a similar mark are preached or taught, two things ought to be examined in them, whereby it is incumbent to investigate and judge heretics. The first is concerning the person asserting, whether he is otherwise suspect of heresy. The other is, whether some of the hearers understood those words according to a heretical sense: and hence were scandalized. And if the latter happened, the assertor of this proposition ought to be summoned and compelled to publicly interpret those words which he said, according to the true meaning of those words: so that every scandal may be removed from the hearers. But

---

cietatis, 1706), vol. 3, col. 23B.

if the person is suspect: but none of the hearers took scandal from his words, then he ought to be summoned secretly, and questioned about the meaning of his words, and if he confesses that he said those words in accordance with the Catholic meaning, he ought to be set free without any punishment: and it is not necessary (as I think) that he be forced to make a public clarification of his words: lest perhaps from the new declaration of his words someone would be scandalized, who before had not been scandalized. Nevertheless, I think that it is right that the Inquisitors admonish such a preacher or teacher that he should not dare to preach or teach similar things without a clear explanation of the words.

A "scandalous proposition," or "proposition offensive to pious ears," is a proposition which gives an occasion of ruin to the pious hearers. I will present some examples of this matter, so that the prudent reader can judge others like these. "Heretics ought to be tolerated, and ought not to be killed." "Almsgiving for the poor is of greater merit than to offer a stipend for the sacrifice of the Mass." "It is silly to offer the salutation of the Virgin as a prayer." "A tyrant can be killed by any subject of his." "Fasting does not pertain to Christian perfection." "There is no precept of receiving Baptism." All these propositions are scandalous: because they all give an occasion of ruin to the hearers.

The first truly opens a very wide path for introducing any heresy whatever: because the facility of pardon gives an incentive for sinning. The second proposition turns away from the Sacrifice of the Mass, and devotion to it: because if people believe that the Sacrifice of the Mass is of less merit than almsgiving: then the people will revere that sacrifice less than they ought, and will not make it to be celebrated as many times as they do now. But they will say that one single Mass (as Luther teachers) is enough for one people. The third proposition takes away the devotion which people have towards the pious Mother of God, Whom God willed to be a

On the difference between a heretical, erroneous, and other propositions

mediatrix between us and Him. The fourth proposition gives an animus and strength to the people so that they would kill their ruler at will: because it will always be alleged that the ruler is a tyrant. The fifth proposition in a certain way deters men from fasting. The sixth proposition renders men tepid for receiving Baptism.

A "temerarious proposition" is that which completely lacks all authority or reason, which is of any weight, by which it could be proved. For those things are said to be done heedlessly[15] (as Blessed Thomas says[16]) which are not guided by any reason, so that that assertion is said temerariously, which cannot be proved by any authority or reason. Thus, that proposition will be called "temerarious in faith," which enunciates about things pertaining to the faith, which cannot be proved by any reason or any authority. Such are the propositions which follows. "Judgment Day will be within a year." "Christ our Redeemer remained for forty days, which intervened between the Resurrection and the Ascension in the Ark of the Covenant." "The disciples of John the Baptist were those who, in the Passion of Christ the Redeemer, said: 'Away with him; away with him; crucify him' (Jn. 19, 15)." "John the Evangelist was sanctified in the womb of his mother." "Everyone living in Rome was in mortal sin." "All bishops are damned." "More of those married are saved, than of the monks." "More women are saved than men." All these propositions ought to be marked for their temerity, and their assertor will rightly be deemed temerarious.

Yet the proposition, and its assertor, will be freed from this note if that which is asserted has some likelihood of being true; even though it lacks both authority and reason, especially if some utility from that assertion can arise. As are many things which contemplative men imagine were plausibly done, and when told to the people can by them stir

---

15 *Temere.*
16 II-II, q. 53, a. 3.

up very good affections. Such are certain injurious words, which contemplative men plausibly imagine were said by the very wicked accomplices and other soldiers, and the crucifiers of Christ our Redeemer said to His face, and preachers of God's word usefully relate them to the people. Whereby, even though they could not be proved by any authority or valid reason, still they ought not on this account be called temerarious: because they are strengthened by a great likelihood, and are related not without utility. If nevertheless they lack all likelihood, no matter how much those propositions have hope of to benefit, they will deservedly be deemed temerarious, and as such ought to be forbidden by those to whom it pertains to do this. Because evil things ought not to be done, so that therefore good things may come: and God does not need our lies.

A "schismatic and seditious proposition" is one which takes away the unity of the members of the Church, either universally or howsoever particularly: these propositions which follow are of this sort. "A bishop is not superior to a simple priest." "The Pope is not the superior to the other bishops." "One ought not obey a wicked prelate." "By mortal sin all authority is lost." "Subjects can correct and punish their rulers at will when they commit some crime."

An "injurious proposition" is one which detracts from some state of the faithful or some illustrious person. Such are the many assertions of John Wycliffe and John Hus which were condemned in the Council of Constance in the eighth and fifteenth sessions. Among them are these which follow. "If anyone enters any private religious community of any kind, of those having possessions or of the mendicants, he is rendered unfit and unsuited for the observance of the laws of God."[17] "Religious living in private religious communities are not of the Christian religion."[18] "All of the order of

---

17 Sess. 8, prop. 21 (Dz., 13th edition, 601).
18 Sess. 8, prop. 23 (Dz. 603).

On the difference between a heretical, erroneous, and other propositions

mendicants are heretics, and those who give alms to them are excommunicated."[19] "The Roman Church is a synagogue of Satan"[20] and "The Pope is the Antichrist."[21] "The cardinals are Antichrist's ministers."[22] All these propositions ought to be called injurious, because they inflict very clear injuries to the states [i. e., the religious state] or to illustrious persons.

Now that I have discussed about every kind of condemnable proposition, I have reckoned it to be worthwhile to admonish the reader not to so think that these types of propositions are distinct and separate from each other such that they cannot belong to the one and the same assertion. The same assertion in fact can be branded with many of these which we have now explained. For this assertion, which is one of the pestiferous assertions of John Wycliffe: "Religious living in private religious communities are not of the Christian religion,"[23] is heretical, scandalous, temerarious, schismatic and injurious. It is heretical: because it gives an opinion contrary to the decision of the universal Church. It is scandalous, because it deters men from entering religion, and it persuades the professed to not fulfil what they have vowed to the Lord. It will be called temerarious, because it is supported by absolutely no reason or authority: but instead contradicts the multitude of all holy men. It is rightly deemed schismatic, because it divides the unity of the Church, since it separates the religious from it. Now that it is

---

19 Sess. 8, prop. 34 (Dz. 614).
20 Sess. 8, prop. 37 (Dz. 617).
21 John Wycliffe, *De potestate papae* (London, Trübner and Co., 1907), c. 12, p. 328.
22 This was another error of John Wycliffe. It is the tenth of the eighteen errors condemned by Archbishop Arundel of Canterbury in 1396. Cf. Edward Brown, ed., *Fasciculus rerum expetendarum ac fugiendarum* (London: Impensis Richardi Chiswell, 1690), vol. 1, p. 216.
23 Dz. 603.

injurious to all religious congregations and their religious is so clear that no one can reasonably doubt it.

Chapter IV

On the various ways by which it can be proved that some proposition is heretical.

Although I have discussed enough, as I think, about the heretical proposition, nevertheless so that I may fully bring the work to a close, I judged that it would be necessary to show the ways by which some proposition can be very clearly convicted of heresy, lest perhaps in the condemnation of some proposition, the judges, upon whom it is incumbent to do this, overturn the sentence, condemning some proposition as heretical which could not rightly be called such, or calling Catholic, that which should have been condemned as heretical. For from many, not only uneducated and ignorant men, but also by otherwise learned men, error was made on this point; when they defamed many propositions in their writings as heretical, which by no means deserved to have been labeled as heretical. For (so that I may omit others) Bishop Philastrius of Brescia, of whom Augustine makes mention in his book, *On Heresies, to Quodvultdeus*, branded many assertions with the note of heresy in that renown work of his, *De haeresibus*, which nevertheless are now defended by all as being Catholic. Also, he proposes to us many propositions as Catholic which we in that work which we published, *Against All Heresies*, listed not without reason among the heresies. Therefore, lest something similar happen to others, I have decided to now show many ways, and they are certain and undoubtable ones, by which some proposition could be convicted of heresy. From which it will be very clearly established that the proposition ought not to be called heretical which by any of those ways which we will just now explain, could not be convicted of heresy.

The first way, and the best of them all, is Sacred Scripture: because everyone who calls himself a Christian, is bound to most firmly believe that everything is true which Sacred Scripture teaches us: and he is not allowed to doubt about them in any way whatsoever. Because otherwise God, Who is believed to be the first author of them all, would be held suspect of a lie: which Christian ears are horrified to hear. Hence Augustine, in a letter to Jerome, says the following: "For I confess to your Charity that I have learned to yield this respect and honor only to the canonical books of Scripture: of these alone do I most firmly believe that the authors were completely free from error. And if in these writings I am perplexed by anything which appears to me opposed to truth, I do not hesitate to suppose that either the manuscript is faulty, or the translator has not caught the meaning of what was said, or I myself have failed to understand it."[1] And these words are found in the book of the Decretals, in the chapter, *Ego solis*, in distinction nine.[2] Though Augustine's words are incorrectly cited there, wherefore I warn the reader, that those words which are cited in the Decretal, ought to be corrected according to this citation. Therefore, since everything which Sacred Scripture proposes to us to be believed, we are obliged to most firmly believe, so that whatever opposes those things, rightly ought to be deemed heretical.

Yet especially in this matter one ought to consider that the testimony of Sacred Scripture, whereby some proposition ought to be convicted of heresy, is so clear and undoubted, that none of the sacred and approved Doctors interprets it to have some other meaning, according to which the proposition could not, according to it, be convicted of heresy. For it often happens that among the sacred Doctors there is not an agreement about the sense of some passage of Sacred Scripture: but one differs very greatly from the

---

1 Letter 82, c. 1, n. 3 (PL 33, 276).
2 *Decretum Gratiani*, pt. 1, dist. 9, c. 5 (PL 187, 49D-50A).

other, when extracting the meaning of that passage. Then, therefore, although the meaning which one or the other of the sacred Doctors gives to that passage of Sacred Scripture, very clearly conflicts with some proposition, such a proposition ought not to be immediately deemed heretical, if it is established that it was explained otherwise by other sacred Doctors: such that according to their meaning, that passage of Sacred Scripture does not conflict with the proposition. For when the propositions on that passage are diverse, it often happens that it is unsure to us, which of those we necessarily ought to hold: and hence it follows that none of them are sufficient for establishing some dogma, or for refuting a heresy. For the testimony of Scripture, which ought to oppose some proposition and convict it of heresy, ought to be certain and manifest. Hence Augustine in his book against the letter of Petilianus,[3] *On the Unity of the Church*, when responding to certain testimonies of Scripture, with which the Donatists were trying to prove that the Church consists of them alone, says these words: "For if it can be interpreted as posited ambiguously for us or for you, certainly it would not help your cause at all, since we, if we should wish to use such things, would use countless pieces of evidence which likewise would not help our cause at all."[4]

Thus that proposition, which contradicts Sacred Scripture, according to the meaning received by the Catholic Church, without a doubt, ought to be deemed heretical. And one ought not to be concerned whether it clearly or latently contradicts Scripture: because it shall be certain that in whatever way that proposition opposes, conflicting in this way with Sacred Scripture, it rightly ought to be branded of heresy. For there are some heresies, the contraries or the

---

3 Petilianus was a Donatist of the fifth century in Roman North Africa.
4 C. 23, n. 67 (PL 43, 440).

contradictories of which were stated in Sacred Scripture, and of this kind are the propositions which clearly conflict with Sacred Scripture. As (for example) that Christ is not God; that the three Persons are not one essence. Their contradictories are stated in Sacred Scripture. There are other heresies, the contraries or contradictories of which, although they are not so stated in Holy Writ, as having that sense of the words found there, still from those things which Sacred Scripture teaches, such contraries, or contradictories, are inferred by a very evident consequence, and such assertions hiddenly conflict with Sacred Scripture: because Scriptures oppose those things which are necessarily derived from them. And such propositions also ought to be deemed heretical, as well as the first: because those things which, from the contents in Sacred Scripture, are inferred by a necessary consequence, have as much firmness of truth, and necessity of faith, as those things from which they are concluded.

For example, these propositions: "The Deity was mortal in Christ's Passion"; "Christ was not at the same time God and man," are called and are heretical. Because even though their opposites, having that sense of the words, are not found in Holy Writ, still from those things which are contained in Holy Writ, they are deduced by an evident consequence. Gregory Nazianzen teaches this opinion, speaking thus: "Those things which are concluded from Sacred Scripture consequently ought to be held as if they were written in Scripture."[5] According to this rule many sacred Doctors

---

5 Francisco Ruiz De Montoya so formulated the thought of St. Gregory Nazianzen in his *Regulae intelligendi scripturas sacras* (Paris: apud Ioannem Ruellium, 1550), rule 74, fol. 37r, where he cites St. Gregory using this summary of his thought. St. Gregory's actual words are: "…so neither, if I found something else either not at all or not clearly expressed in the words of Scripture to be included in the meaning,

very constantly assert and preach, that some things ought to be believed: because they are inferred from the sayings of Sacred Scripture, even though they are not found in it. Hence Origen says: "For the sake of those who hunger and thirst it was written: 'I was hungry; and, I was thirsty' (Mt. 25, 35). And, because of the naked and of those who are strangers, because of the sick, and those who are in prison: 'I was naked'; and, 'I was a stranger'; and, 'I was sick,' and, 'I was in prison' (v. 36). And to this we may also add: 'I suffered afflictions,' 'I was beaten,' 'I was tempted,' and all such things. And as, in the things which are written in the Scriptures, the words of the Lord truly apply, where He says: 'As long as you did it to one of these my least brethren, you did it to me' (v. 40), so when the just man suffers persecution, when evil is spoken of him, or when he suffers anything of this kind, set Christ in the midst of those who do this injury; saying to them: When you do an injury to one of the least of these, it is Me you have assailed, it is against Me you have spoken evil."[6]

Yet here it will be very important that one take care that he deduce very correctly and plainly in deductions of this kind: because if the conclusion is not evident, but doubtful, it also will not be evident that the proposition, which seems to conflict with Sacred Scripture in appearance, is heretical. And certainly, from an error of this kind of deduction, many were deceived, and fell into many errors. For there were many, so that I may put forth one example of many, who tried either to praise or at least excuse some vices: having been moved by this reason alone, because Sacred Scripture relates that those things were perpetrated by some

---

should I avoid giving it utterance, out of fear of your sophistical trick about terms" (Oration 31, or the Fifth Theological Oration, n. 24 (PG 36, 159C)).

6   PG 13, 1601C-D.

men who were otherwise just. Certain men thought that it necessarily follows that every such deed ought to be deemed good, which it is evident was performed by a man praised in Sacred Scripture: or on the contrary, that every single deed be reckoned evil, because Scripture relates that it was done by a bad man. They attempt to excuse Judith from lying, because Sacred Scripture commends her many other virtues. For the same reason they labor to deliver Lot from drunkenness and incest. By this same argument, Faustus the Manichaean long ago accused Sacred Scripture of falsity, because Scripture itself relates that some evil deeds were done by men otherwise just. That reasoning indeed would have been good, and the argumentation valid, if it were proved to be true that he who is just at one time, as Pelagius and after him Luther said, was unable to act wickedly; or he who is bad at one time, could never afterwards become good again. Now since this opinion is very false, it is evidently wrongly concluded that a deed is good, from the fact that its doer was good; or that it is evil, because it was done by an evil man

Hence Blessed Augustine in book twenty-two of his *Reply to Faustus the Manichaean*, responding to the more eloquent calumnies of this kind of the same Faustus, in chapter sixty says these words: "When we find bad and good actions recorded of the same person, we must take warning from the one, and example from the other."[7] And again in chapter sixty-two of the same book, when discussing the fornication of Juda, who had intercourse with Thamar his daughter-in-law, says: "The mistake of Faustus and of Manichaeism generally, is in supposing that these objections prove anything against us, as if our reverence for Scripture, and our profession of regard for its authority, bound us to approve of all the evil actions mentioned in it; whereas the greater our homage for the Scripture, the more decided must be our

---

7 PL 42, 438.

condemnation of what the truth of Scripture itself teaches us to condemn. In Scripture, all fornication and adultery are condemned by the Divine law;[8] accordingly, when actions of this kind are narrated, without being expressly condemned, it is intended not that we should praise them, but that we should pass judgment on them ourselves."[9] And again in chapter sixty-five of the same book he says: "The impiety, therefore, of Faustus' attacks on Scripture can injure no one but himself; for what he thus assails is now deservedly the object of universal reverence. As has been already said, the sacred record, like a faithful mirror, has no flattery in its portraits, and either itself passes sentence upon human actions as worthy of approval or disapproval, or leaves the reader to do so. And not only does it distinguish men as blameworthy or praiseworthy, but it also takes notice of cases where the blameworthy deserve praise, and the praiseworthy blame. Thus, although Saul was blameworthy, it was not the less praiseworthy in him to examine so carefully who had eaten food during the curse, and to pronounce the stern sentence in obedience to the commandment of God.[10] So, too, he was right in banishing sorcerers out of the land.[11] And although David was praiseworthy,[12] we are not called on to approve or imitate his sins, which God rebukes by the prophet.[13] And so Pontius Pilate was not wrong in pronouncing the Lord innocent, in spite of the accusations of the Jews;[14] nor was it praiseworthy in Peter to deny the Lord thrice;[15] nor,

---

8 Cf. Ex. 20, vv. 14 & 17.
9 PL 42, 439.
10 Cf. I Kings 14, 24-45.
11 Cf. I Kings 28, 3.
12 Cf. II Kings 12, 7-12.
13 Cf. John 19, vv. 4 & 6; Mt. 27, 22-23.
14 Cf. Mt. 26, 70-74.
15 Cf. Mt. 16, 22-23.

again, was he praiseworthy on that occasion when Christ called him Satan because, not understanding the things of God, he wished to withhold Christ from His Passion, that is, from our salvation. Here Peter, immediately after being called blessed, is called Satan. Which character most truly belonged to him, we may see from his apostleship, and from his crown of martyrdom"[16]

From all these things it is evident that some proposition ought not immediately to be called heretical, due to the fact that it conflicts with that which seems to be deduced from Sacred Scripture: but before we pass sentence, it is necessary to diligently examine whether that, with which such a propositions conflicts, is correctly or incorrectly concluded from Sacred Scripture. If the conclusion is correct, such a proposition will rightly be deemed heretical. But if the conclusion is incorrect, that proposition will not be judged heretical, on account of such a conclusion. Still, it will be suspect of heresy, to the extent it is established concerning the conclusion, whether it is necessary or not.

Therefore, the first way, and (as we have said) the most important of all whereby we can convict some proposition of heresy, is Sacred Scripture. For this is that "tower of David, which is built with bulwarks: a thousand bucklers hang upon it, all the armour of valiant men" (Cant. 4, 4), because from it arms are taken up, with which we ought to fight against the enemies of the Catholic faith. This is also that brook from which David took the stones, with which slew the proud Goliath, the very fierce enemy of Israel.[17] Hence Paul in his Second Epistle to Timothy says: "All scripture, inspired of God, is profitable to teach, to reprove, to correct, to instruct in justice, that the man of God may be perfect, furnished to every good work" (II Tim. 3, 16-17). Yet here the reader

---

16 PL 42, 441.
17 Cf. I Kings 17, 40.

ought to be admonished not to think that the words of Sacred Scripture, according to every meaning of them, are efficacious for confuting heresies: because unless they are taken in the literal sense, they have little force for disputing. The mystical sense is not valid for refuting heretics: but only the literal sense. And hence when Bishop Petilian of the Donatists wishes to prove in that part of Africa alone, which was providing food for the Donatists, is the true Church, and to support this claim he cited the passage from the Canticle of Canticles: "Shew me, O thou whom my soul loveth, where thou feedest, where thou liest in the midday" (1, 6). Responding to him, Augustine, in his book *On the Unity of the Church*, says these words: "These are mysterious [*mystica*], secret, symbolic; we beg of you something obvious that does not need an interpreter."[18] And in his letter to the Donatist Vincentius he again says: "For what else is it than superlative impudence for one to interpret in his own favor any allegorical statements, unless he has also plain testimonies, by the light of which the obscure meaning of the former may be made manifest."[19]

From which words it is clearly proved that some Catholic men, who dispute against heretics who deny that sacramental Confession is of Divine institution, act imprudently when they try to refute them by those words which Christ said to the lepers: "Go, shew yourselves to the priests" (Lk. 17, 14), or by that which, when speaking of Lazarus, He said to the Apostles: "Loose him, and let him go" (Jn. 11, 44). These quotations are indeed good and useful for strengthening the faithful: yet they are hardly effective for refuting unbelievers: because they are mystical, and doubtful. Still if the mystical sense were such that by other testimonies of Scripture it could be proved that that is the true meaning of

---

18 N. 69 (PL 43, 441).
19 Letter 93, c. 8, n. 24 (PL 33, 334).

the text, then such a sense, as Augustine taught in the words just cited, will be effective for establishing a dogma, and refuting a heresy. About which it is unnecessary to discuss at great length, because in that work which I published, *Against All Heresies*, I recall that I spoke enough:[20] and in another work, which I am now preparing about the correct and genuine understanding of Sacred Scripture, I hope that I hope to speak much more copiously, with God as my guide.

The second way whereby a proposition can be convicted of heresy, is the definition of a general council rightly (as is befitting) assembled. For a general council cannot err: since it is governed by the Holy Ghost, Who always assists them. Hence it is that we are obliged to give full faith to those things which were decreed by a general council rightly assembled, and to those things which are deduced as a necessary consequence, even if those things cannot be proved by clear testimonies of Sacred Scripture. Thus, every proposition asserting something against a definition of some approved council, or against something which by an evident and necessary consequence is inferred from a decree of a council, will be rightly branded with the mark of heresy, and for its refutation the definition of the approved council is enough: even if there is lacking a clear testimony of Sacred Scripture. Many propositions are convicted of heresy in this way, which without the definitions of the councils, nowise, or with great difficulty, could be shown to be heretical. Now lest anyone distrust me on this point due to a lack of examples, I will add some propositions which except by the councils' authority, could hardly be rejected from the bosom of the Catholic faith.

"In the Sacrament of the Altar the material substance of bread and likewise the material substance of wine remain."[21]

---

20 Introduction, c. 3.
21 Dz. 581.

How to prove that a propostion is heretical

"People can at their will correct masters who offend."²² "All are simoniacs who oblige themselves to pray for others who assist them in temporal matters."²³ "Special prayers applied to one person by prelates or religious are not of more benefit to that person than general (prayers), all other things being equal."²⁴ "The rational soul is not truly, and of itself, the form of the human body." "The Epistle to the Hebrews is not Paul's." "The first Epistle of the seven canonical Epistles does not belong to James." All these propositions are heretical, yet their error could scarcely be demonstrated other than by the authority of the councils. The first four were condemned in the eighth session of the Council of Constance. The fifth was condemned in the Council of Vienne, celebrated under Pope Clement V, whose decree is found in the Clementine Decretals, in the chapter *De summa Trinitate, et fide Catholica*.²⁵ The last two were condemned by many councils.²⁶

The third way whereby we can convict an assertion of heresy is the universal consent of the Church, without the testimony of any passage of Sacred Scripture, and without the definition of any general council. For there are many things which even though they are not contained in Sacred Scripture: yet because they have been kept by the very ancient custom of the Church, have no little force for confuting heresies. For those things ought to equally be believed

---

22 Dz. 597.
23 Dz. 605.
24 Dz. 599.
25 "In order that all may know the truth of the faith in its purity and all error may be excluded, we define that anyone who presumes henceforth to assert defend or hold stubbornly that the rational or intellectual soul is not the form of the human body of itself and essentially, is to be considered a heretic" (*Constitutiones Clementinae*, bk. 1, tit. 1, c. 1).
26 Dz. 784.

which were derived from Christ Our Savior Himself: and thence from mouth to mouth reached to our times. For likewise from the Pythagorean philosophers, Archippus and Lysis,[27] who having schools in Thebes in Greece, handed down the Pythagorean teachings by word alone, which their students retaining by memory, were using their intellects and memories in place of books. We read that Christ wrote nothing which has remained: but he taught by word alone, and the Evangelists did not write all the precepts: but some of them were conserved by memory, and they came to us having been transferred to us from mouth to mouth.

Which things however were so kept, that they have the firmest certitude of truth: just as if they had been handed down by writing. For just as God helped the Evangelists by his Divine Spirit, or the other sacred writers, when they wrote something: so He breathed upon the Church with the same Spirit, when she says something to us. For Christ said to His Apostles: "It is not you that speak, but the Spirit of your Father that speaketh in you" (Mt. 10, 20). For it ought not to be believed that God has left His Church without His Spirit, so that He now disdains to speak by her mouth: especially since He says: "I am with you all days, even to the consummation of the world" (Mt. 28, 20). Therefore, just as we believe the divine Scriptures were written by the hands of the Apostles and Evangelists, so also we are bound to believe the Divine words, spoken through the mouth of the Church. For just as not all the things which Jesus did were written (as John the Evangelist testifies[28]), so neither every-

---

27 Aristoxenus of Tarentum reports that two Tarentines, Lysis and Archippus, were the sole survivors when the house of Milo in Croton was burned, during a meeting of the Pythagoreans, by their enemies (Iamblichus, *Life of Pythagoras* (Los Angeles: Theosophical Pub. House, 1918), c. 35, p. 90).
28 Cf. Jn. 20, 30.

thing which He said. Now it ought to be believed that many of these deeds or words of Christ, which were not written, the Apostles told to others by word, and so from mouth to mouth, and were poured out from heart to heart until they reached us, without any other testimony of Scripture. Such are nearly all the things which the Catholic Church keeps regarding the rite of giving the Sacraments, yet one is not allowed to reject them: because either they all, or the greater part of them, proceeded from Christ Himself, their institutor, and going forth from mouth to mouth, until they reached us. Hence it is that if anything be taught against these things, which the Church has so kept and taught until these times, it rightly ought to be deemed heretical.

Hence Origen says: "In the ecclesiastical observances there are some things of this sort, which everyone is obliged to do, and yet not everyone understands the reason for them. For the fact that we kneel to pray, for instance, and that of all the quarters of the heavens, the east is the only direction we turn to when we pour out prayer, the reasons for this, I think, are not easily discovered by anyone. Moreover, who would readily explain the reasons for the way we receive the Eucharist, or for the rite by which it is celebrated, or for the things that are done in Baptism, the words, actions, the order, the questions and answers? And yet, we carry all these things on our shoulders, covered and veiled, when we so fulfill and follow those things; just as we have received things deposited by the great high priest and his sons."[29]

Moreover, the text and composition of words which the Church uses in the consecration of Christ's Body and Blood, is not found in the Gospels of any of the Evangelists: yet it would be wrong to believe that Sacrament ought to be confected by any other words than those with which the Church now confects the Sacrament: because such words,

---

29 Hom. 5 on Numbers (PG 12, 603B-C).

which the Church now uses, came forth (as we believe) from Christ Himself. For Pope Innocent III acknowledges this, speaking thus: "Therefore we believe that the form of words, as it is found in the Canon [of the Mass], was received by the Apostles from Christ, and by their successors from them."[30] These words are found in the book of the Decretals, in the title, *De celebratione Missarum*, in the chapter, *Cum Marthae*.[31] Therefore a most certain way, and a very strong argument for proving that some proposition is heretical, is the universal consent of the Church: such that that proposition may be called heretical, which is against the universal consent of the Church: even though there is no testimony of Scripture, whereby such a proposition could be refuted. Whence the Wise Man in Proverbs, says: "Forsake not the law of thy mother" (6, 20). This third way for refuting heresies was defined in the Council of Trent, celebrated under Paul III, which in the third session declared that the truth of the faith is contained partly in the books of Scripture, and partly in traditions: and after it listed all the books of Sacred Scripture, in which the truth of the faith is contained, it says these words which follow: "If anyone, however, should not accept the said books as sacred and canonical, entire with all their parts, as they were wont to be read in the Catholic Church, and as they are contained in the old Latin Vulgate edition, and if both knowingly and deliberately he should condemn the aforesaid traditions let him be anathema."[32]

The fourth way is the judgment of the Apostolic See: because this See cannot err regarding those things which pertain to faith. But I have decided to instruct the reader about this: what by the name of the "Apostolic See" ought to

---

30 Register 1, bk. 5, letter 121 to Archbishop John of Lyon (PL 214, 1121C).
31 *Decretals of Gregory IX*, bk. 3, tit. 41, c. 6.
32 Dz. 784.

be understood, because by this name, not merely the person of the Pope himself is understood: because he can err as a man, thinking incorrectly, and having incorrect opinions: just as history relates about many Sovereign Pontiffs that they erred. For (so that I may omit many others) Honorius I was condemned in the Sixth Ecumenical Council, because he favored the heresy of Monothelitism. The name of the "Apostolic See" signifies the Sovereign Pontiff himself, not as he does something as a private person: but as he does those things, which pertain to the chair [of Peter], not proceeding only from his own understanding: but from the understanding of good and learned men. Taking the name, "Apostolic See," in this way, as often as it is read in decrees or elsewhere, the Apostolic See cannot err in the faith. Hence Pope Agatho says: "All the sanctions of the Apostolic See should be accepted as though affirmed by the divine voice of Peter himself."[33] [Huguccio of Pisa[34]] when expounding these words in the decree speaks thus: "[This does not happen by reason of the Pope but on account of the authority of the See, hence] he carefully said, 'of the Apostolic See,' and he did not say, 'of the Apostolic man.'"[35] Thus the decrees of the Apostolic See, or a judgment pronounced by the Roman Pontiff, are not understood to be those things which are uttered hiddenly, wickedly, unadvisedly by the Roman Pontiff alone, or also which by him, with few favoring him, others having been

---

33 *Decretum Gratiani*, pt. 1, dist. 19, c. 2 (PL 187, 106C).

34 Huguccio of Pisa wrote these words, though the text here cites *Archdeaconus*. Huguccio was an Italian canonist who died in 1210 A.D.

35 *Summa Decretorum*, ad dist. 19, c. 2. For the sake of clarity, the full quotation of Huguccio has been cited here, which in Latin is: *Hoc non fit ratione papae sed propter auctoritatem sedis, unde caute dixit apostolicae sedis et non dixit apostolici.*

despised or not having been consulted unto self-deception: but which are uttered by the Roman Pontiff, from the counsel of many wise men, especially the eminent Cardinals, having firstly been fully examined.[36]

Now [Pope Nicholas I[37]] explains what sort of examination ought to be made before a decision of the Apostolic See

---

36 Papal infallibility was more correctly explained when it was defined by the First Vatican Council as follows: "The Roman Pontiff, when he speaks *ex cathedra*, that is, when carrying out the duty of the pastor and teacher of all Christians by virtue of his supreme Apostolic authority he defines a doctrine of faith or morals to be held by the universal Church, through the Divine assistance promised him in Blessed Peter, operates with that infallibility with which the Divine Redeemer wished that His Church be instructed in defining doctrine on faith and morals; and so such definitions of the Roman Pontiff from himself, but not from the consensus of the Church, are unalterable" (Dz. 1839). "Papal infallibility is a personal and incommunicable charisma, which is not shared by any Pontifical tribunal. It was promised directly to Peter, and to each of Peter's successors in the primacy, but not as a prerogative the exercise of which could be delegated to others. Hence doctrinal decisions or instructions issued by the Roman congregations, even when approved by the Pope in the ordinary way, have no claim to be considered infallible. To be infallible they must be issued by the Pope himself in his own name according to the conditions already mentioned as requisite for *ex cathedra* teaching" ("Papal Infallibility," *Catholic Encyclopedia* (New York: Robert Appleton Company, 1907-1913), vol. 7, p. 796).

37 "Blessed Gregory" is wrongly cited here, as the author seems to have followed the incorrect reference for this quotation found in the Decretals. Cf. *Decretum Gratiani, causa* 35, q. 9, c. 4 (*Apostolicae*) (PL 187, 1694A).

is pronounced, speaking thus: "The opinion of the Apostolic See is always conceived with such great moderation of counsel, ripened to maturity, uttered with such great gravity of deliberation, that it neither needs to be retracted, nor admits of necessity to be changed, unless perhaps it was so pronounced that it could be retracted, or changed, if it arises according to the tenor of a premised condition."[38] Hence by accepting the name of the "Apostolic See" in this way, I believe that it cannot err in the faith, and that its decrees are completely infallible, certainly not by reason of the person, from whom they proceed: for because he is a man, it follows that he could err: but by reason of the chair, which he governs and rules. For God is accustomed to impart gifts of graces to persons otherwise unworthy, on account of the office, which they administer. For (so that I may pass over others in silence) Caiphas on account of his pontifical dignity with which he was adorned, was given to prophesy about the Redemption of the human race, that it would be accomplished by Christ's death.[39] It was much more fitting that God would grant the privilege of infallible truth to him who is the pastor and ruler of the whole Church. For so Christ promised that He would do, saying: "I have prayed for thee, that thy faith fail not: and thou, being once converted, confirm thy brethren" (Lk. 22, 32). How will Peter's faith fail, that is, the faith of the Apostolic See, when He asked for it, Who is always heard? Or how could He lead back the erring sheep, or strengthen the vacillating, if their pastor and ruler would err, just as they?

---

38 Letter 58 of Pope Nicholas I, to King Charles the Bald (Mansi, *Sacrorum Conciliorum Nova Et Amplissima Collectio* (Venice: Antonius Zatta, 1767), vol. 15, col. 339E; PL 119, 1171B).

39 Cf. Jn. 11, 50-51.

Wherefore, Blessed Leo in his [fourth] sermon [on the anniversary] of his elevation to the pontificate, when discoursing on this promise of Christ, says: "The Lord took a special care of Peter, and prayed expressly for Peter's faith, as if the state of the others would be more certain if the mind of their chief were unconquered. In Peter, therefore, the fortitude of all was guarded, and the help of Divine grace was so ordained that the stability was given by Christ to Peter, and conferred by Peter to the Apostles."[40] If perhaps a Roman Pontiff has ever erred in an explanation of the faith, it could have happened from the fact that he did not exercise as much diligence as he ought to have done before pronouncing judgment: because either he did not fully examine (as he ought), or did not consult those whom it was befitting for him to consult. For in that case he erred as a particular person, not as a governor and ruler of the Chair. The man then erred, who was in the Apostolic See, but the Apostolic See did not: because the Apostolic See (as we showed from [Pope Nicholas I]) judges nothing without careful examination. Now when it so judges, it could not err: because God is in its midst, lest it be moved from the true faith. Thus since by this privilege which God gave to the Apostolic See that it could not err, it follows that all are obliged to believe those matters of faith, which have been defined, and have been judged, after having been thoroughly examined by it: and if something contrary to those things is pertinaciously asserted, it necessarily ought to be judged as being heretical. Hence [Pseudo-] Blessed Jerome when writing to Pope Damasus says: "This, most blessed Pope, is the faith that we have been taught in the Catholic Church. If anything therein has been incorrectly or carelessly expressed, we beg that it may be set aright by you who hold the faith and See of Peter. If, however, this our profession be approved by the judgment

---

40 C. 3 (PL 54, 151B).

How to prove that a propostion is heretical

of your apostleship, whoever may blame me, will prove that he himself is ignorant, or malicious, or even not a Catholic but a heretic."[41]

In this way these following propositions are heretical: "Sacramental Confession is merely of human authority."[42] "The souls of the just dying in the state of grace, do not clearly see the Divine essence before Judgment Day."[43] The Catholic Church rejects these two propositions as heretical: yet their error cannot be demonstrated so easily elsewhere, as from the decisions of the Roman Pontiffs. For Sixtus IV condemned the first, whose decree I inserted in that work which I published, *Against All Heresies*: in the section on "Confession." Benedict X condemned the second and his decree was put in the same work, in the section on "Beatitude," in the sixth heresy.

The fifth way, whereby we can prove that an assertion is heretical, is the concordant opinion of all the sacred Doctors, who wrote about this matter against that proposition. For that which is asserted against the opinion of all such men, will be determined to be heretical. And Athanasius clearly teaches this in that great oration of his magnificent *Oration against Idols*, speaking thus: "For an argument when confirmed by the authority of great men cannot but give credibility."[44] Still, if some proposition were to contradict one or another sacred Doctor, not on that account ought such a proposi-

---

41   Pelagius, *Profession of Faith to Pope Innocent* [*Libellus fidei ad Innocentum papam*], c. 14 (PL 45, 1718).

42   "Peter de Osma and his above-mentioned followers were not fearing to pertinaciously affirm, that the confession of sins in species is to be found really in the statute of the universal Church, not in Divine law" (Sixtus IV, Bull *Licet ea*, August 9, 1479 (Mansi 32, 380A)). Cf. Dz. 724.

43   Dz. 530-531.

44   N. 45 (PG 25, 90B). Also titled, *Against the Heathen*.

tion be deemed heretical: because the writings of such men, no matter how holy and learned they may be, ought not to be received as Divine oracles: because it is not evident that those writings have proceeded from God: but from man, who could be deceived. Now nothing prevents us from saying that he who could be deceived was wrong. And it is not just, or consonant with reason, that we would be obliged to believe him under pain of damnation in hell, who could both be deceived and deceive, such is any mere man: because for this reason it would necessarily happen that we would be very often held to accept what is false as being true, and what is true as being false: which one is not allowed to say.

But even if the writings of individual holy men ought not to be held as law: so that it would be wicked to depart from them: still the concordant opinion of all the sacred Doctors about matters of faith, which was never contradicted with impunity, by the Church or those Catholic men, should be held as the true teaching of the Church. For (as Blessed Paul says) unto this God gave to us "some apostles, and some prophets, and other some evangelists, and other some pastors and doctors... that henceforth we be no more children tossed to and fro, and carried about with every wind of doctrine by the wickedness of men, by cunning craftiness, by which they lie in wait to deceive" (Eph. 4, vv. 11 & 14). If then they were given so that we may not err, it is impossible that all would err at the same time, who were sent so that we would not err.

Moreover, Holy Writ sends us to the old Doctors: so that we may be taught by them, whence it is that we are bound to believe them by the same law. For we would be commanded in vain to go to them, unless we were bound to accept their teaching. For so Moses says: "Remember the days of old, think upon every generation: ask thy father, and he will declare to thee: thy elders and they will tell thee" (Deut. 32, 7). Again, the concordant opinion of all the sacred Doctors, which no one ever contradicted with impunity, very clearly proves that it is also the view of the whole Church. Because if all those sacred Doctors have erred, their error having been protracted through so many centuries, the Church would not have left it unnoticed. Hence it is that the Church always appears silent to the opinion of all those with whom she agreed: because if she had not agreed, neither also would she have been silent. For it could never be said more correctly, that he who is silent, seems to consent; rather since the matter is so serious, that to be silent would be pernicious, but to speak both useful and necessary. "Not to oppose error," as said Pope [Felix III[45]], "is to approve it, and not to defend truth is to suppress it... Indeed, to neglect to confound evil men—when we can do it—is no less a sin than to encourage them. And he who does not oppose an obvious crime is open to the suspicion of secret complicity."[46] These words are found in the chapter, *Error*.[47]

But because I have disputed at great enough length about this matter in the introduction of *Against All Heresies*, in the seventh chapter: wherefore I have judged it superfluous to dispute longer here about this matter. Yet we merely conclude that this concordant opinion of all the sacred Doctors, both present and past, about some matter is as equally effective an argument for refuting heresy as a definition of the universal Church. Because those things, which by all, without contradiction of the Church about matters of faith, seem to have been approved by the same Church, while it was silent: because unless it had approved, it was bound to contradict, lest with the prophet Isaias it would be said: "Woe to me, because I have held my peace" (Is. 6, 5). Jerome fought in

---

45 Pope Innocent is incorrectly cited here as found in Gratian's Decretals.
46 Letter 1 (to Acacius of Constantinople) (PL 58, 898A-B).
47 *Decretum Gratiani*, pt. 1, dist. 83, c. 3 (PL 187, 401A).

this way against Helvidius. For, in order to show against him the perpetual virginity of Mary the Mother of God, since explicit testimonies of Sacred Scripture supporting this matter were lacking, he very powerfully used the testimony of holy men who preceded him.[48] Next, the [Sixth General[49]] Council, gathered against Macarius, Bishop of Antioch, attributed very much authority to the testimonies of the holy Fathers. For so it says: "In all matters we follow the holy Fathers and Doctors of the Church: Athanasius, Hilary, Basil, Gregory the theologian, and Gregory of Nyssa, Ambrose, Augustine, Theophilus, John of Constantinople, Cyril, Leo, and we accept what they have set down on the correct belief and the condemnation of heretics."[50] From which words it is very clearly established that the concordant opinion, without contradiction, of all the holy men who preceded us, has great authority for refuting heresies.

Therefore, there are five ways by which we can prove that some proposition is heretical: besides which I do not believe there to be any other. Hence it is that an assertion, which in none of these ways, which we have treated, can be convicted of heresy, such an assertion (although it may be branded with some other note) cannot rightly be called heretical. And the assertor, although a pertinacious assertor of that proposition, who cannot be convicted of heresy in any of these

---

48 "Might I not array against you the whole series of ancient writers? Ignatius, Polycarp, Irenaeus, Justin Martyr, and many other apostolic and eloquent men, who against Ebion, Theodotus of Byzantium, and Valentinus, held these same views, and wrote volumes replete with wisdom" (*The Perpetual Virginity of Blessed Mary*, n. 19 (PL 23, 202A)).
49 I. e., the III Council of Constantinople. The text here mistakenly cites the fifth council.
50 Mansi 9, 183A-B.

ways, could not be deemed a heretic, and as such be rightly punished.

Chapter V

Who can judge about heresy, and pronounce sentence, which all are obliged to obey?

Although we have set forth the definition of heresy, by which it can be known, which propositions ought to be called heretical, and which not: still often about many propositions, dissentions arise among learned men in pronouncing sentence about them; some saying that they deservedly ought to be branded with the note of heresy, others on the contrary asserting that they are Catholic, or at least could not be called heretical without injury. And this contention does not happen to the faithful against heretics alone: but Catholic and learned faithful themselves disagree with each other, and often fight against each other about this matter. Therefore, it is necessary to know the true judge in this controversy, who has the authority of pronouncing sentence, so that all disputes and dissentions may be eliminated. But if there would not be any judge, with whose decision all about obliged to comply; but rather everyone would be free to think as he wishes: there will be no one willing to lay down his arms in the battle.[1] Thus it would happen in this way, that in many things pertaining to the faith, we would have nothing certain: but the judgment would always be undecided and doubtful: because there would not be agreement about that judgment among believing and learned men. About this matter, even though in that work which I published, *Against All Heresies*, I think that I spoke abundantly,[2] nevertheless I have decided to repeat here some things from there, and also add some things: because those things which we treat in this work, are directed to the judicial forum. And hence I deemed

---

1 *Hastam abjicere*, taken from Cicero, *pro Lucius Murena*, ln. 45.
2 Introduction, c. 8.

that it necessary to complete this matter more fully, so that we may explain before everything else, the full and most firm power of the judge.

Yet I would firstly like to point out to the reader that he ought not think that I discuss in this chapter about the judge of heretics [i. e., the inquisitor], because about this matter the discussion is very different. For there are many men who judge and can punish heretics, who still are not able to pronounce sentence of heresy (as we will say shortly). Nevertheless, everyone who can judge about heresy, can judge and punish a heretic. For after he, to whom it pertains, has determined that some assertion is heretical, he himself, as another to whom this has been committed, can judge the pertinacious assertor of that proposition a heretic, and punish him as such. Luther says that Sacred Scripture is the only judge of heresy, to which alone every summons or appeal ought to be made: because by it alone (as he says) every dispute that has arisen about the faith, ought to be resolved. That sly man perceived, inspired by the serpentine hiss, how clear is the need for a judge, so that no craftiness of words could be concealed, and hence decided to choose such a judge who could not pronounce sentence. For even though Scripture itself rightly understood (as we said in the preceding chapter) is very powerful for refuting heresy, still since there is a dispute about understanding it, it could not be a judge: especially when it lacks another very clear passage in Scripture by which what is doubted could be elucidated. Furthermore, if the question is about Scripture itself, whether it ought to be called sacred [or canonical], it of itself cannot be the judge: because then it will go on *ad infinitum*. No testimony can be valid in its own cause, according to the saying of Christ Our Savior: "If I bear witness of myself, my witness is not true" (Jn. 5, 31). If you say that one writing can be proved by another to be sacred, then it will be for this reason that one must go on immeasurably without end, or it will be necessary that some dispute would lack a judge: for instance, if from the first writing [*scriptura*], upon whose testimony all depend, so that they may be called sacred, a dispute would occur. Add to these things that there are many things which we are compelled to believe, which nevertheless cannot be proved by the testimony of Scripture: due to the fact that (as Blessed John says[3]) there are many other things which the Lord Jesus did, about which the Gospels make entirely no mention: which nevertheless the Catholic Church holds and teaches with a most firm faith.

But it is necessary that we reply to those things which Luther argues to support his view. For he objects to us that which Christ in John's Gospel says: "Search the scriptures, for... they give testimony of me" (Jn. 5, 39). And certainly, if Luther would consider well, he would understand that he slays himself with his own sword. Because from that passage it is merely gathered that the Scriptures are witnesses and not judges. For He did not say: "Search the scriptures: because they pronounce judgment about me," but He said, "Search the scriptures, for... they give testimony of me." Now the role of witnesses is not to give sentence, but merely testimony. But to the judge it pertains to hear the statements of the witnesses, which when heard, according to their testimony, he will pronounce judgment. Wherefore we admit that the judgment ought to be pronounced according to the testimony of Sacred Scripture, because (as we said in the preceding chapter) it is the most effective witness for the condemnation of heresy: but it is necessary that there be a judge who investigates and examines the sayings of this witness. Because when this has been removed, anyone will distort the sayings of this witness: since anyone would presume to interpret Sacred Scripture in favor of his own whim.

Therefore, this insane opinion of Luther having been rejected, I reckon that the true and undoubted judge in

---

3 Cf. Jn. 20, 30.

the judgment of faith is a general council rightly assembled, as is befitting. Now for the confirmation of this view, many and very impelling reasons are at hand. The first is that such a universal council represents the Church, about which all Catholic men reckon it has such great authority that they would say that its judgments and decrees ought to be received as Divine oracles. For Augustine, in his letter to the priest Casulanus, thinks that "the despisers of ecclesiastical customs ought to be punished as prevaricators of the Divine laws."[4] And (so that I may omit others for the sake of avoiding prolixity) Blessed Irenaeus Martyr, in the third book of his *Against the Heresies*, says: "Since therefore we have such proofs, it is not necessary to seek among others the truth, which is easy to obtain from the Church; since the Apostles, like a rich man [depositing his money] in a bank, lodged in her hands most copiously all things pertaining to the truth: so that every man, whosoever will, can draw from her the water of life.[5] For she is the entrance to life; all others are thieves and robbers. On this account are we indeed bound to avoid them, and on the contrary to gather with the utmost care the [truths] belonging to the Church and to embrace the tradition of the truth. For how stands the case? Suppose there arise a dispute relative to some important question among us,

---

4 *Decretum Gratiani*, dist. 11, c. 7 (PL 187, 60A). "In those things concerning which the divine Scriptures have laid down no definite rule, the custom of the people of God, or the practices instituted by their Fathers, are to be held as the law of the Church. If we choose to fall into a debate about these things, and to denounce one party merely because their custom differs from that of others, the consequence must be an endless contention, in which the utmost care is necessary lest the storm of conflict overcast with clouds the calmness of brotherly love, while strength is spent in mere controversy which cannot adduce on either side any decisive testimonies of truth" (Augustine, letter 36, n. 2 (PL 33, 136)).
5 Cf. Apoc. 22, 17.

should we not have recourse to the most ancient Churches with which the Apostles held constant intercourse, and learn from them what is certain and clear in regard to the present question? For how should it be if the Apostles themselves had not left us writings? Would it not be necessary [in that case] to follow the course of the tradition which they handed down to those to whom they did commit the Churches?"[6] Irenaeus the Martyr's authority is so much superior to all the others, inasmuch as he was nearer to the Apostles. For he was a hearer of Polycarp the Martyr, who was a disciple of John the Evangelist, as the histories of many men recall.

Since from the testimony of these and many other men it is evident that the Church's authority is so great, that all the faithful are bound to obey its judgments and decrees in all things, it follows that this same authority is in the general councils rightly (as is befitting) assembled. For the general councils represent the universal Church: because all those, to whom it belongs to define about faith and morals, are summoned to them: and the opportunity of speaking is granted to all such men. For it does not belong to everyone to teach, and to judge about the law: but to the priests alone. The prophet Malachias testifies to this when speaking thus: "The lips of the priest shall keep knowledge, and they shall seek the law at his mouth: because he is the angel of the Lord of hosts" (2, 7). As in the human body not all the members have the same activity, so (as Paul says) "We being many, are one body in Christ, and everyone members one of another. And having different gifts, according to the grace that is given us, either prophecy, to be used according to the rule of faith; or ministry, in ministering; or he that teacheth, in doctrine" (Rom. 12, 5-7). You see how, according to Paul's opinion, the offices in the Church are diverse, according to the diversity of the members.

---

6 C. 4, n. 1 (PG 7, 855A-B).

But when a member exercises the action belonging to itself, the whole body is said to act: even though not all the members do it. As (for example) a man is said to see, although neither the hands or the feet see, but only the eyes; a man is said to hear, although only the ear hears. The same thing therefore regarding the Mystical Body, which is the Church, ought to be said: such that those things have been ordained by a general council rightly assembled, we may say, were decreed and determined by the whole Church: because all those to whom in the Church it belongs to treat about the faith assembled in it, or at least were invited to come. For in this way when the Apostles and the elders assembled in Jerusalem to settle the important question regarding the cessation of the observances of the Old Law, that assembly of the Apostles and elders was called the whole Church, even though many Christians at the time were elsewhere, who did not assemble there. For after the book of the Acts of the Apostles relates what was decreed about that question, it adds these words which follow: "Then it pleased the apostles and ancients, with the whole church, to choose men of their own company, and to send to Antioch" (15, 22). In which words that assembly gathered together in Jerusalem was clearly enough called the whole Church. Thus, since a council rightly assembled represents the universal Church, it is necessary that we believe that that power, which faithful Catholics believe resides in the universal Church, is in a council rightly assembled.

There is yet another, and not less pressing reason, which moves us to believe that the power of judging about heresies is very firmly in the whole Church: namely, because a council legitimately united, cannot err in any way in faith. It is truly fitting that the faith which rests upon the supreme and infallible truth, also have such a judge, who cannot err. Now a general council legitimately convened cannot be deceived in any way in faith and morals: because it is guided in all things which it defines and judges by the Holy Ghost, Who is always assisting it. For Christ Our Savior also promised to the Church this same thing, saying: "I will ask the Father, and he shall give you another Paraclete, that he may abide with you forever" (Jn. 14, 16). Which words ought not to be referred only to the Apostles, but to the universal Church, to which He promises the presence of the Holy Ghost until the end of the world. For the Apostles were not going to live until the end of the world. Next, in the Gospel of Matthew, He again says: "If two of you shall consent upon earth, concerning anything whatsoever they shall ask, it shall be done to them by my Father who is in heaven. For where there are two or three gathered together in my name, there am I in the midst of them" (18, 19-20). And if Christ promised that he would do this, when two or three were gathered in His name: He will do this much more abundantly, when a whole general council has been legitimately assembled.

Now this power of judging about the faith is not in the provincial councils. Because such councils could err in the faith: as we know regarding many from a most true account of history that they erred. For (so that I may omit others) the [VII] Council of Carthage,[7] in which, with the martyr Blessed Cyprian, eighty bishops assembled, declared that heretics, and those baptized by heretics, ought to be baptized again, when they return to the communion of the Church. Yet that this council erred in this opinion, there is no believing Catholic who doubts. When therefore a provincial council can err, their errors are corrected by the authority of general councils. Hence Augustine says: "That even of the plenary Councils, the earlier are often corrected by those which

---

7 "[H]eretics, who are called adversaries of Christ and Antichrists, when they come to the Church, must be baptized with the one baptism of the Church, that they may be made of adversaries, friends, and of Antichrists, Christians" (Mansi 4, 965D; PL 3, 1077A). This council was held in 256 A.D.

follow them, when, by some actual experiment, things are brought to light."[8] But if anyone were to ask me what authority do the definitions or decrees of the faith have, which the provincial councils issued, concerning which councils it is not evident that they had a legate of the Apostolic See, or were confirmed by the Pope, as are many councils of France and Spain: I reply that if the Church never afterwards contradicted their definitions, they ought to be held by all as the true and undoubted faith. Because even though an explicit confirmation does not appear, they were still confirmed by the tacit consent of the whole Church: since they were never corrected by another council. For if those councils erred in the faith, the Church would never have kept silence: but (as is her custom) it would have immediately counteracted their error by contrary decrees.

And the same thing ought to be said on all points about the universities, or schools for studies: that none of them have authority for judging the faith, such that by their judgment all would be obliged to obey. Because such a school, just like a provincial council, can err in the faith. For it is not the body of men for which God asked that its faith would not fail. And hence it often happens that they err. For, so that I may pass over in silence about others, it is manifest that many schools erred in our century in the case of the marriage which was contracted between Henry VIII of England and Catherine, the widow of the same Henry's deceased brother. For about this marriage some schools, one of which was in Paris, was of the opinion it was completely null, because they contended that the laws given in Leviticus, which seemed to speak against this marriage, are obligatory. Yet the contrary is the case: because after having taken the fit counsel of his brothers (as was befitting) about this matter, and having consulted all the schools of the world, and after many disputations about this matter between learned men, Pope Clement VII,

---

8 *On Baptism, Against the Donatists*, bk. 2, c. 3, n. 4 (PL 43, 129).

who then presided over the universal Church, judged that the aforesaid marriage was valid, and the Mosaic laws, which seem to oppose this marriage, ought to be recounted among the judicial precepts, and consequently abrogated by Christ's death. But even though some proposition ought not to be called heretical, which contradicts the definition of some provincial council, or of some school, still it ought to be called suspect of heresy, and its teaching and preaching could rightly be interdicted by those to whom this power belongs: unless perhaps some other school supports it, or it has some truly Catholic Doctor who taught it. For in that case we say that it also ought not to be called suspect of heresy, merely because such or such a school deemed it to be heretical: especially if the Doctor, who defends it, has adduced not light reasons for its assertion.

After general councils, the Sovereign Pontiff holds the highest place in the definitions of the faith: because he represents the whole Church, in that he is the head of the whole body. For so Augustine says when commenting on John's Gospel: "Peter, in receiving the keys, represented the holy Church."[9] These words of Augustine are also found in the chapter, *Quodcumque*.[10] And for this reason a prelate, who takes care of some church, is called a church, as it appears in the chapter, *Scire debes*,[11] and it is found more explicitly

---

9 *Tractates on the Gospel of John*, tract. 50, n. 12 (PL 35, 1762). Cf. Mt. 16, 19.

10 *Decretum Gratiani*, pt. 2, c. 24, q. 1, c. 6 (PL 187, 1267A-B).

11 *Ibid.*, pt. 2, causa 7, q. 1, c. 7 (PL 187, 746B). "Whence you ought to know that the bishop is in the Church, and the Church in the bishop; and if anyone be not with the bishop, that he is not in the Church, and that those flatter themselves in vain who creep in, not having peace with God's priests, and think that they communicate secretly with some; while the Church, which is Catholic and one, is not cut nor divided" (St. Cyprian, letter 68 (to Florentius Pupianus), n. 8 (PL 4, 405B)).

in the Gospel, in that place, where he who does not want to hear two admonitions of his brother, is commanded to be made known to the Church.[12] For a prelate is called in that passage "the Church," and the things which are appropriated to him, as to a judge, are reckoned to have been appropriated to the Church.

I reckon it now ought to be done the same way, so that if he detects some doubt about the faith: the Roman Pontiff would be asked about it, and (because he holds the place of Blessed Peter, and governs the whole Church) those things he shall have replied, we believe to be the faith of the whole Church. For he who has been placed over all, could judge the cases of all, especially those which concern the whole multitude, such is a matter pertaining to the faith. There are very many testimonies of holy men about this matter. [Pseudo-]Blessed Jerome in his letter to Pope Damasus says: "This, most blessed Pope, is the faith that we have been taught in the Catholic Church. If anything therein has been incorrectly or carelessly expressed, we beg that it may be set aright by you who hold the faith and See of Peter. If however this, our profession, be approved by the judgment of your apostleship, whoever may blame me, will prove that he himself is ignorant, or malicious, or even not a Catholic but a heretic."[13] These words are found in the chapter, *Haec est fides*.[14] Pope Innocent I, a man renown for holiness as well as sanctity, in his letter to the [II] Council of Milevum says: "Whenever a question of faith is in dispute, I think, that all our brethren and fellow bishops ought to refer the matter to none other than Peter, as being the source of their name and office, as Your Charity has now referred [to ascertain] what may be for the

---

12 Cf. Mt. 18, 17.
13 Pelagius, *Profession of Faith to Pope Innocent* [*Libellus fidei ad Innocentum papam*], c. 14 (PL 45, 1718).
14 *Decretum Gratiani, causa* 24, q. 1, c. 14 (PL 187, 1269B).

common weal of all the churches throughout the world."[15] Which words are also cited by Gratian in the Decretals, in the same *causa* and question recently given above.[16]

[Pseudo-] Pope Julius I, in his letter against the Oriental [bishops] in support of Athanasius, speaks thus: "I have written to you and to all who in Antioch, against the Apostolic and canonical rule, have gathered together without having consulted us, to rebuke you; firstly concerning the injuries of the letters, next why you have summoned Athanasius and his supporters to your council, when the canons prescribe that nothing ought to be decided without the Roman Pontiff, to whom these and the more important matters of the churches both by the Lord Himself, and by all the Fathers of the general councils, by special privilege (as it is said) were wholly delivered."[17] Finally Pope Innocent III says: "He who notes that Peter replied to the Lord when he asked who the disciples said He was, "Thou art Christ, the Son of the living God" (Mt. 16, 16), and the Lord prayed for him, that his faith would not fail."[18]

By these testimonies which we have cited it is clearly proved that the authority of judging about matters of the faith does not belong to any lower bishop. And reason persuades that it ought to be so done as it has been done, because "What touches all (as the rule of law decrees), must be approved by all."[19] Now there is nothing which pertains to all more than the faith: because for this reason the true faith is called Catholic, meaning universal: because all Christians are obliged to embrace it. For there is one faith of the

---

15 Letter 182, n. 2 (PL 33, 784); Dz. 218.
16 *Decretum Gratiani, causa* 24, q. 1, c. 12 (*Quoties fidei*) (PL 187, 1269A).
17 Letter 2 (PL 8, 983C).
18 *Decretals of Gregory IX*, bk. 3, tit. 42 (*De baptismo et ejus effectu*), c. 3.
19 *Liber Sextus*, bk. 5, tit. 12, rule. 29.

Book 1, Chapter 5

whole Church: as Paul says: "One faith, one baptism" (Eph. 4, 5). Hence since a dispute, in which the faith is treated, is that sort of matter which concerns the universal Church, it is inferred that the judgment, which by lawful right can end disputes arising from the faith, be approved by all, or by him who governs all, who (as we said) can speak for all, and whose pronouncement rightly ought to be reckoned to have been pronounced by all. Thus, no inferior bishop, or the whole college, which he governs, can pronounce judgment in a dispute concerning the faith: since this dispute is of such kind that it pertains to the whole Church. For what shall have been at one time determined to belong to the faith, all will be obliged to believe it under threat of hell.

But if someone were to object to us that which is said in chapter, *Ad abolendam*,[20] namely, that all whom the Roman Church, or bishops in their churches, shall have declared to be heretics are excommunicated, from which words it perhaps might seem to someone that authority was given to bishops for judging about heresy, [then I reply that] it is not so. The authority is indeed given of judging in regard to a person who has fallen into clear and manifest heresy, that he can declare him a heretic, if he does not wish to recant. Yet by those words, the power of judging a dispute that has arisen about the faith was nowise granted, especially when the matter is doubtful. Because this power (as was evident from the aforesaid testimonies) was reserved to the Apostolic See. And a Gloss on the chapter, *Quotiens*, on the words, *Nisi ad Petrum*,[21] supports this opinion of ours. For it speaks

---

20 *Decretals of Gregory IX*, bk. 5, tit. 7 (*De haereticis*), c. 9.
21 "Whenever a question of faith is in dispute, I think, that all our brethren and fellow bishops ought to refer the matter to none other than Peter, as being the source of their name and honor, against whose authority neither Jerome nor Augustine nor any of the holy Doctors defended their opinion" (*Decretum Gratiani*, pt. 2, *causa* 24, q. 1, c. 12 (PL 187, 1269A)).

thus: "This seems to be against the chapter *Ad abolendam*.[22] For it is implied there that those whom bishops have said should be avoided, should be avoided as heretics." And in reply it says, "The response is that that citation should be understood of when they are talking about something that it is certain is heresy; but not where there is a doubt." From which words it is established clearly enough that the power of determining and deciding in a doubtful case regarding the matter of the faith is not within the authority of a bishop lower than the Roman Pontiff.

Wherefore let the inquisitors of heretics beware not to heedlessly arrogate this power to themselves: let them understand that they are inquisitors, not judges. And if they are judges, let them recognize that they are judges of heretics, not of heresies. Assuredly it is firstly incumbent upon them that, having applied all diligence, they consult learned men about that matter, not one or two only, but many. If, when these things have been correctly fulfilled, it has been established regarding the asserted proposition that it is heretical, they themselves are judges, who can proceed against its assertion: and if he disdains to recant, they have power according to the Ecclesiastical regulations to punish him. But if it is not established about the asserted proposition, whether it deserves to called heretical or not, because there is no agreement about the matter among learned and believing men, some claiming it to be heretical, while others defend it as Catholic, then the inquisitors would do wrongly, if they were to pronounce sentence about that proposition: because in that case the matter ought to be referred to the judgment of the Apostolic See, to which it belongs to judge important cases, especially articles of faith.

Regarding this matter Pope Pelagius [II] commanded as follows: "But if," he says, "questions should arise in any province, and among the bishops themselves of the

---

22 *Decretals of Gregory IX*, bk. 5, tit. 7 (*De haereticis*), c. 9.

province their views begin to vary, and there is no agreement between the disagreeing bishops themselves, they ought to be referred to a higher See: and if there in fact they are not easily and justly settled, let them be judged where a synod has regularly assembled, both canonically and justly. But let the greater and more difficult questions (as the holy synod has decreed, and the blessed custom has required) always be referred to the Apostolic See."[23] And the divine Law given through Moses commanded this same thing, speaking thus: "If thou perceive that there be among you a hard and doubtful matter in judgment between blood and blood, cause and cause, leprosy and leprosy: and thou see that the words of the judges within thy gates do vary: arise, and go up to the place, which the Lord thy God shall choose. And thou shalt come to the priests of the Levitical race, and to the judge, that shall be at that time: and thou shalt ask of them, and they shall shew thee the truth of the judgment. And thou shalt do whatsoever they shall say, that preside in the place, which the Lord shall choose, and what they shall teach thee, according to his law; and thou shalt follow their sentence: neither shalt thou decline to the right hand nor to the left hand" (Deut. 17, 8-11). Just as then in the Mosaic Law, a doubtful judgment of leprosy devolved upon the priest and judge, who then was in charge: so now in the Evangelical Law, a doubtful judgment about the faith ought to be decided by the Sovereign Pontiff alone.

But God would not have provided enough for the Church, if He had not left her a judge who would settle the disputes about the faith that arose: and whom she would consult in doubtful matters. Now whether the Pope could err in the definitions of the faith or not, is a controverted matter among theologians, about which matter I will state what I think in the next chapter in a few words. Yet I say and most firmly hold this, that although the Pope could err in the faith, and

---

23 *Decretum Gratiani*, pt. 1, dist. 17, c. 5 (PL 187, 95B-C).

truly has erred: still all ought to embrace his decision, until the Church were to condemn it as erroneous: or it were to be decided through clear testimonies of Sacred Scripture concerning his error. Now the error is not deputed as a sin to those erring and obeying the decision of the Pope in this way: because obedience excuses them. For the Lord said: "And thou shalt do whatsoever they shall say, that preside in the place, which the Lord shall choose, and what they shall teach thee, according to his law; and thou shalt follow their sentence." Yet it ought to be pointed out to the reader that although bishops or inquisitors of heretics could not judge or decide about heresy, especially when the matter is doubtful: they still can, either on account of the doubt alone, which is had about a particular proposition, or for the sake of avoiding scandal, which could arise from its teaching or preaching, or for some other reason, forbid teachers, and preachers, and all others, not to dare teach or publicly preach it in any way. But if someone would act against a prohibition of this kind, he could rightly be punished by them: yet not as heretics, but as disobedient and rebellious. Because since such a proposition is doubtful, and it is not yet evident that it is heretical, its teacher or preacher, or any other assertor of that proposition, although it was forbidden by the inquisitors to assert it, could not be justly punished as a heretic. For someone cannot be punished as a heretic if it is not established that he has asserted a heretical proposition, or favored it in any way. For no one ought to be deemed a heretic merely from the fact that he acted or spoke contrary to the prohibition of the inquisitors. Still this sort of man could deservedly be punished on account of such contempt of the prohibition: and in fact, gravely, after having firstly weighed the gravity of his rebellion.

Chapter VI

Whether the Pope can delegate to someone the power of judging about the faith, such that those things which would be defined by a legate of the Pope about the faith, ought to be necessarily held by all as the true faith?

About those things which were explained in the immediately preceding chapter, a certain doubt of no little importance could arise, to which I decided to reply, so that I may leave this matter, as is befitting, fully resolved. For I said in the preceding chapter, the pow--er of defining about the faith rightfully belongs to the Sovereign Pontiff, and no one is allowed to contradict those things which have been defined by the Sovereign Pontiff about the faith. It can rightly be doubted, whether the Pope could delegate this power of defining to someone else, such that all the faithful would be obliged by the same rule to accept those definitions of the faith, which the legate of the Apostolic See gave, to whom the treatment of the faith was entrusted, as if they were given by the Supreme Pontiff himself, and he who would pertinaciously contradict this sort of legate, would thence be reckoned a heretic, as though he had opposed the definitions and decrees about the faith given by the Sovereign Pontiff? And that the Pope is able to transfer this power of defining to anyone else, could be argued from the fact that there are many other things which the Pope does by delegates, to whom he gives the power of judging, and those things which were decreed by them have the same force, and the same firmness as if they had proceeded from the mouth of the Pope himself. For he settles disputes through the auditors of the Rota. The dispensation of vows, and many other things of the same sort, the Pope commits to the one whom they call the Sacred Penitentiary, so that many persons are pardoned by him. All which concessions and indulgences, even though they came forth from the supreme Penitentiary, are still deemed to have been given by the Pope: and they have as much force and power before all men, as if the Pope had given them by his own mouth. Because what we do through others, we seem to do by ourselves. Therefore, just as all these things, which are of very great importance, the Pope commits to others to be carried out, it seems, that also in a similar way some matter of the faith could be transferred to someone else, so that it might be decided by him.

Furthermore, from a long and ancient custom of the Church the practice has been kept that the Pope has often delegated to others this power of defining. For when in some province disputes about the faith arise, the Pope was accustomed to send a legate, and command that matter to someone of the same province, who having fully known and discussed (as it fitting) the matter, would give a decision, to which all are obliged to obey. In all general, and rightly assembled councils, which the Pope did not attend, legates of the Apostolic See were always present, who in the name of the Pope, would give the definitions of the faith: the judgment of whom was pronounced as though by the voice of the Sovereign Pontiff himself, and was always accepted by all. For in the Council of Nicea, which is reckoned to be the first and most famous of all the councils, the legates of the Apostolic See were Bishop Hosius of Cordoba, and Victor and Vincentius, Roman priests. In the First Council of Ephesus, the legate of the Sovereign Pontiff was Saint Cyril, Bishop of Alexandria. Aimarius[1] in the *Liber de Synodis*, says that a certain Bishop Arcadius from Italy was also in the same council at the same time as Cyril as the legate of the Pope:

---

1 Aimarius Rivalius, jurist and humanist, lived in the reigns of Louis XI and Charles VIII of France and was a professor of law at the University of Grenoble. He is believed to be one of the first Frenchmen who dealt with the history of Roman law.

but this is not evident from the Acts of the same council.[2] In the Council of Chalcedon the legates of Pope Leo I were Bishop Julianus [of Cos] and the priest Renatus [Cardinal of Saint Clement], and after them others were sent, namely, Bishop Paschasinus of Lilybaeum, Bishop Lucentius of Asculum, and the Roman priest Boniface: as is evident from the Acts of the same council. And in all the others, which afterwards, in the absence of the Pope, were rightly assembled, this was observed by perpetual and inviolable custom, namely, that legates of the Pope would be present, who in his name, marked out the most certain rule of faith. From all which things it seems that the Pope delegated to his legates this power of defining the faith.

But if we carefully examine the matter (as ought to be done), all these things, which we have cited, certainly insufficiently support the aforesaid opinion, and there are much stronger and more convincing things which can be brought forth in favor of the contrary opinion. Wherefore I very willingly differ from this opinion, very firmly holding that the Pope cannot delegate to anyone else such power of defining in a matter of the faith, such as he has: such that the things defined by him to whom this power was delegated, are made firm with as great strength, as if they were pronounced by the mouth of the Sovereign Pontiff himself. And so that I may make this matter clearer, it firstly needs to be discussed

---

2   It seems that they were actually present. "The Pope was pleased that the whole East should be united to condemn the new heresy. He sent two bishops, Arcadius and Projectus, to represent himself and his Roman council, and the Roman priest, Philip, as his personal representative. Philip, therefore, takes the first place, though, not being a bishop, he could not preside. It was probably a matter of course that the Patriarch of Alexandria should be president. The legates were directed not to take part in the discussions, but to give judgment on them" ("Council of Ephesus," *Catholic Encyclopedia*, vol. 5, p. 492). Cf. Mansi 4, 555C.

whence the Pope has this privilege: that he would be able to decide in a dispute about the faith, and to pronounce a definitive judgment in doubts that have arisen about the faith, whose decision all are obliged to obey under threat of hell? And whence is it that no other particular person, besides the Pope, but only the universal Church, or a general council fully representing it, enjoys this privilege to such an extent that it can prescribe the rule of the Catholic faith to all?

The certain and indubitable cause of such an excellent prerogative is the multiplex dignity of the Sovereign Pontiff. The first dignity of the Sovereign Pontiff is in fact, that God made him the pastor of the whole flock, when saying: "Feed my sheep" (Jn. 21, 17). For all who, having received Baptism have professed the Christian faith, are Christ's sheep: the care of all of whom God committed to Peter and his successors, and He commanded him, that he feed them all. And all the sheep were not to be fed with bodily food by him who, having left all things for Christ, had been made so poor that he also had not enough similar food for himself: much less for so many of all the rest. Thus, with spiritual food, Peter was ordered to feed the Lord's sheep: namely, with the doctrine of God's word. Therefore Peter, because he is the universal pastor, ought to teach all Christians the Catholic faith, and all Christians, if they doubt anything about the faith, and want to understand, ought to learn from Peter, and not from another, lest they err; because no other is the pastor of all the Lord's sheep.

The second dignity of Peter is the certitude and infallibility of his doctrine: such that when teaching the sheep committed to him, he cannot err, and this is not from himself, but from the gift of God, Who always assists him by reason of his dignity, lest he err in the definitions of the faith. "I have prayed for thee," the Lord said to Peter, "that thy faith fail not" (Lk. 22, 32). And because this certitude and infallibility of the faith, not by reason of Peter himself, but on account of the sheep committed to him, is granted to Peter, he immediately adds, "and thou, being once converted, confirm thy brethren." As though He had said more clearly, "Wherefore I have prayed for you, that your faith would not fail: because you ought to confirm all the rest in the faith. Therefore, so that you may fully exercise this function committed to you, it is necessary that you always be firm in the faith. For otherwise if Peter were to err when defining, it would be necessary that the sheep, which ought to follow him as their shepherd, when he errs, they would all err: or at least they would receive not a small occasion of erring. This is the privilege of the Apostolic See, granted on account of the universal Church, which he accepted to govern, so that when he teaches that same Church the faith, he cannot err. I indeed do not deny that the Pope can err in the faith, and can be a heretic: because it is related concerning some that they erred in the faith, yet this happened to them when they were speaking, or writing, or perhaps teaching, as individual and private persons. Nevertheless, if they spoke, or taught, or wrote as public persons, and exercising the office of prelature, then I believe that God would not permit them to err: lest the Church, His spouse, which He procured to be beautiful for Himself, they would spoil by their error. No one doubts that a very different consideration ought to be had, regarding the Sovereign Pontiff: to the extent that he is a private person, and to the extent that he is a public person. When he speaks, or writes something, as a private person, he does not want all to accept it, or believe that they are obliged. But whenever he speaks, or writes, as a public person, and to the extent that he is the Sovereign Pontiff, he intends to oblige all to those things. For the Sovereign Pontiffs wrote many things, which they did not write with that purpose, namely, that they would be held as decrees and definitions. For (so that I may pass over in silence other things) the response of Innocent IV is widely known, to a man very skilled in Canon Law, who, when he asked whether those things which he had written in Canon Law, he wanted to be held by all as law and firmly decreed, he answered that he nowise wanted it: but left free judgment to each person, so that anyone might think as he preferred. For he said that he had written not as the Sovereign Pontiff, but as any one of the private theologian.[3] Therefore the Pope can, as I think, have an opinion contrary to the Catholic faith: yet God will never permit that what he thinks wrongly, as Pope, he would command to be believed by the whole Church, just as He did not permit Balaam to curse Israel.[4]

---

3 "Our great predecessor, Innocent IV, wrote his Commentaries on the books of the Decretals, when he was the Supreme Pontiff: *while residing in Lyon, after the Council was celebrated there, composed an apparatus on the Decretals*: as Tommaso Diplovataccio testifies in his biography of the same before mentioned Innocent never arrogated this to himself, namely, that whatever he wrote in that work, would be considered definitive regarding the matter; but he readily allowed that his opinion, which he had proposed as a private theologian, to be opposed by other theologian: as it appears from that same biography which we cited; and much more from that later canonists took very broad license in this matter, whilst they often abandoned opinions inserted by Innocent in their commentaries, and they did not hesitate to go to all others" (Pope Benedict XIV, *De Synodo dioecesana libri tredecim* (Rome, Joannes Generossus Salomoni, 1755), p. xvi). Cf. Tommaso Diplovataccio, *De claris juris consultis* in *Studia Gratiana: post octava Decreti saeculari* (Bologna, Institutum Juridicum Universitatis Studiorum Bononiensis, 1953), vol. 10, p. 129. "Has not Our Lord made this constitution, and has he now here expressed his intention, therefore what further do you wish? Reply. He does not pronounce as Pope, but as a theologian, and often we have heard from him that he was not intending that his glosses would make a law" (Hostiensis on *Liber sextus*, bk. 5, tit. 11, c. 2 (*Solet*) in *In Sextum Decretalium librum Commentaria* (Venice, Apud Juntas, 1581), vol. 6, fol. 33vb.

4 Cf. Num. 24.

Whether the Pope can delegate to someone the power of judging

Having prefaced and carefully considered all these things, it is easy to conclude that the Pope cannot delegate this power of defining in matters of faith to anyone else, because he cannot transfer the certainty and infallibility, which he has regarding the definitions to be given, to anyone else. No one ever (as far as I know) was so foolish to this extent, that he would have said that the Pope's legates, or his delegates, could not err. For they could err, since they were not given such a great privilege by God, that they would be infallible in their definitions. For God did not ask for Peter's legates or delegates, that their faith would not fail, as He asked for Peter himself. Now this infallibility is extremely necessary for him who ought to judge about the faith: so that he can oblige all the faithful to accept his definition. Otherwise, it would be necessary that the Church's faith is sometimes not certain, if it were to rest upon an uncertain and fallible rule. For this reason, the power of giving decisions about the faith was never delegated to provincial councils, because they can err. The authority of those provincial councils is extended only to these limits, namely, that therein dissensions be ended, grievances be heard, morals be corrected: yet not that therein something would be decided about the faith. For the Council of Nicea permitted only this to them.

Furthermore, those things which belong to some particular Order, or are connected to a state, and depending upon it, no one can delegate to another order outside of it. To confect the Eucharist, to absolve penitent sinners of sins, no one, even if he be the Pope, can delegate to someone who is not a priest: because these things are annexed to priestly Orders, and necessarily require priestly Orders, in him who ought to perform one of these things. In the same way the Pope cannot delegate to someone who is not a bishop, that he perform ordinations, that is, that he confer the Sacrament of Orders to someone, because, in order that someone can confer the Sacrament of Orders, he necessarily ought to be a bishop. From which things we clearly conclude that the Pope could not delegate the power of defining about the faith to someone else, such that all the faithful would be held to obey his definition, because (as we said) the certitude and infallibility, which are required for such supreme power, were annexed to the papal dignity, and are by no means separable from it: because (as we said) God prayed for this, and for nothing else, that his faith would not fail.

Again, if the Pope could transfer the power of defining about the faith to another, in the same way he could also delegate the canonization of the Saints to someone: because the canonization of the Saints (as Blessed Thomas teaches[5]) is a matter in a certain way pertaining to the faith. The words which the Sovereign Pontiff says in the canonization of some Saint somewhat support this opinion of Blessed Thomas, which were put in the book of the sacred ceremonies of the Church, and are those which follow: "For the honor of the Blessed Trinity, the exaltation of the Catholic faith and the increase of the Christian life, by the authority of Our Lord Jesus Christ, and of the Holy Apostles Peter and Paul, and our own, after due deliberation and frequent prayer for Divine assistance, and having sought the counsel of many of our brother bishops, we declare and define [name] of good memory to be a Saint and we enroll him among the Saints." The Pope says these words when he canonizes someone. In which words one ought to notice that he says that such a canonization is for "the exaltation of the Catholic faith." But if this opinion of Blessed Thomas displeases someone, and he tries to completely deny that the canonization of the Saints pertains to the faith, so much the more does he strengthen our argument, the more he makes the canonization itself of

---

5 "Honor we show the Saints is a certain profession of faith by which we believe in their glory, and it is to be piously believed that even in this the judgment of the Church is not able to err" (*Quodlibetal Questions* IX, q. 8).

less weight than the faith itself. For if that which is greater, namely, the definition of the faith, the Pope can delegate to another; all the more could he delegate that which is less, namely, the canonization of the Saints. Now no one having a sane mind would assent to this, since it is condemned by the perpetual custom of the Church. For even though the Pope commits many preparatory and required things for the canonization to be carried out by others: such as the investigation of the life, the examination of witnesses: still the Sovereign Pontiff himself alone pronounces the judgment, declaring someone to be a Saint, and as such enrolls him in the list of the Saints. And never has it been heard from the very first ages of the Church until the present time that the Pope delegated to his legate the canonization of some Saint.

Finally, what makes the opinion most certain and indubitable to me is the perpetual and inviolate custom of the Church, which never held as certain and undoubted before the definition of the Apostolic See, those things of the faith which had been decided by legates of the same See. And the Sovereign Pontiffs did not ever want those things to be held as certain by the Church, which the very course and progression of past events teaches very clearly. For many disputes about the faith have arisen in various parts of the world, for the dispelling of which the Sovereign Pontiffs sent legates, who, after they put an end to the disputes by the judgments, the sentences of the legates themselves were confirmed by the sentences of the Sovereign Pontiffs, or they were again judged by the Pontiffs themselves. Which thing would not have happened, except that the Sovereign Pontiffs had reckoned that their sentence was necessary. There are so many examples of this thing among the various nations, that it would be wearisome to relate them: nevertheless, lest it seem that testimony is lacking, and consequently I would leave the matter suspect, I will cite one or two examples.

Book 1, Chapter 6

When Berengarius, a deacon of the church of Angers, was spreading his heresy against the wonderful Sacrament of the Eucharist throughout France, Hildebrand,[6] Cardinal of the Holy Roman Church, legate of Victor II who then ruled the universal Church, condemned his heresy. Nevertheless Pope Nicholas II, who succeeded Victor in the Pontificate, having convened a council of one hundred and thirteen bishops in Rome, afterwards condemned the heresy. Which sentence did not need to be given by the Pontiff, if the definition of the legate Hildebrand could do enough for all [the faithful]. After Berengarius, some centuries having elapsed, John Wycliffe arose in England, who taught very many wicked and pestiferous teachings, by word and books published. Knowledge of this case was given by the Archbishop of Canterbury to the legate of the Apostolic See, who having examined the matter fully (as should be done) publicly condemned John Wycliffe himself, and all his heresies. After John Wycliff, some few years having elapsed, John Hus followed after in Bohemia, who pertinaciously defended all the heresies of John Wycliffe. Which having been heard by the Sovereign Pontiff, who, after having diligently examined everything, condemned all his heresies. But afterwards the Sovereign Pontiff and at length the Council of Constance condemned the heresies of both Johns. All of which things are established from the decree of the eighth session of the same council.

Some time ago when a certain Pedro [Martinez] of Osma[7] was teaching some new things in Spain, which seemed heretical by the judgment of many: Sixtus IV, who then ruled the universal Church, entrusted with full powers the investigation of this case to His Grace Alfonso Carillo, Archbish-

---

6 I. e., Pope St. Gregory VII (ca. 1015-1085) was born Hildebrand of Sovana (Italian: *Ildebrando di Soana*).

7 Pedro Martinez de Osma (ca. 1427-1480 was a Spanish theologian and philosopher, known for his views on indulgences, which he retracted at the end of his life. He was born in Osma.

Whether the Pope can delegate to someone the power of judging

op of Toledo, and Primate of the Spains. He, after having fully examined the matter with the council of many learned men, judged many assertions of that Pedro of Osma to be erroneous and heretical. Yet after this judgment, the same matter was referred to the same Sixtus, who, after having fully considered everything (as was befitting), confirmed the sentence of the aforesaid archbishop by a public Bull: which confirmation of sentence we chose to insert in that work which we published, *Against All Heresies*, so that which was hiding in darkness might to known to all.[8]

If those things, which by the above-mentioned, and other legates of this kind of the Apostolic See, were defined about the faith, and were confirmed with firm strength, such that they ought to have been held by all the faithful as being the certain and undoubted faith, it was not necessary that the Pope to have added in addition his sentence, because it would have been to do something already done. But because those things which were decided by the Apostolic delegates were about the faith, they lacked full strength, because it was always believed by all that they could err in the faith: wherefore this was always observed, that after the decision of the legates the Pope would add a distinct sentence, which, proceeding from his mouth, would teach all what ought to be held about the faith. Hence experience itself teaches very clearly, that the Sovereign Pontiffs themselves never thought those things, which had been decided by their legates about the faith, ought to be held as certain and undoubted before the definitions of the Pontiffs themselves.

Perhaps here someone will object to me, speaking thus: "If those things, which are decided by the legates of the Apostolic See about the faith, are not necessarily to be held as certain, why does the Pope send them, since their legation is superfluous and useless?" I reply that they are

---

8 *Against All Heresies* (Camillus, NY: Dolorosa Press, 2021), s. v., "Confession," pp. 323-325.

not sent in vain: because they could investigate and examine the matter, so that afterwards they may report to the Sovereign Pontiff: just as in the canonization of the Saints. Next, even though they cannot pronounce a certain and indubitable sentence about the faith, they still can forbid the assertion of some proposition due to an urgent reason (as we said in the preceding chapter about the inquisitors). He who would contradict their decision will be rightly punished, yet not as a heretic before the definition of the Pope, if the matter is doubtful, especially if he shows that he waits for it: but as rebellious and disobedient. This ought to be observed not only in decisions given privately by the legates of the Apostolic See, but also in the definitions of the councils, in which the legates of the Apostolic See were present. For after a decision has been given about the faith by the same legates with the whole council, the Church always sought the judgment of the Sovereign Pontiff: and not before the confirmation of the Sovereign Pontiff himself has she ever wanted to hold as certain and firm, what had been decided by the legates of the same See.

Concerning which matter I would like to bring forth some testimonies, from which it can be very fully established that what we say is true.[9]

In the Council of Chalcedon the legates of Leo, the then-Sovereign Pontiff, attended: Bishop Paschasinus of Lilybaeum, Bishop Lucentius of Asculum, and the Roman priest Boniface; as it evident from the Acts of the same council, in the first[10] and last session,[11] and from the [eighty-

---

9 The Pseudo-Letter from the Council of Nicea addressed to Pope Sylvester I, and the Pseudo-Rescript of Pope Sylvester to the Nicene Synod cited in the text have been omitted here as they are spurious and somewhat unintelligible.
10 Mansi 6, 566B.
11 Mansi 7, 400E-401A.

ninth[12]] and [ninetieth[13]] letters sent to the Emperor Marcian from Pope Leo: and from the letter of the same Pope Leo addressed to the whole Council in Chalcedon, which is his [ninety-third] letter.[14] Yet the things which were defined in that council were not considered ratified and firm from the council itself, until they were confirmed by the Sovereign Pontiff. On account of which the Fathers assembled in the council wrote to Leo, the Sovereign Pontiff, requesting that he would deign to confirm the decrees made there. In which letter, after they made an account of those things which were defined by them in the council, they adjoin these words which follow: "Accordingly vouchsafe most holy and blessed Father to accept as your own wish, and as conducing to good government, the things which we have resolved upon for the removal of all confusion and the confirmation of Church order. For your holiness' delegates, the most pious Bishops Paschasinus and Lucentius, and with them the very reverend priest Boniface, attempted vehemently to resist these decisions, from a strong desire that this good work also should start from your foresight, in order that the establishment of good order as well as of the Faith should be put to your account. For we duly regarding our most devout and Christ loving emperors, who delight therein, and the illustrious senate and, so to say, the whole imperial city, considered it opportune to use the meeting of this ecumenical Synod for the ratification of your honor, and confidently corroborated this decision as if it were initiated by you with your customary fostering zeal, knowing that every success of the children rebounds to the parent's glory."[15] These words are found at the end of the third session of the same council.

---

12 PL 54, 930B.
13 PL 54, 932A.
14 PL 54, 937B.
15 Letter 98, c. 4 (PL 54, 957B-959A).

Book 1, Chapter 6

Now to this petition the same Blessed Leo replies, by a letter addressed to the whole council, confirming the decrees of the same council, and speaking thus: "I do not doubt that all your brotherhood knows that I embraced wholeheartedly the decrees of the holy council that was held in the city of Chalcedon to confirm the faith, since there was no reason for me, who lamented that the unity of the Catholic faith had been disrupted by heretics, not to rejoice exultantly at its restoration to integrity. This you have ascertained not only from the fact of the achievement of most blessed unanimity but also from the letter which after the return of my representatives I sent to the bishop of the city of Constantinople—if he had been willing to show you the reply of the Apostolic See.[16] Therefore, lest through malign interpretation it might appear uncertain whether I approve what was decreed about the faith at the Council of Chalcedon through your unanimity, I have sent this letter to all our brethren and fellow bishops who attended the aforesaid council—[a letter] which the most glorious and clement prince, as I have requested, will out of love for the Catholic faith deign to bring to your notice, so that both the whole brotherhood and the hearts of all the faithful may know that I, not only through the brethren who represented me but also through approving the conciliar proceedings, have joined my own judgment to yours, in the case evidently of the faith alone (which needs to be constantly repeated) for the sake of which it was decided by decree of the Christian emperors and the consent of the Apostolic See to summon a general council, so that through the condemnation of the heretics who refused to be corrected, no doubt at all should remain about the true Incarnation of Our Lord Jesus Christ. Therefore, if anyone ever dares to support the faithlessness of Nestorius or defend the impious teaching of Eutyches and Dioscorus, let him be cut off from

---

16 Letter 106 (to Anatolius, Bishop of Constantinople; PL 54, 1001A-1009B).

Whether the Pope can delegate to someone the power of judging

Catholic communion, and let him have no share in that body whose reality he denies, most beloved brethren."[17] And in letter [one hundred fifteen] he writes to Emperor Marcian, asking that he would command that this confirmation of his of the Council of Chalcedon to be published: so that he might make known to all those things pleased the Apostolic See, which had been defined about the faith in the Council of Chalcedon.[18]

Furthermore, in the sixth general council, which is the third which was held in Constantinople, one of the most important general councils of the first order which the Catholic Church accepts, in which the legates of Agatho, the then Sovereign Pontiff, were the priests Theodore and George, and the deacon John. Now those things which were defined in that council, were confirmed by Pope Leo [II], who succeeded the deceased Agatho near the end of the council. The letter[19] of Blessed Leo [II] renders a very clear and complete testimony of which affair, sent to Emperor [Constantine IV], which begins thus: "To the King of Kings, under whose rule are all the kingdoms of the world, the little..." Which letter I do not wish to cite in its entirety: lest I burden the reader with its great length. I will only cite some part of it, by which the Sixth Council is confirmed by him, with these words: "Since the holy universal and great Sixth Synod has followed in everything the Apostolic doctrine of the most eminent Fathers, and since it preached the same definition of the correct faith, which the Apostolic See of the Holy Apostle Peter (whose

---

17 Letter 114 (PL 54, 1027B-1029B).
18 "But because by all means your piety and most religious will must be obeyed, the Synodical Constitutions which pleased me about confirming the Catholic faith and condemning heretics, I have willingly approved; which, so that it may come to the knowledge of all the bishops and churches, it will be deemed worthy for Your Clemency to command" (PL 54, 1035A).
19 Dated May 7, 683 A.D.

ministry we perform although unequal) received with veneration, therefore we, and through our exercise of our office of this venerable Apostolic See, give full consent to the things contained in the definition of faith: as upon a solid rock, which is Christ, having acquired firmness from the Lord Himself. Wherefore as we have received, and firmly preach the five holy General Councils: Nicea, [I] Constantinople, I Ephesus, Chalcedon, and [II] Constantinople, which also the whole Church of Christ approves and follows: and so we receive with equal respect and judgment, as following and interpreting them, that sixth holy Council recently celebrated in the royal city with the pious care of Your Serenity, and we rightly deign to number this council with the others, as we perceive that it was gathered as with one and the same grace of God: and the bishops of Christ's Church who faithfully gathered in it, we reckon ought to be equally numbered among the holy Fathers and Doctors of the Church."[20]

Therefore, by these very manifest testimonies, it is very clearly proved that those things which had been decreed by the legates of the Apostolic See, with the rest of the council of bishops about the faith, were not received by all the faithful as certain and indubitable, before the Pope had given his decision. From all these we clearly gather that the Pope cannot transfer to another the kind power of defining about the faith, which he has, such that by the legate's own definition, or judgment, he can oblige all Christians to believe something, as the Pope can.

But here not a small doubt occurs to me, to which I have decided to reply: lest a scruple remains, which could harm the conscience of someone. For on account of these things, which we said concerning the confirmations of the councils, sought from and granted by the Sovereign Pontiffs, someone could rightly doubt whether councils assembled from the

---

[20] PL 96, 405B-D; Mansi 11, 730D-731A. This letter is spurious according to Baronius (cf. PL 96, 399D in footnote a).

whole world by the authority of the Pope, in which the Pope was not present, but only his legates, could err in the definition of the faith? If it is said that such councils could err, the consequence is that it would also be granted that such councils (without the presence of the Pope) ought not to be called general [or ecumenical], or that general councils assembled without the authority of the Pope could err: both of which are absurd. For that general councils, gathered without the authority of the Sovereign Pontiff, could err is the heresy of many heretics, condemned by all Catholics. Now that without the presence of the Pope a general council could be celebrated, is established from the thing itself: because in none of those four famous councils, namely, Nicea, I Constantinople, Ephesus, and Chalcedon, was the Pope present. Nevertheless no one ever denied that they were general. But if such councils without the presence of the Pope, but with his legates, and assembled by his authority could not err, why was a confirmation of those things, which were defined by that whole council, expected? Because if that council could not err, it is unnecessary that the definitions of the councils would be confirmed by the Pope.

Concerning this matter (so that I may speak frankly) I would have preferred to hear an opinion other than mine: but because I have not seen any up until now, who have raised this question, or who had discussed something about it: I am forced to say (with due respect for a better opinion of others) what I think about this matter. I indeed very firmly hold, and do not think that anything else should be thought, that such councils, which were gathered from the whole world by the authority of the Pope, in which, if the Pope is absent, yet his legates are present, ought to be called general councils: and consequently could not err in the faith. Not in fact because the legates of the Apostolic See are infallible in their definitions of the faith, since they of themselves alone could err: but because that whole assembly in which they are, could not err on account of the assistance of the Holy Ghost. But even if those councils could not err in the faith, still not in vain and without reason, but rather for many and very just reasons, those councils always asked for approbation from the Sovereign Pontiff himself, and confirmation of the things which were defined by the whole council. The first reason in fact is that so it would be evident to all that that the Pope thinks the same things as the council, and that his legates have expressed the true mind of the Pope himself. For since someone could doubt whether the legates of the Apostolic See faithfully had fulfilled their office, carrying out their affair according to the will and opinion of the one delegating; it is necessary that the Pope would clearly express his own opinion, uttered by his own mouth, or written by his own hand. For in other public affairs this is commanded by law to be done. If someone contracts marriage through a proxy: even though it is a lawful marriage, and laws declare it to be indissoluble, as it is stated in the paragraph, *Cum dicitur*,[21] and in the law, *Generali*,[22] nevertheless fraud could be concealed in the contract, namely, by the procuration

---

21 "Where it is said, 'women are joined to their husbands by paternal choice,' it is intended to be understood that paternal choice is desired in marriage, and that without it marriage is not legitimate, according to the words of Pope Evaristus: 'Otherwise, unless [the bride] is given by the parents, the marriage is not legitimate'" (*Decretum Gratiani*, pt. 2, *causa* 32, q. 2, c. 12, §7 (PL 187, 1473B)). Later interpreters interpreted the word, "legitimate," in terms of liceity rather than validity, though Gratian originally saw parental consent to be necessary for the legitimacy of the marriage, given the canons that follow.

22 "Where a general commission has been given to a man by someone to seek a husband for his daughter, this is not sufficient ground for the conclusion of a marriage. Therefore it is necessary that the person selected should be introduced to the father, and that he should consent to the marriage, in order for it to be legally contracted" (*Digest of Justinian*, bk. 23, tit. 2 (*De ritu nuptiarum*), n. 34).

being false, wherefore those so contracting are accustomed to repeat again in person such a contract with their own words.

Therefore, so that it may be evident to all that the head is in conformity with its members, that is, the Pope thinks the same thing as the council, it is necessary that not merely by his legates, but that he would express his own opinion by himself. And the same very Blessed Leo clearly states the same things in the aforesaid letter sent to the Council of Chalcedon, in which when giving the reason for his confirmation, he speaks thus: "...so that both the whole brotherhood and the hearts of all the faithful may know that I, not only through the brethren who represented me but also through approving the conciliar proceedings, have joined my own judgment to yours."[23] From which words it is clearly established that the confirmation of the definition is not granted by the Pope, so that by it the Pope would add more strength to the definition: but so that by it, it would be more clearly evident to all about the will and opinion of the Pope, which he had expressed through his legates. And by this it is clearly proved that it ought to be done in this way, because sometimes it was discovered that the legates of the Sovereign Pontiff performed their legation unfaithfully, and in opposition to those things which the Pope committed to them. For Pope Nicholas I in his letter to the bishops stationed throughout Asia and Libya, says that his legates, whom he had sent to Constantinople for the investigation of some important matter, did the whole business contrary to his explicit commands, and said that they did those things in that way by command of the Pope. Thus, lest someone would suspect that in the definitions of the councils some legate did some such thing, it is necessary that the Pope would confirm

---

23 Letter 114, c. 1 (PL 54, 1029A).

by his own mouth and with his own hand, those things which the legates of the Apostolic See said in the council.[24]

Another reason can be that it happened on account of the Pope, lest if perhaps afterwards he forsake the definition of the council, it would be pled that he never consented to such a definition, and his legates nowise expressed his will. Therefore, lest that would afterwards happen, it is necessary that subscribing by his own hand, he would say that he thinks it along with the whole council, and has embraced that same thing, which was declared (by the prompting of the Holy Ghost) by the whole Council. And if the Pope, God permitting, afterwards tries to remove the definition of the council, he would be condemned by his own subscription.

There is a third and strongest reason: it is because although a council could not err in its definitions and decrees about the faith, still in other matters, which do not pertain to the faith, no truly learned man doubts that it could err. For the Council of Chalcedon, which is one of those four very famous councils, which Blessed Gregory says that he venerates as the four holy Gospels,[25] erred by placing the patriarch of Constantinople before the patriarch of Alexandria, who from the ancient custom of the Church, confirmed by the Council of Nicea, always had the second place after the Roman Pontiff. On account of which Pope Leo, although he confirmed those things which had been defined in the Council of Chalcedon about the faith, nevertheless rejected that definition by which it preferred the patriarch of Constantinople to the patriarch of Alexandria, and condemned it by a clear judgment: as it is evident from the [one hundred and fourth] letter of the same Leo, addressed to Emperor Marcian,[26] and from the [one

---

24 The Robber Council of Ephesus in 449 A.D. is an example of the fallibility of councils not approved by the Holy See.
25 Cf. Dz. 349.
26 "Let the city of Constantinople have, as we desire, its high rank, and under the protection of God's right hand, long enjoy

Whether the Pope can delegate to someone the power of judging

hundred fourteenth] letter of the same, which is addressed to the whole Council of Chalcedon.[27]

Therefore the aforesaid councils sent an account of their acts to the Sovereign Pontiff, and asked for confirmation from him, not indeed merely for those things which pertain to the faith: because those things were certain and infallible, and made firm with steadfast strength, since the councils could not have erred in them: but by reason of other businesses, since those councils could have erred in which things, they were asking for certitude as well as confirmation of the decision from the Sovereign Pontiff, as the supreme judge of the Church. And certainly if the words of the letter sent from the Council of Chalcedon to Leo are carefully considered, in that letter the council asked for confirmation of that definition alone, which it had given about the prelature of the Patriarch of Constantinople: and there is not mention about any of the

---

your clemency's rule. Yet things secular stand on a different basis from things divine: and there can be no sure building save on that rock which the Lord has laid for a foundation. He that covets what is not his due, loses what is his own. Let it be enough for Anatolius that by the aid of your piety and by my favor and approval he has obtained the bishopric of so great a city. Let him not disdain a city which is royal, though he cannot make it an Apostolic See; and let him on no account hope that he can rise by doing injury to others. For the privileges of the churches determined by the canons of the holy Fathers, and fixed by the decrees of the Nicene Synod, cannot be overthrown by any unscrupulous act, nor disturbed by any innovation" (N. 3 (PL 54, 995A-B)).

27 "On the matter of preserving also the inviolable decrees of the holy Fathers which were issued at the Council of Nicea, I admonish the observances of Your Holinesses that the rights of the churches must remain as they were laid down by the three hundred eighteen divinely inspired Fathers. Let vicious ambition covet nothing belonging to another, nor let anyone seek his own increase through injuring another" (N. 2 (PL. 54, 1029B-1031A)).

matters of faith.[28] And Leo responding to the same council, says that for this alone was it assembled, so that it might treat about the faith, and not about other judgments.[29] These are the things which seem more certain to me about the matter; if anyone would offer better things, I will receive them (as they say) with open arms, and I will give great thanks to him in return: it is far from the case that I am prepared to repress [a better viewpoint]. For I do not adhere to my view so tenaciously that I would think that it is always the best, and hence would disdain to accept another's.

The arguments, which we have put at the beginning of the chapter, and which seem at first glance to support the opposite view, are very easily resolved. To the first in fact I reply, conceding that there are many things which the Pope rightly, nay, at times necessarily, controls through others, because he alone does not suffice to do everything. Yet it is not right that he would through others decide matters pertaining to him about the faith, which are much more important than all the other public affairs. For even though those things which we do through others, we seem to do ourselves: still we ourselves do not really act. Next, there is a big difference between whether you examine by our own, or another's eyes: because (as Titus Manlius [Imperio-

---

28 "And we further inform you that we have decided on other things also for the good management and stability of church matters, being persuaded that your holiness will accept and ratify them, when you are told. The long prevailing custom, which the holy Church of God at Constantinople had of ordaining metropolitans for the provinces of Asia, Pontus and Thrace, we have now ratified by the votes of the Synod" (Letter 98, n. 4 (PL 54, 955C-957A).

29 "I do not doubt that all your brotherhood knows that I embraced the decrees of the holy council that was held in the city of Chalcedon to confirm the faith" (Letter 114, n. 1 (PL 54, 1027B)).

sus Torquatus] in Livy says very well[30]) that the things that you do through another, hardly ever turn out well. We admit that the Pope can delegate to someone the investigation of a matter pertaining to the faith: namely, so that he may hear the reasons and arguments of disagreeing learned men, yet on this condition, that the thing that he shall understand from those discussions, must be referred to the Sovereign Pontiff: so that he may pronounce judgment on everything investigated. Otherwise, if the legate of the Pope were to pronounce judgment about the faith, it will not so bind someone contradicting, that it would not be allowed to him to appeal to the Pope. Before whose decision, although he contradicts the legate, he will not be deemed a heretic. The solution of the other argument is shown from those things which we have already said.

---

30 "Shameless, he said, was a pilot and a general too, who, when he uses other men's eyes for everything that is to be done, demands that the lives and fortunes of others be entrusted to him" (Livy, *The History of Rome*, bk. 26, c. 22, ln. 6).

Chapter VII

Who ought to be declared a heretic?

Up until this point we have disputed through many chapters about heresy. But now reason itself persuades that we would discuss about the assertor of the heresy itself, who is accustomed to be called a heretic: and that we teach who rightly ought to be deemed such. One ought not (in my opinion) to easily make a pronouncement about this matter: but the judge ought to make a serious and careful examination, before reckoning that someone is a heretic. For since there is no crime more disagreeable that someone can accuse a Christian man of, than if he calls him a heretic, it is befitting to examine the matter carefully, and (as it is said) to "check the stone with the plumb-line," before the judge were to pronounce sentence concerning this matter. The Mosaic Law commanded that a long and careful examination precede before the priest pronounced someone a leper.[1] Hence it is befitting that one would make a much greater investigation [*Inquisitionem*] before someone would be declared a heretic. Because one ought to refer more to the truth for judgment, than to the figure: more to the body, than to the shadow. For a leper carries the figure of a heretical man, as we will show below in the second book, in the eighteenth chapter. Therefore, lest anyone err in the censure of heretics, I will give a very certain rule here, by which it can be shown whether he is a heretic or not.

Yet before all else I have decided to admonish the reader, that the word "heretic" is used in various and multiple ways in the Canons. For sometimes anyone who has fallen into heresy in whatever way is called a "heretic" in a very broad sense, who gave a clear and strong suspicion of heresy. And

---

1 Cf. Lev. 13.

according to this very broad meaning of the word, supporters of heretics, and their harborers are called "heretics": even though it is not evident that they sincerely support the error of those whom they defend or harbor in their house. Schismatics and Simoniacs [are called heretics]: because those who are such, give no little suspicion of heresy. This word "heretic" is not used for heretics according to this very broad designation of "heretic," under those titles which are written in the Decretals of Gregory IX, the Sixth Book of the Decretals and the Clementines: because those, and many punishments, which are commanded through the decretals contained under those titles, to be inflicted upon heretics by the Sovereign Pontiffs, do not agree in all those things, which can be comprehended under its very broad meaning.

Therefore, having put aside this very broad meaning of the word, let us show, following the proper and legitimate meaning of this same word, who truly and deservedly ought to be deemed a heretic: so that the punishments decreed by law may be inflicted upon him. Many things in fact are required, so that someone deservedly ought to be called a heretic. First of all, it is necessary that he shall have received the Catholic faith at one time in Baptism. For he who never put on Christ, will be reckoned a pagan, or Saracen, or Mohammedan, or reckoned by any other name you wish, yet he will never be called a heretic: so that the punishments, which the Church has decreed against heretics, could rightly be inflicted upon him. For the Church does not judge about those who are outside [the Church], as Paul says: "What have I to do to judge them that are without?" (I Cor. 5, 12). But he who has not put on Christ in Baptism, in this way is outside the Church, so that he has never entered its house: because he has not yet come to Baptism, which is the doorway of this house. Hence concerning those who have not received Baptism, the Church does not judge: and consequently these men who are not those whom she punishes by the name of heretics. The second [requirement is] that after Baptism has been received, in order that someone would be called a heretic, there is an error about the faith. A mere exterior deed without an error of the intellect (as we said above in chapter one) is not heresy; also, for the same reason the deed itself alone with an error of the intellect, although it can render one suspect of heresy, still cannot make a heretic. Thus, in order that someone ought to be called a heretic, it is necessary that he hold some error about the faith.

Now not only he who asserts or believes what is contrary to the truth errs: but also he who doubts about the very certain faith itself, or a very firm truth. Hence Augustine, in the *Enchiridion* addressed to Laurentius, when defining error, speaks thus: "To err is just to take the false for the true, and the true for the false, or to hold what is certain as uncertain, and what is uncertain as certain."[2] From which words it is very clearly gathered that not only he ought to be called a heretic, who thinks contrary to the Catholic faith, but also he who doubts about the true faith: he has the other things which, we will say below, are required for being a heretic. For he who doubts about the faith, also errs in this way, just as he who asserts something against the faith: because by his very doubting, he bears witness that he believes that Sacred Scripture can deceive, and the Church can be deceived. But if he did not believe this about those things, he never would have doubted about what they said. Moreover, he who doubts, loses the faith: because he lacks the firmness, which is annexed to the faith: for which reason a strong doubt (we do not now speak about very light doubts) and the faith cannot at the same time be united. This is clearly proved by the testimony of Blessed Bernard, speaking thus: "Faith is free from doubts; if it has doubts it is not faith, but opinion."[3] And Blessed Athanasius, after having given the rule of the

---

2   C. 17 (PL 40, 240).
3   *On consideration*, bk. 5, c. 3, n. 6 (PL 182, 791A).

faith in the Symbol, speaks thus: "This is the catholic faith; which except a man believe truly and firmly, he cannot be saved."[4]

And God, after He had promised through the prophet Habacuc the coming of His Son, in chapter two, adds these words: "Behold, he that is unbelieving, his soul shall not be right in himself" (v. 4). Jerome, when interpreting these words, speaks thus: "If your faith gives in to doubt, and you think that what I promise is not going to happen, you will have for a great punishment the fact that you will be displeasing to my soul. But the just who believes my words and does not doubt concerning those things that I promise, he shall have everlasting life as his reward."[5] And Theophylactus, commenting on the passage in Romans, "The justice of God is revealed therein, from faith" (1, 17), speaks thus: "For when God bestows by His grace those things which exceed human thoughts, faith is rightly necessary for us. For if we shall have begun to be curious scrutinizers of Divine things, we have lost all."[6] From all these things it is very clearly gathered that a doubt is, as it were, diametrically opposed to the faith: and consequently, he who doubts ought not to be reckoned a believer, but a heretic. Finally, [Pseudo-] Pope [Sixtus I] says: "Doubting in the faith, is faithlessness."[7]

But against this opinion perhaps someone will object that he who doubts about the faith, does not deny any article of the faith; and hence it seems to be gathered that he nowise ought to be deemed a heretic. Because every heretic denies some article of the faith. And so that the strength of the argument may appear more, let us propose that Peter doubts about this proposition, "Christ is God": When Peter so doubts, he does not deny any article of the faith: because if it were to be

---

4 PL 88, 586B; PG 28, 1583C.
5 Bk. 1 (PL 25, 1291B).
6 PG 124, 351B.
7 *The False Decretals of Pseudo-Isidore* (PL 130, 102C).

said that he denies something, he would be reckoned to deny this: "Christ is God." But since we have supposed that Peter doubts about it, it follows that he neither affirms nor denies it: because if he does either of these, he will hardly be said to doubt. If he does not deny that article of the faith, concerning which there seemed to be a very strong reason [that he had doubted], it follows that he does not deny any article of the faith. Because if that which seems more probably to be in him, is not in him, then neither that which is less probably. If he denies no article of the faith, undeservedly then he will be deemed a heretic.

To this argument I reply, that Peter in so doubting about the aforesaid article of faith, sins gravely against the precept of the faith. Because as the confession of the mouth is made unto salvation, so the believing of the heart is necessary for justice.[8] In this way then, he who does not believe with the heart in due time and place, sins. Thus in practice when some article of the faith presents itself to the mind of some Christian, that is, as an article that ought to be believed, or as one not to be believed: if he, to whom that article so presents itself, knows that such an article is preached by the Catholic Church as one that necessarily ought to believed, and knowing this doubts; he certainly sins, and against no other precept than that of the faith: because he does not believe at that time in which he was obliged to believe. And this is enough, so that he might rightly be deemed a heretic. But because this omission of credulity in a necessary time, even though it is efficacious enough, and a clear cause of sin, nevertheless, perhaps it is not in this way an efficacious and clear cause, that someone on account of it alone ought to rightly be deemed a heretic.

Wherefore I respond otherwise, and better, conceding it to be correct [to say] that not every Peter so doubting denies this article, "Christ is God," but one of these: "God is true,"

---

8 Cf. Rom. 10, 10.

or "The Church, which Paul says is 'the pillar and ground of the truth' (I Tim. 3, 15), cannot err in the faith." For someone doubts about some article of the faith, which the Catholic Church proposes to us as necessarily to be believed: only because he believes that God, or Scripture handed down from Him, can deceive, or the Church, which is always taught by God Himself, be deceived. If he believes either of which, he will rightly be deemed a heretic. Now these things which we said about someone doubting, we wish to be understood only of him who persists with a determined mind in such doubting, which keeps him tottering between both sides of the doubt. But if he doubts in such a manner because he leans more towards the truth of the faith, than to the opposite side, he ought not be to called a heretic: especially if he has doubted from a certain weakness, as happens in the first movements, and in those who have this by nature, as they are of two minds and doubtful about everything, tormented by incessant scruples of conscience.

But here the reader ought to be warned that he should not think that every doubt, even deliberated and constant, which pertains in any way to the faith is enough such that it can make the man affected by it a heretic. For about what or how someone may doubt differs very much. There are some who doubt about words, or about the Scriptures. There are again some who, even though they give complete faith to words, or to the Scriptures, still they doubt about the meaning of the words or the Scriptures. They believe, I say, that the words are true, and completely lacking all falsity: nevertheless, they doubt about what is meant by those words. The first kind of doubt about those things, which pertain to the faith, is completely forbidden: it is not permitted to doubt about anything concerning the truth of those things which the Catholic faith proposes to be believed. A second kind of doubt can also be had about those things which we are held to believe with a firm and constant faith, without heresy and the note of any other crime. Nicodemus hesitated with the first kind of doubt, concerning Christ's words: "Unless a man be born again, he cannot see the kingdom of God" (Jn. 3, 3). He indeed doubted: because he did not believe that those words could be true in any way, and hence he said: "How can a man be born when he is old? can he enter a second time into his mother's womb, and be born again?" (v. 4). In completely the same way the Jewish disciples doubted, who were in Capharnaum, about the words of Christ saying: "The bread that I will give, is my flesh, for the life of the world" (Jn. 6, 52). For they were saying: "How can this man give us his flesh to eat? (v. 53). They were indeed doubting: because they were not believing the words said by Him. There is clear proof of this, because when they heard Christ's words, they said: "This saying is hard, and who can hear it?" (v. 61). And finally they went away, and for this reason they left Christ's discipleship.

I know of a recent writer,[9] who, in his annotations on John, tries to defend Nicodemus from the fault of incredulity, as though the Catholic faith would be endangered, because he was incredulous. But I prefer here and elsewhere to always follow the footsteps of the Fathers (by whose teaching the Church shines as the sun and the moon[10]), rather than to delight in new opinions. Augustine, when speaking about Nicodemus, says these words: "The Spirit speaks to him, and he thinks of the flesh. He thinks of his own flesh, because as yet he thinks not of Christ's flesh. For when the Lord Jesus had said, 'Except you eat the flesh of the Son of man, and drink his blood, you shall not have life in you' (v. 54), some who followed Him were offended, and said among themselves, 'This saying is hard, and who can hear

---

9 A Gloss on the 1568 edition names the writer as Brother Frans Titelmans (1502-1537), a Flemish Franciscan scholar who later joined the Capuchins.

10 Cf. Bar. 6, 66.

it?' (v. 61). For they fancied that, in saying this, Jesus meant that they would be able to cook Him, after being cut up like a lamb, and eat Him... The Lord, however, expounded to them, and said, 'It is the spirit that quickeneth' (v. 64). After He had said, 'Except you eat the flesh of the Son of man, and drink his blood, you shall not have life in you' (v. 54), lest they should understand it carnally, He said, 'It is the spirit that quickeneth: the flesh profiteth nothing' (v. 64)... This Nicodemus, who had come to Jesus by night, did not savor of this spirit and this life."[11] Augustine compares Nicodemus clearly enough, and makes him similar to the incredulous Capharnaites. And he calls Nicodemus proud and puffed up: because he believed his own judgment more than Christ's words.[12]

Cyril teaches the same things, when interpreting these words: "How can a man be born when he is old?" (Jn. 3, 4), says these words: "Nicodemus is convicted hereby of being still carnal, and therefore no way receiving the things of the Spirit of God. For he thinketh that this so dread and illustrious Mystery is foolishness. And hearing of the birth spiritual and from above, he imagineth the carnal womb returning to birth-pang of things already born, and, not attaining beyond the law of our nature, measureth things Divine; and finding the height of its doctrines unattainable by his own conceptions, he falleth down, and is carried off. For as things that are dashed by mighty blows upon the hard stones again rebound, so too I deem the unskilled mind falling upon conceptions of greater caliber than it, being relaxed returns, and ever glad to remain in the measure that suits it, despises an understanding better and loftier than itself. In which case the ruler of the Jews now being, receives not the spiritual birth."[13]

---

11 *Tractates on the Gospel of John*, tract. 11, nn. 5-6 (PL 35, 1477-1478).
12 *Ibid.*, tract. 12, nn. 6-7 (PL 35, 1487).
13 *On the Gospel According to John*, bk. 2 (PG 73, 243A-B).

Chrysostom says: "For the 'how,' is the doubting question of those who have no strong belief, but who are yet of the earth. Therefore Sara laughed when she had said, 'How?' And many others having asked this question, have fallen from the faith. And thus heretics continue in their heresy, because they frequently make this enquiry, some of them saying, 'How was He begotten?' others, 'How was He made flesh?' and subjecting that Infinite Essence to the weakness of their own reasonings. Knowing which, we ought to avoid this unseasonable curiosity."[14]

Theophylactus agrees with this, saying: "Nicodemus, when hearing a greater than human teaching, is amazed, and being unyielding asks something human, 'How can it be,' which is a sign of disbelief. For where there is no faith, there it is inquired, 'How is this?' and 'Why is this?' Moreover, Nicodemus' words appear ridiculous. For he did not understand the spiritual birth, but instead mentions the birth of the bodily womb."[15] By which words it could be pled more clearly against Nicodemus' faith. I embrace most willingly the opinion of these very illustrious men, rather than the opinion of that recent writer, who tries to excuse Nicodemus not only from incredulity, but also from sin: especially because for no probable reason, which would seem to urge somehow, but by a very ridiculous figment of the imagination, he tries to persuade us of this.

I certainly think that this recent writer, a truly learned and pious man, wanted to excuse Nicodemus from incredulity because he knew that he was otherwise a believer. For I see many who, motivated by this reason, anxiously labor to excuse many of the holy men from sins: because they recognize that they were otherwise just and holy. If this reason urges them to excuse, it is necessary that they would try to

---

14 *Homilies on the Gospel of John*, hom. 24, nn. 2-3 (PG 59, 146).
15 *Ennaratio in Evangelium Joannis*, c. 3 (PG 123, 1203C).

excuse David from homicide and adultery: and Peter from denying his Master. Because both of these men had been much more just before sin than Nicodemus at the time in which we say that he doubted: especially because he (as the Gospel relates) was a hidden disciple of Christ: and hence he had come at night, because on account of the fear of the Jews he dared not to come openly to Him. Therefore, one undeservedly strives to excuse Nicodemus from incredulity at that time: when he first came to Christ's discipleship, not without fear. For it is unlikely that Nicodemus, in the first beginning of his discipleship, was so firm in the faith that at that time he would not have doubted in anything: especially since none of the Apostles were such in the beginning of their Apostleship, so that he never afterwards doubted.

But why do I tarry to make known the doubting of Nicodemus, since Our Lord Jesus Christ Himself branded him in regard to incredulity. For when Nicodemus had said, "How can these things be done?" (Jn. 3, 9), Christ Our Savior, among the other things which He said to him, said this: "How will you believe, if I shall speak to you heavenly things?" (v. 12). From which words it is very clearly established that Christ branded Nicodemus for his incredulity. I am now forced to add all these things, because a certain friend reproached me in writing, because in the first edition of this work, I had branded Nicodemus with the mark of doubt and incredulity, and to prove that he rightly reproaches me, he objects that aforesaid recent writer, who in his annotations on John, defends Nicodemus. I read the words of that writer, which I had not seen before, and I bear witness before God that if that writer had persuaded me of his opinion, I would have immediately recanted my own. But since I found no such thing in his writings, I preferred to follow the opinion of the holy Fathers than to adhere to his new view, and one badly proved by him.

Who ought to be declared a heretic?

The Virgin Mother of God doubted the second kind of doubt, when she replies to the Archangel Gabriel announcing to her that God was to be conceived by her in her womb: "How shall this be done, because I know not man?" (Lk. 1, 34). She inquires, certainly not as those distrusting the Angel's words, but as firmly believing, and not comprehending the way which the words could be fulfilled, and desiring tobe taught about the way. Thus, she did not doubt about the thing itself, but about the way, whereby the thing could be accomplished. For so Theophylactus interprets those words of the Virgin Mother of God, saying: "It was not because the Virgin did not believe that she said, 'How shall this be done?' Rather, it was because she was wise and astute, and sought to understand the manner in which this would take place. For nothing like this had ever happened before, nor would it again. This is why the Angel makes an allowance for her, and does not chastise her as he did Zacharias, but instead explains to her how it would come about. It was fitting that Zacharias was chastised, for he knew many examples of barren women who had given birth."[16] And Blessed Bernard in his fourth homily on the Gospel, *Missus est*, interprets those words of the most glorious Virgin in the same way, speaking thus: "She doubts not the fact, but only inquires about the manner of its accomplishment. She says not 'Will it be done?' but 'How shall this be done?' It is as though she were to say: 'Since my Lord knows, and my conscience bears me witness, that His handmaid has made a vow to know no man, by what law shall it please Him to work this wonder? If I must break my vow that I may bring forth such a Son, I rejoice on account of the Son, but I grieve because of my vow. Nevertheless, His will be done.'"[17]

---

16 T*he Explanation of the Holy Gospel According to St. Luke* (PG 123, 703D-706A).

17 Hom. 4 (On Lk. 1, 32-38), n. 3 (PL 183, 80C-D).

According to this manner, the holy Doctors, by whose teaching the Church shines as the sun and the moon, adhibiting full faith to the words of Sacred Scripture, very often doubted about the understanding of them: as their writings clearly testify. The scholastic theologians also act according to this manner, when they propose very many questions to be discussed, not because they doubt about the matter itself, which is proposed: but about the manner and understanding of it. For far be it that we would believe that they doubt as often as they propose something in the manner or form of a question. For they very often propose questions, not because they themselves doubt: but because they want to obviate the doubts which perhaps could arise in others, and opportunely heal them. Now this happens without any sin, and with great merit; it is far from being the case, that someone could rightly reproach them on this account.

A third thing which (according to the opinion of certain men) is required, so that someone may be called a heretic, is that he would not reject the whole Catholic faith: but only some part of it. For they say that he who has completely abandoned the Catholic faith, ought to be called an apostate, and not a heretic, and in this way they distinguish a heretic from an apostate, due to the fact that heretics contradict some particular article of the faith. But an apostate completely rejects the whole Christian faith. So teaches Guy the Carmelite in his *Summa de haeresibus*.[18] Juan de Torquemada subscribes to the same in that work which is titled, *Summa Ecclesiae*.[19] But on this point I do not agree: because according to this reasoning it would be necessary to concede that a heretical man through the increase and multiplication of heresies would cease to be a heretic. For he who pertinaciously asserts one or two heresies, according to their opinion, is called a heretic, and if this sort of man daily falls

---

18   Fol. 3v, lns. 92 ff.
19   Bk. 4, pt. 2, c. 13, fol. 385r.

into another and another heresy, until he completely denies the whole faith, only then, according to the opinion of the same men, will he be called an apostate, and not a heretic: thus, by adding heresies he ceases to be a heretic.

Now there is no one with a sane mind, who does not understand how absurd it is to claim this, because it is not consonant with reason: that that which received a nomenclature from some form, through the multiplication of the same form, lose the nomenclature. As for example, if a man by reason of his whiteness is called white, however much whiteness is added to him, he will never cease to be called, and to be white: therefore, in the same way, since a heretic is named from heresy, he will never cease to be a heretic through whatever multitude of heresies. An apostate and a heretic are not some two disparate things, which cannot coincide in the same being, just as an animal and a horse: but are like a genus and species, as animal and man. Heretic is the name of the genus, which under it there are as many species as there are species of heresies, which men could pertinaciously maintain. An apostate is the name of a species, such that every apostate ought to be reckoned a heretic; nevertheless, not every heretic, on the contrary, is reckoned to be an apostate. And Blessed Thomas supports this opinion of mine, who says that there are three species of disbelief, namely: pagans, Jews and heretics: and under the name of heretics he reckons however many have left the Catholic faith in whatever way.[20] And he says more explicitly that "apostacy does not imply a special kind of disbelief, but an aggravating circumstance thereof, according to II Peter 2, 21: 'It had been better for them not to know the truth [Vulgate: "the way of justice"], than after they had known it, to turn back' (II Pet. 2, 21)."[21]

---

20 Cf. II-II, q. 10, a. 5.
21 Cf. II-II, q. 12, a. 1, ad 3um.

If apostacy is not a distinct species from heresy, it follows that neither also is an apostate a distinct species from a heretic. William of Ockham subscribes to the same opinion.[22] I have heard that there are some followers of Blessed Thomas, who after the first edition of this work, publicly teaching theology in the University of Salamanca, still contend that apostacy ought not to be called heresy. But certainly (so that I may speak frankly) I cannot but be surprised with what impudence they can deny that an apostate ought to be called a heretic, if they wish to maintain the teaching of Blessed Thomas. For if the species of disbelief, as Blessed Thomas says, are only three, namely, Jews, pagans, and heretics, I ask them, under which of these species is apostacy contained? It is not encompassed under the name of Jews: because it is not possible that one forsakes the Catholic faith that he would fall into any Jewish error: and hence it follows that he could not rightly be called a Jew. Nor could he be called a pagan, because an apostate received the faith at one time, and retains the character of the Lord's flock. A pagan, however, does not have either the latter or the former. An apostate returning to the faith is not obliged to be baptized again: but a pagan, if he wants to enter the Kingdom of God, is obliged to receive Baptism, which he did not receive: an apostate (as it is very clearly evident) is punished by the Church for the crime of apostacy. And whence it follows that he is not completely outside of the Church: because otherwise he would not be punished by her, as Paul says: "What have I to do to judge them that are without?" (I Cor. 5, 12). Now a pagan is not punished by the Church, because he is completely outside her. If an apostate, by reason of his apostacy, ought not to be called neither a Jew nor a pagan, he necessarily therefore ought to be called a heretic, otherwise Blessed Thomas did not fully enumerate the species of disbelief.

---

22 *Dialogus*, pt. 1, bk. 4, c. 13.

Next, if apostasy (as Blessed Thomas says) only implies an aggravating circumstance, and it does not denote a distinct species: I will inquire about this circumstance, what and what kind is it? It is certain that this circumstance is the forsaking of the entire faith, and not only from one or another part. But this circumstance does not aggravate endlessly: because otherwise it would change the species, which Blessed Thomas denies. If that circumstance does not aggravate endlessly, then that circumstance having been added it is needful that it remains in that species, in which that circumstance was set apart. But that circumstance having been laid, all forsaking of the faith would be under the species of heresy: thus it will be put under the same species. I present something similar: if someone has taken by theft two ducats from Peter, and another has stolen from John all his possessions, all admit that the second theft does not differ by species from the first: but by the circumstance alone, which does not change the species. Likewise, therefore one ought to say entirely the same thing about those two, one of whom forsook part of the faith, but the other the whole of it.

Moreover, every punishment which laws decree against heretics, also ought to be inflicted upon apostates of this kind. Therefore, apostates of this kind ought to be comprised under the name of heretics, when laws speak about heretics: because otherwise there would be no canonical law by which apostates of this kind could be punished. For that title, which is inscribed in the fifth book of the Decretals [of Gregory IX], *De apostatis et reiterantibus baptisma*,[23] does not concern these apostates: but only those who have abandoned the clerical or religious state which they had professed at one time. And the Gloss annotates this in the same place, in the first chapter of the same title,[24] and this is more fully

---

23   Title 9.
24   "We do not command that clerics, who, having abandoned their order, habit, and office, live in apostasy like laymen, should

confirmed by chapter, *Contra Christianos*, [in the title,] *de haereticis*, in the *Liber Sextus*.²⁵ For there it is commanded that they (who having abandoned the Catholic faith) revert to the rites of the Jews, are to be punished as heretics. Therefore, moved by these very efficacious reasons, I say that an apostate also ought to be reckoned to be heretical: just as he, who has fallen into only one heresy. Yet in that work which I published, *Against All Heresies*, in chapter nine of the introduction, I followed the opinion of others, due to the fact that at that time I had not considered the matter well (as was befitting). Therefore, I now retract that opinion, and embrace the present one as being more correct.²⁶

The fourth and last thing which makes an absolute and consummate heretic is pertinacity, which if you have removed, even if someone holds or teaches an error contrary to the faith, he ought not to be reckoned a heretic. Hence Augustine speaks thus: "But though the doctrine which men hold be false and perverse, if they do not maintain it with passionate obstinacy, especially when they have not devised it by the rashness of their own presumption, but have accepted it from parents who had been misguided and had fallen into error, and if they are with anxiety seeking the truth, and

---

be freed by ecclesiastical censure if they are held after being seized in the commission of crimes." When Bishop Jocelin of Salisbury had asked if he should protect delinquent clergy from arrest by secular authorities, Pope Alexander III said that he should not, and defined "apostasy" as grounds for withdrawing clerical immunity.
25 "One must proceed against Christians who adopt or revert to the rites of the Jews, even if they were originally baptized as infants or under fear of death—as one would proceed against heretics who had confessed or been convicted on the testimony of Christians or Jews. One should proceed against abettors, harborers, and defenders of these people as one proceeds against abettors, harborers, and defenders of heretics" (Bk. 5, tit. 2, c. 13).
26 The 1543 ((Cologne: Novesianus), fol. 17D) edition of this work still had this opinion which was revised in the later editions.

are prepared to be set right when they have found it, such men are not to be counted heretics."²⁷ And these words are found in the chapter, *Dixit Apostolus*.²⁸

Against these words someone perhaps will object that the Sovereign Pontiff, Innocent III, who when asked by Count [Raymond VI] of Toulouse, whom one ought to call manifest heretics, replies to him by these words: "Upon this we have decided that you should be given the answer that those should be understood to be manifest heretics who publicly preach against the Catholic faith or profess or defend an error, or who have been convicted or have confessed before their prelates, or have been condemned judicially by them on a charge of heretical wickedness."²⁹ These words are also found in the chapter, *Super quibusdam*.³⁰ From these words of Innocent someone perhaps will take up an argument against those things which we said about pertinacity, speaking thus: "Innocent, when explaining who ought to be called a manifest heretic, never mentioned pertinacity: therefore pertinacity is not necessary." But this is not the case, as it is objected, nor is it concluded correctly in the same objection. For Innocent III was not then treating about heretics in general, but only about manifest heretics. For he then merely answers regarding the things asked, but he was not asked about pertinacity: but about evidence, and the manifestation of the offense. There certainly was no doubt about who ought to have been called pertinacious or heretics: but the doubt was about which heretics ought to be considered manifest. And for this reason he was silent about pertinacity, supplying it in thought, and he replies only about the manifestation

---

27 Letter 43 (to Glorius and Eleusius), c. 1, n. 1 (PL 33, 160).
28 *Decretum Gratiani*, pt. 2, *causa* 24, q. 3, c. 29 (PL 187, 1307A).
29 Registry 3, letter 154 (PL 216, 173C).
30 *Decretals of Gregory IX*, bk. 5, tit. 40 (*De verborum significatione*), c. 26.

and about the evidence of it, about which alone he had been asked.

Therefore, from all these things which we said are necessarily required for someone to be reckoned a heretic, I have deduced this definition of a heretic. A heretic is one who after he has received Baptism, and was sufficiently instructed in the Catholic faith, pertinaciously errs against that which he knows from the Catholic Church to be held as the faith, either when asserting the opposite truth, or doubting about the truth itself. It is not necessary to explain this definition more: because it is clear enough from those things which we have said.

Therefore, having considered well all these things it will be sufficiently apparent to anyone, how much Bernard of Luxemburg[31] erred, who, when putting together a list of heretics, put many in it who by no means ought to be called heretics. For he included there some men who never professed the Catholic faith in Baptism, such as Averroes and Avicenna, who according to those things which we have said, nowise could be called heretics. He mixed in some others in that same place, who even though they had received holy Baptism, still they had not fallen into any heresy, such as the Marranos and Mozarabs. And certainly (as I think) he did not understand who and for what reason they are called Marranos, or Mozarabs: hence I thought it worthwhile to explain the meaning of these words, so that from thence it may be manifest, how undeservingly he listed them among the heretics.

---

31 Dominican theologian, controversialist, and Inquisitor of the Archdioceses of Cologne, Mainz, and Trier, who died in 1535 in Cologne. "As the author of the *Catalogus haereticorum*, he has been described as somewhat lacking in critical judgment; but he was otherwise a safe and indefatigable defender of the Faith against the heretics of his time" ("Bernard of Luxemburg," *Catholic Encyclopedia* (1908 ed.), vol. 2, p. 503).

They are called by the Spanish "Marranos," who according to current memory, or from the accounts of others in the past, are known to trace their origin from the Jews. Therefore, a son of Jews, or a grandson, or a great-grandson, although he himself is now a true Christian, and a faithful Catholic, is always called a "Marrano" by the Spanish. Hence it is that not on account of any fault of his own, but only on account of a blot of his parents, he will be called a "Marrano." Thus, there is no reason why someone should list the Marranos among the heretics, since someone could very well be a Marrano, as well as a truly Catholic and believing man.

Still, I recognize that the name "Marrano" is disreputable and injurious, both on account of the parents from whom they descend, and on account of the suspicion of Judaism, which they always carry against themselves, because it is known by experience that many of them reverted to Jewish rites and ceremonies. Now this which he said concerning the suspicion which is nearly always had against the Marranos, I would like it to be said, "according to the common opinion of the people," yet not according to my opinion. For in saying it, I have stated the common custom of the people, that there is always a bad suspicion about the Marranos, and one nearly always thinks so badly about them, that one scarcely ever calls them by another name than Jews. Yet I cannot approve of this custom of the people, and it cannot be approved by any Christian and prudent man: it is truly unjust, and nowise Christian, that we would have bad suspicions about him who of himself gave no occasion for suspicion. For it is determined by Divine and human law, that anyone is presumed good, until the contrary is proved.

But these men, who attack the Marranos with bitter hatred, say that they suspect bad things about the Marranos, not because they of themselves gave some worthy occasion of suspicion: but because they derive their origin from Jewish parents, and hence they say that they can rightly suspect, because those men will sometimes imitate their parents. It is surely an unworthy reason for suspicion: because according to this thinking it would always be allowed to think badly about everyone, or at least to suspect. For there is now hardly any man who parent has not been sullied by some sin. If in other sins it is not lawful to badly opine about any man, because his father was tainted with a similar crime, I do not know why it will be permitted to rather suspect this regarding Judaism, that a son would revert to Judaic worship: because his father, or grandfather, was in the past a Jew. Furthermore, if it be allowed to suspect this about those who derive their origin from the Jews, for the same reason it will be allowed to also suspect about those who take their origin from pagans: because there is no greater reason why it would be allowed to suspect rather about those, than about these men: since it is known by well-known experience that many of the pagans after having received Baptism have returned to paganism. If they would affirm that it is allowed to suspect this about pagans, the consequence is that that they would concede that it is allowed to suspect this about everyone without any distinction: because however many have converted to Christianity, have come either from Judaism or from paganism.

Next, even if this perhaps were allowed to be suspected about those who were born, raised, and taught from parents in Judaism: still this would not be allowed in regard to those who, even though they derive their race from the Jews, yet have many truly Christian ancestors: such that their immediate parents, and grandparents, and great-grandparents, and distant ancestors were truly Christians. I bear witness to all these things before God, and His Angels, that I did not speak so that I might defend my own case. Because I am estranged from all consanguinity with the Marranos, as can be shown to all who wish to thoroughly study my origin, but I have spoken urged on by my conscience, so that I may resist in part a common error of the people, lest if this error spread further, the Church would make ready a schism which would divide those converted from the Gentiles and those converted from the Jews.

The Mozarabs are neither heretics nor suspect of heresy. For they hold no error against the Catholic faith, nor do they support any heresy, nor are they separated from the obedience to the Roman Church: but by the ceremonies alone, which they have in the ordo of the Divine Office and the celebration of the Mass, differing from the common use of the Latins. Even though these ceremonies differ from those used by the Roman Church, still they were never rejected by the Roman Church. For all Spain formerly, in the time of Saint Isidore, Archbishop of Seville, and Saint Ildephonsus, Archbishop of Toledo, who ruled those churches nine hundred years ago, was keeping that Mozarabic custom, the Roman Church approving. Which custom of celebrating from that time until the present day in Toledo, the most opulent city of Spain, in certain parishes has been kept uninterruptedly, and is still observed. There also exists today, in that very magnificent cathedral church of the same distinguished city, a certain very opulent chapel, in which Mass is celebrated daily, and all the rest of the daily and also nightly sacrifice of praise, fixed at the seven hours of the day, is offered according to the Mozarabic ordo, rite and ceremonies. Now he who wants to know at what time, and for what reason this manner is kept in the other parts of Spain, may read the [*Estoria de España*[32]], which the very illustrious and very learned King Alfonso X of Castile and León composed. For this man in the fourth part of the aforesaid history, in the third chapter,

---

32 The *General Estoria* is cited here, but this work was uncompleted and gives the history from the origin of the world merely until the birth of Christ. Alfonso X's other historical work, *Estoria de España*, seems rather to be referred to here.

composed a long and very interesting narrative about this matter.[33]

But because it is very difficult to find this history in other sources, hence I decided to briefly touch upon those things which this very learned king described at length, so that I may make known to all the very interesting affair. Long ago all of Spain, he says, was celebrating the Sacrifice of the Mass according to the Visigothic custom, instituted by Blessed Isidore [of Seville] and Blessed Leander, very differently from the custom and rite of the Roman church. Hence when this custom and rite was kept everywhere in Spain, King Alfonso VI of Spain, who recovered Toledo from the Saracens, married Constance [of Burgundy], daughter of the king of France. Who when she had seen the sacred office of the Mass was celebrated according to a very different custom and rite in Spain, than is celebrated in France, besought her husband, the king, that he would take away that custom, and ceremonies of the Mass completely from all of Spain, and would substitute in its place the French custom, which was conformed to the Roman church. About which matter the king did not want to decide anything: unless firstly (as was proper) consult the Sovereign Pontiff, Gregory VII, who then ruled the universal Church. But the Pontiff after having fully examined the matter (as he ought), replied to the legates that the ancient custom of Spain, which was good and holy, and instituted by the Holy Fathers, ought not to be removed, but rather kept in its entirety.

But the queen again besought the king very insistently to abrogate it, whose wishes the king was desiring to satisfy, convoked a general assembly composed of both ecclesiastics and of laymen. The king made known the queen's wish, and asked that they would consent to satisfy her: to which petition of the queen, although all spoke against it, at length

---

33 Cf. *Las quatro partes enteras de la Cronica de España* (Zamora: Auguston de Paz, 1541), fols. 311r-312v.

Who ought to be declared a heretic?

it was decided from the concordant judgment of all and the king, that this matter would be decided by a conflict of arms of two chosen men, who would fight a duel; one for the Visigothic, or Mozarabic, rite chosen from the whole kingdom, and the other for the French, or Roman, rite, designated by the queen and king. They came to the fight, and he who was fighting for the Mozarabic rite was the victor. But the queen having seen these things, did not want to keep quiet: but, as women are importunate and pertinacious until their wishes are satisfied, harassed the king again more vehemently and insistently, who, to please the queen again exhorted the whole assembly of the kingdom, to remove the Visigothic rite, and want to accept the French, or Roman rite. When they all together, however, spoke out against this, it was decided with the common agreement of all, that when an immense fire had been lit, the two books would be cast into it, one containing the office of Mass according to the French rite, the other according to the ancient custom of Spain. And on the day when this was going to be done, a general fast was appointed by Bernard, Archbishop of Toledo (for this event took place in Toledo) so that through the merit of fasting God having been made sympathetic would deign to reveal, through showing a miracle, what should be done. Those two books were cast into the midst of the fire, and the book, which had the French, or Roman, office, began to make a hissing sound, and immediately by a sort of leap, sprung back out of the fire. But the book, which contained the Visigothic, or Mozarabic office, remained without any harm in the middle of the fire, until that [fire] was completely extinguished.

And not even when such a great miracle had been seen, did the queen want to yield, wherefore the king henceforth did not want to exhort the kingdom (as he had done before): but to command, and force by various threats, that having removed the old office, they would accept the French, or

Roman office. Which not without tears they were forced to do, although in some churches in Toledo the renown custom and ancient rite remains, which has been kept therein until the present day. And hence there arose the common proverb among the Spanish: *Allá van leyes, do quieren reyes*,[34] which in [English] means the same as if one were to say, "The laws go where kings want." We wanted to repeat this lengthy account here, so that we might thence show how much without reason Bernard of Luxemburg inserted the Mozarabs in his *Catalogus haereticorum*.

---

34 *Do* is a literary form of *Donde*, meaning "where."

Chapter VIII

On the solution of certain doubts, which arise from the things said in the previous chapter.

About those things we discussed in the chapter immediately preceding, some doubts of not small difficulty could present themselves, to all which doubts I have decided to respond here: so that I may remove all cause of doubting, and in this way may leave the matter finished.

The first doubt is about a catechumen, who has not yet received Baptism: but only has a firm intention of receiving Baptism, if before he is touched by the water of Baptism, he were to fall into some heresy, whether he ought to be called a heretic. And perhaps it will seem to someone that such a man ought not to be called a heretic, and ought not to be punished as such: because he did not yet receive Baptism, and hence did not enter the house of the Church, and consequently was not yet subject to the Church's judgment. But those who think so, are greatly mistaken, and missed the mark (as they say) heaven-wide.[1] For a catechumen, who has decided with a firm will to be cleansed by the water of Baptism, if persevering in this intention, having been forced by necessity from this light, departs from this life without the sprinkling of water, doubtlessly will be saved: because even though he was not baptized with the Baptism of water, he was still baptized with the Baptism of desire, which happens through the hidden infusion of the Holy Ghost: about which Baptism, Christ when ascending into heaven and promising the Holy Ghost to the Apostles, says: "You shall be baptized with the Holy Ghost, not many days hence" (Acts 1, 5). He

---

1 *Toto errat coelo*, i. e., one errs by the whole extent of the heavens.

said, "baptized with the Holy Ghost," on account of the grace which they were going to receive in the coming of the Holy Ghost, and by which, they were to be cleansed from all filth of sins. Baptism, therefore, which is called by scholastic theologians "of desire," is able to cleanse souls from sins, as also to save.

But outside of the Church there is not salvation.[2] For the Church is (as Blessed Peter interprets[3]) figured by the ark of Noe, outside of which, however many are found, perish: and those alone, who have entered into it, are saved. From these things it clearly follows that he who had determined to received Baptism of water with a firm will, has already at that time entered the Church since he is in the state of salvation, which cannot be had (as we said) outside the Church: and if he openly shows this firm intention of his will to the Church, publicly asking for Baptism from her, by this very fact he subjects himself to the Church: although he has not received the Baptism which he asks for from her. And it is confirmed by the chapter, *Veniens*: where these words are found: "Not only through the Sacrament of faith: but also through faith of the Sacrament, one is beyond doubt made a member of Christ."[4] If a man is made Christ's member

---

2 *Extra Ecclesiam nulla salus.* "He can no longer have God for his Father who has not the Church for his mother" (St. Cyprian, Letter 73, n. 21 (PL 4, 503A)). "Whoever is without the Church will not be reckoned among the sons, and whoever does not want to have the Church as mother will not have God as father" (St. Augustine, *Sermo IV de symbolo*, c. 13, n. 13 (PL 40, 668)). "By the heart we believe and by the mouth we confess the one Church, not of heretics but the Holy Roman, Catholic, and Apostolic (Church) outside which we believe that no one is saved" (Pope Innocent III (Dz. 423)).

3 Cf. I Pet. 3, 20-21.

4 *Decretals of Gregory IX*, bk. 3, tit. 43 (*De presbytero non baptizato*), c. 3. Cf. Letter of Innocent III to the bishop of Ferrara (PL 215, 865A).

On the solution of certain doubts, which arise from the things said

through faith alone without the Sacrament of Baptism, then he is also made a member of the Church, which is His body, thus he can be judged by it, and punished as part of it, and its member. Whence it is that a catechumen, who asked with a firm and constant will for Baptism, if after he has been thoroughly instructed about the right faith, falls into some heresy before he has received the Baptism of water, ought to be reckoned a heretic, and as such, unless he recants, is to be punished: not however (as I think) as severely as if he had received Baptism of water. Nevertheless, I wish that these things be understood only of him who, after the firm intention of receiving Baptism, was sufficiently instructed about the right faith: and after having received the teaching of this kind, changing his mind has fallen into heresy. But if he were to fall into heresy before he was fully instructed about the Catholic faith (as we will say shortly below) such a man ought not to be reckoned a heretic.

The second doubt is about a baptized infant, who before the use of reason was taken by unbelievers, and afterwards when he attains the use of reason, does not want to accept the Catholic faith: but embraced the Mohammedan law, about which he was instructed, whether such a man is a heretic, and ought to be reckoned an apostate, and as such (if he is taken hold of by the Christians) ought to be punished? And that such a man ought to be called a heretic, seems to be proved: because everything, which is contained in the common definition of a heretic, applies very well to him. For he pertinaciously maintains a heresy, or he has completely forsaken the faith, after he had put on Christ through Baptism.

But I think that it ought to be said otherwise: because in order that someone would deservedly be called a heretic (certainly in my opinion) it is not enough that he pertinaciously maintains a heresy after having received Baptism: unless after the reception of the same Baptism he shall have been fully taught about the true faith. Certainly, infused faith alone, which is given through Baptism, without any living voice of a teacher teaching exteriorly, according to the consonant opinion of all theologians, hardly suffices for believing. "How shall they believe him, of whom they have not heard? And how shall they hear, without a preacher? And how shall they preach unless they be sent, as it is written: How beautiful are the feet of them that preach the gospel of peace, of them that bring glad tidings of good things! But all do not obey the gospel. For Isaias saith:[5] Lord, who hath believed our report? Faith then cometh by hearing; and hearing by the word of Christ" (Rom. 10, 14-17). By which words Paul the Apostle very clearly teaches that no man can by himself attain the true faith without any preaching of God's word. Therefore, it is necessary that one not be called a heretic, who has not attained the full faith, which (as we said) he could not attain without any preaching of God's word. It is surely unfitting that one would be condemned because he did not do, what he in no way had been able to do.

I reckon that the same thing ought to be said about the Jews and Saracens, and other unbelievers, who receive Baptism at an adult age, that they ought not to be immediately called heretics: if after having received Baptism, and before they were fully instructed about the faith, they shall have fallen into some heresy. For regarding these men, it rightly ought to be suspected that at that time they erred out of ignorance, and hence when such men shall have been caught, they ought to be taught, and admonished with mercy: and if after admonition and charitable correction they would fall into the same error, it may be rightly believed that they no longer have erred out of ignorance, but out of bad will. Thus, he who having received Baptism, was captured by the Saracens before the years of discretion, and since he was raised by them, worships according to their sect, if afterwards it would happen that he is captured by the Christians (in my opinion)

---

5 Cf. Is. 53, 1.

On the solution of certain doubts, which arise from the things said

he should be admonished and taught about the true faith, yet not be deemed a heretic, and ought not to be punished as such.

The third doubt is about him who was baptized, not with a valid and necessary form, who even though he did not receive a valid Baptism, still on account of the Baptism says and proclaims that he is a Christian, and strives to be thought of as such, if this man pertinaciously maintains some heresy, whether he ought to be called a heretic. William of Ockham says that such a man ought to be called a heretic:[6] yet I greatly disagree with him on this point, and rightly so: because every heretic has left the house of the Catholic Church, which he had at one time entered through Baptism. For Blessed John, when speaking about heretics, after he had said that they are antichrists, says these words: "They went out from us, but they were not of us" (I Jn. 2, 19). Didymus of Alexandria in his exposition of this Epistle explains in what way heretics ought to be called "antichrists," speaking thus: "For it follows that he who separates himself from the fraternity of the faithful, are antichrists. How are they not antichrists, who savor things opposite to what the Church confesses?"[7] These antichrists "went not out from us," because they were separated from the unity of the Church, into which they were implanted in Baptism, "but they were not of us": because they were not numbered among those who were predestined to eternal glory. Now Blessed John proves this in this way. "For if they had been of us," he says, "they would no doubt have remained with us" (I Jn. 2, 19). Hence every heretic departs from the house of the Church. But he who never entered the house of the Church, cannot depart from it. Therefore it follows for the same reason, that he who never entered the Church, could not be a heretic. Now he who was baptized not according to the valid and necessary form of

---

6 *Dialogus*, pt. 1, bk. 3, cc. 2-3.
7 *Ennaratio in epistolam I S. Joannis* (PG 39, 1784C-D).

Baptism, also did not enter the house of the Church. Thus, he who, although he were to fall into some heresy and pertinaciously support it, ought not be called a heretic.

Now I believe that this is true when he knew that he was not baptized with the form which all Christians use, and wanted to so remain. For then he was neither baptized with a Baptism of water, nor with a Baptism of desire. But if he, not knowing that he was baptized in this way, thinking that he was validly baptized, then if he has the use of reason, although he was not baptized with the Baptism of water, yet he was baptized with an interior Baptism, and this (as we said above) is enough, that he could rightly be called a heretic.

There is a fourth doubt: whether he ought to be called a heretic, who holds and teaches the opinion of some man, as though it were an article of faith: and so he is prepared to die for the defense of that man's opinion, as he would do for those opinions which are known to pertain to the faith? And about this matter I would certainly prefer to hear the opinion of others, than to say my own. Yet I will say what I think: lest I appear to have raised the question for no reason. I indeed do not hesitate to call such a man a heretic, because such a man errs in the faith, and pertinaciously. For everyone who, after he has received Baptism, pertinaciously errs about the faith, by the concordant opinion of all sensible men, is rightly deemed a heretic; wherefore he about whom we are speaking at present, ought to be deemed a heretic.

But because someone perhaps will doubt that this sort of man would err in the faith, I will remove the reason for doubting by the testimony of Augustine, who when defining error in his *Enchiridion* addressed to Laurentius, speaks thus: "To err is just to take the false for the true, and the true for the false, or to hold what is certain as uncertain, and what is uncertain as certain."[8] This man, who thinks the

---

8 C. 17 (PL 40, 240).

On the solution of certain doubts, which arise from the things said

opinion of someone is the Catholic faith, and maintains that opinion with as a firm will as the Catholic faith, who holds uncertain things as certain, thus according to Augustine's judgment, errs. Moreover, this man so thinking, by that very fact makes a calumny to the Catholic Church, and thinks that it could err in the faith: because those things, which according to this man's opinion, are certain, the Church holds to be uncertain. Thus the Church errs, in this man's opinion: because, as Augustine said, "To err is just to… hold what is certain as uncertain, and what is uncertain as certain." Now anyone who will think this about the Church, which is always enlightened by the Divine Spirit, will be reckoned a heretic by all Catholics. Rightly, therefore, that man will be called a heretic, who maintains the opinion of some man as the Catholic faith with such an obstinate will.

Now so that we may show what we say more clearly, I have decided to put forth an example before the eyes. The Church has defined nothing up until now about the conception of the Virgin Mother of God, whether she was conceived with original sin or without it.[9] But she leaves everyone free to hold what opinion he wishes about this matter. For so decided Sixtus IV, in the *Extravagantes*, which begins, *Grave nimis*;[10] which decretal of the *Extravagantes*, the Council of Trent confirmed in the fourth session.[11] If anyone, while this decision of the Church remains in effect, were to maintain either opinion with such a firm will that he would suppose that it is the Catholic faith, and having been warned about

---

9 In the Constitution *Ineffabilis Deus* of December 8, 1854, Pope Pius IX pronounced and defined that the Blessed Virgin Mary "at the first instant of her conception, by a singular grace and privilege of Almighty God, in virtue of the merits of Christ Jesus, the Savior of the human race, was preserved immaculate from all stain of original sin" (Dz. 1641).
10 *Decretals of Gregory IX*, bk. 3, tit. 5, c. 29.
11 Dz. 735.

this matter, nonetheless pertinaciously perseveres in the same opinion, so that he would be prepared to undergo death for it, such a man (without any doubt) ought to be deemed a heretic. Because in this way he shuns to submit, such that he pertinaciously believes that she errs: since she holds as uncertain those things which in the judgment of this man are certain. I, in fact, believe that the Virgin Mother of God was conceived without Original sin. Because this is more honorable and more befitting the dignity of the Mother of God, and not detracting even a pin from the dignity and excellence of her Son, the Redeemer of the whole human race. Nevertheless, I do not hold this opinion with such a firm will that I would think that it is the Catholic faith, and hence for the defense of this opinion, I would not be willing lay down my neck to the sword. And I think that one ought to judge in this manner about others: such that whoever when discussing defends some viewpoint about matters of the faith with as firm and certain will just as he would defend the Catholic faith, ought to be deemed a heretic. For anyone is bound to defend the Catholic faith with such a constant will, that if God were to permit the Pope or a universal council rightly assembled to teach the contrary: nay, nor even were an Angel from heaven (as Paul says[12]) to proclaim the contrary, one ought not to believe it. On the contrary, no one is allowed to have, short of heresy, such a constant will about those things, which are treated about matters of the faith subject to controversy. For he who were to defend with such a firm will controverted opinions of this kind, such that he would not be prepared to obey the Church saying it, by that fact alone would think that the Church could err in the judgment of the faith, which is very clear heresy. But if someone when discussing an opinion about matters of the faith, no matter how much he holds the opinion with a firm will: and thinks that it is the Catholic faith, yet is prepared to obey the Church

---

12   Cf. Gal. 1, 8.

On the solution of certain doubts, which arise from the things said

teaching something else, even if he would err, will never be called a heretic on account of this.

Chapter IX

What is pertinacity, and who ought to be called pertinacious, such that on these grounds he can be reckoned to be a heretic?

Although I have made a long and (as I think) sufficiently complete discussion about the definition of a heretic, yet someone perhaps could be uncertain on account of that which was said in that same place about pertinacity, not knowing what pertinacity would be: and who ought to be deemed pertinacious: so that (if the other things are present) one could rightly be called a heretic. Wherefore so that I may leave the matter completely finished, it seemed to me necessary, to undo this knot, regarding which there seems to be not a little obscurity.

The word pertinacity is derived from [the Latin word] *pertendo* [i. e., to persevere]. For (as Marcus [Terentius] Varro said) "In what thing someone ought not to persist, and he persists, there is pertinacity. But in what one ought to hold firm, and if he persists, it is called steadfastness [*perseverantia*]."[1] Seneca said, "Bad men are overcome by unwearying [*pertinax*] goodness,"[2] and Livy says, "Stubborn [*pertinax*] virtue conquers all things."[3] Both said pertinacity [*pertinax*] for perseverance, on account of their great closeness between the themselves. For (as Cicero says in *Officiis*) "pertinacity is very close to perseverance":[4] because both persist in the things begun. Yet they are distinguished by that, with which they deal: because perseverance occurs in something good, pertinacity in something bad.

---

1 *On the Latin Language,* bk. 5, n. 2.
2 *On Benefits,* bk 7, c. 31, n. 1.
3 *Ab urbe condita,* bk. 25, c. 14, n. 1.
4 *De inventione,* bk. 2, c. 54, n. 165

Book 1, Chapter 9

Therefore, having premised this meaning of the word, it is necessary to establish the definition of the thing, according to which anyone ought to be examined regarding pertinacity. One is pertinacious, who persists in an error which under pain of guilt he is bound to forsake. From the first part of the definition, it is gathered that not only he ought to be called pertinacious who asserts something false, but also, he who doubts about the truth. Because (as I said above in the seventh chapter of this book) he errs in this way, who doubts about a certain truth: just as he who asserts something opposed to it. Hence it is that just as someone can be pertinacious by doubting something, about which it is not allowed to doubt: so one would be pertinacious asserting something opposed to that which he is obliged to believe. And for this reason, we taught in the place just cited that a doubt in regard to the faith ought to be called heretical, if one shall have doubted with pertinacity. Now we say that someone then persists in an error, when having been warned, he contemns to revoke his error.

Next, it was added in the definition of pertinacity that one is bound to forsake the error in which he persists: because although someone may err, if he is not obliged to relinquish his error, by no means will he be called pertinacious. Certainly, there are many who are deceived by some error, who so erring, do not sin: because they are not held to know the truth opposed to that error. For someone can err without any guilt about the number and strength of the elements, the movement of the heavens, the effect of the stars, the natures of the animals, and other things of this sort, to knowing which things, the Catholic faith does not compel. For Augustine in *Enchiridion*, when speaking about errors of this kind, speaks thus: "In the case of these and other false impressions of the same kind, we are indeed deceived, but our faith in God remains secure. We go astray, but we do not leave the way that leads us to Him. But yet these errors, though they are not sinful, are to be reckoned among the evils of this life which is made subject to vanity to such an extent, that we receive what is false as if it were true, reject what is true as if it were false, and cling to what is uncertain as if it were certain."[5] And not only in these things, but also in those which are stated in Sacred Scripture, can many err without any stain of sin: because since not all are held to know everything contained there, it is necessary that he who shall err through ignorance about something of them, is (as we taught above) excused from guilt. And he who when erring does not sin, ought not to be deemed pertinacious: because one could not be pertinacious without sin. From which things we conclude that he who persists in some error ought not to be called a heretic, unless he would be held to forsake his error under pain of guilt.

Therefore, it ought to be seen who is bound to renounce the error which he asserts, or supports, and from this one will get a clearer idea about who ought to be reckoned pertinacious. First of all, I lay down a very certain rule about this matter. Whoever knows that his assertion is contrary to Sacred Scripture, or a decree of some general council, or a legitimate definition of the Pope, or against the common opinion of all Catholic Doctors, or against the tacit consent of the whole Church, errs, and sins: and if he desires to be freed from the sin, he is bound to immediately recant his error. Therefore he who knows that he errs in this way, is to be immediately deemed pertinacious without any further monition. Because Sacred Scripture, or the definition of the Church, which he knew very well, avails more than a hundred, not to speak of two or three warnings. For just as he who acts against a precept, the transgression of which is an excommunication adjoined by law, is deemed contumacious: because although no admonition of man preceded, still the caution of the law preceded, which ought to be valued to be

---

5 C. 21 (PL 40, 243).

worth more than three hundred warnings of men: so also, he who errs against Sacred Scripture, or knowing the definition of the Church, even if there were no admonitions given, will be said to err pertinaciously. It is otherwise if someone would assert something opposed to the clear judgment of the Catholic Church, because he is unaware that what he asserts is contrary to the Catholic faith; he is not pertinacious, and consequently, ought not to be considered a heretic.

And I am not motivated to say it without reason: but I assert this having been motivated by very many opinions of the holy Doctors, and by a very pressing reason. It certainly can happen that someone has the Catholic faith in general, believing everything contained in Sacred Scripture, and everything which the Church holds and teaches is true, and nonetheless errs about some particular thing: because he does not know that it is against Sacred Scripture, or against the decision of the Church: nay, rather he believes that the Church thinks just as he does, and he believes because he thinks that the Church so believes, and he is not going to believe if it be established that the Church believes otherwise. No one having a sound mind will say that this man sins: because ignorance excuses him, if the matter is of such sort that he is not held to know it. For Christ, when speaking to the Pharisees, says: "If you were blind, you should not have sin" (Jn. 9, 41). Theophylactus, when expounding which words, says: "You indeed ask about corporeal blindness, I however speak about the blindness of the soul, because if you were blind, that is, ignorant of Scriptures, you would not have such a sin: because you would sin through ignorance."[6] For it is certain that not all are bound by the same law regarding the faith: because more is required from a learned man, than from an uneducated man; more from an ecclesiastical man, and dedicated to sacred things, than from a lay and secular man; a prelate ought to know more

---

6 *Ennaratio in Evangelium Joannis*, c. 3 (PG 124, 63C-D).

things than his subject. "The lips of the priest," says God through the prophet Malachias, "shall keep knowledge, and they shall seek the law at his mouth" (2, 7). Even though ignorance often excuses prelates and preachers from heresy, it does not likewise excuse from sin: because they are obliged to know everything which is necessary for the fulfilling of their office. A preacher ought not to spread abroad anything before the people which he has not thoroughly examined, and about which it is not certain that what he preaches is true, and if he has erred through ignorance, his ignorance will not excuse him from sin: because he was obliged to know [such things]. If nevertheless he was truly prepared to be corrected when the Church shall have taught something else, although he sinned, because what he did not know he tried to teach; still he ought not to be reckoned a heretic: but he should be punished as one who is temerarious.

Other learned men can be excused through ignorance, sometimes in those things which were explicitly condemned: namely, because they did not know that they were condemned. For learned men are not bound to know all the heresies which were clearly condemned: because they are not obliged to know all the decrees of the councils: and hence if they were to say something through ignorance, being prepared to be corrected, they ought not to be reckoned heretics. Uneducated people, and the common man in general, are not bound to know more than those articles of the faith which are stated in the Apostles' Creed, and are not obliged to have a penetrating understanding of them: but it is enough if they understand in a rough way [*grosso modo*], as long as they have this promptitude of the soul, that are prepared to believe anything else the Church shall have taught. If a rural man would be ignorant of whatever else besides these articles, he will not sin: because ignorance will excuse him. From which things it very clearly follows that such a man ought not on this account be proclaimed a heretic. Because his error, to

Book 1, Chapter 9

which there is no malice adjoined, does not avail to make the man a heretic. For no man, who is without sin, ought to be reckoned a heretic: because he who is without sin, is in the state of salvation; a heretic, however, is not in the state of salvation. Because "Without faith," as Paul says, "it is impossible to please God" (Heb. 11, 6). But a common man, who erred through ignorance of those things which he is not held to know, is without sin: therefore, such as he ought not to be reckoned a heretic.

Besides, Augustine confirms this same thing, speaking thus: "If anyone thinks the same opinions which Photinus held about Christ, and was baptized in his heresy outside the communion of the Catholic Church... believing that his view was really the Catholic faith, I consider him as not yet a heretic, unless, when the doctrine of the Catholic faith is made clear to him, he chooses to resist it, and prefers that which he already holds."[7] And [Pseudo-] Blessed Jerome in a letter to Damasus, supports this opinion, speaking thus: "If this, our profession, be approved by the judgment of Your Apostleship, whoever may blame me will prove that he himself is ignorant, or malicious, or even not a Catholic but a heretic."[8] In which words [Pseudo-] Jerome intimates that not every man who thinks against the judgment and decision of the Pope ought to be called a heretic: because he deemed it would be possible that such a man so thinks through inexperience and ignorance. Because if it happened that he did not think that he ought to be called a heretic, but ignorant: and hence he did not say absolutely that that sort of man ought to be called a heretic: but he made a distinction between an

---

[7] *On Baptism, Against the Donatists*, bk. 4, c. 16, n. 23 (PL 43, 169).

[8] *In Expositione Symboli* (Among the supposititious works of St. Jerome). *Decretum Gratiani*, pt. 2, *causa* 24, q. 1, c. 14 (*Haec est fides*) (PL 187, 1269B). Pelagius, *Letter and Confession of Faith to Pope Innocent I*, n. 14 (PL 45, 1718).

ignorant man, a malicious man, and a heretic. From all these things we conclude that no man, even if he holds and teaches whatsoever pestilential error, ought to be called a heretic, if malice being absent, he said it from ignorance alone.

Now positive laws teach how someone can be excused through the claim of ignorance, by which [laws] among other things it is said: "Someone alleging ignorance ought to prove it."[9] The laws also relate by what arguments, witnesses, and judgments ecclesiastical judges can and ought to prove present and past ignorance in the one erring. I have decided to admonish the inquisitors of heretics about this alone, so that when they perceive that someone is erring in the faith, they would carefully consider the quality of the person and the error, and when these things have been carefully examined, they will easily understand who and in what error he could be excused through ignorance from the mark of heresy. Because, if the thing which he asserts is among those things which not everyone is obliged to know, one ought to firstly investigate, whether it can be proved by witnesses, or by another way that he knows that his assertion is against the Catholic faith: and then he will rightly be reckoned pertinacious, and consequently rightly reckoned a heretic. Now if it cannot be clearly proved that he so knew, then it ought to be examined whether he is prepared to accept that faith which the Catholic Church holds. And if he shall have shown that he is truly prepared, then it ought to be believed that he erred through ignorance, and on account of it he will not be pronounced pertinacious. Now if he is not prepared to accept that faith which the Catholic Church holds: on account of that reason alone, he will be pronounced pertinacious and a heretic.

And what we said about ignorance, I reckon that the same thing ought to be said about forgetfulness, because he who

---

9 Gloss on rule forty-seven of the eighty-eight rules that Pope Boniface VIII placed in the final title of *Liber sextus*.

has completely forgotten something, ought to be deemed ignorant at that time. And certainly this sort of man, although he also errs in the faith about those things which he formerly knew, if he could prove clearly in some way that he had now forgotten, he ought to be excused from pertinacity and heresy. But he will prove that he had forgotten, if when that which he contradicts shall have been recalled to his mind, he immediately embraces it without any repugnance, and recants his error. For in this way we may excuse some holy Doctors from heresy, who could nowise be excused except that we may believe that they, when they said some things, forgot other things, which it is certain that they had read. For Jerome, when expounding the words of the Savior in Matthew, "Whom do men say that the Son of man is?" (16, 13), says these words: "He does not say, 'Whom do men say that I am?', lest He seem to ask boastfully about Himself."[10] Which interpretation very clearly contradicts Luke the Evangelist, who when relating the same event said, "Whom do the people say that I am?" (9, 18). Yet it ought to be believed that when Jerome wrote those things, he had forgotten these words of Luke. Likewise Blessed Jerome in his *Commentary on Matthew*, when interpreting the words in Matthew, "Entering into a boat, he passed over the water and came into his own city" (9, 1), says: "We understand 'his own city' to be none other than Nazareth, whence He was called a Nazarene."[11] Yet this interpretation very clearly contradicts Mark the Evangelist, who in the second chapter (v. 1) when relating the same event, says that that city, into which Christ entered at that time is Capharnaum. Blessed Ambrose, when interpreting the ninth chapter of Luke, says that that James, who saw Christ transfigured on the mountain at the same time with Peter and John, was the first bishop

---

10 *Commentary on Matthew*, bk. 3 (PL 26, 115A).
11 Bk. 1 (PL 26, 54D).

What is pertinacity, and who ought to be called pertinacious?

of Jerusalem.[12] Yet this opinion is as it were diametrically opposed to Matthew, who, when relating Christ's transfiguration in chapter seventeen (v. 1), says that that James was the brother of John, who (as it is proved from the account of the Acts of the Apostles[13]) was not the bishop of Jerusalem. Many other similar things are found in the sacred and holy Doctors, and yet not a tittle is detracted by these things from their holy lives and teaching. For it ought to be piously believed that they then wrote not recalling these things, not paying heed to what Sacred Scripture related about that thing elsewhere, and if they would have paid heed, they never would have written those things which they wrote.

But here it needs to be pointed out to the reader that he ought not to reckon someone to be a pertinacious heretic, even though he asserts a proposition which he knows has been condemned by the Church, unless he shall have asserted it in that same sense, in which he knows that it was condemned by the Church. It certainly can happen that a proposition condemned by the Church may have many meanings, a false one, according to which it is rejected by the Church, and a true one, according to which it is by no means condemned. For this proposition: "God created evils" is heretical, and has been condemned by the Church. For Blessed Augustine in chapter sixty-six of his book, *On Heresies, to Quodvultdeus*, says that the Florinians are heretics, solely because they were saying that God created evil things, contrary to Sacred Scripture, which says: "God saw all the things that

---

12 "James was the first to take His place on the sacerdotal throne" (*Expositio Evangelii secundum Lucam*, bk. 7 (PL 15, 1701C-1702A)). Here a footnote states that the Roman edition of this text has: "the first [of the Apostles] who underwent martyrdom." Hence the text in Migne's *Patrologia Latina* has been corrected.

13 Cf. Acts 12, 2: "And he killed James, the brother of John, with the sword."

he had made, and they were very good" (Gen. 1, 31).[14] And in chapter sixty-five, the same Father Augustine counts the Coluthiani among the heretics because they were denying that God created evils, in opposition to that which God says through the prophet Isaias: "I form the light, and create darkness, I make peace, and create evil" (45, 7).[15] Now these cannot stand together, so that both contradictory things may be said to be false and heretical, unless both of them have a twofold meaning, such that according to one meaning it may be reckoned to be a true and Catholic assertion, but according to another meaning false and heretical. For there is a certain evil of punishment, and there is also an evil of guilt. Thus, God creates evils (as Augustine says in that same place) by inflicting very just punishments, which Coluthus was not perceiving: not however by creating evil natures and substances, insofar as they are natures and substances: in which matter Florinus was erring. If someone, therefore, were to assert that this condemned proposition: "God creates evil things," or its opposite: "God does not create evil things," even though he knows that it has been condemned by the Church, he ought not on this account to be considered pertinacious and heretical, unless he would assert it in that sense in which he knows that it was condemned by the Church. As a confirmation of which matter, Hilary says, "Heresy lies in the sense assigned, not in the word written; the guilt is that of the expositor, not of the text."[16]

About the aforesaid matter I wanted to add this one thing, and decided to admonish the reader about it, so that everything that we said in this chapter about him who asserts with a firm will something against the faith, he would think those things ought to be also said about him who doubts, such that he who doubts about some one of those things which

---

14 PL 42, 42.
15 *Ibid.*
16 *On the Trinity*, bk. 2, n. 3 (PL 10, 52A).

he knows are held by the Church as the faith, even if no warning precedes, will be rightly be called pertinacious and (as we said in another chapter) heretical: because such a man as he also errs and persists in an error, which he is obliged to forsake under threat of hell.

The second rule about pertinacity is this: Whoever errs through ignorance against the faith which the Catholic Church holds, if he has been adequately warned, is obliged to recant his error, and if he does not do so, he is pertinacious and reckoned a heretic. This rule is approved by the testimony of Blessed Augustine speaking thus: "Those, therefore, in the Church of Christ who savor anything morbid and depraved, and, on being corrected that they may savor what is wholesome and right, contumaciously resist, and will not amend their pestiferous and deadly dogmas, but persist in defending them, become heretics."[17]

But perhaps against this rule someone will object that he who has erred through ignorance in the faith, thinking what he asserts to be true, is not obliged to recant his error: because he would lie in so revoking, and "He who acts against his conscience" (as the common proverb of theologians says) "exposes himself to damnation."[18] We easily repulse this objection saying that this sort of man who errs in the faith asserting what is false for true: just as he is bound to recant his erroneous words, so he is also bound to mentally change his opinion, and lay aside his conscience: so that what he firstly believed to be true, he afterwards believes to be false. Assuredly he is firstly obliged to change the opinion of his mind, but then to recant his error with his mouth. Which order having been kept, "With the heart, he believes unto

---

17 *City of God*, bk. 18, c. 51, n. 1 (PL 41, 613).
18 *Qui facit contra conscientiam, aedificat ad Gehennam* (Gloss on Rom. 14, 23). Cf. St. Thomas, *Quaestiones Quodlibetales*, quodlibet 3, q. 12, a. 2. Also cited in *Decretum Gratiani*, c. 28, q. 1, c. 14 (PL 187, 1426A).

justice," as Paul commands, "but, with the mouth, confession is made unto salvation" (Rom. 10, 10).

The third rule is this: He who errs through ignorance in the faith after he has been admonished (even though not adequately) about his error, is held to diligently seek after the truth, and to consult learned and Catholic men about that matter, with the intention of embracing that teaching, which has been shown by them to him. Augustine teaches this opinion speaking thus: "But though the doctrine which men hold to be false and perverse, if they do not maintain it with passionate obstinacy, especially when they have not devised it by the rashness of their own presumption, but have accepted it from parents who had been misguided and had fallen into error, and if they are with anxiety seeking the truth, and are prepared to be set right when they have found it, such men are not to be counted heretics."[19] In which words it ought to be considered that he says, "if they are with anxiety seeking the truth." From which words it is clearly concluded that he who errs in the Catholic faith, if he contemns to seek the truth with anxiety, he ought to be deemed pertinacious and a heretic.

The fourth rule is this: Everyone who errs through ignorance against the faith which the Catholic Church holds, and swears that he will never forsake his assertion, immediately without any previous admonition ought to be reckoned pertinacious and heretical. The certitude of this rule is proved as follows. Anyone who is not prepared to be corrected, ought to be deemed pertinacious; but he who swears that he is not going to depart from that opinion which he holds, is not prepared to be corrected: thus, he ought to be reckoned pertinacious.

But against this someone perhaps will argue, saying that this sort of man is not pertinacious: because since this man errs through ignorance, it is not held to recant his error,

---

19 Letter 43 (*To Glorius and Eleusius*), c. 1, n. 1 (PL 33, 160). Cf. *Decretum Gratiani, causa* 24, q. 3, c. 29 (PL 187, 1307A).

What is pertinacity, and who ought to be called pertinacious?

unless he has firstly been warned: from which it seems to be gathered that he ought not to be called pertinacious. For according to those things which we said above, no one ought to be called pertinacious who is not bound to recant the error which he holds. I reply conceding that this sort of man is not bound to the recanting of his error before an admonition: yet he is bound not to so adhere to his error with such a firm will, that he would not be prepared to obey one correcting him. He is indeed bound to revoke that firmness of will, so that he would be prepared to obey those whom he is obliged to obey, and to accept their teaching. But you will say: Could not such a man as this be excused from pertinacity through ignorance? For ignorance excuses him from a lie, who asserts what is false, because he thinks it is true: according to the opinion of Augustine saying: "No one, of course, is to be condemned as a liar who says what is false, believing it to be true, because such a one does not consciously deceive, but rather is himself deceived."[20] I indeed admit that someone can be excused from a lie, who nevertheless can nowise be excused from temerity. On account of which Augustine after those words, which we have just now cited, immediately adds these words: "And, on the same principle, a man is not to be accused of lying, though he may sometimes be open to the charge of rashness, if through carelessness he takes up what is false and holds it as true."[21] So also I say that he who swears that he will not recant his opinion which through ignorance he thinks is true, is excused from error and lying, but he is not excused from the temerity of the oath, and from that firmness of will, which completely excludes all correction. And these words are enough about open pertinacity.

---

20 St. Augustine, *Enchiridion*, c. 18 (PL 40, 240). *Decretum Gratiani, causa* 22, q. 2, c. 4 (*Is autem*) (PL 187, 1130C).
21 *Ibid.* (PL 187, 131A).

Chapter X

What kind of admonition ought to be adequate, so that he who has contemned it, would rightly be deemed pertinacious?

There are many men erring about the Catholic faith who (as we said by way of an introduction in the preceding chapter) before they are adequately admonished, are not held to revoke their error, and hence before the admonition of this sort they ought not to be deemed pertinacious. Thus, since the pertinacity of these men, so that it could be manifested, depends upon the admonition, it is worthwhile and necessary to discuss what sort it ought to be: and whether it ought to be given, and how often repeated, so that it can rightly be deemed adequate. Now so that all this can be done better, one ought to consider before all else the different kinds and qualities of heresies: because according to their differences, it will also be necessary that a different kind of admonition be given. For there are some clearly condemned heresies; others are not clearly condemned, but latently condemned. I call those heresies clearly condemned which were condemned by the express definition of the Church, or the opposites of those things expressed and manifested in Sacred Scripture, or very clear conclusions are deduced from other things contained in Sacred Scripture. If someone, for example, were to say: "David was not a king," the heresy would be clearly condemned: because although it was not condemned in some council, still its opposite was expressed in Holy Writ. Also, if someone were to say, Jacob the Patriarch was not the grandson of Abraham, the heresy would be clearly condemned, because although its opposite was not expressed in Sacred Scripture by the same words, nevertheless the very manifest consequence is deduced from other words contained in the same Scripture. For therein it is said that Jacob was the son of Isaac. And Isaac was the son of Abraham; from which words it is evidently deduced that Jacob is the grandson of Abraham.

A heresy not clearly condemned is one which was not condemned by the express definition of the Church, and its opposite was not expressed in Sacred Scripture, or a very clear and immediate consequence deduced from other things contained in Sacred Scripture, but through many reasonings from other things contained in Sacred Scripture, which are not known to all, is proved to be heretical. Such are all the following propositions. "There are not three parts of penance." "Holy Water has absolutely no more worth than unblessed water." "All blessings, which the Church does or says upon water, wine, bread, salt, wax, and other things of this kind, ought to be mocked and despised." "Christians are not permitted in any way to wage war." "The souls in Purgatory can merit further reward or punishment." "Bishops are not superior to simple priests." All these assertions are heretical, yet were not expressly condemned, so not everyone will easily know that they are heretical: because so that it may appear to be heresy, many arguments are needed. It would be necessary that whoever would want to prove that these propositions are heretical would make many reasonings, and one would need much reading.

The difference of heresies having been premised, I will add some certain conclusions, from which whatever pertains to this matter can be easily concluded. Therefore, let this be the first conclusion: If someone clearly falls into a condemned heresy, he ought to be admonished to revoke his heresy by an express condemnation of his own heresy, by showing him the express definition of the Church, or by showing the opposite of his heresy in Sacred Scripture, or its opposite by deducing the evident and immediate consequence from other things contained in Sacred Scripture. And it is unnecessary that this admonition be repeated, so that he may be said to have been adequately warned: because even if it only happens once, it will be called an adequate admonition. For we call that an adequate admonition by which it is shown so clearly to the one erring that his assertion is opposed to the Catholic truth, that anyone not insane, would acknowledge that he was openly convicted of his error. From these things it follows that he, who does not accept an admonition of this kind, ought to be reckoned pertinacious, and consequently heretical. For this sort of man would not be afraid to oppose the Catholic faith, which was manifestly shown to him: hence it is that (according to those things which we said in the preceding chapter) he is not prepared to be corrected, and in this way ought to be declared pertinacious.

But if someone erring in such a way has some arguments, which motivated him to have that error, will it be permitted for him to ask for the solution of such arguments before the revocation of his error? By no means: because he is bound to bring into captivity his understanding unto the obedience of the faith.[1] And (as Jerome says) "a pure faith and a frank confession does not look for quibbles or circumlocutions."[2] But after he has revoked his error, then it will be permitted to ask for an explanation of the arguments by which he was bound, lest he seek the explanation so that he may acknowledge the truth: so that he may be able to better understand the faith, which he believes, and be more fully strengthened in it.

Perhaps someone will still ask moreover: Whether it is allowed for this man having been admonished in this way after his error, to appeal from the parish priest to the bishop, and from the bishop or inquisitor to the Sovereign Pontiff? I answer that he who has been adequately admonished, or corrected, is not allowed to appeal, and if he should attempt to appeal, his appeal is void and ought to be deemed malign.

---

1 Cf. II Cor. 10, 5.
2 Letter 82, n. 5 (PL 22, 738).

Hence it is that notwithstanding such an appeal, he ought to be reckoned by the Church as pertinacious and heretical. For it is not necessary that those things which have already been legitimately decided once by the Church, be decided again afterwards by new discussions. Hence Pope Leo I, when writing to Emperor Marcian about those things which had been discussed in the Council of Chalcedon, speaks thus: "Through Our Lord Jesus Christ, who is the Author and Ruler of your kingdom, I entreat and beseech Your Clemency, that in the present Council you do not allow the faith, which having been handed down from the Apostles, our blessed Fathers preached, to be retracted as though it were doubtful, and not permit those attempting to raise up the ruins of the things which long ago were condemned by the authority of our predecessors."[3] And Pope Gelasius says the same things in the chapter, *Majores*,[4] and Pope Felix in the chapter, *Achatius*.[5]

The second conclusion is: He who when asserting some heresy not openly condemned, although he has been admonished by a preacher, parish priest, bishop, or by any other man lower than the Sovereign Pontiff, is not bound to revoke his error, unless through manifest and evident arguments it be shown to him that his assertion is against the Catholic faith, especially if he is a learned man, who knows how to understand the arguments which could be asserted against that heresy. For regarding an uneducated man (as we will say below) another evaluation ought to be made. Hence it is that if an admonition, without arguments of this kind were to have been made to him, it ought not to be called adequate. This conclusion is proved [as follows]. No one besides the Sovereign Pontiff (as we said above in the fifth chapter) can so judge about heresy, that all would be held to obey

---

3 Letter 90, c. 2 (PL 54, 933B-934A).
4 *Decretum Gratiani*, pt. 2, *causa* 24, q. 1, c. 2, (PL 187, 1264A).
5 *Ibid.*, c. 3 (PL 187, 1264B).

his censure, wherefore one is not held to the admonition of anyone besides the Sovereign Pontiff to revoke an assertion not openly heretical. For he who is not held to adhibit firm faith to another in those matters which pertain to the faith, is also not held to revoke his erroneous assertion upon his simple admonition alone, because he who revokes an erroneous assertion, ought to hold the contrary with a firm faith: but subjects in those things, which are of the faith, are not held to give firm faith to their lower superiors, because then the faith of the subjects would rest upon the wisdom of men (which Paul denies[6]): therefore subjects are not bound to revoke their errors upon the simple admonition of those men.

Furthermore, whoever is not bound to obey the judgment of someone can appeal his judgment: but from a superior admonishing his subject about an error, and not showing clearly through the rules of faith, that that error is opposed to the Catholic truth, it is allowed to appeal: therefore, he is not bound to obey his admonition, and consequently his admonition ought not be to deemed adequate. The Major of this syllogism is manifest from the definition of an appeal: because from that judgment which someone is obliged to obey, one is not permitted to appeal. The Minor is proved by the authority of Pope Pelagius saying: "But if in any province questions shall have arisen, and among the bishops of the province themselves the views shall begin to be discordant, and among those disagreeing themselves, their views do not agree, let them then be referred to a greater See: and certainly if things are not easily and correctly resolved in that place, let them be canonically and correctly judged where the council has assembled according to law. But the greater and more difficult questions (as the holy synod has stated, and the blessed custom requires) may always be referred to the Apostolic See." And these words are found

---

6 Cf. I Cor. 2, 5.

in the chapter, *Multis*.[7] And Pope [Vigilius] says the same thing in the chapter, *Qui se*.[8] But will it not be permitted for him who errs through ignorance to appeal from the bishop, or the inquisitor, after it has been shown to him by convincing arguments that the assertion is clearly opposed to the Catholic truth? If the arguments are such that according to the judgment of learned men they prove very clearly that his assertion is opposed to the Catholic truth, it will nowise be allowed to appeal. But if the arguments are not so evident, he is not forbidden to appeal. Perhaps you will ask the reason why in this case rather than in the preceding one it would be permitted to appeal. The reason is clear. Because he who appeals after having been admonished with evident arguments has no occasion of an appeal; wherefore appealing in this way he sins, and if he does not abandon his appeal, he ought to be deemed rebellious, audacious, and pertinacious, and ought to be punished as such. But he who has not been admonished by clear arguments, has just reason for an appeal: because it has not yet been clearly shown to him that his assertion opposes the Catholic truth. Also, he to whom the Catholic truth has not been clearly shown, if he has some arguments, even though false, can justly ask for the solution of arguments of this kind, before he revokes his error. Yet this (as we just said) would not be allowed if the truth has already been shown to him through evident arguments.

Again, the same conclusion is proved thus. A bishop ought to be ready (as Blessed Peter says[9]) to give a reason to everyone asking of that faith which is in him: thus, a subject is not bound to revoke his error upon the bishop's simple admonition: unless he gives a reason, by which he proves that such an error contradicts the Catholic faith. This inference is

---

7   *Decretum Gratiani*, pt. 1, dist. 17, c. 5 (PL 187, 95B).
8   *Ibid.*, pt. 2, *causa* 2, q. 6, c. 12 (PL 187, 621B-C).
9   Cf. I Pet. 3, 15.

evident: because if someone, without a reason having been given, would be bound to revoke his assertion as erroneous, the other person would not be bound to give a reason to him: so that by it he may force him to revoke his error. But I reckon that this ought to be done only with learned men: because they understand those arguments which are offered to them for the proving of the Catholic truth. But the uneducated do not understand the arguments which can be offered to them, whence it is that they ought not to be said to him: because it would only stir up the air, and to utter words in vain. For that man (as I think), upon the mere simple admonition of the parish priest or at least the bishop, is bound to revoke his error. If, however, he contemns the parish priest and bishop, because he thinks that they are ignorant, as frequently happens to them, then learned men ought to be used, who with a simple word without any argument, admonishes him again and again: whom if he despises two or three times, he ought to be (certainly in my judgment) reckoned to be pertinacious.

From all these things it is clearly proved that Bartolus [de Saxoferrato][10] erred, who says, "He ought to be reckoned a pertinacious heretic, and to be punished as such, who does not believe the inquisitor asserting something."[11] If all are always held to believe the inquisitor asserting something, it would be true what Bartolus says, that every man ought to be reckoned to be pertinacious, who contemns to believe the inquisitor asserting something about the faith. For then he would be pertinacious in that opinion, from which he is bound to depart, and hence according to the definition of

---

10 Bartolus de Saxoferrato (Italian: Bartolo da Sassoferrato; 1313-1357) was an Italian law professor and one of the most prominent continental jurists of Medieval Roman law.
11 *Commentaria in primam infortiati partem* (Turin: [s. n.], 1590), on *Digest of Justinian*, bk. 26, tit. 10, law 3, §. *Tutores*, fol. 62v.

pertinacity, he will rightly be called pertinacious. But it is not so, that all are necessarily held to always believe the inquisitor asserting something. Otherwise, it would necessarily happen that men would sometimes be held to believe an error or heresy. For it could be that the inquisitor would err in the faith: because by the office committed to him, he was not confirmed in the faith, and was not made inerrant. For these men, who support the Pope's authority very much, admit he could err in the faith, if he does not practice that diligence which he is bound to do regarding the examination of truth. For so teaches [Cardinal] Juan de Torquemada in his *Summa Ecclesiae*.[12] Much more easily could an inquisitor err, since Christ did not ask for him that his faith would not fail, as Sacred Scripture bears witness that He had asked for Peter.[13]

I know an inquisitor who was angry towards a certain preacher, because he publicly preached that confession is necessary by Divine law, and ordered him to publicly revoke his opinion. That inquisitor was in fact an expert in Canon Law, who perhaps had read a comment on the Decretals, on the beginning of the fifth *Distinctio*, on Penance,[14] saying that confession is not of the Divine law,[15] but of human law; and

---

12 "The assistance of the Holy Ghost which was promised by Christ does not regard the person of the Pope but the office or See, and hence since to have an opinion belongs to the person, but to judge belongs to the office: although it would possible to the Pope to have a wrong opinion, still to err by deciding in a judgment about those things which are of the faith is not possible, while the Divine promise stands" (*Summa de Ecclesia* (Venice: Michele Tramezzino, 1561), bk. 2, c. 112, fol. 259v).
13 Cf. Lk. 22, 32.
14 *Decretum Gratiani*, pt. 2, *causa* 33, dist. 5, c. 1 (*Consideret*) (PL 187, 1631B).
15 Peter de Osma in his book, *Tractatus de confessione* (1542). The copies of this book were burnt, and none are available today. Dz. 724. Cf. Alfonso de Castro, O. F. M, *Against All Heresies*, in

Panormitanus[16] commenting on the chapter, *Omnis utriusque sexus*,[17] asserting this same thing, and hence thought that this is an irrefutable opinion. Therefore, I will now inquire of Bartolus, whether such a preacher was then held to believe the inquisitor asserting that confession is not of Divine law, but merely of human law? If he would say that the preacher is not obliged to this, then for this reason what he said is false: "He ought to be reckoned a pertinacious heretic, and to be punished as such, who does not believe the inquisitor asserting something." But if Bartolus were to say that that preacher was obliged by the command of the inquisitor to publicly revoke his opinion: then it is necessary that he grant that that preacher was obliged to recant the Catholic truth, and to preach heresy in its place.

For to say that the confession of sins is not of Divine law, but merely of human law, is heresy, and has already been condemned by the Apostolic See by a clear judgment. Which condemnation we inserted in that work which we published, *Against All Heresies*, in the section on "Confession." And this opinion was not condemned by the Apostolic See alone, but also by a general council legitimately assembled. For the Council of Trent, which was begun under Paul III, and afterwards when he died proceeded under Julius III, in the

---

the section, "Confession," first error.

16 *Commentaria in quartum et quintum Decretalium Librum* (London: Cum privilegio regis Philippo Tinghio, 1586), vol. 3, fol. 256r. Panormitanus (d. 1445) was the abbot of the monastery of Maniace, near Messina, whence his name *Abbas*, to which has been added *modernus* or *recentior* (in order to distinguish him from *Abbas antiquus*, a thirteenth-century canonist who died ca. 1288); he is also known as *Abbas Siculus* on account of his Sicilian origin. He stated that no overt authority indicates that God or Christ explicitly instituted confession to a priest.

17 *Decretals of Gregory IX*, bk. 5, tit. 38 (*De poenitentiis et remissionibus*), c. 12. Cf. Dz. 437.

fourteenth session celebrated under the same Julius, in which it was treated (while I was there present) about Sacramental confession, among many other things, which then issued canons about this matter, namely, it directed the third, sixth, and seventh to this scope,[18] so that it would bind those who would say that that Sacramental confession is not necessary by Divine law for him who has fallen into mortal sin. And we also inserted these canons of the Council of Trent in the section on "Confession" in that aforesaid work which we published, *Against All Heresies*. From which words it is clearly proved that that inquisitor erred very badly, who was trying to force the preacher to recant his own opinion, which when preaching he had publicly said to the people, that confession is of the Divine law. Thus, everyone ought not be to reckoned a pertinacious heretic who does not believe an inquisitor asserting something, because he is not held to believe everything which he shall have said. Now it can be clearly shown when a man ought to be reckoned a pertinacious heretic, who does not want to believe an inquisitor, from the things said and about to be said in this chapter.

Now Bartolus' argument whereby he seems to prove his opinion has no force. For from what is said in that aforesaid law, *Tutor*, §. *Tutores*, namely, that one is said to be pertinacious who does not obey a judge commanding, Bartolus deduces that a man ought to be declared pertinacious who does not believe an inquisitor asserting something. Yet this argument is mistaken in many ways. Firstly, because that law does not speak universally about every command of a judge: but only about the command of an inventory to be made by a guardian, and the tutor who does not wish to obey the judge commanding that such an inventory be made, is said according to the words of the law, to resist the judge pertinaciously. To infer from this particular decree of the law, however, a general law applying to everyone who does

---

18 Dz. 913, 916, 917.

not want to obey a judge, is a very bad inference. For there is not an equal condition of every affair, so that they would all be governed by the same law. For in that affair, about which that law speaks there, the guardian is held to obey the judge commanding, and hence if he does not want to obey, he will rightly be pronounced pertinacious. Yet there are many other affairs in which men are not held to obey the judge: because if they were always, and in all things, held to obey the judge, it would never be allowed for anyone to appeal from a mandate of a judge, and it would then become necessary that the superior judge, to whom he appealed, would be held also to pronounce sentence against the one appealing, because he wrongfully appealed. Now it is evident that the appeals of many are just, and have been declared as such by a superior judge. From which it is manifestly gathered that they then were not obliged to obey the lower judges, from whom it was permitted to appeal, and consequently they then ought not be reckoned pertinacious.

Bartolus secondly erred in his aforesaid argumentation, because even if it were true that every man ought to be deemed pertinacious, who does not want to obey a secular judge, the conclusion ought not to thence be applied to him who does not want to believe an inquisitor asserting something about matters pertaining to the faith. Because matters which pertain to the faith are not of the same sort as secular affairs, and ought not to be measured with the same measure. For affairs which pertain to the faith, rise above all human judgment: and hence Paul says our faith does "not stand on the wisdom of men, but on the power of God" (I Cor. 2, 5). Wherefore in those things a man is not held to obey the inquisitor asserting something: unless it would be evident that those things which he asserts are held by the universal Church, and shine forth by God's wisdom. But secular matters are not so sublime that they surpass all human powers, and hence those matters can depend upon men's wisdom.

The third conclusion is: If someone were to fall into some heresy through ignorance, and after having been admonished by the parish priest, bishop or whatever other believing man by evident arguments, that his assertion is against the Catholic faith, he is immediately obliged to revoke his error: which if he does not do, he will be pertinacious, and reckoned heretical. This conclusion is sufficiently known to anyone, if he would consider that it is unimportant by whom someone is instructed, provided that the truth has been clearly shown to him: because (as all the wise philosophers teach) one ought to consider what is said, and not by whom it is said.[19] Moreover, Paul the Apostle said that our faith does "not stand on the wisdom of men," but it would be the wisdom of men if the same admonition made by a subject were not as powerful than if it were said by a superior. Again, if he who errs through ignorance against the Catholic faith, afterwards when reading by himself in the books of others, discovers arguments which clearly prove the Catholic truth, he would be held without any further admoniser to revoke his erroneous assertion: therefore, if someone else shows him through evident arguments the same Catholic truth, he will also be held to revoke his erroneous assertion.

But someone will say: What difference then will there be between he who has been admonished by a superior, and he who has been admonished by a subject? A great difference indeed. For a superior can also summon an unwilling man who errs against the Catholic faith, to appear before him, and demand from him and account of the faith: he can indeed compel him to hear arguments by which he may try to persuade him of the Catholic faith. He also can bind him

---

[19] St. Augustine, *Expositions on the Psalms*, on Ps. 49, sermon 3, n. 20 (PL 36, 395). *Decretum Gratiani*, dist. 19, c. 8, §3 (PL 187, 110B).

to revoking his error. And if he contemns to obey these and the other things pertaining to his office, he could inflict due punishments upon him, according to the gravity of his crime. But a subject can do none of these things, even though he would be equally bound upon his adequate admonition to revoke his error, just as though he had been admonished by his superior. These things have been said about an admonition made by those inferior to the Sovereign Pontiff. Now whether completely the same thing ought to be said about an admonition made by the Sovereign Pontiff, different persons say different things. For there is no agreement among them all about this matter. For certain men say that the Sovereign Pontiff is measured with the same measure as other bishops, and they say that he also is held by this law, that he ought to be ready to give a reason to everyone asking of that faith which is in him.[20] Unless he gives which, they say that no one is obliged on account of his admonition to revoke his error, which he maintains against the Catholic faith on account of ignorance. William of Ockham supports this opinion,[21] And Jean Gerson discusses [this opinion in a tract entitled,] *Whether it is licit in matters of the faith to appeal from the decision of the Sovereign Pontiff?*[22]

Yet I think the opposite, thinking it to be safer to believe the simple admonition of the Pope is enough so that someone would be held to revoke his error, especially since he, after firstly having consulted with learned men (as he ought), has fully examined the matter. For otherwise it would also be allowed in a dispute which is about the faith, to appeal from a decision of the Pope, which is a horrendous thing to

---

20 Cf. I Pet. 3, 15.

21 *Dialogus*, bk. 1, c. 20.

22 *Quomodo et an liceat in causis Fidei a summon Pontifice appelare seu ejus judicium declinare?* in *Ioannis Gersonii Opera omnia* (The Hague: apud Petrum de Hondt, 1728), vol. 2, pp. 303-308.

say, since there is no one to whom one can have recourse or appeal. The appeal is certainly ridiculous, because in this way we would always be doubtful, and we would languish without any hope of a remedy, since it is very difficult to assemble a legitimate council, which now is nearly impossible on account of the many hostilities among rulers, who fight fiercely among themselves with perpetual and irreconcilable wars. Furthermore, in this way an occasion would be given to anyone to teach with impunity all the heresies they wish, because when he would be condemned by the Pope, he will appeal to a council. Luther certainly did this, when he understood that he had been condemned by Leo X, who nevertheless after hearing a rumor about an assembling a council, withdrew his published books from the council saying that he would not submit to a council, so that he made it plain to all that he would not learn the truth, but in order to cover his pertinacity with some paint, he had appealed to a council which he hoped would never be assembled.

Next, it is ridiculous to say that on account of the doubt in the faith of any man whosoever, a council ought to be assembled, which nevertheless ought to be done according to those who maintain the opposite view. But if you deny this saying that the Pope can without the assembling of a council often refute errors against the faith through evident arguments, wherefore the assembling of such a council will not always be necessary; what if the one erring through ignorance would deny that those arguments are of any value, and were to say that they do absolutely nothing against his assertion? Who then will be the judge, who would judge about the value of the arguments? If you say that one ought to believe the judgment of learned men, who say that such arguments are valid, you will then be forced to say that the Sovereign Pontiff's authority is less in the judgment of the faith, than the authority of learned men, since the former depends upon the latter. Hence it is that as often as there is

What kind of admonition ought to be adequate

a dispute about the strength and evidence of the arguments which are made by the Pope, one necessarily ought to appeal to a council, which no one having a sane mind will say. On account of these and many other inconveniences which can arise if it were permitted to appeal from the decision of the Pope to a future council, the Sovereign Pontiff Pius II issued a special decree against those who interposed appeals of this kind. And because this decree is unknown to many, because it is not found among the other Extravagantes Decretals, which are published together with the other books of Canon Law, I want to insert it all here, so that henceforth it can be known to all.

The Bull of the Sovereign Pontiff, Pius II, by which one is warned under threat of very serious punishments, not to appeal from the decision of a Pope to a future council.

Pius the Bishop, servant of the servants of God, for a perpetual memorial of the matter.

An execrable, and in former ages unheard-of abuse, has sprung up in our time, namely, that some people, imbued with the spirit of rebellion, presume to appeal to a future Council, from the Roman Pontiff, the Vicar of Jesus Christ, to whom it was said in the person of Blessed Peter: "Feed my sheep" and "Whatsoever thou shalt bind on earth shall be bound also in Heaven"; they do not do so because they are anxious to obtain sounder judgment, but in order to escape the consequences of their sins, and anyone who is not ignorant of the laws can realize how contrary this is to the sacred canons and how detrimental to the Christian community. Because—passing over other things which are most manifestly opposed to this corruption—who would not find it ridiculous when appeals are made to what does not exist and the time of whose future existence nobody knows? The poor are oppressed in many ways by the stronger, crimes remain unpunished, freedom is conceded to delinquents, and all ecclesiastical discipline and hierarchical order are confounded.

Wishing therefore to thrust away from Christ's Church this pestilent venom, to take care of the salvation of all those who have been committed to us, and to hold off from the sheepfold of Our Savior all cause of scandal, we condemn appeals of this kind by the counsel of all prelates and juris-consults of Divine and human law adhering to the Curia and on the ground of our sure knowledge; we denounce them as erroneous and detestable, quash and entirely annul them in the event that any such appeals, extant at present, may be discovered, and we declare and determine that they are—like something void and pestilent—of no significance. Consequently, we enjoin that nobody dares under whatever pretext to make such an appeal from any of our ordinances, sentences, or commands and from those of our successors, or to adhere to such appeals, made by others, or to use them in any manner.

If anyone, of whatever status, rank, order, or condition he may be, even if adorned with imperial, royal, or episcopal dignity shall contravene this after the space of two months from the day of the publication of this Bull by the Apostolic Chancery, he shall *ipso facto* incur sentence of anathema, from which he cannot be absolved except by the Roman Pontiff and at the point of death. A university or a corporation shall be subjected to an ecclesiastical interdict; nonetheless, corporations and universities, like the aforesaid and any other persons, shall incur those penalties and censures which offenders who have committed the *crimen laesae maiestatis*[23] and promoters of heretical depravity are known to incur. Furthermore, scriveners and witness-

---

23 Lit., "the crime of injured sovereignty," i. e., high treason against a sovereign.

es who shall witness acts of this kind and, in general, all those who shall knowingly furnish counsel, help, or favor to such appealers, shall be punished with the same penalty.

Therefore, it is not allowed to any man to infringe or to oppose by audacious perversion this charter of our will, by which we have condemned, reproved, quashed, annulled, decreed, declared, and ordered the aforesaid. If anyone, however, shall so attempt, let him know that he shall incur the indignation of Almighty God and of Saints Peter and Paul, His Apostles.

Given at Mantua, in the year 1460 of the Lord's Incarnation, on the fifteenth day before the Kalends of February, in the second year of our Pontificate.[24]

From all these things it is very clearly established that it is nowise licit to appeal from a sentence which the Sovereign Pontiff gave in a previously well-investigated dispute of the faith. Therefore, one doubtlessly (as I reckon) always ought to believe the Pope's simple admonition: especially if he firstly has fully examined the matter together with many learned men. Otherwise, we could have nothing certain in many matters pertaining to the faith: because there are many things pertaining to the faith which we firmly hold through the mere decision of the Pope, in which the Pontiff gave absolutely no reason for his decision. But you will say, then our faith would be in the wisdom of some man, if anyone were to be held to his simple admonition alone to revoke his error. I reply that it will not be in man's wisdom, but in God's power, Who said that He would pray for Peter, that his faith would not fail.[25] Still, if the Pope, after having consulting learned men, but relying upon his judgment alone, attempts to decide something, in which case he without a doubt could

---

24 The Bull *Exsecrabilis* (Dz. 717).
25 Cf. Lk. 22, 32.

err, then I would believe that he ought to give a reason of that faith, to which he attempts to force others: especially if the matter is such that it would require much study, and about which at other times learned and Catholic men hesitate. And I would not think that such a simple admonition of the Pope is enough, so that someone thinking against it, would be by that very fact pertinacious: and consequently reckoned a heretic.

For Peter, although the Sovereign Pontiff, was compelled by the Apostles and the brethren who were in Judea, to give an explanation why he entered the house of the Gentile Cornelius, and conversed with him.[26] A decree published by the Pontiff about the faith, even if an explanation were not given in it, which would oblige to such faith: because (as we taught above) it is enough to refuting heresies, to show it to the one erring, I think that it is enough for an adequate admonition: such that whoever opposes it when it is known to himself, is pertinacious, and consequently ought to be reckoned a heretic. Because even though no explanation is added in that decree, which motivated him to publish such a decree, one still ought to believe that the Church would never have accepted such a decree, unless it had been sure that it was published with strong reasons.

---

26 Cf. Acts 11, 2-3.

Chapter XI

On the declaration of faith made by someone before an assertion of heresy, whether it avails to free him from the mark of heresy.

Learned and believing men, when considering the sublimity of our faith, which often surpasses all the powers of human understanding, when they undertake to treat about the mysteries of faith in either word or writing, fear lest they may fail in the treatment itself and so be stained with the mark of heresy, which they greatly detest. In the beginning of their disputation, they are accustomed to protest that they do not want to depart even a hair's breadth from the rule of faith: but in everything they wish to embrace that faith which the Catholic Church holds, and they say that they subject themselves in all things to the decision of the same Catholic Church. But if afterwards it happens that they say something against the Catholic faith, from the outset they say that they revoke it, and they ask to be held as one who recants. I recall that I did this in the preface of that work which I published, *Against All Heresies*, and in that work both in the preface and also elsewhere, I know that I often said it. Thus, it is wondered by many, and not undeservedly, of what avail are these protestations: whether those who have asserted something contrary to the Catholic faith can, and ought, to be excused from the crime and mark of heresy on account of the protestations of this kind made by them.

Now in order that we bring forth a clearer explanation about this matter, one ought to have a twofold consideration on it. For excusing from that crime of heresy is done in one way before God, Who knows the secrets of the hearts,[1] and another way before men, who only see those things which appear

---

1 Cf. II Par. 6, 30.

outwardly. Someone certainly can be excused before God, who nevertheless will not be excused before the judgment of men, and vice versa. For God does not judge except according to the testimony of our conscience: because knowing what sort of faith lies hidden in our hearts, also knowing what kind of declaration of the same faith was made by us, pronounces such a sentence about us, not caring about the other things which are uttered by us with our voice. Human judgment only considers those things which are done outwardly, and so only notices the works, words and other things which appear outwardly: so that from those things as from a sort of signs it conjectures what lies hidden in the heart. Now it often happens that those things which appear outwardly are not true signs of those things which are in the heart: as is shown in hypocritical men who pretend to be something outwardly, and are in reality something different in their hearts. Hence it necessarily happens that there are many men innocent before God, who human judgment condemns: and on the contrary, there are many men approved by human judgment, who are rejected before God.

Thus, let us firstly speak about excusing before God, and afterwards about excusing before men. Wherefore let there be this sort of conclusion about this matter: A general declaration about the faith, and a conditional revocation of heresy, if done truthfully and sincerely, excuses before God from the crime of heresy him who has fallen into some heresy through ignorance. This conclusion will be apparent to anyone if he were to consider that he who truthfully and from his inmost heart universally professes the Catholic faith, and from the heart condemns every heretical error, is prepared to be corrected (if he should err), and if he were to fall into heresy, revokes and condemns it: when he would be fully taught about it. Otherwise he would not have truly and from the heart made a general declaration about the faith, and would not have sincerely made a conditional revocation of heresy

On the declaration of faith made by someone before an assertion of heresy

into which he could have fallen. But he who was prepared, when he errs, to be corrected, even if it would happen that he falls through imprudence into some heresy (as we taught above) will never be called a heretic: because (as Augustine says) he does "not maintain it with passionate obstinacy."[2]

And on this point I make no distinction whether he errs about those things which he was held to know, or about those things which he was not obliged by any law to know: in whatever way he errs, if he has truly and sincerely declared the faith in general: and with the same truthful heart has revoked all heresy, if he had fallen into it, he is always excused before God. For such man as this, who in this way has declared the faith with a pure heart, and truly revokes heresy if he were to fall into it: if he errs about those things, which he was obliged to know, through the sin of ignorance, that is, because he was ignorant of that which he was obliged to know, he will be held guilty before God, yet not for the crime of heresy. I said, and not without reason, "if he sincerely made that declaration of faith, or conditional revocation of heresy": because if he declared the faith not sincerely, but with words only and a feigned intent, such a declaration of faith or conditional revocation of heresy will not support him at all before God. For there are those who say to God, "Lord, Lord": yet God will say at the Judgment: "Because I know you not, depart from Me all you who work iniquity."[3] These also are they who, the Apostle bearing witness, "profess that they know God: but in their works they deny him" (Tit. 1, 16).

Such was Martin Luther in the beginning of publicizing and spreading of his heresies: because he then declared the Catholic faith by words, and said that he subjects his teaching to the examination of the holy Roman Church: but afterwards he showed by many and very clear evidence that this

---

2 Letter 43, c. 1, n. 1 (PL 33, 160), cited above.
3 Cf. Mt. 7, vv. 21 & 23.

declaration was feigned. Whence it happened that he had no excuse concerning his heresies before God Who searches the reins and hearts.[4] For in that work, which he sent to the Sovereign Pontiff Leo X, he made this declaration: "At the outset I protest that I desire to say or hold nothing which firstly in and from Holy Writ, then from the Ecclesiastical Fathers, and received and kept up until now by the Roman Church, and is found and can be found from the Canons and Decrees of the Pontiff... By this protest I believe it to be made clear enough that I am able to err, but I will not be a heretic."[5] Perhaps by this protestation of his Luther was able to deceive men, who only behold those things which appear, but not God Who penetrates with His eyes the deepest recesses of the heart, and knows most clearly whatever hides in them. Now how true this protestation was, and with what intention it was made, he himself declared not long afterwards, when having been admonished about his errors by the same Leo X, he not only did not submit to the admonition, neither did he revoke his heresies at his command: but he defended the same heresies more pertinaciously, and afterwards having run wild, he attacked with many insults the same Leo X, to whose correction he previously pretended to submit himself. He could not hide his hypocrisies for long: but it was necessary that, boiling over, and headstrong by his pride, and insolent by his arrogance he would burst out at some time.

We think that these things that have been said are enough regarding the excusing before God, but now let us discuss what kind of excuse about heresy a general declaration about the faith can make before men. So that we can do it more openly and clearly, however, it is necessary to firstly point

---

4 Cf. Apoc. 2, 23.
5 M. Luther, *Resolutiones* (1518) in *Weimarer Ausgabe* (Weimar: Hermann Böhlau, 1883) (and hereafter "WA"), vol. 1, p. 529, ln. 33-p. 530, ln. 11.

On the declaration of faith made by someone before an assertion of heresy

out the fact that men can err about the faith and fall into some heresy in two ways. For there are some men who err not knowing. There are again others who knowingly deviate from the true rule of faith. I call those men "knowing," who know something has been defined by the universal Church, or has been accepted by her as the true faith, and nonetheless teach, or are not afraid to express an opinion against the judgment of the same Church. But I call those "unknowing," who are unaware that something belongs to the Catholic faith: and hence think, or teach, against the same faith. Yet if they were to know the opinion which they express is against the Catholic faith, they would immediately revoke their opinion.

These things having been premised, I will add some conclusions from which anyone could very easily understand what pertains to this matter. The first conclusion is: He who unknowingly errs in the faith about those things which he is not obliged to know, is excused by the Church through a general revocation. This conclusion is manifest from those things which we taught in the ninth chapter of this book. For (as we taught in that place) not all are held by the same obligation regarding the knowledge of the faith. He who is ignorant about that which he is not obliged to know, does not sin; but he who does not sin is not a heretic: therefore, he who through ignorance errs about those things which he is not obliged to know is excused before the Church from heresy through a general declaration of faith.

The second conclusion is: He who not knowing errs in the faith about those things which he is obliged to know, even if he is excused before God (as we said), nevertheless is not excused before men by a true general declaration of the faith: unless perhaps he could prove his ignorance. This conclusion is correct, because although he does not know, still the Church presumes, and rightly so, that he knows those things about which he errs. For since he was obliged to know that matter, she very fittingly presumes that he knows it, and therefore so judges about him, as though he had erred knowingly. But he who errs knowingly, as we will soon say, cannot be excused from the crime of heresy by any declaration of faith previously made. Yet if that man wanted to prove his ignorance, so that in this way he could purge himself from the crime of heresy, he ought not to be repelled, but kindly heard.

Now how someone could prove their own innocence, I leave this to be discussed by legal experts. Still, careful consideration is necessary, so that he whose duty it is to judge others about heresy, firstly very diligently pays attention whether that man was obliged to know that about which he erred. For there are also some things pertaining to the faith so recondite, that they often lay concealed from very learned men, as are some things which can very difficultly be elicited from Sacred Scripture, and hence it is permitted to doubt about those things, and learned men often hesitate and vacillate about them. Certainly, in such matters that are doubtful, and not yet clearly decided by the Church, a general declaration made about the faith will avail to excuse the one erring from the crime of heresy, such that if afterwards the Church were to define something about that matter, he who before the definition thinks that opposite, nowise ought to be pronounced a heretic, because he had willingly submitted his opinion to the judgment of the Church. For this reason Abbot Joachim[6] was not condemned as a heretic in the [IV] Lateran Council under Innocent III, even though his teaching was therein branded by the Church of heresy. For he had submitted his teaching to the decision of the Church, as appears through those things which are found in the chapter, *Firmiter*.[7] Regarding these things also, which are against the

---

6 Joachim of Flora (1132-1202) was an Italian Cistercian abbot who had held certain Trinitarian errors.

7 "Yet on this account we do not wish to detract from the mon-

On the declaration of faith made by someone before an assertion of heresy

express definition of the Church, do general declarations of the faith of this kind avail unto him about whom it is unsure whether he had known the definition of the Church? Because on account of that general declaration of the faith, which he had made, it is permitted to doubt that he erred out of ignorance of the Church's definition. Now he has confirmed this suspicion of others, and his own excusing, if when the definition of the Church shall have been shown to him, he immediately recants his error, and condemns the heresy, which he was holding.

The third conclusion is: Whoever asserts something against that which he knows is the faith of the Church, or doubts about it, even though he has made a general declaration of the faith, in no way could such a declaration of the faith support him, and moreover he ought to be reputed by the Church as a heretic. For he is pertinacious: because even though he says that he is prepared to be corrected about his error by the Church, in reality he is not prepared. For how can it be that someone was prepared to obey the one whom he fights in open assault [*aperto Marte*[8]]? But he who knowingly departs from the Church's judgment, clearly opposes the Church: therefore, that man is not ready to correct his error upon the Church's command. Hence it is that he ought to be called pertinacious and heretical: even though he made a general profession of faith. Otherwise, a very wide way would be open to all, through which all would introduce what heresies they will, nay, a very great occasion would be given to heretics to teach with impunity whatsoever heresy.

---

astery in Florence (whose founder is Joachim himself), since both the institution there is regular and the observance salutary, especially since Joachim himself has ordered all his writings to be assigned to us, to be approved or even corrected by the judgment of the Apostolic See" (*Decretals of Gregory IX*, bk. 1, tit. 1 (*De summa Trinitate et fide Catholica*), c. 2; Dz. 433).

8 Cf. Seneca, *Oedipus*, ln. 275.

For any heretic will firstly make a general declaration of faith, and conditional revocation of any heresy into which he might happen to fall, and will think it enough for himself that even though he afterwards asserts a most pestilential heresy, he could excuse himself from the mark of heresy.

For in this century Martin Luther, the most pestilential of all heretics, used deceit and trickery of this kind, who in that work which he sent to the Sovereign Pontiff, Leo X, even though he strewed great and very clear heresies in it, nevertheless he made that declaration in the beginning of that work, which we recently cited above in this chapter. But even though he had made such a declaration, the same Sovereign Pontiff Leo did not hesitate to brand him with the mark of heresy, and rightly so: because he understood that such a declaration of his was feigned and not truthful, as the same Luther himself declared in the text of the same work. For even though someone may want to conceal a lie with many coverings, still the lie itself is of such a sort, that in the end emerges as itself. For in that same work, which he had addressed to Leo X, either repenting or having forgotten this above-mentioned declaration, he was not ashamed to pour out these words very clearly diametrically opposing the above-mentioned declaration: "And so that I may sometimes be daring," Luther says, "I declare that I do not doubt, but rather I am prepared to endure fire and death for, those things which I have said here, and I declare anyone a heretic who thinks otherwise."[9] By these words he revealed himself clearly enough, who previously had lain hidden. What more is needed so that we would reckon him a pertinacious heretic? How can it happen that he is ready to be corrected, who is prepared to endure fire and death for those things which he teaches? The clever serpent certainly thought that by deception of this kind he deludes Catholic men. And so that we may show his diabolical malice more

---

9   WA 1, p. 607, lns. 18-21.

On the declaration of faith made by someone before an assertion of heresy

clearly to the whole world, I will cite other words of his, whereby he revealed more clearly his diabolical spirit. For in the book of the Acts which the same Luther compiled in one volume, and before the very Reverend Thomas de Vio, the renown Cardinal [Cajetan] of Saint Sixtus, sent by the Apostolic See as a legate to pacify the Lutheran hostilities, he included these words which follow: "Now, dear reader, so that you may be in agreement with me. This last reply of mine, even though I have given it with much reverence, as though I left [the matter] to the decision of the Pope: but you must not think, however, that I have done it, because I doubt about the matter myself, or that I will ever change the opinion of my mind. The Divine truth is also the Lord of the Pope. For I do not wait for a man's judgment: when I have known the Divine judgment."[10] Do you now see, honorable reader, how truthfully and how sincerely that first declaration of Luther was made? I now ask you whether you want to exclude Luther from the list of heretics on account of that declaration? I do not think that any Catholic man, unless he be insane and senseless, who by the supports of such a frivolous and empty declaration would want to vindicate a heretical man from the mark of heresy. Therefore I say and hold with a very firm mind, that no one who would oppose the judgment of the Catholic Church, which he knew well, can through absolutely any general declaration of faith previously made by him, be excused from the crime of heresy before the Church. Hence it is that if someone asserted something in his writings contrary to the express definition of the Church, which it is clearly evident from the writings of the same man was known to him, can and also ought after his death, notwithstanding any declaration made by him, to be condemned as heretical: unless it were established that he repented of this sort of error before death. For this reason,

---

10 *Acta F. Martini Luther Augustiniani apud D. Legatum Apostolicum Augustae* (WA 2, p. 17, ln. 38-p. 18, ln. 4).

therefore, I confess that I do not know how I could excuse from the crime of heresy a number of teachers who are held to be Catholics, when I find some opinions in their writings which very clearly and diametrically oppose the definitions of the Church: and it is established from the writings of the same teachers that those same definitions which they opposed, were known to them. If, however, it is not established that he knew the Church's definition which he contradicts, and from thence it appears that he thinks rightly about the faith in other matters, I would believe that the general declaration of the faith previously made by him, ought to support him, so that by it he can be rightly freed from the stain of heresy.

Chapter XII

Concerning blasphemers, whether they ought to be reckoned to be heretics.

After having already completed the general consideration of heretics, and having explained everything which suffices for having a complete knowledge of heretics, now (so that I may leave the same matter clearer) it seemed [worthwhile] to me "to check the stone," as it is said, "with the plumb-line," and to discuss about certain persons, who could perhaps cause doubt, whether they ought to be reckoned heretics. And firstly, regarding a blasphemer, about whom not a small occasion of doubting is had, whether he ought to be pronounced a heretic. For theologians do not reckon blasphemy among the sins of disbelief, and hence deny that blasphemy pertains to heresy. But if blasphemy is not heresy, it follows that neither is a blasphemer a heretic. Yet the opposite somewhat seems to be the case, because inquisitors of heretics punish blasphemers, whom nevertheless they would not dare to punish unless they considered them to be heretics. For a clearer and more certain decision about this matter, it is necessary that we firstly consider about blasphemy, what kind of sin it is, and from thence we will more easily discover what we are inquiring about it.

Hugh of Saint Victor in his book, *De fructu carnis et spiritus*,[1] defines blasphemy, speaking thus: "Blasphemy is evil speech of insulting words hurled upon another with a certain abusive irreligiosity: or it is the belittling of the Divine or a human name made by swearing or reproaching."[2] From which two definitions it is established that blasphemy is properly a reproach or insult with belittling of the Divine

---

1 This work is also attributed to Conrad of Hirsau.
2 C. 6.

honor. And for this reason, those who swear by the private members of Christ or of other holy men, are called blasphemers. Because even though Christ in fact has those private members, as any other true and whole man, and hence in this way those naming them do not lie, still they name those things to dishonor and insult Christ, wishing from this manner of speaking, to intimate that there is something ignominious in Christ and blameworthy. Therefore, those words even though they are not of themselves blasphemous, still the very manner of speaking, which is with insult and mockery, brings about a blasphemy. Now that Hugh put in his definition "evil speech of insulting words hurled upon another," and did not express upon whom, he put it this way because he thought that insults to God are a blasphemy, but also insults which are said to the Saints, from thence devolve in some pass on to God. For just as God is praised in His Saints and He acts through His Saints, so on the contrary when they are insulted or mocked, those things which God does in His Saints are consequently insulted, and God is mocked, Who is the doer of them.

Now this belittlement of the Divine honor can happen in two ways: because either it is on the inside in the heart, or on the outside through words, or other exterior signs. Those things which are interior in the heart, can still happen in three ways: because either it is only in the mind, or only in the heart, or it is simultaneously in the mind and the heart. That blasphemy is only in the mind, by which someone within himself says that which belittles the Divine goodness: and yet not for that reason is he badly inclined towards God. Now God (as Dionysius teaches[3]) is the very essence of true goodness, or goodness itself. From which it clearly follows that whatever is attributed to God, pertains to His goodness: and whatever is foreign to God, is also far from the notion of perfect goodness, which is His essence. Thus, whoever

---

3 *The Divine Names*, c. 1, §5 (PG 3, 594C).

says that something belongs to God, which is opposed to Him, or says what is opposed to Him is proper to Him, and on account of this is not badly inclined towards God, such a man as this blasphemes in his mind only.

For there is no doubt that a blasphemy can be in the mind without a perverse will in the one blaspheming, or the one belittling the Divine goodness. Because although every blasphemy insofar as it is voluntary, is from a bad will: still not every blasphemy is with a will inclined to belittling the Divine goodness. For just as all believing is voluntary, still not all believing is from a will inclined by God's charity: in this way every blasphemy is voluntary, yet not every blasphemy is from a badly inclined will, or from a will wanting to blaspheme. For this malice of the will, about which we now speak, is related to the blasphemy of the mind, as charity to faith. Hence it is that just as faith can be without charity, so also blasphemy of the mind without malice, or without blasphemy of the heart.

That blasphemy is in the heart alone, and a blasphemy by the will alone, by which someone believing about God, that He ought to be believed, yet is badly inclined in regard to God. For it is not contradictory that blasphemy is simultaneous with the faith. For someone can believe that God is almighty, and say within himself, in order to injure God, that God is not almighty, and delights in such a lie. We see that something similar happens regarding injuries, which are said to men, in whom it often happens that someone willing to inflict an injury upon another would say to him that what nowise befits him, as for example when he says that a man is blind, whom he knows sees very well, or says that he croaks, whom he knows sings very well. In this way someone could, in order to injure God, say that He can do nothing, when nevertheless he certainly knows that He is almighty. He can also believe that God is just, knowing, and almighty and not want God to be one of those things: for example, because

He would not want God to be so knowing that nothing is hid from Him, even the most secret thoughts of our heart, or he would not want Him to be so powerful for punishing his sins, so that none can resist Him, or he would not want Him to be so just, that by no prayers or gifts someone can deflect Him even a hair's breadth from uprightness. Such men as these have a blasphemy in their will, although they have the true faith in their minds.

Such are they about whom it is said: "The pride of them that hate thee ascendeth continually" (Ps. 73, 23). Since, as James says, "The devils also believe, and tremble" (2, 19). And the same thing ought to be said about damned men: yet all of them always hate God; because they do not want God to be so powerful, or so just, that He would punish them for their sins. They are sorry for their sins, which they committed, not because they regard the sins themselves as detestable: but because they hate the punishments which they suffer for them. They certainly still have their wills evilly attached to their sins, and would still want, if they could, to wrongly indulge in those things for which they are punished, still they do not want to undergo the punishments for them: and hence they lament, because God is so just, that He always wills to punish, or so powerful, that no one can resist His power. And this is the reason why they have hated God, and why they blaspheme in their wills.

For John in the Apocalypse speaks thus about the damned: "Men were scorched with great heat, and they blasphemed the name of God, who hath power over these plagues" (Apoc. 16, 9). Hence, they blaspheme because they lament that God has such power that He is able to inflict those plagues. A certain Gloss expounds that passage in this way, which Saint Thomas cites,[4] although he does not state who is the author of that Gloss.[5] I certainly thought, when I read in

---

4 II-II, q. 13, a. 4, *Sed contra*.
5 Anselm of Laon, *Glossa Ordinaria* (PL 114, 739B). The *Glossa*

Blessed Thomas, that it would be found in the Gloss which is commonly called the *Glossa Ordinaria*: yet when checking there I found nothing like what he cited. Whosoever it is, if his authority did not suffice, certainly the authority of Blessed Thomas citing and approving it ought to suffice.

Thus, such blasphemy, about which we now treat (as Saint Bonaventure says) is that which in the Gospel is called blasphemy of the spirit. For he says that blasphemy is not completely the same thing as the spirit of blasphemy: for these two things (as he says) are related as genus and species.[6] Every spirit of blasphemy is blasphemy, yet not vice versa. The spirit of blasphemy is "the inclination and wish to vituperate against God."[7] The spirit of blasphemy in this way gives origin to the hatred of God, just as the Holy Ghost gives origin to the love of God. And the theologians say that this kind of spirit of blasphemy, meaning the inclination to vituperate against God, is the greatest of sins and irremissible, not because it would not be forgiven if due repentance is made for it: but because it is such (as Bede says on the third chapter of Mark[8]) that he who has once committed it, never

---

Ordinaria was formerly attributed to Walafrid Strabo.

6 *Commentaria in quatuor libros sententiarum Magistri Peteri Lombardi* (Quaracci (Florence): Ex typographia Collegii S. Bonaventurae, 1885), bk. 2, dist. 43, a. 3, q. 2, dub. 2, p. 997.

7 *Quid ergo aliud videtur spiritus blasphemiae quam affectatio et desiderium vituperationis divinae?* (Richard of St. Victor, *Tractatus de spiritu blasphemiae* (PL 196, 1188A)).

8 "He who shall have sinned against the Holy Ghost... 'shall not be forgiven him, neither in this world, nor in the world to come' (Mt. 12, 32). We do not deny that he also, if he would want to do penance, can be forgiven by Him 'Who will have all men to be saved, and to come to the knowledge of the truth' (I Tim. 2, 4); but because believing the Judge and Giver of pardon Himself, and Who will always accept the repentant, also says that this blasphemy will not be forgiven, we believe that just as this blasphemer will never attain forgiveness by the merits demanded, so neither will

Book 1, Chapter 12

makes adequate repentance for it: because on account of its very great malice God withdraws His help from him, without which he could not attain to repentance. Or according to Alexander of Hales, the reason why it is called irremissible, is because "it provokes the eyes of the Divine Majesty to not having mercy, or to not forgiving." [9]

From all these things it is now evident which is the blasphemy simultaneously in the mind and heart. For the former is that by which someone thinks wickedly about God, and for that reason is badly inclined towards Him and does not fear to vituperate Him. For example, if someone believes that God is not omnipotent, and from thence has the audacity to belittle His honor, and to insult Him, and in contempt of Him contemns all His commandments. This blasphemy certainly is not a very grave sin of itself, because of the ignorance which it has adjoined, and hence its wicked will which arises to some extent excuses from such great gravity of the sin. For the latter is the blasphemy in regard to the Son: because it is through ignorance; the former, however, is blasphemy in regard to the Holy Ghost, because it is out of pure malice and hence worse. These words about blasphemy which occurs in the heart suffice.

There is yet another blasphemy, exterior blasphemy, which is usually called blasphemy of the mouth, not because it is done only in the mouth and only by words, but because it is shown outwardly more by words than through other signs, and the name come from those things which happen more frequently. For blasphemy can be shown outwardly in deeds just as by words. For he who as an insult were to spit upon the image of Christ or the Virgin, or strikes it with his fist, or kicks it with his feet out of contempt, or would do other

---

he attain to the very fruits of worthy penitence" (*In Evangelium S. Marci*, bk. 1, c. 3 (PL 92, 164D)).

9 *Universae Theologiae Summa: In Quatuor Partes* (Cologne: Gymnicus, 1622), pt. 2, q. 131, mem. 5, vol. 2, p. 613.

similar things which would show his contempt of God and His Saints and be an insult, this many indubitably ought to be considered a blasphemer, and punished as such. Hence Bede, when expounding the passage from the Second Epistle of Peter the Apostle, "Through whom the way of truth shall be evil spoken of" (2, 2), speaks thus: "The way of truth is blasphemed by heretics not only in those whom they have led away to associate with them in their heresy, but also in those whom they arouse by their impure deeds and execrable sacrifices or secret rites which they do, in hatred of the Christian name, while the uneducated suppose that all Christians are given over to shameful acts of this sort. Scripture says of men such as these, 'The name of God through you is blasphemed among the Gentiles' (Rom. 2, 24)."[10] From whose words it is clearly established that exterior blasphemy is committed not only by words, but also in deed, although all such blasphemy (as I said) is usually called by the common name of blasphemy of the mouth. For in this way profession and denial are more often done by words, and hence all exterior profession and denial, are usually called profession of the mouth or denial of the mouth, and yet any of these can be done by deeds just as by words. For Paul when speaking about sinners says: "They profess that they know God: but in their works they deny him" (Tit. 1, 16).

Therefore this exterior blasphemy can also be distinguished triply, just as we said above about blasphemy of the heart. For since words and other exterior works are signs of those things which are in the soul, and proceed from them, hence it necessarily happens that words and other signs are distinguished according to the distinction of those things which are their signs, and from which they arise and proceed. And thus there can be an exterior blasphemy which only proceeds from a sole blasphemy of the mind without an evil affection of the will: and another which proceeds from the wicked-

---

10 PL 93, 74D.

ness of the mind and the will at the same time. It necessarily ought to be judged about any such blasphemy as these, what sort is that interior blasphemy from which it proceeds: hence it is necessary to see whether some one of these ought to be called heresy, or whether it has some connection with heresy? And certainly, about that blasphemy which is in the affections alone, although it is a very grave sin, and (as we said) irremissible, still it does not have something in common with heresy or with infidelity. For opposites (as Aristotle says[11]) happen to the same thing. This blasphemy of the affections alone is in the will: thus, it is neither heresy nor disbelief. But regarding the other blasphemy, which is in the intellect, whether malice in the will is conjoined with it or not, the difficulty is whether it pertains in some way to disbelief.

And for a full explanation of this matter, I decided to firstly admonish the reader about this, so that he would consider that it is one thing to say something, and another to believe it. For when one lies, he says something which nevertheless he does not believe to be true, and he does not state whether he says something with his mouth, or his heart. For someone can say something in his heart, and reflect upon it within himself, which nevertheless he does not believe to be true. Next, it ought to be noticed that two things ought to be considered in faith. The first is to believe all the articles of the faith. The second is to say those same articles of the faith with the mouth or heart. The first of these pertains to the faith, and this is truly called faith. But the second is called the confession of the faith, and according to that which Paul says: "With the heart, we believe unto justice; but, with the mouth, confession is made unto salvation" (Rom. 10, 10). On the contrary these two things also ought to be considered regarding disbelief, for instance dissent about those things

---

11 *Categories*, c. 6 (6a15); c. 10 (13a15); cf. Boethius, *Commentary on the Categories*, bk. 4 (PL 64, 269).

which pertain to the faith, and to say something inwardly or outwardly against the faith. The first of these, namely, dissent, pertains to disbelief, and is heresy. But the second, namely, to say in the heart or with the mouth something contrary to the faith, is the crime of blasphemy: so that blasphemy does not consist in believing, but in this, saying something in the heart or with the mouth against God, whether or not he believes what he says is true: provided he says it with the intention of doing an injury to God. Because in order that blasphemy may be called a crime, it is not enough that one say something disparaging the Divine goodness: unless he say that deliberately.

From which it is clearly inferred that blasphemy is not a fault opposed to the faith, but it is a fault against the confession of the faith. And hence it is deduced that a blasphemer, by the mere fact that he has blasphemed, ought not to be declared a heretic: unless from some other source something besides the blasphemy is adjoined, which would make him a heretic. For if someone says or does something which derogates the Divine goodness, and believes it to be so about God, he is called a blasphemer and a heretic at the same time. Insofar as he says something against the Divine goodness, he is a blasphemer: insofar as he believes that which he says, he is a heretic. If someone believes something about God, which is opposed to the Divine goodness, and does not say it: such a man as this would be a heretic, and not a blasphemer. But if on the contrary someone were to interiorly or exteriorly say something about God, which was averse to the Divine goodness, and yet does not believe what he says is so, such a man as this will be called a blasphemer, and not a heretic. There are many such blasphemers, who having been cast down by some passion or weakness, not bearing an assault of tribulation or affliction from God, from Whom they think the tribulation was inflicted upon themselves, desiring to be revenged, because otherwise they would not do this, they say that the injuries ought to be execrated with a foul and cursing mouth: as though those words inasmuch are said as a curse could at least harm God a little. If one would afterwards ask them whether they believe that God is what they called Him, they would certainly deny it. I have known many such men, who after uttering blasphemies with their mouths through passion, would put their necks to the sword before they before they would admit that that which they uttered as a blasphemy were true. Therefore, since there is such a diversity of blasphemies, it behooves that their punishment be diverse, and the judge ought to smite them with due punishment in diverse ways.

The punishment of a blasphemy, which has absolutely nothing in common with heresy, such as the one which is committed in an oath uttered by the private members of Christ or of holy men with reviling and dishonoring, of this kind or of any other similar one, does not pertain to inquisitors of heretics from their ordinary authority nor in any way to him who has the same authority: unless it has been delegated to them from elsewhere, that they can involve themselves, to investigate or judge them. But the punishment of them belongs to ordinary judges both secular and ecclesiastical. Now this blasphemy, which has a certain affinity or connection with heresy, rightly will pertain to inquisitors of heretics, so that they may investigate, judge, and punish about it. Just as he who would say that God unjustly punishes someone, or that He cannot do this or that, or that He had unwisely done something: such a man as this is a blasphemer, and ought to be examined by the inquisitors of heretics. Not merely because he is a blasphemer, but because by such a blasphemy he gave a little suspicion of heresy. "For out of the abundance of the heart the mouth speaketh" (Mt. 12, 34). What sort every man is, that sort is his speech. So great is the connection of words with morals, that on account of this

Solon[12] (as [Diogenes] Laertius[13] relates about him) said, "Speech is the mirror of action": because the nature of the soul is represented in speech, just as in a mirror. Whence it is that we rightly suspected about everyone, that when he speaks about something, he thinks as he says. Because (as it is found in Aristotle's writings) "Spoken sounds are symbols of affections in the soul."[14]

But since everything from which a strong suspicion of heresy arises, pertains to the judgment and tribunal of the inquisitors, it is necessary that every such blasphemy be subjected, even from their ordinary authority, to the examination and judgment of the inquisitors. Yet when they inquire about blasphemy of this kind, it behooves them to diligently consider the quality of the person, as in other crimes, whether he be a person who otherwise has given some or no suspicion of that error uttered or of any other. Next, he ought to consider the circumstance of the time in which he blasphemed, whether he was at that time in some tribulation, or free from all tribulation. Because therefrom he will also be able to surmise the adjoined quality of the person, whether he blasphemed from disbelief or from impatience. If after having considered well the circumstances of the time and person, it is established that he blasphemed out of disbelief, the inquisitor will proceed to punish him as a heretic, especially if he says that he believes what he said. If he denies that he believes that which he said, nay, he says that he believes the opposite, and after having considered the aforesaid circumstances, the suspicion still remains that

---

12 Solon (640-558 B.C.) was an Athenian statesman, lawmaker, and poet.
13 *The Lives and Opinions of Eminent Philosophers*, bk. 1, c. 2, n. 58. Diogenes Laertius (third century B.C.) was a biographer of the Greek philosophers.
14 *On Interpretation*, c. 1 (16a6).

he spoke out of disbelief, an [oath of] purgation[15] may be enjoined upon him, and then a moderate penance. But if he fails to make an [oath of] purgation, I reckon that the same thing ought to be done in his case which Canon Law determines regarding other heretics who fail to make an oath of purgation. But if after having considered well the aforesaid circumstances, it is established that he blasphemed not out of disbelief, but from impatience and some passion: then because he is not reckoned a heretic, but only a blasphemer, the inquisitor of heretics does not have from ordinary law something more he can do regarding him.

Nevertheless, the inquisitors of heretics, especially in Spain, have this authority specially delegated to themselves, that they are able to punish blasphemers of this kind, and rightly so; both on account of the gravity and enormity of the crime, which (as we taught above) is a very grave sin; and also on account of the negligence of those judges, both ecclesiastical and lay, upon whom it is incumbent from their office to punish very severely detestable blasphemies. For since they are negligent in this, it is just that this matter be delegated to others, who punishing blasphemies with more severe correction and harsher discipline, could recall men from this detestable and dreadful vice.

---

15 The "oath of purgation" (*purgatio canonica*) was a testimony to the innocence made by those accused of sins or crimes. The oath of purgation trumped any evidence of guilt and gave the accused a canonical *licentia*, that is, an absolution or non-guilty judgment. The oath of purgation, however, was only allowed for free men who had not demonstrated habitual criminal conduct.

Chapter XIII

Concerning fortune tellers and soothsayers, and other diviners, whether they ought to be called heretics.

The curious desire of knowing is so great in many men that they try to learn with a wicked curiosity, even at the expense of the Catholic faith, those things which would be more beneficial not to know. For which reason it is accustomed not undeservedly to be doubted by many about men of this kind, who are called diviners, whether they all ought to be deemed heretics, and ought to be punished as such by the inquisitors of heretical depravity. For the fuller understanding of which matter, it will be necessary before all to inquire what is divination, and how many kinds are there: and therefrom we will be able to gather whether they who perform it ought to be called heretics or not.

Divination is the telling of those things, the knowledge of which cannot be had naturally, and has not been revealed by God. Now the things are either past, present, or future. The knowledge of past and present things can be had naturally: because present things can be seen; past things, because they were present at one time, were seen at one time: and the knowledge remains from their having been seen, which the philosophers call abstractive, and through which some can from past things certainly know things and tell them to others. But future events, because they do not yet have existence, cannot be seen, and hence nothing certain can be held about them. Due to which divination is accustomed to be considered the foreknowledge of future events: because those things are those which of themselves cannot be naturally known. If, however, someone would tell and assert with certitude present or past things which cannot be naturally known, I would also call it divination.

For instance, if he who is a hundred miles from Rome, were to say what is done at that moment of time in Rome, or were to say to a man whom he never saw, those things which he did during the whole course of his life, he certainly (in my opinion) would also be called a soothsayer, just as if he had seen the future. For just as he who knows past things through revelation, or present things which he could not have otherwise known, is called a prophet, even though more frequently he is called a prophet who foreknows future events through revelation: so also he is properly called a soothsayer who asserts with certitude past or present things which he could not have naturally known without God's revelation. Accordingly, the Samaritan woman, to whom Christ had said that she had five husbands, and he whom she now had, was not her husband, when she heard this immediately exclaimed saying: "Sir, I perceive that thou art a prophet" (Jn. 4, 19). She accordingly reckoned that He ought to be called a prophet, because He knew very well past things, or absent things, which remained hidden. Still even though this is the case, only he is usually called a soothsayer who declares future events with certitude, and without any fear of deception.

Now future events (as Blessed Thomas excellently teaches[1]) can be known in two ways. For they are known either through the knowledge of their causes, or they are known in themselves. Now causes are related to their effects in three ways. For there are some which produce their effects of necessity and always. Such like future effects can be foreknown and foretold with certainty, from considering their causes, even as astrologers are accustomed to know and foretell an equinox, a solstice, an eclipse of the sun and moon. Such foretelling is not called divination: because what properly divine is not usurped by it. Other causes produce their effects, not of necessity and always, yet they rarely fail from

---
1 Cf. II-II, q. 95, a.1.

Concerning fortune tellers and soothsayers, and other diviners

the production of their effects. Likewise, from such like causes their future effects can be foreknown, not indeed with certainty, but by a kind of conjecture. In this way astrologers predict about rains, droughts, earthquakes, about the fertility or sterility of the land: and physicians foretell concerning death, or the recovery of the sick, in which things they sometimes foretell correctly, other times they are mistaken. This foretelling also cannot be called divination: because it does not exceed the limits of natural knowledge.

There are other causes which have absolutely no necessity that they either always or sometimes produce their effects: because they are always doubtful in themselves, and uncertain, they can produce sometimes certain effects, other times the opposite effects. Such causes are called free: as for instance men and Angels. The effects which are to be produced by causes of this kind cannot be foreknown either as always or as in many cases through the knowledge of the causes with any certitude. No matter how much someone knows Peter, he cannot from this knowledge know for certain whether Peter will fast tomorrow or not: whether he will speak, or be silent: because since he is free in regard to these effects, he can do either one or the other. Thus, such effects, which depend upon causes of this kind, no one can know until they happen, for example when he sees Peter eating, or fasting, or being silent, or speaking. To know these things with certitude, or to foretell them before they happen, belongs to God alone, Who (as Paul says) "calleth those things that are not, as those that are" (Rom. 4, 17).

Of future events of this kind ought to be understood that which Solomon says: "Great affliction for man: because he is ignorant of things past, and things to come he cannot know by any messenger" (Eccle. 8, 6-7). When Jerome interpreted these words in his commentaries on Ecclesiastes, he says: "Although many good and bad things befall a man, even a righteous man is not able to know what will befall him, or know the causes and reasons for each thing. For no one can know what will happen, yet he does know that all things are done by God to the advantage of man, and nothing is done without His will. For this is a great affliction for mankind, since as the poet says: 'The mind of man knows not his lot and coming fate.'[2] If he hopes for one thing, then another happens; he expects the enemy to come from one direction and is wounded by a spear from the opposite direction."[3] Therefore anyone who would presume to know or foretell such future events (without God revealing them) is proved to usurp what belongs to God alone, and such a man as this is called a diviner. For as it is said [by Isidore of Seville], "They pretend to be filled with divine inspiration, and with a certain deceitful cunning they forecast what is to come."[4]

But if someone would foreknow or predict future contingent things of this kind, which depend upon free causes, by God revealing, he will not be called a diviner: because not from himself and through himself does he have such knowledge, but from God: and in this way he does not usurp something divine unto himself: but he attributes to God, because he acknowledges that he has received from Him. Otherwise, all God's prophets would be called diviners, in that they predicted many things about the future. None of the holy men, however, called them diviners, but prophets. For he alone is called a diviner who usurps in an undue way unto himself foreknowledge, or the prediction of future events, which depend upon free causes. And such divination is always a sin, and in fact a grave sin: because it is against

---

2 *Nescia mens hominum fati, sortisque futurae* (Virgil, *Aeneid*, bk. 10, ln. 501).
3 PL 23, 1075B.
4 *Etymologies*, bk. 8, c. 9, n. 14 (PL 82, 312B) (translated by Stephen A. Barney, W. J. Lewis, J. A. Beach, and Oliver Berghof, in *The Etymologies of Isidore of Seville* (Cambridge, 2011)). Cf. *Decretum Gratiani, causa* 26, q. 4, c. 1, n. 2 (PL 187, 1342A).

Concerning fortune tellers and soothsayers, and other diviners

the religion and worship due to God, and yet not all divinations are subject to equal guilt: because one is worse than the other, the more it makes use of evil means for foreknowing the future. For there are some who use the invocation of devils so that they can foreknow the future.

But there are others who predict the future without the express invocation of devils, such as Augurs, who from the sounds of birds, or the Haruspices, who from the entrails of birds, or the Chiromancers, who through the reading of palms, are wont to predict many things about the future. And some are the interpreters of lots [*Sortilegi*], who under the name of the Christian religion, through the examination of one passage or another of Sacred Scripture, or through some things which they call they lots of the Saints or of the Apostles (as Isidore says[5]), they practice the skill of divination. And the [former] are properly the interpreters of lots who are reprehended and condemned in Canon Law. For there are many other interpreters of lots nowise reprehended by law, but are tolerated by it, and are they who, although they do something so that by having considered its outcome, they may come to know something hidden, either present or future, yet they gain their knowledge not from the devil, but from God, as happens in the drawing of lots. That divination which happens with the invocation of devils is much worse than that which is practiced without their invocation.

There is yet another, not small difference among the divinations themselves. For there are some which are somewhat mixed with heresy, and cannot be practiced without some support of some heresy. For instance, if one were to baptize the dead, with that form and that rite with which a living man is baptized, or a child is baptized, so that from thence one may have the response of the lots cast, or if the Sacrament of the Eucharist were to be abused for sorcery and performing incantations, or one were to pour out detestable prayers for

---

5 *Ibid.*, n. 28 (PL 82, 313B).

executing his incantations before idols. For such interpretations of lots, or auguries, are not done without an admixture of heresy. For to believe that the dead can be profitably baptized was the heresy of the Marcionites, as we taught in that work which we published, *Against All Heresies*, in the section on Baptism, in the third heresy. To rebaptize children, is the clearly condemned heresy of the Anabaptists. To pray to idols is idolatry, if anyone thinks that in it the gods are deserving of adoration, it is a very apparent heresy. The abuse the Sacrament of the Eucharist for performing sorcery, gives very strong suspicion of heresy. Because doing this, besides the great irreverence which he shows to the most Blessed Sacrament, it is rightly believed that he is of the opinion that the most Blessed Sacrament of the Eucharist can do something for performing sorcery, and has some force and power for the performance of those sorceries: because if he did not believe this, he would not use it for the perpetration of such sorcery. Now to think this is a clear heresy and blasphemy.

If, however, someone would invoke the demons, so that when the lots have been cast, or some drawings have been made, he would be taught by them about some future events, although he would sin gravely, yet he would not be called a heretic if the things which he manages to know from the demons, are such that they could be foreknown well by the demons. For the demons, who know the natures of things, and their powers and movements (as it is stated in the chapter *Sciendum*[6]) better than men, can from the knowledge of causes foreknow the effects which they necessarily and always produce, just we said about astrologers above, regarding the foreknowledge of the eclipses of sun and moon. If someone tries to foreknow from the devil the

---

6 *Decretum Gratiani*, pt. 2, *causa* 26, q. 4, c. 2 (PL 187, 1343B-1344A). Cf. Augustine, *On the Divination of Demons*, c. 3, n. 7 (PL 40, 584-585).

eclipses of this kind, or the sterility of the earth or its future sterility, although he sins very gravely, still he ought not be deemed a heretic.

But if those things, which he could not naturally know, he tries to know through the invocation of demons, this man in my opinion ought to be presumed to be a heretic: because he would not invoke the devils in order to foreknow these things, unless he believed that the devils foreknow them. Now to think this about the devils is a clear heresy: because he who believes that the devils can foreknow with certitude those future contingent things, which depend upon man's free will, believes that they are gods: because that this belongs to God alone is sufficiently proved by that which is read in the books of Isaias the prophet: "Shew the things that are to come hereafter, and we shall know that ye are gods" (41, 23). Concerning such men alone, who invoke the devils so that they may know from them those things which they could only know from God, I reckon ought to be understood the chapter, *Episcopi*, in which interpreters of lots and sorcerers are called heretics.[7] This was said there, not because it is necessary that interpreters of lots and sorcerers are always called heretics: but because sometimes such divinations, cannot be done without the admixture of some heresy. In the same way the chapter, *Non observetis*, also ought to be understood.[8]

There are other divinations which, although they cannot be done without grave sin, still they can be exercised without the admixture of some heresy. For instance, if someone through casting lots or auguries, inquires from the devil regarding future events, those things which he could foreknow through his own nature, either he asks from him, that he do what is certain that the devil can do with God's permission, and does not believe that the devil knows more things than he

---

7 *Ibid.*, q. 5, c. 12.
8 *Ibid.*, q. 7, c. 16.

knows: or more things than he can do, and it is evident that he mixes with his casting of lots and sorceries nothing other than what proceeds from a clear error of the faith. If someone wants and instantly manages to know with the help of the devil what is happening in Rome or in the Emperor's army, or who is the author of some wicked deed in secret, committed without witnesses, or in what place the evildoer hides, he ought not to be reckoned a heretic on account of these things: because such divinations, or such casting of lots, or sorceries, although they are very serious sins, still they do not have any admixture of heresy. For just as other sins can be committed through pure malice, and without any error or ignorance, but deliberately, so also casting lots a(nd auguries, and other divinations can be done out of pure malice, and deliberately, without any error of the intellect, and consequently without any heresy.

Therefore, these things having been premised, I set down such teaching, from which the whole of this entire matter depends. Casting lots and auguries, and the rest of the divinations which cannot be done without the support of some heresy, are subject to the investigation and censure of the inquisitors of heretical depravity, and ought to be punished by them. Such are the works of the necromancers: because they (as we will say later) always think incorrectly about the faith, believing about the devils, that they can do many things which they cannot actually do. But casting lots and auguries, and other divinations which are performed from the malice of the will alone, without any error of the intellect, are not subject from ordinary law to the censure of the inquisitors of heretical depravity: unless from elsewhere it has been delegated to them for this case. This was expressly decreed by Alexander IV.[9] But bishops can investigate and judge about this sort of casting of lots, which does not savor

---

9 *Liber sextus*, bk. 5, tit. 2 (*De haereticis*), c. 8 (*Accusatus*), n. 4 (*Sane*).

Concerning fortune tellers and soothsayers, and other diviners

of heresy: because their authority is broader than the authority of inquisitors.

Now, so that the inquisitor of heretics may know whether the interpreter of lots, or the augur, or any other divinator is subject to his jurisdiction or not, in my opinion he ought to do this. He will interrogate about the power of the devils, about their knowledge, as for instance, what does he believe that they know about the future, what can they do about these lower things. He will also ask whether the devil can find out and perfectly know the secrets of man, which are contained in his heart alone. For that these things are subject to the knowledge of God alone, Sacred Scripture bears witness, saying: "The searcher of hearts and reins is God" (Ps. 7, 10). And the Apostles when praying to God, said: "Thou, Lord, who knowest the hearts of all men..." (Acts 1, 24). From which it is evident that it is heresy to say that the devil knows the secrets of men. Now interpreters of lots are wont to often mix errors of this kind. And if he shall answer about these things according to the rules of faith, one ought to believe that he committed such a sin from pure malice, and not from an error of the intellect: unless the deed itself is such, that it gives strong suspicion of heresy. Such deeds are those which we related above, namely, Baptism of the dead, rebaptism of children, the abuse of the Sacrament, for practicing sorcery. For these deeds and ones similar to them, although they are not heresies, since heresy is not in the deed, but in the intellect (as we taught above in the first chapter), nevertheless they give a very strong suspicion of heresy.

Chapter XIV

Regarding magicians, whether they ought to be deemed heretics, and punished as such.

There are, alas, many men who having abandoned the true God, the Creator of them and of all others, are not afraid to have recourse to the devil, the chief enemy of all men: and although those serving God can certainly hope for everything truly good from Him, they prefer to serve the devil, and obey him in everything, from whom they can receive nothing but evil. For the devil himself, has been cast all the way down to hell from that sublime state in which he was placed by God on account of that madness, and prodigious pride, whereby he tried to equate himself with God; yet he persists in that blind ambition until now, so that he strives to equate himself with God, and does not fear to desire Divine honors. Since he does not now hope that he could obtain those honors, seeing that he has been dispossessed of them in heaven, he daily endeavors to receive them from men, whom he most certainly knows can be more easily deceived. Now, in order to obtain these Divine honors, which he so anxiously desires, he leaves nothing untried. For he deceives some by deceptions, "transforming himself," as Paul the Apostle relates of him, "into an angel of light" (II Cor. 11, 14): he allures others by the various proposed gifts and rewards, accordingly as he knows what each man desires. By deceptions and wiles he has seduced until now many men of both sexes: who highly venerate him, and adore him as God. Yet not all who obey him, venerate him with the same rite and procedures, nor are all known by the same name. For just as the Christian religion contains various rites within it, by which the true God is worshiped: also the various groups of men, which albeit are different among themselves in dress, name, and ceremonies, nevertheless all tend to this same end, that they worship God: and they obey Him: so Satan, that parent of pride, wishing to imitate God in this, has many adherents to his diabolical worship, who although are known by different names, and have different worship, rites, and customs, still there is agreement among themselves in that all praise the devil and venerate him, and they take care to obey him in everything.

Now, their diversity can be considered in various ways. Firstly, in fact, it can be considered from the diversity of means used for obtaining that which they desire. For there are those who say that they raise up the dead by incantations, so that having been taught by them, they could predict, or divine, something about the future. And these men (as Augustine teaches[1]) are called necromancers, because *nekros*[2] means "dead," and *manteî*[3] means "divination." Others are called hydromancers from "water," which in Greek is *hydōr*[4] from the gazing upon which, they thought that they could summon shadows of demons, and see images of them, from which they think (as they themselves say) they are taught. There are other similar diviners called by various names,

---

1 "For Numa himself also, to whom no prophet of God, no holy angel was sent, was driven to have recourse to hydromancy, that he might see the images of the gods in the water (or, rather, appearances whereby the demons made sport of him), and might learn from them what he ought to ordain and observe in the sacred rites. This kind of divination, says Varro, was introduced from the Persians, and was used by Numa himself, and at a later time by the philosopher Pythagoras. In this divination, he says, they also inquire at the inhabitants of the nether world, and make use of blood; and this the Greeks call νεκρομαντείαν [necromancy]. But whether it be called necromancy or hydromancy it is the same thing, for in either case the dead are supposed to foretell future things" (*City of God*, bk. 10, c. 35 (PL 41, 223)).
2 Νεκρος.
3 Μαντεία.
4 Ὕδωρ.

whose names are listed in the chapter, *Episocopi*[5] Because we discussed about whose divination in the chapter immediately preceding, wherefore I have decided to say nothing else about them.

Another difference among those who venerate the devil can also be considered, which is taken from the diversity of things which they do by the devil's help, and which things they wish to ask for from the devil. I have decided to discuss all these things one by one in this order, such that I will firstly show who and of what sort they are, then I will investigate whether they ought to be reckoned among the heretics, and punished as such. Therefore, there are some men who very greatly desire that they can do some marvelous things, so that, by the working of these marvels, they may be accepted by others, and they may be unto them a marvel and astonishment, and for this reason they subject themselves to the devil, so that by his help and power they could do many marvelous things. These men (as Augustine teaches[6]) are called magicians, such as those who before Pharoah (as the history of Exodus relates[7]) resisted Moses trying to do with the help of demons all those marvelous works which Moses was doing by God's power. The well-known Simon [the Magician] was such, who (as Luke relates in the Acts of the Apostles) "thought that the gift of God may be purchased with money" (8, 20). For this man worked so many and such great marvels with the help of the devil, that he was considered by the Samaritans (whence he originated) to be a god, and the Roman government (as Justin Martyr relates in his *Apology*) erected a statue of him as a god.[8]

---

5 *Decretum Gratiani*, pt. 2, *causa* 26, q. 5, c. 14.
6 *City of God*, bk. 10, cc. 8-9 (PL 41, 285-286).
7 Cf. Ex. 7.
8 Cf. St. Justin Martyr, *First Apology*, c. 26 (PG 6, 367A-B). The statue is later mentioned by St. Irenaus (*Against Heresies*, bk. 1, c. 23, n. 1 (PG 7, 671A)), Tertullian (*Apology*, c. 13 (PL 1,

Now, so that we can more certainly and clearly determine whether or not they ought to be called heretics, in the first place it is necessary to take note that no magician performs any of their marvels, without some pact made between him and the devil. For Satan does not teach all these things freely, nor does he impart freely all the more that power of his, but he receives something from that magician, so that he would want to help him perform those marvels. Therefore, it ought to be considered before all else the nature and conditions of that pact: because important knowledge about this pact depends upon it. Now this pact can be made in two ways, for certain pacts are made openly and expressly, but not others, which are only tacitly and hiddenly.

A pact is open and express which is made with the devil himself, and is given to him in his own person. And this again is twofold. For there are some which are made publicly and solemnly, and there are also others made privately, completely without any solemnity. A pact is public and solemn which is made with the devil sitting in a royal throne, surrounded by a multitude of his subjects, in a sort of general assembly, as in certain general assemblies, in which all who fight under the devil, and have given their names to him, gather. For there before them all some men promise (as we will say below at greater length) obedience to the devil, and vow that they will keep all his commands in everything; they renounce God and all His works, and swear that they are ready to commit other countless crimes. After they have made this promise, the devil immediately promises that he will give them those things which he knows they desire. For he does not promise everything to everyone, but the more each man hands himself over to the devil, and promises to do more things in his honor, the more also the devil promises to him, and grants more things.

347A-348A)), and St. Augustine (*On Heresies, to Quodvultdeus*, c. 1 (PL 42, 25)).

A pact is private and express, which is made with the devil himself, given mutually with promises, yet done without any solemnity, and also without any witnesses. Now those things which the devil promises that he will give them, he strives earnestly to give, lest if he be found to be a liar in the things promised, those who had given themselves to him, would again depart from him, and in this way he would lose those whom he now has as servants. Yet there are not a few things which the devil nowise is able to do: either because they exceed his natural powers, or although they do not exceed them, nevertheless God, without Whose permission he cannot do anything, does not permit him to do those things. If the devil promises some one of these things to them, he often deceives with some illusions and deceptions, so that they would think that they had attained what they were hoping for from the devil.

A pact with the devil is tacit, which someone makes not with the devil, but with him who is a disciple and servant of the devil, promising him complete and entire obedience, and renounces God and the Catholic faith; and he promises all the rest of the things which others promise to the devil himself. Now he, to whom these things are promised, in return, promises them that, on account of these things, many great and marvelous things shall be obtained. But this pact, even though it was not made with the devil himself, the devil himself holds it as ratified, and strives to fulfill everything contained in it all the same, just as if those things had been promised by him. Hence it is that not only they who made an express pact, but also those who made a tacit pact with the devil, do or may seem to do many unusual and stupendous things, by the devil helping them. Concerning all these men it cannot unsuitably be said what the Lord said through the prophet Isaias concerning other sinners: "We have entered into a league with death, and we have made a covenant [*pactum*] with hell" (28, 15).

Book 1, Chapter 14

These things, therefore, having been noted, so that we may know regarding some magician, whether he is a heretic or not, two things ought to be considered. The first is the nature and conditions of the pact itself which he made with the devil; whether it be tacit or express makes no difference. If by that pact he promised that he would adore the devil, and would give him other divine honors, and promises this or that other similar thing: because he believed that he ought to do so, rightly, beyond any doubt, he should be reckoned a heretic: because he believes that the devil is God, since he adores, or promises to adore and venerate, him as God. For the true God, the Creator of all things, Who spoke though the mouths of holy men, whose prophets are from the beginning, when speaking through the prophet Isaias, says: "I am the Lord, and there is none else: there is no God, besides me" (45, 5). And again in the same place: "I am the Lord, and there is none else" (v. 6). And again: "Am I not the Lord, and there is no God else besides me?" (v. 21).[9]

If he did not make a pact about something opposed to the Catholic faith, which can very rarely happen, because (as we said) the devil is never accustomed to freely, without some certain hope of gain, impart the power which he has, and by it to serve men at their bidding, then that magician should be examined as to what he believes about the devil's power. If it can be known with certitude that he believes about the devil, that he can do what the Catholic Church teaches belongs to God alone, he without any doubt should be reckoned a heretic. As for example, if he believes that the devil can create something, as the Manichaeans and Priscillianists said, or he believes that the devil can raise the dead: which in reality belongs to the Divine power alone. For just as we believe

---

9 Here there seems to be a mistranslation in the Douay-Rheims Bible, which has the words, "Have not I the Lord..." Whereas the Vulgate reads, *Numquid non ego Dominus*, and not *Numquid non ego habeo Dominum*.

by faith that the human soul can be created by God alone, so also one ought to hold by faith that God alone can unite the same soul of man to the human body. For we evidently know this by certain natural reason, that no substantial form can be united to some matter as its form, except by that agent alone, who can produce it. A cause which cannot produce the substantial form, also cannot unite it to matter. Because by uniting in this way, it would seem to produce the composite itself from the matter and form. But it is quite absurd to say that some cause produces some composite, whose matter or form it cannot produce. Therefore God, Who alone produces, and can create, man's soul, can alone also unite it again to the same body, after it has been separated from its body. For otherwise, he who would unite the soul to the body, would be said to have made that man. It is execrable to say that the devil could do this, because when God said, "Let us make man to our image and likeness" (Gen. 1, 26), He clearly taught us that the productions of man himself is so great, that propagation apart, it can happen by God alone.

Perhaps someone here will object to me that Samuel, who (as it is related in First Book of Kings[10]) was brought up by a woman who had a divining spirit, and when asked, gave responses to King Saul. We can reply to this objection in two ways, as Augustine teaches in his letter to Simplicianus.[11] Firstly, in fact it can be said according to him, that it was not Samuel's soul which appeared and spoke with Saul: but a certain apparition, and imaginary illusion made by the machinations of the devil, which Sacred Scripture calls Samuel,[12] by a figure of speech, whereby images are wont to be called by the names of the things themselves. For the images of Cherubim, placed upon the Ark of the Testament,

---

10 I Kings 28, 11-19.

11 *De diversis Quaestionibus ad Simplicianum libri duo*, bk. 2, q. 3, n. 2 (PL 40, 141-142).

12 Cf. I Kings 28, 15-16 and Eccli. 46, 23

are called Cherubim in Sacred Scripture,[13] even though they were not really Cherubim, but just their images. And when Pharoah's butler was in prison with Joseph, the vine which he said that he saw in a dream, on which there were three branches, although he neither saw the vine nor the branches: but only the images of those things. According to this manner the Angels also, who long ago were sent by God to men: were called gods in the Old Testament, merely on account of the fact that they represented God, by Whom they were sent. For when speaking about the Angel with whom he had fought, Jacob said: "I have seen God face to face, and my soul has been saved" (Gen. 32, 30). For Jacob was not seeing God (as all the holy Doctors concordantly teach), but an Angel sent by God, who, because he was representing God in a special manner, was called "God," or "Lord," by Jacob. So also could that image of Samuel, which the devil put before Saul's eyes, be called Samuel. But if a scruple presses someone to believe that not Samuel's image, but Samuel himself, was brought up, because he who appeared foretold true things to Saul, which could not be said by a wicked spirit, because he cannot foreknow anything certain about the future, which does not happen from necessary causes alone; Augustine takes away this scruple in the aforesaid letter, speaking thus: "It can also appear remarkable that the demons recognized Christ, whom the Jews did not recognize. For when God wishes someone to know true things even through base and infernal spirits, although they are only temporal and pertain to this mortal life, it is convenient and not inappropriate for him who is almighty and just to grant to such spirits so that they may announce to human beings what they hear from the Angels, and thus, for their punishment, those to whom these things are foretold will suffer through foreknowledge the evil that threatens them before it comes.

---

13 Cf. Ex. 25, 18.

But they only hear as much as the Lord and Ruler of all commands and permits."[14]

Secondly, it could be said, according to Augustine's opinion, that he who appeared to Saul, was the true spirit of Samuel brought forth by the devil, God permitting it, on account of some reason hidden to us. For since Christ allowed Himself to be taken up by the devil, and set upon the pinnacle of the Temple, and placed upon a high mountain, it is not surprising that he was permitted to carry Samuel's soul from the lower regions: especially since Samuel's soul itself is of nigh infinitely less excellence than Christ Himself. Or assuming that it was Samuel's true spirit which appeared to Saul, it certainly could be better said that he was brought thither, not by some magical art, or by the devil's power permitted for this, but by the Divine power and direction, which was hidden from the woman with the divining spirit and the devil, so that he might pronounce the Divine sentence to Saul soon to come upon him on account of his faults, just as he himself while he was alive announced to the same Saul that he was removed from the kingdom by God's decree.

If, however, someone would rather wish to approve of the opinion which says that Samuel's soul was brought up by the devil by God's permission from the lower regions, above all he ought to take care not to believe or suspect either that that soul was restored to its own body, or that it was so infused into some other body, such that from that conjoining of the body with that soul, when reunited, he was a true and whole man, just as he had been before death. For such a conjoining of the body with the soul, not even God could permit the devil to do by his own powers. And Augustine, who accepts that man's soul could be brought from the lower to the higher regions by God's permission, certainly does not accept that the devil could infuse it into the body. For only in regard to

---

14 *De diversis Quaestionibus ad Simplicianum*, bk. 2, q. 3, n. 3 (PL 40, 142).

local motion does he say that Samuel's soul could have been subject to the devil's power: so that he could move it from place to place, when it is unwilling. For the example that he cites avails to prove this, which he took from Christ, whom the devil brought from the desert into the city of Jerusalem, and set upon the pinnacle of the Temple. But the soul, even when unwilling, could be brought by the devil whither he pleases, unless the devil would be impeded by God from doing this. Therefore, whoever wants to approve of this opinion, in order that he may say that Samuel's soul was brought by the devil with God's permission before Saul, will need to say one of these, either that soul was not then conjoined to a true body, but rather to an imaginary and apparent one, to which it was not united as its form, but merely assisting it as its mover: or if it is said to have appeared in a true body, to which it was truly united as its form, he will be forced to say that such a union of the soul with the body to it was made by God alone, lest he say that a man could be made by the devil (which is wicked).

But if someone contends that the devil could unite man's soul to the body, he certainly is condemned by the testimony of Blessed Leo I, who in his letter to Bishop Turribius of Asturia when discussing the error of Priscillian saying, "The souls which are placed in men's bodies have previously been without body and have sinned in their heavenly habitation, and for this reason having fallen from their high estate to a lower one alight upon ruling spirits of various qualities, and after passing through a succession of powers of the air and stars, some fiercer, some milder, are enclosed in bodies," speaks thus: "This blasphemous fable they have woven for themselves out of many persons' errors: but the Catholic Faith cuts off all of them from union with its body, persistently and truthfully proclaiming that men's souls did not exist until they were breathed into their bodies, and that they were not there implanted by any other than God, who is the Creator both of the souls and of the bodies."[15] Pope Leo teaches that it must be held by the Catholic faith that souls are infused into human bodies by God alone.

Therefore, when some magician shall say that he raises some dead man, he nowise ought to be believed: because the devil himself, by whom he is helped, cannot do this. He indeed could, when God permits and the devil is favorable, bring the soul alone of some dead man from the lower to the higher regions, and infuse it into some phantom body, as a representation, and into that likeness of the dead body, not indeed as the form joined to it: but as its mover. And because the devil can do this, whence it is that the devil himself, by illusions and deceptions deceives the magicians themselves, and other foolish men, so that they think that he can raise the dead. Nevertheless, anyone who thinks this is wicked and a heretic: because he gives to a creature, that is, the devil, that which belongs to God alone. For one of the main proofs, whereby (as the concordant opinion of all the holy Doctors holds) Christ manifestly demonstrated His Divinity to us was the raising of the dead. But if this raising of the dead could have been done by the power of demons, Christ would not have proved His Divinity well enough by that argument.

There is yet something else to be considered about the devil's power, namely, to change men into beasts, or birds, or whatever other brute animals, about which I reckon that the magician ought to be examined, and very diligently interrogated, whether he believes the devil could do it. For magicians also very often say that they can do this, and long ago about these things the heathens have told that many fabled things were done. All which things were believed by many on account of the unreasonable and thoughtless credulity of the Greeks, which progressed to such an extent, that no lie was so bold-faced that it lacked a witness, and hence

---

15 Letter 15, c. 10 (PL 54, 684C-685A).

Book 1, Chapter 14

belief among them. Lucian [of Samosata][16] writes that when he was in Thessaly for the sake of knowing sorcery, that he was changed into an ass, when he wanted to become a bird.[17] Not because this actually happened to him, but (as I think) as a derision and mockery of the art of magic, the man composed this plot, who mocked no one, and not even the gods themselves. Apuleius afterwards taking up the same plot wrote the book of *The Golden Ass*,[18] to display his eloquence, although according to the opinion of many, he did not achieve that which he desired. Homer dreamt up, rather than related, that the very famous sorceress, Circe, changed Ulysses' companions into beasts.[19] Ovid relates that Diomedes' companions after the Fall of Troy were changed into birds.[20] And Blessed Augustine relates that when he was in Italy, he had "heard such things about a certain region there where landladies of inns, imbued with these wicked arts, were said to be in the habit of giving to such travelers as they chose, or could manage, something in a piece of cheese by which they were changed on the spot into beasts of burden, and carried whatever was necessary, and were restored to their own form when the work was done. Yet their mind did not become bestial, but remained rational and human."[21]

Which unreasonable and thoughtless credulity from the heathens, having arisen especially from renown ancient Greece, has proceeded even to our times, in which there are not lacking men who believe that men can be changed into

---

16 Lucian of Samosata (ca. 125-after 180) was a Hellenized Syrian satirist, rhetorician, and pamphleteer who is best known for his characteristic tongue-in-cheek style, with which he frequently ridiculed superstition and religious practices.
17 Cf. *Lucius, or The Ass*, c. 13.
18 *The Golden Ass* is today ascribed to Lucius of Patras.
19 *Odyssey*, bk. 10, lns. 212 ff.
20 *Metamorphoses*, bk. 14, lns. 498-503.
21 *City of God*, bk. 18, c. 18, n. 1 (PL 41, 574).

beasts, or wolves, or dogs, or cats, by the incantations of magicians and the power of devils. If the magician believes that these things, or similar things, can be done by the devil, he will beyond a doubt be deemed a heretic, because he attributes to the devil those things which surpass all natural powers of creatures, and which can belong to God alone. For (as it is established from the things immediately preceding) just as only God can produce the human soul, so also He alone can unite it to the body: and whence it follows likewise that He alone can transfer it from body to body. Moreover, the human soul is of such and so great nobility, that it can inform and animate none but the human body as its instrument. For just as any substantial form requires some specific dispositions in the matter, so that it can support and inform it; just as the form of fire requires heat in the matter; the form of a tree or plant requires moisture and viridity: so the human soul requires the human form, so that it can animate that body, and it can grow. Yet I do not think that such human form is so required, such that God could not unite man's soul to a brute animal if He wished. Nevertheless, God has decreed never to do this, Who from the beginning when creating man, infused his soul into the body only as an instrument, and He then made it such in the form of the body, as He would continually make afterwards. And for this reason, we say that man's soul, if it be referred to the order and power of the nature, can only grow the human body. Therefore it ought not to be believed that any power of the devils can change men into beasts, or birds, or other brute animals.

But if anyone objects those things which the poets relate which the sorceress Circe did long ago, and which are said today are done by many magicians, Augustine replies eloquently and ingeniously to all these things, speaking thus: "And indeed the demons, if they really do such things as these on which this discussion turns, do not create real substances, but only change the appearance of things created by the true God so as to make them seem to be what they are not. I cannot therefore believe for any reason that not only the soul but also the body, can really be changed into bestial members and features by the art, or power of the demons; but the phantasm of a man which even in thought or dreams goes through innumerable changes may, when the man's senses are laid asleep or overpowered, be presented to the senses of others in a corporeal form, in some indescribable way unknown to me, so that men's bodies themselves may lie somewhere, alive, indeed, yet with their senses locked up much more heavily and firmly than by sleep, while that phantasm, as it were embodied in the shape of some animal, may appear to the senses of others, and may even seem to the man himself to be changed, just as he may seem to himself in sleep to be so changed, and to bear burdens; and these burdens, if they are real substances, are borne by the demons, that men may be deceived by beholding at the same time the real substance of the burdens and the simulated bodies of the beasts of burden."[22]

And to prove this opinion of his, whereby he says that those things are not real, but illusions of the devils, he cites experience, which is wont to teach many true things. Now for verifying the experience itself, he relates two occurrences, in which it is very certainly perceived that what he says is true. After relating these occurrences, he afterwards again explains his opinion, speaking thus: "Therefore what men say and have committed to writing about the Arcadians being often changed into wolves by the Arcadian gods, or demons rather, and what is told in song about Circe transforming the companions of Ulysses, if they were really done, may, in my opinion, have been done in the way I have said. As for Diomede's birds, since their race is alleged to have been perpetuated by constant propagation, I believe they were not made through the metamorphosis of men, but were slyly

---

22 *Ibid.*, n. 2 (PL 41, 574-575).

substituted for them on their removal, just as the hind was for Iphigenia, the daughter of king Agamemnon. For juggleries of this kind could not be difficult for the demons if permitted by the judgment of God; and since that virgin was afterwards found alive, it is easy to see that a hind had been slyly substituted for her. But because the companions of Diomedes were of a sudden nowhere to be seen, and afterwards could nowhere be found, being destroyed by bad avenging angels, they were believed to have been changed into those birds, which were secretly brought there from other places where such birds were, and suddenly substituted for them by fraud."[23] Augustine clarifies the whole matter brilliantly and ingeniously (as is his wont).

According to this way, which Augustine teaches, many other things ought to be understood which unreasonable and thoughtless heathen believed that magicians could do. For (so that I may pass over other ridiculous things) the heathens were persuaded that by the incantations of magicians, the moon is pulled out of the sky, or the sun is darkened. Hence Ovid, when speaking about Medea, said: "She endeavors to charm the reluctant moon from her orb, and involve the chariot of the sun in darkness."[24] And Virgil in *Pharmaceutria* [or "The Sorceress"]: "By magic songs and incantations even the moon can be dragged down from the heavens."[25] They so thought that they could help the moon in eclipse [*laborantem*] by loud noises, so that the voices of those singing incantations could not reach in that place, in order that they might not be heard by it, wherefore they used to beat drums and cymbals. For they thought that all these things were very useful. Hence [Tibullus] says: "Incantation seems to draw the moon down from her car, and would do

---

23 *Ibid.*, n. 3 (PL 41, 575).
24 *Heroides* (or *Eclogues*), Letter 6 (*Hypsipyle to Jason*), lns. 85 f.
25 *Eclogues*, bk. 8, ln. 69.

it but for the blows on the echoing bronze."[26] Juvenal, when speaking about a very loquacious woman, said: "[No need for anyone to sound the trumpet, beat the gong:] She can come to the aid of the moon in labor, all on her own."[27]

All these things could not be done by the power of the devils, who cannot change the order of nature instituted by God. But (as Augustine said about other things) the devil was putting by a diabolical illusion likenesses and phantoms of them before men's eyes so accurately and skillfully so that men would believe that they saw not likenesses and phantoms, but the realities. For the confirmation of whose opinion besides the examples which he brought forth many other could cited, among which I will mention only one, which is related in the lives of the Fathers. A certain youth ardently loved a young lady, and was daily soliciting her to consent to venereal acts with him. Whom, because she never wanted to consent, a certain Jewish magician at the youth's request, turned into a mare, as she was seen to herself and others beholding her. For which reason she was brought to Blessed Macarius, who upon seeing her said, that a woman was seen by him, and not a horse. For the devil could not delude the senses of a holy man, just as he had deluded the senses of others. He therefore, when praying to God for her, freed her by his prayers from such a delusion. Finally, this opinion is confirmed by the authority of the Synod of Ancyra,[28] which gave a very clear explanation about this matter, speaking thus: "Whoever therefore believes that anything can be made, or that any creature can be changed or transformed to better or worse, or be transformed into another species or likeness, except by the Creator Himself, who made all things and through whom all things were made, is

---

26 *Elegies*, bk. 1, poem 8, lns. 21 f.
27 *Satire 6,* lns. 442 f.
28 The Synod of Ancyra was held in 314 A.D.

Whether magicians ought to be deemed heretics

beyond doubt an infidel."[29] These words are cited by Gratian in the chapter, *Episcopi*.[30] For the decrees of this synod are not found among those, which are contained in two large volumes, published in Cologne eight years ago.[31] For the decrees of the Synod of Ancyra [*Concilii Ancyrani*] are there, and having suspected Gratian of a typographical error (as often happens elsewhere in the book of Gratian) such that for Ancyran [*Ancyrano*] was put Ancyra [*Ancyrense*], I thoroughly examined all the decrees of the Ancyran Synod, hoping to find there the aforesaid decree: but I found no such thing in the Ancyran Synod. Yet the editor of those councils added this decree after the decrees of the Ancyran Synod, saying that he found it in a certain manuscript book.[32]

---

29 Mansi 2, 535 f.
30 Pt. 2, *causa* 26, q. 5, c. 12.
31 *Concilia omnia tum generalia tum provincialia*, ed. by Laurentius Surius (translating to Lorenz Sauer).
32 *Concilia omnia tum generalia tum provincialia* (Cologne: apud Geruuinum Calenium, & haeredes Iohannis Quentel, 1567), vol. 1, p. 300.

Chapter XV

On sorcerers, whether they ought to be called heretics, and punished as such.

Among the many men whom the devil has in his power, those who invoke him, and make a pact with him, so that by his help they can bring about those things they wish, some are included who are called sorcerers by their works, because they are of such a wicked and pestiferous disposition, that imitating no one well except the devil himself, they choose to do many things wickedly, and on account of this alone they subject themselves to the command of the devil: so that they may be taught by him, by what pact they can hurt others. For although magicians and enchanters, about whom we discussed in the previous chapter, could also do these evil deeds with the devil's help, still on account of this skill of evil deeds they are not called magicians [*magi*], but by the proper term, sorcerers [*malefici*], as it can be easily established from the very etymology of the word.[1] For in the law, *Nemo*, in the [Theodosian] Code, [in the Title,] *De maleficis et mathematicis et ceteris similibus*,[2] it is said that men of this kind on account of the greatness of their crimes are called sorcerers by the populace.

There are many kinds of sorcerers of this kind, however, which are distinguished not according to the variety of means and of instruments, which the sorcerers use in their art: but according to the diversity of evils which they effect in others. For there is a sorcery which is called amatory, and

---

1 I. e., *Malefici* gradually superseded *venefici* ("givers of poison") as the technical term for sorcerers. Cf. modern Italian, *malia, malefizio*, etc.

2 I. e., "Concerning enchanters, magicians, and other similar persons." Bk. 9, title 18, constitution/law 5.

there is another called noxious; and the latter is also multiple according to the multiplicity of harms which by those sorceries are inflicted upon men. Amatory sorcery is that which is done for inclining the hearts of men or women to lust and filthy love. And those who perform this, in whatever way they do it, sin gravely: because (as it is clearly certain) they solicit to a deed that is evil, and expressly forbidden by God. Now something evil, which cannot be done without sin, no one can advise someone to do without sin, nor solicit to it. For (as Paul says) "Not only they that do such things are worthy of death, but they also that consent to them that do them" (Rom. 1, 32).

Sorcery is noxious, which is done for inflicting some harm upon someone. For sorcerers of this kind are wont to harm men in various ways. For sometimes they harm them in their own persons: sometimes in their possessions, or in things connected to them. For these sorcerers often by the secret working of the devil quickly kill men, without any drink being given. But sometimes they do not take them so quickly from life: but produce death over a long period of time, so that after long and lamentable maladies, and miserable wailing, the person's body, which is infected with the curse, is worn out and weakened little by little, until finally it perishes. On account of these and other harms, which they are wont to inflict upon human bodies, in the last law of the [title of the Theodosian] Code, *De maleficis et mathematicis*, they are called "enemies of the public safety."[3] These men kill sheep, and cattle, and the rest of the brute animals, which perhaps were very fat, in a very short space of time, are made afterwards thin, and utterly so thereafter. These men often so bind married men that they can nowise perform intercourse for the work of generation. These men are they who (as it is said in the law, *Multi*, in the [title of the] Code, *De maleficis et mathematicis*, disturb the elements, change the weather,

---

3 Bk. 9, tit. 18, l. 9.

stir up winds and storms, make hail, and frightful stones to descend from on high, which destroy all the grain and fruit.

Now so that they can do all these things, they use various instruments and means. Sometimes they put clearly harmful things in food, or drink, or clothing, or some other thing which touches that person. Other times they do not give any such thing: but they produce certain images, having observed certain times, and set formulas, and certain rites and signs, which they baptize in the name of Beelzebub, chief of the demons, having employed and uttered certain other words, which it is not even allowed to repeat, and even if it were allowed, I could not do it without great horror and trembling of soul. After these things have been done in this way, they put the aforesaid images into the fire, and there they ask for the sicknesses or other evils, which they wish to happen to that person, whose image they have made. And sometimes with needles, or with other sharp iron rods, they pierce the head of that image, or chest, or abdomen, or thighs, or another part of the body, in which they desire some evil to arise in the person, whom they wish to harm. When all these things have been completed it often happens that that person, whom the sorcerer manages to harm, is gravely tormented, and suffers in the head, or stomach, or abdomen, or suddenly gets some sickness, which none of the doctors can recognize. Other times they harm with just words uttered from their mouth, concerning which Lucan said: "The heart not contaminated with any poison drank, when enchanted perishes."[4]

It can be proved by two arguments that all these things are done by the operation of demons. The first is taken from the fact that in all these things it is necessary that certain figures be drawn, which cannot be naturally known, and certain entirely unknown and utterly dreadful names of demons, although mixed with other holy names, will be written there,

---

4 *Pharsalia*, bk. 6, lns. 457 f.

which it ought to be believed were set down for fulfilling a pact made with the devil. The second argument very plainly proves through the fact that those compositions of images, and touches, or those letters, or words uttered, could not from their own nature cause death, or other sicknesses, or any harm in human bodies. Because if this power of acting had been bestowed upon things of this kind, then every time, and in every place, and in every subject of same quality and disposition, anyone would make similar images or letters, or utter similar words, that power would act. But it is evident that if someone else, who has no pact with the devil, were to make such letters, or utter such words, nothing will happen. From which it is most evidently concluded that such sicknesses, or any other injuries, are in no way produced by the power of the images or words. And hence it is proved that these things are done by the demons themselves, with whom the sorcerers have made a pact either publicly or privately. For the demons themselves, who are very intelligent, know very well the natures and properties of minerals and herbs, and other natural things better than all doctors and physicians, who have lived on earth. For the devil when sinning (as Blessed [Pseudo-] Dionysius teaches[5]) did not lose the substance and properties of his Angelic nature: but retained all his natural and very splendid gifts intact.

Since, therefore, he has a very perspicacious intellect, he quite easily knows those things which can inflict death, or sicknesses, or torments, or any other things harmful to man. He knows how to mix together the ingredients from which poisons are produced, which are able to inflict the harm to man such as he wishes. Therefore, since the devil has great expertise in things of this kind, when such images (as we said) are pricked with needles, or letters are made, or words are uttered, with God's permission, he secretly and invisibly applies the poisons which can harm the man whose

---

5 *On the Divine Names*, c. 4, §23 (PG 3, 723C-727A).

image is pierced through, and in this way the devil does these things, which the sorcerer chooses to do, by the natural power and strength of the poisons. Because the sorcerer is often unaware of these poisons, and does not see the devil apply them, he thinks that all those things which happen, are done by the power of such images, or letters, or words, which nevertheless are not done either by the images, or by the figures, or by any words, or by the devil himself; but by other causes having the natural power to do this, which are hiddenly applied and brought near by the devils themselves, who know the power of those causes: so that those things are effected in the very bodies of men, which the sorcerers desire. And it often happens that those who perform these sorceries, do not know the remedies to apply to these evils which they inflicted: because the devil, their teacher, did not teach them more, or (so that I may speak more correctly) the devil did not promise more to them.

Yet there are others, who know both very well, namely, to harm and to apply the remedy to the injuries inflicted by themselves or others. About this matter I decided to admonish the reader, so that he may understand, that sorcerers of this kind, not only sin gravely when they injure: but also when they give the remedy by the diabolical art of this kind to the harm done by themselves or by another, such that the sorcery performed would not have the power to do harm. For although those so doing benefit the injured neighbor, still (as Paul says) "Evil ought not to be done, that there may come good" (Rom. 3, 8). The invocation of devils is evil. It is also evil and very bad to make either an express or tacit pact with the devil: therefore, it is also evil and very bad to undo the sorcery already applied, if it is to be undone not otherwise than through the invocation of the devil and with his help. For that which is evil in itself, could not be good by any good intention applied, nor by any other good circumstance. Whence it is, that although it is good to remedy the ailments

Book 1, Chapter 15

of neighbors, still it is not good to perform sorcery to remove the neighbors' injuries. "Thou shalt follow justly after that which is just" (Deut. 16, 20).

Still if the sorcery applied is discerned to be such that it can be impeded by any natural power, without any invocation of the devil, and without any pact made with him, then it will be good and meritorious to undo that sorcery; which is far from what could be reckoned a sin. Sorcery can also be taken away through the prayers of holy men so that it would not achieve its effect. Likewise, sorcery can also be licitly impeded, if that image, into which the needle is fastened, or other similar instrument through which the sorcery was done, is found and broken into pieces. For then the devil would no longer vex him, because he does not stand in conformity with the pact, which he made with the sorcerer: except inasmuch as some sign given by him still remains. But it is not a question of small importance, whether it is allowed to ask from him who performs sorcery, and was ready to perform it daily, that he undo the sorcery applied to someone, or prevent that it be able to carry into effect its operation, especially if he believes that he can only undo it with the help of the devil and the doing of sorceries. Angelo [Carletti] di Chivasso[6] in his *Summa [de Casibus Conscientiae]*, in the title, *Superstitio*,[7] cites the opinion of Petrus Aurioli[8] about this matter,[9] and approves of it, who says that

---

6 Blessed Angelo Carletti di Chivasso (1411-1495) was a noted Italian moral theologian of the Order of Friars Minor.
7 *Summa angelica de casibus conscientiae* (Nuremberg: Anton Koberger, 1492), fol. 276r.
8 Petrus Aurioli (1280-1322) was a French Franciscan philosopher and theologian, called on account of his eloquence *Doctor facundus*. He taught theology at Paris and Pope John XXII appointed him Archbishop of Aix (1321).
9 "Thus they say that if he wants to do his sorcery, it being conceded that he would sin in doing so: yet if I use him for the good

this can be licitly requested from any sorcerer, whom it is known is prepared to do sorceries of this kind. Now he tries to argue in support of this opinion of his by the fact that it is permitted for anyone to use the evil of another for one's own benefit. For which matter he cites the testimony of Augustine saying that it is licit for me to use the oath of an unbeliever for my benefit, although I know that the oath is by his false gods which he worships.[10] One could also assert something similar to support the same point in regard to him who asks for a loan from him whom he knows will give only for the interest. Now this request by the consent of all the Doctors is licit. From which it seems to follow that it would also be licit for anyone to ask from him who is ready to perform sorcery, to impede the commenced sorcery.

But notwithstanding all these arguments, I hold the opposite opinion, and say that Petrus Aurioli, and Angelo di Chivasso who followed him, were mistaken on this point, in that they did not consider the matters well, and hence did not see how wide is the difference between the point under discussion and the other examples, which they cited as similar cases. For that he, who asks the sorcerer to undo the sorcery by sorcery, sins, is proved very clearly even from this, that the same sorcerer (as we said shortly before) sins gravely when he takes away the commenced sorcery by diabolical art, lest it attain the effect. Therefore it cannot happen, that he, who asks the sorcerer to undo the commenced sorcery by diabolical art, would not sin. For anyone who asks another to do that which cannot be done without sin, sins: because in so asking he consents to the iniquity of the other by inducing him to sin. Now it is certain, because just as equal punishment, so also equal guilt binds the doer and the one consenting: nor can the

---

of another, for instance in the avoidance of death, it does not seem to be a sin" (*Commentariorum in Quartum Librum Sententiarum* (Rome: Zannetti, 1605), dist. 34, art. 2, p. 182).
10 Ep. 47, n. 2 (PL 33, 184-185).

one asking be excused from sin for this reason, namely, that the sorcerer whom he asks had been prepared to do sorcery upon anyone's request. For even though he was prepared, still he would not have done this particular sorcery, unless he had asked. From which it is evidently proved that his request was the proximate cause, that the sorcerer performed that particular sorcery. For we call the cause that which when placed, the effect is placed, and when that cause is removed, the effect is removed. If there were not someone requesting, the sorcerer would not have done that particular sorcery, and done it for the one requesting: therefore, the one requesting was the cause that another perpetrated sorcery, and hence it is proved that the former sins: because he induced the other to sin, and gave the proximate cause to the sin.

And this can be confirmed by that which is found in the chapter, *Nec mirum*, where after something is said about Necromancers and Hydromancers, these words are added: "To all these above-mentioned things pertain the amulets of execrable remedies, which the medical art condemns, either in incantations, or in [marks which they call] characters to be hung or fastened, in all which things is the art of the devils, arisen from a certain pestiferous association of men and bad angels."[11] These words are ascribed to Augustine's name, but actually they are not Augustine's.[12]

Now the examples of the unbeliever prepared to swear by his gods, and the usurer prepared to loan for interest, which instead of being similar cases, lead one to the opposite opinion, and prove completely nothing. Because all those

---

11 *Decretum Gratiani*, pt. 2, *causa* 26, q. 5, c. 14, n. 4 (PL 187, 1353B).

12 Bishop Burchard of Words ascribes these words to St. Augustine in the marginal note in the *Decretum Gratiani*, which cites the *Decretum Burchardi*, bk. 10, c. 44 (PL 140, 84). Most of it can indeed be traced to the writings of Saint Augustine. Cf. *Christian Doctrine*, bk. 2, c. 20, n. 30 (PL 34, 50).

things related are dissimilar to the point on hand about which we now dispute. For in those cited examples the things which are requested are not evil in themselves: because they can be done well, by those who are going to do them, if they wish. The fact that they are done badly, is not from the wickedness of the thing itself: but from the wickedness of the one acting, who only wants to do badly the thing which he could have done well. For he who requests an oath from an unbeliever, does not ask that he swear by false gods, otherwise he would sin by so asking: because he would ask for that which is clearly a sin: but he only asks that he swear: and if the option were given to the one asking, he would choose that he swear by the true God, triune and one. If, however, the unbeliever swears by false gods, the fault belongs to the one swearing, and not to the one demanding the oath: because he who demands asks for that from him which, if he wishes, he could do well.

Likewise, he who asks from the usurer, does not ask that he give for interest: because so asking he would sin, when he asks it from him, which he could not do without sin: but he asks more precisely, that a loan would be given to him, which could be done not only without sin, but also with merit. If the usurer does not want to give the loan without interest, the fault belongs to the usurer himself, not to the one asking. Because he asks from him for that which he, if he wanted, could do without sin and with merit. Therefore, in all these examples, and other similar ones, he who asks does not induce another to sin: because he asks for that which could be done without sin, but he uses for his own benefit, the iniquity of the other, who does not wish to do that except badly, which if he wanted to, could act rightly. Quite different is the case of him who asks from a sorcerer to undo sorcery by diabolical art, lest it avail to do harm. For he asks from the sorcerer what he cannot do without sin. For (as we said shortly before) not only he sins who performs sorcery, so that it may do harm: but also he who takes away the sorcery by diabolical art, so that it would not do harm. Because to perform the diabolical art, with whatsoever good intention he does it, is a very grave sin. Thus, he who asks the sorcerer to undo the sorcery by the diabolical art, not only uses the sorcerer's iniquity for his benefit: but also induces him to sin and consequently sins: because he asks from him that which he, even if he wished, could not do without sin. Now if there were some such sorcery that could be undone by the sorcerer without sin, for instance, because he knows where is the noose, or image, or some amulets, or characters with which the sorcery has already begun: then just as he could without sin undo the sorcery by breaking into pieces all those things: in this way anyone else could without sin ask from that sorcerer, that he undo the sorcery in that way.

All these things having been noted beforehand, there remains that we inquire whether sorcerers of this kind ought to be deemed heretics, and punished as such. Concerning which matter, so that a certain judgment can be given, there are three things to be inquired about these men. The first is whether they made some pact with the devil, whether expressed or tacit, whereby they promised each other that they would do that which derogates from the Catholic faith. For never, or very rarely (as we said in the preceding chapter), does the devil impend his help to men without some hope of gain. If in the pact made between them and the devil some promise about matters of faith is included, for instance about adoration or reverence to given to the devil himself, or about denying the same reverence to Christ Our Savior, or about the breaking and trampling upon Christ's image, or the Cross upon which when dying He worked our salvation, which the devil is wont to most highly seek after from those with whom he shows himself exorable: there is then no doubt that sorcerers ought to be reckoned as heretics, and punished as such. Because none of those things which we said, can be willingly and deliberately done without manifest heresy. For although there are many things which the will does without the judgment of reason: because to that thing the will is of itself prone, and those things of themselves are like a sort of will, by which they can attract the will itself to love of themselves, yet there are other things which (as we said in the first chapter) the will never desires: unless because the intellect judges them to be good: because those things have nothing in themselves, by which they can attract the will. And hence it follows that if the will desires some one of those things, it is only moved to desiring it by the intellect judging it to be good. Therefore, in all these things, the exterior operation clearly indicates an error of the intellect. From all which things it is evidently concluded that all sorcerers, who bring about through a pact one of those things which we just said, ought to be reckoned heretics, and punished as such.

The second thing about which sorcerers ought to be examined, is the sorcery itself which they practice, about which matter the investigation ought to vary just as we said that the sorceries are various. For one of those we said is called amatory, the other noxious. From those who practice amatory sorceries, it ought to be diligently inquired whether they believe about sorceries, either that the devil can force the will of a man, or of a woman, to some libidinous love, or to have dishonorable love in any way. And because they believe that this can be done, there is a strong suspicion: because unless they would think that these things can be done by the art of sorcerers, or by the devil's power, they would never perform such sorcery for effecting that thing. If it has been ascertained that these men so believe, and they would not depart from it when admonished about this error: but are pertinacious in it, they will rightly be deemed heretics, and will be punished as such: because they pertinaciously maintain a clear heresy.

For to believe that man's will can be forced by the devil to loving something, is a very clear heresy: because that coercion is incompatible with the liberty which God endowed our will. For "God," as the Wise Man says, "made man from the beginning, and left him in the hand of his own counsel. He added his commandments and precepts. If thou wilt keep the commandments and perform acceptable fidelity forever, they shall preserve thee. He hath set water and fire before thee: stretch forth thy hand to which thou wilt" (Eccli. 15, 14-17). From which words of Ecclesiasticus, it is very clearly established that man's will was made free by God, and hence it follows that it cannot be forced by the devil: because otherwise it would not be free. If man could be forced by the devil to loving something, then straightway man would not be placed "in the hand of his own counsel" (as Ecclesiasticus said): but in the hand of the devil's counsel. Thus, he who pertinaciously asserts that man's will can by forced by any sorcery to loving something, ought to be deemed a heretic, and punished as such.

The devils certainly can allure the will by persuasions to loving, by representing some apparent sort of good, although false, in that love. They also can stir up the appetite of the flesh, which is not free, so that it would desire it, and ardently seek after it, even though otherwise it was cold towards it. For as it is written in Job, "His breath kindleth coals" (41, 12). Now the desire of the flesh, after it has been vehemently kindled, will also vehemently solicit the will, and strongly urge it, so that it draws to its desire. Due to this very vehement temptation, it happens that ignorant men say that they are unwillingly forced to have this love, and cannot want to forsake it. But in reality they are deceived: because if they want to resist, they can easily do it with God's help, Who is prepared to help everyone who flees to Him. "God is faithful," says Paul, "who will not suffer you to be tempted above that which you are able" (I Cor. 10, 13).

Next, those who perform these sorceries ought to be examined whether in the performance of them, they mix something which rightly can give a strong suspicion of heresy. Because if these things are not present, the inquisitors of heresies could not by law determine anything about those cases, unless it has been specially delegated to them in that province: because this is specifically forbidden to them in the chapter, *Accusatus*.[13] But if such things mix in their sorceries, so that no light suspicion of heresy can be taken about them, rightly the inquisitor can and ought to diligently and carefully examine about those sorceries. For when the Pope in that chapter, *Accusatus*, §. *Sane*, restricts inquisitors from investigating sorceries or interpreters of lots, he immediately makes an exception of those soothsayings which savor of heresy. In which place the word, "soothsaying," ought to be taken according to its broad meaning, so that it includes all kinds of sorceries. For according to the proper meaning of the word, it only pertains to divinations, as is evident from Isidore, in the chapter *Sortilegi*.[14] But because in the aforesaid chapter, *Accusatus*, §. *Sane*, after the Pope mentioned divinations, he immediately added the interpretation of lots, it is evident that by the word, "interpretation of lots [*sortileges*]," he not only understood divinations, but also sorcer-

---

13 "Certainly those whose high privilege it is to judge concerning matters of the faith ought not to be distracted by other business; and inquisitors deputed by the Apostolic See to inquire into the pest of heresy should manifestly not have to concern themselves with diviners and interpreters of lots, unless these are also heretics, nor should it be their business to punish such, but they may leave them to be punished by their own judges" (*Liber sextus*, bk. 5, tit. 2 (*de hereticis*), c. 8 (*Accusatus*), n. 4 (*Sane*)).

14 "'Interpreters of lots' (*sortilegus*) are those who profess the knowledge of divination under the name of a false religion, using what they call 'lots (*sors*, gen. *sortis*) of the Saints,' or those who foretell the future by examining one passage of Scripture or another" (*Etymologies*, bk. 8, c. 9, n. 28 (PL 82, 313B)).

Book 1, Chapter 15

ies: because he says that they are some of those things which savor of heresy.

Therefore, it ought to be seen, and carefully investigated, what are those sorceries which savor of heresy. Paolo Grillandi,[15] in his *Tractatus de hereticis*,[16] for a knowledge of this matter assigns certain rules, which he relates that he took from Oldrado.[17] Firstly, in fact, he says that if the interpretation of lots, or sorceries, are so done that in them the invocation of the devil is present by way of adoration, then they clearly savor of heresy. Next, he adds that although it is not done by way of adoration, still if by those sorceries it is asked or expected from the devil what belongs to God alone to do, for instance to raise the dead, to reveal the secrets of the hearts, or to predict future things which do not depend upon natural causes, then that petition savors of heresy. Thirdly, he says that if there is an invocation of the devil not through the manner of prayer, and it is asked of the devil only that which he can do by his natural power; although any other things are applied in the performance of the sorceries, he says that it does not savor of heresy. Therefore, he says that to celebrate Mass for the dead for someone living, so that he may quickly die, or to give a consecrated Host to a woman on which are written filthy characters, for provoking libidinous love, it does not savor of heresy. He says the same thing about the relics of the Saints, and about sacramentals, such as a chalice, a portable altar, holy oil,

---

15 Paolo Grillandi (born c. 1490) was an Italian jurist, from Abruzzo, active as a papal judge in witch trials, from 1517. His book *Tractatus de hereticis et sortilegii*, based substantially on his judicial experience, became a standard text on witchcraft and demonology.

16 *Tractatus de hereticis et sortilegiis* (Lyon: Jacobo Giunti, 1536), bk. 2, q. 10, fol. 51r.

17 Oldradus de Ponte, *Consilia seu responsa et quaestiones aureae* (Venice: Damiani Zenari, 1585), counsel 210, fols. 109 ff.

holy water, water from the Baptismal font; all which things, although they may be mixed in the sorceries, he says do not savor of heresy. And he tries to prove this opinion of his by this, that other punishments are imposed by law upon these things, than [those imposed] upon heretics. And for this he cites the chapters, *Quicumque*,[18] and *De homine*.[19] He adds moreover something else, at which I cannot but be surprised that his ignorance is so great. For he says that if someone would have irreverently cast the Cross, or an image of the Virgin Mother of God, or of another Saint, on the ground, and tramples it with his feet, it would not savor of heresy. For which matter he cites the chapter, *Si canonici*.[20]

From all these assertions of Paolo Grillandi, I do not find what I can approve or tolerate, except those first two, one of which is concerning the adoration of the devil: and the other about the request, whereby it is requested of the devil that which only God can bestow. Which two things savor of heresy. And we ourselves also teach this same thing. But all the rest of the things which are contained in the third assertion are manifestly false, and deserving of a sharp reprehension. Now in order that we may make this clearer, it ought to be firstly noticed that the interpretation of lots, or some sorcery,

---

18 *Decretum Gratiani*, pt. 2, *causa* 26, q. 5, c. 13 (*Quicumque*), n. 1 (PL 187, 1352A).

19 *Decretals of Gregory IX*, bk. 3, tit. 41, c. 7 (*De homine*) (PL 215, 1463A-C).

20 *Tractatus de hereticis et sortilegiis*, fol 51r. "We utterly rebuke the detestable abuse and horrible impiety of those who treating with irreverent boldness crucifixes and images or statues of the Blessed Virgin and other Saints, throw them to the ground in order to emphasize the suspension of Divine worship, and leave them under nettles and thorns. We forbid severely any sacrilege of this kind. We decree that those who disobey are to receive a hard retributive sentence which will so chastise the offenders as to suppress the like arrogance in others" (*Liber sextus*, bk. 1, tit. 16 (*De officio Ordiinarii*), c. 2 (*Canonici*), last paragraph).

savors of heresy, and it is the same thing as that which gives strong suspicion of heresy. For otherwise it would not be seen how the interpretation of lots, or sorcery, which consists in the exterior operation, could savor of heresy: since heresy (as we said in the first chapter of this work) consists not in an exterior action, but in the error of the intellect. Now to use sacred things, especially a Sacrament or the sacramentals, for the performance of sorceries, gives clear and forceful suspicion of heresy. Because no one would use those things for the performance of sorceries, unless he believes that they have some power for the performing of similar works. Now such credulity is clearly heresy. Because God, Who did not give to the Sacraments a natural power, but an extraordinary power, not for destruction and ruin of bodies and souls, but He gave it for the salvation of souls.

Yet the devil seeing that he is less powerful for working amatory sorcery, since (as we said) he cannot force someone to love against his will, hence he procures whatsoever more sacred things to mix into the sorceries of this kind, which he rarely uses in other noxious sorceries. Because the devil can, if God permits, work noxious sorceries on a man against his will. Thus, under this guise the devil deceives many by persuading them that the abuse of those Sacraments produces marvelous effects regarding love, which he very well knows cannot be done by those Sacraments or sacramentals. Nevertheless, that father of lies strives to persuade men to contemn the Christian religion, so that they may offend God more gravely. And he does not just procure these things from laymen, but also from those who serve the altar. For I read about a sacrilegious priest, that when he loved a woman with an unbridled and shameless affection, so that he might draw her into the love of himself, half of the Most Sacred Host, which he had consecrated in Mass, he took saying some filthy and detestable words, which at this time did not achieve the effect, but he sent part of the host to the aforesaid woman, not in the shape of the Host, but crushed, and reduced into powder, as apt for taking in a drink. Now the things that are done in this respect by women are so many, and so foul and abominable, that it is better to pass over those things in silence than to make known anything about them.

Therefore, so that we may conclude this whole matter with a brief summary, I lay down the following very certain rule about it. Every sorcery which is performed by a mixing of some Sacrament, or sacramental object, renders that action suspect of heresy. Because unless one believed that such Sacraments or sacramentals have power for the working of sorceries, he would not use them. Thus, when the inquisitor comes to know that some such sorcerer acknowledges that it can do harm, not indeed because of the sorcery, but on account of the mixing of the Sacraments, the sorcerer thereby renders himself suspect of heresy. He will diligently and carefully examine that prisoner about his credulity. If he were to say that he does not believe that the Sacraments have any capacity and power for sorceries, but that he used them to obey the will of the devil who commanded this, then the inquisitor cannot punish him, even though he sins very gravely: because he is forbidden in the chapter, *Accusatus*, §. *Sane* of [the title] *De hereticis* in *Liber Sextus*, but his punishment is deferred to the Ordinary alone. But if the sorcerer were to say that he mixed the Sacraments or sacramentals into his sorcery because he believes that they have some capacity and power for sorceries of this kind, then rightly the inquisitor according to the chapter, *Accusatus*, could punish him, not on account of the sorcery; but on account of the error of faith, from which if, when duly admonished, he does not wish to forsake, he should be treated by him in everything as a heretic. And I reckon that completely the same thing ought to be said about him who irreverently casts upon the ground the Lord's cross, or the image of the Virgin Mother of God, or of some other Saint. For these things could not be done without vehement suspicion of heresy, especially since it is a heresy, condemned in the Seventh Synod,[21] which says that images are not worthy of veneration: but ought to be completely despised.[22]

Now that which Paolo Grillandi cites from the chapter, *Si canonici*,[23] certainly proves nothing: because that citation has completely nothing to do with the present matter under discussion. For those canons, about which that text speaks, neither say that the images are trampled underfoot, nor that they are cast down to the ground due to some irreverence or contempt of them: but they were doing this by a certain ceremony for stirring up a certain horror, abomination, and hatred in the people against the person on account of whose crime the suspension of Divine service was imposed. Although that thing was deserving of reprehension, still it ought not to be branded as heresy. Still if they had cast them to the ground due to irreverence and contempt, without a doubt they would have been reckoned as heretics: because the Seventh Synod (as we just said) declared that those who long ago taught that it ought to be done, are heretics.

---

21 I. e., the II Council of Nicea.
22 "Anathema to the calumniators of the Christians, that is to the iconoclasts. Anathema to those who apply the words of Holy Scripture which were spoken against idols, to the venerable images. Anathema to those who do not salute the holy and venerable images" (Extract from the Acts, Session I (Mansi 12, 1009)).
23 *Liber sextus*, bk. 1, tit. 16 (*De officio Ordiinarii*), c. 2 (*Canonici*), last paragraph.

Chapter XVI

Whether lamiae and Striges ought to be deemed heretics.

Besides those badly ruined worshippers of the devil, about whom we discussed in the two previous chapters, there are still others also serving the devil, so much worse than them all, the more horrible atrocities they commit, by which they give greater offense to God and more clearly abandon the Catholic faith. For they are so evil and wicked that whatever wickedness, or heinous crime, or infidelity can be contrived by other men, who serve the devil in whatsoever way, these men do and perpetrate. These men are called by the Spanish in their language, *Bruxos*.[1] Italians call them *Strigoni* and *Strighe*. But in Latin they are called lamiae and *Striges* on account of the likeness (as I think) which they have with the animals, which are called by names of this kind. For so Apuleius in that work of his which he entitled, *The Golden Ass*, especially in the first book, where when speaking about women of this kind, says these words: "But he smelling the stink wherewith those hags [lamiae] had imbrued me, thrust me away."[2] And Philostratus in the *Life of Apollonius* [of Tyana], who was of the school of Pythagoras, says: "The vampires, that is to say, of those beings whom the many regard as lamias and hobgoblins. These beings fall in love, and they are devoted to the delights of Aphrodite, but especially to the flesh of human beings, and they decoy with such delights those whom they mean to devour."[3] It is necessary that we explain the sect of these men, so that from thence we can reply better to that which we inquire about

---

1 Or *Bruja* in modern Spanish, which means a witch.
2 *The Golden Ass* [or *Metamorphoses*], bk. 1, c. 17.
3 Bk. 4, c. 25.

them, namely, whether such men ought to be reckoned as heretics or not.

About this matter, because faults in different authors are read, who perhaps did not fully examine the matter (as ought to have been done), wherefore omitting them all, I will say those things which were known with very certain experience, and which things the adherents of this pestiferous sect themselves, both men and women, have spontaneously confessed before the judges, from whom I have learned this. Whoever wants to profess themselves as a member of this diabolical sect, is firstly led by the one, by whom he is taught, before the tribunal of the devil, sitting on a throne as for a king. For the devil shows himself to them in a certain visible and bodily form, to persuade them of his false majesty and authority by a fabricated sign. Thus, having been brought before him: he who is prepared to profess this sect, immediately must renounce Baptism, and abandon all the teachings of the Catholic faith. Next, it is necessary that he reject all the ecclesiastical Sacraments. He must throw to the ground the cross and trample underfoot the images of the Immaculate Virgin, and of any others of the Saints. Yet this trampling of images need not be done immediately before the devil: but it suffices that he promise that he will do it afterwards, as soon as the occasion offers. When these things have been done, he gives himself, as perpetually obliged and devoted to the devil, as to a leader or king, vowing in his hands, and promising, as religious are accustomed to profess the vow of their profession in the hands of their prelate, to be forever faithful to him in the future, and to submit to all his commands. After these things having touched the writing on a certain book, containing some obscure and unknown pages, promises by swearing that he will never return to Christ's faith, and not observe the Divine precepts, but only those which will be commanded by the leader himself, namely, the devil. He promises moreover that he will come as many times as he shall be called to the nightly gatherings, and will make sacrifices which he shall see are done at those nocturnal hours, will say the prayers, will show to him the worship of adoration, and finally will do everything else which are done by others there.

Which vow and oath having been made by him, immediately the devil, who had shown himself sitting in the throne as a king, putting on a cheerful face promises to give to the one so persevering, perpetual happiness and immense joy, which he does not have in himself, and to have whatever pleasures he desires in this world, and finally he promises that he will give much greater things after this life. Next, he appoints one devil for his care and teaching, who will continually accompany him, and may serve him in all things, and give him everything he desires. To this demon assigned to care was appointed this special duty among others, so that as often as it shall be necessary to go to the nocturnal games, he will announce this to his little client, and bring him to the place of the gathering. The men themselves, the teachers of this diabolical art, call (as I hear) this demon, who was given as a protector for guarding, Martinetus or Martinellus.

As often as a general assembly of them ought to be made on some night for games and employing themselves in pleasures, two days before that assembly ought to be made this demon announces to his little client, and tells him the hour and place, so that when the time comes, he may be prepared to come. But when the hour of going approaches, immediately that demon, whom we said is called by them Martinetus or Martinellus, calls that same man with a certain human voice, fashioned to be like a human voice. When that voice has been heard, soon that man who is to go, takes a small container of ointment, and anoints certain members of his body with the ointment taken from that container. When this has been done, he leaves the house, and there he finds Martinetus near the door of the house waiting for him in the form of a goat, upon which (as the men themselves relate) he rides, who is to be bought to the games, grasping firmly the hair of goat, lest on account of the very fast movement of the goat, he perhaps fall to the ground. Thus the devil, taking the form of a goat, in this way transports him very quickly through the air, and brings him to the place of the assembly: where a large crowd of men and women gather in front of the devil sitting like a king.

After each of them has arrived there, he firstly makes a reverence to the devil, yet in a different way than we are accustomed to do. For they do not face, but turn their backs towards the devil, and they do not bow the head towards the chest, but bend it towards the shoulders, such that with the chin elevated towards heaven they bend their head backwards. But they genuflect (not as we are wont to do) bending the back side of legs: but the front side they lift from the ground. Which reverence having been shown, they sometimes offer sacrifices to him, yet not always. When these things have been completed, the devil himself, who sits upon a throne of majesty, commands all to dance and sing, taking their pleasures with joy and rejoicing. And every demon takes with the hand his woman, for whose care he was appointed, and dances with her, and makes round dances. When the round dances and the dancing have finished, they thence come to decorated and prepared tables which are found with sumptuous plates, so that each one may enjoy them as he wishes. When the feasts have finished all lights are extinguished, and each demon takes his woman in the form of an incubus. But if there are men present, they each have their own demon in the form of a succubus, that is, in the form of a woman, and thus they have carnal intercourse with each other, and they receive the pleasures of the flesh until satiety with the greatest (as they say) enjoyment. When all these things have been completed, they all return to their homes riding on goats, by which we said they were firstly transported to the assembly. And in doing all these things the greatest care is taken by them all that God be not invoked or named in any way, or that one would make the sign of the Cross either while going, or when remaining in the assembly, or when returning from it: because if any of those things are done, the demons not bearing it immediately flee, and all those illusions done by the devil's art vanish.

Besides all these things there are many other disgraceful things and wicked deeds which those very evil lamiae commit. For it does not seem enough for them that they give themselves over to the devil for the sake of satisfying their lusts, and that they serve him in everything: but they moreover try to bring as many others as they can to the devil's allegiance and away from God's service, so that the devil's empire may by increased by their ministry. For besides the fact that they solicit many to profess the diabolical art of this kind, they strive to kill many children before they have received Baptism, lest by the Baptism received they could attain everlasting glory. At night they enter other men's houses, they enter rooms, no matter how much they are locked, by the devil opening the way for them, they suck the blood of children, sometimes they suffocate them, and commit many other evil deeds regarding them. And for this reason (as I think) they are called lamiae and striges. For a lamia is a certain very cruel animal appearing to have a womanly face, and having horse-like feet. Jeremias speaks about lamiae of this kind in the book of Lamentations, saying: "Even the sea monsters [*lamiae*] have drawn out the breast, they have given suck to their young" (4, 3). The *strix* [or screech-owl], however, is a nocturnal and troublesome bird, so-called from the screech it makes. Lucan speaks about this bird thus: "The screech of nightly owl raising her hoarse complaint."[4] This bird attacks children lacking nurses, and sucks living blood from their small bodies. And from the

---

4 *Pharsalia*, bk. 6, ln. 689.

Book 1, Chapter 16

harm of this bird, women are called *Striges*, about whom we have spoken until now: because they suck children's blood, like that bird.

Thus far are the things which I understood to be more certain about this pestiferous sect of men; part of which is from the reading of some authors, who wrote about this matter; part is from the accounts of some esteemed men, who being judges, carefully examined arrested men of this kind, and received nearly all these things from their confession. And among other things, which about these very evil men are known by certain experience teaching, is the fact that many more are women, who profess this diabolical art, than men. There can be twofold reasons for this (in my opinion in fact). The first is the excessive credulity of women, on account of which this sex is easily deceived. Whose defect the devil knowing very well, attacks them more frequently by deceits and lies than men. For the devil seduced Eve, the mother of all, but Adam her husband (as Paul testifies) "was not seduced" (I Tim. 2, 14). For this reason, Paul himself does not allow a woman to teach, lest she having been deceived, deceive others by her teaching. Theophylactus, interpreting which passage of Paul, says: "The woman taught once, and the whole world was also overthrown: for this reason, this sex may not teach. For it is inconstant, [it easily submits,] and can easily be seduced. For notice that he did not say, 'Eve being seduced,' but 'the woman,' that is to say, as though he were discussing the feminine gender itself. For in the same manner that the whole race perished in Adam, so through Eve inconstancy spread unto all woman; by that inconstancy to be sure that same transgression took place firstly in Eve."[5]

The second reason is the fragility of the same women, and their inclination to lust. For there are women more inclined to lust than men. And especially due to this reason (as I think) the feminine gender is called by Blessed Peter the "weaker

---

[5] *Expositio in Epistolam ad Timotheum* (PG 125, 39A-B).

vessel" (I Pet. 3, 7). Now the first and chief end to which men who profess this diabolical sect tend, is the pleasure of the flesh, due to which for the sake of lust and attaining satiety, they all gave themselves to the devil, and they do all the other things, which we said. Hence for this reason many more women than men profess this diabolical art: because women desire more vehemently the pleasures of the flesh, and more easily succumb to the desire of this kind.

But among the very many things which we said about the sect of these lamiae, there are some things which seem to some to be false, and completely unbelievable. For there are some that hold very firmly and teach that it is false that lamiae of this kind are brought to those amusements, and to take those pleasures, and that the demons have intercourse with them for the pleasure of the flesh: but all these things are mere dreams, from which those women are deceived even when awake, thinking that they truly saw those things, which happened in the imagination alone. And to support this they cite the Synod of Ancyra, whose words are found in the chapter, *Episcopi*. In which place among others these words are said: "That is to say, when Satan himself, who transforms himself into an Angel of light, has taken hold of the mind of each of these women and subdued her to himself by her infidelity, he then transforms himself into the appearance and likeness of various persons and deludes the mind he holds captive during times of sleep, alternating happy visions with sad, and known persons with unknown, leading them through every kind of crooked path; and though the faithless woman experiences all this only in the spirit she believes that it happens not in the mind but in the flesh. For who is there that is not drawn out of himself in sleep and in nightly visions and does not see many things while asleep that he has never seen awake?"[6] They also assert as a confirmation of the same opinion some examples, with which

---

6 *Decretum Gratiani*, pt. 2, *causa* 26, q. 5, c. 12 (PL 187, 1349).

they say that they prove with certain experience that some women, who thought that they were transported to other places, while the same were seen having fallen asleep on the ground during that whole time, in which they were saying that they were transported to other places.

But actually, those who do not believe that lamiae can be transported from place to place by the devil, do not understand the devil's natural power, which Holy Writ and its sacred interpreters have stated so clearly. For in whatever surroundings these inferior bodies may be, they are subject to the command of Angels, either good or bad, as to their local movement, such that the Angels, either good or bad, can move them from place to place as they wish. For if the Angels (as the more common opinion of the theologians and philosophers holds) move those heavenly bodies, which are of immense size: much more easily could they move from place to place human bodies, which are of much smaller size. Moreover, an Angel took the prophet Habacuc by the hair of his head from Judea into Babylon, so that he might give the bread, which he was carrying to the reapers, to the prophet Daniel enclosed in the den of lions.[7] Who after he had given the bread to Daniel, was immediately brought back by the same Angel from Babylon to Judea.[8] If a good Angel could do that, it follows that a demon could also do the same: because (as Dionysius the [Pseudo-] Areopagite teaches[9]) the natural good remained unimpaired in devils. Again, the devil, by whom Christ Our Savior was tempted in the desert, took Christ Himself (as Matthew relates[10]) and transported Him from the desert into the holy city, and placed him upon the pinnacle of the Temple. And again took Him up from there, and brought Him to a very high mountain,

---

7 Cf. Dan. 14, 32-35.
8 Cf. v. 38.
9 *The Divine Names*, c. 4, §23 (PG 3, 725).
10 Cf. Mt. 4, 5.

Whether lamiae and Striges ought to be deemed heretics

where he showed Him all the kingdoms.[11] If the devil could move Christ's holy Body, with God's permission, so easily through very long distances, it follows that he could move any other human body to any great distance. And hence it clearly follows that he could transport lamiae not merely in the spirit, but also in the body, to where he wishes.

Add to all these things the manifest experience, whereby it is most surely known that the lamiae themselves are transported by the devil. For the confirmation of which matter, I could cite many examples, which I heard from those who saw. Yet omitting this I will cite only two, which Paolo Grillandi reports in this tract, *De Haereticis*.[12] For here he relates that in the year of the Lord, 1524, having been himself invited by the abbot of the Monastery of Saint Paul he went from the city to the castle Nazanus, which was under the same monastery. When he arrived there two women were presented to him, who were accused that they were lamiae, and were being held in prison, so that he might examine them. And from one of them, who was more compliant, and of a milder disposition, he says that he learned nearly that whole great number of ceremonies, which we related above, which men professing this sect observe. From the second, whom he says was called Lucretia, he relates that while she was transported from the assembly of the amusements to her house, near dawn the bell rang, which in Italy is accustomed to be rung at that time, so that the people would be reminded for prayer. Which sound having been heard the devil departed, and left her in a certain field full of thorn hedges near the bank of the river. Now a certain young man, whom she knew very well, happened to pass by there near to her, whom she seeing called to herself. But the young man seeing her naked, besides the private parts which were covered with a short garment, and having disheveled hair, he was stunned,

---

11 Cf. v. 8.
12 Bk. 2, q. 7, fols. 41r ff.

and feared to approach her: but finally having been overcome by the charms of the woman he drew near and asked her what had happened to her, and for what reason she remained unclothed. But she wanted to cover the truth of the matter with invented lies, and to pretend: since the young man nowise believed all these things, he said that he would not do anything for her: unless she would clearly reveal the truth. Thus, she seeing that she gained nothing by lies, promised that she would say the truth to the young man, if he promised that he would always keep all those things a secret. Which when the young man promised by swearing, she immediately opened the truth with full confidence, saying that she had been carried by the devil to the nocturnal amusements, from which when she was being brought back by the same devil to her house, when the sound of the bell was heard, the devil departed, and left her there. When the young man heard these things he believed her, and brought her secretly to his house, for which reason he was given many gifts by her. But finally, the young man, having forgotten that he promised, related all these things to one and another person, and thus little by little the matter was divulged, and for which reason she was arrested and brought to jail. The young man, however, having been summoned as a witness before the aforesaid Paolo Grillandi, to whom the examination of this woman was assigned, told all these things which we have now related, and finally the woman herself confessed that all these things are true. From which story, which was confirmed by clear experience, it is manifestly proved to be true that the lamiae of this kind are sometimes transported by demons from place to place, quite far apart.

A certain woman of the diocese of Sabina was professed in the diabolical art, and when her husband had a suspicion about which art, he asked her many times whether she knew and practiced it: which she always denied to know. But the husband persisting in his suspicion anxiously asked for the

Whether lamiae and Striges ought to be deemed heretics

truth, who acted so craftily that he saw her one night anointing herself with a certain ointment; which anointing having been done, he saw the woman departing very swiftly like a bird, and from the upper balcony of the house descending to the lower areas; the husband following her, so that he might see wither she was going, saw her no longer; going to the door of the house found it closed. Which thing gave great wonder to him. But on the next day the husband again asked the wife what he anxiously wanted to know, and she constantly (as before) said that she did not know. But the husband, so that the woman could not now deny, says clearly to her whatever he had seen her do on the previous night, then hit her forcefully with a stick, and threatened harder blows unless she said the truth: which if she would plainly disclose, he promised that he would give pardon to her. The woman therefore understanding that she could not keep secret any longer, disclosed the truth, and sought pardon from the husband, which the husband granted to her on this condition, that she would bring him to suchlike assemblies: but she, to procure pardon, readily promised the things requested, and fulfilled the thing promised with the permission of Satan. When he was brought to the place where the amusements were taking place, he beheld the amusements, the ring dances and everything else, and finally sitting at the table with the others so that he might be fed, when he judged the food to be tasteless, he asked for salt to be given to him, which was missing on the table, and although he asked again and again, it was never given to him. At last, when after an unmannerly request and a long delay the salt was given to him, he said: "May God be praised now, because the salt has now come." When these words were uttered the demons, because they avoid hearing God's praises, immediately went away, and everyone else vanished: the lights having been put out he remained alone naked, until at sunrise he saw some shepherds, whom he asked what was that country in which he was in. But they answered that it was the territory of Benevento in the Neapolitan kingdom. Which place was a hundred milestones from the country of that man, for which reason although he was rich, he was forced to beg along the road so that he could return to his house. After he arrived to which place he immediately accused his wife of the crime of lamiae, and set forth all that happened (as it was related) before the judges. Who fully (as it should be done) examining the whole affair, found all that we said was true, which things were also confirmed by the confession of the same wife.

I could relate many other testimonies among those which I ascertained through very faithful witnesses in Spain: but those things which we have just told seem to me to be enough for proving that those lamiae sometimes are brought by demons from place to place not only in the spirit, but also in the body. Now, that others object that they experienced that those lamiae were brought by demons not in the body, but in the spirit: because while they thought that they were so brought, while others seeing, who gave testimony about this matter, they were lying on the ground as though sleeping: achieves nothing against those things which we have said. For we do not say that they are always bought in the body: but this can happen, and we contend that it sometimes has happened, granting moreover that the opposite also sometimes happens, such that not in the body, but in the spirit alone they are brought by the demons from place to place through an imaginary vision of it. Thus, we concede that their experience is true: but it is befitting that they also believe that ours is true, because one is not opposed to the other: but both could happen at different times.

But it remains that we reply to the chapter, *Episcopi*, which seems to specifically conflict against us: yet if everything contained in it be well examined, it is clearly established that it does nothing against us. For that sect about which it

Whether lamiae and Striges ought to be deemed heretics

is treated in that chapter is quite different from this sect of lamiae, about which we are disputing at present. Firstly, in fact, the professors of that sect believe that a certain woman named Diana, or Herodiana, was changed into a goddess, to have something of the true Divinity. lamiae, however, do not believe this: but know well that the spirit appearing to them is the devil, and God's enemy, and although they know this, still on account of the pleasures they receive in it, willingly subject themselves to him. Secondly, the professors of that sect believe (as is evident from the context of that chapter) that some creature can be changed by someone other than God into a different species, for example a man into an ass, or horse. Now whether all lamiae believe this, is not evident to him up until now: because (as I can conjecture from those things which I have read and heard about them) this is not belonging to their sect: although perhaps some of them believe this, because they profess not only the sect of the lamiae, but also the sect of sorcerers. Thirdly, they differ: because that sect is not said to deny Christ's faith absolutely, and to contemn His Sacraments, to shatter the cross, all of which things we said are done by the lamiae.

Yet about this there is agreement between both sects, that the professors of them both occupy themselves at night with the devil in pleasures: both also sometimes believe that what happens in their imagination alone, happens in the body. Next, I say that even if this sect of the lamiae were the same as that about which that chapter, *Episcopi*, speaks, still that text does nothing against us. For that text does not deny that women can be corporally transported by the devil from place to place, and it does not say that the movement always happens in the spirit, and in the imagination, and never in the body: but it merely says that those women are deceived, supposing that those things happen in their bodies, which happen in the imagination alone. And it certainly so happens often, although sometimes (as we said) it happens that they are not deceived. And if that text would say universally, that it never happens that they are transported by the body, the arguments with which it is attempted to prove this achieve absolutely nothing. Since for the confirmation of their opinion it brings forth as a witness the prophet Ezechiel, who testifies that he saw God's visions not in the body, but in the spirit:[13] and Paul, who did not know, whether in the body, or whether he was out of the body, when he saw God's secrets.[14] I indeed admit that these examples suffice for proving that those visions sometimes happen not in the body, but in the spirit, which we also acknowledge.

Yet if from them one wishes to infer that such things never happen in the body, and always in the spirit: who does not see how weak the argument is? From one thing in fact, or another singular thing, even if it may be permitted to infer a particular proposition, still it will never be permitted to infer a universal one. I say furthermore that there are some things related in that chapter, *Episcopi*, about the carrying of those women, which it is evident never happened in the body, but always in the spirit. For it is said in that place about those women, that they believe that they ride upon certain beasts during the nocturnal hours, and to pass through the spaces of many lands in the silence of the inhospitable night. And concerning the lamiae we also related above that they believe this same thing. For that they are sometimes transported not only in the spirit and imagination, but also in the body, we ourselves concede, and we proved that this can happen by reason and at the same time with experience. Now that they ride upon beasts, and when riding pass through large spaces of land in a very short time, I concede this happens not bodily, and truly, but in the spirit only. For those beasts, by which they say that they are transported, are not true beasts: but certain imaginary bodies made out of the air or from any

---

13 Cf. Ez. 11, 24.
14 Cf. II Cor. 12, 3-4.

other material by the demons for a likeness of the beasts. Or perhaps there are no bodies, but the devil impresses a very strong mental image upon them, so that that happens, which is wont to happen to those sleeping, to those women even while they are awake, especially at night when their bodily eyes can see little or nothing: because those things which happen in dreams, men when awake often afterwards claim to have really seen. And certainly the same thing could happen to women of this kind, when they think that they are carried over long distances in a very brief period of time. For there is not such great agility of any beast, nay, nor of any bird, that in the space of an hour can transverse thirty or forty milestones. And there also is not such great mobility of any beast, that it could through so great a space suspend itself in the air, so that its weight would not weigh it down and cast it down to the ground. And concerning these and other things of the same kind, which are said regarding the movement of those women, I think that that chapter, *Episcopi*, ought to be understood, when it says that those things happen in the spirit alone and in the imagination, and not in the body.

Otherwise, that which is said about the incubus demons, unless reasonably understood, will rightly be judged unbelievable. For it being supposed that the devils (as the more common opinion holds) are spiritual substances lacking bodies, it is necessary that they would be indivisible and impartible. Hence it is that they cannot emit anything from their substance as seed, and hence it follows that they are unable to have intercourse with woman, as men are accustomed to have intercourse with them. And according to this meaning I think some sacred Doctors ought to be understood, who deny that demons can have intercourse with women. Chrysostom openly denies this.[15]   Philas-

---

15 "Is it not a particular hallmark of folly to claim that Angels descended to have intercourse with women, and that their incorporeal nature of theirs was reduced to association with corporeal

trius, Bishop of Brescia, whom Blessed Augustine relates that he saw in Milan,[16] in a small work in which he discusses about all heresies, among the other heresies he includes that opinion which says that devils can have intercourse with women.[17] Blessed Augustine is more doubtful on this matter, which doubt (as I suspect) arose to him from the fact that he thought that devils had bodies, although perhaps not of the nature as ours.[18] This opinion of Augustine, however, has been rejected by all schools of theology, and there is not any theologian, even one, who defends Augustine's opinion on this point. But because (as the same Augustine says in the passage just now cited) it was known by a very certain experience, that women even unwilling were oppressed by demons: hence, it is befitting to inquire about the manner so that we may say according to the faith and in a Catholic way whereby it could be done.

About this matter I will say what I think, being ready to hear someone teaching better things. The devil, who knew the features and properties of any lower nature better than all the wise men of the world, could condense the air, and compose from it, or from some other matter, a body, and fashion it in the form of a man, or an ass, or a horse. Which body having been completed, although he could not give any soul to it, still he could do all those things regarding

---

creatures?" (*Homilies on Genesis*, hom. 22, n. 2 (PG 53, 188)).

16 "A certain Philastrius, Bishop of Brescia, whom I myself saw at Milan with the saintly Ambrose, has written a book on this subject..." (Letter 222 (to Quodvultdeus), n. 2 (PL 33, 999)).

17 *Liber de haeresibus*, n. 108 (PL 12, 1224B).

18 "I dare not determine whether there be some spirits embodied in an aerial substance (for this element, even when agitated by a fan, is sensibly felt by the body), and who are capable of lust and of mingling sensibly with women; but certainly I could by no means believe that God's holy angels could at that time have so fallen..." (*City of God*, bk. 15, c. 23, n. 1 (PL 41, 468)).

Whether lamiae and Striges ought to be deemed heretics

local motion, which the soul would do, if it were in it. For he can move the hands, the feet, the tongue for speaking, raise the genital members, so that they would seem fit for intercourse, and finally move the whole body, as men are wont to move when having intercourse with women. When they have done all these things, still the seed, which the Greeks call *sperma*,[19] they cannot emit from that body. Because that seed (as physicians and doctors teach) is part of the substance which remains from food well digested, namely, that part which is close to being changed into blood. Which doctors assuredly infer from the fact that those who indulge too much in sexual activity after they deplete all the semen that they have, at length they emit blood. Now an imaginary body, since it is completely unanimated, cannot break down the food, nor make any digestion of it. Hence it is that it also does not have any semen: which, when having intercourse with a woman, it can emit. It is thus necessary that the devil, when he has intercourse in an imaginary body with a woman, wrest out that semen from another human body, so that he can emit it into the woman's vagina. Now the woman having been deceived by the illusions of the devil thinks that that semen was emitted from the demon incubus out his own body. And I do not doubt that the woman can conceive from such semen. Which if it happened, the offspring thence born ought not to be called a son of the devil: but the son of him from whom the devil wrested the semen, which was dropped into the woman's womb, and from it such a conception followed.

After all these preliminary remarks, it remains that we reply to that which was firstly asked, namely, whether lamiae of this kind, and *Striges*, about whom we have discussed until now, ought to be deemed heretics, and punished as such. It can be easily replied to this question from these things which have been related about them above. For many

---

19 I. e., σπέρμα.

things are done by the adherents of that sect, on account of which they all rightly ought to be deemed heretics, but also apostates. For they give Divine honors to the devil as to God, adoring him, and offering him sacrifices. Which things by no means can be done without a strong suspicion of heresy. For they would never give such honors to the devil, unless they thought that he has something of divinity. Now believing this they have blasphemed, and fall into open heresy, against that which the Royal Prophet says: "Who is God but the Lord? or who is God but our God?" (Ps. 17, 32). And in Psalm eighty-five: "For thou art great and dost wonderful things: thou art God alone" (v. 10). And God Himself says through the Prophet Isaias: "I am the Lord, and there is none else: there is no God, besides me" (45, 5). And he very often repeats the same thought in that same chapter.

Next, men who are adherents of this pestiferous sect despise the Sacraments, by which contempt they fall into another open and condemned heresy, thinking that the Sacraments are worthless, which from the judgment of the Catholic Church, confer grace to those worthily receiving them. Besides all these things, they smash to pieces the cross and images of any other Saints. Which things give not a small suspicion of heresy. For to say that images ought not to be tolerated, but rather ought to be broken, is a heresy condemned in the Seventh Synod.[20] And the adherents of this diabolical art are not merely heretics, but, so that nothing may be wanting to their diabolical wickedness, they are also very clear apostates. Because they explicitly renounce Christ's faith, and what is worst of all, they promise by swearing that they will never return to the Catholic faith. Rightly therefore these pestiferous men, either men or women, who profess this diabolical art, ought to be deemed heretics, and punished as such. But besides these things, which pertain to the faith, they commit other heinous crimes, on account of which with the sentence

---

20 I. e., the II Council of Nicea.

of the ecclesiastical judge, which would condemn them of heresy, the secular power alone could arrest them, and punish them with the ultimate punishment. For (as we related above) they kill children at night, or make men sick and unhealthy, and commit other similar offenses on account of which they are deserving of death: even if it were not established about their unbelief or apostacy.

Chapter XVII

Concerning those believing, harboring, supporting, and defending heretics, whether they ought to be deemed heretics, and punished as such.

Many and various are the kinds of men, upon whom the laws which speak about heretics, inflict many, and various and serious punishments: for which reason it can be rightly doubted whether they all ought to be deemed heretics, and reckoned as such. Of these men some are called believers of heretics, others harborers, others supporters, and lastly others defenders. It is necessary to speak about each in its turn, and firstly we will state who they are to whom all these things belong, next we will discuss whether they rightly ought to be counted among the heretics. Peter Paludanus says that those who are called "believers of heretics," who although they believe not heresy in particular, yet have a good opinion about the heretics who teach them, believing that they are good men and think correctly about the faith: and for this reason, they believe by a general credulity everything which those heretics assert.[1] There are many such uneducated men of this kind remaining among heretics, and well disposed towards them. About these men there is no reason for doubting that they are heretics, especially if they have pertinacity in their evil credulity, such that although they have been warned that those men are heretics: they nonetheless persist in their credulity and view, believing that those heretics are good men and truly believers. For just as it is not necessary to believe the Catholic faith explicitly and in particular, so that someone may be deemed a true believer: but it is enough that one believe in general, and profess

---

1 *Scriptum in quartum sententiarum* (Salamanca: Andreas à Portonariis, 1552), dist. 13, q. 3, p. 159.

Book 1, Chapter 17

whatever the Catholic Church believes: so on the contrary, so that someone may be called an unbeliever and heretic, it is not necessary that he believe some heresy in particular: but it suffices that he in general believe those things which a manifest heretic, and a man condemned by the Church, believes and teaches.

But although these men, who pertinaciously believe public heretics are good and believing men, ought to be reckoned heretics: yet because none of them believe in a particular error, the Church does not want that they be punished with all the punishments of heretics, but with other much milder punishments, as we will show afterwards in this chapter. For those who believe in some error of the heretics in particular are reckoned clear heretics, as it was explicitly decreed in the next-to-last chapter of *De haereticis*.[2] Still, if that heretic has not been condemned by the Church, and was not a manifest heretic on another account, and the simple man believes in general whatever that heretic believes, solely because he thinks that he believes what the Church believes, in this case that simple man ought not to be reckoned a heretic, and not a believer of heretics, as one can easily establish from the words of Augustine in his letter to Glorius and Eleusius.[3]

---

2 "But if those of the aforesaid [heretics], after they have been apprehended, do not want to return to doing worthy penance, they ought to be cast into prison in perpetuity; believers of their errors, however, we likewise judge to be heretics" (*Decretals of Gregory IX*, bk. 5, tit. 7, c. 15, §1).

3 "The Apostle Paul has said: 'A man that is a heretic, after the first and second admonition, avoid: Knowing that he, that is such an one, is subverted, and sinneth, being condemned by his own judgment' (Tit. 3, 10-11). But though the doctrine which men hold to be false and perverse, if they do not maintain it with passionate obstinacy, especially when they have not devised it by the rashness of their own presumption, but have accepted it from parents who had been misguided and had fallen into error, and if they are with anxiety seeking the truth, and are prepared to be set right when

Regarding those believing, harboring, supporting, and defending heretics

In another way some men are judged believers of heretics, not on account of a verbal confession, whereby they say that they believe what another believes: but on account of the deeds which they do regarding those men, giving or harboring something from them. For it is not important whether someone makes known his will by words or deeds.[4] For from the exterior works it is permitted to suspect about the dispositions of the mind, which are hidden within, as is inferred from the chapter *Qui viderit*[5] and in *The Code of Justinian*.[6] If those who honor heretics, willingly hear their sermons, have excessive conversations with them, have their books, and frequently read them, they ought to be called believers

---

they have found it, such men are not to be counted heretics" (*Decretum Gratiani*, pt. 2, *causa* 24, q. 3, c. 29 (*Dixit Apostolus*) (PL 187, 1306C-1307A)).

4 "What does it matter whether the people declare their will by voting or by the very substance of its actions? Accordingly, it is absolutely right to accept the point that statutes may be repealed not only by vote of the legislature but also by the silent agreement of everyone expressed through desuetude" (*The Code of Justinian*, De legibus senatusque consultis et longa consuetudine (*Digest*, bk. 1, tit. 3, law 32 (*De quibus*))).

5 "'Whosoever shall look on a woman to lust after her, hath already committed adultery with her in his heart' (Mt. 5, 28). For whereas an adulterer is called by the Greek word, *moechus*, whilst not another man's wife, but a woman is forbidden to be looked at, the Truth openly shows that by the mere look alone, when only one that is unmarried is vilely lusted after, adultery is perpetrated. Yet generally speaking the thing is differentiated according to the situation or order of the person lusting, that is to say in this way, that purposed concupiscence in like sort defiles one in sacred Orders, as the sin of adultery defiles that other" (*Decretum Gratiani*, pt. 2, *causa* 32, q. 5, c. 13 (PL 187, 1489B-C)).

6 "Fraud must be proved by convincing evidence" (Bk. 2, tit. 21 (*De dolo malo*), l. 6 (*Dolum*)).

of heretics, reckons the Archdeacon[7] in the chapter, *Quicumque*.[8] Nevertheless, it is necessary (as he likewise says) that they do this frequently, but if on the other hand they did one of these things once it would be clear, he says, that they ought not to be deemed believers of heretical books. For if they who once heard the words of heretics, and never afterwards return to them, or they read books of heretics one time, and afterwards burned them, he says that such men ought not to be called believers of heretics: because they do not seem to have approved of what they later avoided. Likewise, he says that they ought not to be called believers of heretics, who visit heretics, or give support to them, or give guidance to them, or have done some other similar thing, in which nothing explicit is shown which pertains to their heresy: because these things are very often given merely as a monetary wage. Yet I myself think that this is true on this condition, if they who give these things to heretics, have not in the past fallen into heresy: because if they previously fell into heresy, and afterwards have provided these things to the heretics, they will not only be reckoned believers of heretics, but heretics, and relapsed, as was decreed in the chapter, *Accusatus*.[9]

---

7 Guido de Baysio (1246-1313).

8 "Whoever dares to give ecclesiastical burial to such persons, namely, believers, followers, harborers, and defenders of heretics, should be punished by the sentence of excommunication until there is suitable satisfaction" (*Liber sextus*, bk. 5, tit. 2 (*De hereticis*), c. 2 (*Quicumque haereticos*)).

9 "A person accused or suspected of heresy, against whom there is a strong suspicion of this crime, if he abjures the heresy before the judge and afterwards commits it, then, by a sort of legal fiction, he shall be judged to have relapsed into heresy, although the heresy was not proved against him before his abjuration. But if the suspicion was in the first place a small or light one, although such a relapse renders the accused liable to severe punishment, yet he is not to suffer the punishment of those who relapse into heresy."

Regarding those believing, harboring, supporting, and defending heretics

Harborers of heretics are certainly without guilt, and are they who receive those they are unaware are heretics: and about them the laws ought not to be understood, which inflict some punishments to harborers of heretics. For it would be unjust to inflict punishments upon those who lack all guilt. Yet it is necessary to notice that these men, who plead that they have received heretics on account of ignorance, ought to prove their ignorance, in order that they may show themselves free from guilt, especially if before they had manifestly fallen into heresy, or gave vehement suspicion of heresy. Those harborers of heretics are said to be at fault who intentionally and with certain knowledge receive heretics, whether they do it hiddenly or openly. And it does not matter whether such a harborer harbors one or many heretics multiple times, or only once, because if he has harbored only one heretic once, he will be called a harborer of heretics, and will be subject to the same punishments which have been decreed by law against harborers of heretics. For so that someone may be called a harborer of heretics, the multitude of the receptions ought not so much be examined, as the purpose on account of which he harbors the heretic. Because if he harbors the heretic in order to hide the heretic, lest he could be punished by the judge, then he will correctly be called a harborer of heretics: as it can be easily gathered from many other cases described in law. For the laws judge a man to be a harborer, who harbors and hides the wrongdoer, so that thus the one hidden could be delivered from hands of the judge.[10] And he

---

(*Ibid.*, c. 8 (*Accusatus de haeresi*)).
10 "The harborers of criminals constitute one of the worst classes of offenders, for without them no criminal could long remain concealed. The law directs that they shall be punished as robbers. They should be placed in the same class, because when they can seize robbers they permit them to go, after having received money or a part of the stolen goods" (*Digesta*, bk. 47, tit. 16 (*De receptatoribus*), l. 1). "It is proper for every good and worthy Governor

who has hidden a heretic ought to be punished as a heretic. For the one hiding makes the crime his own. And Baldus [de Ubaldis][11] explicitly annotated this on the first law of [the title,] *De his qui latrones vel in aliis criminibus reos occultaverint*, of *The Code of Justinian*.[12] And I reckon this is also true if the heretic were a relative of the harborer: because since children are punished for the father's sin, on account of the atrocity of the crime, as we will say in the second book, it is much more just that one be punished for one's own crime, when they have harbored their own parents.

But if someone has intentionally harbored a heretic in his house, not so that he may hide or defend him, and not

---

to take care that the province over which he presides is peaceable and quiet. This he will accomplish without difficulty if he exerts himself to expel bad men, and diligently seek for them, as he must apprehend all sacrilegious persons, robbers, kidnappers, and thieves, and punish each one in proportion to his crime; he should also restrain those who harbor them, as without their assistance a robber cannot long remain concealed" (*Digesta*, bk. 1, tit. 18 (*De officio praesidis*), l. 13). "When any robbers or other malefactors reside or conceal themselves on the land of another, the owner of the property (if he is present) or his agents (if he is absent), or the persons having the control of the same, are obliged to voluntarily deliver up the said criminals; and if they knowingly should not do so of their own accord, they shall be notified by the civil authorities to surrender those who are sought, in order that they may be tried and punished according to the nature of their offences. Where, however, the owners of the land or their agents, or those having charge of the same, do not promptly give them up, then the Governor of the province, having been applied to, must take all legal measures to arrest them" (*The Code of Justinian*, bk. 9, tit. 39 (*De his qui latrones vel in aliis criminibus reos occultaverint*), l. 2).

11   Baldus de Ubaldis (1327-1400) was an Italian jurist.
12   *In VII, VIII, IX, X et XI codicis libros* (Venice: Giunta, 1577), p. 230.

Regarding those believing, harboring, supporting, and defending heretics

so that he may support his heresy: but only so that he may recall him from the heresy, and convert him to the Catholic faith, even if he has received him many times, he will not be called a harborer of heretics, and he will not be punished with the punishment of a harborer. For he who receives him with this intention, especially if he has some hope about his amendment, carries out a work of true charity, one greater than which he could scarcely render to his neighbor. Hence it is that no judge can exact punishments from him on account of it. But such a man as this on account of the good end he so intends in such a reception, may be held to be just and deserving of a reward before God, yet the Church, which does not know those things which are interior, will rightly punish him on account of such a reception, unless he shall have proved by clear evidence that he did it with a good intention and good purpose. Now no other certain and clear evidence of this good intention (in my opinion) can be given, except a deed done by him, which is established to be a clear means ordained for attaining such an end: as for instance, if he proves by reliable witnesses that he reprehended him on account of the heresy which he maintained, and admonished him, that having abandoned the heresy, he would return to the Catholic faith. If by these, or other proofs of this kind, he shall have proved that he received the heretic in his home with a good intention, the Church will praise him for the good deed, so far from it wanting to punish him as a harborer of heretics.

Some are called "supporters of heretics," others also "defenders of heretics": whose difference seems to me to depend on this alone, namely, that the defender omits by deeds, but the supporter by words, what one is obliged to do against the heretic. A defender is he who supports the heretic by his strength and power. But he will be called a supporter in this regard, who by words alone assists the heretic, or who omits to do something against the heretic, which he was bound by law to do. Let us speak about these two singly, and firstly about the supporters. Someone can be made a supporter of heretics (as we said) in two ways, namely, by words alone, or by their omission. It can happen that someone supports a heretic by words in two ways, because someone can support his teaching, and he can support the person due to ignorance of his teaching: because he does not know of what sort is his teaching. He who supports the teaching of heretics by words, saying that it is good, and argues in favor of it, and asserts reasons, these men are not merely supporters of heretics, but are reckoned heretics, nay, worse than the heretics themselves, whom they strive to support. For Pope Urban says: "He who defends the errors of others is much more condemnable than those who err, because he not only errs, but also prepares and strengthens the stumbling-blocks for others."[13] And Isidore says the same thing in the chapter, *Qui consensit*.[14]

Someone also can support the heretical person by words alone, and this in multiple ways. Firstly, in fact, by excusing the person from the crime of heresy, not out of inconsideration, or as a joke: but seriously, as for instance, if someone were to say that the heretics are not such as they say they are, but are good and believing Catholics. And if those who do these things are not manifest heretics, they are not called supporters of heretics: but they are excused as long as it is not evident that they are heretics: but the suspicion alone is had about them. Yet if from a slip of the tongue or as a joke someone has said some words in favor of a heretic, not on that account ought he to be reckoned a supporter of heretics,

---

13 *Decretum Gratiani, causa* 24, q. 3, c. 32 (*Qui aliorum*) (PL 187, 1307C).
14 "He who consents to those sinning, and defends another transgressing, will be cursed before God and men, and will be corrected with a very severe reproof" (*Decretum Gratiani, causa* 11, q. 3, c. 100 (PL 187, 1875C-1876A)).

so that it would be necessary on account of this to subject him to the punishments of the law. Which can be proved from something similar in the law, *Famosi*, in the *Digest of Justinian* in the title, *On the Julian law relating to the crime of lese majesty*.[15] And it does not matter whether they who so support by words give the support in or outside of a court of justice. For as long as it is established that they are not heretics, lawyers can assist persons who are heretics, by defending them and their possessions in a court of law.

And the chapter, *Si Adversus*, in the title, *De haereticis*,[16] does not conflict with this opinion: because that text ought to be understood of those lawyers, who support manifest heretics, and the same thing ought to be said about notaries, who prepare the documents for manifest heretics, who are by the law itself excommunicated, and infamous, and suspended from every office of theirs. Yet if lawyers assist those whom it is not established that they are heretics, or notaries prepare the documents for them, none of them will be subject to this punishment: even if it would be established that they are heretics after such support has been bestowed upon them. For it is just that for anyone accused of such a crime, that the defense of himself be permitted, until he has been convicted of the crime.

---

15 "The personal character of the accused should be taken in account, and whether he could have committed the offence, as well as whether he had previously done or planned anything of the same nature, and also if he was of sane mind, for a slip of the tongue ought not inconsiderately be held as deserving of punishment" (*Digesta*, bk. 48, tit. 4 (*Ad legem Iuliam maiestatis*), l. 7 (*Famosi*), n. 3).

16 "We strictly prohibit you, lawyers and notaries, from assisting in any way, by council or support, all heretics and such as believe in them, adhere to them, render them any assistance, or defend them in any way" (*Decretals of Gregory IX*, bk. 5, tit. 7, c. 11).

Book 1, Chapter 17

It could happen otherwise that someone would support a heretic by words alone, not indeed by excusing him before others, but by warning him of his arrest, which the judge may try to inflict upon him, so that having been thus warned he may take care to seek safety for himself by flight, and to put himself in a safe place, from which the judge could not seize him. And he who has so advised the heretic, I think that he ought to be punished as a supporter of heretics. For he supports him enough who helps him in such a way, that by the advice of the counsellor he would escape the hands of the judge. And an argument from the lesser to the greater can be taken up in favor of this position, from that which is decreed in the fourth law of the *Digest* [of Justinian] in the title, *On the Julian law relating to the crime of lese majesty*.[17] Now it is evident that to offend the Divine Majesty, which is done by the sin of heresy, is a much graver than to offend earthly majesty, as it is said in the chapter, *Vergentis*.[18] Now I reckon that this is especially true when the heretic, having

---

17 "Persons who are infamous and have no right to bring an accusation are undoubtedly permitted to bring this one" (*Digesta*, bk. 48, tit. 4 (*Ad legem Iuliam maiestatis*), l. 7 (*Famosi*)).

18 "Since, according to the legal sanctions, those guilty of crimes of lese majesty are punished by capital punishment, their property confiscated, and the life of their sons spared with regard to mercy alone, all the more so those who, wandering in the faith, offend Jesus Christ, the Son of God Our Lord, must be, by ecclesiastical discipline, deprived of their goods and separated from our Head Who is Christ, for it is much more serious to offend the Eternal Majesty than to offend temporal majesty" (*Decretals of Gregory IX*, bk. 5, tit. 7 (*De haereticis*), c. 10). In this decretal letter, *Vergentis in senium* (March 25, 1199), that Pope Innocent sent to Viterbo, a city within the Papal States, Innocent declared that heresy was treason against God. Consequently, in pursuing heretics, he applied the sanctions and employed the procedural norms used in ancient Roman treason trials.

Regarding those believing, harboring, supporting, and defending heretics

been advised by another to flee, follows his advice, and thus was delivered from the authority of the judge.

But whether he who advised him ought to be punished as a supporter of heretics, when the heretic did not follow the advice of the counsellor, I dare not decide: but I leave it to others to be disputed. And certainly, he who would want to call the counsellor a supporter of heretics, does not do so without grounds: because in every crime the intention of the offender ought to be examined more than the deed done by him. And laws want the will of the wicked man to be punished with the same severity as the effect, as say the Emperors Honorius and Achadius in the law, *Quidquid*, in the *Code of Justinian*, under the title, *On the Julian law relating to the crime of lese majesty*.[19] Now this man who advised the heretic about fleeing, wanted that the heretic would flee, otherwise he would not have warned him. But the fact that the heretic did not flee, ought to be attributed to the heretic himself, not to the advisor, who did all that he could do to aid his flight. From which it seems to follow that that advisor ought to be punished with the same punishment, with which he would be punished if his advice would have been put into effect.

One could support a manifest heretic by words alone in another way: for instance, if he were to intercede for him before a prince, or another secular authority, so that he would not be punished with the penalty of death, or he would beseech the ecclesiastical judges, upon whom it is incumbent to judge about the heresy of that man, so that they would not give sentence against him. He who gives support or protection of this kind, would rightly be called a supporter of heretics. For although in other crimes it would be permitted for anyone to intercede for another, as it is

---

19 "The laws punish with equal severity the intention to commit a crime and its actual perpetration" (Bk. 9, tit. 8, l. 5).

stated in the law, *Si fuerit*,[20] and the law, *In metallum*,[21] and the law, *Divus*,[22] especially if they have some hope of his amendment, otherwise it would not be allowed without this hope in this forum of conscience, although in the exterior forum it is permitted to them: yet in the crime of heresy on account of its very grave wickedness it is nowise allowed to do this. This can be proved from the fact that intercessions of this kind were interdicted by law, lest they be made for those who committed the crime of lese majesty, as it is stated in the chapter, *Si quis cum militibus*.[23] From which it is most evidently gathered that it also not be permitted for anyone to intercede for a manifest heretic: because it is much more serious to offend Eternal Majesty than temporal majesty.

Finally, one could be called a supporter of heretics in another way, not because he supports by words, but because he omits that which he was bound by law to do against heretics, either as a public or a private person. For some things ought to be done against heretics, which can only be done by a public authority: there are also some which all are obliged to do. The public authority is held to punish heretics condemned by the Church according to the quality of the crime. For this is commanded to it in the chapter, *Ad abolen-*

---

20 *Digest*, bk. 34, tit. 5 (*De rebus dubiis*), l. 10.
21 *Ibid.*, bk. 48, tit. 19 (*De poenis*), l. 22. A Gloss on the words, *adfines habent*, in this law states that parents and guardians can ask for a change or mitigation of a sentence.
22 *Ibid.*, bk. 48, tit. 19 (*De poenis*), l. 15.
23 "Lastly we also command that those who ever attempt to intervene before us are infamous without pardon" (*Decretum Gratiani*, pt. 2, *causa* 6, q. 1 c. 22 (PL 187, 735C)).

dam §. Statuimus,[24] and the chapter, *Excommunicamus,*[25] §. *Moneantur,*[26] found in [the title,] *De haereticis* [in the Decre-

---

[24] "Moreover, we ordain that counts, barons, rectors, consuls of cities and other places, being called upon by the archbishops and bishops, shall bind themselves with an oath that in all matters aforesaid, they will stoutly and effectually aid the Church against heretics and their accomplices, and endeavor faithfully, according to their office and power, to execute the ecclesiastical and imperial statutes concerning the matters herein mentioned" (*Decretals of Gregory IX*, bk. 5, tit. 7 (*De haereticis*), c. 9). The decretal is taken from the bull of Pope Lucius III, written at Verona and issued November 4, 1184.

[25] *Ibid.*, c. 15. N. B. Origen here is citing the Old Latin version of this verse which contains the words, "*Ostenta eos Domino contra solem,*" which in Greek means to hold someone up as an example. Cf. *Bibliorum sacrorum latinae versiones antiquae, seu Vetus Italica* (Rheims: Florentain, 1743), vol. 1, p. 309.

[26] "Secular authorities, whatever office they may hold, shall be admonished and induced and if necessary compelled by ecclesiastical censure, that as they wish to be esteemed and numbered among the faithful, so for the defense of the faith they ought publicly to take an oath that they will strive in good faith and to the best of their ability to exterminate in the territories subject to their jurisdiction all heretics pointed out by the Church; so that whenever anyone shall have assumed authority, whether spiritual or temporal, let him be bound to confirm this decree by oath. But if a temporal ruler, after having been requested and admonished by the Church, should neglect to cleanse his territory of this heretical foulness, let him be excommunicated by the metropolitan and the other bishops of the province. If he refuses to make satisfaction within a year, let the matter be made known to the Supreme Pontiff, that he may declare the ruler's vassals absolved from their allegiance and may offer the territory to be ruled by Catholics, who on the extermination of the heretics may possess it without hindrance and preserve it in the purity of faith; the right, however, of the chief ruler is to be respected as long as he offers no obstacle in this matter and permits freedom of action. The same law is to

tals of Pope Gregory IX]. Therefore, the secular power, known by any name, if it neglect to do these things which are commanded to it in these chapters, will rightly be called a supporter of heretics, and will be subject by that very fact to the punishments decreed by law. For (as [Pseudo-] Pope Damasus says) "He who can resist and confound the wicked, and fails to do this, does nothing else than to give support to their impiety. Suspicion of secret complicity is not out of place where someone who can fails to act against an obvious crime."[27] These words are found in the chapter, *Qui potest*.[28]

Rulers who neglect to resist heretics will not only undergo the punishments of human law, but they will be held guilty before God of all the evils which the heretics will do. Which assuredly is clearly proved from the fact that when long ago the people of Israel fornicated with the daughters of Moab, the Lord having been angered said to Moses: "Take all the princes of the people, and hang them up on gibbets against the sun: that my fury may be turned away from Israel" (Num. 25, 4). Origen, when interpreting these words, says: "The people sin, and the rulers are hung up 'against the sun,' that is, they are brought forward that they may be examined and may be convicted by the light. You see what is the condition of the rulers of the people: they are not merely rebuked for their own sins, but they are also forced to render an account for the sins of the people, that it was not their fault that the people sinned, lest perhaps they did not warn, and were not diligent to rebuke those who gave the beginning of the fault,

---

be observed in regard to those who have no chief rulers (that is, are independent). Catholics who have girded themselves with the cross for the extermination of the heretics, shall enjoy the indulgences and privileges granted to those who go in defense of the Holy Land" (*Ibid.*, c. 12; Mansi 22, 987-988). This decretal is taken from IV Lateran Council, canon 3.

27 Apocryphal letter 2 (PL 13, 431A).
28 *Decretum Gratiani*, pt. 2, *causa* 23, q. 3, c. 8 (PL 187, 1171B).

so that a pestilence might not spread to many. For the rulers and teachers ought to do all these things, for, if they do not and have no concern for the people, the people sin, and they themselves are hung up, and they are brought forth to judgment. Moses, that is, God's law, convicts them as negligent, and indolent, and God's wrath will be turned against them, and will cease from the people."[29] It certainly would behoove all kings, rulers, and all other secular authorities to precisely consider this matter, and always have this history before their eyes, so that thence they would certainly shake off all idleness and drowsiness, and would resist heretics more diligently and strongly, lest having been made more audacious by their impunity, they do more serious harm. But because we will make a longer disputation about this matter below in the second book, wherefore I have decided to say nothing further at the present time.

Now, a private person is not held to do anything (that I know) against heretics: except that he would bear witness against them as to what he knows, so that helped by his testimony the judge could give a just judgment against them. Thus, he who, knowing that someone is a heretic, especially if he has been asked about this matter by the judge, does not want to say the true testimony: but instead intentionally denies that which he knew, so that the heretic would not be condemned: will rightly be called a supporter of heretics, as can be gathered from the chapter, *Quisquis*.[30] In whichever of these ways, someone who supports a heretic sins, and indeed gravely, on account of which he deserves to be

---

29 *In Numeros Homiliae*, hom. 20, n. 4 (PG 12, 735A-B).
30 "Whoever from fear of any political power hides the truth, provokes upon himself God's anger, because he fears man more than God... Both he who hides the truth, and he who tells a lie are guilty, because the former does not want to do good, and the latter desires to do harm" (*Decretum Gratiani*, pt. 2, *causa* 11, q. 3, c. 80 (PL 187, 868A)).

punished with serious punishments. For he who supports a heretic in this way, consents to his crime, whence it is that he becomes a participant of his crime. King Josephat of Juda, an otherwise good man, was reprehended by God on account of the fact that he had aided wicked King Achab, although he had not supported the idolatry, to which he was addicted; but only to his person.[31]

They are called "defenders of heretics," who employ their forces or arms, and power, in resisting, lest they be captured, imprisoned, or punished in whatever way, or finally lest they be examined by the judge. It is written about the defense of this kind in [the *Decretum Gratiani, causa*] twenty-four, question three, in many chapters,[32] and in [*causa*] twenty-seven, question one, chapter, *Si custos*.[33] Such were the defenders of the Lutherans, and there are in our age many princes of Germany, Duke [John] Frederick [I] of Saxony, who firstly defended Luther, and next to this man, Philip [I], Landgrave of Hesse, who support the Lutherans so earnestly, and defend them so whole heartily, that they are not merely prepared to fight for them: but helped by the support of many German cities, in this year of 1546, they have assembled an enormous and very strong army against the most faithful and very zealous defender of the Church, Emperor Charles [V],

---

31 Cf. II Par. 19, 2.

32 *Decretum Gratiani*, pt. 2, *causa* 24, q. 3 (PL 187, 1292 ff.).

33 "Arrest the aforesaid woman, working with our defender, Sergius, and at once not only recall her to the [religious] habit she wrongly despised, without any excuse, but also consign her to the convent, where she can be strictly guarded in every way. Show total care over her, so that from your strictness, she may learn how wicked the sin was which she has committed. In this matter, in any layman, although we do not think it very likely, attempts to prevent you, for any reason, suspend him from participation in the most Holy Communion" (*Ibid.*, pt. 2, *causa* 27, q. 1, c. 18 (PL 187, 1380)).

King of Spain.[34] On account of the defense of these men, this very pestilential heresy of the Lutherans has spread so much, that it has infected nearly all Germany. And certainly we know this from experience, that no heresy lasts long, except that which had powerful rulers who defended its heresiarch with all their might. For the devil instigates not only to provide heretics, but also supporters and defenders of any other wicked men, lest due to a lack of protection the crimes would cease. Hence it is that God, when speaking to holy Job, says to the devil and his members, who are all hostile: "His body is like molten shields, shut close up with scales pressing upon one another. One is joined to another, and not so much as any air can come between them" (41, 6-7).

Blessed Gregory, when interpreting which words, says: "It is said that the body of the dragon is covered with scales, to keep it from being quickly penetrated with shafts. In like manner the whole body of the devil, that is, the multitude of the reprobates, when reproved for its iniquity, endeavors to excuse itself with whatever evasions it can, and opposes, as it were, some scales of defense, that it may not be transfixed with the arrow of truth."[35] And he adds: "These scales of sinners are both hardened and joined together, so as not to be penetrated by any breath of life from the mouth of preachers. For those whom a like guilt associates, the same does a perverse defense also crowd together in obstinate agreement, in order that they may protect each other with mutual defense for their sins. For everyone fears for himself, when he beholds another admonished or corrected, and therefore arises with the like feeling against the words of reprovers, because, in protecting another, he protects himself. It is there-

---

34 This is a reference to the Schmalkaldic War (1546-1547) in which Charles V defeated Elector John Frederick I of Saxony and Landgrave Philip I of Hesse.
35 *Moralia*, bk. 33, c. 29, n. 51 (PL 76, 706B-C).

fore well said: 'One is joined to another, and not so much as any air can come between them' (v. 7); because while they mutually shield each other in their iniquities by their proud defense, they suffer not the breath of holy exhortation in any way to reach them. But He added still more plainly their deadly agreement, saying: 'They stick one to another and they hold one another fast, and shall not be separated' (v. 8). For they who might be corrected if divided, persevere, when united, in the obstinacy of their iniquities: and are day by day the more easily separable from the knowledge of righteousness, the more they are not mutually separated from each other by any reproach. For as it is wont to be injurious if unity be wanting to the good, so is it fatal if it be not wanting to the wicked. For unity strengthens the perverse, while it makes them accord; and it makes them the more incorrigible, the more unanimous."[36] If some German princes, and other authorities of that nation, did not defend Luther and the other heretics so strongly, either they would have recovered their senses, or if they would have remained pertinacious in their heresies, these men having been removed from life, all Germany would already have returned to the true and Catholic faith, which they had known before very well.

Against all these kinds of persons, namely, believers, harborers, supporters, and defenders of heretics, there are many and various punishments decreed by law. For someone designated by any of these names, is by that very fact excommunicated, and if after a whole year has elapsed after this excommunication, without any just satisfaction given by him, from that moment of time he is made infamous, and removed from all public offices, and is not admitted for the election of others, nor as a witness. Still many other penalties are inflicted upon them, which, because they are stated clearly and plainly enough in the chapter, *Excommunicamus*,

---

36 *Ibid.*, nn. 54-55 (PL 76, 708B-709A).

Regarding those believing, harboring, supporting, and defending heretics

§. *Credentes de haereticis*,[37] and in the chapter, *Quicumque*, §. *Haeretici*, in the title, *De Haereticis*, in the *Liber Sextus*;[38]

---

[37] "Moreover, we determine to subject to excommunication believers who receive, defend, or support heretics. We strictly ordain that if any such person, after he has been designated as excommunicated, refuses to render satisfaction within a year, then by the law itself he shall be branded as infamous and not be admitted to public offices or councils or to elect others to the same or to give testimony. He shall be intestable, that is, he shall not have the freedom to make a will nor shall succeed to an inheritance. Moreover, nobody shall be compelled to answer to him on any business whatever, but he may be compelled to answer to them. If he is a judge sentences pronounced by him shall have no force and cases may not be brought before him; if an advocate, he may not be allowed to defend anyone; if a notary, documents drawn up by him shall be worthless and condemned along with their condemned author; and in similar matters we order the same to be observed. If however he is a cleric, let him be deposed from every office and benefice, so that the greater the fault the greater be the punishment. If any refuse to avoid such persons after they have been pointed out by the Church, let them be punished with the sentence of excommunication until they make suitable satisfaction. Clerics should not, of course, give the Sacraments of the Church to such pestilent people nor give them a Christian burial nor accept alms or offerings from them; if they do, let them be deprived of their office and not restored to it without a special indult of the Apostolic See. Similarly with regulars, let them be punished with losing their privileges in the diocese in which they presume to commit such excesses" (*Decretals of Gregory IX*, bk. 5, tit. 7 (*De haereticis*), c. 13, §5 (*Credentes*)).

[38] "But heretics, believers, harborers, defenders, and their supporters, as well as their children until the second generation, may not be admitted to any ecclesiastical benefice or public office. But if it has been done otherwise, we decree it null and void" (*Liber sextus decretalium*, bk. 5, tit. 2 (*De hereticis*), c. 2 (*Quicumque*), §2 (*Haeretici*)). The Constitution, *Quicumque haereticos credentes*, from which this quotation in the Decretals was taken, was promul-

wherefore for the sake of avoiding prolixity, I have omitted them, having thought that I have done enough, because I have indicated the places to the reader, where they all are written out: especially because we will dispute about them all one by one in the second book.

---

gated during the reign of Alexander IV (December 12, 1254-May 15, 1261). The exact date is not known.

Chapter XVIII

That the arrested heretic ought not to be punished immediately: but his amendment ought to procured, and how.

Up until now I have treated about those things which seem to me to be necessary for the complete knowledge of heretics. Just now it is necessary that we discuss what the inquisitor of heretics, or judge, to whom it is incumbent to judge about this crime, ought to do with the heretic after he has been arrested. And assuredly so that the case may be correctly handled according to the canonical laws, this consideration ought to be firstly made: Whether that man, who has been caught in some heresy, had been convicted at another time of this or some other heresy, or had been accused on account of a very strong suspicion, or instead it is known that that he has fallen into heresy for the first time. Regarding those who previously either were convicted or strongly suspected of the crime of heresy, we now say nothing: because, we will discuss this case at length in the following book. We now treat about him, of whom it was never known before in a court of law, that he had fallen into heresy. Even though such a man as this ought afterwards to be punished according to the quality of his crime, still due punishment ought not to be immediately inflicted upon him when he has been apprehended, but one ought to first strive for his amendment, so that if it were possible, he may be firstly recalled to the Catholic faith from error, so his soul may become saved in God's judgment.

Mild and not severe correction is necessary: because excessive severity is wont to shatter, and rarely to straighten out. Hence Paul, when teaching Timothy his disciple how he ought to correct the erring, says: "With modesty admonishing them that resist the truth: if peradventure God may give them repentance to know the truth" (II Tim. 2, 25). [Hervé de Bourg-Dieu[1]], when interpreting these words in his commentaries on the Epistles, says: "For this reason we ought to strive to bring them to repentance, namely, so that we may thence gain a reward for ourselves, lest God give the repentance without us through an internal inspiration, and we would not thence have a reward."[2] Moreover the weakness of the inquisitors themselves, by which they can fall, unless God prevents, into a similar, or another worse heresy, urges them to correct those erring with meekness and goodness: because unless they do so, God will perhaps permit that they fall into a similar or worse heresy, in order that therefrom they may come to know their own weakness. Hence Paul says: "If a man be overtaken in any fault, you, who are spiritual, instruct such a one in the spirit of meekness, considering thyself, lest thou also be tempted" (Gal. 6, 1). The Apostle said this, lest perhaps if a superior would consider the sin of his neighbor, and not attend to his own, he may be moved not to compassion, but to indignation: not to help, but to judge: not to instruct in the spirit of meekness, but to destroy in the spirit of fury. Meekly therefore, that is, in that spirit one ought to aid the man fallen into heresy, with which anyone would desire to be aided when he errs. And, in order that every single judge may know how he should become mild towards the one erring, Paul adds in the same Epistle, saying: "considering thyself, lest thou also be tempted." Because he who in a spirit of rage, and not of meekness, corrects a subject, is permitted by God to be tempted, or deceived: and so that perhaps therefrom knowing his own weakness, he may learn to have compassion on others.

---

1 This quotation is here incorrectly attributed here to St. Anselm of Canterbury.
2 *In epistolam II ad Timotheum* (PL 181, 1464D).

That the arrested heretic ought not to be punished immediately

And Blessed [Rabanus[3]], in his commentaries on the Lamentations of Jeremias, when expounding the passage, "Depart you that are defiled, they cried out to them" (4, 15), speaks thus: "Such is the voice of proud teachers, who accept the animal which is fat from the flock: and the one which is weak they cast out; what is weak they do not make firm, and what is sick, they do not heal. 'Depart,' they say: 'you that are defiled': be gone, go away, do not touch us, do not partake anything from us: your wounds are unhealable, and your injuries are incurable, you are not worthy of the Christian communion; so that the Holy Ghost 'no more dwells among' you (v. 15), 'The face of the Lord hath divided them' (v. 16), and cast them off, and will no more regard them, because you respected not the persons of the priests, neither did you meekly accept the correction of your elders.[4] Such speech does not enlighten the blind, nor heal the sick, nor cure the sick: but rather kills, and sends the one in danger into despair. For the good teachers weighing the weaknesses of others from their own weakness, strive to rescue those sinning from the snare of error through the soothing remedy of humility and kindness, rather than thrust the wavering into the pit of perdition through harshness."[5]

Next, for the sake of the common good, it is necessary that the man who is a heretic be not immediately punished: because it might be possible that he converts, and as much as that he now harms himself through heresy, so much afterwards, and much more after his conversion he may benefit the universal Church through his public profession of faith. Therefore, to remove such too quickly, would yield a great detriment to Christendom. Blessed Gregory [IV] confirms this reason, who when writing to the bishops of France, says:

---

3 This commentary was written under the name of St. Jerome, but it was compiled by Rabanus.
4 Cf. v. 16.
5 *Commentaria in Jeremiam*, bk. 20, c. 4 (PL 111, 1256C-1257A).

"Although it commonly happens to priests, that there are things which ought to be reprehended, still kindness does more towards those who are to be corrected than severity; exhortation, rather than threatening; charity, rather than power: since none of us lives without fault, or without sin. For if the Lord had judged Blessed Peter the Apostle, our teacher, immediately after the triple denial, he would not have received so much fruit from him, as he did."[6] Which words are cited by Gratian, in the chapter, *Licet*.[7] But so that I may state the truth, I was unable to find these words in the whole registry of Blessed Gregory's letters, which Gratian cites in that place under Gregory's name, although I searched for those words with great diligence. But I found in Gregory that which Gratian likewise cites in the chapter, *Quid autem*, in the same Distinction: which words, because they very much agree with our objective, I have decided to quote it here. "Moreover, your Fraternity knows well what the canons say about bishops who desire to inspire fear by blows. For we have been made shepherds, not persecutors. And the excellent preacher says, 'Reprove, entreat, rebuke in all patience and doctrine' (II Tim. 4, 2). But new and unheard of is this preaching, which exacts faith by blows."[8]

The Glossator, when interpreting which words, says that they ought to be understood of him who has not received the Catholic faith: because this man (as he says) ought not to be forced to accept the faith, but that man who had accepted the faith at one time ought to be forced to retain the faith, and in this way he says that those things which are said in the chapter, *Quis [potest]*,[9] do not oppose this text.

---

6 PL 106, 855A; Mansi 14, 515B-C.
7 *Decretum Gratiani*, pt. 1, dist. 45, c. 4 (PL 187, 234B).
8 Bk. 3, letter 53 (PL 77, 649B); *Decretum Gratiani*, pt. 1, dist. 45, c. 1 (PL 187, 233A).
9 "[Christ] not only constrained [St. Paul] with His voice, but even dashed him to the earth with His power; and that He might

That the arrested heretic ought not to be punished immediately

Because he thinks those things which are said there ought to be understood of him who has already once received the faith, so that he ought to be forced to keep it. But actually he is quite mistaken, and he is completely off track: because he neither understood the latter nor the former text. For that the chapter, *Quis [potest]*, does not speak about him who had accepted the Catholic faith, is very clear from the fact that it speaks about Paul the Apostle, whom the Lord struck with blindness when he was going to Damascus, and threw down to the ground, and in this way withdrew him from the persecution of the Christians, and converted him to accepting the Catholic faith. Now who does not know that at that time Paul had not received the faith, nay, so that he would accept it he was somewhat forced by God through those punishments? And the very words of the same chapter say once and again, that Paul was forced by God to accept the Gospel. Thus that chapter, *Quis [potest]*, does not speak about him who has at one time accepted the faith. But how those words ought to be understood we (with God as the guide) will explain below in the second book.

But neither the chapter, *Quid autem*, did he understand well, when he said that it ought to be understood of him who had not received the faith, that he ought not to be forced to the faith by blows. For if the Glossator of the Decretals had read

---

forcibly bring one who was raging amid the darkness of infidelity to desire the light of the heart, He first struck him with physical blindness of the eyes... Towards whom did Christ use violence? Whom did He compel? Here they have the Apostle Paul. Let them recognize in his case Christ first compelling, and afterwards teaching; first striking, and afterwards consoling. For it is wonderful how he who entered the service of the Gospel in the first instance under the compulsion of bodily punishment, afterwards labored more in the Gospel than all they who were called by word only" (*Decretum Gratiani*, pt. 2, *causa* 23, q. 4, c. 43 (PL 187, 1205C-1206A)). Cf. St. Augustine, Letter 185 (to Boniface), c. 6, n. 22 (PL 33, 802-803).

the whole letter of Blessed Gregory, from which the chapter, *Quid autem*, was taken, he would have easily understood that it ought not to have been so understood (as he taught). For Blessed Gregory in that place writes to Bishop John of Constantinople reprehending him because a certain monk of Isauria had been beaten in the church with clubs. And reprehending this sort of punishment, he said: "New and unheard of is this preaching, which exacts faith by blows." He was speaking about a Christian man, and a monk, and not about someone who had not yet received the faith. Next, from the words of the same text the Glossator could have concluded that those words ought to be understood about a man with the faith, and not of someone who has not yet professed the faith. For when reprehending the bishops who want to be feared by blows, he said: "We have been made shepherds, not persecutors." But bishops are not shepherds of the Jews, or of the Saracens, or of others who have never embraced the faith: but they are shepherds of those who have put on Christ through Baptism, whom Gregory teaches ought to be fed as sheep, not persecuted.

Now when Gregory said: "New and unheard of is this preaching, which exacts faith by blows," in that place he takes faith not merely for that assent of the mind, whereby we assent to the things which ought to be believed: but for a certain obedience by which we submit to anyone rightly instructing us, whether he instructs us about things which ought to be believed, or about things to be done. For in this way one is accustomed to speak, who admonishes another about something: "Believe me, and give alms, or fast." Or, "If you believe me, you will not go to such or such a place, lest you should suffer a serious injury." Therefore, Blessed Gregory says that it is not good preaching "which exacts faith by blows," that is to say, obedience. Certainly, in that place he was speaking about every virtue, not merely about faith in those things which ought to be believed, for which

That the arrested heretic ought not to be punished immediately

Blessed Gregory thought reasons and words avail more than blows. Still, I do not wish to deny, nay, I very firmly assert, and afterwards I will assert more clearly, that they who have at one time accepted the faith in Baptism, ought to be forced to keep it, but I say, relying upon the testimony of holy men, that mild things ought to be used, rather than harsh things. Words prior to blows; it ought to be done by love before fear: because many are drawn by love and words alone, who would be repelled from the faith by fear and blows. If the inquisitor profits nothing by words, and he rightly despairs about the salvation of the heretic, then he ought to proceed to blows, and treat him as incorrigible. Now what he ought to do with such a one as this we will discuss below in the second book, which we will devote to this matter.

But regarding him about whose salvation it is rightly not yet despaired of, even though he ought to be punished, still words ought to be employed prior to blows, so that by words and reasons, which can move the intellect more than torments: he may be drawn to the faith, and in this way he may at length become saved. For that this is much better, Blessed Augustine, a most zealous opponent of heretics, teaches clearly enough, who says these words: "For while the Lord, by His servants, overthrows the kingdoms of error, His will concerning erring men, as far as they are men, is that they should be amended rather than destroyed... It is ours, accordingly, to desire in preference the better part, that we might attain our end in your correction, not by contention, and strife, and persecutions, but by kindly consolation, by friendly exhortation, by quiet discussion."[10]

And Blessed Bernard in his sermon on the Canticles teaches this opinion more clearly and copiously, who when interpreting the passage from the Canticles, "Catch us the little foxes" (2, 15), speaks thus: "They are to be caught, not

---

10 *Against the Fundamental Epistle of Manichaeus*, c. 1 (PL 42, 173).

driven away. They are to be caught, I say, but with no other force than the force of arguments wherewith their errors are refuted. For themselves, let them, if it is possible, be reconciled to the Church, let them be brought back to the true faith. Such is the desire of Him 'Who will have all men to be saved, and to come to the knowledge of the truth' (I Tim. 2, 4). Such also is the wish of the Bridegroom, as He signifies in this place where He does not simply say, 'catch the foxes,' but 'catch us the foxes.' Therefore He wants these foxes to be won over to Himself and His Spouse, the Catholic Church, and expresses this desire by saying, 'Catch us the foxes.' Consequently, whenever an experienced and learned member of the Church undertakes to dispute with a heretic, he is bound to make it his aim, not merely to convict his opponent of error, but also to convert him to the truth. For he should bear in mind the words of Saint James, 'He who causeth a sinner to be converted from the error of his way, shall save his soul from death, and shall cover a multitude of sins' (5, 20). But should the heretic be unwilling to return, and, after being once or twice admonished, remains still obdurate in his error, then according to the Apostle's injunction he must be avoided, as one entirely corrupted."[11]

After words, if he does not want to obey, and refuses to admit that he has been conquered by the disputation, then I judge it good, nay, necessary, that one proceed in his regard with blows: because vexation is wont to give understanding.[12] For those who are not naturally inclined to virtue, nor have upright souls, so that they seek to be led by the teaching of words, it behooves them to be put under the yoke of discipline, so that having been forced by the authority of laws they may thereafter understand better. Hence Solomon in the Proverbs says: "Folly is bound up in the heart of a

---

11 Sermon 64, n. 8 (PL 183, 1086D-1087B).
12 "Vexation alone shall make you understand what you hear" (Is. 28, 19).

That the arrested heretic ought not to be punished immediately

child, and the rod of correction shall drive it away" (22, 15). Yet all these things which we say ought to be done lest the heretic's soul be forever damned, not however, because his body should not be punished in this life. For even if he is converted and truly accepts the Catholic faith, still he should be punished with kindness according to the quality of his error and past pertinacity.

Chapter XIX

That one ought not to publicly dispute with a heretic, especially a pertinacious one.

We have said that a heretical man ought not to be punished immediately: but first he ought to be admonished about the heresy, such that having been refuted with reasons and arguments, he may abandon the heresy which he was holding (if it could happen) and accept the true and Catholic faith. Nevertheless, I reckon that this admonition, or disputation, ought to be done in private, and not publicly before the people: because such a public disputation could do more harm than good to the heretic himself with whom it is done, and to the people hearing, and also to the one disputing. For nearly all heretics, especially those who not out of ignorance, but intentionally, depart from the unity of the Catholic faith, acquire popular acclaim and vainglory, and desire to be praised by all, and to be held as learned men. Hence Augustine says: "He is a heretic, who, for the sake of some temporal advantage, and chiefly for the sake of his own glory and pre-eminence, either gives birth to, or follows, false and new opinions."[1] In which words Augustine states not the definition, but what is the specific innate character of all heretics, and what is the parent or origin of all heretics. For he who is desirous of glory, leaves nothing untried for acquiring it, and if no other way appears to be open, so that he may reach his goal, he will not hesitate to concoct a new doctrine, so that he may give an occasion for all to admire himself by the newness of the thing.

Now when, with the devil inciting and God permitting, he has fallen into heresy, he is not ashamed to summon some very learned and Catholic men to a public debate. He asks

---

1 *On the Profit of Believing*, n. 1 (PL 42, 65).

for public disputations, not so that he may be taught about the truth; but so that he may be praised by the people, whom he desires very much to please. Hence Blessed Gregory says: "For neither do heretics try to attain truth by their investigations, but to appear to be the winners; and whereas they desire to show for wise without, they are bound within in their foolishness with the chains of their own pride; hence it comes to pass that they look out for contests of rivalry, and concerning God, Who is our Peace, they know not how to speak with peaceableness, and by the article of peace they become contrivers of strife. To whom it is well spoken by Paul, 'But if any man seem to be contentious, we have no such custom, nor the church of God' (I Cor. 11, 16)."[2] From this immoderate desire for glory arises such brazen contention in the disputation, so that even if the heretic has been refuted through the most manifest arguments, still he would never want to admit the truth: but he always seeks some tiny cracks though which he can escape, lest he admit that he has been conquered in front of the people. Although he may acknowledge to himself that he has very clearly erred, still he will disdain to admit it: because he prefers to publicly defend his error even against his conscience, than to admit that he was conquered in the disputation, lest by this occasion that glory, which he ardently loved, would be lost.

There are so many and such clear examples of this thing, that there would be no need to recount them, if we were writing only for learned men. Arius was refuted and condemned in the Council of three hundred eighteen Fathers celebrated in Nicea: and yet he was not made wiser on account of it, nay, having been made more insane, he increased his pertinacity, and having been made unyielding was never corrected. Berengarius was condemned in many councils. In the Synod of Vercelli Leo IX condemned him for being nowise willing to appear. In the Synod of Tours before the Supreme

---

2 *Moralia*, bk. 8, c. 3, n. 4 (PL 75, 803-804).

That one ought not to publicly dispute with a heretic

Pontiff Victor II, Berengarius likewise sang the palinode, but afterwards repented of this palinode, and returned to the former heresy. Then having been summoned to Rome by the Supreme Pontiff Nicholas II in the general council celebrated at that time, he abjured and anathematized his heresy. The words of which abjuration are found in the chapter, *Ego Berengarius*.[3] But after this abjuration (as Lanfranc recounts about him[4]) he returned again to his vomit like a dog.[5] The same thing happened to John Hus in the Council of Constance, who although refuted with many and evident reasons, still he never wanted to recant his errors.

For the heretic, so that he can preserve the glory which he anxiously desires, is not ashamed to remain in error, and is ashamed to correct the error. Thus it is very difficult that someone would so refute a pertinacious heretic in a public disputation such that he would admit that he had erred. For, acknowledging this difficulty, Solomon says: "It is better to meet a bear robbed of her whelps, than a fool trusting in his own folly" (Prov. 17, 12). [Venerable Bede[6]], when interpreting these words in his commentaries on Proverbs, says: "It was easier for the holy Doctors to go against the fury of paganism, when some nations were robbed from it, and by preaching were converted from its bestial fierceness to the piety of the faith, than to go against any heretic trusting in his own perfidy of doctrine: because without a doubt in the

---

3 *Decretum Gratiani*, pt. 3, dist. 2, c. 42 (*Ego Berengarius*) (PL 187, 1750A-1751A).
4 "Most rightly did the Pope command this statement, most rightly did the synod agree to it, and most rightly would you have properly executed it, that is, if the lying tongue of your heart had not spoken from the heart, and you had not afterwards returned as a miserable perjurer to your former vomit and pig-trough of mud" (*Liber de corpore et sanguine Domini*, c. 4 (PL 150, 415C-D)).
5 Cf. Prov. 26, 11 and II Pet. 2, 22.
6 The text here incorrectly cites St. Jerome.

former case they were doing battle against foreigners, in the latter case against their own bowels."[7] If however this disputation is done in private and only in front of learned men, he would more easily learn the truth. Thereafter when the truth has been known he will more easily be forced to acknowledge it, when there are no people, whom he fears, and before whom he would be afraid to admit that he has been defeated. Therefore, from these things it is evident that a disputation in private can greatly benefit the heretical man for accepting the faith, and a public disputation greatly hinders.

A disputation of this kind also can harm the disputing Catholic himself not a little, if he is not a learned man, and sufficiently instructed in Holy Writ, and well exercised in other disputations. For otherwise it could happen that the truth, which is always victorious, may seem to have been conquered in his mouth. For heretics are often very skillful in disputing, and know well how to set traps, and how to make an unrestrained rambling of rhetoric into a thorn hedge of syllogisms, and to thus often ensnare the contradictor with his arguments: so that unless he is very skillful, he would be unable to disentangle himself. Now if the disputing heretic did this with a Catholic man, perhaps the Catholic man, not knowing how to solve the arguments, will think that the heretic argues very well, and finally having been deceived would follow the opinion of the heretic. Unless Athanasius was skillful in disputing, Arius would have easily deceived him in front of the proper judge. The very many disputations which Augustine had with heretics clearly show how necessary are skill and experience for the disputer, in which unless he was skillful, he would have been often overcome. And due to this Bernard, who (as it was evident at the end of the preceding chapter) said that a heretical man ought to be caught by argumentation and disputation, nevertheless

---

7 *Allegorica expositio in Parabolas Salomonis*, bk. 1, c. 17 (PL 91, 990A).

reckons that the disputation ought to be done by a learned and experienced man: on account of the danger, which could thence happen. Concerning the danger of this kind Solomon spoke, when he says: "He that cutteth trees, shall be wounded by them, if the iron be blunt" (Eccle. 10, 9-10). Jerome, when interpreting these words in his commentaries on Ecclesiastes, says: "Heretics are fruitless trees, and a thicket without the benefit of fruit. Hence also a grove was forbidden to be planted in God's Temple, and arbors of leaves, that is, canopies of merely sounding words are rejected. However learned and wise a man may be therefore who chops these trees with the sword of his speech, he will be endangered by them, unless he is on his guard; especially if the following happens to him: 'if the iron is blunt, and it has troubled his face" (v. 10),[8] that is, if his disputation was found to be weaker, and he did not have sharpness of mind, whereby he cuts down whatever is contrary [to the truth]: then his mind[9] is blunted, he will pass over to the opposing side, and wicked strength will make him firm[10] [in error]."[11]

This public disputation also harms those hearing: especially if they are uneducated, or wavering or weak in the faith. For the uneducated and illiterate common man does not know how to distinguish between what is true and what is false: and hence he is easily deceived in judging, judging

---

8 St. Jerome here quotes from the *Itala*, or the Old Latin version of the verse, i. e., "and it has troubled his face" (*et faciem ejus turbaverit*), instead of "and be not as before" (*et hoc non ut prius*) from the Vulgate.

9 The mind here is called the *principale cordis*, which in Greek is *hegemonikon* (ἡγεμονικόν), and is a Stoic term used to designate a ruling or governing power; specifically the human reason.

10 The *Itala* version of this verse has "And he will be made firm by the strength" (*Et fortitudine confortabitur*), which, as St. Jerome mentions in the next sentence, was taken from the *Septuagint*.

11 *Commentarius in Ecclesiasten* (PL 23, 1095B-C).

what is true as being false, and the false for the true. He will praise the sophistic arguments of heretics as correct reasonings. When the heretic reasons incorrectly, he will say that he has reasoned very well, and made an irrefutable argument. His specious arguments, which, if they were examined from within, have no force, he will judge very convincing, and thus will be drawn little by little into the opinion of the heretic. Thus it will happen that the people who came strong in the faith to hear the disputation, depart weak and vacillating: and if perhaps someone doubting had come, after having heard the disputation he would very firmly and without any doubting embrace the same heresy. The public disputation with Luther a few years ago[12] gave us an example of this thing. It was held in Leipzig, Germany: where the very learned man, [Johann] Eck, publicly disputing with Luther, although he very clearly conquered him with arguments; nevertheless, the people not so judging as was the reality, praised Luther more than the Catholic Eck, wherefore the latter having been disregarded they accepted the teaching of Luther at the expense of their souls.

For this reason Plato reckoned that it ought not to be discussed about the chief laws of the city in the presence of the youth, if thereby difficulty about them would come forth, lest the influence of the chief laws be lessened among the youth, among whom it ought to be greatest.[13] If so much

---

12 The Leipzig Debate took place in June and July, 1519.

13 "For in your case (your laws being wisely framed) one of the best of your laws will be that which enjoins that none of the youth shall inquire which laws are wrong and which right, but all shall declare in unison, with one mouth and one voice, that all are rightly established by divine enactment, and shall turn a deaf ear to anyone who says otherwise; and further, that if any old man has any stricture to pass on any of your laws, he must not utter such views in the presence of any young man, but before a magistrate or one of his own age" (*Laws*, bk. 1, 634d-e).

respect for human laws, in Plato's judgment, is due, it is right that much more be shown to Divine laws, so that among the uncultivated people it would not be disputed about them: lest among them the authority of the Divine laws and the certitude of the faith be diminished, when it sees that those things are called into doubt and question, which it behooved to be considered very true and most firm. Hence Paul, very well recognizing these dangers, and wanting to avert them, admonishes Timothy, his disciple, to abstain from disputations of this kind, speaking thus: "Contend not in words, for it is to no profit, but to the subverting of the hearers" (II Tim. 2, 14). [Ambrosiaster,] when interpreting these words, says: "He advises to avoid contentions, and that precepts should be given under the fear and dread of God; because strife can still generate scruples to those less stable. For in the contention such things are wont to be brought forth, with the polished sword of malevolence, that would disturb the minds of the beginner brothers."[14] And Blessed Pope Leo I, when writing to Emperor Marcian, speaks thus: "For when the restlessness and depravity of a few have been restrained or removed, an amiable unity will easily be strengthened, if in that faith, which having been announced by the Evangelists and Apostolic preaching, we received and have through our ancient Fathers, the minds of all would concur, completely no argumentation of any objection having been allowed, lest through delusive and deceptive craftiness, those things, which were founded upon the Cornerstone Himself and will remain forever, would seem either weak or doubtful"[15]

And certainly for this same reason it is not advantageous, or consonant with reason, that in the public disputations, which Catholic and learned men are accustomed to have in schools or elsewhere among themselves, that heretical or scandal-

---

14 *Commentaria in Epistolam ad Timotheum Secundam* (PL 17, 490B).
15 Letter 94 (PL 54, 941B-942A).

ous propositions, even for the sake of practice, be defended in the presence of the people. For many on account of this have fallen into those heresies which they had seen defended for the sake of debate in schools. For simply because it was defended in the schools, they thought that those things were true, or at least tolerable, which were said there. I truly know a certain man not completely uncultivated or unintelligent, but somewhat educated, called into court by the inquisitors, and put into prison, because he had not been afraid to publicly say that simple fornication was not a sin. Who afterwards, when asked by what temerity had he dared to assert such a pestiferous heresy, answered that he had learned in the schools, in which he had often seen such an opinion publicly defended. Wherefore I reckon that it would have been done more considerately, if those who had overseen such disputations, had removed heretical propositions of this sort from their disputations, and had very constantly forbidden them to be defended in the schools.

And certainly, if I am not mistaken, those who when overseeing disputations of this kind could have driven away such heretical and scandalous propositions from the school, ought to have been punished much more severely than those who were allured by the public defense of such propositions, such that they would dare to say that they are true. And I think that not only heretical and scandalous propositions ought to be driven out from public disputation, but also those which, even if they may be very true, still they exceed the abilities of the people hearing, and in which uncultivated people could very easily err. Such are the matters of grace and free will, predestination, God's foreknowledge, and many mysteries and miracles of the Eucharist. To dispute in front of uncultivated and uneducated people, I reckon is dangerous: because it often happens in them that arguments are made against the truth which seem to the illiterate people to be more evident than the responses, which are given for the defense of the truth. The people often understand the arguments which are made, and rarely understand the solutions to those same arguments. In the matter of predestination and God's foreknowledge, any shoemaker or tailor has come to know how to raise arguments, and to add force to the arguments; yet a very learned man could scarcely answer those men, who would be easily able to answer any other erudite man. And so it can scarcely happen that an uneducated man seeing this would not be scandalized, and waver in the faith. The author of this scandal is he who publicly disputed about things of this kind, and so as such will be punished by God.

So it was foretold long ago in a figure in the Law of Moses: "If men quarrel, and one strike a woman with child, and she miscarry indeed, but live herself: he shall be answerable for so much damage as the woman's husband shall require, and as arbiters shall award. But if her death ensue thereupon, he shall render life for life" (Ex. 21, 22-23). Origen, when interpreting this law as an allegory, says: "Let those two men, who quarrel be two discussing and examining teachings or questions of the Law with one another and, (so we speak with the saying of the Apostle), quarreling 'about strifes of words' (I Tim. 6, 4)... Because, therefore, those who quarrel over questions quarrel 'to the subverting of the hearers' (II Tim. 2, 14), on that account they strike the woman with child and expel her infant either already formed or yet unformed. The soul which has just conceived the word of God is said to be a woman with child...This soul, therefore, which is now called a woman because of its weakness, is stricken and made to stumble by two men quarreling between themselves and bringing forth stumbling blocks in the strife—which a dispute of words is always accustomed to have—so that it casts out and loses the word of faith which it had tenuously conceived. This is a quarrel and contention 'to the subverting of the hearers.' If, therefore, the soul which has been made to stumble cast off the word not yet formed, he who made it stumble is said to suffer loss."[16] And after many interjected words he again says: "'The infant which is formed'[17] can be seen as the word of God in the heart of that soul which has attained the grace of Baptism or which has manifestly and clearly conceived the word of faith. If this soul, therefore, stricken by too much contention between teachers, should cast off the word and be found to be a part of those whom the Apostle said, 'For some are already turned aside after Satan' (I Tim. 5, 15), 'he shall render life for life.' On the Day of Judgment, he is to be taken before that Judge 'that can destroy both soul and body in hell' (Mt. 10, 28), because also elsewhere the Prophet says to Jerusalem, 'I have given Egypt for thy atonement, Ethiopia and Saba for thee' (Is. 43, 3). Or, certainly it probably can be applied, such that he who was conscious to himself of such a great stumbling block may lay down his life for the life of that person whom he made to stumble and may give labor to the point of death how he may turn back, how he may repair, how he may restore that soul to the faith."[18]

If only mature men, and men stable in the faith, were present it would be permitted to dispute not only about these true and Catholic propositions, but also it would be permitted to dispute about propositions howsoever heretical, if it were done merely for the sake of practice, so that from thence the truth of the faith may shine forth more clearly, and the disputants themselves may become, through such an exercise, instructors and more prepared for refuting heretics. For just as hastiludes, and other games among friends are wont to be

---

16 *Homilies on Exodus*, hom. 10, n. 3 (PG 12, 371C-D; 372A-B).
17 "But if the infant be already formed, he shall render life for life" (*Si autem formatum fuerit, dabit animam pro anima*) is the Old Latin translation for Ex. 21, 23. Cf. Sabatier, *Bibliorum Sacrorum latinae versiones antiguae* (Rheims: apud Reginaldum Florentain, 1743), vol. 1, p. 178.
18 *Homilies on Exodus*, hom. 10, n. 4 (PG 12, 373B-C).

done in an arena, so that thence they may be instructed how they may fight in war against an enemy; so also it is fitting that among learned and Catholic men, practices of literary work, and disputations about the faith be held, so that thence they may learn how they ought to fight against the heretics of the Church, and the bitterest enemies of the Catholic faith.

And what Alexander IV says in the chapter, *Quicumque*,[19] does not conflict with this opinion, where he forbids all laymen under pain of excommunication, that they dare not dispute publicly or privately about the Catholic faith. For there the Pope forbids a true disputation, and not a pretended one. It is a pretended disputation, which is done with words only, and not minds; such [a disputation] is among those who although they are concordant in the same opinion argue and reply, so that the they may more clearly discover the truth of the matter. Just as also a war is pretended among those who make use of hastiludes. A true dispute is among those who contradict each other not only with words, but also with their minds, and defend complete opposite opinions. Catholic men make a pretended disputation, when they dispute about matters of faith: because they think the same thing with concordant minds, and they contradict each other with words only. Catholic men hold a true and not pretended disputation against heretics when they dispute about the Catholic faith: because just as they fight outwardly with words, so they inwardly disagree in their minds. The Pope forbids this true disputation, which is held with heretics about the faith, to lay-persons, namely, lest they dare to publicly or privately dispute with heretics about the Catholic faith. And he rightly forbade it: because even though there were some

---

19 "We inhibit also that it should be lawful for any lay-person publicly or privately to dispute about the Catholic faith. Whosoever shall do otherwise, let him be bound with the cord of excommunication" (*Liber sextus decretalium*, bk. 5, tit. 2 (*De hereticis*), c. 2 (*Quicumque*), §1 (*Inhibemus*).

learned laymen, who could dispute with heretics well and without danger, still laws do not decree about things which happen rarely, but about those things which happen in most cases. Now it rarely happens that laymen are learned in the faith, and skillful in disputing about it: and hence lest they, in being defeated in the disputation, receive an occasion of ruin to themselves, or give an occasion [of ruin] to others listening, such a disputation was rightly forbidden to them.

But the other disputation about the faith, which is performed feignedly between Catholics, was not forbidden to the laity by that chapter, *Quicumque*, because a feigned disputation is not properly a disputation; just as neither is a feigned war properly a war, nor is a picture of a man properly a man. And if the Glossator had adverted well to this, in that chapter, *Quicumque*, §. *Inhibemus*, he would not have been pressed with such difficulties with which he is there pressed, and would have easily loosened the snare, with which he thought that he was held. Thus, to laymen alone was it interdicted, lest they dispute publicly or privately about the Catholic faith. It was not so absolutely forbidden to ecclesiastical men, however, for them to dispute against heretics about the faith: but it is permitted for them to dispute against heretics about the faith, provided that it be done in the presence of men who are learned and stable in the faith.

And sometimes it will not only be allowed, but rather necessary, to publicly dispute against heretics, even in the presence of simple people, for instance, when the people are assailed by heretics, or by other unbelievers, and incited to abandon the Catholic faith. For then it is incumbent upon the prelates of the churches, to defend their believing subjects against the infestation of the heretics, and they are bound to dispute against the heretics, through themselves or at least through learned men, who are skillful in disputing, so that God's glory may be manifested, and the Catholic truth defended, and the heretics confounded. For on account of this (as Paul says) a bishop must be learned so "that he may be able to exhort in sound doctrine, and to convince the gainsayers" (Tit. 1, 9). And Blessed Peter commands the bishops that they be "ready always to satisfy everyone that asketh you a reason of that hope (and faith) which is in us" (I Pet. 3, 15).[20] Otherwise if when heretics are crying out and challenging to a public disputation, Catholic men were to keep silent, an occasion of suspicion would be given to the people, to suppose that the Catholic men are distrustful about the certitude of the faith, due to the fact that they dare not to go into battle against the heretics, or to suppose that they think like the heretics, because they are silent when those men are crying out. Assuredly it could not be said more truthfully, that he who is silent, seems to consent, than to say, when a matter is very serious, to be silent is pernicious, but to speak is useful and necessary. It will then be necessary to dispute with the heretic, because an error which is not contradicted, is approved; and "Truth is struck down when it is not defended."[21] The reason is that to neglect to confound the wicked, is nothing other than to support them. And he is not free from a suspicion about a secret alliance, who forbears from resisting a manifest evil deed.

Now the decrees and law which seem to absolutely prohibit a disputation about the faith are directed to heretics alone, who are forbidden from every disputation by which they presume to oppose the Catholic faith, or doubt about it. For about this disputation ought to be understood the command of Emperor Marcian, which is found in the law, *Nemo*. "He commits an injury," he says, "against the most reverend Synod who publicly contradicts what has once been

---

20 This verse is cited according to the Old Latin version.
21 Pope Felix III, letter 1 (to Acacius of Constantinople), although cited in Gratian as written by Pope Innocent (*Decretum Gratiani*, pt. 1, dist. 83, c. 3 (*Error*) (PL 187, 401A); Mansi 7, 1029E; PL 58, 897B).

decided and properly established."[22] But a Catholic, who disputes against a heretic in support of those things which were defined in the Synod, does no injury to the Synod, nay, shows honor. But a heretic, who fights against the Synod, does an injury to the Synod: because he contends that it has erred. Thus he inhibits heretics to dispute about the faith, because they think against the faith: but he does not forbid Catholics, who fight for the faith, to dispute about the faith. Hence, so that we may understand more clearly all the decrees and laws which forbid disputations about the faith, it ought to be noticed that in a true disputation about the faith, which is between a Christian and a heretic, there are two distinct prohibitions, according to the two persons who enter upon a disputation of this kind, namely, the Christian and the heretic.

The prohibition of the Christian is limited to lay persons, for to laymen alone, in that paragraph, *Inhibemus*, was a disputation interdicted. A disputation about the faith was also interdicted to heretics: and this prohibition is general: because it is not allowed for any heretic to dispute about the faith, wanting to undermine the faith, or to doubt about it: especially in those matters which by an explicit definition of the Church have already long ago been decided. For what is found in the chapter, *Majores*,[23] ought to be referred to

---

22 "No one, whether he belongs to the clergy, the army, or to any other condition of men, shall, with a view to causing a tumult and giving occasion to treachery, attempt to discuss the Christian religion publicly in the presence of an assembled and listening crowd" (*Code of Justinian*, bk. 1, tit. 1 (*De summa trinitate et de fide catholica*), l. 3 (*Nemo*)).

23 "Our ancestors foreseeing by Divine inspiration, did most earnestly pray the faithful that whatsoever was at one time decreed by any council against any heresy, and promulgated for the communion of faith and the Catholic and Apostolic truth, did not allow thereafter it to be mutilated by new reconsiderations, lest a per-

heretics alone. For that chapter was taken from a letter of Pope Gelasius [I], which he sent to the bishops of Dardania, who were asking Gelasius why Acacius,[24] a supporter of the Eutychian heresy, was condemned without a general Council. The bishops indeed wanted that Acacius, having firstly been summoned to the Council, and there heard, and if he did not give a reasonable explanation for his opinion, nay, were to assert that heretical opinion, then he would be rightly condemned, and not before. Pope Gelasius writes to these bishops, judging that they are asking for a wrongful thing, and that Acacius was justly condemned without the assembling of a council: because since the Eutychian heresy was long ago already condemned, it was not necessary to assemble a new Council in order to condemn a supporter of the same heresy.

And among the many things which Gelasius eloquently discusses in that letter for supporting this point, shortly after the beginning he says in reply those words which are cited in that chapter, *Majores*. By which words (as it is easily established from the text of the letter) he teaches that heretics, who in a clear heresy, and especially one that was condemned long ago, ought not to be admitted to a disputation: but it is necessary that they revoke their error without any discussion. "Because," as Gelasius says in the same letter, "if it were permitted to anyone to [decide] again those things which have been salubriously decided, absolutely no ordinance of the Church against whatever particular errors would remain stable, and every irreproachable decision would always be

---

verse occasion be given of disturbing those things which had been medicinally decreed, but by the author of whatever madness, as well as the error having been condemned, they judged to suffice, that whosoever at any time would be a spreader of this error, would be bound by the original sentence of his condemnation" (*Decretum Gratiani*, pt. 2, *causa* 24, q. 1, c. 2 (PL 187, 1263C-1264B)).

24 Acacius was the Patriarch of Constantinople from 472 to 489.

disturbed by the same recurring follies. For even though the pests have at one time been expelled by the fixed boundaries of the synodal rules put in place, when battles have been resumed, they would remove the very foundation of truth, and strike whatever upright heart. What if faithless men were to be hereafter allowed to enter a Council? When whatever truth has been shown to them, pernicious falsity would never cease to pour forth, even though reason or authority are not wanting, yet not giving up the single aim."[25] Which words themselves sufficiently indicate that they are directed against heretics, who spurred on by various ravings strive to oppose the firm faith with their disputations, and are not directed against Catholics, who bustle about defending the same faith.

The Supreme Pontiff, Blessed Leo I also keeps only heretics away from a disputation. For when writing about the then-recent Eutychian heresy, he speaks thus: "The hope, therefore, of heavenly aid being increased through the Emperor's friendship, I venture with the greater confidence to appeal to your Grace on behalf of the mystery of man's salvation, not to allow any one in vain and presumptuous craftiness to inquire what must be held, as if it were uncertain."[26] And when writing to the same Emperor Marcian about those things which were treated in the Council of Chalcedon, he says: "Through Our Lord Jesus Christ, who is the Author and Ruler of your kingdom, I entreat and beseech Your Clemency, that in the present Council you do not allow the faith, which having been handed down from the Apostles our blessed Fathers preached, to be retracted as though it were doubtful, and not permit those attempting to raise up the ruins of the things which long ago were condemned by the authority of our predecessors."[27] In which words it is

---

25 Letter 13 (PL 59, 62A-B); Mansi 8, 50B-51A.
26 Letter 82 (PL 54, 917B-918A).
27 Letter 90, c. 2 (PL 54, 933B-934A).

very clearly evident that he only wished to forbid that disputation whereby the firm faith is put into doubt, and what is certain is investigated in it as being uncertain.

But since there are heretics, who strive to make the certitude of the faith uncertain by their disputations, and there are Catholics, who strive to defend the firmness of the faith with their disputation, it follows that only the heretics are they who are forbidden to dispute about the faith, and not the Catholics. For these men alone are they who do injury to the authority and dignity of the faith, when they strive to amputate its certitude from it, and are not afraid to call it either false or doubtful. Hence Blessed Maximus [of Turin] in a certain sermon on several martyrs says: "It is a matter of great danger, if after the oracles of the prophets, after the testimonies of the Apostles, after the wounds of the martyrs, you would presume to discuss our old faith, as if it were new, if after such expert guides, you nevertheless will remain in error: if after the combats of such as did struggle unto death for the defense thereof, you will yet oppose it with idle disputation."[28] Thus heretics are they to whom it was interdicted to dispute about the faith, which if at any time they, having despised every prohibition, would not be ashamed to oppose by their disputations, the defense of the same faith is not interdicted to Catholics. Nay, sometimes (as I said) it is necessary and enjoined by precepts to ecclesiastical prelates, who (as shepherds) have the responsibility of warding off the wolves, lest they harm the sheep by their bites. For when it is feared that the people would fall into heresy, because there is no one who refutes the heretics by their disputation, then it would be necessary to dispute against the heretics.

On account of this Blessed Athanasius disputed with Arius, so that he might refute him, or at least strengthen the people in the faith. On account of the same reason, Blessed Augustine many times publicly disputed with various heretics:

---

28 Sermon 88 (PL 57, 707C).

Book 1, Chapter 19

with Felix the Manichaean, with Felicianus the Arian, with Pascentius, an Arian royal official, and with Emeritus [of Caesarea], a Donatist. Led by the same reason Archbishop Lanfranc of Canterbury chose to publicly dispute with Berengarius: so that having been publicly refuted and confuted he could not secretly deceive the people (as he was doing). But Berengarius did not want to have this disputation with Lanfranc, greatly fearing the shame of [Lanfranc's] victory. This is evident from the preface of a certain tract, which the same Lanfranc wrote against Berengarius.[29] For the same reason Blessed Bernard did not hesitate to come from the cloister and quiet of his monastery located in Burgundy all the way to Sens in France, to dispute against the very pestilent heretic Peter Abelard in favor of the Catholic faith. For even though he was called to the event by the Archbishop of Sens, he then refused to come, because he thought that it was not his concern, but the bishops', whose ministry it is to judge about doctrine: nevertheless, when he heard that the heretic was made more proud because of this, and more audacious to reproach the hosts of Catholic men, he acquiesced to his friends' counsel, and came to the disputation: but the heretic himself fled from this disputation: and so it happened by God's will that the heretic, who challenged Blessed Bernard to a one-on-one combat, fled firstly himself from the combat.

And so that this matter may be clearer, it seems good to insert here the words which Bernard wrote about this matter. For he speaks thus: "But I gave in (not easily, indeed I wept)

---

29 "[Y]ou therefore avoid me and you avoid religious persons who can pass judgment between your words and mine. And I would have preferred in the presence of such persons to hear you and confer with you about no other matter than the opinions that, with an audacity that should be punished, you pretend are compatible with your own opinions..." (*Liber de corpore et sanguine Domini* (PL 150, 413C)).

to the advice of my friends, who, seeing how everybody was getting ready as for a show, were afraid that our absence would cause scandal among the people and make my adversary's horns grow. And as error was growing stronger, there being no one to reply or contradict, I turned up at that place and day, unprepared and unprotected, save that in my mind I meditated on the texts: 'Take no thought how or what to speak: for it shall be given you in that hour what to speak' (Mt. 10, 19), and, 'The Lord is my helper: I will not fear what man can do unto me' (Ps. 117, 6). Now besides the bishops and abbots, there had assembled very many religious, and from the cities, masters of schools, and many educated clerics; and the king was present. And so, in the presence of all, my adversary standing face to face with me, there were produced headings excerpted from his books. When they began to be read, he went out, not wanting to listen, appealing against the appointed judges."[30] From whose words it is very clearly evident when and where it may be permitted to dispute with a heretic. For when from the lack of a disputer, who contradicts, the heretic grows stronger, scandal threatens the people, then a disputation is necessary so that the heretic may be confounded, and the people strengthened in the true faith. But then one ought to dispute in the presence of learned men, and not in front of uncultivated people: because it is not expedient that the lofty disputation would be made before uneducated judges. Where, however, from the lack of a disputation no danger threatens the people, I think that it would be more advisable if every disputation would be cut off, and it be done according to the counsel of the Wise Man, who speaks thus: "Answer not a fool according to his folly, lest thou be made like him" (Prov. 26, 4).

---

30 Letter 189, n. 4 (PL 182, 356A-B).

Chapter XX

Although it is not absolutely good to dispute with a heretic, it is still good and holy to write against heretics.

Perhaps from those things which we said in the preceding chapter someone will conclude that it is also not good, nor permitted, to write against heretics, thinking that the nature of a vocal disputation and writing is the same, and with the same measure both ought to be measured. For long ago I had dispute about this matter with a certain man not a little educated in Greek and Latin. For when he was living in Bruges in Flanders, where I was at the time, and I was then preparing the book, which I published, *Against All Heresies*, he was secretly detracting my labor, saying that I had taken up a completely useless business and that it would have been more advisable if I had never begun the work. But (as is often wont to happen) those things he thought he was saying secretly and which I would never know, my friends having heard, and at length relating to me, I came to know. I went to the man and asked him whether he himself had said such things. He could not deny it, who was aware that he had said it before many people, by whose testimony it could be proved. I next asked him what motivated him to so think, so that he would detract such a holy work. "Because many men," he replied, "when reading this work will perhaps praise the heresies themselves, against which you dispute, than the Catholic truth, and when reading those things preached now long ago by others, more bold by this very fact they will take up defending the same heresies, which you attempt to oppose. And in this way, although you wish to extinguish the heretics, you will raise up heretics: because you place a scandal before them, and give an occasion for heresy. 'But he that shall scandalize one of these little ones,' that believe in Christ, as the Savior says, 'it were better for him that a millstone should be hanged about his neck, and that he should be drowned in the depth of the sea' (Mt. 18, 6)." Behold you see the very pressing reason by which he was motivated, so that he thought it not merely useless, but even harmful, to write against heretics. And yet he was a man who strove very much to be seen as a theologian, when actually he was not.

Then when the book, which I had prepared, *Against All Heresies*, was completely finished and published, when I returned to my native land of Spain, there were not wanting those who likewise reproached me as that man had done in Flanders. But neither were these men theologians, nor were they going around thinking that they were theologians (as he did). These men were in fact learned men, but they had only learned human laws, which they call either pontifical or civil: and one ought to be a little more sparing to this judgment, because it is not surprising if they erred in a matter which does not pertain to their law. For if they were learned theologians, they would not have disapproved of my labor, whereby I took up the disputation against all heresies in favor of the Catholic faith; nay, they would have rather strongly praised it, just as now (God being the Author) to Whom I give immense thanks, as many soever as there are learned theologians in the world praise it, and express marvelous praises. For if they had known well what and what kind of scandal ought to be avoided, and what kind ought to be contemned, they would not have fallen into such an error, whereby they thought that one ought not to write against heretics or heresies, lest someone reading would be scandalized, and fall into those same heresies.

Our Savior taught that there is a scandal that rightly ought to be contemned, for when the Apostles were saying to Him, that the Pharisees were scandalized because He had said that a man is not defiled by the food which enters into the mouth, He responded: "Let them alone: they are blind, and leaders of the blind" (Mt. 15, 14). By which words Our Savior very clearly despised that scandal of the Pharisees. Therefore, so that we may show forth the truth of this matter more clearly, it is necessary that we treat the variety of scandals and in passing what sort of difference there is between them. "Scandal" in Greek,[1] in Latin is *offendiculum,* and when applied to morals, signifies an occasion of evil. Hence Jerome when expounding that passage of Matthew, "Dost thou know that the Pharisees, when they heard this word, were scandalized?" (v. 12), speaks thus: "And because 'scandal' is frequently used in the Church's Scriptures, we should briefly speak about what it signifies. We can express *scolon* [σκῶλον] and *scandalum* as 'little obstacle' or 'falling and striking against the foot.' So then when we read: 'Whoever "scandalizes" any of the least of these,'[2] we understand this: the one who by word or deed gives to anyone an occasion for falling."[3]

Now such a scandal is wont to happen in two ways, because either it is given by someone, or it is taken with no one giving; and due to this it is named with two names. For the one is called scandal given [or active scandal], and the other is called scandal taken [or passive scandal]. Scandal given is something said or done which of itself gives to another an occasion of a fall, that is, an occasion of a sin. Such a scandal is always a sin, and in fact a mortal sin, if it entices to mortal sin. Concerning this scandal Christ spoke when he said: "He that shall scandalize one of these little ones that believe in me, it were better for him that a millstone should be hanged about his neck, and that he should be drowned in the depth of the sea" (Mt. 18, 6). And again: "Woe to that man by whom the scandal cometh" (v. 7). Scandal of this kind must always

---

1 Ancient Greek: σκάνδαλον (*skándalon,* "a trap laid for an enemy, a cause of moral stumbling").
2 Cf. Mt. 18, 6; Mk. 9, 42; Lk. 17, 2.
3 *Commentaria in Matthaeum,* bk. 2 (PL 26, 107B-C).

be avoided, by that law and reason whereby we are bound to avoid other sins. There is another scandal, which is called taken, and it is not given, and it is a fall, or collapse, that is, a sin coming forth from a good deed or saying of another, or at least from a saying or deed which is not evil. This scandal is called taken and not given, because someone takes an occasion of sin from a thing which is not apt for giving an occasion of evil. No one is obliged to avoid this kind of scandal in another.

Sometimes scandal arises from something good, and necessary for salvation, as are all those things which have been enjoined to us under precept. For if someone is scandalized because you abstain from meat in Lent, or you hear holy Mass on Sunday, you are not able to omit any of these things with impunity; nay, you are held to do any of them, having despised that scandal. For the law of charity which commands that you love yourself more than your neighbor, also commands that you avoid sin more in yourself than in your neighbor. You would sin, however, if you were to omit those things which were commanded to you. Therefore, you ought not to omit those things which have been commanded to you, in order to prevent another from sinning through the scandal. About this scandal is understood the saying of Bede which is put in the "Rules of Law" [*Regulae Juris*]: "It is better to allow the birth of scandal, than to abandon the truth."[4] Which rule of law, according to the opinion of all Doctors, theologians, and canonists, ought to be understood of the triple truth, namely, of life, justice, and doctrine, such that neither the truth of life, nor of justice, nor of doctrine ought to be omitted on account of avoiding our neighbor's scandal; especially if such a truth is necessary for the soul's

---

4 *Decretals of Gregory IX*, bk. 5, tit. 41 (*De regulis juris*), c. 3, §1 (*Qui scandalizaverit*). Ven. Bede, *Homiliae*, bk. 3, hom. 67 (PL 94, 442C). Cf. Gregory I, *Homiliae in Ezechielem*, hom. 7, n. 5 (PL 76, 842C).

salvation. Otherwise, if that truth is not necessary, as happens in the truth of life, which is not enjoined under obligation of precept, but only given as a counsel, then on account of avoiding the neighbor's scandal, which will arise in him out of ignorance, it would be permitted to omit for a time such a truth of life, until he is taught that such a thing is good, and is not any occasion of scandal.

But when the neighbor has already been thoroughly taught, and it has been clearly shown to him that such a thing is good, which has completely no reason for scandal in it, if the neighbor is still scandalized, such a scandal is now malicious, having arisen from pure malice, and not from ignorance; on account of which no truth ought to be ever be abandoned for avoiding which scandal. Alexander of Hales;[5] Richard of Middleton on the fourth book of the Sentences;[6] Pope Adrian [VI] in *Quaestiones quodlibeticae XII*[7] interpret the aforesaid rule of law in this way. A Gloss expounds that rule also in the same way, although not as clearly, plainly, and distinctly as they.[8] It differs from the others in that the Gloss calls "the truth of discipline," that which the above-mentioned Doctors call "the truth of doctrine": for otherwise it would be necessary to assert that the Gloss did not fully assign in its division all the parts of truth, since it omitted the truth of doctrine, which ought not to have been omitted: but rather it ought to have been put in the first place, as faith is prior to charity. Therefore it necessarily happens, lest we say

---

5 *Summa Universae Theologiae* (Venice: Franciscus Francisci-um, 1575), pt. 2, q. 189, mem. 6, a. 3, §4, fol. 415v.
6 *In... sententiarum questiones...: In quartum sententiarum...* (Venice: Soardus, 1509), vol. 4, dist. 38, a. 10, q. 2, fol. 174v.
7 *Quaestiones quodlibeticae XII* (Paris: Claude Chevallon, 1527), q. 1, fol. 7v.
8 Cf. *Decretales Gregorii IX pont. Max. suis commentariis illustratae* (Paris: apud Gulielmum Merlin... & Gulielmum Desboys..., ac Sebastianum Nivellium, 1561), col. 2132.

that the division which the Gloss assigns is defective, that by "the truth of discipline" we would understand "the truth of doctrine." Thus, it is a Christian rule, that "It is better to allow the birth of scandal, than to abandon the truth."

Therefore, having premised all these things, I ask those who think that it is not good to write against heresies, because someone when reading that work will perhaps be scandalized, thinking that the heresy that is rejected is truer than its rejection: The scandal of this scandalized man will be of what sort, given or taken? If they say that it is scandal given, it will be necessary for the same reason that they would say that to write against heresies is a mortal sin: because (as we said) all such scandal, which of itself gives an occasion of mortal sin, is a mortal sin. Hence since heresy is a mortal sin, and (as we showed in the first book) very grave, it follows that writing against heresies, if (as they say) scandal is given, it is also a mortal sin, and the one writing against them sins mortally. If they concede this, then I will again ask them if the favorer of that [writing] were to keep it so secret so that no one would see it, or if others have read it, and no one was scandalized from it, but rather on the contrary many who were doubtful in the faith, or otherwise heretical, were recalled to the faith by it, and strengthened in it: whether then also that writing against heresies ought to be called a scandal. If they then say that it ought not to be called a sin, nor a scandal, because no one was scandalized and it edified many, it thence follows that neither it is a sin, nor should be called scandal given, although many would be scandalized from its reading. This conclusion is thence very manifest, because a deed, so that it may be called scandal given, does not depend on the fact that another is scandalized from it: because if that deed is evil when done before others, whether someone is scandalized from it or not, it will always be called scandal given. Whether or not someone takes an occasion of blasphemy when he sees another blaspheming, when the blasphemy has been done publicly it is always called scandal given. Thus it is a necessary consequence that the writing against heresies be not called scandal given: even though many take from it the occasion of a fall, if it ought not to be called scandal when no one is scandalized from it.

But if they say that such writing against heresies ought to be called a mortal sin (even if no one reads it) and it is scandal given, even though those reading it are not scandalized from it, it would be necessary to say that those men, Blessed Augustine, Blessed Jerome, and Blessed Irenaeus, sinned mortally, due to the fact that they published many writings against heresies, and it will be necessary to say that such tracts of theirs, which they published against heresies are scandalous: because someone could also have been scandalized by those tracts, such that he would choose [to embrace] those very heresies which those holy men condemned, rather than the Catholic truth. He who would not hesitate to concede this, would also be forced to condemn the whole Catholic Church, because it did not ever condemn such tracts, nor did it forbid the faithful from reading them. I do not believe that anyone is so foolish that he would say that holy men sinned mortally on account of the fact that they wrote against heresies, and that the Church erred, because it allowed the tracts of holy men, which they wrote against heresies, to be read.

Yet if someone would be so brazen, that he would not be ashamed to concede this, I will lead him into much more difficult straights, and into the greatest inconsistency which we could conceive for a Christian man. For he who says these things will necessarily be forced to say that the Evangelists erred in the writing of their Gospels, and Paul in his Epistles: because they all wrote down some heresies of wicked men; and although the Evangelist or the Apostle had condemned them, still there were not lacking those who afterwards have defended them. The heresy of the Sadducees, denying the

Resurrection, is clear, which was condemned by Christ Our Savior, as Matthew, Mark, and Luke relate. Yet it is certain that there were many heretics who afterwards fell into the same heresy, and would that there were not also many men, who support the same heresy, thinking that nothing remains after this life. Paul the Apostle condemns two heresies in the First Epistle to Timothy: one which forbids marriage; the other which forbids some certain types of food:[9] no believer (that I know of) had taught those heresies before Paul's time: but because he foresaw by a prophetic spirit that there would be some men who would teach them, wherefore he fittingly forewarned, so that we would beware of them. If Paul forewarned about future heresies, writing them down, and condemning them before they arose, he wrote much more efficaciously and strongly against those which had already arisen, just as he also did against those which arose in his time. In the Epistle to the Galatians he deliberately disputes against those who were saying that the ceremonies and sacrifices of the Old Law are necessary for salvation in the Evangelical Law. He argues against this same thing in the Epistle to the Hebrews. Yet it could happen that someone reading the Epistles of Paul, would choose [to embrace] the heresies which Paul condemns there, rather than the Catholic truth. For Ebion, Cerinthus, and the Sampsaean and the Elcesaite heretics, notwithstanding Paul's opinion, said that the ceremonies of the Old Law are necessary in the Evangelical Law. Who then will be so foolish that he would reckon that Paul's Epistles ought to be destroyed, the Gospels ought to be erased, lest perhaps someone reading them would fall into the heresies which are condemned therein, or into other vices, which are there reprehended?

From all these things I conclude that he who writes against heresies not merely does not sin in doing this, but he acts well; and such writing is not a sin, nay, rather a good work,

---

9   I Tim. 4, 3.

and consequently ought not to be called scandal given, even though some may be scandalized by it. Moreover just as someone can be scandalized by a writing of this kind, taking from it the occasion of assenting to some heresy, so on the contrary many can through that writing be recalled to the Catholic faith from the heresy into which they had perhaps fallen, and those who perhaps were doubtful and wavering in the faith can be strengthened, and it is likely that the latter would happen more frequently than the former: because in such writing the Catholic faith is praised, heresy is reprehended and condemned; therein the Catholic faith is fought for, and heresy is refuted. Wherefore since good and Catholic men cannot only be persuaded from a writing of this kind for the strengthening of their faith, but in addition they are urged by this, and as it were compelled to this, and it follows that if someone reading this writing which disputes against the heresy falls into any of those heresies condemned therein, it ought not to be attributed to the wickedness of the writing, but rather to the wickedness of the one reading, who has abused the writing, since he approves and judges as being good that which he reads there to be evil and disapproved. If a snake when devouring a hen or a capon or a ram turns it into poison, who will say that it is its own fault, and not rather the snake's, which on account of the evilness of its association, that which by its nature was salutary, it turns into poison? Completely the same thing ought to be reckoned about him who when reading those tracts, which are written against heretics, chooses [to embrace] those same heresies which he sees there reprehended and condemned, rather than the Catholic truth.

From all these things it is clearly concluded that he who writes against heresies, does not merely not sin, but does well, and such a writing ought not to be called a sin, but a good and meritorious work, and consequently ought not to be considered a scandal given, even though someone may be scandalized by it. Because such a scandal does not arise from the writing, which of itself is good, although the heresy is evil which is reprehended by it: but it proceeds from the malice of the reader, who abuses the good. Thus, such a scandal ought to be reckoned a scandal taken, and not given: because he by his own fault wanted to stumble, even though he was forewarned about the stumbling block. He through his own malice wanted to adhere to that opinion, about which he had been warned is heretical, so that he would beware of it. No one is obliged to avoid such a scandal as this, because that rule of Christian law (as we said) is understood about this, which says: "It is better to allow the birth of scandal, than to abandon the truth." For if someone having been taught by me about the Catholic faith and about a heresy, so that having been warned he would beware of it, falls into that same heresy, the fault will be his, not mine, who warned him.

From which it is very clearly gathered that one nowise ought to omit the teaching of the Catholic faith, so that error may be avoided in one's neighbor who errs due to his own fault. For otherwise for the same reason preachers of God's word should not reprehend vices in a public sermon, and confessors not ask penitents about them in a private confession: since it could happen that someone would take an occasion of desiring sins, which perhaps he did not know, learning therefrom, and at length committing those sins which he had never committed before. For the same reason a doctor ought not to warn a sick man about harmful foods, so that he would beware of them: because it often happens that after the prohibition men desire those foods more ardently, which if they eat, they will perhaps die. Nevertheless, if this had happened, no one in his right mind would blame the doctor on account of this: because he warned the sick man, nay, rather he having been inculpable will put the whole blame upon the sick man himself; because he did not want to obey the doctor advising him, but relying upon his own prudence, brought death upon himself. If a corporal doctor when warning a sick man to beware of harmful food acts well, it follows that a spiritual doctor when warning others to stay away from harmful teachings acts so much better, as the soul is better than the body, and as the sicknesses of the soul are more serious than those of the body.

Again, something good never ought to be omitted on account of avoiding the neighbor's scandal, which arises in him by his own malice: although (as we said) it may be permitted for a time to omit, for the sake of avoiding scandal, what arises from ignorance; because then one ought to omit the good deed for so much time until he may be taught about the truth. That this is so is proved by the testimony of our Redeemer, Who after He had taught the Pharisees that the Apostles do not sin by eating without washing their hands, and when the Apostles said to Him that the Pharisees were scandalized by this, He replied: "Let them alone: they are blind, and leaders of the blind" (Mt. 15, 14). By which words Christ our Redeemer very clearly despised such scandal of the Pharisees, in that it arose from their pure malice, since having been taught about the truth by Him, they did not want to understand that same truth. Hence Theophylactus, when interpreting the aforesaid words of the Savior, says: "Here we learn that it is not to our detriment to give offense to those who willingly take offense and are incorrigible."[10] And likewise on Luke, when explaining the miracle of the man who had the dropsy,[11] whom the Lord healed on the Sabbath day, he speaks thus: "Then when the man that had the dropsy had come in the midst, the Lord cared naught about how He might not offend [the Pharisees], but how He might heal him who needed His care. For when a great good is expected, we must not care if the foolish are scandalized."[12] The

---

10 *Ennaratio in Evangelium S. Mattheum* (PG 123, 307B).
11 Cf. Lk. 14, 2.
12 *Ennaratio in Evangelium S. Lucae* (PG 123, 930A).

scandal of those who, when reading tracts published against heresies, fall into the same heresies, arises from their own wickedness, and not from ignorance; because when the truth of the faith has been plainly explained to them, they despise it and choose [to embrace] the error condemned in the same place. Therefore, it follows that (according to Our Savior's teaching) such scandal of these men, who are scandalized of their own accord, ought to be contemned, and one ought not to omit writing against heresies for the sake of avoiding it.

Next, how empty and frivolous is this unsuitability, that these men stumble against these books which are written against heresies, Paul shows very clearly in the Epistle to the Romans, in which he disputes about the Mosaic Law, showing that it was not as good as the Jews thought: because it could not justify men, as they believed. And at length when showing what good the Law had, he says: "By the law is the knowledge of sin" (3, 20). He said this because there are some sins which we would not know are sins, unless the Law had taught us that they are sins. Wherefore again in chapter seven of the same Epistle, he says: "I do not know sin, but by the law; for I had not known concupiscence, if the law did not say: Thou shalt not covet" (v. 7). Thus, this Law having been given, and through it having obtained the knowledge of sin, from thence it arose that men would desire more the very sins which they understood to have been forbidden through the Law. And hence he in the fifth chapter of the same Epistle said: "The law entered in, that sin might abound" (v. 20). In which words the [adverbial phrase beginning with] "that" ought not to be understood in the meaning of the final cause: but as signifying the resulting effect. For God did not give the Law for this purpose, but so that better things would be done. Yet when the Law was given men were enflamed with a greater desire for those same things, which had been forbidden to them by the Law. For (as the poet [Ovid] says) "We are ever striving after what is forbidden, and coveting what is denied us."[13]

And similarly Paul says this same thing in the same Epistle in chapter seven, speaking thus: "Sin taking occasion by the commandment, wrought in me all manner of concupiscence" (v. 8). And after many other words he says there on the same subject, he argues against himself, speaking thus: "What shall we say, then? Is the law sin?" (v. 7). Paul makes this objection to himself, because someone could perhaps think that the Law is bad and it would have been better if such a Law had not been given, since from it many (as it has been said) took the occasion of sinning more. But Paul replies to this objection, "God forbid. But I do not know sin, but by the law" (v. 7). And shortly afterwards he says, "For without the law sin was dead. And I lived some time without the law. But when the commandment came, sin revived, and I died. And the commandment that was ordained to life, the same was found to be unto death to me. For sin, taking occasion by the commandment, seduced me, and by it killed me. Wherefore the law indeed is holy, and the commandment holy, and just, and good" (vv. 8-12). [Hervé de Bourg-Dieu,] when interpreting these words in his commentaries on the Epistles, says: "Thus sin using the Law improperly, grew more desirable because of its prohibition and became sweeter, and it deceived and caused a fall."[14] And Theophylactus, when expounding the same words of Paul, says: "For the goal [of the Law] was to lead to life, and it was also given for that purpose. But if however death came from it, it certainly was not its fault: for sin, meaning the impulse towards the worst, and a corrupt and sin-loving heart, or so that I may

---

13 *Amores*, bk. 3, poem 4, ln. 17.
14 *Commentaria in epistolas Pauli—In Epistolam ad Romanos* (PL 181, 687C). Cf. Augustine, *De diversis questionibus ad Simplicianum*, bk. 1, n. 5 (PL 40, 104).

speak more rightly, pleasure, killed and deceived me through the commandment."[15]

Paul therefore thinks that the Law was good, and that it was good to have established such a Law, although from it men many times took an occasion of sinning, and of sinning more ardently; because the Law, which was good, did not give this occasion of evil to them: but they by their own malice took by their own wickedness an occasion from the Law. And hence Paul spoke cautiously in the aforesaid words, saying: "taking occasion by the commandment," and he did not say, "the occasion was given by the commandment." Because the Law, which was good, could not give an occasion of any evil to them: but men themselves, because they were evil, took an occasion of evil from that which was good. Let us say in the same way regarding the published writing against heresies, just as Paul said about the Law: The occasion having been taken, heresy seduces the foolish through the Catholic writing, and deceives them. What shall we say, then? Is that writing a sin? God forbid. But the writing is holy, and the work holy, just and good. Finally, so that we may conclude, if to avoid the spontaneous scandal by the foolish, writing against heretics ought to be avoided, it will be necessary for the same reason to avoid all the works of holy men: because you will scarcely find any middling-size work in which some heresy is not repeated and condemned. For they persecuted heresies with such great hatred, that they seem to have always sought an occasion whereby they could fight against some one of them.

Perhaps someone will object to me that which we said in the preceding chapter, that a public vocal disputation against heretics it not good, unless where necessity would urge, and in this way perhaps for the same reason he will conclude that it is also not good to dispute by writing against them. But anyone will easily understand that this objection is of

---

15   *Commentarius in Epistolam ad Romanos* (PG 124, 423D).

completely no importance, if he considers how great is the difference between a vocal and a written disputation. For all can attend a vocal and public disputation; and all eagerly come together to hear it, both the uneducated as well as the educated. But no one but educated men read a written disputation, and hence a written disputation will be considered private, and not public. We concede, however, that a vocal disputation in private, and in front of only learned men can be done, just as now we concede about a written disputation. Next, in the vocal disputation the uneducated, who are present, even though they do not understand the opinions, still strive to judge about the disputation. Rarely, however, does anyone judge about a written disputation, except learned men. But hardly anyone (as I said) unless he be educated, cares to read it, and if someone would read it, he will not understand: and therefore, he also cannot judge. In this manner holy men distinguished the teachings which were given by voice or by writing: because when preachers of God's word advise that teachings be tempered according to the capacity of the listeners, such that they would not discuss about sublime matters before an uncultivated people: still those who consult these writing, often wrote about sublime things in their works: because they thought that those works would not be read by uneducated men, and so they did not think that the same danger threatens from writing which it was sure that could arise from vocal preaching. On account of this same reason, I reckon that those books ought to be avoided, which dispute against heretics in the vulgar language: because such written disputation published in the vulgar tongue is already public, and hence exposed to the judgment of uneducated men, just as though it were to be done with a public voice. Rightly therefore ought the general assembly of the Kingdom of Castile to be praised, which forbade by a public edict that such books against heretics would be translated into the common language, and commanded those which had already been translated may not be sold under grave penalties.

Chapter XXI

That the heretic if he repents, ought to be mercifully received by the Church.

Holy Mother Church, which follows in the footsteps of her most sweet Spouse, is accustomed to receive with open arms (as they say) a heretical man if he recovers. For she in fact imitates her Spouse, Who (as Paul says) "will have all men to be saved, and to come to the knowledge of the truth" (I Tim. 2, 4). "He that shall come to me," Our Savior says, "I will not cast out" (Jn. 6, 37). It is right then that His spouse the Church would not cast out those who wish to return to Christ. God promised through the prophet Jeremias to the Jewish synagogue, which had fornicated with many lovers through the worship of various idols, that He would receive it, if it would return to Him. Thus it is fitting that the Church would receive her children who had departed from her fold, when they returned to her. Yet long ago Novatian thought the contrary, who broke forth in such great madness, that he feared not to teach that the forgiveness or remission of sins ought not to be given to those who had fallen. But the Church enlightened by God's Spirit, understands well how cruel and how foreign to the Divine mercy is this opinion, and wherefore when condemning Novatian, promised and gave forgiveness to those fallen. Nay, she rejoices more affectionately like a pious mother, than about those whom she had never lost. For she knows that her Spouse is the Good Shepherd, Who did not kill, and did not strike the erring sheep: but rejoicing put it upon His shoulders, and led it to the sheepfold, and finally having called together His friends, asked them to rejoice with Him, because He found the sheep which He had lost.[1]

---

1 Cf. Lk. 15, 4-6.

Book 1, Chapter 21

Next, the father in the Gospels did not reject his prodigal son returning to him from the feeding of swine and a faraway region into which he had gone away, nor did he reproach him for his prodigality, or did he afflict him with any insult: but when the father saw him a great way off, he was "moved with compassion, and running to him fell upon his neck, and kissed him" (Lk. 15, 20): and he "said to his servants: Bring forth quickly the first robe, and put it on him, and put a ring on his hand, and shoes on his feet: and bring hither the fatted calf, and kill it, and let us eat and make merry: because this my son was dead, and is come to life again: was lost, and is found" (vv. 22-24). So the heavenly Father judges, so He corrects, and so He gives kisses to the sinning son, not lashes, as one who does not want the death of the sinner: but that he be converted, and live.[2] Although this parable of the prodigal son is wont to be understood of every sinner, yet to me it seems that it ought to be understood more about him who has fallen into heresy, than a believer, who has committed some mortal sin. For the believer is still in the Father's house, because he has not yet left the Church, which (Paul bearing witness[3]) is the house of God. But the heretic, who has separated himself from the fellowship of the Catholic Church, has left the Father's house, and went so much farther away, the more that when the faith was forsaken he immersed himself in many vices. He returns to the Father's house when having abandoned the error by which he was previously deceived, he accepts the Catholic faith, whereby he enters again into the Church, whence he had gone out. But the heavenly Father receives such a son as this with joy, and rejoices over him more than over the older son, who had remained in the house.

Is there one who would not receive a returning son as a mother with the same joy as the Father receives him? Will

---

2 Cf. Ez. 18, 23.
3 Cf. I Tim. 3, 15.

the bride be contrary to her Spouse, such that him whom the Spouse receives kindly and with joy, she would reject with harshness? God forbid. For the Church does nothing in matters pertaining to faith and morals, except as directed and taught by God, her Spouse. It is proved therefore that they act badly who reproach heretics returning to the fellowship of the Church, or Jews or Saracens converted to the true faith, for their past unbelief, and afflict them with insults for this, when they should rather treat them kindly, speak to them sweetly, and attend to them with charity and love, so that by these bonds they may keep them better in the faith received. And perhaps those who treat them bitterly and with harshness, do this so that they might regret having accepted the faith. Wherefore the Lord in the Old Law, under a certain figure, just as the rest of the things which were said in that Law, commanded that men of this kind would not be insulted, and one may not reproach them for their past error. For so He says in Leviticus: "If a stranger abide among you, do not upbraid him" (19, 33). He commanded that one would not upbraid him for his error, but rather that he should be reckoned by them as a native-born. A stranger among Christians is anyone who comes to Christianity from the Jewish or Saracen religions. The Lord commanded that no one may reproach this sort of person with the reproach of being a foreigner, and that no one may insult him due to the fact that he previously was a Jew or a Saracen: no one ought to consider, just as the God also does not consider, what he was before: but what he is now.

Hence Ambrose says: "Once wickedness is renounced, virtue finds immediate entrance. The departure of evil brings about the introduction of virtue and the same effort that banishes crime leads to an adherence to innocence."[4] And these words are found in the chapter, *Cum renuntiatur*.[5] But

---

4 *On Cain and Abel*, bk. 2, c. 4, n. 16 (PL 14, 348C-D).
5 *Decretum Gratiani*, pt. 2, *causa* 32, q. 1, c. 9 (PL 187,

the Lord reprehends through Ezechiel the prophet those who, acting against this law of the Lord, treat the newly converted harshly and improperly, saying: "They oppressed the stranger by calumny without judgment" (22, 29). Jerome, when interpreting these words in his commentaries, says: "They were oppressing with calumnies the stranger and the sojourner, who had not yet been made a member of His Church, but only a supporter and someone having the beginnings of the faith: just as afterwards they went round about the sea and the land to make one proselyte, and make him a child of hell."[6] It is more correct that those who convert to the faith of the Catholic Church from the Jews, Saracens, or heretics, after having abandoned their errors, ought to be received kindly, treated sweetly, lest deterred by excessive harshness, they depart from their beginning faith: but rather drawn by kindness and holy blandishments, they may gladly persevere in the faith which they at some time received.

And if someone among these recent Christians, and newly converted from Judaism or from the Saracens, would happen to err in the faith, and afterwards recognize his error being prepared to be corrected, I say that such a man as this ought to be received with greater mercy and less penance than another among the old Christians: especially if it be established that he erred out of ignorance, and not from malice: for instance, because he had not been fully instructed about the faith. And the chapter, *Contra Christianos*,[7] does not stand in the way, because it is understood of the pertinacious, and those who are not prepared to be corrected from their error. Nevertheless, if they show signs of true contrition, and want to return to the unity of the Church, they ought to be received kindly: because ignorance, and sometimes weakness, excuses them.

1465C-1466A).

6 *Commentaria in Ezechielem*, bk. 7 (PL 25, 214B). Cf. Mt. 23, 15.

7 *Liber sextus*, bk. 5, tit. 2 (*De haereticis*), c. 13, also cited above more fully.

Wherefore lest under this veil of excuse they manage to always conceal their malice, it would be necessary that a certain time be given to the newly converted Christians, and not too short a time be set, during which they may be obliged to learn those things which pertain to the Catholic faith, and teachers who would teach them: because unless it be done, even if they would err afterwards, they could rightly excuse themselves, saying: "No man hath hired us" (Mt. 20, 7).

But lest someone take from these things which we said an occasion of error, thinking that a heretical man as often as he recovers always ought to be received with mercy, it was befitting to admonish the reader about this matter, so that he understood that it could happen in two ways that a heretic after converting to the faith is received by the Church. In one way, that he is received only for the salvation of his own soul: in another way, he is received not only for the salvation of his soul, but also of his body. In the first way we say that at whatever time a heretic repents, even if he has relapsed, he always ought to be received to penance: so that he can attain the salvation of his soul. "For penance," as [Pseudo-] Augustine says, "even if it arrives at the last moment of life, saves and liberates."[8] And in the chapter, *Super eo*,[9] it is taught that when a heretic has relapsed he ought not to be denied the Sacraments of Penance and the Holy Eucharist, if he humbly asks for them and manifest signs of repentance are seen in him.

In the second way, that is, for the benefit of body and soul, it behooves one not to always receive heretics, and the Church does not always want to receive them. And rightly does the

---

8 *Concordia discordantium canonum, causa* 3, dist. 7, c. 6 (*Nullus expectet*). "For penance, if it arrives in the last opening of life, heals and liberates in the washing of Baptism..." (*De vera et falsa poenitentia*, c. 17, n. 33 (PL 40, 1127). This work has often been incorrectly ascribed to St. Augustine and is of unknown authorship.
9 *Liber sextus*, bk. 5, tit. 2 (*De haereticis*), c. 4.

Book 1, Chapter 21

Church do this: because if she would always receive them, so that she would keep them unharmed in life, and in other temporal goods, this would give place to the destruction of many (as we will teach at greater length in the second book). Now we will teach in the following chapter which heretics, and when, does the Church receive for the welfare of body and soul.

Chapter XXII

That heretics returning to the faith for the first time, ought not to be received all equally, and with equal mercy.

Although we said that all heretics, who have been caught only one time for having fallen into heresy, ought to be received when they return to the Catholic faith; nevertheless, one ought not to treat all of them with the same kindness, but according the diversity of the crime and person, the diverse mercy will be applied to them. For "According to the measure of the sin," God commanded, "shall the measure also of the stripes be" (Deut. 25, 2). This diversity ought to be considered in many things, and firstly: Whether he who has erred in the faith, comes spontaneously, and without any accusation, or after he had been accused. For it is of great importance whether you do something freely or from fear. If someone has erred in the faith, and afterwards acknowledging his sin without someone's accusation or denunciation, but of his own accord shall have approached the inquisitors of heretics, and shall have asked for mercy, he doubtlessly should be received with kindness and mercy. And without any mark of infamy, some private penance, according to the quality of the heresy and person, is imposed upon him. And in such a case as this, one ought not to take into consideration any difference from the time of his trial and confession: for instance, if he came before or after the time of grace granted by the inquisitors. For inquisitors of heretics are wont as soon as they visit a town, so that they may inquire about heretics, publish edicts and instruct the people through preachers, that if anyone in that place shall have fallen into some heresy (by the devil's persuasion), within such or such a time, for example within a week or month, they may recognize their errors, and humbly admit in the presence of the inquisitors that they have erred: otherwise if they shall be caught after this period presignified to them has already ended, they will be punished as heretics. This preset period granted to them is accustomed to be called the "time of grace": because from a favor [*ex gratia*] and not from necessity the time of pardon and mercy was granted to them; because if they shall come in that time, pardon and mercy will be given to them. Thus, in whatever time someone comes, whether that man comes within the time of grace or afterwards, in a voluntary way, and without any accusation or summons, he always ought to be received with mercy.

And this can also be proved from something similar that is written in the chapter, *Si tibi absenti*.[1] But if someone shall come not of his own accord, but when he has been accused and summoned to the Inquisition, and has confessed his sin before them, one ought then to have this foremostly in consideration, namely, whether he came within the time of grace, or afterwards. If someone accused of heresy acknowledges his sin before he is summoned to the court of justice, and humbly confesses it within the time of grace, I say that he ought to be mercifully received, and with pardon of his sin, whether he knows that he was accused or not. For otherwise I cannot understand whom that time of grace can benefit: because it certainly nowise benefits those who come of their own accord, and completely freely; since these men even if they were to come after the time of grace has already elapsed (as we just said), ought to be admitted. Thus, it ought to be said that the time of grace either is completely unimportant, or it necessarily avails those who come after an accusation.

---

1 *Liber sextus*, bk. 2, tit. 4 (*De praebendis*), c. 17 (*Si tibi absenti*), §4 (*Antequam*). The law says that when a benefice has been assigned to someone, it cannot be given to someone else, unless a period of time has been granted for its acceptance, and then after the end of that period, before it has been assigned to someone else, the one to whom it was first assigned can still accept it.

How heretics returning to the faith for the first time ought to be received

Yet an appropriate penance will be imposed upon these men according to the qualities of their crimes.

If, however, after the time of grace has elapsed someone having been accused and summoned comes and then confesses his crime before the inquisitors, there is a doubt among the canonists, whether he ought to be received. For the Archdeacon[2] says on the chapter, *Ut commissi*,[3] that this sort of man ought not to be received,[4] and he refers to a law of *The Code of Justinian*, [in the title,] *De his qui latrones vel in aliis criminibus reos occultaverint*.[5] Dominicus[6] in the same place quotes this opinion of the Archdeacon, and neither opposes nor confirms it: but he goes on, being content with merely its quotation.[7] But Hostiensis in his *Summa*, on the title, *De haereticis*, says that a heretic, before he is convicted, always ought to be received. For in the paragraph, *Qualiter deprehendatur*, he speaks thus: "If the one summoned confesses from fear of the trial, and the judge sees that he is contrite, and has hope about his conversion, he can spare him, having enjoined a salutary penance... But if he denies [his error], and was convicted, he ought to be condemned by the ecclesiastical judge, to whom this pertains, as it is said in the chapter,

---

2 I. e., Guido de Baysio.
3 *Liber sextus*, bk. 5, tit. 2 (*De haereticis*), c. 12, §. *Necnon*.
4 "For if after the time of grace he is personally interrogated and heard, although he reveals his error, he is unworthy of pardon" (*Super Sexto Decretalium* (Lyon: Jacobus Giunta, 1547), fol. 110v).
5 "When any robbers or other malefactors reside or conceal themselves on the land of another, the owner of the property (if he is present) or his agents (if he is absent)... do not promptly give them up, then the Governor of the province, having been applied to, must take all legal measures to arrest them" (*The Code of Justinian*, bk. 9, tit. 39, l. 2).
6 Domenico da San Gimignano (1375-1424) was an Italian canonist who compiled the *Liber sextus*.
7 *Lectura super sexto libro decretalium: cum apostillis clarissimorum virorum* (Trino: Piston, 1520), fol. 250v.

Ad abolendam."[8] And on the phrase, *Quando et qualiter Ecclesiae reconcilietur*, he says that immediately after the condemnation without any interval he can be reconciled by the bishop's authority, but during the interval [he cannot be reconciled] except by the Pope's authority.[9] And the Lord Cardinal [Hostiensis] on the chapter, *Ad nostrum*,[10] says that if he is convicted after he shall have denied [his error], he may not be admitted to the revocation of this kind of error, so that by it he may avoid death. Because he who waited to be convicted, and when convicted recants, does not do this within allotted time, nor spontaneously: because he seems to have made his confession [of his error] out of fear. Now the Glossator of the Decretals teaches that one ought to be received even after the condemnation, if he then is known to spontaneously recant. He says this on the chapter, *Ad abolendam*, §. *Presenti*, on the word, *recurrere*,[11] and in the second to last chapter of *De haereticis*,[12] §. *Si qui autem*, on

---

8   *Summa aurea*, bk. 5, cols. 1359-1360. "Whom the same church of Rome, or the individual bishops in their dioceses, with the advice of their clergy, or the clergy themselves, in case of a vacancy of the see, with the advice, if need be, of neighboring bishops, shall judge to be heretics" (*Decretals of Gregory IX*, bk. 5, tit. 7 (*De haereticis*), c. 9).

9   *Summa aurea*, bk. 5, col. 1367.

10 *Constitutiones Clementinae*, bk. 5, tit. 3, c. 3. The reference to the commentary given here is *In Clemen.*, *Ad nostram*, §. *penult. de hereticis*.

11 "But it seems that he also ought to be compelled to keep the faith (*Decretum Gratiani*, pt. 1, dist. 45, c. 5 (*De judeis*)), after the heretic has been condemned, he is not compelled: but if he wants to spontaneously recant, he ought to be received when he has renounced his error (*Decretum*, pt. 2, c. 24, q. 3, c. 29 (*Dixit Apostolus*)) and cast into prison in perpetuity to do penance (Bernard of Compostella, Gloss following *signat contrarium et soluit* [on the word, *Audientia*])."

12 *Decretals of Gregory IX*, bk. 5, tit. 7, c. 15 (*Excommunicamus*),

the word, *deprehendi*, and he tries to prove this opinion of his there [from *The Code of Justinian*], speaking thus: "But as the Church never closes her heart to those who return to her"[13] and "We pardon those who repent."[14] Although these words are related in the Gloss of Panormitanus[15] on the chapter, *Excommunicamus*,[16] §. *damnati*, in the same title, nevertheless he relates the opinion of the Archdeacon which he prefers.[17] And to support this opinion he cites the text in the chapter, *Accusatus*.[18] On which chapter he says that only the relapsed ought to be punished without mercy. Therefore Panormitanus says that this opinion ought to be held: because it is milder, and he proves [his view] by the rule, *Odia*,[19] and by the rule, *In poenis*,[20] from the *Rules of Law* of *Liber Sextus*.

Notice that you see three opinions of the most learned men, of which two are extreme, the other, namely, Hostien-

---

§1 (*Si qui autem*).
13 Bk. 1, tit. 1 (*De summa Trinitate*), c. 8 (*Inter claras*), n. 35.
14 *Ibid.*, tit. 5, c. 4 (*Manichaeos*), n. 6.
15 Panormitanus (1386-1445), or Nicolò de Tudeschi, also known as *Abbas Modernus*, was an Italian Benedictine canonist. He was the Archbishop of Palermo.
16 *Decretals of Gregory IX*, bk. 5, tit. 7, c. 15 (*Excommunicamus*).
17 "A heretic wishing to return to the faith does not evade the punishment of death. For to do penance for the crime committed he ought to be cast into prison in perpetuity. But today this punishment can be commuted into another if it seems proper to the superior" (*Lectura super quinque libros Decretalium* (Basel: Johann Amerbach, 1488), vol. 5).
18 *Liber sextus decretalium*, bk. 5, tit. 2 (*de hereticis*), c. 8 (*Accusatus*), n. 3 (*Licet*).
19 Rule 15 in *Liber sextus*: *Odia restringi, et favores convenit ampliari* ("It is fitting that burdensome things be restricted and favorable ones extended").
20 Rule 49: *In poenis benignior est interpretatio facienda* ("In penalties the milder interpretation is to be adopted").

sis', which somewhat divides in the middle. What therefore will I, a man who is a theologian, do where so many great men fight? For I could say what that rustic Virgil said: "'Tis not for us to end such great disputes."[21] I will frankly say, nevertheless, that none of these opinions absolutely and in every respect please me. And let not anyone be surprised, or say that I am arrogant and proud because I, a man who is a theologian, would dare to contend in a juridical matter against experts in Canon Law: but let him rather consider, I beseech, that there is no one, or never was a learned man, who writing with purely human understanding, did not err at some time, according to that which is said in the common proverb: "Sometimes even good Homer nods off."[22] Let him also take into consideration what Juvenal says: "From the togate plebeians will come one that can solve the knotty points of law, and the enigmas of the statutes."[23]

But passing over these things (so that I may return to our subject) for a clearer illustration of this matter, it will be necessary to consider this threefold process according to the three stages by which judges are accustomed to proceed for the punishment of a heretic. For firstly the heretic is accused and summoned. Secondly, he is convicted of heresy by reliable witnesses. Thirdly, he is condemned, and then punished with those punishments to which he had been condemned.

If before the accused and summoned heretic has been convicted of his crime, he acknowledges his sin after the time of grace, I say with Hostiensis that such man as this ought to be received to mercy with a salutary penance, if the

---

21 *Bucolics*, bk. 3, ln. 108.
22 This proverb is derived from the quote by Horace in *Ars Poetica* (ln. 359; c. 18 B.C.), *indignor quandoque bonus dormitat Homerus* ("I become annoyed when the great Homer is being drowsy").
23 *Satire 8*, lns. 49 f. I. e., the common people, who wore togas at that time more frequently than the aristocracy.

How heretics returning to the faith for the first time ought to be received

judge perceives that he is sorry for his past sin, and has good hope about his amendment. For this sort of person, since he has not actually relapsed, neither has he relapsed by any fiction of law nor could he truly be called incorrigible since he does not defend his error with any pertinacious animosity, there is no reason why he could be condemned to death, or handed over to a secular judge. For the laws command that no one ought to be handed over to a secular judge unless he is incorrigible and has relapsed. Hence, since mercy is not refused by law to this person, it is understood to have been granted. Still, a salutary penance will be imposed upon him, in the imposition of which, so that full justice may be kept, one ought to take into consideration the heresy and the quality of the person, namely, whether the heresy into which he fell is contrary to an article of faith which he was obliged to know explicitly. For (as I recall to have said elsewhere above) not all men are obliged to believe everything with an equal legal obligation. If he was not obliged, according to the quality of his person, to know the teaching of faith that he had opposed, and wherefore it is evident that he erred out of ignorance, then he ought to be taught with moderation and charity about the true faith, which if he immediately accepts, he ought to be received with mercy and without any mark of infamy. Because since he does not defend his error with any pertinacious animosity, it follows that (according to Augustine's opinion in the chapter, *Dixit Apostolus*[24]) he ought not be reckoned a heretic, and ought not to be punished as such. But if some penance is imposed upon him as a precaution [*ad cautelam*], namely, so that he may be henceforth more cautious in speaking, it ought to be light, since there was no or nearly no sin.

But if he erred about those things which he was bound to know, then it ought to be investigated whether he erred

---

24 *Decretum Gratiani*, pt. 2, *causa* 24, q. 3, c. 29 (*Dixit Apostolus*) (PL 187, 1306C-1307A). See its full quotation above in c. 7.

deliberately and knowingly, or out of ignorance. For it is possible that he was negligent in learning those things which he had been obliged to know: and because he was negligent in learning, he erred on some particular point, thinking that what he believes, is believed by the Catholic Church. If it is established that he erred out of ignorance of those things which he was held to know, and when admonished about his error he immediately retracts it, and accepts the true faith without any rebellion, he will be admitted with mercy, and a penance will be imposed upon him, and not a light one: but somewhat heavier than the preceding one: yet he will not be punished as a heretic: but because he was negligent in learning those things, which he had been obliged to know under threat of hell. Still the inquisitor ought to be cautious in this place, so that he can look well into whether he who erred about these things, which he had been obliged to know, erred out of ignorance. Because he who is ignorant of those things which he was bound to know, ought to prove his ignorance, if thereby he procures to be excused. But if it is established that he erred deliberately and knowingly, even though he comes after the accusation, he will be admitted to mercy if he immediately abjured his heresy: yet a penance will be imposed upon him, and a much heavier one than the two preceding ones. Because as Our Savior says: "The servant who knew the will of his lord... and did not according to his will, shall be beaten with many stripes" (Lk. 12, 47).

And what the Archdeacon cites from the annotations on *The Code of Justinian,* [on the title,] *De his qui latrones vel in aliis criminibus reos occultaverint,* does not apply to the matter at hand. But the heretic, who having been summoned when the time of grace had transpired denied his crime, and afterwards when convicted by reliable witnesses admits his crime and asks for mercy, it ought to be given to him, so that he may evade the punishment of death: but he ought to be put into prison in perpetuity. And it is very clearly proved

How heretics returning to the faith for the first time ought to be received

by the chapter, *Excommunicamus*, §. *Si qui autem*.[25] And the chapter, *Ad abolendam*, §. *Praesenti*,[26] does not conflict, where it is said that he ought to be left by the judgment of the secular authority to be punished, who does not immediately return to the Catholic faith after the detection [*deprehensionem*] of the error. For not everyone who was accused of heresy is said to be caught [*deprehensus*] in it, but only he who was legitimately convicted of heresy. For otherwise it would be necessary that everyone who was accused of heresy, and denies his crime, should have been handed over before the legal trial to the secular authority: because that text says that he who after the detection of the error does not hasten back to the unity of the Catholic faith, should be handed over to the secular judge to be punished according to his judgment. Now to say this is most absurd.

And it does not suffice for someone to be said to have been caught in heresy, because he was convicted by witnesses to have taught or firmly asserted some proposition, which is [said to have been] truly heretical: but it is necessary that it also be proved by true proofs that such a proposition is heretical. For although he persists in some heresy (as we taught above in this first book, in chapter ten) before he has been duly admonished about his heresy, he will not be called pertinacious, and consequently not a heretic, if he was prepared to retract the heresy, when the true faith was shown to him. Otherwise, it would be necessary to say that as often as the inquisitor of heretics commands some preacher or teacher to abjure some proposition as heretical, he would be

---

25 "If those caught in heresy should wish to return to the faith, they are to be cast into prison in perpetuity, to do appropriate penance" (*Decretals of Gregory IX*, bk. 5, tit. 7, c. 15 (*Excommunicamus*), §1 (*Si qui autem*)). The decretal has a typographical error, *noluerint ad agendam* which should be *voluerint...*, which has been corrected here. Cf. Mansi 23, 73B.

26 *Decretals of Gregory IX*, bk. 5, tit. 7 (*De haereticis*), c. 9.

obliged to do this. For the inquisitor would say that unless he immediately abjures according to the chapter, *Ad abolendam*, he will immediately hand him over to the secular court. And so he would sometimes force someone to recant and abjure a Catholic proposition. Therefore he ought not to be called caught, unless he has been convicted. Now how and by what proofs a proposition ought to be convicted of heresy, we clearly explained above in chapter four. And certainly (as I think) the Archdeacon was deceived from the false understanding of this word, "caught," supposing that every accused man who comes forward after the time of grace has ended ought to be sent away, and handed over to the secular authority. And the Lord Cardinal [Hostiensis] was also deceived, who thought that everyone who has been convicted, even if he returns [to the faith] before condemnation, ought to be handed over to the secular authority: because (as he says) he did not return at once and immediately. But he is in fact mistaken: because the text in the chapter, *Ad abolendam*, did not say absolutely, "unless they return immediately," but it said, "immediately after the apprehension of the error."

Someone is said to have been apprehended in some crime, when it is known by the evidence of a deed that he has committed such and such a crime, or it has been proved by witnesses, or he has confessed by his own public confession that he did it. Hence it is that if someone convicted of heresy immediately confesses it, and abjures the heresy, it ought to be said that he abjured immediately after the apprehension of the error, and consequently ought not to be handed over to the secular judge, to be punished according to his judgment. Because the chapter, *Ad abolendam*, commands that a heretic who immediately after the apprehension of the error wants to return to the unity of the Catholic faith, may not be handed over to the judgment of the secular authority. And in the chapter, *Excommunicamus*, §. *Si qui autem*, it is commanded that this sort of man, who after he has been

How heretics returning to the faith for the first time ought to be received

apprehended returns, ought to be put into prison in perpetuity: therefore, in order that someone may evade the death penalty, it is not necessary that he admit his crime before he has been convicted: because even if after he has been convicted, that is, caught in error: if nevertheless before he has been condemned by sentence, he admits his error, having been put into prison he may avoid the death penalty. Not only Panormitanus and the other Glossators of the Decretals, who hold the other extreme and very mild opinion, support this position of mine: but also Gonzalo García de Villadiego,[27] in his tract on heresies.[28]

It now remains that the third case be examined, namely, about him who even after he has been convicted, denied, and hence was condemned, so that he would be punished by the judgment of the secular authority, and after this sentence of condemnation, admitted his crime, believing that in this way he would obtain mercy. I very firmly believe that this sort of man nowise ought to be admitted, so that such a pardon would be given to him, which would release him from the judgment of the secular authority. Because such a man as this ought to be presumed to have come forth fictitiously. The text of the aforesaid chapter, *Ad abolendam*, clearly supports this, where it is commanded that the heretic "is to be handed over to the judgment of the secular authorities to receive due punishment, unless immediately after the detection of his error he spontaneously hastens back to the unity of the Catholic faith." But he who comes after the condemnation does not return spontaneously, but having been forced as it were by fear of punishment: and he who, having been convicted, still waited for the sentence, does not return immediately. And in both chapters [both entitled], *Excom-*

---

27 Gonzalo García de Villadiego (1438-1487 or 1488) was a Spanish jurist and religious, bishop of Oviedo who studied at the University of Salamanca.

28 *Tractatus contra haereticam pravitatem.*

municamus, §. *Damnati*,[29] entirely no indulgence is given to the condemned: but it is commanded that the heretic be handed over to the secular authority to be punished with due punishment.

Now what Panormitanus argues by the chapter, *Accusatus*,[30] in which pardon is only denied to the relapsed, has little weight. Firstly, because what he says is in that chapter is not found there. For in that place the Pope declares who ought to be called "relapsed," and who ought to be punished with the punishments of those relapsed into heresy, yet he does not state the punishments by which they ought to be punished. Next, although pardon is denied only to the relapsed in that place, still it is not granted to all the rest, which was most necessary, especially since previously it had been denied to them in many places, as appears through the chapter, *Ad abolendam*, and the chapter, *Excommunicamus*, in the first and the second [chapters with this same name]. Also, the argument which he brings forth, that his opinion ought to be accepted as being more mild according to the rule, *Odia*, and the rule, *In poenis*, avails nothing. Because those rules are understood in a doubtful matter, when it is not evident what ought to be held from the law, in which case the punishments and burdensome things ought to be restricted, but when the laws very clearly assign punishments, then they ought not be restricted. Also, those things which the Gloss cites in support of this opinion are of no importance. For it is sufficiently replied to them in the chapter, *Super eo*.[31] For in that text it is declared that the Church does not close its heart to anyone, such that it would deny to him what she sees to be necessary for his soul: and hence she does deny the Sacraments of Penance and the Eucharist to the condemned and the relapsed, if they show signs of repentance. Yet she often

---

29 *Decretals of Gregory IX*, bk. 5, tit. 7, cc. 13 & 15.
30 *Liber sextus*, bk. 5, tit. 2, c. 8.
31 *Ibid.*, c. 4.

How heretics returning to the faith for the first time ought to be received

closes her heart in those matters which pertain to the health of the body: because when these things are denied they are wont to benefit the salvation of the soul.

Next, the Glossator was deceived in the aforesaid, §. *Si qui autem*,[32] on the word, *Deprehensi*,[33] where he expounds, speaking thus: "Publicly, such that of the notorious, or also of the condemned." I indeed admit that that the condemned ought to be called "caught": but in that section, *Si qui autem*, because in the same chapter, in the section, *Damnati*, the word had been said concerning the latter, those who were "caught" through condemnation. Otherwise, if it were understood concerning all those caught, §. *Si qui autem* will be contrary to the preceding section, §. *Damnati*. Now such contrariety in the context of the same chapter ought not to be imagined; which contrariety is very easily taken away if we notice that there are others besides those condemned, who by the law are called "caught." For they are caught, who were apprehended in the very perpetration of the crime, as for instance: because they were seen to so preach, or teach, and those who were convicted by reliable witnesses, and those who publicly confessed their crime in a judicial court. Thus §. *Si qui autem* is understood concerning these men, and not of the condemned; but §. *Damnati* is understood of the others, who were condemned by the sentence of the ecclesiastical judge. If the Glossator observed carefully the difference of words, he would not have been so mistaken.

There yet remains that we discuss about another kind of heretics, namely, about those who admit their error, but do not wish to abandon it: because they say that it is not an error, but the true faith. But we will dispute about this below in the second book, all of which we will devote to this matter; for we now in this first book dispute about only those heretics

---

32 *Decretals of Gregory IX*, bk. 5, tit. 7, c. 15 (*Excommunicamus*), §1.
33 I. e., "caught."

who after the darkness return to the Light, and after having abandoned their errors, return to the Catholic faith.

Chapter XXIII

Regarding apostates, whether they ought to be received kindly and with mercy when they return to the Church, just as other heretics.

Although it has already been said about every heretic, that if he repents of his sin at a suitable time, he will be received unto mercy: yet some men doubt about apostates, whether they also ought to be measured with the same measure, so that pardon would also granted to them if they return of their own accord to the Catholic faith. Now the cause of this doubt arises from the fact that Civil Law does not give the same kindness and mercy to apostates, as to other heretics. For in the law, *Ii qui*, in *The Code of Justinian*,[1] the emperor commanded that apostates, even if they wish to return to the Catholic faith, are punished with the ultimate punishment: even though it does not say that other heretics would be punished by the penalty of death. To settle this question one ought to call to mind what we said above in the first chapter of this first book, that apostates are included under the name of heretics, and there is no other difference between apostacy and heresy, except that which is between species and genus. For as we taught in that placed from Blessed Thomas, apostacy is a species of unbelief, which is included under heresy, and adds nothing to heresy besides a certain aggravating circumstance, which is the opposition to the whole faith, while other heresies oppose not the whole faith, but only part. But if apostacy is a species of heresy, and not distinct from it in another way, it is a necessary consequence that an "apostate" is also a certain species of "heretic," and having no other difference with "heretic," except such as there is between species and genus.

---

1   Bk. 1, tit. 7 (*de Apostatis*), l. 3.

Book 1, Chapter 23

Thus, this having been premised, I will firstly lay some very firm foundations, relying upon which the judgment of this question may remain constant and firm against all the darts of the adversaries. Here is the first foundation. Regarding the crime of heresy no one can judge another except an ecclesiastical judge alone. This foundation is proved by the chapter, *Ut inquisitioni*,[2] where the Pope explicitly restrains every secular authority, lest it examine in any way about heresy, or judge and try a case, because the crime of heresy is purely an ecclesiastical matter. For no secular judge can decide about any purely ecclesiastical matter, which if someone would attempt to do, his decision would be null and void, as it is explicitly stated in the chapter, *Bene quidem*,[3] and in the chapter, *Ecclesia Sanctae Mariae*.[4] And for the same reason the examination and judgment in a matrimonial lawsuit are completely inhibited to secular judges, and reserved to ecclesiastical judges alone: because Matrimony, in that it is a Sacrament, is reckoned a purely ecclesiastical matter. Furthermore, a secular judge cannot investigate about heresy, nor judge about it, that is, he cannot judge whether this or that assertion is heretical or Catholic: thus he cannot on account of it punish some crime. The conclusion is obvious: because it is unjust that someone could judge a crime, about which he does not know.

Now that a secular judge cannot investigate about the faith or heresy, is clearly proved from these things which we said above in chapter five. And it is further proved, because the secular authority ought to be enlightened by the Church, and it ought to be taught by her, and not vice versa. For (as it is said in the chapter, *Solicitae*[5]) ecclesiastical power is like the

---

2 *Liber sextus*, bk. 5, tit. 2, c. 18.
3 *Decretum Gratiani*, dist. 96, c. 1, §§6-7 (PL 187, 455B-456A).
4 *Liber sextus*, bk. 1, tit. 2 (*De constitutionibus*), c. 10.
5 *Decretals of Gregory IX*, bk. 1, tit. 33 (*De majoritate et obedientia*), c. 6.

sun, but the secular power is like the moon, which receives its light from the sun. Next, in the Old Law[6] not the king, or prince, or duke, or doctor; but only the priest had the right of examining and diagnosing lepers, and he alone judged the lepers, and from his judgment depended whatever the law commanded ought to be done about the leper: therefore it ought to be done in the same way in the New Law, that not the king or prince, or any other secular authority, but the priestly order alone has the power of diagnosing and judging heresy. For the leper (as the holy Doctors interpret) was a very pronounced figure of heresy.

Hence Augustine, when discussing about the ten lepers cleansed by Christ Our Savior, speaks thus: "For none of those to whom He bestowed corporeal benefits, is found to have been sent to the priests, except lepers. For He also said to him whom He had cleansed from leprosy: 'Go, shew thyself to the priest, and offer for thy cleansing according as Moses commanded, for a testimony to them' (Lk. 5, 14)... We ask then, of what leprosy was a figure, whereof they that were ridded were called, not 'healed,' but 'cleansed.' It is a disease which doth first appear in the skin, but destroyeth not immediately the strength, nor the use of feeling and the limbs. We may not absurdly suppose the lepers, therefore, to be figured as such who have not the knowledge of the true faith, but profess diverse-colored teachings of error. They hide not their witlessness, but do use all such wit as they have to make it manifest, and proclaim it in high-sounding phrases. There is no false doctrine but hath some truth mixed up with it. A man's discourse then, with some truths in it unequally mingled with falsehoods, and all confounded in one mass, is like to the body of one that is stricken with

---

6 Cf. Lev. 13, 2: "The man in whose skin or flesh shalt arise a different colour or a blister, or as it were something shining, that is, the stroke of the leprosy, shall be brought to Aaron the priest, or any one of his sons."

leprosy, whereon all manner of foul colors do appear in this and that place along with the true color of skin."[7] In which words it ought to be noted that since he said that among those, whom the Christ had given health of the body, only lepers were sent by Him to the priests, in consequence of this he said that lepers bear the figure of heretics. From which things it is clearly concluded that it will be necessary that just as at that time only priests were examining and judging lepers, so now only the sacerdotal order, that is that ecclesiastical authority, may examine and judge heretics.

Here is the second foundation. When a secular judge punishes heretics, he does this by way of permission and a handing-over made by the ecclesiastical judge, namely, when the ecclesiastical judge has completed all that he could do about the heretic, he leaves him and hands him over to the lay authority, permitting it to do about that man what it sees to be expedient. This is explicitly stated in both of the two chapters, *Excommunicamus*, §. *Damnati*.[8] From these two foundations it is inferred clearly enough that the lay authority cannot punish a heretic in any way, before this is permitted to it by the ecclesiastical authority.

Here is the third foundation. Canon Law never commands in any statute for an apostate from the faith, who spontaneously returns to it, to be handed over to a secular judge to be punished according to his judgment. From which it manifestly follows that the secular authority cannot punish an apostate, who spontaneously returns to the Catholic faith, with death. For an apostate (as we said before) is truly a heretic. But the secular authority cannot punish a heretical man: except when he has been handed over by the ecclesiastical authority. The ecclesiastical authority has not yet handed over apostates, who spontaneously wish to return:

---

7 *Quaestiones Evangeliorum*, bk. 2, c. 40 (PL 35, 1354-1355).
8 *Decretals of Gregory IX*, bk. 5, tit. 7, cc. 13 & 15 (*Excommunicamus*).

thus, the lay authority cannot punish them with death, nay, nor judge about them.

From all which things I conclude that Master Jean Nicolas of Arles erred, who in his tract on heresies,[9] tenaciously holds that an apostate even spontaneously wanting to return, ought not to be admitted to pardon, motivated from that aforesaid law, *Ii qui*.[10] For that law is of no importance: because even if there were no canonical law, which decreed the opposite about apostates, that general canonical prohibition is enough, and more than enough, for its overturning, whereby it is forbidden to secular judges to presume to investigate or judge about heresies in any way. Thus Gonzalo García de Villadiego holds a much better opinion than this [Master Johannes Nicolaus] of Arles, whom he opposes; who in his book on heresies is of the opinion that apostates are to be judged in this regard by the same law whereby heretics are judged.[11] Furthermore (so that I may confirm my opinion more strongly) Canon Law not only did not decree that apostates spontaneously willing to return ought to be handed over to the secular authority, nay, it explicitly commanded the opposite in the chapter, *Contra Christianos*.[12] For in that chapter the Pope commands that those who revert to the rites of the Jews, ought to be punished as heretics.

---

9 *De haereticis aureus tractatus* (Lyon: Vincent de Portonariis, 1536), bk. 2, *notabile* 44, fol. 80. Gonzalo García de Villadiego wrote the first book which is divided into twenty-five questions and Jean Nicolas of Arles added a second book containing fifty *notabilia*.

10 "Assistance is given to those who have fallen and wandered, but no aid will be accorded to those who are lost; that is to say, those who profane the sacred rite of baptism, for they will find no remedy in repentance which usually is beneficial in other crimes" (*The Code of Justinian*, bk. 1, tit. 7 (*de Apostatis*), l. 3, §3).

11 *De haereticis aureus tractatus*, bk. 2 (*Tractatus contra haereticam pravitatem*), q. 20, fols. 48v-49r.

12 *Liber sextus*, bk. 5, tit. 2 (*De haereticis*), c. 13.

But Canon Law (as we said in the immediately preceding chapter) grants pardon to heretics when they spontaneously return to the faith, and receives them to mercy, not handing them over to the secular authority to be punished according to their judgment: thus, it will be necessary to likewise receive apostates just as heretics.

Now that which García de Villadiego cites in his favor, so that he may establish this view, from the text of the chapter, *Quidam* [*sicut accepimus*],[13] little or not at all supports this position. For those about whom Innocent III speaks in that chapter, were not apostates such as about whom we now are speaking. For those men about whom the Pope speaks in that text have not entirely abandoned that Catholic faith, and they are not reprehended by the Supreme Pontiff on this account; but rather because they were observing the rites of the Jews at the same time with the faith of Baptism. For on this account the Pope for their condemnation cited there from Sacred Scripture, cursed is the man "that goeth on the earth in two ways" (Eccli. 2, 14), calling the two ways Christianity and Judaism. True apostates, about whom we now speak, have abandoned the whole Catholic faith, and about these men was the question directed. Hence it is evident that that text cited by García de Villadiego hardly confirms his opinion.

But the chapter which we cited, *Contra Christianos*,[14] very clearly confirms our opinion, so that nothing clearer could be said. For that chapter clearly speaks about those who having left Christianity had reverted to the rites of the Jews, as is evident from the *Casus*[15] of the chapter in the inserted Gloss.

---

13 *Decretals of Gregory IX*, bk. 5, tit. 9, c. 4.
14 *Liber sextus*, bk. 5, tit. 2, c. 13.
15 Élie Régnier, a French jurist (fl. 1483-1494), wrote the *Casus longi Sexti et Clementinarum* which was frequently quoted among the Glosses or marginal notes in *Sextus Liber Decretalium Casus litterales & Notabilia domini Helie regnier complexus*, each time

How repentent apostates ought to be received by the Church

Again, Canon Law decreed absolutely nothing in particular about apostates regarding with what sort of punishment they should be punished: which thing it would not have omitted to do, unless because it wanted them to be included under the category of heretics, and it reckoned that they ought to be punished with the same punishment with which heretics themselves are punished. For it ought not to be thought that the holy Fathers, who decreed very many laws for the punishment of heresy and other crimes, were so remiss about apostacy, which is a very pestilential crime, that they would reckon that it ought not to be punished, or so negligent, that they would not have decreed absolutely anything regarding the remedy and punishment of them. Therefore, since one ought to believe that the Church decreed something about apostates, and this is not found elsewhere than when it decreed about heretics, it should necessarily be acknowledged that apostates ought to be judged by the same laws, with which other heretics are to be judged.

Next, those things which were decreed and ordained about some matter in general, ought to be brought to bear upon every species of that genus, and attributed and applied to every species of that genus: unless there be some species of that genus expressly excepted from that generality. If a law decreed that a thief should restore fourfold those things which he took by theft, there is no doubt that that law ought to be interpreted regarding every thief, for instance a robber, a committer of sacrilege, and other kinds of thieves, such that any of them ought to be punished with that punishment, namely, that he be forced to restore fourfold the things taken: unless the law would determine something about some type of theft elsewhere. For then "The genus is abrogated by the species," as it is said from the Rules of Law.[16] But "heretic" is a sort of genus (as we said above in this chapter), whose

---

following the word, *Casus*, which indicates this source.
16 *Generi per speciem derogatur* (*Liber sextus*, rule 34).

quasi-species is "apostate." Thus it necessarily happens that those things which Canon Law decrees about heretics, also ought to be extended to apostates, and understood [to be] concerning them: unless elsewhere Canon Law determines that something else ought to be done by a special decree. Therefore, since Canon Law has not decreed anything specifically about apostacy, it necessarily behooves that those things which it had decreed about the punishment of heretics, also ought to be understood about apostates. Canon law commands that a heretic who wishes to return to the faith at the suitable time, ought to be received unto pardon: hence the same things necessarily ought to be done about an apostate.

Now those things which Johannes of Arles asserts for the establishment of his opinion are of no weight, and undeserving that they would give us the obligation of a reply: but still it is befitting to reply to them. Firstly, he says that we ought not to allege a disagreement between Canon and Civil Law, unless there is a clear opposition between them: but rather one ought to harmonize those laws. To support this he cites the law, *Praecipumus*,[17] and the first law of *De inofficiosis dotibus*,[18] and the text from the chapter, *Quum expediat*.[19] I reply to this argument by the same text which he himself

---

17 "We order that hereafter there shall be no recourse to Us by appeal from the decisions of judges of distinguished rank, lest the rights of others may seem to be infringed if We are called upon to consider them, and are called away from the occupations which We are pursuing for the general welfare" (*Code of Justinian*, bk. 7, tit. 62 (*De appellationibus et consultationibus*), l. 32).

18 "As all the property of your mother is said to have been exhausted by a dowry, and since it is proper for laws to agree with one another..." (*Ibid.*, bk. 3, tit. 30, l. 1).

19 "Since it is expedient that laws harmonize with laws, and to avoid their corrections, if they are able to be upheld..." (*Liber sextus*, bk. 1, tit. 6 (*De electione et electi potestate*), c. 29).

cites. For there it is said, "It is expedient to harmonize laws with laws, and to avoid their corrections, if the laws themselves can be upheld," where the Gloss on the word, "upheld (*sustineri*)," says: "They are here reprehended, who want to uphold laws, which have been completely corrected: thus, where it is clear regarding the correction, they may not be upheld." Thus Johannes of Arles is himself reprehended in the text which he cites: because he want to uphold the law, *II qui*,[20] even though it is very clearly reduced to nothing by Canon Law, in the chapter, *Ut inquisitioni*,[21] where it is commanded to every secular authority not to examine or judge in any way about the crime of heresy.

Next, he argues thus: nowhere in Pontifical Law is it found explicitly written that penitent apostates ought to be pardoned, such that they may avoid bodily death: thus the decision of the Civil Law ought to be maintained explicitly ordering that apostates ought not to be pardoned. I reply to this argument that he has erred twice in it. For firstly, in fact, he assumes what is false, namely, that it was nowhere explicitly written in Pontifical Law that penitent apostates ought to be pardoned. For (as we already said) in the chapter, *Contra Christianos*,[22] and in the chapter, *Ad abolendam*,[23] and in both chapters, *Excommunicamus*,[24] for even though it orders nothing about it under the name "apostate," still that which is said about heretics suffices, since it is evident from those things which we said above, that an apostate is a heretic. Secondly, that argument is mistaken because even though it were assumed to be true, the conclusion is faulty and weak. Because even though Pontifical Law had decreed nothing about apostasy, it does not follow that one ought

---

20 *The Code of Justinian*, bk. 1, tit. 7 (*de Apostatis*), l. 3, §3.
21 *Liber sextus*, bk. 5, tit. 2 (*De haereticis*), c. 18.
22 *Ibid.*, c. 13.
23 *Decretals of Gregory IX*, bk. 5, tit. 7 (*De haereticis*), c. 9.
24 *Ibid.*, cc. 13 & 15.

to act according to the ruling of Civil Law. Nevertheless, he tries to prove this conclusion by the rule: Where nothing explicitly decided by Civil Law is found, nor is the opposite found in Canon Law, the Civil Law ought to be maintained, even in the ecclesiastical forum. Certainly if this rule is true anywhere, it avails only those matters which can be subject to Civil Law, and about which Civil Law can examine and judge: but in those matters which are completely foreign to Civil Law, and in which Civil Law can decide absolutely nothing, his rule has no shred of truth. For according to this reasoning it would be necessary to assert that everything decreed is valid and firm which Civil Law has decreed about Confirmation, or the revocation of Matrimony in cases in which Canon Law decreed nothing definite, as for instance in the chapter, *Litteras*.[25] In which case the Pope decreed nothing definite. Thus, Civil Law could, according to this rule, decree any of those three positions which the Pope there deems probable, as a separate law. It could also determine a certain form of the Sacrament of Extreme Unction, and if Civil Law has decreed it, it would be necessary to act in conformity to it: even though the Church has never fixed (as Saint Bonaventure says[26]) the certain and precise form of that Sacrament. For in these and similar matters, in which Civil Law cannot decide anything, if it were to decree something, it would be completely worthless, even though nothing had been decided about them by Pontifical Law. Since it is said that the crime of any heresy, and consequently of apostacy, is foreign to the authority Civil Law, it is necessary that whatever Civil Law would decree about it is completely worthless, even if nothing has been decreed about it by Pontifical Law.

---

25 *Ibid.*, bk. 2, tit. 13 (*De restitutione spoliatorum*), c. 13.
26 *Commentaria in quatuor libros sententiarum*, dist. 23, art. 1, q. 4, concl.

Chapter XXIV

If a heretic recants, what ought to be required of him, before he may be received to the communion of the Church?

Although we said above that every heretic, if he recovers his senses at the appropriate time, ought to be admitted by the Church, yet I think that it ought not to be done as soon as he asks for it. For firstly he ought to be tested, whether he truly wishes to hold and embrace the Catholic faith, or to pretend [to do so], and only from fear of punishments. Next, [he ought to be tested] whether he wishes to accept the Catholic faith with an inconstant and short-lived intention, or with a constant and firm intention: it is indeed unfitting that he who with a lukewarm and vacillating mind says that he wishes to return to the Catholic faith, would be received into the communion of the Church, lest (if perhaps he would return to the vomit like a dog[1]) he have the occasion of sinning more gravely. "No man putting his hand to the plough, and looking back," Our Savior says, "is fit for the kingdom of God" (Lk. 9, 62). That very strong and illustrious warrior, Gedeon, when he was girded for war against the enemies, (by the Lord's command) said to his people, and announced to everyone listening: "Whosoever is fearful and timorous, let him return" (Judges 7, 3). I think that it should be done likewise in the Church, which is like "an army set in array" (Cant. 6, 3), and which is in continual readiness for war, so that he who is doubtful in the faith, and is hesitating, is not received in it, but is rejected: especially [him] whose weakness had been fully known from his own departure from the faith to another [belief].

For otherwise, he who would easily receive him to the fellowship of the Church exposes the other faithful, with

---

1 Cf. II Pet. 2, 22.

whom he will intermingle, to the danger of contagion, if he would return to his former error. Hence Blessed Gregory in his Register [of Letters] says: "Whenever the eye of the heart, covered with a cloud of error, becomes serene in the light of enlightenment from above, one ought to take great care lest the author of disunion hiddenly make an assault, and with the weapon of error again cut off from the root of unity those who have returned to it."[2] Therefore, one ought to know that he is constant and firm in the faith, who when returning from heresy, is to be received into the fellowship of the Catholic Church. A leper according to the Old Law,[3] was not received within the camp, or within the city, whence on account of his leprosy he had been cast out, unless his clothes were changed[4] and his hair shaved, even though he was held to be clean by the judgment of the priest. It is clearly enough evident that that leprosy was a figure of heresy, from the testimony of Augustine, which we just cited in the preceding chapter: and hence it is also proved that the leper bore the figure of the heretic. Thus, one ought to use much greater diligence lest we receive the heretic, whose figure the leper bore, as soon as he has been declared clean enter the city, that is, the Church: but firstly he ought to remove his clothes, that is, his outward associations with heretics, and shave all his hair, that is, all his thoughts of heresy, which hang from the heart, just as those [hairs] hang from the head, so too he may appear to us firm and constant in the faith.

But because this constancy of mind and firmness in the faith can only be known through outward signs, so the Church has reckoned that it ought to be proved by two proofs before

---

2 *Decretum Gratiani*, pt. 2, *causa* 1, q. 7, c. 9 (PL 187, 572B-C); PL 87, 1347C.
3 Cf. Lev. 13
4 N.B. The Scriptural passage cited here (cf. v. 6) rather has "wash" instead of "change," as found in some Greek manuscripts and Old Latin versions.

communion with the Church is given to the heretic recovering his senses and returning to the Catholic faith. The first proof is the public abjuration and detestation of the past error in a court of judgment. For he who returns to the Catholic faith from heresy is bound, before he may be received, to publicly abjure and detest the aforesaid heresy before the bishop or inquisitor. This is commanded to be so done in the chapter, *Ad abolendam*, §. *Presenti*.[5] In past times this abjuration and detestation of heresy was done only in a common council of bishops, as appears in the chapter, *De eo*,[6] and in the chapter, *Si quis Episcopus*.[7] But now when either general or provincial councils are assembled with difficulty and rarely, lest in so great delay of time, either he unmindful of this true thought would return to the vomit, or remaining in the true faith having been prevented by death he were to depart [from this life] without the communion of the Church, it was decreed, and rightly so, that this abjuration ought to be done before the bishop and according to his direction.

---

5 "Nonetheless we decree by the present ordinance that whosoever has been caught in manifest heresy... he is to be left to the judgment of the secular authority, to be punished with due punishment, unless after the detection of the error he spontaneously returns to the unity of the Catholic faith, and consents to publicly abjure his error according to the direction of the bishop of the region" (*Decretals of Gregory IX*, bk. 5, tit. 7 (*De haereticis*), c. 9).

6 "But I put off deciding what was to be arranged about the case of the lapsed, so that when quiet and tranquility should be granted, and the divine indulgence should allow the bishops to assemble into one place, then the advice gathered from the comparison of all opinions being communicated and weighed, we might determine what was necessary to be done" (*Decretum Gratiani*, pt. 1, dist. 50, c. 35 (PL 187, 274C-275A)).

7 "If any bishop or deacon, or any cleric shall have been accused before the bishops (because it is not fitting elsewhere)..." (*Ibid.*, pt. 2, *causa* 2, q. 7, c. 50 (PL 187, 660A)).

Next, when inquisitors were given against heretics, this authority and power of receiving heretics was also delegated to them: yet such that they may not do it without the bishop's counsel and assent. But how the formulation of this abjuration ought to be constituted, is had in the chapter, *Ego Berengarius*.[8] Yet about these things it can be doubted whether he who has been caught in some heresy, when he spontaneously wants to return to the Catholic faith, ought to be forced to abjure and detest every heresy: or whether it will be enough to abjure only the one in which he has been caught. The Gloss on the chapter, *Accusatus*, §. *Eum vero*,[9] on the word, *Simpliciter*, holds that he is not obliged to abjure every heresy: but only the one about which he had been accused, and the Gloss says there that its opinion is taken from its text, §. *Eum vero*; because that text speaks conditionally, if he generally abjured every heresy. If, however, he were held to abjure every heresy, the text would not have left it under condition. The Gloss on the aforementioned chapter, *Ego Berengarius*, teaches the same thing, on the words, *Omnem haeresim*,[10] and this Gloss proves this its opinion by the chapter, *Presbyter, si a plebe*.[11]

I indeed willingly accept the opinion of these men in this sense, that a heretic is not bound by any express law when he returns to the Church, to abjure and detest every heresy:

---

8 *Ibid.*, pt. 3 (*De consecratione*), dist. 2, c. 42 (PL 187, 1750A-1751A).
9 *Liber sextus*, bk. 5, tit. 2 (*de hereticis*), c. 8, n. 1.
10 "He does this out of abundance, because he is only held to purge himself from the heresy, about which he was accused; it is proved from *Presbiter si a plebe*, although it is a contrary proof, because he who sins in one thing, is become guilty of all [cf. James 2, 10]; in [*Decretum Gratiani*, pt. 2, *causa* 33, q. 3 (*De penitentia*),] dist. 5, c. 8, and he errs in the whole Trinity, who errs in one Person; [*Ibid.*, pt. 3,] dist. 4, c. 83."
11 *Ibid.*, pt. 2, *causa* 2, q. 5, c. 13.

because (as I think) no such law has yet been decreed which obliges a heretic accused of one heresy to abjure every heresy. But even though this is the case, still nothing prevents that the inquisitors of heretics can for a just reason compel the heretic to abjure and detest not merely that heresy which he had been accused of, but every heresy in general. For according to various circumstances and events a man can be compelled to many things by his superior, to which otherwise he would not be compelled. And certainly (so that I may express my opinion more clearly) I reckon that it always ought to be done in this way, and I think it better, that he be compelled to abjure every heresy. Because this is more in accordance with the public utility, lest an occasion be given to any heretic of falling innumerable times into one and another heresy, when he understands that he can do this without danger of death. For (as from that law, [*Accusatus*,] §. *Eum vero*,[12] it is clearly inferred) he who has not fallen into the same heresy which he had previously abjured, but into another, is not called "relapsed," and will not be punished with the punishment of the relapsed, if he had not previously abjured every heresy: but that only into which he had previously fallen.

Moreover, nearly all heresies are connected to each other, because although they have different faces, still they have tails tied to each other, as it is said in both chapters, *Excommunicamus*.[13] When one thing is inappropriately given (as Aristotle says), many other things follow. From one error

---

12 *Liber sextus*, bk. 5, tit. 2 (*de hereticis*), c. 8, n. 1.

13 "They have different faces indeed but their tails are tied together inasmuch as they are alike in their pride." (*Decretals of Gregory IX*, bk. 5, tit. 7, c. 13); "We excommunicate and put under anathema... the Cathars, Patarenes, the Poor Men of Lyon... and others by whatever name they shall be described, who indeed have different faces, but who are bound together to each other by their tails" (*Ibid.*, c. 15).

admitted, many falsities follow.[14] From one error many others are necessarily derived, as streams from a spring. We have clearly learned this from experience in the case of Luther. For this man began to despise all the indulgences of the [Supreme] Pontiff, and from thence he began the preaching of his errors. Then, not being content with this, he acted like a mad man to the point that he was not afraid to deny Purgatory. Hence, he was forced to deny that any satisfaction is necessary for sins, and he admits only two parts of penance. After all these things, seeing the very strong arguments which were impelling him to abandon his error, he said that nothing is held to remain in the sinner after the remission of guilt, for the absolving of which when the guilt has been remitted. You now see how the heresies are connected and linked together. And for this reason, it is necessary that whoever abjures a particular heresy, would also abjure all those which are derived from it, and which are conjoined to it by an invariable association: because it cannot be easily known immediately, what evil can be drawn out of a particular heresy, it is hence better that he who ought to abjure one heresy, would abjure absolutely every heresy.

Yet if someone would argue against these things by the text of the chapter, *Presbyter, si a plebe*,[15] the argument will be completely useless: because this and that matter are quite dissimilar. For there it is treated about the purgation of sin, in which matter I admit that it is true that no one is bound, nor ought to be forced to admit his guilt except about that sin alone about which he had been convicted. Here however we are now not at all treating about purgation: but about

---

14 "With one unfitting thing given, the others follow" (Aristotle, *Physics*, bk. 1, c. 2 (185a11-12)). Cf. Jacques Lefèvre d'Étaples, *In hoc opere continentur totius philosophiae naturalis paraphrases* (Alcalá de Henares: Johannes Brocarius, 1540), fol. 7v.
15 *Decretum Gratiani*, pt. 2, *causa* 2, q. 5, c. 13 (PL 187, 607B-608A).

the abjuration of heresy, which is a very different matter. For I also likewise admit that no one can be forced to purge himself[16] of a heresy about which he had not been convicted. Then even if the reason why an abjuration and a purgation ought to be done were the same, that text does nothing against us: because other crimes are not so connected and joined together as heresy, and hence in other crimes it is not necessary that he would purge himself of all: but only about the one of which he was convicted.

The second proof of his constancy of mind, and not a simulated but a true return to the faith, is a public promise, confirmed by an oath, of not departing from that faith which he then confesses, but rather of continually persevering in it until death. For he who swears that he will do something, testifies sufficiently that it is his intention, and that he truly, and not insincerely, promised it. For, as Paul says, an oath is the end of every controversy.[17] The form of this promise and oath is found in the chapter, *Quoties*.[18] And (so that no place may be left for suspicion) he will moreover swear that that abjuration and this promise, which he confirmed by oath, he does not make from fear of death, or of any temporal punishment: but only out of hatred and detestation of heresy, and out of love for the Catholic faith. All which things having been rightly carried out, the heretic, who having abandoned his former error wishes to return to the Catholic faith, and asks for mercy at the appropriate time, will be received in the communion of the Church.

Now this rite of abjuration and manner of receiving heretics to the fellowship of the Church, is not recent, neither devised in the last three hundred years, nor a purely human invention, as Luther is wont to say: but more than a thousand years old, and coming down (as it permitted to

---

16 I. e., admit his guilt.
17 Cf. Heb. 6, 16.
18 *Decretum Gratiani*, pt. 2, *causa* 1, q. 7, c. 9 (PL 187, 572B-573C).

suspect) from the very times of the Apostles, and God inspiring it to His Church (as one ought to believe) having been ordained in various councils. The Second Synod of Arles in chapter nine of its decrees, ordered this rule of discipline: "A Novatian must not be received, unless he has shown a spirit of penitence and has condemned his error."[19] The Council of Nicea celebrated under Constantine the Great in chapter eight of its decrees when speaking about the same Novatian heretics, says: "If he wishes to come to the Catholic Church from the Novatians, it has pleased the holy synod, that they be ordained, and in this way may remain in the clergy. But before all things they ought to make a confession, which ought to be demanded to be in writing, that they declare that they will follow the things decreed by the universal consent of the Catholic Church, namely, that they will be in communion with those who perhaps have entered into a second marriage, and with those who have lapsed in time of persecution, yet for whom a manner and period of penance has been fixed, so as in all things to follow those things which are observed in the Catholic Church."[20] Much clearer are those things which are found in the Council of Ephesus celebrated under Theodosius the Younger and Pope Celestine [I], and they state more fully the way which the Catholic Church now keeps in receiving heretics. For in the letter which the aforementioned council sent to the heretic Nestorius, Bishop of Constantinople, these words which follow are found: "Now it does not suffice, even to your revered self, merely to confess the symbol of faith, which was set forth at the same time (the Holy Ghost bestowing) when the venerable and great council in Nicea was assembled: for this you have neither understood nor rightly interpreted, in fact wrongly, although you pronounced the same words with the

---

19 PL 84, 242C; Mansi 7, 879D. The synod was held in 452 A.D.
20 PL 84, 95B; *Decretum Gratiani*, pt. 2, *causa* 1, q. 7, c. 8 (PL 187, 572B); Mansi 2, 688C.

sound of the voice. But it is also fitting that by swearing you would confess that you indeed anathematize your foul and unholy doctrine: and on the contrary you think and teach those things which we, all the bishops and teachers and rulers of the nations throughout the east and west, believe and teach."[21] In which words it is clearly shown the way whereby heretics, who wish to return to the faith, ought to be received, which the Catholic Church now holds. Yet the precise form which the inquisitors of the faith now enjoin upon the heretic returning to his senses after the confession of his heresy, and before the infliction of punishment, is much fuller and copious: for it precludes to the heretic all freedom of erring in the future, in this set of words: "I, N., recognize and confess before Your Excellencies, that I have erred in things said before, and about these things with a contrite and humbled heart I request absolution and penance, and I abjure this heresy and any other known by whatever name: and I promise that for the future I will keep inviolate the faith which the Roman Church holds and proclaims: and that I will persecute with all my strength heretics, and those believing them: and both them and their supporters, harborers and benefactors, in good faith and without deceit, I will disclose to the Church, or to the prelate, without delay: and I will wholly keep and complete the penance which will be enjoined upon me for my fault: and I both want and allow that if from this hour it would happen in the future that I relapse into the same or another error of any heresy known by whatever name, perhaps by erring in some occasion, either by believing or trusting those erring, or by knowingly receiving, or defending them or those believing them, either by supporting by word or deed, or by doing good to them in whatever way, or by hiding them, or by not showing good faith; and I should not complete without delay, or if I shall not keep and perfectly complete the penance enjoined by

---

21 Pseudo-Isidore (PL 130, 294D-295A); Mansi 4, 1087D-1088A.

you, by that very fact I would thence be excommunicated and a perjurer and a manifest heretic: and I judge myself, such that without further thought and judgment may those punishments which by law are appointed to the lapsed and manifest heretics be imposed upon me. Furthermore, I assert and profess that I have said the pure and whole truth about myself and others as far as I know: and if perhaps it could be established that I have maliciously suppressed and was silent about something of the truth, the penance to be imposed or enjoined upon me by you, or the forgiveness obtained or to be obtained would be of no benefit to me." This is the form of abjuration inquisitors of heretics for the most part now enjoin by word or writing upon a heretic returning to his senses at the due time, so that from it and by it he may testify that he is firm in the faith, and that no crack remains in him, by which, if he would afterwards err, he could escape from undergoing the appropriate punishments for his crime.

BOOK TWO

Preface

So hardened is the pertinacity of some heretics, that if someone wished to turn them back from the crooked and distorted errors in which they deviated at some time to the straight path of the faith, he could sooner shatter than straighten them. For there are many heretics who hold so fast to their heresies, that if the definitions of the Catholic Church, or her most ancient customs kept from the Apostles until today, or the concordant opinions of all holy men about some matter, or the clearest testimonies of Sacred Scripture were presented to them, they would remain more obstinate in them, so far from wanting to depart from them. One ought not, nay, nor is it befitting, to punish them with the same clemency of law, in which manner they would have been punished had they wanted to come to their senses (as we said in the first book). An educated doctor certainly does not anoint the eyes of all men with the same eye salve: nor does a surgeon treat all wounds with the same gentleness. For it is necessary that wounds be cut off with iron, that do not respond to the remedy of a poultice. I discussed in the first book of this work only about those heretics, who have not been completely given up, and I showed the mild medicaments for them, by which I hoped their wounded consciences could be healed. Now therefore, so that I may leave the matter completely finished, I thought it would be necessary to discuss in this second book about those heretics, who are afflicted with an incurable sickness, so that I may teach who they are, and with what law they ought to be treated.

Chapter I

Who deservedly ought to be reckoned an incorrigible heretic?

Because I decided to discuss in the second book about him, who maintains a heresy with a very obstinate mind, so that having been rightly judged to be already incorrigible: wherefore, before examining everything, I considered it necessary to say who is incorrigible, so that we may fully know who he is about whom we have taken up the present disputation. Now in order that we may do this better, it will be necessary to say something about correction, because (as Aristotle says) "By means of the straight line we know both itself and the curved."[1] The correction which the incorrigible man rejects means emendation of some error. Now an error can be in the will, and in the intellect. The will errs when it desires that which it should have hated, or hates what it should have loved: or when it loves more that it ought, that which it should have loved; or when it pursues with hate more than is allowed, what it could justly hate. The intellect errs when it judges false things as true, or true things as false, or certain things as uncertain.[2] When someone corrects his error, either it is an error of the will or the intellect that is then said to be corrected. Yet it is unnecessary to discuss now about the correction of the will: but about the correction of the intellect because heresy, about the correction of which we are now treating, as we said in chapter one [in book one] of this work, is an error of the intellect, and not of the will.

Yet something ought to be said about any correction: in the first place it ought to be noted that someone is not said to be incorrigible because he cannot be corrected, but

---

1 *De anima*, bk. 1, c. 5 (411a5).
2 St. Augustine, *Enchiridion*, c. 17 (PL 40, 240).

because he does not want to be corrected. For free will can be turned around, and changeable from this to that, so much so that what it had loved ardently; it may now pursue very impatiently, and that which it had very bitterly hated, it may now love unrestrainedly; that which it now reckons to be true, afterwards judges to be false, and vice versa, by the intellect always yielding to the will in these alternations. And from this it necessarily happens that no one adheres to some opinion so tenaciously that he cannot depart from it: because the will, to which the intellect is subject and is very often ruled at its pleasure, receives new and contrary dispositions to those which it had before. Accordingly, the intellect frequently makes its judgments according to the choice of the will: because it judges those things to be good, towards which it knows the will is disposed, and on the other hand it judges those things to be bad, which it knows that the will hates. Hence it necessarily happens that just as the will is changeable about its affections, so the intellect about its judgments: such that what it previously called good, afterwards it could call bad, and call bad what is good. Otherwise, it would be necessary to say that he who has at some time fallen into an error, could not be justly punished, because he was not revoking his opinion: because no one is actually punished for that which he could not avoid. Thus, much less would it be just that someone be punished by a man, because he does something which was not in his power not to do. But he who has fallen into some heresy, unless he recover his senses, abjuring the pestilential assertion, will be very justly punished by men in this life, and by God in the future life. Therefore, it necessarily happens that man's intellect is often changeable about its judgments, such that he now thinks and could teach things contrary to those which he previously thought. Because even though the intellect is the natural and not free cause in its operations, still in many things it is subject to the command of the will: such that by it commanding it turns now to knowing these things, now to knowing things; now it believes these things, now those things: and it judges them to be good or evil.

From which things it is most evidently gathered that a heretic ought not be called incorrigible because he could not cease to defend the heresy which he previously maintained: but because he does not want to do so when he could: and yet not everyone who does not want to be corrected ought to immediately be called incorrigible, even if he has been admonished one time: because it is not enough to be admonished once, but it is necessary to admonish many times, so that he would deservedly be reckoned incorrigible. Now how many times and by whom ought he be admonished, so that he could deservedly be reckoned incorrigible, that now ought to be discussed. For explaining which matter fully (as it should be done) it is necessary to have a threefold consideration, according to the threefold ends to which the admonition ought to be directed. Firstly, in fact, he who has fallen into heresy is admonished lest he become a heretic. For not everyone who falls into some heresy, by that very fact is made a heretic: because unless pertinacity is present in him, even though he errs he will not be called a heretic, as Augustine teaches; and his opinion is found in the chapter, *Dixit Apostolus*.[3] Thus for this reason he who errs in the faith is firstly admonished so that he would not become a heretic: if he despises that admonition, he will now deservedly be called pertinacious, and consequently a heretic.

Now how and by whom this admonition ought to be done, and how often repeated, I have already at length and clearly enough stated above in book one, chapter ten, and hence this need not be repeated here. After he has now been made a heretic, it is necessary to still admonish him many times, so that he may deservedly be called incorrigible. For not every

---

3 *Decretum Gratiani*, pt. 2, *causa* 24, q. 3, c. 29 (PL 187, 1307A). The quotation is found above in bk. one, c. seven.

heretic ought to be reckoned incorrigible: since it is evident that many of them have been corrected, who nevertheless in the past had been very pertinacious in their heresies. It is one thing to be pertinacious, and another to be incorrigible. How, and for what reason someone ought to be reckoned pertinacious we explained above in book one, chapter nine, but we intend to explain when, and for what reason someone ought to be reckoned incorrigible. Thus, the heretic ought to be admonished, and not lightly, before he be handed over to the secular authority as incorrigible. For Blessed Paul said that a heretic ought not to be avoided before two corrections, lest some heretic be immediately reckoned incorrigible, because having been admonished by them once and perhaps very lightly, he does not want to acquiesce to their admonition. They ought to labor more, so that a few be justly punished, than that many be unjustly punished. They will not glory, even if it were permitted to glory, that they have condemned many for heresy: but because they justly condemned, and pronounced a just sentence against them. For a good judge ought not to care about how many, but how justly he punishes heretics. The matter ought to be carefully examined, and it is necessary to "leave no stone unturned" (as it is said[4]), before it be despaired about the correction of someone. It behooves the inquisitors of heretics to use all diligence regarding the correction of the heretic, before they reckon him incorrigible, and hand him over to the secular authority as such.

Yet I do not want that on this account anyone would suppose that I think that the admonition of the heretic ought to be protracted endlessly, or repeated innumerable times, so that the heretic always ought to be admonished until death, and one always ought to hope for his correction, so that he never ought to be reckoned incorrigible before death, because he can always recover from the heresy before death.

---

4 Euripides, *Children of Heracles*, ln. 1002; Plato, *Laws*, bk. 10 (890d).

Who deservedly ought to be reckoned an incorrigible heretic?

I do not think so: because (as I said) someone ought not to be reckoned incorrigible because he cannot be corrected: but because he does not want to be corrected when duly corrected. Now what sort ought to be deemed due correction, so that if the heretic despises it, he may deservedly be called incorrigible, that ought to be treated by me now. Abbas,[5] commenting upon the chapter, *Cum non ab homine*,[6] relates the opinion of Don Antonius [de Butrio] saying that a triple admonition necessarily ought to precede, so that someone may be called incorrigible.[7] Whose opinion although in other things pertaining to this matter Abbas rejects, yet on this point he willingly embraces it.

But this opinion of theirs, though it is true in other crimes, still it does not have true judgment in the crime of heresy. For Blessed Paul reckons two admonitions to be sufficient, so that a heretic can rightly be reckoned incorrigible, and hence after two admonitions he commands to cease from further warnings. Surely because he did not hope for any correction by the heretic. "A man that is a heretic," he says, "after the first and second admonition, avoid: knowing that he, that is such an one, is subverted, and sinneth, being condemned by his own judgment" (Tit. 3, 10-11). He wanted that two warnings be given, so that by them a test may be made of the correction of the heretic, when they have been carried out, if he neglects to be corrected, he commands to abstain from the warning and discussion with him, and this is what he said:

---

5 I. e., Panormitanus (d. 1445) who was the abbot of the monastery of Maniace, near Messina, whence his name *Abbas*, to which has been added *modernus* or *recentior* (in order to distinguish him from *Abbas antiquus*, a thirteenth-century canonist who died about 1288); he is also known as *Abbas Siculus* on account of his Sicilian origin.

6 *Decretals of Gregory IX*, bk. 2, tit. 1 (*De judiciis*), c. 10.

7 *Commentaria seu lectura in quinque Decretalium libros* (Jacobus de Giuncta, 1527), vol. 3, n. 27, fol. 40r b.

"avoid." Now the reason why he ought to be avoided is his irremediable incorrigibility, and Paul expressed this by the other words speaking thus: "knowing that he, that is such an one, is subverted." He called the incorrigible man "subverted," and about whose correction no hope is rightly had. Now that the above-mentioned words of Paul ought to be understood of an incorrigible heretic, Theophylactus bears witness, who when interpreting those words says: "How then did he say elsewhere, 'if peradventure God may give them repentance' (II Tim. 2, 25)? There he speaks about those who show some hope for their correction: but here he calls the heretic incorrigible, who has been completely subverted, and who has been condemned by himself, that is, who is unable to defend himself. For he cannot say: 'No one corrected me, no one taught me.' Therefore, when after the admonition he has remained in these things, he has condemned himself by his own judgment."[8] Notice that you see according to Paul's opinion, that a heretical man, who contemns the first and second admonition, ought to be reckoned incorrigible, and hence one ought not to correct him again.

Perhaps someone will object to me, saying that Christ Our Savior commanded at least a triple admonition, who commanded that a brother offending against us be admonished three times before he be held as the heathen and publican.[9] It can be easily replied to this that Our Savior is not speaking about a public and juridical correction, but of a secret and fraternal one, which precedes the juridical correction. Now the correction which is given to the heretic, about which we now speak, ought neither to be called secret nor fraternal, but juridical: because it ought to be made by command of the judge, or else made for him, so that he from the twofold admonition can judge whether he is corrigible, or not. And from this it is concluded that the threefold admoni-

---

8 *Expositio in Epistolam ad Titum* (PG 125, 170A).
9 Cf. Mt. 18, 15-17.

Who deservedly ought to be reckoned an incorrigible heretic?

tion need not be given to the heretic: but it is enough that according to Paul's opinion he be admonished twice. And so having been admonished twice, if he does not want to be corrected, he may be reckoned incorrigible. Yet these two admonitions ought not to be given quickly one after the other without an interval: because then it ought to be reckoned not two but rather one admonition.

If someone objects to me the chapter, *Ad abolendam*,[10] where the Pope commands that the heretic who after he has been caught in error, does not immediately abjure his heresy, is handed over to the secular authority to be punished by it, from which it seems to follow that a further admonition is unnecessary: I reply that he who renounces [his errors] after the first or second admonition ought to be said to immediately recant. Since the intervals and periods of time are not punctually prefixed, they ought not to be taken very strictly in a moral matter, as in logic or philosophy. Next, custom (which is the best interpreter of laws) teaches us that those words ought not to be so understood. For the Church was always wont to set some limit in advance to heretics, and yet not brief, within which if they would come to their senses, she will receive them to her bosom as a kind mother. When that time has transpired, she closes the door, just as the Evangelical history relates that the Lord closed the door to the foolish virgins who had come untimely to the celebration of the wedding.[11]

And the beginning of this laudable ecclesiastical custom is not recent: but it is evident that it is very old, since in fact it is known to have been observed a thousand years ago. For long ago when Nestorius concocted a new heresy against the Catholic faith, denying that the Blessed Virgin Mary ought to be called the Mother of God, Pope Celestine, who then governed the universal Church, sent a letter to him: in which

---

10 *Decretals of Gregory IX*, bk. 5, tit. 7 (*De haereticis*), c. 9.
11 Cf. Mt. 25, 1-12.

he rebuked him about the error, and gave him the period of ten days in which he could reflect well within himself. And if within that time he would not want to accept the true and Catholic faith, he knew that he would be deprived of his episcopate and the communion of the faithful. The deacon Liberatus [of Carthage] gives testimony about this matter, who lived during the pontificates of Silverius and Vigilius, in a work which he called the *Brevarium [causae] Nestorianorum, et Eutychianorum*,[12] speaking thus: "But Pope Celestine sent a letter of chiding with an exhortation and blaming, that he should not have erred from his ordination. And the beginning of it is, *Aliquantis diebus vitae nostrae*,[13] giving the period of ten days to him, that is, from the first day of the reception of that letter, until the last day, so that if Nestorius nowise corrects his explanations and turns back to the Church, which on account of Christ, Who is her Head by Whom they had been rejected, he would know that he has been separated from her communion and the communion of all the holy bishops, making known to him that he had given away his place in the council by his letter, the beginning of which is, *Tristitiae nostrae sanctitatis vestrae litterae*, whereby he instructed Cyril that if Nestorius nowise corrects his teaching within those ten days, he determines that he would be removed from the general communion of the bishops, or fellow bishops, and from looking after that church [of Constantinople]."[14]

And the letter from the Council of Ephesus sent to the same Nestorius mentions this postponement granted by Pope Celestine out of mercy, in which after the monitory words these words are added: "Or if thy Piety do not so,

---

12 I. e., *A Short History of the Case of the Nestorians and Eutychians*.
13 I. e., "In the considerable days of our life..." PL 50, 469B-485A; Mansi 4, 1026A ff.
14 PL 68, 977B-C.

according to the postponement set forth in the letters of the aforementioned most holy and pious Bishop and our co-minister of our Roman Church, Celestine, know that thou hast no lot with us, nor place nor communion with God's priests and bishops."[15] Pope Benedict II also kept this same custom after a number of years with the heretic Macarius, Bishop of Antioch,[16] granting to him the period forty days for recovering. Now it is evident that that this was done in this way from the Acts of the [Sixth General] Council,[17] a part of which is related in the chapter, *Convenientibus*, in which among the other words, these are found: "Likewise Peter the delegate of the Pope said: 'The heretic Macarius was exiled to Rome by the holy Synod, and our father, Pope Benedict, gave him a delay of forty days, and he was daily sending his advisor, Boniface, to him, and he was instructing him with admonitory words from Sacred Scripture: but he by no means wanted to be corrected. Now he was doing this so that he might receive him in his Order [of the Episcopacy]."[18] In which words it ought to be especially noticed that after Macarius was already condemned by the Council for heresy, a postponement of forty days was given for him to come to his senses. From which words it is very clearly proved that it is one thing to condemn someone, and something quite different to condemn him as being incorrigible. Therefore, not everyone who is a heretic will be deemed incorrigible, unless after it has been established that he is a heretic, he shall in addition be sufficiently admonished. Next the Council of Constance decreed to observe this same thing with Jerome of

---

15 PG 77, 107B; PL 130, 294C; Mansi 4, 1087C.
16 Macarius I of Antioch was the patriarch of Antioch and he was deposed in 681 A.D. for professing Monothelitism.
17 I. e., III Council of Constantinople.
18 *Decretum Gratiani*, pt. 2, *causa* 1, q. 7, c. 4, §9 (PL 187, 569A). Cf. PL 129, 227B.

Prague,[19] whom (as it is evident from the twenty-first session of the same Council) having been detained for many days in prison the Council waited, so that led by repentance for his former error, he might recover from the snares of the devil, by which he was being held captive.

Thus after some time, even if short, has been given to the heretic, the inquisitors and judges of heretics ought to use within that time all the diligence can so that the heretic may depart from his error. At one time they may gently admonish him, at another time they may send learned and pious men to him, who may teach him how much he has departed from the Catholic faith, by testimonies of Sacred Scripture, or by the decision of the Church, or they may refute him by the other ways, as we taught above, by which heresies ought to be subdued. They ought to show that this is, and always was, the opinion of the Church by testimonies of the holy Doctors. If the heretic shall have been so hardened in his error, that within the prefixed time after having been sufficiently admonished he does not want to abandon the heresy, then he could rightly be reckoned incorrigible, and punished as such. And if after the time set for him has elapsed, and after having used all due admonition in that time, being repentant he shall truly recover from the error, his soul will be saved: yet he will be punished as incorrigible, and will not be received unto pardon and forgiveness, such that by that conversion and repentance, he would avoid the punishment of death, especially if he has already been condemned by sentence. For otherwise if before the condemnation, although after the set time has ended, he were to recover (as we taught above in the first book[20]) he would be put into prison in perpetuity, as it is commanded to be done in the chapter, *Excommu-*

---

19 Jerome of Prague (1379-1416) was a chief follower of Jan Hus and was burned for heresy at the Council of Constance.
20 Cf. c. 22 above.

Who deservedly ought to be reckoned an incorrigible heretic?

nicamus, §. *Si qui autem*.[21] But if he would want to return after the condemnation, he will not be received at that time. Because even if he then repents, still he would seem to do it not from love of the truth, but from aversion to the punishment.

And such suspicion ought not to be judged to be far afield from Christian piety: nay, rather on the contrary it is very similar to the Divine will. For God judges sinners in the same way, who if they [do not] wish to repent during the time given to them for repentance, when the time of the present life has finished, even if they would ask with tears and groans, still they will never obtain it. For the damned in hell (as the book of Wisdom testifies[22]) grieve that they acted wickedly, and repent on account of the sins which they committed in this world, which nevertheless nowise benefits them towards salvation. Because not from a love of virtue and justice, but from aversion to the punishment which they undergo, they grieve that they have sinned. Even if it be granted that they repent of their evil deeds from love of justice, such repentance will obtain nothing from God, due to this alone: because it was done outside of the time given by God for repentance and pardon. "The night cometh," Our Savior says, "when no man can work" (Jn. 9, 4). In which passage according to the interpretation of Augustine,[23] Our Savior called the time after this life "the night when no man can work," that is, merit either for life or for never-ending death. But why can they not merit? Do they not have the full liberty of will? They have it indeed. What therefore impedes that they cannot merit glory or punishment? Certainly, as it is the opinion of Doctors of not little authority, only the

---

21 *Decretals of Gregory IX*, bk. 5, tit. 7 (*De haereticis*), c. 15, §1.
22 Cf. c. 5.
23 "Let man, then, work while he lives, that he may not be overtaken by that night when no man can work" (*Tractates on the Gospel of John*, tract 44, n. 6 (PL 35, 1716).

state impedes, namely, because they are in that state in which God has decreed that they cannot merit either any glory or punishment, no matter how well or badly they act. The Church imitates this when she fixes a time for repentance, within which if they withdraw from the heresy, she receives them and grants them pardon.

Now the time granted by the Church for avoiding the punishment of death, as we said in book one,[24] is the whole time before the sentence has been pronounced: because if they return in that whole time, even if after they shall have been convicted by witnesses, they may evade the punishment of death. But when this time has elapsed, even if they were to say that they repent, she does not receive them unto pardon: because she presumes they repent from aversion to the punishment and not from love of justice: and hence she deems them incorrigible, and hands them over to the secular authority so that they may be punished based upon that due investigation. Similarly, a heretic is called incorrigible who has defended a heresy which he knew has been condemned by the Church, and perseveres in it until death: because the definition of the Church, which he knew well, was for him equivalent to a double or triple admonition. Thus since he did not wish to listen to the Church's admonition: but having despised it persevered in heresy until death, he is rightly judged to be incorrigible, and will be punished with the same punishments if after death it is established about his heresy, with which a living man, and remaining incorrigible, is punished, as it is stated in the chapter, *Accusatus*, §. *In eo*.[25]

---

24 Cf. c. 22 above.
25 "But in the case in which the heirs of an inheritance ought not to be admitted on account of the heresy of its author, notwithstanding that when the author himself was alive this was not the case, when his death intervened, by the sentence pronounced, one ought to proceed to the confiscation of the goods after the death of the same" (*Liber sextus decretalium*, bk. 5, tit. 2 (*De haereticis*),

Who deservedly ought to be reckoned an incorrigible heretic?

Likewise, for the same reason he is also reckoned an incorrigible heretic, who, when accused of heresy, denied his fault the whole time which had been given to him for pardon, if he had confessed. But when he sees that he has been convicted by witnesses, the time given for pardon having elapsed, he admits his crime, and says that he repents. Such a man as this ought to be considered incorrigible: because even though he says that he repents, he ought not to be believed that he says this from a zeal for the faith and hatred of heresy: but rather from the fear of punishment, which he greatly abhors. But even if such a man is rightly reckoned incorrigible, still the Church has decreed to treat him more mildly than if he had remained pertinacious in heresy until the end. For this man, who after he has been convicted by witnesses, returns to his senses before the pronouncement of the sentence, and wants to return to the communion of the Church, the Church commands to cast into prison in perpetuity to do suitable penance: as it is stated in the penultimate chapter of *De haereticis*, §. *Si qui autem*.[26]

And yet not because someone is already condemned as incorrigible ought the inquisitors of heretics to cease from admonishing him: but they ought to use further diligence to recall him from error to the true faith, and in this way they may save his soul from the fires of hell, if they can: even though they cannot now deliver his body from death. And this is now the third end for which the last admonition is directed. Many remedies ought to be tried, so that they may at least deliver his soul from the devil. If Pope Benedict was daily admonishing the heretic Macarius for the period of forty days (as it was said above), so that he might receive

---

c. 8, §7).

26 "Now if any of the aforesaid, after being seized, do not wish to do appropriate penance, they shall be imprisoned for life, but we similarly judge believers of their errors to be heretics" (*Decretals of Gregory IX*, bk. 5, tit. 7, c. 15 (*Excommunicamus*), §1).

him in his Order of the Episcopacy, it ought to be done much more earnestly and importunately so that his soul having been delivered from the devil's power, Christ may receive him among the choirs of the Angels. Let the inquisitors often admonish him, and if they themselves do not succeed in their exhortations, then let them use other learned, and truly pious, and respected men, who may admonish him. And although these men do not prevail at all against the heretic, still they ought not to disdain to use other men: because everyone cannot do everything.

In fact, many were converted to the Catholic faith in consequence of Paul's words, who perhaps would not have been converted by the words of Peter and of the other Apostles. Many also did penance upon the preaching of Peter, and were baptized, who perhaps would nowise have done penance by the preaching of the other Apostles. For God has not decreed to draw all men to Himself by the same minister of the word: but certain men through Peter, others through John, others through Bernard, others through Francis, and others through Dominic. "There are diversities of graces," Paul says, "but the same Spirit; and there are diversities of ministries, but the same Lord; and there are diversities of operations, but the same God, who worketh all in all" (I Cor. 12, 4-6). And after Paul lists the various kinds of graces, he immediately adds: "But all these things one and the same Spirit worketh, dividing to every one according as he will" (v. 11). If God divides His particular gifts according as He wills, then he does not bestow them all upon everyone: therefore, it is not surprising if He gave grace to Peter, so that he can convert Francis, and did not give this to John.

Next, if the heretical man contemns to recant his opinion through learned men, procure to offer him some pious man illustrious for holiness of life, even if he be uneducated. Because it is possible that the speaking of a holy, simple, and uneducated man is more powerful for confounding the heretic, than a thousand arguments of learned men. "The foolish things of the world hath God chosen," as Paul says, "that he may confound the wise" (*Ibid.* 1, 27). So that God would cast down Pharoah's pride, and break his hardness, He did not choose great and savage beasts, but very small living things, namely, flies, sciniphs, and locusts.[27] God also often wants the words of some simple and uneducated man to be more powerful than the syllogisms and logical arguments of all learned men, so that our faith may not seem to be "on the wisdom of men," as Paul says, "but on the power of God" (*Ibid.* 2, 5).

A very clear and most appropriate example to support this is that which is told in the *History of the Church*. And so that great trust to my words may be had, I decided to insert here the words which the same *History* relates: for when reporting what things occurred in the Council of Nicea, it speaks thus: "Now we may learn how much power there is in simplicity of faith from what is reported to have happened there. For when the zeal of the religious emperor had brought together the priests of God from all over the earth, rumor of the event gathered as well philosophers and dialecticians of great renown and fame. One of them who was celebrated for his ability in dialectic used to hold ardent debates each day with our bishops, men likewise by no means unskilled in the art of disputation, and there resulted a magnificent display for the learned and educated men who gathered to listen. Nor could the philosopher be cornered or trapped in any way by anyone, for he met the questions proposed with such rhetorical skill that whenever he seemed most firmly trapped, he escaped like a slippery snake. But that God might show that the kingdom of God is based upon power rather than speech, one of the confessors, a man of the simplest character who knew only Christ Jesus and Him crucified,[28] was present with the other

---

27 Cf. Ex. 8 & 10.
28 Cf. I Cor. 2, 2.

bishops in attendance. When he saw the philosopher insulting our people and proudly displaying his skill in dialectic, he asked everyone for a chance to exchange a few words with the philosopher. But our people, who knew only the man's simplicity and lack of skill in speech, feared that they might be put to shame in case his holy simplicity became a source of laughter to the clever. But the elder insisted, and he began his discourse in this way: 'In the name of Jesus Christ, O philosopher,' he said, 'listen to the truth. There is one God Who made heaven and earth, Who gave breath to man whom He had formed from the mud of the earth, and who created everything, what is seen and what is not seen, with the power of His Word, and established it with the sanctification of His Spirit. This Word and Wisdom, whom we call "Son," took pity on the errors of humankind, was born of a virgin, by suffering death freed us from everlasting death, and by His Resurrection conferred on us eternal life. Him we await as the Judge to come of all we do. Do you believe that this is so, O philosopher?' But he, as though he had nothing whatever that he could say in opposition to this, so astonished was he at the power of what had been said, could only reply to it all that he thought that it was so, and that what had been said was the only truth. Then the elder said, 'If you believe that this is so, arise, follow me to the church, and receive the seal of this faith.' The philosopher, turning to his disciples and to those who had gathered to listen, said, 'Listen, O learned men: so long as it was words with which I had to deal, I set words against words and what was said I refuted with my rhetoric. But when power rather than words came out of the mouth of the speaker, words could not withstand power, nor could man oppose God. And therefore if any one of you was able to feel in what was said what I felt, let him believe in Christ and follow this old man in whom God has spoken.'

Who deservedly ought to be reckoned an incorrigible heretic?

And thus the philosopher became a Christian and rejoiced at last to have been vanquished."[29]

From which words it is very clearly established that Christian simplicity is more powerful for breaking the hardness of heretics, than a thousand clever uses of words of learned men. Hence it is that it is not enough for the inquisitors of heretics, if for the conversion of some heretic, they make use of one or two learned men: but it is befitting that they use for him many and more learned men whom they know, and this is not enough so that they would consummately carry out their office: but it is necessary that they offer him men excelling in holiness, even though uneducated, if they know them. Because (as we said) it could happen that God through the merits of a holy and simple man would convert the heretic, whom learned men could not cover by their arguments. Yet I decided to point this out to the reader, lest he suppose that I think that a very exact and very lengthy admonition is so needed before the condemnation of the heretic, that (unless it has preceded) the heretic could not be rightly condemned, and handed over to the secular authority. For (as I recall that I have often said) if he has been once and again duly admonished, and he does not obey that warning, it suffices so that he can be condemned by the inquisitors, and handed over to the secular authorities, as is evident from the chapter, *Ad abolendam*.[30] But I say that this very lengthy and very exact admonition is necessary so that at least the heretic's soul may be saved, if he returns to his senses: when his body has been condemned to death.

Perhaps the inquisitors of heretics will expostulate me, that I want to impose upon them something difficult and full of hardships. To whom I respond: much greater and much

---

29 Rufinus, *History of the Church*, bk. 10, c. 3 (PL 21, 469B-470B) (translated by Philip R. Amidon, S. J., *The Church History of Rufinus of Aquileia: Books 10 and 11* (Oxford, 1997)).

30 *Decretals of Gregory IX*, bk. 5, tit. 7 (*De haereticis*), c. 9.

more grievous is the hardship, which the heretic on account of the heresy, and those on account of an office negligently administered, will undergo in hell. Many things ought to be endured so that the shepherd and leader may deliver even one soul from the jaws of hell. The Son of God, to free us from the power of the devil, assumed our flesh with nearly all its miseries, and deigned to suffer death in it. Thus is it not equitable that the inquisitors and bishops, upon whom this matter is imposed as a duty, would refuse the aforesaid labors of admonitions for recovering the soul of the heretic, whom which Christ the Son of God did not refuse to undergo death.

Chapter II

That the relapsed heretic is rightly reckoned incorrigible, and who ought to be called "relapsed."

Because the Church punishes heretics who are called "relapsed" as incorrigible heretics, wherefore I thought that it will be necessary to examine here who should be called "relapsed." It can happen in two ways that someone is called "relapsed." For a certain man has clearly relapsed. A second, however, has relapsed not clearly and manifestly; but he is reckoned to be relapsed on account of a presumption of the law, which is of such kind and so great, that against it no investigation may be admitted. Now so that someone may be called "manifestly relapsed," two things are necessary. The first is that someone has fallen at one time into a heresy, and having been accused of it and condemned on account of it, and after that condemnation, he abjured the heresy in court. The second is that after the abjuration of this kind, he falls again into heresy. Which two things, if they apply to someone, then he will be called, and will be "manifestly relapsed." If either of these are absent, although he could be perhaps called "relapsed": but not "clearly and manifestly relapsed."

There are still others (as we said) who even though they have not manifestly relapsed, and have not been clearly convicted of that same relapse, yet by a presumption of the law they are reckoned to be relapsed. Now this can happen in two ways. For he who gave such great suspicion of heresy that he required canonical purgation, although he was not convicted of the crime, if after having abjured the heresy again falls into heresy, this man by the presumption of the law is reckoned relapsed, as appears in the chapter, *Accusa-*

tus, §. *Eum vero*.[1] For Canon Law represents him as having fallen, who gave very strong suspicion of heresy, so that if afterwards he were to relapse, he rightly would be called "relapsed." Now these things ought to be understood about a man strongly suspected: because he who gave small and light suspicion of heresy, although afterwards he falls into heresy, will not be called "relapsed." Still he will be punished more severely than if without any preceding suspicion, he would then fall into heresy for the first time. These things are found in the aforementioned chapter, *Accusatus*. And it does not matter whether he falls into the same heresy or into another: because he who has simply abjured heresy, that is, not expressing this or that one, but heresy absolutely, or he who abjured heresy generally, that is, every heresy, if afterwards he shall fall into heresy (although not the same one), is rightly judged to be relapsed, as it is expressly stated in the same chapter, *Accusatus*, §. *Eum vero*.

Yet a not a small difficulty arises here about him who abjured limitedly and restrictedly, such that he only abjured about that heresy which he was accused of, or had been greatly suspected of: if afterwards he would fall not into the same, but into another heresy, whether he ought to be called "relapsed." The Glossator on that same §. *Eum vero*, on the word, *Simpliciter*, says that he thinks that such a man ought not to be called "relapsed." I also both subscribe to his opinion, and follow it with might and main, as it is said: because if the Pope would have wanted that such a man as this to be deemed relapsed, he would not have spoken with that specification and restriction: but he would have said that he, who at one time abjured heresy in any way, if he were to afterwards fall into heresy, ought to be called "relapsed." But since he says that he ought to be called "relapsed" who abjured heresy simply, or generally, and afterwards falls into the same or another heresy, by that very fact he seemed by

---

1 *Liber sextus decretalium*, bk. 5, tit. 2 (*De haereticis*), c. 8, §1.

the word "relapsed" to exclude him who after he abjured one single heresy, fell into another. But inquisitors of heresies actually free themselves from this difficulty in another way, because they compel a heretic caught one time, to abjure not merely that heresy about which he has been accused of, or greatly suspected of, but rather every heresy. Now whether this is done justly, we discussed above in the first chapter of this book.

Someone is said by a legal fiction to have fallen in another way, namely, when after having abjured a heresy he receives, brings, visits, or associates with heretics; or gives or sends gifts or presents to heretics; or grants a favor to them: which man cannot be excused. For in this case the law presumes that he, who at another time had fallen into heresy, does some one of these things which we have just said, because he again approves of the previous heresy which he abjured. But these things ought to be understood of him, about whose prior fall it was at some time established: either this fall was established before or after the abjuration. For the text in that same chapter, *Accusatus*, §. *Ille quoque*,[2] speaks only about that man. But about those things said in that section, two doubts arise to me, which have not a small difficulty. The first is whether he, who on account of great suspicion of heresy, abjured every heresy, if after that abjuration receives heretics, or sends gifts, or does any one of those things which are listed in that section, ought to be called "relapsed." And perhaps it will seem to someone, that he should: because after the general abjuration of heresy, he again falls into great suspicion of heresy by receiving heretics, or by giving or sending them gifts. But I, moved by two reasons, think that the contrary ought to be said.

The first is that there is no text wherein that statement can be proved, nay, if it is permitted here to act by conjectures from the text of that section, it would rather be allowed to

---

2 *Liber sextus decretalium*, bk. 5, tit. 2 (*De haereticis*), c. 8, §2.

conjecture such a man as this, about whom we now dispute, ought not to be called "relapsed": because if the Pope had judged him to be called "relapsed," he would not have added those words, by which he clearly exempts him from that general rule: but he would have spoken in general terms: but when saying, "About whose fall into heresy before the abjuration it had been established, or is now established," he states clearly enough that he whose fall is never established, ought not to be called "relapsed." The second reason is that that everyone who is judged according to the laws "relapsed," must have clearly and manifestly fallen into heresy at least once, and must have been convicted of it. And so on account of one clear fall and another from a fiction, or presumption of the law, he will rightly be judged "relapsed": as appears in the two cases, about which *Accusatus* speaks [in] §. *Eum vero* and also §. *Ille quoque*. Now where there was only suspicion, even if it gave strong suspicion of heresy once and again, in my opinion he will not be called "relapsed": because the suspicion, which does not arise from the law and a legal right, that is, which laws do not approve and confirm, will never be sufficient, so that someone could rightly be condemned by it. Thus, since there is no law which commands him to be suspected, who abjured on account of the suspicion of heresy alone, if afterwards he receives heretics, or gives them gifts, and he did this in support of the heresy, it is established that he ought not to be reckoned relapsed on account of this: but a canonical purgation ought to be enjoined upon him, and in my opinion he ought to be judged more severely on account of the second suspicion which he gave, than he was punished when he gave the first.

The second doubt, and in my opinion certainly much more difficult, is about him whose fall into heresy, either before the abjuration or afterwards, was manifest and notorious, and who afterwards receives heretics, or gave them gifts: but such heretics, to whom he gave gifts, were not suspected of the heresy, into which this man who gives the gifts fell, nay, it is evident that such heretics are very far from that heresy, whether he who gave gifts to heretics of this kind, after he abjured the heresy, ought to be called "relapsed" by the text of §. *Ille quoque*. And it seems not: because when something is sanctioned by law, on account of some reasoning stated in the law itself, which moves the legislator so that he would decree in this way, if such a thing occurs, to which the reason for the law could nowise be applied: it ought to be believed that such a thing as that is not encompassed by the law. Because a law (as Panormitanus says on the last chapter of *De rescriptis*[3]) is nothing other than the reason for the law itself.[4] Now the reason which that text asserts, so that he who after an abjuration of heresy received or visited heretics, or gave or sent gifts to them, ought to be called "relapsed," is that (as it says) "by following an error previously accepted there is no doubt that he did it." This reasoning, since it proceeds from a mere suspicion or presumption, and from the evidence of a fact, seems to have force only about him alone who after having abjured a heresy has communicated with a heretic fostering the same heresy, into which it is established that he has fallen, or at least he has communicated with a heretic fostering another heresy, which has a very close connection with it, into which he had previously fallen. For then from such a communication with the heretic he rightly ought to be presumed to have returned to the same heresy which he had previously abjured: because he receives that heretic by defending him, visits or gives or sends gifts to him. Nevertheless, if he who abjured the heresy communicates with the heretic about whom it is established that he maintains some very different heresy, and not the same one which the other man abjured: I do not see how from an

---

3   *Decretals of Gregory IX*, bk. 1, tit. 3 (*De rescriptis*), c. 43.

4   Cf. *Commentaria super prima parte primi Decretalium* (Turin: apud haeredes Nicolai Beuilaquae, 1577), fol. 90v a.

association of this kind it is permitted to be suspected that he returned to the same heresy: since it is evident that such a man as he, with whom he conversed, clearly contradicts that heresy, about which this man was formerly convicted.

Perhaps here someone will respond to me that although he ought not to be suspected from this association that he returned to the same heresy which he had previously held, and afterwards abjured, yet it correctly ought to be presumed that he fell into another heresy, and this is enough so that he may deservedly be called "relapsed." Nevertheless, against this response the text itself seems to argue: because the reason why the text says that he who after the abjuration of heresy communicated with heretics ought to be called "relapsed" is because it is presumed that he returned to the aforesaid error. From which words it ought to be inferred that he who did not give suspicion that he returned to his former error, ought not to be called "relapsed." Nor does that which is said in §. *Eum vero* make any difference, namely, that he who abjured heresy in general, if afterwards he falls into it or another heresy, ought to be called "relapsed": but that text does not speak about him who from a legal fiction or by a presumption is called "relapsed": but about him who clearly and manifestly, and without any fiction, has relapsed. And certainly, he who has been once convicted of heresy, if after a general abjuration of heresy, shall have fallen into that heresy or another one, will be called "relapsed." He who has not been twice convicted of heresy, but is called "relapsed" from a legal fiction, in order that the legal fiction against him be valid, it is necessary that he fall into the same heresy, about which he had previously given a strong suspicion. For the text expressly so teaches about this in the chapter, *Accusatus*, §. *Eum vero*.

And so that my opinion may appear clearer, I decided to quote the words of the text. "A person accused or suspected of heresy," it says, "against whom a great and very strong suspicion has arisen, if he abjured the heresy in a court of law, and afterwards offends in the same [heresy], ought to be reckoned to have relapsed by a certain legal fiction."[5] In which words it ought to be noted that which is said, "and afterwards offends in the same [heresy]." From which words it is clearly enough gathered that he who after the abjuration offends in some other heresy, and not in that one concerning which he had previously given suspicion, ought not to be called "relapsed." And I reckon that the words which are had in §. *Ille quoque*[6] ought to be understood according to this manner. For as in the case which is set forth in §. *Eum vero*, very strong suspicion precedes, and afterwards the open commission follows: so on the contrary in the case about which §. *Ille quoque* speaks the open commission precedes, and afterwards the very strong suspicion. Thus as in the first case, so that someone may be called "relapsed," it is necessary that he offend in that heresy, about which he had been previously strongly suspected: so also in the second case, so that he may be called "relapsed," it will be necessary that he be very strongly suspected about the same heresy, about which he had previously been clearly convicted.

And certainly, reason itself persuades that it be done in this way, because it is not fair that he who was twice clearly convicted of heresy, and he who was only one time convicted and a second time greatly suspected of heresy, be of completely equal condition in the court of law. For by this in my opinion they are distinguished, because he who was twice clearly convicted of heresy, whether he falls back into the same heresy or into another, will be called "relapsed," especially if after he was firstly convicted of heresy, he abjured every heresy. But he who was only once convicted of heresy, and at another time greatly suspected, whether the open commission precedes, and afterwards the very great

---

5 *Liber sextus decretalium*, bk. 5, tit. 2, c. 8.
6 *Ibid.*, §2.

suspicion, or vice versa, he will not be called "relapsed": unless he were to return to the same heresy, about which he had been firstly convicted, or greatly suspected. And I certainly think that it ought to be so said: unless some decision of the Church is made, which clearly opposes this opinion of mine. For if by a decree of the Church which openly contradicts this opinion of mine, whenever it shall have been made, I ask that this opinion of mine be considered recanted. Because I esteem the decision of the Church to such an extent that I would not want to deviate even a hair's breadth from her in any matter.

Someone can in yet another way be called "relapsed," on account of vehement suspicion, for instance, if firstly having been convicted of heresy he had abjured every heresy, and was put into prison for life, as it is commanded to be done in the chapter, *Excommunicamus*, §. *Si qui autem*,[7] and afterwards escaped from the prison. He certainly will be rightly called "relapsed" because he was convicted of his first fall, and he gave vehement suspicion by the mere fact that he escaped from the prison. For due to this alone we can rightly suspect that he did not truly repent, because he despised to fulfill the penance enjoined, and hence it happens that we may rightly suspect that he returned to his original error. And Abbas favors this opinion, who in the chapter, *Cum non ab homine*,[8] when discussing who ought to be called incorrigible, among others whom in that same place he lists under this name, also adds him who neglects to perform the penance imposed. And he specifically speaks about him who escaped from the prison in which he had been imprisoned on account of a crime, especially if when summoned by a judge he does not want to appear. And Abbas proves his opinion

---

7 *Decretals of Gregory IX*, bk. 5, tit. 7 (*De haereticis*), c. 15, §1.
8 *Ibid.*, bk. 2, tit. 1 (*De judiciis*), c. 10.

by the chapter, *Ut fame*,⁹ and the chapter, *Litteras*,¹⁰ and the chapter, *Accedens*,¹¹ and the chapter, *Testimonium*.¹² "For he is said to be corrected," as Abbot says, "who did penance for his sin."¹³

But there is not a small difficulty about him who has already abjured every heresy, either because he had truly fallen into heresy, or because he had given vehement suspicion of heresy, if such a man as this after that abjuration again falls into heresy: but afterwards acknowledging the error, of his own accord, and without any accusation comes to the inquisitors, and humbly confesses his sin before them, and asks pardon, whether such a man as this ought to be considered "relapsed," and consequently "incorrigible," and ought to be punished as such. And that he ought to be called "relapsed" could be proved by this: because he has twice fallen into heresy. Yet I reckon that he ought not to be called "relapsed," if it is true that he comes of his own accord, and from a true knowledge of the sin. For no one can be judged to be "relapsed," unless he has been twice convicted of heresy, or at least convicted once of a fall and a second time convicted of vehement suspicion. But this man who comes of his own accord, ought not be said to have been convicted a second time, therefore cannot be called "relapsed," and consequently cannot be called "incorrigible." Hence, it is that he necessarily ought to be received for pardon. Nevertheless, it is necessary that the inquisitor diligently investigate whether he actually came of his own accord, and confessed his sin. For if from fear of the trials which perhaps he had known were against him, it was established that he came, then he

---

9   *Ibid.*, bk. 5, tit. 39 (*De sententia excommunicationis*), c. 35.
10 *Ibid.*, bk. 2, tit. 23 (*De praesumptione*), c. 14.
11 *Decretum Gratiani*, pt. 1, dist. 50, c. 10 (PL 187, 258B-C).
12 *Decretals of Gregory IX*, bk. 2, tit. 20 (*De testibus*), c. 54.
13 *Abbatis Panormitani Prima interpretationum in secundum decretalium librum* (Leiden: Senetonii fratres, 1547), fol. 35.

will rightly be called "relapsed": because he admitted his sin not from zeal for the faith, but from fear of the punishment, and it deservedly ought to be believed that he does not truly repent.

After having already explained who ought to be called "relapsed," it is now necessary that we show that he rightly ought to be called "incorrigible," and should be punished as such. In this matter I see that there is no need for many words, since there is a clear decision of the Church to this effect about this matter. For Pope Lucius III speaks thus: "But those who after having abjured their errors, or cleared themselves upon examination, (as we said), to their Bishop, shall be found to have relapsed into their abjured heresy; we decree, that without any further hearing they be forthwith delivered up to the secular power."[14] But many heretics mock and deride this decision of the Church, and gainsay with some reasons that it is contrary to Christian piety: but all of their reasons, by which they strive to plead this we will demonstrate (with God as my guide) to be completely worthless and (so that I may speak more clearly) irrational. They firstly object to us the mercy of God, Who is always prepared to the sinner relapsing even a thousand times into sin, if he recovers his senses each time and does true penance. Thus it would behoove the Church (as they say), which is His spouse, to act in imitation of her Spouse, such that as many times a heretic comes to his senses, and gives signs of true repentance, she would receive him, and give pardon to him.

To this objection Pope Alexander IV responds in the chapter, *Super eo*,[15] whose words I decided to explain at somewhat greater length because they are obscured on account of their excessive brevity. We certainly admit what they object, that pardon for a fault always ought to be given

---

14 *Decretals of Gregory IX*, bk. 5, tit. 7 (*De haereticis*), c. 9.
15 *Liber sextus decretalium*, bk. 5, tit. 2 (*De haereticis*), c. 4.

to the sinner, as often as he does true penance for the sin; and always he ought to be received into the communion of the Church, if he shows true signs of repentance. For nothing of those things which the Church grants to all the Catholic faithful, ought to be denied to him. The sins assuredly ought to be heard, which he would wish to disclose to the priest in an auricular confession; which when heard, unless something impedes, the absolution of his sins ought not to be denied to him. If he would ask for the Sacrament of the Eucharist, it ought to be administered to him. Yet the Sacrament of Extreme Unction will not be administered to him, because according to the opinion of Blessed James a Sacrament of this kind ought not to be administered except to those who suffer from some bodily illness.[16] After his death, ecclesiastical burial would be granted to him as to the rest of the Catholic faithful. Still, it does not follow that death, or some other punishment ought not to be inflicted on account of the offense of the heresy into which he relapsed. For it ought not to necessarily happen that as many times the forgiveness of a fault be given, the forgiveness of the punishment, to which he had been appointed on account of the guilt be given. For God also after He forgave a sin, was accustomed to inflict punishments immediately after. For which matter (so that I may omit others) that is a very clear proof which the Second Book of Kings relates about King David. For when he acknowledged the gravity of the fault which he had committed in the adultery and homicide, he besought from God the forgiveness of the same fault. The prophet Nathan rendered testimony of which when saying: "The Lord also hath taken away thy sin" (12, 13). Yet after this remission of the fault, the same prophet predicted to him that he would suffer many calamities and punishments on account of the offence committed, all of which he afterwards underwent, although he had already been forgiven the

---

16 Cf. James 5, 14.

sin. Christ's spouse, the Church, has deemed that it ought to be done in this same way, who receives unto penance the relapsed heretic if he regains his senses, yet she does not fear to inflict the punishments to which he had been appointed on account of the crime of heresy.

Furthermore, the heretics secondly object to us that to Peter asking Our Savior how many times one ought to forgive a brother sinning against him, and with a question bringing forth his opinion, "till seven times?" (Mt. 18, 21), Our Savior replies: "I say not to thee, till seven times; but till seventy times seven times" (v. 22). By which words He very clearly taught that we always ought to forgive a brother sinning against us. This objection changes absolutely nothing, and does not do anything against us: because by those words, Christ merely teaches us that we always ought to forgive the offenses we receive, that is, which are done against us, such that as many times as someone sins against us, so many times we ought to forgive him. Yet another procedure ought to be made use of in the punishment of those crimes which are openly against the Divine honor, teaches [Pseudo-] Augustine speaking thus: "Attend diligently brothers, and know that it is one thing to sin against God, and another against a man. For when men sin against us, if we do not pardon those repenting, we commit a sin, but when some men sin against God, if we would want to forgive without great difficulty, we make ourselves partakers of their sins."[17]

Hence it happens that a judge, whosoever he may be, when he punishes not his own offenses, but those of God or of the Church or of another government, he is not held to the execution of this same precept: such that when he punishes not private, but public offenses, he could punish according to the quality of the crime even with capital punishment, and is not obliged to remit the punishment of this kind, nay, very often he would be obliged not to remit. Now a heretic

---

17 Sermon 225 (*De Martyribus II*), N. 5 (PL 39, 2162).

Relapsed heretics are reckoned to be incorrigible, and who they are

does not sin against the judges alone, or the prelates, whom he scandalizes by his error: but he offends in many ways against God and His spouse, the Church. Firstly, because he supposes that they can either deceive or be deceived, and for this reason he refuses to obey their orders. Secondly, because they strive to infect the faithful, who are members of Christ, with their pestiferous error and tear them away from Christ's body. In the chapter, *Vergentis*,[18] it is said that a heretic offends the Divine Majesty.

Again, heretics thirdly argue against us speaking thus: Let it be granted that it is permitted to condemn a heretical man, and punish an incorrigible man, yet not after he has relapsed the first time ought he be reckoned incorrigible: because Paul the Apostle when writing to Titus admonishes him, "A man that is a heretic, after the first and second admonition, avoid" (3, 10). From which words they conclude that the Church acts against Paul's opinion, since she condemns a heretic after the first admonition, and hands him over to the secular authority, so that he may be punished by it as it seems expedient. And certainly (so that I may frankly state the truth) those words of Paul seem to have not a little weight against us: if it would be established that they were said in this way by Paul, as they were now cited by us, and are found in the vulgate Bibles.[19] Yet it is not established that such is the writing of Paul: because many holy men cite, read, and interpret those words of Paul otherwise. And that different reading of Paul is not found only in recent authors: because this would insufficiently take away the authority from the published and common Bibles: but since among the very old, not only Latin authors but also Greek authors

---

18 *Decretals of Gregory IX*, bk. 5, tit. 7 (*De haereticis*), c. 10.

19 An official Vulgate Bible was not yet officially promulgated until 1590 A.D. The words, "after the first and second admonition, avoid," were later included in the officially approved Latin Vulgate version of the text.

are found, it makes us uncertain of how those words of Paul ought to be read.

[Ambrosiaster] in his commentaries on the Epistle to Titus, reads the passage in this way: "A man that is a heretic, after the first admonition, avoid."[20] Which reading is certainly different from that which is found in the vulgate Bibles. Blessed Cyprian cites this passage of Paul in these words: "A man that is a heretic, after the first admonition, avoid."[21] In which words he made no mention of the second admonition. Tertullian in his book, *Prescription against Heretics*, citing these same words of Paul, says that a heretic ought to be avoided "after the first admonition."[22] Next, Blessed Irenaeus the martyr, a neighbor enough to the Apostles, speaks thus: "Such was the horror which the Apostles and their disciples had against holding even verbal communication with any corrupters of the truth; as Paul also says, 'A man that is a heretic, after the first admonition, avoid: Knowing that he, that is such an one, is subverted, and sinneth, being condemned by his own judgment.'"[23] In which words he relates that Paul said that a man that is a heretic, after the first admonition, ought to be avoided, and one ought not to wait for a second. Now which is the more correct text, whether this which is found in the vulgate Bibles, or that which these four illustrious and very ancient authors cite, I am not so great that I could decide, nor so arrogant that I would dare to attempt this. For Blessed Jerome in his commentaries on the Epistle to Titus when interpreting this passage of Paul

---

20 PL 17, 504A.
21 *Ad Quirinum, Testimonium contra Judaeos*, bk. 3, c. 78 (PL 4, 772).
22 C. 6 (PL 2, 18A).
23 *Adversus Haereses*, bk. 3, c. 3, n. 4 (PG 7, 853B-854A). Note that the Greek text has "and the second," and in bk. 1, c. 16, n. 3 he also says, "and the second," although these words are not found in the *Vetus Italica* version of the Scripture.

says that these words of Paul are found differently in the Greek codices than in the Latin codices; in the Greek he says that only "after one admonition" is found. But in the Latin codices he says that it is read, "after the first and second admonition." Now which of these is the truer Jerome does not decide: because he does not reject either one.[24]

Now, so that I may reply to the argument which is proposed to us from that passage of Paul, I say that Paul in that place does not speak about him who after he departed from some heresy, returns to it or another: but about him, who persists in the same heresy, even though he was admonished once and again to abandon the heresy, and such a man as this ought to be avoided, and one ought not to communicate any more with him: because he who having been admonished once and again about his error, does not want to be corrected, and thinks that the one correcting him errs, and it ought to be feared that he would destroy him by whom he is admonished and taught. Hence Chrysostom when interpreting this passage of Paul, after he had cited other words of Paul from the Second Epistle to Timothy,[25] which apparently seem to oppose these words, wishing to conciliate all those words, he speaks thus: "In the former passage he speaks of the correction of those of whom he had hope, and who had simply made opposition. But when he is known and manifest to all,

---

24 St. Jerome in fact favors the Latin version which includes the second admonition saying in his said commentary: "In the Latin codices it is read (which the Pope and Athanasius truly approve): 'after the first and second admonition'; namely because to correct or admonish him, who is depraved by some error, only once does not suffice: but also a second teaching ought to be given to him, so that 'in the mouth of two or three witnesses every word shall stand' (Deut. 19, 15)" (PL 26, 597C).

25 "With modesty admonishing them that resist the truth: if peradventure God may give them repentance to know the truth" (2, 25).

why do you contend in vain? Why do you beat the air? What means, 'being condemned by his own judgment'? Because he cannot say that no one has told him, no one admonished him; since therefore after admonition he continues the same, he is 'condemned by his own judgment.'"[26] From whose words it is established clearly enough that those words of Paul ought to be understood of him who persists in the same heresy, whom he says has been admonished once and again, and if he does not want to believe, he ought to be avoided. Yet if such a heretic as this (by God's inspiration) recovers his senses, and afterwards (by the devil's suggestion) falls again into heresy, what ought to be done about that man Paul does not teach in this passage. Hence it is that Paul's opinion, even according to the words which are found in the Vulgate Bibles, in no way contradicts the decision of the Church.

---

26 Hom. 6, n. 1 (PG 62, 696).

Chapter III

That it is just and necessary to punish heretics.

Although the crime of heresy is so pestilent and intractable, so that among all human iniquities there is none which can harm all Christendom more, and which is less able to be cured, still supporters of heretics were not lacking, who fight for their impunity, saying that heretics ought not to be punished as heretics: but left to the Divine judgment. I believe that those who teach these things, if there is any place in this matter for conjectures, speak in this way so that they could preach the heresies that they wish, more freely to the whole people. They certainly desire to pour out in public those heresies which they perceive to be contrary to the teaching of Catholic Church: but from fear of punishment, which they are very much afraid of, they dare not whisper them. They who teach these things plead their case: because they fear to be castigated by the avenging punishments, when they see others like themselves confounded by unrestrained punishment, and reckon that they acquire impunity for themselves, if they prove that others, whom they know to be guilty of the same crime, nowise ought to be punished.

Now, so that we may banish this teaching far and a very long way away from the Church, it is necessary that we prove with many very impelling reasons, that the punishment of heretics is just and necessary. Thus, firstly I ask those who teach these things whether what they teach about heretics they reckon also pertains to all iniquitous men, such that they believe that no evildoing man however villainous ought to be punished: but rather they think that every such man ought to be left to the Divine judgment. I do not believe that any man, unless he be insane, thinks so: because this very clearly opposes the natural law. For there neither is nor ever was a nation so barbaric which does not very sharply punish thieves, robbers, and murderers because otherwise the possessions of no one would safe, the life of no one secure, and no country would last long: but all would perish very quickly. For men would be as fish in the sea, the bigger ones of which devour the smaller ones. Keeping that order of things, it would be necessary that only the powerful would live, and there would be no place in the country for the poor and weak.

Besides this natural law which is implanted in the hearts of all, the written Divine law very manifestly condemns such an opinion: because it commands not only in a few passages that malefactors ought to be punished. I omit those punishments which the rigor of the Old Law long ago decreed ought to be inflicted upon sinners. Paul the Apostle, when speaking about the power given to rulers by God, says: "But if thou do that which is evil, fear: for he beareth not the sword in vain. For he is God's minister: an avenger to execute wrath upon him that doth evil" (Rom. 13, 4). And the Prince of the Apostles confirms the same opinion saying: "Be ye subject therefore to every human creature for God's sake: whether it be to the king as excelling; or to governors as sent by him for the punishment of evildoers, and for the praise of the good" (I Pet. 2, 13-14). There are many other testimonies for this matter: but it is irksome to quote them, because I see that these suffice and more than suffice, and many are unnecessary.

Therefore, if it is necessary to admit that a wrongdoer ought to be punished, I ask for the reasons on account of which he ought to be punished: which having been assigned, since the same reasons that militate against heretics, militate against wrongdoers, we thence conclude either that no wrongdoer ought to be punished, or it is also necessary that a heretic be punished. It is evident that there is a twofold reason which greatly urges that wrongdoers be punished according to the various qualities of their crimes. The first reason is the correction and amendment of the wrongdoer himself. For unto this the sinner is firstly punished (so that by the punishment bearing down) he may learn to act rightly. "Vexation alone," as it is written in Isaias, "shall make you understand what you hear" (28, 19). And Solomon says in the book of Proverbs: "Folly is bound up in the heart of a child, and the rod of correction shall drive it away" (22, 15).

Now if someone perhaps contends that this saying of the Wise Man refers only to children according to their age, so that they alone ought to be taught with the rod of discipline, and not old men, nor young men, let him hear [Venerable Bede[1]] interpreting these words of Solomon in his commentaries on Proverbs. "We have known many children endowed with wisdom; for the child Jeremias also received the ministry of prophecy. And Daniel writes: 'God gave to the children knowledge, and understanding in every book, and wisdom' (1, 17). Hence to understand that the children in this passage signifies the young holds true, not by age but by understanding; the Apostle was forbidding them to be suchlike, to whom he says: "Do not become children in sense: but in malice be children" (I Cor. 14, 20). For it is necessary that children of this kind, that is, souls given to foolishness, or licentiousness, or idleness, be castigated with juvenile discipline, and brought to a righteous path of life by force of sensible men."[2]

On account of this reason the most good God Who does not want the death of the sinner, but rather that he be converted and live,[3] often punishes sinners in this world with various tribulations and calamities, so that even so He may instruct them, so they may recognize the evils they have done, and

---
1   The text incorrectly cites St. Jerome here.
2   *Super parabolas Salomonis allegorica exposition*, bk. 2 (PL 91, 1004A-B).
3   Cf. Ez. 18, 23.

long for the goods which by their fault they have lost. For there are many who, having been vexed by afflictions, were forced to understand that the vices, by which they have been ensnared, are very bad: and thus giving up their former life, they began a new one, and putting off the old man with his actions, they put on a new man, who was created according to God in justice and holiness of truth.[4] And (so I that may omit many others) the prodigal son, of whom Luke makes mentions in his Gospel, supports us with not a small example. He in fact having received the portion which fell to him by hereditary law, "went abroad into a far country: and there wasted his substance, living riotously": but afterwards after having been forced by bitter hunger, returned to himself, and learned how great were the goods he had lost, which he had when staying in his father's house. And in this way having been made wiser, he returned to his father, acknowledged his sin, and when begging for mercy, he immediately obtained his request. (15, 20)

Paul the Apostle although he previously was a devastator and a very fierce persecutor of the Church, when he was going to Damascus was struck with blindness of the body by the Lord: so that at least in this way he might be forced to desire the true light of the heart.[5] Thus Paul, who in prosperity had blindness of the mind, was healed by the eye-salve of scourges, so that he might receive the eyesight of the mind, and might offer himself to the prompt obedience of God. And hence after the imposition of hands of Ananias, scales are said to have fallen from the eyes of his body, so that through those scales we may understand the falling away of the blindness from the mind.

For this reason Paul admonishes us all that the tribulations, which are a sort of scourge, with which God instructs us when striking us as a father, we ought to bear with a patient

---

[4] Cf. Eph. 4, 22-24.
[5] Cf. Acts 9.

soul. "For whom," he says, "the Lord loveth he chastiseth: and he scourgeth every son whom he receiveth. Persevere under discipline. God dealeth with you as with his sons. For what son is there whom the father does not correct? But if you be without chastisement, whereof all are made partakers, then are you bastards and not sons. Moreover, we have had fathers of our flesh for instructors, and we reverenced them. Shall we not much more obey the Father of spirits and live? And they indeed for a few days, according to their own pleasure, instructed us: but he, for our profit, that we might receive his sanctification" (Heb. 12, 6-10). Wherefore in the Second Epistle to the Corinthians he glories about tribulations received, speaking thus: "Gladly therefore will I glory in my infirmities, in reproaches, in necessities, in persecutions, in distresses, for Christ" (12, 9-10). And the Royal Prophet, when acknowledging the advantage of Divine scourges, gives thanks to God for them, speaking thus: "It was good for me that thou hast humbled me, that I may learn thy justifications" (Ps. 118, 71): when elated by prosperity he had not fully learned God's precepts, so that he would fulfill them in deed: but afterwards he was humbled by fierce punishments, and in this way he learned to obey God's precepts. For, as Solomon says, "Where humility is, there also is wisdom" (Prov. 11, 2).

These things having been prefaced, it is necessary to ask those who teach that heretics ought not to be punished, whether heretics forsaking the Catholic faith do well or badly. I do not think that any Christian man has lost his reason to such an extent that he would say that heretics do well, and are without crime on account of the heresy which they maintain. For since heresy is a sin, and so great that it overturns the foundation of the whole Christian order, it thence follows that a heretic, due to the fact that he embraces and defends heresy, acts badly and very badly. If heresy is evil, and the heretic acts badly by adhering to it, the consequence is that it is a good thing to convert a heretic from heresy to the Catholic faith. Now heretics are often (as experience has proved) converted to the Catholic faith by punishments and by tormenting afflictions. Thus it is a good and a very good thing to punish heretics with pains and afflictions, so that by their urging they may be forced to uphold the faith which they once received in Baptism. For (as [Augustine] said): "Happy is the necessity that compels us to do the better things."[6] Moreover, if someone does a good deed and draws out a man from the deep water so that he may live, into which he had cast himself wishing to die: and if he were to neglect to rescue him from death, when he could, even using whatever violence, he would act badly, and be held guilty of the death before God. For (as Pope Symmachus says) "There is not a great difference, whether you cause or permit a death. For he is proved to inflict death, who does not prevent it when he can."[7] Hence a judge does much better, to whom power was given from God for the vengeance of evildoers, if he forces heretics, so that they may be converted to the Catholic faith, though harsh punishment as great as you please. For he delivers the soul from death, which is so much more bitter than the death of the body, as the soul excels the body by a vast distance.

This argumentation, by an argument proceeding from the less to the greater, because in my opinion it presses upon the adversary very much, in order that it may come out clearer, I thought that it will be worthwhile to confirm with the various examples and comparisons which Augustine adduces in his letter to the officer Boniface when speaking on this matter saying: "For both the physician is irksome to the raging madman, and a father to his undisciplined son—the former because of the restraint, the latter because of the chastisement which he inflicts; yet both are acting in love. But if they were

---

6 Letter 127 (to Armentarius and Paulina), n. 8 (PL 33, 487).
7 *Decretum Gratiani*, pt. 1, dist. 83, d. a. c. 1 (PL 187, 399B).

to neglect their charge, and allow them to perish, this mistaken kindness would more truly be accounted cruelty. For if the horse and mule, which have no understanding, resist with all the force of bites and kicks the efforts of the men who treat their wounds in order to cure them; and yet men, though they are often exposed to danger from their teeth and heels, and sometimes meet with actual hurt, nevertheless do not desert them until they restore them to health through the pain and annoyance which the healing process gives—how much more should a man refuse to desert his fellow-man, or a brother to desert his brother, lest he should perish everlastingly, being himself now able to comprehend the vastness of the boon accorded to himself in his reformation, at the very time that he complained of suffering persecution?"[8]

Again, just as a father conducts himself towards his family, so a king, or priest, or any other ruler [conducts himself] in regard to whatever kingdom, or province, or nation under his authority. For Blessed Augustine teaches this when commenting on Psalm fifty, where when addressing the father of the family, he says these words: "Just as it is our responsibility to talk to you in church, so it is yours to dispose matters in your homes in such a way that you may give a good account of those under you."[9] But the householder is obliged to correct his children, and all others subject to him by word and scourges, so that even so they may become wiser, and they may be forced to convert from evil to good. Wherefore Solomon says: "He that spareth the rod hateth his son: but he that loveth him correcteth him betimes" (Prov. 13, 24). From which words it is clearly inferred that a king is obliged to correct a heretical man with words and scourges, so that at least in this way he may be forced to return to the Catholic faith, which he had received in Baptism: because if he neglects to do this, he is not a lover of the heretic from

---

8 Letter 185, n. 7 (PL 33, 795).
9 *Expositions of the Psalms*, Ps. 50, n. 24 (PL 36, 599).

charity: but will be reckoned a hater of the heretic opposed to charity. For as Solomon says, "Better are the wounds of a friend, than the deceitful kisses of an enemy" (*Ibid.* 27, 6). Finally (so that we may conclude this first reason for the punishment of bad men) if it is good that bad men be punished for the correction of the bad men, the consequence is that is so much better is the punishment of some sinner, the worse is the sin that he commits. Because the worse the sin is, the better will be its correction, and consequently so much better (all other things now being equal) will be the punishment which is ordained to compel such correction. But the crime of heresy (as we taught above) is the worst crime. Thus the punishment of a heretic is very good, which forces him in a certain way to the revocation of the heresy and making an abjuration.

The second reason on account of which it is good and necessary to punish wrongdoers is the public and common utility of the whole nation, namely, so that others, who observe such punishments, may be struck with fear, which may force them to turn away from evil. For (as the distinguished poet says) "By reason of their fear of punishment, bad men hate to sin."[10] Now after sinners become no longer accustomed to evil through the fear of punishment, they begin to be horrified of it, and then little by little what is good becomes sweet from custom. Hence Augustine says: "When through the fear of hell a man refrains from sin, justice becomes a custom, and what was hard is loved, and fear begins to be excluded by charity, and chaste fear takes its place, by which we fear that [the Spouse] would delay, that He would depart, and we

---

10 The original wording is *Oderunt peccare boni virtutis amore. Tu nihil admittes in te formidine poenae*, which in English is: "The good hate to do wrong out of love of virtue: you will admit nothing against you in fear of punishment" (Horace, *Letters*, bk. 1, poem 16, lns. 52 f.).

would be without Him. The former is useful: but it does not remain in eternity, as the latter."[11]

Wherefore Christ Our Savior often threatened sinners with God's harsh judgment: so that through the fear of hell He might recall them from their sins to repentance. For even though those are better who are motivated by love, still there are many who are forced by fear to the good: and these are not wicked. For "The fear of the Lord is the beginning of wisdom" (Ps. 110, 10) and prepares the way to charity. For this reason Paul when writing to Timothy says: "Them that sin reprove before all: that the rest also may have fear" (I Tim. 5, 20). Assuredly Paul wanted to turn men away from evil by the fear of punishment, and lead them to the good, and for this reason he commands that he reprove those that sin before all, so that the punishment of some may deter many from evil. Now if those sinning publicly were left unpunished, from this a very great occasion is given for committing whatsoever bad deeds. Ease of pardon certainly gives an incentive to committing faults. And the very wise Solomon says: "For because sentence is not speedily pronounced against the evil, the children of men commit evils without any fear" (Eccle. 8, 11). For this reason Aristotle reckons it just that some punishments be decreed by the government for transgressors of laws: so that through fear of them men

---

[11] This modified quotation of St. Augustine's *Exposition on the Psalms* is taken from *Decretum Gratiani*, pt. 2, *causa* 23, q. 6, c. 4 (PL 187, 1241C-1242A). St. Augustine's original wording is: "Through fear they refrain themselves from sin. They indeed fear, but they do not love justice. Now when they refrain themselves from sin through fear, the custom of justice begins, and what was hard begins to be loved, and God becomes sweet: and man already begins for that reason to live justly, not because he fears punishments, but because he loves eternity. Therefore fear is excluded from charity, but it follows after chaste fear..." (*Expositions on the Psalms*, Ps. 127, n. 8 (PL 37, 1861-1862)).

might be forced to the observance of the laws. "The mass of men," he says, "are amenable to compulsion rather than reason, and to punishment rather than to a sense of honor. And therefore some men hold that while lawgivers should employ the sense of honor to exhort and guide men to virtue, under the notion that they who have been well trained in virtue will then obey; they should impose chastisement and penalties on those who disobey and are of less promising nature; and they should entirely expel the incurable: because the good man and he who lives under a sense of honor will be obedient to reason; and the baser sort, who grasp at pleasure, will be kept in check, like beasts of burden by pain."[12]

And from this second reason for just punishment we clearly gather that it is good and necessary to punish heretics, lest their impunity provide an occasion to others to preach and teach whatever heresy they wish. For this is learnt by a manifest proof that those regions in which severe justice is in force, are much more free from heresies than those in which unbridled liberty of teaching and preaching whatever one pleases has been granted. A very trustworthy witness of this is our Spain, regarding which, on account of the harsh rigor of discipline against heretics enforced in it, scarcely anyone has dared to undertake preaching or teaching the Lutheran doctrines: although many from this pestiferous faction rove through nearly all the regions of the Christian world. If Germany had used even some mediocre rigor of discipline against the heretics, it would not have experienced such great harm to the Catholic faith, and would not have suffered a very troublesome and very dangerous infestation of heretics, as it now suffers. Because fear of harsh punishment would have repressed their exceedingly unbridled audacity. They having been terrified by fear, even if they would not have been corrected and improved, at least Germany would not have spurned this opportunity it had thereafter lost, that the

---

12 *Nicomachean Ethics*, bk. 10, c. 9 (1179b).

poison of its heresy, which it had conceived in the mind, would not have dared to spew forth into the people, and in this way so many people would not have been corrupted with their pestiferous doctrine. Rightly therefore the very wise Solomon says: "The rod and reproof give wisdom: but the child that is left to his own will bringeth his mother to shame" (Prov. 29, 15). [Venerable Bede[13]] when interpreting these words says: "For the child whom he admonishes to be very frequently corrected and instructed, is God's people, who if they are not castigated with assiduous warnings and rebukes of the priests, generate disorder in the Church, lowering their esteem for those things which outwardly belong to the religion of the Christian faith."[14] Thus the German people now bring their mother, the Church, to shame: because left to their own will, who if they had been instructed with the rod and correction, they would have received wisdom from her (as Solomon says).

From all these things we very clearly conclude that either not a single wicked man ought to be punished, or a heretic also ought to be punished: because it is good to procure the amendment of a heretic just as the amendment of any other sinner through punishments, and it is good to incite fear in others, lest they dare to spew out the poison of heresy, by which the people can be infected, far and wide among them. If he who transgresses against the government can rightly be punished, it follows that a heretic may also justly be punished: because a heretic also transgresses against the government. Hence the very pious Emperor Theodosius in the law, *Manichaeos*, says: "Whatever is committed against the Divine religion is productive of injury to all persons."[15]

---

13 The text incorrectly cites St. Jerome here.
14 *Super parabolas Salomonis allegorica exposition*, bk. 3, c. 29 (PL 91, 1022A-B).
15 *The Code of Justinian*, bk. 1, tit. 5 (*De haereticis*), l. 4. Cf. *Theodosian Code*, bk. 16, tit. 5, l. 40, §1.

Furthermore, if a king or bishop or any other public authority is able to punish those transgressing against his neighbor, and against the government, it is a consequence, and a necessary one, that much more can they punish those who transgress against God and against the Church. Because the latter sin much more seriously than the former, and on account of this they also ought to be punished more severely. For Heli the priest says, "If one man shall sin against another, God may be appeased in his behalf: but if a man shall sin against the Lord, who shall pray for him?" (I Kings 2, 25). Now heretics, because they pertinaciously think contrary to the teaching of the Catholic Church, believe that the Church herself can err. But he who believes that the Church can err necessarily believes either that God errs, by Whom she is governed and taught, or that God has so abandoned His Church that He does neither wants to govern nor teach her, contrary to that which He Himself had often previously promised. Now whichever one of these heretics think about God, thinking in this way they will gravely sin against Him: because by these things they make God a liar, or ignorant, or nowise faithful to His promises.

Since therefore heretics inflict a very grave injury to God, it is befitting that they ought to be punished more gravely than if they had injured some man or the whole nation. For on account of no other reason the Roman rulers and all the rest of the Gentile rulers inflicted the Apostles and the rest of the martyrs with such an atrocious persecution: than because they despised their idols, and were publicly disparaging them. They did not persecute the Apostles on account of disturbing the peace, or on account of betraying the nation, or on account of any other crimes. Because the Apostles were peaceable men, attempting nothing against the nation, harming no one, and beneficent to all. They were never accused as evildoers of doing anything opposed to welfare of the nation: but merely because they did not want to burn incense to idols, and they despised them. Hence the rulers and the kings as being zealous for their false gods, raged in the vindication of them. They certainly and rightly thought that offenses against God ought to be punished more severely than offenses against a man. For this reason I do not doubt that they, if they had known the true God, would have been much more furiously incensed at the defense of heretics, than they then raged against the Apostles.

Again every person or nation having coercive power, can oblige their subjects to those things which are necessary for the observance of peace and tranquility. Now if someone neglecting to observe those things, disturbs the peace, he can justly punish him according to the quality of the crime. But there is nothing which takes away the peace and unity of the Church than heresy. Because by it a heretic separates himself from the truth of the faith. And on account of this all heretics are called schismatics, that is, dividers: because they divide the unity of the faith and of the Church. Thus heretics are justly punished as disturbers of ecclesiastical peace. Next, Paul (as he bears witness in II Corinthians) was ready to punish all disobedience of the Corinthians. Why then will it not be allowed for Christian rulers to punish the disobedience and rebellion of heretics, who with shameless and pertinacious audacity rise up against the Church's teaching, and contemn to obey her very reasonable commands? Moreover heretics, as Paul says, "grow much towards ungodliness. And their speech spreadeth like a canker" (II Tim. 2, 16-17). Because daily it takes possession of, and devours, and pollutes the minds of those who hear them, and live with them. Therefore, lest they go about more, having been made more audacious by licentious impunity, and daily do more harm, it is good to restrain them with harsh punishments, so that having been frightened by the fear of punishments they may cease to do harm.

Add to all these things the consent of the whole Catholic Church, which for many centuries has reckoned that heretics ought to be punished, so that she might make them wise by the punishments, and she might keep the wolves away from the sheep. Paul, a vessel of election,[16] struck a certain false prophet with blindness, because he was seeking to turn Sergius Paulus away from the faith. For, as the Acts of the Apostles relates, "Paul, filled with the Holy Ghost, looking upon him, said: O full of all guile, and of all deceit, child of the devil, enemy of all justice, thou ceasest not to pervert the right ways of the Lord. And now behold, the hand of the Lord is upon thee, and thou shalt be blind, not seeing the sun for a time. And immediately there fell a mist and darkness upon him, and going about, he sought someone to lead him by the hand" (13, 9-11). If Paul used such great severity on the false prophet, because he was trying to turn the proconsul from the faith, it ought to be believed that he would use much greater severity against Luther, and the other heretics of this time, who turn not merely one proconsul, but many proconsuls, dukes, marquises, bishops, archbishops, many cities, and many regions from the faith. Pope Innocent I condemned the Cataphrygians to exile.[17] Pope Gelasius punished the Manichaeans discovered in the city [of Rome] with exile.[18] King Reccared [I] of the Spains long ago excluded all the Arians living in Spain from the army.[19] And he did not allow

---

16 Cf. Acts 9, 15.
17 "[Pope Innocent I] found many Cataphrygians in the city whom he constrained to exile in a monastery" (*Liber Pontificalis*, n. 42). The *Theodosian Code* (bk. 16, tit. 5, l. 40, §5) contains a law of Honorius dated February, 407, against the Manichaeans, Cataphrygians and Priscillianists. The term Phrygian is used as a synonym for Montanist.
18 *Liber Pontificalis*, n. 51.
19 "[Recaredus] converted the Arian bishops, and obliged them to become Catholics, more by reason than by authority, and with

them to hold any post of a freeman. The emperors Theodosius and Martianus decreed various punishments against heretics, which are found in the *The Code of Justinian*.[20]

It is now very clearly established (as I think) that they greatly err, who argue in favor of the impunity of heretics: and it is much worse regarding the heretics themselves, for whom they desire impunity: because they give to them an opportunity to preach and teach freely all the heresies that they wish. Hence Blessed Gregory when expounding the passage in Job, which speaks about the devil under the name of Behemoth saying: "The shades cover his shadow" (40, 17), speaks thus: "For all the wicked are in truth shadows of the devil: for while they give themselves up to imitate his iniquity, they derive, as it were, a form of resemblance from his body. But as the reprobate are his 'shadows' in the plural number, so each separate sinner is his 'shadow' in the singular. But when the wicked gainsay the teaching of the just, when they do not permit any wicked person to be corrected by them, the shadows of this Behemoth cover his shadow; because sinners, whenever they are conscious to themselves of sin, support another sinner in the same course. His shadows cover his shadow, when the more wicked support by their misdirected patronage the doings of the most wicked. And this they doubtless do with this object, that, while the fault, with which they themselves are bound, is corrected in others, they may not at last be reached themselves. They cover themselves therefore, when they protect others, because they foresee that their own conduct is

---

them the whole nation of the Visigoths in Spain; not suffering any heretic to serve in his army, or to hold any post in the state.—Thus heresy was abolished in Spain, where it had prevailed from the beginning of the fifth century, for about one hundred and eighty years" (Claude Fluery, *Histoire ecclésiastique* (Paris: Pierre Emery etc., 1727), vol. 7, p. 643).

20 Bk. 1, tit. 5 (*De haereticis*).

attacked, by the same means as they see others confounded with bold reproof. And thus it happens, that while the aggregate of sins is defended, it is also increased, and that the guilt of each person is more easy of commission, the more difficult it is of punishment. For the evil doings of sinners derive so much greater increase, the longer they are permitted, through the defense of the powerful, to remain unpunished. But such persons, whether they seem to be within or without Holy Church, display themselves more openly as the enemies of God, the greater patrons they are of sins."[21]

---

21 Bk. 33, c. 4 (PL 76, 675A-B).

Chapter IV

It is replied to the objections of those who argue in favor of the impunity of heretics.

There is hardly any lie so evident, that it cannot be covered by him who lies and wishes to deceive with an appearance of truth. So also there are not lacking to those who want heretics to be unpunished, certain arguments, although false, by which they strive to persuade others of their error by some color of truth. Hence, so that the Catholic truth may remain clearer and more firm, it is necessary to meet and completely overthrow their objections and arguments by which they oppose the Catholic truth. They firstly therefore object that forced service does not please God: but one ought to sacrifice freely to him,[1] and from this they conclude that no one ought to be forced to the faith, or to some other good. For no one (as they say) ought to be forced to that, from which no benefit can be obtained. Now from the good which someone does, having been forced, he does not merit to receive any reward from God. For the Apostle when he exhorted the Corinthians to give alms says: "Everyone as he hath determined in his heart, not with sadness, or of necessity: for God loveth a cheerful giver" (II Cor. 9, 7). From which it is given to be understood that he who gives against his will, loses both the thing and the reward.

To this objection Blessed Augustine replies speaking thus: "If a bad will ought always to be left to its own freedom, why was Paul not left to the free use of that most perverted will with which he persecuted the Church? Why was he thrown to the ground that he might be blinded, and struck blind that he might be changed, and changed that he might be sent as an Apostle, and sent that he might suffer for the

---

1 Cf. Ps. 53, 8.

truth's sake such wrongs as he had inflicted on others when he was in error? If a bad will ought always to be left to its own freedom, why is a father instructed in Holy Scripture not only to correct an obstinate son by words of rebuke, but also to beat his sides, in order that, being compelled and subdued, he may be guided to good conduct?[2] For which reason Solomon also says: 'Thou shalt beat him with the rod, and deliver his soul from hell' (Prov. 23, 14). If a bad will ought always to be left to its own freedom, why are negligent pastors reproved? And why is it said to them, 'That which was driven away you have not brought again, neither have you sought that which was lost' (Ez. 34, 4)? You also are sheep belonging to Christ, you bear the Lord's mark in the Sacrament which you have received, but you are wandering and perishing. Let us not, therefore, incur your displeasure because we bring back the wandering and seek the perishing; for it is better for us to obey the will of the Lord, who charges us to compel you to return to His fold, than to yield consent to the will of the wandering sheep, so as to leave you to perish."[3] And these words are found in the chapter, *Displicet*.[4]

But because in these words Augustine seems to speak absolutely and without any distinction, so that everyone without any distinction could be forced to any good, lest someone having misunderstood his words be deceived, I decided to remind the reader to understand that not all can be justly forced to the faith: but the condition of him who is forced ought to be considered. If someone never received Christ's faith in Baptism, such as the Jews, Saracens, or pagans, he certainly ought not to be compelled with threats and terrors: because to believe belongs to the will. But if

---

2 Cf. Eccli. 30, 12.
3 Letter 173, n. 3 (PL 33, 754).
4 *Decretum Gratiani*, pt. 2, *causa* 23, q. 4, c. 38 (PL 187, 1198C-1199B).

someone has already once received the faith in Baptism, and afterwards abandoned it, as apostates and the rest of the heretics do, he rightly ought to be compelled to hold the faith that he at one time accepted. Now the reason for this difference is that by the law of Nature anyone is obliged to give what he has once promised: and in this way from the same law arises that the public authority can force him to keep the things promised. For although everyone is free to promise or not promise something, still after he has promised it, it is no longer in his power to keep or not keep the promise. For by his promise he subjected himself to the public authority, so that he could be compelled by it to keeping the promise.

Completely the same thing ought to be said about a vow, and the fulfillment of a vow. For to vow belongs to liberty, but to fulfill the vow belongs to necessity. No one indeed is forced to the first, but to the second anyone is justly compelled. For the Jews, Saracens and the other unbelievers one is free to want or not want to accept the faith. I certainly do not say free as to acquiring beatitude, such that without faith, just as with it, they could acquire everlasting beatitude. But I say free, regarding the human public authority: because they are not subject to the public authority regarding this, so that they could be compelled to accepting the Catholic faith. But once they have received the faith in Baptism, because they promised at that time to keep it afterwards, they can rightly be compelled to hold on to what they received and keep what they promised. This opinion of ours is confirmed by the authority of the Fourth Synod of Toledo, which in the fifty-seventh chapter of its decrees after it had ordered that Jews and Saracens ought not to be forced to the Catholic faith, speaks thus: "[Jews] are to be induced by the free use of their will to convert rather than impelled by force. But, whoever has already been compelled to come to Christianity, as was done in the time of the most religious prince Sisebut,[5]

---

5   In 615, the Catholic King Sisebut ordered the forced Baptism

because they have already been associated with the Divine Sacraments—having received the grace of Baptism, been anointed with the chrism, and shared the Lord's Body and Blood—it is fitting that they be compelled to keep the faith which they have received by force or by necessity, lest the Lord's name be blasphemed and the faith which they received deemed worthless and contemptible."[6] Which words are found in the *Liber decretorum* in the chapter, *De Judaeis*.[7] From which words it very clearly appears that heretics are to be forced to the Catholic faith, which they abandoned.

Now I admit what they object, namely, that no one ought to be forced to that to which he is uselessly forced. But is a heretic uselessly forced to accepting the faith? Hardly so. Because multiple benefits come from this compulsion. The first is the amendment of the heretic himself, which can easily arise from the punishment: because something often begins by fear, and finally is completed with perfect love, and then (as Blessed John says) "Perfect charity casteth out fear" (I Jn. 4, 18).

But they object that these things do not benefit many men: but by such punishments many become false Christians, who even though they publicly say that they have the faith, still they deny it in their hearts. To this objection I reply following Blessed Augustine, that medicine ought not to be despised, because an uncurable disease of some men is not cured by it. For it is not a flaw of the medicine, but of the sickness, when that medicine which aids other maladies, does not cure some malady of the same kind. Next, even though compulsion to salvation does not profit some men of this kind, still it ought not then be reckoned to be useless: because then the public utility ought to be considered, which is much more import-

---

of Jews. The text of Canon 57 of the Fourth Synod of Toledo (633), a work of Isidore of Seville, is a correction of that royal decision.
6 Mansi 10, 633B.
7 *Decretum Gratiani*, pt. 1, dist. 45, c. 5 (PL 187, 235A-B).

ant than the private utility. For by such punishment heretics are restrained from publicly preaching and teaching their heresies: in which way they would infect the whole country with their pestiferous doctrine. It is truly a great benefit for the whole country, if it is kept unstained from the pestiferous teachings of the heretics. Hence we gather that it is better, that is, less evil, to tolerate hidden heretics, than to permit public ones: because the latter by their unbridled and licentious audacity become much more harmful than the former, who from fear of punishment, as though restrained by a sort of bridle, dare not to become manifest in public.

Secondly, they argue thus: heretics ought to be refuted by words and reasons, thus they ought not be forced to the faith by punishments and afflictions. They say that the valid inference is known to be true, and they prove the assumption by saying that because Blessed Peter teaches that "we all ought to be ready to satisfy everyone that asketh you a reason of that hope which is in us" (I Pet. 3, 15). I certainly admit (and this same thing I have already taught above) that it is good to firstly admonish heretics with words, giving reasons according to the condition of each heretic, to convince them of their heresy: but because there are many men so pertinacious and hardened, that they are more easily broken than corrected, it is necessary to do regarding them that which Blessed Isidore says: "It is necessary that one be confronted more sharply who is not set right when he is chastised by a mild word. For those things must be cut off with pain that cannot be healed by gentleness."[8]

A shepherd, who sees the wolf entering the flock of sheep, firstly shouts at him, so that by just doing this he may be kept out of the flock: and if he sees that he is nowise deterred by the shouting, he attacks him with a staff, a hand-sling, a sword, and an arrow, if it is necessary, so that he may drive him out of the flock, and in this way keep the sheep

---

8 *Sententiae*, bk. 3, c. 46, n. 11 (PL 83, 716B).

unharmed. The shepherds of the Church are the prelates, who watch over their subjects, as over sheep entrusted to them, for whom they are to give an account to God. Now the wolves, which harm these sheep very much, are heretics, about whom Our Savior says: "Beware of false prophets, who come to you in the clothing of sheep, but inwardly they are ravening wolves" (Mt. 7, 15). And Paul in the Acts of the Apostles called heretics "wolves," speaking thus: "I know that, after my departure, ravening wolves will enter in among you, not sparing the flock" (20, 29). Therefore, lest heretics harm others, it is befitting to strike them like ravening wolves with scourges and cudgels, if perhaps they are not restrained by a mild admonition. Doctors are forced to seek after many and different medicines when they see that the usual and common remedies do not help, and the more the maladies grow worse, the more efficacious antidotes ought to be sought, which can more quickly and better drive them out from the human body. Of course the most suitable and best medicament of salvation in regard to heretics for leading them back to the faith is gentleness and kindness, through monitory words, and mildness of speech. But when these medicines, on account of the indurate malice of heretics, are known to do no good for them, those to whom the curing of such maladies has been committed, ought to use on them harsher and more bitter medicaments. For Our Lord and Redeemer Jesus Christ, an exemplar of all mildness and meekness, after having made a scourge of little cords, drove all the moneychangers, their sheep also and the oxen out of the Temple, poured out the money of the changers, and overthrew the tables.[9] If He did this to the moneychangers, He would have shown Himself much more severe to heretics: because the sin of heretics is much more grave than that of the moneychangers, and heretics can do much more harm to the Church than moneychangers.

---

9 Cf. Jn. 2, 15.

Replies to those arguing in favor of the impunity of heretics

Thirdly, these men, who ask for the impunity of heretics, argue as follows. The perfect manner of living, which all Christians ought to have, is very fully contained in the holy Gospels, and in the Epistles of Paul and of the other Apostles. Now the Gospels, or the Epistles of the Apostles, do not teach that Christians ought not to implore the support of rulers against heretics, nor ought rulers to give any trouble to heretics: therefore the rulers who punish heretics, and those who appeal to rulers for assistance regarding this punishment, act contrary to the teaching of Christ and of the Apostles. To this objection I reply twice. Firstly, I certainly deny that there is no teaching in the holy Gospels and the Epistles of the Apostles about the punishment of heretics. For Christ Our Savior, when speaking about a reprehended and unamended sinful brother, says: "If he will not hear the church, let him be to thee as the heathen and publican" (Mt. 18, 17). And a little before in the same chapter He said: "Woe to that man by whom the scandal cometh. It were better for him that a millstone should be hanged about his neck, and that he should be drowned in the depth of the sea" (vv. 6-7). But there are no men, through whom a more serious scandal arise than through heretics; thus it is better "that a millstone should be hanged about his neck, and that he should be drowned in the depth of the sea." And Paul the Apostle commanded that a heretical man after having been admonished once and again should be shunned from the fellowship of men. And when writing to the Galatians he makes known clearly enough that heretics ought to be driven from the communion of men speaking thus: "I would they were even cut off, who trouble you" (5, 12). Now there are no men who stir up more serious and more harmful troubles among the faithful than heretics: who daily contrive new teachings, by which they strive to separate God's people from the unity of faith.

Next, even if no clear teaching about the punishment of heretics were to be found in the sacred Gospels, or in the Catholic Epistles of the Apostles, still not on that account does it follow that their punishment is unjust. Because the reason why the punishment of heretics was deliberately and on purpose unmentioned was lest the faith of the sacred Gospels be attributed to human power. For since those things which are believed by faith surpass all human understanding, it is befitting that the faith of the Gospel be attributed to Divine power, and not to human wisdom or power. On account of this Christ Our Savior did not choose philosophers or learned men to be His first disciples, through whom the faith of the Gospel was to be preached, but simple, uneducated and completely illiterate men. So also lest the same faith be imputed to human power, it was indeed befitting that it be preached through the whole world, not by emperors, kings, dukes, or any other authorities of the world that you wish: but through power, weak, and powerless men. But now after the faith of the Gospel has already been preached throughout the world, the rulers of the earth carrying the banner of the vivifying Cross under the name of Christ began to fight, submitted themselves with the diadem of kings to the obedience of the faith, it was by this time then fitting that the faith itself be supported with arms and be made firm with their authority and majesty against the very fierce enemies of the same faith, of kings and of rulers. For just as of old although David was the king, and by God's command was anointed by Samuel the prophet, he patiently waited and acted meekly with Saul, until God took away Saul from the midst of all, and when he was taken away from this life, he exercised all the royal prerogatives, so also the Church did not use at the beginning the power of the material sword upon her subjects: but instead she waited with all meekness, until God subjected the necks of the kings of the earth to her yoke.

Replies to those arguing in favor of the impunity of heretics

Fourthly, they argue against us from the example of the Apostles and the other rulers of the Church, who at the beginning of the nascent Church, very perfectly taught the Catholic faith by word and example. For (although at that time there were many heretics, namely, Simon Magus, Menander, Saturninus, Cerdo, Ebion, Cerinthus, Marcion, Valentinus, and many others whom it is unnecessary to name) it is never read that they had implored the support of rulers or help against the heretics, and did not ask of them that they would punish the heretics with some punishment, with which they might be compelled to return to the Catholic faith. Therefore it is not permitted to Christians now to persecute heretics with the support of the rulers, otherwise they would greatly deviate from imitating the Apostles, which ought to be reprobated very much. The Donatists raised this objection (as Augustine testifies when commenting on John[10]) against those who were persecuting heretics. But Blessed Augustine easily refuted this objection saying that in the beginning of the nascent Church the Apostles and their successors did not ask for the support of the rulers against heretics: because no emperor at that time, or king, was obeying the Gospel; none of them at that time had accepted the faith of Christ our Redeemer.[11]

---

10 "But they wonder that Christian powers are roused against detestable scatterers of the Church. Should they not be moved, then? How otherwise should they give an account of their rule to God? Observe, beloved, what I say, that it concerns Christian kings of this world to wish their mother the Church, of which they have been spiritually born, to have peace in their times" (*Tractates on the Gospel of John*, tract 11, n. 14 (PL 35, 1483)).

11 "Mark, now, how it was said in regard to those who came first, bring them in; it was not said, compel them to come in—by which was signified the incipient condition of the Church, when it was only growing towards the position in which it would have strength to compel men to come in. Accordingly, because it was right that when the Church had been strengthened, both in power and in

In fact in those times the Roman rulers were Nero, Domitian, Trajan, Decius and other similar cruel tyrants, who all very fiercely persecuted the Catholic faith. It had not yet been fulfilled at that time what the Holy Ghost, through the mouth of David, had predicted. "And now, O ye kings, understand: receive instruction, you that judge the earth. Serve ye the Lord with fear: and rejoice unto him with trembling" (Ps. 2, 10-11). "And all kings of the earth shall adore him: all nations shall serve him" (Ps. 71, 11). How is it possible that the Apostles, and those who lived soon after them, would ask for support and help at that time from those whom they knew were very clear enemies of the Christian faith? For the Apostles were not so stupid and mindless that they would seek from these men, whom they knew very well very passionately persecuted the Catholic faith, support for the defense of the same faith against the heretics. Thus the fact that the Apostles, and those who lived soon after them, did not ask for the support of the rulers against the heretics, was not because the heretics were not deserving of punishment: but because the sword of the Gentile rulers and emperors was not yet serving the Gospel.

But after the emperors were washed by sacred Baptism, they gave their names to Christ, and began to glory concerning His name: the Christians then at that time did not hesitate to ask for the support of the rulers against the heretics. For Catholic men asked for help from Constantine the Great in the Nicene Council, whereby they could extirpate the heretics, whose petition the most pious emperor very willingly granted, and so he condemned Arius with his followers to exile: because they did not wish to accept the faith of the Nicene Council. Emperor Theodosius punished the Manichaean heretics with the privation of all their possessions: and he deprived them of all inheritances. The other emperors and

---

extent, men should be compelled to come in to the feast of everlasting salvation" (Letter 173, n. 10 (PL 33, 757)).

Christian kings having followed their examples, issued various laws in the succession of time against the heretics: so that by the severity of the laws, they might repress the insane audacity of the heretics.

For this reason also (as Augustine says[12]) when many of the seventy disciples departed from Our Lord and Savior, and He permitted them the choice of their wicked and impious departure, He said to the other twelve who had remained: "Will you also go away?" (Jn. 6, 68). Certainly Our Savior did this at that time because although He also then had great power, which He could have used for punishing and restraining them, nevertheless He firstly choose to commend humility. For Christ at that time was scorned, and the kings of the earth were not yet adoring Him, nor were the nations serving Him, as the Royal Prophet had predicted about Him.[13] "It is in proportion to the more enlarged accomplishment of this prophecy that the Church (Christ's spouse) wields greater power, so that she may not only invite, but even compel men to embrace what is good."[14] For that man who had made the great supper, when they who had been invited refused to come, said to the servant: "Go out quickly into the streets and lanes of the city, and bring in hither the poor, and the feeble, and the blind, and the lame. And the servant said: Lord, it is done as thou hast commanded, and yet there is room. And the Lord said to the servant: Go out into the highways and hedges, and compel them to come in, that my house may be filled." (Lk. 14, 21-23). In regard to those who firstly came, it was said, "Bring them in." But in regard to those

---

12 "I hear that you have remarked and often quote the fact recorded in the Gospels, that the seventy disciples went back from the Lord, and that they had been left to their own choice in this wicked and impious desertion, and that to the Twelve who alone remained the Lord said, 'Will you also go away?'" (*Ibid.*).
13 Cf. Ps. 71, 11.
14 St. Augustine, Letter 173, n. 10 (PL 33, 757).

who came afterwards it was said, "Compel them to come in." What was said to the first ones, ought to be referred to those times in which the kings and rulers of the earth had not yet received the faith. For at that time everyone was left to the choice of his own will. That which is said afterwards, regards the subsequent times, when the sword of kings and emperors began to serve the Gospel. And in the latter times, heretics ought not to be merely invited, but compelled so that the Catholic faith, which they once received in Baptism, they may believe unto justice, and confess with the mouth unto salvation.[15]

---

15 Cf. Rom. 10, 10.

Chapter V

Concerning the punishments of heretics, and firstly regarding the bodies, and then it is treated regarding the spiritual punishments individually, and now firstly about the confiscation of temporal goods.

We have already clearly shown by very manifest (as I think) arguments that the punishment of heretics is just and necessary: it remains that we discuss individually the punishments, which laws decree for heretics and prove that they rightly decreed, so that in this way we may put to silence the impudent audacity of certain men, who accuse the Popes and kings of excessive severity against heretics. There are many and diverse punishments with which ecclesiastical ordinances and laws of emperors command heretics to be punished. For there are some spiritual punishments, which pertain to the soul alone. Others are corporal, which afflict the body. We will speak about them individually, and firstly about the corporal ones.

Among the corporal punishments, one, and which does not vex heretics a little, is the proscription and confiscation of all goods. For he who is a heretic is deprived of the ownership of all his goods by the law itself, and the government treasury assumes ownership in his place if the heretic is a layman and in lands of lay rulers. But if the heretic is a layman in lands of the Church, or is a cleric, his goods are assumed by the treasury of the Church: unless the goods of the clerics belonged to the Church, or they themselves have revenues from the Church, because they will be applied to the church to which they belong, or from which they had received revenues.[1] Punishments are certainly just, and

---

1 "As to the property of the condemned, if they are laymen, let it be confiscated; if clerics, let it be applied to the churches from

rightly decreed against so grave a crime, so that by fear of so harsh a punishment, heretics will dread to openly present their heresies to others. Accordingly the desire and love of riches runs so deep in the souls of many men that for the protection of those riches they do not omit any labor, and leave nothing untried, even to expose themselves to danger of death if it would be necessary for preserving them. Now one's love of riches is as great as the amount of joy and pleasure that he takes from them when they are possessed, and so great also is the sorrow that comes when after having possessed them they are lost. For by an equal scale on the balance are weighed hate and love: joy and sorrow: joy and sadness. As much as someone loves something, rejoices and delights about its presence, so much does he hate the deprivation of the same thing, grieve and is sad about it. And from this it happens that as many as ardently love riches, they are made suspicious and fearful. Assuredly, in every affair a rich man is more fearful than a poor man; he fortifies his buildings more securely from fear of thieves. He dreads storms on account of the crops which he has in the fields, and on account of the merchandise he has on the sea. He fears friends, least perhaps he be forced to give them something when they ask. He fears enemies, lest by force or some deceit inflicted, they would partly harm some things. Being more timid and stingy, he is reviled for his fear of loss. Finally, he does everything more circumspectly, and he speaks with a fear of calumny, which especially is wont to be contrived against the rich: because they have what could be taken away by them.

For this reason, wise legislators, when they made some laws which they desire to be observed very well, decreed some penalty of money for the transgressors of the same laws. Solon, who is now numbered among the Seven Sages

---

which they received revenues" (*Decretals of Gregory IX*, bk. 5, tit. 7, (*De haereticis*) c. 13 (*Excommunicamus*), §1 (*Damnati*)).

First bodily punishment of heretics: the confiscation of temporal goods

of Greece,² to some of their laws, which he gave to the Athenians, so that they might be better observed, he added a certain fine of money. For (as Plutarch relates in *The Life of Solon*) if someone spoke ill of the living in sacred temples, courts-of-law, the public offices, and at festivals; he commanded that the transgressor be fined five drachmas, three drachmas to the person injured, and two more into the public treasury.³ If a man committed rape upon a free woman, he commanded that he was to be fined a [hundred] drachmas.⁴ Now in the Roman Empire many and various are the laws which decree a certain monetary fine to the perpetrators of some crimes. There are also many others which, on account of other more serious crimes, those who perpetrated them, were deprived of the ownership and possession of all goods. For if someone was sullied with the crime of high treason, the law commands that by that very act he be deprived of all his goods.⁵ Which punishment so extends its force and power that it also is effective after death. Because, even if the criminal was not accused of this crime during his life, he can be accused after death, and if he was convicted at that time, then his goods would be taken back from those who possessed them. For so it was enacted in the last two

---

2   Plato, *Protagoras*, 343a.
3   C. 21, n. 1.
4   C. 23, n. 1.
5   "Anyone who joins an infamous faction composed of either soldiers, private persons, or barbarians, whether he himself, as its head, receives the oath, or takes it as an individual, shall be put to death as guilty of high treason, and all his property shall be confiscated to Our Treasury, whether he has plotted the death of illustrious men who are members of Our Council and Consistory, and of the Senate (as they form part of Our government), or finally, of anyone else who is in Our service; for the laws punish with equal severity the intention to commit a crime and its actual perpetration" (*The Code of Justinian*, bk. 9, tit. 8 (*Ad legem Iuliam maiestatis*), l. 5 (*Quisquis*).

laws of the same title.⁶ Counterfeiters of money by that very act lose the possession of all their goods.⁷ The goods of a man contracting an incestuous marriage were put by that very act into the government treasury, as appears in the chapter, *Incestas*.⁸ The ravisher of a free woman, whether she was

---

6 "It should be remembered that, where any act is alleged to have been committed against the majesty of the Emperor, it is customary for the crime to be prosecuted even after the death of the culprit, since the Divine Marcus ordered the property of the Senator Druncianus, who was the accomplice of Cassianus in his conspiracy, to be confiscated to the Treasury after his death; and, during Our reign, many heirs have been deprived of their right to estates under similar circumstances" (L. 7 (*Meminisse*)). "After the enactment of the Constitution of the Divine Marcus, We have adopted the rule that the accusation of this crime can be made even after the decease of the culprits, so that, if the offender should be convicted after his death, his memory may be condemned to infamy, and his heir deprived of his estate" (L. 8 (*Post*)). This translation was made from D. Godefroy, *Corpus juris civilis, Pandectis ad Florentinum archetypum expressis, Institutionibus*... (Amsterdam: Johannes Blaeu, 1663), as these two laws were omitted in some other editions.

7 "When anyone makes counterfeit money, We order that his entire property shall be confiscated to Our Treasury, for We wish that money shall be coined only in Our mints. Those who are guilty of counterfeiting have committed high treason, and a reward is promised to their accusers. Whenever a counterfeiter of solidi, or anyone who has placed them in circulation, is convicted, he shall instantly, and without delay, be put to death by fire" (*The Code of Justinian*, bk. 9, tit. 24, l. 2 (*Si quis nummum*)).

8 "This Authentic adds another punishment; namely confiscation, not only of the dower, but of all goods, namely of the separation from legitimate children, likewise deportation, and corporal chastisement, if the person is of inferior rank: also forfeiture of military rank [*spoliatio cinguli*] is added, and children (namely, legitimate ones) on account of this transgression are freed from parental authority: nevertheless the duty of feeding the parent is

then a virgin, or whether she has been betrothed or a widow, and those who were present when the crime took place, are deprived of the ownership of all their goods, and their goods are transferred to the ownership of the said ravished freeborn woman.[9] I omit other municipal laws, which are many and various, scarcely any of them from so many will be found, which for restraining of some crimes did not decree some monetary fine, to those who committed such crimes.

And if in all these and others laws of this kind, which were approved by the common consent of the whole people, fines of a certain amount of money, or the privation of all goods, is said to be justly decreed for the restraining of such crimes, it is much more just that heretics, whose sin is much more serious than others' sin, be restrained by the proscription of all their goods. For (as it is very well said in the law, *Gazaros*[10]) "It is much more serious to offend an eternal than a temporal majesty."[11] From which it is clearly gathered, that it is much more just to punish heretics, because they offend Divine Majesty, with the proscription of all goods, than those who offend human majesty with any other crime you wish. Likewise, if counterfeiters of money are justly deprived of ownership of all their goods, it is much more just that heretics be struck with a similar punishment, who are much worse counterfeiters than they. Because heretics disseminate false and erroneous teachings in place of true ones, and they distort Sacred Scripture to a false meaning, quite alien from the Spirit of God. Is not Sacred Scripture much more precious than whatever and however much money of the world? Thus, he is much more wicked, who attempts to

---

incumbent upon these children" (An Authentic in *The Code of Justinian* after bk. 5, tit. 5, l. 6 = Collation 6/7, Tit. 2, [Nov. 12.1]).
9 *The Code of Justinian*, bk. 9, tit. 13, l. 1, §1 (*Et si quidem*).
10 This word is a distortion in the Authentics of *Catharos*, or Cathars.
11 An Authentic in *The Code of Justinian* after bk 1, tit. 5, l. 19.

falsify Sacred Scripture, applying a false meaning to it, than he who forges false money. Hence it is that he ought to be punished much more severely.

Moreover, it is just that the punishment correspond to the guilt, and someone is punished in that thing in which he sinned, or in that whence he took an occasion of sin. For by this reasoning Solomon in the book of Wisdom proves that the plagues whereby God afflicted the idolatrous Egyptians were just, speaking thus: "Because some being deceived worshipped dumb serpents and worthless beasts, thou didst send upon them a multitude of dumb beasts for vengeance. That they might know that by what things a man sinneth, by the same also he is tormented. For thy almighty hand, which made the world of matter without form, was not unable to send upon them a multitude of bears, or fierce lions, or unknown beasts of a new kind, full of rage: either breathing out a fiery vapour, or sending forth a stinking smoke, or shooting horrible sparks out of their eyes: whereof not only the hurt might be able to destroy them, but also the very sight might kill them through fear. Yea and without these, they might have been slain with one blast, persecuted by their own deeds, and scattered by the breath of thy power: but thou hast ordered all things in measure, and number, and weight" (11, 16-21). In which words it ought to be noticed that he says: God punished the Egyptians by flies, sciniphs, and locusts, not because other punishments were lacking to Him, by which He could have afflicted them: but because none was more befitting the guilt, that they would be punished by the same living things, which they were venerating with very great honor. From this same argument we gather that although there may be many other punishments whereby heretics could be punished, still they are justly punished by the proscription of all their goods, so that they may be punished in that which gave them an occasion for their heresy.

First bodily punishment of heretics: the confiscation of temporal goods

For among the many causes of heresy, one, and it is not insignificant, is avarice (as we will show in book three, chapter one), which opens a very wide door to introducing heresies. Hence Paul in the First Epistle to Timothy says: "They that will become rich, fall into temptation, and into the snare of the devil, and into many unprofitable and hurtful desires, which drown men into destruction and perdition. For the desire of money is the root of all evils; which some coveting have erred from the faith, and have entangled themselves in many sorrows" (6, 9-10). And in the Epistle to the Colossians he says that avarice is "the service of idols" (3, 5). Our Savior also taught this in the parable of the marriage feast,[12] which a king made for his son, and sent his servant to call those invited to it, and they would not come. Now among those who neglected to come, there was one who went to his merchandise. For because he loved riches, he was doing work with merchandise to acquire them, and thus he preferred this to the joy of the marriage feast. The marriage feast which the king makes for his son, according to the interpretation of all the holy Doctors, is a figure of the Incarnation of the Son of God.[13] To this marriage feast God invites through His servant, when he calls through his preaching to faith in the Incarnation. But he neglects to come, who loves riches, and attends to business. For he who loves riches unrestrainedly, will despise the Son of God made poor for us, and will give no faith to His Gospel, which extols poverty, and highly recommends it to us. For this is, I think, one of the chief reasons why many of the Jews refuse to accept the Catholic faith: namely, because they love riches very much, and employ usury for acquiring them, which, if

---

12 Cf. Mt. 22.
13 "God the Father made a marriage for God, his Son, when he united human nature with him in the womb of the Virgin" (St. Gregory the Great, *Homilies on the Gospels*, hom. 38, n. 3 (PL 76, 1283B)).

they convert to the faith of the Gospel, they know ought not to be allowed to them. Next, he who ardently loves riches, even if he has already once received the faith in Baptism, which obliges him to believe the Gospel, still whatever he reads in the Gospel as a recommendation of poverty and the contempt of riches, he will twist into another meaning: because his will having been exceedingly infected with the love of riches, directs and draws his whole mind in favor of them. And in this way the mind having been blinded thinks about them, speaks about them, commends and teaches about them. Whence [Pseudo-] Blessed Jerome when expounding Psalm one hundred forty-three, in the verse: "Their oxen fat" (v. 14), speaks thus: "The Israelite people are slender, the Egyptians fat. For you see the teachers of heretics do nothing else except to strive after riches. They strive after riches, and they despise the poor Christ."[14]

But besides these testimonies of the Scriptures, there exist not a few examples which clearly prove that heresies often arise from avarice. For (so that we may bring forth a few from among the many) the renowned Jeroboam, who raised up as the king of Israel over ten tribes, when fearing that if the people of Israel would go up to Jerusalem for the sake of adoring the true God, and thus the heart of the people would be turned to their lord Roboam the king of Juda, and in this way Jeroboam himself would lose the kingdom that he then had, and finding out a device he made two golden calves, and he said to the people of Israel: "Go ye up no more to Jerusalem: Behold thy gods, O Israel, who brought thee out of the land of Egypt. And he set the one in Bethel, and the other in Dan" (III Kings 12, 28-29). From which deed we learn that the avarice of the same Jeroboam flung himself and his whole kingdom not merely into heresy, but into apostacy and idolatry. And Angelomus[15] testifies in his

---

14 *Brevarium in Psalmos* (PL 26, 1245C).
15 Angelomus of Luxeuil (d. ca. 895) was a monk from Luxeuil,

commentaries of the books of Kings that this Jeroboam is a type of all heretics, when expounding this crime of the same Jeroboam which we just said.[16] Blessed Jerome also teaches the same thing on the seventh chapter of the prophet Amos.[17] That heresy of the Pharisees, teaching the people that it is better and more pleasing to God to offer sacrifices in the Temple than to distribute them to needy parents, is also manifest, and severely condemned by Christ.[18] Now this heresy of the Pharisees proceeded from their very clear avarice. Also from this pestiferous root is the error of the Greeks, who (as Guy the Carmelite relates[19]) teach that usury is licit. Finally (so that I may pass by many other examples) I will bring forth only one and a second, which will be enough to show how powerful unrestrained avarice is for subverting the faith, and for giving rise to heresy. Isidore [of Seville] in his book, *De viris illustribus*, which he made after Jerome and Gennadius,[20] when discoursing about Bishop Hosius of Cordoba, relates these words which follow:

Franche-Comté, and Biblical commentator. He was influenced by Alcuin.

16 "But Jeroboam who separating the ten tribes from the house of David and God's Temple led them into idolatry, signifies heretics who love dissension, and tear apart the unity of the Catholic faith by heresies, and in this way they hand over those following them to the worship of wicked spirits" (*Enarrationes in libros Regum*, on bk. 3 (PL 115, 471B)).

17 "Their priest Amasias is accustomed to send once in a while to King Jeroboam, a heretic, and the patron of heretics, and to accuse holy men and preachers of the faith before him, and to order teachers not to preach in Israel so that they might not act contrary to the will of the king" (*Commentary on Amos* (PL 25, 1076A)).

18 Cf. Mt. 15.

19 *Summa de haeresibus et earum confutationibus*, fols. 23r-24r, c. 9.

20 Jerome and Gennadius of Marseilles also wrote similar works bearing the same title.

Hosius, Bishop of the church of Cordoba, wrote a letter to his sister on the praise of virginity composed of beautiful and eloquent speech...[21] Also in the Synod of Sardica he published very many canons. He, however, after a long decline of old age was summoned by Emperor Constantius and having been frightened by threats, fearing that he would suffer exile or the confiscation of his goods as an old and wealthy man, consented right away to the Arian impiety... A cruel death immediately ended his life in fact, as he deserved.[22] For after the wicked prevarication of Hosius, as a certain man says, while the holy Bishop Gregory of the city of Elvira was brought in according to the imperial decree, and nowise wished to be in communion with him, Hosius having been disturbed, tells Clement, the vice-mayor, to send him into exile. But he says, 'I do not dare to send a bishop into exile, unless you firstly cast him out of the episcopate.' But when holy Gregory saw that Hosius wanted to give the sentence, he appealed to Christ, crying out from the depths of his whole faith: 'Christ, our God, Thou who art going to come to judge the living and the dead, suffer not today that human sentence be declared against me, the least of your servants, who for the faith of Thy name, as though being guilty, am made a spectacle: but Thou Thyself, I beseech Thee, pass judgment on Thy cause, Thou Thyself deign to declare the sentence in vengeance. Not as though I being fearful desire to escape from exile, since no affliction is hard to bear for Thy name: but so that many may be freed from the error of prevarication, when they see the present vengeance.' These words having been said, behold immediately Hosius sitting back with scornful contempt as though he were a regal emperor, when he tried to declare the sentence, his face contorted, his neck likewise twisting, and he fell from his seat to the

---

21 *De viris illustribus*, c. 5, n. 6 (PL 83, 1086A)).
22 *Ibid.*, c. 5, nn. 6-7 (PL 83, 1086A-1087A).

First bodily punishment of heretics: the confiscation of temporal goods

ground, and immediately expired. Then, as everyone was marveling, even that pagan Clementine became terrified, and though he was the judge, fearing that judgment with a similar punishment might also be passed against him, he prostrated himself at the feet of so great a man, begging him to spare one who had sinned against him in ignorance of the Divine law, and not by his own opinion so much as by the command of someone ordering him. For this reason, Gregory alone having complete confidence among the number of those upholding [the faith], neither turned to flight nor suffered exile, since everyone was afraid to judge him further.[23]

Whose words I have cited in great length and without changing a word, because they contain a history very much worth knowing, and an example worth remembering, so that all may clearly see that what Paul said about avarice is true, that certain men desiring it have erred from the faith. See that long ago Hosius, an illustrious man and renowned in the Catholic faith, who in the [I] Council of Nicea and the Synod of Sardica, fought very well for the faith, finally when old lest he be without the riches which he acquired when young, fell into the Arian heresy, which formerly he clearly condemned.

A great part of Germany gave to us another example in these times which cannot be related without great sorrow of the heart, which envying ecclesiastical men, because they possessed many riches, and desiring to procure them for

---

23 *Ibid.*, c. 14, nn. 16-18 (PL 83, 1091A-1091C). St. Isidore took this account from the *Libellus precum*, which Victor Cyril De Clerq in *Ossius of Cordova* (Washington D. C.: Catholic University of America Press, 1954) calls "a typical Luciferian document, full of manifest exaggerations and partisan distortions, and as such deserves little credence," and in particular, "the narrative on the death of Ossius is obviously fictitious and written with malicious intent" (pp. 485 & 517).

themselves, so that they could do it by some entitlement, although not real or just, they raised up from hell a heresy invented by the Audians,[24] but rejected by the Church, and long buried, saying that ecclesiastical men cannot possess any riches, neither lands, nor possessions: but the poverty of Christ and of His Apostles ought to be imitated by all.

Long ago there rose up a certain man in Egypt teaching it to the Audians under Pope Damasus and Theodosius the Elder: but it quickly perished. The Waldensians, or the "Poor Men of Lyons," revived it a long time later. Marsilius of Padua,[25] known solely for the fact that he bitterly hated ecclesiastical men, taught the same error at about the same time. But Pope John XXII clearly condemned this man along with his error. Then after a few years had elapsed John Wycliffe, who seems to have sworn to the words of the Waldensians, revived this error saying that it is contrary to Sacred Scripture that ecclesiastical men would have possessions: but this error was condemned with many others in the eighth session of the Council of Constance.[26]

Nevertheless, Luther raised up from hell this heresy many times condemned and now buried for a long time, who seems to have been born only for this, so that he might revive the venomous teachings of nearly all the old heretics. For when he began to spread abroad some errors, all of Germany did not immediately adhere to him: but the greater part was contradicting him, and was execrating his errors. Now the sly man, inspired by a serpentine spirit, in order to gain the favor of the people toward himself, thought up a way whereby he could easily achieve this. He began to criti-

---

24 The Audians disapproved of wealthy bishops. Cf. St. Augustine, *On Heresies, to Quodvultdeus*, c. 50 (PL 42, 39).
25 Marsilius of Padua was a physician born at Padua about 1270 and died about 1342, unreconciled to the Church.
26 "It is contrary to Sacred Scripture that ecclesiastical men have possessions" (Dz. 590).

cize ecclesiastical men, whom he very well knew were very much disliked by the people, and he said that it was nowise allowed for them to have properties or lands, nor to have any riches at all. Because (as he said) neither the Apostles whom the prelates of the Church succeed, nor the other disciples of Christ Our Savior, whose place the other lower parish priests take, possessed any properties or any lands, and if some of these things were given to them, they sold them and the price from them they divided among the poor. For this reason (which in that large work which we published, *Against All Heresies*, we showed is of no weight) Luther taught that ecclesiastical men are unjust possessors of all the lands and properties which they possess. Thus, for this reason and on this pretext, the people given over to avarice were easily persuaded otherwise to seize by force and violence the riches of the ecclesiastics, which they were avidly desiring, as from unjust possessors. Thus it happened that all the properties in many regions of Germany were taken away from the Church. Many cloisters, when the monks were cast out of them, were plundered, and their fields, gardens, vineyards, and houses, even if those properties are in another place, they were divided among themselves, or arrogated for the common benefit of the country.

The English followed this example some years later. The king either permitting, or (what I think is truer) commanding, in order that they may satisfy their voracious cupidity, all the monasteries, which in that kingdom were very wealthy, they destroyed, and they divided among themselves their annual revenue. And certainly it ought to be feared that that accursed hunger for gold, which was the cause of such great evils, also may be the cause that what was wrongly begun by him, may never cease. I truly fear, and with reason, that that part of Germany, which (by Martin Luther teaching) was separated from the Church, motivated by their avarice, may never wish to return to the unity of the Church. Because they all understand very well, that they never ought to be received by the Church, unless they firstly restore the properties which they unjustly snatched from the Church. Thus I fear (which may the most benevolent God will to avert) that they will prefer to lack that most sweet concord of the whole Church, than to be deprived of the riches now held.

When I first published this work, I conceived this fear not only about Germany, but also about England: but now there is not something which we fear about England, because God in His immense mercy, impelled by the prayers, as it is piously believed, of many faithful who were hiding in that kingdom, opened a way by which the whole kingdom, which had departed from the union of the Church, might return to her fellowship. For King Henry VIII of England, who had been the cause and origin of this departure, left only one male child, Edward as the successor to his kingdom, who after completing six years in the possession of the kingdom, died in the sixteenth year of his age before he had married a wife. Mary, his sister, a very Christian woman, succeeded this man in the kingdom by hereditary right, and who was so constant in the Catholic faith that her father Henry was never able to cause her to deviate even an inch either by flattery or great fears to accept his heresy. When she first received the rule of the kingdom, she began to think about bringing back the kingdom to the Catholic faith, and she employed all her efforts to achieving this. But because she knew she is a woman, and hence she did not believe that she would be able to accomplish the very arduous work without an also very Christian husband, she married Philip, King of Spain, son and heir of Charles V, a truly Catholic and pious man, who always held religious matters in highest veneration. When the marriage agreements were given and accepted, immediately he set out to England for its execution, accompanied by many Spanish from every rank. After he arrived there he united himself to Queen Mary by the bond of matrimony

First bodily punishment of heretics: the confiscation of temporal goods

on the feast of James the Apostle in the year 1554. Having performed the solemn celebrations of marriage the king and queen gave themselves entirely to this business, so that they might lead back the kingdom of England, which they now held under their rule, to the fold of the Catholic Church, from which it had departed for many years. To rightly accomplish this they commanded to be gathered in London the Assembly of the whole kingdom, which the English call the Parliament, on the twelfth day of the month of November of same aforesaid year. This Parliament having been assembled, the king employed very great diligence so that he might win over the whole kingdom to the acceptance of the Catholic faith, so that he left nothing undone for the sake of this matter. Therefore, by the king inducing in this way, and God specially helping, it happened that on the next occurring day of Saint Andrew the whole kingdom, through his overseers gathered in assemblies, publicly gave the obedience to the Roman Pontiff, which they had withdrawn many years before. Which having been done, a few days later the king and queen sent their ambassadors to Rome, who would show every reverence to the Pontiff in their name and of the whole kingdom. Thus the kingdom of England is in that state, in which it had been before Henry separated himself and it from the union of the Church.

We have now proved by many testimonies of Sacred Scripture and of the holy Doctors, by very clear examples, that one of the greatest causes of heresies is and always was wanton avarice. Therefore, this punishment is justly decreed to heretics, that they be deprived of all their possessions by the law itself. For by fear of this punishment, he who ardently loves riches, even if he be a heretic, still will be afraid to spread his heresy to others. And if he were not afraid to make manifest the heresy, which he mentally conceived, it would happen (as according to the opinion of the Wise Man) he would be punished in that whereby he sinned.[27]

But here someone perhaps will object that there are many heresies which do not at all originate from avarice, nay, they are somewhat diametrically opposed to avarice. Such was the heresy of the Apostolics saying that no one who keeps anything of his own can reach eternal life. Thus such heresies ought not to be punished with such a punishment, lest in that which they did not sin they would be punished. I certainly admit that there are some such heresies, which have entirely no agreement with avarice: yet a law does not regard particular cases, but those which happen for the most part. Next, even if such heresies do not originate from avarice, still they will be justly punished by the proscription of all goods. Because not for this reason alone is this punishment imposed upon heretics: but also, namely, because heresy (as we showed above) is a very serious crime, he is punished in that which is believed to very severely afflict nearly all men, and so that by fear of such punishment, they may dread to fall into the crime of heresy. And if they do not avoid heresy from fear of this punishment, it is just that they suffer that same punishment which they disregarded out of love of heresy.

---

27 Cf. Wis. 11, 17.

Chapter VI

That a heretic, from the time of the crime committed, loses all ownership of his goods, even before the declaration of the judge: yet the government treasury cannot seize the goods, except after the declaration of the judge.

A heretic is punished, and indeed justly (as we proved from very evident arguments), with the privation of all his goods: but it is necessary that we inquire whether by the very fact that he is a heretic he may be stripped of the ownership of all his goods, or whether it is necessary that a declaration of a judge precede, whereby it may become known that he is a heretic. About this matter there is a variety of opinions among jurists. The Archdeacon commenting upon the chapter, *Cum secundum leges*,[1] says that a heretic ought not to be deprived of the ownership of all his goods immediately after the crime has been committed: but in order that the heretic lose such ownership, he says that the sentence of the judge is necessary.[2] Not actually because such a sentence which condemns him to punishment is necessary, since he admits that this is not necessary: but because, he says, a declarative sentence of the crime committed, that is, whereby it is declared that he was a heretic, is prerequired. Until this sentence is pronounced, he says that the heretic is the true owner of all his goods, and can dispose of them as though they were really his. But when such a sentence has been given, whereby he is condemned of heresy, he says that the effect of that condemnation is drawn back to the day of the crime committed, such that by virtue of this declarative sentence, he is deprived (from the day of the

---

1 *Liber sextus decretalium*, bk. 5, tit. 2 (*De haereticis*), c. 19.
2 Guido de Baysio, *Lectura super sexto libro decretalium* (Venice: Juntae, 1577), col. 117r a.

crime committed) of ownership of all his goods, and from that time all alienation of his goods is forbidden to him. And he holds this opinion based upon what is said in the aforesaid chapter, *Cum secundum leges*, in §. *Confiscationis*.³ For there the Pope commands that the execution of the confiscation may not be done by the government treasury, unless firstly by some ecclesiastical authority having authority over this, shall have promulgated sentence upon this same crime.

Now this opinion of such a great man (allow me to say) seems to me completely absurd, and very clearly contrary to the text. Firstly, in fact against this opinion is that which Aristotle says: "God is bereft of this alone, to make undone what has been done."⁴ From which words it is very clearly gathered that if the heretic before condemnation was the true owner of his goods: the consequent condemnation is unable to make that he was not that owner. Otherwise, the consequent condemnation will do what God cannot do. Furthermore, if before the condemnation he was the owner of his goods: then before the condemnation he could sell or exchange his goods, or in any other way transfer to the ownership and power of someone else. For these are the effects proceeding from true ownership, namely, to give, sell, and exchange. For he who is the owner of something can sell, exchange, or give away that thing: unless perhaps he is impeded by law, so that he could not do this, as happens in someone younger than twenty-five years old who can do none of these things in regard to his own things. Certainly not because he is not the owner of those things, but because he is prohibited by

---

3 "Yet the execution of this kind of confiscation or seizure of the same goods ought not to occur by the heads of state or other temporal rulers according to the declaration of our predecessor, Pope Gregory, before the sentence on the same crime has been promulgated by the bishop of the place, or another ecclesiastical person who has authority over this."

4 *Nicomachean Ethics*, bk. 6, c. 2 (1139b), citing Agathon.

law so that he cannot do any of those things in regard to his own things. The same thing happens in the case of a married woman, who although she has true ownership of her dowery, still without her husband's permission and assent, she can nowise transfer it to the ownership and power of another. If the heretic before condemnation is the owner of his goods, the consequence is that before condemnation he can give away, sell, or exchange them: because he is not impeded by any law, as the ownership over them remains, from being able to do any of these things.

Next, if the heretic before condemnation has true ownership of all his goods, it follows from this that when he has died before condemnation, his Catholic son succeeding him will also have true ownership of those goods: because he succeeds to all the goods of which the father was the owner. If he concedes this, as it is necessary for him to concede, it follows from it that although afterwards it is established about the heresy of the father, and on account of it he is condemned after death, those goods which the son now has, should not be taken away from him, and be confiscated by the government treasury: because it is not just, that someone be deprived of his goods without his guilt, whose true owner he was. This, however, is disproved by the chapter, *Accusatus*, §. *In eo vero casu*.[5] Again this opinion is clearly opposed to the text of the chapter, *Cum secundum leges*.[6] For there it is decided that the goods of heretics ought to be confiscated by the law itself. If for the confiscation of the heretic's goods

---

5 "But in the case in which the heirs of an inheritance ought not to be admitted on account of the heresy of its author, notwithstanding that when the author himself was alive this was not the case, when his death intervened, by the sentence pronounced, one ought to proceed to the confiscation of the goods after the death of the same" (*Liber sextus decretalium*, bk. 5, tit. 2 (*De haereticis*), c. 8, §7).

6 *Ibid.*, c. 19.

(as this opinion says) a judge's declaration is required, those goods then are not confiscated by the law itself. For "by the law itself" is not other than to say that they are confiscated by power of the law alone, without the sentence of any man.

And (so that we may make our opinion more firm) let us bring forth an example in a similar case and affair, by which the same matter may be more clearly known. For an argument from a similar case has great force and power among jurists. He who commits a crime for which an excommunication is inflicted by law, although for this, because he ought to be shunned by others, according to the edict of the Council of Constance, a declaration of a judge is required, still, so that this man may fall into the excommunication, no sentence or declaration is required. For an excommunication inflicted by law differs from an excommunication inflicted by man, in that the first requires no sentence of a man to take effect, but no one can incur the second without the sentence of a judge. A heretic is excommunicated before condemnation: thus before condemnation he is also deprived of the ownership of his goods. The reasoning is correct, because this punishment is also inflicted by the law itself: therefore also before the declaration of the judge he will fall into the latter as into the former, since for no other reason does he immediately fall into the excommunication without the declaration of a judge, except because it was inflicted by the law itself.

Next, if the government treasury before the condemnation of the heretic, did not acquire ownership of his goods, it follows that the treasury commits a fault before such a sentence, when it asks from the judge to be given the goods of someone, whom it intends to prove is or was a heretic: this, however, no one having a sane mind will concede. Now that this follows from that is manifest by the fact that the treasury so asking asks not for what is its own but another's: thus it asks unjustly, especially when it asks him for the goods for no other reason except merely on account of the crime of heresy, in which it very certainly knows that he whose goods it asks for has fallen. Now what this opinion asserts in its favor, supports its opinion little or (so that I may speak more truly) not at all. For what is said in §. *Confiscationis*, does not pertain to the heretic, but to the treasury; and in that part of the text, the Pope does not speak about the heretic, whether he loses ownership of his goods before the declaration of the judge: but it speaks about the laying hold of or seizure of the goods to be made by the treasury, which it completely forbids to be done before the declaration of the judge. And it rightly forbids it: because it does not pertain to a layman, or secular authority to judge about the crime of heresy: because it could very often err in its judgment.

Now so that we may show more clearly what we say, it is necessary in this case to consider the two persons, also two very different operations according to the diversity of persons, one of which befits one person, the other the other person. The heretic and the treasury are certainly very different in the matter. Ownership and possession are also things quite different between themselves, either of which can be separated from the other. For there can be ownership without possession, and possession without ownership, as is well known to anyone. According to these two persons, and those two qualities of the things, there are also two parts in the chapter, *Cum secundum leges*.[7] The first part is the beginning of the chapter. The second part is in §. *Confiscationis*. In the first it is treated about the ownership of the goods of the heretic, and it takes it away from the heretic, and gives it to the treasury: determining that the heretic's goods are confiscated by the law itself. But because when the ownership has been taken away from the heretic, the possession was not immediately taken away: and similarly, because the ownership was conferred upon the treasury, it was understood that the possession was not immediately conferred to it: where-

---

7 *Ibid.*

fore, in the second part of that chapter, in §. *Confiscationis*, it is treated about the conferral of the possession. And it says that the treasury cannot take this possession, unless firstly the sentence upon the crime shall have been promulgated by some ecclesiastical person, who can do this. For no one can by force and violence take hold of his own property kept back from him by an unjust possessor: but it ought to be done by the authority of the judge [according to the laws] *Si quis ad se fundum*[8] and *Omnibus per civitates*.[9] Therefore,

---

8 "When anyone asserts that a tract of land, or any other property, belongs to him, and thinks that he is entitled to restitution of possession of the same, or institutes civil proceedings to obtain it or brings an accusation of violence, after having complied with the legal formalities, he is hereby notified that if he cannot prove the commission of the crime, he shall suffer the same penalty which the defendant would have undergone, if guilty. But if, having failed to serve notice upon the party in possession, he should employ force against him, We order that the case involving violence shall be heard before any others, and whatever has happened to the party in possession should be ascertained, so that the right to possession of the property which he lost may be restored to him; and that, when this has been done, if a criminal accusation should be brought, the penalty for violence shall not be inflicted, but the decision of the entire case shall be postponed, so that the principal matter may be disposed of; and if judgment should be rendered against him, he shall be deported to an island, after the confiscation of all his property" (*The Code of Justinian*, bk. 9, tit. 12 (*Ad legem Iuliam de vi publica seu privata*), l. 7).

9 "We desire that all persons, both in the towns and in the country, shall be deprived of permission to harbor thieves, vagabonds, and armed fugitive slaves. If anyone, in violation of this law which We have promulgated for the public welfare, should attempt to entertain armed slaves, vagabonds, or robbers on his premises, or near his person, We order that he shall be punished severely, after having been sentenced to pay a fine of a hundred pounds of gold. The illustrious Governors of provinces should see that no one dares to violate this law in any respect, and if they do so knowing-

Judicial sentence required before actual confiscation of heretic's goods

because the Pope in the first part of the chapter had taken away ownership of the heretic's goods from the same heretic, and had conferred them to the treasury, he forbids in the second part that one would, on the pretext of this ownership, seize possession of such goods on his own authority: but he should wait for the public authority to give him possession of the goods. Now he says that such a public authority is an ecclesiastical person authorized to judge regarding the crime of heresy, and when his declaration on the crime of heresy has been promulgated, he says that it is enough for this, namely, that the treasury can confiscate the heretic's goods. Hence the text of §. *Confiscationis* says that the declaration of the ecclesiastical judge is necessary for this, namely, that the treasury can confiscate the heretic's goods, and take possession of them, not however for this, namely, that it can acquire ownership of those goods: because the ownership of such goods had already been granted to him before such a sentence in the first part of the chapter. Thus by such a sentence, whereby someone is condemned as a heretic, he is not deprived of the ownership of his goods: but by that sentence it is declared, and it becomes known that he has already been deprived of such ownership, which privation actually before such a sentence had not been manifested in this way to others, and by such a sentence he can be dispossessed.

And certainly, if the Archdeacon, a man otherwise learned, had averted to this distinction of things, he would have thought differently. Therefore, this opinion having been rejected as false, another opinion is truer: Giovanni

---

ly, they shall be stripped of their rank and office, and, after having been condemned to pay a fine of a hundred pounds of gold, shall be put to death, and their principal retainers, as well as the attendants attached to their persons, shall also be condemned to death, in addition to the confiscation of their property" (*Ibid.*, l. 10).

d'Andrea[10] commenting upon this same chapter, *Cum secundum leges*, which says that a heretic loses ownership of all his goods from the day of the crime committed.[11] Many other men learned in Canon Law maintain this opinion. Abbas on the first chapter [of the two bearing the same name], *Excommunicamus*.[12] Dominicus a San Geminiano[13] on the above-mentioned chapter, *Cum secundum leges*.[14] Pietro d'Ancarano[15] on the same chapter.[16] All these men reckon that the heretic from the day of the crime committed is deprived of the ownership of his goods. Now that they say from the day of the crime committed ought to be understood, not only regarding the crime of heresy. Because not by the very fact that someone falls into the crime of heresy does he lose the ownership of his goods, but only after he is so pertinacious in his heresy, that then deservedly (according to those things which we said in book one) he ought to be reckoned a heretic. For just as not everyone who falls into

---

10 Alias, Johannes Andreae (ca. 1275-1348) was an Italian canonist.

11 "The goods of heretics are confiscated by the law itself, which is proved by a triple legal argument. But the apprehension of the goods ought not to be done by the secular authority, unless firstly it was pronounced upon the crime by the ecclesiastical judge, who can do this" (Gloss on *Liber sextus decretalium* (Venice: Juntas, 1595), bk. 5, tit. 2, l. 19, p. 436b).

12 "After having been condemned of heresy, they are punished by the judge, and the goods of heretics are confiscated" (Gloss on *Decretals of Gregory IX*, bk. 5, tit. 7 (*De haereticis*), c. 13).

13 Dominicus a San Geminiano (d. 1424) was a vicar general of the bishop of Modena and Italian jurist.

14 *Lectura super Libro Sexto*, pt. 2, fol. 144r.

15 Alias, Petrus Ancharanus. Pietro d'Ancarano (ca. 1333-1416) was an Italian jurist.

16 *Super Sexto Librum Decretalium acutissima Commentaria* (Bologna: apud Societatem typographiae Bononiensis, 1583), p. 396a.

Judicial sentence required before actual confiscation of heretic's goods

heresy, unless pertinacity be present, ought to be reckoned a heretic; so neither does every such man, pertinacity having been excluded, lose the ownership of his goods. For in the chapter, *Cum secundum leges*, the Pope does not decree that the goods of those fallen into heresy are confiscated: but the goods of heretics, from which follows that he who has fallen into heresy, if when admonished about it immediately revokes his error, is not by the law itself deprived, nay, and he ought not to be deprived, of all his goods: which ought to be noted not only in this punishment, but in all the others, which laws decree for heretics, whether they are inflicted by the law itself, or ought to be inflicted by the judge. For since none of the punishments has the law decreed ought to be given to him who only has fallen into heresy: but to him who is a heretic. Now to those who when admonished immediately revoke and condemn their error, the punishment ought to be imposed at the discretion of the judge, taking into consideration a previous error, and the quality of the person. Therefore, from that moment of time alone, in which he can be rightly deemed a heretic, it ought to also be reckoned that he loses all ownership of his goods.

The heretic, from that time until the condemnation of his crime, has mere, bare possession of his goods, without any ownership of them. But the treasury has the opposite condition about those goods: for it has only ownership without any possession regarding them before the condemnation of the crime. And whence two things necessarily follow, one by reason of the lost ownership, the other by reason of the possession retained. From the latter, that he retains possession, although (as we will say afterwards) not conferred by law to himself, it follows that the heretic at that time cannot be exempted from paying his own debts by the exception of heresy: because before he has been deprived of his possessions, just as he retains possession of the goods, so also their administration, and consequently as an administrator he can pay his own debts. By reason of the ownership lost, it follows that all alienations of those goods at that time made by the heretic are of no strength, or importance, and can be easily revoked by the treasury. And from this also it necessarily follows that the treasury can claim those goods alienated in this way from the hands of any possessor, yet on this condition, that the price, by which those goods had be sold, be restored to the buyer, if such a price, or something equivalent to it is found with the heretic. If, however, neither the price of those goods, nor something else in place of the price is found with the heretic, the treasury could now claim those goods also when no price was given: although the buyer bought them in good faith. Giovanni d'Andrea teaches this in the place cited above, and after him Dominicus a San Geminiano in the same place. And for a confirmation of this matter they assert as proof the laws, *Si cum dotem*, §. 13,[17] and the following law, *Dotium causa*;[18] and the law, *Imperator*, of the title, *De legatis et fideicommissis*,[19] and the following law.[20]

---

17 "When a woman makes a mistake as to the condition of her husband, and thinks that he is a freeman while, in fact, he is a slave, some preference must be shown her with respect to the property of her husband; for example, if there are other creditors, she must be preferred in case an action *de peculio* is brought, and if the slave owes anything to his master, the woman shall not be preferred to him, except with reference to what was either given by way of dowry, or purchased with money forming part of it, since property of this kind is dotal" (*Digest of Justinian*, bk. 24, tit. 3, l. 22, n. 13 (*Si mulier*)).

18 "And where anything has been expended on property belonging to the dowry, and no account is given of the same by the woman, an exception on the ground of bad faith will be available" (*Ibid.*, l. 23).

19 *Ibid.*, bk. 31, tit. 1, l. 70.

20 *Ibid.*, l. 71.

Judicial sentence required before actual confiscation of heretic's goods

I, however, adduce something similar, which greatly confirms the point. If Peter buys from John something stolen in good faith, which John had snatched away from Francis, and afterwards Francis finds the thing stolen from him in Peter's possession, he will justly claim it from Peter, even though the price is not found in the possession of the thief, or something else having the same value. Now he justly will do this for no other reason than because he can demand back and claim his property from any possessor. Therefore, since a heretic from the day the crime was committed, is deprived of ownership of his goods, it thence follows that he, if he has sold something from among his goods, sold not his own property, but the treasury's. And consequently, the treasury can claim it from any possessor before the legal time of prescription has elapsed. For those possessing the goods of heretics can prescribe: even against the Roman Church during the period of forty years, as is evident in the chapter, *Si qui, exigentibus*.[21] From which text it is clearly gathered that he who bought something from a heretic in good faith, thinking that he is a Catholic, after the period of forty years has elapsed, the treasury cannot claim it from the buyer. For that text grants prescription not only to the children of heretics, but also to others not belonging to his household: provided they are Catholic, and possess in good faith, believing in good faith that they had received from a Catholic man, although before such receptions he had become a heretic.

From this lost ownership of goods, it also follows that a heretic cannot make a last will, and if he perhaps had made a will at death, it is of no force, or importance: because a will ought to be made regarding one's own goods, not regarding another's. For just as he cannot sell or exchange those goods, so also he can nowise transfer ownership and control to some other person, or do this as a gift during his lifetime: because

---

21 Bk. 2, tit. 12 (*De praescriptione*), c. 2.

all such transfers of goods, so that they may stay valid and firm, require that there be true ownership in the transferer, of which since the heretic is deprived, it follows that he not justly make any such transfer of goods. From this ownership of goods lost before the sentence of the judge, it also follows that a heretic is obliged to give to the treasury all the goods which he had when he became a heretic to be possessed: and if he does not give, he sins mortally.

Because I know that this All these things having been considered is contrary to the opinion of many jurists, I intent to prove it by very manifest and evident reasons, so that anyone who reads them, may whole-heartedly[22] go over to my opinion. Firstly in fact it is proved by this, that those goods do not now belong to the heretic (as we manifestly showed, and the majority of jurists concede) but to the treasury: thus the heretic retaining those goods, retains what is not his own, but another's: therefore, by retaining he sins, especially when he retains against the will of the treasury. These consequences are proved by Blessed Augustine in his letter to Macedonius saying: "If the offense committed has involved theft, and restitution is not made, although it is possible to make it, there is no repentance but only pretense."[23] And these words are found in chapter, *Si res*.[24] Perhaps someone here will reply: Augustine's words do not apply to our point of discussion: because Augustine speaks (as it is established from his words) about property belonging to another, from the acquisition or possession had of which, a sin is committed: the heretic's goods are not such: because the heretic did not sin (as I presuppose) in acquiring such goods. Hence it is that such goods of the heretic are not of such a kind that, according the saying of Augustine, the heretic would be obliged to give them back.

---

22 Lit., manibus ac pedibus ("by their hands and feet").
23 Letter 153, n. 20 (PL 33, 662).
24 *Decretum Gratiani*, pt. 2, *causa* 14, q. 6, c. 1 (PL 187, 966A).

Judicial sentence required before actual confiscation of heretic's goods

Therefore, I will prove in a different way and more clearly this opinion of mine as follows. By the precept, "Thou shalt not steal," not merely the taking of another's property is prohibited: but also any detention of another's property, when the owner is unwilling. Otherwise, it would be necessary to say that a thief only sins, when he takes away (contrary to the will of the owner) another's property, and not when he retains contrary to the will of the owner, which is clearly erroneous. For [Venerable Bede], when commenting on the verse from the book of Proverbs, "He that is partaker with a thief" (29, 24), etc., speaks thus: "For not only the thief, but also he is held to be guilty, who being aware of the theft, does not want, when he is able, to reveal the money to the owner who is looking for it."[25] These words are found in the chapter, *Qui cum fure*.[26] Which words ought to be so understood, that one is obliged to reveal not the thief, but what was stolen: and this when the thing stolen can be recuperated. If he who does not reveal the thing stolen, when he can, is held guilty of theft: much more will he be held guilty, who truly detains it in his own possession. And in this way it follows that not only the taking of the thing, but also the detention is prohibited by Divine precept. From which it is very clearly established that a heretic sins when he keeps in his possession goods formerly his own, and does not give them to the treasury: because he keeps what is not his own against the will of the owner.

If someone perhaps with an obstinate mind wants to hold the opposite position, he would reply, admitting that the keeping of someone else's property is forbidden by that Divine precept, yet not every detention: but only the detention of property taken by theft. This statement is clearly refuted and proved to be false: because according to it one

---

25 *Allegorica expositio in Parabolas Salomonis*, c. 29 (PL 91, 1022D).
26 *Decretals of Gregory IX*, bk. 5, tit. 18 (*De furtis*), c. 4.

ought to admit the heir does not sin, when he does not give back and can give back the legacy left in the last will to the legatee: for he, even though he keeps what belongs to another, still not what was taken by theft, and so according to the aforesaid reply one ought to say that he when so keeping, does not act contrary to that precept: "Thou shalt not steal." Likewise for the same reason one ought to concede that he who does not give back to its owner asking for it what was entrusted to his keeping, does not sin even though the owner of what was entrusted is a wise man, and asks for the thing entrusted for use in an upright business. For he does not detain a thing taken away by theft, whence it is (as according to the things conceded) he does not act against that precept: "Thou shalt not steal." And hence it follows that he does not sin since he does not act against that precept. Now this is very clearly false, so that no man of a sound mind would dare to concede it: because a man is bound by the natural law to give back what has been entrusted, especially when giving back in this way he does not inflict greater harm upon the owner than if he would keep it. Many other absurd and incompatible incongruities would follow from that erroneous interpretation of the Divine precept: which because it would take a long time and be tedious to consider them all, therefore I pass over them.

Therefore, let them acknowledge that it is necessary by that precept, "Thou shalt not steal," that all retention of another's property is forbidden (when the owner is unwilling), which is not granted by Divine or human law. Hence it is that anyone who retains another's property against the owner's will sins by such retention: unless perhaps such retention of another's property has been either commanded or granted to him by law, or by a judge rightly judging. For if he retains by the authority of the law, or of the judge judging rightly, by so retaining he does not act against the Divine precept, and consequently does not sin. For then it is permitted to retain another's property against the actual will of the owner: yet not against the due will, which the owner himself is obliged to have. For the owner himself ought then to want his property to be detained by someone else when such detention has been commanded by law or by a judge rightly judging. And if then he would want his property to be given back to him, he would want wrongly: and would sin by so willing. For this reason he who does not give back to the owner full of rage the sword entrusted by him, does not sin: because he is prohibited by natural law to give it back. For the same reason if the judge commands him who keeps a deposit, not to give it back to the owner: but to keep it in his name, because the creditor asks for payment of a debt to be made to him from that deposit, which he distrusts will be made from elsewhere, if the deposit is returned to the owner; in which case he who does not return the deposit, does not sin: because by the authority of the judge judging correctly, who justly looks out for the indemnity of the creditor, he does this.

I said, "by the authority of the judge judging correctly," because if it were evident to me that the judge judges unjustly, when he commands the detention of another's property against the will of the owner, I would act badly if I retain it. From which it follows that if I were to dispute before a judge with the owner about a thing, which I know really belongs to him, and the judge, being deceived either by love, or by hatred or by inexperience, judged in my favor, deciding that the thing is mine, then I will detain that thing unjustly: even though I keep it by the authority of the judge, because the judge then judged unjustly. Still if the matter were doubtful to me, about which I dispute with another before a judge, and the judge decides that it is mine: then I can justly retain it, even though it belonged to another: because I do not know that it belongs to someone else, and I retain it by the authority of the judge, whom I believe judged correctly. As often as someone without the authority of law or of a judge retains another's property against the will of the owner, he sins and acts against that precept: "Thou shalt not steal," by which it is prohibited not only the taking of the property of another, but also its detention when the owner is unwilling.

From these things it is very clearly proved that a heretic is bound to give the goods which he now has, and which were previously his own, to the treasury, and if he does not give, he will sin mortally: because he retains property of another against the will of the owner. For the goods, which the heretic retains (as we have already proved) are not his own, but the treasury's, to which by the law itself were attached to the treasury: which goods the heretic when the treasury was unwilling retains without any authority of law: therefore, he unjustly retains them until he gives them to the treasury, which is their true owner. For there is no law which grants to the heretic with privation of ownership possession of the goods formerly his own until the judge's condemnation. For if some such law is shown, I will voluntarily cede the battlefield, and will willingly recant the things that I have said. Yet I know that there is no such concession of law in the whole Canon Law, from which judgment of this case ought to be sought.

Perhaps here someone will object to me the text of the chapter, *Cum secundum leges*,[27] in which the treasury is forbidden to seize the goods of the heretic before his condemnation. But certainly, if the text of this edict is considered carefully (as it should be done), it nowise contradicts my opinion, nay, instead it supports it. For that edict certainly deprives (as we said before) the heretic of the ownership of his goods: yet it does not grant confiscation of the goods until the aforesaid condemnation. Because even though in §. *Confiscationis* the treasury is forbidden to seize his goods before the heretic's condemnation, still not by this does it

---

27 *Liber sextus decretalium*, bk. 5, tit. 2 (*De haereticis*), c. 19.

concede to the heretic the retention of those goods until the aforementioned condemnation. For from the fact that the treasury cannot seize, it does not follow that the heretic is not obliged to give them. For these two things often cohere in many things, so that Peter cannot seize something from me by his own authority: and yet I am obliged to give it to him. Firstly, the case is expressed in the laws, *Si quis ad se fundum*,[28] and *Omnibus per civitates*.[29] Next, the legatee cannot seize the legacy left to him in a last will on his own authority, and yet the heir is obliged to give it to him. Again, he who by some fraud injures another in the sale of something, is obliged to the recompensation of the damage to that man: yet the same man cannot take recompensation from him, especially if he can obtain it from the judge. There are many other similar examples, which are not necessary to enumerate, by which it is shown that it does not follow that a heretic is not bound to give his goods before the condemnation to the treasury, from the fact that the treasury before such condemnation cannot seize them.

Therefore, since there is no law which grants to the heretic deprived of his goods the possession of his goods, until he has been condemned of his crime by a competent judge: it is thence proved that the heretic is obliged to give his goods to the treasury, without any condemnation of the judge, such that if he does not give them, he would sin mortally. Yet I believe that this is true only when he is sure that he is or was a heretic: because before this he was perhaps excused through ignorance. This opinion can also be proved by all those reasons, by which it is proved that a penal law inflicted by the law itself obliges the guilty man in conscience to the punishment decreed by law, without undergoing any sentence of the judge. About which matter, because I will

---

28 *The Code of Justinian*, bk. 9, tit. 12 (*Ad legem Iuliam de vi publica seu private*), l. 7.
29 *Ibid.*, l. 10.

treat copiously enough in that small work which I am now preparing to publish on penal law,[30] wherefore I decided to say nothing more now. Thus I send the reader to that work, so that he may draw from it the things suitable to this point. From these things therefore it is evident that all those err who teach that the heretic before the condemnation of his crime, is not bound to give the goods formerly his own to the treasury which, by the law itself from the day of the crime committed, is the owner of them.

And certainly (as I frankly admit), I am unable to understand how these two things can be consistent, namely, that the treasury is by the law itself the owner of all the heretic's goods, and that the heretic when retaining his goods, is not obliged to give them to the treasury, which is now their true owner, especially since by no law has it been granted to the heretic the possession of those goods. For these two things are as it were diametrically opposed to each other: the heretic without any authority of law or of the judge retains the goods of the treasury, and he is not held to give them to the treasury. Hence it is necessary that just as the heretic has been deprived of the ownership of his goods, and the treasury is made their owner: so also the heretic by the law itself is bound to give the goods to the treasury: especially when the law does not grant to the heretic that, although he has been deprived of the ownership of his goods, he could retain them, until he has been condemned of the crime of heresy by the competent judge. And Abbas holds this opinion of mine, when commenting on the chapter, *Delecti*.[31]

Now whether a heretic coming to his senses, and repentant of his crime, recuperates ownership of such goods which he had then lost through heresy, seems to me to be a question

---

30 *De potestate legis poenalis libri duo.*
31 *Decretals of Gregory IX*, bk. 1, tit. 43 (*De arbitris*), c. 4; *Commentaria seu lectura in quinque Decretalium libros*, vol. 2, fol. 253v a.

of little difficulty: since it has been very expressly decided about it in the chapter, *Vergentis*.[32] For having considered the quality of the person and the error, also taking into account the past obstinacy of the same heretic, and the present repentance, which can be inferred in one way or another from exterior signs: the judge could mercifully give either all the goods or at least some part of them to him. The obstinacy of the heretic could also be so long and so ironlike that even if he afterwards repents, the judge acts justly if he decides that none of his goods are to be left to him. For although the repentant heretic escapes from the death penalty, still not on that account does it follow that he is by the law itself absolved from all the rest of the punishments.

---

32 "Nor should their properties revert to heretics in the future, unless someone voluntarily takes pity upon them when they experience a change of heart and reject the company of heretics" (*Decretals of Gregory IX*, bk. 5, tit. 7 (*De haereticis*), c. 10; Innocent III, *Registrorum sive epistolarum*, bk. 2, letter 1 (PL 214, 539A).

Chapter VII

On the second punishment of heretics, which is the privation of all rule over subjects of whatever kind.

Another punishment of heretics is the privation of any jurisdiction of a prelate, and the authority which they previously had over men of whatever condition. For he who is a heretic, is deprived of all such things by the law itself: just as it is clearly decreed in the chapter, *Absolutos*.[1] But because there appear many things worth noting: I decided to publish the words of the text, so that those who would read them could consider the difficulty of the matter, and they may understand those things about that text we said are worth noting. The words of that chapter are as follows: "Let them know that they are absolved from the obligation of fealty [i. e., fidelity], homage, and all duty, whoever were held bound by any covenant, strengthened by whatsoever band, to such as are manifestly lapsed into heresy." By the word, "absolved," it is clearly shown that the sentence has been passed by the law, and is not to be imposed by the judge. For it does not command that they be absolved, but is says to precisely those liable through guilt, that they should know that they are absolved. Hence it is that the guilty man is obliged in conscience to undergo this punishment, even before every other sentence of the judge, just as we said above about the privation of other goods.

By this that it says, "from the obligation of fealty," it is clearly shown that he who keeps something entrusted by the heretic to him for safekeeping, ought not to return the thing entrusted to the heretic asking for it. For even though all are obliged by the natural law to be faithful in returning something entrusted: nevertheless, anyone who has

---

1 *Decretals of Gregory IX*, bk. 5, tit. 7 (*De haereticis*), c. 16.

received something entrusted from the heretic is freed from this obligation of fealty, so that once his heresy has been manifested, he is not obliged to give it back to the heretic. Whence it is that if after the heretic has been condemned by the Church, the treasury wishes to seize his goods in the possession of someone else having been entrusted under the guaranty of fealty, he who was keeping the thing entrusted would be bound to give it to the treasury, and could not excuse himself from giving through the excuse of something entrusted or of fealty: because he has then been absolved from this debt of fealty by the Church.

For the same reason the commander of some town or fortress, who received it from some ruler under fealty and oath, if such a ruler would become a heretic, he will not be obliged to restore the castle or fortress: nor give it to anyone else upon his command besides the treasury, to which by the law itself belongs the ownership of such things. There are also many things which everyone is obliged to give to a ruler to whom he has sworn fealty, namely, safe, secure, honest, useful, easy, possible: because all these things are related and declared in the chapter, *De forma fidelitis*.[2] Whoever is

---

[2] "Since I was asked to write something about the oath of fealty, I have noted for you these things which follow from the authority of books. Whoever swears fealty to his lord should always have six things in mind: safe, secure, honest, useful, easy, possible. Safe, namely, lest he injure his lord with his own body. Secure lest he injure his secret interests or his defenses through which his lord can be secure. Honest lest he injure his lord's justice or in other matters which seem to pertain to his honesty. Useful lest he injure his lord's possessions. Easy or possible, lest that the good, which his lord could easily do, he would make difficult, and that what would be possible, he would make impossible for his lord. A faithful man should pay heed to these examples. It is not sufficient to abstain from evil, unless he may do what is good. It remains that he faithfully give his lord counsel and help in the aforementioned matters, if he wishes to be worthy of his benefice [fief] and safe in

Second bodily punishment of heretics: privation of all rulership

obliged to keeping fealty to another is absolved by the law itself from all these parts of fealty, after he, to whom he was bound, has become a heretic. Unless perhaps in some case he were obliged by Divine law to giving some of these things, which cannot be taken away by human law. For I believe that the duties of humanity in the case of extreme necessity are also due to the heretic by Divine law. For necessity is not subject to law.

On account of this same absolution from the debt of fidelity, a believing spouse is not bound to render the [conjugal] debt to the heretical spouse: because by the heresy of the other spouse he has been freed from this debt of fidelity. Yet not from every debt: but only from that which is expressed by an affirmative precept, for spouses, on account of the Sacrament of Matrimony, by which they are joined together, are bound to each other by a double bond of fidelity: one affirmative, and the other negative. For each one of the spouses is held to render the debt to the other. He is also held not to give his body to anyone else than to his spouse. From this fidelity, which is expressed by a negative precept, neither of the spouses is ever free, no matter how much the other spouse may sin, even if he were to fall into the crime of heresy. Because even if on account of the adultery or heresy of the other, the innocent spouse can ask for and obtain a divorce, nevertheless after a divorce has been made between them, neither of them could be joined in any way to anyone else beside his spouse, as it is clearly taught in the chapter, *Quasivit*,[3] and in the chapter, *Quanto*,[4] of the

---

the fealty that he has sworn. The lord also ought to render his duty to his faithful man in all things. If he does not, he may be thought of as faithless, just as he, who in consenting or telling lies will be perfidious and perjurious" (*Decretum Gratiani*, pt. 2, *causa* 22, q. 5, c. 18 (PL 187, 1156C-1157B)).

3 *Decretals of Gregory IX*, bk. 4, tit. 19 (*De divortiis*), c. 2.
4 *Ibid.*, c. 7. Innocent III's letter cited here is actually titled, *Quo-*

title, *De divortiis*. Thus from that fidelity alone, which is expressed by an affirmative precept, is the believing spouse freed by the law itself, after the other has fallen into manifest heresy, such that he would no longer be held to render the debt to the other.

But this absolution of fidelity and of the debt is not only confirmed by human and Canon Law, but also by Divine law. For just as the adulterer through corporal adultery is deprived by law of demanding the debt: so also through spiritual adultery, which is heresy, is he deprived by the same law: because spiritual adultery is worse than corporal adultery. Now whether the heretic coming to his senses recuperates though repentance this right of asking for this debt, which he had lost through heresy: the question seems doubtful to some. Urban III in the chapter, *De illa*,[5] decided that the woman who was separated without the Church's judgment from the husband fallen into heresy, ought to render to the husband after he has returned to the Catholic faith, and commands her to be compelled if she does not want to return to the husband. But if she departed from him by the Church's judgment, he says that she nowise ought to be compelled to receive him.

But the Glosses[6] on the chapters, *Quanto*[7] and *Mulier quae*,[8] are not afraid to opine contrary to that text, saying: the woman, who departed from the heretical husband, if he returns to the faith always ought to be compelled to receiving

---

niam te novimus, and not *Quanto te novimus*, as mistakenly written in this decretal.

5   *Ibid.*, c. 6.

6   Gloss on the words, *judicio ecclesiae*, in the chapter, *Mulier quae* (*Decretals of Gregory IX*, bk. 3, tit. 32, c. 20/21) and on the words, *redire cogatur*, in the chapter, *Quanto* (*Ibid.*, bk. 4, tit. 19, c. 7).

7   *Decretals of Gregory IX*, bk. 4, tit. 19, c. 7.

8   *Ibid.*, bk. 3, tit. 32 (*De conversione conjugatorum*), c. 20/21.

her husband, even if she departed from him by the judgment of the Church. And if she does not want to return to the husband, it says that she ought to be forced to take the vows of the monastic state. To prove this opinion it cites *Mulier quae*. Abbas on the same chapters does not entirely approve of the judgment and opinion of the Gloss: but howsoever he departs from it, still he does not bring forth any reason, by which he shows to us that he rightly departed from it.[9]

But I will bring forth reasons, by which I will prove that the Gloss is completely off track. And firstly, I will pierce the Glossator with his own sword: because that chapter, *Mulier quae*, which the Glossator cited to support himself, fights very clearly against him. For that chapter (as it can be very easily gathered from its words) does not speak in favor of the heretic who came to his senses, and does penance: but supports the woman, who had been separated from her heretical husband by the judgment of the Church, and grants to her that when the same husband is unwilling to allow her to freely enter the religious state of monastic vows, she can do so if she wills. In which words that especially ought to be noticed that it says, "freely enter": therefore she ought not to be forced to enter religion, even if she is unwilling to return to her husband. Otherwise, if she ought to be forced to enter the religious state (as the Gloss teaches), she will not then enter the religious state freely, as that text says. Furthermore, if the woman freely, and not having been forced, can enter the religious state when her husband is unwilling, then she can also remain outside of the religious state separated from him when the husband is unwilling. This consequence will thence clearly be proved to be correct if we show the cause and origin from which it arises, namely, that the believing

---

9 Panormitanus, *Commentaria seu lectura in quinque Decretalium libros* (Jacobus de Giuncta, 1527), vol. 6, fol. 163r b, & vol. 7, fol. 52r a.

woman, who had been separated from her husband by the judgment of the Church, is able to enter the religious state.

The reason is certainly no other than because by heresy, as by spiritual adultery, he lost the right of asking for the debt from the wife, and in this way she was made free from this debt. For if he had not fallen into heresy, the woman could not (when he was unwilling) enter the religious state, as it is explicitly decreed in the chapter, *Quidam*,[10] and in the chapter, *Cum sis*.[11] Thus the reason for that separation made by the entrance into religion having been clearly shown, I will inquire of the Glossator whether the heretical husband when returning to the faith recuperates through repentance that right of asking for the debt, which he had lost through heresy, or not. If he says that the heretic recovered that right, it will be necessary to assert that his wife (when he is unwilling) cannot freely enter religion: because by such an entry she would deny to the husband what was then belonging to him by right. But if he says that the heretic did not recuperate through repentance such a right once lost through heresy, it follows that the wife is not bound to render him the debt after repentance, just as she also was not bound before the repentance: because (as it was conceded) the heretic after repentance does not have a greater right for asking the debt from the wife than he had before the repentance. Wherefore just as after the repentance of the husband, formerly a heretic, his wife can freely enter religion when he is unwilling: so also she can freely remain in the world against his will, and without rendering of the debt: for the reason for both separations is completely one and the same.

But (so that I may speak more plainly) it is not necessary to give a choice to the Glossator: because whether he will or not, he is obliged to admit that a heretic after repentance

---

10 *Decretals of Gregory IX*, bk. 3, tit. 32 (*De conversione conjugatorum*), c. 3.
11 *Ibid.*, c. 4.

does not recuperate the right of asking the debt from the wife: because once an obligation has extinguished it does not revive. For on account of this the heretic after repentance does not necessarily (as we said above) recover the goods which he had lost though the obstinacy of heresy, as it is specified in the chapter, *Vergentis*:[12] thus also for the same reason he will not recover the right of asking the debt, which he had lost at some time. And hence it necessarily follows that his wife could freely deny him the conjugal debt, and consequently she will not be compelled to receive the man, returning from unbelief, from whom she had been separated by the judgment of the Church.

And I am truly astonished why the Glossator would have fallen into such a clear error, especially when he has such a very explicit decision of the Church opposed to his opinion, in the above-mentioned chapter, *De illa*.[13] Now that which he says, that that chapter is corrected by the following chapter, is not so: because the following chapter in no way contradicts, firstly, since they speak about different things. For the chapter, *De illa*, speaks about the woman who has been separated by the judgment of the Church: who ought not to be forced to return to the man returning from heresy; the following chapter, however, speaks at the end about her who by her own judgment was separated from the unbelieving husband, who after the man's repentance ought to be forced to return to him, although this is not clearly enough expressed in that same place: but it ought to be drawn from it by reasonable inferences.

Now the reason for this difference comes from (in my judgment) the fact that the Church does not want any punishment inflicted upon the heretic, before he has been condemned of his crime by her, as is it clear in the chapter,

---

12 *Ibid.*, bk. 5, tit. 7 (*De haereticis*), c. 10.
13 *Ibid.*, bk. 4, tit. 19, c. 6.

Ut inquisitionis,[14] and in the chapter, *Cum secundum leges*.[15] And if something has been attempted contrary to this, by the law itself it is considered as not done. Thus the woman who by her own judgment separated herself from her living unbelieving husband: because she punished her husband with the penalty of a heretic, before he had been condemned by the Church, wherefore the Church judges such separation as not done: and hence as though she had never been separated from him, she is compelled to stay with him. Now she who was separated by the judgment of the Church, punishes her husband after he has been condemned of his crime by the ecclesiastical judge. For I do not think that that judgment of the Church, which is said to be needed so that that woman could (when her husband is unwilling) enter religion, is anything else but the sentence of the ecclesiastical judge, whereby it is declared that that man is a heretic: by which sentence having been given, without a further sentence of separation, I reckon it to suffice, so that the woman could be separated from her husband, and that having been separated she could not be compelled to receive her husband returning from heresy.

But it is now necessary that we go on to the explanation of rest of the parts of that aforesaid chapter, *Absolutos*.[16] For it not only says that those who have been bound by some obligation to heretics, are absolved from all duty of fidelity: but also from all duty of obedience [*debitas dominii*].[17] For a clearer understanding of the phrase, it is befitting firstly to instruct the reader about the multiplicity of dominion. For there is a dominion over men, another over the other things, irrational things serving men, such as

---

14 *Liber sextus decretalium*, bk. 5, tit. 2 (*De haereticis*), c. 18.
15 *Ibid.*, c. 19.
16 *Decretals of Gregory IX*, bk. 5, tit. 7 (*De haereticis*), c. 16.
17 The chapter, *Absolutos*, uses instead the phrase, "debt of obedience" (*debito obsequii*).

Second bodily punishment of heretics: privation of all rulership

money, clothing, houses, fields, vineyards, animals, other things similar to these. We do not speak about the dominion of these things in this chapter, because we have discussed about it above, according to what was explained about the chapter, *Cum secundum leges*. Dominion over men is still multiple: because there is a natural dominion; one is civil, and the other is Evangelical. There is no natural dominion over some man except the dominion of parents, that is, that which the parent has over the children. For all were children in the natural law, and there was no other dominion in the state of innocence than that of parents. For the father and the mother, then as now, had the power of teaching, admonishing, and of correcting their children, and the children, then as now, were obliged to obey their parents, and to serve them in their needs, if they suffered any. This dominion then is called "natural," because natural reason teaches that a child should assist his parent, and serve him from whom he received existence, and obey the one to whom it belongs to admonish and correct him. This dominion, even though it is natural, is not so fixed and immovable that it cannot be removed, as is the rest of natural dominion, which any man has over the things needed for the conservation of his life. For (as Blessed Thomas correctly teaches[18]) the first and greatest natural inclination is to exist: and hence man has natural dominion over anything necessary for the preservation of his life.

This dominion a man neither can cast away from himself: nor on account of any crime can it be taken away by a court of justice. Hence the same Blessed Thomas says, "If a man were condemned to die of hunger, he does not sin if he

---

18 "In man there is first of all an inclination to good in accordance with the nature which he has in common with all substances: inasmuch as every substance seeks the preservation of its own being, according to its nature: and by reason of this inclination, whatever is a means of preserving human life, and of warding off its obstacles, belongs to the natural law" (I-II, q. 94, a. 2).

partakes of food brought to him secretly, because to refrain from taking it (as he says) would be to kill himself."[19] The dominion of the father over the children is not so firm and fixed: because the son in reality is not as necessary to the father for the preservation of his life, as other things. Whence it is that the father can cast off from himself that dominion: and a superior can take it away from the father in punishment for some misdeed. The first part is evident in emancipation, because by it the father constitutes the son to be his own master, and he renounces the authority and dominion which he has over the son. The second part is evident in *The Institutes of Justinian*, [in the title,] *Quibus modis ius potestatis solvitur*, where among other words these are found: "If a man, convicted of some crime, is deported to an island, he loses the rights of a Roman citizen; whence it follows, that the children of a person thus banished cease to be under his power, exactly as if he were dead."[20] It happens in the same way in the sin of heresy, because on account of this crime the father loses the dominion, which he had over his children, and the children are made to be their own masters. For the children who were otherwise subject to the father, by him falling obstinately into heresy, are by the law itself absolved from all duty of obedience, [the right to] which the father had over them before, as it is said in the aforesaid chapter, *Absolutos*[21]

But because many could have thought that this was not very clearly decreed in that chapter, whence the Church willed to make a special decree about this matter: whereby that which we have just now said was declared. Such a decree is found in the chapter, *Quicumque*, §. *Illorum*.[22] And hence it follows that the heretical father cannot make

---

19 II-II, q. 69, a. 4 ad 2um.
20 *The Institutes of Justinian*, bk. 1, tit. 12, l. 1 (*Cum autem is*).
21 *Decretals of Gregory IX*, bk. 5, tit. 7 (*De haereticis*), c. 16.
22 *Liber sextus decretalium*, bk. 5, tit. 2 (*De haereticis*), c. 2, §4.

a pupillary substitution for his child under puberty. Because among the other things requisite for a pupillary substitution this is the main one, namely, that the testator have the child under puberty under his control.[23] This corollary can also be elsewhere deduced from the fact that a heretic is not competent to make a will. Now no one can make a pupillary substitution, unless he firstly made a will for himself.[24] But the question can be raised about this matter, if the father before he became a heretic needed the son for the preservation of his life, and afterwards the same need perduring he were to fall into heresy, whether the son would be held to give him those works, and attend to him according to his need. To which question I reckon it ought to be replied thus, namely, that the son in this case is held by a greater obligation to the father than he is held to another who is in need: because even though the son has been freed by the law itself from the father's dominion and authority, still he is not freed regarding the works of mercy that ought to be shown to him, in which the father though a heretic ought to be preferred. The Gloss on distinction thirty, chapter one,[25] and Panormitanus on the chapter, *Si quis*,[26] teach this same opinion.

Another dominion is over persons not naturally, but civilly, that is, that which is not from nature, but received its beginning from human statutes. And this is also diverse and multiple, according to the various authorities and powers which rulers have over those whom they rule. For there is a domin-

---

23 *Digest of Justinian*, bk. 28, tit. 6 (*De vulgari et pupillari substitutione*), l. 2.
24 *Ibid.*, §1.
25 *Decretum Gratiani*, pt. 1, dist. 10, c. 1 (*Si qui filii parentes*) (PL 187, 164C). Cf. *Decretum Gratiani: cum Glossis*, edited by Oudin Petit (Paris: Dudinus Parvus, 1542), fol. 49r.
26 *Decretals of Gregory IX*, bk. 5, tit. 7, c. 5. Cf. Nicolaus de Tudeschis, *Commentaria In Quartum, & Quintum Decretalium* (Venice: apud Juntas, 1617), vol. 7, fol. 117r b.

ion which induces servitude in him whom someone rules. By this dominion the power is possessed of using a slave for everything he wishes: except for crimes, which cannot be perpetrated without offense to God. By this dominion the master has full power over his slaves of using them for his benefit: and not for their benefit. And by this, this dominion differs from regal dominion: because a king, unless he wishes to be a tyrant, does not use the subjects for his own benefit: but for the benefit of the subjects. Now a master uses a slave not for the benefit of the slave: but for his own benefit, just as he uses his cattle. For the master can sell, exchange, give away, lease the slave, just as he could do with a beast of burden. Which certainly miserable slavery, even though it was introduced on account of sin, nevertheless was approved by the law of nations, as is found in the chapter, *Jus gentium*.[27]

Whoever has fallen into manifest heresy immediately loses this dominion, and his slave, if he does not consent to the master's heresy, by that very fact is absolved from his duty to his master. But the difficulty could arise, whether the ownership of his slave is transferred to the government treasury, just as of other things, such that after the master's heresy, his servant would become the slave of the treasury, or rather the slave would become his own master, and would be freed by the law itself. With all deference to better judgment, I reckon that the slave who did not want to consent to the master's heresy ought not to be included among the other goods, so that he would pass over into the ownership of the treasury with the other goods: but by that very fact he ought to be given his liberty, such that he could justly and without any sin flee from the heretic who had been his master, and deny him all obedience. For in the above-mentioned chapter, *Absolutos*,[28] all who were bound in any way to heretics, are

---

27 *Decretum Gratiani*, pt. 1, dist. 1, c. 9 (PL 187, 32A).
28 *Decretals of Gregory IX*, bk. 5, tit. 7 (De *haereticis*), c. 16.

Second bodily punishment of heretics: privation of all rulership

absolved from every obligation: therefore also slaves are freed, and consequently become free men.

Furthermore about this matter an explicit decree is found in Roman law. For in the law, *Manichaeos*,[29] Emperor Theodosius decreed that a slave, who did not want to obey a heretical master, becomes free by the law itself. It is certainly a just law, whereby a punishment is given to the heretical master, and a reward to the Catholic slave. Now Roman law, even if it could not decree about the faith or heresy, still can apply a punishment to heretics and a reward to believers. Hence it is that at least in the lands which are subject to the emperor, the slave who refused to obey the heretical master, and did not want to accept his heresy, is given freedom by the law itself: because so it is commanded in the aforesaid law, *Manichaeos*. And I reckon that the same thing ought to be done in the lands of the Roman Church, which nowise are subject to the emperor. Because, even if in those places the laws of the emperors do not have force: that chapter, *Absolutos*, still has its force, by which it is commanded to all, that they know that they are absolved from all duty to the master, who were bound in any way to those manifestly fallen into heresy.

There is another civil, and political, dominion which does not bring into slavery him over whom it is had: but merely confers to the one having dominion, the authority and power of commanding those things which are necessary, or at least advantageous and fitting, for the good rule of the country which he rules, and of punishing the transgressors of those things which were commanded by him. Kings, dukes, counts, and other rulers who govern nations have this dominion. These men over whom such dominion is possessed, are not called slaves, but subjects, and by the words now accepted by all, are called vassals. This domin-

---

29 *The Code of Justinian*, bk. 1, tit. 5 (*De haereticis*), l. 4, §8. Cf. *Theodosian Code*, bk. 16, tit. 5, l. 40, §6.

ion is also lost by manifest heresy, such that when a king has become a heretic, by the law itself it ought to be said that he is deprived of his kingdom, the duke of his dukedom, the count of his territory, and likewise concerning other rulers of nations called by any other name: for the chapter, *Absolutos*, speaks generally about every dominion. And no one ought to be surprised that the Pope on account of the crime of heresy would depose a king from his royal dignity, and deprive him of the kingdom: because in the matter of faith even kings, just as also others who are inferior, are subject to the Supreme Pontiff.[30] Whence it is that he could punish them just like any other. For Pope Zacharias deprived the king of France of his kingdom on account of a much lesser reason, as it is related in the chapter, *Alius*.[31] The Apostolic See transferred the Roman Empire from the Greeks, because

---

30 St. Thomas Aquinas and Suárez concur with this opinion. "Nevertheless this right of dominion or authority can be justly done away with by the sentence or ordination of the Church who has the authority of God: since unbelievers in virtue of their unbelief deserve to forfeit their power over the faithful who are converted into children of God" (II-II, q. 10, a. 10); "Consequently, [the Pope] can, through this power, deprive such a prince of his dominion; he can prevent the latter from injuring the subjects; and he can release those subjects from their oath of allegiance, or declare them to be released, since such an oath is always understood to carry with it the condition that it may be thus dissolved" (Suárez, *A Defense of the Catholic and Apostolic Faith*, bk. 3, c. 23, n. 21 (translated by Gwladys L. Williams, Ammi Brown, and John Waldron, in *Selections from Three Works* (Liberty Fund, 2015))).

31 "And another Roman Pontiff deposed from the kingdom the king of the Franks not so much for his iniquities as for the reason he was not useful for so great a power, and substituted in place of him Pippin the father of the Emperor Charlemagne and absolved all the Franks from the oath of fealty that they had taken to him" (*Decretum Gratiani*, pt. 2, *causa* 15, q. 6, c. 3 (PL 187, 983C)).

Second bodily punishment of heretics: privation of all rulership

they were not defending the Church, to the Germans, as it is found in the chapter, *Venerabilem*.[32]

It is therefore much more just that on account of the crime of heresy kings would be deprived of their kingdom: if the king becomes a heretic, to whom does the dominion and authority of his kingdom devolve? Certainly not to the emperor, especially if the king was not subject to the emperor, which sort are the kings of Spain, France, and England. For the goods of lay heretics, which by Canon Law and Roman law are assigned to the treasury, are not understood to be assigned to any treasury without distinction: but to the treasury of that which has dominion and supreme secular jurisdiction over the heretic. Thus it follows that the kingdom, and the rest of the goods of a heretical king who is not subject to the emperor, are not by the law itself assigned to the emperor's treasury. And it ought not to be said that that kingdom by the law itself belongs to the Church: because by the law itself the goods of lay heretics are not assigned to the Church: only except the goods of those who live in the lands of the Church, as it appears in the chapter, *Vergentis*:[33] and in the chapter, *Excommunicamus*.[34] To whom then will that kingdom belong by law? If that king has a legitimate and believing heir, I would say that he is the rightful and legitimate successor of the kingdom. Because since there is nothing determined in law about a heretical king, it follows that the same thing be reckoned about him which it is said about the man dying intestate. For since he by heresy is deprived of the kingdom by the law itself, inasmuch as regards the possession of the kingdom he ought to be reckoned dead: and because regarding his kingdom, to whom it ought to be given, the laws do not decide anything, it necessarily befitting that the kingdom devolve to the legitimate heir. And it seems to me that the

---

32 *Decretals of Gregory IX*, bk. 1, tit. 6 (*De electione*), c. 34.
33 *Ibid.*, bk. 5, tit. 7 (*De haereticis*), c. 10.
34 *Ibid.*, c. 13.

same thing ought to be said about any other dominion over whatsoever thing, to which there is annexed the bond of primogeniture, such that if its possessor becomes a heretic, those goods ought not to be assigned to the treasury, but to its legitimate successor of his primogeniture. Still I do not wish to determine anything certain about this matter, but I leave it to the experts of civil law, to be determined by them whose proper office this is. If a heretical king has no heir, or he whom he has is also a heretic, then if the kingdom is also not infected with heresy, I would say that the kingdom itself has the right and the power of choosing a king for itself, according to that which is said in the [Fourth] Book of Kings: the people "made themselves a king" (8, 20). But if the kingdom is also infected with the same pestilence as the king, the kingdom will also be deprived by the law itself of the power of choosing a king for themselves, and then the business will devolve to the Supreme Pontiff, so that he as the highest judge of the Church may decide what ought to be done, just as it can be easily gathered from those things said in the chapter, *Excommunicamus*, §. *Moneantur*.[35]

Finally, another dominion is Evangelical, and it is the power granted to someone from God's Gospel, and not from elsewhere, which is the power of absolving the sinner from sin, and the power of excommunicating, and of absolving from excommunication. Only those ecclesiastical men having the care of souls have this dominion, as do the bishops, archbishops, and the Pope. And this said power is called Evangelical dominion, because it is had from the authority of the Gospel alone. This power is also called by theologians the power of ecclesiastical jurisdiction. A very difficult question about this dominion is considered among theologians: whether a heretic is also deprived by the law itself of this dominion as other men, that is, whether any ecclesiastical prelate, either the Pope or any other, after

---

35 *Ibid.*, c. 13, §3.

Second bodily punishment of heretics: privation of all rulership

having become a heretic is by the law itself deprived of the power of prelature? There is no agreement about this matter among all theologians. For some say that when an ecclesiastical prelate has become a heretic, by Divine law he is deprived of his prelature. But others on the contrary think that whatever ecclesiastical prelate pertinacious in heresy, is not deprived by any Divine or human law of the power of prelature. And those who think in this way, are forced to say that this Evangelical dominion is not comprehended under that general statement, which is said in the chapter, *Absolutos*: "Let any know who were duty bound by any agreement, however strongly confirmed, to individuals obviously fallen into heresy, that they are released from the debt of human obedience and from any respectful deference whatever."[36] For one ought to exclude there Evangelical dominion: from whose obligation (according to the opinion of these men) those who had been obligated to [prelates] who fell into heresy by that dominion, are not absolved by the law itself. We defer the solution of this knotty question, because it is difficult and requires long treatment, to another chapter, all of which we will spend upon this business alone, when we will treat about spiritual punishments. For such powers and such dominions ought to be reckoned as being more spiritual than corporal.

About all these spiritual punishments of heretics, about which we have discussed in this chapter, it is doubted by some whether a hidden heretic would fall into these punishments. The cause of the doubt is this: because that often-cited chapter, *Absolutos*,[37] seems to apply only to manifest heretics. For it absolved only those from the duty of fealty and obedience, who were bound in any way to those manifestly fallen into heresy. Philippe [de Dexio?[38]] says that this is also true

---

36 *Ibid.*, c. 16.
37 *Ibid.*
38 Philippe de Dexio, or Phillipus Decius, (1454-1536) was an

in a hidden heretic, if his heresy can be proved: because then it can be manifested, even though it is not actually manifest. Giovanni d'Andrea teaches this same opinion yet with this added condition, that there be a trial for proofs: because a trial (as he says) then makes the fault manifest, as it is said in the chapter, *Quum olim [pro canonicis]*.[39] Still he thinks that it ought to be said otherwise, if there is no trial for proofs: because the Church does not judge about hidden things. And Angelo [Carletti] di Chivasso[40] in his *Summa [angelica de casibus conscientiae]*[41] subscribes to his opinion: Sylvester Mazzolini[42] embraces the same in his *Summa [Summarum, quæ Sylvestrina dicitur]*.[43]

Yet I think (I pray that hostility may be absent from my words) that all those men, no matter how very learned in law, did not understand the true and genuine meaning of that text. For the fact that that text speaks about those manifestly fallen into heresy, ought not to be understood about the manifestation which belongs to the heretic, such that he asserted his heresy in public, or openly. For someone can publicly, and in front of a thousand witnesses, assert some heresy, and not be a heretic: because he could have asserted it out of ignorance, thinking that such an assertion is Catholic. He could also assert without any pertinacious animosity,

---

Italian jurist.

39 *Decretals of Gregory IX*, bk. 5, tit. 40 (*De verborum significatione*), c. 24.

40 Carletti di Chivasso, or Angelus de Clavasio, (1411-1495) was a noted moral theologian of the Order of Friars Minor from Piedmont, Italy.

41 *Summa angelica de casibus conscientiae* (Leiden: Scorpio de Gabiano, 1534), fol. 193v.

42 Sylvester Mazzolini, in Italian Silvestro Mazzolini da Prierio, in Latin Sylvester Prierias, (1456/1457-1527) was a theologian born at Priero, Piedmont.

43 *Summa Summarum, quae Sylvestrina dicitur* (Strasbourg: Grieninger, 1518), fol. 219r.

but be prepared to obey the Church teaching something else. If either of which occurs, even if he would err in the faith, he will nowise be reckoned a heretic: as it is found in the chapter, *Dixit Apostolus*.[44] If he is not a heretic, it necessarily follows from this that he ought not to be punished with the punishment of a heretic, and consequently the punishment of that chapter, *Absolutos*, does not apply to him. Otherwise, it would necessarily happen that someone without his own fault, and without suspicion of a fault, nay, and without any just reason would be punished, which is against the natural law, Divine law, and human law. For that text releases those who had been bound by obligation to those manifestly fallen into heresy from the duty of fealty and dominion. And yet (as we said) someone could without any sin manifestly fall into some heresy. Therefore, the fact that that text speaks about those manifestly fallen into heresy, ought not to be understood of the manifestation, which is the case on the part of the one asserting: because whether he falls into heresy secretly or publicly, he does not incur the punishment if he is not a heretic.

Therefore, the words of that text ought to be understood of the manifestation which belongs to heresy, such that one may be said to manifestly fall into heresy, who falls into a manifest heresy, which he knows has been condemned by the Church, even though he asserts it hiddenly, and without any witness. But he who falls into heresy due to ignorance, will not be said to have manifestly fallen into heresy, even though he asserted it in the public forum before a thousand witnesses: because such an assertion was not manifest to himself that it is heretical, and has been condemned by the Church. He, however, who according to this manner of understanding manifestly falls into heresy, that is, into a manifest heresy, by that very fact necessarily ought to be deemed a heretic. Because he (as we taught above in the first book,

---

44 *Decretum Gratiani*, pt. 2, *causa* 24, q. 3, c. 29 (PL 187, 1307A).

chapter ten) without any further admonition already ought to be reckoned pertinacious: because he is not prepared to correct his error. Which is concluded very easily, or it can be concluded from him: because he (by open war[45]) opposes the Church, by which he ought to have been corrected, when he does not hesitate to assert that proposition, which he knows has been condemned by the Church. But if someone out of ignorance has fallen into heresy, and afterwards having been duly admonished disdains to obey, then he will first be said to have fallen manifestly into heresy, when he refuses to heed the due warning. Therefore he, who according to this understanding falls manifestly into heresy, since he ought to be reckoned a heretic according to the aforesaid words, will deservedly incur the punishment of heretic, no matter how hidden he is, if nevertheless he has expressed the heresy, which he has mentally conceived, by some word.

And of such men manifestly fallen into heresy in this way, ought to be understood the words of that chapter, *Absolutos*,[46] by which it is said, that those who had been under some obligation towards such men having so fallen manifestly into heresy, are released by the law itself from every such obligation. For by those words, "to those having manifestly fallen into heresy," the same thing is understood, as if it had said, "to heretics." And just as such men as these, even though they may be hidden, fall into the punishment of the chapter, *Cum secundum leges*:[47] so also by the law itself fall into the punishment of the aforesaid chapter, *Absolutos*, if they outwardly manifest (even though hiddenly) their heresy. "For," as Abbas says on this chapter, *Absolutos*, "the punishment bears upon the transgressor himself, no matter how hidden."[48] To support which opinion he cites a Gloss

---

45 *Aperto Marte*.
46 *Decretals of Gregory IX*, bk. 5, tit. 7 (*De haereticis*), c. 16.
47 *Liber sextus decretalium*, bk. 5, tit. 2 (*De haereticis*), c. 19.
48 Niccolo Tedeschi, *Abbatis Panormitani Commentaria in*

Second bodily punishment of heretics: privation of all rulership

which he said is noteworthy in the *Constitutiones Clementinae*, in the first chapter of *De haereticis*, on the words, *Eo ipso*.[49] From which things Abbas concludes that a heretic, even though hidden, by the law itself loses all dominion, just as he also loses all the rest of his goods by the law itself: but such absolution of dominion could not (as he says) be employed unless firstly the manifest case is proved.

In which words, even though he speaks correctly, yet he seems to me to have erred like the others regarding the understanding of that word. There is moreover something else in which Abbas' opinion does not please me, which he seems to judge in that place. For when saying that "the punishment imposed by the law itself bears upon the transgressor himself no matter how hidden," he seems to speak about the hidden thing not only in an incidental manner, but also about that which by its nature is hidden, such as he who when mentally considering his heresy gave no sign of his heresy by which it could be known by others. For it is clearly evident that Abbas thought this, from the fact that to prove his opinion he cites that Gloss on the *Constitutiones Clementinae*, which clearly teaches that the punishment inflicted by the law itself bears upon that transgressor who transgressed in his mind alone, exhibiting no exterior sign of his transgression, by which it could be known to others with certitude. Now this opinion has never pleased me, and nearly the whole school of theologians rejects it. But I do not wish to dispute about it at the present time, because in that work, which I am preparing, *De potestate legis poenalis*, in the second book of that work, I will make a longer disputation about this matter. Now therefore I speak only about the man hidden in an incidental manner, that is, about him who

---

quartum et quintum decretalium librum (Venice: apud Joannem de Gara, 1570), fol. 120v b.

49 *Clementinarum*, bk. 5, tit. 3 (*De haereticis*), c. 1 (*Multorum*), footnote *n*.

brought forth his heresy exteriorly, and outside of the hidden recesses of the heart, yet if he did it hiddenly, so that it was scarcely known to one or two. From this therefore such a man, no matter how hidden, if he has fallen into a manifest heresy, I say that he has incurred all of those punishments which have been imposed by the law itself against heretics.

Chapter VIII

The punishment of heretics about which was treated in the preceding chapter is proved to be just by manifest reasons.

Because the object of this work, and first goal towards which we have directed this fight of ours, is so that we may show that the punishment with which the Church smites heretics is just, it is necessary that we prove that the punishment, about which we disputed in the previous chapter, was deservedly inflicted upon heretics. Whoever would carefully consider how much the examples of superiors avail to influence their subjects will understand how just, nay (so that I may speak more truly), how necessary it is to take away all power of preeminence from heretics. Scipio Africanus[1] was saying that he was not motivated to virtue by anything more than by the examples of his superiors: whose images he saw depicted in the forum.[2] Plutarch relates concerning Julius Caesar that when he perceived some things depicted of Alexander, "he was lost in thought for a long time, and then burst into tears. His friends were astonished, and asked the reason for his tears. 'Do you not think,' said he, 'it is matter for sorrow that while Alexander, at my age, was already king of so many peoples, I have as yet achieved no brilliant success?'"[3] And from this he was

---

1 Publius Cornelius Scipio Africanus (236/235-183 B.C.) was a Roman general and statesman. His greatest military achievement was the defeat of Hannibal at the Battle of Zama in 202 B.C. This victory in Africa earned him the epithet "Africanus."
2 This anecdote is also told with the same words by Duns Scotus (*Scotus academicus, seu Universa Doctoris subtilis theologica dogmata...* (Paris: Edmundus Couterot, 1676), vol. 3, p. 372b), who gives Plutarch's biography of Scipio in his *Parallel Lives*, but this part of the work has been lost for many centuries.
3 Plutarch, *Caesar* (Bernadotte Perrin, ed.), c. 11, §3.

made more ready and stronger for doing remarkable feats. If the examples of those men who have passed away can move the minds of the living so much, all the more it ought to be believed that the examples of those who are superiors, especially those examples which are not merely heard, but seen with the eyes [can move the minds of the living]. For things seen move much more than things heard. For the example of Miltiades helped Themistocles[4] very much towards virtue. For when Themistocles was an adolescent, he wallowed in drinking and other allurements of the flesh.[5] But after Miltiades was made a general, after he defeated the Barbarians at Marathon,[6] no one ever saw him do anything

---

4 Themistocles (ca. 524-459 B.C.) was an Athenian politician and general.

5 "It is said, indeed, that Themistocles was so carried away by his desire for reputation, and such an ambitious lover of great deeds, that though he was still a young man when the battle with the Barbarians at Marathon was fought and the generalship of Miltiades was in everybody's mouth, he was seen thereafter to be wrapped in his own thoughts for the most part, and was sleepless o' [at] nights, and refused invitations to his customary drinking parties, and said to those who put wondering questions to him concerning his change of life that the trophy of Miltiades would not suffer him to sleep. Now the rest of his countrymen thought that the defeat of the Barbarians at Marathon was the end of the war; but Themistocles thought it to be only the beginning of greater contests, and for these he anointed himself, as it were, to be the champion of all Hellas, and put his city into training, because, while it was yet afar off, he expected the evil that was to come" (Plutarch, *Lives*, Themistocles, c. 3, §§3-4.) The author seems to be following here an academic oration from the law faculty of the University of Salamanca written in 1538-1539. Cf. Diego De Covarrubias, *Five Academic Orations from the University of Salamanca, 1538-1539* (Biblioteca Universitaria de Salamanca Ms. 2038), fol. 36. N.B. An "oration" (*oratio*) was given on the occasion for seeking a doctoral degree.

6 490 B.C.

unseemly. But to the many men asking him what was the cause that he was changed so suddenly, he answered that the trophies of Miltiades stirred him from sleep. Cicero relates that Demosthenes used to watch, who said that it gave him pain if any mechanic was up in a morning at his work before him.[7] The examples especially of those who are superior to others by some authority have such great force and power that they not merely urge, but as it were seem to force, the inclinations of the subjects to imitating them.

Wherefore Paul when reprehending Peter, in that on account of the Jews who had come from Bishop James of Jerusalem, feignedly withdrew from the Gentiles, being unwilling to eat with them, said to him: "Thou dost compel the Gentiles to live as do the Jews" (Gal. 2, 14). For because Peter was the supreme pastor and ruler of the whole Church, others ought to follow in his footsteps: hence Paul held Peter's example was of such great value that he said that by his example he not merely persuaded, but forced others to live as the Jews. And deservedly he spoke in this way, thinking that examples influence much more that words. On account of which the Son of God made man for us and being willing to show men the most certain way whereby they may reach eternal glory: firstly by examples, and afterwards by words equipped us for it. For firstly, as Luke says, "He began to do and to teach" (Acts 1, 1). When Chrysostom discourses on that passage he says: "The Apostles first taught by their conduct, and then by their words; nay, rather they had no need of words, when their deeds spoke so loud."[8] Whence it arises that public sins are deemed more grave than hidden ones, and all the more grave the more they have been committed by a person of greater authority, and who is more obliged to give a good example to others. Wherefore the Lord says through the prophet Ezechiel about bad priests: "They were a stumbling

---

7 *Tusculan Disputations*, bk. 4, §44.
8 *Homilies on the Acts of the Apostles*, hom. 1, n. 3 (PG 60, 18).

block of iniquity to the house of Israel" (44, 12). Blessed Gregory when discussing those words says: "For certainly no one does more harm in the Church than one who has the name and rank of sanctity, while he acts perversely. For him, when he transgresses, no one presumes to take to task; and the offense spreads forcibly; for example, when out of reverence to his rank the sinner is honored."[9]

Now the reason for this derives from the fact that he who sins publicly, encourages others to do the same thing by his example, and for this reason he is said to scandalize: because by his example he puts a stumbling block before others for their ruin. On account of which Our Savior harshly threatens him who scandalizes in this way, speaking thus: "But he that shall scandalize one of these little ones that believe in me, it were better for him that a millstone should be hanged about his neck, and that he should be drowned in the depth of the sea" (Mt. 18, 6). He who so scandalizes another will not only render an account for his own sin, but also for the sin of someone else who was motivated to sinning by his example. Which would not happen unless because he was the cause of the other's sin, vehemently impelling him by his example to sin. Everything which we have said is leading up this conclusion: that by these examples it becomes known to all how great is the power of examples. And if the examples of just any man avail so much to motivate the desires of other men: much more will the examples of those who are superior to the rest, by some authority and power.

And hence it can be very clearly established that it is just that all power of superiorship and dominion may be taken away from heretics. For it is justly feared that by these things he who is superior to his subjects may draw them to the same heresy by his example. Children nearly always strive to imitate their parents: and they very frequently lead their lives according to their example. For it is implanted by

---

9 *Pastoral Rule*, bk. 1, c. 2 (PL 77, 16A).

nature in children, that they love their parents, and hence it comes about that whatever they see in their parents, they would deem to be good. But everyone desires and tries to imitate what he considers to be good; besides this mutual love between parents and children, there is still another, and assuredly a very strong reason which very strongly impels to the imitation of their parents. This is the continual mutual association of parents and children. For children see their parents, when they eat, when they drink, when they play, when they joke, when they are angry, when they mock. They see their gluttonies, drunkenness, prodigality, tenacity, fornications, adulteries, and other vices of this sort. They hear them detracting, flattering, lying, swearing, perjuring, blaspheming, and saying many other things which are unbecoming for an upright man. And it rarely happens that parents do or say at home a thing of some importance which is hidden from the children.

Now Sacred Scripture teaches how much the manners of bad men can harm those who have continual familiarity with them. "He that walketh with the wise," says Solomon, "shall be wise: a friend of fools shall become like to them" (Prov. 13, 20). And again: "Be not a friend to an angry man, and do not walk with a furious man: lest perhaps thou learn his ways, and take scandal to thy soul" (*Ibid.* 22, 24-25). And Ecclesiasticus explains this same thing with an excellent comparison saying: "He that toucheth pitch, shall be defiled with it: and he that hath fellowship with the proud, shall put on pride" (13, 1). Lastly, the Royal Prophet says: "With the holy, thou wilt be holy... and with the perverse thou wilt be perverted" (Ps. 17, 26-27).

If associating with good men can benefit, associating with bad men could harm much more, because we are all more inclined to evil than to good. It is very difficult that someone would live innocently among evil men. For these two reasons children imitate their parents more than other men:

because they love them more, and have a longer association with them. And they more easily imitate their bad deeds than their good deeds, because nature now somewhat corrupted by sin impels more strongly to evil than to good. And hence it rarely happens that a hardworking son comes from a depraved father. I certainly know that sometimes it so happens: but this is rare, and marked with a white stone:[10] but I speak about those things which frequently, and nearly always happen. If the father is a businessman, he has sons in business; if the father plays games, he has sons playing games; if he is a fornicator, he raises sons who are fornicators; if he is an idolator, he teaches his sons idolatry; finally, if he is a heretic, he infects his children with the same heresy.

This is many times proved by clear experience, that men have drawn their children into the same heresy into which they themselves have fallen. Bohemia is a witness, which after being under their King Wenceslaus and the Roman Emperor Sigismund, the Catholic faith ceased, and still to this day has not returned to it, for no other reason than because their children imbibed from their tender years the same error by which they saw their parents influenced. I certainly fear that (which may God design to avert by His goodness) the same thing may happen to Germany. Because if the children are imbibed with the same Lutheran heresy by their parents, with which they are now infected, tardily will that region be converted to the Catholic faith. "A young man," as Solomon says, "according to his way, even when he is old, he will not depart from it" (Prov. 22, 6). And the illustrious poet said, "Censers, even if they have been completely emptied, retain their fragrance for a long time."[11]

---

10 *Notatum albo*, i. e., is very exceptional. The Romans used a white stone or piece of chalk to mark their lucky days with on the calendar. Those that were unlucky they marked with black charcoal.

11 Horace, *Epistulae*, bk. 1, n. 2, ln. 69.

Reasons justifying the punishment of privation of all rulership

It is just therefore, and necessary, to take away all paternal power from heretical parents, and to make their children masters of themselves, lest the parents by their authority and by their example draw the children into the same heresy, and the children, supported by the authority of law, could, if they wish, resist the parents, as those who have already been released by the law itself from their power. For this reason many theologians, among the number of whom is Saint Thomas, teach that it is not allowed to baptize the small children of infidels when the parents are unwilling: because such baptizing (as they say) would afterwards produce vilification of the Christian faith, because the parents would raise the children in their error: who having been so raised in childhood, never afterwards would fully hold the Catholic faith which they have received in Baptism. Yet other theologians, among whom is counted the *Doctor Subtilis*, [Duns] Scotus, who maintain the opposite opinion, reckon for the same reason that children of unbelievers, who had been baptized against the parents' will by order of the ruler, ought to be separated immediately after Baptism from the care and charge of the parents, lest if they remain with them, they might be drawn into the same error of disbelief by which they are infected.

If it is just that the dominion of parental power be taken away from heretical parents, lest they infect their children with the same heresy, it is much more just that any other civil and political dominion be taken away by the law itself from heretical rulers. For those who have this dominion could harm very many more than those who have only a small dominion, because political, or regal, dominion is more vast than paternal dominion. And a king, or duke, or marquis, or any other ruler commands many more than he who merely is a father. Next, a king has more power over his subjects than a father has over his children, and hence it happens that subjects often try to imitate their king more than children their parents. Assuredly, kings can give many rewards because they possess riches, and because they are so powerful that none of the subjects can resist them, they can afflict their subjects with various punishments when it pleases them. From the first arises among base men the hope of receiving some reward. From the second arises in the subject fear of the ruler, namely, lest he exercise the power of punishing when he chooses towards them. These two things, namely, fear and hope, are wont to impel the minds of men towards flattery, for some men flatter so that they could obtain the things which they ardently desire: but other men lest they incur punishments, which they greatly fear, take care to please their rulers in every way. And they say and do those things which they hope will be pleasing to their ruler, and omit to say and do those things which they know displease their ruler. "They that are clothed in soft garments," Our Savior says, "are in the houses of kings" (Mt. 11, 8). For in the houses of rulers there are flatterers and those who strive to please men. Very well, therefore, and elegantly the poet Claudian said, "The world shapes itself after its ruler's pattern, nor can edicts sway men's minds so much as their monarch's life; the unstable crowd ever changes along with the prince."[12] And in the first book of the praises of Stilicho he says: "Of a truth their leader's pattern passes to the crowd, and the soldier follows not only the standards but also the example of his general."[13]

Therefore, from all these things it is very clearly allowed to conclude how much a heretical king could harm his subjects in the faith. For his example will turn away many from the truth of the faith: because some from fear, others from love of him or of his goods, will assert, teach, and preach the same thing he does. When the Wise Men from the East came to

---

12 *Panegyric on the Fourth Consulship of the Emperor Honorius*, lns. 299-302.
13 *On the Consulship of Stilicho*, lns. 169 f.

Reasons justifying the punishment of privation of all rulership

Jerusalem, seeking the king of the Jews then recently born, King "Herod was troubled, and all Jerusalem with him" (Mt. 2, 3). It is not surprising that Herod, who was a foreigner and a tyrant was troubled at hearing the name "king," and would want to destroy him. For so it is that if someone, while that king is reigning, calls someone else "the king" of that place, he exposes him to a thousand dangers, and hands him over to unobstructed destruction. But that Jerusalem when having heard the name of its king then born is troubled, the matter is worthy of astonishment: because it should rather have rejoiced and exulted on account of that thing, than be troubled: because it knew that Herod was a foreigner, and had no right to the kingdom. Hence it is that it should have rejoiced concerning the casting out of the tyrant and the coming of the king. But if we recall Claudian's words, we will easily understand that it ought to have happened in this way, that when the king was troubled, all of Jerusalem was troubled at the same time with him. Because, as Claudian said, "The unstable crowd ever changes along with the prince." Thus when there is a heretical king it will necessarily happen that the people will be drawn into the same error. Which, if it disdain to do, with many torments, and various tortures, will it be compelled to do.

There exist more very manifest examples than I wish to bring forth of this thing, from which I have decided to bring forth some so that we may prove by their testimony the things which we have said. There were many idolatrous kings in the nation of Israel, such as Jeroboam, Baasa, Ela, Zambri, Amri, Achab, and Ochozias. When these men reigned, the people did not cease to sacrifice to idols, because they followed the insane perfidy of their kings. In the New and Evangelical Law there were many heretical kings, who fiercely vexed the Catholic Church, to such an extent that by reason of them many deserted the Catholic faith. Julian the Apostate, after he deserted the faith, persecuted the Catholic

Church more than any other pagan king. He forced many to deny the faith, and led many to martyrdom. The kings of the Goths, because they had been infected with the Arian heresy, made for this reason a great slaughter of Christians in Italy and Spain. About the atrocious cruelty which Vandals employed on the Christians, there is the history divided into two books, and written by Bishop Victor [of Vita].[14]

I will cite only one of the Gothic [persecutions] which occurred in Spain: which Blessed Gregory mentions, which I think is enough to show how harmful is a heretical king to the Catholic Church. Leovigild, King of Spain[15] and originating from the Goths, having been infected with the Arian heresy, tried to infect his children and his kingdom with the same heresy. Hermenigild, however, the firstborn son of the king, and hence heir of the whole kingdom, urged by Blessed Leander, the then Bishop of Seville, abandoning the Arian heresy, was converted to the Catholic faith, whom the Arian father, to call him back to the same heresy, firstly acted towards him with allurements and rewards, then with threats and tortures. Since all these things could not turn away that most constant soul from the Catholic faith even a little, the angered father having firstly deprived him of the hereditary right to the kingdom, cast him into chains and prison. Now when the feast of Easter was come, and by decree of the universal Church Christians are accustomed to receive the Sacred Body of the Lord, the faithless father sent an Arian bishop to the son, so that he might receive Communion from his hand, so that by this the father would reconcile him with himself. But the man of God Hermenigild refused to do this, and reproached the bishop coming, and with great constancy

---

14 *Historia persecutionis Africanae Provinciae, temporibus Geiserici et Hunirici regum Wandalorumy* (PL 58, 127-260. This version is divided into five books, but modern versions are commonly divided into three books.

15 He reigned from 568 to 586 A.D.

repelled him from himself with strong rebukes. When the Arian father heard this, he fell into a rage: and immediately, forgetful of parental affection, sent his executioners to kill his son, which they did.[16] What, I ask, would the heretic not refrain from doing to the faithful, who to maintain the Arian heresy did not spare his own son, but handed him over to executioners? Do you think that he who was so atrociously persecuted his own son would attend the rest of the faithful with a more equable spirit?

But it is necessary, so that we bring forth examples from this century of ours: because these more than the other which we have already mentioned, could move the minds of those observing. When Martin Luther began to spread abroad his errors thirty years ago, Fredrick, Duke of Saxony immediately gave assent to him, the people moved by whose example and authority fell into the same heresy. The same thing happened with Philip [I], Landgrave of Hess. Therefore it was rightly decreed that a king, or any other secular ruler, having become a heretic, lest he could harm the believing people subject to him, is by the law itself deprived of the dominion of the kingdom, and any other secular power.

---

16 *Dialogues*, bk. 3, c. 31 (PL 77, 289C-293A).

Chapter IX

Concerning another punishment of heretics, which is infamy, and of the others which follow from it.

Among the other punishments with which the Church rightly decreed heretics should be punished is numbered infamy, which ought to be deemed so much greater than the other punishments, as one's reputation is rightly set before all other transitory goods: "A good name," Solomon says, "is better than great riches" (Prov. 22, 1). Now whoever is a heretic is deprived of this good name, whether he be a secret or manifest heretic. Still there is this difference between a secret and a manifest heretic: namely, that a secret heretic is deemed infamous merely by infamy of law, and not by infamy of fact: because his crime, since it has not yet been manifested, does not avail to take away his reputation. A manifest heretic, however, is judged infamous both by infamy of fact and by infamy of law. Anyone incurs infamy of fact through the manifestation of his crime, and he incurs so much graver infamy, the graver the crime which he has committed; and so much greater, or wider, the more the sin has been manifested to many. For the gravity of infamy ought not to be measured with the same measure as its breadth, or extension. For if Peter commits a grave sin manifested to a few, and John has perpetrated a light crime known to many, Peter's infamy is graver, but John's is greater or wider.

Wherefore infamy of fact, which the heretic incurs from the manifestation of his crime, ought to be reckoned very grave: because heresy (as we taught in the first book, in the second chapter) is reckoned among the gravest sins. Infamy of law is that to which from the decree of the law someone is condemned. For there are some sins, any one of which, if someone commits, by the law itself is reckoned infamous, such as he who exercises the disgraceful occupation of usury, and unlawfully collects interest on interest.[1] And he who contracts [marriage] at the same time with two spouses, or who has two spouses at the same time is [infamous] by law.[2] And in common language anyone condemned by the sentence of a judge of a public crime, by the law itself is deemed to be infamous. Now this last statement is reckoned true only when he has been condemned by a definitive sentence, not however by an interlocutory sentence,[3] and when he has been condemned by the ordinary judge, and if he is not condemned by a decision of an arbitrator.[4] Now heresy by both laws, civil and canon, is called a "public crime": because a crime in civil law is called "public," if the denunciation or accusation of it can be made not solely by the person who has suffered some loss from the crime: but also by any citizen. For there are some offenses designated by law, which on account of their gravity can be accused by everyone, lest they remain unpunished: for instance, homicide, parricide, adultery, and the crime of high treason. And hence they are called "public crimes": because it pertains to the public utility, that such crimes be punished: because unless it be done, many troubles would thence befall the country.

Now there is no crime more harmful than heresy, and which could trouble more seriously a country. On account of which Paul when speaking about heretics, said: "Their speech spreadeth like a canker" (II Tim. 2, 17). Deserv-

---

[1] Cf. *Decretum Gratiani*, pt. 2, *causa* 3, q. 7, c. 2, §20 (*Porro*) (PL 187, 692B-C); *The Code of Justinian*, bk. 2, tit. 11, l. 20.
[2] *Digest of Justinian*, bk. 3, tit. 2 (*De his qui notantur infamia*), l. 13 (*Quid ergo*); *Decretals of Gregory IX*, bk. 1, tit. 21 (*De bigamis non ordinandis*), c. 4 (*Nuper a nobis*).
[3] I. e., made or done during the progress of an action especially when delay would cause irreversible injury.
[4] *Digest of Justinian*, bk. 3, tit. 2 (*De his qui notantur infamia*), l. 13 (*Quid ergo*), §5 (*Ex compromisso*).

Third bodily punishment of heretics: infamy and its consequences

edly therefore anyone among the people can accuse about the crime of heresy: lest it go about further with licentious impunity, and the whole country be infected with its poison. For "Whatever is committed against the Divine religion is productive of injury to all persons."[5] Now those things which inflict an injury to all, can be accused by all. Wherefore the crime of heresy can be accused by all, and hence it follows that according to the rules and precepts of civil law, it ought to be numbered among the public crimes. Now Canon Law shows it much more clearly: because according to Canon Law every crime is called "public," because it pertains to the common utility, that no crime be unpunished, as it is evident by the chapter, *Crimina*.[6] Hence, it is a logical consequence that anyone condemned by an ecclesiastical judge of some crime, is by that very fact infamous, as if he were condemned of a public crime. Which (as Angelo Gambiglioni,[7] notes[8]) is only true in the case when such a man has been condemned on account of intent [*dolus*], not on account of negligence [*culpa*]. Anyone therefore condemned of heresy is deemed by both laws infamous, and all the more as heresy is worse than other sins.

But there is a doubt whether the heretic, before he is condemned of the crime of heresy, would be infamous by the law itself, or it is required that he firstly be condemned of the crime of heresy, so that he would incur infamy of law.

---

5 *The Code of Justinian*, bk. 1, tit. 5 (*De haereticis*), l. 4 (*Manichaeos*).
6 "Gregory nowise passed over crimes once heard unexamined, even if the accused and the accuser had reconciled" (*Decretals of Gregory IX*, bk. 5, tit. 22 (*De collusion detegenda*), c. 2).
7 Angelo Gambiglioni (d. 1461), or Angelus de Aretio in Latin, was an Italian jurist.
8 *In quatuor Institutionum* (Venice: *Ad Candentis Salamandra Insigna*, 1574), on bk. 1, tit. 26 (*De suspectis tutoribus et curatoribus*), §5 (*Suspectus*), fol. 58r b.

And perhaps it will seem to someone that a heretic before condemnation ought not to be called infamous: because it is said to be a rule in public crimes that infamy of law is never incurred in them except after the definitive sentence of the ordinary judge.[9] But these objections notwithstanding, it seems to me that it ought to be said that the heretic before condemnation is by the law itself infamous. I am persuaded to say this by some reasons. Firstly, in fact, I am motivated from the fact that believers of heretics, and their receivers, who are excommunicated because they neglected to render due satisfaction within a year, are reputed as heretics: as it appears in the chapter, *Quum contumaciam*.[10] It is one among the other punishments whereby believers of this kind and receivers of heretics are punished by law, that they are infamous by the law itself, as appears in the chapter, *Excommunicamus*, §. *Credentes*.[11] By which words it is clearly implied that every heretic is by the law itself infamous. Furthermore, whatever causes a thing to be in a certain way, as Aristotle says, is that and more so:[12] thus if believers and receivers of heretics are by the law itself infamous on account of the heretics, it is necessary that the heretics themselves, on account of whom this punishment was inflicted upon them, are also infamous by the law itself.

---

9 *Digest of Justinian*, bk. 3, tit. 2 (*De his qui notantur infamia*), l. 1.
10 *Liber sextus decretalium*, bk. 5, tit. 2 (*De haereticis*), c. 7.
11 *Decretals of Gregory IX*, bk. 5, tit. 7 (*De haereticis*), c. 13, §5.
12 "A thing has a quality in a higher degree than other things if in virtue of it the similar quality belongs to the other things as well" (*Metaphysics*, bk. 2, c. 1 (993b)). Whatever is the cause of any formality or perfection in other things, itself possesses that formality or perfection in a greater, more eminent degree. If water is made hot by a fire, then the fire possesses heat more perfectly than the water, let alone the other things made hot by means of the hot water.

Third bodily punishment of heretics: infamy and its consequences

On the contrary, everything which belongs to those who are by the law itself infamous (as it will appear from the following), belong also to heretics. Thus it is a logical consequence that heretics are reckoned by the law itself infamous. And there is no need for a declaration or condemnation of the crime: but by the fact itself that they became heretics, they incur infamy of law. Just as we said above about the ownership of all goods, which from the day the crime was committed, without any other condemnation or declaration, we showed that the heretic lost [all his goods]. And it was certainly just that heretics would incur by the law itself such infamy: because heresy is a much graver crime than all the others which we have enumerated above, on account of any of which infamy is incurred by the law itself: therefore, it was much more just that on account of heresy infamy is incurred by the law itself, than on account of all the rest.

Now what is said to be a rule in public crimes, that infamy is never incurred on account of them except after the sentence of the ordinary judge: although it holds true for all other crimes, still does not apply to those which were designated by law, which if someone would commit, he is by the law itself infamous. Among the number of these (as we said) is the crime of heresy. Wherefore the heretic before condemnation is infamous by the law itself. This punishment punishes not only the heretics themselves, but also their children, such that children of heretical parents, although believers, are deemed by the law itself infamous. And rightly in fact was it determined that this punishment ought to be extended even to the children. Because just as children enjoy their parents' glory and nobility, so it was just that on the contrary they would feel in themselves the parents' ignominy, disgrace, and infamy in themselves. "The glory of children," Solomon says, "are their fathers" (Prov. 17, 6). For he who was begotten by good parents, receives a natural inclination to good in many things from those parents. Because from them he

Book 2, Chapter 9

derives the physical constitution of his body, which if it is good, is no little help and stimulus for virtue. Hence Aristotle says in his *Politics*: "As a man begets a man, and a beast a beast, so from a good man, a good man should be descended; and this is what nature desires to do, but frequently cannot accomplish it."[13]

Besides this inclination which children receive from their parents, there is also in these children a natural imitation of the parents, which is great in many, and was always an aid to virtue. For youth, who have some innate qualities, are wont to emulate the dignity of their elders, to aspire to the felicity of paternal praises. So the name of Philip [II of Macedon] excited Alexander; so the glory of the [Scipio] Africanus the Elder, Scipio the Younger; so the fame of Julius Caesar, Octavian [or Augustus]. Finally in this way Pyrrhus [or Neoptolemus] was spirited by imitation of his father Achilles. Hence the suspicion arises about children, that they are, or will be, like their parents were. And this is that glory of the children, which arises from the nobility and virtue of their parents, namely, that they are thought to be good and assiduous: because they are the children of good men. It is a support of this position that Aristotle says in the aforesaid place: Helen of Theodectes said in praise of herself: "Who dares reproach me with the name of slave, when from the immortal gods, on either side, I draw my lineage?"[14] And Blessed Paul says in the Epistle to the Romans: "If the root be holy, so are the branches" (11, 16). In this way from Abraham arose Isaac, from this man was begotten Jacob. From Tobias the Elder proceeded Tobias the Younger, a man as good and holy as his father.

In the same manner it ought to be thought about bad men: because from wicked parents proceed nearly always evil children, imitators of the paternal iniquity, just as from

---

13 Bk. 1, c. 6 (1255a).
14 *Ibid.*

hemlock arises a poisonous fruit, or from bilge-water flows some putrid and filthy water. And this same thing is proved by Solomon's testimony, who in the book of Wisdom says: "For the children that are born of unlawful beds, are witnesses of wickedness against their parents in their trial" (4, 6). The opinion was always reputed to be so true that it is made renown by the old adage, which says: "A bad egg from a bad crow."[15] Yet all these things are not made firm by a very constant and unvaried law, so that the contrary cannot happen. For it sometimes happens that from good parents bad children come forth, just as an infected fruit may come from a good tree, or very bitter water flowing from a sweet fountain. So from Adam arose Cain: from Noe, Cham: from Isaac was born Esau. And (so that we may come to secular history) the son of Scipio Africanus (as Valerius Maximus[16] relates about him[17]) was insane and lazy. The son of the most illustrious Counsul Quintus Fabius Maximus led such a reckless life of luxury (as related by the same Valerius[18]), that he was deprived of all his father's estate by the *praetor urbanus*.[19]

On the contrary from wicked parents likewise sometimes come good men, and industrious children of virtue, just as roses come from thorns. For from the very wicked and idola-

---

15 *Mali corvi malu ovum.*
16 Valerius Maximus was a first-century A.D. Latin writer and author of a collection of historical anecdotes.
17 *Factorum et Dictorum Memorabilium*, bk. 3, c. 5, n. 1.
18 "Quintus Fabius Maximus, son of the renowned citizen and general Quintus Fabius Maximus Allobrogicus: how doomed with luxury was the life he led! His other shameful deeds are erased; however, his character is able to be exposed abundantly through this disgrace, namely, that the city praetor Quintus Pompeius deprived him of his father's estate" (*Ibid.*, n. 2).
19 The *praetor urbanus* presided in civil cases between citizens.

trous King Achaz (as the history of IV Kings relates[20]) the faithful and holy King Ezechias was born. And the renowned holy King Josias, who removed the abominations of impiety, whose remembrance (as Ecclesiasticus says[21]) "shall be as sweet as honey," was the son of the wicked and idolatrous King Amon. But these examples are rare, because on the other hand it frequently and nearly always happens that wicked men are begotten of wicked parents, and good men from good ones. The examples of this are so many and clear that it is unnecessary to enumerate them. But the reason for this, if anyone desires to know, we willingly offer to him. It is certain that various inclinations of the soul arise from various temperaments of the body. For he who abounds in bile [*colera*] is easily angered, and easily pardons. In him whom phlegm flourishes, he suffers from being sleepy and sluggish. He who is strong with blood [*sanguine*], joyfully rejoices, and is easily prone to all pleasures of the flesh. He who has more than enough black bile, or melancholy, is slowly angered, slowly forgives, flees nearly all happy things, enjoys sad things, mulls over worries, avoids crowds of men. Temperaments and features of the body so varied, nearly always arise from the temperaments of the parents. Because out of the seed detached from parents, the body is coagulated, joined together, and then it is formed little by little from the mother's blood, and nourished, and in this way at the same time as the body, it receives the inclinations from the parents. Baptista Mantuanus[22] elegantly embraced this opinion in two verses speaking thus:

---

20 Cf. IV Kings 16, 20.
21 Cf. Eccli. 49, 2.
22 Baptista Spagnuoli Mantuanus (Italian: Battista Mantovano; English: Battista the Mantuan or simply Mantuan; also known as Johannes Baptista Spagnolo (1447-1516) was an Italian Carmelite reformer, humanist, and poet.

The moisture which is green in the leaves, comes from the roots,
And the manner born in the children go forth with the seed of the parents.[23]

And hence the infamy arises, which the children contract by law from the parents. For the law presumes, and rightly so, that the children will be such as their parents were, as is verified by experience. For in the chapter, *Si quis*,[24] it is said that in the children, the examples of the paternal, that is hereditary, crime is feared. Justly therefore the children of heretics are reckoned infamous: because it is deservedly suspected about them, that (unless they be helped from elsewhere) they would slip into that error with which the parents have been infected. Yet children of those heretics, who reviving from heresy, have returned to the Catholic faith, and were attached to the unity of the Church will not undergo this infamy of law.[25]

A heretic cannot be a witness, as is evident in the first chapter of *De haereticis*,[26] and the chapter, *Ipsa pietas*.[27] And deservedly a heretic is rejected from giving testimony, because among the many things which are required in a witness, is reputation. See the chapter, *Testimonium*,[28] and

---

23 *Qui viret in foliis, venit a radicibus humor, Et patrum in natos adeunt cum semine mores.* These lines are from one of the dedicatory poems in Fr. Baptiste's *Sylvarum*, bk. 1 (in *I. Baptistae Mantuani Carmelitae Theologi, Philosophi, Poetae & Oratoris clarissimi Operum* (Antwerp: apud Joannem Bellerum, 1576), vol. 3, fol. 247r).
24 *Decretum Gratiani*, pt. 2, *causa* 6, q. 1, c. 22 (PL 187, 735A).
25 *Liber sextus decretalium*, bk. 5, tit. 2, c. 15 (*Statutum*).
26 *Decretals of Gregory IX*, bk. 5, tit. 7 (*De haereticis*), c. 1 (*Dubius in fide*).
27 *Decretum Gratiani*, pt. 2, *causa* 23, q. 4, c. 24 (PL 187, 1186B-1188B).
28 *Decretals of Gregory IX*, bk. 2, tit. 20 (*De testibus et attestationibus*), c. 54.

the chapter, *Praeterea*.²⁹ And Isidore in his book, *Etymologies*, when speaking about the qualities of a witness says: "If good conduct is missing, a person is not trustworthy, for justice cannot keep company with a criminal."³⁰ And these words are found in the chapter, *Forus*.³¹ Next (as it is said in the *Rules of Law*³²): "Once wicked, he is always presumed wicked": especially in the same kind of wickedness. Thus a heretic, who gave false testimony about the Catholic faith, is justly presumed that he will give false testimony about anything else.³³ Moreover, the Wise Man of Ecclesiasticus says: "What truth can come from that which is false [*mendace*]?" (34, 4). By which words the Wise Man teaches clearly enough that trust ought not to be given to a liar. Therefore trust ought not to be given to a heretic: because once he has been caught in a serious and pernicious lie, from this it logically follows that he ought not to be accepted as a witness.

Yet this ought not be to accepted absolutely and universally: because from this source the lawsuit of heresy ought to be accepted, in which a heretic can give testimony against a heretic.³⁴ For just as the rule, whereby it is taught that the accomplices of a crime ought not to be admitted as witnesses, has an exception in the crime of high treason and simony, so also there is an exception in regard to the crime of heresy.

---

29 *Ibid.*, bk. 2, tit. 21 (*De testibus cogendis*), c. 7 (*Dubius in fide*).
30 Bk. 18, c. 15, n. 9 (PL 82, 651A).
31 *Decretals of Gregory IX*, bk. 5, tit. 40 (*De verborum significatione*), c. 10.
32 *Semel malus semper praesumitur esse malus* (rule 8 in *Liber sextus decretalium*).
33 *Decretum Gratiani*, pt. 2, *causa* 2, q. 7, c. 24 (*Non potest*) (PL 187, 644B-C).
34 *Liber sextus decretalium*, bk. 5, tit. 2 (*De haereticis*), c. 5 (*In fidei favorem*); *Decretum Gratiani*, pt. 2, *causa* 2, q. 7, c. 26 (*Si haereticus*) (PL 187, 645B-C).

Third bodily punishment of heretics: infamy and its consequences

Thus a heretic can testify against a heretic, yet not against a believer. From which I infer that an oath by a heretic partially proving may not be brought forth against a Catholic Christian to supply for partial proof: even though the opposite is stated in the law. For by the law it is commanded that an oath necessary as a supplement of proof may be brought forth for what has been partially proved.[35] Such an oath, however, ought not to be granted to a heretic partially proving against a Christian: because such an oath supplies the place of any testimony. Now since a heretic is rejected by law from giving testimony, it follows that an oath ought not to be taken from him as a supplement for a partial proof. Furthermore, before an oath is taken from someone to supply for a partial proof, the quality of the person ought to be firstly inspected and carefully examined, namely, whether he be a good man, truthful, trustworthy, and God-fearing, who would not dare to commit perjury for any great price. All which things since they are far from the heretic, it follows that an oath ought not to be taken from him as a supplement for a partial proof. Also, for the same reason a heretic cannot accuse a Catholic.[36] It is necessary that he who would want to justly accuse or reprehend the crimes of another, be himself extraneous to the same crimes.[37] And the distinguished poet elegantly taught this same thing, speaking thus: "[Let the straight-limbed man deride the one with deformed foot,] let the white man deride the black African."[38]

---

35 *Digest of Justinian*, bk. 12, tit. 2 (*De jurejurando*), l. 31 (*Admonendi*); *The Code of Justinian*, bk. 4, tit. 1 (*De rebus creditis*), l. 3 (*In bonae fidei*); *Decretals of Gregory IX*, bk. 1, tit. 40 (*De his, quae vi metusve causa fiunt*), c. 10 (*Super eo quod adversarius*).
36 *Decretum Gratiani*, pt. 2, *causa* 2, q. 7, c. 24 (*Alieni*) (PL 187, 644B); *Ibid.*, c. 25 (*Pagani*) (PL 187, 644C-645A).
37 *Ibid.*, pt. 2, *causa* 3, q. 7, c. 3 (*Qui sine*) (PL 187, 693A-B); *Ibid.*, c. 6 (*Postulatus*) (PL 187, 694C).
38 Juvenal, *Satire 2*, ln. 23.

There is yet another punishment of heretics, which also is derived from the aforesaid infamy of law, and it is the privation of whatsoever dignity and public office, and whatever ecclesiastical benefice, and unworthiness and inability to receive any of these thereafter. Nevertheless it ought to be pointed out to the reader that these two things, namely, the privation of things received, and unworthiness of receiving, ought not to be equated. For heretics do not incur the privation of the office or benefice received by the law itself: but only after they have been condemned by the judge to that privation. For the words, which are used in the chapter, *Ad abolendam*, in the section, *Praesenti*,[39] do not state that the sentence has been passed by law, but that the sentence is to be passed by the judge, for it is said in that place as follows: "He may be stripped of the privileges of every ecclesiastical order"; for if it had said that he was stripped *ipso facto*, or by the law itself, it would have expressed that the sentence has been passed [*latae senteniae*], but when saying, "He may be stripped of the privileges of every ecclesiastical order," it clearly stated that the sentence is to be passed by the judge [*ferendae sententiae*]. And in the chapter, *Excommunicamus*, §. *Credentes*,[40] words of the same character are used, which express that the sentence is to be passed and has not been passed. Hence it is that before a heretical priest has been stripped of the privileges of his ecclesiastical order by the ecclesiastical judge, and degraded by the bishop, he could not be punished on account of the crime of heresy, or on account of any other crime, by the secular authority. And if some secular judge, before the stripping of the privileges of this sort, were himself, or through another, to lay violent hands upon such a heretical priest, he would fall into the

---

39 *Decretals of Gregory IX*, bk. 5, tit. 7 (*De haereticis*), c. 9, §. *Praesenti*.
40 *Ibid.*, c. 13, §5.

judgment of the canon: *Si qui suadente diabolo*.[41] Because such a man, however much a heretic, enjoys the privileges of the ecclesiastical order, until he has been deprived of them by the sentence of the competent ecclesiastical judge.

It also thence follows that a heretic, who holds such a public office, before his is despoiled of the office, makes the fruits, which proceed from such an office, his own, which [after he has been despoiled of his office] immediately come under the legal right and power of the treasury. The first part of this corollary is clear from the fact that that heretic still retains the office, and has in it true and full possession, and consequently also has the right to take possession of the fruits. For such a right for receiving the fruits arises from the profession of the office: thus since he has not been impeded by any other right he can take possession of such fruits, whence it necessarily follows that when the office is retained, he also retains the reception of the fruits, which arise from the profession of such an office. For when the principal is granted all the subordinate matters are granted,[42] unless it is taken away on another account. Now this would not happen if the heretic had been deprived of every office by the law itself. For then he could not acquire the fruits of the office: because he would not have any right to take possession of those fruits.

I prove the second part of the corollary: that a heretic is deprived by the law itself of the ownership of all his possessions, and the treasury is substituted in his place.[43] And hence it follows that the fruits which the heretic acquired, by the very fact that they were acquired by him, are transferred to

---

41 Or *privilegium canonis*; *Decretum Gratiani*, pt. 2, *causa* 17, q. 4, c. 29 (PL 187, 1071A-B).
42 *Decretals of Gregory IX*, bk. 1, tit. 29 (*De officio et potestate judicis delegate*), c. 5 (*Praeterea*).
43 *Liber sextus decretalium*, bk. 5, tit. 2 (*De haereticis*), c. 19 (*Cum secundum leges*).

the ownership and control of the treasury. It can also be said otherwise, that although the heretic is not deprived by the law itself of his office and dignity, nevertheless he is deprived by the law itself of the right of taking possession of the fruits, which proceed from such an office, and that right passes over to the treasury, just as the rest of the goods. And according to this manner of speaking, although the heretic retains the office, he does not acquire its fruits: but the treasury by reason of the right, which belongs to itself on account of the heretic, acquires them for itself. And perhaps the latter is more consonant with the law, because in the chapter, *Absolutos*,[44] it is said that those who had been under obligation in any way to heretics, are released from all debt of obedience, fidelity, and service. And hence it follows that he who owed some returns by reason of some public office or dignity, is released from paying such a debt, and so the heretic will not have the right to exact such returns: and consequently will never acquire its fruits, even though he retains the office or dignity. Therefore, although the heretic is not deprived by the law itself of the office or dignity, still he is deprived by the law itself of the right of exacting the fruits, or returns, which could have belonged to him by reason of the office or dignity.

Another penalty, which is unworthiness, or ineligibility for public offices, or ecclesiastical benefices, is shackled with a harsher and more bitter law. For so that the heretic may incur this punishment, a sentence of the judge is not necessary, which reckons him to be unworthy or unable: but after he has become a heretic, he is reckoned by the law itself unable and unworthy of receiving such public offices or ecclesiastical benefices. This is very clearly taught in the chapter, *Quicumque*, §. *Haeretici*.[45] For there the Pope decrees that "if it is done otherwise, it is null and void." Not only is he unworthy

---

44 *Decretals of Gregory IX*, bk. 5, tit. 7 (*De haereticis*), c. 16.
45 *Liber sextus decretalium*, bk. 5, tit. 2 (*De haereticis*), c. 2, §2.

and unable: but also every ecclesiastical man, who at the entreaties of the heretic or his supporter, acquired dignities, pre-eminences, and any other ecclesiastical benefices, is deprived of them all by the law itself, and is made unworthy and unable to receive others thereafter. Which penalties apply only to those who knew that such benefices were conferred upon him through the entreaties of the heretic. For he who was unaware that the benefice was conferred upon him at the entreaties of the heretic, although he is to be deprived of such a benefice by the law itself, still he is not reckoned unable to receive others thereafter. All which things are taught in the chapter, *Quicumque*, §. *Ad haec*.[46] These penalties of unworthiness and ineligibility apply not only to the parents, but extend unto their children, and sometimes also apply more extensively to the grandchildren. Which diversity arises only from a distinction of parents: because if the father is a heretic, he radiates his inability and unworthiness to his children and unto his grandchildren. But if mother alone is a heretic, she affixes inability only to the children, and not to the grandchildren. And if the father or mother after either of them was made a heretic, thereafter repented, and abandoning the heresy, firmly joined himself to the unity of the Church, neither the grandchildren, nor the children are in any way deemed unworthy or unable regarding ecclesiastical benefices. All these things are contained in the chapter, *Statutum*.[47]

---

46 *Ibid.*, §3.
47 *Ibid.*, c. 15.

Chapter X

Whether it is just that on account of the father's heresy that the Catholic son be punished?

There are many who think that it is unjust and too harsh that the Catholic children of heretics are punished on account of the heresy of their parents with the same punishments with which their parents are punished, such that they are infamous just as they, unable to receive offices or benefices the same as they, deprived as they are of all inheritances which could come to them by hereditary laws. For I saw many in Flanders, when I lived there ten years ago, who although they deemed it just that heretics are punished, yet they took it badly that the punishment of heretical parents were extended to their children, and they complained about that punishment of heretics, which is prescribed by canon and civil law: and they were accusing Spain, because they had heard that all the laws, which were decreed by the Supreme Pontiffs, or by the emperors, are observed to a man in Spain, and they were inveighing against me as a defender of the laws. For they were saying that it is unbecoming that someone would be punished without guilt, since God (as they were saying) does not afflict anyone beyond his guilt. They were confirming this same point with the testimony of Augustine saying: "God is not an avenger before someone is a sinner."[1] Next they corroborated their view by adding that which God said though the prophet Ezechiel speaking thus: "The soul that sinneth, the same shall die: the son shall not bear the iniquity of the father, and the father shall not bear the iniquity of the son: the justice of the just shall be upon him, and the wickedness of the wicked shall be upon him" (18, 20). By which words he clearly (as they were saying)

---

1 *On Genesis*, bk. 11, c. 17, n. 22 (PL 34, 438).

teaches us that no one ought to be punished for someone else's sin, but everyone for his own. Therefore, motivated by these reasons, which seemed to themselves to be like an indissoluble Herculean knot, they were saying that it is unjust that the children of heretics would be punished for the iniquity of their parents.

But certainly they, and however many others who think this way, are completely off course, and seem to argue more for their own rather than the Catholic cause. The error of these men is proved from the fact that in so thinking, they not merely accuse and incriminate human laws and decrees, but also God, Who often punishes children for the sins of their parents, He Himself bearing witness, Who says: "I am the Lord thy God, mighty, jealous, visiting the iniquity of the fathers upon the children, unto the third and fourth generation of them that hate me" (Ex. 20, 5). He said, "Visiting," meaning "punishing," or "beating," or "chastising": for when the Lord does one of these things towards us living in this life for our sins, then He is said to visit our iniquities. For so He Himself says through the prophet David: "If they profane my justices: and keep not my commandments: I will visit their iniquities with a rod: and their sins with stripes" (Ps. 88, 32-33). According to this manner of speech the Lord says that He "visits the iniquity of the fathers upon the children, unto the third and fourth generation": because for the iniquity of the fathers God punishes the children, unto the third and fourth generation. For children are a kind of possession belonging to the parents, and among all the external possessions that are more connected with the parents themselves, and approach more personally to themselves. And hence it happens that they are more troubled by their sicknesses, as though they were their own, and they lament over their adversity, as about their own, they mourn their death more vehemently, than the loss of any goods.

Whether a Catholic son ought to be punished for his father's heresy

Next, children are constituted under the governance and authority of the parents, and are as it were a possession of the parents. Hence it follows that just as the sickness and death of a servant falls unto the injury of the owner, whose servant he is: so also the affliction of the son falls unto an injury to the father himself: for the father can make use of the son's labor, and lease it out, just as the labor of a servant. And from this it necessarily follows that when the son has either died or is sick, the father suffers an injury, and in this way the father is punished in the death or sickness of the son, just as he would be punished in the sickness or death of a servant. Thus when God sends sicknesses, wounds, famine, injuries, or any other adversity to the children, he punishes not so much them as their parents in them. David was so punished in the death of his son born in adultery, so that he would feel sorrow and pain in him whom he had begotten from illicit and condemned intercourse.[2] For the son is not punished: but rather God being merciful he was taken before the use of reason, lest wickedness should alter his soul.[3] Thus the death of the son insofar as it pertains to the son himself, was not a punishment, but a work of mercy: but insofar as it pertains to David himself, it was a work of punishment and vengeance, by which he was punished by that in which he had sinned. So also the children of Sodom without any sin of their own having been consumed with fire at the same time as their parents,[4] and the Lord did not punish the children swallowed up by the earth with Dathan and Abiron without any sin of their own:[5] but instead He had pity on them, when He compelled them while they were innocent to depart from this life: lest if they had abode longer in this life, they would

---

2 Cf. II Kings 12, 18.
3 Cf. Wis. 4, 11.
4 Cf. Gen. 19.
5 Cf. Num. 16, 30-33.

have been made imitators of their fathers' iniquities, and so would have afterwards underwent more severe punishments.

 Sometimes also God afflicts children of older age for the sins of the parents, by which affliction He does not punish the children, but the parents. Such an affliction becomes something good for the children: because by it they become more cautious in avoiding future sins, and by it their virtue and merit grows, if it is patiently borne. Hence it is that, although such an affliction is burdensome and bitter to them: still it will never be called a penalty in respect to them, nor a punishment, according to that in respect to which a penalty or punishment implies an order or reference to guilt. Yet such an affliction of the children in connection with the parents will be called a punishment: because it was inflicted upon the children for the sin of the parents themselves, in whom the parents are also afflicted at the same time. Whence it is that when Cham sinned by sin of irreverence towards his father, Noe cursed the son of the same Cham, namely Chanaan, speaking thus: "Cursed be Chanaan, a servant of servants shall he be unto his brethren" (Gen. 9, 25). Noe cursed the boy Chanaan, the son of Cham, so that by that curse he might afflict and punish Cham more severely, since he saw that not only he, but also his son, was cursed by his father.

 And according to this manner not only sons, but also grandsons, and thereafter until the fourth generation the Lord afflicts for the sins of the parents, so that in them He may punish their grandfather, or great-grandfather, or great-great-grandfather. "Visiting," God says, "the iniquity of the fathers upon the children, unto the third and fourth generation."[6] He did not say beyond the fourth generation, because a parent's life rarely extends so long that they would see another generation after the fourth, by whose affliction they themselves could be punished. For because the afflic-

---

6 Gen. 20, 5.

tion of children for the parents' sins is inflicted by God for the punishment of the parents themselves: wherefore it is befitting and necessary that it be done only in those children or generations the one sinning could see. Nicholas of Lyra when interpreting this sentence of Divine vengeance, after giving the exposition which we have just now related, afterwards adds another, speaking thus: "'Unto the third and fourth generation': it was said sometimes bad men see their children to such a number of generations, and so shape them by their bad examples, or they imitate what they saw in their fathers."[7] And Saint Thomas seems to approve of the same opinion, who when enumerating the reasons on account of which one man can be punished for a time for the sins of another, speaks thus: "Secondly, when one person's sin is transmitted to another, either by 'imitation,' as children copy the sins of their parents, and slaves the sins of their masters, so as to sin with greater daring; or by way of 'merit,' as the sinful subjects merit a sinful superior, according to Job, 'Who maketh a man that is a hypocrite to reign for the sins of the people?'[8] Hence the people of Israel were punished for David's sin in numbering the people.[9] This may also happen through some kind of 'consent' or 'connivance': thus sometimes even the good are punished in temporal matters together with the wicked, for not having condemned their sins, as Augustine[10] says."[11]

With all respect which is due to such great men, their opinion displeases me, nor could it please anyone considering the matter well: unless perhaps he be led more by affection

---

7 *Biblia sacra cum Glossis, interlineari & ordinaria, Nicolai Lyrani postilla et moralitatibus...* (Lyon: Gaspar Trechsel, 1545), vol. 1, fol. 164r C.
8 Job 34, 30.
9 Cf. II Kings 24.
10 *City of God*, bk. 1, c. 9, n. 3 (PL 41, 22).
11 II-II, q. 108, a. 4 ad 1um.

Book 2, Chapter 10

than by reason. For a son who imitates his father's iniquity, if he is punished by God for his imitation, is not punished for the father's sin, but for his own: because such imitation is the son's own sin. Now had this sin of the son not been done in imitation of the father, it nonetheless would be punished by God in the son himself its perpetrator: thus when it was committed following the father's example, it should also be punished in the son himself. For by the fact that the son, by his father's example perpetrated some crime, the whole guilt of the crime is not taken away from him: although it may be lessened somewhat. Therefore the conclusion is that if God punishes a son on account of the imitation of his father's iniquity: He may be said to punish him for his own sin, and not for the father's: because such imitation (as we said) is the son's own sin. Hence such a literal interpretation of the text from the book of Exodus cited above is unbefitting, which says: "Visiting the iniquity of the fathers upon the children, unto the third and fourth generation." For then (as it was shown) God does not visit the iniquity of the fathers: but the iniquity of the sons upon the sons themselves.

Furthermore, if according to that manner God punishes the sins of the fathers upon the sons, He ought to punish not only until the third and fourth generation, but unto a thousand generations: because as many as have imitated the father's iniquity will be punished by God, even if that imitation of the father's iniquity goes on for a thousand generations. For it is evident that sons often are imitators of their father's iniquities beyond the fourth and fifth generation: because by the talk and account of others they know that their parents, grandparents, great-grandparents, great-great-grandparents, and others before them so acted. For instance, a father either by a word or bad example instructed his son, and the latter passes down in the same way to his son the bad teaching which he received from his father, and this son to another, and so forth unto many generations. Now these sins are always accustomed to be called the sins of the first man who did such things, as it is easily seen in the Third and Fourth Book of Kings, in which books when the deeds of the kings of Israel are related, it is said about the many wicked idolatrous kings: "And he departed not from all the sins of Jeroboam the son of Nabat, who made Israel to sin, but he walked in them" (IV Kings 13, 11). Which order of succession extended beyond the tenth generation of Jeroboam, far beyond the fourth.

Someone perhaps wishing to defend Nicholas of Lyra will say that the end of the punishment of the sons for the sin of the parents ought not to be limited by God to the fourth generation, such that such punishment never proceeds further: because in the same place it is not said that God visits the iniquity of the fathers unto the third, and finishes with the fourth generation. Hence it is that although the imitation of the father's iniquity extends beyond the tenth and twentieth generation, every such imitation, according the God's sentence, is punished for the sin of the father. The words which immediately follow in the same text clearly overpower this exposition. For this is what He afterwards said: "I am the Lord thy God, mighty, jealous, visiting the iniquity of the fathers upon the children, unto the third and fourth generation of them that hate me: And shewing mercy unto thousands to them that love me, and keep my commandments" (Ex. 20, 5-6). By which words He taught clearly enough that there is a great difference between the punishment of the wicked, and the reward of the good. Because He punishes the sins of the fathers unto the third and fourth generation. But [He rewards] the fathers' virtues, Who remunerates in the sons unto a thousand generations, that is, unto very many. For He signified this by those words, "And shewing mercy unto thousands to them that love me, and keep my commandments." Assuredly God, because He is more inclined to sparing, than to punishing, makes a shorter punishment of the fathers' evil deeds: because He does not punish the sons for the fathers' iniquity beyond the fourth generation. But He gives rewards for the fathers' good deeds for a much longer time: because He blesses the sons for the fathers' virtues for many generations, and gives various gifts.

But if God visits the iniquity of the fathers upon the sons, not only to the third and fourth generation, but even to a thousand: there would then be no difference between the punishment of the wicked, and the recompense of the good: since also the former (according Lyra's exposition) ought to be extended unto a thousand, and innumerable generations, just as the latter. Again, just as we are taught by the Divine law that no one is to be saved for the good of someone else, so also we are instructed that no one will be perpetually condemned for another's sin. For Paul when speaking about the retribution of all men, whether evil or good, says: "He will render to every man according to his works" (Rom. 2, 6). Thus [He will render] not according to the works of the fathers. And again: "Every one of us shall render account to God for himself" (*Ibid.* 14, 12). Notice that He says, "for himself." And so the son will not render an account to God for his fathers. And the Wise Man says: "By what things a man sinneth, by the same also he is tormented" (Wis. 11, 17). Hence it follows that sons ought not to be tormented forever by those things in which their fathers sinned.

Therefore this opinion of Nicholas of Lyra, whereby he says that eternal punishment is inflicted upon the son for the father's iniquity, insofar as he is an imitator of the father's crime, ought nowise to be tolerated: but those things which he said incorrectly, or at least less cautiously on Exodus, he corrected on the tenth chapter of the prophet Ezechiel, saying that the son is occasionally punished with a spiritual and eternal punishment for the father's sin: because the father's sin gave an occasion of sin to the son, for which the son was at length punished. For in that place Nicholas of

Lyra says these words which follow: "Nevertheless it ought to be known that sons of bad fathers are frequently imitators of their fathers' wicked deeds, because they are raised in their midst, and the actions of the fathers are deemed to have greater weight, and in this way they are frequently also punished corporally and spiritually for the fathers' sin, yet occasionally insofar as they follow their example, but simply for their own sins."[12] In which words he corrected what he either has said incorrectly on Exodus or he here expounded clearly what he had said obscurely there.

Blessed Thomas spoke more carefully: and hence his words do not require as much excusing, or interpretation. For the holy man in the place cited above, clearly asserts that no one ought to be punished with a spiritual punishment for the sin of another. Yet there is agreement between him and Nicholas of Lyra about this, namely, that he also teaches that the son ought to be punished for the father's sin with a temporal punishment, when the son derives the father's sin through imitation, that is, when the son is an imitator of the father's sin. But because (as we said) that imitation of the father's iniquity is the son's own sin: although the father gave its occasion, consequently then the son is punished for his own sin even temporally, and not for the father's sin. And in the same way it ought to be said about another's sin, which passes on to someone else by reason of consent, or disregard, for which reason (as Saint Thomas says) the good are sometimes punished with the wicked: because they did not reprove their sins. He who consents to the sin of another, commits his own sin: and hence requires his own punishment, and similar to that which he who perpetrated the crime merited. Hence Paul, when speaking about sinners, says: "They who do such things, are worthy of death; and not only they that do them, but they also that consent to them that do them" (Rom. 1, 32). He also commits his own sin, who disre-

---

12 *Biblia sacra cum Glossis*, vol. 4, fol. 252v A.

gards the sin of another, and does not correct or rebuke, when he is obliged to rebuke: because he is reckoned as someone consenting before God and men. For the *Glossa Ordinaria* on that passage of Paul, which we have just cited, says: "To keep silent, is to consent, when you could reprove."[13] And Pope Leo [I] wrote: "He who does not reclaim others from error shows that he himself has gone astray."[14] If those consenting and disregarding consent and disregard by their own sin, it is thence proved that they are punished for their own sins, and not for others'.

Yet this opinion of Blessed Thomas can also be excused and very well explained, so that he who would wish to defend him could easily do so, saying that Blessed Thomas does not deny that the son who is an imitator of his father's sin ought to be punished for his own sin. But he further says that he also ought to be punished for his father's sin, such that the son who imitates the father in the crime is punished at the same time for his own and for the father's. And Augustine favors this opinion in the first exposition (for he made two) on Psalm 108, on the verse, "May his posterity be cut off" (v. 13), speaking thus: "Just as emulation of those who are good causes one's own sins to be expunged, so emulation of those who are evil causes not only one's own sins but also those of the ones who are emulated to result in their own just consequences."[15] Although Augustine speaks merely of the imitator, he who nevertheless desires to defend Blessed Thomas ought to say the same thing about the one consenting and the one disregarding, such that the one either consenting or disregarding is not only punished for his own sins, but also for those to which he consents, or which he disregards. But according to this exposition the question of the son imitating

---

13 PL 114, 474.
14 Letter 15, c. 15 (PL 54, 688B); *Decretals of Gregory IX*, bk. 5, tit. 7 (*De haereticis*), c. 2 (*Qui alios*).
15 *Enarratio in Psalmum CVIII*, c. 15 (PL 37, 1437).

the father's iniquity will still remain difficult. Why is he not punished for the sin of another whom he imitates, just as he is punished for the father's sin? But if someone also concedes that man is punished for the sin of others, whom he imitates: just as for the father's sin, he will very difficultly sustain the cause to be supported. Because this having been granted, it will also be necessary to concede that if someone imitates a thousand men in some crime, he ought to be punished not only for his own sin, but also for the sins of them all, whom he imitated in the same crime. Which if someone would want to concede, he certainly will make Divine justice hard, and very harsh. Hence, in order that we may be freed from all these difficulties, we think that it ought to be better said that the innocent son is punished for the father's sin for this reason alone, because the son is a sort of thing of the father belonging to him, and a sort of possession of his, in whose affliction the father is punished as in his property, and so much the more, the more the father loves the son than all the rest of his temporal possessions. For it is certain that the father is punished more bitterly, when he knows that his son was deprived of the inheritance of his goods, than if he knew that those goods, which he himself was deprived, were to pass on to the son's ownership and possession. For although the father severely laments, because he is deprived of the ownership and possession of all his goods, still he receives some solace, when he knows that his son will inherit the ownership of all his goods, and such solace somewhat alleviates the bitterness of his sorrow. For one of the sorrows that bitterly grieves dying parents, is when they foreknow the want, or injury, or whatever other misfortune which their children will suffer after their death. But if their children are safe and sound, and they leave them having in abundance of all temporal things, they bear death itself more easily. Thus although the sons of heretics are afflicted by the privation of the parents' goods, and the infamy, and other similar penalties: nevertheless, because the parents are tormented by the sons' affliction of this kind, whence by it the parents are punished according to the deserts of their own crimes. Therefore in no other way ought it to be admitted that an innocent son is punished for the sin of the father, or (so that I may speak more correctly) afflicted, except because the father disagreeably undergoing such an affliction of the sons, is afflicted and punished in that.

Perhaps against this opinion someone will object to me the Church's decision given in the chapter, *Accusatus*, §. *In eo vero casu*.[16] For in that place the Pope decreed that the heir of any heretic, whose heresy was not declared before death, ought to be deprived of the whole inheritance which he had from the heretic, if he at that time consents to the heresy of the deceased. If the son according to this decree, after the father's death, is deprived of the father's goods, there is no doubt that he then is tormented for the father's sin: and yet by that torture of the son, the father is not punished, since he has already passed from this world, and the punishments of the children, which they suffer in this life, he can no longer feel. Therefore it is false that an innocent son is never afflicted for the father's sin, unless because by that affliction the father is punished.

Yet we can easily refute this objection in many ways. Firstly in fact, it is not absolutely certain that deceased parents, or other relatives, who are in Purgatory, or in hell, do not feel those pains which their relatives suffer in this life. For Blessed Augustine when discussing this matter did not dare to decide anything, but left this matter as doubtful and uncertain, speaking thus: "Someone objects, 'But can we really believe these consequences to have been part of Judas' punishment, that after his death his wife and children were reduced to poverty, and displaced, and thrown out of their homes; that a creditor sought out all his property, and strangers seized all

---

16   *Liber sextus decretalium*, bk. 5, tit. 2 (*De haereticis*), c. 8, §7.

his work; that no one supported or pitied his children, and that they all died off swiftly without issue? Can we really suppose that the dead experience any grief over things that happen to their nearest and dearest after their own demise? Do they even know about it, when their perception is engaged elsewhere in accordance with their deserts, whether good or bad?' In reply I must say that it is an enormous question, and one that cannot be dealt with now because it needs extensive treatment, whether, or in what measure, or in what way, the spirits of the dead are aware of things that happen to us... It was thus a terrible fate for Judas that after his tragic death his wife should remain so defenseless as a widow and his children as orphans that a creditor could search out all his property and strangers seize his work, that his family should be expelled from their homes and his children find no one to take pity on them, and that they should perish in one generation leaving no posterity. If the dead are conscious of all this, it is the culmination of their woes; if not, it is a fearful warning to the living."[17] Augustine dared not decide whether the dead know the misfortunes of their dear children. If the deceased heretic knows the miseries and calamities, which happen to their children due to their own heresy, there is no doubt that he is tormented by those miseries.

---

17 *Enarratio in Psalmum CVIII*, c. 17 (PL 37, 1437-1438). St. Peter applied the words of Psalm 68, "Let their habitation be made desolate: and let there be none to dwell in their tabernacles" (v. 26) and Psalm 108, "His bishopric let another take" (v. 8), to Judas the traitor, in Acts 1, 20. Psalm 108 continues with these curses, "May his children be fatherless, and his wife a widow. Let his children be carried about vagabonds, and beg; and let them be cast out of their dwellings. May the usurer search all his substance: and let strangers plunder his labours. May there be none to help him: nor none to pity his fatherless offspring. May his posterity be cut off; in one generation may his name be blotted out" (vv. 9-13). Following St. Peter, St. Augustine here applied these additional curses of Psalm 108 to Judas also.

Next, even if what is done regarding the living relatives would be hidden from the deceased, still what is cited in *Accusatus*, §. *In eo vero casu* opposes no part of our opinion. For the heretic (as we already taught above) not only from the time of condemnation, but from the time when the crime was committed, loses ownership of his goods, and from that same time the son also is deprived of the right of inheriting the father's goods. Hence it necessarily follows that a hidden heretic, whose heresy was declared after his death, ought to be said to have been punished by law before death in himself and his children, albeit he did not experience this punishment before death. It indeed would have been undeserved to deprive the son of a heretic now deceased of the inheritance from his father who did not deserve this through any fault of his own, if he had acquired true ownership of it by his father's death. Just as it would also have been unjust to deprive the son on account of the father's heresy of other goods, which he had received not by any hereditary right, but he had procured by his own labor. The son of the deceased heretic, however, after it was declared that the father was a heretic, is justly deprived of the possession of the father's goods: because not he, but the treasury, had ownership of them: because from the day that the crime was committed (as we said) he was deprived of all those goods, and the treasury assumes ownership in his place.

And certainly from this place a very strong (in my opinion) argument can be made for proving our opinion, which we stated above against the Archdeacon saying that a heretic is not immediately after the offense deprived of the ownership of his goods: but it is necessary that there be a sentence of a judge, which declares him to be a heretic. If this were true, it would thence follow that a heretic dying in a hidden heresy would have ownership of his goods until the moment of his death, since before that time he was never condemned of heresy. This having been granted, it thence necessarily follows that the heir, who inherits such an inheritance, has after the death of that man true ownership of those goods, of which the dying heretic was the owner. And it thence further follows that although it were declared that the dead man was a heretic, the heir ought not to be deprived without his own guilt of those things, of which he had then been made the owner: just as he is not deprived of other things which he by his own labor had acquired. But since the heir is deprived by law of the goods which the deceased heretic had possessed, after he was declared to have been a heretic, and he is not deprived of the goods which the heir himself previously possessed, it is thence proved that the heretic's heir never had ownership of those goods as he had of the others, and this for no other reason except because the heretic, whom he succeeds, lost such ownership from the day and the hour of the committed crime.

Chapter XI

It is replied to the objections, which in the beginning of the preceding chapter were put forth for the opposite stance.

It now remains that we reply to those reasons and arguments, upon which those who maintain the opposite view (as we said in the beginning of the previous chapter) rely. Firstly in fact, they argue that it is unjust that a son be punished for the parent's sin: because God (as they say) does not punish anyone for another's guilt, but for his own. What kind of and how much force this argument has can be easily shown to anyone from those things which we said: because we showed by clear testimonies of Scriptures that God visits the iniquity of fathers on the sons. Wherefore we could easily turn back this argument on them, so that we may transfix them with their own sword, speaking thus: It is just that the son would be punished for the father's sin: because God, Who is the most just, and cannot err, often in this life punishes children for the sins of parents. But they confirm this opinion of theirs with the testimony of Augustine saying: "God is not an avenger before someone is a sinner."[1] But this saying of Augustine does not disturb us: because his words, if considered carefully, do not argue against us. For although God never takes vengeance on someone before he is a sinner, nevertheless He often afflicts and torments many without any fault of theirs. For vengeance, or punishment, and affliction are not entirely the same thing. Since vengeance has a certain reference to a previous injury, without which no punishment can be called revenge, or vengeance.

Also, both "punishment" and "castigation," if taken according to the true and proper meaning of those words, imply a reference to guilt, without which no one is properly said to be

---

1 *On Genesis*, bk. 11, c. 17, n. 22 (PL 34, 438).

punished, or castigated: even though he may be very severely tormented: but neither "affliction" or "torment" imply any reference to guilt. For if someone suffers tribulation in whatever way, either on account of his guilt, or without it, he is always said to be afflicted. For just men, to whom God gives various tribulations in this life to increase their merit, are indeed afflicted and tormented: but they are not punished, nor are they castigated: because there is no guilt in them, which ought to be punished or castigated, and if there were some, it would not deserve such great castigation. And God does not take revenge, or vengeance, on them: because He does not find an offense in them, which ought to be avenged. Thus Augustine spoke very well when he said: "God is not an avenger before someone is a sinner": for God only avenges sin, which is an offence against Him: and God does not take revenge, except on a sinner, who inflicted an injury upon Him by sin. Still "punishment" is often accustomed to be used not according to the proper meaning of the word: but it is extended more broadly for any affliction, either that one that is inflicted on account of sin, or without sin. And in this way the word "punishment" is used in the chapter, *Vergentis*, §. *Nec hujusmodi*.[2] For it is said there "that many times, according to Divine judgment, children also are punished temporally for the sake of the parents." In which quotation it is very clearly evident that the word, "punishment," was put for "affliction." For the children, who did not sin are not properly said to be "punished," but "afflicted": but the

---

2 "And this punishment must not be omitted under the apparent pretext of mercy towards those children of those who have lost their goods, even if they follow the true faith, since many times according to Divine judgment, children are also punished temporally for the sake of the parents, and sometimes in accordance with the canonical penalties, the punishment falls not only on the perpetrators of the crimes, but also on their descendants" (*Decretals of Gregory IX*, bk. 5, tit. 7 (*De haereticis*), c. 10).

parents who sinned are punished by the children's affliction. Wherefore it said, "are punished," instead of, "are afflicted."

But although God does not punish or castigate anyone without fault, still He often afflicts, or torments, without fault: but He never does this without numerous, and indeed very just, reasons, although the reason for those afflictions is frequently hidden from men: so also human laws often inflict some punishments upon men without guilt, yet never, if they are just laws, do they inflict them without cause. For there are many reasons why someone could be justly afflicted with some temporal suffering. Firstly in fact, someone by no fault of his own could by an accident be made unsuitable and unworthy for having or acquiring something good. For many things could be lacking to someone without his fault, which by law are required for obtaining or performing rightly some office. For the priesthood, or episcopate, due age is required, sufficient learning, the soundness of some members of the body, all of which anyone could lack without his own fault, and so without his own fault would be justly rejected from the episcopate and the priesthood. In this way a leper is removed without any fault of his own from office in the Church. And on account of a second marriage [after the death of a spouse],³ or a handing down a death sentence,⁴ a man is hindered from the reception of Holy Orders, and impeded from exercising an Order received. For this reason the son of a heretic without any fault of his own is disqualified from an office and benefice: because by the law itself he is infamous, even without guilt. But for suitably acquiring an office or benefice, good fame is especially necessary.

The second reason could be: because the good of which someone is deprived is not his own good, but a common one: and it is just that someone for the sake of obtaining or

---

3 *Bigomia.*
4 *Judicium sanguinis.* Cf. the canonical irregularities in 1917 *Codex Jur. Canon.* 984, 4 & 6; II-II, q. 108, a. 4, ad 2um.

preserving the common good would suffer in himself some loss. [For example,] that an episcopal see be attached to a certain church belongs to the good of the whole city, and not only to the good of the clerics, and on account of the poverty of the city the episcopal see could justly be taken away from it: and no matter how rich, if the people were to kill their bishop, even though the clergy were resisting and contradicting, the whole city ought to be deprived of the dignity of the episcopate. Which having been done all the clergy will be afflicted by the punishment, and will suffer harm without their fault, yet not unreasonably: because the good of which the clergy is then deprived, was not their own, but the common good of the whole city. But when the city was punished, and deprived of such a good, the clergy are consequently afflicted, and deprived of such a good: because it is part of that body. For it is unjust and not consonant with reason that part of the city would have a bishop, while the rest would lack the same dignity. Also for this reason the children of heretics without their own guilt are not admitted to a public office, nor to a benefice, nor to taking part in an election, nor to serving as a witness: because any of these things is not the particular, but the common good of the whole city. Because it pertains to the whole state that public offices and benefices be held by good persons, and those persons without absolutely any suspicion of evil.

Blessed Thomas assigns yet a third reason,[5] on account of which someone could be justly punished without any fault of his own, or (so that I may speak more correctly) afflicted or tormented, namely, because the good of one person may depend on the good of another, and an example occurs in the crime of high treason, where a son loses his inheritance through the sin of his parent, and the same thing could likewise be said of the crime of heresy, in which also the son (as we said) loses the inheritance due to the father's sin.

---

5   Cf. II-II, q. 108, a. 4 ad 2um.

For the father, on account of crimes of this kind, is deprived of all his goods, which by the law itself are appropriated to the treasury: wherefore the consequence is that the son loses the inheritance, which he would have had from the father's goods. For the son could not be the heir of him, who when dying had completely nothing.

Heretics secondly argue against this opinion of ours, objecting to us that which the Lord says through the prophet Ezechiel: "The soul that sinneth, the same shall die... the son shall not bear the iniquity of the father, and the father shall not bear the iniquity of the son" (18, vv. 4 & 20). Which words seem to be diametrically opposed to our opinion, nay, they seem to conflict with other words of God Himself, by which He said that He visits "the iniquity of the fathers upon the children, unto the third and fourth generation" (Ex. 20, 5). This argument certainly seems to have difficult enigmas, and many very learned men have worked quite hard to resolve them. For some men (as Jerome relates[6]) said that those words of Exodus, in which the Lord says that He visits "the iniquity of the fathers upon the children, unto the third and fourth generation," ought not to be understood literally, but parabolically, such that they have a different meaning than what they sound forth.[7] But it is evident that it is not a parable, even just by the fact that the Lord was then making a law, when He said those words, and He was threatening a

---

6 "You wish to know, he says, that this which is said, 'I will visit the iniquity of the fathers upon their children unto the third and fourth generation' (Deut. 5, 9), does not express what many think: and it is not similar to this sentence [or proverb], 'The fathers have eaten a sour grape, and the teeth of the children are set on edge' (Jer. 31, 29)" (*Commentaria in Ezechielem*, bk. 6 (PL 25, 171B)). Cf. Peter Lombard, *Sententiae*, bk. 2, dist. 33, n. 10 (PL 192, 732).

7 Cf. St. Isidore of Seville's *Etymologies*, where he says, "Allegory is 'other-speech,' for it occurs when one thing is said and another is understood" (bk. 1, c. 27, n. 22 (PL 82, 115B)).

punishment to one transgressing the law, whereby He greatly urges the observance of the law. Now in making laws there is no place for parables: but rather laws ought to be simple and clear, so that they can be understood by everyone.

And Blessed Jerome says that he was never convinced that those words ought to be considered parabolical. Notwithstanding (so that I may speak frankly) neither does he give a sufficient explanation of those words. For Blessed Jerome twists so greatly that apparent dissonance of the Divine words, that he began to say that children are never punished for the parents' iniquities: except because they are imitators of the parents' iniquities. For when expounding chapter eighteen of the prophet Ezechiel, after he had said that the words which are found in Ezechiel fly in the face of those which were cited from the book of Exodus, he says these words which follow: "And we, until the present day, have thought that the two passages from Exodus, which we cited above, were not a parable, but a simple explanation of a sentence. And although we did not dare to say anything—nor the clay vessel to speak against the potter, 'Why hast thou made me thus?'[8]—yet we were secretly scandalized, because it seemed to be an injustice of God, that one man sins, and someone else pays for the sins. For if he visits 'the iniquity of the fathers upon the children, unto the third and fourth generation,' it seems unjust that one should sin and another should be punished. But from what follows: 'of them that hate me,' the scandal of the threat, or precept, is removed. For they are punished in the third and fourth generation, not because their fathers have sinned: since the fathers, who were the sinners, ought rather to have been punished; but because they were imitators of the father, and hated God, by a hereditary wickedness, and impiety growing also into the branches from the root."[9]

---

8 Cf. Is. 29, 16; Rom. 9, 20.
9 *Commentariorum in Ezechielem Prophetam Libri Quatuordec-*

Yet regarding this exposition he did not remain so secure and silent, that by it he believed it sufficed for himself, or for others: but some scruple about this matter always seems to have disturbed him. Because after he had said the aforesaid exposition, and expended many words about this matter, at length he added these words which follow: "In the meantime," he says, "let it suffice to have said about the proverb, or parable, that the Law and the prophets, Exodus and Ezechiel, nay, God Himself Who spoke both in the former and the latter, do not seem to differ in their views, or to correct in the latter what He said incorrectly in the former. But if anyone has been able to find either a better or another meaning, which removes the stumbling block of the conflicting passages, his opinion rather ought to be accepted."[10] From whose words it is very clearly established, how difficult the solution of this perplex question is, which tortured Blessed Jerome so severely, a man indeed renowned for doctrine as well as holiness. For pressed by the various difficulties of this question (as he himself clearly testified) he was secretly scandalized, not knowing on which side he might stand, without being blocked by the other side. Finally, professing the opinion which seemed more secure to him, and not completely sure of it, he said that one ought to accept the opinion of him who had discovered the better understanding. Hence it is that according to his point of view, we are obliged to believe other Doctors on this subject who came after him and penetrated the meaning of this text more correctly than he, and very clearly explained that there is no contradiction between those two passages. And it is not surprising, because (as it is said in the proverb) "Sometimes even good Homer nods off," that the things which he related in this above-mentioned exposition (I pray that no ill-will be

---

im, bk. 6, c. 18, vv. 1-2 (PL 25, 167D-168A).
10 *Ibid.* (PL 25, 169C).

present in these words) are neither correct nor agree in any way with the passage of Exodus.

There are very clear passages in Holy Writ, which state that children are punished for the sins of their parents, so that it could not be concealed by any subterfuge. For Cham sinned against his father, Noe, showing his uncovered nakedness to others,[11] for which sin his son Chanaan was cursed by his father. That this curse proceeded from God's sentence and decree is proved from the fact that God afterwards accomplished in deed the execution of his curse in the same Chanaan and his sons: but because some think that Chanaan was cursed not merely for his father's sin, but also for his own, due to the fact that he first saw, and told his father, and hence it is necessary that I bring forth another much clearer and stronger passage. The small infants, who were burned by fire in Sodom at the same time as their parents,[12] yet it is evident that this happened to them not for their own sins, as they had not yet committed any, but for the sins of the parents. Also that David's son who was born to him from adultery, was taken away by death for the father's sin, the words which the prophet Nathan said to him prove very clearly. For after David confessed his sin, saying: "I have sinned against the Lord" (II Kings 12, 13), the prophet Nathan immediately said to him: "The Lord also hath taken away thy sin: thou shalt not die. Nevertheless, because thou hast given occasion to the enemies of the Lord to blaspheme, for this thing, the child that is born to thee, shall surely die" (vv. 13-14). The sons and daughters of Achan who stole of the anathema of Jericho contrary to the Lord's command, were killed at the same time with Achan himself, their father, by order of Josue. Once this was done the Lord was appeased, who had been angered about the sin of Achan.[13] The sons of Giezi, the

---

11 Cf. Gen. 9, 22.
12 Cf. Gen. 19, 24-25.
13 Cf. Josue 7.

servant of the prophet Eliseus were struck with leprosy,[14] on account of the father's sin, who against the will of Eliseus, accepted gifts from the leprous Naaman on account of the healing conferred upon him. Thus from these testimonies it is very clearly proved to be false what Blessed Jerome says: namely, that children are never punished by God unto the third and fourth generation, because their fathers sinned: but because they were imitators of their fathers.

Moreover, if children are never punished for the sins of the fathers, but only those who imitate the fathers in the crime, it would be false what the Lord says in Exodus, that he visits the sins "of the fathers upon the children, unto the third and fourth generation" (20, 5): because then He visits not the sins of the fathers, but merely the sins of the children themselves, when he punishes them for their sins alone, and not for the fathers' sins. Next, it is evident from the very context that Blessed Jerome incorrectly understood that passage of Exodus, and did not correctly analyze that text. For Jerome says that those words, "of them that hate me," ought to be referred, such that the children are they who hated God, and on account of this are punished by God. Now, so that we may clearly show that those words ought to be referred not to the children, but to their parents, it is necessary that we cite the words of Exodus, which are much clearer than those which Blessed Jerome cites from the fifth chapter of Deuteronomy. For in both places God gave the same sentence in somewhat different words. The text of Exodus is the following: "I am the Lord thy God, mighty, jealous, visiting the iniquity of the fathers upon the children, unto the third and fourth generation of them that hate me" (20, 5). For it is evident that the relative pronoun, "that," ought to be referred to the fathers, and not to the sons: because this relative pronoun ought to be referred to exactly the same thing to which the possessive

---

14 "But the leprosy of Naaman shall also stick to thee, and to thy seed for ever" (IV Kings 5, 27).

prepositional phrase, "of them," refers. Now that possessive prepositional phrase can nowise be referred (as it is very clearly evident) to any else but to the fathers: because the third and fourth generation, which is expressed there, are not the sons' offspring, but the fathers' offspring. Thus the fathers themselves, from whom are the third and fourth generation, which God visits on account of the sins of the fathers, are they that hate God, not the sons. From which we conclude that also in the text of Deuteronomy, which Blessed Jerome cites, the demonstrative pronoun, "to them," refers not to the sons, but to the fathers: such that the fathers are those who hate God, not keeping His commandments: for which reason God punished not only the fathers themselves, but also their third and fourth generation.

Now when God makes this threat in Exodus, He premises these words: "I am the Lord thy God, mighty, jealous." Wherefore it ought to be understood that those words were said to show us by them that He has such great power that He can afflict not merely the sinning fathers themselves, but also the sons for the fathers. Theophylactus, when interpreting in the ninth chapter of John's Gospel those words with which the Apostles asked about the man born blind, whether that blind man sinned, or his parents, so that he would be born blind, gave this same exposition which Jerome gave; so that by it he could reconcile the words of Ezechiel and Exodus, which seem at first glance to be opposed to each other. Moreover, he added a second exposition which I have not found in the writings of any other sacred Doctor. For he says these words: "For it is not just that children who do not act unjustly be afflicted on account of the fathers' sins: and God teaches this through Ezechiel saying, 'This parable shall be no more, whereby it is said, The fathers have eaten sour grapes, and the teeth of the children are set on edge' (Ez. 18, 2-3). And He likewise makes a law through Moses, 'The fathers shall not be put to death for the children' (Deut.

24, 16). But someone will say, 'How is it written that He visits the iniquity of the fathers upon the children, unto the third and fourth generation?'[15] Therefore it first of all ought to be said that this is actually not a universal judgment, and was not decreed against everyone, but only against those who went out from Egypt."[16]

But this opinion of Theophylactus does not please me at all, because it is clearly proved to be false from the punishment which was inflicted upon Giezi due to the gifts which he stealthily received from Naaman after he had been cleansed from leprosy. For after this misdeed Eliseus said to him: "The leprosy of Naaman shall also stick to thee, and to thy seed forever" (IV Kings 5, 27). Now this Giezi was not among the children of Israel who went out from Egypt, but although he was born many centuries later, his children were punished for the sins of the father, even though they were not imitators of the father's iniquity. It is also evident that David was not among the number of those who went out from Egypt. And yet for his sin God punished his son with death whom he had begotten of Bethsabee, just as the prophet Nathan had forewarned him, speaking thus: "Because thou hast given occasion to the enemies of the Lord to blaspheme, for this thing, the child that is born to thee, shall surely die" (II Kings 12, 14).

Moreover, if we consider the circumstances of those words we would clearly know that those menacing words ought to be referred not merely to the children of Israel who went out from Egypt, but to all other men. For those words were then said by God, when He brought forth the Decalogue: and He applied those threats to the transgressors of the first Commandment, saying that He would "visit the iniquity of the fathers upon the children, unto the third and fourth generation." But those precepts of the Decalogue were not given

---

15 Cf. Ex. 20, 5.
16 *Enarratio in Evangelium Joannis* (PG 124, 42B-C).

only to those who went out from Egypt, but to all men in general. Thus the consequence is that the words, whereby He threatened those transgressing His precept, are understood to likewise have been said to all men. For it is not plausible that God when giving the precept would speak to all men, and immediately afterwards when He threatens the transgressors of the precept, does not speak to all the same men, but only to some: especially when He did not give any indication in His words whereby He clearly showed that He firstly spoke to all, and afterwards only to some.

The author of that work which is called the *Antikeimenon*,[17] that is, of contrary or antithetical things, whoever he may be,[18] for its author is not evident, strives to conciliate in some way those words of Exodus with the words of Ezechiel, speaking thus in Question twenty-[eight]: "How is it written in Exodus: 'Who renderest the iniquity of the fathers to the children, and to the grandchildren' (34, 7), when on the contrary it is said by Ezechiel: 'What is the meaning that you use among you this parable as a proverb in the land of Israel, saying: The fathers have eaten sour grapes, and the teeth of the children are set on edge. As I live, saith the Lord God, this parable shall be no more to you a proverb in Israel. Behold all souls are mine: as the soul of the father, so also the soul of the son is mine: the soul that sinneth, the same shall die' (Ez. 18, 2-4). Response. The sins of the fathers are punished in the sons, when for the guilt from Original sin, the souls of the offspring are stained: and again the sins of the fathers are not punished in the sons, because when we are freed from Original sin through Baptism, we do not

---

17 *Antikeimenon, id est, Contrapositorum: sive contrariorum in speciem utriusque Testamenti locorum...* (Venice: Ad Signum Spei, 1552). This book was written to explain a considerable number of apparent Biblical discrepancies.
18 St. Julian of Toledo (642-690).

thereafter have the faults of the parents, but those which we ourselves commit."[19]

But the response certainly errs twice. Firstly in fact in that which it says, that any man before Baptism is stained for the sin of the first parents. For even though the sin of the first parents is the root and origin whence all our evils proceed, still not from it as though by nature are we stained or called sinners. For everyone has his own sin, even when we were children before Baptism, from which one is called a sinner. The reason why it is called original is because from it the sin of our first parents drew its origin. For that sin of the first parents no longer exists, and when it occurred, ought not to be called original, but actual: thus each person is stained not from it, but from his own sin. Concerning which matter, because it is far away from the main goal of our disputation, it is unnecessary to discuss further: because the Council of Trent celebrated under Paull III, in the fifth session, in the third canon, defines clearly enough, and in every single man before Baptism there is his own Original sin.[20]

Next, the author of that book errs in that he thinks that the word "iniquity" in those words of Exodus ought to be taken for guilt, when actually in that passage it only ought to taken for the punishment whereby sins are punished. For to visit the iniquities of the fathers upon the children, is the same thing in that passage as to give the punishments to the children by which the sins of the fathers are punished. For there is there a synecdochical figure, by accepting the cause for the effect, which Sacred Scripture often uses. The Royal Prophet used this meaning of sin when he said, "I was conceived in iniquities" (Ps. 50, 7). For since in every man

---

19 Bk. 1, q. 28 (PL 96, 609A-B); *Decretum Gratiani*, pt. 2, *causa* 23, q. 3, c. 13 (PL 187, 1628A).

20 "If anyone asserts that this sin of Adam, which is one in origin and transmitted to all is in each one as his own by propagation, not by imitation..." (Dz. 790).

there is only one single original sin, it is evident that King David was not conceived in iniquities which have true guilt. And yet because there are many punishments which follow from Original sin itself, he said that he was conceived in many iniquities. For the same reason Paul called the concupiscence of the flesh sin, because it was caused by Original sin, as a punishment from the guilt.[21]

Next, even if we were to freely grant that in those words of Exodus sin is taken for guilt, that interpretation cannot agree with the context, because God says the He visits the iniquities of the fathers upon the children unto the third and fourth generation. But Adam's sin is not transmitted unto only the third and fourth generations, but unto all generations (as Paul says), because all men have sinned in Adam.[22] Furthermore, those words of God, as it is very clearly evident, are a warning, so that by the fear of threats men might be prevented from transgressing the commandment. Now it would be ridiculous to threaten someone with an evil that they will necessarily suffer, whether he acts either well or badly. But no one can avoid Original sin (Christ being excepted[23]), but at some time he falls into it. Thus it is not Original sin, which God threatens that He will visit upon their children unto the third and fourth generation.

It now remains that we give the true meaning of that text, and that we show that Ezechiel nowise disagrees with Exodus. Firstly therefore I say that those words which the Lord says through the prophet Ezechiel, "The soul that

---

21 Cf. Rom. 6, 12: "Let no sin therefore reign in your mortal body, so as to obey the lusts thereof."
22 Cf. Rom. 5, 12.
23 The Immaculate Virgin Mary has always been free from the stain of Original sin, but still contracted the debt of Original sin, such that had she not been preventively redeemed by her Divine Son, she was due to contract Original sin since she descended from Adam.

sinneth, the same shall die... the son shall not bear the iniquity of the father" (18, vv. 4 & 20), ought to be understood of eternal punishment, which awaits sinners after this life. And certainly if the aforesaid words of Ezechiel are understood of that punishment alone, the opinion of those words is very true. Because no one is eternally damned except for his own sin. For He did not say, "The soul that sinneth, the same shall be punished," but He said, "the same shall die." From which words it is apparent that the Lord did not speak about any punishment, but only about death. Now the death, which is given by the Law for every mortal sin, is eternal, and not temporal. Those words of Ezechiel can also be understood, not only of eternal punishment, but also of temporal and spiritual punishment, of which kind is the privation of God's grace, the loss of the right to receive glory. For no one is punished by these punishments, except for his own sin.

And certainly, if those things which surround the words of the prophet Ezechiel were fully considered, anyone easily, even moderately educated, would come to know that those words ought to be understood of spiritual punishment, either eternal or temporal. Now what the Lord says in Exodus, namely, that He visits "the iniquity of the fathers upon the children, unto the third and fourth generation," ought to be understood of corporal and temporal punishment. Thus God punishes with corporal punishment in this life the children for the sins of the fathers: but eternal punishment, and any other spiritual punishment, even though temporary, He never punishes the son for the sin of the father, but the soul which sinned, the same shall die.

Hence Augustine on the book of Josue when treating why for the sin of Achan, his sons were punished, speaks thus: "Nor is it to be believed, even with the punishments which are imposed after death, that one person can be condemned for another; but this punishment is only to be inflicted in those things, which would have had an end, even if they did not end in that way."[24] Shortly after these words Augustine gives the reason why God punishes one person for another with the bodily punishments of this life, speaking thus: "Thus the visible afflictions of men: because they can be both beneficial and harmful to those who are inflicted with them: the Lord knew in the secret depths of His Providence, how He would distribute them to each person, even when He seems to avenge the sins of some men upon others. But the invisible punishments, which harm, and cannot benefit, just as no one pays (God being the judge) for another's sins, so no one ought to pay, when man is the judge, these visible punishments except for his own fault."[25] In which words he gave a very complete and sufficient reason why God corporeally punishes in this life the son for the sin of the father: namely, because such punishment of the son, both harms the father and benefits the son for the salvation of his soul. For on account of augmenting the salvation of the same soul, God often corporally afflicts the just without their guilt in this life. Hence it is not surprising if God torments the just children of wicked fathers with corporal and transitory punishments, and procures the spiritual salvation of the sons.

Now, although they may be temporary, God never punishes children for the sins of the fathers with spiritual punishments. Hence Blessed Augustine reprehended a certain bishop named Auxilius, because he struck a certain nobleman, Classicianus, along with his whole household with excommunication on account of a certain crime of the same Classicianus. For when writing to the same bishop after he had said that the same Classicianus had informed him by his own letter that such a sentence of excommunication had been conferred against him and his household, he says these words which follow:

---

24 *Quaestiones in Heptateuchum*, bk. 6 (*Quaestiones in Jesum Nave*), q. 8 (PL 34, 778).
25 *Ibid.* (PL 34, 779).

Defense of punishing a Catholic son for his father's heresy

"On reading this letter from him, being very much troubled, the thoughts of my heart being agitated like the waves of a stormy sea, I felt it impossible to forbear from writing to you, to beg that if you have thoroughly examined your judgment in this matter, and have proved it by irrefragable reasoning or Scripture testimonies, you will have the kindness to teach me also the grounds on which it is just that a son should be anathematized for the sin of his father, or a wife for the sin of her husband, or a servant for the sin of his master...

"For this is not one of those judgments merely affecting the body, in which, as we read in Scripture, some despisers of God were slain with all their households, though these had not been sharers in their impiety. In those cases, indeed, as a warning to the survivors, death was inflicted on bodies which, as mortal, were destined at some time to die; but a spiritual judgment, founded on what is written, 'Whatsoever thou shalt bind upon earth, it shall be bound also in heaven' (Mt. 16, 19),—is binding on souls, concerning which it is said, 'As the soul of the father, so also the soul of the son is mine: the soul that sinneth, the same shall die' (Ez. 18, 4)...

"But if, perchance, the Lord has revealed to you that it may be justly done, I by no means despise your youth and your inexperience, as having been but recently elevated to high office in the Church. Behold, though far advanced in life, I am ready to learn from one who is but young; and notwithstanding the number of years for which I have been a bishop, I am ready to learn from one who has not yet been a twelvemonth in the same office, if he undertakes to teach me how we can justify our conduct, either before men or before God, if we inflict a spiritual punishment on innocent souls because of another person's crime, in which they are not involved in the same way as they are involved in the Original sin of Adam, 'in whom all have sinned' (Rom. 5, 12)."[26]

---

26 Letter 250, nn. 1-2 (PL 33, 1066-1067).

Still another exposition can be given of those Divine words, which were cited from the book of Exodus and from the prophet Ezechiel, which also are from Blessed Augustine on the book of Josue. The words of the prophet Ezechiel ought to be referred to human judgment, such that by human judgment it would not be allowed to punish a son for the father's sin, or the father for the son's sin: but each one for his own. But those things which are said in Exodus, pertain only to the Divine power, which alone can visit "the iniquity of the fathers upon the children, unto the third and fourth generation." For in that aforementioned place Blessed Augustine, responding to this question with a doubt, speaks thus: "Is there is another precept for human judges, that they should not punish anyone for someone else? but are there not judgments of God of that kind, Who by His deep and invisible plan knows how far He must extend even men's temporal punishment and salutary fear?... But if Achan were found by someone, and arrested, and the guilt of his crime had been brought to Josue's judgment, in no wise ought it to be supposed that a human judge would have punished either someone in place of him, or anyone else with him, who was not at all an accomplice in his deed. For he was not allowed to go beyond the mandate of the law which gave him the order or the permission to punish one of his fellow men, but without sentencing someone to be punished for someone else's sin. Now God judges by a far more secret judgment, Who is also able to deliver or destroy after death, which man cannot do... For God commanded the human judge, in those matters which pertain to be judged by human judgment, because in His own judgment He Himself makes [a judgment] to which human ability cannot come near."[27]

From whose words, that which he said, namely, that human judgment cannot punish one man for another's sin, ought

---

27 *Quaestiones in Heptateuchum*, bk. 6 (*Quaestiones in Jesum Nave*), q. 8 (PL 34, 778-779).

not to be taken universally and understood of every punishment: but only of the punishment of death. Because about this punishment alone I find in the Divine law that judges were forbidden to punish one man for another. For these are the words of the Law, which God decreed about this matter: "The fathers shall not be put to death for the children, nor the children for the fathers, but every one shall die for his own sin" (Deut. 24, 16). When He forbade killing here, He made completely no mention of another punishment. To keep this law of the Lord Amasias, the son of Joas king of Juda, even though he killed those who had killed his father: still he did not want to kill their sons, as it is related in the Fourth book of Kings in chapter fourteen.[28]

Wherefore I cannot but be astonished how Emperors Honorius and Arcadius in the law, *Quisquis cum militibus*,[29] were not afraid to say that they by imperial indulgence grant life to the children of them who committed treason, as though without this imperial indulgence, they could have justly killed the sons for the sins of the fathers. Since by the Divine law, which we have cited above, it was forbidden to them to kill the fathers for the sons, or the sons for the fathers. Now the reason which they assert in the same law, that they could also justly kill the sons, has entirely no weight. "For they should be put to death," they say, "by

---

28 "But the children of the murderers he did not put to death, according to that which is written in the book of the law of Moses, wherein the Lord commanded, saying: The fathers shall not be put to death for the children, neither shall the children be put to death for the fathers: but every man shall die for his own sins" (v. 6).

29 "The sons of a person convicted of such an offense, to whom by special Imperial indulgence We grant the privilege of life (for they should be put to death by the same punishment as their father, as in their cases his example, that is, the inclination to commit a crime, is inherited)..." (*The Code of Justinian*, bk. 9, tit. 8 (*Ad legem Juliam majestatis*), l. 5, §1).

the same punishment as their father, as in their cases his example, that is, the inclination to commit a crime, is inherited." What a completely worthless argument! A judge will then be allowed to kill Peter, because he justly feared that he would become a thief, or a murderer, or some other similar thing. For the punishment never ought to precede the crime, but follow it. It is indeed just to fear that which the fathers committed in their sons. It is also just to cure this fear, such that by having applied some just remedy so that that which is feared would not happen. Still it is unjust, and very unjust, that on account of the fear of a future crime someone would be punished with the same punishment with which he would be punished if he had actually committed that crime. Thus not from mercy alone or from imperial indulgence (as they say) but from mere justice is life granted to the sons of those who are guilty of treason.

And completely the same thing ought to be said about the Catholic sons of heretics, who even though they could be justly struck with other punishments for the heresy of their parents, still they will never be punished with the punishment of death for them. Because as the Divine law says, "Every one shall die for his own sin." Now that which the Pope says in the chapter, *Vergentis*,[30] that the life of the children of those who are guilty of treason is spared merely through mercy, Pope Innocent, who is the author of that text, did not

---

30 "For since, according to lawful sanctions, those guilty of committing treason are executed, their good confiscated, the life of their children spared merely through mercy; how much more ought those who, deviating in the faith of God, offend against God [and] Jesus and Christ the Son of God, to be cut off from our Head, which is Christ, by ecclesiastical censure, and deprived of [their] temporal goods, since it is far more serious to commit treason against that which is eternal than that which is temporal" (*Decretals of Gregory IX*, bk. 5, tit. 7 (*De haereticis*), c. 10, §. *Quum enim*).

speak by defining or approving it: but merely related that the laws of the emperors decreed about those guilty of treason: and hence he argues from the less to the greater concerning the confiscation of goods that something similar, to what the laws of the emperor decreed about those guilty of treason, ought to be done in regard to heretics. Therefore let this be the most certain and infallible opinion, that no human judge is ever allowed to kill one man for the sin of another.

Which rule ought to be extended not to death alone, but also to other scourges and wounds of the body, and the rest of the tortures of the body, such that it is also understood to be forbidden to the human judge to scourge, or wound, or punish with any other similar punishment of the body, one man for the sin of another. For illustrious theologians so think, namely, Alexander of Hales,[31] and after him Blessed Thomas.[32] And indeed deservedly they thought that that Divine law ought to be so extended, because just as by the precept, "Thou shalt not kill," not only death is forbidden, but any other striking of the body; so also it follows that by that precept, "The fathers shall not be put to death for the children, nor the children for the fathers" (Deut. 24, 16), scourging, or any other striking of the body, is also forbidden to the judge, such that he cannot either scourge or beat anyone for the sin of another. Thus regarding this punishment which included death, and other tortures of the body, which Alexander of Hales and Blessed Thomas call an inflictive punishment [*poenam flagelli*], Augustine understands (as from the whole context of his writing may be easily gathered) when he said that it is not permitted to a human judge to punish one man for another. He also says that spiritual and invisible punishment, such as excommunication, never ought to be inflicted by a human judge, except for a man's own sin: just as God

---

31 *Universae Theologiae Summa: In Quatuor Partes* (Cologne: Gymnicus, 1622), pt. 3, q. 41, mem. 4, a. 1, pp. 303 f.
32 II-II, q. 108, a. 4.

never punishes with spiritual and invisible punishment one man for the sin of another. The other punishments, which are neither spiritual nor directed towards the death of the body, a human judge can rightly inflict upon someone, when a just reason is at hand, for the sin of another. And not only for the sin of another, but even without any sin: yet a judge can never licitly inflict punishments of this kind without a just cause. For the son born of fornication, merely on account of the sin of the father, is not admitted to the priesthood, as God so commands. "A mamzer, that is to say, one born of a prostitute, shall not enter into the church of the Lord, until the tenth generation" (*Ibid.* 23, 2). Likewise a judge on account of a death sentence very justly given, and the command for execution, is punished with an irregularity.[33] Therefore there are two ways (as is evident from the aforesaid things) by which we showed that the words, which are found in Exodus, very well agree with those which were said through the prophet Ezechiel, and there is no contradiction between those two passages.

---

33 An irregularity is a canonical impediment directly impeding the reception of tonsure and Holy Orders or preventing the exercise of Orders already received, among which is voluntary homicide. Cf. 1917 CIC °985 §4; 1983 CIC °1041 §4

Chapter XII

That heretics ought to be punished with the penalty of death, whether it be that such a death is inflicted upon them by the sword, or fire, or any other way.

The last punishment now presents itself, namely, death; with which, we will prove very clearly with God's help, that heretics, unless they come to their senses in time, justly ought to be punished. And so that we may treat the matter more clearly, firstly before everything else, I wish to interrogate those who think the opposite, whether it is lawful to kill a man for a just reason? Perhaps they will say as the Waldensian heretics formerly taught, that there is no reason so just such that on account of it someone could be deservedly and justly killed, even if it would be done by the command of the judge. And certainly (if some place ought to be given to suspicions and conjectures) I suspect that some of the Lutherans think this way. For Otto Brunfels[1] in his *Pandects of Sacred Scripture*,[2] wanting to convince that heretics ought not to be killed, among the other things which he cites, quotes Isaias saying: "They shall not hurt nor kill in all my holy mountain, saith the Lord" (65, 25). Which words do not speak any more about heretics than about anyone else, that they are more forbidden to be killed than others. Wherefore I conjecture from this citation, and deservedly, that he thought that no one ought to be killed even for any reason. If they so think, they will fall into another much more pestilential error. For such an error

---

[1] Otto Brunfels (1488-1534) was a German Protestant theologian.
[2] *Pandectarum Veteris et Novi Testamenti, Libri XII* (Strasbourg: Schottus, 1528), fol. 50v, where he gives a series of quotations from the Bible under the heading, "That heretics are burned, is contrary to the Spirit."

besides this one, which opposes with Holy Writ, takes away human social intercourse, disturbs the peace of the whole nation, and completely perverts all decent government. For even if the precept of not killing had been given in the Old Law, still there were many other laws, which ordered men to be punished with death for some particular wicked deeds. He that shall go aside after magicians, and soothsayers was ordered to be killed.[3] He that cursed his father, or mother was condemned to death.[4] There are many others of this kind, which it is not now necessary to enumerate.

Leaving aside the Old Law, which has now been abrogated by Christ's death regarding the judgments and ceremonies, let us come to the time of the Evangelical Law. Blessed Peter the Apostle punished Ananias and Saphira with death,[5] because having sold land they kept back part of the price by fraud, keeping part of it for themselves, and not bringing the whole price (as they were bound to do from a vow) before the Apostles. Furthermore, the Teacher of Truth Himself taught that the man who had killed another man on his own authority, justly ought to be killed, when speaking thus: "All that take the sword shall perish with the sword" (Mt. 26, 52). By which words the Savior clearly taught that he ought to be punished with death, who killed another. I know that there are some who think that these words which we have just cited from Matthew, nowise are able to prove that a murderer can justly be killed. For they say that those words ought to be understood not according to the apparent meaning of the words: because if those words are interpreted according to it, clear falsity (they say) will be found in them: which would be wicked to assert. For it is evident that not everyone who strikes someone with sword, perishes by the sword of justice: because many such men, are either devoured by the

---

3 Cf. Lev. 20, 6.
4 Cf. *Ibid.*, v. 9.
5 Cf. Acts 5, 1-10.

Fourth bodily punsihment of heretics: death by various means

sea, or drown in the waves, or end their lives by a fever or some other disease, or are killed by enemies.

But this argument does not actually impede those words from being understood literally without any mystical meaning: because this argument presented just now proceeds from a mistaken understanding of the text. For in this way it seems that one comprehends those words as though they had been said by Christ for preaching future events, and not rather as a command of those things which one ought to do. For Christ in these words, "All that take the sword shall perish with the sword," did not intend to warn us about the future happening of things, so that we would understand by what death all those who had taken up the sword would die: but He decreed a precept, and showed the law by which He taught what punishment they deserved, who killed another by the sword. And so that I may make this opinion clearer and more probable, I wish to put forth similar words as an example, from the correct consideration of which words, these words which were said may be understood more easily. One of the Divine precepts contained in the Decalogue is expressed by these words: "Thou will not make to thyself a graven thing" (Ex. 20, 4). And again, "Thou will not adore them" (v. 5). And in another precept, "Thou will not kill" (v. 13). And again in another, "Thou will not commit adultery" (v. 14). For if the words of all these precepts ought to be examined by the rules of grammar alone, they would seem to predict future events: because they are all in the future indicative mood,[6] which is used not for commanding, but only for indicating what will happen. Thus if those words were to be interpreted according to that indicative mood, who does not see that they all give very false meanings. For

---

6 N. B. The indicative mood is used in Latin to express actual events which happen or will happen in the future, whereas the imperative mood is used to express a command of what should be done.

the children of Israel, to whom those words were said, made graven things, and adored them, and killed many men, and often committed adultery. Far be it however that we say that something false is in God's words: and hence we are forced to understand that those words do not express the outcome of future events, as the rules of grammar require: but we may only interpret them as stating God's precepts, such that we acknowledge that the indicative mood was used for the imperative. In this way in every respect one ought to understand those words of Christ: "All that take the sword shall perish with the sword," such that we may think that those words are not of a person predicting the future, but of a person commanding and decreeing a law, whereby He gave the power to the public authority, so that it could punish with the sword him who has killed another privately and without public authority.

Peter was at that time such a man, who having no public authority struck the servant of the ruler with a sword. Theophylactus supports this interpretation of ours, who in his commentaries on Matthew when interpreting the above-mentioned words, after he had given another explanation to those words of Christ, says these words which follow: "Then Christ gives the dictum of the Law, that he who slays will himself be slain. For the Law says that 'they who take the sword shall perish with the sword.'"[7] From whose words it is evident that those words of Christ pertain to the Law. Now the function of the Law is not to predict future things, but to command that which one ought to do, or forbid that from which one ought to abstain. And certainly, if the context itself of the words is properly examined, one will clearly know that those words pertain to a precept. For after Peter had struck the servant of the priest, Christ said to him: "Put up again thy sword into its place" (Mt. 26, 52). Now that

---

7 Cf. Gen. 9, 6 and Jer. 15, 2. *Enarratio in Evangelium Matthaei* (PG 123, 454A).

those words pertain to a precept, no one could rightly doubt: because they were enunciated in the imperative mood. Now in order to urge Peter to the execution of this command, He puts at that time before his eyes the penal law given long ago against all murderers, so that at least by fear of punishment He might avert him from the use of the sword, speaking thus: "All that take the sword shall perish with the sword."

And the concordances very clearly support this opinion which are published in common Bibles, in which are often noted in the side margin, other passages of Scripture agreeing with that sentence which was written close by on the side. But on the side of these words of Christ in Matthew's Gospel are found cited in the margin: Genesis 9 and Apocalypse 13.[8] By which notes it is indicated to us that a sentence similar to that which is found in Matthew 26, is found in those two places. Now the words which are found in Genesis 9 are these: "Whosoever shall shed man's blood, his blood shall be shed" (v. 6). Against these words the same argument could be formed, which was made above against those words of Matthew understood according to my meaning. For many shed human blood, whose blood was never shed. But on account of this argument none of the sacred Doctors ever (that I know) was forced, in view of these words to abandon the literal meaning, and seek the mystical meaning: because in these words all understood that the future indicative was used for the present imperative. Thus the same thing in every respect ought [to be understood] in those words in Matthew: "All that take the sword shall perish with the sword," but the words are clearer which are said in the Apocalypse, where these words are found: "He that shall kill by the sword, must be killed by the sword" (13, 10). For speaking clearly (as it is befitting) He showed that this passage is not a prediction of future events, but rather is a law stating that a murderer

---

8 *Biblia: cum Concordantiis Veteris et Novi testamenti* (Koberger, 1501).

ought to be killed. For that which He says, "must [*oportet*] be killed," is the same as if He had said, "ought [*debet*] to be killed." Or, he ought to be killed according to the law.

I know that there are some Doctors who interpret the above-mentioned words of Christ figuratively concerning a spiritual sword. But because Augustine teaches that one never ought to depart from the literal sense, and seek after a figure, except when necessity obliges, that is, when according to the literal sense an absurd meaning is obtained.[9] Hence it is proved in these words one ought not to depart from the literal sense, by interpreting them of a spiritual sword: because by using the word "sword," according to the proper meaning of that word, there will be no (as we have clearly shown) absurdity in those words. I wanted to speak at such great length about the correct meaning of these words because I see that there are some men to whom it is very displeasing that by the testimony of those words I would wish to prove that a murderer can be lawfully killed. I will perhaps discuss elsewhere at greater length about the meaning of these words, if God grants me life, in another work which I am now preparing.[10]

Again from this opinion yet another is very clearly derived. For if there is no just reason on account of which it is lawful to kill a man, it necessarily follows that for no reason is it lawful to wage war: because it is nearly impossible that wars would be waged without the killing of some man. But how much this opinion is foreign to the truth of the Catholic faith, it is not necessary to show now: because we have already overcome it by very clear arguments in that work which we published, *Against All Heresies*, in the section on "War"

---

[9] "When the words taken literally give an absurd meaning, we ought immediately to inquire whether they may not be used in this or that figurative sense..." (*On Christian Doctrine*, bk. 3, c. 29, n. 41 (PL 34, 81).

[10] Cf. *De potestate legis poenalis*, bk. 1, c. 7.

Fourth bodily punsihment of heretics: death by various means

[*Bellum*]. Next, if man is never permitted for any reason to kill any wicked men, no state could remain safe: because unless the most wicked men are killed, there will be no quiet in the nation, no peace will remain in it. Evil men will afflict all just men so much more boldly, the more certain they know that they cannot be killed for any crime. And the death, which it is unlawful to inflict on the most wicked men according to the sentence of the judge, it will be permitted to inflict upon all just men with impunity by all the most wicked men themselves. If it were not permitted to the judge ruling the nation to kill any man, the land would be full of thieves and robbers, the sea with pirates, and nothing would be safe: but men would be like, according to the saying of the prophet Habacuc, the fish of the sea, whose larger ones often devour the smaller ones.[11] On account of which there never was (that I know of) a nation so barbaric and uncultivated which did not decree for the sake of some crimes that death be inflicted on evildoers. Thus, so that there be due peace and tranquility in a nation, it is expedient that whatever very wicked men, especially about whom there is no hope of amendment, be killed, lest on account of them the whole government collapse.

If someone however were to object to us the Divine precept, which says: "Thou shalt not kill," we would reply that by that precept, only that killing is forbidden which is done by a private person: not however that which is determined to be inflicted by a judge for some just reason. In proof of which Blessed Jerome speaks thus: "To punish murderers, profaners, and poisoners is not shedding blood but administering the law."[12] Blessed Augustine says that some men are excepted from the precept, "Thou shalt not kill," whom he asserts can be justly killed. Finally after having enumerated those

---

[11] Cf. Hab. 1, 14: "And thou wilt make men as the fishes of the sea, and as the creeping things that have no ruler."
[12] *Commentary on Jeremias*, bk. 4, c. 22 (PL 24, 811C).

men, he says the words which follow: "With the exception, then, of these two classes of cases, which are justified either by a just law that applies generally, or by a special intimation from God Himself, the fountain of all justice, whoever kills a man, either himself or another, is implicated in the guilt of murder."[13]

Perhaps having been convinced by these reasons (as is befitting), these men who contend that heretics ought not to be killed will say that it is licit and just to kill a man for some just cause, yet they will deny that heresy is a just cause on account of which a heretical man ought to be killed, even if he be very pertinacious. Now so that we may very clearly show that they err very pertinaciously, one ought to investigate and carefully examine what are the just causes on account of which some can be justly condemned to death. I do not wish at the present time to list all of these causes individually or one by one, but only the types of causes. Galen,[14] a man very illustrious besides the science of medicine, in every type of philosophy, in the small work which is entitled, *The Soul's Traits Depend on Bodily Temperament*,[15] gives some reasons on account of which some men are deservedly punished with death, speaking thus: "For three reasons consonant with reason we take away deplorable and wicked men from this life, namely, lest surviving they insult us: [secondly] that they should bring about that men like themselves would be terrified, that they would receive the same punishment if they would perpetrate anything against the law. The third reason is that they themselves are destined to die, being so depraved in mind, that they have incurable malice, from which they indeed cannot be corrected by the Muses themselves, nor

---

13   *City of God*, bk. 1, c. 21 (PL 41, 35).
14   Galen of Pergamon (129-216 A.D.) was a Greek physician, surgeon, and philosopher in the Roman Empire.
15   *Quod animi mores corporis temperamenta sequantur*.

Fourth bodily punsihment of heretics: death by various means

could they be made better either by Socrates or Pythagoras."[16] But because many men will perhaps not fear to contemn the opinion of Galen as a pagan and nowise Christian, it is necessary that we confirm all three reasons assigned by him from natural reason, with testimonies of Sacred Scripture, and then we will show on account of the same three reasons that the death of an incorrigible heretic is just.

He said that the first reason is namely lest the deplorable and very evil men being alive, would insult others. It is indeed just that the innocent always be kept unharmed, and he who has the office of governing the nation ought to nowise permit anyone to insult or injure another. Wherefore if some very harmful man, after having been warned once and again by the judge not to harm another, does not want to reform his bad life, but being always persistent in his malice, harms many daily, the judge may be forced to take him from this life, lest he could harm others more. For a ruler of a nation is bound to provide more for the whole nation than for one or another citizen, to conserve the whole body, than one member. Yet these things ought to be understood, if the harm were great: because not for any light harm is he allowed to kill, even if the man were pertinacious in it. Thus he may grant that any wicked man be killed, rather than that the whole nation perish. Now it would perish, if any evil men were allowed to live. For, as Solomon says, "Corrupt men bring a city to ruin: but wise men turn away wrath" (Prov. 29, 8). Wise men turn away wrath when they take away pestilent men from this life, lest those men be able to demolish the city. It is this reason which justifies the laws which command thieves, pirates, assassins, murderers, and other men of the same sort to be killed.

If there be just cause to take away the life of a wicked man, then there would also be just cause to take away the life

---

16 *Galeni opera omnia* (Leipzig: Car. Cnoblochii, 1822), vol. 4, pp. 815 f.

of an incorrigible heretic: because if the latter were allowed to live, he would greatly harm other Catholics. For Paul expressed well enough how much harm a heretic could do when saying: "But shun profane and vain babblings: for they grow much towards ungodliness, and their speech spreadeth like a canker [*cancer*]" (II Tim. 2, 16-17). Commenting upon which words Theophylactus says: "It is an evil, says Paul, which cannot be restrained, and does not allow any further treatment: for it devastates everything, and is incurable. For cancer is a disease producing rottenness, and to such an extent that it devours everything surrounding it."[17] And because the harm is so clear, which heretics confer upon Catholics, Paul when writing to the Galatians about the false prophets who had seduced them, says: "I would they were even cut off, who trouble you" (5, 12). And Blessed Jerome says: "Cut off the decayed flesh, expel the mangy sheep from the fold, lest the whole house, the whole paste, the whole body, the whole flock, burn, perish, rot, die. Arius was but one spark in Alexandria, but as that spark was not at once put out, the whole earth was laid waste by its flame."[18] That which the distinguished poet said echoes with this opinion: "An unhealable body part [*corpus*] must be cut away by knife, lest the healthy part be drawn in to infection."[19]

A second reason for inflicting death, which Galen teaches, is so that others through fear of a similar punishment may be deterred from perpetrating similar crimes. The previous reason had to do with the peaceful life of the citizens among themselves, and the preservation of the entire nation by this, namely, that no one harms another. But this second reason regards the good morals of the citizens themselves, namely, so that no one would dare to commit atrocious crimes, even

---

17 *Expositio in Epistolam II ad Timotheum* (PG 125, 110B).
18 *Commentaria in Epistolam ad Galatas*, bk. 3 (PL 26, 403B). *Decretum Gratiani*, pt. 2, *causa* 24, q. 3, c. 16 (PL 187, 1302C).
19 Ovid, *Metamorphoses*, bk. 1, lns. 190 f.

Fourth bodily punsihment of heretics: death by various means

if no neighbor would be harmed by them. For there are many men prone and inclined to some crimes, but through fear of death, which they greatly dread, and which they know has been inflicted upon others for committing similar wicked deeds, they are deterred from those crimes, and they fear to commit them. For the wise Solomon says in Proverbs: "The wicked man being scourged, the fool shall be wiser" (19, 25). For this reason just men (as the Royal Prophet says) rejoice about the punishment of evil men: because they recognize that they themselves have benefitted from such punishment not a little regarding virtue, or hope that they will increase [in virtue] afterwards. "The just shall rejoice," the prophet says, "when he shall see the revenge: he shall wash his hands in the blood of the sinner" (Ps. 57, 11). Upon which passage Cassiodorus says: "How can this be, that He Who has bidden us pray for our enemies maintains that the hands of the holy will be washed in the blood of sinners? If we look at this more carefully, it will afford an example of correction rather than savagery; for when the blood of a sinner is shed, the hands—in other words the deeds—of the most just man undergo correction. When the guilty man perishes, the innocent man is warned to behave more carefully and more diligently. So it happens that the blood of the sinner cleanses the just man's hands in a holy rather than a cruel way. As Solomon says: 'The wicked man being scourged, the fool shall be wiser.'"[20]

From this root arises a very numerous number of laws commanding men to kill on account of crimes which harm no one except the perpetrator himself. He who shall have gone aside after magicians, and soothsayers, in the Mosaic Law is commanded to be killed.[21] Although by these crimes no one besides the perpetrator of them himself is harmed, still to inspire horror for those crimes in others, the punish-

---

20 *Explanation of the Psalms* (PL 70, 408D-409A).
21 Cf. Lev. 20, 6.

ment of death was decreed by the Law for such crimes, namely, so that others would understand how serious those crimes are, for which such a severe punishment is inflicted, and so that others by the dread and fear of similar punishment may be deterred from perpetrating similar wicked deeds. For this is the reason, on account of which in the Old Law God commanded the one rebelling against the priest to be killed. "He that will be proud, and refuse to obey the commandment of the priest, who ministereth at that time to the Lord thy God, and the decree of the judge, that man shall die, and thou shalt take away the evil from Israel: and all the people hearing it shall fear, that no one afterwards swell with pride" (Deut. 17, 12-13). In which words God gave this reason alone for killing, which we now treat. Hence to punish an incorrigible heretic with death can now appear to be very just, not to speak of it being just. Whence it is that to engender dread and hatred of such a great crime in others, it is just to inflict the punishment of death upon an incorrigible heretic, so that at least from this, other men may know how serious the crime of heresy is, for which such a sad sentence is decreed, and so that others by fear and dread of a similar punishment may be afraid to be heretics. If it is just through the punishment of one man to inspire dread of the same crime, the more the crime was more serious, so much the more will it be more just through a greater and more severe punishment, to instill greater dread of the same crime in others. But there is no more serious sin (as we taught above in the first book) than the sin of heresy, therefore there is no crime, the hatred of which ought to be more instilled in a Christian man, and hence it consequently follows that there is no crime for which someone could be more justly killed than for fixed and incurable heresy.

If Martin Luther, when he first began to pour out his venom, and after having been duly admonished did not want to recover his senses, had been punished (as he ought) with

Fourth bodily punsihment of heretics: death by various means

capital punishment, others would have had fear, and so many and such pestiferous sects of heretics would not have gushed forth, such as Germany, alas, undergoes today. But because Luther escaped unpunished, the heresies of Oecolampadius, Zwingli, Carlstadt, and the worst of all the heretics, the Anabaptists, would not have dared to go forth in public and babble their heresies.

And hence the response appears to a certain argument, whereby those who deny that heretics, no matter how incurable, cannot be killed for the crime of heresy, defend themselves and imagine that they conquer us. For they say that a punishment and correction of a delinquent is worthless and foolish, by which the delinquent cannot be corrected. But after death the heretic cannot be corrected, therefore it is unjust to kill him. O what a beautiful argument! If this argument were of any weight, it would also prove that it is never licit to kill someone for any other grave crime, not theft, not adultery, not homicide, not sacrilege. For none of these can be corrected after death, just as neither can the heretic. Thus, according to their opinion it would be necessary that none of them could be justly killed.

We therefore reply that not every punishment is solely for the correction of the delinquent, but also for caution of others, namely, so that others terrified by fear may avoid such crimes. Wherefore Blessed Augustine says: "None of us wishes any heretic to perish. But the house of David did not deserve to have peace, unless his son Absalom had been killed in the war which he had raised against his father... Thus if the Catholic Church gathers together some by the perdition of others, she heals the sorrow of her maternal heart by the delivery of so many nations."[22]

The third reason on account of which, as Galen says, it is just to kill a wicked man, is the evil man himself: because it is despaired, and indeed rightly (as it can be conjectured

---

22 Letter 185, c. 8, n. 32 (PL 33, 807). Cf. II-II q. 10, a. 8, ad 4um.

from his way of life) about his amendment, and it is feared that if he were to continue to live, he would get worse daily. Thus lest he go further on to some very grave misdeed, it is just that having been taken away by death, he be precluded from the liberty of sinning. The two first reasons regard the utility of the whole nation, but this third reason regards the advantages for the delinquent himself. For it is preferrable to die than to live badly, and it is also preferable that a wicked man die, than to become worse day by day. But so advancing, as Paul says, according to his hardness and impenitent heart, he treasures up to himself wrath, against the day of wrath, and revelation of the just judgment of God.[23] For which reason God, Who is rich in mercy[24] and long-suffering in patience, snatches away many in this life in childhood, or adolescence, or youth, lest the crimes, from which they are then free, afterwards when living commit; for so says Solomon: "He pleased God and was beloved, and living among sinners he was translated. He was taken away lest wickedness should alter his understanding... For his soul pleased God: therefore he hastened to bring him out of the midst of iniquities" (Wis. 4, vv. 10-11 & 14).

If this cause could be just, so that on account of it someone could be killed, it could not be more just than when killing an incorrigible heretic, lest being allowed to live he be more insane each day, and become worse. For it is typical of heretics that unless they were forbidden, they would daily increase their malice, by always stirring up new errors. For Paul was speaking about these men when he said: "Evil men and seducers shall grow worse and worse: erring, and driving into error" (II Tim. 3, 13). Even though many examples of this could be given, still the example of the one man, Martin Luther, will be enough for them all, whose deeds, because they happened in our time, and are happening, and many

---

23 Cf. Rom. 2, 5.
24 Cf. Eph. 2, 4.

Fourth bodily punsihment of heretics: death by various means

of them are very well known to nearly the whole Christian world: will be able to give testimony in favor of our opinion much more strongly than any examples of the old heretics, which we have not seen. Examples seen certainly move more than those heard.

For this Martin Luther had small beginnings of his errors, from which he developed into so many, and so pestiferous (as we now see) errors. In fact, in the beginning he only erred about the indulgences, which by the Bulls of the Supreme Pontiffs were wont to be granted to sinners for the remission of punishment: and he did not then rave about anything more. Since at that time he thought rightly about the Sacraments of the Church, he acknowledged the whole order of the ecclesiastical hierarchy, the Pope, that is, he recognized that the Bishop of Rome is superior to all the other bishops, and is the ruler of the whole Christian world. For in a letter to Leo X, the Supreme Pontiff at that time, he wrote these words which follow: "Therefore, Most Holy Father, I prostrate myself at your feet, placing myself and all I am and have at your disposal, to be dealt with as you see fit. My cause hangs on the will of Your Holiness, by whose verdict I shall either save or lose my life. Come what may, I shall recognize the voice of your Holiness to be that of Christ, speaking through you."[25] Proceeding shortly after these words he denied that any satisfaction is necessary for sins: but when the guilt is remitted, he said that completely all the punishment is remitted. Thence compelled he denied Purgatory, which nevertheless he had confessed very clearly and publicly in the disputation held in Leipzig in the beginning of his error. When he had been admonished about these errors by the Supreme Pontiff, Leo X, and he did not want to sing the palinode[26] (as

---

25 Letter to Pope Leo X dated May 30, 1518, taken from: *The Letters of Martin Luther* (Margaret A. Currie, London, Macmillan & Co., 1908) pp. 30 f. WA vol. 1, p. 529, lns. 22-25.

26 I. e., a recantation or to unsay what he had said. A palinode is

he was obliged): Leo X declared him a heretic, and publicly excommunicated him as such. At last Luther seeing himself declared a heretic, and condemned, burst forth as many and suchlike heresies, as no heretic ever before him had taught.

Regarding the errors to be investigated of all heretics (as from that work which I published, *Against All Heresies*, can be easily inferred) I have used as much diligence (far be it from me to brag) as anyone else ever used about this matter. Yet I have not found one among so many, even though they were many, who taught so many at the same time, and such pestiferous heresies. Thus it would have been better for him that immediately from the beginning, when he contemned to obey when duly admonished, to have been punished by the sword or fire, than being alive to fall into so many heresies, by which he daily increased the Divine wrath against himself, and keep it treasured against the day of the just judgment of God,[27] so that thereupon he would then be punished more severely. In fact in my opinion no one could be a more cruel enemy to Martin Luther, than he who being able to justly take away his life, permitted him to live so long. Unless perhaps led by good zeal although indiscrete, he wished to imitate the Divine mercy in this matter, which often gives to sinners (as Job says[28]) time for repentance, although they abuse the time granted to them, and do not wish to do penance. But these are certain secret dispensations of the Divine goodness, since men do not know the reasons for which, it is not necessary to imitate God in them.

What shall I say about the Anabaptists, who under the skin of sheep, that is, under the name of the Gospel and fraternal charity, all of which words they always have in their mouths,

---

an ode in which the writer retracts a view
or sentiment expressed in an earlier poem.
27 Cf. Rom. 2, 5.
28 Cf. Job 24, 23: "God hath given him place for penance, and he abuseth it unto pride."

Fourth bodily punsihment of heretics: death by various means

they put on the character of a wolf filled with wickedness and impiety? Since these men when they first began to rave, erred in no other matter (that I know of), except about Baptism, and hence they were saying that those who had been baptized in infancy, ought to be rebaptized when they reached the age of reason. Yet because they were not restrained from this error (as they ought) and punished, going on by a licentious savageness to worse things, they threw themselves headlong over to the most pestilential heresies. Thus it would have been better for the Anabaptists themselves to have been killed, than to have been kept to imbibe or swallow down so many very pestilential dregs of heresies.

Notice that you have now seen, fair reader, three reasons on account of which an incorrigible heretic can justly be killed. The first, lest when living he harm others deceiving them by his error. The second, so that by his peril others may be made more cautious, and be deterred from heresy by fear of such a great punishment. The third, lest continuing to live they become worse daily, and stir up greater Divine wrath against themselves. From which three reasons we very clearly conclude that if any man can be justly killed, no one ought to be killed with greater reason than an obstinate and incurable heretic. Long ago by Divine law it was commanded that a blasphemer would be brought out of the camp, and stoned by the whole people.[29] Much more therefore ought a heretic be justly killed, since heresy (as we taught in the first book) is a much more serious sin than blasphemy. Furthermore, in Deuteronomy God commanded that a false prophet and contriver of dreams be killed. For after he forewarned that they ought not to listen to such a prophet, he added these words: "And that prophet or forger of dreams shall be slain: because he spoke to draw you away from the Lord your God, who brought you out of the land of Egypt, and redeemed you from the house of bondage" (Deut. 13, 5). Now who ought

---

29 Cf. Lev. 24, 14.

to be reckoned more truly a false prophet, and who turns the people away from God more than a heretic, who turns [the people] away from the faith, "without which it is impossible to please God" (Heb. 11, 6)? He therefore deservedly according to God's law ought to be killed, so that he could no more turn away the people from God.

Again we have known by Scripture relating that Semei received the sentence of death because contrary to the prohibition of King Solomon he went out of the city of Jerusalem.[30] Much more just therefore would it be to kill a heretic, who against God's precept goes out of the Church, within which he should have constantly stayed. Next, the famous King Josias, to whom neither before him nor after him was there a king in Juda similar,[31] slew all the priests who contrary to the Lord's law sacrificed victims to idols on the altars, on which they were sacrificing.[32] Mathathias also, that illustrious priest of the Law, and propagator of the faith, boiling with zeal, slaughtered upon the altar him who had come to sacrifice [to idols] upon the altar.[33] What do you think this Mathathias, or the famous Josias would do to heretics, if either of them were now alive? I do not doubt that both of them for God's honor, and being zealous for the faith of His Church, would punish every single heretic with capital punishment, to take away the evil from the Church. Justly therefore have emperors decreed by their laws that obstinate heretics ought to be killed.[34]

---

30 Cf. III Kings 2, 36-46.
31 Cf. IV Kings 23, 25.
32 Cf. *Ibid.*, v. 20.
33 Cf. I Mach. 2, 24.
34 "Manicheans must be expelled from towns, and delivered up to *extreme punishment,* for no place should be left them in which they may cause any injury even to the elements" (*The Code of Justinian,* bk. 1, tit. 5 (*De haereticis*), l. 5 (*Ariani*)); joined with "We understand the *extreme penalty* to mean only death." (*Digest of*

Fourth bodily punsihment of heretics: death by various means

We have shown clearly enough (as I think) that it is just that a heretic would be killed, but by what kind of death he ought to be killed, has little bearing on the matter. For in whatever way he is killed, it is always taken in good part by the Church: because the harm is always taken away, which when alive he could give to others, and fear is instilled in others, lest they dare to teach or say in any way similar things. On account of which in different countries, heretics are killed by different and various kinds of death, because there is no kind of death decreed by civil and imperial law. In Flanders, and in other lower parts of Germany, when I lived there ten years ago, I saw heretics punished by decapitation. Yet in Guelders heretics bound hand and foot by order of Charles [II], Duke of Guelders, and cast alive into a river, so that they may be drowned in the river. By the same kind of death (as I heard from many witnesses) a prominent Lutheran was punished in Antwerp by order of [Archduchess] Margaret [of Austria], aunt of Emperor Charles [V], who then governed that country. I also heard in Bruges in Flanders from many trustworthy eyewitnesses that it is the custom in that city to cast heretics alive into boiling oil, so that they may be very quickly burned by it: but then when I was there, they perished only by decapitation. In other kingdoms or provinces of the Christian world, the new, constant, and inviolable custom is to burn heretics with fire: so I saw happen in France, especially in Paris. So also in Spain, and I believe that it was always so done in Italy. For Blessed Gregory relates that Basil, a magician, was burnt in Rome, and he praises the thing done.[35] And (so that we may go back to more ancient times) Bishop Dioscorus of Alexan-

---

Justinian, bk. 48, tit. 19 (*De poenis*), l. 21 (*Ultimum supplicium*); emphasis added).

35 "[Basil] was burned to death as a magician as a result of the fervent zeal of the Christian people of Rome" (*Dialogues*, bk. 1, c. 4 (PL 77, 168D)).

dria, who preceded Gregory by a number of centuries, in the first session of the Council of Chalcedon, when it was treated about the errors of Eutyches in the same place, said: "If Eutyches holds notions disallowed by the doctrines of the Church, he deserves not only punishment but even the fire."[36] From which words it is very clearly established that it is not a recent invention, but a very old opinion of wise Christians that heretics ought to be burned with fire.

Panormitanus commenting on the chapter, *Ad abolendam*,[37] relates that Hostiensis[38] and Giovanni d'Andrea[39] on the same chapter say that heretics ought to be burned with fire.[40] To support this they cite that which Our Savior said

---

36 Mansi 6, 634C.

37 *Decretals of Gregory IX*, bk. 5, tit. 7 (*De haereticis*), c. 9.

38 "...although regarding heresy the law imposes the punishment of the extreme penalty [*Ultimum supplicium*], as the *Code* [*of Justinian*] in the same law, *Ariani* [bk. 1, tit. 5 (*De haereticis*), l. 5] which the other law interprets to be death (*Digest of Justinian*, bk. 48, tit. 19 (*De poenis*), l. 21), yet from the custom such men are burned, because the burning of a living man is also the extreme penalty" (*Summa aurea*, col. 1366).

39 "[*Debitam*] here and above the same due punishment is understood to mean the burning of fire; which is proved in John 15, where it is said, "If any one abide not in me, he shall be cast forth as a branch, and shall wither, and they shall gather him up, and cast him into the fire, and he burneth" (v. 6). Human law imposes the ultimate punishment. *Code* [*of Justinian*] in the same law, *Ariani* [bk. 1, tit. 5 (*De haereticis*), l. 5], which another law interprets to be death. *Digest* [*of Justinian*, bk. 48, tit. 19 (*De poenis*), l. 28 (*Capitalium*)] and the general custom interprets this to be the due punishment, regarding this see also the response on the chapter, *Firmissime*, [*Decretals of Gregory IX*, bk. 5, tit. 7 (*De haereticis*), c. 5] and in this way the Divine, human, and customary law agree to this punishment" (*In quintum Decretalium librum novella Commentaria* (Venice: apud Haeredem Hieronymi Scoti, 1612), fol. 48r b).

40 "But I ask about the aforesaid, with what punishment ought

Fourth bodily punsihment of heretics: death by various means

in John's Gospel: "If any one abide not in me, he shall be cast forth as a branch, and shall wither, and they shall gather him up, and cast him into the fire, and he burneth" (15, 6). Panormitanus seems to likewise favor their opinion in the above-mentioned place: and when commenting on the chapter, *Excommunicamus*.[41] But all these men, although they are very learned, err multiple times. Firstly, because even though heretics ought to be killed, still it is not necessary to burn them, because this (as we said) is not commanded by any law. Next, even if there were some law which commanded that heretics be burned by fire, still those words of the Savior cited from John's Gospel do nothing to prove that law. For the Savior did not speak there about the fire of this world, which we now see with these eyes of the body; but he spoke about the fire of hell, with which sinners will burn forever. And that saying of His is not directed to them alone, who are separated from Christ through their error of faith, as are the heretics; but Christ is speaking there about all sinners, who on account of the lack of charity are separated from Christ, and do not remain in Him: and He says that all those men will burn with the everlasting fire of hell, unless they repent. If anyone would ask why are heretics burned, I reply that this is not founded on any law, but merely custom.

---

heretics to be punished; Hostiensis and Giovanni d'Andrea teach that they thus ought to be burned with the punishment of fire, as is gathered from the Gospel of John, where it is said, 'If any one abide not in me, he shall be cast forth as a branch, and shall wither, and they shall gather him up, and cast him into the fire, and he burneth' (15, 6)" (Niccolo Tedeschi, *Abbatis Panormitani Commentaria in quartum et quintum decretalium librum* (Venice: al segno della Fontana, 1571), fol. 118r b).

41 *Decretals of Gregory IX*, bk. 5, tit. 7 (*De haereticis*), c. 15. "... today they are burned with fire" (*Abbatis Panormitani Commentaria*, fol. 120v b).

Which custom, if anyone would want to demonstrate that it is just, he will better prove it by the fact that it is befitting to the Divine law, given long ago through Moses, and by the punishments with which long ago God punished similar sinners. In the sedition stirred up by Core, Dathan, and Abiron, two hundred fifty men of the leading men of Israel, who adhered to them, were consumed by the fire sent by God from above, because they were schismatics, and attempted to usurp the sacerdotal office contrary to law and custom.[42] For every heretic is reckoned a schismatic, and rightly so, because he separates himself from the unity of the faith, which the whole Church of Saints holds, Next, when on account of the aforesaid punishment made by God, the whole multitude of the children of Israel murmured against Moses and Aaron, saying that they had killed the Lord's people, and a sedition arose, the tumult increased to such an extent that Moses and Aaron fled to the tabernacle of the covenant to save their lives: God from above sent a fire upon the people, which made a great massacre in the people. For fourteen thousand and seven hundred men perished in that conflagration (as Sacred Scripture relates[43]), besides them that had perished in the sedition of Core.

If God were now the God of revenge,[44] as of old, He would burn the Lutherans with fire sent from above, because they have made a sedition and daily make a sedition against the Christian rulers, and they say that they are tyrants, because they make heretics to perish by burning. Not without reason therefore are schismatic heretics burned, since God obliterated so many schismatics by burning. For due to this reason the law is said to be just, which in some kingdoms, such as in Spain, decrees that those who act with perverse lust should be burned with fire; because by a similar punishment

---

42 Cf. Num. 16, 35.
43 *Ibid.* v. 49.
44 Cf. Ps. 93, 1.

Fourth bodily punsihment of heretics: death by various means

God long ago punished Sodom and Gomorrha on account of the same sin. Among other laws given by God through Moses, one was that by which it was commanded that "If the daughter of a priest be taken in whoredom, and dishonour the name of her father, she shall be burnt with fire" (Lev. 21, 9). The soul of any Christian is reckoned the daughter of that High Priest about Whom the Royal Prophet said: "Thou art a priest forever according to the order of Melchisedech" (Ps. 109, 4). For the soul was regenerated by the grace which was bestowed on him in Baptism through the merits of Christ's Passion. But this soul is taken in whoredom, when it loses that integrity of faith, which it received in Baptism, through heresy. For heresy is a kind of spiritual fornication. Having perpetrated whoredom of this kind, His Father's name is said to have been violated: because when a man received from Christ a name through Baptism, by which that man is called a Christian, after he has fallen into heresy, he now does not deserve to be called a Christian, but an Arian, and Nestorian, or a Lutheran, or he will be reckoned by some other name. Such a man as this will be rightly handed over according to the law to be burned by flames.

We have expounded this law by an allegory, not in fact so that by it we suppose that we prove that a heretic necessarily ought to be burned. For I am not so ignorant, that I would think this: because I certainly know according to Augustine's teaching that a proof ought not to be taken from the mystical sense of Sacred Scripture for confirming some doctrine: but only from the literal sense.[45] Therefore for this reason alone was it pleasing to play for a short time with an allegory, so that I might show that this punishment of heretics by

---

45 "For what else is it than superlative impudence for one to interpret in his own favour any allegorical statements, unless he has also plain testimonies, by the light of which the obscure meaning of the former may be made manifest" (Letter 93 (Against Vincent the Donatist), c. 8, n. 24 (PL 33, 334)).

burning has an example in Sacred Scripture whereby one could somewhat confirm it. Still, that this custom of obliterating heretics by burning is just, can be proved another way: namely, because that kind of death greatly terrifies the minds of those seeing it. Hence it is that it instills a terrible fear in those seeing and hearing, and hence it follows that by this kind of death others are more deterred from heresies. Therefore, so that I may briefly conclude those things which I have said at length: I say and most firmly hold that it is just that an incorrigible heretic be killed. By what kind of death, however, he ought to be killed, this or that, I reckon matters little: but each kingdom or province will be free to kill the heretic by what kind of death it wishes, since there is no type of death fixed by universal law.

Chapter XIII

It is replied to the objections of those who say that heretics ought not to be punished with death.

After now having shown our and the Catholic opinion about the killing of incorrigible heretics by very firm (as I think) reasons, so that its truth may be made know to all more clearly, and it may be established more firmly, I thought that it will be necessary to respond to those things which the adversaries object against us, and to show that they have completely no strength. A certain Otto Brunfels from the family of Lutherans in the fourth book of a certain work, which he called *Pandects of Sacred Scripture*, in the place, "Concerning heretics ought not to be burned": he cites here and there testimonies of Sacred Scripture, by which he tries to prove that heretics ought not to be killed, but convinced by reasons. Some of which when considered either superficially or thoroughly nowise support his view of them. But others, even though they only on the surface show that they support them, yet when thoroughly and carefully examined (as is befitting), they will clearly show that they give no testimony for their opinion. Firstly therefore (so that I may begin from the Old Testament) they object to us that passage of the prophet Isaias: "They shall turn their swords into ploughshares, and their spears into sickles" (2, 4). Which words I do not see how they could apply to the punishment of heretics. For whether you regard the literal meaning, which alone is capable of establishing some doctrine, in those words, or you also consider the mystical meaning hidden under the literal meaning, you will find nothing which pertains to the matter at hand.

For according to that true meaning of that passage, the prophet promises the peace which was to come into the world when Christ became incarnate, and had been born of the Virgin's womb, at which time so many and so frequent wars had preceded, that scarcely a way was open to men, wanting to pass from one province to another. In fact, before Christ's Incarnation, wars were raging everywhere, the Gentiles were fighting fiercely among themselves, and they often waged wars against the people of Israel with productive and prosperous success. But when Christ was born of the Virgin, Who came to teach true peace to men by word and deed, peace was then given to the whole world. On account of which (as Bede relates in the book, *De ratio temporum*[1]) in Rome the Temple of Peace, which until that time had always been closed, at that very moment, God so disposing, opened of itself, to indicate the novelty of such a great thing.

Now that these words of Isaias ought to be referred to the time of Christ, those words which precede very clearly prove. "And in the last days the mountain of the house of the Lord shall be prepared on the top of mountains, and it shall be exalted above the hills, and all nations shall flow unto it. And many people shall go, and say: Come and let us go up to the mountain of the Lord, and to the house of the God of Jacob, and he will teach us his ways, and we will walk in his paths: for the law shall come forth from Sion, and the word of the Lord from Jerusalem. And he shall judge the Gentiles,

---

[1] "In the forty-second year of Augustus Caesar, in the twenty-seventh from the death of Antony and Cleopatra, when Egypt became a Roman province, in the third year of the 193rd Olympiad, and in the 752nd from the building of the city, in the year when all commotions of nations were stilled throughout the whole world, and, by the appointment of God, Caesar established real and durable tranquility, Jesus Christ consecrated by his advent the sixth age of the world" (*The Reckoning of Time* (PL 90, 545B)). According to tradition, the doors of the Janus Quirinus shrine were closed when Rome was at peace. Augustus boasts in his *Res Gestae* (13) that these doors had been closed only twice before his time, but three times while he was *princeps* (cf. Livy 1.19.2-3; Suet., Aug. 22).

and rebuke many people" (vv. 2-4). Which words ought to be referred to the time when Christ was born (as it is evident). And after the above-mentioned words Isaias immediately adds: "And they shall turn their swords into ploughshares, and their spears into sickles: nation shall not lift up sword against nation, neither shall they be exercised any more to war" (v. 4). Which words were fulfilled when He came, Who was to judge the Gentiles and many nations.

If, however, anyone contends that those words ought to be referred to the whole time that would come after Christ was born: I am not opposed to it, as long as he understands that Christ Our Savior Himself, commended by His teaching not merely peace to us: but took away every occasion of war. For He commanded that we love our enemies, and do well to those who hate us, and pray for those who persecute us, and endeavor to calumniate us.[2] Next, so that He might establish a more perfect peace among ourselves, He counseled that no one seek the repair of an injury, nor fight in court with a neighbor for something: because these two things are things which often are wont to disturb peace between neighbors. "You have heard," said the peacemaking King Himself, "that it hath been said, An eye for an eye, and a tooth for a tooth. But I say to you not to resist evil: but if one strike thee on thy right cheek, turn to him also the other: and if a man will contend with thee in judgment, and take away thy coat, let go thy cloak also unto him. And whosoever will force thee one mile, go with him other two" (Mt. 5, 38-41). All of which things, even though they are not reckoned precepts, but counsels, by all Catholics: still they remove all occasion of war from those who rightly observe them. Thus those who have observed the whole of Christ's Law, both in the precepts and in the counsels, loving perfect peace, "shall turn their swords into ploughshares, and their spears into sickles."

---

2 Cf. Mt. 5, 44.

Nothing is said therefore in these words, which pertains to the punishment of heretics. Unless perhaps by those words of Otto Brunfels, or any other Lutheran, would say that all revenge, or any punishment by whatever authority, is forbidden. Which if perhaps, due to his unbridled and impudent license of speaking, he is not ashamed to say, let him hear, I entreat, Paul condemning his opinion, who when speaking about public political power, says: "But if thou do that which is evil, fear: for he beareth not the sword in vain. For he is God's minister: an avenger to execute wrath upon him that doth evil" (Rom. 13, 4). By those words of Isaias, even if perhaps (which I do not think is true, since they say nothing about this matter) war made by private authority is forbidden, or revenge, or punishment, which is made by private authority: still none of these things are inhibited, if it is done by the public authority for a just reason. And we ourselves also acknowledge that a heretical man howsoever pestilential cannot be killed by any man: unless he has been commissioned by the public authority. Now concerning the mystical understanding of those words of Isaias, which can be given in multiple ways, I have nothing to say against it, because it (according to the teaching of all the sacred writers) has little efficacy for proving some doctrine.

Secondly, Otto Brunfels asserts in his favor another testimony from the same prophet Isaias speaking thus: "They shall not hurt, nor shall they kill in all my holy mountain" (11, 9). And certainly (as I frankly admit) I cannot understand how from those words that Otto can conclude that heretics ought not to be killed, since not specifically about heretics alone, but by general speech the prophet Isaias says about all men: "They shall not hurt, nor shall they kill in all my holy mountain." Unless perhaps Otto contends that God through those words of Isaias the prophet forbids every killing of any man. But we will show that this is false, and foreign to the Catholic faith, in the next chapter. Furthermore, if Otto says that God by those words forbids any man to be killed within the Catholic Church, it follows that he would also admit that God forbids that after the Gospel was given, an authority would inflict some harm upon any man. For just as in those words God said: "Thou shalt not kill," so also He said: "They shall not hurt." Wherefore according to this opinion, neither king, nor emperor, nor any other authority could kill a very wicked man, on account of whatever very grave crimes, nor scourge, nor beat, nor fine, nor banish from a nation or kingdom, nor finally inflict any other harm on him, because God through the prophet Isaias said: "They shall not hurt, nor shall they kill in all my holy mountain." Now this is not merely an error and a heresy, but great madness and savagery, which since it is unworthy of being assailed by arguments against it, it ought to have been put out of the way by fire and death.

But it is necessary that we show the true and genuine meaning of those words, and then it will become clearer how far away those words of Isaias are from the subject of the present disputation. Those words of Isaias do not contain any precept or prohibition, but are certain promises of those goods, which after Christ's coming in the flesh, God was going to give to His Church. And (so that we may show what we say more clearly) it is befitting to repeat the words which precede: because the context of Scripture is that which is especially wont to manifest its true meaning. Now those words which immediately precede are these: "And there shall come forth a rod out of the root of Jesse, and a flower shall rise up out of his root. And the spirit of the Lord shall rest upon him: the spirit of wisdom, and of understanding, the spirit of counsel, and of fortitude, the spirit of knowledge, and of godliness. And he shall be filled with the spirit of the fear of the Lord. He shall not judge according to the sight of the eyes, nor reprove according to the hearing of the ears. But he shall judge the poor with justice, and shall reprove with equity for the meek of the earth: and he shall strike the earth with the rod of his mouth, and with the breath of his lips he shall slay the wicked. And justice shall be the girdle of his loins: and faith the girdle of his reins" (Is. 11, 1-5). There is no one who is Catholic who would not interpret all these words of Isaias of Christ Our Savior: because all the sacred Doctors attribute them to Christ our Redeemer. And Paul interprets part of those words in the Second Epistle to the Thessalonians concerning Him.[3]

Now after these words the prophet Isaias immediately adds many good things, which were to be given to us through Christ, speaking thus: "The wolf shall dwell with the lamb: and the leopard shall lie down with the kid: the calf and the lion, and the sheep shall abide together, and a little child shall lead them. The calf and the bear shall feed: their young ones shall rest together: and the lion shall eat straw like the ox. And the sucking child shall play on the hole of the asp: and the weaned child shall thrust his hand into the den of the basilisk. They shall not hurt, nor shall they kill in all my holy mountain, for the earth is filled with the knowledge of the Lord, as the covering waters of the sea" (vv. 6-9). It is evident that these words of Isaias are promises of those good things which were to be given through Christ our Redeemer to the human race. For just as by those words it is not commanded to us that we make that wolf to dwell with the lamb, and the leopard with the kid: so also by those words it is not commanded to us that we not kill, or not hurt. For all those words are of the same condition, which are in the same context joined to that above-mentioned passage, such that all those words are called promises, or precepts. Now when He says: "They shall not hurt, nor shall they kill in all my holy mountain," not about men: but He is speaking about those

---

[3] "And then that wicked one shall be revealed whom the Lord Jesus shall kill with the spirit of his mouth; and shall destroy with the brightness of his coming, him" (2, 8).

poisonous snakes, namely, the asp and the basilisk, which He had just named. Since He promised about the basilisk and the asp, that they will not kill, and will not hurt in all His holy mountain. Which words never ought to be taken according to the mere superficial sense of the words, but according to the spiritual sense.

But if someone does not trust me on this point, let him listen to Blessed Jerome, who in his commentaries on the prophet Isaias, when interpreting all the aforesaid promises of Isaias, speaks thus: "The Jews and our Judaizers contend that these things will also happen literally, so that in the brightness of Christ Whom they think will come at the end of the world, all the beasts will become tame, both the wolf, having put off the former ferocity, and the lamb will feed together, and others with others which we now see are inimical to each other... But we will also ask them this, why would it be becoming to God's majesty that the wolf and lamb feed together, and the leopard dwells with the kid, and the lion eats straw, and the weaned child thrusts his hand into the hole of the asp? Unless they plan to restore the golden age of Saturn to us, after the fables of poets, in which wolves will feed together even with the lambs, rivers will run full of honey wine, and from the leaves of the tree will trickle very sweet honey, all places will be filled with springs of milk...[4] We have briefly said these things, so that we may convict our Judaizers of snoring from a very deep sleep. Otherwise according to the vivifying Spirit the meaning is easy..."[5]

---

4 Cf. Ovid, *Metamorphoses*, bk. 1, lns. 107-112: "Spring was eternal, and placid breezes [*Zephyri*, the west wind] caressed with warm breath the flowers having been grown without being seeded. And soon the unplowed earth brought forth crops, and the field, not having been replanted, grew white with heavy grains. Sometimes rivers of milk flowed and sometimes streams of nectar, and golden honey was distilled from the verdant oak tree."

5 *Commentaria in Isaiam*, bk. 3 (PL 24, 147B-148A).

Book 2, Chapter 13

And finally, when giving the spiritual meaning, he says these words: "But he who has been weaned is by no means nourished with the milk of infancy, but is now fed with solid food. He thrust his hand into the den of the basilisk, that is, into the abode of Satan himself, and draws him out from there. Whence also power was given to the Apostles, to 'tread upon serpents and scorpions, and upon all the power of the enemy' (Lk. 10, 19). But the animals filled in former times with poison will in no way be able to harm and kill those who shall dwell on the holy mountain of God, which is interpreted as the Church, of which it is said in the Gospel: 'A city seated on a mountain cannot be hid' (Mt. 5, 14)."[6] From whose words it is very clearly established that those words of Isaias, which the Lutheran Otto objects to us, contain completely nothing which pertains, even remotely, to the punishment of heretics. I now entreat you, O reader, to consider the kind of proofs from Scripture the Lutherans attempt to prove their heresies. For by these and other testimonies of the same sort they deceive uneducated people, and draw them into very pestilential errors.

Thirdly, they object to us, that Our Savior says about a brother offending against us who, having been admonished once and again neglects amendment: "If he will not hear the church, let him be to thee as the heathen and publican" (Mt. 18, 17). By which words He gave the power of excommunicating to the Church, not of killing: thus heretics are (that Otto says) unjustly killed. What a beautiful argument! which errs not only once, but again many times. Firstly, in fact it is well-known to everyone, who has dabbled even a little in logic, that it is a clumsy way of arguing from a citation of an authority, by negating, just as though one would argue in this way: Christ Our Savior did not say on Monday that one must fast, or pray, or study Sacred Scripture: therefore it is not permitted to do any of these things on that day. For

---

6 *Ibid.* (PL 24, 148C).

if the conclusion of this argument were valid and effectual, in the same way it would be allowed to conclude from the opposite, arguing thus: Christ our Redeemer did not say that on Monday one must not fast, or not pray, or not study Sacred Scripture: therefore it is not allowed to omit any of these things. Thus from the same citation of the argument two contradictory things are proved. But just as Christ Our Savior did not command one thing, so neither did He command the other. Such is the present argumentation, whereby Otto argued that a heretic ought not to be killed: because Christ did not command to kill: but to excommunicate. This is the logic of the Lutherans, which they very often use, supposing that they deceive the world by fallacies of this kind: but in vain do they cast the net before the eyes of the birds.

They also err in the same way when they argue thus from the words of Paul said to Titus: Paul says that we should avoid a man that is a heretic, after the first and second admonition:[7] not however, that we should kill [such a man]. I admit that Paul did not say this, but neither did he forbid that they be killed, and hence it is not allowed to conclude one or the other. They commit the same fallacy in many other arguments, which they make on this point, especially when they argue from that saying of the Savior, which He says: "Take heed and beware of the leaven of the Pharisees" (*Ibid.* 16, 6). He did not say: "Kill the heretical Pharisees": but He merely said, that we ought to be beware of them. To which things I reply, that if He did not say: "Kill," neither also did He say: "Do not kill."

Next, there is yet another error in the above-mentioned argument: because even if that conclusion were correct arguing negatively from the citation, nothing else could be concluded therefrom, than that the ecclesiastical authority cannot kill a heretic. Because to it alone, and not the secular

---

7 Cf. Tit. 3, 10.

authority, was Christ then speaking, and to it He gave the power of excommunicating. Thus by the fact of when giving the power of excommunicating, He was silent about the power of killing: it can only be concluded (yet if the conclusion were good) that the power which can excommunicate, cannot kill. Although many Catholics deny this, who give both swords to the Church, still the Church herself shows in her deeds that she has only one sword. Because she only uses the spiritual sword, shutting up the other one in the sheath. For ecclesiastical judges do not kill heretics: but the secular authority, which according Paul's saying, "beareth not the (corporal) sword in vain" (Rom. 13, 4), and orders them to be killed. And there is no decree in the whole Pontifical Law, which orders heretics to be killed: but only commands that they be handed over to secular authority to be judged by it, according to its judgment.

But here the Lutherans attack us saying: Bishops, and other inquisitors of heretics are like unto priests of the Jews, who although they were actually the authors of the death of Christ Our Savior, were nevertheless saying to Pilate, the Prefect of Judea: "It is not lawful for us to put any man to death" (Jn. 18, 31). The ecclesiastical judges of heretics show themselves in every respect (as the Lutherans say) to be such. For these men (as the Lutherans calumniate) are the authors of the death of heretics, and yet they say that they are not permitted to kill heretics, and with that end in view they hand them over to the secular authority, to be condemned by it to death. But in reality here, as they are mistaken elsewhere, they err very miserably blinded by their malign affection.

Now so that I may make known to all how hatefully they speak against the inquisitors and the other ecclesiastical judges, it is necessary that I show very clearly that there is a very great difference, and hence the comparison is unsuitable, between ecclesiastical judges of heretics and the Jewish priests. The Pharisees, and the other priests of the Jews,

Replies to objections about the death penalty for heretics

although they did not kill with their hands, nevertheless killed with their tongues, and by many and various ways, when procuring His death. And firstly, as John the Evangelist testifies, "The chief priests and the Pharisees, gathered a council, and said: What do we, for this man doth many miracles?" (11, 47). And at length when the counsel was given by Caiphas, the priest of that year, that it was expedient that Christ die, lest the whole people perish,[8] the other acquiesced to his counsel, and from that day they thought to kill Christ, the Redeemer of all men.[9] Next they handed him over to Pilate, and before him accused Christ unto death: and because they could not do this with truthful witnesses, they brought in false witnesses who would give false testimony against Christ. Moreover when Pilate had examined Christ's case, and wanted to release Him, because he found no cause of death in Him, he said to the people: "Whom will you that I release to you, Barabbas, or Jesus that is called Christ?" (Mt. 27, 17). When these men, the high priest and the ancients, heard these things, as Matthew relates, "They persuaded the people, that they should ask for Barabbas, and take Jesus away" (v. 20). Again when Pilate showed Christ scourged, and bearing the crown of thorns on His head, and clothed with a purple garment to the people, so that at least in this way he might provoke the people to mercy towards Him: "The priests and the servants," as Blessed John relates, "cried out, saying: Crucify him, crucify him" (19, 6). After these things when Pilate tells the priests and the people to take and crucify Christ, the Jews responded: "We have a law; and according to the law he ought to die, because he made himself the Son of God" (v. 7). Next, when Pilate sought to release Christ, the Jews cried out saying: "If thou release this man, thou art not Caesar's friend. For whosoever maketh himself a king, speaketh against Caesar" (v. 12). Finally,

---

8 Cf. Jn. 11, 50.
9 Cf. *Ibid.*, v. 53.

when Pilate sat down in the judgment seat, he showed Christ to the people, and said: "Behold your king" (v. 14). The Jews (among whom without a doubt were the priests) cried out: "Away with him; away with him; crucify him" (v. 15). And when Pilate said to them: "Shall I crucify your king? The chief priests answered: We have no king but Caesar" (*Ibid.*).

Notice, I beseech you, and consider carefully, how many times the priests asked for Christ's death before the judge: and yet not casually, but urging the judge very importunely, and seducing the people with various lies to ask for the same thing. On account of all of which things they are reckoned to have crucified Christ Our Savior: because even though they did not crucify with their hands, still they did this by their counsel. In this way Blessed Augustine harmonizes the dissonance which there seems to be between the Evangelists, one of whom says that Christ was crucified at the third hour, while the other at the sixth. For the Jews, as Augustine says, killed Christ at the third hour, with so many and such words (as we said) by procuring His death: but the soldiers killed with their hands at the sixth hour.[10]

Let us now see whether the inquisitors, or other ecclesiastical judges, do some of these things with heretics. What is most certain, and we know by experience teaching us, is that ecclesiastical judges after they have condemned someone for heresy, and determined that he is an obstinate heretic, immediately declare that he is not under their authority and dominion, and they hand him over to the secular authority, as a man who on account of his obstinacy of heresy, has left the Church, and has put himself under the lay authority alone. Now when the ecclesiastical judges hand him over to

---

10 "We understand, accordingly, that it was the third hour when the Jews cried out that the Lord should be crucified. And thus it is intimated most truly that these persons did really crucify Christ at the time when they cried out" (*Harmony of the Gospels*, bk. 3, c. 13, n. 42 (PL 34, 1184)).

the secular authority, they do not ask from it that it would kill the heretic, and they do not say in any way that he is condemned to death. And if the secular authority does not want to kill the heretic, the ecclesiastical judges neither force or urge it in any way to kill the heretic, nor ever give any counsel of inflicting death to the heretic, nay, on the contrary they always ask the same secular authority not to impose the punishment of decapitation, or another death penalty. All these things since they are most certain, and well-known to the whole (as I think) Christian people, I am surprised that the impudence and unbridled evil-speaking of the Lutherans is so great, that they are not afraid to say that the inquisitors of heretics are similar to the priests of the Jews, who killed Christ: since there is a vast difference (as is established by the reality itself) between the latter and the former.

I certainly could much more correctly and suitably say that Luther and his followers are similar to the priests of the Jews. Because they sought false witnesses, when they could not have truthful ones, so that they could hand over Christ to death: the Lutherans truly eagerly search for false testimonies of Sacred Scripture, when they do not have true ones, so that they might completely kill Christ's Body which is the Church. They say that Christ did and taught many things which He never dreamed of. They attribute many things to the Apostles which were very alien to them. And they contrive a thousand fabrications, for no other reason than so that they may make the Church, which is Christ's body, to perish, and may give us another, the assembly of the malignant, which the Royal Prophet proclaimed that he hated.[11]

The Lutherans, and those who support them on this matter, fourthly object to us the parable about the wheat, over which the enemy sowed cockle, which the servants of the goodman of the house seeing, said to him: "Wilt thou that we go and gather it up? To which he said: No, lest perhaps gathering

---

11 Cf. Ps. 25, 5.

up the cockle, you root up the wheat also together with it. Suffer both to grow until the harvest" (Mt. 13, 28-30). If God forbids the cockle to be rooted up, then they act unjustly and against God's precept (as it seems to the Lutherans), who root up heretics, signified by the cockle, from the field of this world by death. This is the Lutherans' strongest argument, on which they rely more, and by which they think that they triumph over us. But we (with God as my leader) will very easily show that this objection proceeds from a false understanding of the text. Firstly in fact, it is unnecessary to explain the persons or the other things put in the parable, since the Teacher of Truth Himself has given the interpretation of all those things to the Apostles asking, speaking thus: "He that soweth the good seed, is the Son of man. And the field, is the world. And the good seed are the children of the kingdom. And the cockle, are the children of the wicked one. And the enemy that sowed them, is the devil" (vv. 37-39). From which interpretation it is established that the word "cockle" better fits the heretics themselves than their heresies. I said this on account of those who raise the doubt about whether the parable befits heresies or heretics. "The cockle," Christ says, "are the children of the wicked one." But it is necessary that the rest be carefully examined. When the servants of the goodman of the house want to gather up the cockle, the goodman of the house forbade them speaking thus: "No, lest perhaps gathering up the cockle, you root up the wheat also together with it." In which words it ought to be especially noticed that he did not absolutely and generally, and without any reason, forbid the gathering of such cockle: but rather he immediately gave the reason, on account of which he forbade it to be done. "Lest perhaps," the goodman of the house said, "gathering up the cockle, you root up the wheat also together with it." The fear of rooting up the wheat, therefore, is the reason why the cockle are allowed to grow with the wheat. On the other hand, therefore, one ought to gather it up when there is no reason for so fearing, for example, because the distinction is clearly and very well known; and one is not so joined and connected to the other, that one could not very easily root up one without the other: then the goodman of the house does not forbid the rooting up of the cockle to be done. If he had not expressed any reason for the prohibition, but instead had spoken absolutely, although there actually were some reasons for the prohibition, and all of them were absent: I acknowledge that the full force of the prohibition would always exist. Yet if the legislator expresses principle and final motive, on account of which he bears witness that he commands or forbids something, it follows that when that reason ceases, the precept or prohibition would also cease. For when expressing such a reason the legislator clearly declared that if that reason were absent, he would not have commanded or forbidden any such thing. For if when the reason is excluded he nonetheless would have commanded or excluded, it follows that it was not the single and only reason for the precept or prohibition. Thus by those above-mentioned words, just as the goodman of the house forbade the servants, that when the fear of uprooting the wheat remains valid the cockle ought not to be gathered, so on the contrary he granted to the same servants that when no just cause exists for fear, they could gather the cockle. I reckon that it ought to be done in completely the same way (so that we may apply the parable to our proposition) in performing the punishment of heretics. If it is doubted about some man whether or not he is a heretic, because it is not fully established that he said some heretical assertion, or it is not established that he is pertinacious, or if it is established that he had taught some such proposition, yet it is not established that that proposition is heretical, then the inquisitors would certainly act very unjustly if they would declare him a heretic, and the secular authority would act unjustly and cruelly if it were to order him to be killed. For then God says to it: You may not gather up the cockle, "lest perhaps gathering up the cockle, you root up the wheat also together with it." But if it is very certainly known that some man is a heretic, because the assertion, which he defends, is diametrically opposed to the Catholic faith, and he has been duly admonished several times, then he licitly ought to be killed; because it is not feared that a Catholic may be killed as a heretic.

Now that this is the correct and real meaning of that text, Blessed Jerome in his commentaries on Matthew when interpreting the aforesaid parable says: "Now he leaves room for repentance in the words: 'Lest perhaps gathering up the cockle, you root up the wheat also together with it' (Mt. 13, 29). Here we are admonished not to cut off a brother quickly. For it can happen that the one who today has been seduced by a harmful doctrine, tomorrow may come to his senses and begin to defend the truth. Now the words that follow: 'Suffer both to grow until the harvest' (v. 30), seem to contradict the command: 'Put away the evil one from among yourselves' (I Cor. 5, 13) and the command that we are by no means to have fellowship with those who are called brothers and are adulterers and fornicators.[12] For if uprooting is prohibited and patience is to be preserved until the harvest, how is it that certain ones must be expelled from our midst? There is a remarkable likeness between wheat and the cockle that we call darnel. As long as it is a seedling and its stem does not come to ear, it is just about impossible, or at least extremely difficult, to discern any distinction between them. Therefore, the Lord is warning us in advance that we must not quickly make a judgment when the matter is doubtful. Rather, we should reserve the conclusion to God the Judge, so that when the Day of Judgment comes, He may cast out from the assembly of the Saints not the mere suspicion of sin, but

---

12 Cf. I Cor. 5, 11.

manifest guilt."[13] Jerome so clearly confirms our opinion that nothing clearly for its assertion could be said.

Augustine subscribes to the same opinion, who in the third book of *Against the Letter of Parmenian* speaks thus: "The Lord Himself when He said to the servants wishing to gather the cockle: 'Suffer both to grow until the harvest.' He premised the reason saying, 'Lest perhaps gathering up the cockle, you root up the wheat also together with it.' Where he sufficiently shows that when this fear is absent: but a sure security completely remains of a sure stability of the grain, that is, when a man's crime is so publicly known, and is so hateful to all, that he has either completely no defenders, or such defenders none such as might cause a schism, the severity of discipline should not slacken, in which the emendation of the depravity is so much the more effective, the more diligent is the confirmation of charity."[14] Augustine very clearly supports our opinion.

---

13 *Commentary on Matthew*, bk. 2 (PL 26, 93D-94A).
14 Bk. 3 (PL 43, 92).

Chapter XIV

Whether it is permitted to attack heretics by war, after it is fully established about their pertinacity, and rebellion.

At the time when I was writing this work, *On the Just Punishment of Heretics*, I was in Trent, where by the ever august Emperor Charles V, and King of Spain being the first of this name [i. e., Charles I], urging and instigating, the Supreme Pontiff Paul III, had convoked a general council, to which by the command of the Most Serene Prince Philip of the Spains, who then was ruling the Spains on account of the absence of Charles, his father, I had come. During which time the same Emperor Charles, decided to declare war against some German princes due to many and very just reasons. Thus while the war was proceeding, when it had then had such beginnings so that they gave great hope of victory, I on account of the sickness which plagued me in that same place for a long time and severely, by the exhortation of the doctors who were taking care of my health, was forced to return alone from Trent to my native Spain. When I was returning there, I heard on the way many and various men who prided themselves as being faithful Catholics, who interpreting the war which the emperor was waging begun by him for the sole reason of the Christian religion, were wrongly and irreligiously accusing the same emperor, saying that it is hardly a Christian affair to attack heretics by a war: because they (as they were saying) should be conquered not by arms, but with reasons. Therefore motivated by this occasion, I decided to insert this controversy into this work, which I had just completed [*ad umbilicum perduxeram*], so that I might show they who so think err by the whole extent of the heavens [*toto coelo*].

Now so that we can show this more clearly, it is necessary first of all to establish that not every war is evil and condemned by Divine law, as the Manichaeans and other heretics think: but some wars are not merely permitted by Divine law, but are also praised, namely, that war in which everything is present, which is required for a just war. For John, the Precursor of the Lord, no greater than whom has risen up among those that are born of women,[1] to the soldiers asking him what they ought to do to attain eternal life, did not command them to lay down their arms, to quit the army, to strike no one, to kill or wound no one in battle: but he only commanded this, that they do violence to no man, neither calumniate any man; and be content with their pay.[2] Now if every war were deserving of condemnation, John the Baptist would not have been content with this alone: but it would have been befitting that he forbid every war to them. Since, then, he said no such thing, by that very fact he is seen to think that there is something worthy of praise in war. Next, the Teacher of Truth Himself, Christ Our Savior, admonishes that tribute be given to Caesar,[3] which for that reason (according to Paul's opinion) is commanded to be given, so that necessarily therefrom pay may be given to the soldiers for the preservation of peace. For Paul, when discussing about the obedience to be given to rulers, says: "Wherefore be subject of necessity, not only for wrath, but also for conscience' sake. For therefore also you pay tribute. For they are the ministers of God, serving unto this purpose" (Rom. 13, 5-6). From all of which things it is very clearly established that some wars can be just.

Now what things are necessary and sufficient so that a war may be just, it is necessary now to explain, so that thence it may be established whether to attack heretics by war is just. So that a war be just by that justice, which alone excludes the obligation of restitution of those things which were taken

---

1 Cf. Mt. 11, 11.
2 Cf. Lk. 3, 14.
3 Cf. Mt. 22, 21.

Whether one may war against pertinacious and rebellious heretics

in war, only two things are necessary: namely, the authority and power to make a war, and a necessary cause. Yet if a war ought to be just, by that justice which excludes sin, that is, so that it may be done without sin, two other things in addition are necessary. The first of these is that the war be begun with a good purpose and a good intention. The second, that the person who ought to fight in the war is legally eligible for war, that is, such a person who is not prohibited by law to fight in war. Some men add a third, namely, the thing for which the war is waged, such that the war is done for recuperating things or for the defense of the country. But this third thing (as I reckon) is superfluous, because it is contained under the second of the first two, namely, under the just cause. Therefore it is befitting that we discuss one by one all these four things which we said are required, and thence it will be clearly established that a war can be just, which happens to be done against heretics.

Thus the first thing necessary for a just war is the authority of making a war. For not anyone by his own judgment can declare war: but only he who does not have a superior, from whom reparation of the injuries or harm inflicted upon him could be sought. For he who has a superior, to whom he could have recourse for reparation, of obtaining vengeance, cannot declare war. For the Lord clearly forbade this when saying: "Revenge is mine, and I will repay" (Deut. 32, 35). And he who asks for vengeance from the superior, who rules in God's place, asks from God, Who constituted him His minister for this, so that those, of whom he has care, he may defend and protect from all who want to harm them, whether the invaders be his subjects or foreigners. For Paul was speaking about subjects, when writing to the Romans he says: "If thou do that which is evil, fear: for he beareth not the sword in vain. For he is God's minister: an avenger to execute wrath upon him that doth evil" (Rom. 13, 4). For unto this Paul reckons that the sword, that is, the power of punishing, is given by God to rulers, so that they can punish malefactor subjects, and in this way avenge the injuries of those so injured. But regarding foreigners it ought to be understood that which the Royal Prophet says: "Rescue the poor; and deliver the needy out of the hand of the sinner" (Ps. 81, 4). The prophet Jeremias also says these same things, when saying: "Execute judgment and justice, and deliver him that is oppressed out of the hand of the oppressor" (22, 3).

An inferior, therefore, who has a superior to whom he can have recourse for reparation of the harm, or for requesting vengeance, would act unjustly, if for some one of these reasons he were to start a war, because when acting in this way he would transgress God's precept, which forbids revenge. A ruler, however, who has no superior in civil affairs, just as for the kingdom or nation which he accepted to rule or protect, can declare war, so also for himself insofar as he is a common and public person: because he does not have a superior to whom he ought to have recourse for obtaining vengeance. For Augustine clearly teaches this when speaking thus: "The natural order which seeks the peace of mankind, ordains that the monarch should have the power of undertaking war if he thinks it advisable, and that the soldiers should perform their military duties in behalf of the peace and safety of the community."[4]

Now by the name of monarch here I understand not only the emperor, and those kings who are nowise subject to the emperor: but all those rulers, who have jurisdiction and full dominion in deciding the disputes of their subjects, such that when their sentence has been heard, their subjects cannot appeal to any else as a higher judge. Some rulers in Italy today are such; for instance, the duke of Florence, the duke of Ferrara, the duke of Mantua, and the Marquess of Montferrat. For all these men from ancient custom have this jurisdic-

---

4 *Reply to Faustus the Manichaean*, bk. 22, n. 75 (PL 42, 448).

tion and power over their subjects, so that their subjects may not appeal from their civil judgment to any other superior. And I do not know whether any German dukes or marquesses today have this authority and power of declaring war. The reason for which doubt arises in me from the fact that each of them coins his own money, which belongs by right only to the superior ruler. But this notwithstanding I reckon that this power of declaring war is denied to them by law, because they are all subject to the emperor, by whom whoever of them has given an injury or caused harm to another can be punished.

The Imperial Diet[5] provides a very clear proof of which matter, which is propped up by the authority of the emperor in Germany, to whom as many as believe themselves unjustly harmed by other rulers from all the German cities have recourse. Thus since they all recognize the emperor, from whom any of them can ask for reparation of an injury or harm, it thence follows that none of them can justly without the authority of the emperor declare war against any other. Because war is only declared when forced by necessity, and hence is always reckoned unjust, when the matter for which the war is waged can be suitably dealt with otherwise than by war.

Now regarding other dukes or marchionesses, or other rulers even if they are given the name of monarchs, having rulership under the power of a king, in the kingdom of Spain, or of France, or of Naples, or in any other kingdom, there is no reason why one ought to doubt, whether they can declare war without the authority of the king to which they are subject. For even though they can give rights and laws to their subjects, nevertheless in declaring them, they are so subjected to the king, that they cannot decree anything against the laws established by the king. And hence it is established that

---

5 I. e., *Reichsstand*. The Latin name used here is the *Senatus publicus*.

they are not truly the head of the provinces, or towns, which they oversee and rule: and hence they do an injury to the kings, to whom they are subject, if they usurp to themselves their authority by declaring war, as if they were the true and supreme heads in their dominions. Likewise by the name of monarch in Augustine's letter cited above, ought to be understood those nations which from ancient custom have full jurisdiction in the lands subject to them: such that they recognize no other superior. For I believe that such nations have the authority of declaring war, as kings: because there is also in them (as Aristotle teaches[6]) sovereignty, although it is not praised equally by the same Aristotle, as royal sovereignty.

Yet this which we now say about nations, and just said above about certain dukes and marchionesses of Italy, Cardinal Thomas de Vio, commonly called Cajetan, reckons that it ought to be understood with this condition, if they with good faith were and are in peaceful possession of such authority of declaring war.[7] For if they usurped it from the greatness of power, due to which they audaciously rebelled against their superiors, so that they could not, nor now cannot be controlled by them, he reckons that they do not have the authority to declare a just war. To whose opinion I wholeheartedly subscribe. Because it is unseemly that what had its beginning in bad faith, without any just cause following thereafter, would afterwards be made firm by just possession.

---

6 "Another mode is for all to assemble in a body, but only for the purpose of electing magistrates, enacting laws, considering the declaration of war and the conclusion of peace and holding the audit of magistrates, but for all other matters to be considered by the magistrates appointed to deal with each respectively and elected by suffrage or by lot from all the citizens" (*Politics*, bk. 4, c. 11 (1298a)).

7 *Summula Cajetani* (Leiden: apud haeredes Iacobi Iuntae, 1561), p. 35.

For (as the rule of law in *Liber sextus decretalium* teaches[8]) "A possessor in bad faith never prescribes."

The second thing which we said is necessary for a just war, is a just cause. There can be many and various causes of a just war, all of which Augustine includes in a general statement saying that a just cause of war is an injury inflicted, the avenging of which, since it cannot be had except by war, the ruler, or he who has authority to declare war, could justly undertake a war.[9] For in the questions on the book of Josue he says: "A just war is usually defined as one that avenges wrongs, when a people or city must be punished for neglecting to make amends for the wrongs inflicted by its own people, or to restore what has been seized unjustly."[10]

But because it could be doubted what by the word, "wrongs," is understood, and hence it will necessarily be reasonable that the judgment of the justice of the war, which depends on the cognizance of the wrong, is also doubtful, wherefore so that every reason of doubting from this source may be removed: I decided to review all the causes of a just war, and prove them all by the testimony of Sacred Scripture, so that no one could rightly doubt about any of them, whether it be just or not.

The first cause of war, therefore, is idolatry, from which those who are unwilling to abandon, can justly be conquered. For due to this cause God commanded the children of Israel to destroy and demolish many nations, speaking thus: "Destroy all the places in which the nations, that you shall possess, worshipped their gods upon high mountains, and hills, and under every shady tree: overthrow their altars, and break

---

8 Rule 2.
9 Cf. Clemente Dolera, *Catholicarum institutionum ad christianam theologiam compendium* (Rome: Antonio Blado, 1565), p. 501.
10 *Quaestiones in Heptateuchum*, bk. 6, n. 10 (PL 34, 781); *Decretum Gratiani*, pt. 2, *causa* 23, q. 2, c. 2 (PL 187, 1166C).

down their statues, burn their groves with fire, and break their idols in pieces: destroy their names out of those places" (Deut. 12, 2-3). Nicholas of Lyra reckons that all these things were commanded, "lest from the remaining shrines, or temples, of the idols, an occasion of idolatry would be given to the Jews, and so that the memory of idolatry might be completely obliterated,"[11] and in this way a great injury in His people be avoided. And relying on the evidence of this Divine precept, I think that the war is just which the Catholic kings of the Spains have waged for a number of years and even now wage against the barbarous and idolatrous nations, which do not know God, found in the east and the west. Yet I think that that war is just on this condition, if before the kings declare war against them, they diligently and faithfully take care to admonish them to abandon the worship of false gods, and adore the true God, Who is the Creator and Ruler of all things.

Now this admonition ought not to be light and perfunctory, such as men are wont to do in matters of small importance: but it ought to be a strong and assiduous admonition such as Paul commanded Timothy to make, speaking thus: "Preach the word: be instant in season, out of season" (II Tim. 4, 2). Interpreting which words Theophylactus says: "As it were to speak with insistence and importunity, not once but always. There is not a fixed time for this, but both 'in season,' that is, when in peace and you are without fear, and in the Church: but also 'out of season,' when you are in dangers, speak and preach outside the Church."[12] Thus it is not enough to admonish once and lightly about the Christian religion, but one ought to announce to them again and again the Evangelical Law; and hence for its confirmation to offer some probable reasons, the greatest of which, besides miracles, is wont to be the upright and blameless life of those who preach.

---

11 *Biblia sacra cum Glossis*, vol. 1, fol. 334v F.
12 *Expositio in Epistolam II ad Timotheum* (PG 125, 127A).

Whether one may war against pertinacious and rebellious heretics

For if the preaching is light, for instance because it was only done once, and without any persuasive reasons, they would perhaps not be immediately obliged to believe, lest they be reckoned light of heart. For Christ the Savior Himself said about the unbelievers to whom He preached: "If I had not done among them the works that no other man hath done, they would not have sin" (Jn. 15, 24). And Augustine says that if the Gentiles had believed the Evangelical Law, the enemy of flesh and blood, without any miracle, it would have been a great miracle.[13] Now it would be absurd to say that these Indians found in the New World, to whom the Gospel had never been made known, would be held to believe more quickly that those to whom Christ Himself preached.

Next, that admonition ought to be kind, and show that it proceeds from an affection of charity, and not harsh, full of threats and terrors, because such should rather be called force than an admonition. Hence Blessed Gregory says: "Those who with pure intent desire to bring to the true faith aliens from the Christian religion should study kindness, and not asperity; lest such as reason rendered with smoothness might have appealed to should be driven far off by opposition. For whosoever act otherwise, and under cover of such intention would suspend people from their accustomed observance of their own rites, are proved to be intent on their own cause rather than on God's."[14] And the [IV] Synod of Toledo says: "The holy synod commanded concerning the Jews that none hereafter shall by force be compelled to the faith; for

---

13 "Miracles were necessary before the world believed, in order that it might believe... How is it that in enlightened times, in which every impossibility is rejected, the world has, without any miracles, believed things marvelously incredible?" (*City of God*, bk. 22, c. 8, n. 1 (PL 41, 760)).

14 *Register of Epistles*, bk. 13, letter 12 (To Paschasius, Bishop of Naples) (PL 77, 1267C-1268A); *Decretum Gratiani*, pt. 1, dist. 45, c. 3 (PL 187, 233B-C).

'God hath mercy on whom he will; and whom he will, he hardeneth' (Rom. 9, 18)."[15]

Now that it is said by [John Duns] Scotus on the fourth book of the *Sentences*,[16] in the last question of the fourth distinction, that Christian rulers act conscientiously if by threats and terrors they force infidels to accept the faith: I think that it ought to be understood only of those rulers who have charge of infidels in other places, whom they rule and govern as being subject to themselves. And they could drive these men away from their property and authority, and perhaps inflict other punitive damages upon them, unless they wish to live according to the Christian religion. Now Christian rulers cannot force by threats and terrors all other men who are not subject to their authority to accept Christ's faith: but they can and ought to diligently and frequently, and kindly as Gregory teaches, admonish them. Which admonition if they accept it, although they do not wish to receive Baptism: I do not think that war can be justly declared against them. If, however, they do not wish to comply with

---

15 C. 57 (Mansi 10, 633); *Decretum Gratiani*, pt. 1, dist. 45, c. 5 (PL 187, 235A).

16 "The obligation of rulers ought to be seen so that they care for the true worship, which belongs to the natural law, and keeps away blasphemies and public errors, which provoke God's anger to the detriment of public peace, because religion is useful for the infidels themselves, etc., and why the civil power extends more to heretics than to infidels, etc., for example sacrileges, which are done against the faith publicly and privately, whether they have the right of vindicating them, or forbidding the use of superstition, from which a danger of subversion of the other faithful can redound, as also many other sins against the natural law itself. About these things I say nothing at present, lest I be too lengthy: but I say that the Teacher [Peter Lombard] ought to be understood only regarding threats and terrors in civil matters, not however in those threats, which regard bodily death" (*Opera omnia* (Paris: Ludovicus Vivès, 1891), vol. 16, p. 497).

Whether one may war against pertinacious and rebellious heretics

such an admonition, but instead obstinately persist in their error, especially if they impede the preaching of God's word, then it will be just, on account of this cause that war is waged against them, because all these nations (as it has been proved by experience) practice idolatry, and many other nefarious vices are committed against the law of nature.

For just as God long ago commanded the children of Israel that war be made against the Jebusite and the other idolaters, so now it is expedient that it is to be made also against these nations infected with similar vices and crimes. And Cyprian clearly teaches this speaking thus: "But if before the coming of Christ these precepts concerning the worship of God and the despising of idols were observed, how much more should they be regarded since Christ's advent."[17] If war is just, as Augustine says above in the place cited, which rulers wage for avenging injuries to men, war ought to be much more just which rulers wage for avenging injuries to God: because they are held to love God more than themselves, and hence it follows that they can and ought to do more for God's honor than their own. But the greatest injury is inflicted upon God through idolatry, because by it the supreme honor, which is due to God alone, is taken away from Him, and rendered to a creature, which nowise befits it. And certainly there is no sin, as Holy Writ often bears witness, which enrages God more, and on account of which God shows more that He was offended. Furthermore, if those barbarians found by the Spanish in the New World blasphemed Christ and did not wish to refrain from blasphemy, the Christians rulers were able for this reason (as Saint Thomas teaches[18]) to wage war

---

17 *Exhortation to Martyrdom*, c. 5 (PL 4, 659B); *Decretum Gratiani*, pt. 2, *causa* 23, q. 5, c. 32 (PL 187, 1227B).

18 "Among unbelievers there are some who have never received the faith, such as the heathens and the Jews: and these are by no means to be compelled to the faith, in order that they may believe, because to believe depends on the will: nevertheless they should be

against them: therefore much more could they wage war against them on account of idolatry, because this is a much graver sin than blasphemy.

Perhaps here someone may object to me, that hatred of God is a much more serious sin than idolatry, and yet on account of it one may not begin a war against someone. Again, if on account of idolatry it is permitted to fight against these barbarians, then on account of adulteries and thefts, and other sins of that kind it would be permitted to wage war against them: and hence it would further follow that one could also wage war against Christians on account of similar sins; even though those who wage war were not harmed by such sins: because by those sins an injury is also inflicted upon God: although not as grave, and God declares that He is offended by men through those sins. I reply that although hatred of God is a much more serious sin than idolatry, still because it does not so much appear to men, because it remains hidden in the mind, therefore it cannot be justly punished by men, nor can the haters of God themselves be fought against by war by men on account of it. For, as Solomon says, "He that speaketh that which he knoweth, sheweth forth justice" (Prov. 12, 17). Now even though other sins are more serious, and appear to men's eyes, still they do not give a sufficient

---

compelled by the faithful, if it be possible to do so, so that they do not hinder the faith, by their blasphemies, or by their evil persuasions, or even by their open persecutions. It is for this reason that Christ's faithful often wage war with unbelievers, not indeed for the purpose of forcing them to believe, because even if they were to conquer them, and take them prisoners, they should still leave them free to believe, if they will, but in order to prevent them from hindering the faith of Christ. On the other hand, there are unbelievers who at some time have accepted the faith, and professed it, such as heretics and all apostates: such should be submitted even to bodily compulsion, that they may fulfill what they have promised, and hold what they, at one time, received" (II-II, q. 10, a. 8).

cause, so that on account of them war can be waged against their authors. Because even though God is gravely offended by them, still God Himself Who was offended, did not grant the faculty to rulers, that on account of them they could wage war against their perpetrators by whom they were not injured, as He granted to them against idolaters in those words cited from the Deuteronomy.

But to this argument perhaps a patron of the Indians will reply, that God in those words cited from Deuteronomy did not command war to be waged against the Amorrhites and the other six nations on account of their idolatry: but because God had promised their lands to Abraham and to his seed after him. I reply that these things nevertheless do not weaken the force of my argument at all. For when God promised that land to Abraham and to his seed, He had then already decreed to take it away from the Amorrhites on account of their iniquities, and after He decided to take it away from those unworthy possessors, He then promised Abraham that He would give that land to him. He certainly ought to take it away from them before He would give it to others, because the corruption of one thing ought to be brought about before the generation of another. Now God would never have determined to take away that from the Amorrhites, unless these foreseen sins had required this, because "God is not an avenger," as Augustine says, "before someone is a sinner."[19]

And God's words themselves, by which He promised that land to Abraham and to his seed, very manifestly indicate this. For God says these words to him: "Know thou beforehand that thy seed shall be a stranger in a land not their own, and they shall bring them under bondage, and afflict them four hundred years. But I will judge the nation which they shall serve, and after this they shall come out with great substance. And thou shalt go to thy fathers in peace, and be buried in a good old age. But in the fourth generation they

---

19 *On Genesis*, bk. 11, c. 17, n. 22 (PL 34, 438).

shall return hither: for as yet the iniquities of the Amorrhites are not at the full until this present time" (Gen. 15, 13-16). From these last words it is very clearly established that the Amorrhites were deprived of that land by God on account of their iniquities. But much clearer are the words which are found in Deuteronomy: "Say not," Moses says, "in thy heart, when the Lord thy God shall have destroyed them in thy sight: For my justice hath the Lord brought me in to possess this land, whereas these nations are destroyed for their wickedness. For it is not for thy justices, and the uprightness of thy heart that thou shalt go in to possess their lands: but because they have done wickedly, they are destroyed at thy coming in: and that the Lord might accomplish his word, which he promised by oath to thy fathers Abraham, Isaac, and Jacob" (9, 4-5). In which words it is very clearly said that those nations were wiped out on account of their iniquities.

In those words which he adds: "and that the Lord might accomplish his word," the conjunction, "that," does not denote the cause, but the attainment of the effect, as it is often wont to be understood in Holy Writ. "Now the law entered in," Paul says, "that sin might abound" (Rom. 5, 20). Far be it that someone would so think about God. But God gave the Law, so that by it men would become good and just: and nevertheless it did not so happen, nay, on the contrary when the Law was given, men abounded in offenses, because they desired all the more the things forbidden. There is something else similar in John where he says: "For these things were done, that the scripture might be fulfilled: You shall not break a bone of him" (19, 36). The fulfillment of Scripture certainly was not the reason why those things were done. Nay, rather on the contrary, the reason why Scripture predicted those things was because they would happen. For otherwise that prediction of Scripture would seem casual and fortuitous, and not prophetic. Thus the meaning which John intends in those words is that by those things having happened, the Scripture saying, "You shall not break a bone of him," was fulfilled. Completely the same thing ought to be said about the promise to Abraham, that when those particular tribes were destroyed on account of their impious acts, God gave those lands, which He had promised to Abraham that He would give them to his seed, to the people of Israel. Now if someone would want to contend that the conjunction, "that," does not mean in that passage the attainment of the effect, but the true cause, I do not wish to argue on account of this: yet I will then say that it is evident from the text itself that two reasons on account of which those nations were destroyed are stated there. The first and the greatest is the impiety of those nations. The second, which depends on that reason and is posterior to it, is the fulfillment of the Divine promise.

The second cause of a just war is the abandonment of the true worship of God, such that a people knowing the true God, and worshiping Him (as it should be done), were to abandon such worship of God, and give it to another, to whom it is not due; on account of this they can be attacked with war by him who has the authority of declaring war. For long ago God commanded the children of Israel, that the city which had fallen into this crime, be destroyed by war, as when speaking in Deuteronomy: "If in one of thy cities, which the Lord thy God shall give thee to dwell in, thou hear some say: Children of Belial are gone out of the midst of thee, and have withdrawn the inhabitants of their city, and have said: Let us go, and serve strange gods which you know not: inquire carefully and diligently, the truth of the thing by looking well into it, and if thou find that which is said to be certain, and that this abomination hath been really committed, thou shalt forthwith kill the inhabitants of that city with the edge of the sword, and shalt destroy it and all things that are in it, even the cattle. And all the household goods that are there, thou shalt gather together in the midst of the streets thereof, and shalt burn them with the city itself, so as to consume all for the Lord thy God, and that it be a heap forever: it shall be built no more. And there shall nothing of that anathema stick to thy hand: that the Lord may turn from the wrath of his fury, and may have mercy on thee" (13, 12-17). In which words, among other things it ought to be noticed what He lastly said: "that the Lord may turn from the wrath of his fury, and may have mercy on thee." For by those words we are taught that this crime is so serious before God, that on account of only one city infected with that crime, God's anger is often provoked against the whole kingdom: especially if such a sin is neglected to be punished.

On account of this sin all the children of Israel gathered in Silo so that they might fight against the tribe of Ruben, and the tribe of Gad, and half of the tribe of Manasses.[20] For the children of Israel had heard that they had built an altar in the land of Chanaan along the Jordan: and they thought that they had built this altar for this purpose, so that on it they would offer sacrifices and victims to the gods of the Gentiles. Now because they were fully informed by the messengers whom they had sent to those tribes on account of this matter that the affair was different from what they had thought, they refrained from the war which they had decided to wage against those tribes. But here one ought to note that although this cause about which we now treat, is a just cause for war, still not account of it is it permitted to anyone to declare war on those departing from the true worship of God, but this is granted only to him who at another time was so governing these abandoning men as their supreme ruler. For just as only this man is he who can by right punish them, so by his authority he can declare war against them.

The third cause of a just war is when someone impedes someone else, so that he may not obtain what is due to him by law. Hence Julius Caesar in the writings of [Marcus

---

20 Cf. Jos. 22.

Annaeus] Lucanus seems to me to have said very well: "The one who refuses what is just, surrenders everything to an enemy in arms."[21] Which words Caesar said so that he might show the just cause of the war which he was beginning against the Roman Republic: because admittance to Rome, which was due to him as a true and well-deserving citizen of the Republic, from which the government of the Roman Republic was endeavoring to impede him. But leaving aside profane examples, let us bring forth a sacred example, which has much greater strength. The children of Israel (as the book of Numbers testifies) fought against Sehon and Og, kings of the Amorrhites, because they did not want to permit them to pass through their land, even though the children of Israel promised that they would not go aside into the fields, or their vineyards, nor drink waters from their wells: but would go on the king's highway, until they passed their borders.[22] Augustine when treating this story says: "It certainly ought to be noted how just wars were waged. For a harmless passage was denied, which very justly should have been allowed by the right of human society."[23]

The fourth cause of a just war is when one's own things are sought, which are kept by force and violence by the enemy, and cannot otherwise be recovered except through war. For on account of this cause when Saul died, David waged war against Isboseth, Saul's son, who was trying to take control of the kingdom of Israel, which God had already bestowed upon David through the prophet Samuel.[24]

---

21 *Arma tenenti omnia dat, qui justa negat* (*Pharsalia*, bk. 1, lns. 348 f.).
22 Cf. Num. 21, 21-23.
23 *Quaestiones in Heptateuchum*, bk. 4 (*Quaestiones in numeros*), q. 44 (PL 34, 739); *Decretum Gratiani*, pt. 2, *causa* 23, q. 2, c. 3 (PL 187, 1167A-B).
24 Cf. II Kings 2.

The fifth cause of a just war is the defense of the ruler himself or his subjects. For everyone has the right to defend himself, so also the ruler has the right to defend those who are his subjects, because just as everyone ought to take care of himself, so the ruler ought to take care of all his own subjects. And if they are bothered by the enemy, the ruler can justly begin a war against the enemy for their safety, so that he may force him to not bother his subjects. For (as laws bear witness) it is permitted to repel force with force. For this was the main reason, sacred history asserts, why David waged so many wars against the Philistines. For this reason also, and on account of the immediately preceding reason, the children of Israel with the Machabees as their leaders happily fought against Kings Antiochus and Demetrius.

The sixth cause of a just war is against him who supports the enemy unjustly pursuing. For just as it is permitted to repel an enemy unjustly pursuing, so also it is permitted to repress him, through whom the power of the enemy is increased, so that he having been repressed and humiliated, the power of the enemy may be lessened. For this reason King David struck Syria of Damascus, because it was giving help to Adarezer, king of Soba.[25]

The seventh cause of a just war can be if anyone shall have inflicted a public injury to the ruler, and he, or he who rules him, does not want to make worthy recompensation. This was the only cause on account of which King David began a war against Hanon king of the Ammonites.[26] For he had inflicted a public injury upon King David, when he ordered one half of the beards of the messengers whom David had sent to him, and one half of their garments even to the buttocks to be cut off. For this injury was inflicted not only upon the messengers who suffered, but also upon the king, by whom they had been sent. Thus it is permitted for

---

25 Cf. II Kings 8.
26 Cf. II Kings 10.

the king, who suffered the injury, to himself get compensation for the same injury: because he does not have a superior from whom he may ask for it. But when he attempts to obtain this, he ought to keep this before his eyes, that he not by the occasion of vengeance satisfy his own anger, but rather that he do it being concerned for the common utility. Namely, so that public justice be preserved, and henceforth everyone would take care not to inflict an injury upon another person.

The eighth cause of a just war can be the rebellion of subjects, who rise up against their ruler, and having been admonished by him contemn to obey him. For the ruler so contemned can justly begin a war against the rebellious subjects. King David gives to us reliable testimony of which matter, who began a war against Seba the son of Bochri:[27] because he stirred up the people to leave David for himself. Hence Augustine says: "When force is required to inflict the punishment, that, in obedience to God or some lawful authority, good men undertake wars, when they find themselves in such a position as regards the conduct of human affairs, that right conduct requires them to act, or to make others act in this way."[28] But he who wishes to reduce the number of these causes could ascribe this eighth cause to the fourth. Because he who wages war against rebels, seeks after what belongs to himself, that is, obedience, which was withdrawn from him by his subjects.

The ninth cause of a just war is if someone protects a wicked man who ought to be punished by law, so that he would not pay the just penalties. For the ruler, who has the right to punish the wicked man, can justly begin a war against his unjust defender. About this matter the book of Judges provides for us clear evidence which relates that the eleven tribes of Israel (the leader of whom by God's command was Juda) began a war against the city of Gabaa, and the whole

---

27 Cf. II Kings 20.
28 *Reply to Faustus the Manichaean*, bk. 22, n. 74 (PL 42, 447).

tribe of Benjamin, because they did not want to hand over for punishment the men of Gabaa, who when molesting with an incredible fury of lust, killed the wife of the Levite husband, but defended them as though they did something just. For which reason all the eleven tribes fought so wholeheartedly against the tribe of Benjamin, that they nearly completely wiped out the tribe of Benjamin.[29]

The tenth cause of a just war is the violation of an agreement made and undertaken. For on account of this cause, he who was injured from the violation of such an agreement can justly begin a war against the violator of the agreement. For this reason Joram the king of Israel with Josaphat king of Juda helping him, made a war against Mesam the king of Moab, because he did not want to give the tributes of lambs and rams which he was held to pay yearly from an old agreement.[30] Now if anyone would wish to find fault with this war, because it was waged by King Joram, this accusation will be quickly removed by the fact that the just King Josephat of Juda gave assistance to this war, which he would not have wanted to give unless he firstly consulted the Lord through a prophet, whether he ought to be wage the war or not. Therefore the prophet Eliseus, who even though he disdained King Joram on account of his wickedness, still out of reverence for the just King Josephat gave responses by God's inspiring, making them constant and strong for war through the certain promise of victory.

Here are all the just causes of war which I was able to gather from Holy Writ, besides which I think no other could be found which could not be reduced to some one of these. Still I decided to point this out to the reader, so that he may understand that he who helps that first instigator of the just war has the same causes of a just war, which the first instigator of the just war himself has. Hence it is that anyone who

---

29 Cf. Judges 20.
30 Cf. IV Kings 3.

supports the one justly waging war by fighting in the war, is said to have a just cause of war, unless something else would impede, which impedes the justice of the war. For the just cause of war is to support justice, on account of the defense of which the war is reckoned just. For Abraham justly fought against the four kings, who made Lot, the son of his brother, a captive, and he delivered him from their hands.[31] If Lot had a just cause of war in fighting against those kings, and resisting them, lest he be taken captive by them, Abraham also had a just cause of war by coming to the assistance of Lot himself, so that he might deliver him from the enemies, who had unjustly seized and carried him off. King Josephat of Juda also justly waged war against the King of Moab, in support of King Joram, because King Joram himself, to whom he was giving assistance, had a just case of war (as we said).[32]

We said that there are four things necessary for a just war, two of which, which we said are the most important, we have disclosed so far, namely, the authority and the cause: there remains that we set forth the other two. A good intention in war is required, so that it can be called just. Augustine teaches this speaking thus: "The real evils in war are love of violence, revengeful cruelty, fierce and implacable enmity, wild resistance, and the lust of power, and such like; and it is generally to punish these things, when force is required to inflict the punishment."[33] But this good intention is not a special condition of a just war, but one common for every good work. For no work can be called good, if it is done with a wicked intention. Still this wickedness of the work does not arise from the work itself, but from the one doing the work, who does wickedly that which is good. Hence it is that when it is inquired about the justice of a war, that only

---

31 Cf. Gen. 14.
32 Cf. IV Kings 3.
33 *Reply to Faustus the Manichaean*, bk. 22, n. 74 (PL 42, 447).

ought to be investigated which is intrinsic and connatural to the war itself; but not that which is extrinsic to it.

The last thing which is said to be required in a just war is that the person who wages the war is not forbidden to make war. For he is forbidden to fight in this way, by that very fact would sin when acting contrary to the prohibition, and so he would make the war, which is otherwise just, unjust. War has been interdicted to ecclesiastical person by a public decree: for the [IV] Synod of Toledo established such a decree about this matter: "Clerics who have been discovered to have willingly took up arms in any sedition, after having been degraded from their order, are to be confined to a monastery to do penance there all their lives."[34] And the Synod of Meaux[35] cited by Gratian speaks thus: "Any of those who are perceived to belong to the clergy, may not take up military arms: nor may they march armed, but they may give the designation of their profession by their religious manners and religious habit: which if they disdain, as contemners of the holy canons, and profaners of ecclesiastical authority, they are punished by the loss of their own order, because they cannot minister to God and the world at the same time."[36]

But here one ought to point out to the reader that he ought not to think that war is prohibited to ecclesiastical persons, because it is evil in itself: but only because war is unbefitting to such persons: because they are deputed to doing something better, to which war clearly conflicts. For some things are simply and absolutely good, which nevertheless are not good for some people. For instance it is good to contract marriage, yet for those who have vowed chastity, it is not something good. But although to wage war is

---

34 C. 45 (Mansi 10, 630D).
35 The Synod of Meaux-Paris met from 845 to 846 A.D.
36 *Decretum Gratiani*, pt. 2, *causa* 23, q. 7, c. 37 (PL 187, 1247B-1248A); Synod of Meaux, c. 37 (Mansi 14, 827).

forbidden for ecclesiastical persons, still it is not forbidden to them to take part in them, such that they would spiritually assist those justly fighting, by praying for them, exhorting them to virtue, and by hearing the confessions of their sins. For in the Old Law God commanded Josue that in the war against Jericho the priests would sound the trumpets.[37] And it ought to be further noted that if this condition of a just war be lacking in some particular person, who joins in the public and general war, although it can make the war unjust as to that particular person, still the public war itself will not be called unjust on account of this. Because the reputation of the war ought to be taken from the majority and not from the minority; unless perhaps the same persons, by whose authority the war was declared, is among those persons to whom war is forbidden by law, unless when perceiving the common necessity forces or permits one to go to war. For then he who starts the war sins, and for this reason makes the war unjust: not in fact on account of an injustice which he inflicts upon the enemy, but on account of that injustice which he renders to the Church, by sending an ecclesiastical person to war against her prohibition.

See that we have now explained everything which is reckoned to be required for a just war: all these things ought to be understood not only regarding a public and general war, but also of a private war. Hence all those things also ought to be required in a private war, so that it can be called just, which we said are required for the justice of a public war. Still I decided to point out to the reader in this place, that he ought to understand that here we are not speaking about a defensive war, in which someone defends himself from some unjust invader, but about that war which someone firstly starts against someone else. For in a defensive war, whether it be public or private, authority ought not to be waited for: because this is granted to all by nature, that men

---

37 Cf. Jos. 6, 4.

would defend themselves against an unjust invader. Because all laws concede that, as it is said in the chapter, [*Tua nos duxit*], "It is lawful to repel force with force."[38]

And hence it appears how unjustly Sylvester Mazzolini in his *Summa*,[39] reprehends the *Summa Angelica*,[40] because it said that the same things are required for a private just war, which are required for a public just war. For because he argued that a cleric unjustly assaulted can defend himself, and a private man unjustly assaulted can defend himself without permission of the superior, this same thing can be proved about a city unjustly assaulted, which without permission of the ruler can wage war only so that that it may defend itself from the unjust invader. Wherefore just as a private person is not obliged to wait for the ruler's authorization so that he could defend himself, so also any nation is not obliged to wait for the authorization of the ruler, so that it could defend itself from an unjust invader, especially if

---

38   *Decretals of Gregory IX*, bk. 5, tit. 12 (*De homicidio voluntario vel casuali*), c. 19. The text here has the chapter *Significasti* (c. 16 or 18), but the phrase mentioned is found in this title only in the chapter, *Tua nos duxit*; hence this chapter has been substituted in the translation.

39   "Regarding the justice of a particular war, which is neither a duel or a reprisal, according to the *Angelica Summa*, the five things which have already been listed are required, but it is wanting in many things. Firstly, because if, as it says, authorization of the superior is required for the justice of a private war, the private war will then be a general and public war. Secondly, because if it is required that he not be a cleric, it follows that a cleric cannot defend himself" (*Summa Summarum, quae Sylvestrina dicitur* (Antwerp: Petrus Bellerus, 1578), vol. 1, p. 90b).

40   Alias, *Summa de Casibus Conscientiae*, which is mentioned above in book one. "In a war, however, so-called in the second way [i. e., improperly speaking, not authorized by the ruler] five things are required..." (*Summa angelica de casibus conscientiae* (Mantua: Giorgio Arrivabene, 1492), fol. 31r).

from such a delay danger of the nation is near at hand. And thus, so that we may avoid this inconsistency, we said that those things, which are required for a just war, ought not to be understood of a defensive war, but of a war wherein someone attacks another.

Therefore, after having explained everything, it is necessary that we answer the main question, and show that it is licit to attack heretics by war after it has been established about their pertinacity and rebellion. Which we will easily do, if we show that all those things are present in a war of this kind, which we said are required for a just war. It is unnecessary to discuss about the last two, because those two things (as we said) are adventitious and extrinsic to war itself. Wherefore, the wickedness, which a war would have on account of a lack of them, is not from the nature and distinctive characteristics of war itself, but merely from the wickedness of the one fighting, for instance because he had bad intention, or because he is forbidden to fight. And if someone were to contend about these two conditions of war, we may suppose that those things are in this war, which can be present or absent in every war. For what prevents starting a war against heretics with a good intention? For it is a good intention to want to convert heretics to the faith, and to force them to maintain the faith which they at one time received in Baptism: which we know many have done from fear of the evils which are inflicted through wars. It is a good intention to want to exalt and spread the Catholic faith, which heretics easily hem in by their pertinacious rebellion, unless, having been restrained by war from their pestilent errors, they return to their senses. It is a good intention to want to force the rebellious and disobedient to render the due obedience to which they are obliged.

Now the success itself of the war of Emperor Charles [V] mentioned above very clearly shows that this, or some other equally good intention, was in the war, so that whoever wishes to rightly consider it, unless he has been corrupted by rapacious envy, can very clearly know. For after the Emperor (with God's favor) obtained the victory, he was not ardently desiring to take vengeance upon the enemy. After obtaining such a great victory he showed leniency and kindness to the enemy; he did not want to punish John Fredrick [I], Duke of Saxony, and Philip [I], Landgrave of Hess, with decapitation which they deserved to suffer according to the laws, who persuaded many people in Germany to rebel against the same emperor, and gathering an immense army, with audacious temerity attacked the same emperor, often hurling war missiles into his camp; but mercifully granted to them their lives, which they did not deserve. Even though many conjoined cities of Germany raised troops for these dukes against the emperor, still the emperor did not sack any of them. He has not harmed until now any of those who admitting their guilt asked pardon; but the emperor very mercifully granted pardon to them all. If there were those things in the emperor which (as Augustine says) are wont to vitiate the just intention of war, namely, "love of violence, revengeful cruelty, implacable enmity,"[41] towards those who had gravely offended His Majesty, after he had brought them back under his control, he would not have so easily and quickly spared them. Concerning the second thing which is required for the justice of a war, there is nothing which someone could justly dispute. Since it is a matter very well known to the whole world, that the emperor gathered not ecclesiastical persons, but laymen from many and various regions, namely, from Germany, Spain, and Italy, so that he might subdue the Germans rebelling against the Catholic Church and him.

Two other things remain to be discussed, namely, the authority and the cause. Regarding the authority no one, unless he is completely ignorant and witless, can doubt. Because if authority for starting a war is in a man, there is

---

41 *Reply to Faustus the Manichaean*, bk. 22, n. 74 (PL 42, 447).

Whether one may war against pertinacious and rebellious heretics

no one who has more certain and greater authority than the emperor, who alone truly does not have a superior in temporal matters of this kind. For he is (as Pope Innocent [III] says[42]) the "lesser light to rule the night."[43]

There remains, therefore, that we investigate about the cause, which if we show to be just, we will thence clearly prove that it is just that pertinacious heretics be fought against in war, and how very wrongly they think who were finding fault with Emperor Charles on account of the war of this kind. If we wish to recall to memory some of the just causes of war which we enumerated above, we will find many which clearly demonstrate that this war is just. We put the just cause of war, the abandonment of the true worship of God, in the second place. But heretics, who do not believe the things which ought to be believed about God or about His spouse, the Church, do not worship God truly and as they ought. Therefore, heresy is a just cause of war, which those who do not wish to abandon, can justly be conquered.

---

42 "Even as God, the Creator of the universe, has set two great lights in the firmament of heaven, the greater light to rule the day and the lesser light to rule the night, so for the firmament of the universal Church, which is called by the name of heaven, He has appointed two great dignities: the greater to rule over men's souls, as it were the day, and the lesser to rule over men's bodies, as it were the night. These are the authority of the Pope and the King. Further, as the moon derives its light from the sun, which indeed is less than the sun both in bulk and in importance, though alike in place and power, so the power of the King derives the splendor of its dignity from the authority of the Pope; and the more the former keeps within view of the latter, so much the more is it adorned by a lesser light, and the further it is removed from the view of the other, so much the more does it excel in splendor" (Letter to the nobleman Acerbus and to the other leaders of Tuscany and of the Duchy (1198) (PL 214, 377A-377B)).

43 Cf. Gen. 1, 14.

A second cause of a just war, which we listed in the eighth place, is if someone were to rebel against a superior, to whom he is obliged to give complete deference. And certainly for this motive also it is very clearly proved that the war is just which is waged against pertinacious heretics. For all heretics are clearly rebels against the holy Catholic Church, whose teaching all the faithful are obliged to accept. But heretics, blinded by pride, prefer their own opinion to the teaching of holy Mother Church, and hence in order to defend their opinion, they do not hesitate to contradict the teaching of the Catholic Church, and despise her precepts. Hence Job when speaking about heretics speaks thus: "They have been rebellious to the light, they have not known his ways, neither have they returned by his path" (24, 13). Blessed Gregory reckons that these words ought to be understood of heretics.[44]

Furthermore, pertinacious heretics (as we clearly proved above in the third chapter of this book) deservedly ought to be punished. And we showed in the twelfth chapter of the same book, that they ought to be punished with the punishment of death, if they do not wish to come to their senses. And wherefore it very clearly follows that if they want to resist this just punishment, the ruler, under whose authority they are, could on this account justly fight a war against them. For he who refuses to undergo a just punishment decreed by the ruler's command, and lest he suffer it resists the ruler, is a rebel. We have already clearly shown above from the testimony of Sacred Scripture and from the opinion of Blessed Augustine that rebellion is a just cause of war.

Again, if a pertinacious heretic was justly condemned to death, it makes no difference (as showed in the twelfth chapter of this book) with which death, namely, by the sword, or by fire, or by water, or in whatever other way death is inflicted upon him: it follows that it is just that pertinacious and rebellious heretics be vanquished by war, so that they

---

44 *Moralia*, bk. 16, c. 57, n. 70 (PL 76, 1154B-C).

Whether one may war against pertinacious and rebellious heretics

may perish, and in this way the ruler can punish them with death, as they have deserved. For the wars waged for this reason by Moses, all of which Faustus the Manichaean was reproaching, Blessed Augustine defends: because by them he was inflicting the death which they had deserved at other times. For when speaking in this way, he says: "The account of the wars of Moses will not excite surprise or abhorrence, for in the wars carried on by Divine command, he showed not ferocity but obedience; and God in giving the command, acted not in cruelty, but in righteous retribution, giving to all what they deserved, and warning those who needed warning."[45] Therefore in a similar manner, the emperor, or any other ruler, when he fights a war against pertinacious heretics, who are subject to him by law, ought not to be said to act cruelty, but in righteous retribution, to give to all what they deserved, and to warn those who needed warning.

Finally, after the necks of rulers subjected themselves to Christ, holy and learned Pontiffs often exhorted that they would undertake a war against pertinacious and rebellious heretics, and in this way curb their obstinate passion for harming. The Supreme Pontiffs were not content with mere exhortations to war, but to all who, marked with the cross, went forth against heretics, they often granted an indulgence for the punishments which they deserved for their sins, so that at least drawn by a very great reward soldiers would have willingly gone forth to wars. Blessed Gregory, when writing to Gennadius, Patrician and Exarch of Africa, exhorted to war against the Donatist heretics, speaking thus: "As the Lord has made your Excellency to shine with the light of victories in the military wars of this life, so ought you to oppose the enemies of the Church with all activity of mind and body, to the end that from both kinds of triumph your reputation may shine forth more and more, when in public wars, too, you firmly resist the adversaries

---

45 *Reply to Faustus the Manichaean*, bk. 22, n. 74 (PL 42, 447).

of the Catholic Church in behalf of the Christian people, and bravely fight ecclesiastical battles as warriors of the Lord. For it is known that men heretical in religion, if they have liberty allowed them to do harm (which God forbid), rise strenuously against the Catholic faith, to the end that they may transfuse, if they can, the poison of their heresy to the corrupting of the members of the Christian body. For we have learned that they are lifting up their necks against the Catholic Church, the Lord being opposed to them, and desire to pervert the faith of the Christian profession. But let your Eminence suppress their attempts, and subdue their proud necks to the yoke of rectitude."[46] Shortly afterwards he prays to God that this Gennadius would be strong for waging war of this kind, speaking thus: "Furthermore, bestowing on you, as is due, the affection of our paternal charity, we beseech the Lord to make your arm strong for subduing the enemies, and to sharpen your soul with zeal for the faith like the edge of a quivering sword."[47]

Next, when the Albigensian heresy arose in France near Toulouse, the Supreme Pontiff, Innocent III, a man renowned for his conduct and learning, after he understood that they did not wish to forsake, for the sake of the many reasons and proofs offered to them, their error, he decided (as Platina relates[48]) that they should be attacked. [Pope Innocent III[49]], seeing this sect of the Albigensians still obstinate in

---

46   Bk. 1, letter 74 (PL 77, 528B-C).
47   *Ibid.* (PL 77, 529B).
48   Alias, Bartolomeo Sacchi. "At this time sprung up a heresy at Toulouse, which by Innocent's means, the blessed Dominic (who was afterwards made a Saint) repressed with the aid of Simon Montfort; for it had gone so far, that not only disputations of words, but also arms were needed" (*The Lives of the Popes* (London: C. Wilkinson, 1685), p. 256).
49   Blessed Antoninus relates that Pope Innocent III, and not Honorius III gave this indulgence for those taking part in the Al-

their error, granted indulgences and condonations of sins (as Blessed Antoninus relates[50]) to those who went forth to war against heretics of this kind.[51] Finally when the heresy

---

bigensian Crusade.

50 "At that time a Crusade began to be preached in France, in the region of Toulouse, against the Albigensians by command of the Lord Pope Innocent [III]. And firstly the monk, [Blessed] Pierre de Castelnau, was sent as a Legate from the Pope, who excommunicated the count of Toulouse [Raymond VI] as a supporter of heretics: when the sentence was pronounced the count publicly threatened him with death. Now when the Legate was returning from the town of Saint-Gilles two squires followed him: and finding him not far from the river, one them thrust a lance into his side. Who having received a mortal wound having turned his head towards him looked at and said to him, repeating many times: 'May the Lord forgive you, brother: and I forgive you.' Having said this he expired. The Lord Pope having heard these things sent Gualon [or Guala Bucchero], Cardinal-Deacon of Santa Maria in Portico, a jurist and a man of great prudence, and very zealous for the Christian faith; ordering the king, and all the rulers of the kingdom that as true Catholic believers and defenders of the faith, that they would attack the regions Toulouse and Narbonne, and the other cities which the attackers and subverters of the Christian faith had seized for the remission of their sins. Having sent twelve abbots of the Cistercian Order by Innocent III to the same legate, who were then leading lives of holiness and learning: who would preach the Crusade against the Albigensians: granting a plenary remission of sins to those taking up the cross and waging war against the heretics; even if they would happen to die on the way before the war after the cross has been taken up" (*Chronicorum opus* (Leiden: Ex officina Juntarum, et Pauli Guittii, 1586), vol. 3, tit. 19, c. 1, sect. 3, p. 90).

51 *Ad sponsae suae* (1204): "Thus may your Royal Greatness assist you also with our dear sons… the Cistercian abbot, and Peter and Ralph monks of Fontfroide, legates of the Apostolic See, whom we destine specially to this, that the material sword may be sanctioned to supply the defect of the spiritual sword, and you,

of the Hussites spread through Bohemia, and its upholders could not be recalled from it by arguments and reasons, at the urging of Giuliano [Cesarini], Cardinal[-Deacon] of Sant'Angelo, Legate of the Apostolic See, indulgences of sins having been given for this reason (as Aeneas Sylvius relates[52]), went out to war against the same heretics. If war against heretics ought not to be undertaken, God, Who rules His Church, would not have permitted the Supreme Pontiffs who govern her, having promised remissions of sins, to encourage the faithful so many times to war. Therefore from all these things it is now very clearly established that it is just, that pertinacious and rebellious heretics be attacked by war, so that assailed by war, they may receive the deserved avenging of their crime.

Yet it is befitting to warn rulers, that they not think that they so possess this power of waging war against heretics, that as often as it pleases them, they could start a war against heretics. For it is not allowed for them to do this, unless after it shall have been declared by an ecclesiastical judge that they are heretics. For it is not equitable that a punishment would be inflicted upon someone, before it be established that he has guilt, which demands such punishment. Now one cannot establish a heretic's crime except through a declaration of an ecclesiastical judge, to whom alone laws grant to pronounce definitive sentence of pertinacity in him. For

---

besides the temporal glory which you will attain from so pious and praiseworthy a work, may obtain that pardon for sins, which we grant as an indulgence for those crossing the sea to bring aid to the Holy Land" (PL 215, 362C); *Etsi nostri navicula* (1204): "...and enjoining them for the remission of their sins, since we want those who faithfully shall have labored against the heretics to rejoice in the same indulgence as we grant as an indulgence for those crossing the sea for the aid of the Holy Land" (PL 215, 360A)).

52   Pope Pius II, *De Bohemorum origine ac gestis historia* (Solingen: Johannes Soter, 1538), c. 48, pp. 62 & 91.

Whether one may war against pertinacious and rebellious heretics

Pope Boniface VIII in the chapter, *Ut inquisitionis*,[53] forbids any secular authority to dare judge about this crime: because this crime (as he says) "is merely Ecclesiastical." Next, in the chapter, *Cum secundum leges*,[54] in the section, *Confiscationis*, the Pope forbids that the goods of heretics be seized by secular rulers before the ecclesiastical justice, to whom this belongs by law, has promulgated the sentence upon the crime of heresy. And completely the same thing ought to be said about death, which a ruler can by no means inflict on the heretic for the crime of heresy, unless after the ecclesiastical judge, to whom it pertains, shall have declared him to be pertinacious. And hence it follows from what has been said that a ruler cannot begin a war against heretics solely on account of heresy, except after the ecclesiastical judge, to whom this befits by law, shall have declared by public sentence that they are heretics.

It remains that we reply to the objections of the adversaries, who believe that their objections are so strong that no one can stand up against them. But we shall easily show, with God as the guide, that they have no force, and thence we will make our opinion stronger. Firstly, therefore, they object to us that heretics ought to be convinced by arguments and not by force, because faith ought to be free, and not forced. Even though they brought forth no testimony to me to support their argument, so that there would be nothing to which I ought to respond, I offer Blessed Bernard for supporting them, who when expounding the words, "Catch us the little foxes that destroy the vines" (Cant. 2, 15), says these words: "But if we interpret the Bridegroom's words allegorically, taking the vines to mean churches and the foxes heresies, or rather heretics, then the sense will be that heretics are to be caught, not driven away. They are to be caught, I say, but with no other force than the force of arguments wherewith their

---

[53] *Liber sextus decretalium*, bk. 5, tit. 2 (*De haereticis*), c. 18.
[54] *Liber sextus decretalium*, bk. 5, tit. 2 (*De haereticis*), c. 19.

errors are refuted. For themselves, let them, if it is possible, be reconciled to the Church, let them be brought back to the true faith. Such is the desire of Him 'Who will have all men to be saved and to come to the knowledge of the truth' (I Tim. 2, 4). Such also is the wish of the Bridegroom, as He signifies in this place where He does not simply say, 'Catch the foxes,' but 'catch us the foxes.' Therefore He wants these foxes to be won over to Himself and His Spouse, the Catholic Church, and expresses this desire by saying, 'Catch us the foxes.'"[55]

To this objection I reply that what they say is true, that a man ought to freely invited, and not by force, to the Catholic faith. Nevertheless this is not universally true, but it holds true for those who have never received Baptism, who nowise ought to be forced to the faith. But those who have at one time put on Christ in Baptism (as we showed above in the fourth chapter of this book) ought to be forced, so that they would hold the faith, which they at one time received. Now what Bernard says, "with no other force than the force of arguments wherewith their errors are refuted," ought to be understood of those heretics alone, who have not yet been duly admonished about their errors, and to whom arguments have not yet been presented to them, by which their errors are refuted: and hence it is not established that they are pertinacious. For concerning these men I acknowledge that they ought not to be opposed by force, before they have been duly admonished about their errors. Yet when this due admonition has been shown to them, if being obstinate in their errors they contemn to accept the Catholic faith, they could be justly conquered, so that the death which is due to their crime, and which through power they strive to avert, even unwillingly they may be forced to undergo. And Blessed Bernard also teaches this same thing, who after the above-mentioned words added in the same place these words which follow: "Conse-

---

55   Sermon 64, n. 8 (PL 183, 1086D-1087A).

quently, whenever an experienced and learned member of the Church undertakes to dispute with a heretic, he is bound to make it his aim, not merely to convict his opponent of error, but also to convert him to truth. For he should bear in mind the words of Saint James, 'He who causeth a sinner to be converted from the error of his way, shall save his soul from death and shall cover a multitude of sins' (5, 20). But should the heretic be unwilling to return, and, after being once and a second time admonished, remains still obdurate in his error, then according to the Apostle's injunction he must be avoided, as one entirely corrupted. Thenceforth it will be better, at least in my opinion, to drive away such a fox, or even to put him under restraint, than to permit him to go on destroying the vines."[56] Bernard clearly confirms our opinion, far from it being the case that he could support the contrary opinion.

Secondly they object to us that one ought to spare the multitude, and one ought to treat it mildly, even if it all, or the majority of it, has fallen into a crime. For this they also brought forth no proof to me, yet I bring for a testimony, which when fully explained, whence it is established that they, who think the opposite, have spoken very foolishly on this point. Augustine in a letter to Boniface says: "When, owing to the serious ruptures of dissensions in the Church, it is no longer a question of danger to this or that particular individual, but whole nations are lying in ruin, it is right to yield a little from our severity, that true charity may give her aid in healing the more serious evils."[57] And they are cited by Gratian in the chapter, *Ut constitueretur*.[58] Alexander III

---

56 *Ibid.* (PL 183, 1087A-B).
57 Letter 186, c. 10, n. 45 (PL 33, 813).
58 "But in cases of this kind, where through serious tearing of dissensions, danger lies of slaughters, not of this or that man, but of the people, severity ought to be somewhat lessened, so that genuine charity may come to the aid of curing greater evils" (*Decre-*

also commanded the same thing in the chapter, *Latores*.[59] And Gratian cites another saying of Innocent [III] in the chapter, *Quoties*, speaking thus: "As often as a fault has been committed by the people or by a mob, because they cannot all be punished, it is wont to pass unavenged."[60] And Blessed Augustine in a letter to Bishop Aurelius again says: "These offenses are taken out of the way, at least in my judgment, by other methods than harshness, severity, and an imperious mode of dealing—namely, rather by teaching than by commanding, rather by advice than by denunciation. Thus at least we must deal with the multitude; in regard to the sins of a few, exemplary severity must be used." And these words are cited by Gratian in the chapter, *Comessationes*.[61] These testimonies of the sacred Doctors all seem on the surface to prove that a multitude always ought to be spared, and hence they, who are opposed to us on this point, perhaps will think that they prove that it is not just that a war be undertaken against heretics, howsoever pertinacious and rebellious.

I certainly admit that a sinning multitude ought to be spared, and treated more mildly: yet this cannot always be so done: but only when such a multitude acknowledges its sin, and is prepared to correct it, and good hope is had about its correction. Otherwise if the same multitude when sinning, does not acknowledge its sin, nay, rather wants to pertinaciously defend it as something done well: then they

---

tum Gratiani, pt. 1, dist. 50, c. 25 (PL 187, 267A)).
59 "But because they were saying that a great multitude sinned with them in this, and it could not be known to which of them offended more or less, we have brought the same matter back to you to be relaxed according to your judgment" (*Decretals of Gregory IX*, bk. 5, tit. 27 (*De clerico excommunicato, deposito vel interdicto ministrante*), c. 4).
60 *Decretum Gratiani*, pt. 2, causa. 1, c. 14 (PL 187, 574C).
61 Letter 22, n. 5 (PL 33, 92); *Decretum Gratiani*, pt. 1, dist. 44, c. 1 (PL 187, 229A).

ought to be forced with a severe punishment to abandon their error, lest excessive indulgence give them an occasion of obstinacy, especially if the same multitude trusts in its own might, whence it becomes more bold regarding sin. [Pseudo-] Augustine expressly teaches this in the book, *De vera et falsa poenitentia,* when speaking thus: "For when there are so many who fall that [some priests] defend their former dignity and use it as an excuse, as it were, to sin themselves, that hope ought to be cut down."[62] And certainly, even if Augustine would not teach [this], reason itself clearly shows, that the multitude sinning, which refuses to acknowledge its sin, ought to be punished gravely. Because if the sin of many remaining in obstinacy were to be left unpunished, the sin itself will be for others an example, so that they think that as often as one wishes it is licit for them to perpetrate something similar. For this reason the jurist[63] commenting on the law, *Aut facta,* in the last section, says: "It sometimes happens that the punishments of certain malefactors are rendered more severe whenever an example is necessary, as for the suppression of many persons engaged in highway robbery."[64] Which opinion I think ought to be understood, when a sinning multitude refuses to acknowledge its sin, and to depart from it. For otherwise if the multitude itself acknowledging its sin would abandon it, I reckon that it ought to be done what is said in the chapter, *Comessationes,* and in the other chapters cited above.

---

62 C. 18, n. 34 (PL 40, 1128); *Decretum Gratiani,* pt. 2, *causa.* 33, *de poenitentia,* dist. 6, c. 1 (PL 187, 1640A). This work has often been incorrectly ascribed to St. Augustine and is of unknown authorship.
63 I. e., Claudius Saturninus.
64 *Digest of Justinian,* bk. 48, tit. 19 (*De poenis*), l. 16, n. 10.

Chapter XV

That the books of heretics ought to be burned.

It seems to me that one does not take well enough care of Christendom if when heretics have been removed from life, and their property proscribed, their books still remain preserved, by which even when dead they could greatly harm all Christendom. Paul when writing to Timothy, assuredly a holy and learned man, admonishes that he keep away from speaking with heretics, lest by their words, which he knew are very influential towards evil, he be corrupted. "But shun profane and vain babblings: for they grow much towards ungodliness. And their speech spreadeth like a canker" (II Tim. 2, 16-17). If heretics' words can harm so much, that for this reason they are compared to a canker, much more without a doubt will their writings do harm. For even though "Spoken words," as Jerome says, following Pliny [the Younger], "possess an indefinable hidden power,"[1] yet for many reasons writings often have more of an effect than words. For there are many who when speaking have no effect, because they lack the teeth, which are chiefly necessary for correct pronunciation, they lack a loud and peaceful voice, which greatly holds the attention of the hearers: or if they have all these things, they have very bad and dreadful gestures, so that they rather repel than attract the listeners from the speech. But writing without all these things can have an effect: because it does not require any of these things, so that it can instill and foster the sympathy of the reader.

---

1 St. Jerome, letter 53, n. 2 (PL 22, 541). Pliny the Younger, *Letters*, bk. 2, §3, ln. 9: "There is something in the voice, the look, the carriage, and even the gesture of the speaker, that makes a deeper impression upon the mind."

Next, things which are written are pondered more attentively, and are arranged much more accurately before they appear in public, than those things which we discuss in ordinary conversation, which often, as they present themselves to the mind, are brought forth without much examination. And hence it necessarily follows that written speech often has stronger force, and finer prickles, which as soon as it has been said, once the mind of the reader has been pricked, it is so strongly stuck in, that even when one wishes to do so, he cannot free himself from it. Also those who read, in many cases consider at length about what is read, and read it much more attentively and with longer examination, than they listen to the words of one speaking. Something written has moreover something special, by which it can harm much more far and wide, than uttered speech: even though it has been so anxiously premeditated, so that at every juncture of it, the orator has scratched his head a thousand times, and worn out all his nails. As a result, once it has been spoken by the mouth, it flies away irretrievably: for once it has been uttered by the mouth, it can benefit or harm no one but those who then heard it. But those things which have been written, are kept for many centuries, and are read by various men during many centuries. Hence it happens that written things kept for many centuries can do good or harm for many centuries. Therefore the conclusion is, that books of heretics, containing in themselves errors against the Catholic faith, ought to be reckoned as though they were perennial fountains perpetually spewing forth venom, or as some deep roots perpetually producing a certain poison from themselves, which can easily destroy the unwary. It is therefore necessary that all heretical books be burned, lest some pestilential root may remain, which at any time could produce from it new heretics.

The prophet Jeremias was appointed by Our Lord not merely to cut off the branches, but also pull up the roots, and

That the books of heretics ought to be burned

destroy them.[2] For when the root is kept, the branches may easily spring forth from it. For heretics take care to leave behind their heresies, wherefore they leave behind their writings in published books, so that by those books they may transmit their heresies not only among those who at that time live in foreign countries, but also to coming generations. Thus on two accounts it is established that books of heretics are very harmful. For by them, as through as it were canals, heresies pass over from one nation to another, and from kingdom to kingdom, and from province to province: the heretical authors can easily transmit all these heresies, not through their own voice, nor through speaking ministers, into very remote regions. Next, after having already spread the heresies through many nations, some other much more serious trouble arises from the books of heretics, that the heresies do not ever die from any oldness of age, and no teaching is so harmful, which is never covered over by time, or buried by being forgotten. Because the heresies will necessarily last as long as the books, which were published for their defense remain in existence.

All these things are proved by manifest experience, as we have as many examples as we wish for their confirmation. And it is unnecessary to repeat old examples, whose number is many: since enough, and more than enough, is that which nearly the whole Christian world, alas, now knows by experience teaching. When Luther deserting from the Catholic faith, firstly began to be insane, he published for the defense of his error a number of books, whereby he tried to also persuade others, if he could, of his heresies. Many read these books, and having been allured by them were brought over from the truth to falsehood, so that many worse heretics, and much more pestilential than Luther, immediately arose in Germany, who took care to also confirm their heresies by published books. Thus by these means within a few years

---

2 Cf. Jer. 1, 10.

nearly the whole of Germany nearly perished, which was of old a considerable part of the Christian world. And this pestilence did not contain itself with Germany alone, which ought not to be said without a sigh and tears: but diffused itself and spread through nearly the whole of Europe. Accordingly, rare is the region in the whole Christian world in which there are not some Lutherans, either open or hidden. It is certainly evident that this did not come forth from another source than because books of Luther, and of other men of the same sort, were transported through nearly every region with impunity, and were shown to whomsoever to read. And hence this pestilence acquired such great strength by going around, that unless God in His goodness and clemency deigns to heal this widely spreading disease, there then will surely be no hope left. If nevertheless from the beginning such books had been forbidden, with that earnestness which was befitting, and their carriers, sellers, readers, detainers had been punished with harsh severity, this plague would not have become so great. For a certain distinguished poet commanded it ought to be so done, saying: "Resist beginnings; too late is the medicine prepared, when the disease has gained strength by long delay."[3]

Thus whoever shall diligently examine what serious harm the recent heretics have caused by their books, will lament with the prophet Jeremias, and will say: "Sea monsters have drawn out the breast, they have given suck to their young" (Lam. 4, 3). For [Rabanus[4]] interprets these words as pertaining to the exceedingly atrocious cruelty of heretics, speaking thus: "A sea monster has a human face, but the body of an animal... Heretics can be understood in the 'sea monsters,' who indeed have a human face, but have animal hearts through ungodliness. These men 'draw out the breast' when they freely preach their error. They 'give suck to the young,'

---

3 Ovid, *Remedia Amoris*, lns. 91 f.
4 St. Jerome is incorrectly cited here.

That the books of heretics ought to be burned

when they wrongly strengthen the minds of the little ones following them by nourishing, when they publish wicked things, unto ungodliness."[5] Since therefore it is established by very evident reasons, and by most certain experience of things, that heretics' books greatly harm Christendom, it necessarily follows from this that such books ought to be burned, or obliterated from the world in any other way, so that they could not be read by anyone.

If a water well, or public fountain, from which the people are accustomed to draw drinking water were to be spoiled with poison, he who governs the people, ought to block up the well, lest some incautious person perhaps drinking from it were to perish. If the governor of the people would not want to block the well, but wants it to lie open to everyone, by that very fact he should be deservedly reckoned an enemy of the whole people. It is very clearly certain that nothing different ought to be said about heretics' books. For their books serve as it were like public wells, after they have been brought into the public: which since they are infected with the poison of heresy, it will be necessary to remove them from the entire world lest someone perhaps going to them, draw the poison of heresy from them, by which he may be infected and perish. Whoever then when he could forbid them, permits them, will be justly reckoned an open enemy of all Christendom. Because he wants to destroy all the faithful whom he could, and draw into pestiferous errors, when he does not remove heretical books from them, which offer an occasion of heresies. For as Pope Symmachus said very well: "There is not a great difference whether you inflict death or allow it to be done. For he is proved to have inflicted death upon the weak, who did not prevent it when he could have done so."[6]

---

5 *Commentaria in Jeremiam*, bk. 20, c. 4 (PL 111, 1249B-C). Cf. St. Gregory, *Moralia*, bk. 20, c. 6, n. 15 (PL 76, 116A).
6 *Decretum Gratiani*, pt. 1, dist. 83, pars 1 (PL 187, 399B).

Book 2, Chapter 15

And certainly (so that I may speak frankly) every king, or governor, or mayor, or any other authority deliberately allowing heretics' books to be sold to subjects in the lands of his jurisdiction, besides the fact that he sins gravely, solely on account of this he gives great suspicion of heresy against himself. This can be proved by a very clear testimony of Blessed Pope Innocent III, who in a letter says these words: "Certainly to neglect to act against the wicked when one can, is nothing else but to support them. And it does not lack an indication of secret complicity with them on the part of those who refrain from impeding a manifest crime."[7] There is certainly no better way whereby one can prevent heresies from arising among the people, and stop them from spreading further when they have risen up, than if the books of heretics, from which an incautious man can easily drink the venom of heresy, are prohibited. Hence it is that according to the opinion of Innocent III, a king or any other authority does not lack an indication of secret complicity, who refrains from impeding heresies by the burning of books. And one is not merely suspect of heresy, who allows heretics' books to be sold when he could forbid this: but he will be guilty before God of all the heresies into which the readers of those books, having taken the occasion from them, shall have fallen. For Paul when speaking about such men, says: "They who do such things, are worthy of death; and not only they that do them, but they also that consent to them that do them" (Rom. 1, 32). The Ordinary Gloss, when interpreting this verse, says: "To keep silent, is to consent, when you could reprove."[8] And [Pseudo-] Blessed Pope Damasus says: "He who can obstruct and perturb the wicked, and does not do so; it is nothing other than to support their impiety."[9] If heretics

---

7 *Ibid.*, c. 3 (*Error*) (PL 187, 401A); Innocent III, Register of letters, bk. 5, n. 4 (PL 214, 952A).
8 PL 114, 474.
9 *Decretum Gratiani*, pt. 2, *causa* 23, q. 3, c. 8 (*Qui potest*) (PL

That the books of heretics ought to be burned

harm believers by their books (as we said), it necessarily follows that every ruler is a partaker of the same harm, who, when he could, does not want to avoid such harm, especially if the ruler was admonished about the harm, which could arise from the reading of such books.

We find a prefigurement of which opinion very perfectly delineated in the Old Testament: where about the owner of an ox pushing with his horn, who having been warned did not want to shut him up, God made this law: "If the ox was wont to push with his horn yesterday and the day before, and they warned his master, and he did not shut him up, and he shall kill a man or a woman: then the ox shall be stoned, and his owner also shall be put to death" (Ex. 21, 29). God then ordered the owner of the ox pushing with his horn to be killed for no other reason except because he judged him to be a murderer, even though he had killed no one with his own hands. Yet because the owner did not want to shut up the ox, and in this way he could have prevented the man's death, the death is imputed to him, just as though he himself had killed him with his own hands. It is indeed just that he be held guilty of that harm, on account of whose guilt and negligence it is evident that that harm occurred. It is evident that the ruler who when admonished that some books are pernicious and troublesome to the Catholic faith, does not want to forbid them, ought to be bound by a similar punishment. For if afterwards some men from the reading of those books would incur the death of their souls, their death will be imputed to the ruler, who when he could, did not want to remove the occasion of death. Wherefore Our Savior says: "He that shall scandalize one of these little ones that believe in me, it were better for him that a millstone should be hanged about his neck, and that he should be drowned in the depth of the sea" (Mt. 18, 6). Without any doubt he scandalizes

---

187, 1171B); cf. Pope Damasus, *Opera apocrypha* (PL 13, 431A).

believers in Christ, who give them an occasion of departing from the faith which Christ and his Apostles taught.

He who writes a book in favor of some heresy, clearly scandalizes believers in Christ: because he gives an occasion to others to depart from the true faith. But he who neglects to prohibit books of this kind when he could, has the same guilt as if he had written the books. Certainly he has the guilt of the doer, who neglects to correct what he could: wherefore he also is said to have scandalized believers in Christ, who neglects to forbid heretics' books. Thus it would be better for this man (according to the Savior's saying) "that a millstone should be hanged about his neck, and that he should be drowned in the depth of the sea." On account of these same very pressing reasons not only the Supreme Pontiffs, upon whom this business is incumbent, but also emperors and kings, who wanted to have some advantage from the Catholic faith, have legislated by laws and decrees that heretics' books ought to be burned for many centuries. For the famous Constantine, who firstly subjected the majesty of the empire to Christ's humility, ordered that all the books of the Arians be burned, having threatened with the punishment of death all who kept such books. And so that greater trust may be given to my words, I decided to insert here the letter of the same Constantine, which he wrote about this matter to the bishops and the people, which is the following.

Victor Constantine Maximus Augustus, to the bishops and people

Since Arius has imitated wicked and impious persons, it is just that he should undergo the like ignominy. Wherefore as Porphyry, that enemy of piety, for having composed licentious treatises against religion, found a suitable recompense, and such as thenceforth branded him with infamy, overwhelming him with deserved reproach, his impious writings also having been destroyed; so now it seems fit both that Arius and such as hold his sentiments should be denominated Porphyrians, that they may take their appellation from those whose conduct they have imitated. And in addition to this, if any treatise composed by Arius should be discovered, let it be consigned to the flames, in order that not only his depraved doctrine may be suppressed, but also that no memorial of him may be by any means left. This therefore I decree, that if anyone shall be detected in concealing a book compiled by Arius, and shall not instantly bring it forward and burn it, the penalty for this offense shall be death; for immediately after conviction the criminal shall suffer capital punishment. May God preserve you![10]

More than a hundred and fifty years after Constantine the Great, the Emperors Valentinian [III] and Marcian[11] decreed various punishments against the followers of Eutyches and Apollinaris, and then against those who kept books containing the teachings of these men: they made a law containing these words: "Nor shall it be lawful for any of them either to say or write, publish or distribute anything against the Holy Synod of Chalcedon, or to repeat what has been said or written by others on this subject. No person of this kind shall dare to have the books, or preserve the sacrilegious memorials of writers, and if they are convicted of such crimes, they shall be condemned to perpetual deportation. We order that those who, desiring to be informed of these unfortunate heresies, discuss them, shall be sentenced to pay a fine of ten pounds

---

10 *Historia tripartite* (Socrates), bk. 2, c. 15 (PL 69, 934B).
11 Valentinian III was the emperor of the West from 450 to 455 A.D., and Marcian was the Roman Emperor of the East from 450 to 457 A.D.

of gold to Our Treasury, and those who have attempted to teach them these unlawful doctrines shall be condemned to death. All treatises of this kind, and all books which contain the dangerous dogmas of Eutyches and Apollinaris, shall be committed to the flames, so that every trace of their wicked perversity may be destroyed by fire. It is only just that a penalty of equal severity should be imposed for the commission of this monstrous sacrilege, therefore let the Governors of provinces and their officers, as well as the defenders of cities, know that, if they either fail to obey these rules which We, by the most religious sanction of this law, have decreed shall be observed; or if they permit them to be violated by a display of rashness, they will be compelled to pay a fine of ten pounds of gold to Our Treasury, and, in addition to this, will incur Our resentment."[12] Emperors Theodosius [II] and Valentinian [III] also decreed the same thing, as is evident from the law, *Damnato*.[13]

Behold, you see the emperors' holy diligence about the prohibition of heretical books, and rigor in their burning. But have not the supreme and holy Pontiffs acknowledging this condemned the severity of these laws? Not at all, nay, rather they have commended it by words and deed,

---

12 *The Code of Justinian*, bk. 1, tit. 5 (*De haereticis*), l. 8 (*Quicumque*), nn. 9-13.

13 "Let no one venture to either have in his possession, read, or copy, the impious books of the wicked and sacrilegious Nestorius, written against the venerated sect of the orthodox, and the decrees of the Holy Convocation of bishops at Ephesus, and which We order shall be diligently sought out and publicly burned; so that no one may mention the above-stated name in any religious discussion, and these sectaries have any opportunity of holding any assembly in their city, country, or suburban houses, or anywhere else, either secretly or openly. We have determined to deprive all such persons of the right to hold assemblies, and they all are hereby notified that any violator of this law will be punished with the confiscation of his property" (*Ibid.*, l 6 (*Damnato*)).

That the books of heretics ought to be burned

themselves doing the same thing, and commanding others to do the same thing by their decrees. For Pope Leo I, in a letter to Bishop Turibius of Astorga speaks thus: "Care must be taken, and the priestly diligence exercised to the uttermost, to prevent falsified copies that are out of harmony with the pure Truth being used in reading. And the apocryphal scriptures, which, under the names of Apostles,[14] form a nursery-ground for many falsehoods, are not only to be proscribed, but also taken away altogether and burnt to ashes in the fire. For although there are certain things in them which seem to have a show of piety, yet they are never free from poison, and through the allurements of their stories they have the secret effect of first beguiling men with miraculous narratives, and then catching them in the noose of some error. Wherefore if any bishop has either not forbidden the possession of apocryphal writings in men's houses, or under the name of being canonical has suffered those copies to be read in church which are vitiated with the spurious alterations of Priscillian, let him know that he is to be accounted a heretic, since he who does not reclaim others from error shows that he himself has gone astray."[15]

Now what Pope Gelasius reckoned ought to be done with heretics' books, the *Liber Pontificalis* declares, which when describing the life of this Gelasius relates these things among others: "In his time Manicheans were discovered in the city of Rome, whom he transported into exile and whose books he burned with fire before the doors of the basilica of Holy Mary."[16]

Furthermore two archbishops, legates of the Apostolic See, firstly ordered the books of John Wycliffe to be burned: then the universal Church in two general councils gathered

---

14 Viz., the Manichaeans.
15 Letter 15, c. 15 (PL 54, 688A-B).
16 *The Book of the Popes* (New York: Columbia University Press, 1916), n. 51 (Pope Gelasius), p. 111.

in Rome and Constance ordered the same thing to be done, as it is very clearly established from the acts of the Council of Constance, in the eighth session, where after it is said that the books of the aforesaid John Wycliffe were condemned to the fire in the Roman Synod, a decision of the same Council of Constance is moreover added, which expressed by these words, follows shortly afterwards: "This holy synod, therefore, in the name of our Lord Jesus Christ, in ratifying and approving the sentences of the aforesaid archbishops and of the council of Rome, repudiates and condemns forever, by this decree, the aforesaid articles and each one of them in particular, and the books of John Wycliffe called by him *Dialogus* and *Trialogus*, and the same author's other books, volumes, treatises and pamphlets (no matter what name these may go under, and for which purpose this description is to be regarded as an adequate listing of them). It forbids the reading, teaching, expounding and citing of the said books or of any one of them in particular, unless it is for the purpose of refuting them. It forbids each and every Catholic henceforth, under pain of anathema, to preach, teach or affirm in public the said articles or any one of them in particular, or to teach, approve or hold the said books, or to refer to them in any way, unless this is done, as has been said, for the purpose of refuting them. It orders, moreover, that the aforesaid books, treatises, volumes and pamphlets are to be burnt in public, in accordance with the decree of the synod of Rome, as stated above. This holy synod orders local Ordinaries to attend with vigilance to the execution and due observance of these things, insofar as each one is responsible, in accordance with the law and canonical ordinances."[17]

And although these testimonies which we have presented could be enough for the confirmation of our opinion, still so that we may leave it more firm, I will to recall older and more ancient examples, and cite the Acts of the Apostles in which

---

17   Mansi 27, 634-635.

we will find the clearest testimony for this matter. For about the miracles Paul performed at Ephesus, that history when discussing these things says these words: "Many of them that believed, came confessing and declaring their deeds. And many of them who had followed curious arts, brought together their books, and burnt them before all; and counting the price of them, they found the money to be fifty thousand pieces of silver. So mightily grew the word of God, and was confirmed" (Acts 19, 18-20). These are Luke's words in the Acts of the Apostles. If at that time the books of curious arts were burned due to Paul's command, much more should heretics' books be burned, which could harm more. But it ought not to be passed by without notice that which Luke added to exalt that burning of the books, speaking thus: "So mightily grew the word of God, and was confirmed." For by those words Luke clearly teaches us that the burning of such books is very rich evidence of an increase and confirmation of God's word in them. Wherefore it is also permitted to conclude on the contrary that strong evidence of a decrease and collapse of faith is in those who do not wish to burn heretics' books when they could.

Next, Origen testifies that after the times of the Apostles this was observed in the whole Church, who says: "If this case were judged today among men and if an examination were held among the rulers of the churches concerning those who have endured the penalty of Divine vengeance, because, for instance, they teach things that are different from the churches, would it not be judged that, whatever they have said, whatever they have taught, whatever they have left behind in writing, all of it should utterly perish equally with their own ashes?"[18] From whose words it is established that at his time it was the opinion of the whole Church that heretics' books ought to be burned. Add to all these things, that Eusebius of Caesarea in a book concerning his times

---

18 *Homilies on Numbers*, hom. 9, n. 2 (PG 12, 624D-625A).

relates that the books of the sophist Protagoras were burnt by the Athenians.[19] Although Eusebius in that place does not explain the reason for this burning, still one ought not to believe that it was for any other reason than so that they might provide for their nation and avoid the harm that such books could inflict upon readers. If heathen men had such great concern for their nation, which they had assumed to govern: it is much more just that Christian rulers would take greater care of the Catholic Church, for which the Son of God deigned to undergo death, and consign heretics' books, which can harm the Church much more than those of the sophist Protagoras, to the avenging flames. For it is not equitable that Christian rulers would be inferior to the rulers of heathens in the right governing of a nation.

But if, as we proved it ought to be done, heretics' books ought to be burned: a punishment worthy of his crime will doubtlessly be given thereby to any heretical author: because according to the saying of the Wise Man, "By what things a man sinneth, by the same also he is tormented" (Wis. 11, 17). For all heretics sin by a desire for vainglory, from which pestilent root, just as many other wicked deeds arise, so also heresy, which is the most serious evil of them all. For he who seeks too much after popular glory, will leave nothing untried to attain it, and direct all his actions to it as to a goal. When he speaks, when he writes, when he disputes, or when he does whatever other action, he will always have before his eyes the glory of the people, because this is the highest of all his desires. But if he loses hope that he can attain this glory which he very ardently desires in any other way, then he tries to fabricate a new doctrine so that by its newness he may draw others to the admiration of himself. Next, from the same powerless desire for popular glory arises pertinac-

---

19 "This man the Athenians punished by banishment, and burned his books publicly in the middle of the marketplace" (*Preparation for the Gospel*, bk. 14, c. 19).

That the books of heretics ought to be burned

ity which is so inflexible, that although he is overcome in a dispute in everyone's judgment, he never wants to give up. For he prefers to persist in error, than to admit himself conquered, lest by this occasion he lose even a very small part of the glory which he immoderately desires.

For heretics are very well represented in those very proud men, who said: "Come, let us make a city and a tower, the top whereof may reach to heaven: and let us make our name famous" (Gen. 11, 4). Since in fact heretics want to make their names famous in the world, and for this reason construct towers of proud vanity, and compose books full of heresies. So ingrained is the desire for vainglory in all heretics, that by it, as by the proximate cause Augustine decided to give the definition of a heretic, speaking thus: "A heretic is one who either devises or follows false and new opinions, for the sake of some temporal profit, especially that he may lord and be honored above others."[20] For this reason Paul when wishing to induce the Philippians to the unity of faith, admonishes them to abstain from all vainglory, which he knew can harm very much this unity of the faith. "Being of one accord, agreeing in sentiment, let nothing be done through contention" (2, 2-3). Thus it is just that as through the heretic's writing of books he procured popular glory, he would not attain this when his books have been burned, and in this way he will be punished in that in which he sinned. Long ago a wicked man (as [Valerius Maximus[21]] relates[22]) burnt with fire and destroyed in a short time the temple of Diana in

---

20   *De utilitate credendi*, c. 1, n. 1 (PL 42, 65).
21   Strabo seems to be incorrectly cited here.
22   "A man was found to plan the burning of the temple of Ephesian Diana so that through the destruction of this most beautiful building his name might be spread through the whole world" (*Factorum et Dictorum Memorabilium* (*Memorable Deeds and Sayings*), bk. 8, c. 14, n. 5). Cf. Strabo, *Geography*, bk. 14, c. 1, n. 22.

Ephesus built with marvelous workmanship, which had been built over a long period of time, and at great expense. When that man was arrested, and asked why he had dared to do such a serious and such a sacrilegious crime, he answered that he wished to leave to posterity the remembrance of himself, which because he could not attain this by brilliant deeds done by himself, he hoped that he would attain this by a very wicked crime. The judges understanding this, by a public edict forbade any writer who wrote that sacrilegious crime, to divulge its perpetrator by his own name, so that having suppressed his name, the remembrance which he so intemperately and unbridledly wished to transmit to posterity, would be very quickly obliterated. Whoever shall consider the matter well, will easily understand that no sheep is similar to another sheep, as any heretical man is to that wicked man. He overturned and destroyed the temple of Diana: and the heretic tries to tear apart, turn upside down, and throw into disorder God's Church, which is His temple. That wicked man was motivated by the feeble desire for vainglory to perpetrate that impious crime, and a heretic is led from the very ardent love of the same vainglory, to fabricate a new doctrine, and in this way to depart from the unity of the Church. It is fitting that a similar punishment fall upon the heretic, namely, that he not attain that glory, which he so anxiously desired through the publication of books, when all his books have been completely obliterated.

Something similar to this is that which Judas Maccabaeus did with Nicanor, the commander of the army of King Antiochus. For after he was killed in war, Judas ordered Nicanor's tongue to be cut off and given to the birds. Why so? Ought one to suppose that Judas Maccabaeus commanded it without cause? By no means. Nicanor had in fact blasphemed against Almighty God, arrogating to himself to such an extent, that he feared not to say that one ought to rather obey him than God. For this reason Judas commanded that his tongue be cut off even after his death, so that he might punish him in that member, by which he had sinned so impiously.[23] All heretics are blasphemers, because they do not hesitate to call the Church, which is always taught by God, a liar, or at least deceived. They are also arrogant, to such an extent that they attribute more to their own judgment than to the opinions of all the holy Doctors. I have said too little, unless I say that they attribute to themselves even more than to the ruling of the whole Church. These men through books as through quasi-tongues still speak when dead, and by them spread abroad their blasphemies against God and His Church. Therefore one ought to cut off these tongues, that is, their books, and not merely to be plucked to pieces by birds, but consigned to be burned with flames: so that no trace of them could remain.

To any of the heretics doubtlessly befits that which by God's command the prophet Jeremias spoke to Edom, speaking thus: "Thy arrogancy hath deceived thee, and the pride of thy heart: O thou that dwellest in the clefts of the rock, and endeavourest to lay hold on the height of the hill: but though thou shouldst make thy nest as high as an eagle, I will bring thee down from thence, saith the Lord. And Edom shall be desolate: every one that shall pass by it, shall be astonished, and shall hiss at all its plagues. As Sodom was overthrown and Gomorrha, and the neighbours thereof, saith the Lord" (49, 16-18). The assembly of heretics no matter how many and frequent it is at times will, by God dispersing it, be forsaken: because when the true faith has been uncovered and fully understood, their heresy will be abandoned by all, and there will not be anyone who adheres to it. Long ago the heresy of Arius was very frequent, and extended through various regions, but now it is become a desert like Edom: because all rejected it and withdrew from it. That heresy was abandoned to such an extent, that not only there are no

---

23 Cf. II Mach. 15, 33.

Arians, but there also there are no books of the Arians, which would teach and defend that heresy.

Today Luther's heresy is very common and full with many people, who like an eagle made high its nest, deceived with so much pride and arrogance, that it does not fear to set its mouth against heaven,[24] and say that the Church was in darkness until his preaching: but I am confident in the Lord,[25] that at length it shall be desolate as Edom. But how shall the assembly of heretics be desolate? "As Sodom was overthrown and Gomorrha, and the neighbours," the Lord says. Now these cities, as sacred history relates, were overthrown by fire and perished by burning.[26] Thus it is befitting to burn with fire not only heretics, but also their books, so that every heresy would be desolate like Edom, and there would be no one dwelling in it. The city of Jericho was not only destroyed by the children of Israel, but burnt with fire, and totally destroyed, so that when the foundation was removed no occasion of rebuilding would remain.[27] However much a heresy has been destroyed, refuted with reasons, and completely effaced from the Christian world: still if the books which teach and defend it remain, its foundations seem to remain, upon which that heresy could easily be rebuilt. Whoever wishes that Christendom be well cared for, should make all the heretics' books, if he can, to burn, lest perhaps a believer by reading, be wounded by them, and perish. If communications with heretics, according to Paul's precept,[28] ought to be avoided lest we be injured by their fellowship, and the writings of heretics (as we previously said) can harm

---

24 Cf. Ps. 72, 9.
25 Cf. Ps. 10, 2.
26 Cf. Gen. 19, 24-25.
27 Cf. Jos. 6.
28 Cf. II Tim. 2, 23: "And avoid foolish and unlearned questions, knowing that they beget strifes"; I Cor. 15, 33: "Be not seduced: Evil communications corrupt good manners."

That the books of heretics ought to be burned

us more than words: it follows that books ought to be avoided with greater care than words, and one ought to be watchful with much greater diligence about their prohibition.

And completely the same thing that we said about heretics' books, ought to be done regarding the books of Jews and other infidels, who happen to live among Christians and under the rule of Christians. Yet there is a difference among Jews' books that ought to be considered: because not all are on the same level, and hence also ought not to be judged by the same law. For some are absolutely good, such as are the all the books of the Old Testament, and other which contain true explanations of those books, and these ought to be permitted to the Jews, just as they are permitted to those, so that they may keep the rite and ceremonies of the Mosaic Law. Because in all of them is found some evidence of the Catholic faith, which is represented in them, as the truth in a figure, and a body in a shadow. There are other books composed by the rabbis of the Jews, full of lies and nonsense, and fables; and (what is much worse) many blasphemies against Christ and His Law.[29] By these books their ordinary

---

29 Pope Innocent IV: "To THE KING of France: The wicked perfidy of the Jews, from whose hearts our Redeemer has not removed the veil of blindness because of the enormity of their crime, but has so far permitted to remain in blindness such ·as in a measure covers Israel, does not heed, as it should, the fact that Christian piety received them and patiently allows them to live among them through pity only. Instead, it commits enormities that arouse shock in those who hear them and horror in those who mention them. For, ungrateful to the Lord Jesus Christ Who, in the abundance of His kindness, patiently expects their conversion, they, displaying no shame for their guilt nor reverence for the honor of the Christian faith, throw away and despise the law of Moses and the prophets and follow certain traditions of their elders. On account of these same traditions, the Lord reproves them in the Gospel saying: 'Why do you transgress God's commandment and render it void in the interest of your traditions, teachings: doc-

men are seduced, and nourished, encouraged, and detained

trines and commands of men?' In traditions of this sort they rear and nurture their children. These traditions are called 'Talmud' in Hebrew. It is a large book, exceeding in size the text of the Bible. In it are often found blasphemies against God and His Christ, obviously entangled fables about the Blessed Virgin abusive errors and unheard-of follies. But of the laws and the doctrine of the prophets they make their children altogether ignorant. They fear that if the truth which is found in the law and the prophets, indicating clearly that the only begotten Son of God is to appear in the flesh, be furnished these children would be converted to the Christian faith and humbly return to their Redeemer.

Not content with these things, they make Christian women nurses for their children, in insult to the Christian faith, and with these women they commit many shameful actions. On account of this, the faithful must beware lest they incur divine indignation, since they shamefully suffer them to do things which bring confusion upon our faith.

Indeed our beloved son the chancellor of Paris and the doctors, the regents of Paris, after having at the command of our predecessor, Pope Gregory of blessed memory, as expressed in a decree, read the abovenamed book of abuse and others, along with all their glosses, taken from them by force, and after having examined them, consigned them to the flames, in the presence of clergy and laity, to the confusion of the perfidy of the Jews, as we have seen in their letters. You, also, Catholic king and most Christian prince, have given fitting help in these matters and extended your favor, and on account of this we recommend the Royal Excellency with fitting praise to God and bestow our gratitude upon you. Nevertheless, because the blasphemous abuse of these Jews has not yet ceased, nor their troubles as yet given them understanding, we asked your Royal Highness and we beseech you in the name of the Lord Jesus Christ to strike down with merited severity all the detestable and heinous excesses of this sort which they have committed in insult of the Creator and to the injury of the Christian name and which you have with laudable piety begun to prosecute. You should order that the above-mentioned abusive books, condemned by these doctors, as well as all the commentaries which have been exam-

That the books of heretics ought to be burned

in their perfidy, lest they be converted to Christ's faith. Such books as these rightly ought to be burned: because just as they ought to be compelled not to impede Christ's faith by evil acts of persuading, so it is just that they be compelled not to impede by published books, so that at least some of them may be converted to the faith of the Gospel. And just as they ought to be compelled, not to blaspheme Christ and His holy Law by words, so also that they would not blaspheme by things written. Now all these things are removed if such books are burned, which Christian rulers can legitimately do, since the Jews as a punishment for the sin which they committed in Christ's death, were made slaves.[30]

---

ined and condemned by them, be burned in fire wherever they can be found throughout your kingdom. You should stringently forbid them hereafter to have any Christian nurses or other Christian servants, lest the children of the freeborn serve the children of the maidservants. As slaves reproved by the Lord, whose death they sinfully plotted, they must acknowledge themselves, as a result of this act, as slaves of those whom the death of Christ set free, while condemning them to slavery. Thus henceforth we may with fitting praise be able to commend to God the zeal of your sincerity.
Given at the Lateran, on the ninth of May, in the first year [1244]" (Solomon Grayzel, *The Church and the Jews in the XIIIth century* (Philadelphia: The Dropsie College for Hebrew and Cognate Learning, 1933), pp. 251 ff).
30 "...Jews, in consequence of their sin, are or were destined to perpetual slavery" (St. Thomas Aquinas, *On the Government of the Jews: To the Duchess of Brabant*, in *Selected political writings* (Oxford: Blackwell, 1974), p. 85. "Jews are slaves of rulers by civil slavery" (III, q. 68, a. 10 ad 2um)).

Chapter XVI

Some arguments whereby some try to prove that heretics' books ought to be permitted are answered.

Even though I have proved with very pressing and very evident reasons that heretics' books ought not to be permitted: but ought to be burned, or destroyed in some way: nevertheless there are not lacking, even among those who boast that they are Christians, who are not afraid to oppose this Catholic truth. For when, some years ago, I was in Flanders, I frequently was involved in a dispute with a learned and Catholic man, according to external appearances, yet I was suspecting that he was a heretic. And some years later I found in Paris and elsewhere men of the same sort, who although they wanted to look like Christians, still they were very pertinaciously maintaining that heretics' books ought not to be burned. For there are now many such men everywhere, whom Christ Our Savior foretold would come, wearing "the clothing of sheep, but inwardly they are ravening wolves" (Mt. 7, 15). I will relate here the general arguments of them all, and when I refute them very easily, I will show that they are not even supported by a staff of a reed.[1] Firstly in fact they say that many truly Catholic and well-discussed things are in heretics' books, many knotty questions of Sacred Scripture are very well-explained, many obscure things elegantly elucidated, which are completely not found in Catholic authors, or they are not as well explained and arranged. Now they say that it is unjust to deprive the Catholic Church of all these things, and hence they conclude that it is also unjust to burn such books of

---

1 Cf. Ez. 29, 6: "And all the inhabitants of Egypt shall know that I am the Lord: because thou hast been a staff of a reed to the house of Israel."

heretics, from the burning of which such grave detriment clearly arises to Christendom.

This argumentation, which they consider very forceful, is lame in both feet: because both premises, by which it attempts to proceed to the conclusion, are false. For that which it firstly assumes, namely, that many good and well-discussed things are found in heretics' books which can nowise be found in Catholic authors, is false, and clearly injurious to Divine Providence. I certainly admit that there are some true and Catholic, and beautifully explained things in heretics' books, otherwise no one would want to believe them, if they all were full of lies. But that those true and Catholic things which are well discussed, can nowise be found in the Catholic Doctors, this is what I very steadfastly deny. For even though God has granted to bad and unbelieving men the function of prophesying, still He did not want those things which they predicted by prophesying, to be predicted by them alone: but He decided that those same things to be manifested to the world much better and more clearly through the mouths of other prophets. The well-known wicked Balaam prophesied about the coming of the Messias:[2] but other prophets predicted this much better and more clearly than he. The well-known Caiphas, who was the priest in the year in which Christ Our Savior suffered, prophesied that Jesus was going to die for the salvation of all.[3] Yet David, Isaias, and many other holy prophets predicted more extensively and more clearly that this salvation of the human race was to be had through Christ's death.

When God firstly willed to reveal some truth necessary for the salvation of the soul, He never did it except through

---

2 "I shall see him, but not now: I shall behold him, but not near. A star shall rise out of Jacob and a sceptre shall spring up from Israel" (Num. 24, 17).
3 "...one man should die for the people, and that the whole nation perish not" (Jn. 11, 50).

Replies to objections that heretics' books ought to be permitted

just and holy men. Long ago God gave the Old Law, but He handed it down to the people of Israel through the hands of the very holy man, Moses. A long time afterwards He instituted the Evangelical Law; yet He did not want its preachers to be thieves, assassins, murderers, or adulterers, but only very holy men, namely, His Apostles, whom He had chosen for this work. Christ Our Savior commanded them, "Go ye into the whole world, and preach the gospel to every creature" (Mk. 16, 15): yet He did not want them to do this immediately, for He commanded them "that they should not depart from Jerusalem, but should wait for the promise of the Father" (Acts 1, 4): and firstly "receive the power of the Holy Ghost coming upon them" (v. 8). Why so? Namely, so that through the coming of the Holy Ghost He would make them worthy heralds of the Gospel, without Whom they would have been unworthy to announce such a sublime law to the world. For because Paul had understood that this grace of the Holy Ghost is necessary for worthily announcing the truth of the Gospel, he said concerning himself and the other Apostles: "Our sufficiency is from God, who also hath made us fit ministers of the new testament" (II Cor. 3, 5-6). Thus it ought not to be believed that God, Who at another time did not will to reveal to the world the truth of the Gospel except through men filled with the Holy Ghost, now would want to make known through schismatic heretics some part of the Gospel hitherto unknown.

And it also ought not to be believed that the Church, which long ago was copiously instructed by Christ, and now daily is abundantly taught by Him, would be ignorant of something among those which necessarily ought to be believed. Otherwise Christ would not have sufficiently fulfilled His promise, whereby obliging her confidence, He said: "But the Paraclete, the Holy Ghost, whom the Father will send in my name, he will teach you all things, and bring all things to your mind, whatsoever I shall have said to you" (Jn. 14, 26). If Christ necessarily taught everything that ought to be believed, and the Holy Ghost gave the understanding of all those things, it follows that the Church does not lack knowledge of any of those things. "Can I hide from Abraham what I am about to do?" (Gen. 18, 17). If God did not want to hide from Abraham what He was about to do on account of friendship, much less did He hide from the Church those things which are necessary for salvation. Because He has embraced her with a much more ardent love, since she is His spouse. And God teaches us this same thing through the prophet Amos speaking thus: "The Lord God doth nothing without revealing his secret to his servants the prophets" (3, 7). He did not say to any prophets whatsoever, but only to His servants. Therefore from the believers of whom the Church consists, we ought to learn, if we desire to know something, and not from heretics. Because the Church in those things which pertain to piety and religion, is much more amply taught by Him, Who can neither deceive nor be deceived.

And the martyr Irenaeus teaches this same thing speaking thus: "Since therefore we have such proofs, it is not necessary to seek the truth among others which it is easy to obtain from the Church; since the Apostles, like a rich man [depositing his money] in a bank, lodged in her hands most copiously all things pertaining to the truth: so that every man, whosoever will, can draw from her the water of life.[4] For she is the entrance to life; all others are thieves and robbers. On this account are we bound to avoid them, but to make choice of the thing pertaining to the Church with the utmost diligence, and to lay hold of the tradition of the truth. For how stands the case? Suppose there arises a dispute relative to some important question among us, should we not have recourse to the most ancient Churches with which the Apostles held constant intercourse, and learn from them what is certain and clear in regard to the present question? For how should it be

---

4 Cf. Apoc. 22, 17.

if the Apostles themselves had not left us writings? Would it not be necessary, [in that case,] to follow the course of the tradition which they handed down to those to whom they did commit the Churches?"[5] So speaks Irenaeus the martyr and disciple of the martyr Polycarp. From whose words it is evidently established that the Church is very full of every teaching of truth, and not needing the teaching of any of the heretics.

Next, even if the Church were not to know something pertaining to the faith, it ought not to be believed, nor is it probable, that it was revealed by God to heretics. "I confess to thee, O Father," Christ Our Savior says, "Lord of heaven and earth, because thou hast hid these things from the wise and prudent, and hast revealed them to the little ones" (Mt. 11, 25). God reveals to little ones, I say, the things which He had hid from the wise and prudent, not to the proud, not to those who are very great in their own estimation, so that they would not hesitate to prefer their own opinion to the opinion of everyone else. God reveals, I say, to the little ones, that is, to the humble, who consider their own qualities to be of very little worth, who never wish to rely upon their own prudence, and who do not hesitate to bring into captivity their understanding unto the obedience of Christ.[6] God often reveals mysteries to little ones of this kind, which He hid from the wise and prudent; not to heretics, who are so great in their estimation of themselves, that they think that they surpass all other men by their wisdom and they are not afraid to attribute their own judgment more than to the definitions of the whole Church.

Moreover, albeit we would grant that some things are treated in a Catholic manner and faithfully in heretics' books, which are not found in Catholics' books, still those things ought not to be taken from heretics. Because heretics mix

---

5 *Adversus Haereses*, bk. 3, c. 4, n. 1 (PG 7, 853B-855B).
6 Cf. II Cor. 10, 5.

together with those true things many other false things at the same time; and it ought to be feared that the readers, having been allured by the sweetness of the truth, being incautious swallow down the poison of falsity. It is preferable therefore to lack however much good food, than to eat it mixed with fatal poison. And hence it is established to be false, that which was assumed in the second place in the aforesaid argumentation, where it is said, that it is unjust to deprive the Church of those true and well-arranged things, which are found in heretics' books. It is certainly not unjust, nay, it is on the contrary very just and very holy, and hence also necessary, that we remove however much good food from our Mother Church, in which we were begotten through Baptism, and from our brother believers, if we know that they are mixed together with deadly poison. The teaching of heretics is such in every respect, which always has false things mixed together with true things: wherefore it ought to be avoided by everyone.

Now Gregory so teaches this very clearly, who in his *Moralia* speaks thus: "Heretics have this especial peculiarity, that they mix good and evil, that so they may easily delude the sense of the hearer. For if they always said wrong, soon discovered in their wrongheadedness, they would be the less able to win a way for that which they desire. Again, if they always thought right, then, surely, they would never have been heretics. But whilst with artfulness of deceiving they engage themselves with either, both by the evil they vitiate the good, and by the good they conceal the evil, to the end that it may be readily admitted; just as he that presents a cup of poison, touches the brim of the cup with honied sweets, and while this that has a sweet flavor is tasted at the first sip, that too which brings death is unhesitatingly swallowed. Thus heretics mix right with wrong, that by making a show of good things, they may draw hearers to themselves, and by setting forth evil they may corrupt them with a secret pesti-

Replies to objections that heretics' books ought to be permitted

lence."[7] Behold, you see proved by Gregory's very clear testimony, that heretics' teaching is always like a poisoned drink. And hence it necessarily follows that whoever has some care of Christendom, is also obliged to destroy such a drink lest it avail to ever harm the same Christendom. For it is better for the Church to be without such a drink, than to drink something poisoned.

Pope Leo I teaches the same opinion, who (as we showed in the preceding chapter) in a letter to Bishop Turibius of Astorga when commanding that the books of the Priscillianists, and other apocryphal writings, be avoided and burned, that which could be objected to this opinion, he rejects, speaking thus: "For although there are certain things in them which seem to have a show of piety, yet they are never free from poison, and through the allurements of their stories they have the secret effect of first beguiling men with miraculous narratives, and then catching them in the noose of some error."[8]

For this reason Christ Our Savior rebuked the demons crying out and saying that He is the Son of God, forbidding them to say such things.[9] The things that they were saying were and are very true; nevertheless He forbade them to speak, and yet not without cause: but it ought to be believed that He did so on account of a very just reason. It was namely so that He might take away from the people an occasion of believing the demons again when they were speaking false things. For Bede testifies that this is the reason of His prohibition, when speaking thus: "Now the Psalmist makes clear why the Lord Himself forbids the demons, who says: 'But to the sinner God hath said: Why dost thou declare my justices… in thy mouth?' (Ps. 49, 16). A sinner is forbidden to preach the Lord, lest anyone listening to his

---

7 Bk. 5, c. 11, n. 28 (PL 75, 693B-694A).
8 Letter 15, c. 15 (PL 54, 688B).
9 Cf. Lk. 4, 41.

preaching should follow him in his error, for the devil is an evil master, who always mingles false things with true, that the semblance of truth may cover the witness of fraud."[10] If Christ Our Savior on account of that reason forbade the demons crying out, it is just that the Church which ought to conform herself to Him, as a body to the head, should forbid heretical authors, who are the offspring of demons, so that demons could not do harm with words. Therefore, the Church acts prudently, when it prohibits heretics' books, and decrees that they ought to be burned: because she justly fears that what the Wise Man says may happen: "He that toucheth pitch, shall be defiled with it" (Eccli. 13, 1).

Secondly moreover, those who were disputing with me that heretics' books ought not to be burned were objecting to me, speaking thus: "Granted, heretics' books contain some false things, which we cannot deny: because otherwise they would not be heretics, yet the injury which such books could inflict upon Christendom can be obviated by another way without their burning. For if those books are cleansed of all errors, then all the rest will remain clean, and then the good things could be offered to those reading without any danger of poison. It is thus bad to burn heretics' books: because by that burning the Church would be deprived of those things which in heretics' books are treated well and in a Catholic manner, without which can be had without any danger from it." It can be easily replied to this objection by those things which were said in response to the previous argument. For there we showed both by reasons taken from Holy Writ, and from the testimony of Saint Irenaeus, that there is nothing true and Catholic in heretics' books, which is not much better and faultlessly treated in Catholics' books. From which it is most evidently concluded that the Church is not deprived of the knowledge of any Catholic truth, even if all the heretics' books would be burned.

---

10 *Expositio in Evangelium S. Lucae*, bk. 2 (PL 92, 381B).

Replies to objections that heretics' books ought to be permitted

There are still two others things by which we can easily refute an objection of this kind. For even if we were to grant that there are some true and Catholicly discussed things in heretics' books, which are not found in Catholics' books, nevertheless it would not be profitable to try to obtain them for two reasons, even though their books would be accurately corrected, and were defecated of all error. Firstly in fact, one ought to consider that the dignity of Sacred Scripture is so great, that it would not be permitted to let anyone touch it, and much less interpret it, and dispute about its meaning: but it ought to be believed that this is allowed only for those who are truly believers, and who accept Sacred Scripture with that reverence becoming to it. Now anyone may easily understand this, if he firstly bears in mind by what name Sacred Scripture is known by. Paul the Apostle who knew the secret things of God,[11] calls Sacred Scripture the Divine Testament, such that he calls the Old Law the Old Testament, but the Evangelical Law he calls the New Testament. For in the Epistle to the Hebrews when speaking about the superiority of the Evangelical Law over the Old Law, which was unable to give grace to sinners, speaks thus: "And therefore he is the mediator of the new testament: that by means of his death, for the redemption of those transgressions, which were under the former testament, they that are called may receive the promise of eternal inheritance" (9, 15). In which words Paul first named the Evangelical Testament and Law "the new testament." Which names came into use to such an extent that among all Catholics, that those two laws are not called otherwise than by the names of the New and the Old Testaments.

God in this Testament did not command any part of His riches for heretics, nor did He make them heirs of His possessions. If it was unbefitting that the son of the bondwoman be made an heir with the son of the free woman, much less

---

11 *Arcana Dei.* Cf. II Cor. 12, 4.

is it fitting that a stranger such as a heretic would receive an inheritance along with the son of the free woman. If the bondwoman, that is, the synagogue (as Paul says[12]) had to be cast out, it is much more just that a stranger and enemy be cast out, that is, the church of the malignant[13] with its heretical children. Because this does not serve, and does not bring any benefit to the Church, just as of old the bondwoman synagogue: but as an enemy and rebel it always persecutes it with a hostile design. Thus having disinherited heretics as very bad children, it necessarily follows that they have no right of beholding the paternal testament, which is Sacred Scripture. If they cannot behold, how is it that they could interpret? Therefore it is nowise fitting to seek from a heretic the interpretation of Sacred Scripture, since it is not allowed for him to interpret it.

Tertullian clearly teaches this opinion speaking thus: "Thus, not being Christians, they have acquired no right to the Christian Scriptures; and it may be very fairly said to them, 'Who are you? When and whence did you come? As you are none of mine, what have you to do with that which is mine? Indeed, Marcion, by what right do you hew my wood? By whose permission, Valentinus, are you diverting the streams of my fountain? By what power, Apelles, are you removing my landmarks? This is my property. Why are you, the rest, sowing and feeding here at your own pleasure? This (I say) is my property. I have long possessed it; I possessed it before you. I hold sure title-deeds from the original owners themselves, to whom the estate belonged. I am the heir of the Apostles. Just as they carefully prepared their will and testament, and committed it to a trust, and adjured [the trustees to be faithful to their charge], even so do I hold it. As for you, they have, it is certain, always held you as disinherited, and rejected you as strangers—as enemies.' But on what ground

---

12 Cf. Gal. 4.
13 Cf. Ps. 21, 17.

Replies to objections that heretics' books ought to be permitted

are heretics strangers and enemies to the Apostles, if it be not from the difference of their teaching, which each individual of his own mere will has either advanced or received in opposition to the Apostles?"[14] And there is no need for the testimony of men, for that which God Himself, Who has spoken through the mouths of the prophets, has given clear testimony. For the very patient Job, when speaking about the theft and violence of heretics, says: "They reap the field that is not their own, and gather the vintage of his vineyard whom by violence they have oppressed" (24, 6). Blessed Gregory in his *Moralia* reckons these words ought to be understood of heretics, speaking thus: "By the name of a 'field' may be denoted the wide compass of Holy Scripture, and heretics 'reap' it not being their own, in that they carry away from it sentences which are infinitely removed from their own notions; which same is furthermore described by the title of a 'vineyard,' in that through the sentences of truth it puts forth the clusters of the virtues; the owner of which vineyard, that is, the originator of Holy Scripture, they as it were 'oppress with violence,' because they endeavor violently to twist because they endeavor to violently distort His meaning in Holy Writ; as He saith, 'But thou hast made me to serve with thy sins, thou hast wearied me with thy iniquities' (Is. 43, 24). And they 'gather the vintage of that vineyard,' in that they heap together therefrom clusters of sentences after the bent of their own understanding."[15] In which words it especially ought to be noted that he says that Sacred Scripture is a field not their own, and hence heretics can neither sow nor reap in it.

But much clearer are those words which God, David being the witness, spoke: "But to the sinner God hath said: Why dost thou declare my justices, and take my testament in thy mouth?" (Ps. 49, 16). Cassiodorus in his commentaries on

---

14 *Prescription against Heretics*, c. 37 (PL 2, 51A-B).
15 Bk. 16, c. 49, n. 62 (PL 76, 1150B-C).

the Psalms speaks thus: "'Testament' refers to both to the Old and the New, for when one is mentioned indeterminately both are being cited. This verse can also refer to heretical teachers presuming to teach God's law, for to 'take' signifies the presumption of the unappointed. It does not seem that He was forbidding believers to read Scripture, regarding which He deigned to admonish sinners especially."[16] Cassiodorus reckons that those words of God said in general to sinners, ought to be interpreted of heretics alone. And if some would contend that those things ought to be understood of all sinners, I will easily concede; because this meaning will not oppose our prior opinion, but will help it very much. For if God is enraged by the sinner, because he dares to declare His justices, and take up His covenant in his mouth, much more for the same reason He will be enraged by the heretic, since he is the worst of all sinners.

There is still another reason, and not less, but perhaps more compelling, on account of which it is not advantageous, nay, and not permitted, especially for the uneducated, to seek the interpretation of Sacred Scripture from heretics' books, even though they may have been cleansed of the dung of heretics. For these things which we are obliged to believe, always ought to be accepted with a firm, and nowise hesitating mind. Otherwise, if such a doubt would have been present, which would hold the mind in suspense and in doubt, this (as we taught above in the first book, in the seventh chapter) would be enough for making a man a heretic. Those things which are said or written by a heretical man always ought to be suspected by a Christian man, because they were said by such a man; unless he already knew their certain truthfulness from another source. Diogenes Laertius in his book, *Lives and Opinions of Eminent Philosophers*, when he discusses about Aristotle, relates that to someone asking, "What do people gain by telling lies?" he answered in this way:

---

16 *Expositio in Psalterium*, pt. 1 (PL 70, 355A).

Replies to objections that heretics' books ought to be permitted

"Just this, that when they speak the truth," he said, "they are not believed."[17] For it is presumed, and justly so, that he always lies. For as the *Rules of Law* says: "Once wicked, he is always presumed wicked."[18] The jurists teach, and correctly so, that this rule ought to be understood of the same kind of malice. For it would be unjust that because someone was caught in the crime of adultery or whatever other crime, merely on account of this, one would be permitted to suspect him of every crime. Yet regarding him who was once caught in some particular crime, it is rightly allowed to suspect him to remain in that crime, until it is fully established about his amendment.

Now it is evident that the heretic erred, and at least at some time he was incorrect, otherwise he would not be a heretic. Thus anyone can justly suspect that he errs or is incorrect in everything he says or writes, unless from another source the truth of those things were fully established. Hence it is that firm trust never ought to be given to him on account of his personal fault: but everything which has not been proved from elsewhere, will also be suspected merely on account of the fact that they were said by him. And it seems to me that the Wise Man thought this when he said: "What truth can be said by a liar?" (Eccli. 34, 4).[19] He does not teach that he necessarily lies, or cannot say the truth: but that he is always suspected to have lied, who was once caught in a lie. For this reason, Blessed Augustine in a letter to Blessed Jerome does not admit that there is in Holy Writ even the least falsehood: because that alone, he says, would take away trust and authority in all the rest.[20]

---

17 Bk. 5, c. 1, n. 17.
18 Rule 8 in *Liber sextus decretalium*.
19 *A mendace, quid verum dicetur?* which the Douay-Rheims Bible translates, "What truth can come from that which is false?"
20 "For it seems to me that most disastrous consequences must follow upon our believing that anything false is found in the sa-

From all these things it is clearly and evidently gathered that one ought not believe a man who has been proved to have erred and is a heretic: unless those things which he says or writes have been corroborated by more certain testimony of others. Therefore it is unreasonable that we seek from heretics the explanation of Sacred Scripture, since they have been caught elsewhere to have distorted the same Scripture, or twisted it into another meaning alien from the Catholic faith. No one would dare to take corporeal food (yet if he cares at all about his own life) from the hand of him whom he knew had offered him poison even one time. Thus is it much more reasonable that whoever wants to take care of his salvation and the life of his soul, would dread to accept a teaching about the faith from heretics, who are notorious for having many times mixed poisonous teaching into their writings. The man in the Gospel who on account of the unexpected coming of his friend when asking for a loan of bread,[21] knocks at the deserted door of his neighbor. We ought to ask for the bread of true doctrine only from a Christian: because a Christian man is a neighbor to another Christian, both dwelling in one and the same city, namely, the Church. Nothing however ought to be asked from heretics,

---

cred books: that is to say, that the men by whom the Scripture has been given to us, and committed to writing, did put down in these books anything false. It is one question whether it may be at any time the duty of a good man to deceive; but it is another question whether it can have been the duty of a writer of Holy Scripture to deceive: nay, it is not another question—it is no question at all. For if you once admit into such a high sanctuary of authority one false statement as made in the way of duty, there will not be left a single sentence of those books which, if appearing to any one difficult in practice or hard to believe, may not by the same fatal rule be explained away, as a statement in which, intentionally, and under a sense of duty, the author declared what was not true" (Letter 28, c. 3, n. 3 (PL 33, 112-113)).

21 Cf. Lk. 11, 5.

who like foreigners, have departed from the dwelling of the Church.

A Catholic son of the Church would certainly injury his mother, if he were to ask for the bread of doctrine from heretics, whom she considers very despicable, just as she says in Job when speaking about the same heretics, "Whose fathers I would not have set with the dogs of my flock" (30, 1). Blessed Gregory when interpreting these words says: "Who is the 'flock' of Holy Church, but the multitude of the faithful? Or who else are called 'the dogs' of this flock, but holy teachers, who became the guardians of those believers? Which same whilst in behalf of their Lord they cried aloud, given up to daily and nightly watchings, uttered, so to say, loud barks of preaching. Concerning whom it is said to that Church by the Psalmist, 'The tongue of thy dogs be red with the same' (Ps. 67, 24). Since there are some that being recalled from the worshipping of idols are made the preachers of God... Now we speak of the fathers of heretics meaning those whom we style 'heresiarchs,' by whose evil preaching, that is, by the seed of speaking, the peoples following them were begotten in error. So then Holy Church 'would not have set the fathers' of heretics 'with the dogs of her flock,' because she rejects the founders of errors by judging, and disdains to number them among the true fathers. Which persons though they seemed to have recalled some from the erroneousness of heathenism, to have trained the practices of some to the doing what is right, yet due to the fact that they did not think right things of God, she does not 'set them with the dogs of the flock,' because she does not reckon them among right preachers."[22]

And it seems to me that the prophet Ezechiel thought the same thing, when he spoke by God's command to the false prophets of Israel, speaking thus: "Woe to the foolish prophets that follow their own spirit, and see nothing" (13, 3). Blessed

---

22 *Moralia*, bk. 20, c. 6, n. 15 (PL 76, 145C-146B).

Jerome when explaining these words in his *Commentaries on Ezechiel*, speaks thus: "Since according to the pattern of the Scriptures, the term 'prophets' is used of good and bad alike, they differ from each other in that the good prophets are said to be 'wise men,' whereas evil prophets are said to be 'fools and 'senseless.'"[23] The former refer to men of the Church, the latter to all heretics who forsake the Spirit of God and 'follow their own spirit. For they prophesy not from a Divine impulse, but 'out of their own heart.'"[24] But why the prophet said, "Woe," the words that follow clearly explain. "They see vain things," says Ezechiel, "and they foretell lies, saying: The Lord saith: whereas the Lord hath not sent them: and they have persisted to confirm what they have said" (v. 6). Behold the reason on account of which he said to the heretics, "Woe." Thus after having manifested the reason for the threat, the prophet finally states what God resolves to do with them, speaking thus: "Because you have spoken vain things, and have seen lies: therefore behold I come against you, saith the Lord God. And my hand shall be upon the prophets that see vain things, and that divine lies: they shall not be in the council of my people, nor shall they be written in the writing of the house of Israel, neither shall they enter into the land of Israel" (vv. 8-9). Although Blessed Jerome refers these words to the final day of judgment,[25] on which God will put the heretics outside of the council of His people; still nothing prevents that they also may be understood of this present life, in which heretics are already separated from the council of God's people: because they are outside the Church, which alone is God's people.

But because the words of the prophets are more obscure, and not always ought to be taken according to the surface of the text, but often according to their mystical meaning, which

---

23 Cf. Ps. 48, 11.
24 *Commentaria in Ezechielem*, bk. 4 (PL 25, 109A-B).
25 *Ibid.* (PL 25, 111A-C).

is wont to be insufficiently effective for the confirming of some teaching: hence I will cite another very clear testimony from the wise Ecclesiasticus which very clearly testifies that the exposition of Scripture ought not to be received from heretics. "The word of the law shall be fulfilled without a lie, and wisdom shall be made plain in the mouth of the faithful" (34, 8). Certainly nothing could be said more clearly in favor of our opinion, which we maintain. If wisdom shall be made plain in the mouth of the faithful, then from a heretic, who is not faithful, but unfaithful, it will not be made plain, but will be filled with a thousand difficulties. If "the word of the law shall be fulfilled without a lie," it necessarily follows that the word of the law is not fulfilled in the writings of heretics, in whose writings are found so many falsehoods.

Chapter XVII

Whether it is permitted for someone who has heretical books to read them.

Heretics' books are not always (as we taught in the last chapter necessarily ought to be done) burned, nay, sometimes on account of the negligence of judges, to whom this pertains, sometimes on account of very wicked avarice of merchants, they are offered for sale indiscriminately so that anyone who wishes, could read them. For this reason it is doubted by many Catholic men, whether anyone who wishes to read heretics' books could licitly do this, and without sin. Concerning this matter (as I think) a certain and universal judgment cannot be given: but one ought to make various considerations, according to which one ought to give various replies. Firstly in fact, it ought to be considered whether there is a prohibition of a superior having authority for this, whereby it is forbidden to all to read heretics' books. If there is such a prohibition decreed by law, which forbids to all without distinction the reading of heretics' books, without any doubt I believe that every person who reads such books forbidden by law, sins. Since in fact the disobedience, by which he refuses to fulfill the precepts of a superior, very clearly makes him guilty of sin. "He that despiseth you," Our Savior says to prelates and superiors, "despiseth me" (Lk. 10, 16). And again: "The scribes and the Pharisees have sitten on the chair of Moses. All things whatsoever they shall say to you, observe and do" (Mt. 23, 2-3). When He said, "whatsoever they shall say to you," it ought not to be taken absolutely, so that Christ would have taught everything which they would will at pleasure to enjoin upon their subjects, the subjects are forced to do all those things. But that saying, "whatsoever…," ought to be referred to all, and only those things, which pertain to the chair on which they sit. For everything pertaining to the chair, and not other things, which prelates command their subjects, their subjects are bound to do. But nothing can pertain more to the priestly chair than to admonish the subjects to remain in the true faith, and to remove every occasion of error far away from them: therefore a prelate could not command anything more just to his subjects, than if he were to forbid to them the reading of heretics' books, from which a very great misfortune could arise to them. And I think that it matters not whether the law, whereby heretical books are kept from being read, was sanctioned by the ecclesiastical authority, or by the secular authority, because we are bound to obey the former as the latter.

Paul is so teaching who, when speaking about every power without distinction, says: "Let every soul be subject to higher powers: for there is no power but from God: and those that are, are ordained of God. Therefore he that resisteth the power, resisteth the ordinance of God. And they that resist, purchase to themselves damnation... Wherefore be subject of necessity, not only for wrath, but also for conscience' sake" (Rom. 13, vv. 1-2 & 5). From which words Blessed Thomas concludes that not merely pontifical, but also imperial and regal human laws oblige the consciences of subjects to their observance.[1] And certainly Theophylactus seems to support Blessed Thomas' opinion, who, when interpreting the aforesaid words of Paul, speaks thus: "It is necessary that to be subject, not only so that you do not undergo God's and the magistrate's wrath for being disobedient, and suffer intolerably; but also on account of one's conscience."[2]

Nevertheless this ought not to be understood of every law, but one ought to consider the matter of the law, that is, the

---

[1] "And he says indefinitely 'higher powers' so that we may subject ourselves to them by reason of the sublimity of their office" (*Commentary on Romans*, c. 13, lect. 1).

[2] *Commentarius in Epistolam ad Romanos* (PG 124, 515C).

issue itself, about which the law deals. If the issue is light, and one which can benefit the State very little, one ought not to believe that the maker of the law wants by such a law to oblige his subjects under pain of guilt; and if he perhaps wanted this, and expressed it by his law, I do not believe that he could do this. For, as Paul says, power was not given to superiors for destruction, but for edification.[3] Now it would be a very great destruction, and a very dangerous snare of them, if superiors could make a law for any light issue, for the transgression of which the subjects would incur some guilt or sin, especially mortal sin. If the issue is of great importance, from which some great advantage or disadvantage could arise to the State, I do not doubt that the high authority, whichever it may be, either ecclesiastical or civil, can make a law which will oblige its transgressing subjects to guilt, even mortal. I believe that Paul indeed spoke about such matters when he said: "Wherefore be subject of necessity, not only for wrath, but also for conscience' sake." But since the reading of heretical books is a matter of great importance, from which Christendom can received very serious harm (as we showed in the previous chapter), it is thence proved that not only Pontiffs, but also kings, and all other secular authorities without distinction, could make a law prohibiting the reading of heretics' books, and make the transgressors of which law liable to serious guilt.

Now it is not evident to me whether a general prohibition of not reading heretics' books of this kind, has been hitherto legislated either by the Supreme Pontiff or by the emperor. Some perhaps will say that such a prohibition was imposed in the chapter, *Fraternitatis*, where it is said that the chapters of the heretics, Celestine and Pelagius, ought not to be accepted, because it is necessary that when the author has been condemned, his books have also been condemned.[4] But

---

3   Cf. II Cor. 10, 8.
4   "Since Coelestius and Pelagius were condemned in the Synod

this text says nothing (as I think) which would pertain to the matter at hand. For due to the fact that a book has been condemned, it does not necessarily follow that its reading has been prohibited. Now this is indeed proved from the fact that in the chapter, *Excommunicamus*, §. *Credentes*,[5] it is said that instruments drawn up by a notary, who is a believer, or harborer, or defender, or supporter of heretics, are condemned when the author has been condemned. It is certain that the Pope through such a condemnation of the instruments does not forbid the reading of the same instruments: but forbids this alone, namely, that they would have any force for giving testimony, and would have weight in a trial. In the same way ought to be understood regarding heretics' books, which when their authors have been condemned, are immediately reckoned to have been condemned. Condemned, I say, not such that they could not be read by anyone, but rather that no one can use their testimony for the confirmation of an opinion, and no one could confirm his opinion supported by their judgment. Thus by that text it is not proved that the reading of heretics' books has been forbidden by Canon Law: and I do not know of another text which clearly states this view.

And it certainly would be just, that a universal decree would be laid down in Canon Law whereby it would be prohibited under pain of excommunication incurred ipso facto, and under other grave penalties, that anyone would sell the books of a publicly condemned heretic, or dare to read them, or keep them in his house, without the special

---

of Ephesus, how can those chapters be accepted, whose authors are condemned?" (*Decretals of Gregory IX*, bk. 5, tit. 7 (*De haereticis*), c. 4).

5 "If he be a notary, let the instruments drawn up by him be considered worthless, for, the author being condemned, let them enjoy a similar fate" (*Decretals of Gregory IX*, bk. 5, tit. 7 (*De haereticis*), c. 13, §5).

permission of the Apostolic See, or the inquisitor of heretics having authority in that country. I know of particular prohibitions about this matter in various regions. In Spain, the inquisitors of heretics have prohibited many individually named books of heretics, who apply diligence concerning this matter. And for this reason among others, Spain remains so cleansed of heretics. Where such a prohibition is had, I do not doubt that he who, without the permission of the superior who could grant it, ventures to read forbidden books of heretics, is guilty of mortal sin.

But if there is no prohibition, then one ought to consider the various qualities and conditions of the persons, because according to their variety, the censures to be given for this matter are different. For there are some entirely uneducated men, who know nothing besides that language in which the book was written by the heretic, for instance the Latin language, Greek, Spanish, Italian or German. For heresies could be written in any language, and we have known, by experience teaching, that heresies have been written in any one of these which we have just listed. Others are sciolists, who besides the language, understand a little more: yet they do not understand to the extent that they could distinguish between leprosy and leprosy,[6] they do not know how to differentiate the beautiful from the ordinary, or make a distinction between the holy and the profane. Whosoever among these, whether he be an uneducated man or a sciolist, shall intentionally and on purpose read a book of a heretic condemned by the Church, sins mortally: unless perhaps the reading was so small, that it could not of itself do harm, because then on account of the incompleteness of the matter he will be excused from sin.

This assertion is indeed very clearly proved to be true, because any of these men reading such books exposes himself to a manifest danger of a mortal sin, and certain

---

6 Cf. Deut. 17, 8.

a very serious one, which is heresy. Now everyone who exposes himself to the danger of mortal sin (as the concordant opinion of all theologians bears witness) sins mortally. "He that loveth danger," says the Wise Man, "shall perish in it" (Eccli. 3, 27). And the supreme Teacher of Truth Himself clearly commands us to avoid every occasion of sin, speaking thus: "If thy right eye scandalize thee, pluck it out and cast it from thee. For it is expedient for thee that one of thy members should perish, rather than that thy whole body be cast into hell. And if thy right hand scandalize thee, cut it off, and cast it from thee" (Mt. 5, 29-30). By which words, according to all the sacred interpreters of them, Our Savior taught us that every occasion of sin ought to be avoided, if we wish to be delivered from the fire of hell. Those sin mortally who accept a manifest occasion of a very grave sin, such as heresy, when reading books of heretics, which they know have been condemned by the Church.

But because someone perhaps will boldly deny with shameless temerity that an uneducated person, or a sciolist, such as we said above, exposes himself to the danger of heresy when he deliberately reads heretics' books, wherefore this now ought to be proved with very convincing arguments. Firstly in fact, it is certain and undoubtable that he sins mortally, who deliberately associates with men, whose morals are corrupt and perverse. Which happens for no other reason except on account of the danger to which he occasions himself, by associating with such bad men. It is certainly rare that one who is near to danger could be safe for a long time. It is rare that one living uprightly could say: "I was the brother of dragons, and companion of ostriches" (Job 30, 29). "Few, very few, whom righteous Jove did bless, or quenchless virtue carried to the stars,"[7] who having dwelt among the wicked, themselves lived as just and innocent men. Hence the Wise Man says: "He that toucheth pitch,

---

7 Virgil, *Aeneid*, bk. 6, lns. 129 f.

shall be defiled with it: and he that hath fellowship with the proud, shall put on pride" (Eccli. 13, 1).

Since indeed from the mutual familiar intercourse of men between themselves, the behaviors of both are very easily exchanged between themselves. Whence Seneca says: "Phaedo[8] says: 'Certain tiny animals do not leave any pain when they sting us so subtle is their power, so deceptive for purposes of harm. The bite is disclosed by a swelling, and even in the swelling there is no visible wound.' That will also be your experience when dealing with wise men: you will not discover how or when the benefit comes to you, but you will discover that you have received it."[9] And what Seneca said concerning the benefit, which is had from the association with the good, completely the same thing, and using the same comparison, ought to be said of the harm which arises from associating with bad men, and all the more so: because since men are more inclined to evil, bad men allure, and draw them to themselves, more strongly than good men. "With the holy," says the Royal Prophet, "thou wilt be holy... and with the perverse thou wilt be perverted" (Ps. 17, 26-27). How strong is the association of good or bad men is shown by the very clear example of King Saul, who (as the Book of Kings relates[10]) was prophesying with the prophets, and he was raving with the wicked.

For this reason Blessed Thomas reckons that those who are simple people and weak in the faith about whose subversion it can rightly be feared, should be forbidden to communicate with Jews and other unbelievers, especially not to be on very familiar terms with them, or to communicate with them without necessity.[11] If associating with men is so strong

---

8 Presumably Phaedo the friend of Plato and pupil of Socrates, author of dialogues resembling those of Plato.
9 *The Epistles of Seneca*, letter 94, n. 41.
10 Cf. I Kings 10, 10
11 II-II, q. 10, art. 9.

that it can changes men's morals from good to evil, and overthrow from virtue to vice, much more could the reading of books do this. Because when we read a book, we associate with its author, who discloses his thoughts to us, and shows his desires, and often moves a reader more through writing (as we said in the immediately preceding chapter) than a hearer through spoken words. Furthermore, it is very certain that books full of piety can benefit the readers. Thus for the same reason books of the ungodly could harm those reading, especially those who do not have much knowledge and learning, so that they could recognize the poison of heresy very often hiding in them, and beware of them. Often such men become like the books they read.

There are other men, learned in theology and sufficiently instructed in it, who understand very well the Sacred Doctors whom they read, and the condition of these men is also diverse. For there are some men by their nature lovers of new things, unstable, who have not the skill to continue steadfastly in anything to which they adhered at one time: but are more changeable than the wind, turning now this way, now that way by the least breeze. They now love, and in an hour, they hated what they previously loved: men in fact (as it is said) not of many hours, but of scarcely one hour. I reckon that about these men completely the same thing ought to be said, which I said about the ones above. Because these latter men, just as the former, also put themselves in a manifest danger of heresy, when they read heretics' books. For just as he who knew that he was so weak, that when put in any very slight occasion of sin, could not restrain himself from fornication, sins mortally as often as he voluntarily places himself in such an occasion of sin: so with like reason, he who has known from experience that he is so fickle and inconstant in character, that he very easily falls from any, even very little persuasion, or he always enjoys new things, whatever they may be, and applauds them, it is necessary that he sins, and indeed mortally, if he reads heretics' books, from whose fallacious arguments he very easily could be persuaded due to his fickle disposition. If John Hus had never read the books of John Wycliffe, he would not have fallen into so many, and such pestiferous heresies. For Aeneas Sylvius relates about him that he was a lover of novelties, and hence when reading the books of John Wycliffe, as something new brought into Bohemia, he very easily drank the poison of all the heresies which John Wycliffe had left in his books.[12] The same thing happened to Martin Luther, who when reading the books of the same John Hus willingly accepted all his errors.

There are again other learned men, knowing how to distinguish between good and evil, who are constant and firm in the faith: but they are oppressed by incessant temptations of disbelief, and are tormented by the proddings of heresies not without their great and heavy sorrow. These men if compelled by some just or very pressing reason read books of heretics, I do not believe that they sin. Because since they knew by long experience that they are stable and firm in the faith, it ought not to be said that the put themselves in danger from heresy, when they read heretics' books: because trusting in the Lord, and they do it, not presuming about their own strength, to remedy some occurring need. For example, if a learned man, especially one having the care of souls, living among or near heretics, who fears that his people might read heretics' books, to detect their feigned assurances, to reply to their fallacious arguments, and in this way protect the people entrusted to him from every heresy; such a man as this, no matter how many temptations of heresies he may be goaded by at other times, not only will not sin, nay, rather merits. Because in so doing he does not place himself in danger of heresy, but when necessity is obliging, he commends himself to the Divine mercy, in which he trusts, which on account of the people committed to him, for which alone

---

12 Pope Pius II, *De Bohemorum origine*, c. 35, p. 58.

he reads such books, will not permit him to be deceived by the heretics' books. But if there is no just reason urging, but merely for the sake of his own inordinate desire he would read heretics' books, I do not believe that he is free from mortal sin. Because since he was at other times goaded by many temptations of disbelief, when reading heretics books he adds (as it is said[13]) fuel to the fire, and in this way will be attacked by many and more pressing temptations of disbelief: whence it will happen that he will necessarily at some time be conquered. For because Paul feared this, wherefore he admonishes men of this kind, speaking thus: "He that thinketh himself to stand, let him take heed lest he fall" (I Cor. 10, 12).

There are finally other learned men amply instructed in theology, and in any other discipline necessary for it, firm and constant in the faith, not vexed by any or very weak temptations of unbelief. Regarding these men I do not doubt that they, provided there not be any prohibition of a superior, could read heretics' books without any sin. And if they were to do it with an upright intention (as it should be done), for instance, because they want to fight against their heresies, or respond to their fallacious arguments, not only will they not sin when so reading, but they will receive a great reward on this account. For by doing this they make themselves a wall of the house of Israel, and wage war against the enemies of God and His Church: wherefore it is just that they receive a recompense for their labor from God, Whom they serve. For those who read heretics' books for this cause alone, so that they may be able to fight against them, these men are rightly figured by Phinees, who entered into a brothel house, not to consort with a harlot, but to pierce through the Israelite fornicator with his sword, and for this he was highly praised by God, and given a great reward.[14]

---

13 *Addere oleum camino* (Horace, *Satires*, bk. 2, satire 3, ln. 321).
14 Cf. Num. 25.

Hence the Fourth Synod of Carthage granted bishops that they could read heretics' books. For in chapter sixteen of its decrees the aforesaid council says these words: "A bishop may not read the books of the pagans, but in times of need he may examine those of heretics."[15] When forbidding books of pagans, it allowed the reading of heretics' books, and rightly so, because the reading of heretics' books is necessary, so that they could know the heretics' trickery, and hence it is granted to bishops: because they have the care of souls, and it is rightly presumed that they are learned men, and constant in the faith. For on account of a similar reason Blessed Thomas, when speaking about communion to be had with Jews and other unbelievers, says these words: "For some are firm in the faith; and so it is to be hoped that their communicating with unbelievers will lead to the conversion of the latter rather than to the aversion of the faithful from the faith. These are not to be forbidden to communicate with unbelievers who have not received the faith, such as pagans or Jews, especially if there be some urgent necessity for so doing."[16] If communication with Jews is permitted to those who are firm in faith, when some benefit from such communication is hoped for: also for the same reason it will be permitted for them to read books of heretics, when the need arises, and some benefit is hoped for, especially if there is no probation of the superior, which forbids doing it.

Although this opinion is manifest to anyone even slightly educated, still for its greater confirmation I decided to insert here a very weighty example, deserving to be told, which Eusebius of Caesarea relates. For he when discussing about Dionysius of Alexandria, after he extolled up to heaven by wonderful praises his teaching, holiness, and constancy in torments for Christ's sake in book six of his *Church Histo-*

---

15 *Decretum Gratiani*, pt. 1, dist. 37, c. 1 (PL 187, 201A); Mansi 3, 952D.
16 II-II, q. 10, a. 7.

ry, finally in book seven, he relates things which follow about that Dionysius of Alexandria: "In the third epistle on Baptism," Eusebius says, "which this same Dionysius wrote to Philemon, the Roman presbyter, he relates the following: 'But I examined the works and traditions of the heretics, defiling my mind for a little time with their abominable opinions, but receiving this benefit from them, that I refuted them by myself, and detested them all the more. And when a certain brother among the presbyters restrained me, fearing that I should be carried away with the filth of their wickedness (for it would defile my soul)—in which also, as I perceived, he spoke the truth—a vision sent from God came and strengthened me. And the word which came to me commanded me, saying distinctly, "Read everything which you can take in hand, for you are able to correct and prove all; and this has been to you from the beginning the cause of your faith."[17] I received the vision as agreeing with the Apostolic word, which says to them that are stronger, "Be skillful money-changers."'"[18] In which words I admonish the reader to take notice of the reason why that Divine oracle permitted Dionysius to read heretics' books. Because, he said, "You are able to correct and prove all."

From which words what we said above concerning uneducated and sciolist men is very clearly proved to be true, namely, that they cannot embark on the reading of heretics' books without sin: because they cannot test and discern each one. Yet if a prohibition about this thing was given at one time, I reckon that he sins who reads heretical books, no matter how learned he may be, if he did it without permission. Thus whoever reads books of the Lutheran heresy without permission of the Apostolic See, will sin mortally, and he will be ipso facto excommunicated: because in the

---

17 Cf. I Thess. 5, 21-22: "But prove all things; hold fast that which is good. From all appearance of evil refrain yourselves."
18 C. 7, n. 1 (PG 20, 647B-C).

Bull, *Coena Domini*,[19] issued by Paul III[20] all are excommunicated, who read the books of Martin Luther, or of others of the same sect, without permission of the Apostolic See. Nevertheless this excommunication does not extend to those who read books of other heretics, because they alone are mentioned in the Bull.

When I first published this work, *On the Just Punishment of Heretics*, there was no other decree prohibiting the reading of heretics' books, besides that which we just said was issued by Paul III. After a number of years Paul died, and Julius III succeeded him in the pontificate, who understanding very well how much the reading of heretics' books could harm the Christian people, issued a decree much more copious, whereby under very grave penalties, he interdicted to all the reading of the books of any heretic without any distinction.[21]

---

19 Or, *In coena Domini*, a Papal Bull, so called from the feast on which it was annually published in Rome, viz., the feast of the Lord's Supper, or Maundy Thursday.

20 In 1536. *Magnum bullarium romanum* (Luxemburg: Henrici-Alberti Gosse, 1742), vol. 1, p. 718, §1. The number of heretics listed expanded in later years. Cf. "*In Coena Domini*," *Catholic Encyclopedia*, vol. 7, p. 718.

21 "Censorship was gradually becoming systematized. It was quite time, if the faithful were to be preserved from heresy, for Alfonso de Castro, writing in 1547, feels obliged to argue at much length to prove the danger arising from such books and the need of prohibitive legislation. There were no laws, he said, either papal or imperial, to punish the possession and reading of wicked books. In Spain the inquisitors had prohibited many works of heretics by name and had made diligent exertions to suppress them, to which was attributable the freedom of Spain from heresy, but many people held that the condemnation of a book merely declared that it was not to be regarded as authoritative, and that there was neither sin nor crime in owning or studying it. To be sure, the bull *In Coena Domini* of Paul III (1536) had excommunicated all who read Lutheran books without a papal license, but as it was limited to

Now so that this prohibition may be made known to all, I decided to put it here in its entirety, which follows:

Julius Bishop, Servant of the Servants of God, in perpetual memory of the matter now decreed.

Since the thoughts of our minds especially reflect on how the Catholic faith may everywhere increase and flourish, We willingly endeavor that every occasion of deviating from it may be removed. Certainly since, as it has recently been made known to us, from the faculties which were at one time granted to some, so that they could keep and read heretical books or also those suspected regarding the faith, for the purpose of refuting the errors of those same books, the fruits which were hoped for have not come until the present time, but on the contrary, various inconveniences have followed. We, desiring to obtain the aforementioned, to take care of the salvation of souls of Christ's faithful, on our own initiative, not at the bidding of any request brought before us about this matter, but from our sure knowledge and mature deliberation, of reading each and every faculty and permission to keep Lutheran or other heretical books, or those suspected regarding the faith, to any persons of whatever rank or state, even if they shine forth with episcopal or archepiscopal or other higher ecclesiastical dignity or secular preeminence, with the sole

---

these, all other heretical books were regarded as free. Soon after this the heart of de Castro was gladdened by the bull *Cum meditatio* of Julius III (April 29, 1550), prohibiting the possession and reading of all heretic books under the full penalties of heresy, and he made haste to print it in a subsequent edition of his treatise" (Henry Charles Lea, *Chapters from the Religious History of Spain Connected with the Inquisition* (Philadelphia: Lea Brothers, 1890), p. 59).

exception of the inquisitors, or commissaries appointed for a set time by the Apostolic See concerning heretical depravity during that same period, by whichever predecessor of ours and us and the said Apostolic See or its Legates, even *De latere*, or our Major Penitentiary, or anyone else, under whatever forms and expressions of words, and with all the modifying clauses and irritating clauses of repeals and other decrees that have been granted up to now by any similar motion and knowledge, by this decree, We revoke, make void and annul with Apostolic authority, and We consider and wish to be considered by others as revoked, made void, and completely undone in respect to all things. Restraining more strictly the persons mentioned under judgments, censures, and punishments inflicted and promulgated by Us and the Apostolic See against possessing or reading similar books, lest they henceforth presume to use in whatever way the aforementioned faculties and licenses, or the pretext of them or others, to possess or to read the aforesaid books hitherto condemned, or whatever others which shall be condemned in the future. And moreover, each and every printer of books, librarian, and those selling in whatever way and any other persons having in his possession Lutheran or heretical books, or those containing Lutheran or other false doctrine in them, or those condemned in any way by Us and the said See, for any reason even from Our and the said See's special license or permission, of whatever state, rank, order, condition, or preeminence they may be: even if they shine forth (as mentioned before) with pontifical, or any other higher ecclesiastical or secular dignity, the said inquisitors and commissaries (as mentioned before) excepted, We require and admonish by the said Apostolic authority and by this same decree, both them and each one of them, in virtue of holy obedience, and under threat of incurring the branding of heresy and everything enjoined and promulgated against heretics by law, both by ecclesiastical and secular judgments, censures, and punishments, We command by strictly ordering, that within the period We assign to them, and to any of them of sixty days from the date of publication of this decree, in the manner and form of the computations to be made as written below, twenty days of which for the first period, and another twenty for the second period, and the remaining twenty days from the third and final period, and by canonical admonition, that these writings, each and every Lutheran or other heretical book, or those containing Lutheran or other false teaching in it, condemned in any way by us or the said See, in their possession for whatever reason including trade, and even with our special permission and license, or of the same See (as mentioned before) being in their possession, ought to be physically and actually delivered up to the inquisitors of heretical depravity in the cities in which the books of this kind are. And nevertheless We command, with the same initiative by Apostolic letters, venerable Bishop Gian Pietro of Frascati-Naples,[22] our beloved sons Juan of Saint Clement of Burges,[23] and Marcello of the [Basilica of the] Holy Cross of Jerusalem,[24] and Francesco Sfondrato,[25] named Cardinal-Priest General Inquisitors, deput-

---

22 Gian Pietro Cardinal Carafa of Frascati (*Tusculana*) and Naples, who was also an inquisitor, and later became Pope Pius IV. Cf. Gams, *Series episcoporum Ecclesiae catholicae* (Regensburg: Josef Manz, 1857), pp. XX & 905; L. Pastor, *The History of the Popes* (London: various, 1891-1899), vol. 14, pp. 56-424.
23 Juan Cardinal Álvarez de Toledo, O. P. (1488-1557), who was appointed the bishop of Burgos, Spain, in 1537, and in 1547 was appointed Cardinal-Priest of San Clemente. Cf. Gams, p. 17.
24 Marcello Cardinal Cervini degli Spannocchi of Montepulciano, who became Pope Marcellus II in 1555. Cf. Pastor, vol. 14, pp. 1-55.
25 Francesco Cardinal Sfondrato, bishop of Sarno, archbishop of Amain. Cf. Pastor, vol. 13, pp. 6, 10, 12, 17, *passim*.

Whether it is permitted to read heretical books

ed by the Apostolic See, that they themselves or through another or others, after having examined, and warned the same persons not obeying our command by our decree, that they would retroactively incur the mark of heresy, and other judgments, censures, and aforesaid punishments on account of this kind of disobedience, publicly declare, and have declared by others, that they are heretics, bound with censures and punishments, until they have delivered up each and every one of the same Lutheran or other heretical books of this kind to the above-mentioned inquisitors in the cities, in which the books of this kind (as mentioned before) are, and have obtained the favor of being restored to their former standing; violators shall be stricken with ecclesiastical censure without the right of appeal, notwithstanding any constitution and Apostolic ordinance or other provision to the contrary. Even if the said See has granted an indult to any, jointly or singly, that they may not be interdicted, suspended, or excommunicated by Apostolic letters not making full and express mention, word for word, of such indult.

Moreover, in order that all the foregoing may be brought to the notice of those concerned, and that ignorance of them may not justly claim or legitimately excuse itself, We desire and decree, with the said Apostolic authority, that this decree be read openly and clearly in a loud voice by some couriers of our Curia in the Basilica of the Prince of the Apostles of Rome and Lateran Church, at a time when large numbers of people are wont to gather there to hear the Divine services, and be affixed to the doors of the Basilica and the Church, as well as to the door of the Apostolic Chancellery and in the front of the *Campo de' Fiori*,[26] where it may hang for some time for the reading

---

26 *Campo de' Fiori* is a rectangular square south of Piazza Navona in Rome, Italy. It is diagonally southeast of the *Palazzo della Cancelleria* and one block northeast of the *Palazzo Farnese*.

and notice of all, and when it has been removed from there, let copies of it remain posted in the same places. And that by the reading, posting and publication of this kind each and every person comprehended by this decree, after sixty such days, in this way shall be individually obliged and bound, as if they had been read and published in their presence and in person. And their transcriptions signed with the hand of a public notary and secured with the seal of some person constituted in an ecclesiastical dignity, that the trust ought to be completely given, which would be given to the original if it were to be exhibited or displayed. We will however that those who have delivered up Lutheran books or other aforesaid books to the said Inquisitors within such an interval and period of time: and unless they will be heretics or suspected regarding the faith, otherwise than from the retention of books of this kind, they are deemed by Us to be, and are ipso facto, absolved from censures and punishments in both forums, even without an abjuration being done in addition. We absolve them in the aforesaid occurrence retroactively (provided they completely perform the penance which the confessor, to be chosen them, reckons ought to be enjoined upon them on that account). Let no man therefore infringe, or boldly and rashly oppose this Our Letter of revocation, voiding, annulment, restraining, examination, warning, command, decree and will, or contravene it. But if any one shall presume to attempt it; let him know that he shall incur the displeasure of Almighty God, and of His Blessed Apostles Peter and Paul.

Campo de' Fiori, translated literally from Italian, means "field of flowers." The name dates to the Middle Ages when the area was a meadow.

Given at Rome by Saint Peter, in the year 1550 of Our Lord's Incarnation, the twenty-ninth day of April, in the first year of our Pontificate.[27]

Which decree, to show that it is authentic, was procured from the archive of the Judiciary House of the Holy Inquisition in the city of Valladolid by the Lord Fiscal Promoter[28] of the Inquisition, hence it is contained verbatim, copied form the aforesaid decree.

---

27 Bartolomeo Fontana, *Documenti vaticani contro l'eresia Luterana in Italia* (Rome: Società Romana di storia patria, 1892), pp. 412-414. N.B. The Sacred Congregation of the Index on December 5, 1895 commented that this Bull of Julius III, *Cum meditation*, restricts only bishops who are not also Ordinaries from possessing heretical books. "It must be noted, then, that jurisdiction as episcopal is not to be confused with ordinary; for the latter is extended to more people than the former; for there are many who enjoy ordinary jurisdiction, for example, Parish Priests, Directors of local Congregations, etc. without, nevertheless, exercising jurisdiction as though they were episcopal" (AAS 30 (1897-98), 395). This decree is also found among the unofficial collection of decretals entitled, *Septimi Decretalium* (bk. 5, tit. 4, c. 2).

28 Or the Promoter of Justice, or Public Prosecutor.

Chapter XVIII

Concerning the spiritual punishments of heretics, and firstly concerning excommunication, from which arise another, which is the deprivation of burial.

Up to this point we have disputed about corporal punishments, which laws decree for heretics, and we have proved that they were justly and deservedly decreed: it remains that we discuss about spiritual punishments, and we will prove that they are no less deserved by heretics than corporal punishments. These men have certainly transgressed with their soul, by thinking falsely about the Catholic faith, and with the body, by writing, or preaching against it, or teaching differently in any way, or by doing anything else against the ordinances of the faith, and hence it is just that they would be punished in body along with the soul, at least in that way by which the soul can be punished in this world. The first punishment which pertains to the soul is excommunication, by which they, as infected sheep, are driven away from the flock of the Church, lest they infect the rest of the sheep by their association, whereby it is also forbidden to other Catholics to have any association with them, lest perhaps having associated with them they be infected by them. This punishment is described in the chapters both entitled, *Excommunicamus*, in *De haereticis*.[1] Every heretic undergoes this punishment, by the very fact that he is a heretic, even though he was never condemned by a judge for heresy: whether he be relapsed, or then became a heretic for the first time, as long as he assents to his heresy as a heretic, that is, as pertinacious although he afterwards returns to his senses.

---

1 *Decretals of Gregory IX*, bk. 5, tit. 7 (*De haereticis*), cc. 13 & 15.

Yet if someone without any pertinacity assents to some heresy, being prepared to accept and hold that faith which the Catholic Church holds, just as he ought not to be declared a heretic, so also he ought not to be declared excommunicated. For those Decretals which we have just now cited do not inflict all who have fallen into some heresy with the sentence of excommunication, but only heretics. Because even though it is very clear by the reality itself, still on account of many, who fear where there is no fear, I decided that it ought not to be omitted.

And also not every heretic is subject to the sentence of excommunication, but only those who manifest in any way the heresy which they have mentally conceived, so that if someone were then present, he could know that he has fallen into such a heresy. If someone, for example, contemplates within himself some heresy, which he pertinaciously believes, and expresses it in words, without anyone hearing: just as those men are wont to do, who are going to teach the people by a public reading or exhort by a discourse, who (so that they may afterwards be without impediments in the pronunciation) firstly say alone by themselves, what things they are afterwards going to say to the people: such a man will doubtlessly be reckoned excommunicated. Because his heresy is already virtually manifest and exposed to human judgment, even though from a lack of witnesses it happens to be hidden.

Now he who has mentally conceived a heresy, and has never put it forth, such a man is not excommunicated, nay, and the Church cannot excommunicate him. How can the Church excommunicate him whose sin, on account of which the excommunication ought to be imposed, she cannot know? It is indeed necessary that she who ought to justly punish him, should know very well the crime, on account of which he rightly ought to be punished. "He that speaketh that which he knoweth," Solomon says, "is a judge of justice" (Prov. 12,

First spiritual punishment: excommunicaiton and denial of burial

17).[2] But neither the Pope nor the whole Church militant can perceive heresy hidden in the heart: because only God is the searcher of hearts.[3] "For man seeth those things that appear, but the Lord beholdeth the heart" (I Kings 16, 7). Thus the Church, which cannot perceive heresy hidden in the heart, also cannot solely on account of it penalize someone with the punishment of excommunication. And what is said in the chapter, *Cogitationis poenam*,[4] confirms this opinion. "Nobody undergoes punishment," as the text says, "for a thought," and in the chapter, *Cogitatio*, in the same distinction [of Gratian]: "A thought does not deserve punishment."[5] And this is what the common opinion of theologians says: "The Church cannot oblige interior acts."

Yet a Clementine Gloss on the section, *Verum*, of the first canon of the title, *De haereticis*,[6] teaches the opposite, having been deceived by a certain phrase of these *Constitutiones Clementinae* misunderstood by the Gloss itself. Since in fact that Clementine canon excommunicates by the law itself inquisitors of heretics, who do not do or omit something against heretics, due to hatred or love, which they ought to have done. From which statement that Gloss deduces that there is now no reason for doubting that which the Archdeacon had said is a doubtful matter, namely whether a hidden heretic is excommunicated by the law itself: because it is very clearly established from the text of this Clementine canon (as the Gloss says[7]) that the Church can punish interi-

---

2 *Judex justitiae est*, which is translated in the Douay-Rheims Bible as "sheweth forth justice."
3 Cf. Wis. 1, 6.
4 *Decretum Gratiani*, pt. 2, *causa* 33, q. 3 (*De poenitentia*), dist. 1, c. 14 (PL 187, 1522C).
5 *Ibid.*, c. 20 (PL 187, 1525C).
6 *Clementinarum*, bk. 5, tit. 3, c. 1, §4.
7 *Liber sextus decretalium D. Bonficii Papae VIII, Clementis Papae V Constitutiones...* (Venice: s. n., 1591), vol. 2, pp. 188 f.

or acts of the soul, and hence it is very clearly proved that any hidden heretic is excommunicated by the law itself. And to confirm its opinion, it then cites many texts of the law, which do not in the least support its proposition.

And (so that I may speak frankly) it did not correctly understand the text of that Clementine canon, and it did not consider well its meaning. For that Clementine canon does not only punish the interior acts of the soul, over which the Church (as we said) has no jurisdiction in the exterior forum, but she punishes the exterior actions, which proceed from those interior ones. For the Pontiff there does not excommunicate the inquisitors who have merely hatred or love: because he could not excommunicate anyone merely for hatred in the heart, even if the hatred were very ardent: but the Pontiff there excommunicates the inquisitors, who on account of hatred, or love did something in the court of the Inquisition against reason. After having carefully considered these words, it is very clearly established that hatred or love are not punished there, but the exterior work is punished, or the omission of the exterior work proceeding from hatred or love. Certainly hatred and love are very different from a work proceeding from hatred or love. Those first two things are interior acts of the soul, but the latter is an exterior act. The Church does not and cannot punish those first things. For the Apostle forbids the judgment of these things when speaking thus: "Judge not before the time; until the Lord come, who both will bring to light the hidden things of darkness, and will make manifest the counsels of the hearts" (I Cor. 4, 5). This last thing, however, namely, the exterior work arisen from hatred or love, the Church can justly punish, even if it is hidden due to a lack of witnesses: because by its nature, it will soon come forth from the interior recesses of the heart, or at least it is manifestable. Thus, every text which the Gloss cites imposes the punishment for exterior actions, and no decree will ever be found in the law, which determines some

First spiritual punishment: excommunicaiton and denial of burial

punishment for someone merely on account of an interior act of the soul, such as hatred or love.

From this punishment of excommunication arises another, as a river from a fountain, namely, the deprivation of ecclesiastical burial. For no one dying in an excommunication can be buried in a holy place, as is evident from the first canon of the title, *De sepulturis*.[8] But lest any undereducated person perhaps doubt about this matter, it seemed deserving to the Church that a special decree about this matter be made, which forbade ecclesiastical burial to all heretics. And it is found in the chapter, *Quicumque*.[9] And it was certainly rightly so decreed. Because he, for whom it is not permitted to pray, does not deserve to be buried in a holy place. For bodies are buried in holy places simply because (as Augustine says) those who enter the holy places may pray to God for those who are buried there. And for this reason (as Augustine says in the book, *On the Care of the Dead*,[10] ought to be done) the graves of the dead are called "monuments," because they admonish the minds of the living to remember the dead. But since no remembrance could benefit the dead, it follows that neither could the burial benefit them.

This punishment, as we have just explained it, that is, the sentence of excommunication inflicted by the law itself upon heretics, some theologians, not of the lowest sort, consider it so just, that they reckon that it has been inflict-

---

8 *Clementinarum*, bk. 3, tit. 7, c. 1 (*Eos qui*).
9 *Liber sextus decretalium*, bk. 5, tit. 2 (*De haereticis*), c. 2.
10 "But then the only reason why the name 'Memorials' or 'Monuments' is given to those sepulchers of the dead which become specially distinguished, is that they recall to memory, and by reminding cause us to think of, them who by death are withdrawn from the eyes of the living, that they may not by forgetfulness be also withdrawn from men's hearts. For both the term 'Memorial' [*memoria*] most plainly shews this, and 'Monument' is so named from 'monishing,' that is, putting in mind" (C. 4, n. 6 (PL 40, 596)).

ed not merely by human law, but also by Divine law. For Josse van Clichtove[11] in his assertion of the defined truths at the Synod of Sens[12] holds this opinion: Jacques Masson[13] in his assertion of the judgment given by the University of Louvain against Luther,[14] clearly subscribes to the same opinion. Johann Eck in his *Enchiridion [of Commonplaces] against Luther [and Other Enemies of the Church]*, in the chapter, "Concerning the Burning of Heretics,"[15] seems to

---

11 Josse Van Clichtove (1472-1543) was a theologian, born at Nieuport (Flanders), who published his *Compendium veritatum* in 1529.

12 "The Church obtains the power of imposing an excommunication from Christ: which on account of the serious spiritual penalties (which it inflicts), ought to be feared very much. Which we strive to support by the testimony of Holy Writ, and also of the holy sanctions: so that we may clearly bring to light that that same excommunication comes forth from Divine and human law" (*Compendium veritatum ad fidem pertinentium contra erroneas Lutheranorum assertiones ex dictis et actis in concilio provinciali Senonensi apud Parisios celebrato* (Paris: in officina Henri Estienne Simon de Colines, 1529), c. 12, fol. 57v).

13 Jacques Masson (or *Jacobus Latomus*) (ca. 1475-1544) was a Flemish theologian, a distinguished member of the Faculty of Theology at the University of Louvain. He was a theological adviser to the Inquisition. The general focus of his academic work centered on opposing Martin Luther and the Protestant Reformation.

14 "And [an excommunicated man] ought not to be avoided by reason of the precept of the one excommunicating, but of Christ Who commanded that such a man ought to be held as a heathen and publican" (*Articulorum doctrinae fratris M. Lutheri per theologos Lovanienses damnatorum ratio ex sacris literis et veteribus tractatoribus* (or *Foundation from Sacred Scriptures and Ancient Writers of the Condemnation of the Doctrinal Sentences of Friar Martin Luther Done by the Louvain Theologians*) (Antwerp: Michael Hillenius, 1521)).

15 *Enchiridion of Commonplaces against Luther and Other Enemies of the Church* (Grand Rapids, Michigan: Baker Book House,

think the same thing. All these three illustrious theologians concordantly think that the punishment of excommunication is inflicted upon heretics by Divine law, far removed from them thinking that it is unjust. And this is not without cause, and without any reason, but they assert it motivated by many testimonies of Sacred Scripture. Since in fact Paul when writing to Titus says: "A man that is a heretic, after the first and second admonition, avoid: knowing that he that is such an one is subverted, and sinneth, being condemned by his own judgment" (3, 10-11). And Blessed John says: "If any man come to you, and bring not this doctrine, receive him not into the house nor say to him, God speed you. For he that saith unto him, God speed you, communicateth with his wicked works" (II Jn. 1, 10-11).

Yet other theologians, although they assert that the sentence of excommunication imposed by law upon heretics is just, still they deny that it has the force of Divine law: because (as they say) when Paul and John were saying these things, they did not say that such a thing was commanded by God, just as elsewhere Paul when he discusses something similar, is wont to say: "Not I but the Lord commandeth" (I Cor. 7, 10), and again, "I speak, not the Lord" (v. 12). But Paul could not (as they say) impose the sentence of excommunication on all heretics by his own authority. But certainly someone will think to prove that this response has no force, by that which Paul says to the Thessalonians: "And we charge you, brethren," Paul says, "in the name of our Lord Jesus Christ, that you withdraw yourselves from every brother walking disorderly, and not according to the tradition which they have received of us" (II Thess. 3, 6). Notice that Paul forbids association with those who do not walk according to the tradition which they had received from him, and he commands it not in his own name, but in the name of Our Lord Jesus Christ. Theophylactus when explaining these

---

1979), c. 27, pp. 178 f.

words says: "More than once we have pointed out that Paul calls a more severe ordinance a precept. Thus now when making a more formidable exhortation, he says, 'For we do not enjoin this thing, but Christ Himself. For the things that I say, He actually says.'"[16]

Which of these opinions is truer, I do not decide, since it suffices for me in this discussion that those who deny that the punishment of excommunication is inflicted by Divine law, could not deny that it is consistent with the Divine law, to excommunicate pertinacious heretics. For he who time and again despises a brother correcting a sin, and moreover does not want to listen to the Church, Christ Our Savior commanded that he ought to be held as a heathen and a publican.[17] By which words according to the concordant opinion of all Catholics, Our Savior gave to the Church's prelates the power of excommunicating him who neglects to be corrected after having been admonished thrice. For it is the same thing to say, "Let him be to thee as the heathen and publican," as if He would have said, "Have completely no association with him." For just as association with the Gentiles was of old forbidden to the people of Israel, so likewise the Savior now forbids the Christian people, or He gave the power to prelates of forbidding association with him, who contemns to hear the Church, saying: "Let him be to thee as the heathen and publican." For Blessed Chrysostom when interpreting these words of Matthew says: "Do you see how He has bound him down with twofold constraint, both by the vengeance here, and by the punishment hereafter? But these things has He threatened, that these circumstances may not arise, but that fearing, at once the being cast out of the Church, and the

---

16 *Commentarius in Epistolam II ad Thessalonicenses* (PG 124, 1351B-C).
17 Cf. Mt. 18, 17.

First spiritual punishment: excommunicaiton and denial of burial

danger from the bond [of excommunication], and the being bound in Heaven, he may become more gentle."[18]

Now so that no one would dare to contemn the prelate's sentence of excommunication, but may reckon it to be firm and ratified, He added, "Amen I say to you, whatsoever you shall bind upon earth, shall be bound also in heaven; and whatsoever you shall loose upon earth, shall be loosed also in heaven" (Mt. 18, 18). Jerome when explaining these words says: "Because He had said: 'If he will not hear the church, let him be to thee as the heathen and publican,' a secret response or unspoken thought of this brother who despises [the Church] could be: 'If you despise me, I also will despise you. If you condemn me, you too will be condemned by my sentence of judgment.' Because of this possibility, He gave authority to the Apostles to ensure that those who are condemned by such measures may know that the human verdict is corroborated by a Divine verdict, and whatever is bound on earth is equally bound in heaven."[19] From which words it is very clearly established how ratified and confirmed by God is the excommunication which is imposed upon him who, having been twice admonished, afterwards contemns to listen to the Church. Now who listens to the Church less than the heretic, who prefers his own opinion to the definition of the whole Church, and departs by his own judgment from that faith which he knows the whole Church holds? And perhaps those three above-mentioned very learned men understood this same thing, that the punishment of excommunication imposed on heretics is by Divine law, because the human law, which inflicts it on heretics, rests upon the Divine law.

Again, this excommunication of heretics is shown to be just by the fact that the Lord God long ago, when commanding the people of Israel to destroy the Jebusite, the Canaan-

---

18 *Homilies on Matthew*, hom. 60, n. 2 (PG 58, 586).
19 *Commentary on Matthew*, bk. 3 (PL 26, 131D).

ite, and the five other nations, added: "Thou shalt make no league with them, nor shew mercy to them: neither shalt thou make marriages with them. Thou shalt not give thy daughter to his son, nor take his daughter for thy son: for she will turn away thy son from following me, that he may rather serve strange gods" (Deut. 7, 2-4). Please notice the reason why He forbade them to contract marriage with the Gentiles. "For she will turn away," He says, "thy son from following me." Is there not a similar danger in associating with heretics, whose "speech spreadeth like a canker" (II Tim. 2, 17)? Thus for the same reason it is just that association with heretics is forbidden to all Christians, lest they turn away their hearts by their fallacies, when they associate with them. Hence Paul says: "What part hath the faithful with the unbeliever?" (II Cor. 6, 15). This reason is so strong that Paul reckoned that on account of it alone a believing woman married to an unbelieving man, who does not allow her to remain in the faith, but daily solicits and urges to unbelief, can be separated from her husband. For so says Paul: "But if the unbeliever depart, let him depart. For a brother or sister is not under servitude in such cases. But God hath called us in peace" (I Cor. 7, 15). Theophylactus when explaining these words says: "For instance if he were to command you, that you become a partaker of his unbelief, or else you leave the marriage, leave. It is better to dissolve the marriage than piety. If he quarrels with you, he says, because you do not partake with him in unbelief, separate. For you are not 'under servitude in such cases,' that is, in matters of this kind you are not be forced to tolerate the man. For it is better to depart than to wrangle. And certainly that is not the Divine will; for 'He hath called you in peace.' Therefore if he quarrels, he has given you cause for divorce."[20]

Next, that which God long ago commanded to be done in the Mosaic Law with the leper, is a manifest example

---

[20] *Commentarius in Epistolam I ad Corinthios* (PG 124, 646).

proposed to us, so that when it has been examined well, we may thence learn what ought to be done in the Evangelical Law regarding heretics. "All these things," as Paul says, "were done in a figure of us" (I Cor. 10, 11).[21] Among the many other things which they were commanded in the Mosaic Law necessarily to be done regarding lepers, was this one, that the leper should be cast out of the camp. "All the time," the Law says, "that he is a leper and unclean, he shall dwell alone without the camp" (Lev. 13, 46).

Now the leper described holds the manifest figure of heretics. For Blessed Augustine, when expounding the passage of the Gospel about the ten lepers says: "We must try, then, to find out what the leprosy itself signifies. They who were without it are called 'clean,' not 'sound.' Leprosy is a defect in color, not an organic ailment or a failure in the power of senses or members. It is not, therefore, beside the mark to understand by lepers those who, not having the knowledge of the true faith, hold various doctrines of error. They do not hide their ignorance, but bring it forth to the light as the greatest cleverness, and boast about it in their speech. There is not one single false doctrine which has not in it something of truth. True doctrine, therefore, which is confused with an undue amount of false doctrines in the mouth of one man, like that which becomes apparent on the human body by color, signifies leprosy, a leprosy composed, as it were, of healthy and unhealthy dyes, spots, and stains; mortal bodies with various hues of color."[22] Bede subscribes to these words in a homily on the passage of Luke's Gospel

---

21 This wording of the quotation is found in the Clementine Vulgate of 1598.
22 *Quaestiones Evangeliorum*, bk. 2, q. 40 (PL 35, 1354-1355).

which according to the practice of the Roman Church is read in the Mass of the [Tenth]²³ Sunday after Pentecost.²⁴

There are still many other things to be considered in the leprous man, from which can be gathered that he was a true figure of the heretic. For the leprous man infects others by contact with him, and a heretic harms believers by association with him. The leper's breath was harmful, and for this reason his mouth was ordered to be covered with cloth.²⁵ And the heretics' speech, Paul bearing witness, "spreadeth like a canker" (II Tim. 2, 17), and for this reason he is forbidden to preach. Because as Solomon says: "He that putteth a fool to silence, appeaseth anger" (Prov. 26, 10). Since, therefore, the leper, lest he could harm others by his association with others, was commanded in the Mosaic Law that he be cast out of the camp²⁶ and of association with all men, by this exemplar and under the veil of this figure it is shown to us that it is just, nay, necessary, that that the heretic be excommunicated, and in this way cast out of the camp of the Church, lest when associating with Catholics, he would be able to harm them by his association.

Add to these things that heretics are always contentious, and never want to embrace the peace which the living and dying God so strenuously commended to us, but having been made inventor and upholders of new teachings they eager-

---

23 Lk. 17, 11-19. The text here cites the fourteenth Sunday after Pentecost, but this Gospel is now found in the tenth Sunday's Gospel of the *Missale Romanum*.

24 "And whosoever lacks Christ's grace through heretical depravity, or Gentile superstition, or Jewish perfidy, or also fraternal schism, as it were, having difference of color (cf. Lev. 13, 2), it is necessary that he come to the Church, so that he may have the true color of faith, which he will receive" (*In Evangelium Sancti Lucae*, bk. 5, c. 17 (PL 92, 542D-543A)).

25 Cf. Lev. 13, 45.

26 Cf. Num. 5, 2.

First spiritual punishment: excommunicaiton and denial of burial

ly seek after contentions, and stir up strifes and dissentions within the Church. Wherefore it is just and necessary to cast out heretics from the communion of the Church, so that at least in this way peace may be rendered to the Church. For Solomon says: "Cast out the scoffer, and contention shall go out with him" (Prov. 22, 10). Bede when expounding these words says: "Expel the heretic, whom you cannot correct, from the Church; and when you take away from him the liberty of preaching, you render assistance to Catholic peace."[27]

Finally, from the very beginning of the Church true Catholics always fled away from consorting with heretics, and completely withdrew from associating with them, and they did not want to have any conversation with them, except perhaps for the sake of correction, to such an extent that they did not want to enter a house in which there was a heretic. As a very certain and irrefragable testimony of which matter, I give just one example which Blessed Irenaeus relates. For he, a true martyr of Christ, when speaking about the bishop and martyr Polycarp, a disciple of John the Apostle, says these words: "There are also those who heard from him that John, the disciple of the Lord, going to bathe at Ephesus, and perceiving Cerinthus within, rushed out of the bath-house without bathing, exclaiming, 'Let us fly, lest even the bath-house fall down, because Cerinthus, the enemy of the truth, is within.' And Polycarp himself replied to Marcion, who met him on one occasion, and said, 'Do you know me?' 'I do know you, the first-born of Satan.' Such was the horror which the Apostles and their disciples had against holding even verbal communication with any corrupters of the truth; as Paul also says, 'A man that is an heretic, after the first and second admonition, reject; knowing that he that is such is subverted, and sins, being condemned by his own judgment'

---

27 *Allegorica expositio in Parabolas Salomonis*, bk. 2, c. 20 (PL 91, 1003C).

(Tit. 3, 10-11)."[28] And nearly the same words are cited under the name of Bede in the chapter, *Omnis*.[29]

Since therefore we have shown by so many compelling reasons that the excommunication of heretics is just, it is necessary so that whoever chooses to be and be considered a believing Catholic would avoid consorting and conversing with any manifest heretic, lest doing the contrary, he give to others the just occasion of suspecting that he also has been stained with the same crime of heresy, as he with whom he converses.

---

28 *Adversus Haereses*, bk. 3, c. 3, n. 4 (PG 7, 853-854).
29 *Decretum Gratiani*, pt. 2, *causa* 24, q. 3, c. 24 (PL 187, 1275C-1276B).

Chapter XIX

Whether a heretic could be excommunicated after death.

It is very clear to any theologian, even one only moderately understanding Sacred Scripture, that a dead man cannot be excommunicated, because the power of jurisdiction, which is granted by Christ Our Savior to the prelates of the Church for excommunicating someone, was granted only for those living and existing on earth, but not for the dead, who are located above the earth, or below the earth. For Christ Our Savior granted the power of excommunicating the incorrigible and contumacious (as we just taught in the preceding chapter by the testimony of the holy Doctors) by these words, speaking thus: "If he will not hear the church, let him be to thee as the heathen and publican" (Mt. 18, 17). Now those words, as it is very easily established from the text of the Gospel itself, are referred to those alone who having been corrected once and again by a brother, and a third time by a prelate, refuse to amend, being as it were contumacious and rebellious. From which process of the Gospel, all theologians conclude with a concordant opinion that the sentence of excommunication cannot be given for any sin, even mortal; but contumacy needs to be annexed, without which the sentence of excommunication cannot be made. But since a dead man cannot be admonished once either by a brother or by the Church, he could never be called contumacious or rebellious after death, wherefore he cannot be excommunicated after death.

Perhaps someone will say that the dead man is not excommunicated on account of the contumacy which he had after death, because such contumacy of this kind cannot befall him, but rather the dead man is excommunicated on account of the contumacy he had before death, which was not known while he was alive, but after his death. But that this could not

Book 2, Chapter 19

happen, the words, which Christ Our Savior said immediately after the preceding ones for the confirmation of excommunication, very clearly prove. For after those words, "Let him be to thee as the heathen and publican," He immediately added: "Whatsoever you shall bind upon earth, shall be bound also in heaven; and whatsoever you shall loose upon earth, shall be loosed also in heaven" (v. 18). By which words (as we showed in the immediately preceding chapter from the testimony of Jerome) Our Savior further explained the same power of excommunicating, and He showed that it is ratified and firm.

Still if someone does not trust Jerome alone in this matter, and is not content with his testimony alone, I could cite many others from among the holy Doctors as a testimony for this matter. Nevertheless, lest I burden the reader by excessive prolixity in a very clear matter, I will cite only two other very reliable witnesses, and (as it is said) beyond all exception,[1] who rely on the above-mentioned words of Our Savior to prove that the power of excommunication was given to the Church. The first is [Pseudo-] Pope and martyr Urban [I] in a letter concerning the common life and offering of the faithful written to all bishops, who after he inhibited Church goods from being taken to be converted into other uses and threatened anyone looting them with excommunication, lest anyone dare to contemn such an excommunication, he proves the same power of excommunicating by the Savior's words, whereby He says: "Whatsoever you shall bind upon earth, shall be bound also in heaven."[2] Pope Gelasius in the

---

1 *Omni exceptione major.*
2 PL 130, 139A. This passage is said to be apocryphal and a product of the *False Decretals of Pseudo-Isidore.*

Whether a heretic could be excommunicated after death

chapter, *Legatur*,[3] and in the chapter, *Nec quisquam*,[4] proves by those same words that the power of excommunication was given to the Church.

Now those words of Our Savior speak only about those who are on earth, that is, about those who are alive in this world, not however about the dead, who are either above the earth or below the earth. Thus the Church can bind or loose only the living, but not the dead. And not merely all theologians uphold this opinion, but also the experts of Canon Law. Yet some canonists except from this law a heretical man, who although he has died to this world, nevertheless on account of the gravity of the crime, they say that he can also be excommunicated after death. For the Glossator of the Decretals on the chapter, *Si quis episcopus*,[5] on the words, *Post mortem*, after he cited the chapter, *Sane*,[6] as

---

[3] "And He Who alone had such great power, commands Blessed Peter the Apostle: 'Whatsoever you shall bind upon earth, shall be bound also in heaven; and whatsoever you shall loose upon earth, shall be loosed also in heaven.' 'Upon earth,' He said. For He never said that the dead are absolved from the binding" (*Decretum Gratiani*, pt. 2, *causa* 24, q. 2, c. 2 (PL 187, 1288C-1289A)).

[4] "And let no one at all persuade you that Achatius was freed from the crime of his transgression, because he who, after falling back into an association of depravity, by law deserved to be excommunicated from the Apostolic communion, died persisting in this same damnation, and the absolution which he neither sought nor deserved at all, being dead he no longer can obtain. Indeed, it was delegated by the voice of Christ to the Apostles themselves: 'Whatsoever you shall bind upon earth,' etc. Moreover, concerning him who has been assigned a permanent abode in the Divine judgment, it is not right for us to decide otherwise than that in which his last day finds him" (*Ibid.*, c. 4 (PL 187, 1289C-1290A)).

[5] *Decretals of Gregory IX*, bk. 5, tit. 7 (*De haereticis*), c. 5.

[6] "*It is not necessary to withhold alms after death from those we did not cease to communicate in life. Urban II to Bishop Guitmund of Aversa.* Of course, we praise Your Fraternity for dealing

a confirmation of his opinion, then objects to himself, and replies by these words: "On the contrary, because crimes are extinguished by death, [*Causa*] twenty-three (twenty-four according to others), question two, chapter one,[7] and the crime was extinguished with the punishment.[8] Yet this

---

with Richard, the son of Borellus, out of zeal for God and charity for souls. But it ought not to be feared, you are not so much to abstain from alms for him. Indeed, among the other Fathers of our faith, Blessed Leo, the eminent Doctor, says: 'We cannot be in communion with those, when dead, with whom when alive we were not in communion' [Letter 167]. It is clear, therefore, that since those with whom we have communicated when they were living (to speak from the contrary), we can also communicate with them when dead. We are clearly placed between two oppositions, that is, between the ungodly and the schismatics. We cannot communicate with schismatics in any way, or we may: but we communicate dispensationally with sinners and robbers, because they have supported the Church up to now, and promise themselves to be faithful in the future. Otherwise we must leave the regions of this world. Under which pledge we also granted him absolution recently on the birthday of Blessed Peter. Because then the aforesaid man was neither excommunicated by name, nor did he go forth with the excommunicated by name, but remained in the faith and service of his Lord, although dispensationally for us, that is, as long as we suffer them, to communicate by alms for him, and to help the soul of the deceased in all ways of the Christian religion" (*Decretum Gratiani*, pt. 2, *causa* 24, q. 2, c. 3 (PL 187, 1289A-C)).

7 "Now that after death no one can be excommunicated or absolved, is shown from the words of the Gospel, in which it is said: 'Whatsoever you shall bind upon earth,' etc. Above the earth, he says, not under the earth; showing that we can loose or bind the living according to the diversity of their merits; but we cannot pass judgment on the dead" (*Ibid.*, c. 1 (PL 187, 1288A-B)).

8 "Even if Marcellus, who was accused of the crime of forgery, is dead, and for this reason the crime is extinguished in his person, still the accusation is not annulled, so far as you are concerned, as you state that his wife, as well as yourself, has also been accused of

Whether a heretic could be excommunicated after death

is special in the crime of heresy unto the detestation of the crime, so that after death he could be accused and excommunicated."[9] Abbas in expounding the aforesaid chapter, *Si quis episcopus*, subscribes to the same opinion, also saying that this is special for a heretic, that after death he could be excommunicated.[10]

But actually (so that I may speak frankly) both erred miserably, because they neither understood the power of the Pontiffs in this matter, nor did they consider the power of excommunication, nor Gratian's words, and penetrate more deeply those things which he cites in that same place from other authors. Certainly someone could be condemned of heresy after death, that is, sentence be given by which it is declared that he was a heretic, and fell into heresy in this world, because the deceased heretic showed no signs or repentance. For (as we said in the preceding chapter) a heretic is excommunicated by the law itself even before the declaration of a judge. Because even if someone were a heretic so secretly, that it never reached the knowledge of the judge, still if he outwardly manifested his heresy in any way, and did not merely ardently love his heresy with zeal in his heart, still not on account of this will he be free from the excommunication, since such excommunication does not depend on man, so that it might have its force, but it was inflicted by the law itself. Thus he who is condemned of heresy after death, is not then excommunicated, but is declared that he was excommunicated before death, so that thereafter it is not permitted for anyone to pray for him as for others, and all understand that he who was condemned for

---

complicity in the same offence" (*The Code of Justinian*, bk. 9, tit. 6 (*Si reus vel accusator mortuus fuerit*), l. 2).
9 *Decretales Gregorii IX. Pont. Max suis commentariis illustratae* (Paris: Merlin & Desboys, 1561).
10 *Commentaria seu lectura in quinque Decretalium libros*, vol. 7, fol. 134r.

heresy does not have part in the prayers which the Church makes for the deceased.

And I wish to prove incontestably that nothing else can be said by an authority and by a very convincing reason. Pope Leo in his letter to Rusticus, bishop of Narbonne, speaks thus: "[Question: *Concerning those who on their deathbed promise repentance and die before receiving communion.* Reply:] Their cause is reserved for the judgment of God, in Whose hand it was that their death was put off until the very time of communion. But we cannot be in communion with those, when dead, with whom when alive we were not in communion."[11] From which words it is evident that Pope Leo's opinion is that no one can be absolved after death from the excommunication, in which he died. And hence it is deduced that in the same way no one, who died without excommunication, can be excommunicated after death. Now this reasoning is proved to be good by the testimony of Pope Urban in the letter to Bishop Guitmund, who from those words of Blessed Leo forms the same conclusion, speaking thus: "Indeed, among the other Fathers of our faith, Blessed Leo, the eminent Doctor, says: 'We cannot be in communion with those, when dead, with whom when alive we were not in communion.' It is clear, therefore, that since those with whom we have communicated when they were living (to speak from the contrary), we can also communicate with them when dead."[12]

Pope Gelasius in the chapter, *Legatur*,[13] very clearly says that no one after death can be absolved from the excommunication in which he died, and in confirmation of his opinion he cites those words now often repeated, which Our Savior

---

11 Letter 167, q. 8 (PL 54, 1205C-1206A); *Decretum Gratiani*, pt. 2, *causa* 24, q. 2, c. 1 (PL 187, 1288C-1289B).
12 *Decretum Gratiani*, pt. 2, *causa* 24, q. 2, c. 3 (PL 187, 1289A-B).
13 *Ibid.*, c. 2 (PL 187, 1288C-1289A).

said to Blessed Peter: "Whatsoever you shall bind upon earth, shall be bound also in heaven; and whatsoever you shall loose upon earth, shall be loosed also in heaven" (Mt. 18, 18). Gelasius when very learnedly commenting on these words says: "'Upon earth,' He said. For He never said that in the binding the dead are absolved."[14] From which words it is very clearly established that Pope Gelasius was motivated by this reason to say that a dead man cannot be bound or absolved, namely, because he is not on earth. Now this reason equally persuades about a deceased heretic, as about all the other deceased: because the deceased heretic is not more upon the earth than the other dead. Therefore since the same reason ought to apply to the deceased heretic, which applies to the other deceased, it is necessary that deceased heretics be judged by the same law, by which the other deceased are judged about an excommunication. Because either that reason given by Gelasius does not prove well about the other deceased, that they cannot be loosened or bound, or it also applies to a heretic just as to the other deceased.

Furthermore, Solomon says: "If the clouds be full, they will pour out rain upon the earth. If the tree fall to the south, or to the north, in what place soever it shall fall, there shall it be" (Eccle. 11, 3). The tree about which Solomon speaks in this passage, is then said to fall (as Jerome interprets on the same place[15]) when a man dies. "In what place soever it shall fall, there shall it be," because just as death laid hold of him, so afterwards he will be found. From which opinion of Solomon it is proved that he who is not excommunicated at death, likewise cannot be excommunicated after death. What Pope Gelasius says in the chapter, *Nec quisquam*, confirms this argumentation of ours, where when discussing about the

---

14 *Ibid.* (PL 187, 1289A).
15 "For wherever you have made your home and seat for the future, whether to the south or facing the north, when you die you will remain there" (*Commentarius in Ecclesi*asten (PL 23, 1102A).

deceased whether he could be absolved from an excommunication, or be bound by it, says these words: "Moreover, concerning him who has been assigned a permanent abode in the Divine judgment, it is not right for us to decide otherwise than that in which his last day finds him."[16] These words are very manifestly consonant with those which we cited from Solomon.

Again in the same way the Pope, or any other bishop, can excommunicate a deceased heretic, just as he can absolve a man unjustly condemned of heresy, as it was decreed in the first session of the Fifth Council,[17] which Gratian cites in the chapter, *Sane profertur*.[18] But when he absolved him who had been unjustly condemned for heresy, he did not absolve from the excommunication, because it is evident that it was null, and was not inflicted upon him, but he merely declares that he was not excommunicated: thus when he condemns or excommunicates a heretic after death, he is merely declaring that he is a heretic, and was excommunicated on account of the heresy, and hence he ought not to be prayed for thereafter.

Next, that they say that this is something special for heretics, that on account of the gravity of the crime they could be excommunicated after death, very clearly shows that they do not know to whom the power of excommunicating granted to the Church extends. For if they had understood this well, they never would have said this. Who would

---

16 *Ibid.*, c. 4 (PL 187, 1290A).
17 I. e.. the Second Council of Constantinople.
18 "It is reasonably brought forward by some, who say that it is necessary to anathematize heretics after death, and to follow in this the teaching of the holy Fathers, who not only condemned heretics when they were alive, but also their death inasmuch as they died in their impiety, just as they recalled after death those who were unjustly condemned, and wrote them in sacred diptychs" (*Ibid.*, c. 6, §6 (PL 187, 1292A)).

Whether a heretic could be excommunicated after death

ever say that the ruler of a city can punish evildoers staying in that city, in which he has completely no jurisdiction? The rule of law is indeed clear which condemns and invalidates such a sentence and punishment. "The sentence is void," the rule says, "if pronounced by another than the proper judge."[19] Nevertheless, if a king on account of the gravity of a crime, which is committed in a city, were to grant a new authority to the ruler of another city, so that he could punish the evildoers, and very wicked men, who he knew would otherwise not be subject to his jurisdiction in the city, then with the new authority granted to him he could give a firm judgment on them, against whom he previously could do nothing at all.

The power of excommunicating, which we learn from the Gospel was given to the Church, extends only to the living, as it is clearly established from the words of the Gospel, and from the interpretation of the holy Doctors, whom we cited above. Therefore if a bishop attempted to excommunicate a dead man, he will give sentence on him who is not subject to him, and it will necessarily happen that that sentence, because it was not pronounced by the proper judge, according to the rule of law, ought to be reckoned to be void. If God granted to the Church, in addition to the general authority given over the living, some other special authority so that she could also excommunicate heretics after death on account of the gravity of heretics, then I would concede.

But because they cannot show that any other special authority over heretics was granted by God, I do not know by what audacity they dare to say that this is special for

---

19 Cf. *Liber sextus Decretalium*, rule of law n. 26: "Everything that the judge does outside of his official duties is null and void"; *The Code of Justinian*, bk. 7, tit. 48 (*Si non a competenti judice judicatum esse dicatur*), l. 4; *Decretum Gratiani*, pt. 2, causa 6, q. 3, c. 2 (PL 187, 738A); *Decretals of Gregory IX*, bk. 2, tit. 1 (*De judiciis*), c. 5 (*At si cleri*). Peter Lombard, *In IV Sententiarum*, dist. 17, q. 3, art. 3, ad 2um; Suppl., q. 8, a. 2, Obj. 2.

heretics, on account of the gravity of the crime, to be excommunicated after death. For there is something special in that crime, whereby it surpasses in wickedness that other vices: but there is not something special in the power of excommunicating granted by Christ to the Church, such that He would have granted her a broader power over heretics than over other men. Now it is necessary that they consider this power more than the gravity of the crime, so that they could correctly decide about this question: because an excommunication itself, so that it be valid, depends more on the power granted to it, than on that gravity of the crime. Therefore, motivated by these very convincing arguments, I say that a heretical man can be condemned after death, that is, by the sentence being declared that he was a heretic, and persevered in heresy until death, and consequently had died in the excommunication: yet I deny that he could then after death be firstly excommunicated, since by death he was then placed beyond the judgment of men.

And Gratian does not say anything else in Part two, *Causa* twenty-four, Question two: because here he says that a man could be accused and condemned for the crime of heresy after death, which we also assert, but he never says that he, or anyone else, could be excommunicated after death. If you ask why someone could be condemned for heresy after death, but not excommunicated, I reply that this is the reason, namely, that the sentence condemning the deceased heretic is as it were declaratory of past deeds, declaring that he had embraced this or that heresy with a pertinacious mind, and consequently was excommunicated by that fact: which (as it is clearly evident) can happen even after death. But an excommunication is not so much a sentence, as an execution of a sentence. For just as it is one thing to decide that a thief deserves hanging, and another to hang the thief, so likewise it is one thing to decide that someone is deserving of excommunication, and something quite different to

Whether a heretic could be excommunicated after death

actually excommunicate him. In fact the first is called the sentence, but the second is not the sentence but the execution of the sentence. Granted, an excommunication ought to be called a sentence, yet it will not be merely a declaratory one of a past deed, but an inflictive one of a present punishment. For by the excommunication it is not merely declared that he upon whom it was inflicted committed some deadly crime, on account of which alone the excommunication was inflicted: but in addition to this a punishment is inflicted, whereby the excommunicated man is excluded from participation and association with the faithful. Now this punishment cannot be inflicted upon the dead, since they are now placed beyond men's judgment.

When, however, someone is condemned of heresy, and judged a heretic, no spiritual punishment is inflicted upon him: but merely a declaratory sentence is pronounced about a deed done long ago while he still was alive, which declares that he was a heretic, and had died in heresy. Which sentence is not of little importance, nor is it given in vain and uselessly: but it greatly causes many things which thence occur to be done by law: namely, to all corporal punishments, which can befall the heretic's body, because this body and those things which befall it are on earth, and subject to men's authority.

Firstly in fact, it avails for making a confiscation of the possessions of the same heretic. For the possessions of him who when hid while living in heresy, if after death it is evident that he was a heretic, by that very fact are confiscated, as decreed in the chapter, *Accusatus*, §. *In eo*.[20] Such a sentence also brings about making known the infamy of the children to others. The children of a heretical parent were indeed (as we taught above) by the law itself infamous: but because the parent's crime, whence the infamy is transmitted to the children, was hidden: wherefore the infamy of the children was not known to others. Now the deceased man

---

20 *Liber sextus decretalium*, bk. 5, tit. 2 (*De haereticis*), c. 8, §7.

is condemned so that by that very fact, it makes known the children's infamy to everyone knowing this condemnation. Next, the deceased heretic's condemnation does a third thing: namely, it manifests to others that the body of that man is unworthy of the ecclesiastical burial-place in which he was buried. For (as we showed in the preceding chapter) a heretic is by law deprived of ecclesiastical burial. Wherefore after it is established about his heresy after death, his body, if it can be distinguished from the others of the faithful, ought to be disinterred as from something unjustly possessed, and cast out of the Church. For so the Council of Constance decreed ought to be done with the heretic John Wycliffe's body, then already buried. For in the eighth session, after the same Council declared that he was a heretic, and his repentance never took place, it added these words: "And this holy Synod decrees and orders that his body, and bones (if they can be distinguished from the other bodies of the faithful), to be exhumed, and cast far away from the Church's cemetery, according to the canonical and legal ordinances."[21]

Finally, this sentence, by which someone after death is condemned of heresy, brings about by that very fact that all would understand that it is wicked and impious to pray to God for him, just as for an excommunicated man, who died in the excommunication. The sentence, whereby someone is condemned of heresy after death brings about all these things, yet it does not have the power to inflict an excommunication upon him.

---

21 Mansi 27, 635-636.

Chapter XX

It is replied to the objections which could be adduced in favor of the opinion of Abbas and the Gloss.

Here nevertheless perhaps some supporter of Abbas or the Gloss will object to me that many heretics have been anathematized after death. For the Council of Constance in the eighth session anathematized John Wycliffe already deceased at that time. And in the Fifth Council,[1] in the first session, Dioscurus[2] and Eutyches,[3] and many other heretics, who had already been dead long before for many years. In the Sixth Council,[4] in the last session, Theodore of Pharan, Sergius, Pyrrhus, Paul, and Honorius, and many other heretics were anathematized, who were all already dead. And in the chapter, *Si quis episcopus*,[5] it is commanded that an anathema be pronounced after death for a bishop who appointed heretics or pagans as heirs.

I certainly admit that someone could be anathematized after death, yet not excommunicated. For to anathematize and to excommunicate, or an anathema and an excommunication, are not entirely the same things. Now it can indeed be established that this is so from the fact that there are

---

1 I. e., the Second Council of Constantinople.
2 Both Dioscurus and Eutyches were anathematized by the Lateran Synod in 649 A.D.
3 Cf. Can. 11 (Mansi 9, 383; Dz. 223). Dioscurus was not anathematized by the Fifth Ecumenical Council, the Second Council of Constantinople.
4 The Sixth Ecumenical Council was the Third Council of Constantinople which took place in 680-681 A.D., but the author seems rather to be referring to the Lateran Synod of 649 A.D., which was called by some the Sixth Council, but is now generally not accepted to be an ecumenical council. Cf. Dz. 271.
5 *Decretals of Gregory IX*, bk. 5, tit. 7 (*De haereticis*), c. 5.

many who anathematize heresies and heretics, who have completely no power of excommunicating. For everyone who abandons the heresy which he was previously holding, when he is received into the communion of the Church (as we taught above) is obliged to firstly abjure and anathematize the heresy by which he had been stained: as it appears in the chapter, *Ego Berengarius*.[6] Yet not every such heretic returning to his senses has the power of excommunicating. Moreover the Church often in her sentences after the word, "excommunication," adds the word, "anathema," saying: "We excommunicate and anathematize," as it appears in both of the chapters, *Excommunicamus*.[7] And in the chapter, *Cum non ab homine*,[8] it is firstly commanded that the incorrigible cleric be "excommunicated," and then, "struck with the blade of anathema." From all which things it is very clearly evident that an excommunication and an anathema are not entirely the same thing: but an anathema adds something more to the excommunication especially because consistently, where these two words are joined together, the word "anathema" is always placed after the word "excommunication," and is never put before it. Again when Peter was warming himself in the court of the high priest, Mark the Evangelist says about him that "He began to curse (*anathematizare*) and to swear, saying; I know not this man" (14, 71). Now it is certain that Peter was not them excommunicated, although he anathematized.

From all these things it is established clearer than light, that there is difference between these two words, "anathematize" and "excommunicate." Therefore it is befitting to explain the meanings of these words, because thereupon the

---

6 *Decretum Gratiani*, pt. 3 (*De consecratione*), dist. 2, c. 42 (*Ego Berengarius*) (PL 187, 1750A-1751A).
7 *Decretals of Gregory IX*, bk. 5, tit. 7 (*De haereticis*), cc. 13 & 15.
8 *Ibid.*, bk. 2, tit. 1 (*De judiciis*), c. 10.

whole sum total of this question depends, and from the want of knowledge of these things many have taken an occasion of error, thinking that the meaning of both words is completely the same, while nevertheless it is very different. "Anathema" is a Greek word, and it means the votive offerings, which are offered to God and His Saints, and are hung in the temples for the sake of honor. And according to this bare meaning of the word, it is very often found in Holy Writ, especially in the Old Testament. For (so that I may omit others) that is very manifest, which is read in the book of Josue about the storming of the city of Jericho, where these words are had: "And when in the seventh going about the priests sounded with the trumpets, Josue said to all Israel: Shout: for the Lord hath delivered the city to you: And let this city be an anathema, and all things that are in it, to the Lord" (6, 16-17). He commanded that the city and all things which were in it to be an anathema to the Lord, because He wanted everything which was in it to be kept for the Lord, and offered in sacrifice to Him, such that no one would dare to keep from among those things for themselves any of those things. Now when Achan, the son of Charmi, had taken from the spoils of the city, and had kept it for himself, the Lord was angered, and said to the sons of Israel: "The anathema is in the midst of thee, O Israel: thou canst not stand before thy enemies, until he be destroyed out of thee that is defiled with this wickedness" (*Ibid.* 7, 13). He called the spoils in this passage "anathema," which Achan, the son of Charmi, had kept for himself, because they had been consigned to be dedicated to God. Now just as it is not permitted to touch those things which have been offered to God, so also it is not permitted to associate with those who have been cut off from the Church through excommunication.

And for this reason, by a similitude drawn through the contrary, he who has been excommunicated, is called by analogy "anathema." For so Paul uses the word when he says: "If any one preach to you a gospel, besides that which you have received, let him be anathema" (Gal. 1, 9), that is, excommunicated, and separated from God. All these things are confirmed by the testimony of Blessed Chrysostom, who speaks thus: "For as in the case of a thing dedicated, which is set apart for God, no one would venture so much as to touch it with his hand or even to come near it; so too with a man who is put apart from the Church, in cutting him off from all, and removing him as far off as possible, he calls him by this name in a contrary sense, thus with much fear denouncing to all men to keep apart from him, and to spring away from him. For the thing set apart, no one, from respect of it, ventures to come near to. But from him who is cut off, all men separate themselves from a very opposite feeling. And so the separation is the same, and both the one and the other are equally removed from the generality. Still, the mode of separation is not the same, but in this case it is the opposite to what it is in that. For from the one they keep back as being dedicated to God; from the other as being estranged from God, and broken off from the Church."[9]

And Theophylactus after him says the same thing, when interpreting the passage of Paul to the Romans: "I wished myself to be an anathema from Christ, for my brethren" (9, 3).[10] And the Fifth Council[11] asserts this same thing, whose testimony is cited by Gratian, in which these words are found: "Anathema means nothing other than separation from God."[12] This ought to be understood, according

---

9 *Homilies on Romans*, hom. 16 (PG 60, 549).
10 *Commentarius in Epistolam ad Romanos* (PG 124, 459A).
11 I. e., the Second Council of Constantinople.
12 *Decretum Gratiani*, pt. 2, *causa* 24, q. 3, c. 9 (PL 187, 1299B). "Or do they not know, or rather knowing do they pretend not to know, that the judgment of anathema is nothing other than separation from God? Even though the wicked did not receive the word [anathema] from anyone, nevertheless he in reality inflicts

to that meaning, according to which anathema is joined to excommunication, and about it alone the Fifth Council[13] was speaking, as is evident from the context of the quotation, which always is wont to uncover the true and genuine meaning of the text. Since in fact elsewhere, according to the full meaning of that word, it signifies many more things than separation from God, as is clearly evident from the testimonies of Sacred Scripture and of the holy men, which we cited above. "Anathema" is taken according to this manner, whenever it is said in the Councils' definitions or the Pontiff's decrees: "If someone says or does this or that, let him be anathema," that is, cursed, and alienated from the society of the Church. For the word, "Anathema," as by analogy is joined to excommunication, expressed not merely a lesser excommunication, but a greater, by which the one excommunicated is cut off and separated from the Church. For so it is expressly taught in the chapter, *Hengiltrudam*.[14] From this noun, "anathema," is derived the verb, "anathematize," which means to curse, detest, and execrate. As evidence of which thing (so that I may omit the pagan authors) I cite only Blessed Augustine, who says these words: "Whence it is that the anathema is seen to be something detestable and abomi-

---

the anathema upon himself, by his impiety separating himself from the true vine. Now what do they say, and again what do they say to the Apostle saying: 'A man that is a heretic, after the first and second admonition, avoid: knowing that he, that is such an one, is subverted, and sinneth, being condemned by his own judgment' (Tit. 3, 10-11)?" (Mansi 9, 371B).

13 I. e., the Second Council of Constantinople.

14 "Know that Engeltrude, wife of Boso [III Count of Turin and Arles] is not only under the ban of excommunication, which separates her from the society of the brethren, but under the anathema, which separates from the body of Christ, which is the Church" (*Decretum Gratiani*, pt. 2, *causa* 3, q. 4, c. 12 (PL 187, 677A)). She was excommunicated in 866 A.D. after deserting her husband and fleeing to France with Wanger, her vassal.

nable. For just as a conqueror would not take anything for his own use, but would vow all for paying the punishment, and this was 'to anathemize,' which in common language means 'to dedicate.' The origin of this word is in the Greek language, from those things which were vowed and fully discharged, that is, having promised and given up, are put on high in temples: ἀπὸ τοῦ ἄνω τιθέναι, that is, to place a thing on high, either by fixing or hanging."[15] Thus "anathema" according to Augustine, is the same as something abominable and detestable.

Now "to anathematize," or (as he says) "to anathemize," is to abominate, curse, and detest. And this word is taken according to this meaning in the writing of Mark the Evangelist in that place cited above, when he said that Peter "began to curse and to swear, saying; I know not this man" (Mk. 14, 71). For Peter then swore with an oath by an execration, which (as Augustine teaches[16]) is the most serious of all oaths. When Peter was swearing he was cursing himself, and imprecating maledictions, so that greater faith would be adhibited to his oath; as though he were to say: "May I be cursed by God, and may God add such and such things to me, may these or those things come upon me, if I knew this man." This certainly is to swear and to anathematize. And it ought to be believed that Peter when denying said this, or something similar, on account of which he was said "to curse [*anathematizare*] and swear": for when swearing he anathematized not another, but himself. From all these things it is now very clearly established that there is a difference between to anathematize and to excommunicate,

---

15 *Quaestiones in Heptateuchum*, bk. 4 (*Quaestiones in Numeros*), q. 41 (PL 34, 738).
16 "When someone says, 'If I have done this, may I suffer that,' he seems to swear by solemn oath and imprecation, which is the strongest form of oath" (*Expositions of the Psalms*, Ps. 7, n. 3 (PL 36, 99)).

namely, the same which is between to curse, or detest, and to excommunicate. For those two things have such an order between themselves, that they are neither always separated from each other, nor always necessarily follow each other, so that they fit with the same thing. For although it could be the same thing to be excommunicated and to be anathematized, still it does not follow that everyone whom we anathematize or curse, is by that very fact excommunicated, nor on the contrary does it follow that every excommunicated person is by that very fact anathematized, or cursed.

And on account of this reason the Church, after she excommunicated publicly and by name, she was accustomed to anathematize. She then anathematizes, when she pronounces certain words of a curse and imprecations against the one excommunicated, for instance by saying Psalm one hundred and eight, full of curses, which in some churches is wont to be read at that time. In other churches certain ceremonies full of horror, are accustomed to be done after the excommunication has been given. Lit candles are extinguished with water poured from above before the people by the priest, who then says these words: "As this candle is extinguished in the water, so may the soul of this excommunicated man be perish in hell." Then as a sign of sadness for the soul thus perishing, a raised crucifix is covered with a black veil. When the Church does these and other similar things against the one excommunicated, she then anathematizes him. And the Pontiff commands this or any other similar thing to be done with an incorrigible cleric, whom in the above cited chapter, *Cum non ab homine*, after he has been excommunicated, he commands, if he does not wish to amend, ought to be "struck with the sword of anathema."[17] From all which things it is

---

17 "If, after having been deposed from office, he is incorrigible, he should first be excommunicated; but if he perseveres in his contumacy he should be stricken with the sword of anathema; but if plunging to the depths of the abyss, he reaches the point where

very clearly established in the decrees of the councils and Pontiffs that not in vain and without reason after the word "excommunication" is added the word "anathema." For after the excommunication, to incite greater horror and fear in others, it is right to add a curse, which the word "anathema" means.

Hence it is evident that Sylvester Mazzolini erred miserably, who in his *Summa [Summarum]*, in the first title of *Excommunicatio*,[18] says that an anathema is completely the same thing as a major excommunication, and to anathematize is also the same thing as to excommunicate with a major excommunication. For the persuasion of his opinion he cites the chapter, *Hengiltrudam*.[19] But actually (so that I may speak frankly) he did not understand the text: because if he had understood it well, he would have known very well that it does not support his opinion in the least. For that text says that an anathema states a major excommunication, which ought to be understood when it is taken according to that meaning, according to which it is applied to an excommunication. Yet that text never says that an anathema does not mean anything other than an excommunication. Next, that which the text says, an anathema signifies a major excommunication, ought to be so understood, because a curse which the word "excommunication" signifies, is not given except when preceded by a major excommunication. Therefore an anathema signifies a major excommunication, because when an anathema is said, it is given to be understood that a major excommunication has preceded, after which alone an anathema is won to be said, that is, a curse. I omit the very beautiful etymology of the word "anathema" which Sylvester gives. I

---

he despises these penalties, he should be given over to the secular arm" (*Decretals of Gregory IX*, bk. 2, tit. 1 (*De judiciis*), c. 10).

18 *Summa Summarum, quae Sylvestrina dicitur* (Antwerp: Petrus Bellerus, 1578), vol. 1, p. 355a, n. 23.

19 *Decretum Gratiani*, pt. 2, *causa* 3, q. 4, c. 12 (PL 187, 677A).

certainly am not surprised that he did not know these things, but I am very surprised that he was not afraid to teach with such great authority things which he did not know.

And certainly I would not have said these things against him, if he had been even a little forbearing with others. For he often treated injuriously Angelo [Carletti] di Chivasso,[20] a man renown, besides for learning which he had not a little, for many miracles, even though he frequently stole many words, and not one having been changed, from him: as one could easily detect very many thefts of his, whoever wishes to compare his *Summa* with the *Summa Angelica*, although he seems to have taken pains to hide his thefts, because those things which Angelo put under one word [or heading], he took care to transfer to another word, lest perhaps he who might read both *Summa* on the same subject, could detect the theft. Thus it was befitting to be done with Sylvester, that since he had blamed so many times, he might also be blamed.

Therefore we acknowledge that not only deceased heretics, but also deceased Catholics, can be anathematized by the living, yet not excommunicated. For we very often see living children curse their dead parents, and detest and abominate them, wickedly imprecating them, because perhaps the parents while they lived, were prodigals of those things, or because they divided wrongly the inheritance with them, or on account of some similar reason. Whence it so happens that children anathematize their deceased parents, yet not in the same manner do they excommunicate them, because not all are able to do this, since to excommunicate is an act of authority and jurisdiction, which it is very clear not all have. Still the Church was not wont to anathematize, that is, curse,

---

20 Blessed Angelo Carletti di Chivasso (1411-1495) was a moral theologian of the Order of Friars Minor; born at Chivasso in Piedmont he wrote the *Summa de Casibus Conscientiae*, called after him the *Summa Angelica*.

except him whom had firstly been excommunicated. Thus although the Church sometimes uses the word "anathema" (as we said) for "excommunication," still she does not always do this. Hence the Council of Constance anathematized the deceased John Wycliffe: the Fifth Council[21] anathematized many heresiarchs already dead: the Sixth Council[22] anathematized many other deceased heretics, that is, it cursed them, and said imprecations on them, yet it did not excommunicate them. And neither a council in its definitions nor a Pontiff in his decrees ever used the word "excommunication" against those heretics, but only the word "anathema." Since in fact both the councils and the Supreme Pontiffs understood well that they did not then have authority and jurisdiction over them, and they knew that there is not a small difference between anathema and excommunication.

Also that which is cited from the African synod in the chapter, *Si quis episcopus,*[23] ought to be interpreted in the same way, such that there the anathema is taken as a curse and not as an excommunication. For if it were to be used as an excommunication, he would have said, "Let him be anathema," that is, "Let him be excommunicated," and it would not have said, "Let an anathema be said to him." Because such a manner of speech is not used in the Church, so that instead of "to excommunicate," one would put, "To say an excommunication to someone." Therefore the council orders that an anathema be said to the bishop who appoints heretics or pagans as heirs, that is, he be cursed by all, all imprecate him, and all call him accursed.

Also let it be granted that the anathema there is put for excommunication, still nothing will hinder our opinion: because (as it is proved from the context of the words) that sentence which is pronounced there against such a bishop, is

---

21 I. e., the Second Council of Constantinople.
22 I. e., the Lateran Synod of 649 A.D. Cf. Dz. 271.
23 *Decretals of Gregory IX,* bk. 5, tit. 7 (*De haereticis*), c. 5.

Refutation of objections of Abbas and the Gloss

merely declaratory of the punishment already inflicted, and not an execution of a new excommunication. If the council had said, "Let him be anathema," it would have seemed to have thought that the excommunication was firstly inflicted after death, because when commanding there to be an anathema clearly seems to insinuate that previously there was not an anathema. But since the council commands that the anathema be pronounced, it is shown clearly enough that the sentence is declaratory. Because that which it says, "Let the anathema be pronounced," it is the same as though it were to have said, "Let him be declared to have been excommunicated," "Let him be called accursed." And that this is the true meaning of the text, the words which follow very clearly show. For after the council had said, "Let an anathema be said," it immediately added, "and his name be nowise listed among the priests of God."

There was in fact long ago the custom, that a list of all deceased bishops would be kept in the church, who were its pastors, and such sort of list was publicly read before the altar in the presence the people, so that the people would commend them to God. The African Synod therefore commands that the bishop who appointed heretics or pagans as heirs, would not be written in the list of bishops, and his name not recited among the names of the other bishops. That this was the Church's custom long ago is very clearly proved by that which Blessed Pope Leo [I] says in a letter to Anatolius, Bishop of Constantinople. For in that letter the same Blessed Pope Leo answers to certain questions proposed by the aforesaid Anatolius, and when replying to the third question, he speaks thus: "Concerning the reading out of the names of Dioscorus, Juvenal, and Eustathius at the holy altar, it beseems you, beloved, to observe that which our friends who were there present said ought to be done, and which is consistent with the honorable memory of Saint Flavian, and will not turn the minds of the laity away from

Book 2, Chapter 20

you. For it is very wrong and unbecoming that those who have harassed innocent Catholics with their attacks, should be mingled indiscriminately with the names of the Saints."[24]

And another, also [Pseudo-] Blessed, Pope Leo, the [second[25]] of this name, in a letter for the confirmation of the Sixth Council,[26] which if found in the last session of the same Council, shows the same custom and clearly explains the text of that chapter, *Si quis episcopus*,[27] when he says: "Furthermore," [Pseudo-] Leo [II] says, "we anathematize and hence execrate all heresies and all their authors, and supporters, who have tried to introduce errors into the Church against the Apostolic and orthodox faith having been deceived by diabolical fallacies of falsities, that is, Arius, Sabellius, Macedonius..." And after having listed many names of heretics, he finally adds: "Whom the holy, Catholic and Apostolic Church casts out of the list of believing Fathers, just as cockle ought to be taken away from the barn floor of the Lord's Church by the fan of Divine judgment."[28]

---

24 Letter 80 (PL 54, 914C-915A).
25 Pope Leo III was incorrectly cited here.
26 I. e., the Third Council of Constantinople. "Pope Leo II responded to the wish of the Emperor in a letter addressed to him, which at the same time contains the papal confirmation of the sixth Ecumenical Synod. The Pope in this letter first commends the Emperor as indeed worthy of commendation, and then remarks that the legates who had been sent by Agatho to the Synod had arrived in Rome in the July of the past 10th Indiction, i. e., in the July of 682. From this it is clear that the concluding note of this letter, as found in one of the two old Latin translations, representing it as written *Nonis Maii Indict. x.,* i. e., on the 7th of May 682, cannot possibly be genuine; for the Pope wrote after the return of his legates" (Charles Joseph Hefele, D.D., *A History of the Councils of the Church* (Edinburgh: T. & T. Clark, 1896), vol. 5, p. 180). Baronius considers this letter "suspect" as well. Cf. PL 96, 387.
27 *Decretals of Gregory IX*, bk. 5, tit. 7 (*De haereticis*), c. 5.
28 Mansi 11, 731; PL 96, 408A.

Refutation of objections of Abbas and the Gloss

From which two very reliable witnesses the correct and original meaning of that chapter, *Si quis episcopus*, is clearly established, since the council commands that that sort of bishop who appoints heretics or pagans as heirs, be not be called a bishop or priest of God after death, but an anathema be pronounced, that is, a detestable and abominable curse, and his name not be recited in the list of deceased bishops.

Secondly, it seems to me that someone could object the second chapter[29] which begins, *A nobis*,[30] where Pope Innocent [III] defines that after death absolution can be given to the deceased dying in excommunication,[31] and next he says that the Church in certain cases could bind and loose the dead. This text at first glance seems to completely destroy our opinion, but when well considered and intelligently examined it will speak in favor of our opinion, very far from even remotely wanting to oppose us. For the clearer understanding of which I advise the reader to consider that an excommunication, which is inflicted upon one person, extends its effects to many people. For an excommunication pertains not merely to the one excommunicated, but also to others: because when the Church excommunicates someone, by that very fact it obliges others not to publicly and solemnly pour out prayers before God, or give public alms, or offer sacrifices for him, or finally dare to have any association with him. It strikes that excommunicated man with not merely one lash, but with many, some of which pertain to the body, others to the soul. For since the excommunicated man has been cut off as a putrid member from the body, and separated far away: for which reason the common

---

29 There are two chapters in this title which begin with *A nobis*, and so the author is here referring to the second of these two.
30 *Decretals of Gregory IX*, bk. 5, tit. 39 (*De sententia excommunicationis*), c. 28.
31 The Pope here speaks of an excommunicated man "in whom there were manifest indications of repentance" when he died.

prayers of the Church, and her other good works, which the rest of the living members, united to the head, communicate with each other, can nowise benefit the one excommunicated. And this is the wound or lash which is inflicted upon the soul through excommunication. And about this the Church can do absolutely nothing regarding the deceased, because the soul, which ought to be struck with this lash, after the separation from the body is completely separated from the Church's judgment.

Besides this lash of the soul, there are other things which pertain to the body, namely, the privation of ecclesiastical burial, he cannot speak in a trial after a legitimate and valid sentence, and many other things decreed by law against those excommunicated. Regarding these corporal punishments I do not doubt that the Church could inflict them on the deceased, because the body of the deceased, and those things which could affect it, are still subject to the authority of the Church. Thus the Church can excommunicate, for a just reason, not only a heretic, but also any other wicked dead man, for this purpose, so that his body may lie outside of the Church as being unworthy of ecclesiastical burial. For a just urgent reason she can absolve another man who died in excommunication for this purpose, so that an ecclesiastical burial may be granted to him, of which he had been deprived on account of an excommunication.

Next, when the Church (as we said) excommunicates someone, she binds others so that they are unable to publicly pray to God for that man or perform other acts of piety on his behalf. Which having been done it harms him somewhat indirectly, when it deprives him of the suffrages both of body and of soul, which could come forth from others for him. And I do not doubt that the Church can do this regarding the deceased, because although that dead man has been put outside of the judgment of the Church, still other living men, to whom such a command of the Church is directed, are

Refutation of objections of Abbas and the Gloss

subject to the Church's authority. But because a certain harm is inflicted from such a command, wherefore the Church is then said to excommunicate: even though not the deceased but the living are bound by such an excommunication. And in this way it also ought to be asserted that the Church can absolve the dead from excommunication, who died in it. By which absolution, if the matter is considered well, both the dead man and others who are living are absolved; since the living were indeed bound, so that they could not pray for him who had died in excommunication. But after the benefit of absolution has been granted, the living are absolved, so that they can freely pray for the deceased, and exercise other works of piety for him. Nevertheless, because when such liberty has been granted to the living, it becomes beneficial for the deceased, the deceased man himself is said to be absolved.

And I reckon that the second chapter which begins, *A nobis*,[32] ought to be understood in this fashion, where the Pope decrees that the Church can loose and bind the dead. For (as it is evident from the context of the same text) the Pope in that place speaks not only about that benefit of the absolution which gives liberty to the living so that they can with impunity pray to God for the dead man, and exercise other works of piety for him. And he stated this same thing when he said that someone has been absolved before God Who is not deceived, who nevertheless is excommunicated. How can he be bound before the Church, who has been absolved before God, except because he is said to be bound simply because others have been bound by the Church, so that they could not pray for him, and on account of this he is said to be bound, because such binding of others redounds to his detriment? For otherwise the Church cannot excommunicate that dead man, so that she would separate and cut off

---

32 *Decretals of Gregory IX*, bk. 5, tit. 39 (*De sententia excommunicationis*), c. 28.

him from God, who was absolved before God, and consequently is joined to Him. I have drawn out the very long discussion about this matter, because I knew very well that those things which I have said are highly necessary, so that I can pull up by the roots this error, and in its place plant the firm truth.[33]

---

[33] "Although during the first centuries the anathema did not seem to differ from the sentence of excommunication, beginning with the sixth century a distinction was made between the two... At a late period, Gregory IX (1227-41), bk. 5, tit. 39, c. 49, *Si quem*, distinguishes minor excommunication, or that implying exclusion only from the Sacraments, from major excommunication, implying exclusion from the society of the faithful. He declares that it is major excommunication which is meant in all texts in which mention is made of excommunication. Since that time there has been no difference between major excommunication and anathema, except the greater or less degree of ceremony in pronouncing the sentence of excommunication. Anathema remains a major excommunication which is to be promulgated with great solemnity" ("Anathema," *Catholic Encyclopedia*, vol. 1, p. 456). "Anathema is a sort of aggravated excommunication, from which, however, it does not differ essentially, but simply in the matter of special solemnities and outward display" ("Excommunication," *Catholic Encyclopedia*, vol. 5, p. 680).

Chapter XXI

Whether a bishop, or any other priest, having become a heretic loses that ecclesiastical power which is called by theologians the power of Order.

That there are two ecclesiastical powers, one which is called the power of Order or Sacramental power, the other which is called the power of jurisdiction, the whole school of theologians teaches and many testimonies of the Fathers confirm. Saint Thomas defines the power of Order or Sacramental power, which is the same thing, when speaking thus: "The sacramental power is one that is conferred by some kind of consecration."[1] Now it is called "Sacramental" from the end to which it is ordained: because every such power is ordained to the granting and ordering[2] of the Sacraments. Such power can also be called "Sacramental," because it is always given to someone through the conferral of some Sacrament, especially according to the opinion of those who think that the episcopacy is another order distinct from the priesthood. For those who hold the contrary opinion say that the bishop has many Sacramental powers after his consecration, which nevertheless were not conferred upon him through the conferral of a Sacrament. This power is also called "the power of Order," because no one can have it, unless he be constituted in some certain grade and order.

Saint Thomas says that the power of jurisdiction is that which is conferred from the simple injunction and commis-

---

1 II-II, q. 39, a. 3.
2 I. e., the use and manner of celebrating the Sacraments. Cf. Manuel Useros Carretero, *'Statuta Ecclesiae' y 'Sacramenta Ecclesiae' en la Ecclesiologia de St. Tomás* (Rome: Gregorian University, 1962), n. 24, p. 53.

sion of man,³ such as the power of excommunicating or absolving from excommunication and the power of judging in public causes. Juan de Torquemada in his *Summa ecclesiastica*⁴ says that this power of jurisdiction is twofold according to two forums, namely, of conscience and of causes. The power in the forum of conscience is that which the pastor of souls has, through which he can absolve his subjects from their sins. The power in the exterior forum is the power by which someone in affairs and causes which are between men, has the right of deciding, and of pronouncing sentence even against the unwilling. The powers of Order are diverse, just as the Orders to which they pertain are diverse. For certain powers of Order or Sacramental powers befit only the bishops, as are: to be able to confer Orders, to confirm, to consecrate Churches or altars or chalices, to bless the rest of the sacramentals, such as priestly vestments, all which things the bishop alone can do. There are other powers of Order which befit all priests. Accordingly, the power of consecrating Christ's Body, and the power of absolving from sins, are powers of Order, any of which are transmitted to the priest in his consecration, when the bishop ordains him. The bishop confers the power of consecrating when after the chalice is handed over he says: "Receive the power to offer sacrifice to God, and to celebrate Mass, both for the living and the dead, in the name of the Lord." The bishop transmits the power of absolving with these words: "Receive the Holy Ghost. Whose sins you shall forgive, they are forgiven them; and whose sins you shall retain, they are retained."⁵ But because

---

3 II-II, q. 39, a. 3.
4 Bk. 1, c. 26, fol. 109v.
5 Pope Pius XII issued the Apostolic Constitution *Sacramentum Ordinis* in 1947 in which he determined the essential matter of Holy Orders as follows: "The matter of Holy Orders of the diaconate, priesthood, and episcopate, and this alone, is the imposition of the hands... the tradition of the instruments at least for the future

through this power of absolving, the priest cannot act unless he has some jurisdiction, wherefore according to Blessed Thomas' opinion it necessarily follows that the two powers of Order and jurisdiction would concur at the same time in the absolution of the sinner, and if the priest lacks one of these, he is not able to effect anything at all.[6]

Nevertheless, others divide and define these two ecclesiastical powers otherwise. For Alfonso [de Madriga] of Ávila[7] in chapter sixty-two of the book which he called *Defensorium* [*trium conclusionum*],[8] he distinguishes these two powers, not by the fact that one is conferred through consecration, and the other without consecration: nor by the fact that one is given by God immediately, the other by man: but by the diversity of things, about which they are exercised, which are two, namely, Christ's Real Body, and Christ's Mystical Body. He says that the power of Order is that which is over Christ's Real Body, directly or indirectly. He says that the sacerdotal Order directly regards Christ's Real Body: because the first things towards which this Order is directed is the consecration of the Eucharist. The Order of Deaconate and Subdeaconate, and the other minor Orders also are ordained to the Eucharist: because all subminister in something or are of service to the confecting priest, as can

---

is not necessary for the validity of the Holy Orders of the diaconate, priesthood, and episcopate" (Dz. 2301).

6 "It is essential to this sacrament [of Confession] not only for the minister to be in Orders, as in the case of the other Sacraments, but also for him to have jurisdiction" (Suppl., q. 8, a. 4).

7 Alonso Tostado (ca. 1400-1455 A.D.) was a Spanish theologian, councilor of John II of Castile and briefly bishop of Ávila, whence his title *Abulensis*. "In his *Defensorium*, written on this occasion against Torquemada and other critics, he gave utterance to views derogatory to the authority of the Pope" ("Alonso Tostado," *Catholic Encyclopedia*, vol. 14, p. 788).

8 *Defensorium trium conclusionum* (Cologne: Johann Gymnich & Anton Hierat, 1613), pt. 2, p. 60B.

be manifest to anyone considering the acts of the individual Order, which Isidore describes, as is found in the chapter, *Cleros et Clericos*.[9] This power of Order is granted by Christ to the priest through the ministry of the ordaining bishop. The power of jurisdiction according to [Alfonso] of Ávila pertains to Christ's Mystical Body, which according to Paul's teaching is the Catholic Church of the believers. And this power [Alfonso] of Ávila teaches is also twofold, one in the forum of contention [or litigation], the other in the forum of conscience, accordingly as we just now divided them based upon the opinion of Juan de Torquemada.

Yet there is this difference between them, namely, that Juan de Torquemada says that the power of jurisdiction in the forum of conscience is not conferred to the priest in virtue of his ordination, when he is ordained by a bishop: but is conferred afterwards by man, when the Pope, or the bishop, gives him the care of souls. From which he deduces that simple priests, who have completely no care of souls, do not have any power of jurisdiction. [Alfonso] of Ávila maintains the opinion contrary to this, who teaches that the power of jurisdiction in the forum of conscience is conferred to any priest in his ordination, when he was ordained by a bishop. For at that time he says, because from the condition of the Order, and Christ's institution, the power of jurisdiction in the forum of conscience over all the faithful of the whole world belongs to any priest: yet the Church, for a just reason, to avoid schism and confusions which could thence arise, restricted this jurisdiction, by distinguishing the subjects. Wherefore concerning a simple priest, who has no care of souls, he says that he has the power of jurisdiction over all the faithful; yet such power is not actually taken away by the Church, but bound. Therefore, when the ordinator, either the Church, or any prelate, gives jurisdiction to any ordained man in the forum of conscience, or in the contentious forum,

---

9 *Decretum Gratiani*, pt. 1, dist. 21, c. 1 (PL 187, 115D ff.).

he says that nothing new is granted to him, but the Church merely removes the impediment, or takes away the ligature whereby she had bound his power.

But actually I can nowise approve of this opinion of [Alfonso] of Ávila, nay, I am forced by some very pressing reasons to depart from it. The first is because the power of jurisdiction is a correlative term, which relates not merely to itself, but to another, namely, to those over whom is such power. Thus there are these two correlative things, the power of jurisdiction and subjects, just as a superior and an inferior. But the nature of correlative things, according to the teaching of Aristotle,[10] is such that when one of them ceases to exist, the other necessarily perishes. As for example, when a son has died, it is necessary that he who was previously his father, is no longer his father, because there is no longer him to whom he could be referred. From which it is very clearly proved that a simple priest, who has no care of souls, also has no power of jurisdiction, because he does not have a subject upon whom he could exercise it.

The second reason is that this power of absolving from sins is not conferred to the priest by a man, but principally from God, even though in such a conferral of power the bishop is God's minister, through whose hands God transmits that power to the priest: and [Alfonso] of Ávila admits this same thing in chapter sixty-three. From which it clearly follows that the Church cannot take away, restrict, lessen, or bind this power of jurisdiction in the forum of the conscience from the priest. Because what was granted by a superior, an inferior cannot remove or lessen. From which it would further follow that a simple priest can truly absolve anyone, although he would sin by absolving, yet the other would remain truly absolved. Now to admit this is against the teaching of all theologians. Now that this follows therefrom is manifestly proved from his teaching. Because in chapter sixty-two he

---

10 Cf. *Categories*, c. 7 (7b15-34).

proves by a similar argument that the Church cannot take away from a priest the power of confecting the Eucharist, namely, because such power was not given to the priest by the Church, but by God, Who is greater than the Church. But Blessed Thomas, and those who follow his opinion, are easily freed from these incongruities. For a simple priest, who does not have the care of souls, even though he may have that power of absolving, which according to their opinion, is called the power of Order: still he does not have the power of jurisdiction, and hence cannot validly absolve anyone.[11]

The third reason which impels me very much is that if the power of jurisdiction in the forum of conscience and the power of jurisdiction in the contentious forum over all the faithful of the whole world belong to any priest (as [Alfonso] of Ávila says), two very great and absolutely intolerable incongruities thence follow. The first is that by Divine institution all priests are equal in the power of jurisdiction, and so the Pope would not be superior to all others by Divine law, but merely by human law. Now this opinion has been condemned by the authority of many councils. The other, and not less incongruous, is that if this were so, it would thence be very clearly proved that Christ badly and very badly organized Christendom, since He left in it so many rulers, equal in authority, any one of whom would have equal authority over all the faithful. For such a great multitude of rulers without any order could rather (as it is very manifest in this same matter) harm than benefit the Church. Now to admit this would be manifest heresy: because Sacred Scripture commends the order of the Church to such an extent

---

11 "It is essential to this Sacrament not only for the minister to be in Orders, as in the case of the other Sacraments, but also for him to have jurisdiction: wherefore he that has no jurisdiction cannot administer this Sacrament any more than one who is not a priest" (Suppl., q. 8, a. 4).

Whether heretical bishops and priests lose their power of Order

that on account of its extraordinary order, it says that she is formidable to her enemies. "Terrible," it says about her, "as an army set in array" (Cant. 6, 3).

The fourth reason is: All the power which is given to a priest in his ordination, is the sacerdotal character, or something so necessarily connected to that character, that it cannot be separated from it: but the sacerdotal character is not the power of jurisdiction, but the power of Order: therefore no power of jurisdiction is conferred to the priest in his ordination, but only the power of Order. It is unnecessary to prove the major premise and the conclusion, because they are known: yet the minor, from which the whole force of the argument depends, I prove in this way. The power of jurisdiction is limitable, which can be increased and decreased, and be completely removed. The character, however, can have none of these things, as is manifest from the very nature of the character: therefore the character is not the power of jurisdiction.

The fifth reason against [Alfonso] of Ávila is this: Every power which is conferred through some Sacramental ordination, is the power of Order: but the power of absolving was given to the priest in his ordination of this kind: therefore it is the power of Order, and not of jurisdiction. The conclusion and the minor are known of themselves, but the major is proved: because for no other reason it is called the power of Order, except because it is conferred through the conferral of an Order. Furthermore, such power of absolving from sins, which is transmitted to the priest in his consecration, is ordered to the administration of the Sacrament: therefore it is called a Sacramental power rather than the power of jurisdiction.

The last reason, which (certainly in my opinion) greatly fetters [Alfonso] of Ávila is that it is accepted with the consent of all theologians that for giving Sacramental absolution the power of Order is required, such that the power of jurisdiction alone without the power of Order would not suffice for this, that someone could absolve another from sins: just as it is manifest in him who has the care of souls, but is not a priest. For even though he may have the power of jurisdiction, still, because he lacks the power of Order, he cannot absolve anyone. No other power of Order however is required, except the power of absolving: therefore it ought not to be called the power of jurisdiction, but the power of Order. And (so that we may fetter the man more strongly) let us suppose that it happened, which can very easily happen, namely, that when a bishop ordains a priest as a curate, or bishop, after he gives to him the power over Christ's Real Body, immediately dies, before he transmits to the same priest the power of Christ's Mystical Body. In the case no one having a sane mind will say that such a priest can absolve from sins. Therefore what is lacking? Certainly not the power of jurisdiction, because he has it by reason of the care committed to him: therefore the power of Order is lacking, but the power of Order over Christ's Real Body is not lacking, because that was already given to him by the bishop, before he passed away: therefore the power of Order over Christ's Mystical Body is lacking, which is nothing other than the power of absolving from sins. From which it is very clearly gathered that such power is not the power of jurisdiction, but of Order: and hence it consequently follows that not every power, which is over Christ's Mystical Body, ought to be reckoned the power of jurisdiction.

On account of these reasons, which seem to me to be very pressing, I reckon that these two powers of the Church, namely, of Order and jurisdiction, ought not to be distinguished, and not defined in that way, as we said [Alfonso] of Ávila distinguished them. Having imitated Blessed Thomas on this point, I say that these two powers are distinguished by the fact that the power of Order, or (as Saint Thomas says[12])

---

12 Cf. Suppl., q. 36, a. 2 ad 1um.

Whether heretical bishops and priests lose their power of Order

the Sacramental power, is conferred through the conferral of some ecclesiastical Order, whether it be over Christ's Real Body, or over His Mystical Body. The power of jurisdiction is that which is given over others by an injunction or commission of some man. Thus one ought to discuss regarding these powers, whether he who has them, if he becomes a heretic, immediately loses them. In this chapter we will discuss only about the power of Order: and in the next chapter we will inquire about the power of jurisdiction. The powers of Order, according to the variety of Orders, we said are various: some of which belong to all priests, others belong only to bishops. We will thus dispute firstly about the sacerdotal power of Order, but soon about the episcopal power of Order.

Regarding the sacerdotal power of Order, Peter Lombard, who is called the "Master of the Sentences," teaches that that power, which is over Christ's true Body, does not remain in him who has become a heretic, nor in him who has been excommunicated. And so that anyone may easily know his mind, I will cite his words, which he says about this matter: "But those," he says, "who are excommunicated, or publicly known to be heretical, do not seem to be able to confect this Sacrament, although they are priests, because no one says in his consecration: 'I offer,' but: 'We offer," as if in the name of the Church. And therefore although other Sacraments can be celebrated outside the Church, it does not seem that this Sacrament can be."[13] It seems that Gratian also thought the same thing. For he says these words: "Thus whoever is alienated from the unity of the Church, which is understood by Peter, can anathematize, but is not able to consecrate; he has no power of excommunication or reconciliation."[14] Whose error the Gloss openly recognizing, decided to correct him. For on the words, "not able [*non valet*]" the Gloss says these

---

13 *In IV Sententiarum*, dist. 13, q. 1 (PL 192, 868).
14 *Decretum Gratiani*, pt. 2, *causa* 24, q. 1, c. 4 (*Audivimus*), part 2 (*Si autem*) (PL 187, 1265C).

words: "Yet he also confects outside of the Church, if he observes the form: because this belongs to the Order, which he retains when withdrawing from the unity of the Church, [cf. *causa*] one, question one, [c. 97,] *Quod quidam*. But he cannot excommunicate: because this belongs to jurisdiction which he who withdraws has lost as [it is said in *causa*] one, question one, [c. 39,] *Remissionem*."[15] But the same Glossator on the chapter, *Accedens*,[16] concerning a degraded priest, thinks the opposite when saying that he does not "believe that he confects because," as he says, "he has lost all power."[17] And I am certainly surprised that men so learned and so good would have fallen into such a manifest error.

The falsity of this teaching is very clearly proved from the fact that the power of consecrating is nothing other than the sacerdotal character, which is imprinted on the priest by God, when the bishop ordains him, and says, "Receive the power to offer sacrifice to God, and to celebrate Mass, both for the living and the dead..." When these words have been completed, God imprints the character of the priest on the soul, and the priest through that character receives from God the power of consecrating the Eucharist.[18] Whence it is that the power of confecting the Eucharist perdures as long as the sacerdotal character remains in him. But this character, since it is imprinted by God alone, only God can

---

15 *Decretum Gratiani: cum Glossis*, fols. 470v b-471r a.
16 *Decretum Gratiani*, pt. 1, dist. 50, c. 10 (PL 187, 1265C).
17 *Decretum Gratiani: cum Glossis*, fol. 81v a.
18 Pope Pius XII determined the form for the ordination of priests are the following words which are said in the preface of the Mass of priestly ordinations, "Bestow, we beseech, Almighty Father, upon this thy servant the dignity of the priesthood; renew in his vitals the spirit of sanctity, that he may obtain the gift of good merit acceptable to Thee, O God, and may by the example of his conversation introduce rigid judgment of morals" (Apostolic Constitution, *Sacramentum Ordinis*, November 30, 1947, n. 5).

Whether heretical bishops and priests lose their power of Order

efface it from the soul. Therefore it follows that the power of consecrating cannot be taken away from a priest, through any crime, howsoever grave, even if he were degraded. For through such a degradation, although the Church takes away from the priest the execution of the Order, such that he cannot without sin confect the Eucharist, still she does not take away from him, nor could she take away from him, the power of Order, so that he could not confect, even if she were to attempt to do so. Furthermore, the Church does not give the priest the power of confecting, but God alone. Because that power, since it is so great and so excellent that it exceeds the power of all the Angels, let alone of men, can only be conferred by God, although for the conferral of that Order there is a bishop, as the minister, exercising something about the priest, without which God never grants such power to a priest. Therefore it is necessary that the Church could not take away from the priest the power of consecrating, which it is evident that God alone gave him.

Again, if the teaching of the Master of the Sentences were correct, it would thence follow that the priest, who recovers his senses from the heresy into which he had fallen, ought to be reordained so that he could confect Christ's Body in the Eucharist. But to assert this would be very erroneous, and against the definition of the universal Church. For the Council of Florence when transmitting the very certain rule of faith to the Armenians, which they ought to hold, when discussing about the Church's Sacraments, says these words: "Among these sacraments there are three, Baptism, Confirmation, and Orders, which imprint an indelible sign on the soul, that is, a certain character distinctive from the others. Hence they should not be repeated in the same person. The remaining four do not imprint a sign and admit of repetition."[19] In which words one ought to especially note two things, which very strongly confirm the two arguments just

---

19 Dz. 695.

adduced. The first thing is that it says that the character is indelible, and this is of service to the former argument. The other is when it says that the Sacrament of Orders ought to be connumerated among those Sacraments which do not admit reiteration. Thus we say that according to the opinion of the whole Catholic Church, every priest rightly ordained, even if he were to become a heretic, and be degraded, can confect the Eucharist, although he would sin by doing so. Hence [Blessed Thomas][20] says: "Such as, being within the Church, received the power of consecrating the Eucharist through being ordained to the priesthood, have such power rightly indeed; but they use it improperly if afterwards they be separated from the Church by heresy, schism, or excommunication."[21]

Perhaps someone will object to us against these things the chapter, *Degradatio*.[22] For in that chapter it is decreed that when a bishop degrades a priest he would use this formula: "By the authority of Almighty God, Father, Son, and Holy Ghost, and by our own authority, we take the clerical habit from thee, and we depose, degrade, and deprive thee of every Order, benefice and clerical privilege." From which words it seems to be inferred that the man degraded has no power of Order, and consequently is deprived of the sacerdotal character. Otherwise the formula of degradation would contain falsity, when it says, "we deprive thee of every Order." And the Gloss on that chapter says that evidence is thence obtained against those who say that the one degraded can confect. But actually that Glossator was mistaken, and did not fully understand the meaning of those

---

20 St. Augustine in the second book of his letter, *Contra epistolam Parmeniani*, is incorrectly cited here, but the words are found in the *Summa Theologica*, just after a quotation from this work of Augustine.
21 III, q. 82, a. 7.
22 *Liber sextus decretalium*, bk. 5, tit. 9 (*De poenis*), c. 2.

words. For by those words the Pope understands that the one degraded is deprived and despoiled of the execution of the Order, not however the power of the Order. Because he could not be deprived of this, since the character is indelible. And *Cardinalis* supports this exposition of ours, who on the chapter, *Accedens*,[23] says that wherever it is found in the law, that the one deposed or degraded "loses" or "does not have the Order," it ought to be understood of the execution and the privileges of the Order. His Holiness Pope Adrian [VI] teaches the same opinion in his commentary of the fourth book of the *Sentences* in the question on Confirmation, article three.[24] And so it necessarily ought to be said, lest we would say that the Pope erred when defining.

Concerning the power of absolving from sins, however, a certain opinion cannot be given without distinction: but according to the diversity of powers various definitions will also be given. For (as we said in the beginning of this chapter) the power of absolving from sins is twofold. One is called the power of Order, and this is the sacerdotal character; whether one effect is greater or the same as the other, has little bearing on the present discussion. And this power is transmitted to the priest when the consecrating bishop says: "Receive the Holy Ghost. Whose sins you shall forgive, they are forgiven them; and whose sins you shall retain, they are retained." There is another power of absolving from sins which is called the power of jurisdiction in the forum of conscience. This is not transmitted in the consecration of the priest, but afterwards, when the care of souls is given to him;

---

23 *Decretum Gratiani*, pt. 1, dist. 50, c. 10 (PL 187, 1265C).

24 "On the contrary, [the Doctors] say that however much a priest was degraded, and if intending to confect on due matter he pronounces the Sacramental form, he validly consecrates" (*Quaestiones in quartum sententiarum praesertim circa sacramenta* (Paris: Jodocus Badius, 1516), fol. 22r).

Book 2, Chapter 21

and it is not transmitted immediately from God, but from the man, who commits to him the care of souls.

Neither of these two things without the other (as we said before) can exercise the act of absolution of sin. For a priest who has no care of souls, neither ordinary or delegated (except in the case of extreme necessity) can absolve anyone. On the contrary, he who has the care of souls, and is not a priest, can also absolve no one. Therefore a priest who has become a heretic can lose the power of jurisdiction: because, since he receives it (as we said) from a man, the man who gave it, or another superior, can take it away from him. But the power of absolving, which is called the power of Order, or Sacramental power, just as a man did not give it to the priest, so neither can a man take it away from him. For this power is also indelible from the soul, just as the power of confecting the Eucharist: because both of these things are deemed to be nothing other than the sacerdotal character imprinted by God in the soul of the priest. From which it is very clearly gathered that a heretical priest, if the Church does not take away from him the care of souls which he had before, can absolve his subjects from their sins: because he would retain the power of Order and jurisdiction for doing it. Now, however, because the Church deprives heretics of every benefice, although they would have the power of Order, nevertheless after they were deprived of it, they could not absolve, because they lack the power of jurisdiction.

Therefore this whole discussion of ours can be expressed by two very certain rules. The first rule is that a heretical priest does not lose, nor can lose, any power of Order, because it is indelible and given by God alone. The second rule is that a priest who has become a heretic can lose the power of jurisdiction, because he did not receive it in the consecration, but afterwards from the commission of a man. And because the Master of the Sentences and Gratian did not consider well the difference of these two powers, they were mistaken when supposing that the completely same thing ought to be said about both of them, because nevertheless they would very easily come to know, that it ought not to be so said, if they had considered well that there is a great difference between those two powers, and that the circumstances of those two powers are diverse.

But it is now necessary that we see what the Master of the Sentences brought forth for the confirmation of his opinion. For it ought not to be thought that such a great man would even have said it gratuitously, and without any reason, although false. The consecrating priest (he says) does this in the person of the Church, and not his own: because when he offers the host, he does not say, "I offer," but he says, "We offer." But he who is outside the Church cannot do something in the name of the Church. Therefore a heretic, or an excommunicated man, since he is separated from the Church, could not consecrate in the name of the Church.[25] This reasoning is certainly very weak, and which any man even moderately educated, by no means a master of the *Sentences*, could very easily hurl back, if he had well considered that there is a wide difference between the consecration of the Eucharist and the prayers which precede or follow it in the canon of the Mass. The priest says those prayers in the name of the Church, in the unity of which he remains as her member. In the consecration, however, when he confects the Eucharist, he speaks not in the person of the Church, but in the person of Christ, whose place he takes through the power of Order. Now that he speaks in the person of Christ, the very context of the words, which proximately precede the words of consecration very clearly show. For the priest at the time when he is prepared to consecrate, when speaking about Christ Our Savior, says these words which follow: "Who, the day before He suffered, took bread into His holy and venerable hands, and with eyes lifted toward heaven, unto

---

25 *Libri Quatuor Sententiarum*, dist. 13, q. 1 (PL 192, 868).

Thee, O God, His Almighty Father, giving thanks to Thee, did bless, break, and give unto His disciples, saying: Take, and eat ye all of this: For this is My Body." From which context of words it is very clearly established that the priest pronounces the words of consecration in the sole person of Christ, and not in his own person. Therefore an excommunicated or heretical priest, or cut off in another way from the unity of the Church, if he were to celebrate Mass, because he keeps the power of Order, truly confects the Lord's Body and Blood: yet because he has been separated from the unity of the Church, his prayers, which he offers in the name of the Church, have completely no power, and no merit, such that they cannot benefit either the heretic himself or those for whom they are said.

Chapter XXII

Whether a bishop having become a heretic, by that very fact, loses the power of episcopal Order.

We have said in the preceding chapter that the powers of Order are diverse, some of which belong to all priests: and we discussed about them then, whether they would be lost on account of heresy. Some only belong to bishops, and about these it ought to be inquired now, whether a bishop, having become a heretic, by that very fact loses or could lose them all. Now so that we may be free from the difficulty of the question, it is necessary that we firstly discuss another question, upon which (as I think) the whole difficulty of this question depends. Thus it ought to be inquired whether the Pope or a general council could take away the power of Order from a bishop, which was granted to him through ordination. For if the Church could do this, it ought to be believed that she has already taken away such power from heretics: because when she prosecutes them with supreme and very just hatred, it ought to be piously believed that she took away from them whatever she could take away. If on the other hand the Church could not take away this power of Order from a bishop, it could them be established clearer than light that a bishop does not lose such power, even if he were to become a heretic, especially since it would be established that by Divine law it is not taken away from a bishop on account of heresy.

Pope Innocent [IV] on the chapter, *Quanto*,[1] says that it was the opinion of certain men saying that the Pope can prohibit bishops from administering the Sacrament of Order or Confirmation: which prohibition having been made, if the bishop were to attempt to confect such Sacraments, they

---

1 *Decretals of Gregory IX*, bk. 1, tit. 4 (*De consuetudine*), c. 4.

say that he would do nothing. "Because although the Pope cannot take away the Sacrament of Baptism, or other necessary ones: he could still (as these men say) ordain about them either by giving the form, or by ordaining about the persons, by which and to whom they would be conferred, as it is noted in chapter one [of the title], *De baptismo*.[2] For the Pope, according to these men, ought to be obeyed in all spiritual things, in matters concerning the danger of the soul: unless those things are found to have been explicitly forbidden, or are opposed to the faith."[3] After Innocent [IV] relates the opinion of these men, he neither absolutely approves nor entirely reprehends it: but after having firstly given a certain distinction, he says that either "the Pope makes a law, whereby he takes away this power of the bishop, and then he says that the bishop does absolutely nothing by conferring such a Sacrament contrary to the prohibition: or the Pope simply forbids the bishops to act; and such a simple prohibition," as he says, "would not impede the impression of the character."[4] Panormitanus on the same chapter, *Quanto*, relates this opinion of Innocent, and says that his opinion is very good, far from reprehending it.[5]

Alexander of Hales also says that this was the opinion of some, yet he branded it with a very different mark, asserting that it is false and erroneous.[6] Not only Alexander of

---

2 "Certainly if someone immerses a child in water three times in the name of the Father, and of the Son, and of the Holy Ghost, Amen, and did not say: 'I baptize you in the name of the Father, and of the Son, and of the Holy Ghost, Amen': the child is not baptized" (*Ibid.*, bk. 3, tit. 42, c. 1 (*Si quis*)).
3 *Abbatis Panormitani Commentaria*, fols. 112v b-113r a. Cf. Innocent IV, *In Quinque Decretalium libros* (Venice: Bernardinus Majorinus Parmenses, 1570), fol. 23r.
4 *Abbatis Panormitani Commentaria*, fol. 113r a.
5 *Ibid.*, fol. 113r b.
6 *Uniuersae Theologiae Summa* (Venice: apud Franciscum Fran-

Hales, but all scholastic theologians who treat about this matter, very clearly condemn it. I, subscribing to Innocent's and Panormitanus' judgment of their opinion, reckon that that opinion is not merely false, but heretical. Yet not for this reason do I think that they ought to be called heretics: because I do not think that they so thought with pertinacious animosity, so that they would have wanted to maintain their opinion against the teaching of the Catholic Church. Nay, on the contrary, I very firmly believe that they, if they had been admonished about this matter (as was befitting), would have immediately revoked their opinion. Next, the matter itself does not belong to the first principles of the faith, regarding which a Christian man is not permitted to be ignorant: and it is not a matter so clear in itself, that one could not be excused through ignorance, especially since it pertains more to the realm of theologians than of canonists.

Now so that we may show the certain and indubitable opinion about this matter, it is necessary to firstly point out some things which could help very much for showing the clarity of the matter. Firstly in fact, one ought to consider that (as Augustine says) "it is one thing to lack something utterly, and another to have it improperly"; and in like fashion, "it is one thing not to bestow, and quite another to bestow, but not rightly."[7] One also ought to consider that there are various powers in a bishop of his Order, all of which ought not to be weighed by an equal scale on the balance. Accordingly, a bishop has power about the conferral of some Sacraments, such as Order and Confirmation, which can only be conferred by bishops. They also have power from their Order for blessing and consecrating some things which are not Sacraments, but are called sacramentals, such as churches, chalices, vestments, and other things which are conse-

---

ciscium, 1575), pt. 4, q. 10, member 5, n. 6, fol. 147r b-v a.
7 *Against the Letter of Parmenian*, bk. 2, n. 28 (PL 43, 71), as reworded by St. Thomas in III, q. 82, a. 7.

crated by bishops alone. All these things, and other similar things, are called sacramentals because they all are ordained to the consecration of some Sacrament, or its administration. For the consecration or blessing of a church, the consecration of a chalice, the blessing of vestments, and many other things of this sort, are ordained to making consecration of the Eucharist with due devotion and reverence. The consecration of chrism is directed to the conferral of the Sacraments of Baptism, Confirmation, and Extreme Unction.

All these things and other things of this kind can also be called sacramentals for another reason, namely, because they have some similarity with the Sacraments. For God conferred this power to all the Sacraments, so that they would confer grace to those worthily receiving them. And all these things, which are called sacramentals, even though they were not given by God with power so that they could confer grace to those receiving them, still to all of them after they have been consecrated or blessed by the Church, a special power has been given by God to effecting something in the one devoutly receiving them, which would not have been effected without the blessing: for instance holy water, blessed ashes, candles, palms, or bells. The blessing of all of which things ought not to be thought to be worthless (as the wicked Waldensians thought), and ridiculed as such: but according to the teaching of the whole Catholic Church, God grants some special power to all these things on account of the Church's blessing, which they would not have without the blessing. I recall that long ago I spoke about this matter in that work which I published, *Against All Heresies*, in the section on "Water" [*Aqua*], in the second heresy, and in the section on "Exorcism."

All these things having been considered, I will put forth some conclusions in their order, from which whatever pertains to this matter, can be very easily understood. First conclusion: "The Pope cannot take away from the bishop the power of conferring those Sacraments which are reserved to bishops, as are Confirmation and Orders, such that the Pope could make the conferral of those Sacraments invalid and worthless." It is necessary to prove this conclusion by very many and very evident reasons, so that it may thence be very clearly established that the opinion of Innocent [IV] and Panormitanus is false and heretical. Firstly in fact this conclusion of ours is proved to be true, because the power about the conferral of the Sacraments of Confirmation and Orders, which a bishop has, was granted to him by Divine law and by God: from which it is very evidently gathered that the Pope cannot take it away from a bishop: because an inferior cannot take away from another which was granted to him by a superior. I wish to prove the premise of this argument, from which its whole force depends, with many reasons. For if I were to show that that power was granted by God to the bishop, no one could think thereafter that the Pope could take it away from the bishop. For this is one of the main reasons whereby theologians prove that the power of consecrating cannot be taken away from a priest even though he has been degraded: because since he has received it from God and not from men, it follows that no man can take it away from a priest.

Now, that such power, especially regarding the conferral of Orders, has been granted by God alone to the bishops is firstly proved from the fact that the power of confecting the Eucharist, even ministerially, surpasses the proper and native strength of the whole Church, because unless God had given this power to priests, so that as ministers they could confect the Eucharist, the whole Church could not transmit it to any priest. From which it is clearly proved that the power which a bishop has for conferring this power in their ordinations, likewise surpasses the whole strength and power of the Church. Hence it necessarily follows that a bishop received such power, not from man, who could not give it, but from God alone. For otherwise if the power of consecrating a priest could be given by a man, the Divine power having been excluded, to anyone, it would thence very clearly follow that the power of confecting the Eucharist, which is conferred through that prior power, could also, the Divine power having been excluded, be given to anyone. For it is certain that if I by human strength (not excluding God's general concurrence) could place Peter in some Order and dignity, whatever Peter does by that Order and dignity, will be doable by human strength. Accordingly, there is a well-known rule of philosophers, which is: "Whatever is the cause of a cause is the cause of what it causes."[8] But if Peter did something through such an Order and dignity that could not be effected by human strength, it most evidently thence follows that no one could place by human strength Peter in such an Order and dignity. Thus, since the power of a priest is above all human power, it follows that the power of making priests which a bishop has, also exceeds all human strength. Therefore what a man cannot give to a bishop, he likewise cannot take away from a bishop. And just as the Pope cannot take away from a priest the power of consecrating, so neither from a bishop the power of ordaining: because both surpass human strength.

Secondly the above premise, namely, that the power of Order which is in bishops regarding the conferral of the Sacraments belongs to them by Divine law, is proved. Because unless this were so, it would thence follow that bishops are superior to other priests merely by human law, whence by Divine institution alone, bishops would not have any power greater than other priests. For a bishop has nothing else which another priest could not have except the conferral of

---

[8] Cf. St. Thomas, I-II, q. 79, a. 1, obj. 3; *De veritate*, q. 27, a. 3, obj. 16; *De malo*, q. 3, a. 1, obj. 4; *In II Sentences*, dist. 37, q. 2, a. 1, obj. 2; Scotus, *Lectura 2*, dist. 37, n. 17; *Ordinatio*, bk. 2, dists. 34-37, q. 4, n. 21.

the Sacraments of Order and Confirmation. But if this power corresponds to bishops merely by human and not Divine law, it most evidently follows therefrom that nothing corresponds to bishops by Divine law, which does not correspond to other priests. Now it is the heresy of Aerius to assert this, which Augustine condemns with the name of heresy in his book on heresies.[9] And Blessed Epiphanius [of Salamis] in his book on eighty heresies, when discussing the seventy-fifth about Aerius, enumerates this one among his heresies.[10] And we in that work which we published, *Against All Heresies*, in the section on "Bishops" [*Episcopus*], proved with many very evident reasons that such an opinion is heretical.

That antecedent assumed above in the first argument is again proved for a third time to be heretical. If the power which a bishop has regarding the conferral is not from Divine law, but granted to him from human law alone, it follows that the Pope could also confer such power to priests. Because if it was granted to him by human law alone, just as the Church decreed about the bishops, so it could decree about the priests, so that they also could ordain others as priests. But Panormitanus thinks that there is no unsuitability, because in the passage previously cited he spontaneously, and without being forced by any argument, says that the Pope could delegate this power to any priest, so that he could confer Orders. If he was speaking about minor Orders, which are not deemed sacred, I would not contradict him, as I will

---

9 *On Heresies, to Quodvultdeus*, c. 53 (PL 42, 40).
10 "But his teaching was more insane than is humanly possible, and he says, 'What is a bishop compared with a priest? The one is no different from the other. There is one Order,' he said, 'and one honor and one rank. A bishop lays on hands,' he said, 'but so does a priest. The bishop administers Baptism, and the priest does, too. The bishop performs the Eucharistic liturgy, the priest likewise. A bishop occupies the throne, and the priest also occupies one'" (*Panarion* ["Medicine Chest"], bk. 3 (PG 42, 506C)).

explain more clearly afterwards. But because he speaks absolutely about every Order, then I cannot pass over what he says, since his opinion is manifestly erroneous. For if the Church could do this, it thence follows that the Church could make all priests equal to bishops, because it could give the power of ordaining to priests, and consequently the power of confirming, which having been given, they will be equal in every respect. For Blessed Jerome in the letter to Evangelus says: "For what function, excepting ordination, belongs to a bishop that does not also belong to a presbyter?"[11] If by this alone a bishop rises above other priests, it follows that when that power has been given to priests, they would be equal to bishops. But as we just said, we are taught by the Catholic faith that bishops by Divine law are superior to the rest of the priests: thus we are held to believe from the Catholic faith that the Pope cannot delegate to priests the power of conferring Orders, especially the priesthood.

Furthermore, Paul says: "And without all contradiction, that which is less, is blessed by the better" (Heb. 7, 7). Thus the greater is the bishop, who blesses and consecrates the priest, than the priest who is consecrated by him. Hence it is that one cannot be made a priest by a mere priest, because they are equal to each other. Again the Council of Florence, when giving a very sure rule of faith to the Armenians, which it was necessary that they follow, when it discussed about the Sacrament of Orders, said that its true minister is the bishop: therefore the Church cannot institute another minister, and consequently the Pope could not delegate this to a different priest. Because just as he could not institute a different matter or form from that instituted in the Sacraments, so neither can he institute a different minister than Christ instituted. Thus the power which the bishop has regarding the conferral of the Sacraments, is granted to him and not to someone else by

---

11 Letter 146, n. 1 (PL 22, 194).

Divine law, and so it is neither removeable from him by the Church nor givable to anyone else.

From which is deducible a clear answer to that which was firstly asked in this chapter, whether a bishop having become a heretic loses the power of episcopal Order. To which question we reply that a bishop, even though he is a heretic, or degraded, never loses such a power. Because such a power is given to him by God, and not by man: it is also given through his consecration when he is consecrated. Now every power of Order or Sacramental power (as we taught from Blessed Thomas above), because it is given through a consecration, it is indelible, just as the consecration itself is also indelible. Furthermore, the Church was not accustomed consecrate heretical bishops again if they came to their senses: but always received them in their dignity, as appears from the Acts of the Seventh Council, which was the Second Council of Nicaea, in which many bishops, who had departed from the Church on account of heresy, after they came to their senses, asking for mercy were received in their ranks and honors, without new ordination as it is found in the chapter, *Convenientibus*.[12] Nevertheless, if they were to lose the episcopal Order through heresy, it would be necessary to consecrate them again, when they return to the Church.

Again, the Church commands that those ordained by heretical bishops who had kept the correct form of the Church in the ordination, ought not to be reordained, but would remain in their ranks: as it is very clearly found in the chapter, *Ordinationes*.[13] And this was more explicitly explained in the Seventh General Council, whose pronouncement is found in the chapter, *Convenientibus*. For the Church would not have decreed this unless she thought that the bishop, although he

---

12 *Decretum Gratiani*, pt. 2, *causa* 1, q. 7, c. 4 (PL 187, 568A-571A).

13 *Ibid.*, q. 1, c. 113 (PL 187, 534C).

becomes a very obstinate heretic, always retains the power of Order. Because although the rite of consecration by which the bishop was consecrated was instituted by human law, still the power which is given to the bishop in that consecration is given by God alone and not by man.

Finally, this is proved by the testimony of Blessed Augustine, who, when disputing about this matter against Parmenian, speaks thus: "If even their leaders have been received for the good of peace when they have come from the [Donatist] party, once the error of schism has been corrected, and, if it has seemed to be necessary that they exercise the same offices that they used to exercise, they are not ordained again. Rather, just as the Baptism in them has remained integral, so has their Ordination, because in their schism there had been a defect that was corrected by the peace of unity; [the defect] was not in the Sacraments, which are identical wherever they are. And, when it is judged to be advantageous to the Church that their leaders who have come into the Catholic community not fill their posts there, the Sacraments of Ordination are nonetheless not removed from them, but they remain upon them. Therefore no hand is imposed upon them in the presence of the people, lest an offense be committed against the Sacrament."[14] These words of Augustine are cited by Gratian in the chapter, *Quod quidam*.[15]

Perhaps against these things someone will object to me the chapter, *Daibertum*,[16] in which Pope Urban [II] says that Daibert [of Pisa][17] when ordained by the heretical bishop, Wezilo,[18] received nothing, and was ordained again. And

---

14 *Against the Letter of Parmenian*, bk. 2, n. 28 (PL 43, 70-71).
15 *Decretum Gratiani*, pt. 2, *causa* 1, q. 1, c. 97 (PL 187, 523B-C).
16 *Ibid.*, q. 7, c. 24 (PL 187, 58A-B).
17 Daibert of Pisa was the bishop (1088-1092) and archbishop (1092-1105) of Pisa, leader of the first Pisan crusader fleet, and subsequently Latin patriarch of Jerusalem (1099-1102 or 1105).
18 Wezilo was the archbishop of Mainz (1084-1088), a leading

Whether heretical bishops lose their power of episcopal Order

when giving the reason, the same Pope says: "Because he who had nothing, could give nothing to him on whom he imposed hands." Hence it clearly follows that that Bishop Wezilo when he became a heretic lost the power of episcopal Order. The Gloss there in the beginning of the chapter replies to this argument that the reason why the Pope decreed this was because this Daibert "was not [ordained[19]] using the form of the Church," and hence he rightly reckoned that he had received nothing, and ought to be ordained again. By this response although the Gloss seems to satisfy by those words, in which the Pope gives the reason of his repetition, speaking thus: "Because he who had nothing, could give nothing to him on whom he imposed hands." From which words it is evident that the Pope knew that the heretical Bishop Wezilo did not have the power of conferring Orders. Wherefore I say that the heretic Wezilo was never a bishop, because he had been consecrated by another heretical bishop outside of the form of the Church. And the affair happened in this way, relates whoever he was who described the case of that chapter before the words of the Glossator. In which event, it is evident that that Wezilo received nothing from the other bishop: and hence has nothing, which Daibert could confer.

The second conclusion: "The Pope can forbid the use of the episcopal Order to bishops in regard to the Sacraments: he may do this either by a particular prohibition, or by a general law not to give Orders, or administer the Sacrament of Confirmation. When this prohibition has been made, a bishop ordaining or confirming contrary to that prohibition, would sin by so doing, although he did those things which ought to be held to be valid, and one ought not to

---

supporter of the emperor in the Investiture Controversy and of the Antipope Clement III. In 1085, Wezilo was excommunicated for simony by the pro-Papal synod of Quedlinburg.

19 The text here has "baptized," but the Gloss cited as the source uses the word "ordained."

repeat them." That reason ought to avail for the proof of this conclusion, which we cited above from Innocent [IV] and Panormitanus, which can be greatly useful for this proposition, even though it does nothing for the other. One ought to obey the Pope in everything which is not contrary to the faith and God's law: that the use of the episcopal Order be forbidden to a bishop, is not contrary to faith, nor against God's laws. Because even though it is of Divine law (as we said) that a bishop rightly ordained has episcopal power, still it is not of Divine law that that he always exercise that power. Whence it is that it can be forbidden to him by a superior that he not exercise it.

This argumentation cannot help in any way to prove the opinion of Innocent [IV] and Panormitanus. Because it ought to be held by Catholic faith that a bishop keeps the power of Order once received, since it has been granted to him by God: wherefore the Pope's precept does not avail to do anything regarding that matter. Now to always exercise is not commanded by Divine law, and hence about it the Pope can do whatever he wishes concerning it. Next, it is not within the bishop's power to have or not to have the power of episcopal order: because this depends on God's will, Who as He alone gave this power, so He alone can remove it. Thus the obedience of the bishop does nothing for this matter: because just as the Pope cannot command a bishop what is not within his choice, so neither is a bishop held to obey in those things which are not subject to his will. But to exercise, or not to exercise, the power of episcopal Order is within the bishop's choice: because when he wishes he can exercise it, and when he wishes he can omit it. And hence it follows that the Pope can forbid this power to the bishop, and the bishop is held to obey the Pope forbidding.

Yet in this Innocent [IV] ought to be praised, that (as Panormitanus relates about him in the above-mentioned chapter) he says that such a prohibition ought not to be tolerated if the

Pope without a weighty reason would wish to make a universal law whereby he were to forbid the use of the Sacraments of Order and Confirmation. Because such a prohibition would be unsuitable to all Christendom, and would disturb its whole condition, and in such things which disturb the whole state of the Church, Pope Innocent [IV] says ought it not to be heeded, but it ought to be resisted throughout the universal Church.

From this second conclusion is deduced that a heretical bishop cannot rightly use the power of episcopal order regarding the administration of Orders and Confirmation, because it is forbidden to him by the Church, as is evident in the chapter, *Dicimus*,[20] and the chapter, *Pudenda*.[21] If however against the Church's prohibition, yet the due form having been kept, and the right intention applied, he would either confirm someone or consecrate to the priesthood; even though the ordination or confirmation done by him would be valid, still he would sin, and certainly gravely by administering such Sacraments.

The third main conclusion: "The Pope can take away from bishops that power of Order, which they have regarding sacramentals, for instance consecrations of altars, consecrations of chalices, blessings of vestments necessary for the celebration of Mass." To do all these things, although it was granted to each and every bishop, still this does not belong to them by Divine, but human law. For Christ did not institute any of these things, but with the passage of time they were gradually instituted by the Church. Now that which rests merely on human law, could be taken away by the men who established that law, or by those who succeeded in their place and authority. Now it is evident that the Pope who now lives does not have less power in the Church than the

---

20 *Decretum Gratiani*, pt. 2, *causa* 24, q. 1, c. 31 (PL 187, 1279C-1280C).

21 *Ibid.*, c. 33 (PL 187, 1281A-1282A).

Supreme Pontiffs who preceded him. Therefore just as the preceding Popes decreed all those things to be done by the bishops, so the subsequent Pontiffs could decide that bishops could do none of them. Furthermore, just as the Church long ago established all those consecrations and blessings, so also now she could abrogate them all in general, such that Mass would be celebrated without them all. Which things having been abrogated, it is evident that the bishops' power in this matter has been completely abrogated. Because then a bishop would then do nothing more than any other priest, if both did and said the same things over the altar and chalice. For a bishop now by consecrating or blessing those things, merely makes those things to be suitable instruments for doing some work through them, without which consecration of blessing they would not be suitable for it. But when those consecrations and blessings have been abrogated by the Church, those instruments, all those things having been precluded, would be suitable for doing that work. Thus a bishop would then not make those things by consecrating or blessing, more than any other priest. From this same reason it is proved that the Pope can grant to all other priests this power about the sacramentals which is now reserved to bishops alone: such that they could from the Pope's concession consecrate churches, altars, high altars, chalices, patens, and the rest of things of this kind which are reserved to bishops alone. Because since all these things depend on human law alone, the Pope, who has full power over the whole Church, could dispense as he wishes to anyone he pleases, although he would act wrongly if he were to want to completely remove such an inveterate custom of the Church. For the same reason it is also deduced that (according to the opinion of those who say that minor Orders are not Sacraments, and not instituted by Divine law) the Pope could also take away the conferral of those Orders from bishops, and grant them to other priests.

Whether heretical bishops lose their power of episcopal Order

Concerning heretical bishops, what ought to be known on this point can be very easily established from the things that have been said. It is indeed certain that the Church can take away this power from them: and according to the power which she has, it is evident that she did from the chapter, *Ecclesiis*,[22] and the two following chapters.[23] For there it is commanded that the churches consecrated by the Arians be again consecrated. Nevertheless, the Gloss there on the chapter, *Ecclesiis*, says that this ought to be understood, if the form of the Church had not been kept, because if they had kept it, [the Glossator] says that they ought not to be consecrated again. But the Gloss is actually mistaken, because in the chapter, *Ecclesiis*, the text clearly says that a church ought to be consecrated again which had been consecrated by him who does not have faith in the Trinity. I certainly believe that the Glossator was deceived from the fact that he thought that completely the same thing ought to be done regarding the sacramentals, as regarding the Sacraments, even though there is a vast difference between them. Because the consecrations of Sacraments depend on Divine law: and hence it happens that the power which priests or bishops have over them cannot be taken away from them. Now the power over the sacramentals depends on human law alone, and hence the Church which decreed this law, could remove that power from bishops, such that their consecrations would effect nothing, especially on account of such a serious crime as is heresy. And it seems to me that the same thing ought to be said about the other consecrations and blessings of other sacramentals, such as the consecration of a chalice, the blessings of ornaments and vestments. For the judgment is the same for similar things: and that which is said in the chapter, *A nobis*,[24] does not withstand this opinion.

---

22 *Ibid.*, pt. 3, dist. 1, c. 20 (PL 187, 1712A).
23 *Ibid.*, cc. 21-22 (PL 187, 1712B-C).
24 *Decretals of Gregory IX*, bk. 1, tit. 16 (*De sacramentis non*

For there the Pope decrees that altars ought not to be consecrated again, or vestments blessed again, on which or with which degraded priests have celebrated, because all those things had been truly consecrated or blessed, and hence he does not want that they be consecrated or blessed again. But because it was done by heretics in regard to those sacramentals, the Church reckons it to be of no force and importance: and hence it is necessary that all those things be done by him who is able to do them.

But then someone could rightly ask by what name ought this power of bishops be called, which bishops have regarding the consecration and blessing of sacramentals. It certainly ought not to be called the power of jurisdiction, because by it one can neither punish someone nor pronounce a sentence. If it be called the power of Order, it will be necessarily admitted that there is a power of Order which is removeable by the Church, which Blessed Thomas says that the power of Order is indelible.[25] That the power of Order is indelible ought to be interpreted of only the power of Order which is about the Sacraments, about which alone he was treating in that question.

---

iterandis), c. 2.
25 II-II, q. 39, a. 3.

Chapter XXIII

Whether a bishop who has become a heretic is by that very fact deprived of all power of jurisdiction, even if he be the Pope.

We began an inquiry and dispute about ecclesiastical power, whether such is taken away from a heretic through heresy by that very fact, and we have already sufficiently discussed about the power of Order in the last two chapters. It now remains to treat about the power of jurisdiction, whether a bishop or Pope loses it by the law itself, if he became a heretic. This question certainly presupposes one thing, and it asks another. It presupposes in fact that a bishop and Pope could become a heretic. Concerning a bishop, no one has ever doubted: because it has been ascertained by manifold and very certain experience that many bishops were archheretics, let alone heretics. But concerning the Pope whether he could be a heretic, it is a disputed question among theologians, and each side has Catholic and very learned supporters. Now I do not wish to treat this question at this time, and I do not wish to decide anything about it, besides that which I said above in chapter six of the first book, namely, that the Pope cannot err as he is a public and communal person and become a heretic. For (so that we may omit others) regarding Honorius I it cannot be avoided that he was a heretic, since in the Sixth General Council[1] he was condemned of manifest heresy, and proclaimed a heretic. For which reason the same Sixth Council in the Supreme Pontiff's legates, the priests Theodore and George, and the deacon John, pronounced an anathema to him many times, as it is evident from the final session of the same Sixth Council; which sentence in fact Leo II ratified, as is very

---

1 I. e., III Council of Constantinople.

clearly evident from his letter, which he wrote back about this matter to Emperor Constantine [Pogonatus], in which he calls him a heretic not just once.[2] He who wishes to read this letter will find it in the second volume of the *Conciliorum generalium*, immediately after the last session of the Sixth Council.[3]

Yet I know that there are some who, taking up the cause of Honorius, try to excuse him. Among whom one and the chief is [Albert] Pighius of Kampen[4] in that very large work

---

[2] "Before anything else, this much is absolutely sure: Honorius was not condemned as guilty of preaching heresy in his official capacity (*ex cathedra*). Something more, he was not even condemned as being privately a heretic. Strictly speaking, he was condemned for being a helper of heresy. Whatever might have been the intention of the fathers of the Sixth Ecumenical Council, this much is certain: the decree of the council would be of no value except insofar as it was ratified by the Apostolic See. Now Leo II, who had succeeded Agatho as Pope before the end of the council, in his ratification of the fathers' decree either explained the decree in such fashion or so mitigated it that the upshot was that Honorius was to be stigmatized not as a heretic, but as a helper of heresy. Here are Leo's words to Constantine Pogonatus ratifying the council's decree: 'We anathematize the inventors of the new error, that is, Theodosius, Cyrus, Sergius, Pyrrhus, Paul, Peter... and also Honorius who did not enlighten this Apostolic See with the doctrine of Apostolic tradition, but allowed its immaculate faith to be soiled by profane betrayal.' A short time later, Leo wrote to the bishops of Spain explaining the matter. Honorius was condemned along with the others: 'because instead of extinguishing the incipient flame of heretical doctrine, as befits the holder of Apostolic authority, he rather fanned it by his negligence'" (Van Noort, *Dogmatic Theology: Christ's Church* (Westminster, Maryland: Newman Press, 1959), vol. 2, pp. 306 f.).

[3] *Concilioru Generalium Graecorum et Latinorum* (Paris: Galioti a Prato, 1524), fols. 105v-107r; PL 96, 400A-412B.

[4] Albert Pighius (ca. 1490-1542) was a Dutch theologian born in Kampen, archdeacon at Utrecht and opponent of Luther. At

of his on the ecclesiastical hierarchy,[5] and in a certain disputation which he made on the Acts of the Sixth Council.[6] The certainly learned man does nothing else regarding the true defense of Honorius than to plow the sand, or to wash [the color out of] a brick.[7] For in order to defend Honorius, he says that the sixth session of the council was distorted and corrupted by the Greeks, in whose tongue the Acts of that council were firstly written. Now he says that the reason for this distortion was that the Greeks always envied the Roman Pontiff, and for this reason he says that many lies against Pope Honorius were mixed into the Acts of that council by them, so that in this way they might detract the authority of the Roman See. But actually he supports Honorius more by these fictions and dreams than if he had kept silent.

Firstly in fact that which he says, that the Acts of the Council were distorted by the Greeks, is said merely arbitrarily, nay, temerariously, because it is not founded upon a likely reason. For if the Greeks out of envy wanted to detract the Roman See by Honorius, it is very likely that they would have tried the same thing against other Roman Pontiffs, who condemned other heresies of the Greeks; for instance, it was Leo I who condemned Eutyches and Dioscorus, and he wrote many very learned letters against them to various people. If it is likely that on account of envy of the Roman See the Greeks wanted to distort the Acts of the Sixth Council, it is much more likely that on account of the same envy they would have distorted the Acts of the Council of Chalcedon, in which Dioscorus and Eutyches were condemned, especially since on account of this condemnation the Armenians and a

---

Ratisbon in 1541 he took part in the efforts at reunion with the Protestants.
5 *Hierarchiae ecclesiasticae assertio* (Cologne: Melchior Neuss, 1538).
6 *Diatriba de actis VI et VII Synodi.*
7 "To wash a brick" (πλίνθον πλύνειν), i. e., to labor in vain.

large part of the Greeks began to withdraw from obedience to the Roman Pontiff. I do not wish to argue more in favor of the veracity of the Acts of the Sixth Council, because a learned man, Francisco Torres,[8] Spanish by birth, published a book[9] in which he fights in favor of this matter against Albert Pighius, and in my opinion he certainly triumphs over him on this point.

Furthermore, even if we freely concede to Albert Pighius that the Acts of the Sixth Council were distorted in other matters, still Honorius will not be thus saved from infamy, because there is still one other legitimate witness, and approved by all, who accuses him of this crime. For the holy and very learned man, Bede, a quasi-eyewitness because he was a contemporary of Honorius, in the book *De ratione temporum*, when discussing about Emperor Constantine IV, says these words: "Pope Agatho, at the request of the most pious rulers Constantine, Heraclius, and Tiberius, sent envoys to the royal city, amongst whom was John, then a deacon, but not long after Bishop of Rome, to bring about the unification of the holy churches of God. They were received very graciously by Constantine, the most reverend defender of the Catholic faith, and were ordered to lay aside all philosophical debates in order to search for the true faith in peaceful discussion, and all the works of the Fathers that they asked for were given to them from the library of Constantinople. One hundred and fifty bishops were present there, under the presidency of the Patriarchs George of the royal city [Constantinople] and Macarius of Antioch. And those who asserted that there was one will and one operation in Christ were convicted that they had falsified very many statements of the Catholic Fathers. With the conflict

---

8   Francisco Torres, known as Turrianus (ca. 1509-1584), was a Spanish Jesuit Hellenist and polemicist.
9   Cf. *De actis veris Sextae Synodi, deque canonibus, qui ejusdem Sextae Synodi falso feruntur...* (Florence: s. n., 1551), pp. 78 ff.

settled, George was corrected, and Macarius, together with his followers and their predecessors Cyrus, Sergius, Honorius, Pyrrhus, Paul, and Peter, were anathematized."[10]

In which words one ought to especially note two things. The first is that he says that those heretics were convicted that they had distorted the writings of the Catholic Fathers. For this was always, and now is, the continual and inviolable custom of heretics, to fabricate lies and falsify Scriptures, so that they can defend their heresies before the people, whom they wish to deceive before all else. The other thing is that it serves the present proposition, where he reckons Honorius among those who were struck with an anathema on account of the Monothelite heresy. Thus we suppose that the Pope can fall into heresy, and be a heretic. Now the question rightly presents itself worthy of careful examination: Whether the Pope, or any other bishop, having become a heretic, loses all power of jurisdiction such that he ought not to be then reckoned the Pope or the bishop? This question certainly ought to be decided in one way according to Divine law, and another according to human law.

If this question is investigated according to human law, it will be necessary to reply in one way regarding the Pope, and another regarding the other bishops. For the Pope ought not to be measured by the same law and measure as other bishops are. Because all other bishops are subject to human law, and are obliged to bear the punishments decreed by human law due to some crimes if they were to fall into those crimes. From which it is very clearly concluded that every bishop after he has become a heretic is excommunicated. And hence it is also concluded that he is deprived by that very fact of his episcopate, if the Church had inflicted by a perpetual decree this punishment to a heretical bishop. Now the Church has never (that I know of) decreed this until the present time. For

---

10 *De ratione temporum*, c. 66 (*Chronicon sive de sex hujus saeculi aetatibus*) (PL 90, 567C-568A).

although there are many holy men, whose testimonies I will cite below, who say that heretics have no honor or dignity, still they did not say this as decreeing a law. For since they were not Supreme Pontiffs, it is certain that they could not make laws which would bind all bishops. But the Pope, since he is the head of the whole Church, what he decrees for all the other members, administering sensation to them all, just as he can judge all, so he cannot be judged by anyone, as it stated in the chapter, *Si Papa*,[11] in the chapter, *Nemo*,[12] and in the chapter, *Oves*.[13] For which reason it is concluded that the Pope is not bound by any human precepts, because he does not have a superior on earth by whom he can be bound.

Now it is certain that no one can be bound by an inferior or by an equal: because (as it is a common proverb of

---

11 "If the Pope, remiss in his duties and neglectful of his and his neighbor's salvation, gets caught up in idle business, and if moreover, by his silence (which actually does more harm to himself and everyone else), he leads innumerable hordes of people away from the good with him, he will be beaten for eternity with many blows alongside that very first slave of hell. However, no person can presume to convict him of any transgressions in this matter, because, although the Pope can judge everyone else, no one may judge him, unless he, for whose perpetual stability all the faithful pray as earnestly as they call to mind the fact that, after God, their own salvation depends on his soundness, is found to have strayed from the faith" (*Decretum Gratiani*, pt. 1, dist. 40, q. 1, c. 6 (PL 187, 214C-215A)).

12 "No one could judge the first See, since all Sees wish to be judged by the first See. The supreme judge could be judged neither by Augustus, nor by all the clergy, nor by kings, nor by the people" (*Ibid.*, pt. 2, *causa* 9, q. 3, c. 13 (PL 187, 798B)). This quotation is falsely ascribed in the *Decretum* to Pope Innocent I, but is taken from an apocryphal *Constitutum Silvestri*, or *Council of Silvester* (Cf. c. 20 in Mansi 2, 631).

13 "The sheep cannot accuse their shepherd, unless he would deviate from the faith" (*Ibid.*, pt. 2, *causa* 2, q. 7, c. 13 (PL 187, 640C).

jurists) "An equal has no authority over an equal."[14] And hence our theologians conclude that the Pope is not obliged to making a yearly auricular confession of his sins, because such annual confession was commanded merely by human law, namely, by the famous chapter, *Omnis utriusque sexus*.[15] It is very aptly proved that the Pope who has full authority over all Canon Law, is not obliged to it. From the same root arises that the Pope cannot fall into a censure of any ecclesiastical canon, such as excommunication, interdict, suspension, or irregularity. For all these censures, since they were decreed by human law alone, cannot bind the Pope, who it is certain, is not even equal to those by whom those canons were decreed. From all these things it necessarily follows that a Pope having become a heretic is not by the law itself excommunicated, by that kind of excommunication which is called an ecclesiastical censure.

I deliberately spoke about an excommunication which is an ecclesiastical censure, because there is a certain other broader and milder excommunication against heretics, which according to the opinion of many (as we said above in chapter eighteen of this second book) is inflicted by Divine law. But this is nothing but a certain separation from the exterior association with the faithful: such that all the faithful are forbidden by Divine law not to associate with heretics, according to that saying of Paul: "A man that is a heretic, after the first and second admonition, avoid" (Tit. 3, 10). Which saying John echoes speaking thus: "If any man come to you, and bring not this doctrine, receive him not into the house nor say to him, God speed you" (II Jn. 1, 10). And with this excommunication the Pope, as any other Christian if he becomes a heretic, will be by that very fact immediately excommunicated. Because after it has been established about

---

14   *Cum non habeat imperium par in parem* (*Decretals of Gregory IX*, bk. 1, tit. 6 (*De electione*), c. 20 (*Innotuit*).
15   *Ibid.*, bk. 5, tit. 38 (*De poenitentiis et remissionibus*), c. 12.

his heresy, all Christians are held to abstain from associating with him. There is still another much more harsh excommunication, which not merely separates from exterior association, but also sequesters from the participation of spiritual goods, and inflicts many other inconveniences, which need not be enumerated here. Therefore regarding this excommunication, which is an ecclesiastical censure, and inflicted by the Church, I reckon that the Supreme Pontiff, even if he becomes a heretic, is not excommunicated with this excommunication by the law itself, unless from a source other than from human law it would be established that he by the very fact that he was made a heretic, has been deposed from the Papal dignity.

Such an excommunication, since it was inflicted by human law, cannot bind the Pope, who beyond any doubt is above every human law. This opinion in fact seems so true to Saint Thomas that he says that the Pope cannot delegate this power to anyone, so that he could excommunicate the Pope.[16] And Saint Bonaventure and Albert the Great teach the same thing, as Juan de Torquemada relates about them, who approves of the opinion of all these men.[17] Thus they opine incorrectly who teach that all laws which decree something about heretics bind also the Pope, if he becomes a

---

16 "Outward judgment is according to men, but the judgment of confession is directed to God, before whom a person is rendered less by the fact that he sins, but not among the rankings of men. And therefore in outward judgment just as no one can give the sentence of excommunication to himself, so neither can he commit it to another, nor excommunicate himself. But in the forum of conscience he can commit his own absolution to another, which he cannot use for himself" (*In IV Sentences*, dist. 19, q. 1, a. 3, qc. 3, ad 3).

17 *Summa de Ecclesia una cum eiusdem apparatu nunc primum in lucem edito, super decreto Papae Eugenii IIII in concilio Florentino de Unione Graecorum* (Venice: Michele Tramezzino, 1561), bk. 2, c. 104, fol. 244v.

heretic. For while he is the Pope, he is subject to deposition, that is to say, he can be deposed on account of heresy; he is not, however, subject to any other censure of law. But after he has been deposed, then at that time he will be subject to all ecclesiastical punishments, as all the rest of men. And hence it is that the Pope having become a heretic, unless impeded by Divine law, and still before he is deposed, could keep all his rank and jurisdiction. Because although he is not bound by excommunication, no other human law impedes him from binding and loosing others.

Against these things which we said, perhaps someone will object to me a certain Gloss on the chapter, *Achatius*,[18] which relates these words: "Here is a case where a Pope can bind a pope, when a pope incurs a sentence already pronounced [*latae sententiae*] in a canon. The rule, 'An equal cannot bind or loose an equal,'[19] does not stand in the way because, if a Pope is a heretic he is less than any Catholic."[20] I very easily refute this objection, when frankly saying that that Glossator does not have such great authority that he can stop me by his authority, especially since in other places he teaches many very evidently false and erroneous things, so that he has rightly lost all authority on account of those things. Next, if we examine carefully the words themselves which he now quotes, they very clearly show how little solid teaching they contain in themselves. For he says, "If a Pope is a heretic, he is less than any Catholic." If a heretical Pope is less than any Catholic, then any Catholic is greater than a heretical

---

18 *Decretum Gratiani*, pt. 2, *causa* 24, q. 1, c. 1 (PL 187, 1263B).
19 Cf. *Decretals of Gregory IX*, bk. 1, tit. 33 (*De majoritate et obedientia*), c. 16 (*Cum inferior*).
20 *Decretum Gratiani: cum Glossis*, s. v. *In heresim*, fol. 470v. The Glossator is John of Wildeshausen, called Johannes Teutonicus (ca. 1180-1252), who was the Master General of the Dominican Order.

Pope. This manifest conclusion is given from that, because "greater" and "lesser" are correlative terms.

Let us see therefore how this "greater" and "lesser" ought to be reckoned. And it is certain that "greater" ought to be said in the same way whereby "lesser" is said: because otherwise they will not be comparative or relative opposites. If the Gloss speaks about "greater" and "lesser" in regards to jurisdiction, it is evident that his words are false. For it is very clearly evident that it is false that every Catholic is greater in jurisdiction than a heretical Pope. Because there are many Catholics who have absolutely no more jurisdiction than a heretical Pope, as they are all just laity, to whom it does not pertain to examine a heretical Pope, nor to evaluate about it, nor to punish him on account of this. But if he is speaking about greatness or littleness regarding merits, grace, or charity, even if he is speaking in this way, still he will not be able to conclude anything from this which could support his position. For according to that meaning of "lesser" and "greater," it will also be said that a Pope being in mortal sin is less than any Catholic and just man. But does it follow that equal can bind or loose equal, or that the Pope ought to fall into the canon of a sentence already pronounced? Because in order that someone can bind or loose, greatness of sanctity is not required, but rather greatness of jurisdiction. Thus it badly corresponds to the objection of the rule which says: "An equal cannot bind or loose an equal," by saying that a heretical Pope is less than any Catholic.

Wherefore I say that, secluding every Divine law about this matter, if this question ought to be decided merely according to human law, a Pope who has become a heretic, although he rightly ought to be deposed due to this, still he is not by that very fact deposed, or by that very fact excommunicated. Because as long as he is the Pope, he cannot be excommunicated, nor bound by any other ecclesiastical censure, since he is above every human law, whereby

Whether heretical bishops lose all power of jurisdiction

those censures have their firmness and their strength. But he will be Pope as long as shall be tolerated by the Church. But the Church doubtlessly tolerates him until it is evident that he has been deposed, or rightly ought to be deposed, by Divine law. Because Paul III, who now lives, although he is the Pope by the election of men, has full authority over the whole Church, not from men, but from God. And from this it is very evidently gathered that he cannot be deposed by the Church for whatever crime, unless it is evident from the same Divine law that the Church can depose the Pope on account of such a crime.

Hence having put aside human law, from which we cannot say anything certain about this question, let us turn to the Divine law, as the source of all truth, so that we can be plentifully taught therefrom. Let us thoroughly examine therefore the Divine Scriptures, and let us seek after those things which are necessary for being the Pope, and from this we will easily understand whether the Pope, if he becomes a heretic, has immediately lost the Papal dignity or not. For by very certain philosophical reasoning we know that something is necessarily destroyed when those things are lacking which are necessary for its existence. On the other hand, if all things which are necessary for something's existence are present, if the thing is naturally and not freely caused, it is impossible for it not to exist. For since blood is necessary for man's life, wherefore when blood is wanting, man cannot live. Otherwise, if man were to live without blood, by this one piece of evidence it would be very evidently proved that blood is unnecessary for his life. Heat is necessary for there to be a fire, and hence it follows that when the heat has been completely destroyed, the fire also perishes.

Thus this foundation having been firstly laid, it is necessary that we carefully examine from the same Divine Scriptures those things which are necessary for being Pope. I omit here the other things which outside of the Pope himself, such as the voluntary election of the electors themselves, and the aptitude in those electing, namely, so that they would be capable of electing. Having omitted these and other things of this kind, if we speak about those things which are in the one to be elected or the elected one himself, it is necessary to distinguish. Because certain things are necessary for simply being, others are necessary for being well. Those things which are required for being well are such things that without them one could be the Pope, but not a good Pope: and these are knowledge of Divine things, prudence about things to be done, very fervent charity; and other such things without which, even though one could be the Pope, still he will not be a good Pope. Now those things which are necessary simply to be the Pope are two. One of which is merely necessary for becoming, and not after it has been done: and this is the will of the one elected, whereby he consents to the election made of him. For this is necessary so that one may become the Pope: because when he is unwilling, he cannot become the Pope. Yet once he consents to the election, and has been made the Pope, his will is then not necessary for being the Pope: because even though he may repent of his past choice, and does not want to be the Pope, and renounces the Papacy, nonetheless he is still the Pope until his renunciation has been accepted by those to whom it pertains, as it appears in the first chapter of *De renunciatio*.[21] If anyone

---

21 "Since some men in their curiosity, disputing about matters which are not very useful, and boldly seeking to know more than they ought, against the teaching of the Apostle (Cf. Rom. 12, 3), seemed to be imprudently calling into troublesome doubt whether the Roman Pontiff, especially when he recognizes himself to be inadequate to govern the universal Church, and bear the responsibilities of the supreme pontificate, can renounce the Papacy and its responsibility and honor: Pope Celestine V, Our predecessor, while he presided over the rule of that same Church, wishing to remove grounds for any hesitation concerning this matter, having

seeks after a reason for these things, we willingly present it now, which is this. Anyone can renounce his own right, yet not the right of another. The Church when electing Paul as the Pope, still has not a right on account of this regarding Paul until he consents. After he consents, however, to the election made of him, just as she acquired a right over him, so that she could ask from him for doctrine and the rest of the things which he is bound by the Papal office to give to the Church. For there is in fact a mutual contract between the electors and the one just elected, whereby they are mutually obligated to each other. The one elected assuredly to rendering the due office of pastor for which alone the Church elected him. But the Church, which elected him as a prelate, by this very fact obliged herself to rendering due obedience to him. And hence it happens that when he has been firstly elected, he could renounce the election made of himself, because only then may he renounce his right. However, once he has consented to the election, and has been made the Pope, he can no longer renounce the Papacy without the consent of the Church: because if he did this, he would renounce not only his own right, but the right of the Church, which he cannot do. From which things it is very clearly established that the will of the one elected as the Pope, although it is necessary for becoming the Pope, still it is not necessary for

---

consulted with his brothers, the cardinals of the Roman Church, among whose number We then were, following the agreed council and consent of ourselves and all of them, established and decreed by Apostolic authority that the Roman Pontiff can freely resign. Lest it happen that this decree be forgotten over the course of time, or such doubt be further protracted, We have therefore decided that it should be placed among the other constitutions for a perpetual reminder of the matter, following the council of our brothers" (*Liber sextus decretalium*, bk. 1, tit. 7 (*De renunciatione*), c. 1 (*Quoniam aliqui*)).

the conservation of the Papacy: because (as I said) he could be [or remain as] the Pope against his will.

The other thing is necessary for becoming the Pope, and for being the Pope, and this is faith. And here I do not speak about formed faith, about which Paul says that it "worketh by charity" (Gal. 5, 6). Because this is unnecessary for being the Pope, since the Pope when being in [the state of] mortal sin can be elected Pope and remain as the Pope. Otherwise one would fall into the error of the Waldensians and John Hus, saying that every ecclesiastical dignity is lost through any mortal sin. Which error was condemned in the Council of Constance, in the fifteenth session.[22] Hence the faith which I say is necessary to be the Pope is habitual faith distinct from hope and charity, which is given in Baptism, and about which Paul says that without it "it is impossible to please God" (Heb. 11, 6). This faith, I say, is necessary to be the Pope, such that without it one cannot become the Pope, or remain in the Papacy. And because this is the principle foundation, upon which nearly the whole fabric of this teaching of ours consists, wherefore it ought to be elaborated for its firm stability, and proved by many reasons.

For which matter it is especially conducive to carefully investigate the whole process whereby Christ came to give the Papacy to Peter. For He did not immediately and without any intervals grant him this power: but firstly He promised it, deferring this giving to another time. Next, before He gives, He admonished about the dignity promised to him, so that he would understand what was being enjoined upon him by it. Finally, when Christ granted to Peter the authority promised, He then stated more openly the power of the dignity, and what things are necessarily required for it. If someone wishes to carefully consider all these things, he will certainly very clearly learn from it how necessary Christ Our Savior wanted the faith to be for the Papacy.

---

22 Cf. Dz. 488 & 656.

Firstly in fact Christ Our Savior promised this power to Peter, speaking thus: "I will give to thee the keys of the kingdom of heaven. And whatsoever thou shalt bind upon earth, it shall be bound also in heaven: and whatsoever thou shalt loose upon earth, it shall be loosed also in heaven" (Mt. 16, 19). But when He gave the keys to Peter, He did not say "heaven" in the singular: but He signified by the plural number that those things which he would loose or bind on earth would be loosen and bound in the heavens, so that even by this difference of words He would teach us that He would grant something greater to Peter than to the rest of the Apostles.[23] Before Christ promised this to Peter, He asked all the Apostles what they thought about Him, and what opinion they had about Him. To which question Peter alone answering said: "Thou art Christ, the Son of the living God" (v. 16). In which place Theophylactus notes that those words for expressing Peter's greater faith ought to be recited with an article signifying a certain emphasis, for so Theophylactus says: "He did not say, 'Thou art the anointed one, a son of God,' without the article 'the,' but with the article, 'the Son,' that is, He Who is the One and the Only, not a son by grace, but He Who is begotten of the same essence as the Father. For there were also many other christs, anointed ones, such

---

23 "It is no small difference that Peter received the keys not of one heaven but of more, and in order that whatsoever things he binds on the earth may be bound not in one heaven but in them all, as compared with the many who bind on earth and loose on earth, so that these things are bound and loosed not in the heavens, as in the case of Peter, but in one only; for they do not reach so high a stage, with power as Peter to bind and loose in all the heavens. The better, therefore, is the binder, so much more blessed is he who has been loosed, so that in every part of the heavens his loosing has been accomplished" (Origen, *Commentary on the Gospel of Matthew*, bk. 13, n. 31 (PG 13, 1182A)).

as all the priests and kings; but "the Christ," with the article, there is but One."[24]

When this confession of faith had been made by Peter, Christ immediately said to him: "Blessed art thou, Simon Bar-Jona: because flesh and blood hath not revealed it to thee, but my Father who is in heaven. And I say to thee: That thou art Peter; and upon this rock I will build my church, and the gates of hell shall not prevail against it" (vv. 17-18). These words clearly show a certain remuneration exhibited to Peter for the confession of his faith. Theophylactus very clearly teaches this when speaking thus: "The Lord remunerates Peter, giving him a great reward, that the Church will be built on him. Since Peter confessed Him as Son of God, the Lord said that this confession which he made shall be the foundation of those who believe, so that every man who intends to build the house of faith shall lay down this foundation. For even if we should put together innumerable virtues, but do not have the correct foundation, we build uselessly."[25] Cyril [of Alexandria] teaches the same opinion, who when interpreting the aforementioned words of Matthew, says: "To my mind it appears evident that the rock here intended by Christ, is nothing else than the disciple's unshaken faith, on which the Church was built, that it might not be in danger of falling or surrendering to the powers of darkness."[26]

In these words of the two Doctors it especially ought to be noted that they teach us through Christ's words, and not from their own brain, that faith is the foundation of the whole structure of the Church. But where this foundation is absent, nothing can be built thereon, and if something has been built on it, it is necessary that when that foundation has been taken away it would collapse. The conclusion therefore is that when the Catholic faith, which is the foundation

---

24 *Enarratio in Evangelium S. Matthaei* (PG 123, 318D).
25 *Ibid.* (PG 123, 319A-B).
26 *Dialogues on the Trinity*, bk. 4 (PG 75, 866B-C).

of the whole Catholic structure, fails in someone, the Papal dignity cannot be made firm in him, which is the first stone in that structure, after the faith. Nay, no other ecclesiastical dignity instituted by Christ, such as the episcopal authority, could be established in him who does not have the Catholic faith. Because this [ecclesiastical dignity], since it was instituted by Christ, having been placed in the structure by the same, could not have another foundation than that which was placed by Christ Himself, namely, the faith. And from this it also follows that when this foundation of the faith has been taken away from him, who was the Pope or bishop, by that very fact the Papal or episcopal dignity, which previously was in him, falls from him.

Perhaps someone wishing to escape from the force of this argumentation will say that the Baptismal character, which is called the "sacrament of the faith," is enough, so that the Papal dignity could be placed and conserved in someone who does not have the faith. But these words are mere nonsense, as can easily be evident to one even mediocrely considering the matter. For when Theophylactus states Christ's words, he does not say that the Baptismal character is the foundation, but only the confession of the faith. Even if Theophylactus would not interpret, one could very clearly establish this point, from Christ's words themselves and their circumstances. For there was no mention there of Baptism, neither of the Baptismal character, nor could there be merit in Peter, so that on account of it Christ would give him such a great reward. But in the confession of faith, which Peter made, there was much merit, and hence it was held by Christ to be worthy, for which He promised such a great reward, as He decided to give to no other except Peter, whom He instituted the head of the whole Church.

And it can be clearly proved that faith is the foundation of the whole of religion, and of the whole ecclesiastical structure. For Paul when writing to the Corinthians says: "Other foundation no man can lay, but that which is laid; which is Christ Jesus" (I Cor. 3, 11). Augustine when interpreting which words says: "If Christ is the foundation, then there is no doubt whatsoever that we must have faith in Christ, since it is by faith, as the same Apostle teaches,[27] that Christ dwells in our hearts."[28] And Paul, when writing to the Colossians, again says: "He hath reconciled you in the body of his flesh through death, to present you holy and unspotted, and blameless before him" (1, 22). In which words Paul very clearly said that faith is the foundation, and from this it is concluded that when faith has been taken away the whole rest of the building collapses.

And certainly (so that I may speak openly) this reasoning, which was now made from the notion of the foundation, urges me very much to think that the Pope, if he becomes a heretic, by that very fact is deprived by Divine law of the Papal dignity. For another [reasoning], which some make from the notion of members, which are connected to each other by faith, is not as effective, so that by that notion someone could prove that the Pope, if he becomes a heretic, is then not the head of the whole Church: namely, because he is then not a member of the Church, since he lacks the faith. For Cardinal Thomas de Vio, in his small work on the authority of the Pope and a council,[29] easily resolves this argument, saying that the Pope, even if he becomes a heretic, is still a member of the Church. Because although he lacks faith, he still has the Baptismal character, by which, as also by faith, someone can be made a member of Christ's Church, as Innocent [III] expressly teaches in the chapter, *Veniens*,[30]

---

27 Cf. Eph. 3, 17.
28 *On Faith and Works*, c. 16, n. 27 (PL 40, 215).
29 *Auctoritas Pape et Concilii sive Ecclesie comparata* (Rome: Marcellus Silber, 1511), c. 22, fol. 114r.
30 *Decretals of Gregory IX*, bk. 3, tit. 43 (*De presbytero non baptizato*), c. 3.

whose word are these: "Not only through the Sacrament of faith [i. e., Baptism], but also through the faith of the Sacrament is someone made beyond all doubt Christ's member."

Perhaps someone will also reply to me from the words of the same chapter, saying that in that same chapter, Baptism is also called the foundation. I certainly admit that Baptism is also called the foundation: but it ought to be carefully examined, in respect to what it is called the foundation, and it will be found that it is called the foundation in respect to the other Sacraments. For the question of this chapter was about an unbaptized priest, whether he had received the Order of the priesthood, and in order to persuade that he had not received the priesthood, he says that by lacking Baptism, which is the foundation of the other Sacraments, no other Sacrament could be built thereupon. Albeit the Pontiff said these words not when defining, but disputing, as one can easily establish by examining the text. But the Pontiff did not say there that Baptism is the foundation of the Papal dignity, and there was not a discussion then about it. Let it be granted that he had also said this; still he would not have said that Baptism is a sufficient foundation, such that faith would not also be a necessary foundation. Because this would clearly oppose Christ, Who said that He would found His Church upon the confession of faith, and Who on account of that confession of faith promised that He would give Peter as a reward the keys of the kingdom of heaven.

And this is the other thing which in the words of Theophylactus lastly cited ought to have been noted, when he said that Christ remunerated Peter's confession, when He promised him that He would build His Church upon his confession, and on account of that same confession He would give him the keys of the kingdom of heaven. For because when all the other Apostles were silent Peter alone confessed that Christ is the Son of God, wherefore He promised to him alone the keys of the kingdom of heaven, and the power of binding and loosing over all men. If on account of the confession of faith as on account of a certain merit, Christ promised the Pontifical dignity over all men, by this same fact He declared that he who does not have faith is unworthy to be preeminent to the others. Thus who is so mindless that he would want to rightly attribute the Papacy to anyone without the faith, which Christ did not want to promise to Peter without the confession of the faith, and hence much less give it?

And the opinion of those who say that Peter then answered for all, and expressed the faith of the others, does not please me. For the other Apostles did not delegate this duty to Peter, that he would answer for all. And Peter was not so arrogant that he would answer for all not having been commissioned, especially because at that time he not only had not been given authority over the other Apostles, but it also had not yet been promised. Now if someone would say that Peter could have done this, because he was older than the other Apostles, I beseech him to consider that Andrew is senior to Peter in the apostolate,[31] which ought to have been esteemed much more than any seniority of age.

Next, Peter himself by his own words testifies that he answers not for all, but for himself only. For he spoke not in the plural (as was befitting) but in the singular, speaking thus: "I say to thee: Thou art Christ" etc.[32] If he had wanted to speak for all, he should have spoken in the plural with these words: "We say" etc. For elsewhere after Christ had at that time instituted him a prelate over all: when on the day of Pentecost all the Apostles, because when the Spirit from heaven was received they were speaking in all languages, they were falsely accused before the people of drunkenness,

---

31 Cf. Jn. 1, 40-41.

32 The author seems to have confused Christ's words in verse 18 with Peter's words in verse 16 here, but Christ did address Peter alone as verse 17 indicates. For there He said, "And Jesus answering, said to him," and not "…said to them."

Peter understanding that he has the care of all, and hence wanting to accept the cause of all, spoke not in the singular but in the plural, speaking thus: "Ye men of Judea, and all you that dwell in Jerusalem, be this known to you, and with your ears receive my words. For these are not drunk, as you suppose, seeing it is but the third hour of the day" (Acts 2, 14-15). If he had wished to reply for himself alone, he would have said: "I am not drunk." But because he then had the care of all, he decided to reply for all saying: "These are not drunk." Therefore he answers for himself alone when he said: "I say to thee: Thou art Christ, the Son of the living God." He alone answers, although all had been asked, because the faith which he had in his heart, could not restrain itself within the depths of his heart, just as the faith of the other Apostles, which because it was more tepid, did not break forth in a public confession.

But because perhaps we have already said enough about this, it is necessary that we go on to investigate the rest of Peter's progression. Christ Our Savior when near to His Passion, foreseeing that the souls of the Apostles would be troubled after His death, enjoins upon Peter that he confirm them in the faith, speaking thus: "Simon, Simon, behold Satan hath desired to have you, that he may sift you as wheat: but I have prayed for thee, that thy faith fail not: and thou, being once converted, confirm thy brethren" (Lk. 22, 31-32). Behold the first duty of the Pope, which God then committed to Peter; this is, to strengthen all the others in the faith. But it is impossible that he who is weak in the faith could confirm the rest in the same faith. Whence it is that the Pope if he becomes a heretic, could no longer be the Pope: because he is completely inept for that which firstly belongs to him by his office, namely, to confirm the rest in the faith.

Finally, when Christ granted to Peter the Papal dignity previously promised, He spoke thus: "Feed my sheep" (Jn. 21, 17). By which words, by the concordant opinion of all

Catholic Doctors, He said that all Christians are the sheep, and Peter is the shepherd of them all, so that He declares by the very name of the office what is incumbent upon Peter and any Supreme Pontiff, successor of Peter, to do from the office: namely, to feed the flock committed to them with a spiritual food, namely, the doctrine of the Catholic faith. He who has the Catholic faith, if he is uneducated, or vitiated by bad morals, even though he does not exercise his office well, nevertheless he is still the Pope: because he has nothing opposing the Papacy. But he who is a heretic has heresy, which completely opposes the Papacy. For he who is a heretic cannot give to others the true doctrine of the faith: and hence it follows that he who is a heretic, cannot be the Church's shepherd. What Augustine says confirms this, when he expounds the passage of the Canticles: "Feed thy goats" (1, 7),[33] speaking thus: "To Peter staying inside [the Church] it is said, 'Feed my sheep.' To the heretic going outside it is said, 'Feed my goats.'"[34] And again in the letter to Vincent the Donatist, when discussing the same words he says: "'And feed thy goats,' not as Peter, to whom it is said, 'Feed My sheep'; but, 'Feed thy goats beside the tents of the shepherds' (*Ibid.*), not 'beside the tent of the shepherd,' where there is 'one fold and one shepherd' (Jn. 10, 16)."[35] In which words Augustine very clearly teaches that he who is the shepherd of Christ's flock, if he becomes a heretic, is no longer the shepherd of Christ's flock, but of his goats.

There are still many other arguments proceeding from these conditions and qualities which necessarily belong to heretics, from which not less evidently it is proved that the Pope, if he becomes a heretic, is immediately by Divine law deprived of the Papal dignity. For every heretic has

---

33 The Douay-Rheims translation is "feed thy kids [*haedos*]." *Haedus* in Latin means a young goat or kid.
34 Sermon 46 (*On the Pastors in Ezechiel*), n. 37 (PL 38, 292).
35 Letter 93, n. 29 (PL 33, 336)

been separated and cut off from the body of the Church, because he divides himself from the faith which the whole Church holds, preferring to rely on his own prudence than to be subject to the judgment of the whole Catholic Church. Now it follows that he who is separated from the Church's faith is also separated from the body of the Church herself, because just as according to Paul's saying, the faith is one:[36] so the Church is one, and the Church's unity depends on the unity of faith, as Hugo of Saint Victor says: "We obtain union by faith, vivification by charity."[37] But whoever has been separated from the body of the Church, is no longer the head of the same body, because it is incompatible that what has been separated from the body, is its head. From which things it is necessarily inferred that if the Pope becomes a heretic, he is no longer the Pope: since by heresy he has been separated from the body of the Church by Divine law.

Whatever other sins, however grave, corrupt the Pope, and make him like a languid head. Only the sin of heresy, however, cuts off the head from the body, and consequently only it deprives the Pope by Divine law of his Papal dignity. Furthermore, heretics are called wolves by Our Savior, Who when warning us that we beware of heretics says that they ought to be fled from like wolves, speaking thus: "Beware of false prophets, who come to you in the clothing of sheep, but inwardly they are ravening wolves" (Mt. 7, 15). Notice that you see that heretics, who are the false prophets, are called wolves, not by anyone else but by Christ Himself, the Teacher of Truth. Therefore lest a wolf become the shepherd of the flock, it is necessary that the Pope and any other bishop, having become a heretic, immediately cease to be a shepherd: whence it necessarily follows that he be neither the Pope nor a bishop. And it is not believable that Christ would want a

---

36 Cf. Eph. 4, 5.
37 *On the Sacraments of the Christian Faith*, bk. 2, pt. 2, c. 1 (PL 176, 416B).

heretical man to be the shepherd of His sheep, whom He certainly knew is a wolf, lest it be said that He committed the sheep to a wolf (which is an indication of extreme insanity). Thus if a prelate from being a shepherd becomes a wolf, it is also necessary that by that very fact he ceases to be a prelate and shepherd, lest even for a short period of time, the sheep be said to have been committed to a wolf.

Again: we proved by many testimonies of Sacred Scripture that every heretic by Divine law ought to be avoided by men, as we already discussed when we discussed about excommunication. Now it is impossible that someone be the prelate of those who by Divine law are held to separate themselves from him, nowise to associate with him, nor receive him in their house, nor greet him; because his subjects are certainly also held to bestow, even with reverence, everything contrary to these things to a prelate, bad in himself. For Peter teaches that obedience ought to be shown to superiors, "not only to the good and gentle, but also to the froward" (I Pet. 2, 18).

Finally, there are very many testimonies of the holy Doctors, which assert that a heretical man has completely no power of jurisdiction in the Church. Firstly in fact, I cite Blessed Thomas, as more recent, who says that the power of jurisdiction "does not remain in heretics and schismatics; and consequently they neither absolve nor excommunicate, nor grant indulgence."[38] And Gratian agrees with this opinion, who immediately after the chapter, *Audivimus*, speaks thus: "Since just as he who blesses is greater than he who is blessed,[39] so he who officially curses is greater than he who is cursed. It is certainly evident that he who abandons the fulness of the Catholic faith nowise has the power of cursing or blessing. For he is unable to curse a Catholic, since that person is superior to himself; he cannot pass judgment about someone who is estranged from the faith, as he cannot give

---

38 II-II, q. 39, a. 3.
39 Cf. Heb. 7, 7.

judgment about someone equal to him."⁴⁰ And Bede says: "All who in any manner separate themselves from the unity of the faith, or from communion with Peter the Apostle, such should neither be able to be loosed from the bonds of sin, nor to enter the gate of the heavenly kingdom."⁴¹ Blessed Ambrose says: "The Lord willed that the power of binding and of loosing should be alike, and sanctioned each by a similar condition. So he who has not the power to loose has not the power to bind."⁴² And below: "It is certain that although the Church has both, heresy does not have either one."⁴³ And Blessed Augustine says that the keys of binding and loosing were given to the Church in Peter, speaking thus: "Peter, in receiving the keys, represented the holy Church."⁴⁴ From which words it is very clearly gathered that he who is outside the Church, has not power of binding or loosing. Cyprian in a certain letter [to Antonianus about Cornelius and Novatian] says: "He then who neither maintains neither the unity of the Spirit nor the bond of peace, and separates himself from the bond of the Church, and from the assembly of priests, can neither have the power nor the honor of a bishop, since he has refused to maintain either the unity or the peace of the episcopate."⁴⁵ These words are found in the chapter, *Novatianus*.⁴⁶ And in another letter, which is to

---

40 *Decretum Gratiani*, pt. 2, *causa* 24, q. 1, c. 4 (PL 187, 1266B-C).
41 Homily 16 (*In natale beatorum Apostolorum Petri et Pauli*) (PL 94, 223B).
42 *Concerning Repentance*, bk. 1, c. 2, n. 7 (PL 16, 468A).
43 *Ibid.* (PL 16, 468B). Cf. *IV Sentences*, dist. 18, n. 2 (PL 192, 885); *Decretum Gratiani*, pt. 2, *causa* 33, q. 3 (*De poenitentia*), dist. 1, q. 3, c. 51 (*Verbum Dei*), §1 (*Dominus*) (PL 187, 1536B).
44 *Tractates on the Gospel of John*, tractate 50, n. 12 (PL 35, 1763).
45 Letter 10 (*alias* letter 51), n. 24 (PL 3, 791A).
46 *Decretum Gratiani*, pt. 2, *causa* 7, q. 1, c. 6 (PL 187, 746A).

Magnus, he again speaks thus: "I answer, that no heretics and schismatics at all have any power or right."[47] And these words are found in the chapter, *Dicimus*.[48]

Add to all these things that the Church has not made any decree up until now, by which it explicitly stated that a heretical Pope is deposed by the law itself, or by which it commanded him to be deposed; which certainly would not have happened except because she understood that the Pope, who would become a heretic, is deprived by Divine law: and hence she did not wish to legislate. It certainly ought not to be believed that the Church, which was always very solicitous about making a separation of heretics, lest they could harm others by their association, would not have hitherto decreed anything about a heretical Pope: since he could harm the Church so much the more than all other heretics, the more he has greater power for harming, and the more other Catholics stand in awe of him, whom as one might expect they ought to regard as the teacher of the faith.

If someone objects to me the chapter, *Si Papa*,[49] I will reply very easily that the text of that chapter, even though was written by a holy man and martyr,[50] still it was not written by a man who could command the whole Church. Whence it is that his words ought to be accepted as a sort of counsel of a holy man, yet they ought not to be held as an obligatory decree. And it ought not to be thought that those words have any obligation, because they were inserted into the body of an ordinance, unless perhaps someone were to show that that the whole *Decretum* of Gratian was approved by the Apostolic See, and everything which is contained in it, are commands to be observed. Nevertheless, that was never done. Therefore, since it is evident from all these very

---

47 Letter 76 (*alias* letter 69), n. 1 (PL 3, 1138A).
48 *Decretum Gratiani*, pt. 2, *causa 24*, q. 1, c. 31 (PL 187, 1279C).
49 *Ibid.*, pt. 1, dist. 40, q. 1, c. 6 (PL 187, 214C-215A)
50 I. e., St. Boniface.

evident reasons that the Pope who has become a heretic is by Divine law deprived of the Papal dignity, whence also it is evident that he who has been deposed is subject to every ecclesiastical censure which has been decreed by law, as any other heretic. Still not on account of this does the rule of law fail which says: "An equal cannot bind an equal." Certainly not due to the fact that the Pope is a heretic is he less than any Catholic, as we related above that the Gloss on the chapter, *Achatius*,[51] says. But from this it happens that he who has become a heretic then ceases to be the Pope, and hence can be excommunicated, and is forced to undergo the other punishments, which have been decreed by law for heretics. Yet if he would remain the Pope, he would not have been subject to them. On account of which we rightly said above that the judgment of this case is by Divine law, and ought not to be sought from a man.

---

51 *Decretum Gratiani*, pt. 2, *causa* 24, q. 1, c. 1 (PL 187, 1263B).

Chapter XXIV

It is replied to the reasons which are objected by those who maintain the contrary opinion.

Although with evident (as I think) arguments I have proved in the preceding chapter that the Pope, if he becomes a heretic, by that very fact is deprived of the Papal dignity by Divine law, nevertheless I thought it to be necessary to reply to the arguments of those who maintain the contrary opinion, so that by their weakness having been shown very clearly, at least from this the truth of our opinion may be more firmly strengthened, and understood more clearly. And I will put forth the first of all the arguments, as it were the standard bearer of the battle line, which the adversaries think to be so powerful and strong that no one is able to resist it. For so it is argued. A bishop, if he becomes a heretic, is not by that very fact deprived of his dignity by Divine law; therefore a Pope even though he is a heretic, is not by that very fact deprived of the Papal dignity by Divine law. They say that the conclusion is known, because (as they say) the Pope is not of worse condition than any other bishop. They prove the antecedent in respect to a bishop, who has a heresy in his mind, to which he pertinaciously adheres, and never manifested it outwardly. For he (as they assert) is truly and properly a heretic, and yet he is not by that very fact deprived of the episcopacy, because a bishop has that episcopal power (as they say) from a human or ecclesiastical commission. And this they say is very certain from the consent of all Catholic Doctors, according to that saying of the very Blessed Pope Leo [I], in the chapter, *Ita Dominus*: "The Lord so wished the sacrament of this office to pertain to all the Apostles in such manner, as that He placed it principally in the Blessed Apostle Peter, the chief of all the Apostles, and wishes His gifts to flow unto the whole body, from him as from the head."[1] And from this as from something very certainly accepted they conclude that a bishop, who has pertinaciously fallen into mental heresy, is not deprived of the episcopate: because the Church cannot inflict any punishment for interior acts. Thomas de Vio Cardinal Cajetan, in his small work, *Auctoritas Pape et Concilii* [*sive Ecclesie comparata*],[2] makes this argument with many words and at great length, which he esteems so highly, that he says that his mind was convinced by it to thinking that a Pope if he pertinaciously falls into heresy is not deprived of the Papal dignity by the Divine law itself.

But I certainly am surprised that a man so great, and who at other times is not wont to give way to much stronger arguments, now by such a weak argument, of which he could refute many things, would admit that he has been conquered. For that reasoning is incorrect whereby he proves that a heretical Pope is not deprived by Divine law of the Papal dignity, by the fact that a heretical bishop is not deprived of the episcopacy by Divine law. It certainly could happen that God would decree this about the Pope, and not about the other bishops, especially because the reason for such a great difference is well-known: namely, because the Pope could harm all Christendom more than any other bishop, if both of them were heretics. For this reason God could rightly deprive a heretical Pope, when no other heretical bishop has been deprived. And it ought not to be thought for this reason that the Papal dignity is of a worse condition, nay, much greater, because it does not permit heresy with itself as the episcopal dignity does.

Next, what has been assumed in that reasoning is false, namely, that a heretical bishop is not deprived of the episcopal dignity by Divine law: because I reckon that the same thing ought to be said about a bishop, which is said about a Pope.

---

1 *Ibid.*, pt. 1, dist. 19, c. 7 (PL 187, 109A).
2 C. 19.

Refutation of those who hold that heretical bishops lose jurisdiction

Now to prove this assumption, he assumes something else, which he thinks is certain, and he says that it proceeds from the opinion of all the holy Doctors, namely, that episcopal authority, or jurisdiction, is from the commission of a man or the Church, and not from God: but this premise assumed by him is false, and falser than falsity itself, and opposed to the opinion of all the holy Doctors, and against the words of Leo [I], which he cites from the chapter, *Ita Dominus*. Because even if the rite of consecration of a bishop was established by the Church, still the episcopal authority was granted to them not by man, but by God. For all the holy Doctors teach that the bishops succeed the Apostles, for which matter I could cite many testimonies, which I prudently admit, lest I burden the reader with excessive prolixity. Still if anyone desires to see them, he will find them in that work which I published, *Against All Heresies*, in the section on "Bishops" [*Episcopus*], in which place I heaped together many testimonies supporting this point, and hence I do not wish to repeat here lest I do what has been already done.

Nevertheless I will not pass over here one from the Council of Florence, which I do not know whether by accident it was left out by me in that place. The Council of Florence stating the certain rule of faith for the Armenians, when it discusses about the Sacrament of Confirmation, says these words: "The ordinary minister is a bishop. And although a simple priest has the power in regard to other anointings only a bishop can confer this Sacrament, because according to the Apostles, whose place the bishops hold, we read that through the imposition of hands they conferred the Holy Ghost."[3] Now the Apostles (as it is very clear) were ordained Apostles and bishops by God, not by any man, as it is established from many from many passages of Sacred Scripture. "As the Father hath sent me," Christ said, "I also

---

3   Dz. 697.

send you" (Jn. 20, 21).[4] It is expressly taught that Christ gave to them the office of Apostles. And He confirmed this again after His death, when He commanded them: "Go ye into the whole world, and preach the gospel to every creature" (Mk. 16, 15). Next, He granted to all the Apostles the power of jurisdiction, when He said to them all together: "Whatsoever you shall bind upon earth, shall be bound also in heaven; and whatsoever you shall loose upon earth, shall be loosed also in heaven" (Mt. 18, 18). For by those words (as all the sacred Doctors teach) Christ granted the power of excommunicating, which could not be without some jurisdiction. If Christ gave the power of preaching to the Apostles, and the power of binding and loosing, and the bishops succeeded in the place of the Apostles, the conclusion is that bishops also have all these powers from God and not from man. For by this sole and very efficacious reason we prove against the heretics that the Roman Bishop is the superior of all the other bishops, because Peter the Apostle was the superior of the rest of the bishops, whose successor the Roman Bishop is proved to be. Whence it is that it is necessary that the Roman Pontiff possess the same authority over the other bishops, which Peter possessed over the rest of the Apostles. Thus by the same conclusion one ought to gather that the same power, although not as broad, belongs to bishops by Divine law, which was given to the Apostles: because they are successors of these men.

Furthermore, the governance of the Church belongs to the bishops by Divine law. For Paul when he was in Miletus, having summoned the bishops from Ephesus to himself, said: "Take heed to yourselves, and to the whole flock, wherein the Holy Ghost hath placed you bishops, to rule the church of God, which he hath purchased with his own blood" (Acts 20, 28). Behold, you see the bishops given the governance of the Church, not by man, but by the Holy Ghost. But he

---

4 Cf. Mt. 10, 1; Mk. 3, 14; Lk. 6, 13.

Refutation of those who hold that heretical bishops lose jurisdiction

who does not have any power of jurisdiction is unable to govern. Therefore the bishops who were instituted by God for the governance of the Church, also have from Him the power of jurisdiction. I certainly admit that the division of bishops, whereby each bishop has particular subjects, was introduced by human law: and rightly for avoiding confusion, and also for avoiding dissensions, which easily could have arisen unless such a division had been made, whereby each can know his own sheep, and keep away foreign ones. But it depends solely on Divine law, not human law, that a bishop has the power of jurisdiction. From Divine law he has this power when made a bishop, but by human law this power is fixed in regard to these or those sheep committed to him, which is sometimes more extensive, other times is more limited, depending solely upon whether more or less subjects are allotted to him. And if it happens on account of some crime the bishop is deprived of his episcopacy by the Pope, which he on account of many crimes could rightly do, then the bishop will be deprived of his subjects, but he will not be deprived of that power of jurisdiction which he received in his consecration. Just as we would say about a priest having a benefice, if he is deprived of the benefice, he cannot absolve, not on account of the lack of power, but because he does not have a subject over whom he may exercise it. Add to all these things, that when bishops are chosen and confirmed,[5] there is no conferral of jurisdiction

---

5 "In canon law the confirmation of a bishop is the act by which the election of a new bishop receives the assent of the proper ecclesiastical authority. In the early centuries of the history of the Church the election or appointment of a suffragan bishop was confirmed and approved by the metropolitan and his suffragans assembled in synod... From the 13th century onwards it was effectively exercised, though the all but universal practice of the Popes of reserving and providing to vacant bishoprics, initiated by Clement V, obscured the issue, since in the case of Papal nominations

to them by the Church: which the Church certainly would not omit to do, if she thought that bishops have this jurisdiction from it. But because the Church holds as certain that bishops after they have been elected and confirmed, have by Divine law jurisdiction over the people committed to them, wherefore she never confers this to them.

Finally, let us discuss Pope Leo [I]'s words, which Cajetan cited in favor of himself: and from them it will clearly appear that Blessed Leo confirms our opinion, so far from his word could support Cajetan. But so that the true meaning of his words may appear more clearly, it is befitting to repeat the beginning of his chapter, whose words are these: "Our Lord Jesus Christ, the Savior of mankind, so instituted, that the truth, which had previously been contained in the Law and the Prophets, should, by means of the Apostolic trumpet, go forth unto the salvation of all men, as it is written: 'Their sound hath gone forth into all the earth, and their words unto the end of the world' (Ps. 18, 5). But the Lord willed the sacrament of this office to belong to all the Apostles in such manner, that He placed it principally in the Blessed Apostle Peter, the chief of all the Apostles, so that from him as from the head His gifts would be diffused throughout the body, so that he who has dared to separate himself from Peter's solidity, might know that he has no share or lot in the Divine mystery."[6]

In which words it especially ought to be noted that he said that the Lord willed that those gifts would belong to the office of all the Apostles. If they have those gifts by the Lord's will, then it is not by Peter's conferral alone. Next, he says that the Lord Jesus Christ, and not Peter, diffuses

---

no confirmation was required" ("Confirmation of Bishops," *Encyclopaedia Britannica* (Cambridge: University Press, 1910), vol. 6, p. 906).

6 *Decretum Gratiani*, pt. 1, dist. 19, c. 7 (PL 187, 109A). Cf. Leo I, letter 10, c. 1 (PL 54, 629A).

these gifts of ministry to the whole body of the Church: but by a certain order, such that from Peter himself as from the head would make the beginning. Which Blessed Leo said because Christ Our Savior firstly granted these gifts to Peter, and afterwards to the other Apostles. For the granting made to Peter is described in Matthew, chapter 16, but which was given to the other Apostles is related by the same Evangelist Matthew, chapter 18. From which order Blessed Leo wishes to conclude that the authority of the other Apostles, although it was given by Christ, still is subject to Peter, and they have that authority as long as they are united to him, their head, and as long as they rest upon the foundation of the ecclesiastical building, from which if they are separated, just as they do not belong to Christ's Church, which was built upon that foundation, so by that fact they all lose the ecclesiastical jurisdiction which they had.

Although Juan de Torquemada regarding the first chapter of this discussion thinks with us saying: When a Pope has become a heretic he is deprived of the Papal dignity by the law itself:[7] yet in this present discussion he opposes us saying: The Apostles were not ordained by Christ, but by Peter. To support his position he cites in the second book of his *Summa de Ecclesia*[8] many texts from Canon Law, which cannot support his opinion one bit: wherefore desiring to avoid prolixity I decided to omit them, especially because this matter is not the main point of our discussion, but merely said in passing.

But it is now necessary that we discuss the other parts of the first and principal argument made by Cajetan, and examine what truth they contain. For he says that he who has mentally conceived heresy and pertinaciously adheres to it, which he has not shown to anyone by an exterior action, is a true heretic. Albert Pighius tries to deny this, yet he does

---

7 Cf. *Summa de Ecclesia*, bk. 4, pt. 2, c. 20, fol. 396v.
8 *Ibid.*, c. 32, fols. 144r-146r.

it unsuitably: because even though heresy proceeds from a choice of the will (as he says[9]), it is not necessarily a consequence on that account, that an exterior utterance of the mouth is required for making a full heretic. For in other sins, which depend more on the will than heresy, which are located in the intellect, only the choice of the will without any exterior operation suffices for effecting the complete notion of the sin. Whence it is that completely the same thing ought to be said about heresy and a heretic: because it is not established that this is required more for heresy, than for other sins. On account of which they who say that the Pope, if he falls into heresy, is by Divine law deprived of the Papal dignity, think that this same thing ought to be said if he falls into mental heresy, because they think that he is no less a heretic than another. And they say that we ought not be to doubtful and uncertain about those things which are done by the Pope: because even though his interior faith is unknown to us, still, as long as his unbelief does not appear to us, we always are held to consider him a believer. Because (as the rule of law says[10]) "Anyone is presumed good until the contrary is proved."

They also deny that confusion of the whole Church is produced by troubling the whole ecclesiastical Order, reputing men to be bishops or priests who were not: because God Who takes care of the Church as His spouse would provide a remedy for her. Just as if an unbaptized man would be ordained a priest, as it is established has sometimes happened from the title entitled about this matter in the decretals,[11] and afterwards he was made a bishop, and finally the Pope, and consecrates many bishops, and ordains priests, and then

---

9 *Hierarchiae ecclesiasticae assertio*, bk. 6, c. 16, fol. 249v.
10 Cf. Gloss on *Decretals of Gregory IX*, bk. 1, tit. 12 (*De scrutinio in ordine faciendo*), c. 1, s. v. *Aestimare*.
11 *Decretals of Gregory IX*, bk. 3, tit. 43 (*De presbytero non baptizato*).

Refutation of those who hold that heretical bishops lose jurisdiction

since he was not a priest, so neither a bishop nor the Pope, even though he was reputed as such. Nevertheless it ought to be believed (as Blessed Thomas teaches[12]) God would then come to the aid of the Church, and give her a suitable remedy. Just as when a woman lied that she was a man, was elected the Pope, and was reputed as such for some years.[13] So also they think that nothing also prevents that the Pope, having fallen into mental heresy, would be deprived of the Papal dignity, although it would then be befitting that he be revered as the Pope. Because lest the Church fall into a Labyrinth of this kind, God would provide a remedy for it. So replies Juan de Torquemada.[14]

Still it can be said, and perhaps better, by asserting that he who has fallen into mental heresy, is a heretic, but not such a heretic that on that account he would be deprived of the Papal dignity by Divine law by it self. For it will be said that interior faith is not necessarily required for the Papal dignity, but the exterior confession of the faith is enough: he who has which, although he lacks interior faith, could keep the Papal dignity which he has. And the Gloss on the words, "and upon this rock I will build my church," seems to favor this opinion, which expounds the word, "rock," not by "faith," but by "the confession of the faith."[15] By which

---

12 "And if he were even promoted to the episcopate, those whom he ordained would not have Holy Orders. But nevertheless it can be piously believed that as to the ultimate effects of the Sacraments, the High Priest would supply the defect, and that he would not permit this to remain so hidden that it could threaten danger to the Church" (*In IV Sentences*, dist. 24, q. 1, a. 2, *quaest.* 3, ad 2um).

13 The author is referring to the now rejected legend of a Popess Joan (r. 855-857). Cf. "Popess Joan," *Catholic Encyclopedia*, vol. 8, p. 407.

14 *Summa ecclesiastica*, bk. 4, pt. 2, c. 20, fol. 394.

15 "*That thou art Peter*, i. e., He became a confessor of the true Rock which is Christ. *And upon this rock*, i. e. on Christ, whom thou hast confessed" (*Biblia sacra cum Glossis*, vol. 5, fol. 52r b).

words it seems to suggest that Peter's Pontificate and the dignity of his successors was founded solely upon the confession of the faith. And if this is the case, it will be necessarily be befitting to say that only an exterior or manifest heretic is deprived of the Pontifical dignity by Divine law, and not an occult heretic who hides his heresy in the depths of his heart. And the reason for this distinction can be given, namely, that God instituted this Pontifical dignity, not for the honor of the Pontiffs themselves, but for the utility of the people. And whence it necessarily happens that the more someone can harm Christian governance, so much the more ought he to be reckoned unworthy, and on the contrary, all the more ought he to be tolerated, the less he could harm the Church. Since then he who retains heresy in his heart, and did not manifest it by any exterior sign, does no harm to the Church by it alone, God does not deprive him of his dignity. But he who publicly says his heresy, because by it he can do much harm to the Catholic Church by it, God willed that by that very fact he was deprived of his dignity, lest his "speech," with Paul as a witness "spread like a canker" (II Tim. 2, 17), spread more powerfully receiving strength from his dignity.

But let us go still further, and examine another part of that argument made by Cajetan. For he says that on account of a purely interior act of the soul, a man can never be subject to human jurisdiction: because God alone is He who beholds the heart, but men those things which appear,[16] and hence they can judge only about those things, and consequently punish only those things. Albert Pighius also denies him this assumed proposition, who teaches with Adrian [VI] and holds as established that the interior acts of the soul are subject to human judgment. Still I myself do not wish to embrace the opinion of Albert or Adrian [VI], but rather agree with Cajetan, as I clearly stated when I discussed about excommunication. Therefore having now examined and

---

16 Cf. I Kings 16, 7.

ly discussed all these parts, Cajetan produced a very bad argument. For even if we were to freely concede to him all those propositions, some of which we have denied, it would merely be permitted to infer from them that other bishops, on account of mental heresy, are not by that very fact deprived of the power of jurisdiction.

But it does thence not follow that the Roman Pontiff is not also by that very fact deprived of his Papal dignity. For regarding the other bishops, even if everything assumed in the argument were to be granted, nothing would be proved, except that from human law on account of mental heresy alone they are not deprived of their dignity. Now so that one would be able to infer that the Roman Pontiff also is not deprived of Papal power on account of mental heresy alone, one ought to prove that the Roman Pontiff also has his power from a human conferral, and not from God. For then it would be rightly inferred that the same things ought to be reckoned about him which are reckoned about the others, because his interior action is also not subject to human judgment, from which he had received power. Or one ought to add in the argument that the Roman Pontiff is not subject to Divine judgment regarding interior acts, just as the other bishops are not subject to human judgment concerning them. Then that inference would also be correct. Because just as other bishops are not deprived by human law of the power of jurisdiction for mental heresy alone, because for it they are not subject to human law: so also it would be befitting that the Roman Pontiff, for mental heresy alone, is not deprived by Divine law of Papal power, if he for such heresy would not be subject to Divine judgment. Otherwise, if these two things are subtracted from that argument, as they necessarily ought to be removed: because we are indeed held to believe by faith that the power of the Roman Pontiff is not from men, but from God, and he is subject to Divine judgment for interior acts, that argument will have completely no strength or weight. For to infer from the fact that other bishops on account of mental heresy alone are not deprived by human law, to which they cannot be subject, that the Roman Pontiff also on account of mental heresy alone is not deprived by Divine law, to which he is truly subject, is such a bad inference, that there is no one who does not understand.

I have made such a detailed examination of Cajetan's argument, so that I may plainly show how weak the argument was, by which he admitted that his understanding was conquered. Thus this argument, which the adversaries esteem before all, having been enervated, we may easily cast down the rest because they are weaker. Secondly it is argued thus: A heretical king or an emperor is not by that fact deprived of his kingdom or empire by Divine law: because it is evident that many kings in the Old Law were idolators, and also many unbelieving kings commanded believers, concerning whom God Himself says: "They have reigned, but not by me" (Osee 8, 4). And again: "I will give thee a king in my wrath, and will take him away in my indignation" (*Ibid.* 13, 11). Thus in the same way the Pope, or any other bishop, although he becomes a heretic, could rule Catholic believers. I reply that it is not the same reason for them all, neither are emperors or kings or other secular rulers governed by the same law by which ecclesiastical prelates are governed. Because temporal rulership or secular power does not have for its foundation, upon which it rests, the faith: and for this reason even if faith is lacking, the rulership and powers of those men can subsist, whether they govern believers or unbelievers. For nothing prevents that an unbelieving man can rule and govern believers in purely secular matters.

And I think that the same thing ought to be said about the priesthood of the Old Law, which although it dealt with spiritual things, still because the faith was not given as the foundation, when the faith was removed it could remain: such that although one was a heretic, he was not by that fact

Refutation of those who hold that heretical bishops lose jurisdiction

deprived of the priesthood. But ecclesiastical power in the Evangelical law is quite different. Because it was founded upon a firm rock, that is, the Catholic faith. Thus when this is overturned, it is necessary that all ecclesiastical power, which rests upon it, would fall. Wherefore although in temporal and corporal matters an unbeliever can govern and rule believers, still in spiritual matters an unbeliever cannot have the power of jurisdiction over a believer.

Thirdly it is argued against us from the fact that [Pope] Marcellinus, who in the horrible persecution raging under Diocletian, allured by the violence of the executioners, succumbed to [offer] wicked sacrifices, and offered incense to idols and cast it upon altars:[17] and yet he was not on this account cast down from the Papacy, but rather persevered in it until death. To this argument it is very easily replied, by denying that Marcellinus was a heretic, because although he was not constant enough in the confession of faith against the then prepared and threatened torments, still he did not lose

---

17 Cf. "At that time was a great persecution, so that within 30 days 17,000 Christians of both sexes in divers provinces were crowned with martyrdom. For this reason Marcellinus himself was haled to sacrifice, that he might offer incense, and he did it" (*Liber Pontificalis*, n. 30 (PL 127, 1467)). St. Augustine, however, wrote: "It is no affair of ours. For they have borne their own burden, whether it was good or whether it was evil. We ourselves believe it was good; but whatever it was it was theirs" (*Answer to Petilian the Donatist*, bk. 2, n. 208 (PL 43, 328)). "Now what need is there of our clearing the bishops of the Roman Church from the accusations and incredible slanders that [Petilian] brings against them? Marcellinus and his priests, Melchiades, Marcellus, and Silvester, are charged by him with surrender of the Sacred Scriptures and offering of incense. But are they on that account convicted of it or are they convicted only through some palpable distortion of the documents? He says that they were wicked and sacrilegious; I reply that they were innocent" (*Concerning the One Baptism, Against Petilian*, c. 16 (PL 43, 610)).

the faith which he was keeping in his mind. But an exterior action (as we said above in first chapter of this work) is not heresy: but only the agreement or disagreement of the mind, even though strong suspicion of heresy sometimes arises from an action itself. As it is supposed that as a man mentally believed, so his action outwardly shows. But these suspicions are of men, who cannot pronounce a certain judgment about hidden things. But that Marcellinus did not lose the faith, is proved clearly enough by that which is found in the chapter, *Nunc autem*.[18] For there it is said that, compelled by pagans, he put grains of incense upon the coals. If he was compelled, then he did not do this by free choice, but to avoid torments. Now he was avoiding torments enough by a mere exterior action, without an error of the intellect: because the heathens, whom he then endeavored to please by those things alone, could not perceive the interior faith of the mind, but the exterior action. Next, even if we were to freely grant that he then lost the faith, still he ought not on that account to be reckoned a heretic: because pertinacity was absent in him, which is most necessary so that someone may rightly be called a heretic, as it is supported from the chapter, *Dixit Apostolus*.[19] Since when he had a change of heart, very bitterly repenting of his fault, he confessed his inconstancy in the general council of bishops, and willingly subjected himself to the judgment of the priests, who seeing his humble confession, dared not to pronounce any sentence on him.

In the fourth place the adversaries argue against our opinion, by that which is said in the chapter, *Cum ex injuncto*[20] [wherein it is said]: "To whom the appointment of some man pertains, to the same belongs the removal of the

---

18 *Decretum Gratiani*, pt. 1, dist. 21, c. 7 (PL 187, 120D-121B).
19 *Ibid.*, pt. 2, *causa* 24, q. 3, c. 29 (PL 187, 1307A).
20 *Decretals of Gregory IX*, bk. 5, tit. 7 (*De haereticis*), c. 12.

same man."[21] From which words they wish to conclude that the Pope, if he becomes a heretic, ought to be deposed by men, and is not deposed by Divine law: because since he was elected by men, he also ought to be deposed by them. This argument is so weak, that it is unworthy of any reply being given to it. For that rule, which was decreed by law for restraining the attempts of temerarious men, they wish to apply to the Divine authority, as though it would extend to something which is not allowed, and on account of it the authority would be confined to certain limits fixed by human judgment. Who, I ask, is the Catholic man, who would not laugh at this conclusion? The Pope is elected by man, therefore he cannot be deposed by God. And he should be laughed at much more who goes on to prove by that rule of law, "To whom an appointment pertains, to the same belongs the dismissal."

Next, even if we were to freely grant to them that the rule is true everywhere, still it is not accepted in that sense which is taken by them. For that rule (as it can be easily established from the context of that chapter) was given in this sense, namely, that no inferior can remove him who was appointed by a superior: and hence the Pope concludes that a priest, if he were bad, ought not to be deposed by the people, which has absolutely no authority over him, but by the bishop who appointed him. And so I would agree that the Pope, who was elected by the Cardinals, cannot be deposed by another authority lower than the Cardinals themselves. But is it permitted to conclude from that rule that a man appointed by someone cannot be removed by a superior? By no means. For a priest appointed by the bishop for the care of souls,

---

21 "Because if perhaps necessity demanded that a useless or unworthy priest should be removed from the care of his flock, it should be done in the proper manner by the bishop, whose duty is known to pertain to both the instituting and removing of priests" (*Ibid.*).

can be deposed by the Pope from the same care: nay, even by the metropolitan archbishop, if the reason on account of which he rightly ought to be deposed, was devolved to the archbishop. Thus since that rule grants to the appointer of someone the power of removing him, by that very fact it seems to have granted the same power to anyone having full authority over the appointer. And hence it follows (I certainly wish to speak according to the aforementioned rule) that God Who is superior to the Cardinals and the whole Church, can by His will and the law produced by Him, remove the Pope who was elected by the Cardinals. Now He removed that heretic from the Papacy, when He established by a most firm decree that His Church is founded upon the faith, or upon the open confession of the faith.

Fifthly the adversaries argue against us by the fact that bishops having pertinaciously fallen into heresy, if they return to the faith, are restored to their dignities: it is therefore a sign that they were not deprived of them, otherwise it would be necessary to make a new election. They prove the antecedent by the chapter, *Maximum*.[22] And hence they argue that the same thing ought to be said about a heretical Pope, because if he returns to the faith, he would not be shackled, but kept in his former dignity. And Cajetan also highly esteems this argument, which nevertheless (so that I may speak the truth) does not disturb me at all. I certainly admit that heretical bishops when they return to the unity of the Church, are wont to be received at their Sees: although Cajetan wrongly proves that by that chapter, *Maximum*. Because that Maximus, about whom is the discussion there,

---

22 "Maximus, also, although he was culpably ordained when a layman, yet if he is now no longer a Donatist, and has abjured the spirit of schismatic depravity, we do not depose from his episcopal dignity, which he has obtained irregularly, on condition that he declare himself a Catholic by sending an attestation to us" (*Decretum Gratiani*, pt. 2, *causa* 1, q. 7, c. 19 (PL 187, 577C)).

was ordained a bishop: he was not in that rank when he fell into heresy. But because he had been ordained a bishop wrongly, and against the ecclesiastical canons, from being a layman without any interval of time having been kept in minor Orders: wherefore there was a doubt, whether he ought to remain in the episcopal dignity. To which question Leo replies that although he was reprehensibly ordained, he should not be deposed from the episcopal dignity, as long as he sends an attestation to the Pope, in which he testifies that he is a Catholic. Therefore that chapter nowise serves our topic of discussion. Which can easily be established by reading Leo's letter,[23] from which the chapters, *Maximum* and *Donatum*,[24] were taken. It certainly makes a great difference whether you read those sources, or the patchwork citations badly extracted.

What Cajetan wishes to prove, would have been much better proved by the chapter, *Convenientibus*,[25] which was taken from the Acts of the Seventh Council, which was the Second Council of Nicaea. For there it was decided that those who had defected from the Catholic faith, when returning to their senses, would then be received in their Sees. But this was done not by the necessity of law, but from a certain dispensation of mercy, as is very clearly established by the chapter, *Si quis haereticae*.[26] For even though heretical bishops are deprived by Divine law of their episcopal dignity, still the Church for a reasonable cause sometimes dispenses, so that having returned to the faith the former dignities are restored. And such a restoration is considered as a new election, or a new appointment. And no one ought to be surprised about this, because the same thing necessarily ought to be said in

---

23 Letter 12, n. 6 (PL 54, 653A).
24 *Decretum Gratiani*, pt. 2, *causa* 1, q. 7, cc. 19-20 (PL 187, 577C-578A).
25 *Ibid.*, c. 4 (PL 187, 568A-571A).
26 *Ibid.*, q. 1, c. 42 (PL 187, 501A-B).

many other matters. For a murderous cleric by the very fact that he has committed murder, incurs an irregularity, and is deprived of the benefice which he has, yet if from a certain mercy he is dispensed from it by the Pope, and the benefice is restored to him, such a restoration is considered as a new appointment.

Sixthly they object to us the chapter, *Audivimus*, where these words are said: "However, if someone invents a new heresy out of his heart, he cannot condemn anyone from the moment when he begins to preach such things, [since a person who already is thrown to the ground cannot overthrow anyone]."[27] From which words they wish to infer that before a heretical bishop preaches or teaches, he can excommunicate and condemn, and from this it is very evidently gathered that not by the very fact whereby he became a heretic was he deprived of his dignity.

This manner of arguing is very weak, because by the fact that one thing is denied, it is not necessary that we say that the other thing is conceded. Next, those words just cited do not belong to Alexander II, whose words are found at the beginning of the chapter. For the words beginning with, "if someone invents a new heresy out of his heart…," are Gratian's, and hence arises the second part of this question. Gratian's authority is not of such great weight that they can overcome me, and force me to abandon my view: especially since he himself teaches very many things elsewhere, in which he ought to be necessarily abandoned by everyone. Nevertheless if we wish to freely accept the aforesaid of Gratian, they could support that opinion above, whereby we said that the mental heretic is probably not deposed by Divine law: because (as we said it is probable in the reply to the first argument) the foundation upon which ecclesiastical authority is founded, is not interior faith alone: but the exterior confession of the faith. But because by this it is necessary

---

27 *Ibid.*, pt. 2, *causa* 24, q. 1, c. 4 (PL 187, 1265A).

to say that he who lacks the confession of exterior faith is deprived by the law itself, which we have openly denied when we discussed what was done by Pope Marcellinus: hence the opinion seems better to me, that the mental heretic is also deprived by the law itself. Yet if the other opinion seems better to someone, he could say that Marcellinus, although he mentally retained the faith, on account of the exterior infidelity, by that very fact was deprived by Divine law of his dignity: and yet, he was tolerated by the whole council, before which he confessed his fault, by that fact by silent votes he was again elected as the Supreme Pontiff.

These are all the things that are wont to be objected by the enemies against the aforementioned opinion of ours: yet there are some other things that have been thought up by me, which seem to me to impel a little more, to which I have also decided to reply, so that thence the truth of our opinion may be more clearly known to all. The first argument that presents itself to me arises from evaluation of the two powers of Order and jurisdiction compared to each other. For the power of Order is much more outstanding and nobler than the power of jurisdiction: but the power of Order does not have faith as the foundation, and it does not require it for its existence: thus the power of jurisdiction, which is less, also does not have faith as the foundation, and does not require it for its existence. And hence it is evidently concluded that it is nowise lost through heresy. From which it clearly follows that neither the Pope nor a bishop, by the very fact that he has become a heretic, loses his dignity. The logical inference of this argument seems known through the negative argumentation from the major to the minor. The minor is manifest from those things which we said above in chapter twenty-one of this book, namely, that the power of Order is founded only on the sacerdotal character, and hence it is deduced that a priest, even if he becomes a heretic, can never lose it. I prove the major of this argument, which perhaps will seem to someone that it ought to be denied more: that the power of Order is over Christ's true Body, but the power of jurisdiction is only over Christ's Mystical Body. Furthermore the power of Order, because it is so great, can only be given by God, whereas the power of jurisdiction often depends on the will of men. And hence another superiority of the power of Order over the power of jurisdiction arises: that the power of Order is indelible and less amissible, but the power of jurisdiction will often be lost.

Add to these things that if someone who is not a priest has a benefice to which the care of souls is attached, by that very fact he has the power of jurisdiction, yet which notwithstanding, he ought to be reckoned as having less dignity than any other priest not having the care of souls. Which could not be the case except because the power of Order is more excellent than the power of jurisdiction. I reply by admitting that the power of Order is absolutely more noble and of greater dignity than the power of jurisdiction, because it deals with a much more excellent object than the latter, because (as it was correctly said in the argument) the former pertains to Christ's Real Body. Yet if those two powers are referred to the people, on account of whom alone they were instituted by God, the power of jurisdiction is known to be much greater than the power of Order: because by it for many reasons the people are provided for more than by the other. For through it the people are taught about the faith and morals. From it, he who is uneducated ought to ask from teaching: as the Lord bears witness through the prophet Malachias, speaking thus: "The lips of the priest shall keep knowledge, and they shall seek the law at his mouth: because he is the angel of the Lord of hosts" (2, 7). Through the power of jurisdiction peace is preserved among the people, justice is retained and to each man is given his due, vices are restrained, the morals of wicked people are corrected: finally whatever goodness there is in ecclesiastical governance would easily go to ruin

Refutation of those who hold that heretical bishops lose jurisdiction

without this power, and if there is something wicked, it would more easily increase without it. None of these things pertain to the power of Order. Wherefore through the power of jurisdiction he who has it can do more good, if he is good: and do more harm, if he is bad. Thus for this reason Christ Our Savior established the power of jurisdiction upon the foundation of the faith, lest he lack faith who by his office is obliged he teach the faith and recall the erring to the faith. But the power of Order, because no teaching or discipline of the people is necessarily enjoined upon him, Our Savior did not want to found the same upon the faith, and did not require the faith for its existence. Because that which ought to be done through it, even when the faith has been excluded, can be done without any harm to others.

The second argument, which to me (so that I may speak frankly) is not a matter of little importance, is that even though a heretic loses the faith through heresy, still not by that very fact is he completely separated from the Church: but is still part of that body and its member: therefore while the heresy remains he could still keep in himself the Papal dignity. Because since he himself has not been cut off from the Church, it seems that he also has not been deprived of the power of jurisdiction, whether it be episcopal or Papal. Now that the heretic has not been completely cut off from the Church, but is still part, and her member, is very clearly proved from the fact that he is still subject to the judgment of the Church: because he is punished by her and afflicted by her with various punishments. Now the Church would not do this unless she knew that a heretic is within her fold, and is a part of it, although a putrid part. For Paul says: "What have I to do to judge them that are without?" (I Cor. 5, 12). And again elsewhere: "Who art thou that judgest another man's servant?" (Rom. 14, 4). I certainly admit and (assuredly by my own judgment) it cannot be denied that a heretic is part of the Church, and its member, and is not altogether separated from her: because even though he does not have the faith, he still has the Baptismal character, whereby he was firstly made a member of the Church, he will always be her member as long as it lasts, as it is supported in the chapter, *Veniens*.[28] But although he is a member of the Church, he still cannot be the head: because since the head is the principal member of the whole body, much more is required for the head, than for the other members. Thus the Pope if he becomes a heretic, will no longer be the head (as before), but the foot: or if there is some other lower or more worthless member.

For the rest regarding the punishment whereby the Church punishes heretics, one ought to distinguish a little, and examine its cause. And certainly one ought to assert that a heretic is within the Church, lest we were to say that she judges about those that are without.[29] And yet not simply because they retain the Baptismal character ought it to be said that she punishes heretics. For on this account one should say that a heretic cannot, as long as he lives, be outside of the judgment of the Church, since he always has the Baptismal character in him. This having been granted, it will also be necessary to assert that after the Church has handed over a man to the secular authority to be punished by it, if the secular power does not want to punish him, and releases him, the Church nonetheless can still punish that heretic, and the same ought to be said of a degraded priest. Yet this ought not to be said because the Church through such a handing over of the heretic, and through degradation, seems to renounce its right, as can be gathered from the words of the same degradation, which are found in the chapter, *Degradatio*.[30]

---

28 *Decretals of Gregory IX*, bk. 3, tit. 43 (*De presbytero non baptizato*), c. 3.
29 Cf. I Cor. 5, 12.
30 *Liber sextus decretalium*, bk. 5, tit. 9 (*De poenis*), c. 2.

Refutation of those who hold that heretical bishops lose jurisdiction

Now so that I may clearly set forth the reason for this punishment, I advise the reader to consider that when someone is baptized, he then enters the Church, just like a new inhabitant who is received in a city. Now when someone is so admitted in some country, from the nature of the reception a certain contract is entered into between the admitted inhabitant himself and the country, such that the inhabitant is obliged to keep the laws and statutes of the country, to obey it, to assist it when endangered, to adhere to its judgment, and the country is held to keep him unharmed in it and to protect him from calumniators. Now so that this contract may be rescinded, the choice of either one of them does not suffice, but both are required: because although anyone can renounce his own right, still not the right of another, especially a right already acquired. Yet if the country and the inhabitant afterwards agree with a concordant will, the inhabitant can remain within the city without any mutual obligation between them, such that neither the inhabitant would not be obliged to country, nor the country to the inhabitant.

Between the one baptized and the Church, from the day of Baptism such a contract is entered upon: because the one baptized from that day is held to keep the customs, laws, and statutes of the Church, to obey her, and submit to her judgment if he commits a fault: and the Church is held to teach him, nourish him with the Sacraments, and protect him with all her strength. A heretic segregating himself from the union of the Church, although he seemed by this same act to renounce his rights: still he cannot deprive the Church, to which he subjected himself in Baptism, of her rights. And for this reason she can punish him, because she preserves the right that she received over him through his Baptism. When the Church degrades someone, or hands over a heretic to the secular authority, she then renounces her rights. Whence it is that if the secular authority does not punish him, the Church can no longer punish him, even though he is within the

Church and her member by reason of the Baptismal character. And if he implores the help of the Church after this, the Church is not held to give this to him: because he renounced his rights, and although the Church has not renounced, she can deprive him of his rights on account of the sin.

Chapter XXV

Whether a witness, who knew that someone has fallen into heresy, is held, although he has not been questioned, to report him to a judge, even before his fraternal correction.

We have up until now discussed the punishments, which have been decreed by Canon and civil law against heretics, over many chapters. But because a judge, although he solicitously desires it, cannot inflict some of them upon a heretic, because he does not know the heretic: thus it is necessary that a witness, who knew the heretic's crime, reveal it to the judge, so that he, having been informed of the crime, can remove the evil from the community: and in this way keep the whole country unharmed. Otherwise the sin would always remain unpunished, unless there was a witness, who would reveal it to a judge. For although the judge may know by himself another's offense, for instance, because while he was watching, that man committed it; he still cannot justly punish him: unless a witness is present, whose testimony could establish his sin. Because the judge himself cannot perform the function of two different persons, such that he would be the judge and witness at the same time. But although the judge could not punish the sin which he alone saw, still he can inquire whether another perhaps knows this same thing, which he saw: so that if there are others who know it very well, then helped by their testimony, he could punish him. Therefore witnesses are necessary for the execution of justice.

For God when speaking about the order of justice says: "One witness shall not rise up against any man, whatsoever the sin or wickedness be: but in the mouth of two or three witnesses every word shall stand" (Deut. 19, 15). Which law

Our Savior seems to have approved.[1] From which words it is clearly gathered that a word cannot stand firm in a judgment, which even though it is probable, it still lacks the testimony of two witnesses. Therefore since witnesses are no less necessary for rightly making a judgment than judges, it thence follows that witnesses by an equal necessity are bound to give testimony, as judges for making a judgment. Certainly a judge would sin if, having been requested in some case, he would disdain to do judgment and justice; and likewise a witness who when requested, either by the judge or by anyone else for whom he could have benefited by his testimony, would sin if he refuses to give testimony: especially about a matter by no means secret, and which not only he knew. And he not only sins, but if by his taciturnity he harms his neighbor, he is held to make compensation for the damage which by his silence he inflicted upon the neighbor. For he who through taciturnity hides a thief, Solomon deems guilty of theft, when speaking thus: "He that is partaker with a thief, hateth his own soul: he heareth one putting him to his oath, and discovereth not" (Prov. 29, 24). [Venerable Bede] in his commentaries on Proverbs when interpreting these words says: "For not only the thief, but also he is held to be guilty, who being aware of the theft, does not want... to reveal the money to the owner who is looking for it."[2]

But there is a doubt whether a witness not asked by someone is held to reveal, either by testifying or denouncing, to a judge the sin of another which he knew. About this matter a certain and universal judgment cannot be given: but firstly the quality of the crime ought to be considered. For if the crime is such that it can easily harm the country, one is bound to reveal it either himself or through anoth-

---

[1] Cf. Jn. 8, 17: "In your law it is written, that the testimony of two men is true."
[2] *Allegorica expositio in Parabolas Salomonis*, c. 29 (PL 91, 1022D).

er to a judge, whether he knew it publicly or it was told to him in secret. For the common good ought to be preferred to the individual good, and hence it happens that someone ought to look out for the safety of the people, rather than the reputation of one man. And concerning a crime of this kind ought to be understood what Augustine says: "Both he who conceals the truth and he who tells a lie are guilty, the former because he is unwilling to do good, the latter because he desires to hurt."[3] And I confirm this opinion of mine by the testimony of Blessed Thomas who speak thus: "As regards matters committed to man in some other way under secrecy, we must make a distinction. Sometimes they are of such a nature that one is bound to make them known as soon as they come to our knowledge, for instance if they conduce to the spiritual or corporal corruption of the community, or to some grave personal injury, in short any like matter that a man is bound to make known either by giving evidence or by denouncing it. Against such a duty a man cannot be obliged to act on the plea that the matter is committed to him under secrecy."[4] There are other crimes which neither harm the multitude, nor inflict serious harm to an individual person, someone is not held to reveal, especially if they were entrusted to him in secret.

From all these things it is very clearly gathered that he who knew someone is a heretic, is bound to reveal his crime to a competent judge, even if he was not specifically asked about this, and even though the heresy of the other was revealed to him in secret. For heresy is a very pestilential poison, which can quickly and easily infect any great multitude. Wherefore for this reason Paul when speaking about heretics said: "Their speech spreadeth like a canker [*cancer*]" (II Tim. 2, 17). It can also be not unsuitably adduced here for the confir-

---

3 *Decretum Gratiani*, pt. 2, *causa* 11, q. 3, c. 80 (*Quisquis*) (PL 187, 868A). Cf. Isidore, *Sententiae*, bk. 3, c. 55, n. 3 (PL 83, 727B).
4 II-II, q. 70, a. 1 ad 2um.

mation of this opinion, what the Lord long ago commanded to be done about a seducer and one persuading to idolatry when speaking thus: "If thy brother the son of thy mother, or thy son, or daughter, or thy wife that is in thy bosom, or thy friend, whom thou lovest as thy own soul, would persuade thee secretly, saying: Let us go, and serve strange gods, which thou knowest not, nor thy fathers, of all the nations round about, that are near or afar off, from one end of the earth to the other, consent not to him, hear him not, neither let thy eye spare him to pity and conceal him" (Deut. 13, 6-8). In which words what especially ought to be noted is that even though such words of seduction were said privately and in secret, still the Lord commanded that the secret ought not to be kept for him: but his crime ought to be revealed, so that afterwards he might be stoned by the people.

Therefore since a witness bound by such a great necessity and obligation to reveal the heretic, although known to him in secret, if someone rather wants to conceal him by his silence than to reveal him, especially if he had been requested to give testimony through an individual command or by a general edict, he will rightly be suspected merely on account of this to such an extent that a canonical purgation can be required of him, in which even if he does it well he will be certainly be punished, not as a heretic, but as being negligent in revealing that which he was held to reveal. But if he fails in the purgation, I reckon that he ought to be punished as a heretic, just as if for some other reason he had been marked with a strong suspicion of heresy, and failed in the purgation appointed to him by the judge and the law. For if he who hides a thief with silence is deemed guilty of theft, it is much more just that he who covers a heretic with silence, be reckoned strongly suspected of heresy. For an error (as Pope Blessed Leo says) which is not contradicted, is approved.[5]

---

5 "He who does not reclaim others from error shows that he himself has gone astray" (Leo I, Letter 15, c. 15 (PL 54, 688B)); *Decre-*

And Blessed Paul says: "Not only they that do them, but they also that consent to them that do them" (Rom. 1, 32). The Gloss, which is called Ordinary, when interpreting these words, says: "To keep silent, is to consent, when you could reprove."[6] And on the words, "I will cut off both him and all that consented with him, to commit fornication" (Lev. 20, 5), the Gloss says: "Those consenting, who could accuse, rebuke or warn, and do not do so, do not escape judgment."[7]

One question of no little importance about this matter still remains to be discussed, which is this: whether a witness who knew some heretic, is held to admonish him with fraternal and secret correction, before he manifests his crime to the judge. For there are some things which seem to urge us to say that a witness is obliged by a precept to admonish the heretic, before he denounces his crime to the judge. Firstly in fact that Our Savior commands that a certain order be kept about everything without any distinction, when saying: "But if thy brother shall offend against thee, go, and rebuke him between thee and him alone. If he shall hear thee, thou shalt gain thy brother. And if he will not hear thee, take with thee one or two more: that in the mouth of two or three witnesses every word may stand. And if he will not hear them: tell the church" (Mt. 18, 15-17). Furthermore, Paul orders that a heretical man after the first and second admonition to be avoided.[8] By which words he clearly taught that a heretical man ought to be admonished twice: and from this it is gathered that before such an admonition no one is allowed to reveal him to a judge. Again, such an admonition of a heretic

---

tals of Gregory IX, bk. 5, tit. 7 (*De haereticis*), c. 2 (*Qui alios*). "An error which is not opposed is approved, and truth is struck down when it is not defended" (Innocent I, *Decretum Gratiani*, pt. 1, dist. 83, c. 3) (PL 187, 401A).

6   *Glossa Ordinaria* (PL 114, 474B).
7   *Ibid.* (PL 114, 354A).
8   Cf. Tit. 3, 10.

is a work of charity and mercy: thus a witness knowing the misery of the erring heretic is held to come to help his misery through his correction. It is hence evident that this inference is good, because, as the Wise Man says, "He gave to every one of them commandment concerning his neighbour" (Eccli. 17, 12). And certainly, he who thinks that the contrary is licit, especially in the case of great necessity, is similar to Cain, who when asked by the Lord where his brother Abel was, replied: "Am I my brother's keeper?" (Gen. 4, 9). Now the antecedent of that conclusion is proved by the testimony of Blessed James saying: "My brethren, if any of you err from the truth, and one convert him: he must know that he who causeth a sinner to be converted from the error of his way, shall save his soul from death, and shall cover a multitude of sins" (James 5, 19-20). And among the three great alms which are enumerated in the chapter, *Tria*,[9] one is "to correct those sinning and to lead back those erring onto the road of truth."

There are also, on the contrary, a number of reasons no less pressing, which support the opposite opinion. And firstly in fact it is proved that there is no necessity of a witness, who knew very well that someone is a heretic, to secretly admonish before denunciation. Because among other things, which the sacred Doctors teach are necessary, so that someone would be held to correct a sinning brother, one is the hope of the sinner himself amending. For to this end is directed the whole order of fraternal correction assigned by Christ Our Savior in the Gospel, namely, so that by that order the brother lost through sin can be gained. "If he shall hear thee," He says, "thou shalt gain thy brother" (Mt. 18, 15). Thus for this reason he is commanded to be corrected, so that he may be amended through the correction. And hence it follows that when someone rightly despairs of the amendment of the sinner, he is not held to correct him secretly, or admon-

---

9 *Decretum Gratiani*, pt. 1, dist. 46, c. 12 (PL 187, 239B).

ish him fraternally. For the admonition of the one correcting is vain and useless, about which no fruit can rightly be expected. Now no one is obliged to vain and useless things: "That he that plougheth, should plough in hope; and he that thrasheth, in hope to receive fruit" (I Cor. 9, 10). Now it is not more reasonably permitted to despair about the amendment of a sinner, than about the amendment of a heretic: because a heretic has pertinacity adjoined to the crime, without which no one is said to be a heretic. Now he who is pertinacious, is not prepared to be corrected: nay, rather he is prepared to contradict the one accusing, and reproaching. Therefore him whom someone clearly knows is a heretic, one is not held to secretly correct, or fraternally admonish: because such a man as this, as Paul says: "is subverted, and sinneth, being condemned by his own judgment" (Tit. 3, 11). Accordingly, so great is the pertinacity of many heretics, that the more they are corrected, the worse they become: and the more that they are admonished about their error, the more tenaciously do they try to defend their error. Wherefore for the good of the heretic himself, even if there were no other reason, one ought to forego his correction and admonition, namely, lest when corrected and admonished he become worse. And I confirm this opinion by the testimony of Augustine, who speaks thus: "If any one forbears to reprove and find fault with those who are doing wrong, because he seeks a more seasonable opportunity, or because he fears they may be made worse by his rebuke, or that other weak persons may be disheartened from endeavoring to lead a good and pious life, and may be driven from the faith; this man's omission seems to be occasioned not by covetousness, but by a charitable consideration."[10] And according to this meaning those words of Solomon ought to be understood when he said: "Rebuke not a scorner lest he hate thee" (Prov. 9, 8). For the Gloss, which is called the

---

10 *City of God*, bk. 1, c. 9, n. 2 (PL 41, 22).

Ordinary, when expounding these words says: "You must not fear lest the scorner insult you when you rebuke him: rather you should bear in mind that by making him hate you, you may make him worse."[11]

Furthermore, that order of correction, or fraternal admonition, set down by Our Savior (as all theologians along with the canonists concordantly teach) ought not to be kept about those sinners, who sin unto the ruin of the country. The opinion of all of these men will thence be clearly established to be true if one would consider the reason why that order of correction is commanded to be kept. For the reason why that order of correction ought to be kept is firstly so that the neighbor's reputation, if it is possible, may be preserved. Afterwards if it has been preserved, and his conscience cannot be cleansed, it is better that his reputation is diminished than his conscience remain injured, or sick: because the spiritual good ought to be preferred to the corporal good. But then when it is unavoidable to diminish his reputation on account of his conscience, one ought to proceed little by little, and try, if it can be done, to take care of his conscience with a small lessening of his reputation. And hence in the second stage one or two witnesses are commanded to be employed, so that before them, who did not know the sin, the sinner may be corrected, and having been confounded in this way by their presence, he may perhaps come around to recovering his senses. But if he does not however amend in this way, then there is no longer any reason to aid his conscience, which is greatly preferrable to his reputation. And for this reason, in the third stage, the neighbor's reputation having been put aside, his sin is commanded to be revealed to the Church, that is, to his prelate.

---

11 *Biblia latina* [*cum glossa ordinaria*] *Walafridi Strabonis aliorumque*... (Basel: Johann Froben and Johann Petri de Langendorff, 1498), vol. 3.

Whether heretics ought to be denounced without fraternal correction

Since therefore the good of the society is greater than, and preferable to, the reputation of one particular man, it thence follows that the neighbor's reputation ought to be put aside for the sake of preserving the common good, and from this it is proved that a sinner, who sins unto the ruin of the nation, ought not to be corrected, or admonished fraternally, before the denunciation. For (as we said above) even if there were something entrusted to someone under the obligation of a secret, he would be held to reveal it to the judge, so that in this way he may avert harm to the nation. Now there is no crime more serious, and can harm a nation more quickly, than heresy: because it harms in religion, which is much more excellent than all corporal things. And because the operations of the soul are much more swift and quick than any actions of the body: hence this crime can likewise harm more quickly than any other corporal evil. From all which things it is very clearly established that he who secretly knows a heretic, is not held to keep that order of fraternal correction set down by Christ Our Savior.

About this question, so that we may bring forth a certain opinion, one ought to firstly consider the great difference between these two things, namely, that a man falls into heresy, and that a man is a heretic. For not everyone who falls into heresy is by that fact a heretic: but it is necessary that he have pertinacity adjoined, which if it is lacking (as we taught above in chapter seven of book one) he cannot be called a heretic. Therefore when this difference has been considered, according to the difference between those two things, I put forward two different, yet certain conclusions, by which it is fully replied to the proposed question.

The first conclusion is that a witness, who secretly knew that someone is fully a heretic, as for example, because he knows his pertinacity, and he knows that he errs, not from ignorance of the Catholic faith, but from his own malice: namely, because he knows that he prefers his own opinion to the opinion of the whole Church: is held to denounce his crime before he corrects, or fraternally admonishes him. This conclusion is proved by those two arguments which we have just presented, the first of which is about the hope of amendment necessarily required, so that someone necessarily ought to be admonished. The other is from the common good, which necessarily ought to be preferred to the particular good. Nevertheless that which we said about averting a common harm through the denunciation of the particular crime, Blessed Thomas treats when saying these words: "[And since he that sins thus in secret, sins not only against you in particular, but also against others, it is necessary to take steps to denounce him at once, in order to prevent him doing such harm,] unless by chance someone was firmly persuaded that this evil result would be immediately prevented by admonishing him secretly."[12] Which limitation is certainly very prudently added, and it is necessary so that the reader not be deceived by it, he ought to carefully examine each part of it. For because it can very rarely happen that a private man can remedy evils of this kind; wherefore not assertively, but under condition he said, "unless by chance." And because a light admonition does not suffice, which could correct him: hence he said, "someone was firmly persuaded." And a firm persuasion does not suffice, because he will attempt to change his mind during a long period of time, because in that long delay the country could suffer harm: hence Saint Thomas prudently said, "that this evil result would be immediately prevented by admonishing him secretly."

And hence no one ought to trust a fraternal, secret, and private correction, so that on account of it he would desist from revealing the heretic: unless perhaps he certainly knew that he has so much influence and power over the heretic that by his mere monition he could call him back from error. But because this happens to heretics very rarely, hence I reckon

---

12 II-II, q. 33, a. 7.

Whether heretics ought to be denounced without fraternal correction

that it is safer that in the crime of heresy one would proceed immediately without any admonition to denunciation, especially if the heretic is not a common and uneducated man, but a teacher, who manages to teach others those things which he thinks. For unless the man is immediately reprimanded through a public denunciation, he will very certainly secretly and hiddenly infect many with the poison of his heresy. For there are many men, who, because they fear to be reprehended and accused about their teaching, do not dare to come forth in public, and because they act wrongly, they hate the light, and do not want to preach upon the housetops according to the Savior's precept,[13] but in the corners. Lest therefore they be so powerful in darkness, it is necessary that their crime be immediately denounced in public and in this way the country will be preserved unharmed.

This first conclusion of ours can still be proved otherwise from the very words of Our Savior, by which He set down for us the order of fraternal correction. For Our Savior does not command a sinning brother, who would not listen to the Church, to be corrected or admonished more: but that he be held as a heathen and a publican. A heretic does not listen to the Church, because he disdains to accept her opinion, and he wants to rely only upon his own judgment. Otherwise, if he would listen to the Church, he would nowise be a heretic. From which it is very clearly proved that a heretical man ought not to be secretly admonished before he is publicly denounced. For when he firstly became a heretic, he leaps over the whole order of fraternal correction instituted by Christ Our Savior, and places himself in the last stage of that order when he so pertinaciously wants to maintain his heresy, that on account of it he does not fear the sentence of the whole Catholic Church.

Moreover that order of correction instituted by Christ Our Savior is commanded to be kept about brothers alone, for

---

13 Cf. Mt. 10, 27.

which reason it is accustomed to be called by everyone the order of fraternal correction. "If thy brother shall offend against thee," Our Savior says, "go, and rebuke him between thee and him alone" (Mt. 18, 15). By which words (as it is very clear) He does not command us to correct everyone sinning against us, but only a brother. Heretics however are not reckoned brothers to the Christian faithful, but foreigners, because by their own choice when departing from God's house which is the Church, they are no longer God's children, just as Christians are called and are: but children of the devil, who is called the father of lies by the Supreme Truth Himself.[14] And certainly he who examines well the Gospels and the epistles of the Apostles clearly understands that only Christians are called brothers among themselves, for they have the same father, namely, God, Whom they worship, and the same mother, that is, the holy Church in which they were reborn through Baptism.

And (so that I may omit many other testimonies) that is very clear which Paul says: "If any man that is named a brother, be a fornicator, or covetous, or a server of idols, or a railer, or a drunkard, or an extortioner: with such a one, not so much as to eat" (I Cor. 5, 11). After which words he immediately added: "What have I to do to judge them that are without?" (v. 12). By which words he described non-Christians because all those without, are outside of the Church. And hence on the contrary it follows that he called only the Christians "brothers": because to differentiate the brothers whom he named before, whom he had first named, in order that he might say that they who are not Christians, ought not to be reckoned among the Christians, he added: "What have I to do to judge them that are without?" Hence Theophylactus when interpreting the aforesaid words of Paul, says: "'That is named a brother.' Accordingly anyone who is guilty of the enumerated vices has merely the name

---

14 Cf. Jn. 8, 44.

of 'brother,' but in fact is not a brother... 'What have I to do to judge them that are without?' Those who are without, he calls 'pagans,' or 'Gentiles': those within, 'Christians.' 'I care not,' he says, 'about those who are without': for it is as though he were to say, 'They are outside of my laws.' It would be superfluous to make laws for those who are outside of Christ's palace and royal court. 'What things soever the law speaketh, it speaketh to them that are in the law' (Rom. 3, 19)."[15] Thus since only Christians are brothers to the Christians themselves, it is thence proved that the order of fraternal correction, which Our Savior commanded to be kept in regard to a brother sinning against us, ought not necessarily be kept in regard to a heretical man. For since he is not a brother of the Christian man, it is not necessary that the Christian man apply this mercy to him, which Our Savior commanded to be shown to sinning brothers.

Of course I do not wish to say that the Christian man is not held to giving any correction to a Jew, or a Gentile, or a heretic. Because correction of a sinner taken absolutely, and without any circumstances, is from the natural law, and hence it is necessary that it obliges everyone, and in regard to all men whether Christians or infidels. For just as a Christian is held, if he can, to deliver an infidel from the danger of corporal death, so also he is held to free him, if he can, from the danger of spiritual death. For we all, whether we are Christians or pagans (as it is inferred from the parable of the Samaritan[16]), are reckoned neighbors to one another: and hence it follows that all are held to help each other, because God "gave to every one of them commandment concerning his neighbour" (Eccli. 17, 12). But even though this correction taken absolutely obliges all men when great necessity urges and there is hope of success: still that order of correc-

---

15 *Commentarius in Epistolam I ad Corinthios* (PG 124, 627A-B).
16 Cf. Lk. 10, 30-35.

tion which Our Savior expressed in the Gospel, a Christian man is not obliged to keep towards unbelievers, because they are not his brothers.

But lest someone think that I have said these things from my brain alone, I will cite testimonies of some holy Doctors of an authority not to be contemned, who taught this opinion. For Theophylactus, when interpreting those words of Christ Our Savior in Matthew whereby He stated that order of fraternal correction, says: "Having spoken strong words against those giving scandal, now He corrects those who have been offended. Lest you, O reader, who have been offended, should utterly fall into error, imagining that the 'woe!' was spoken only to him who gave offence, He said, 'I want you who have been offended, to reprove those who have dealt unjustly with you and harmed you, if they are Christians.' See what He is saying: 'If thy brother,' that is, a Christian, 'shall offend against thee.' But if an unbaptized man wrongs you, then renounce to him even what is yours. If it is a brother, admonish him."[17] By which words he clearly said that unbelievers are not brothers of the Christians.

Tertullian says: "Our faith owes deference to the Apostle, who forbids us to enter on questions, or to lend our ears to new sayings,[18] or to consort with a heretic after the first and second admonition,[19] not after a disputation. He has inhibited a disputation in this way, by designating correction as the purpose of dealing with a heretic, and the first one too, because he is not a Christian; in order that he might not, after the manner of a Christian, seem to require correction again and again, and before two or three witnesses,[20] seeing that he

---

17 *Commentary on Matthew* (PG 123, 342C-D).
18 Cf. I Tim. 6, 3-4.
19 Cf. Tit. 3, 10.
20 Cf. Mt. 18, 16.

ought to be corrected, for which reason that he is not to be disputed with."[21]

And Augustine when interpreting those words of the Savior, "If he will not hear the church, let him be to thee as the heathen and publican" (Mt. 18, 17), says: "Reckon him no more among the number of your brethren. But yet neither is his salvation on that account to be neglected. For the very heathen, that is, the heathens and pagans, we do not reckon among the number of brethren; but yet are we ever seeking their salvation."[22] If the heathens (as Augustine reckons) ought not to be counted among the brothers, it is necessary that neither should heretics be included among the brothers, because the latter are also outside of the Church as the former. And hence it necessarily follows that that order of correction ought not to be kept in regard to heretics which Christ commanded to be kept in regard to brothers alone.

The second conclusion is that a witness who secretly knew that someone has fallen into heresy, and does not know whether he is a heretic, for instance because he does not know whether he erred from ignorance or from malice, and he also does not know whether he is pertinacious in his error, or perhaps if he were admonished he would abandon his error, is held to secretly correct him before he denounces him to the judge. This conclusion is approved. If it is established to the witness that he erred out of ignorance and not out of malice, he is held to secretly correct and admonish him before he denounces: because no one ought to denounce to the judge him by reason of or by the name of the crime whom he certainly knows did not sin in the deed, or doubts about the sin of which man: until he becomes more certain about it, unless perhaps the suspicion is very strong, and from the silence some harm could threaten the country. For then he could denounce his suspicion and his reasons to the judge,

---

21 *Prescription against Heretics*, c. 16 (PL 2, 29A-B).
22 Sermon 82 (PL 38, 509).

so that when the matter has been thoroughly examined, he could provide for the best interest of the country.

Nevertheless, if there is not such fear, he would act unjustly who certainly knows that he who has not sinned in action, or doubts about whose sin, were to report him to the judge as being guilty. For one ought to be sure of the crime of him who is being accused or denounced. For the Wise Man says: "Before thou inquire, blame no man" (Eccli. 11, 7). From which it is clearly inferred that he acts unjustly who denounces to the judge one fallen into heresy, if he certainly knows that he erred out of pure ignorance and not out of malice, but rather he is held to teach him, so that he may turn him away from the error. And hence it further follows that the witness is held to do completely the same thing, when he is entirely ignorant about whether the man erred out of ignorance or out of malice. For the Christian rule and the rule of law teaches us,[23] that about any neighbor we ought to presume the good and not the bad, until the contrary is evident to us. Thus he who has fallen into heresy, especially if he is an ignorant man, or little educated, ought to be presumed to have erred through ignorance, and hence ought to be corrected secretly and fraternally admonished.

If he accepts the correction, and plainly corrects himself, and immediately revokes his error, acknowledging his ignorance, the witness will have gained his soul which he turned away from error. But if he disregards the correction, and does not want to comply with the admonition, then his pertinacity and malice have already been manifested to the witness, especially if the heresy is manifest and the admonition was sufficient, according to those things which we said above in chapter ten of book one, where we treated about the legitimate admonition. Since therefore after his admonition the witness understood him to be such, it is unnecessary that

---

23 Cf. *Decretals of Gregory IX*, bk. 2, tit. 23 (*De praesumptionibus*), c. 16 (*Dudum*).

the witness proceed to the second stage of fraternal correction, employing one or two witnesses, but will immediately denounce him to the judge. Because since it is evident that he is pertinacious, it is also ought to be evident at the same time that he is not prepared to obey the Church, and hence it follows that he ought not to thereafter consider him as a brother, but as a heathen and publican.

The aforesaid second conclusion is further proved. Everything which according to the common opinion of theologians is required on the part of the one correcting, so that fraternal correction is obligatory for him, is present with a witness of this kind: thus that witness is held to secretly correct him whom he knows has fallen into heresy, not knowing whether he has erred out of malice. There are three things which all theologians teach are required on the part of the one correcting, so that the fraternal correction would be obligatory for him, namely, knowledge of the sin, hope of amendment, and opportunity of time. All these things are present with that witness. The first is evident, because the knowledge of the sin which is required and suffices, so that he knows that he is in sin, or in danger of sin, and some say that it is enough that he doubts about his sin. Howsoever it may be, the witness has such knowledge who knows that his brother has fallen into heresy. The second, which is the hope of amendment, is certain to belong to the witness: because since he does not know the other's pertinacity, there is no reason why he ought to despair of his amendment. Finally, the third, which is opportunity, ought to be put back in the choice of the witness himself: because if he chooses to correct, he could easily take an opportunity of correcting.

From all which things it is clearly proved that that witness who secretly knew that someone has fallen into heresy, not knowing whether he erred from ignorance or from malice, is held to correct and admonish him secretly before he denounces him to the judge. But this correction and admonition ought not to be put off for a long time, but ought to be done as quickly as possible, lest if it is put off for a long time perhaps harm to the country may thence happen, for instance if he about whom the witness does not know, was a true heretic and was secretly and hiddenly (as they are often wont to do) spreading his heresies among the people.

Chapter XXVI

Whether the son accusing one of his parents of heresy ought to be on account of this freed from those penalties, which on account of the parent's heresy, ought to be inflicted upon him by law.

After I had completed this whole work, *On the Just Punishment of Heretics*, it happened that a I heard a certain young man telling his sins in Sacramental Confession, whom I questioned about things pertaining to the faith and the Christian religion, and I found that he has the correct and Catholic faith: I then asked him whether he knew some hidden heretic, and whether he had a conversion with someone of this kind. He openly said that he knew that his father is a heretic, due to the fact that he had seen that he errs so pertinaciously, that when admonished by him, he never wanted to abandon his error: nay, rather on the contrary the father was trying to draw the same son into his own error. When I heard this, I exhorted the son to reveal any hidden crime of the father to the inquisitors, and although I proved with many evident reasons that it necessarily ought to be done, still I was unable to persuade him to want to do it. For he was defending himself with this shield, that it was unfitting, and natural reason was not allowing, that a son would lead a father to death. Next, he said that he would harm himself, if the father's crime were revealed, because he could not (as he said) reveal the father's crime without inflicting an injury upon himself, and in this way he would pierce himself through with his own sword. Since in fact all of his father's possessions would be apprehended by the treasury, and he reckoned that he would be deprived of his paternal inheritance. He feared that the infamy which would have been contracted from the paternal crime, would be fixed not only on the father, but would be brought upon himself, his children, and his grandchildren. Therefore he was saying that he would willingly reveal the father's heresy, except that in this way he would get as serious injury for himself. Hence for this reason, he said that he wanted to cover the father's heresy with his silence, so that he might take care of his honor. Nevertheless, I countered saying that it is unlikely that a son who, enkindled with zeal for the Christian faith, had accused the father of the crime of heresy before the judge, would be punished with the same punishments with which he would have been punished if he had not given any testimony of his faith. But he nowise trusting my words, persisted in his opinion saying that he would never reveal his father's heresy, unless firstly he were sure that he would be freed for this reason from all infamy and from all harm.

Therefore taking the occasion, I determined that from that time within myself, to add a special chapter for this, in which I would discuss about this matter as best as I could. For even though this matter should be discussed by canonists, to whom it pertains more than to theologians, still nothing prevents me, a theologian, from attempting to do what I can on my part from the reading of them. About which matter, it seems that two (I reckon) doubts ought to be discussed. The first is, whether such a father, produced in this way by the son to the judge, ought to be punished with the same punishment with which he would have been punished if he had been accused by anyone else. The other is, whether this son when accusing and convicting his father of heresy, due to this ought to be freed from all the punishments which are to be inflicted by law upon sons of heretics.

Concerning the response to the first doubt, this foundation ought to be laid before all else, that it is decreed by law, that the son who should have been condemned to death, if he is produced by the father to the judge, ought not to be punished with death, but with some other more lenient punishment. For the jurists conclude this from that which Emperor Martianus says in the law, *Milites agrum*, §. *Desertorem*, speaking thus: "The Divine Pius ordered a deserter, who had been produced by his father, to be placed in an inferior corps, in order to prevent his father from appearing to have surrendered him to undergo the extreme penalty."[1] And the same thing is said in the law, *Qui cum uno*, §. *Qui filium*.[2] Now it is evident that he who deserts the army in time of war, ought to be punished with capital punishment: as it was decreed in the law, *Non omnes*, §. *Desertor*.[3] From all which things the jurists gather that as often as a son should have been punished with death on account of some crime, if he is produced to the judge by the father, he ought to be punished not by death, but by some more lenient punishment, even if the crime which the son committed was the crime of high treason. For so teaches [Bartholomaeus da] Saliceto[4] on the law, *Propter insidias*.[5] And Felino [Maria Sandeo][6] in the chapter, *Accusasti*,[7] says that "If a father accuses a son of the crime of high treason,

---

1 *Digest of Justinian*, bk. 49, tit. 16 (*De re militari*), l. 13, n. 6.
2 "He who, in time of war, withdraws his son from the army, should be punished with exile and a loss of a part of his property; if he does this in time of peace, he is ordered to be whipped with rods; and if the young man who was conscripted is afterwards surrendered by his father he should be placed in an inferior corps, for he does not deserve pardon who allowed himself to be solicited by another" (*Ibid.*, tit. 16, l. 4, n. 11).
3 "When a deserter is found in a city, it is usual for him to be punished with death; if he is caught elsewhere, he can be reinstated after a first desertion, but if he deserts a second time, he must be punished capitally" (*Ibid.*, l. 5, n. 3).
4 Bartholomaeus de Saliceto, or Bartholomaeus a Saliceto in Latin, was an Italian jurist who lived from 1335-40 to 1411.
5 *The Code of Justinian*, bk. 9, tit. 1 (*Qui accusare non possunt*), l. 14.
6 Felino Maria Sandeo (1444-1503), or Felinus Sandaeus in Latin, was an Italian canonist.
7 *Decretals of Gregory IX*, bk. 5, tit. 1 (*De accusationibus*), c. 8.

the ruler ought to spare him."⁸ Which saying of Felino ought to be discreetly interpreted, such that the ruler ought to spare him, by inflicting a lesser punishment upon him: not however by removing the whole punishment from him. Hence Saliceto spoke guardedly (as I reckon), when saying that "the son ought to be punished more leniently."⁹ Bartolomeo Cipolla¹⁰ in his *Cautelae*, confirms the same opinion.¹¹ Hippolytus de Marsiliis¹² subscribes to the same opinion, when commenting on the law, *Ad quaestionem*.¹³ And these last two cite Raniero [Arsendi] da Forlì¹⁴ and Paolo di Castro¹⁵ on the above-mentioned law, *Propter insidias*, teach the same

---

8 *Commentaria Felini Sandei Ferrariensis in Decretalium libros V* (apud Iacobum Picaiam, 1570), vol. 3, col. 696.

9 "Yet the son ought to be punished more leniently, lest the mother see the son led away to punishment" (*In VII, VIII & IX Codicis libros commentaria* (Venice: sub insigne Aquilae renovantis, 1586), fol. 182r).

10 Or Bartholomew Cepola in Latin, was an Italian jurist who lived from 1420 to 1475.

11 *Varii Tractatus* (Venice, 1580) containing *Tractatus cautelarum*, *Cautela* 1, fol. 250v.

12 Hippolytus de Marsiliis (1451-1529) was an Italian canonist and jurist.

13 "Those whom the accuser produces from his own house should not be tortured, for it is not easy to believe that a substitution has been made for one whom both parents consider their dear daughter..." (*Digest of Justinian*, bk. 48, tit. 18 (*De quaestionibus*), l. 1, n. 3).

14 Raniero Arsendi, or Raynerius de Arsendis de Forlivio in Latin, was an Italian jurist who lived from 1290 to 1358.

15 Paolo di Castro (d. 1441), or Paulus Castrensis in Latin, was an Italian jurist.

opinion, and they thought that it ought likewise to be done in various cases. [Andrea] Alciato[16] teaches the same opinion.[17] Therefore having laid this foundation, from which (as I think) one ought to conclude that the same thing also ought to be done with a father guilty of high treason, whom the son presents to the judge, such that the father produced in this way to the judge, ought not to be punished with death, but ought to be punished with some more lenient punishment. Now this consequence is then manifest because the reasoning is the same here and there. For the reason which is given in that paragraph, *Desertorem*, so that the son ought to be spared, is this: lest the father seem to have surrendered the son for punishment. But an equally just, namely more just, reason is so that the son may not seem to have produced the father for punishment. For it is much more serious, and harder, that the son offers the father for punishment, than that the father does so to the son. Since the son received existence from the father, and for this reason is held to love the father as the source of his existence: and to assist him when he is in need. The father, however, receives nothing from the son which pertains to his being. For this reason, the son is held to obey the father, but the father is not held to obey the son. I certainly acknowledge that parents from a natural inclination, which proceeds from their feelings rather than from natural reason, love their children more than their own parents: nay, more than themselves: because the natural inclination of a thing is more for the conservation of the species than the preservation of another individual. Now the human species is conserved through the life of children, who are more apt for generation, can live longer, and can generate: than through the life of the parents, who according to the usual lifespan will live a shorter time. And this happens so

---

16 Andrea Alciato (1492-1550), commonly known as Alciati (Andreas Alciatus in Latin), was an Italian jurist.
17 *Tractatus de praesumptionibus*, praesumptio 4, pp. 51 f.

that parents always want a longer life for their children than for their parents, nay, often than for themselves.

And this is what is accustomed to be said, that love descends rather than ascends.[18] And for this reason the father (as Paul says) lays up for the children,[19] so that if perhaps they are small when the father dies, he may leave to them the means whereby they can support themselves. A son however does not lay up for the father, because it is not presumed that he will live longer than the son, whom the son is always held to assist as long as he lives. But even though everyone is more inclined to love their children than their parents, notwithstanding the son is more obligated to help his parent in extreme necessity, than his own son who would suffer the same need. For even though there is a greater inclination to the son, still there is a greater obligation to the parent. Because the obligations of the Commandments are not measured by the natural inclinations to the things which are commanded, such that everyone is more obliged to that thing to which he is more naturally inclined, especially if it an inclination proceeding from feelings and not from reason.

For there are many things to which integral nature, and not vitiated by sin, inclines us which nevertheless we are not obliged by any obligation to do, nay, it will be much better and more blessed to omit them. For (so that I may omit other things) integral and unvitiated nature inclines to intercourse on account of the preservation of the human species, which cannot be naturally preserved except men having intercourse with women generate other humans. Yet not all are obliged to this intercourse, but only they who, joining themselves though matrimony, have pledged fidelity to each other in regard to this act. It is also a natural inclination that every-

---

18 Cf. Carlo Chiappini, *Repertorium axiomatum, sententiarum regularumque utriusque juris locupletissimum...* (Macerata: ex praelo Aloysii Viarchi, 1844), p. 34, s. v. *amor*.
19 Cf. II Cor. 12, 14.

one would have compassion on his suffering neighbor, and help the needy. For (as the wise Ecclesiasticus says): "Every beast loveth its like" (13, 19). Yet no one is obliged to have compassion on each and every suffering neighbor, or help each and every needy person, unless he suffers extreme, or at least serious misfortune, which rightly forces other to help him if they can, and if not, they can at least have compassion. Rightly therefore Blessed Thomas says that although for just reasons a father loves his son more than his own father, still he reckons that for a much greater reason, everyone is more obliged to the love of his father than to the love of his son, and is more obliged to aiding the same father, than to the aiding of his son, if both suffer need.[20]

On account of which I cannot not be surprised that Bartolus, an expert in both laws,[21] would have fallen into such a serious error, so that he would have said that a son is not obliged from the natural law to support his parents. For since the jurist Ulpian,[22] on the law, *Si quis a liberis*, §. *Parens*,[23] reckoned that a son by natural reason ought to support his parent, Bartolus when explaining this opinion of the jurist, distinguished natural reason from the natural law, and says that a son is not held by the natural law to supporting his parent, but only from natural reason, that is, from the law of the pagans, as he interprets. Now he is motivated to saying this from the fact that reason (as he says[24]) is not in other

---

20 Cf. II-II, q. 26, a. 9.
21 I. e., Canon and civil law.
22 Ulpian was a celebrated Roman jurist under the emperor Septimius Severus.
23 "It is stated in a rescript that, although a parent should, according to the dictates of nature, be supported by his son, still the latter ought not to be required to pay his debts" (*Digest of Justinian*, bk. 25, tit. 3 (*De agnoscendis et alendis liberis vel parentibus vel patronis vel libertis*), l. 5, n. 16).
24 Cf. *Commentaria in primam infortiati partem*, fol. 35v.

animals. By which words he clearly intimates that he thinks that the natural law is not natural reason which pertains only to men, but a common law, which also befits other animals, or there could be some law dealing with brute animals just as about men. For it is called the natural law because it proceeds from an instinct of natural reason. And in the law, *Non quemadmodum*,[25] in the same title, he repeats and confirms the same opinion, adding that if a person has a rich father and a rich son, he ought to ask for support from the father rather than the son. Because (as he says) it is from the natural law that the father would provide for the son, rather than that the son would provide for the father.[26]

Anyone will easily understand how far all these things are from the truth, if he carefully considers the fourth precept of the Decalogue, which is about the honor of parents; the force and obligation of which assistance of parents, Blessed Jerome teaches, ought to be especially understood.[27] Christ Our Savior, when teaching against the Pharisees teaching the opposite, declared that the obligation of which support is so great, that when the father's need for his support urges, every offering which the son wanted to freely offer to God necessarily ought to be omitted.[28] Now the precepts of the Decalogue, even though they are not all, as it were, very well-known principles of the natural law, still they all are (as all theologians concordantly think) from the natural law; some of which are so to speak conclusions of the natural law, derived from its first principles. And from this it is clearly deduced that the son who is held to assist the needy father

---

25 *Digest of Justinian*, bk. 25, tit. 3, l. 8.
26 Cf. *Commentaria in primam infortiati partem*, fol. 35v.
27 "In consideration of the parents' frailty, age, or poverty, the Lord had commanded that the sons should 'honor' their parents, namely, by ministering to them the necessities of life" (*Commentary on Matthew* (PL 26, 106A)).
28 Cf. Mt. 15.

from the precept of the Decalogue, is obliged to do this from the natural law.

Now the argument which Bartolus makes for the confirmation of his opinion, has no strength. For from the fact that in the aforementioned law, *Si quis a liberis*, §. *Parens*, it is said that it proceeds from natural equity, that children are held to support their parents, he argues that by that fact they are not held by the natural law. If the law would have said that it proceeded from natural equity alone, perhaps his argument could to some extent prove that it is not by the natural law. Nevertheless, since it says that it proceeds from natural equity, and not from it alone, it is evident that his argument does not prove anything. Because equity and law are not so distinguished, that they differ by genus, as separate things which cannot belong to the same thing. And perhaps the reason why Bartolus was deceived, was because he thought that there is a difference between law and equity, so that it would not be permitted to infer from one, the opposite of the other. Concerning which matter, because it would require a longer discussion, and is very foreign to our subject, I do not want to discuss anything at present: still I admonish the reader, that he read about this matter the annotations of Guillaume Budé[29] on the *Pandects* [or Justinian's *Digest*],[30] where he treats this matter at length and elegantly.

Next, that Bartolus says that man is held by a greater obligation to supporting his son than to supporting his father, ought to be understood to be false, if for no other reason, or at least it could be clearly known from it, than because the father for obtaining the wherewithal for life, can sell his son: as it is stated in the second law of *De patribus qui filios*

---

[29] Guillaume Budé (1468-1540), or Guilielmus Budaeus in Latin, was a French scholar.
[30] *Annotationes in XXIV Pandectarum libros* (Paris: Badius, 1524), c. 1, fol. 1r ff.

distraxerunt.[31] When the son, however, is pressed by any necessity, he is nowise allowed to sell his father. It is evident that this diversity only arises from the fact that the son is held by a greater obligation to support the father, than the father to support the son. And from this it is clearly proved that that which Bartolus said on the above-mentioned law, *Non quemadmodum*, is false, namely, that a poor man can ask for the necessities of life rather from a rich parent than from a rich son. For anyone ought to ask for aid rather from him who is more obligated to assist him. Now every man (as we said) is more obligated to support a needy parent than an equally needy son. Thus every needy man ought to ask for the necessities of life more from his son than from his father, if both of them have the means wherewith they can assist him.

We have said all these things in passing upon a favorable opportunity, so that thence it may be established that it is much more just that a son would not see his father handed over to punishment, than that the father would not see the son offered to the same punishment. Because a son is held to love his father, from whom he had received that which he is: than a father to love his son. For the Divine precept, from which the force of the obligation ought rather to be taken than from the natural inclination, obliges the son more than the father. Because it can be easily established even from the fact that the son is more gravely punished by God, who lacks due obedience or piety towards his father, than

---

31 "If any heartless person, induced by extreme poverty and want, should sell either his son or daughter for the purpose of obtaining means wherewith to live, in a case of this kind the sale shall only be valid where the purchaser had a right to the service of the person sold, and he who made the sale, or the one to whom the child was alienated, shall have the right to restore it to its freeborn condition, provided he tenders its value to the owner, or furnishes him another slave in its stead" (*The Code of Justinian*, bk. 1, tit. 43, l. 2).

a father who was excessively harsh or severe towards his son. "He that curseth his father, or mother," the Lord says, "shall die the death" (Ex. 21, 17). Which curse (as Jerome says[32]) ought to be considered not only in words, but also in deeds. A rebellious and stubborn son, who contemned to hear the father's warnings, is also commanded in the Mosaic Law to be stoned.[33] A father, however, even if he has cursed his son, or treated him very severely and sternly, is not so fiercely punished on account of this by God. Therefore a son will sin much more gravely killing his father, than a father his son. And hence it clearly follows that if punishment of death ought to be remitted for a son guilty of high treason, whom the father produced to the judge, lest it seem that the father had surrendered him for punishment, as it is said in the aforementioned §. *Desertorem*, for the same reason the punishment of death ought to be remitted for the father guilty of high treason, whom the son produced to the judge. Because (as we said) it is much more just that the son would not seem to have surrendered the father than the father to have offered the son.

Another reason occurs to me besides this one assigned in the paragraph, *Desertorem*, which movers me much more strongly, so that I would believe that it is just that the punishment of death be remitted both for the son and the father guilty of high treason, if one offers the other to the judge. It is certainly just that the outstanding merit of any man, not only him who did the good deed, but also the other man for whom he offered it, be helped. For God Himself, the source and origin of all justice, often on account of the merit of one man, spares many, let alone one man, from the death which they merited, when forgiving them. For the sake of ten who

---

32 "In the Scriptures, 'honor' is understood to refer not so much to greetings and the duties that must be given, as to alms and the offering of gifts" (*Commentary on Matthew* (PL 26, 105C-106A)).
33 Cf. Deut. 21, 18-21.

were good in Sodom, God would have spared them, so that He would not completely destroy it.[34] Next "When God destroyed the cities of that country, remembering Abraham, he delivered Lot out of the destruction of the cities wherein he had dwelt" (Gen. 19, 29). Again for the prayers of Moses God spared the people of Israel, so that He would not destroy it, or inflict the death which it had merited on account of the sin of idolatry.[35] Paul the Apostle relates that two hundred seventy-six souls in the ship were spared by God for his sake, who were all caught in the fierce sea storm, and were saved on account of Paul's merits.[36]

And the merit of one man avails before God for impetrating not only for the life of the body, but also the life of the soul, which is much more precious, of another man. For God often spares him who, not out of malice, but out of a certain weakness, remains in sin: especially if he wants to depart from it, and according to his weakness disposes himself to virtue, and grants the grace whereby he can attain everlasting life. Which is clearly proved by that which Matthew says about a certain paralytic whom others offered to Christ Our Savior: "Jesus, seeing their faith, said to the man sick of the palsy: Be of good heart, son, thy sins are forgiven thee" (Mt. 9, 2). Notice that you see the paralytic's sins forgiven on account of the faith of those bringing the man. Now whether the faith of those bringing alone, or also the faith of the paralytic himself was in the merit, I do not now wish to discuss, because it is enough, for proving that which I intend, namely, that on account of the faith of those bringing, God pardoned the sin of the paralytic.

Next, Augustine relates that Paul the Apostle was converted to the faith on account of the prayers and merits of Blessed Stephen praying to God for him. And regarding Blessed

---

34 Cf. Gen. 18, 32.
35 Cf. Ex. 32, 11-14.
36 Cf. Acts 27.

Augustine at the time when he was a Manichean heretic, for whom, so that he might be converted to the faith, his mother was making assiduous prayers, and pouring out innumerable tears, Blessed Ambrose is reported to have said: "It is impossible that the child of so many tears should perish."[37] At the prayers of the Canaanite woman, God freed her daughter from the devil, by whom she was grievously troubled, and restored to perfect health.[38] The centurion's servant, who was lying at home sick of the palsy, and was grievously tormented, on account of his lord's prayers and merit, Christ the Savior restored to pristine health.[39] All these (as the holy Doctors think) were healed by Christ not only in body but in soul, the Savior Himself testifying Who said: "I have healed the whole man on the sabbath day" (Jn. 7, 23).

If one man's merit avails before God for impetrating pardon for another, it is just that it also avail among men, especially among those who rule the people in God's place. And if the merit of any man can avail for another who acknowledges his guilt, it is just that a father's merit for his son, and a son's merit for his father, could benefit for pardon, when either of them committed the crime of high treason. For God Himself, Whose example we now treat, often on account of the parents' merits, not only confers many rewards, but remits death and many other punishments which were merited. Which is proved even from the fact that God, Who says that He "will visit the iniquity of the fathers upon their children unto the third and fourth generation" (Deut. 5, 9), Himself says, that on account of the parents' merits, He "will show mercy unto thousands to them that love Him" (Ex. 20, 6). But no one could rightly deny that there is outstanding merit of the father towards the ruler, when he offers to the same ruler his own son, who on account of the high treason

---

37 *Confessions*, bk. 3, c. 12, n. 21 (PL 31, 693-694).
38 Cf. Mt. 15, 22-28.
39 Cf. Mt. 8, 6-13.

towards the same ruler, was worthy of death, so that he may punish if he wishes according to his own judgment and the son's deserts. For such a father actually shows himself more inclined towards the ruler, than towards his own son, and enflamed with such great zeal for justice, that he preferred to have surrendered his own son for punishment, than that justice, which reckons that wicked men ought to be punished, may on his part appear.

For nothing is wanting, that a father who ventures to do this may be equated with [Lucius Junius] Brutus, the founder of Roman liberty, who, "when he assumed the supreme power, he learnt that his sons were attempting to restore Tarquinius, whom he himself had expelled. He caused them to be arrested, and to be whipped with rods before his tribunal; and after that, he caused them to be tied to a stake, and beheaded." In which matter, Valerius Maximus says, "He put off the affections of a father, that he might act like a consul: and rather chose to live childless, than to be remiss in public discipline."[40] He who has undertaken such an outstanding deed for the king or republic, so that having put aside the piety of a father, he did not hesitate to offer his son guilty of high treason to the judge, to be punished by him according to his judgment, is certainly worthy that he may be heard when interceding for his son, and he may at least procure life for his son, who certainly had deserved death for his crime. And if it is just that a father when presenting his son may procure life for the son: it is much more just that the son for the same reason when presenting his father, would merit the father's life. Because (as it is evident from the things which have been said) the deed is much more excellent and of much greater merit, if the son by zeal for justice, or moved by an affection for the royal majesty, presents the father, than if the father would offer the son.

---

40 *Memorable Deeds and Sayings*, bk. 5, c. 8, n. 1.

Now Angelo [Gambiglioni] teaches this opinion concerning a son presenting his father when commenting on the law, *Adulterium cum incestu*, §. *Liberto*,[41] but he merely proves this by the reason given in the often cited §. *Desertorem*. Alberico [de Rosate][42] nevertheless on the aforesaid §. *Desertorem* says that although this is the common opinion of all Doctors, still he is doubtful whether it is so judged.[43] Therefore what ought to be done concerning the necessity and firmness of civil law, I being a theologian do not dare to decide, nor do I wish to decide, but I leave it to be decided by the jurists themselves. Nevertheless, I firmly assert this, that it is equitable and consonant with reason, that to the son whom the father, or to the father whom the son, presents on account of the crime of high treason, ought to be conceded a pardon from death, and mercifully granted life.

The question can be raised about this, whether the same thing ought to be said if a husband turns in his wife or the wife her husband to the judge on account of the same crime of high treason. The reason for which doubt arises from the fact that a husband and wife are reckoned as one flesh, and hence there is a doubt whether both of them ought to love the other more than a father or son. If someone were to say that a husband is more obligated to his wife than his father or

---

41 *Digest of Justinian*, bk. 48, tit. 5 (*Ad legem Juliam de adulteriis coercendis*), l. 39, n. 9. *De appelationibus et relationibus* (Venice: Vindelinus de Spira, 1473),

42 Alberico de Rosate, or Albericus de Rosate in Latin, (or Rosciate; ca. 1290-1354 or 1360) was an Italian jurist.

43 "From this ordinance the Doctors commonly teach that if a father seizes a son declared an outlaw and condemned to death, and hands him over to the authorities of the state, by which he was declared an outlaw according to the custom of the state, that the son ought not to be punished unto death, least the father seem etc.; nevertheless, I doubt whether I would so judge" (*Commentarii in secundam digesti novi partem* (Venice: A Forni, 1585), fol. 225r a-b)).

son, it would be necessary to also assert that it is a graver sin, if someone kills his wife, than if he kills his father or son. And from this it would clearly follow that death, which she deserved, ought to be remitted to a wife whom her husband produced to the judge due to the crime of high treason. Because it would be more just, according to this opinion, that the husband not seem to have surrendered the wife for punishment, than the father his son, or the son his father. About which question I decide nothing at present, but leave it to be disputed by others.

Therefore returning our discussion to what I firstly asked, I say that it is equitable and just, that a heretical father whom the son produced to the judge on account of the crime of heresy, into which he had relapsed, ought to be punished more leniently than if he had been accused by someone else, and if consequently a pardon from death ought to be granted to him, if he has given signs of true contrition. A well-educated jurist with whom I was discussing this matter objected to me, saying that it is an excessive remission of justice, that the sentence of the above-mentioned law §. *Desertorem*, would be extended also to the crime of heresy, just as to the crime of high treason. Because to offend the Divine Majesty is much more serious than to offend human majesty, as it is said in the chapter, *Vergentis*,[44] and in the chapter, *Sicut qui Ecclesiam*.[45] Next, because even if Canon and civil law mutually help each other, and often one supports the other,

---

44 *Decretals of Gregory IX*, bk. 5, tit. 7 (*De haereticis*), c. 10.
45 "Just as he who lays waste God's church, and plunders and invades its estates and gifts, becomes sacrilegious, so also he who persecutes its priests, is guilty of sacrilege, and is judged to be sacrilegious. And below: §. 1. Therefore, fornication is not a more serious sin than sacrilege. And just as a sin committed against God is greater than one committed against man, so it is more serious to commit sacrilege than to commit fornication" (*Decretum Gratiani*, pt. 2, *causa* 17, q. 4, c. 12 (PL 187, 1065B)).

as it is said in the chapter, *Intelleximus ex litteris*,⁴⁶ still the Church did not so accept the laws of the emperors, such that ecclesiastical lawsuits ought to be decided through them, and hence it follows that because it is evident that the crime of heresy is ecclesiastical, it ought to be judged by ecclesiastical ordinances, and not by the laws of the emperors.

I reply granting that it is much more serious to offend the Divine Majesty than human majesty, yet the laws do not punish more seriously, nay, often more leniently those who offend the Divine Majesty, than those who offend human majesty: and they do not punish heretics more seriously than those who have offended human majesty. Now that it is objected that the crime of heresy, because it is ecclesiastical, ought not to be judged by the laws of the emperors, but by ecclesiastical ordinances, proceeds from a wrong understanding of things. For it is evident that in the crime of heresy, two things ought to be considered. The first is the crime itself of heresy, the other is the punishment which is due to that crime. Concerning the first there is no doubt that the matter is entirely ecclesiastical, and hence (as it was decreed in the chapter, *Ut inquisitionis*⁴⁷) no one but an ecclesiastical judge can judge about this crime. No judge besides an ecclesiastical judge can declare by a definitive sentence that an assertion is heretical.

Regarding the other thing, that is, regarding the punishment to be imposed for the crime, it is evident that there are various judges, according to the variety of punishments, which are inflicted upon heretics. For there are (as we showed above through many chapters of this book) certain spiritual punishments decreed for heretics, for instance excommuni-

---

46 "Because human laws should not disdain from following the holy canons, so also the statutes of the holy canons are helped by the constitutions of previous rulers..." (*Decretals of Gregory IX*, bk. 5, tit. 32 (*De novi operis nuntiatione*), c. 1).

47 *Liber sextus decretalium*, bk. 5, tit. 2 (*De haereticis*), c. 18.

cation, the deprivation of ecclesiastical burial, and unworthiness for ecclesiastical benefices. And about these or other similar ones, because they were decreed by ecclesiastical ordinances alone, only the ecclesiastical judge can judge. Others are corporal punishments among which some can be inflicted both by the secular authority and by the ecclesiastical authority, such as infamy and the confiscation of temporal goods. For concerning such punishments both the secular and the ecclesiastical authority can make laws: and they can command that they be carried out against heretics, after it has been established about their pertinacity. In inflicting these and similar punishments, Canon and civil law mutually help each other, and one is supported by the other, and supplies what happens to have been lacking to the other.

Again there is a punishment about which the Church until now has not decreed anything, because it was not fitting to be decreed by ecclesiastical ordinances. Such is death, which is never commanded by ecclesiastical ordinances to be inflicted upon someone, because God repels men of blood from His altar. For David, a man otherwise holy, because he had shed human blood, was forbidden to build the Temple.[48] For this reason ecclesiastical men are forbidden from not only pronouncing or writing a sentence of death, but also from being present at its execution, as it is said in the chapter, *Sententiam*.[49] And if perhaps somewhere in Canon Law death is imposed for some crime, Abbas on the chapter, *Si quis per*,[50] says that it ought to be understood of spiritual death, that is, of excommunication, or of civil death, or of deposition.[51] From all which things it is established that the death

---

48 Cf. I Par. 22, 8.
49 *Decretals of Gregory IX*, bk. 3, tit. 50 (*Ne clerici vel monachi saeculariis negotiis se immisceant*), c. 9.
50 *Ibid.*, bk. 5, tit. 12 (*De homicidio*), c. 1.
51 *Commentaria seu lectura in quinque Decretalium libros novis illustrate*, vol. 7, fol. 143v b.

which is inflicted upon a heretic for the crime of heresy, is an entirely civil and secular matter, and in no way ought to be called an ecclesiastical matter: even though the same crime of heresy for which death is inflicted, is called an ecclesiastical matter. And the ecclesiastical judges themselves assert by their actions what we say. Because after they have judged a heretic to be pertinacious, they hand him over to the secular courts, as those who have nothing more which they could judge about him, and they ask the judge to treat him mercifully, and not pronounce the sentence of death against him.

And thence is it very clearly proved that in the sentence of death to be declared against heretics, the above-mentioned §. *Desertorem*[52] also ought to be viewed just as it is viewed according to the opinion of the jurists in crimes of high treason. Because the sentence of death which is declared against the heretic, is not pronounced by the ecclesiastical judge, but by the secular judge. Furthermore, even though in that sentence of death the matter is mixed, inasmuch as it pertains both to the ecclesiastical and the secular authority, the §. *Desertorem* necessarily ought to be viewed, and the sentence ought to be given according to its decision. Because where for deciding some case ecclesiastical canons are lacking, it is permitted, and sometimes one ought, to use the imperial laws, as it is expressly decreed in the chapter, *Intelleximus ex litteris*.[53] And it suffices to have said these things about the first part.

It remains that about the second part, that is, about the son accusing the father whether he ought to be exempted from all the punishments which the laws decreed against children of heretics, and whether the paternal possessions also ought to be given to him. About which matter, I will explain what I think by two conclusions. The first conclusion is this: A son

---

52 *Digest of Justinian*, bk. 49, tit. 16 (*De re militari*), l. 13, n. 6.
53 *Decretals of Gregory IX*, bk. 5, tit. 32 (*De novi operis nuntiatione*), c. 1.

who accused his father of the crime of high treason or heresy before a judge ought to be freed from infamy, and the other punishments contained in the law, *Quisquis*, §. *Filii*,[54] and in the chapter, *Si quis cum militibus*.[55] Because when the reason for the law ceases, it is necessary that the command and the ordinances of the law itself also cease. For (as [Andreas de Barbatia[56]] says on the chapter, *Quia nonnulli diversis*[57]) "a law is nothing other than the reason for the law,"[58] which is like its mind. And [Andreas] cites for the confirmation of his opinion, Baldus on the law, *Non dubium*.[59] And hence he infers that the law's ordinance ought to be extended to all those things in which the reason for the law itself is found.

And hence also it necessarily follows that when the reason for the law ceases, the ordinance of the law also ceases, especially since the law itself expresses the reason on which it is based. For where a law does not express any reason for its command or prohibition, even if that which we think is the reason for the law is lacking in some instance, we ought not to immediately reckon that the ordinance of the law is not in force. Because perhaps the legislator was motivated by a reason other than we thought, to make such a law. Or when that reason which the legislator stated is absent, then the ordinance of that law ought to be reckoned to also be

---

54 *The Code of Justinian*, bk. 9, tit. 8 (*Ad legem Juliam majestatis*), l. 5, § 1.

55 "If any person in conspiracy with soldiers, private citizens, or foreigners, kills any person of senatorial rank, or a soldier, he shall be condemned for high treason, put to death, and his property confiscated" (*Decretum Gratiani*, pt. 2, *causa* 6, q. 1, c. 22 (PL 187, 735A)).

56 Andrea de Barbatia (ca. 1400-1479) was an Italian canonist.

57 *Decretals of Gregory IX*, bk. 1, tit. 3 (*De rescriptis*), c. 43.

58 *Repertorium principalium... Super prima part principali* (Venice: Georgius de Arrivabenis, 1508), fol. 258v b, n. 82. Abbas seems to be incorrectly cited here.

59 *The Code of Justinian*, bk. 1, tit. 14 (*De legibus*), l. 5.

absent. Because if another reason motivated the legislator, he would have expressed it as another reason in the same law. The reason on account of which Emperors Honorius and Arcadius in the aforementioned law, *Quisquis*, decreed that the children of those who offended the royal majesty deserve infamy and the other punishments that are enumerated there, is this: because the pattern of the paternal, that is, hereditary, crime is feared in them. But in a son accusing his father before a judge of the crime of high treason, or the crime of heresy, there is no reason why the example of the paternal crime ought to be feared; because when accusing his father, he proves and demonstrates by very clear proof and a very evident argument, that he is very distant from the father's crime. And hence it very clearly follows that in such a son the ordinance of the law, *Quisquis*, ought not to be applied to him in whom the reason for the same law is manifestly proved to be absent.

Perhaps here someone will reply that it is true that when the reason for the law ceases the ordinance of the law also ceases, but one will say that this only ought to be so when the effect of the law is not already consummated. For otherwise, if the law has already obtained its effect, even if the reason for the law ceases, still the ordinance of the law ought not to also cease, as Filippo Decio[60] remarks on the chapter, *Cum cessante*.[61] In this case, however, before the son accuses the father of a crime, the above-mentioned law, *Quisquis*, has already obtained its effect. Because it is evident from the context that all those punishments decreed in that law, death only excepted, are inflicted by the law itself, and hence it follows that from the day on which the father commit-

---

60 Filippo Decio (1454-ca. 1535), or Philippus Decius in Latin, was an Italian jurist.

61 *Decretals of Gregory IX*, bk. 2, tit. 28 (*De appellationibus*), c. 60. *Super decretalibus* (Leiden: Petrus Fradin, 1559), fol. 333 r a, nn. 4-5.

ted the crime, before the son accuses him, those punishments obtained their effect. And hence it further follows that although by the son's accusation the reason for the law, *Quisquis*, seems to cease, still the ordinance of the law itself ought not to cease: because its effect had already been commanded for execution.

But this reply is not sound, because that which is said, namely, that by the effect of the law having been consummated, the ordinance of the law ought not to cease, even if the reason for the law ceases, will only be true when the law proceeds from manifest knowledge of the matter to the execution. For then if it is established that the suspicion is false, and from the false suspicion it had proceeded to the effect of the law, necessarily the precept of the law ought to be revoked, and in this way by the reason ceasing, the law necessarily ought to cease. In the father, who has been clearly proved to have committed high treason, even if afterwards he would openly repent of his crime, and would prove his fidelity by manifest proofs, he will never be free on account of this from infamy of law and the other punishments which he had already incurred by the law alone: because through the clear knowledge of the misdeed that law obtained its effect. But, not so in the son, who, even though from the day on which the father committed the crime, falls into those punishments, yet not on account of manifest knowledge of his crime, but he suffered them all merely on account of the suspicion of the law. It is befitting therefore that after accusing his father of the same crime, he proved that the law was mistaken in such suspicion, it would be declared that he is unaffected by those punishments to which he had been condemned on account of the suspicion alone.

Nevertheless, I wanted to admonish the reader about this matter, so that he would not think that completely the same thing ought to be said about infamy and the other punishments which are inflicted on the son on account of the father's crime. For in the children of him who has committed high treason, there is this difference, namely, that he who was born before the father's sin was committed does not contract any infamy from the paternal crime, and does not receive any punishment by law on account of it: but all those punishments decreed by law concern only those who were born after the sin was committed, as it is indicated in the law, *Si manumissus*.[62] For from that place Baldus concludes a general law, that the sin of a father never harms a son who was born before his offense, but only him who was born afterwards. Because this alone (as he says) contracts the stain from the root of the father "infected by this time," but not however another, from a healthy root.[63] The same opinion can be gathered (as I think) from the law, *Emancipatum*, §. *Si quis*.[64]

And about this matter there is in Spain in the kingdom of Castille a special law. For in the book, *Septem partitionum*, which in Spanish is called, *Libro de las siete partidas*,[65] it is

---

62 "Any children that may have been subsequently born to him shall also be reduced to slavery, as the crimes of their parents do not affect those who were proved to have been born at the time that the former obtained their freedom..." (*The Code of Justinian*, bk. 6, tit. 7 (*De libertis et eorum liberis*), l. 2).
63 Cf. *Super Sexto Codicis Justiniani libro commentaria* (Leiden: Trechsel, 1539), fol. 24v a.
64 "Anyone whose father and grandfather have been senators is understood to be both the son and the grandson of a senator; if, however, his father lost his rank before the conception of the former, the question might arise whether he should not be considered the grandson of a senator, even though he was no longer regarded as the son of one? It is the better opinion that he ought to be, so that the rank of his grandfather may be of advantage to him, rather than he should be injured by the condition of his father" (*Digest of Justinian*, bk. 1, tit. 9 (*De senatoribus*), l. 7, n. 2).
65 The *Siete Partidas* ("Seven-Part Code") or simply *Partidas*, was a Castilian statutory code first compiled during the reign of

said: "*Pero no se entienda...*"⁶⁶ Which text (as I think) either from a mistake of the writers, or by an error of the printers, is clearly corrupted, because as it found there, it makes absolutely no sense. But its clear and true meaning is gleaned from the Gloss of [Alonso Díaz de] Montalvo,⁶⁷ added there in Latin, which after he had spoken about the punishments of the kind that should be inflicted upon a traitor, immediately after when speaking about his children, he says: "And his descendants from among the children afterwards procreated are banished, the children previously had, are not punished on account of this or another paternal offense."⁶⁸ From which Gloss I conjecture that the text of that law cited above, which it is evident that it was corrupted, ought to be corrected in this manner: "But it is not understood of the children whom they had before they erred. But of the children whom they later had, since the ancients of Spain ruled whenever they punished the children because of their parents, they always kept this [rule], that there would be no penalty for those who had been engendered by their parents, before they had done the evil deed."⁶⁹ And that this text ought to be so corrected

---

Alfonso X of Castile (1252-1284), with the intent of establishing a uniform body of normative rules for the kingdom.

66 "But this is not understood of the children they have before committing the offense, unless they are accomplices" (Pt. 2, tit. 27, l. 6).

67 Alonso Díaz de Montalvo (1405-1499) was a Spanish jurist and commentator.

68 *Las siete Partidas del sabio rey Don Alfonso el nono...: con la Glossa del insigne Dotter Alfonso Diez de Montalvo...* (Lyon: Gomez, 1550), fol. 74r a.

69 "*Pero no se entiende de los hijos que hubiesen fecho ante que errasen. Mas de los que después ficiesen, siendo ellos fallaron los antiguos de España en todas las cosas allí donde pusieron pena à los hijos por razón de sus padres, siempre guardaron esto, que no hubiesen pena los que sus padres avían engendrado, ante que el fecho malo hubiesen.*" The author here uses Old Spanish, which

can be clearly proved by another law which is had in the same book, where, after the law commanded that a pregnant woman, even if the punishment of death is merited, ought not to be killed until she gives birth, when giving the reason, it subjoins these words: "Because if a son who has been born should not receive punishment for the fault of the father, much less the one who is in the womb for the fault of the mother."[70] From all which things it is established that there is a great difference between the children of those who were stained with the crime of high treason, such that only those who were born after the crime was committed incur infamy and the other punishments of law, and those who had been born before, have been exempted from all these punishments.

Now whether the same thing also ought to be said about children of heretics, I am in doubt. [Giovanni] Caldarino,[71] in his *Consilia*,[72] raises this question, and after many citations from all directions, he finally says that Catholic children of heretics, who were born before the father fell into heresy, ought not to be punished by those punishments which were decreed against the children of heretics. But notwithstand-

---

has been modernized above, as follows: "*Pero no se entiende de los fijos que oviessen fecho ante que errasen. Mas de los que despues fiziessen, siendo ellos fallaron los antiguos de España en todas las cosas alli do pusieron pena à los fijos por razon de sus padres, siempre guardaron esto, que no oviessen pena los que sus padres avian engendrado, ante que el fecho malo fiziesen.*"

70 "*Porque si hijo que es nacido no debe recibir pena por la falta del padre, mucho menes el que está en el vientre por la falta de la madre*" (Pt. 7, tit. 31, l. 11). The Old Spanish wording used here is: "*Ca si el fijo que es nacido que es nacido no deve recebir pena por el yerro de padre, mucho menos la merece el que esta en el vientre por el yerro de la madre*" (*Las siete Partidas*, fol. 70v a).

71 Giovanni Caldarino (1300-1365), or Joannes Calderinus in Latin, was an Italian canonist.

72 *Consilia, sive Responsa* (Venice: Bernardo di Giunta, 1582), *De haereticis*, concilium 3, fols. 92v b-93r a.

ing all these things, which Caldarino asserts in favor of this opinion, I am more inclined to believe that no difference ought to be made among the children of heretics, by the fact that they were born before or after the father's heresy. Because Canon Law, which imposes infamy and other punishments upon children of heretics, makes completely no distinction between them, as is clearly established by the chapter, *Statutum*, §. *Hoc sane*,[73] and the chapter, *Filii*.[74] For in those two places, the Pope, when speaking about the children of heretics, makes no distinction between them, by the fact that there were born before or after: but only by the fact that their parents were pertinacious until death in their heresy, or were corrected in their error and incorporated in the unity of the Church.

But Caldarino replies to this argument saying that although Canon Law speaks indistinctly about children of heretics, still because it is not the same reason for the particular persons contained under that general ruling, the children before birth ought to be distinguished from those who were born afterwards. Now he says that the reason for the diversities is this. It is because those who are born afterwards, descend from condemned blood: and hence it is rightly suspected that they will be like their parents were. But children who were previously born, because they do not descend from infected blood, wherefore it is unjust that a copying of the paternal, that is, hereditary crime be feared in them. But this reply has completely no strength. Firstly, because where the law does not distinguish, we also ought not to distinguish, as it is said in the chapter, *Quod si dormierit*,[75] and the chapter, *Solitae*,

---

73 *Liber sextus decretalium*, bk. 5, tit. 2 (*De haereticis*), c. 15.
74 *Ibid.*, c. 3.
75 *Decretum Gratiani*, pt. 2, *causa* 31, q. 1, c. 13 (PL 187, 1458C-1459A).

Whether a son accusing his father of heresy should be exempted

§. *Nobis autem*,[76] and in the law, *Praeses provinciae*.[77] And hence although that distinction ought to be made in the crime of high treason, still it ought not to be made in the crime of heresy. Because imperial laws, to which it pertains to decree about the former crime, make a distinction between children of the father who commits royal or imperial high treason. Canon Law, however, regarding the punishments which it decreed ought to be imposed upon children of heretics, made no distinction between children themselves of heretics, by the fact that they were born before or after the crime was committed by the father. And by this it is clearly proved that all those laws, which Caldarino cites for the confirmation of his opinion cannot help him at all. Because even though in other crimes civil law determines what ought to be so done, still in the crime of heresy, Canon Law, to which this matter pertains, did not command that any such thing to be done.

Furthermore, the reason for the diversity between the children of heretics born before or after the crime committed by the father, which Caldarino assigns, is null. Because even if the father's infected blood could harm the children in whatsoever way, so that they would thence have an inclination and a certain proneness for committing some sins, still this is not true in those sins which are reckoned purely spiritual, and do not at all originate in the flesh, as are all kinds of envy and many kinds of pride, namely, regarding confidence in one's own merits, to rely only upon one's own prudence, to despise all others in comparison with oneself. All these types of pride are reckoned among spiritual sins, which do not at all originate in the flesh. Now heresy, even though it sometimes arises from carnal vices, nevertheless its chief cause (as we will say in the following book) is pride. Because this is the true parent of all heresies, from which

---

76 *Decretals of Gregory IX*, bk. 1, tit. 33 (*De maioritate et obedientia*), c. 6, n. 6.

77 *Digest of Justinian*, bk. 1, tit. 18 (*De officio praesidis*), l. 3.

especially all heresies are generated. Wherefore although there are some heresies which in some way arise from the concupiscence of the flesh, still there are many others which have nothing in common with the flesh, and concupiscence of the flesh does not solicit to them, but every error of theirs proceeds from the malice of the will. Therefore in regard to heresies, the father's blood, no matter how infected, cannot harm the son at all, so that in him a copying of the paternal heresies is feared: since such heresies do not arise from the concupiscence of the flesh (as other crimes) but from the pride of the soul. And from this it is very clearly proved that no sure distinction among the children of heretics can be given by the mere fact that the crime committed by the father was committed before or after they were born.

But perhaps someone will object to me those things which we said above in chapter nine of this book, when we were speaking about infamy. For in that place we proved, when treating about the infamy of heretics, which also passes on to Catholic children, that that infamy justly passed on to the children, because children often derive their physical constitution of the body, and bodily inclinations, from their parents: and hence the suspicion arises that the children would fall into the same errors, into which their parents fell. I admit that in many heresies, namely, in those which have arisen from concupiscence of the flesh, this reason of suspicion is just, although it is not the only or main reason. If a heretical father believes that one ought not to fast on certain days, as Aerius taught,[78] or that fasting is not virtuous, as Luther reckons,[79] or virginity is not more excellent than matrimony, as Jovinian

---

78 Cf. Philastrius, *Liber de Haeresibus*, c. 72 (PL 12, 1186).
79 "For those who are tempted fasting is a hundred times worse than eating and drinking" (qtd. in Hartmann Grisar, S. J., *Luther* (translated by E. M. Lamond, London: Kegan Paul, Trench, Trübner & Co., 1914), vol. 3, p. 226).

said,[80] or he has fallen into some similar heresy having been drawn by the pleasures of the flesh, it is justly feared about the son due to this that he will at some time fall into similar errors which arise from the flesh. Nevertheless, if the father has fallen into the heresy of Arius, or Sabellius, or Nestorius, or Dioscorus and Eutyches, simply because he received his father's physical constitution, it is not justly feared that the son would fall into the same heresy, into which the father has fallen. Because those heresies have arisen not from the concupiscence of the flesh, as the others, but merely from the mind's pride. The children, however, receive not the rational soul, but only the flesh from the parents.

And for this reason I, in chapter nine of this book, when I was treating about the infamy of heretics, which is passed down to their children, did not say that the only reason why it is passed down to the children is because they inherited the physical constitution, and hence the inclinations to vices, from the parents; but I added another reason, which seems better to me. Namely, because from the love whereby they are affected towards their parents, they nearly always imitate their parents, and often they strive to lead their lives in imitation of theirs. And for this reason, in chapter eight of this book, I proved that the parental authority which parents have over their children, justly ought to be taken away from heretical parents, lest the children from the love whereby they are affected towards their parents, and from the long association had with them, would become imitators of the parent's crime. Now this imitation of the parents is not distinguished in the children by the fact that they were born before or after, and hence it is proved that in the crime of heresy, which does not always arise from the flesh, the distinction ought not to be made between the children of heretics by the fact that they were born before or after the sin of the father: especially since Canon Law, to which this matter pertains, makes no

---

80 Cf. St. Jerome, *Against Jovinianus*, bk. 1, c. 3 (PL 23, 224B).

distinction between the children of heretics, as civil law had made between the children of those who committed royal or imperial high treason.

Next, it is evident that the avenging of the parents often is passed on to the children, merely on account of the gravity of the misdeed, to incite terror in others, as in an illegitimate son, who without his fault, yet not without reason, is prohibited from the ministry of the altar. And I think that this is the better reason why children of heretics, even though Catholic, are inflicted with so many punishments by the law; namely, for denoting the gravity of the misdeed, and instilling fear in others by this. Since this reason equally serves in all the children of heretics, it is thence also proved that no distinction ought to be made among them.

The second conclusion is that the son who revealed the father's heresy to the judge, openly demonstrating his perfidy, deserves that the goods which could have belonged to him from the father by hereditary law, be not taken away from him, but everything would be given to him as a reward of his virtue. Now whether it ought to be so done by the rigor and necessity of the written law, as this conclusion says, it not evident to me, and hence I speak only about the fittingness and a certain natural equity: so that it is equitable and congruent with natural reason to be so done just as it is said in our conclusion. Yet none of the jurists who teach that it ought to be so done cite a text whereby this conclusion can be clearly proved from the law. *El Doctor*, [Juan López de] Palacios Rubios,[81] in his *Repetitio* [*Rubricae*], on the chapter, *Per vestras*,[82] says that the goods of a father ought to be given to a son who revealed the fault of the father, even

---

81 Juan López de Palacios Rubios (1450-1524) was a Spanish jurist called *El Doctor* for his expertise in Canon Law.
82 *Decretals of Gregory IX*, bk. 4, tit. 20 (*De donationibus inter virum et uxorem*), c. 7.

if the father is condemned by the law, *Quisquis*.[83] Yet for a proof of this opinion, he does not cite either any law from civil law or any canon from Canon Law, but only a constitution of Emperor Fredrick [II].[84] The *Repertorium inquisitorum* teaches the same opinion, on the word *Filii*, §. *Sed circa supradictas*.[85] And for the confirmation of his opinion, he also only cites that constitution of Fredrick, in which after he decreed various punishments against heretics and their children, at length he adds these words which follow: "It certainly ought not to be excluded from the limits of mercy that if those who, not following the paternal heresy, reveal the hidden perfidy of the fathers, whatever the punishment whereby their guilt may be punished, the innocence of the children is not subject to the aforesaid deprivation."[86]

Which constitution, if it has any force, it will have its force only in those lands which are subject to the Emperor. Now that which the *Repertorium* says, namely, that the constitution of Frederick is confirmed by the Church in the chapter, *Ut inquisitionis*,[87] is mistaken. Because even though that constitution is praised and confirmed in that place, still not absolutely and universally, but instead it is confirmed with a limitation by these words: "To the extent," says Pope Boniface [VIII], "they advance the honor of God and His

---

83 *The Code of Justinian*, bk. 9, tit. 8 (*Ad legem Juliam majestatis*), l. 5.
84 Cf. *Repetitio Rubricae* (Leiden: Philippus Tinghus Florentinus, 1576), pp. 200b-201a.
85 *Repertorium inquisitorum pravitatis haereticae* (Venice: Damianus Zenarum, 1575), pp. 359 f.
86 Constitution of Fredrick II, *Contra haereticos*, dated 1223, *Commissi*, §. *Vere scientes* (*Monumenta historica ad provincias Parmensem et et Placentinam pertinentia* (ex officina P. Fiaccadori, 1855), vol. 9, p. 248; *Monumenta Boica* (Munich: Typis Academicis, 1834), vol. 3, pt. 1, p. 187).
87 *Liber sextus decretalium*, bk. 5, tit. 2 (*De haereticis*), c. 18.

Book 2, Chapter 26

holy Church, and they continue the destruction of heretics, and do not obstruct the canonical statutes." Behold, you see by what limitation the Supreme Pontiff confirmed those constitutions of Frederick. Thus where those things are decreed in Frederick's constitution, which are contrary to other sacred canons, it is proved that those things were not approved by the Pope in that same place. Now the children of heretics, even if they are Catholics, without any distinction are excluded by Canon Law from the inheritance of paternal goods, as appears in the chapter, *Vergentis*.[88] Wherefore Frederick's constitution for that part, in which he commands that paternal goods be given to the son who revealed the father's hidden heresy, is not confirmed by the Pope, because it opposes that which is said in the chapter, *Vergentis*, where, without any limitation, the children of heretics are excluded from that paternal inheritance. Since therefore it is not established from the rigor and the necessity of the law that the goods of the heretical father ought to be given to the Catholic son, who revealed the hidden heresy of the father, I merely want to show the equitability of this matter, and to prove that it is equitable and congruent with reason that it be so commanded to be done. For it is equitable and just that a reward would be given to one acting well and zealously, especially if in the work which he does zealously, he serves the ruler or the country.

Otherwise, there would be few who are motivated to works of virtue, if every hope of a reward would be taken away from good deeds. Because even though it is much better to do zealous deeds solely from the love of virtue than from the hope of a reward, still there are many more who are moved to what is good through the hope of a reward than those who are moved by the love of virtue alone. Hence Paul, acknowledging such a condition of men, that they are very rare who are motivated to virtue when every reward of virtue has been

---

88 *Decretals of Gregory IX*, bk. 5, tit. 7 (*De haereticis*), c. 10.

excluded, said: "He that cometh to God, must believe that he is, and is a rewarder to them that seek him" (Heb. 11, 6). It is evident that Paul said this because unless men would believe that God gives a reward to those who serve Him, there would be no one, or very few, who would wish to want to serve Him freely. For David, the epitome of the prophets, "inclined his heart to do God's justifications, for the reward" (Ps. 118, 112). And the renown Moses, whom God made the leader and legislator of the Israelite people, and with whom God spoke as a friend with a friend,[89] "looked unto the reward, rather choosing to be afflicted with the people of God, than to have the pleasure of sin for a time" (Heb. 11, 25-26). If such and so great men as these men of God were looking unto a reward, which they were hoping would be given for their merits, who will already be so great that, all hope of a reward having been excluded, he would wish to serve God and obey Him in everything?

And from this it is very clearly proved that no ruler, and no country, could justly arrogate this to themselves, that it would want its subjects to deserve well of it without any hope of a reward, but it is fitting that they be promised various rewards according to the diversity of their merits: so that anyone would long for greater service to the ruler, the more he hopes for a greater reward therefrom. Whence Blessed Gregory when writing to Maximian, the Syracusan bishop, says: "For it is just that they should get payment in the places where they are found to lend their services."[90] And Emperors Honorius and Arcadius acknowledged this same thing in that law, *Quisquis*, §. *Sane*,[91] where they promise

---

89 Cf. Ex. 33, 11.
90 *Decretum Gratiani*, pt. 2, *causa* 12, q. 2, c. 45 (PL 187, 914B); Letters of Gregory I, bk. 4, l. 11 (PL 77, 681A).
91 "If any one of these persons, at the very beginning of the organization of the faction, being animated by a praiseworthy intention, should betray the conspiracy, he shall be honored and

him who betrays a conspiracy a reward from them, and he is to be decorated with honor. If he who accuses another man, nowise joined to him by the bond of blood, proving him to be guilty of high treason, deserves to be decorated with a reward and honor, he will certainly be much more deserving of a reward and honor, who being animated with the zeal of virtue does not shrink from accusing his own father of the same crime. For he gave up being the son, so that he might act as a faithful subject, and preferred to live as an orphan, rather than abandon the safety of the ruler.

Furthermore, if he who "being animated with zeal for true praise," as those emperors say, reveal the traitor, so that they may keep the royal majesty unharmed, is worthy of a reward and honor: it is much more just that he who being animated with zeal for the Catholic faith reveals a heretic be decorated with a reward and honor, because he wishes to keep the Catholic Church, which is greater and better than all emperors, unharmed, so that all poison of heretics having been kept out, none of those members, which are united to her through faith, may be cut off from her through heresy. For just as it is much more serious to offend Divine Majesty than human majesty, as it is said in the chapter, *Vergentis*,[92] so on the contrary, it is much better to serve Divine Majesty than human majesty, and to have zeal for Divine Majesty than human majesty. Again, he who reveals a conspiracy begun against the Roman Pontiff, even if he is a participant in the crime, is not only purged from guilt, but also is commanded in the chapter, *Si quis Papam*,[93] to be encouraged by a remuneration, of which he is not unworthy. And from this it is very clearly gathered that it is much more just that the Catholic son revealing the father's heresy be given a reward,

---

rewarded by Us" (*The Code of Justinian*, bk. 9, tit. 8 (*Ad legem Juliam majestatis*), l. 5, §7).
92 *Decretals of Gregory IX*, bk. 5, tit. 7 (*De haereticis*), c. 10.
93 *Decretum Gratiani*, pt. 1, dist. 79, c. 2 (PL 187, 380C-381A).

since he is not a participant of the paternal crime, as the father.

If someone perhaps would say that heresy is a greater and more serious crime than conspiracy against the Pope: and hence it is not equally just that this man be given a reward as that: he certainly when so speaking concludes our opinion from his own words, than his own [opinion]. For just as heresy is a more serious sin than conspiracy, or any other crime of high treason: so on the contrary he who resists heresy does a greater good, than he who resists a conspiracy: and in this way is worthy of a greater reward. Perhaps someone will say, admitting that such son is worthy that a reward be given to him: but he will say that a great enough reward was given to him by the fact that he was freed from the punishments which by law were to be inflicted upon him due to the father's misdeed, and it is unnecessary that the paternal goods be given to him as a reward.

But he who would so speak, will greatly err from the truth, and show that he does not understand how great the difference is between declining from evil and doing good.[94] For these two things are very different, and separable from each other: to be freed from punishment, and to be given a reward. To this beginning of good, which is to decline from evil, corresponds to the other, which is to be freed from punishment. For someone is not freed from punishment merely because he acts well, but by the fact that he declines from evil. For otherwise he who neither acts well not acts badly, such a sleeping man, is not freed from punishment. Thus the reward corresponds only to a good action. And hence it is clearly established that a son, who accuses the father of heresy, by this alone is freed from the punishments which would otherwise have been inflicted upon him, because it is evident that that he is not an imitator of the paternal crime, and a copying of the paternal iniquity ought not to be

---

94 Cf. Ps. 36, 27.

feared in him. But because he is not only free from the paternal guilt, but also moreover added an outstanding deed by revealing the father's heresy: wherefore it is necessary that he be deemed not merely free from punishment, but worthy of a reward. And in this way he is proved to be worthy, that the paternal goods would be given to him.

Add to all these things that which all theologians teach with a concordant opinion, that every just man in any good deed, which he did for another, merited more for himself than for the other, and he cannot merit for another, who does not merit for himself. And hence the theologians conclude that he who persists in mortal sin and with the willingness to sin, even though he would pray to God most importunately and very fervently for another sinner, he merits nothing for him regarding the soul's salvation, because being in this way, he can merit nothing for himself. The son who revealed the father's crime (as we showed above in the first part of this question) merits that the father produced by him would be punished more leniently, than if he were to be brought forth by another: thus it is just that he merit something for himself: since it is much easier to merit for oneself, than for another.

These are the things that seem to me able to be said about this matter in favor of the equity and fittingness of the aforementioned second conclusion: although those things (as I said) nowise can be proved from the rigor and necessity of the law. And from this I infer that a son, no matter how Catholic he is, is not secure in conscience, by taking and retaining the father's goods for himself which could have belonged to him by hereditary right. Because, since this is not granted to him by law, it is necessary that he wait for the sentence of a judge, from whom the inheritance from the father, or another similar thing, would be granted as a reward for his virtue, as it is decreed to be done in another case, in the first law of *Pro quibus causis servi praemium accipiunt libertatem*.⁹⁵ Therefore before the granting of the judge, the son who had revealed the father's crime would act wrongly, by retaining the father's goods.

There are many other things pertaining to the punishment of heretics I could have treated in this second book, all of which, motivated by many reasons, I have omitted. For some of them are so clear that they could not hide from one even moderately educated. Next, if which things are perhaps difficult and hidden, about which I did not discuss at all in this second book, those things did not pertain (as I think) to punishments: but I think that they only pertain to the processes by which the judge advances to pronouncing the sentence. Which things since they are far apart from that which I determined at the beginning of this work to say, were necessarily omitted by me, lest I be accused by many to have digressed far from the topic. Add to these things the quality and nature of those things. For those things which we omit are such that jurists can discuss about them better than theologians, and for this very important reason I reckoned that they necessarily ought to be left to them.

---

95 "Since scrupulous care as well as the authority of the law should be exercised for the purpose of increasing and encouraging the practice of fidelity by slaves, if you can establish by undoubted proof that you have strenuously exerted yourself to avenge the death of your master, the freedom which was long since ordered by Decrees of the Senate and Laws of the Emperors to be granted to slaves who avenge the death of their masters cannot be conferred upon you, even after having rendered so great a service, merely through the performance of your act, but you must obtain it by appearing before the tribunal of the Governor, and in consequence of his decree" (*The Code of Justinian*, bk. 7, tit. 13, l. 1).

BOOK THREE

Preface

Anyone having the responsibility of governing the people, if he justly and holily desires to execute his ministry, should above all choose this, and should not leave anything untried in achieving it, namely, that no such wicked deeds be perpetrated, unless he wants to be regarded as remiss and completely negligent, and for which he will necessarily be punished. For he who wishes for and seeks after shameful deeds, which he can punish in his subjects, will deservedly be reckoned not a king but a tyrant, not a shepherd but a wolf, not a judge but an executioner. And it is not enough for a king or a bishop, or anyone having the care of the governance of anyone else, that he wish that no crimes or wicked deeds be committed: but it is necessary that he diligently endeavor to expend all his strength for this matter, so that this very thing which he hopes for, would happen. For if on account of his negligence some one of these would happen, it all will be rightly imputed to him, and it will be necessary that he render a very exact account to God regarding every such thing. For it is necessary that all the rulers of the world, by whatever name they are reckoned, understand that they were not placed by God unto this alone, that they punish crimes: but rather that they firstly procure this, that no wicked deeds be perpetrated. For a ruler and governor of the people ought to imitate a good and pious doctor in this regard, who, if he undertakes the care of the health of some man, he not merely try to restore him, after he became ill, to his former health: but that he applies all diligence so that he does not fall into any sickness. If the princes or bishops, or any other rulers of the world, disdain to imitate a doctor, there is no reason why they would disdain to imitate at least

God Himself, Who is the most wise ruler of the whole world. Therefore let all the Christian rulers of the world look upon Him: and if they desire to correctly administer the things which were committed to them, let them act according to the Divine example, which Sacred Scripture shows to them. Since God in fact (as Holy Writ teaches us), "Who will have all men to be saved, and to come to the knowledge of the truth" (I Tim. 2, 4), certainly does not want anyone to perish, or depart from the straight line of justice even a hair's breadth, Who, lest anyone (unless of his own accord and willingly) could ever err, showed a most certain way to all whereby they could attain everlasting life, and furthermore is always prepared to help all who, when deprived of His help, would try in vain to attain it. God teaches what is good, exhorts to it, draws by promises, urges by compelling rewards, helps the beginners, accompanies and encourages those advancing. He very often admonishes about whatsoever sin, lest we being unguarded fall into it. If He sees us close to sin, He deters us by very severe threats of punishments. If he perceives that we are now collapsing, He places His hand under us, so that we are not bruised. Because enemies surround us, who always try to impel us to sin, He employs friends, not to say pedagogues, the Angels, to us, who help us against the enemies, and to the extent that they can protect us from them. Finally God has such a fervent will of conserving us in goodness and averting us from wickedness, that for this matter He seems to omit nothing. Therefore it is necessary that we all assert with the prophet, and so that we may give credit to God, that unless the Lord had helped us, we probably would have fallen into every sin.[1] Thus this immense mercy of God and most vigilant perpetual care which He has for us, as many as rule in His place ought to imitate at least somewhat, whom He instituted to be the various ministers for the government of His people, so that just as He is

---

1 Cf. Ps. 93, 17.

How heresy can be prevented

imitated in preferment, so also they may imitate in care and diligence, so that they exercise all the strength they can so that they may keep their subjects in virtue, and may avert them from vices. But if it is necessary that rulers apply exact diligence in regards to all other wicked deeds, so that they take pains lest they arise: it is so much the more just that they apply that same diligence lest new heresies arise or old ones be called back, the more heresy, which does more harm than all other sins, is worse, and moreover is more pestilent. If rulers ought to watch diligently lest thefts, murders, adulteries, or other crimes of this kind be done in the people, it is much more just that they diligently attend lest heresies arise in the people, which can inflict much more harm on the whole people. For heresy alone is that which attacks and completely overthrows the foundation of the whole Christian religion, which is faith, which having been removed, it is necessary that all other good things, if they were present, immediately collapse. Wherefore since the Christian rulers of the world are compelled by such a great necessity to not merely extinguish heresies, but to prevent them from rising up, lest I seem to have proffered only a bare warning to the same rulers, I have decided in this third book to show them a sure way whereby, if they wish, they can easily attack heresies, lest they arise.

Chapter I

It is taught that there are many ways, whereby heresies can be duly impeded, lest they arise, and it is specially discussed about one of them.

Because it is necessary for princes and all other rulers of the whole of Christendom by whatever name they are reckoned, that they all diligently, according to the obligation of their rulership and ability, watch over and labor that no heresies ever arise; wherefore I thought that it would be something worthwhile for me to do, if I showed to them some ways by which this could be properly done: yet I will show a very broad and most sure way, which nevertheless afterwards is divided into various ways. For it is necessary to take away all occasions which can give an opportunity for heresies, and to pull up all the roots from which it is clear that heresies can be born. This seemed to me to be the most sure and most correct way by which heresies can be impeded lest they arise. For having taken away the cause, it is also necessary that the effect is taken away, which should have come forth from it. And something cannot be better impeded from arising than if you would remove all the causes which could produce it. Thus since this is so well known that no one can deny it, it remains to show the roots of heresies, so that they having been clearly shown, all rulers may be equipped for uprooting them, and in this way bring about that they would not be born.

The roots and causes of heresies are various, and are put into two categories. We can say that some are intrinsic, namely, those which are hidden and affixed to the souls of those who hold heresies. Other causes and roots are called extrinsic, or if you prefer, external, and are those which are without, and outside the person who has fallen into heresy. We will discuss about the intrinsic causes only in this chapter: because the removal of them pertains more to certain individual persons, rather than to princes and rulers. But we will thoroughly discuss in many chapters regarding the other extrinsic causes, which are many and various, and can be easily taken away by princes.

Thus, beginning from the intrinsic causes, I say that the most certain, indubitable, and principle cause of heresies is a man's own sin. And Solomon clearly stated this, who when speaking about a just man taken from this life before the time says: "He was taken away lest wickedness should alter his understanding" (Wis. 4, 11). By which words he teaches us that malice is so powerful that it can change man's understanding from one true judgment to another false and perverse judgment. For the will (as experience teaches us) often draws the judgment of reason to itself, such that the intellect judges those things good which it sees that the will loves, and says that those things are evil, which it knows that the will hated. Wherefore Aristotle reckons that all wrongdoing is [a result of] ignorance.[2] It ought not to be thought that he said this because he thought that every wickedness of the will arises from the will's ignorance; but rather on the contrary, because from every wickedness of the will some ignorance arises, which grows or diminishes according to the measure of the affection of the will itself. Although the will (as Augustine says[3]) can only will or not will that which has been foreknown by the intellect, still it is not necessary that before the will wills or does not will something, that the intellect would judge it to be good or evil: but it is enough that it foresaw it by simple knowledge, with absolutely no

---

2 "Now it is true that all wicked men are ignorant of what they ought to do and refrain from doing, and that this error is the cause of injustice and of vice in general" (*Nicomachean Ethics*, bk. 3 (1110b)).

3 "Yet the will is moved to action by what can be seen" (*On Free Choice of the Will*, bk. 3, c. 25 (PL 32, 1307)).

The intrinsic means of prevention of heresies: The avoidance of vices

consideration of goodness or wickedness: as happens daily in those men who act without counsel or deliberation: not considering whether that which they decide to do is good or evil. After this choice of the will, the intellect often judges according to the command of the will, and hence it arises, that the man so judging, would sin. For although sin cannot be in the intellect, because it does not act freely: still there is sin in the will, by command and affection of which the intellect is moved, so that it would judge this or that.

The will's violent and unbridled affection certainly is able to completely overturn the reason's judgment. And this is what [the Wise Man[4]] says: "A soul that is hungry shall take even bitter for sweet" (Prov. 27, 7). And this is that blindness of soul which is caused by the malice of the will. For Solomon when speaking about the Jews who, motivated by hatred and envy, killed Christ Our Savior, says: "Their own malice blinded them" (Wis. 2, 21). Certainly at first they understood well from Sacred Scriptures, and from the prophecies of the times, and from the miracles performed by Him that Christ Our Savior is the true Messias promised in the Law, namely, when (according to the Savior's parable) they were saying: "This is the heir: come, let us kill him, and we shall have his inheritance" (Mt. 21, 38). But afterwards, because He was reproving and rebuking their evil ways, they were persecuting Him with irreconcilable hatred: and because they saw that the people were very fond of and full of confidence in Him, they burned with envy towards Him. Which [envy] took possession of their minds to such an extent that it completely blinded them so that they could not judge the truth about Him, or think anything good about Him. And according to this time it ought to be understood what Paul says: "If they had known it, they would never have crucified the Lord of glory" (I Cor. 2, 8). For they knew

---

4 Prov. 6, 6 is cited here, which in some codices contains words very similar to those found in Prov. 27, 7.

Him (as I said), but when they crucified Him, they were not then knowing: because their malice (as the Wise Man said) "blinded them."

And it seems to me that the philosophers and poets meant this when, wishing to depict love, they depicted it as being "blind." By which depiction they wished to teach us that our affections are a very clear reason why we often err and are impaired in our judgments.[5] From which blindness of mind heresies very easily arise. Hence [Hervé de Bourg-Dieu[6]] when expounding Paul's words, "That we be no more... carried about with every wind of doctrine by the wickedness of men" (Eph. 4, 14), says: "He said, 'By the wickedness of men,' because there is no heresy except in the soul subject to sins: because the sins committed are the causes for which God permits them to err into the abyss of heresy."[7] For this reason the demons, the very fierce enemies of the human race, wanting to lead men into various errors and heresies, firstly tempt their wills to sins, so that they, having been ardently affected, may afterwards make their intellects to come into the same opinion. For David had understood this very well, when speaking to the demons themselves, he was saying: "Depart from me, ye malignant: and I will search the commandments of my God" (Ps. 118, 115). He was in fact fearing to err in the investigation of God's Commandments, if the temptations of the malicious spirits had driven his will into sin. Which also we know was figured in those Philistines who (as sacred history relates[8]) were stopping up with a heap

---

5 "For the lover is blind in his view of the object loved, so that he is a bad judge of things just and good and noble, in that he deems himself bound always to value what is his own more than what is true" (Plato, *Laws*, bk. 5 (731e)).

6 The text here incorrectly cites St. Anselm.

7 *Commentaria in epistolas Pauli, In Epistolam ad Ephesios* (PL 181, 1248D).

8 Cf. Gen. 26, 14-15.

of dirt the wells which Isaac had dug, so that Isaac could not draw any clear water from them. Those wells seem to me to have represented the deep mysteries of Sacred Scripture, due to the fact that Solomon says: "Words from the mouth of a man are as deep water: and the fountain of wisdom is an overflowing stream" (Prov. 18, 4). Therefore a man digs wells with Isaac, who seeks after the hidden meanings of Sacred Scripture and the deep mysteries of God. But the Philistines secretly fill up those wells with earth: because to us seeking after Divine mysteries the demons throw in earthly thoughts, by which they could either allure or impel us if they could to sins, so that, having been filled with the love of earthly things, we could not draw out the water of true doctrine.

Since therefore from the aforementioned things it now becomes clear that an error of the intellect arises from sin and the malice of the will: whence it is that, just as there are various vices and sins in men, so also there are various roots and various seeds in them, from which various heresies can also arise. Sometimes heresies arise from pride and ambition, sometimes from avarice, and other times from the enticements of the flesh. Regarding pride it is unnecessary to make a long discussion so that we may show that it is the root of heresy, since the Wise Man clearly called it "the beginning of all sin" (Eccli. 10, 15). But although pride is the parent and origin of all sins, still for a special reason it can be called the mother more of heresies,[9] than of all other sins, because heresies arise more proximately from pride, than from all the other vices. For pride makes a man to think more highly of himself than he should, that he knows more than he actually knows, to think that he can do more than he

---

9 Cf. St. Augustine, *Against the Fundamental Epistle of the Manichaeus*, c. 6, n. 7: "What do we suppose to be the reason of this, but that pride, the mother of all heretics, impelled the man...?" (PL 42, 177).

can, and hence it happens that trusting too much his abilities and his prudence, he very easily errs, thinking that he by his abilities can understand every very difficult matter, and penetrate the hidden mysteries of Sacred Scripture by his own strength. Yet David was thinking the contrary, who says: "Give me understanding, and I will search thy law" (Ps. 118, 34). And again: "Open thou my eyes: and I will consider the wondrous things of thy law" (v. 18). Hence those men who when building the tower of Babel wanted to rise up to heaven,[10] seemed to some sacred Doctors to have signified heretics: who also like them strive to rise up to heaven, when relying on their own abilities strive to be able to lay open heavenly secrets. For [Pseudo-] Eucherius [of Lyons][11] interprets this history according to that meaning.[12]

It is assuredly great pride to walk among the great, and marvelous men above oneself: to contemn the judgment and opinions of all others, to attribute so much to one's own judgment so that one trusts only it, more than all others. In punishment of such great pride God strikes them with blindness of ignorance, so that they do not understand many things: but err very badly in those things which, if they would think humbly about themselves, they could very easily understand. For concerning this pride, which imagines many things about oneself, Paul says: "Their foolish heart was darkened. For professing themselves to be wise, they became fools" (Rom. 1, 21-22). And Solomon in Proverbs

---

10 Cf. Gen. 11, 4.

11 St. Eucherius, Bishop of Lyons, theologian, was born in the latter half of the fourth century; died about 449.

12 "Its tower is the pride of this world, or the wicked teachings of heretics, who after having moved away from the East, that is, having departed from the light, they immediately build the tower of their impiety against God, and they concoct the teachings of pride with nefarious boldness, wanting to penetrate the heights of heaven by an unlawful curiosity" (*Commentarii in Genesim*, bk. 2, c. 11 (PL 50, 941B-C)). Cf. St. Isidore of Seville, *Quaestiones in Veterum Testamentum*, c. 11 (PL 83, 237C-D).

says: "Where humility is, there also is wisdom" (Prov. 11, 2). By which words he seems to have attributed by opposition ignorance and error to pride. And Blessed Gregory says: "The light of truth is concealed from elated [and overbusied] minds."[13] Hence God threatens elated heretics, who are not afraid to prefer their own judgment to the judgment of the whole Church, through the prophet Ezechiel speaking thus: "Woe to the foolish prophets that follow their own spirit, and see nothing" (13, 3). He here called heretics "foolish prophets," to whom, because they follow their own spirit and not God's, blindness is given as punishment, so that they would see nothing. For Blessed Jerome in his commentaries on Ezechiel reckons that the aforesaid words ought to be understood of heretics, when speaking thus: "Although the name of 'prophets' according to the rule of Scriptures is common to the wicked and the good, they differ in that the good prophets are said to be wise, but the bad prophets stupid and foolish. One of which refers to ecclesiastical men, the other to all heretics, who, leaving the Spirit of God, follow their own spirit, because they by no means prophesy by a Divine instinct, but by their own heart: hence they also see nothing."[14] From which words it is very clearly established that the heresies of all heretics arise from the fact that they having been elated by pride want to follow their own spirit. For if they had wished to follow the spirit of the Church, which is certainly the spirit of God, they never would have wandered away from the correct rule of faith.

But these things have been said about pride in general. Wherefore it is necessary to add something about a certain species of it, which is called ambition, or the immoderate desire for honor, so that we may show in particular that it is the clear cause of heresy. Nearly all heretics, especially heresiarchs, desire the honors of the world, want to be

---

13 *Moralia*, bk. 27, c. 14 (PL 76, 414B).
14 *Commentaria in Ezechielem*, bk. 4 (PL 25, 109A-B).

esteemed by all, and to be held in high repute: which, since they do not hope that they may attain in another way, they take pains to concoct new heresies, so that by them they may be called teachers and leaders of the people. Moreover, it is very well known that ambition was the cause of many schisms: because many men wanting to rule others, and not wanting to be subjects, withdrew from obedience to those to whom they should have been subject, and in this way they made a schism. "But there is no schism" (so that I may use [Hervé de Bourg-Dieu's[15]] words) "that does not devise some heresy for itself, that it may appear to have had a reason for separating from the Church."[16] Going from the first to the last step by step, we may evidently gather that heresy often is born of ambition, because from ambition arises schism, and from schism heresy.

Ambition gave birth to the first heresy that arose after Christ's Ascension into heaven. For the well-known Simon Magus, whom Luke mentions in the Acts of the Apostles,[17] was (as Eusebius of Caesarea relates[18]) the inventor of the first heresy, agitated with such wild ambitions that he tried to be held as God by the people and adored as such, which afterwards he attained by the devil soliciting and God permitting. For Justin Martyr, in the Apology which he wrote in support of our faith to Emperor Antoninus [Pius], relates that under Claudius Caesar he was declared in Rome a god, and as such was given the honor of a statue. "Which statue," as Justin says, "was erected on the river Tiber, between the

---

15 The text here incorrectly cites St. Anselm.
16 *In epistolam ad Titum*, c. 3 (PL 181, 1503C-D).
17 Cf. Acts 8, 9 ff.
18 "We have understood that Simon was the author of all heresy... Simon was at that time so celebrated, and had acquired, by his jugglery, such influence over those who were deceived by him, that he was thought to be the Great Power of God" (*Church History*, bk. 2, c. 13, n. 6 (PG 20, 170A) & c. 1, n. 11 (137B)).

two bridges, and bore this inscription, in the language of Rome:—*Simoni Deo Sancto*, 'To Simon the holy God.'"[19] Whom Justin likewise relates almost all the Samaritans, and a few even of other nations, adored as the most high god.[20] From this so unbridled and Luciferian ambition arose that wish of buying (as Luke says in the Acts[21]) the gift of God for money, and from this wish arose the error of the intellect, whereby he believed that it could be lawfully done. On account of this alone, this Simon wanted to buy the power of communicating the power of the Holy Ghost, so that at least by this occasion the people would eagerly flock to him for God's gift to be imparted by him, and so having seen the novelty of such a great thing, the people would venerate him as God, to which he was very ardently aspiring.

And from this same root also arose the heresy of Aerius [of Sebaste] saying that a simple priest is entirely equal to a bishop, and there is no difference between them. For Epiphanius [of Salamis], in his book of eighty heresies when discussing about this Aerius, says that he seeing a certain Eustathius, his fellow student arrived at the episcopacy, which he could not attain, he thence began to disturb everything, and say that a bishop is not superior to a simple priest, so that at least in this way he could make himself equal to bishops.[22] The same thing happened to John Wycliffe, who (as Thomas Netter relates about him[23]) sought to gain the bishopric of Worchester in England, which because he could not attain, fell into the same error of Aerius, saying that there is completely no difference between a bishop and any other priest. I believe that exactly the same thing happened in our

---

19 *The First Apology*, c. 26 (PG 6, 142A).
20 *Ibid.*
21 Cf. Lk. 8, 18.
22 *Panarion*, bk. 2, heresy 55, nn. 1-2 (PG 42, 503B-506C).
23 *Doctrinale antiquitatum fidei Catholicae Ecclesiae*, vol. 1, bk. 2, art. 3, c. 60.

age to Luther, and to the many other heresiarchs who rose up after him, who although they are divided among themselves in many other doctrines, still they concordantly all think with Aerius and Wycliffe that all priests are equal, and they do not even acknowledge any bishop, nay, not even the Pope, to be superior by power and Order. Certainly those men all want to be bishops, and even Supreme Pontiffs, which if they would attain, they would not humble themselves, and would not so submit themselves that they would make priests of a lower order equal to themselves. Yet because they despair that they could attain this, lest they might seem to be subject to those whom they persecute with an irreconcilable hatred, they broke forth into this most pestilential heresy saying that neither is the Pope superior to the bishops, nor the bishops to the other priests.

Dathan and Abiron seem to me to have figured all these heretics, who longed for the priesthood which could not belong to them by the Law:[24] and for this reason they rose up against Moses and Aaron, and made a schism among the people. In this way the Lutherans and the other recent heretics strive to disunite the body of the holy Church, while they do not cease to lacerate, dishonor with wicked curses the head, which God gave to this body, that is, the Supreme Pontiff, and (what is the worst) to remove the head from the body. And nothing else is now done by these heretics than what was then attempted by Dathan and Abiron against Moses. Still the just God, just as He then punished those men with a horrendous and unusual death, will also cast all these men into hell, to be buried in perpetual oblivion.

The other root of heresies is avarice, as Paul very clearly taught when speaking thus: "They that will become rich, fall into temptation, and into the snare of the devil, and into many unprofitable and hurtful desires, which drown men into destruction and perdition. For the desire of money is

---

24 Cf. Num. 16.

the root of all evils; which some coveting have erred from the faith, and have entangled themselves in many sorrows" (I Tim. 6, 9-10). In the midst of the vessel which Zacharias the prophet saw going forth, a woman was sitting, who was called wickedness:[25] that that vessel signifies avarice, the Angel who was speaking to the prophet very clearly demonstrated by the name which he called the vessel. "This is," the Angel said to Zacharius, "their eye in all the earth" (Zach. 5, 6). Now there is nothing men have more in view than avarice. "From the least of them even to the greatest," says Jeremias the prophet, "all are given to covetousness" (6, 13). Thus wickedness [*impietas*] sits in the midst of the vessel, signifying the same thing to us as though he had more clearly said that in the very bowels of avarice sits the lack of religion and faith. For just as piety pertains to religion, so on the contrary impiety signifies the lack of religion. From this very wicked root, namely, avarice, that heresy of the Pharisees was born, whereby they were teaching the Jews that it is better to offer something in the Temple, than to provide for needy parents.[26] From the same pestilent root also arose the heresy of the Greeks who (as Guy the Carmelite relates about them[27]) said that usury is licit. Whence also arises the heresy of those who say that simony is licit.[28]

And avarice is not content by this alone that it generates heresies: but as a good mother it nourishes and fosters them,

---

25 Cf. Zach. 5.
26 Cf. Mt. 15, 5: "But you say: Whosoever shall say to father or mother, The gift whatsoever proceedeth from me, shall profit thee."
27 *Summa de haeresibus et earum confutationibus*, fols. 23r-24r, c. 9.
28 The Greeks fall into the same error, who, Guy the Carmelite bearing witness, say that it is permitted to buy ecclesiastical prelatures, and he asserts that it is done by their patriarch (Cf. *Summa de haeresibus*, c. 12, fol. 24v).

Book 3, Chapter 1

lest from a lack of nourishment they necessarily be forced to perish. For Blessed Job among the many things which he salubriously treats by a certain figure (as he is wont) about heretics, admixes this one, that "the root of junipers was their food" (30, 4). Blessed Gregory when interpreting these words says: "What then is there denoted by the 'root of the juniper' saving avarice, from which the thorns of all the sins are produced? Concerning which it is said by Paul, 'For the desire of money is the root of all evils' (I Tim. 6, 10). For that springs up covertly in the mind, and brings forth openly the prickles of all sin in the practice. Which same prickles arising from this root the great preacher immediately implies, when he subjoins, 'Which some coveting have erred from the faith, and have entangled themselves in many sorrows' (*Ibid.*). For he who spoke of 'many sorrows' made known as it were the prickles arising from this root. So by 'junipers' we understand sins, but by 'the root of junipers' what else do we understand, but avarice, that is, the material of sins? So then because heretics in their words generally go after external gains alone, yet are not ignorant that they concoct what is wrong, but do not abandon the preachings of error, whilst they wish to receive their emoluments as teachers, it is well said of them now by the voice of the holy man, 'and the root of junipers was their food,' because whilst they think of avarice with all the faculties of their minds, they are as it were fed by that nourishment, wherefrom assuredly the prickles of sins ensuing are used to be produced. Which persons if ever in Holy Writ they seemingly discover things with sagacity, which while they do not understand, they fancy make for their statements, they directly scatter these, vociferating them to their wretched hearers, whom they covet not the souls of but the substance."[29]

And as it is certainly permitted to suspect from many reasonable inferences, I am of the opinion that many of these

---

[29] *Moralia*, bk. 20, c. 10 (PL 76, 150A-C).

The intrinsic means of prevention of heresies: The avoidance of vices

recent heretics, who now reside in Germany, are held back solely by avarice from not recovering their senses. For (as I hear) public, and not small, stipends are assigned to them in the cities. And I have read about some of them that for this reason alone are they greatly enriched, who nevertheless previously did not have enough for their living. Therefore lest they lose these riches which they desire very much, they do not want to depart from the heresies, although they inwardly recognize that they have erred. And it is not my intention to say many things now about this root, because I have made a longer discussion about this matter above when I discussed about the punishment of heretics.

Lastly, the third parent and origin of heresies is the pleasure of the flesh, which by a certain gentle and sweet violence draws the intellect to the affection of the will, although before it vehemently resisted the will. For the enticements of the flesh are wont to be much more powerful in this matter, than honors and riches. The prophet Isaias clearly teaches that the pleasure of the flesh lessens the intellect's sharpness, and often darkens it, so that the carnal man is unable to understand the hidden mysteries of the faith, when saying: "Whom shall he make to understand the hearing?" Now responding to this question the prophet himself says: "Them that are weaned from the milk, that are drawn away from the breasts" (28, 9), that is, separated from the pleasures of the flesh. But because God makes only these men to understand the mysteries of the faith, which are said to them, it necessarily follows that those who are not weaned from the enticements of the flesh do not understand the things which they have heard: because those enticements dull the intellect, and sometimes completely darken it. "The bewitching of vanity," Solomon says, "obscureth good things, and the wandering of concupiscence overturneth the innocent mind" (Wis. 4, 12). Thus from this it happens that he who excessively loves the pleasures of the flesh, and runs after them without restraint, says that they are good, and thinks that they are licit, and in this way falls into heresy.

Wherefore Paul when writing to the Romans says: "Now I beseech you, brethren, to mark them who make dissensions and offences contrary to the doctrine which you have learned, and avoid them. For they that are such, serve not Christ our Lord, but their own belly" (16, 17-18). Theophylactus when interpreting these words says: "All heresies then are born from this, that their authors are attached to their affections and their belly."[30] And again in the Epistle to the Ephesians he does not request this same thing, but commands when speaking thus: "This then I say and testify in the Lord: That henceforward you walk not as also the Gentiles walk in the vanity of their mind, having their understanding darkened, being alienated from the life of God through the ignorance that is in them, because of the blindness of their hearts. Who despairing, have given themselves up to lasciviousness, unto the working of all uncleanness" (4, 17-19). Behold you see Paul saying that ignorance, obscurity, darkness, and finally blindness of heart happened to the Gentiles from lasciviousness and uncleanness. For which reason he admonishes the Ephesians and testifies in the Lord, that they abstain from those vices, lest they fall into similar darkness and blindness of heart.

Furthermore, among the many species of lust which Blessed Gregory enumerates, one is blindness of the mind;[31] which he would not have done unless he certainly knew that blindness of the mind is generated from the lust of the flesh as from a most certain mother. The very wicked old men who burned with the desire of Susanna (as sacred history

---

30 *Commentarius in Epistolam ad Romanos* (PG 124, 555B).

31 "From lust are generated blindness of mind, inconsiderateness, inconstancy, precipitation, self-love, hatred of God, affection for this present world, but dread or despair of that which is to come" (*Moralia*, bk. 31, c. 45 (PL 76, 621B)).

The intrinsic means of prevention of heresies: The avoidance of vices

teaches) "perverted their own mind and turned away their eyes that they might not look unto heaven, nor remember just judgments" (Dan. 13, 9). The renowned Samson, the strongest of all men, would never have been blinded by the Philistines unless he had firstly lost his fortitude in the arms of Dalila.[32] So likewise our soul, which through the power of the will was made so strong by God, that it could not be forced by anyone, and succumb to anything except when willing, because firstly when deviating towards the pleasures of the flesh, it becomes soft, it does not make use of its native strength, wherefore it is blinded, so that it cannot distinguish true and false things: but it thinks that the pleasures of the flesh are not merely licit, but are good in the highest degree.

Although there are so many examples of this matter, it is necessary to bring forward some, so that at least from this we may persuade the reader that what we say is true. Without a doubt from this root came forth Basilides, who taught that any foul lusts are lawful. For he was (as Epiphanius relates about him[33]) a lustful man and loving every depravity of the flesh. Thence also the heresy of Cerinthus, who taught that there would be the pleasures of the flesh in the promised beatitude;[34] from this root the sect of the Adamites came forth. Whence also the Anabaptists in our age, who, along with the other older heretics, permit the promiscuous and

---

32 Cf. Judges 16.
33 "Basilides gives his disciples permission to perform the whole of every kind of badness and licentiousness, and gives his converts full instruction in the promiscuous intercourse of an evil kind between men and women" (*Panarion*, bk. 1, heresy 24, c. 3, n. 7 (PG 41, 314A)).
34 "The flesh dwelling in Jerusalem will again be subject to desires and pleasures. And being an enemy of the Scriptures of God, he asserts, with the purpose of deceiving men, that there is to be a period of a thousand years for marriage festivals" (Eusebius of Caesarea, *Church History*, bk. 3, c. 28, n. 2 (PG 20, 274)).

indeterminate union of the sexes. Hence the renowned heresy of Aerius was completely rejecting the obligation, virtue, and merit of fasting. From the same root came forth Jovinian equating marriage to virginity. From the same was born the heresy the Beghards and Beguines teaching that all coition, with burning lust of the flesh, is licit. Thence also, as it can be known to all, arise the greater part of the heresies which exist today in Germany. For nearly that whole region is given over to drinking parties, surfeiting, and other excessive pleasures of the flesh. And thus Martin Luther, their false prophet, having been persuaded by the old enemy of the human race, decided to preach and teach those things, which he knew was pleasing to them, and hence would be willingly accepted by them.

Notice that we have now shown the three roots from which, just like all the other sins (as John says[35]), heresies also arise. These are honors, riches, and pleasures. Add to this that these sins are not only the causes why the sinners themselves, their perpetrators, err: but also some good teachers err from those things they ought to teach. For just as on account of the sins of the people God permits bad rulers, so also false teachers.

Concerning bad rulers it is said in the book of Job: "He maketh a man that is a hypocrite to reign for the sins of the people" (34, 30). Blessed Gregory when interpreting this passage says: "The conduct of rulers is so ordered with reference to the characters of their subjects, that frequently the conduct of even a truly good shepherd becomes sinful, in consequence of the wickedness of his flock. For that Prophet David, who had been praised by the witness of God Himself, who had been made acquainted with heavenly mysteries, being puffed up by the swelling of sudden pride, sinned in numbering the people. And yet, though David sinned, the

---

35 "All that is in the world, is the concupiscence of the flesh, and the concupiscence of the eyes, and the pride of life, which is not of the Father, but is of the world" (I Jn. 2, 16).

The intrinsic means of prevention of heresies: The avoidance of vices

people endured the punishment.[36] Why was this? Because in truth the hearts of rulers are disposed according to the deserts of their people. But the righteous Judge reproved the fault of the sinner, by the punishment of those very persons, on whose account he sinned."[37]

Concerning the bad teachers and false prophets, who on account of the sins of the people are sent by God to them, Paul clearly teaches when speaking thus: "Because they receive not the love of the truth, that they might be saved. Therefore God shall send them the operation of error, to believe lying" (II Thess. 2, 10). And God not only sends bad teachers to the people on account of their sins, but what is more astonishing, He permits otherwise good and true teachers to err on account of the iniquity of the people or a particular man seeking teaching. About this matter God Himself gives testimony through the prophet Ezechiel speaking thus: "The man that shall place his uncleannesses in his heart, and set up the stumblingblock of his iniquity before his face, and shall come to the prophet inquiring of me by him: I the Lord will answer him according to the multitude of his uncleannesses... And when the prophet shall err, and speak a word: I the Lord have deceived that prophet: and I will stretch forth my hand upon him, and will cut him off from the midst of my people Israel. And they shall bear their iniquity: according to the iniquity of him that inquireth, so shall the iniquity of the prophet be" (14, vv. 4 & 9-10). And just as God threatened with words, so Holy Writ testifies that He also carried it out in reality. For when Achab the king of Israel asked about four hundred prophets whether he should go out to attack Ramoth Galaad, he next consulted Micheas the prophet of the Lord about the same thing, who said to the king: "I saw the Lord sitting on his throne, and all the army of heaven standing by him on the right hand and on the left: and the Lord said: Who shall

---

36 Cf. II Kings 24, 1-17.
37 *Moralia*, bk. 25, c. 16 (PL 76, 344B-C).

deceive Achab king of Israel, that he may go up, and fall at Ramoth Galaad? And one spoke words of this manner, and another otherwise. And there came forth a spirit, and stood before the Lord, and said: I will deceive him. And the Lord said to him: By what means? And he said: I will go forth, and be a lying spirit in the mouth of all his prophets. And the Lord said: Thou shalt deceive him, and shalt prevail: go forth, and do so" (III Kings 22, 19-22). There could not be clearer and more certain testimony for confirming those things which we have asserted. Achab certainly was a wicked king, and hence according to his iniquity God gave prophets similar to him who would deceive him. Wherefore I reckon that God, on account the many sins of Germany, whether public or hidden, which He knew very well, gave so many heresiarchs to that region, who would teach it so perversely and lead it into such detestable errors. And I can persuade myself of nothing else except that according to its iniquity (as He had threatened through the prophet Ezechiel) He gave wicked and deceptive teachers.

From all these very clear testimonies of Sacred Scripture it is established that it is most evident that the principle and most certain cause of all heresies is sin. Yet this cause of heresies the rulers of the Christian world, whether they be ecclesiastical or secular, cannot completely remove. Because the sin of any man, since it depends upon his will, so that it can be called sin, no ruler, whoever he may be, cannot completely prevent it from being committed by another: because he cannot force the will of another, to pursue good and depart from evil. He certainly can encourage to the good by words and rewards, and dissuade from evil by many reasons, and call away from it by threats: yet it is not possible to force the will to either of these. He can also force that men would not do many sins exteriorly in deed, yet no ruler, no matter how powerful, is able to effect that they would not interiorly desire those sins. Thus all men themselves, because

The intrinsic means of prevention of heresies: The avoidance of vices

they have power over their own free will, can with God's help remove this cause of heresies in themselves. Therefore whoever desires to keep himself unharmed from heresies, ought to firstly strive to avoid vices, lest having been blinded he stray through any deviant errors, and stumbling fall into the pit of heresies.

But if he has already been blinded, and fallen into heresy, no other way lies open for recovering his sight except that with the blind man sitting by the wayside he would cry out to the Lord and say: "Jesus, son of David, have mercy on me" (Lk. 18, 38). Heretics, however, will not be lacking who will rebuke him so crying out that he be silent, and would say that prayer is not necessary for him, since those who have the right faith, also ought to persist in it. But to those so rebuking, he all the more (as the blind man sitting by the wayside) ought to cry out to the Lord, and suppliantly and importunely implore His mercy. Now in order that he may be heard by God, it is necessary that he forsake all past vices, that he flee ambition, avoid avarice, cast far away from himself the pleasures of the flesh as an instantaneous poison. He ought to lament past sins, and every night, imitating the Royal Prophet, wash his bed, and water his couch with his tears.[38] Then he will exchange his life for a better one, so that henceforth he would strive to keep the Divine Commandments until the last one. Because if he does, God is compassionate Who will not abandon him in his blindness, but will enlighten his eyes, so that he may acknowledge his former error, and having forsaken it, return very quickly to the Catholic faith which he had previously abandoned. For Paul teaches this when saying: "Rise thou that sleepest, and arise from the dead: and Christ shall enlighten thee" (Eph. 5, 14). He demands that the sinner rise first, and then He promises enlightenment.

Whence it is that when the Law was given to the children of Israel, and to others not understanding the miracles which

---

38 Cf. Ps. 6, 7.

the Lord had done, and was daily doing for them, Moses was saying to them: "Keep therefore the words of this covenant, and fulfill them: that you may understand all that you do" (Deut. 29, 9). By which words Moses taught clearly enough that a transgression of God's Commandments is the chief reason why the Jews did not understand, and did not see how much God had done for them, wherefore he recalls them from the transgression to the fulfillment of God's Commandments, so that the cause of blindness and ignorance having been removed, they could understand those things which one ought to understand. The prophet Jeremias says that he was instructed [*eruditum*[39]], not by his own intelligence, but by the fire sent from above by God into his bones. [He was instructed] by that fire, I say, which the Lord Jesus Christ came to cast on the earth.[40] And John the Evangelist testifies that the anointing of the Spirit is that which instructs us about all things necessary for salvation.[41] And Christ Our Savior, so that He might open the Scriptures to the two disciples going to Emmaus, firstly enflamed their hearts. About which matter they bear witness themselves, when they were saying: "Was not our heart burning within us, whilst he spoke in this way, and opened to us the scriptures?" (Lk. 24, 32). He who desires to penetrate the Divine Scriptures certainly ought to be ardent and inflamed with Divine love. Therefore, can those sinners who have been ensnared by many vices, who have made their malice cold like cistern water, without any spark of Divine love penetrate the profound mysteries of Sacred Scripture? About John the Baptist, than whom among

---

[39] The Douay-Rheims translation here has "chastised" as the translation of *erudivit*, but the verb *erudio* can also mean to educate or instruct. Cf. Lam. 1, 13: "From above he hath sent fire into my bones, and hath chastised me."
[40] Cf. Lk. 12, 49.
[41] Cf. I Jn. 2, vv. 20 & 27.

those born of women no greater prophet has risen,[42] John the Evangelist says that "He was a burning and a shining light" (Jn. 5, 35). First "burning," then "shining." He was burning by his affection: he was shining by his understanding. He was burning to himself and within himself: he was shining to others and himself. Unless he were burning within himself, he could not have shone, neither to himself nor to others.

Therefore all you Germans who have given your names to Luther and to others of the same sort, and have shown by his words, I exhort in the bowels of charity, and I adjure you through the wounds of Christ Our Savior, that if you have any regard for your salvation, "Do penance therefore for this thy wickedness; and pray to God, that perhaps this thought of thy heart may be forgiven thee. For I see thou art in the gall of bitterness, and in the bonds of iniquity" (Acts 8, 22-23). We, as supplicants for you, implore God Himself that He would deign to lead you back as erring sheep to His sheepfold. But unless you yourselves have a concern for your salvation, and labor for obtaining it through prayer, we alone distrust to obtain through prayer your salvation from God. For God said through the prophet Isaias concerning others very similar to you: "For they seek me from day to day, and desire to know my ways, as a nation that hath done justice, and hath not forsaken the judgment of their God: they ask of me the judgments of justice: they are willing to approach to God" (58, 2). If you then wish to know the true faith from God, you firstly ought to do justice, and keep God's Commandments, and it is necessary to draw your steps near to God through good works, otherwise God will mock you and say, "They ask of me the judgments of justice: they are unwilling to approach to God."

---

42 Cf. Lk, 7, 28; Mt. 11, 11.

Chapter II

The first extrinsic cause of heresies, which is the lack of preaching God's word, which if it is taken away, it opens the door for many heresies to arise.

There are many other causes of heresy besides sin, which we can say are extrinsic or (if you prefer) external, because they do not give an occasion of heresy to the same person in which they are in, but to others. Which because rulers and Pontiffs can more easily and conveniently preclude, hence I decided to discuss about these individually and to make a longer treatment about each one. The first cause of heresies from these external things is the lack of preaching of God's word. For the preaching of God's word is highly necessary, without which no one, even though baptized, could attain the true Catholic faith, and persevere in it without error. For those things which God obliges us to believe are so lofty that they exceed all power of the human intellect. For Paul when defining faith gave this as a sort of characteristic of it, namely, that those things which it proposes to be believed by us cannot be comprehended by the intellect by its own strength. For he speaks thus: "Faith is the substance of things to be hoped for, the evidence of things that appear not" (Heb. 11, 1). Theophylactus when interpreting these words says: "'Evidence,' that is, a demonstration of things that are not apparent. For it makes it so that we may perceive these things with our mind, not otherwise than if they were present. If, therefore, faith can accomplish such things, why would you want to actually see them, so as to fall away from faith?"[1] Furthermore, the Apostle teaches the same thing in the First Epistle to the Corinthians in other words, when speaking thus: "My speech and my preaching

---

1 *Expositio in Epistolam ad Hebraeos* (PG 125, 342A).

was not in the persuasive words of human wisdom, but in shewing of the Spirit and power that your faith might not stand on the wisdom of men, but on the power of God" (2, 4-5).

If we can attain solely by our own power of the intellect those things which we believe by faith, our faith certainly would be in the wisdom of men. Thus, since Paul says that our faith was not in the wisdom of men, by this same thing he teaches us that the mysteries of our faith surpass all power of human understanding. Moses' rod devoured the rod of the Egyptian magicians.[2] In which thing it is given to us to understand by a mystery that faith and the Evangelical teaching surpass the knowledge of all philosophers. And this is what God foretold through the prophet Abdias speaking thus: "I shall destroy the wise out of Edom" (1, 8). From which things it is very evidently gathered that anyone relying on merely the natural power of the intellect, who would want to penetrate the mysteries of the faith, would necessarily err. For the sun by its bright shining beams (as the Wise Man says) blinds the eyes.[3] Whence it is that in the Mosaic Law it was avoided that anyone would lift up a tool upon the altar.[4] By which figure of things (as the sacred Doctors interpret) it was figured that we ought not to want to penetrate by the acumen of ingenuity the mysteries of the Catholic faith, which were signified by the word "altar," as Gregory teaches, speaking thus: "To make an altar of earth for the Lord is to trust in the Incarnation of our Mediator. For then our gift is received by God, when our humility has placed upon His Altar, that is, upon the belief of our Lord's Incarnation, all the works that it performs."[5] Upon this altar a tool ought not to be lifted up, otherwise the altar would be polluted,

---

2 Cf. Ex. 7, 12.
3 Cf. Eccli. 43, 4.
4 Cf. Ex. 20, 25.
5 *Moralia*, bk. 3, c. 26 (PL 75, 624C).

because the Catholic faith ought not to be scrutinized by the natural acumen of the intellect alone, otherwise the faith of him who would want to penetrate with the acumen of his ingenuity will be contaminated.

Nevertheless, if the intellect was helped by the faith, it will easily penetrate all the mysteries, no matter how hidden: because faith raises up the intellect on high, and gives light to it, by which it can see and understand. Hence Blessed Basil when interpreting Psalm 115 says: "Faith is superior to rational methodologies when it comes to drawing the soul to assent. It is not the logical necessity of deductive proofs that engenders faith, but the activity of the Spirit. 'In the name of Jesus Christ of Nazareth, arise, and walk' (Acts 3, 6). What followed this command was the work of the Spirit, and those who witnessed this miracle were compelled to admit the Divinity of the Only-Begotten. Tell me, what is more compelling for assent, a complicated set of syllogistic premises entailing the logical conclusion, or a clearly seen miracle so great that it surpasses all that is humanly possible?... So then, in this way too the mystery of theology requires assent based on unquestioning faith."[6] And Blessed Augustine teaches the same opinion more clearly, speaking thus: "Believers firstly seek the mysteries and secrets of the kingdom of God, that they may understand. For faith is understanding's step; and understanding faith's attainment. This the prophet expressly says to all who prematurely and in undue order look for understanding, and neglect faith. For he says, 'Unless ye believe, ye shall not understand' (Is. 7, 9).[7] Faith itself then also has a certain light of its own in

---

6 *Homilia in Psalmum CXV* (PG 30, 103B & 106A).

7 St. Augustine uses the Old Latin translation, which is closer to the Septuagint version—μὴ πιστεύσητε, οὐδὲ μὴ συνιῆτε. In the Vulgate this verse is translated as: *nisi credideritis, non permanebitis* ("If you will not believe, you shall not continue"). Cf. *On Christian Doctrine*, bk. 2, c. 12, n. 17 (PL 34, 43) for St. Au-

the Scriptures, in prophecy, in the Gospel, in the Apostolic readings... You see then, brethren, how exceedingly unregulated and disordered in their haste are they who like immature conceptions seek an untimely birth before the birth; who say to us, 'Why do you ask me to believe what I do not see? Let me see something that I may believe. You ask me to believe while I still do not see; I wish to see, and by seeing to believe, not by hearing.' Let the prophet speak. 'Unless ye believe, ye shall not understand.' You wish to ascend, but you forget the steps. Surely, out of all order. O man, if I could show you already what you might see, I should not exhort you to believe."[8]

But here it is necessary to warn the reader not to think that this virtue should be attributed to all faith, namely, that it can help the understanding to perceiving that the secrets and mysteries of the kingdom of God, as we have now stated, according to the testimony of the holy Doctors, are in agreement with faith. For we reckon that this ought to be understood only about acquired faith. For infused faith alone, which is given through Baptism, without the living voice of some teacher exteriorly teaching, according to the unanimous opinion of all theologians, does not suffice for understanding those Divine mysteries, nor for believing them. For the preaching of God's word is necessary, through which the hearers may be instructed about those things which they are obliged to believe. Infused faith, however, gives to the hearer only this, that he may more easily believe those things which he heard from the preacher or teacher. "How shall they believe him," Paul says, "of whom they have not heard? And how shall they hear, without a preacher? ...as it is written: How beautiful are the feet of them that preach the gospel of peace, of them that bring glad tidings of good things!"[9] But

---

gustine's reconciliation of these two different translations.
8 Sermon 126, c. 1, nn. 1-2 (PL 38, 698).
9 Cf. Is. 52, 7; Nah. 1, 15; Rom. 10, 14-15

First extrinsic cause of heresies: The lack of preaching God's word

all do not obey the gospel. For Isaias saith: Lord, who hath believed our report?[10] Faith then cometh by hearing; and hearing by the word of Christ" (Rom. 10, 14-17). By these words Paul very clearly teaches that the preaching of God's word is necessary for obtaining faith in the Divine mysteries. Thus I reckon that the eunuch of Queen Candace spoke wisely, who, when reading the prophet Isaias, was asked by Philip whether he understood what he read, responded: "And how can I, unless some man shew me?" (Acts 8, 31). For he reckoned that those mysteries are so deep that he thought that no one without a teacher could comprehend them.

And not only is preaching God's word necessary for firstly receiving the faith: but also for nourishing and keeping it after it has been received, especially in those who are uneducated and very forgetful. For these require the constant preaching of God's word, or other frequent teaching, so that they could say well the mysteries of faith, and retain what they have learned. Otherwise they will neither learn completely nor fully retain, and in this way faith once begun will easily perish merely on account of the lack of preaching. Now anyone will be convinced of this if he understands the characteristics and conditions of God's word. For God's word is so to speak the food of the soul, which nourishes, increases, and perfects it in faith and the other virtues. For that God's word is so to speak the spiritual food of the soul, Truth Itself taught us, for when rejecting Satan's temptation, He said: "Not in bread alone doth man live, but in every word that proceedeth from the mouth of God" (Mt. 4, 4). In which words the Savior showed that there are various foods of man according to the variety of the parts of which the same man is composed. For it is evident that man is composed of body and soul: the food of the body is material and corporeal bread: but the food of the soul is God's word.

---

10 Cf. Is. 53, 1.

For this reason many of the sacred Doctors think that God's word was figured in the manna, which God gave to the hungry children of Israel in the desert. For the nature of that food was of such and so great strength, that it supplied every need, and satisfied the appetite of all, giving to everyone whatever taste, whether meat, or fish, or eggs, or fruit he desired.[11] And in this way God's word now has the taste of every virtue, and relieves the needs of all.[12] For to the proud, the haughty, the ravenous, the gluttons, those who feast, the lustful, the greedy, and all other sinners by whatever name they are called, God's word gives the necessary remedies by which they can save their souls. That manna was also soothing and sweet; and God's word seems very sweet to those who rightly savor it. For the Royal Prophet, who had good taste, was saying: "How sweet are thy words to my palate! more than honey to my mouth" (Ps. 118, 103).

Origen moreover assigns another comparison between these two things when speaking thus: "It is written about the manna of that time that if one received it in the way God had commanded, he would be nourished by it; but if one wanted to receive it contrary to God's command and contrary to the Divinely established manner, he would not enjoy it as life-giving food, but worms would spring forth from it.[13] And thus it came to pass that one and the same kind of manna generated for some worms and putrefaction, but for others it gave food that was health-giving and necessary for life. Now then, our manna is God's word, and with us God's word is effective for salvation for some, but for others

---

11 Cf. Wisdom 16, 20; St. Cyril of Alexandria, *In Joannis Evangelium*, bk. 4, c. 2 (PG 73, 582-583), cited in *Against All Heresies*, s. v., *Eucharistia*, p. 415.

12 Cf. Wis. 16, 25: "Therefore even then it was transformed into all things, and was obedient to thy grace that nourisheth all, according to the will of them that desired it of thee."

13 Cf. Ex. 16, 20.

it yields punishment."[14] Blessed Ambrose shows still many more comparisons between God's word and manna in his letter [sixty-four[15]], all of which I prudently omit, for the sake of avoiding prolixity, thinking that I have done enough, that I have indicated the place to the reader, when he could lay hold of them if he wishes.

Sacred Scripture calls the word of God not only by the name of food, but also by the name of drink, so that assuredly by these two names it would show that it is the complete nourishment of the soul: since drink is no less necessary than food for nutrition. For Christ Our Savior very clearly shows that God's word is drink when preaching to the people, and calling all to His teaching, He cried out, saying: "If any man thirst, let him come to me, and drink" (Jn. 7, 37). He said that they "thirst," who had desired the Savior's doctrine, and He invites them to "drink," that is, to hear the words which He was preaching, whence anyone could be abundantly taught. Then those who had heard Christ preaching, could afterwards say, as the same Savior relates: "We have eaten and drunk in thy presence" (Lk. 13, 26). Now in order to express what food they had eaten and what drink they drank, they immediately subjoin: "Thou hast taught in our streets." By which words they clearly declare that God's preached word

---

14 *In Numeros*, homily 3 (PG 12, 593C-D).
15 Letter to Irenaeus (PL 16, 1219B-1222A). St. Ambrose replies herein to Irenaeus, who had asked why the manna, which was given to the children of Israel, was not given now that the Body of Christ, Which has been given to Christians, is the true Manna, of which the other was a type; as it was also of Divine Wisdom, which is the food of souls. The text cites according to the references of his time, "letter 62 in book 8" of St. Ambrose's letters. Cf. *Omnia quotquot extant D. Ambrosii episcopi Mediolanensis opera, primum per Des. Erasmum Roterodamum* (Basel: per Hieronymum Frobenium, et Nicolaum Episcopium, 1555), pp. 163-165.

is the soul's food, and also is its drink. Indeed, from this we may understand that the preaching of the Word of God is just as necessary for the salvation of the soul as corporeal food and drink are necessary for preserving the life of the body. For Blessed [John] Chrysostom stated this reason, who speaks thus: "For as we eat the bread of this world daily, so he means, let us be continually receiving discourses concerning the faith, and ever be nourished with them."[16] If God's word is deemed to be the food and drink of the soul, it follows that when those who cannot receive doctrine from elsewhere lack its preaching, they will be without the Catholic faith which (as Paul said above[17]) without the preaching of God's word no one can by himself acquire.

There can be still another consideration of God's word from which it can also be easily proved that its removal is a most certain cause of heresies. For God's word is the light, by means of which, whoever wishes to see what to do and wither to direct his steps, can easily see. "Thy word is a lamp to my feet," says the Royal Prophet, "and a light to my paths" (Ps. 118, 105). If you take away a lamp from him who walks in darkness, that absence of light will effect that the one walking also would stumble every third step. As Aristotle says, the absence of the pilot is the cause of the ship's sinking.[18] Because if he were present, by his diligence he could have kept the ship intact. In the same way it ought to be said about God's word, which, if it were preached, would have enlightened the hearers, so that they would not stumble or wander from the path. From which it necessarily follows

---

16 *Homiliae XVIII In epistolam primam ad Timoteum*, c. 4, hom. 12, n. 2 (PG 62, 559).

17 Rom. 10, 14-17.

18 "Thus, if the pilot's presence would have brought the ship safe to the harbor, we say that he caused its wreck by his absence" (*Physics*, bk. 2, c. 3 (195a14), in *Aristotle: The Physics* (Cambridge: Harvard University Press, 1970), p. 133).

First extrinsic cause of heresies: The lack of preaching God's word

that when its preaching has been removed, all wayfarers, who are in this world, will deviate from the path of salvation.

Hence Paul understanding well this need of preaching God's word, writes to Bishop Timothy and his disciple exhorting and encouraging to frequent preaching of the word of God, speaking thus: "I charge thee, before God and Jesus Christ, who shall judge the living and the dead, by his coming and his kingdom, preach the word: be instant in season, out of season" (II Tim. 4, 1-2). Now why he commands to act "in season and out of season" in preaching God's word, he states a few words later, speaking thus: "For there shall be a time, when they will not endure sound doctrine; but, according to their own desires, they will heap to themselves teachers, having itching ears: and will indeed turn away their hearing from the truth, but will be turned unto fables. But be thou vigilant, labour in all things, do the work of an evangelist" (vv. 3-5). Paul indeed had known that there would be many who would err in the faith: hence he admonishes Timothy not to cease from preaching, but instead preach the Gospel very frequently, so that heresies could be better hindered, so that they would not arise.

God also commands that same thing to the prophet Isaias when speaking thus: "Cry, cease not, lift up thy voice like a trumpet, and shew my people their wicked doings, and the house of Jacob their sins" (58, 1). For preachers are in some way like God's dogs, who ought to guard God's flock, which is the Church, by their barking. If they bark very much the wolves will be afraid to attack the flock: but if the dogs sleep, or are silent, the wolves then become more bold from the dogs' silence, and attack the flock with so much more confidence, the more they think that they can harm more securely. I reckon that entirely the same thing ought to be said about the preachers of God's word, which if they cry out continually and from the heart (as is befitting) against heresies and other vices, by their barking they would drive away not only heretics and heresies, but all the rest of the vices, which lay waste to the Lord's flock: yet if they would be silent, and not want to preach, they will harm the Lord's sheep by their silence. For then the demons and their ministers, the heretics, attack them more boldly, and they can harm all the more easily, the more there is lacking one who strikes them with terror, warns them about fleeing, so that they may take care of themselves. And God Himself stated though the prophet Isaias that long ago this was the main reason for the evils of the synagogue, speaking thus: "All are dumb dogs, unable to bark" (56, 10). Jerome when interpreting these words speaks thus: "But those about whom the prophet now speaks are not only 'blind watchmen,' but they are also called 'dumb dogs,' unable to bark. For those who ought to have protected the Lord's flock, and drive away the wolves, and bark for the Lord, love dreams, and delight in demonic visions."[19]

About this matter, which I believe is very clear, it does not seem to me to be necessary to bring forth many examples, because even if the matter were doubtful, and would need to be proved from examples, so many could be at hand, that there is no kingdom which cannot give examples in support of this matter. For I, who have traversed many and various regions of the Christian world, and spent a long time in some of them, taught by experience, I have known that those men who live in mountainous and sparsely populated places, and very rarely hear the preaching of God's word, were infected with many more errors and superstitions, than those men to whom God's word is frequently preached. From which it is very evidently gathered that the lack of preaching of God's word is the main cause that they were falling into such errors: because if they were instructed as the others, they would also be free from those errors, just as those are free from them, who frequently hear sermons of God's word.

---

[19] *Commentaria in Isaiam prophetam*, bk. 15, c. 56 (PL 24, 544B).

First extrinsic cause of heresies: The lack of preaching God's word

It would be just that rulers of both ranks, that is, ecclesiastical and secular, would very diligently obviate this very manifest cause of heresy. But this is more incumbent upon ecclesiastical prelates, to whom the care of souls was given by God. For these are they who are held to teach God's people, and from whom God's people can by right ask for God's doctrine, as the Lord says through Malachias the prophet: "The lips of the priest shall keep knowledge, and they shall seek the law at his mouth: because he is the angel of the Lord of hosts" (2, 7). And so no one (as I will say in another chapter of this third book) ought to be appointed the pastor of souls, except he who has been instructed with at least a moderate education, so that he could teach the people the correct faith and good morals and exhort them. But so great is the unhappiness of our age, that learned pastors, when compared to other unlearned and completely ignorant ones, are like gems in comparison to a number of cheap stones. And if some are educated pastors, who can instruct well the flock committed to them in the faith and morals, still the greater part of them are led by so great and such blind pride, that they disdain to do it, as if the office of preaching were something vile and ignominious. There certainly is not a higher and more honorable function in the Church than the function of preaching, by which the preacher, if he rightly exercises that duty, represents God more. For it is the true function of Apostles, to whom Christ Our Savior, when ascending from this world to the Father, commanded nothing else in like manner as the preaching of the Gospel. "Go ye," He says, "into the whole world, and preach the gospel to every creature" (Mk. 16, 15).

What I consider should be done in this regard, that is, to address the rampant disease, or at least in some part, I will explain briefly. Bishops may oblige the pastors of souls, if there are any who are learned, that they themselves feed the flock committed to them, teach it about the things that ought to be done and believed, and always exhort and admonish it. If the pastors of souls are unlearned, they should oblige them to hire preachers from their revenues, who may supply for their deficiency. If bishops are negligent in this (as very many of them are wont to be), then the secular rulers ought to come to the aid of such gross negligence of the bishops. For they ought to exhort the bishops to appoint good pastors, who can feed the flock committed to them, to distribute preachers, and provide for each people according to the need: if the bishops neglect to do this, I reckon that one ought not to proceed further, lest perhaps if forced, and they do it not from the heart, they may present such preachers to the people, that it would be perhaps better to lack them, than to have them. For they may not seek after (as we see very many of them to do in other matters) the more learned and better, and who could benefit the people more: but those whom they could hire for a small wage.

And still I still do not consider that this matter is completely hopeless, on account of the negligence of the bishops or the other pastors, and ought to be left as such. For then (as I think) the princes and other secular rulers ought to take care of this matter, lest those whom they govern lack the Catholic faith and Christian morals. For one hand helps the other, and one arm ought to assist the other. Members ought to assist each other, when one of them needs the other. If the right arm is not able, or perhaps does not want, to hold up food to the mouth to preserve the life of the body, ought not the left arm take up this labor? Certainly it ought, lest the whole body, and along with the body the arm itself, perish for want of food. For there are as it were two arms of the body, two Christian powers in the world, one ecclesiastical, the other secular and lay. Therefore if the ecclesiastical power, as it is incumbent upon it to do from its office, neglects to offer the food of God's word to the people, then the secular princes and other lords, and rulers of the people in the face of

First extrinsic cause of heresies: The lack of preaching God's word

such great need, ought to provide assistance to the extent they are able, so as not to allow souls to perish due to a lack of spiritual nourishment. They ought to diligently seek after good and learned men, and if it were possible, those who are eloquent, to whom from the public treasury of the city or town, according to the merit of the person or labor, they may assign the wages, so that they may instruct the people on some fixed number of days of the year on faith and morals. And I reckon that what especially ought to be procured, is that common teachers for children, hired from the public treasury, ought to be assigned, who may correctly instruct them in faith and morals. For, as Solomon says, "A young man according to his way, even when he is old he will not depart from it" (Prov. 22, 6). And the distinguished poet said: "Once a fresh jar is imbued with a scent, it will long retain the fragrance."[20]

If the secular authority carries out all these things, it could rightfully say to the ecclesiastical authority, "Be thou ashamed, O Sidon, the sea speaketh" (Is. 23, 4). The ecclesiastical authority certainly ought to be ashamed, if due to its negligence, secular lords take upon themselves that care of souls which it was obliged to have by Divine law. Nevertheless, regarding the negligence of prelates, because I decided to defer to another whole chapter, where I will show that it is the main cause of heresies, wherefore I do not wish to now make a long discussion about this matter. For we presently are treating only about the lack of preaching, pointing out that it is the cause of many heresies; we do not now inquire into who is to blame for this deficiency, but we defer that matter to another chapter, in which we will discuss the negligence and unworthiness of the prelates.

But about those things which we said in this chapter, I decided to warn the reader not to think that I make the lack of preaching to be of such great importance that I would

---

20 Horace, *Epistles*, bk 1, letter 2, lns. 69 f.

think that it is the first cause of heresies, or that I reckon that it to be so great and so powerful that they themselves, who suffer the want of preaching of God's word, cannot prevent it from producing some heresies in themselves. For even though they cannot acquire the true Catholic faith (as we said) without the preaching of God's word, still if they abstain from all vices, so that they would adore the one God (as natural reason shows), and then entrust themselves entirely to Him, God would not allow them to fall into some heresy, but either God Himself would interiorly teach them, or He would send preachers and teachers to them, who would instruct them in the Catholic faith, and all the other things needed for attaining eternal life. For a confirmation of which matter the example of Cornelius the centurion can be enough, who although he was a Gentile, still because he was a foreigner to the vices of the Gentiles, he was heard on account of his alms and prayers, and Peter the Apostle was sent to him, who instructed him.[21]

Yet if they are immersed in various sins, it is not surprising that God would not give preachers to them, since he often withdraws from peoples those whom they had, as their sins demand it. For when Ezechiel the prophet was sent to the people put in the Babylonic captivity, the Lord withdrew the word of preaching on account of the people's sins, so that he would not preach to them. For God said to him (as the prophet himself testifies) these words: "And thou, O son of man, behold they shall put bands upon thee, and they shall bind thee with them: and thou shalt not go forth from the midst of them and I will make thy tongue stick fast to the roof of thy mouth, and thou shalt be dumb, and not as a man that reproveth: because they are a provoking house" (3, 25-26). Jerome when interpreting these words says: "Now the fact that the tongue of the Prophet clings to the palate or throat and becomes mute, [shows that] he does not have the

---

21 Cf. Acts 10.

First extrinsic cause of heresies: The lack of preaching God's word

mandate to reprove; the reason is clear: because, as it says, the house is provoking. And the meaning is this: There is such great bitterness and such contention against God that they do not deserve to hear the reprover. From which it is clear that where there is a multitude of sins, the sinners are unworthy of correction by the Lord."[22] From which words it is evident that sin is the reason (as we said in the preceding chapter) that God not only permits false teachers, and wicked preachers for the people, but also that he removes the good ones which the people have, from them, lest they have those who could teach them.

Thus those who lack the preaching of God's word, if they hunger for it, and desire to be instructed, ought to take care to abstain from vices, and to love and fear God: and God, Who never despises anyone taking refuge in Him, will not drive them away: but He will send them teachers, by whom they can be taught, or He Himself will interiorly teach them. "I have not seen the just forsaken," says the Royal Prophet, "nor his seed seeking bread" (Ps. 36, 25). Cassiodorus proves very well that these words ought to be understood not of material bread, by which the body is fed, but of spiritual bread, which is God's word, when speaking thus: "We read that Abraham, Isaac, and Joseph changed their lands owing to hunger, so there is no doubt that they were in need of bread, for clearly they made for foreign regions because of the indigence of their native areas.[23] But let us turn back to the inner man, and the true pronouncement will become clear to us in a salutary way. We said that the seed was the work of each individual which he sows and reaps, whether good or evil. So the work of the just has no need of bread, that is, of God's word with which he is filled and renewed and by which he lives and is inwardly fed."[24] And yet we do

---

22 *Commentaria in Ezechielem*, bk. 1 (PL 25, 42A-B).
23 Cf. Gen. 12, 10; 26, 1.
24 *Explanation of the Psalms* (PL 70, 265C).

not say these things to excuse the bishops and other pastors, because I reckon that they nonetheless sin because they do not feed God's sheep with His word; unless perhaps they were to have a special prohibition about this matter from God, just as was given to the prophet Ezechiel, as we showed above. For although God may permit, when the sins of the people demand it, that the shepherds of souls would not feed their sheep with God's word, yet He does not command these same shepherds to abstain from preaching God's word.

Chapter III

Concerning the second cause, from which heresies arise, which is the indiscriminate preaching of God's word by anyone without any distinction, and without any examination.

There certainly is a great shortage of the preaching of God's word in the whole Christian world: because (as Our Savior predicted) "The harvest indeed is great, but the labourers are few" (Mt. 9, 37). The great harvest, as Blessed Jerome interprets, is the whole multitude of believers:[1] but "the labourers are few," both the Apostles, and their imitators, that is, the preachers who are sent to the harvest. From the scarcity of whom it happens that some part of the harvest is lost: because the harvest is so great, that so few workers do not suffice. Which matter gives not a small occasion of sorrow to those who have some rule of Christendom. But it especially ought to be lamented that the greater part of these few preachers are so unfit for exercising the function of preaching, that they dishonor and fill with disgrace the function itself, which is very honorable, by their unworthiness. For although there are two things, according to the testimony of all holy men, most necessary for correctly fulfilling the office of preaching, namely, goodness and doctrine, yet there are many preachers of God's word, who lack one of these things; many also who lack both.

For learning is most necessary in the preacher, because the first goal to which preaching ought to tend is to teach the hearers. But, he who has not been taught, cannot teach others. A spring that lacks water, is unable to give drink to another. A body which is not luminous, cannot illuminate others. Therefore it is necessary that a preacher be learned,

---

1 *Commentary on Matthew* (PL 26, 60C).

who receives the care of teaching others. And it is not enough, in order that he may rightly execute his office, that he be learned: unless he is also good, and a lover of virtue, so that not only by word, but also by example he could benefit his hearers. For often examples are more powerful than words. Plato and Aristotle, and the whole multitude of philosophers, diverging in different directions, have received more from Socrates' way of life than from his words. The Apostles, and the other disciples of Christ Our Savior, likewise benefitted more from His example, than from His words for laying hold of virtue. For which reason Christ, the Supreme Teacher of all, Who greatly desired the profit of His disciples, firstly (as Luke relates) took pains to do, and then to teach.[2] Thus after Christ's example, whose place they take in preaching, it is befitting that preachers order very well their lives, so that they would take care to preach by deed and at the same time by word. For it is befitting that he who ought to cleanse others, be firstly clean himself.

He who wishes to make others fervent, and burning with the love of God, it is necessary that he have the heavenly fire in himself, whereby he can inflame the hearers. For it cannot happen that he who is cold and tepid would make others warm. If to extinguished coals someone joined coals of the same condition, they will never be kindled: yet if one moves them next to other coals that are burning, they will easily burn. So likewise, he who hears a preacher whom he knows is infected with vices, unless God be present, Who makes Him burn inwardly, he will never be set on fire by that preacher. Wherefore the Royal Prophet said about Christ the greatest preacher of all preachers: "A fire flamed from his face: coals were kindled by it" (Ps. 17, 9). Isaias the prophet, because he had unclean lips (as he himself lamenting and sighing admits[3]), needed to be purified before he was sent to

---

2 Cf. Acts 1, 1.
3 Cf. Is. 6, 5-7.

Second cause of heresies: Unauthorized and unqualified preachers

preach. For making this purification an Angel was sent, who, taking a coal of fire from the middle of the altar, touched his lips, and tongue, and in this way purified them, which having been purified, he was immediately sent to preach. As long as he had unclean lips, the burden of preaching was not enjoined upon Isaias. However, once his lips were cleansed, he was considered fit for the task, to whom preaching could be rightly entrusted.

Christ Our Savior ascending to heaven, whence He had descended for us, sends the Apostles into the whole world, to preach the Gospel to every creature.[4] And yet He did not permit them to immediately go away, and fulfill the command, but "He commanded them, that they should not depart from Jerusalem, but should wait for the promise of the Father" (Acts 1, 4), so that before they went away they would "be endued with power from on high" (Lk. 24, 49), and enflamed with the fire of the Holy Ghost, by which they could make others fervent in the love of God. Whence it is that David, so that he could rightly teach others God's ways, firstly asked for the threefold Spirit to be given to him, namely, the right, holy, and perfect Spirit. "Renew," he says, "a right spirit within my bowels" (Ps. 50, 12). And again, "Take not thy holy spirit from me" (v. 13). And afterwards, "Strengthen me with a perfect [*principali*] spirit" (v. 14), or as Jerome translates, "powerful" [*potenti*] spirit.[5] And after he asked for this triple Spirit, he immediately adds: "I will teach the unjust thy ways: and the wicked shall be converted to thee" (v. 15). By which order of petitions he shows that that triple Spirit is necessary so that someone could rightly teach God's ways. The Holy Ghost is certainly necessary so that one may teach the hearers to go by the right way to the heavenly country; the Holy Ghost is able to make the hearers

---

4 Cf. Mk. 16, vv. 15 & 19.
5 Cf *Liber Psalmorum* (PL 28, 1166C). St. Jerome follows here the Hebrew text, and not the Greek Septuagint.

holy and fervent in God's love. The perfect or powerful Spirit always makes the soul to be constant and unyielding against the attacks of all temptations, such that it is not terrified by threats, not swayed by gifts, not cast down by adversities, and not raised up and inflated by prosperity. For there are the two very strong artifices, by which preachers are always attacked and often conquered, namely, flatteries and great fears. The latter shakes the soul with fear, the former invades by hope. The latter absorbs the mind by the gravity of sorrows, and often casts into the abyss of despair, the former makes us badly secure by a false sweetness, whereby they can kill more easily. Against both artifices there ought to be present a powerful spirit, which teaching the preacher, so confirms him in good, and makes him constant, so that he is neither terrified by threats, nor led astray by flatteries, but being intrepid always rightly executes the office of preaching committed to him.

Therefore these two things, namely, goodness and learning, (as is evident from these things which we said) are highly necessary for every preacher, so that he rightly executes his office. Which two things in the heavenly fire, which on the day of Pentecost descended upon the Apostles, was plainly designated. For fire is by nature luminous and warm: and hence in the figure of fire the Holy Ghost was pleased to come upon the Apostles, so that by this same thing He might teach us, that to them by His coming, He gave the light of teaching, and the burning of God's love. Yet they are rare (so that I may speak frankly) who have these two things, whence it is that rare are the preachers who handle the office of preaching according to its dignity and merit. For there are some who have accommodated themselves badly, who, even if they are learned, still by their morals impede the powers of preaching. There are others, at least in those things which appear outwardly, truly studious and cultivators of virtue, nevertheless are so uneducated that they ought to be taught

Second cause of heresies: Unauthorized and unqualified preachers

rather than teach. Due to which they give no small suspicion of ambition, because they are not afraid to accept a burden, which it is very well known by far surpasses their strength. This is accustomed to cause not a little, as we will show, harm to the Catholic faith. There are again others so shameless, that although they are neither learned nor good, still with brazen temerity do not hesitate to teach. It is unnecessary to bring forth a few examples of these men, because we all see more than we wish daily and everywhere. For there are other preachers so uneducated, that they have had hardly a smattering of grammar, completely ignorant of the Latin language, and who are unable to even slightly understand the Gospel which is read in Mass.

I indeed know, God as my witness, many such men having certain sermons translated into the vernacular language by others, were delivering them to the people with such daring and grandeur, that he who had not known them, would have thought that they were very learned men. Yet because they speak a foreign tongue after the manner of parrots, they immediately betray themselves, because they often repeat the same tune [*cantilena*], and if anyone would ask about those things which they said, they will reply like parrots. But if you were to ask them to speak about another matter, they will be silent, as though completely ignorant, or perhaps lest they admit that they do not know, before the people among whom they want to seem wise, they will not hesitate to babble a thousand absurdities. And when so speaking with shameless audacity, they betray their own ignorance, who when silent could have been considered learned. To this sort of men pertain nearly all greedy preachers of indulgences, among whom you will find scarcely one or two learned men, who know about the matter which they preach, or give a mediocre explanation. They never intend to teach faith or morals by their preaching, but the only aim of their preaching is not merely to impress many of their hearers, but to extort money from them. To attain this they exaggerate the indulgences which they preach to the people more than is due, whichever way they turn, they beat their breasts, wail, threaten, laugh; in fine they leave nothing untried for extorting money, even if they would do it with danger to the faith. For often they desire to extol the indulgences which they preach to such an extent, that for the praise of them they pour out from their mouths detestable heresies.

Now how much harm has been inflicted upon Christendom from this kind of men, all of Germany can be a witness. Because this was the first root whence this whole pestilence of the Lutherans arose. For when Luther heard some preachers of indulgences, who said about indulgences tabulations which were more than was suitable, they seemed so horrendous to him that he considered it as wicked and iniquitous to keep silent, and not to withstand or impede them. Thus with zeal, and not moved according to discretion he went out in public, and preached against them all, not explaining the true meaning of indulgences (as was befitting), but completely throwing them out, and saying that they are completely useless. When some learned men fought against him, and advised him to sing the palinode,[6] he was so much against it, that he did not hesitate to pour out things much worse than before. Therefore from these greedy preachers of indulgences Luther received the first occasion of his heresy. Which word has now fallen into such a bad reputation among upright and wise men, that non-existent or rare is the good and learned man who deigns to preach indulgences, not on account of the indulgences themselves, but on account of their preachers, who have dishonored and rendered infamous the office of preaching them. I certainly consider that indulgences, if rightly dispensed, are holy and very valuable, yet I abhor

---

6 I. e., a recantation or to unsay what he had said. A palinode is an ode in which the writer retracts a view or sentiment expressed in an earlier poem.

Second cause of heresies: Unauthorized and unqualified preachers

their preachers as being as it were, monsters of Christendom. I would indeed advise the authorities that they would not permit them to be preached except through upright and learned men, and thus they may firstly provide well for religion and then revenue. For the people would give more and more willingly (as I think) to good and learned men, than to these babblers, to whom rarely someone, and then only reluctantly, contributes for an indulgence, inasmuch as he thinks that they are liars.

There are other preachers not so ignorant, of whom we now spoke, but mediocrely learned, who if they wish to be content with their own sort, they could satisfy the people according to their ability, and instruct them in faith and morals. But because they desire to be esteemed by the people above their merit, wherefore they strive to preach to the people the higher and more weightier opinions, than they themselves are able to interpret: the preaching of which things often harms the people more than it can benefit them. For since they preach things which they do not understand well, it is necessary that they interpret wrongly, or leave obscure things without any interpretation. When this happens, even if many of the hearers turn away their minds due to reverence for the mystery from scrutinizing it, many who are more curious and revere the mysteries less, however, will interpret them according to their own judgment and will wander in error.

And the prophet Jeremias deplores this inadequacy in preaching when saying: "The little ones have asked for bread, and there was none to break it unto them" (Lam. 4, 4). He does not say that the little ones asked for milk, but bread. Because they were not content with only the clearest precepts of the Law, but just as though they had already grown up, they were asking for bread, that is, some hidden mysteries, to be revealed to them. He does not say there is no one to give bread, but to break bread for them. For there were those who offered bread, that is, weighty statements, but there was not one who would break, that is, who would interpret and rightly explain them. Hence [Rabanus[7]] when interpreting the abovementioned words says: "Allegorically [this verse] signifies that those who are still weak in discerning, and less able to receive stronger food, to such men the Apostle says: 'I gave you milk to drink' (I Cor. 3, 2), who, on account of the unskillfulness and slothfulness of the teachers, lack the nourishment of spiritual understanding. 'The little ones have asked for bread, and there was none to break it unto them,' that is, any weak men who ask that stronger statements of Sacred Scriptures be broken up into small pieces for them by expounding, but those who would take pains to expound cannot be found."[8]

There are again other preachers, men indeed learned and truly educated, who interpret and expound very well those things which they preach to the people, although they are sublime and hidden mysteries; yet they lack discretion and prudence, by which they may know how to temper their words according to the capacity of the hearers, but they always endeavor to say grandiose things even before uneducated people. To whom it could rightly be said that which the poet [Persius] says: "The Muse provides our poet with grand material."[9] With what intention they do it, I cannot divine, because I am unable to behold their hearts. Nevertheless, if someone here allows place for suspicion, I would suspect that they preach such sublime things before uneducated people, so that they may be considered by the people to be learned men, and be in great admiration before them. They do not seek God's glory or the people's utility, but only their own reputation, and hence they do not preach to teach the people, but to be esteemed by them. And yet I do not think this about all the preachers of this kind, but

---

7 St. Jerome is incorrectly cited here.
8 *Commentaria in Jeremiam*, bk. 20 (PL 111, 1251D).
9 *Satires*, satire 1, ln. 68.

Second cause of heresies: Unauthorized and unqualified preachers

I believe that there are some who when preaching always want to treat about sublime things, because their abilities are of such a nature that the smallest and most obvious things are despised by them, and therefore they disdain to discuss them. Whatever their motives may be, I do not care, nor do I think it concerns us: I do, however, know this for certain, and therefore I will confidently affirm it without hesitation, that all of them deviate far from the purpose of preaching, and although they may be learned, they are unfit for the duty of preaching, as they are unaware of how to adjust their speech according to the capacity of the listeners.

For who would not consider insane the person who attempted to pour an immense amount of water or wine into a small vessel? Thus, certainly in my opinion, a preacher ought to be considered at least indiscreet or imprudent, who preaches the sublime and hidden mysteries of the faith to uneducated people, utterly incapable of such great mysteries. For nature itself teaches that one ought to act otherwise, which created for each animal its own food both of the same nature and proportionate to itself. A lion is fed by some foods, a bear by others, and finally birds by others. And all men themselves do not desire the same food, but everyone seeks the food suitable for himself according to his own physical constitution, and the body's age and health, and adequate for his strength. Thus from these examples of corporeal things, let us lay hold of the understanding of spiritual things. Every rational nature ought to be nourished with its own and suitable foods. Now the true food of the soul (as we showed in the previous chapter) is God's word. But just as in the nourishments of the body there are many differences, so also not every man, whose soul is fed with God's word, is nourished by one and the same word. For some are given to drink only the milk of God's word, that is, simpler and clearer doctrine, as is customary regarding morals, which is usually given to those who first engage in Divine studies. But others who are stronger, and more advanced in learning, need stronger food with which they are fed, that is, the explanation of some sublime mysteries of our faith. Now if a preacher disrupts this order, such that he gives stronger food, that is, he would propose sublime mysteries, to little ones for whom milk alone ought to be enough, it not only could not feed, but the excessive strength of the food may kill, because by this very thing he will give not a small occasion of error. Thus, so that he may not do harm by his preaching, it is befitting that he dispense the word according to the capacity of the hearers.

And this is what Blessed Job, when speaking by a certain (as he is wont to do) mystical expression, said: "He bindeth up the waters in his clouds, so that they break not out and fall down together" (26, 8). Blessed Gregory when interpreting these words says many excellent things which are conducive to our purpose, and I will now cite some of them. "But that uninstructed hearers," Gregory says, "might be comforted not by an inundation of knowledge, but by the tempered dropping of preaching, God 'bindeth up the waters in his clouds, so that they break not out and fall down together.' Because He tempers the preaching of the teachers, that so the infirmity of the hearers, being nourished by the dew of the things spoken, may be made strong... And so water is bound up in the clouds, because the knowledge of the preachers, speaking to the minds of the frail, is forbidden to teach as much as it is able to see. Since, for the most part, if the heart of the hearers is spoilt by the vastness of the utterance, the tongue of the persons teaching is mulcted in the damage of indiscretion. Whence it is written: 'If a man open a pit, and dig one, and cover it not, and an ox or an ass fall into it, the owner of the pit shall pay the price of the beasts' (Ex. 21, 33-34). For what is it 'to open a pit,' saving with strong understanding to penetrate the mysteries of Holy Writ? And what is understood by an 'ox' and an 'ass,' namely, a clean and an unclean animal, save every believer and unbeliev-

Second cause of heresies: Unauthorized and unqualified preachers

er? Accordingly, let him that diggeth a pit cover it, lest an ox or an ass tumble headlong therein, that is, let him, who already makes out deep things in Holy Writ, by silence cover over his lofty perceptions before those that do not reach that compass, lest by a stumbling-block to the soul he kill either the believing little one, or the unbelieving, who might have been led to believe. For upon the death of the beasts of burthen there is a price due, plainly because he is convicted of having done that, whereby the guilty man is held to do penance. Accordingly, the pit must be covered, in that before little minds, deep knowledge requires to be veiled, lest by the same cause that the heart of the teachers is lifted up to the highest things, the infirmity of the hearer fall away to the lowest."[10] Gregory says many other things about this matter in the same place, but it suffices to have cited these words.

We have hitherto the indiscrete dispensing of God's word: it now remains to discuss about the harm which they inflict by reason of their bad life, which they prominently display to the people. For some of them are imbued with the worst morals, who, whether they teach true or false things, are wont to very often harm the hearers. For from their wicked life can arise (as we said above) that their mind is blinded, thinking those things to be good in which they are engrossed, and those things bad which they abhor. And just as they think, so they teach the people: and hence it necessarily happens what Our Savior says: "If the blind lead the blind, both will fall into the pit" (Mt. 15, 14). If the preacher, who is the leader of others, is blinded, it will be surprising if the people who listen to him do not err: especially if the people are attached to him, and hold him in great esteem. For then the people accept his every word as, so to speak, oracles, and there is no one who would dare to depart from his teaching, even a hair's breadth. This matter is so clear, that it would be needless to want to prove it with arguments. For "To seek reasons,"

---

10 *Moralia*, bk. 17, c. 26 (PL 76, 27D-28C).

Aristotle says, "where the senses flourish is a weakness of the intellect."[11] And there is no need to bring forth very few examples, since many are now very well known to the whole world. What a great cesspool there is from the preaching of Luther, Zwingli, Carlstadt, Martin Bucer, and others of the same sort, has been poured out through the whole Christian world, there is no one who does not know. All these heresies would have been completely taken away, if at the beginning when they began to rave, had the preaching of them been completely forbidden.

Yet the negligence of the rulers, who did not want to restrain them when they could, gave them so much audacity in harming that they seemed to vie among themselves in rivalry, which of them would harm the Church more, and he who harmed more was held to be among them more illustrious. Thus every ruler who desired his country to be safe from heresies, did not allow anyone who gave even the least suspicion of heresy to preach in it. It ought to be established regarding the preacher's faith, before he would be permitted to preach to the people. Pope Damasus in the life of Pope and martyr Evaristus, relates that he decreed that seven deacons should monitor a bishop while preaching for the sake of the purity of the truth.[12] O holy statute and worthy of

---

11 Pseudo-Bede, *Sententiae, sive axiomata philosophica ex Aristotele et aliis praestantibus collecta...*, §1 (*Sententiae ex Aristotele collectae*) (PL 90, 1038D); cf. Aristotle, *Physics*, bk. 8, c. 3 (253a30): "...to disregard sense-perception and attempt to show the theory to be reasonable, would be an instance of intellectual weakness..." (translated by R. P. Hardie and R. K. Gaye, in *The Complete Works of Aristotle: The Revised Oxford Translation* (Princeton University Press, 1984), vol. 1, p. 423).

12 "But we return to Evaristus, who, as Damasus tells us, divided the city of Rome among the presbyters into parishes; ordained that seven deacons should attend the bishop whoever he preached, to be witnesses of the truth of his doctrine" (Platina, *The Lives of the Popes* (Cambridge: Harvard University Press, 2008), vol. 1,

Second cause of heresies: Unauthorized and unqualified preachers

such a martyr! If this diligence in scrutinizing the words of a preacher had been kept among everyone until the present day, it would have been easy to resist such a great crowd of heretics as we now (alas!) see. And I certainly fear that this easy permission of preachers, unless it be counteracted very quickly, may cause a swift downfall of nearly all of Christendom. Not without reason, but as the most significant cause of unrest, and indeed a well-known one, I fear this, especially because I know that many preachers in various regions, who time and again gave no small scandal of heresy in their preachings to the people, and yet by a scanty and trifling excuse given by them, were permitted to preach again and again, and if they have seduced some, they gave scandal to all whom they could. However, the outcome itself showed what kind they had been before when they excused themselves, for in the end, they did not hesitate to openly reveal themselves as public heretics. And I would not have been surprised if these things had been permitted by heretical rulers alone, but I am very surprised that by those rulers, and other authorities who are distinguished by the Christian name, permission for suspected preachers is so easy. Therefore I beseech them all, and I implore by the wounds of Christ, that they would not permit anyone who gave even

---

p. 61). Bartolomeo Platina, the author of the *Lives of the Popes* written in 1475, incorrectly believed that Pope Damasus was the author of the *Liber Pontificalis*, where the following is written: "He divided the parish churches in the city of Rome among the priests and ordained seven deacons to keep watch over the bishop when he spoke, for the sake of the word of truth." The thirteenth canon of the apocryphal council of Sylvester is the following, which sheds some light on the passage here: "There shall be seven deacons to watch over the officiating bishop for the sake of the word of truth and Catholic dogma and the wisdom of age, lest in speaking we say Father in place of Son or Holy Ghost in place of Father" (Mommsen, *Gestorum pontificum romanorum* (Berlin: apud Weidmannos, 1898), p. 9).

a slight suspicion of heresy to preach to the people, until he fully cleared the suspicion before the people whom he has scandalized.

Now besides these very unfit and harmful preachers, there are others who even though they are bad, still their malice is not so great that their disposition corrupts their understanding. And these men are certainly wont to corrupt in yet two ways. For there are some of them who believe very well, and think rightly about things to be done, yet they teach otherwise than they think, either influenced by the hope of a reward, or frightened by fear of punishment. For both of these things are accustomed to turn away preachers and other teachers from the preaching of the truth, who can be allured with rewards and deterred with tortures. For Peter the Apostle is a witness that by fear of punishment many speak contrary to what they think, who in the house of the high priest, when questioned by a servant maid, denied that he was a disciple of Christ Our Savior.[13] And I certainly believe that many more are in the courts of rulers, who imitate Peter in this matter, than those who follow the example of his later life, boldly saying to the rulers: "We ought to obey God, rather than men" (Acts 5, 29). Other men are allured by the hope of the reward they greatly desire, so that they teach and preach otherwise than they think. They indeed think correctly, but so that they may please kings or rulers, or finally, the people, they teach and preach those things which they know are pleasing to them. Such were those four hundred false prophets, who advised King Achab to go attack the city of Ramoth Galaad.[14] They certainly were saying that which they knew pleased the king more, and yet none of them fully knew. In which matter although the preachers themselves declaring false things sin gravely, nevertheless greater guilt (as I think) ought to be cast back to the kings and rulers themselves, who only want

---

13 Cf. Mt. 26, 69 ff.
14 Cf. III Kings 22, 6.

Second cause of heresies: Unauthorized and unqualified preachers

to hear those things that please themselves, and if a good and faithful preacher of God's word shall have taught true things, they will hate him and refuse to listen. About which matter King Achab could give full proof to us, who, when asked by Josephat, king of Juda, (as the four hundred false prophets had been sent away) to consult a true prophet of the Lord about making war, replied: "There is one man left, by whom we may inquire of the Lord: Micheas the son of Jemla; but I hate him, for he doth not prophesy good to me, but evil" (III Kings 22, 8).

These adulators are wont to greatly harm in faith and morals: because when they say evil is good, and darkness is light, others believe, and from this belief arises in the hearers a certain love and desire of that evil, which has been praised by the adulator. And if one does that evil, so much the less will he depart from it, the more he believes that what he does is good. Whence it is that he could never attain the true salvation of the soul. Because (as Blessed Gregory says) "One neglects to heal the wound, which is found worthy of the reward of praise."[15] The first step to recovering salvation is to acknowledge that one is sick. For it is very difficult for a sick person to attain health, who does not know that he is sick: because he will neither call the doctor, nor, if the doctor comes of his own accord, will he accept the medicines offered to him: especially because he firmly believes that he nowise needs them. The preacher saying to the ruler, or to anyone else, that the evil that he does is good, does this by his adulation, so that the ruler would never repent that he has acted badly: and hence it follows that he never attains salvation.

And this pestilence of adulation of preachers was harmful at every time. For long ago Jeremias deplores that this was cause of many errors in the synagogue, when speaking thus: "Thy prophets have seen false and foolish things for thee:

---

15   *Moralia*, bk. 4, c. 27 (PL 75, 663A).

and they have not laid open thy iniquity, to excite thee to penance: but they have seen for thee false revelations and banishments" (Lam. 2, 14). [Rabanus] when interpreting these words says: "For the one who promises security of impunity to the one engaged in sinful and unjust deeds shall be subject to prophetic condemnation."[16] And God Himself complains through the same prophet about these flattering preachers, that they have greatly harmed His people, speaking thus: "They healed the breach of the daughter of my people disgracefully, saying: Peace, peace: and there was no peace" (Jer. 6, 14). A preacher heals the breach, who quickly promises security to one sinning and not repenting. And God again says through the prophet Ezechiel: "Her princes in the midst of her, are like wolves ravening the prey to shed blood, and to destroy souls, and to run after gains through covetousness. And her prophets have daubed them without tempering the mortar, seeing vain things, and divining lies unto them, saying: Thus saith the Lord God: when the Lord hath not spoken" (22, 27-28). And those things that then happened to the people of Israel, we now see the same things also now happen in the Christian people. For these false prophets, that is, adulators, preachers, and teachers, are the main reason that kings and rulers impose intolerable taxes on their subjects, and do many other evil things, which unless they were praised by them, they would nowise do. For they applaud them, and say that it is allowed for them to do what they want.

Finally, there are certain other wicked preachers, who believe rightly, and think very correctly about morals, and they teach as they think: but their morals are not in harmony with what they teach, because when teaching well they live badly before the people. And the teaching of these men, even though it is true, not only does not benefit the people, but

---

16 *Commentaria in Jeremiam*, bk. 18 (PL 111, 1209A). St. Jerome is incorrectly cited here.

Second cause of heresies: Unauthorized and unqualified preachers

greatly harms them. For (as Gregory says) "He whose life is despised, it remains that he preaching is condemned."[17] For by his wicked life this sort of preacher greatly detracts the faith by the teaching which he preaches. For he does the same things that he condemns: and in this way he gives not a small occasion of suspicion to the hearers, that the things that were taught by him are not true. They will be persuaded to believe this by this argument, namely, that it is unlikely that someone is so heedless of his salvation, that he would badly care for himself, but for others well. If the things that he teaches are good, why does he not do them? If the things that he does are good, why does he not teach them? Thus whichever way he turns, he is proved to be bad, either teaching badly or living badly. But because men always believe more with their eyes than their ears, wherefore the teaching of one living badly, however good, is despised. Next, it is just that one believe that any man has greater concern for his own salvation, than for others; and hence it necessarily happens that anyone would believe more by examples than by words.

How great an evil it is, when the preacher's life does not agree with his teaching, Blessed Job taught us with mystical words when to confirm those things he was saying, using an oath of execration, he imprecated this as the greatest evil upon himself, unless the things he says are true. "If a spot hath cleaved to my hands then let me sow and let another eat: and let my offspring be rooted out" (31, 7-8). When interpreting these words Gregory says: "After the manner of Holy Writ we call it to 'sow' to preach the words of life... But to 'eat' is to be filled to the full with good works. Hence the Truth Himself saith: 'My meat is to do the will of him that sent me' (Jn. 4, 34). So then, if the things that he gave forth, he forbore to do, he says: 'Then let me sow and let another eat.' As though he said in plain words: 'What my

---

17 *Homilies on the Gospels*, hom. 12, n. 1 (PL 76, 1119A).

mouth utters let not me but another man do.' For of course the preacher who in his ways is at variance with his own words, sows going hungry what another may eat; because he is not himself fed by his own seed, when by wrong conduct he is made void of the rightness of his word. And because it very often happens that the disciples hear what is good to no purpose, when by the life of the master it is destroyed by the example of actions, it in rightly subjoined: 'And let my offspring be rooted out.' For 'the offspring' of the teacher is 'rooted out,' when he who is born by the word, is killed by the example, because him whom the heeding tongue begets, heedlessness of the life kills."[18]

And not only to men is the office of teaching and preaching permitted, but also to women themselves, which is the most absurd of all. I have seen and heard in various regions of the Christian world women, who even though they were not preaching in the Church upon the chair [cathedram], still in their and others' houses, they were making sermons about sublime things; and however many came and wished to hear, they were not afraid to teach. Nevertheless, from these preachings many errors arose, as the outcome showed. And because there are particular examples of diverse countries, and those things which I saw were punished and corrected by those to whom it was incumbent, wherefore I do not now wish to make them known at the present time. I indeed, having been taught by Paul,[19] reckon that no woman ought to be permitted to teach, but it ought to be enjoined that she be instructed. Because after Eve was seduced by the serpent, every teaching uttered by the mouth of a woman righty ought to be suspected; for it ought to be feared that she is a vessel prepared for deception, whereby the devil is accustomed to deceive others.

---

18 *Moralia*, bk. 21, c. 10 (PL 76, 198C-199A).
19 Cf. I Tim. 2, 12: "But I suffer not a woman to teach, nor to use authority over the man: but to be in silence."

Second cause of heresies: Unauthorized and unqualified preachers

Hence since the preaching of God's word ministered through men unfit for so great an office is a well-known cause of many errors and of many heresies (as is established from the things said), it would be fitting that no one be permitted to preach to the people, unless he has been firstly fully examined and approved about faith and morals by his superior. For this business, which is of such great importance, ought not to be committed to all without distinction, but only to those fit to do so. For Paul when writing to Timothy about this matter admonishes him, speaking thus: "The things which thou hast heard of me by many witnesses, the same commend to faithful men, who shall be fit to teach others also" (II Tim. 2, 2). And Blessed Francis, the first institutor and father of all the Friars Minor, having followed the footsteps of Paul the Apostle, commanded all his brothers this same thing in his Rule, speaking thus: "Let no friar at all dare preach to the people, unless he will have been examined by the minister general of this fraternity and approved, and there be conceded to him by the same the office of preaching."[20] I, although unworthy, serve in his Institute.

And the General Council of [IV] Lateran, celebrated under Innocent III, made a special decree about this matter, whereby all of Christ's faithful are forbidden the same thing which Saint Francis forbade his brothers. For in the third chapter of the decrees of the same council these words are found: "Because some indeed 'having an appearance indeed of godliness, but denying the power thereof' (according to what the Apostle says) (II Tim. 3, 5), assume to themselves the authority of preaching, when the same Apostle says: 'How… shall they preach, unless they be sent?' (Rom. 10, 15), let all who, being prohibited or not sent, without having received authority from the Apostolic See, or from the Catholic bishop of the place, shall presume publicly or privately to usurp the duty of preaching be marked by the bond of excommuni-

---

20 C. 9 in Pope Honorius III's Bull, *Solet annuere*.

cation; and unless they recover their senses, the sooner the better, let them be punished with another fitting penalty."[21] Which words are had in the chapter, *Excommunicamus*.[22]

And in another general Council of [V] Lateran, which was celebrated under Leo X, the same decree was renewed, and made more copious. For in the eleventh session of the same council the following decree is contained: "Leo, bishop, servant of the servants of God, with the approval of the sacred council, for an everlasting record. Under the protection of the supreme majesty by whose ineffable providence things in heaven and on earth are guided...We decree and ordain, with the approval of the sacred council, that nobody—whether a secular cleric or a member of any of the mendicant orders or someone with the right to preach by law or custom or privilege or otherwise—may be admitted to carry out this office unless he has first been examined with due care by his superior, which is a responsibility that we lay on the superior's conscience, and unless he is found to be fit and suitable for the task by his upright behavior, age, doctrine, honesty, prudence and exemplary life. Wherever he goes to preach, he must provide a guarantee to the bishop and other local Ordinaries concerning his examination and competence, by means of the original or other letters from the person who examined and approved him."[23]

O truly holy decree and worthy of a general council, in which nothing regarding this matter could be reckoned necessary was omitted. For it has commanded that preachers be examined, and it declares what kind should be approved, and it has prescribed that a testimony of approval be given, so that no one who claims to be approved can lie with impunity. Still only one thing is desired by all, and it is the

---

21 Dz. 434.
22 *Decretals of Gregory IX*, bk. 5, tit. 7 (*De haereticis*), c. 9, §6 (*Quia vero*).
23 Mansi 32, 944A & 946A-B.

execution of such a holy decree. For I do not know that it has even once been commanded for execution, nor have I heard from someone who has seen this to have been done at some time. But this ought to be imputed to the negligence of the bishops, just as also many other things are attributed to their inactivity, about which we will discuss in the following chapter, and there we will show that their very bad negligence is the cause of many evils.

Chapter IV

Concerning the third cause, which is the negligence of the bishops, and of other pastors of the Church.

We begin to explain the third cause of heresies, which if we have fully (as it ought) examined its force and power, we will say that it is the main and first of all the causes, from which it is evident that all the others arise. This is the very great negligence of prelates, many of whom do not take more care of their subjects than of things nowise pertaining to them, and so they abandon the sheep committed to them, as though they were not going to give any account about them to God. And certainly all those things which we discussed above in two chapters, about the shortage of God's word, and about the wickedness of preachers redounds unto the prelates, to whom it pertains to oversee all these things. There are some bishops who could, if they wanted to, fulfill their office: but many others, too preoccupied with matters outside their state and order, refuse to render what they owe. About the negligence of the latter, therefore, we will show how many and how great heresies their negligence begot, and begets until the current day. But firstly it will be necessary to show what those things are which Divine law requires from bishops and other pastors of souls, and in this way bringing the stone to the son (as it is said[1]), we will make it plain to all that there are many among

---

1 According to Thucydides, Diodorus, and Polyaenus, Pausanias, a betrayer of his country, pursued by the ephors, took refuge in the temple of Athena "of the Brazen House" (located in the acropolis of Sparta). Pausanias' mother Theano immediately went to the temple, and laid a brick at the door saying: "Unworthy to be a Spartan, you are not my son" (according to Thucydides, *History of the Peloponnesian War*, bk. 1, c. 1). Following the mother's example, the Spartans blocked the doorway with bricks and forced

them, who now fulfill a very small part of those things, which they are held to do according to their office.

Now if someone wishes to know what those things are which bishops are held to fulfill, he may easily learn from the name of the office which was committed to them: if he would accurately consider its virtuousness and particular nature. For bishops and others to whom the care of souls have been committed are called "shepherds" of souls, and they are. For when Christ Our Savior set Peter over all other Christians, He made him the shepherd of His sheep, saying to him: "Feed my lambs" (Jn. 21, 15). By which words He declared that all Christians are his sheep, and made Peter the shepherd of them all, when He gave him the care of feeding them. And Christ Himself our Redeemer, to show us with what great love He loved us, and with what great concern He had for all of us, called Himself a "shepherd," saying: "I am the good shepherd. The good shepherd giveth his life for his sheep" (*Ibid.* 10, 11). Let us see then what are those things which shepherds are obliged to do for the sheep entrusted them: because bishops, and others having the care of souls, will be bound to perform those same things for the souls committed to them.

Shepherds are firstly obliged to give food to their sheep, lest they perish through hunger and starvation. Both bishops, and all others who have received the care of souls, are obliged to feed the souls of those whom they rule. Now with what food they ought to feed the souls, God Himself, Who made them shepherds, clearly stated through the prophet Jeremias saying: "I will give you pastors according to my own heart, and they shall feed you with knowledge and doctrine" (3, 15). Thus bishops and other pastors of souls are obliged to teach all those whose care they keep. Wherefore Christ Our Savior when sending His Apostles into the whole world, said to them: "Teach ye all nations" (Mt. 28, 19). Since the

---

Pausanias to die of starvation.

Apostles were those shepherds whom God had previously promised to give, according to His heart, and hence to fulfill His promise, He commanded them that they feed all nations with knowledge and doctrine.

Now so that they would be worthy of such a great office, the Holy Ghost descended from heaven upon them in fiery tongues.[2] Not in hands, with which they could conquer the world, nor in feet, by whose agility they would escape the persecutions of tyrants: but in tongues, with which they would teach others who are ignorant. Nature has given us other organs of the body so that by them we can derive knowledge of many things, which we did not know, from the same things. Yet our tongue does not give us knowledge of anything: but those things which we previously knew, we manifest to others by the tongue. Therefore the tongue was not given to us for learning, but rather for teaching. And for this reason the Holy Ghost, when descending upon the Apostles, descended not in eyes, or ears, which are organs apt for learning, but in fiery tongues, so that He might make them fit for teaching, who had already been made teachers and pastors of the whole world.

Hence from these things bishops may learn by how great an obligation they are obliged to teach the people subject to them, and may imitate the examples of the Apostles, of whom due to the episcopal dignity alone they may glory that they are the successors. Otherwise they will be held guilty before God of a duty badly fulfilled, and will undergo due punishments for their silence. And those little bells mixed with pomegranates, which long ago God commanded to be put on the vesture of the priest,[3] with which the priest when entering was obliged to make a sound under pain of death, seem to me to signify this. "And Aaron shall be vested with it in the office of his ministry, that the sound may be heard,

---

2 Cf. Acts 2, 3.
3 Cf. Ex. 28, 33.

when he goeth in and cometh out of the sanctuary, in the sight of the Lord, and that he may not die" (Ex. 28, 35). In which words we ought to consider not only the surface of the letter, as the Jews do: because (as Paul says) "The letter killeth, but the spirit quickeneth" (II Cor. 3, 6). It is necessary then that we examine the hidden mystery under that hard shell of the letter, especially since Paul says that everything happened in a figure for the Jews, and the Law had a shadow of future things. That priestly vesture was signifying the perfect life of the priest, as the Royal Prophet interprets it for us, who says: "Let thy priests be clothed with justice" (Ps. 131, 9).

The little bells put on the vesture signify the voice of preaching conjoined with works. The sound of the little bells ought to be heard, when he enters and leaves the sanctuary, so that he would not die. Because a bishop incurs the death of damnation, if he goes about without any sound of preaching. Hence [Gregory[4]] when expounding that passage says: "The priest, when he goes in or comes out, dies if a sound is not heard from him, because he provokes the wrath of the hidden judge, if he goes without the sound of preaching."[5] Now the nature of the priest's preaching is indicated by this, that they are instructed to mix pomegranates with the bells, in which the unity of faith is symbolized. For just as in a pomegranate, many seeds are contained within one outer peel, so the unity of the faith covers countless peoples of the holy Church, who inwardly have diverse manners. Hence pomegranates are commanded to be joined to the little bells, so that in everything which the priest preaches and teaches, he may diligently strive to maintain the unity of faith through careful observance.

Wherefore Paul understanding very well that the preaching of God's word is highly necessary for a bishop wrote to Timothy, whom he had appointed a bishop and shepherd of

---

4 Venerable Bede is incorrected cited here.
5 *Pastoral Rule*, bk. 2, c. 4 (PL 77, 31B).

souls, exhorting him and vehemently urging him to frequent preaching of God's word by these words: "I charge thee, before God and Jesus Christ, who shall judge the living and the dead, by his coming, and his kingdom: preach the word: be instant in season, out of season" (II Tim. 4, 1-2). These terrible words of adjuration with which Paul adjured Timothy, indicates his very ardent desire, by which he wished to express that a bishop is held by a very great obligation to preach God's word, not on one day or another only, but often. Wherefore he said: "Preach the word: be instant in season, out of season." Theophylactus when expounding these words says: "What is it that I charge? Preach the word, do not withhold the gift that is in you. We would shake with fear if we did not preach. 'Be instant in season, out of season.' As it were, speak with persistence and perseverance, not once but always. The time is not determined for you, but speak and preach both 'in season,' that is, when in peace and you are without fear, and when in the Church: and also 'out of season,' that is, when you are in dangers, and outside the Church. He said 'in season and out of season' according to the opinion of the people: for they consider a time of ease and relaxion to be 'in season,' but a dangerous time as 'out of season.'"[6] Because Theophylactus was a bishop of Bulgaria, he lamented the negligence of all bishops in his own name, saying: "We would shake with fear if we did not preach."

Finally, so that bishops may understand how necessary the preaching of God's word is for them, let them look upon the Shepherd of all souls, Christ Our Savior, with what great care He fed with knowledge and doctrine the sheep to whom alone He testifies He was sent.[7] For He was put before all as an example, so that everyone could learn from His deeds,

---

6 *Expositio in Epistolam II ad Timotheum* (PG 125, 127A-B).
7 Cf. Mt. 15, 24: "I was not sent but to the sheep that are lost of the house of Israel."

what is useful for himself. For (as [Innocent III] says) every action of Christ is a lesson to us."[8]

Now Matthew relates about Our Savior Himself, that He "went about all Galilee, teaching in their synagogues, and preaching the gospel of the kingdom: and healing all manner of sickness and every infirmity, among the people" (4, 23). And again Matthew says the same thing: "And Jesus went about all the cities, and towns, teaching in their synagogues, and preaching the gospel of the kingdom, and healing every disease, and every infirmity" (9, 35). Let the bishops look upon this, and following Christ's example let them go about all the towns and villages of their dioceses, teaching in their temples, and preaching the Gospel of the kingdom, and let them take care to heal the diseases and infirmities of the souls, from which the people everywhere suffer. And certainly unless the bishops, and the other pastors of souls, are obliged to teach the people, since there is no one else whom God commanded this task of instructing, it will be consequently necessary to say that Christ Our Redeemer failed to looked after His Church properly, if He did not provide for the matter of utmost necessity, namely, the teaching of faith and morals. Yet far be such a wicked thought from the hearts of the faithful. For the pastors of souls, who think this way, while they want to remove all guilt from themselves, they make God unjust, saying that He failed to provide food for His family, and left His sheep without any food. For He Himself says through the prophet Isaias, that there is nothing that He could have done which He did not do.[9] Hence it follows that He provided food for His sheep, because He could do this very easily. And He did not appoint anyone else to do this, except the priests whom He appointed the pastors of souls, to whom by this name alone it seems that

---

8 *Sermones de tempore*, serm. 22 (PL 217, 411C). St. Augustine is incorrectly cited here.
9 Cf. Is. 5, 4.

Third cause of heresies: Negligence of bishops and pastors

He commanded that His sheep be fed with knowledge and doctrine.

Yet there are few bishops, or other pastors of souls, who feed His sheep with knowledge and doctrine. I do not want to say that there are none, since I know some, both among the bishops and among the other lower priests, who were teaching the peoples subject to them with frequent preaching. But all these are rare, so that relative to the other innumerable multitude they are comparable to the sun and moon to all the other stars. I also admit that there are some pastors of souls, who even though they themselves do not preach, they still diligently take care to supply for their defect through other fit preachers, lest their sheep perish through hunger for God's word. And certainly if the bishops and others having the care of souls do not know how to preach, they may fully fulfill their office, if they diligently procure that it be done by other fit preachers. But actually (so that I may speak frankly) they are very few who do these things. And hence had not this negligence of the pastors been supplied for by the monks, due alone to the scarcity of God's word, nearly the whole of Christendom would already have perished.

But even though these men are obliged to help the bishops and other pastors of souls to the best of their abilities, still they could not supply for all their defect: because "The harvest indeed is great," as Our Savior says, "but the labourers are few" (Mt. 9, 37). Therefore the sheep are forced to buy their food twice. Firstly in fact, when they gave the tithes of their fruits to the priests, on account of which by Divine law they owed them the food of doctrine. Then they pay again, when they hire at their own expense the labors of other preachers. And (what is worse) the bishops or other preachers often do not want to allow others, although hired by the people, to preach: except those who please themselves. If the bishops would do this so that at least in this away they would better take care of the people, by rejecting the unfit, and accepting the fit, I could not but praise their diligence in this matter. Yet they often do not do this to take good care of the people, but to favor a certain preacher. For which reason I know that it often happens that the people were forced to accept a less fit preacher hired at their own expense. Such men as these, even if they are truly bishops, are nevertheless unfit, who are designated by this name; although it is evident that they were not placed by God, but by men over God's family. For the servant whom the Lord appointed over His family is faithful and prudent, who gives food to the family in season.[10] These therefore, who are placed as bishops over God's family, and do not give food of God's word to the family, were not appointed by the Lord over it.

And because the negligence of all the pastors, especially of the bishops, in this matter was so clear, the general [IV] Council of Lateran, venerably celebrated under Innocent III, issued a special decree about this matter placed in the tenth chapter, whereby it commanded all the bishops, "to appoint suitable men to carry out with profit this duty of sacred preaching, men who are 'powerful in word and deed'[11] and who will visit with care the peoples entrusted to them in place of the bishops, since these by themselves are unable to do it, and will build them up by word and example."[12] Now this decree is found in the chapter, *Inter cetera*.[13] The Council of Trent, celebrated under Paul III, recognizing very well that the lack of preaching of God's word is the cause of many heresies, in the fifth session, issued a much more lengthy decree about this matter, which is expressed in the following words:

---

10 Cf. Mt. 24, 45.
11 Cf. Lk. 24, 19.
12 Mansi 22, 998D-E.
13 *Decretals of Gregory IX*, bk. 1, tit. 31 (*De officio judicis ordinarii*), c. 15.

Third cause of heresies: Negligence of bishops and pastors

But seeing that the preaching of the Gospel is no less necessary to the Christian commonwealth than the reading thereof; and whereas this is the principal duty of bishops; the same holy Synod hath resolved and decreed, that all bishops, archbishops, primates, and all other prelates of the churches be bound personally—if they be not lawfully hindered—to preach the holy Gospel of Jesus Christ. But if it should happen that bishops, and the others aforesaid, be hindered by any lawful impediment, they shall be bound, in accordance with the form prescribed by the general Council [of Lateran], to appoint fit persons to discharge wholesomely this office of preaching. But if any one through contempt do not execute this, let him be subjected to rigorous punishment.

Archpriests, curates, and all those who in any manner soever hold any parochial, or other, churches, which have the cure of souls, shall, at least on the Lord's days, and solemn feasts, either personally, or if they be lawfully hindered, by others who are competent, feed the people committed to them, with wholesome words, according to their own capacity, and that of their people; by teaching them the things which it is necessary for all to know unto salvation, and by announcing to them with briefness and plainness of discourse, the vices which they must avoid, and the virtues which they must follow after, that they may escape everlasting punishment, and obtain the glory of heaven. And if any one of the above neglect to discharge this duty,—even though he may plead, on whatsoever ground, that he is exempt from the jurisdiction of the bishop, and even though the churches may be, in whatsoever way, said to be exempted, or haply annexed or united to a monastery that is even out of the diocese,—let not the watchful pastoral solicitude of the bishops be wanting, provided those churches be really within their diocese; lest that word be fulfilled; "The little ones have asked for bread, and there was none to break it unto them" (Lam. 4, 4). Wherefore, if, after having been admonished by the bishop, they shall neglect this their duty for the space of three months, let them be compelled by ecclesiastical censures, or otherwise, at the discretion of the said bishop; in such wise that even—if this seem to him expedient—a fair remuneration be paid, out of the fruits of the benefices, to some other person to discharge that office, until the principal himself repenting shall fulfil his own duty.

But should there be found to be any parochial churches, subject to monasteries which are not in any diocese, if the abbots and Regular prelates be negligent in the matters aforesaid, let them be compelled thereto by the metropolitans, in whose provinces the said dioceses are situated, as the delegate for that end of the Apostolic See.[14]

But to produce decrees of this kind for many bishops of this time, is to talk to the wind.[15] Now how many errors and what a multitude of heresies may arise from this dearth of God's word, which happens on account of the negligence of the bishops, we have just show in the preceding chapter.

There is another duty of a shepherd, to guard the sheep from wolves, which often attack them. And if there were no shepherd to deter and restrain them, all the sheep would be killed and devoured, not leaving a single one unharmed. Therefore lest the wolves could harm the sheep, their protection is entrusted to the shepherds. The wolves are tyrants, who strip their subjects beyond what is due, and they demand more taxes from them than they can bear, and they cruelly

---

14 C. 2 (Mansi 33, 30D-31C).
15 *Surdo canere fabulum*, lit. to sing a story to a deaf man. Cf. Terence, *Heauton Timorumenos*, act 2, scene 1, ln. 10: "He certainly does not know how deaf I am at the moment when he's telling his stories" (*nae ille haud scit, quam mihi nunc surdo narret fabulam*).

Third cause of heresies: Negligence of bishops and pastors

command them not with meekness and mildness, but very harshly. Hence God says about the evil rulers of Juda when speaking through Ezechiel the prophet: "Her princes in the midst of her, are like wolves ravening the prey to shed blood, and to destroy souls, and to run after gains through covetousness" (Ez. 22, 27). For they all are also "wolves" who persecute just men, even though they are neither kings nor rulers. These are those wolves about whom the Savior when speaking to the Apostles says: "Behold I send you as sheep in the midst of wolves" (Mt. 10, 16). For He sent His Apostles not only among rulers and kings, nor did the Apostles undergo persecutions from them alone, but from many others, all of whom the Savior designated by the name of "wolves."

Heretics are crueler wolves than all these men; because under the appearance of piety and religion they very often kill the souls of others. These men are those wolves of whom Our Savior warns us all to beware when saying: "Beware of false prophets, who come to you in the clothing of sheep, but inwardly they are ravening wolves" (Mt. 7, 15). From all these wolves bishops ought to guard their sheep, lest they be hurt by them. They ought to defend them from tyrants and other persecutors, not permitting them to unjustly maltreat their subjects, or to impose insupportable burdens upon them, or exact immoderate taxes, or inflict any other unjust vexations. And if kings, rulers, or any other superiors attempt to do any of these things, the bishops are obliged to resist them, to reprimand their audacity, and they ought to resist their harsh endeavors, by reproving, entreating, and rebuking (as Paul says) "in all patience and doctrine" (II Tim. 4, 2). They also ought to defend the sheep entrusted to them, lest having been seduced by those men they would lead them into various errors and heresies. For due to this reason Paul teaches that a bishop must be learned "that he may be able to exhort in sound doctrine, and to convince the gainsayers" (Tit. 1, 9). He ought to exhort the people to remain in the truth of the faith, and refute the contradicting heretics with clear arguments.

Yet what now is the number of bishops who now do this? Every such bishop is so rare, that about him it could deservedly be said the saying of the satirical poet: "A rare bird in the lands and very much like a black swan."[16] Thus to all the rest, who either neglect or fear to do it, can be said that which the Lord long ago reproached through the prophet Ezechiel, saying: "You have not gone up to face the enemy, nor have you set up a wall for the house of Israel, to stand in battle in the day of the Lord" (13, 5). Blessed Gregory, when interpreting which words, says: "Now 'to go up to face the enemy' is to go with free voice against the powers of this world for defense of the flock; and 'to stand in the battle in the day of the Lord' is out of love of justice to resist bad men when they contend against us. For, for a shepherd to have feared to say what is right, what else is it but to have turned his back in keeping silence? But surely, if he puts himself in front for the flock, he opposes 'a wall' against the enemy 'for the house of Israel.'"[17] The prelates of this time do not go up against the enemy, nor do they set up a wall for the house of Israel: because for the defense of the flock they do not dare to contradict the powers of this world. I dare not say that there is now no bishop who rebukes the rulers, and dares to publicly resist their evil endeavors, lest perhaps God say that to me which long ago, when affairs were very desperate, He said to the prophet Elias: "I will leave me seven thousand men in Israel, whose knees have not been bowed before Baal" (III Kings 19, 18).

Yet I being undaunted will say this, that a bishop similar to Blessed Ambrose is now rare, who when he was the bishop of Milan, was not afraid to excommunicate Theodosius, the very powerful emperor of the East and West, on account of

---

16 Juvenal, *Satires*, bk. 2, satire 6, ln. 165.
17 *Pastoral Rule*, bk. 2, c. 4 (PL 77, 30B-C).

Third cause of heresies: Negligence of bishops and pastors

the slaughter made in Thessalonica. And he did not bind him with an excommunication for a short time, but for the space of eight months (as Cassiodorus' *Historia Tripartita* relates[18]) he placed him under excommunication. Which time having passed, when the emperor greatly lamented and groaned that he was excommunicated, Rufinus, a man well beloved by the emperor, went to Ambrose and asked him to absolve him from the excommunication, and open the doors of the church to him, and allow him to enter. Yet Ambrose now wanting to do this, sharply reprehended the same Rufinus, because he dared to ask such things from him. "And when Rufinus pleaded and said that the Emperor would come, Ambrose, inflamed with heavenly zeal, said, 'Indeed, Rufinus, I tell you in advance that I will prohibit him from entering the sacred thresholds; but if he transforms his power into tyranny, I will willingly undergo death.'"[19] The emperor came after Rufinus, and found Ambrose staying in front of the doors of the church, and waiting for the emperor. Who after he drew near, besought Ambrose that he would absolve the bond of excommunication. Thus when many words had been said back and forth, he still never wished to absolve him, until he had made full amends for his sin. Which severe rebuke benefitted Emperor Theodosius so much that after-

---

18 "Therefore, retreat, retreat, lest you strive to increase the former wickedness with a second sin. Accept the bond by which the Lord has now bound you of all things; for it is the greatest medicine of health. The emperor, obedient to these words (for he had been nourished by Divine teachings and clearly knew what belongs to priests and what belongs to kings), groaning and weeping, returned to his royal duties. And when a continuous period of eight months had passed, the celebration of the Nativity of Our Savior drew near. However, the emperor, residing in the palace with constant lamentations, incessantly shed continuous tears" (Bk. 9, c. 30 (PL 69, 1145C)).

19 *Ibid.* (PL 69, 1146A-B).

wards when the emperor was in Constantinople he greatly praised Ambrose on account of this and other things, saying: "Hardly have I found a teacher of truth. For Ambrose alone, I know, deserves to be called a worthy pontiff."[20]

Certainly if there were now many bishops like Ambrose, wars between Christian rulers would not be so great and so frequent, so many slaughters of Christians would not have occurred, all Christendom would not be shaken with so many disturbances, neither would so many tragedies be stirred up in it, nor would as many heresies have arisen as we see now. For the greatest part of these things have arisen from the bishops' negligence and timidity, who, when the tempest of heresies arose, did not stand up as a wall for the house of Israel, so that they would dare to openly contradict the kings, princes, and other rulers, who support the archheretics of the present time. Nay, what is worse, in some kingdoms all the bishops except one or two subscribe to the opinion of their heretical kings. Now that all the bishops of that kingdom came into the same heretical opinion, is proved by this evidence, that the one who contradicted the king, was publicly beheaded, and made a true martyr of God. If all the other bishops had truly wanted to imitate this martyr bishop, I do not doubt that the otherwise good king would have continued in the Catholic faith. For it is unlikely that the otherwise good king would have wanted to contradict all the bishops solely by his own prudence. But because he was firstly stirred up to heresies by one or several bishops, and then when the other bishops kept silence or acquiesced, the heresy was so confirmed in the king, that it thence proceeded to nearly the whole kingdom. It is evident that the bishops' negligence was the first cause of such a great evil as that.

I also heard that there is another kingdom in upper Germany, which was nearly completely infected by the Lutheran heresy, yet I knew that no bishop until now has died

---

20 *Ibid.* (PL 69, 1147C).

for the Catholic faith, because all wanted to submit to the royal command rather than to God. And it is evident that the same thing happened to the other German princes, who accepted Luther's heresy, and until the present time maintain it. Because if those bishops (as they were held to do) had resisted them, and openly cried out for the Catholic faith, it is likely that they would not have so easily subscribed to Luther's heresies, and gone headlong after him. Regarding the heresy of the Hussites arisen long ago among the Bohemians, the cause was the negligence of a certain archbishop of Prague, as Aeneas Sylvius bears witness in his book, *De origine Bohemorum*, that it did not perish quickly. For when it firstly arose, Archbishop Sbinco of Prague acted very diligently against John Hus, for the cause of the faith. But when he died an untimely death, [Sigismund] Albicus was appointed in his place, "a singular abyss of extreme greed," about whom, among other things, the same Aeneas Sylvius reports these things. "Once asked, among all sounds, which he would hear with more annoyance, he said, 'The sound of those breaking jaw bones.' Indeed, a suitable pontiff, who would provide fuel to the rising heresy."[21] And finally he says on account of the death of the previous archbishop, and the inactivity and idleness of the successor, the heresy of the Hussites persisted.

The things which we said are required of bishops so far, we have inferred from merely from the notion of "shepherd." Moreover, there is another name bestowed upon them in Holy Writ, by virtue of which it is clearly evident that they are assigned another work. For bishops are called "dispensers" by Paul. For when describing to Titus the virtues with which a bishop ought to be endowed, he says: "A bishop must be without crime, as the steward [*dispensatorem*] of God" (1, 7). And in I Corinthians he says about himself and the other Apostles, who were all bishops: "Let a man so account

---

21 C. 35, p. 62.

of us as of the ministers of Christ, and the dispensers of the mysteries of God" (4, 1). The "mysteries of God" are not merely those which pertain to the doctrine of the faith, but all the Sacraments: because under those things, and the signs, which we see, they inwardly contain some hidden grace, rightly called "mysteries." For Matrimony, which is one of the seven Sacraments which the Catholic Church celebrates, when Paul wished to praise it, he called it a mystery.[22] For in that passage where we read, "This is a great sacrament": the Greek word for "sacrament" is "mystery," when saying as follows: τὸ μυστήριον τοῦτο μέγα ἐστίν. Now the interpreter understanding very well that all Sacraments inwardly contain something of much greater importance than are those things which they outwardly show, rightly reckoned them to be mysteries, and hence translated "sacrament" for "mystery." Only the bishop is the dispenser of all the mysteries. Because even though the other lower priests can administer some of the Sacraments, namely, Baptism, Penance, Eucharist, Matrimony, and Extreme Unction; nevertheless the other two, namely, Confirmation and Orders, can only be administered by bishops. This work then is incumbent upon bishops, that they dispense those Sacraments, which can only be administered by bishops, to their subjects according to each one's need and merit.

Yet "Here it is required," as Paul says, "among the dispensers, that a man be found faithful" (v. 2). For there are many of them, even though they were bishops for a long time, who nevertheless never have dispensed any one of these Sacraments to their subjects, nor have they taken care (which is much worse) to dispense them through other bishops. For this reason I know there are many men and women of advanced age in many dioceses, who have never received the Sacrament of Confirmation; very many also, who have departed from this life in an advanced age without it. And indeed, since

---

22 Cf. Eph. 5, 32.

Third cause of heresies: Negligence of bishops and pastors

it is certain from the testimony of holy men, that this Sacrament gives a certain fortitude to those who worthily receive it, whereby they are made stronger, and they can more easily resist the temptations of the devil: it ought not to be doubted that many due to weakness and fragility have fallen into many vices, and moreover heresies, who, if they had been strengthened by the Sacrament of Confirmation, would have manfully resisted, and would have been free from all these things. Whoever rightly perceives the fault and destruction of all of these people, will attribute it to the negligence of the bishops, who, if they had been faithful dispensers, would have delivered them all from eternal death.

Regarding the Sacrament of Orders, how faithfully many bishops dispense it, it is unnecessary to make a long discourse, since on the contrary they distribute it very profusely. Thus they are stingy with Confirmation, but prodigal with Holy Orders. For all without any distinction are today promoted to the priesthood. And I have not seen or heard of anyone, so uncouth and uneducated, and infected with the worst morals, who if he seeks after the priesthood, he would not attain it. Because if he is rejected by his bishop on account of unworthiness, he is not lacking "a lid that fits the dish" (as it said in the proverb[23]), namely, another bishop, who promotes him to the priesthood from a dispensation of the Pope. We will show, with God as our helper, how great an occasion of heresies is the unworthiness of many priests in the next chapter. Now to whom these evils ought to be imputed, it is not necessary to search much, since it is very clearly established from Paul's teaching that all those things ought to be attributed to bishops who promote unworthy men. For when admonishing Timothy, his disciple and bishop, that he would not

---

23 Cf. Erasmus, *Adagia chiliades* 1.10.72 (alias n. 972; cf. *Adagiorum Chiliades iuxta locos communes digestae* (Sumptibus haeredum Andreae Wecheli, Claudii Marnii, et Io. Aubrii, 1599), p. 1650).

lightly confer ecclesiastical Orders, says: "Impose not hands lightly upon any man, neither be partaker of other men's sins" (I Tim. 5, 22). Theophylactus says in his commentaries on Paul: "'Not lightly,' that is, not from the first examination, nor from the third, but often and accurately examining. For the matter is not without danger. But listen how this is so. 'Neither be partaker of other men's sins.' For of those things which he will commit, you are the cause, and for that reason just as you are a partaker of the good works, so also of the sins. Moreover, you are guilty of past sins, because you neglected them, and you made darkness light."[24] From the words of Theophylactus it is very clearly established that the sins of unworthy priests, according to Paul's opinion, ought to be blamed back upon the bishops, who temerariously promoted them to the priesthood.

From all the aforesaid it is evident that there are three things highly necessary for all bishops, so that they rightly perform their ministry, all which things they are held to administer to their subjects. These are the food of doctrine, the diligent guarding of the sheep, and the dispensation of the Sacraments. Now so that the bishop may be able to fully carry out all these things, it is necessary that he know his sheep, and always watch over them lest they lack any of the things which he is obliged to give to them. It is firstly befitting that he know them, so that he may know those whom he ought to feed. For if he did not know them, it could not happen that he could suitably feed and manfully defend them. Wherefore the Wise Man says: "Be diligent to know the countenance of thy cattle, and consider thy own flocks" (Prov. 27, 23). [Bede] when interpreting these words in his commentaries on the Proverbs, says: "The pastor of a church is bidden to take diligent care of those committed to him. He must know their doings, and he must remember to correct the vices which he may observe among them. For you will

---

24 *Expositio in Epistolam I ad Timotheum* (PG 125, 74A-B).

Third cause of heresies: Negligence of bishops and pastors

not always have the authority to feed the Lord's sheep, but the crown that you will receive is eternal if you have served well the position entrusted to you in your time."[25] It is also necessary that the sheep know their pastor, so that they may know him whom they ought to follow, and by whom they can safely receive food. These two things Our Savior stated in one passage, Who, when He said that He is the good shepherd, to prove this he immediately, added the qualities of the good shepherd, when saying: "I know mine, and mine know me" (Jn. 10, 14). By which words He clearly taught us that he is not the good shepherd who does not know his sheep, and whom the sheep do not know.

Bishops are also held to watch over the sheep committed to them, and take care that they do not lack anything necessary for salvation. For the word "bishop [*episcopus*]" means the same thing in Greek as "overseer."[26] Thus the name itself by which they are called teaches them they ought to take care to guard and watch over their subjects. For which reason Paul reckons that subjects are held to giving obedience to their prelates. "Obey your prelates," he says, "and be subject to them. For they watch as being to render an account of your souls" (Heb. 13, 17). And hence it is that when Christ the true and best shepherd of all was born, "There were... shepherds watching," as Luke relates, "and keeping the night watches over their flock" (Lk. 2, 8). For at the time when He was born, He instructed the pastors of the Church to watch, and keep the vigils of the night, over the flock committed to them. And the wise Ecclesiasticus commends this diligence to every ruler, as the thing most necessary for him, speaking thus: "Have they made thee ruler? be not lifted up: be among them as one of them. Have care of them, and so sit down, and when thou hast acquitted thyself of all thy charge, take

---

25 *Allegorica expositio in Parabolas Salomonis*, bk. 3 (PL 91, 1019A). St. Jerome is incorrectly cited here.
26 I. e., ἐπίσκοπος (*epískopos*).

thy place: that thou mayst rejoice for them" (Eccli. 32, 1-3). Not immediately after a little care has been taken does he permit to rejoice, but when he has acquitted himself of all his charge. And truly if the Wise Man exacts such diligent care from every ruler, it certainly ought to be believed that much greater is necessary for bishops, who are held to do more things for the welfare of their people than other rulers.

Yet there are many bishops, who, having completely forgotten their name, do not have more concern for them, than if they were not going to give an account for them to God. They work diligently to suckle the milk from them and to remove the wool, but they completely disregard looking out for them. They do not consider that they were appointed unto this, namely, that they would take care of the sheep, but that they could collect the fruits from them. And hence they very diligently do the latter, but when it comes to the former, it is remarkable how negligent and lazy they are. Although for ten, twenty, and thirty years they have wrested away fruits from the sheep, many of them do not know their sheep, nor are they known by them. For while they are occupied in the courts of princes and focusing on many things that are far removed from their own duties, they disregard visiting their own sheep and giving what they owe to them. Bishops of this kind ought not to be called bishops, because Christ Our Savior says that such men ought not to be called shepherds, but hirelings. "The hireling, and he that is not the shepherd, whose own the sheep are not, seeth the wolf coming, and leaveth the sheep, and flieth: and the wolf catcheth, and scattereth the sheep: and the hireling flieth, because he is a hireling: and he hath no care for the sheep" (Jn. 10, 12-13).

By many reasons assigned here by Christ Our Savior bishops, and other rulers of souls, who reside outside the flock of sheep, and perpetually, or for a long time, remain outside their dioceses are convicted that they ought not to be called shepherds, but "hirelings." They "leave" the sheep,

Third cause of heresies: Negligence of bishops and pastors

as long as they do not have their association. They "flee," when they depart from the care and duty which they are obliged to fulfill. Finally they think that nothing pertains to them concerning the sheep. Hence these men seem to me to be similar to ostriches, whose nature is such, Job being the witness, that they leave their eggs on the earth, and forget that the foot may tread upon them, or that the beasts of the field may break them, and they hardened against their young ones, as though they were not theirs.[27] Now what follows from this absence of the shepherd, and very crass negligence, the Savior stated in the aforementioned words, saying: "The wolf catcheth, and scattereth the sheep" (Jn. 10, 12). Whether you wish to understand by the word "wolf" tyrants or heretics, anyone of them attacks the sheep more boldly, and kills them more securely, the more he sees that the shepherd is far away, who could assist the sheep. But it seems truer to the literal meaning if in this passage we would understand by "wolf" the heretic, simply because He said that he "scattereth" the flock. For no one else scatters the flock as does the heretic, who, when deceiving them by his false teaching, separates them from the one flock of the Church, and compels them to wander astray through the paths of errors.

From which things it is very clearly established that often the absence, and very great negligence, of bishops and other rulers is the chief reason that some heresies circulate among the people, and the people are seduced by heresies. For when those men are absent, it thence easily happens that anyone may think as he wishes, and what things he thinks he may teach with impunity. For something similar happened long ago due solely to the fault of a ruler in the book of Judges, where these words are had: "In those days there was no king in Israel: but every one did that which seemed right to himself" (21, 24). The parable of the man sowing good seed

---

27 Cf. Job. 39, 14-16.

in his field comes to the same thing, in which an enemy, having taken the occasion that the guards of the field were asleep, oversowed cockle. For the devil, who is the clear enemy of the whole human race, seeing such negligence of the rulers, that they seem to sleep, often oversows the cockle of heresies in God's Church, which is His field in which He firstly had sown good seed, that is, the true doctrine of the faith.[28] And since Paul says that everything was done to the Fathers in a figure,[29] it will not be absurd if we say that the woman, about whom it is read that her son, whom she was nursing when awake, when sleeping at night she overlaid, and killed, signifies this same thing.[30] For while the pastors of souls keep awake, and take that care of those which they are held to do: then they nurse their subjects, whom they ought to love as children, with true doctrine and good examples. Yet if they sleep with the sleep of negligence and of the body, they kill the same children by their laziness and idleness.

But lest anyone object to me that an argument for proving a doctrine ought not to be taken from the parabolical or mystical sense, I wish to present clear testimony of Sacred Scripture for this matter. "Where there is no governor, the people shall fall" (Prov. 11, 14). And God Himself when speaking through the prophet Ezechiel about the shepherds states this more clearly, speaking thus: "Woe to the shepherds of Israel, that fed themselves: should not the flocks be fed by the shepherds? You ate the milk, and you clothed yourselves with the wool, and you killed that which was fat: but my flock you did not feed. The weak you have not strengthened, and that which was sick you have not healed, that which was broken you have not bound up, and that which was driven away you have not brought again, neither have you sought

---

28 Cf. Mt. 13, 24-30.
29 Cf. I Cor. 10, 6.
30 Cf. III Kings 3, 19-20.

Third cause of heresies: Negligence of bishops and pastors

that which was lost: but you ruled over them with rigour, and with a high hand. And my sheep were scattered, because there was no shepherd: and they became the prey of all the beasts of the field, and were scattered" (34, 2-5). Thus since the scattering of the sheep, which signifies a departure from the faith, arises from the negligence of the shepherds, it is evident that the guilt of them all ought to be imputed not only to the sheep themselves, which were scattered and erred, but also to their shepherds on account of their negligence.

For the prophet Jeremias laments the condemnation of both the peoples and of the rulers in one context of words, speaking thus: "From the daughter of Sion all her beauty is departed: her princes are become like rams that find no pastures: and they are gone away without strength before the face of the pursuer" (Lam. 1, 6). When saying that all beauty has departed from the daughter of Sion, he indicated the sins of the people. But when saying that the princes have gone away without strength, he expressed the negligence of the prelates, from whom the evil of the whole people arose. For [Rabanus[31]], when expounding these words of Jeremias in his commentaries on the Lamentations, says: "Also by this opinion, negligent leaders of the Church of God are accused, through whose carelessness all the beauty of the Christian people perishes, as they do not strive in the meditation of Divine law, nor in the worship of piety, nor in the exercise of sacred virtues. Instead, they are driven away by the allurements of pleasure and through various crimes, according to the suggestion of the tempting enemy, whose danger primarily affects those who are placed in positions of authority. They have chosen to follow secular desires rather than the commandments of God. Hence, they do not deserve to receive the glory of the heavenly kingdom with the holy

---

31 St. Jerome is incorrectly cited here.

Doctors, but rather they are forced to endure the punishment of Gehenna with the devil and his angels."[32]

But God teaches us this opinion more clearly, Who after He had said through the prophet Ezechiel that His sheep were scattered, and became the prey of all the beasts of the field, then He threatens very grave punishment to these shepherds for this reason, speaking thus through the same prophet: "As I live, saith the Lord God, forasmuch as my flocks have been made a spoil, and my sheep are become a prey to all the beasts of the field, because there was no shepherd... Therefore, ye shepherds, hear the word of the Lord: Thus saith the Lord God: Behold I myself come upon the shepherds, I will require my flock at their hand... Behold I myself will seek my sheep, and will visit them. As the shepherd visiteth his flock in the day when he shall be in the midst of his sheep that were scattered, so will I visit my sheep, and will deliver them out of all the places where they have been scattered in the cloudy and dark day" (Ez. 34, vv. 8 & 11-12). Certainly God could say nothing harder and clearer against the shepherds, than that He was going to require the lost sheep at their hand, so that they would give an account for them, which account since they would not be able to give a good one, it will be necessary that they be punished for their sin.

The Lord willed to teach us this same thing, not only by word, but also by deed, so that the shepherds and rulers would understand that His threat is not empty, which they would know has already been commanded for execution, even if only once. For since long ago the people of Israel had fornicated with the daughters of Moab, and had adored their gods, the Lord being angry said to Moses: "Take all the princes of the people, and hang them up on gibbets against the sun: that my fury may be turned away from Israel" (Num. 25, 4). Origen, in his twentieth homily on the book of Numbers, says: "If men would think about this, they would never

---

32 *Commentaria in Jeremiam*, bk. 18, c. 1 (PL 111, 1188D-1189A).

Third cause of heresies: Negligence of bishops and pastors

desire or seek after rulership of the people. For it is enough for me to be convicted for my own offenses; it is enough for me to give account for myself and for my sins. What need is there for me to be menaced with sins of the people as well, and to be 'hung up against the sun,' before which nothing can be hidden, nothing concealed?"[33] Therefore whoever has received the care of souls, if he does not want God be angry with him, ought to always take care of their guidance; he ought to always dwell with them, and diligently consider what things are needful, and never, unless forced by great necessity, leave the association with his sheep: but with the prophet Isaias say: "I am upon the watchtower of the Lord, standing continually by day: and I am upon my ward, standing whole nights" (21, 8).

From all these aforesaid things it is very evidently established that the negligence and absence of prelates and other rulers is a cause of heresies, and moreover of many evils. All these things ought to be blamed upon the rulers themselves, from whose negligence they have proceeded. Yet there are many whose mouths have declined to evil words, to make excuses in sins.[34] For some of them want to defend their absences from their bishoprics and parishes with this excuse, that they have substituted for themselves other persons who are good and worthy of the great duty, by whom they do everything which they are obliged to do: and they say that this is enough, because (as they say) the owner of sheep does not always himself feed the sheep, nay, he uses the work of other shepherds, to whom he entrusts them. And hence it is concluded that he fulfilled his duty very well, when he substitutes good vicars for himself.

But this excuse of theirs cannot help them at all, nay, it turns into a greater sin for them, when they seem to arrogate more to themselves than one ought by it. For God is the

---

33 *In Numeros Homiliae*, n. 4 (PG 12, 735B).
34 Cf. Ps. 140, 4.

owner of them, Who says: "All souls are mine" (Ez. 18, 4). And the sheep themselves acknowledge this same thing, saying: "We are the people of his pasture and the sheep of his pasture" (Ps. 94, 7).[35] And they would certainly understand very clearly that they are not the owners of those sheep, if they wish to heed the words by which Christ appointed Peter the shepherd of souls. "Feed," He says, "my sheep" (Jn. 21, 17). And again, "Feed my lambs" (v. 16). He did not say, "Your sheep," but "my." And He did not say, "Your lambs," but "my." Thus God says that He is the owner of the sheep and lambs. Bishops, however, and other rulers of souls, are shepherds, to whom God entrusted them, so that they would take care to feed and protect them, for a promised wage of the labor, if they did it correctly. Otherwise, if God would reckon that they are the owners, He would not ask from them any account of the sheep, nor require the sheep lost from the hand of the prelates, as He Himself warned that He was going to do this through the prophet Ezechiel:[36] but no one is an owner of sheep who entrusts his sheep to a shepherd, so that he could substitute another for himself, unless perhaps with this condition, that he would be obliged to give an account for all. And God did not entrust his sheep to the bishops, or to the other shepherds, so that they would substitute vicars for themselves, to whom they would entrust the sheep. And if contrary to God's will he would entrust God's sheep to another, nonetheless those which perish due to the negligence of the vicar, God will require from the shepherd, to whom He committed them. And he could not defend himself by this reason, that the sheep perished while he was unaware: because (as it is stated in the chapter, *Quamvis*[37])

---

35 This translation is found in the Roman Psalter. The Vulgate translation of this verse is "...the sheep of his hand."
36 Cf. Ez. 34, 10.
37 *Decretals of Gregory IX*, bk. 5, tit. 41 (*De regulis juris*), c. 10.

Third cause of heresies: Negligence of bishops and pastors

"There is no excuse for the shepherd, if the wolf eats the sheep, and the shepherd is unaware."

Furthermore, even if we would freely concede that pastors of souls ought to be regarded as the owners of the sheep, still not in such a way that they could dispose of anything concerning them against God's will, Who is their supreme master. Now God does not will that the rulers of souls commit them to others, since others do not equally take care of them, as they would if they were the owners. For Christ Our Savior says: "The hireling flieth, because he is a hireling: and he hath no care for the sheep" (Jn. 10, 13). Rarely are things belonging to another as well cared for as one's own.[38] The saying of Manlius Torquatus in Titus Livy has been praised, in which he said that what anyone does with someone else's eyes hardly ever succeeds.[39] And so I reckon that the care of sheep can hardly ever succeed which is done by vicars, because they are often not as they should be; but they are "more intent," as Bernard says, "on emptying the purses of his people than on purifying their souls of their vices."[40] They are often such that about any of them it can be said what Virgil said that a shepherd reproachfully said about another shepherd: "This hireling shepherd here wrings hourly twice their udders, from the flock filching the life-juice, from the lambs their milk."[41]

---

38 "And moreover to feel that a thing is one's private property makes an inexpressibly great difference for pleasure; for the universal feeling of love for oneself is surely not purposeless, but a natural instinct" (Aristotle, *Politics*, bk. 2, c. 5 (1263a)).

39 Cf. Livy, *The History of Rome*, bk. 26, c. 22, ln. 6: "Shameless, he said, was a pilot and a general too, who, when he uses other men's eyes for everything that is to be done, demands that the lives and fortunes of others be entrusted to him."

40 *Sermons on the Canticle of Canticles*, serm. 77, n. 1 (PL 183, 1156A).

41 *Eclogue 3*, lns. 5-6.

Next, subjects themselves respect vicars less, and fear them less: hence it follows that vicars can less keep them in virtue, and deter them from vices. Moses, the first prelate of the synagogue, when forced to leave the people, was going to spend a short enough time with the Lord, lest people be unsupervised [*Acephalus* or "headless"] while he was absent, he substituted a vicar for himself, a truly upright man, namely, his brother Aaron. Yet he could not deter the people from making and adoring a golden calf: which nevertheless, when Moses was present, they never attempted to do. Thus the people who when Moses was present had been faithful, when he was absent, fell into idolatry.[42] Moreover, even though he may be a very good man whom the bishop appoints as a vicar in his place, still he will perform his ministry much better and more diligently when the bishop is present, than when he is absent. And hence I think it is unsuitable that a matter of such great importance, as is the care of souls, would be performed by vicars alone, since it would entail great danger to the souls, because (as we said) what anyone does with someone else's eyes hardly ever succeeds.

The Samaritan who set the man wounded by robbers on his own beast, and brought him to an inn, himself took care of him as long as he remained in the inn. But when it was necessary to leave, he entrusted him to the host, because he could not be present. And as (let us say something clearer) Our Savior and Master Himself never, while He lived on earth, entrusted His sheep to Peter or to anyone else, lest He give an occasion to another shepherd by His example, so that He would take care of the sheep through them, to which care He was obliged. After He rose from the dead, and not before, He said to Peter: "Feed my sheep" (Jn. 21, 17). Even though before death He promised that he would give the keys to Peter, still He did not give them until after His death, when

---

42 Cf. Ex. 32, 1 ff.

Third cause of heresies: Negligence of bishops and pastors

it was already close that He was going to depart from us in a bodily and visible form to the Father. When alive He never entrusted His mother to John or another, but only when near to death, when He could not minister or provide any assistance to her.[43] Otherwise, while he was alive, and was able, He did not want to entrust her to another. Therefore, by His example Christ Our Savior taught the bishops not to completely rely upon vicars, but what they could perform themselves, they would not entrust to others.

There are still other rulers of souls who think that they are excused for this reason from residing in their own parishes and associating with their sheep, namely, because they have obtained a dispensation from the Supreme Pontiff, whereby he grants them unrestricted permission, so that they could be absent from their parishes as long as they wish, and live anywhere they choose. But this excuse is so futile and empty that it is unable to defend against not only the fire of hell, but also the slightest breeze or gentle warmth. For since the residence of pastors among their sheep was commanded to the pastors by Divine law, the Pope cannot without an urgent necessity, that is, for the sake of some greater good, dispense from it. For even though he is the supreme pastor of the Church, still authority was given to him, as Paul says, "unto edification, and not for destruction" (II Cor. 10, 8).

Thus since we now leave standing this very clear opinion, that many evils and moreover heresies are from the negligence of pastors, it is necessary to remove this cause, and uproot from the very start this root of so many evils, lest poisonous branches arise from it, and heresy arise from the negligence of the shepherds. Bishops are compelled to continually reside in their dioceses, such that they cannot depart from them, except by a great urgent necessity. Other rulers of souls are very strictly bound to do the same, which if they neglect to do, it will be befitting to deprive them of

---

43 Cf. Jn. 19, 26-27.

their benefices, so that at least the fear of punishment would compel those whom the love of virtue does not draw to the good. If all these things are carried out rightly without any dispensation, I expect that with God's help many evils and moreover heresies are avoided, which, without these remedies, we now often see to have arisen elsewhere.

Chapter V

Concerning the fourth cause of heresies, which is the unworthiness of bishops and other priests.

Bishops, and other rulers of souls, are not merely negligent in feeding and guarding the sheep entrusted to themselves, and fulfilling the other things which are obligatory for them by law: but many of them are so idle and lazy that they also do not seem to take care of their own souls. Wherefore they ought to be reckoned unworthy that such a sublime office should rightly be conferred upon them. For (as Ecclesiasticus says) "He that is evil to himself, to whom will he be good?" (14, 5). He did not say this because he deemed it to be impossible: but because he thought it is difficult and rarely happens, that he who is evil to himself would be good to others. For these two things, namely, to be good to oneself and to others, are different from each other, such that one of them can be separated from the other, and it is not repugnant that both are found together in the same man, nay, sometimes it is necessary. For two things are required of bishops and other priests of the lower order, of which if either one is lacking, it can be the cause of many evils. We have just discussed about the negligence of the shepherds and of other rulers in the previous chapter, where we showed by many very clear reasons that it is the cause of many heresies. It now remains that we also show that the unworthiness of bishops and of other priests, even if they otherwise take due care about the sheep entrusted to them, is a very clear cause which up until now has produced many heresies, and can produce many more, unless it be attended to soon.

Now so that we may be able to accomplish this, it is necessary to firstly show from Holy Writ what sort of men bishops, and other priests of the lower order ought to be, so that they may be rightly reckoned worthy and capable of fulfilling such a duty. Concerning which matter it is not necessary to consult another besides Paul, who delineated very well what sort of men bishops and other priests ought to be, when writing to Timothy and Titus. "A bishop," he says, "must be without crime, as the steward of God: not proud, not subject to anger, not given to wine, no striker, not greedy of filthy lucre: but given to hospitality, gentle, prudent,[1] just, holy, continent: embracing that faithful word which is according to doctrine, that he may be able to exhort in sound doctrine, and to convince the gainsayers" (Titus 1, 7-9). Paul wrote nearly the same words to Timothy.[2] It is necessary to briefly examine each part of this passage, and afterwards it will thence be evident how many priests there are who lack some of these qualities, and how many lack all of them.

The first part of the bishop's role, which encompasses almost all the others, Paul says, is that the bishop should be free from every crime. It is not required that he be without sin, because this is nearly impossible for a man, as John the Evangelist teaches. "If we say," John says, "that we have no sin, we deceive ourselves, and the truth is not in us" (I Jn. 1, 8). Thus Paul says that a bishop ought to be without crime, which is not of any sort, but a grave and mortal sin. This which Paul says is now necessary for a bishop, God commanded to Aaron the priest long ago in a figure and under a veil in the Old Testament, when saying: "Whosoever of thy seed throughout their families, hath a blemish, he shall not offer bread to his God. Neither shall he approach to minister to him" (Lev. 21, 17-18). The Gloss, which is called

---

1 "A Latin translator of the Greek word, σώφρονα, by an ambiguity, translated "prudent [*prudens*]" instead of "chaste [*pudicus*]" (*Bibliorum sacrorum latinae versiones antiquae, seu Vetus Italica*, vol. 3, p. 896). This word is translated as "sober [*sobrius*]" in the Vulgate.
2 Cf. I Tim. 3, 2 ff.

Fourth cause of heresies: The unworthiness of bishops and other priests

the Ordinary, when interpreting these words, speaks thus: "These words taken literally seems to be quite absurd. Such blemishes are not within the power or will of a person. Therefore, he describes the vices of the soul through the blemishes of the body. For when he assumes the role of the people's leader, he approaches as a physician to a sick person. If he himself is sick, with what presumption does he want to heal? Therefore, he should lead by example, who, being dead to all passions, lives spiritually. With such intention, he does not entirely yield to the weakness of the body, nor is greatly shattered by insult."[3]

From the words of this Gloss one reason is established, on account of which a priest ought to be without crime, and without blemish: namely, because he is put forth as an example to the people. Therefore lest the people striving to imitate him fall into vices after him, it is necessary that he be completely clean and without crime. But there can be another not lesser reason for that precept, namely, lest the bishop be less able to rebuke a sinning subject, if he himself is infected with the same crime, about which he rebukes another. Wherefore Paul when writing to Timothy said: "It behoveth a bishop to be blameless" (I Tim. 3, 2). Which ought not to be so understood that Paul reckons that a bishop ought to be completely blameless, but rather that he be not subject and addicted to any public sin, about which he could be rightly reprehended by others, lest it be said to him: "Thou hypocrite, cast out first the beam in thy own eye, and then shalt thou see to cast out the mote out of another's eye" (Mt. 7, 5). It is certainly unworthy that someone would reprehend in another what he himself, with others knowing, did. For Paul rightly rebukes such a man, when saying:

---

3 *Biblia sacra cum Glossis*, vol. 1, fol. 236r D. This quotation was slightly modified and clarified according to a similar passage found in Rabanus' *Expositiones in Leviticum*, bk. 6 (PL 108, 484D-485B).

"Wherein thou judgest another, thou condemnest thyself" (Rom. 2, 1). And again: "Thou therefore that teachest another, teachest not thyself: thou that preachest that men should not steal, stealest: thou that sayest, men should not commit adultery, committest adultery" (vv. 21-22). For this reason Our Savior said to the Jews accusing the adulterous woman: "He that is without sin among you, let him first cast a stone at her" (Jn. 8, 7). With these words, He intended to indicate that someone who is subject to sins is unworthy to either punish or reprimand others. For he casts stones against one sinning, who punishes him for sin, or reprehends him for sin. But no one ought to cast stones at another except he who is free from crime.

After having now explained in general and universally speaking the bishop's perfection, it is necessary that we briefly discuss in particular the rest of the qualities which Paul enumerated. For after Paul said that a bishop ought to be without crime, he then set forth some specific crimes from which he ought to especially abstain, and he firstly says: "Not proud." The vice of pride, even though it is forbidden to all, it still ought to be much more interdicted to an ecclesiastical ruler, from whom all arrogance of pride and all desire for ruling should be completely absent. For Christ Our Savior when instructing the first bishops of the Church said to them: "You know that the princes of the Gentiles lord it over them; and they that are the greater, exercise power upon them. It shall not be so among you: but whosoever will be the greater among you, let him be your minister: and he that will be first among you, shall be your servant. Even as the Son of man is not come to be ministered unto, but to minister" (Mt. 20, 25-28). And Blessed Peter teaches the other bishops the same thing which he had learned from Christ the Teacher of all truth, when speaking thus: "Feed the flock of God which is among you, taking care of it, not by constraint, but willingly, according to God: not for filthy lucre's sake, but voluntarily:

Fourth cause of heresies: The unworthiness of bishops and other priests

neither as lording it over the clergy, but being made a pattern of the flock from the heart" (I Pet. 5, 2-3).

Next, Paul adds: "Not subject to anger." One is not subject to anger who is angered now and again, but he who is frequently moved by anger, and who when given a very slight occasion is always stirred up. No worse vice could befall a bishop, who ought to teach and govern others. For through anger the judgment of reason is sometimes so thrown into disorder that one does not at all know what he is doing, nor does he remember afterwards (as is wont to happen to drunkards) those things which he had then done. "My eye is troubled," David says, "through indignation" (Ps. 6, 8). And a certain wise man said: "Anger so clouds the mind that it cannot perceive the truth."[4] Furthermore, all men shun social interactions with angry men. Solomon also advised all to do this, speaking thus: "Be not a friend to an angry man, and do not walk with a furious man: lest perhaps thou learn his ways, and take scandal to thy soul" (Prov. 22, 24-25). Now it is unbefitting that a bishop would have this vice, due to which he rightly ought to be avoided by everyone.

Paul afterwards says: "Not given to wine." One is not given to wine (as we said about the angry man) who drinks a little wine. And this evil also destroys the sharpness of intellect and provokes the passions of the flesh, which often lead people into many vices. "Wine and women make wise men fall off" (Eccli. 19, 2). It then follows in Paul's words: "No striker," that is, lest in reprimanding and reprehending he would be so severe and harsh, that the reprehension becomes an insult. For the Greek wording used there, μὴ πλήκτην, (as Jerome noted[5]) does not mean a striker of hands, but of

---

4 Dionysius Cato, *Distichs of Cato*, bk. 2, n. 4.
5 "Now after wine drinking, he commands this, that he should not be a striker. This, of course, edifies the hearer when understood literally, that he should not readily stretch forth his hand to strike; he should not burst out in a rage to punch someone else

the tongue; it is thus the same as if he would have said: "Not insulting, or biting." Or, if you wish to extend that word to the striking of the hand, as Theophylactus seems to extend,[6] "No striker," that is he who neither by words nor by lashes strikes violently, but with kindness and leniency let him punish his subjects. Paul says that a bishop ought to be "Not greedy of filthy lucre." By which word Paul understood not only that profit which is unlawful for everyone, but also all forms of business or trade altogether, so that he wished that to be also removed from a bishop, which was permitted to others who are laymen. For all temporal business of profit is sordid to a priest.

After having recounted the crimes which a bishop ought to avoid, he then recounts the virtues with which he ought to be endowed: because (as Gregory says) "It is a small thing not to do evil if one does not also apply oneself, by diligent effort, to good deeds."[7] Paul therefore says: "But given to hospitality," that is, he not merely ought not to desire what belongs to others, like those who covet, but he also generously give to those in need from his own possessions. For which reason the sacred Doctors said that the goods of bishops and

---

in the mouth. But it is better to say that one is 'not a striker' who is gentle and patient so that he knows what should be said at the moment, what should be held in silence; not to 'strike' the conscience of the weak with unhelpful words. For the Apostle, when forming the ruler of a church, forbids him to be a boxer and a pancratiast (which is reproached even among the common people and in heathens if it happens), but as I have said [pay heed to] this: let not the abusive and garrulous man ruin one whom he was able to correct with modesty and mildness" (*Commentary on Titus* (PL 26, 567B-C)).

6 "Neither striking with hands nor using bitter and exasperated words importunately. For he is a physician. Indeed, a physician treats wounds, but he himself does not inflict them" (*Expositio in Epistolam ad Titum* (PG 125, 150D)).

7 *Homilies on the Gospels*, hom. 13, n. 1 (PL 76, 1123D).

other priests are the goods of travelers, and other poor men, whom they are necessarily obliged to assist. Afterwards he says, "Gentle," that is, not envious, but (as Theophylactus says[8]) endowed with moderation, or (as Jerome interprets[9]) a lover of good works. Then he adds, "Prudent," and rightly so because the Teacher of truth Himself said: "The faithful and wise [*prudens*] servant, whom his lord hath appointed over his family" (Mt. 24, 45). And Solomon says: "A prince void of prudence shall oppress many by calumny" (Prov. 28, 16).

Afterwards Paul puts "Continent," which word (according to Jerome's opinion[10]) does not only refer to lust, but pertains to all affection, anger, ambition, envy, fear, so that the bishop would conquer all these.

Finally he says: "Embracing that faithful word which is according to doctrine, that he may be able to exhort in sound doctrine, and to convince the gainsayers." In which words he describes the proper function of a bishop. For the things which he enumerated up until now are also required of the subjects, just as of the bishop. For it is necessary that a bishop, and any other ruler of souls, be learned, so that he may know very well those things which pertain to the faith, and pertain to morals. And the utterance of these things is the "faithful word," which a bishop ought to embrace. Otherwise, if he does not know these necessary things, it will necessarily happen what Solomon says: "An unwise king shall be the ruin of his people" (Eccli. 10, 3). Hence Blessed Gregory says: "No one presumes to teach an art till he has first, with intent meditation, learned it. What rashness is it, then, for the unskillful to assume pastoral authority, since the government of souls is the art of arts! For who can be ignorant that the sores of the thoughts of men are more occult than the sores of the bowels? And yet how often do men who have no

---

8   *Expositio in Epistolam ad Titum* (PG 125, 150D).
9   *Commentary on Titus* (PL 26, 568A).
10 Cf. *Ibid.* (PL 26, 568C-569A).

knowledge whatever of spiritual precepts fearlessly profess themselves physicians of the heart, though those who are ignorant of the effect of drugs blush to appear as physicians of the flesh!"[11] Wherefore the Lord in the Old Law did not permit him who was blind, or blear-eyed, or had a pearl in his eye to approach the sacerdotal ministry.[12] For examining the truth from this shadow or image of things, we are taught that no one completely ignorant, or very little educated, is worthy to receive the episcopal office.

Now the teaching which a bishop ought to possess, ought to be not doubtful, or vacillating, but firm and constant, especially in matters of faith, in which matters one is not allowed to hesitate at all, but to hold all as most certain. And Paul indicated this when he said: "Embracing that faithful word which is according to doctrine." For not everything which we perhaps somewhat grasp, are we said to embrace: only those things which we take hold of with both arms, and tightly squeeze. Hence [Ambrosiaster[13]], so that he might express a greater firmness and constancy of teaching, did not translate [this word as] "[embracing[14]]," but as "holding firm," so that one should hold very firmly the teaching of the faith, and nowise allow oneself to be torn away from it.

And it is not enough for Paul that a bishop would retain very constantly the teaching of the faith, unless it be such and so great that by it he may be powerful "to exhort" and "to convince" those who gainsay. For the teaching by the bishop is not required only for this, that he make take care of merely his own person, but that he may look out for his subjects,

---

11 *Pastoral Rule*, bk. 1, c. 1 (PL 77, 14A).
12 Cf. Lev. 21, vv. 18 & 20.
13 *Commentaria in Epistolam ad Titum* (PL 17, 499A).
14 The text here has *apprehendentem*, or "grasping," which probably was meant to be *amplectentem*, or "embracing," as found in Titus 1, 9, the verse upon which the author is currently commenting. Hence the latter word has been substituted here.

Fourth cause of heresies: The unworthiness of bishops and other priests

not only teaching the ignorant, but also by consoling the afflicted. And this same Greek word seems to mean more, as one can establish from the testimony of Jerome, who for that which we have "to exhort," he translates, "to console."[15] And this is not enough, but moreover it is befitting that the bishop's teaching be so great, that by it he can "convince the gainsayers." That is, he could convince heretics by testimonies of Sacred Scripture, and other reasons pertaining to this matter, and stand up against their arguments. For these men from among those who gave their names to Christ in Baptism, are alone those who are wont to gainsay the faithful word and sound doctrine.

And that Paul was speaking about heretics, the order of the words teaches very clearly. For after he said that it is fitting that a bishop be able to convince those who gainsay, immediately giving the reason for the said words, he added, "For there are also many disobedient, vain talkers, and seducers: especially they who are of the circumcision: who must be reproved, who subvert whole houses, teaching things which they ought not, for filthy lucre's sake" (Titus 1, vv. 10-11). Notice everything which Blessed Paul requires of bishops, all which things are also necessary for the priests of the lower Order, especially for those who have received the care of souls, one ought to understand from Paul's words. For about this matter Chrysostom clearly admonishes us, who speaks thus: "Discoursing of bishops, and having described their character, and the qualities which they ought to possess, and having passed over the Order of priests, he proceeds to that of deacons. The reason of this omission was, that between priests and bishops there was no great difference. For priests also have received the office of teaching and rule over the Church, and what he has said concerning bishops is applicable to priests."[16]

---

15 *Commentaria in Epistolam ad Titum* (PL 26, 568A).
16 *Homilies on I Timothy*, hom. 11, n. 1 (PG 62, 553).

Book 3, Chapter 5

But now it is necessary that we see whether all bishops and priests are such as Paul reckoned they ought to be. About this matter I was desiring to say nothing, lest I seem to have incurred the curse of Cham, due to the fact that I would want to reveal openly the nakedness of the fathers to all.[17] But because the unworthiness of many bishops and priests is so manifest, that even if I were to keep quiet, I could not by my silence hide it, hence it was necessary for me to bring forth some things from very public matters, so that afterwards I could clearly show that which I determined to say from the beginning of this chapter, that their unworthiness was the cause of many heresies.

There are many bishops and other young guides of souls, and many of such a young age that they have barely passed puberty. Which matter is so clearly bad that it is condemned not only by holy men, but by the testimony of the heathen philosophers. For Aristotle says: "No man chooses the young to guide him, because he does not expect them to be prudent."[18] For prudence is highly necessary for him who ought to rule and correct others. The young, however, not to say adolescents and children, (as Aristotle said) cannot be prudent, because they have no experience of things, or very little, without which prudence can hardly be had. "What doth he know," Ecclesiasticus says, "that hath not been tried? A man that hath much experience, shall think of many things: and he that hath learned many things, shall shew forth understanding. He that hath no experience, knoweth little" (34, 9-10). Since therefore it is evident that adolescents and children have very little experience of things, it also ought to be evident that they are not prudent. "In the ancient," says Job, "is wisdom, and in length of days prudence" (12, 12). From which it is clearly gathered that in the shortness of days of children and adolescents, there cannot be prudence.

---

17 Cf. Gen. 9, 21-25.
18 *Topics*, bk. 3, c. 2, n. 5 (117a25).

Fourth cause of heresies: The unworthiness of bishops and other priests

Whence it is that when God decided to gather helpers for Moses, who would help him to carry the immense burden of ruling, He commanded that they be not children, or adolescents, or young men, but ancients, when speaking thus: "Gather unto me seventy men of the ancients of Israel, whom thou knowest to be ancients and masters of the people" (Num. 11, 16). When saying, "whom thou knowest to be ancients," He expressed that not only oldness of age is necessary, but it is befitting that oldness of mind be conjoined to them. For if only oldness of the body is sought in them, as many as could see them would be able to know it. But when it is said, "whom thou knowest to be ancients and masters of the people," it is clearly evident that not only oldness of the body but also, along with it, oldness of the mind is to be chosen. And it is certainly something monstrous and greatly to be deplored, that he who has been appointed for ruling others would need another ruler or (or so that I may speak more clearly) teacher. For he who does not know how to rule himself, how is he able to rule others?[19] Hence the Wise Man sympathizes with the land which has a child as king, speaking thus: "Woe to thee, O land, when thy king is a child" (Eccle. 10, 16). What a great evil it is to put children in rulership, indeed from it can be easily understood that the Lord threatens this as a very great punishment for the people of Juda, through the prophet Isaias saying: "I will give children to be their princes, and the effeminate shall rule over them" (3, 4).

But although the matter is very clear, and very evil, and exceedingly pernicious, to appoint children or adolescents in the rulership of souls, nevertheless those who have appointed them, or have procured that they are appointed, strive to defend it with this excuse, that a good hope is had about those children or adolescents, that they would become very good and perfect men. The excuse is indeed laughable, which is

---

19 Cf. I Tim. 3, 5.

proven to be vain by so many reasons. For hope of this sort can promise nothing certain, since we see so many young men and ancients today entangled with many and various crimes, who gave good hope about themselves in childhood. Thus it will belong to a prudent man not to trust children who it is evident have often disappointed. Next, even if the hope were certain that they would afterwards correspond to their good native qualities, still not for this reason ought such a heavy burden to have been entrusted to them, when only hope is had: but they should wait until they know that they have become such as they hoped. Otherwise, put on a mule or donkey an extremely heavy burden of two measures, exceeding its strength greatly, precisely because the best hope is held for it, that it will eventually become an excellent beast of burden, capable of carrying a much heavier load. If you dare not entrust this to a small mule or donkey solely on account of the hope of the future, why do you dare to entrust the rulership of souls, which is a thousand times heavier burden, to a child solely on account of the hope of future things? Do you value your beast more than the life of a child, to whom you do not hesitate to impose such an immense burden? Although a novice tailor or cobbler may give very good hope of him sometime becoming an expert, still you do not entrust to him to make clothes or shoes for you until you know that he has become such as you hoped: and you wish to entrust so many souls to a child solely based on the good hope you have for him? O unhappy souls which have come into such misery, that clothes and shoes are preferred by you. Christ Our Savior valued them so greatly that for them He did not refuse to shed His Blood; now they are valued less by many Pontiffs than clothes and shoes.

But they bring forth yet another not much better excuse saying that the child was appointed to be a bishop, or the rector of some benefice with the care of souls by a dispensation of the Pope, and thus, every occasion for doubt has

Fourth cause of heresies: The unworthiness of bishops and other priests

been removed. If I were to say what kind of excuse this is, and of what weight it has, they will not believe me, because I am not such that I can turn a staff into a serpent, or a serpent back into a staff, or perform any similar sign according to my teaching. Let them therefore hear Blessed Bernard, a man both renowned for miracles and rich in learning, who when writing to Pope Eugene says: "I am not so ignorant as not to know that you have been made stewards; but if so, it is 'unto edification, and not unto destruction' (II Cor. 13, 10). In a word, it is required among stewards 'that a man be found faithful' (I Cor. 4, 2). When necessity requires you may be excused for exercising your dispensing power; if there is some manifest usefulness, such exercise may deserve commendation. 'Usefulness,' I say, of the community, not your own. For when no good is done either to the community or to yourself, we certainly have not a faithful dispensation, but a cruel dissipation."[20] And in his letter to Count Theobald[21] he again says: "But I would certainly offend God were I to do what you want me to do. For I know quite well that ecclesiastical honors and preferments are due to those who are able and willing to administer them worthily for the honor of God. So to obtain them by my influence for your young son would not be just to you or yours and would be dangerous for myself."[22]

Now if anyone asks for doctrine from bishops and other priests, there are few who could correspond with this duty and obligation. For even though some bishops are learned, there are still so many more so uneducated that they scarcely know how to speak Latin, and (what is much worse) some of them do not even know Latin well. I have not seen an example of which thing (so that I may speak the truth) in Spain, where I was born: but in the other regions, especially in that one

---

20 *On Consideration*, bk. 3, c. 4, n. 18 (PL 182, 769A-B).
21 I. e., Theobald II, Count of Champagne.
22 Letter 271 (PL 182, 475B-C).

which glories that it is the founder of Latin eloquence. For in Spain, with the support of its Catholic King and most Christian Emperor Charles [V], there is not a single bishop today who is not at least moderately learned, and many are truly highly learned. Regarding the ignorance of other priests it is unnecessary to make a long discourse, since unlearned and completely uneducated priests are so frequent everywhere, even among those who have received the care of souls, that a learned priest is rare and considered like a jewel, who is devoted to the care of souls. The number of unlearned priests is so great that it can now be reproached to the Church, what the Lord long ago reproached to the synagogue through the prophet Isaias saying: "His watchmen are all blind" (56, 10). Those who have the care of souls, are the watchmen of the people, who ought (as Paul says[23]) to watch, as for something about which they will render an account to God. Yet He says that all these men are "blind," that is, ignorant. Because even though there were some learned men among the Jews, still these were very rare. How many bishops or other priests as rectors of souls are there now who, according to Paul's precept, are "able to exhort in sound doctrine, and to convince the gainsayers" (Titus 1, 9)?

Now one can certainly establish how much harm can arise from this ignorance of the priests from that which Christ Our Savior says: "If the blind lead the blind, both will fall into the pit" (Mt. 15, 14). And Blessed Gregory when expounding the saying of the Psalmist, "Let their eyes be darkened that they see not; and their back bend thou down always" (68, 24), says: "For, indeed, those persons are eyes who, placed in the very face of the highest dignity, have undertaken the office of spying out the road; while those who are attached to them and follow them are denominated backs. And so, when the eyes are blinded, the back is bent, because, when those

---

23 Cf. Heb. 13, 17.

Fourth cause of heresies: The unworthiness of bishops and other priests

who go before lose the light of knowledge, those who follow are bowed down to carry the burden of their sins."[24]

If we wish to undertake examining the morals of priests, we will find more in them which we condemn, than what we can approve. For we scarcely meet with something in them, which does not greatly differ from those things which are commanded them by law. I know that there are some bishops and priests endowed with very good morals, who according to human frailty strive to fulfill those things which they are obliged to do. But these men are very rare and are pointed out by the people, about whom we do not make this present discussion: but we are presently speaking about others, who have departed very far from those morals which were befitting the sacerdotal dignity. What sort they are inwardly, God knows, Who beholds their hearts: we judge exterior things, which are so wicked that they cannot please any prudent man who thinks rightly about the Christian religion. If from the clothing with which they are clothed, one ought to judge many of them to be neither priests nor clerics, but we will reckon them to be worldly laymen and soldiers. Their animals are adorned with such extravagance and arranged with such meticulousness that it can rightly be said about them what the Royal Prophet said about the daughters of the Gentiles: "Their daughters decked out, adorned round about after the similitude of a temple" (Ps. 143, 12). If only they took such care in adorning and arranging the churches, as they are troubled by the concern of arranging the mules on which they should ride. Their excessive luxury in this matter has been so great for many years, that Blessed Bernard having been exasperated said to them: "Tell us, priests, what is gold doing on a bridle?"[25]

---

24 *Pastoral Rule*, bk. 1, c. 1 (PL 77, 15B).
25 *De moribus et officio Episcoporum*, c. 2, n. 7 (PL 182, 815D). The context is: "Truly the naked cry out and the famished too, they protest, saying: Tell us, priests, what is gold doing on a bri-

Their dining table is extremely luxurious, the feasts excessively extravagant, yet many poor people, whom they are obliged to support, perish from hunger. Many of them are devoted to hunting and wildfowling, they feed hawks, they nourish dogs having deserted the poor, all which things many laymen greatly fear to do out of fear of the Lord God, and yet these things are forbidden not to laymen, but to the bishops and priests themselves. They take part in many games and are more devoted to frequent gambling than to praying or reading. Some of them are so base and hold such a low regard for their own priestly dignity that many of the lower-ranked priests do not hesitate to enter public taverns, leaving their own houses deserted, and there engage in drinking bouts and compete with others in consuming larger quantities of wine, and seek the victory of drinking the most. Regarding their chastity there is no need for us to speak, since their incontinence is so clear to everyone that if we wanted to keep silent, their children would cry out. Many of them openly keep concubines, which brings great disgrace to the Christian religion, from whose embraces they often approach the reception of the Eucharist, fearing neither men nor God. And, so that no wickedness would be lacking to them, they are not afraid to enter known brothels. The incontinence of priests is now so frequent and so public, that if one of them is known to be chaste, although he be wanting in many needful things, for this reason alone he is deemed holy by the people.

---

dle? Does the gold keep the bridle from hunger and cold? Of what use to us, working in wretched conditions of cold and hunger, are all those spare clothes stretched over hangers or folded in traveling chests? ...It is our substance that goes to make your superabundance. Every addition to your vanities is subtracted from our necessities." St. Bernard has adapted here a phrase of Persius: "Tell me, oh pontiffs, what is gold doing in the sanctuary?" (*Satires*, satire 2, ln. 69).

Fourth cause of heresies: The unworthiness of bishops and other priests

Now all these vices make clear that those who do such things are unworthy of the sacerdotal honor. And not only secular priests, but also monks who are held to a much stricter obligation to virtue, are very far removed from their manner of living. For many of them have degenerated to such an extent from the Fathers by whom they were founded, that they have next to nothing which corresponds to their profession, besides their outer clothing, by which they are distinguished from others. In these men, however, necessarily occurs what Augustine says, namely, "I have not found any men worse than monks who have fallen."[26] And actually (so that I may speak frankly), although there are many who observe the rule of their institute which they promised, still, rare are those among them who have not descended from that summit of perfection, on which their Fathers were. From this unworthiness of all priests, as from the greatest cause of the evils, many evils and moreover heresies have arisen long ago, and now, alas, daily arise and are nourished.

For God clearly taught this to us through the prophet Jeremias, saying: "Because the pastors have done foolishly, and have not sought the Lord: therefore have they not understood, and all their flock is scattered" (10, 21). Upon which passage Jerome says these words which follow: "By the translation of the shepherds and the sheep, the guilt of the rulers and the dispersion of the people are described. For because the rulers acted foolishly, and did not seek the Lord, Whom they ought to have sought after with their whole heart, wherefore both they did not see the coming evils, or understand the Lord, and also the whole multitude of Jerusalem was scattered here and there."[27] And God again teaches the same opinion through the prophet Ezechiel speaking thus: "They were a stumblingblock of iniquity to the house of Israel" (44, 12). Blessed Gregory when expounding these

---

26 Letter 78, n. 9 (PL 33, 272).
27 *Commentary on Jeremias*, bk. 2 (PL 24, 751A-B).

words speaks thus: "For certainly no one does more harm in the Church than one who has the name and rank of sanctity, while he acts perversely. For him, when he transgresses, no one presumes to take to task; and the offense spreads forcibly, for example, when out of reverence to his rank the sinner is honored."[28]

The priests' wickedness and unworthiness was not merely the cause of those sins which pertain to morals, but also of many heresies. For Aeneas Sylvius in his book, *De origine Bohemorum*, says: "Almost all the clergy followed John [Hus], burdened by debt, notorious for crimes and seditions, who thought to evade punishments by means of the revolution. To them were joined not a few men renowned for learning, who, since they could not obtain a dignity in the Church, begrudgingly put up with the priesthood, having been committed to those of great wealth, who, although they excelled in nobility, nevertheless seemed lower class in knowledge."[29] And when relating those things which were done in the Council of Constance with the Bohemians John Hus and Jerome of Prague, he says: "They remained obstinate in their stance, neither conquered nor wanting to be conquered with logic. They considered themselves truthful, followers of the Gospel, disciples of Christ; they considered that the Roman Church and the other churches scattered throughout the world have deviated from the traditions of the Apostles, have pursued wealth and pleasures, have sought dominion over people and the highest seats at banquets, have nurtured dogs and horses, have squandered the goods of the churches, which should have belonged to the poor of Christ, through extravagance and luxury, either completely ignorant of Divine Commandments or knowingly disregarding them."[30] From which words it is established

---

28 *Pastoral Rule*, bk. 1, c. 2 (PL 77, 16A).
29 C. 35, p. 59.
30 *Ibid.*, c. 36, p. 64.

Fourth cause of heresies: The unworthiness of bishops and other priests

clearly enough that the bad morals of the priests gave an occasion for heresy to the Hussites, by which they departed from the obedience of the Roman Pontiff.

The same thing is happening in this age of ours to the Lutherans, whose heresies the unworthiness and wicked lives of priests have begotten as the first mother, and now as a wetnurse feeds, supports, and nurtures them. For when seeing the excessive multitude of priests, their unworthiness, and their wicked lives, they began to rave like the Bacchantes against priests and bishops, and against the Roman Pontiff, that is, the Supreme Pontiff of the whole Church, and what they could perhaps justly say against the persons, they twisted back against the priestly dignity itself, and against its hierarchical orders, as though the unworthiness and life of the person, howsoever wicked, could detract even a hairsbreadth from the sacerdotal dignity, or any other authority. If they had been rightly wise, they ought to have labored for the amendment of the persons and the reform of morals, and not remove the pontifical dignity in general. They certainly heal badly who kill.

Otherwise, if these things seem to be sound remedies to them, let them also remove marriages for the same reason, because many spouses do not keep fidelity. Let them remove all ministers and rulers of governments, because many of them perform their ministry unjustly. Let them finally take away tailors, shoemakers, metalworkers, goldsmiths, stonemasons, and all the other artisans, because many of them make a thousand frauds, and they often contrive a thousand lies. If it is not permitted to completely take away these arts, even though the artisans of those things exercise them unjustly, much less was it fitting to totally abrogate the pontifical dignity on account of the unworthiness of the priests and bishops, and any wicked life of them, especially since it was not instituted by men, but by God, and hence it depends not on men's choice, but God's will. But in reality they were blinded by hatred and envy of the bishops, especially of the Roman Pontiff, so that they would not understand the matter: and not now, even if the truth is very clearly shown to them, do they understand. For if something is objected to them in favor of the Supreme Pontiff's or other bishops' authority, since they do not know what they can correctly reply, they immediately cry out: "See the taxes of the pontiff, consider the morals of the bishops." I in fact speak from experience, and not those things which I have learned from the narration of others, but I relate those things which I have seen with my own eyes, and heard with my ears.

And it is certainly difficult, unless God Himself protects, when there is such great unworthiness of priests, and their very wicked lives, for the Christian religion to be everywhere intact. For the Divine law, religion, and the true worship of God have a certain connection with the priesthood, which can be easily proved from Paul's testimony, who says: "The priesthood being translated, it is necessary that a translation also be made of the law" (Heb. 7, 12). If the priesthood and the law would not be connected to each other, what would be this reasoning of Paul, to infer from the translation of the priesthood to the translation of the law? But because Paul reckoned that the priesthood cannot exist without the law, nor the law without the priesthood, such that to any priesthood corresponds its law, and religion, and to any law or religion fits with its priesthood, wherefore it seemed to him that from the translation of the priesthood, one can very well infer the translation of the law. If these two things are so connected, and are dependent upon each other, for the same reason and inference, from the contempt and scorn of the priesthood, contempt of the law and religion necessarily follows. For among all the nations of the whole world, among whom either some true or false religion was ever practiced, the dignity of the priesthood and the esteem and reverence among the people for the priests was always

Fourth cause of heresies: The unworthiness of bishops and other priests

as great as the esteem and reverence for religion itself, and vice versa. Therefore, it is not surprising that in these times, when the priesthood of the Christian religion is neglected and so little esteemed that it is conferred on all without any just merits, the Divine law, Divine worship, and ultimately the entire Christian religion itself are also despised and brought to ruin.

Since therefore it is established that this is the greatest root of all the heresies of the present time, whoever wishes to oppose the heresies and completely remove them ought to greatly labor with all his strength that this very bad root be pulled out, and the priesthood be restored to its dignity. Now this will easily happen if firstly the causes from which this whole contempt of priests arose is removed. It is very well known that the contempt of priests arose firstly from the exceedingly great number of priests, then from their ignorance, and finally from their wicked lives. Certainly the exceedingly great number of anything breeds scorn and contempt: just as on the contrary, the rarity of anything begets the value and esteem for the thing. Next, the great unworthiness of priests shown on many accounts increased the contempt for them. Because many on account of a deficiency of age, others on account of imprudence, others on account of ignorance, others due to their wicked life manifest to all, are unworthy who were promoted to such sublime dignity, and hence contempt for them arose. Thus in this way the priesthood, which has now fallen into such great disdain and great contempt, will easily be restored to its former value and honor, if no one would be promoted to it except one worthy. No one except someone advanced in age should be made a bishop or priest, and who is prudent for undertaking of such an office, and a learned man who would be able to teach others; and good, virtuous, and studious, who may exhort others by his example for striving after virtue. If such men are bishops and priests, I doubt not that the rest of the people in a short time will return to the correct observance of the Christian religion. If the reform of this priesthood is neglected, it is necessary for those who are responsible for carrying it out to bear patiently the contempt of the same priesthood and consequently the throwing overboard of the Divine law and the Christian religion. It will certainly be necessary that to bad priests would happen that which God long ago threatened them through the prophet Malachias, saying: "Therefore have I also made you contemptible, and base before all people, as you have not kept my ways, and have accepted persons in the law" (2, 9).

Chapter VI

Concerning the fifth cause of heresies, which is the translation of Sacred Scripture into the vernacular language.

The translation of Sacred Scripture in the vernacular language can be the cause of many heresies for many reasons and is convincingly proven by many irrefutable testimonies, and the matter itself clearly demonstrates. Now so that we may be able to prove this more clearly, it is befitting to establish the fact before all else, that the first and most powerful root of all heresies is the deformed understanding of Sacred Scripture. For because the things contained in Holy Writ some think ought to be understood not according to the teachings of the Catholic faith, but according to a meaning very far away from the Catholic faith, wherefore they maintain very firmly their opinions even though opposed to the Catholic faith, as if they were Divine oracles. Because those things which they think, they suppose are fortified and strengthened by quotations of Sacred Scripture, and hence hold those things with as constant and firm mind as the other things which are truly contained in Holy Writ. Hence Hilary says: "There have risen many who have given to the plain words of Holy Writ some arbitrary interpretation of their own, instead of its true and only sense, and this in defiance of the clear meaning of words. Heresy lies in the sense assigned, not in the word written; the guilt is that of the expositor, not of the text."[1] And Blessed Augustine says: "Their error, to be sure, could not spring up clothed with the name 'Christian' except from a failure to understand the Scriptures."[2]

---

1 *On the Trinity*, bk. 2, n. 3 (PL 10, 51B-52A).
2 *Eighty-Three Different Questions*, q. 69, n. 1 (PL 40, 74).

If heresies arise from a deformed understanding of Sacred Scripture, it hence follows that the uneducated common people when reading Sacred Scripture thence take a great occasion of falling into various heresies: because they read that which they cannot understand sufficiently. Now that there are many things in Holy Writ, which cannot be understood sufficiently by the common people, is so manifest that it needs no proof besides Luther, and the other men of the same ilk, saying that Sacred Scripture, especially the New Testament, is very easy to understand, such that it can be understood by all, and for this reason it ought to be translated into that language in which it can be read by all. Yet it is clearly proved that Luther, and all those who support him in this matter, err very badly: because there are many things greatly necessary for understanding Sacred Scripture, all which things it is evident the uneducated common people lack. For all the natural sciences, Augustine bearing witness, are very necessary for the correct and accurate understanding of Sacred Scripture. For (as he says in the book, in chapter forty of book two, *On Christian Doctrine*[3]) just as of old God's tabernacle was constructed, by God's command, from the gold and silver which the children of Israel had received from the Egyptians,[4] so in this way the structure of theology which take rise from sciences of the heathens, which are in some way like their silver and gold. The same Augustine in the book, *On Christian Doctrine*, testifies that the knowledge of various histories are necessary for the correct understanding of Sacred Scripture, who shows that some due to ignorance of history have erred about Sacred Scripture.[5]

And not merely for trivial and unimportant matters, but for the establishing of the first foundations of the Evangelical faith, is the knowledge of history necessary. For the first

---

3 PL 34, 63.
4 Cf. Ex. 35, 21-22.
5 Bk. 2, c. 28 (PL 34, 55).

Fifth cause of heresies: Translation of Scripture into the vernacular

foundations of the whole Evangelical teaching is that Jesus the Son of the Virgin Mary was the Messias promised in the Law, and foretold by the prophets. For the confirmation of which faith, many of the most important testimonies which can be cited from Sacred Scripture, can in no wise be understood without knowledge of history. The first is from the book of Genesis, where Jacob, when blessing his son Juda, says these words: "The sceptre shall not be taken away from Juda, nor a ruler from his thigh, till he come that is to be sent, and he shall be the expectation of nations" (49, 10). Now so that these words may be applied to the coming of Christ in the flesh, it is necessary to know from history when the scepter was taken away from Juda, and when a ruler from his thigh ceased to exist. The other is the prophecy of Balaam, who after he said that a star would rise out of Jacob, and a scepter would spring up from Israel, which shall strike the chiefs of Moab,[6] so that he might designate the time when this prophecy would be fulfilled, he said these words: "Alas, who shall live when God shall do these things? They shall come in galleys from Italy, they shall overcome the Assyrians, and shall waste the Hebrews, and at the last they themselves also shall perish" (Num. 24, 23-24). He who would want to prove that this prophecy was fulfilled in Christ Our Savior, ought to know when the Romans overcame the Assyrians, and wasted the Hebrews.

Much more knowledge of history is required for the correct understanding of the prophecy of Daniel about the shortened seventy weeks, after which the Saint of saints was then to be anointed.[7] He who is completely ignorant of history, as many of the common people are wont to be, by no means could apply these prophecies which we said to Christ, about Whom these things were predicted.

---

6 Cf. Num. 24, 17.

7 Cf. Dan. 9, 24.

Next, Augustine in chapter twenty-nine of book two of the same work, *On Christian Doctrine*, teaches that knowledge of the tropes and figures is completely necessary for the knowledge of Scriptures, which ought to be sought from the grammatists and rhetoricians. From the ignorance of this matter it is evident that many heresies could arise, because the figurative speech is not recognized, and believed to be not figurative. For from this root arose long ago in Egypt the heresy of the Anthropomorphites, those thinking that God is corporeal, because Holy Writ often attributes human members to God.[8] For if they had understood the notion of the metaphor, those men would not have fallen into such a heresy. From the same ignorance the heresy of Cerinthus came forth, and of others teaching that the pleasures of the flesh are in heavenly beatitude.[9] For these men were deceived from that which the Savior says in Luke: "I dispose to you, as my Father hath disposed to me, a kingdom; that you may eat and drink at my table, in my kingdom" (22, 29-30). And there are many other things of the same kind in Holy Writ, about all of which it is not possible to discuss in this place. It is certain that unlearned people do not know to distinguish figurative from non-figurative speech, and hence it is necessary that the common people frequently fall into errors, if they wish to understand those passages without any figure, and without any trope.

There are many things in the Gospels said by hyperbole by Christ Our Savior, and thereafter by the Apostles in their epistles. The Apostles and Evangelists often use a synecdochical figure,[10] which he who did not understand, it is

---

8 Cf. St. Jerome, *To Pammachius Against John of Jerusalem*, c. 11 (PL 23, 364B); St. Isidore, *Etymologies*, bk. 8, c. 5, n. 32 (PL 82, 301A).
9 Cf. St. Isidore, *Etymologies*, bk. 8, c. 5, n. 8 (PL 82, 299A).
10 I. e., a figure of speech that uses the name of a part of something to represent the whole, or the whole to represent a part.

necessary that he would err. For he who was ignorant of this, it is necessary that he would err regarding the time of Christ's death and Resurrection, supposing that Christ incorrectly said that that He would be "in the heart of the earth three days and three nights" (Mt. 12, 40). For the same reason they will deride the literal sense of Exodus, where it says that Moses' rod devoured the rods of the magicians.[11] For they will say within themselves: "How is it that a rod, which has neither a mouth, nor teeth, nor throat, nor stomach, nor lastly senses, could devour something?" They will also necessarily say that Paul is a liar, who says that the Holy Ghost "asketh for us with unspeakable groanings" (Rom. 8, 26). "If the Holy Ghost cannot groan, how could He ask 'with unspeakable groanings'?" Therefore a common man when reading, and nowise understanding this, will either say that Paul erred, or he will think wrongly about the Holy Ghost, supposing that He groans, or grieves in some way.

There are many others, and very frequent, figures in Holy Writ, for the explanation of which there is a small book of Bede, which is titled, *De schematibus et tropis sacrae Scripturae*.[12] Furthermore, there are many things in the Sacred Codices, which nowise ought to be understood according to the mere surface meaning of the text, but ought to be interpreted according to the mystical meaning hidden under it. About these things Paul says: "He hath made us fit ministers of the new testament, not in the letter, but in the spirit. For the letter killeth, but the spirit quickeneth" (II Cor. 3, 6). If someone would want all these things to be interpreted literally and not according to the hidden mystery, there is no doubt that he would fall into many heresies. Suchlike are many things which the prophets foretold about Christ. Such is that which the Patriarch Jacob foretold with a prophetic spirit about Christ's Passion: "He shall wash his robe in

---

11 Cf. Ex. 7, 12.
12 PL 90, 175A-186D.

wine, and his garment in the blood of the grape" (Gen. 49, 11). And such is that which is said in Isaias: "His empire shall be multiplied, and there shall be no end of peace: he shall sit upon the throne of David, and upon his kingdom; to establish it and strengthen it with judgment and with justice, from henceforth and for ever" (9, 7). "And of his kingdom there shall be no end" (Lk. 1, 33). Since the house of Jacob is not eternal, but temporal, someone could rightly doubt, how Christ would reign in it forever, especially since Christ Himself afterwards said that His kingdom "is not of this world" (Jn. 18, 36).

There are many other things of the same sort, which if they were understood merely according to the literal sense, there is no doubt that many heresies would thence be begotten, as for instance about Christ's kingdom in this world, and about the perpetuity of this kingdom. And there also is no doubt that that common uneducated man, because he does not know how to penetrate mysteries, thinks that all these things ought to be understood according to the bare literal sense, for which reason it is necessary that he would fall into many inextricable errors. Again, a change of one person for another very frequently suddenly happens in Holy Writ, without any indication, such that Scripture presently speaks about Christ, Who is the Head of the Mystical Body, and at once without any indication of the person speaks about His body, which is the Church, or about His particular members, which are all the faithful. If someone would wish to attribute all which things to the same thing, for instance, to apply everything to the Head, or everything to the body, or to the members, he often cannot do it without manifest heresy: because often those things which befit the Head, are opposed to His body and members; and those things which are proper to the other members, often cannot befit the Head.

Such are the things which the prophet Osee says when speaking about Christ, saying: "Israel was a child, and I

Fifth cause of heresies: Translation of Scripture into the vernacular

loved him: and I called my son out of Egypt as they called them, they went away from before their face: they offered victims to Baalim, and sacrificed to idols" (11, 1-2). The first part of these words ought to be understood about Christ, Matthew testifies,[13] who expounds it about Christ returning from Egypt into Judea. Nevertheless, although the rest was said under the name of the same Israelite people, cannot befit Christ, but only His body, whether true or false, that is, the mixed Church which contains within itself the good and the bad. It is certain that the common man cannot distinguish the diversity of persons, about whom that text speaks as though about one person: but he will apply everything to the same person, especially in Psalm twenty-one, which all ought to be attributed to Christ, and there is nearly no part in it which could belong to the Psalmist itself. And the prophet Isaias, when speaking about Christ under His own name, [says,] "The spirit of the Lord is upon me, because the Lord hath anointed me: he hath sent me to preach to the meek, to heal the contrite of heart" (61, 1). And Isaias says many other things under His own name, which nevertheless cannot befit himself, but Christ. For (as Luke relates[14]) Christ Our Savior taught that those words of Isaias were fulfilled in Himself. Yet the common and ignorant man when reading these things will think that they ought to be understood not about Christ, but about the same prophet, who said them in his own name, and in this way he will fall into very pernicious heresies. I omit many other things necessary for the understanding of Sacred Scripture, about which Blessed Augustine in the book, *On Christian Doctrine*, makes a long discussion, and all those things cannot be included in this chapter. Since the people are ignorant of all those things, it is necessary that they would err in many passages, misunderstanding Sacred Scripture.

---

13 Cf. Mt. 2, 15.
14 Cf. Lk. 4, 17-21.

Besides all these things, parables are very frequent in Holy Writ, whose understanding (as Blessed Thomas and the other Doctors of theology teach) ought to be sought not from the first meaning of the words, that is, by the similitude of one thing to another. It is certain that the people cannot apply these similitudes, and are ignorant of another meaning besides the first. Hence it is necessary to happen, that they would not know how to understand the parables: nay, they would not know how to distinguish between the parables and the clear elocutions. Whence it will necessarily happen that those things which were said parabolically, they would suppose ought to be understood simply and according to the first meaning of the words. I leave to the prudent reader to consider the following matter: What things and how many heresies this can generate. What will I say about the many passages of Scripture, which seem to be opposed to each other, in reconciling which a very learned, and diligent and penetrating interpreter is necessary? When a common and ignorant man reads the superficial opposition of these passages, not knowing how to harmonize them, he will be forced either to admit a falsehood in Holy Writ, or to exclude one of those passages from the Sacred Codices, saying that those words do not belong to Sacred Scripture. Neither of which can someone do without the mark of manifest heresy.

Finally because Blessed Jerome understood that the difficulties are many regarding the understanding of Sacred Scripture: whence in a letter to Paulinus, which is about all the books of Sacred Scripture, after many things which he had said there about this matter, at length when concluding the point, he speaks thus: "These instances have been just touched upon by me (the limits of a letter forbid a more discursive treatment of them) to convince you that in the Holy Scriptures you can make no progress unless you have a guide to show you the way."[15] And certainly from Sacred

---

15 Letter 53, n. 6 (PL 22, 544).

Fifth cause of heresies: Translation of Scripture into the vernacular

Scripture itself it is evident that in former times there were some special interpreters of the same Scripture, whose office it was to interpret Holy Writ. For Paul says that he learned the Law at the feet of Gamaliel,[16] and he praises Timothy because he had learned Holy Writ from his infancy.

From all these things it is very clearly established that Luther deviated very far from the truth, saying that Sacred Scripture is very easy to understand, so that it can be understood by any common man. For something cannot be truly called "easy," for acquiring which many difficult things are necessary: moreover, Luther himself, whether he wants to or not, must admit that he has been mistaken multiple times in the interpretation of Sacred Scriptures, since he often changed his opinion concerning doctrines of faith and morals, now approving a certain opinion, now rejecting the same, and accepting its contradictory. It is evident that the same thing also happened to Erasmus of Rotterdam, who nevertheless also with Luther thinks that Holy Writ ought to be translated into the vernacular language. For he often changed his opinion in his *Annotations on the New Testament*, recanting in the later editions those things which he had taught in a previous edition. Therefore it follows that both of them admit that they were mistaken, as often as he passed from one position to its opposite and embraced a conflicting viewpoint. If Sacred Scripture was very easy to

---

16 Cf. Acts 22, 3.

understand (as Luther[17] and Erasmus[18] say) one ought to ask them how they erred in a very easy matter. I do not believe that it could be replied by them other than that they had been so blinded at that time, that they could not see a very clear matter. And in this way also I believe that they were then blinded when they said that Sacred Scripture is so easy, that by no one it could be misunderstood.

Still, I am very surprised regarding Erasmus, because he is so little consistent with himself, that he very clearly opposes himself. For in his *Ecclesiastes: On the Art of Preaching* he says that Sacred Scripture is obscure in many places, and he shows many causes of the obscurity. Now so that his mind might be known to all, I wish to cite here the words which he

---

17 "No one wants to deal with Scripture, teach people, and bring them faith... But if someone among them attacks you and says: 'One must have the interpretation of the Scriptures, they are obscure,' you should respond that it is not true. There is no clearer book written on earth than the Holy Scriptures; it is unlike any other book as the sun is unlike all other light. They speak such things only to lead us away from the Scriptures and to elevate themselves above us as masters, so that we should believe in their faith" (WA 8, 236, lns. 4 f. & 7-13).

18 "'If Holy Scripture,' they say, 'were translated into the language of the people, laypeople would still not immediately understand it.' I grant it, not everything, not fully; but they will understand a great deal, especially if they have been trained. And Scripture has its milk with which it nourishes those of a tender age and it also has its solid food when you are more advanced [Cf. Heb. 5, 13-14]; in Scripture, as some pious person elegantly said, 'An elephant swims, a lamb walks'" (*Clarifications Concerning the Censures Published at Paris in the Name of the Theology Faculty There*, in *Controversies* (Toronto: University of Toronto Press, 2012), p. 143). Cf. St. Gregory the Great, *Moralia*, Letter to Leander, c. 4 (PL 75, 515A): "Scripture is like a river again, broad and deep, shallow enough here for the lamb to go wading, but deep enough there for the elephant to swim."

Fifth cause of heresies: Translation of Scripture into the vernacular

says in that place, and they are these which follow: "There are those who deny that there is any obscurity in the canonical books, provided that there be learning and sound judgment. And surely hitherto I have so ever favored this opinion, that I have wished it to be most true, but all the Doctors of the Church cry against it with one voice: and also among those who neither lack good judgment, nor expertise in languages."[19] Immediately after these words Erasmus shows various reasons of the obscurity. If Sacred Scripture is obscure in many places, then it is not expedient that it be translated into the vernacular language, so that it may be handed over to uneducated people and to be temerariously read, who would interpret it according to their own judgment, and would contend that it necessarily ought to be so understood. Again, very learned men often have erred about the interpretation of Sacred Scripture, as their very many dissonances among themselves very clearly prove. For since they are often fighting about the meaning of Sacred Scripture, and hold irreconcilable views, it is necessary that one of them errs. If those very learned men, whom God brought into His cellars,[20] after long and enduring study, after fervent and extended prayer, have erred in many things, how can it happen that the ignorant masses, devoted to carnal desires and often enslaved by numerous vices, without any examination would not err far and wide in countless matters?

If the common and uneducated man errs so easily in the interpretation of Sacred Scripture, and from his false understanding (as it is evident from the testimonies of Hilary and Augustine cited above) heresies arise, it is very clearly proved that the translation of Sacred Scripture into the vernacular language gives a very great occasion of heresies to uneducated men. For when they read things which they

---

19 *Ecclesiastae sive de ratione concionandi libro quatuor* (Leipzig: In Libraria Weidmannia, 1820), bk. 3, c. 173, p. 622.
20 Cf. Cant. 2, 4.

cannot understand, they will interpret Sacred Scripture according to their own judgment, and not according to the rules of the holy Doctors, which they never read, and in this way they will fall into countless errors. And to support this we have more examples than we would wish, namely, of many heresies which have been stirred up by uneducated men, because they read and did not understand Holy Writ translated into the vernacular language.

I will present some of them as sufficient evidence for proving this point. The Albigensian heretics rose up some time ago in the time of Pope Innocent III, intertwined with many abominable errors. Now those who stirred up these errors are so called, because they originated in the district of Albi near Toulouse in France. All these men were uneducated, and because they read things which they did not understand, wherefore they fell into many abominable errors. After these men, a few years later, the "Poor Men of Lyons" also rose up in France, from whom the greater part of those heresies which now attack the Church, drew their origin. For Waldo, their leader, from whom they received the name and are called Waldensians, after having given away all his possessions, loved poverty more than was just, and because he was uneducated, he had both some sacred and other books translated into the vernacular language for himself, which when reading and not understanding, he fell into the most pestilential errors, which afterwards the Wycliffites and then the Hussites defended, and now finally the Lutherans defend. After these men in nearly the same century the Beghards and Beguines, all uneducated men, arose, whose eight heresies were condemned in the Council of Vienne under Clement V.[21] Next, the very pernicious heresies of the Taborites,[22] the

---

21 Cf. Dz. 471-478.
22 Cf. Aeneas Sylvius (Pope Pius II), *De Bohemorum origine ac gestis historia*, c. 40

Fifth cause of heresies: Translation of Scripture into the vernacular

Orebites,[23] and the Adamites.[24] Aeneas Sylvius relates the history of all these men in the book, *De origine Bohemorum*, and he says that their authors and defenders were uneducated men, although he does not say that that they had Holy Writ translated into the vernacular language, yet it is probable that they had it, because otherwise there was no other way how uneducated men could have stirred up those heresies, or how so many men would have accepted them once they had arisen. Finally, the Lutherans' heresy, even if it did not arise from this cause, it is still evident that it was spread by it, and that it had thence acquired greater strength to destroy the people. For the people when reading those passages whereby Luther tried to prove his heresies in the Sacred Codices rendered in the Germanic language, were easily persuaded to consent to Luther.

Next, we are taught from the common opinion of all sacred Doctors, that the high and profound mysteries which uneducated people cannot understand, ought not to be conveyed to them, lest by this occasion they would fall into error, but a sermon ought to be tempered according to the capacity of the hearers. For Paul when writing to the Corinthians says: "And I, brethren, could not speak to you as unto spiritual, but as unto carnal. As unto little ones in Christ. I gave you milk to drink, not meat; for you were not able as yet. But neither indeed are you now able; for you are yet carnal" (I Cor. 3, 1-2). [Hervé de Bourg-Dieu[25]], when interpreting these

---

23 *Ibid.*, c. 43. The Orebites or Lesser Taborites, later known as Sirotci, officially "Orphans' Union," were followers of a radical wing of the Hussites in Bohemia. The founders took part in the procession on Mount Oreb, near Třebechovice pod Orebem and Hradec. Founded in 1423 originally under the name Lesser Tábor, it consisted mostly of poorer burghers and some members of the Czech nobility who joined with the commander Jan Žižka.
24 *Ibid.*, c. 41.
25 The text here incorrectly cites St. Anselm.

words in his commentaries on Paul's epistles, says: "For the minds of those hearing ought not to be taught beyond their capacities, but any high and eminent things ought to be concealed from many hearers, and disclosed to scarcely a few. And to beginners or the weak, not lofty and mystical things, but rather things that they can comprehend should be preached, but to the perfect, deep and mystical things should be spoken."[26] And [Pseudo-] Blessed Chrysostom says: "Just as the food of infants changes with their age, so the teaching needs to be tempered in accordance with the people's virtue."[27] And Origen says: "Just as in the nourishment of the body, we have just granted many differences, this also applies to the rational nature, which feeds, as we have said, on reason and the Word of God. Not every nature is nourished by one and the same word. That is why, as in the physical illustration, the food some have in the word of God is milk, that is, the clearer and simpler doctrine. This normally consists in moral instruction, which is customarily given to those who are starting out in Divine studies and who are receiving the first elements of a rational education."[28] Blessed Gregory also teaches the same thing much more clearly and more copiously when expounding the passage: "He bindeth up the waters in his clouds, so that they break not out and fall down together" (Job 26, 8). Which words of Gregory, because they were cited by us above in chapter three of this book, it is now not necessary for us to repeat.

From all these testimonies we gather that to uneducated people high and profound mysteries ought not to be preached, which they cannot understand. And hence it is very clearly proved that Sacred Scripture ought not to be handed over to the uneducated people, to be read by them. For it matters not whether something be handed over by word or writing, if by

---

26 *Commentaria in epistolas Pauli* (PL 181, 837D).
27 *Opus imperfectum in Mattheum*, hom. 51 (PG 56, 927).
28 *Homilies on Numbers*, hom. 27, n. 1 (PG 12, 780C-D).

Fifth cause of heresies: Translation of Scripture into the vernacular

neither way they are able to understand it. If that word which when they could not understand when heard ought not to be delivered to uneducated people, it follows that to the same people Sacred Scripture ought not to be delivered, which it is certain they could not understand. And certainly this reasoning and argumentation has such force (in my opinion) that there is nothing which can truly answer it. For no true and evident distinction can be given between words and writing, by which it is made known that it is wrong that obscure and difficult to understand words be preached to the people, but on the contrary, it is good that an obscure and very difficult to understand writing be handed over to be read by the same people. And this reasoning compels the readers themselves, if they are uneducated, to abstain from reading those books of Sacred Scripture, which they cannot understand.

For this same thing, if they want to correctly understand it, Blessed Peter commands them when saying that they ought to be content with things very easy to understand. "As newborn babes," he says, "desire the rational milk without guile, that thereby you may grow unto salvation" (I Pet. 2, 2). By the word "milk" he meant clear and easy to understand doctrine, whether it be delivered by word or by writing, and Peter commands the uneducated and beginners to desire only this, and by it they can grow unto salvation. For so that some doctrine may be meant by the word "milk," it matters not whether it be written or spoken, but this alone ought to considered, whether it is easy or difficult to understand. Thus Sacred Scripture in those passages where it is understood with difficulty, ought not to be deemed "milk," but "strong meat,"[29] and hence it follows that the uneducated, who try to read it, act against Blessed Peter's precept, who commands them to be content with milk, and not desire stronger meat. For when saying to them that they should desire milk, by this very fact he seems to command them to abstain from

---

29 Cf. Heb. 5, 14.

other solid foods, because (as Paul says): "Every one that is a partaker of milk, is unskillful in the word of justice: for he is a little child. But strong meat is for the perfect; for them who by custom have their senses exercised to the discerning of good and evil" (Heb. 5, 13-14). Theophylactus teaches that those words of Paul ought to be understood about the reading of Sacred Scripture, who, when expounding those words in his commentaries on Paul, says these words: "Thus he who is firm in morals and life, also has his senses of the mind exercised in the Divine Scriptures, discerning lowly and sublime teachings, sound and corrupt ones. For it is not spoken about life here: for everyone discerns it, and comes to know that a bad thing is wickedness, and a good thing is virtuousness. Notice, however, that study, meditation, and expertise of Scriptures is necessary, if we are going to discern which teachings are heretical, and which are not, and not simply lend our ears to everyone. For the palate tastes the food, but the mind examines the words."[30] And there is still something else worthy of consideration in Peter's words, where he gives the reason on account of which the imperfect and the weak ought, as newborn babes, to desire milk. "That thereby you may grow," he says," unto salvation." By which words he clearly intimates that solid food is not given to newborn babes unto health, but unto sickness. From which things it is clearly proved that those who hand over Sacred Scripture translated into the vernacular language to be read by uneducated people, do not provide the salvation of souls, but rather to procure their sickness, because they give them food, which exceeds their strength.

Add to all these things the prohibition of the Church, whereby it is forbidden to laymen to dare to dispute about the Catholic faith in any way. For in the chapter, *Quicumque*, §.

---

30 *Expositio in Epistolam ad Hebraeos* (PG 125, 250A). Cf. Job 12, 11.

Fifth cause of heresies: Translation of Scripture into the vernacular

Inhibemus,[31] Pope Alexander forbids all laymen under pain of excommunication to dare to dispute publicly or privately about the Catholic faith. And rightly indeed did the Supreme Pontiff inhibit this, because he weighed carefully of what great danger the matter is, to permit such a disputation to laymen without any distinction. For although there are some learned laymen, who could dispute well, and without any danger, with heretics, still laws and decrees never deal with what rarely happens, but always with what more frequently occurs. Now it rarely happens that laymen are fully instructed about the higher mysteries of the faith, and skillful in disputing about them, and hence, lest unlearned laity, being overcome in the disputation, take an occasion of ruin for themselves, or give an occasion of ruin to others listening, such a disputation rightly was interdicted to all of them. Now so that this so holy and pious decree may be able to effect that which it intends, it is necessary that Sacred Scripture be taken away from uneducated laymen, lest when reading it, any of them dare to dispute about the more hidden mysteries of the faith with great danger to religion. For he who prohibits something to his subjects, unless he would wish to prepare a snare for them, ought to also prohibit that which gives a great occasion for pursuing a course of action.

Now the very experience of things very clearly teaches how greater the occasion is given to unlearned laymen of disputing about the faith, when Sacred Scripture translated into the vernacular language is handed over to them. For in those regions in which Sacred Scripture translated into the vernacular language has been granted to be read indiscriminately by all laymen, such as in France, Germany, and Italy, not

---

31 "We inhibit also that it should be lawful for any lay-person publicly or privately to dispute about the Catholic faith. Whosoever shall do otherwise, let him be bound with the cord of excommunication" (*Liber sextus decretalium*, bk. 5, tit. 2 (*De hereticis*), c. 2 (*Quicumque*), §1 (*Inhibemus*)).

only very uneducated men, but also women indiscriminately dispute about the Catholic faith, and are not afraid to quarrel with very learned men about the more hidden mysteries of the faith. Jerome reprehends this perversity very much in his letter to Paulinus, which is about all the books of Sacred Scripture, speaking thus: "[As Horace says:] 'Doctors alone profess the healing art, and none but joiners ever try to join.'[32] The art of interpreting the Scriptures is the only one of which all men everywhere claim to be masters. [To quote Horace again:] 'Taught or untaught we all write poetry.'[33] The chatty old woman, the doting old man, and the wordy sophist, one and all take in hand the Scriptures, rend them in pieces, and teach them before they have learned them. Some with brows knit and bombastic words, balanced one against the other philosophize concerning Holy Writ among weak women. Others—I blush to say it—learn of women what they are to teach men; and as if even this were not enough, they boldly explain to others what they themselves by no means understand."[34] And certainly what Jerome testifies and laments happened at his time, we see is now happening (as we said) in many regions. Which abuse, unless it be very quickly removed from those regions, I do not doubt, will certainly bring about a great loss of the Catholic faith in these regions, as we already see is arising to a certain extent that evil, which we have now foretold, and fear.

And there is yet another very pressing reason which ought to force the rulers of the Church to nowise make a translation of Sacred Scripture into the vernacular language, namely, reverence and esteem for Sacred Scripture itself, which, there is no one who doubts, daily lessens, if it be handed over haphazardly to be read by all. For there is nothing which increases more the price and value of something than

---

32 *Epistles*, bk. 2, epistle 1, lns. 115 f.
33 *Ibid.*, ln. 117.
34 Letter 53, nn. 6 f. (PL 22, 544).

Fifth cause of heresies: Translation of Scripture into the vernacular

its rarity and hiddenness: and nothing on the contrary diminishes more all these things than the numerosity of the same thing, and its excessive display. And this is the reason (as all the sacred Doctors teach) on account of which God wanted the ceremonial mysteries of the Old Law to be hidden from the people, and not displayed haphazardly to all, lest from their easily accessible viewing they would be deemed valueless by all. For those things, which were in the tabernacle of the covenant, when the camp was moved, were wrapped up by Aaron and by those who served in the tabernacle, and were not seen by the people, nor also by those who carried them on their own shoulders.[35] The necessity of covering over was not small, namely, the fear of death. If such great reverence was then employed for the shadow, much more ought it to be exercised for the body, so that Sacred Scripture, in which the more hidden mysteries of our faith are contained much more clearly than in those ceremonies, should not be handed over haphazardly to be read by the whole people. Otherwise, Scripture itself, which ought to be most highly valued by all, will quickly be considered contemptible and worthless.

For this reason the Pontiff, Gregory VII, when writing to Wratislaus [II], Duke of the Bohemians (for Bohemia did not then have a king, as now, but a duke) in a certain letter, did not want to grant to him that the Divine Office could be celebrated in the [Old or Church] Slavonic language. For the above-mentioned Gregory in that letter after some words speaks thus: "But because Your Nobility asked that we assent to the Divine Office being celebrated in the Slavonic language in your country, you should know that we are in no way able to give favor to this petition of yours. Certainly about this matter it becomes clear to those who often ponder it, that it was pleasing to God Almighty, and not undeservedly, that Sacred Scripture should be obscure in certain places, lest, if it were freely open to all, it would

---

35 Cf. Num. 4, 5-12.

perhaps become worthless and would be subject to scorn, or it would perversely lead the mind into error due to mediocre translations. Nor is helpful as an excuse that certain religious men have patiently produced this translation simply because the people asked for it, or that they have dismissed it as incorrect, since the primitive Church concealed many things which were later corrected with subtle examination by the holy Fathers, which made Christianity strong, and allowed the religion to grow. Thus, we prohibit by the authority of St. Peter that which is requested imprudently by your people, so that it does not actually occur, and we order you to resist, for the honor of God Almighty, this vain temerity in all men."[36]

Even though Gregory VII expressly speaks only about the Divine Office, still he mentions clearly enough that the same thing ought to be said about the other Divine Scriptures. And it is certainly necessary, that the same thing be said about both: because the greater part of those things which are said in the Divine Office were taken from the Sacred Codices: the rest, however, which were not taken from there, even though they are holy and ought to be duly revered, yet they ought not to be held with greater reverence than those things which were taken from Sacred Scripture. And from this it is clearly proved that if Sacred Scripture ought to be translated into the vernacular language, for the same reason the Divine Office ought to be celebrated in vernacular language. And if this is denied about the Divine Office, as Gregory VII denies, it follows that the same thing ought to be denied about Sacred Scripture. Because Sacred Scripture ought not be esteemed and valued less than all those things which are said in the Divine Office, and hence no less reverence ought to be shown to Sacred Scripture than to the Divine Office, so that it ought not to be handed over to that language in which is can be haphazardly read by all without any distinction. And certain-

---

[36] *Registerum*, bk. 7, letter 11 (*Hujusmodi salutationis nostrae*), written in 1079 (PL 148, 555B-C).

Fifth cause of heresies: Translation of Scripture into the vernacular

ly it ought to be greatly feared that if Sacred Scripture having been translated into the vernacular language is handed over to uneducated people, the people, having thence been made more insolent, would ask that the Mass and the rest of the Divine Office be celebrated in the vernacular language, as now we know is done by the Lutherans in Germany. But if this is granted to them, it would undoubtedly lead to great contempt of the whole Christian religion.

Furthermore, Pope Innocent III, in a letter which he wrote to all of Christ's faithful, both in the city of Metz and in its diocese, who had made Sacred Scripture to be translated into the French language, and for this reason they were making hidden meetings, in which common men were interpreting and teaching it, after he reprehends them about the aforesaid secret meeting, and permits to them some open and clear things of Sacred Scripture, he says these words which follow: "The hidden mysteries of the faith should not be explained everywhere to everyone, since they cannot be understood everywhere by everyone, but only to those who can conceive of them by their believing mind. Because of this the Apostle said to the simpler people: 'As unto little ones in Christ I gave you milk to drink, not meat' (I Cor. 3, 1-2). For 'Strong meat is for the perfect' (Heb. 5, 14), as he said to others: 'We speak wisdom among the perfect' (I Cor. 2, 6); 'For I judged not myself to know anything among you, but Jesus Christ: and him crucified' (v. 2). Such is the profundity of Divine Scripture, that not only simple and illiterate men, but even prudent and learned men do not fully suffice to investigate its wisdom. Because of this Scripture says: 'They have failed in their search' (Ps. 63, 7). From this it was rightly once established in Divine law that the beast which touches the mountain should be stoned;[37] that is, so that no simple and unlearned man presumes to concern himself with the sublimity of Sacred Scripture, or to preach

---

37 Cf. Ex. 19, 12-13; Heb. 12, 20.

it to others. For it is written: 'Seek not the things that are too high for thee' (Eccli. 3, 22). Because of this the Apostle said: 'Not to be more wise than it behoveth to be wise, but to be wise unto sobriety' (Rom. 12, 3)."[38] Innocent III very clearly teaches that more of Sacred Scripture ought not to be delivered to laymen and the uneducated than they could understand.

Finally, since Erasmus of Rotterdam often taught the opposite of this opinion, the faculty of theology of the University of Paris declared by public censures that he had erred on this point. Erasmus in fact in a preface on Matthew says these words: "I desire that Holy Writ be translated in to all languages."[39] About which assertion the University of Paris gave its censure by these words: "Although Holy Writ, which is good and holy by its very nature, may be translated into any language, it is nevertheless a great risk to allow the indiscriminate reading of these translations in the vernacular language without any explanation to the unlearned and simple-minded, abusing them and not reading them piously and humbly, as many are found to do, as evidenced by the Waldenses, Albigenses, and Turlupins[40] who, having taken an occasion from this, spread many errors. Wherefore having perceived the malice of men in this tempest, such translation is perilous and destructive, by speaking without distinction about all the books of Scripture. And even where it might be beneficial to a few, it should not be heedlessly permitted to all. In matters that are not necessary for salvation, it is better to promote the well-being of many by prohibiting it, than to

---

38 *Regesta sive epistolae 1*, letter 141 (*Cum ex injuncto*), written in 1199 (PL 214, 696C-D).
39 Preface to *Paraphrases in Novum Testamentum* (Berlin: Sumtibus Huade et Speneri, 1778), vol. 1, p. xxiv.
40 I. e., "The Rascals," from the French word *Turlupin*. The sect was active mainly in the second half of the fourteenth century around Paris.

Fifth cause of heresies: Translation of Scripture into the vernacular

allow it for the benefit of a few, with grave inconvenience of the multitude. Thus, this kind of translation has been rightly condemned."[41]

Next, in the same preface on Matthew, Erasmus added this proposition: "They cry out, 'It is shameful crime, if a woman or a cobbler speaks about Holy Writ!'"[42] The University of Paris also gave a censure about this proposition, speaking thus: "Having duly considered the impudent temerity of many men of this time, it ought to be reckoned a shameful crime that uneducated and simple men would read Holy Writ translated into the vernacular language according to their own judgment, and discourse or treat about them, deciding about their difficulties. And yet not by this are they forbidden to discuss among themselves about those things which they have heard in public speeches for the correction of morals, and for the exciting of compunction and devotion: so that charity may grow more and more in themselves, humility become more solid, and works of the flesh may be mortified."[43] Yet I know that there are some, who arrogating to themselves more than is just, who mock those Parisian censures, saying, "The Parisian articles do not cross over the mountains." By which words they wish to say that they are not subject to the Parisian censures, but that they are free to think otherwise than they censured. I certainly admit that we have not sworn on the words of the University of Paris, and are nowise obliged to accept its decrees: still I do not deny

---

41 Chérubin de Saint-Joseph, *Bibliotheca criticae sacrae circa omnes fere sacrorum librorum difficultates* (Brussels: Joannes de Smedt, 1706), vol. 4, p. 483; and Carolus Du Plessis D'Argentré, *Collectio judiciorum de novis erroribus... Censoria etiam judicia insignium academiarum* (Paris: Andreas Cailleau, 1728), vol. 2, pp. 60 f.
42 Preface to *Paraphrases in Novum Testamentum*, vol. 1, p. xvi.
43 *Bibliotheca criticae sacrae*, vol. 4, p. 483; and *Collectio judiciorum*, vol. 2, p. 61.

this, which also no one having a sane mind could deny, that the opinion of that university, for which nearly a hundred Doctors of sacred theology gathered, who fully examined the matter (as it ought) by a long and thorough examination, ought to be valued much more than the judgment of any other very learned man about the same matter. And for this reason I reckon that anyone would act more prudently to embrace their opinion on this point, than having despised so many very learned men, to want to rely only upon his own prudence.

Chapter VII

The objections are answered, which are made by those who contend that Sacred Scripture ought to be translated into the vernacular language.

It does not suffice for him who wishes to defend a certain opinion and make it known to others, to bring forth a number of reasons by which he may persuade others: but it is necessary to reply to those things which are objected against it. Which if he does rightly (as is befitting), he will confirm the truth of the opinion so much more strongly, the more he shows more clearly how of completely no strength are those things which are objected against it. For there is hardly any truth so certain and clear about those things which pertain to faith and morals, which lack enemies who try to oppose it with many and various arguments. For the father of lies, who (as Our Savior says) "stood not in the truth" (Jn. 8, 44), but he was a liar from the beginning of human existence, considered the truth so odious, and pursues it with such an irreconcilable war, that he always seeks after soldiers, and equips them with various arguments, by which they could oppose the truth. For we know this to be true, both in other matters, and in this one about which we discussed in the preceding chapter. For even though it is known from reality itself that it is bad to translate Sacred Scripture into the vernacular language, so that it could be read by uneducated people without any distinction, still there are not lacking even Christians and Catholic men who contend that this is good, and bring forth various reasons in favor of it, with which they strive to persuade others of the opinion of Luther and Erasmus. To all which things I decided to reply one by one, so that by the weakness of them all, the truth of our opinion may thus appear clearer and firmer.

They firstly in fact object to us the lack of spiritual food, that is, of God's word, which the whole Christian people suffers not without its great harm. For the shepherds of souls, whom God commanded to feed His sheep with knowledge and doctrine, either do not know how to teach, or neglect to do it. Since then the shepherds are so idle, that they neglect to feed the sheep, that is, the souls committed to their care, with God's word, it seems necessary, or at least expedient, to some men, to give Sacred Scripture translated into the vernacular language to the people, so that the people when reading it may get food for their souls, lest they perish from starvation, or be greatly endangered. To this objection we reply, admitting that the negligence of the shepherds in this regard is very bad, who care so sluggishly for the sheep, that is, the souls committed to them, that they neglect those bleating and asking for the food of God's word: and although they perceive that they perish from hunger, in no wise have compassion for their pitiable need. For we also showed the idleness above in the fourth chapter of this book, and as much as lies in us we grieved over their misery. Thus one ought to come to the aid of such a dearth of God's word, yet not on that account ought food be given to all, but that alone which is needed for each one, which could not inflict harm on the one eating, but rather on the contrary could help him to nourish and foster the spiritual life.

For it is evident (as for example from those things which we just cited in the previous chapter from Origin, Chrysostom, and [Hervé de Bourg-Dieu]) that according to the condition of those who are to be taught, the teaching ought to be tempered, whether it be delivered by words or writing. For just as hard food ought not to be handed over to an infant which he cannot break no matter how much he hungers, or strong food which he is unable to digest by his own strength, so listeners or readers ought not to be instructed above their abilities, but only those things ought to be handed over to them which they can grasp and understand. For which reason I consider it to be a good thing, that in any region of Christendom some catechism be on hand in the vernacular language of that region, which explains very well, by a short and clear way of teaching, everything which pertains to the Catholic faith and Christian morals, so that from it the people may learn by their reading, those things which are necessary for them to attain eternal life. And I do not consider it a shameful crime, if those parts of the Gospels also be handed over to the people in the vernacular language, which through the course of the year holy Mother Church puts forth to be said in the sacrifices of the Masses on Sundays and other feast days. Yet I think that this is permitted on this condition, that the translation of those Gospels into the vernacular language be firstly duly (as is befitting) examined unto the last word by learned and Catholic men, lest from a distorted translation some error could snatch away those reading. For I have knowledge of many errors in various regions sown from Holy Writ translated wrongly and unfaithfully.

Next, these Gospels themselves ought not to be handed over to them bare, but one ought to add to them some brief and clear exposition, which unties the knots, if they occur, and faithfully and very clearly explains the obscure passages, so that all doubt, which could spring up from the text to the uneducated reader, may be removed by that exposition. In clear matters, and those which can contribute to morals, it may roam and explore as one pleases: but in difficult and hardly necessary matters, it should treat briefly and succinctly. And these things will suffice, so that the people could thence be fed, and know those things which are necessary for attaining eternal life. But regarding the epistles of Blessed Paul, it does not seem to me that the same freedom should be allowed, because (as Blessed Peter says) there are many things in them "hard to understand" (II Pet. 3, 16). But regarding the Apocalypse of John the Apostle, I do not see how it could be handed over to the people when translated into the vernacular language, since the most learned men have often wandered in their minds about its meaning on account of its hidden mysteries. I very firmly assert that the Old Testament, however, ought not to be translated into the vernacular language, so that it may be handed over to the uneducated people, because this very handing over cannot serve any need of the people, but merely their curiosity. For those things which pertain to the faith and morals, and are necessary for attaining beatitude are much more clearly and fully expressed in the New Testament, than in the Old; but all the rest which pertained to the judgments and ceremonies in that Old Law, were abrogated by Christ's death. Whence it is that the reading of the Old Testament cannot serve any necessity for uneducated and ignorant people, but for curiosity alone. Since the people could take an occasion of many heresies from which reading, when reading that which they are nowise able to understand, we rightly say that this very reading of the Old Testament ought not to be permitted to the uneducated people, especially since it is not necessary for them for attaining eternal life.

It is secondly argued as follows, so that they may prove that Holy Writ ought to be translated into the vernacular language. Sacred Scripture is preached to the whole people: therefore with equal reason it could be handed over to them to be read. For it matters little whether it be delivered to the people by words or writing. To this argument anyone can very easily reply by those things which we said in response to the immediately preceding objection. And, so that it may appear more clearly, how little this argumentation urges, I have decided to turn it back against those who make it against us. Sacred Scripture can be rightfully translated into the vernacular language, so that it may be handed over to the people to be read, only for that part which can be rightfully preached to the same people by words. Now not everything which is contained in Sacred Scripture ought to be preached to the uneducated people by words, as we have proved in the preceding chapter from the testimonies of Origin, Chrysostom, Gregory, and [Hervé de Bourg-Dieu]. Thus it is thence very evidently concluded that not everything which is contained in Sacred Scripture ought to be translated into the vernacular language, so that it may be delivered to the uneducated people to be read without any distinction.

They thirdly object to us the goodness of Holy Writ, which (as they think) clearly proves that the Writ itself ought not to be denied to the people. For it is unjust (as they say) to deny those things which are good to the people in general. To this objection we ourselves reply that there are many things which when considered absolutely and in themselves are good and useful, which nevertheless when related to some one particular person, are not good, but bad for him: not beneficial, but harmful. It is certainly good to punish murderers, assassins, adulterers, thieves, sorcerers, and the rest of men of that sort. But it is not good for a private man, who has no power of the sword,[1] to punish whatever very wicked men. For a private man is not "an avenger to execute wrath upon him that doth evil" (Rom. 13, 4): and hence, has neither the power of killing, nor of punishing in another way. "For all power is from God" (v. 1).[2] Whence it follows that power which is not from God ought rather to be called "tyranny," rather than "power." Therefore to a private man, and one lacking this power, who would punish someone,

---

1 "The 'power of the sword' in Roman law was the power of the government to enforce the laws and administer justice and punishment, including the death penalty. This was also termed *jus gladii* ('the right of the sword')" (Aaron X. Fellmeth and Maurice Horwitz, *Guide to Latin in International Law* (Oxford: Oxford University Press, 2021), p. 236).

2 This is a variant Old Latin translation of: "For there is no power but from God," as found in the Vulgate.

it could deservedly be said that which Paul says: "Who art thou that judgest another man's servant?" (*Ibid.* 14, 4). There are many foods that are excellent and highly suitable for the nature of the body, such as capons, partridges, veal, kid, and lamb. However, they are not beneficial for infants who have not yet been weaned because the weak digestion of children is unable to properly digest them. A sword is certainly good on account of its many uses, by which it can serve the human nature, especially for cutting apart those things man is wont to eat, which without a knife can scarcely be cut apart, so that they may be prepared to be eaten. A sword is also good for the for the punishment of bad men. For this reason Paul says: "He beareth not the sword in vain" (*Ibid.* 13, 4). Nevertheless, a sword of this kind is not good for children, because not knowing how to use it, they could easily hurt themselves: nor also is it good for an insane man and a furious man, because they when agitated by fury, can inflict death on many by the sword.[3] In this manner I reckon it ought to be said about Holy Writ. For even if it is translated into any language, it is good and holy, still for ignorant and uneducated men, and those who are imbued with bad morals, it is not good, because since many things in it are difficult to understand, it is certain that it cannot be understood by such men, but each one of them will interpret Sacred Scripture according to that which he loves, by the intellect obeying the will, and will pertinaciously contend that it ought to be understood according to that meaning. Just as a sword in the

---

3 Cf. Plato, *Republic*, bk. 1 (331c): "To take an example of what I mean: I think everyone would agree that if one were to take weapons from a friend who is a man of sound mind, and if he were to go mad and demand them back, one ought not to return them. The one giving them back would not be 'just' to do so, and again one should not be willing to tell the whole truth to somebody in that state" (translated by Chris Emlyn-Jones and William Preddy, in *Plato: Republic, Books 1-5* (Harvard University Press, 2013)).

Replies to those who contend for Sacred Scripture in the vernacular

hand of a child, or a furious man, so Holy Writ seems to me to be in the hands of an ignorant man, especially the badly behaved.

In the fourth place they object to us the benefit of good men, who, when reading Holy Writ translated into the vernacular language, have drawn not a little advantage, daily profiting for the better by it for the salvation of the soul. Which when it is ascertained in reality, they want to thence conclude that it ought not to be totally denied to the good and the humble who could profit from Sacred Scriptures, on account of those who abuse them; but on the contrary, lest the progress of good men be taken away, it is expedient to grant them to all. This argumentation has completely no strength, and proceeds from pure ignorance. For so that this argument would have some weight, it ought to have firstly assumed that in all things, without absolutely any distinction, the profit of some few men always ought to be considered rather than that the detriment to many others ought to be averted. For otherwise if this universal proposition is taken away from that argument, nothing could be concluded by it. Now how much this universal proposition deviates from the truth, there is no one who does not see. Because even though no one ought to omit things necessary for the soul's salvation, so that one would avert by this the harm of many others, still from the common opinion of all theologians, things which are not necessary for the soul's salvation, anyone is held to omit, so that by this he may avert the spiritual harm, which they could inflict upon others. For Alexander of Hales says that every man is obliged to put aside anything howsoever good, if it is not necessary for the salvation of his soul, so that he may avert the scandal which will come to his neighbor owing to that neighbor's weakness or ignorance.[4] Bless-

---

4 *Summa Universae Theologiae* (Venice: Franciscus Francisci-um, 1575), pt. 2, q. 169, mem. 6, fols. 413v-415r.

ed Thomas teaches the same thing.[5] Richard of Middletown subscribes to the same opinion.[6]

Therefore let us see whether for any common and private man to read Holy Writ is something necessary for the salvation of his soul. I think that no one is so foolish that he would want to impose this necessity upon everyone. For so thinking, he would condemn every rustic, and all who are completely uneducated. If this thing is not so necessary for everyone, then any good man of the people, although he might draw great profit from the translation of Holy Writ into the vernacular language, he is obliged to want that Holy Writ not be translated into the vernacular language, and to abstain from the reading of it, if he perceives that many take scandal to their souls from its translation and reading: if each person is held, in this matter not necessary for the salvation of his soul, to put aside his own benefit, so that by this he may avert the spiritual harm of a neighbor, it is thence clearly gathered that he upon whom the governance of the whole people is incumbent can justly, nay, is held to, impede such particular benefit of some men by forbidding the translation into the vernacular language, so that by such a prohibition he may avert the spiritual harm which could come forth to others from such a translation.

Next, one also ought to consider that the profit of many ought always to be preferred to the utility of a few. Now it is evident that many more are they who the translation of Sacred Scripture into the vernacular language can harm, than are they who profit from it. The number of fools is much greater than the number of the prudent, and the number of

---

5 II-II, q. 43, a. 7.
6 "Works necessary for salvation ought not to be omitted to avert the scandal of a neighbor on any grounds, because no one ought to omit his own salvation to avert a neighbor's damnation" (*Super sententias Petri Lombardi* (Brescia: Vincentius Sabbius, 1591), bk. 4, dist. 38, a. 10, q. 2, p. 522a.

sinners is much greater than the number of the just. Therefore it follows that one ought to be more mindful of the advantages of the many by forbidding the translation of Sacred Scripture into the vernacular language, than the benefit of a few by permitting it to all without any distinction, with the disadvantage of many. And the Academy of Paris stated this very well in that censure which it issued about this matter against Erasmus' assertion, which we cited at the end of the previous chapter. For among other things which are contained in that censure, it tacitly replies to the aforementioned argument of the adversaries, when speaking thus: "In matters that are not necessary for salvation, it is better to promote the well-being of many by prohibiting it, than to allow it for the benefit of a few at the grave inconvenience of the multitude. Thus, this kind of translation has been rightly condemned."[7]

In the fifth place they object the multitude of heretics now existing within the Church, who daily attack Catholic and believing men with various reasonings, and try to draw simple and uneducated men to themselves by diverse arguments and fallacious persuasions. From this perspective, those who defend the opposing side want to conclude that at least in this wretched time, when there is such a surge of heretics, it may be good, indeed necessary, to translate the Holy Scriptures into the vernacular language, so that the people, by reading those very words, may learn how to respond to the heretics. This argument presses us so little, that we can turn it back against them more powerfully with these words. It is not good that the people would have Sacred Scripture translated into the vernacular language, lest when reading it, they would thence take up arms by which they could take up combat with the heretics about the faith. For (as we said in the previous chapter) disputations of this kind are forbidden by law to lay and common men in the chapter,

---

[7] *Bibliotheca criticae sacrae*, vol. 4, p. 483; and *Collectio judiciorum*, vol. 2, pp. 60 f.

Quicumque, §. Inhibemus. If they are forbidden to dispute about the faith, it is just that that which could give a very great occasion of disputation to them be not permitted to them. Thus, lest the whole people without distinction could take up combat with heretics about the faith, it is necessary that Sacred Scripture, from which the weapons of the disputation ought to be taken up, be completely taken away from them.

In the sixth and last place they argue against us in this way. Sacred Scripture long ago was translated into the vernacular language. For all the Hebrew people, to whom alone the Old Law was given, understood very well the Hebrew language, in which that Testament was established: because that language was then used by all that people. Also the Greek language, in which the whole New Testament, besides the Gospel of Matthew and the Epistle to the Hebrews, was written, was the common language, which all of the common people certainly understood. If Holy Writ was at that time translated into those languages which all of the common people could read and understand, it seems to those who maintain the opposite position, that Holy Writ was handed over to each people in that language in which they could read and understand it. Our adversaries make so much of this reasoning that they think that by it alone they triumph over us. But we, with God's help, will show that it has not more force than all the rest of those reasonings.

If this reasoning has some force, it would be proved by the same manner of reasoning that it is not forbidden by the law of nature that someone would unite his sister to himself in matrimony. For when the human race was founded by God, it was made by Him such that men would take their sisters as wives. For Cain took his sister as his wife. If the human race was founded by God in such a state in which it was not merely licit for it, but necessary to do this, then the same thing also will be licit for men, especially for those who are not subject

Replies to those who contend for Sacred Scripture in the vernacular

to the laws of the Church, as are heathens, Saracens, and Jews. For all those marriages are licit to these men, which were not prohibited by the law of nature. Now if someone would grant that such a marriage of a brother with a sister is legitimate among heathens, it will be necessary to acknowledge that if a heathen who had contracted matrimony with his sister would convert to the Catholic faith, he ought not to be afterwards separated from the same sister by a dissolution of the marriage. Because a marriage which was at one time contracted by a legitimate contract, cannot be dissolved by the Church. "What God hath joined together, let no man put asunder" (Mt. 19, 6). Nevertheless the Church, when a marriage of this kind has been contracted before Baptism, reckons that after Baptism has been received it ought to be dissolved, as is evident in the chapter, *Gaudemus*.[8] For in that chapter the Pontiff decrees that infidels having converted to the Catholic faith are permitted to remain in those marriages alone, which they had contracted before conversion in the second or third degree.[9]

Now if someone would ask, "Why a marriage of a brother with a sister is now detestable, putting aside all human law, which nevertheless of old, when God instituted the human race, was licit?": Blessed Augustine replies to this question speaking thus: "As, therefore, the human race, subsequently to the first marriage of the man who was made of dust, and his wife who was made out of his side, required the union of males and females in order that it might multiply, and as there were no human beings except those who had been born of these two, men took their sisters for wives—an act which was as certainly dictated by necessity in these ancient days as afterwards it was condemned by the prohibitions of religion." And after having interjected a few words, by which he teaches that otherwise wives ought to be taken

---

8 *Decretals of Gregory IX*, bk. 4, tit. 19 (*De divortiis*), c. 8.
9 I. e., first and second cousins.

from among sisters, he afterwards adds: "But there was then no material for effecting this, since there were no human beings but the brothers and sisters born of those two first parents. Therefore, when an abundant population made it possible, men ought to choose for wives women who were not already their sisters; for not only would there then be no necessity for marrying sisters, but, were it done, it would be most abominable."[10]

We also reply in the same way to the above reasoning objected to us, regarding the translation of Sacred Scripture into the vernacular language. When Sacred Scripture was made, it was delivered in the vernacular language: because there was not then any other language in that people in which it could be delivered. For even though after the construction of the Tower of Babel, the languages were divided according to the diversity of regions, still there was not diversity of languages in the same people, such that one would be vernacular, which the whole people would understand, and which the whole people used, and there would be another which only learned men would understand. For this Latin language, which now is learned through study by a few, in former times (as the common opinion of learned men holds) it was common to the whole Roman people, and at that time that people used no other language. But because that people ruled various regions, to all of which it took pains to hand over its language, and also various nations afterwards occupied Italy: from the mixture of these languages, the purity and peculiarity of the Roman language little by little

---

10 *City of God*, bk. 15, c. 16 (PL 41, 457-458). A number of Fathers and theologians concur with St. Augustine on this point, such as Tertullian, Sts. Bonaventure and Thomas, Fr. Cajetan, Bl. Scotus, etc. (Cf. *De Civitate Dei libri XXII. Ex vetustissimis manuscriptis exemplaribus per theologos Lovanienses ab innumeris mendis repurgatus... Cum commentariis nouis & perpetuis R. P. F. Leonardi Coquaei... & Ioa. Lud. Vivis* (Paris: s. n., 1636), p. 929C.)

began to be corrupted, and from such corruption emerged among the Latin peoples the diverse languages: all of which are very widely different from that ancient language which formerly was common to the people, and now is learned by study. The same thing also happened to the Greek people, to all of whom that Grecian language was formerly known which now is learned by a few through study, from which the language which the Greek people now use is widely different.

Therefore the New Testament was then given in the vernacular language, because there was at that time no distinction of languages in the same people, such that one language would have been common to the whole people, another would have been known only to learned men. Therefore, to hand over Sacred Scripture in the common language (as Augustine says regarding matrimony between brother and sister), the more nature compelling is more ancient, the more it later becomes condemnable, as experience itself teaches. Now if someone would object that God could have then created another language, which would have been known only to learned men, in which He would have delivered Sacred Scripture, so that it would not have been known to the whole common people; I acknowledge that God could have done this, but why He did not do this, does not belong to us to ask. For otherwise, you could also object the same thing against Augustine's opinion about the marriage of a brother with a sister, which he said was licit in times past by force of necessity: although he says that it is now condemned. For God could have made besides Adam and Eve, who would beget sons, whom Adam's daughters would take as their husbands, and daughters whom Adam's sons would take as their wives. Which having been done, no necessity would compel brothers to take their sisters as wives. Yet who will dare to reprehend God about this matter, or ask Him why He did so? It is certainly more suitable that everyone would humbly and reverently acknowledge his own ignorance, and say with the prophet: "Thy judgments are a great deep" (Ps. 35, 7).

But putting aside this reply to the aforesaid main reason, I decided to reply still otherwise to the same reasoning: so that thereby it may become plain to all that that reasoning is very weak, by which our adversaries suppose that they triumph over us. I acknowledge that Sacred Scripture was firstly composed in that language which was then the common and mother tongue. Yet the writing itself was not accessible to all, so that it could be read by all without distinction: but only priests and lawyers had it in their possession. For (as it is stated in Deuteronomy) "After Moses had wrote the words of this law in a volume, and finished it: he commanded the Levites, who carried the ark of the covenant of the Lord. saying: Take this book, and put it in the side of the ark of the covenant of the Lord your God: that it may be there for a testimony against thee" (31, 24-26). And it certainly ought not to be believed that Holy Writ was then so common to all, as it is now, which can indeed be easily proved from that which the sacred history relates happened in the time of King Josias in the Fourth Book of Kings.

For in the twenty-second chapter of that book it is related that Helcias the priest found the book of the Law in the Lord's house, which the same priest sent to King Josias through Saphan the scribe. Now "When Saphan had read this book of the Law before the king, and the king had heard the words of the law of the Lord, he rent his garments" (vv. 10-11): namely, because, having heard the book of the Law, he very clearly perceived that none of those things, which God had commanded in His Law, were being observed. Now the king did not understand this well before the book of the Law was found by Helcias the priest: because there was not another book, by which the very faithful and very holy king could have been taught about God's Law. If the book of the Law, that is, the Pentateuch, was then common for the whole people: such that any common man could have it in his possession, it could hardly have happened that the book of the Law would be destroyed among the possessions of all, even among the possessions of the king, and that there would be no one who possessed it or could summarize it. But because only the priests of the Levitical race and the scribes had the whole Law in their possession, wherefore it happened that when the priests and scribes fell away from the true worship of God into idolatry, and despised the Lord's Law, the book of the Law was nowhere to be found: except in the Lord's Temple, in that place where perhaps Moses ordered it to be stored.

It ought to be believed that Paul's epistles, which he wrote to the cities, were given not to the people, but to the bishops alone, and the clergy of that city, so that they could afterwards disclose those things to the people, which Paul had advised them through the epistles. Now this can be easily surmised from that which Paul himself says in the First Epistle to the Thessalonians: "I charge you by the Lord, that this epistle be read to all the holy brethren" (5, 27). If the epistle was given to the whole people, whom then does he "charge"? He certainly charges the bishop and the clergy, to whom it was given, that it be read in the presence of "all the holy brethren," that is, in the presence of all the Christians, who were in that nation. But this was special in this epistle, that he ordered it to be read in the presence of all: because those things which Paul wrote in it were very clear, and which things could be understood by all. Regarding the Epistle to the Romans, and to the Galatians, and to the Hebrews he commanded no such thing, that they would be read in the presence of all: because there were many difficult things in them, which could not be understood except by learned men. If Paul had considered it to be certain and indubitable that his epistles, which he was sending to the cities, were going to be read before the people, it was unnecessary for him to give a special command to the Thessalonians about this matter. But because he had known very well that those epistles, which are sent to the cities, were wont to be given only to the rulers of the cities: wherefore he wanted to make a special command about it, so that it would be read in the presence of all.

Next, even if Sacred Scripture at that time would have circulated through the hands of all, as now, nevertheless the people were not at that time so presuming, as now, about understanding it; nor were the people rashly and insolently daring to dispute about it: but the people were being taught by the priests, according to that which the Lord says through the prophet Malachias: "The lips of the priest shall keep knowledge, and they shall seek the law at his mouth: because he is the angel of the Lord of hosts" (Mal. 2, 7). If some doubt arose, it was necessary to ask the priest, whose responses all were held to obey, according to the Lord's precept, which He had given about this matter through Moses in Deuteronomy.[11] But now with insolent temerity the people claim for themselves the understanding of Sacred Scripture, and do not fear to argue about it with very learned men. And for this reason, even if one could establish that formerly Holy Writ was handed over to the whole people, so that it could be read by any common man without any distinction, which I very firmly deny, still it would be more advantageous to be done otherwise, on account of the shameless temerity and arrogance of the people. For we know that many things long ago were licit, which now nowise are expedient, and if someone now would try to do those things, he would be deemed not merely somewhat bad, but wicked and faithless. For long ago Christ's Body was given to each person asking in the hands, which each one was carrying him with him, so that he could receive at home when he chose. Which thing

---

11 Cf. Deut. 17, 8-13.

can be easily gathered from Eusebius' *Church History*.¹² Yet that which was permitted long ago, would not be expedient to do in our times, because by experience teaching it is feared that there would be some who would handle [the Blessed Sacrament] unworthily, and [It] would be abused for the magical arts. Thus, it is not necessary that all things, which it is evident were permitted in former times, would be now permitted or expedient. Therefore it does not follow that Holy Writ translated into the vernacular language, should now be handed over to the people to be read, however much it might be established that in former times it was handed over to the whole people in the vernacular language. These are the things that I am aware of which are objected by some men against our opinion: to all of which I think that I have replied amply enough. But if there are others which exist, I think that it is undeserving that we spend time answering them, and fill up pages.

---

12 "'Swear to me by the body and blood of our Lord Jesus Christ that you will never forsake me and turn to Cornelius.' And the unhappy man does not taste until he has called down imprecations on himself; and instead of saying Amen, as he takes the bread, he says, 'I will never return to Cornelius'" (Bk. 6, c. 43, nn. 181-189 (PG 20, 627A)). The text cites c. 33, according to an older numbering of the chapters. Cf. *Ecclesiastica Historia divi Eusebii. et Ecclesiastica Historia gentis* (Haguenau: Rynmann, 1506).

Chapter VIII

Concerning the last cause of heresies, which is the constant and incautious reading of books of heathens.

The last cause of heresies now presents itself to me (from among those which rulers can easily remove), which is the constant and indiscriminate reading of books of heathens, especially if someone applied himself from a tender age to reading them, and spent all his labor on them. For it can be established that this thing is powerful for producing various heresies from the fact that whatever pertains to the Christian religion, relates either to morals or to the faith of those things to be believed; all that is rejected and mocked in the writings of heathen authors. Because if some of them teach the virtues, these men nevertheless, who are very rare among them, strive with all their strength to convince others of things which are as it were diametrically opposed to the Catholic faith. And concerning the very virtues whose promoters they claim to be, they have woefully erred in providing instruction, those whom the Gentiles themselves regard as a marvel and venerate as sources of wisdom. And regarding the teaching of the same virtues, whose promoters they profess to be, these men, whom heathenism itself takes for a miracle, and are venerated as sources of wisdom, very miserably erred, teaching those things, which according to the Gospel truth completely turn away from the attainment of eternal happiness, which they being blind were seeking. For many of them determined virtue and the ultimate happiness of man from their own inclination, teaching that to be virtue and happiness, which they very ardently desired.

For Epicurus, wanting to imitate the brute animals, said that the end of all good things is pleasure, led by this reason alone, that animals desire (as he says) it alone.¹ Some said riches, others honors, are the supreme good. Aristotle, whom the whole school of recent philosophers received as a teacher: even though he philosophizes much better, still he erred not a little on this point. For although he places happiness in knowledge, still he says that this is to be had in the present life,² leaving nothing to the other life, in which he supposes there is no activity. He erred to such an extent in which matter, that Paul reckons that we are more miserable than all men, if in this life only we hope to attain happiness.³ For who does not see that no one ever could live or has lived in this life without some misery, or need, or unhappiness? But he who suffers misery, or needs something good, Aristotle asserts in many places, is not happy. And using that reasoning, we may easily pierce through Aristotle with his own sword, when proving that no one in this life can be happy:

---

1 Cicero, *De Finibus Bonorum et Malorum*, bk. 2, c. 10, n. 31 ((Cambridge: Harvard University Press, 1914) p. 117): "For the origin of the chief good, he [Epicurus] goes back, I understand, to the birth of living things. As soon as an animal is born, it delights in pleasure and seeks it as a good, but shuns pain as an evil. Creatures as yet uncorrupted are according to him the best judges of good and evil…"

2 Cf. *Nichomachean Ethics*, bk. 10, c. 7 (1177a11-18): "If happiness is activity in accordance with excellence, it is reasonable that it should be in accordance with the highest excellence; and this will be that of the best thing in us. Whether it be intellect or something else that is this element which is thought to be our natural ruler and guide and to take thought of things noble and divine, whether it be itself also divine or only the most divine element in us, the activity of this in accordance with its proper excellence will be complete happiness. That this activity is contemplative we have already said" (translated by W. D. Ross and J. O. Urmson, in *The Complete Works of Aristotle: The Revised Oxford Translation*, vol. 2, p. 1860).

3 Cf. I Cor. 15, 19.

and hence supreme happiness ought not to be expected in this life, but in the other. For we can argue thus. All men desire happiness: thus this desire is natural, and hence it follows that such a desire is not in vain and in error. Now no one (as reality itself teaches) in this life, which evidently is full of a thousand miseries, attains happiness: therefore it should be hoped for in the other life.

Next, he said many things belong to happiness, which nowise pertain to it, such as nobility, riches, good offspring, a comfortable old age, and goods of the body, such as health, beauty, strength, tallness, strength for fighting, glory, honor, prosperity, power, and fortune. Now all these things (as Holy Writ teaches us) are very far apart from the true and full happiness which we hope for. And if this greatest of all philosophers erred about happiness so miserably, what will be hoped for from the other much lesser ones? Hence Solomon when speaking about philosophers rightly says: "The labour of fools shall afflict them that know not how to go to the city" (Eccle. 10, 15). Jerome, when interpreting these words in his commentary on Ecclesiastes, says: "Read Plato, peruse the subtleties of Aristotle, look more closely at Zeno and Carneades, and you will prove the truth of the saying: 'The labour of fools shall afflict them.' Those men did seek truth with all earnestness, but because they did not have a guide and a pathfinder for the journey, and thought they could grasp wisdom through the human senses, they totally failed to reach the city about which it is said: 'O Lord; so in thy city thou shalt bring their image to nothing' (Ps. 72, 20). For in His city, the Lord will scatter all the shadows, and the various illusions, and pretenses they have put on in their various doctrines. About this it is also written elsewhere: 'The stream of the river maketh the city of God joyful' (Ps. 45, 5)."[4]

---

4 PL 23, 1097B-C.

Book 3, Chapter 8

Besides this common error of them all, whereby they have so falsely discussed about happiness, when treating about the virtues and vices, they taught many other errors. For none of them condemned simple fornication. They all taught that honors ought to be desired, not shunned. Some of them so valued riches, that they placed happiness in them, about which the Royal Prophet says: "They have called the people happy, that hath these things" (Ps. 143, 15). Others (among whom is Aristotle) even though they did not place happiness in riches, still they valued them more than poverty, they said that they could be more useful for virtue, than poverty. And I certainly believe that Vigilantius,[5] John Wycliffe, and John Hus drew their heresy therefrom when saying that voluntary poverty absolutely has no merit before God: even though Our Savior, the Teacher of Truth, said: "If thou wilt be perfect, go sell what thou hast, and give to the poor... and come follow me" (Mt. 19, 21). Others, namely, the Stoics (among the number of whom is our Seneca, and with whom on this point Cicero wished to be numbered in his [*Stoic] Paradoxes*[6]), teach that all sins are equal, and one is not graver than another.[7]

But putting aside the philosophers, who even though they erred in many things, they still taught many true and honor-

---

5 Vigilantius was born in about 370 A.D., at Calagurris in what is now southern France. He opposed the veneration of relics, the sending of alms to Jerusalem, the vow of poverty, and the high esteem of virginity. He was opposed in writing by St. Jerome.

6 Paradox 3, nn. 20-26.

7 Cf. Diogenes Laertius, *The Lives and Opinions of Eminent Philosophers*, bk. 7, c. 1 (Zeno), n. 120: "It is one of [the Stoics'] tenets that sins [ἁμαρτήματα] are all equal: so Chrysippus in the fourth book of his *Ethical Questions*, as well as Persaeus and Zeno. For if one truth is not more true than another, neither is one falsehood more false than another, and in the same way one deceit is not more so than another, nor sin than sin" (translated by R. D. Hicks (Harvard University Press, 1931)).

Last cause: Constant and incautious reading of books of heathens

able things about the virtues: let us come to their poets, the public enemies of all virtues and very skilled and very diligent instigators of vices. For there is scarcely any vice which was not praised very much by the poets. Because no greater praise could be given to the vices, than to give them to their gods, who ought to be the highest in goodness, and the parents and nourishers of all virtues. For when they narrate the deeds of those whom the people worshipped as gods, they describe their tyrannies, parricides, adulteries, incests, rapes, frauds, lies, and unmentionable crimes: such that they ascribe among the honors that the boy Ganymedes was carried off by Jupiter, the greatest of the gods, for unmentionable embraces.[8] Finally they attribute those vices to their gods, which no wise man would allow to be said about himself. Now since they say that these things appertain to the gods, by that very fact they persuade men to do the same things which they hear that the gods do. For examples avail for much greater persuasion, as Claudian elegantly teaches, when speaking thus: "Of a truth their leaders' pattern passes to the crowd, and the soldier follows not only the standard but also the example of his general."[9] If men's examples can move the souls of others to vices or virtues, it is clearer than light that the examples of the gods can do it much more easily.

And not only by examples do the poets entice the minds of readers to pleasures and wantonnesses, but they also do so by words, which they strive to be obscene and disgraceful with so much intent that a poet who uses modest words is not considered to be one of them. Regarding which matter I cite one of them, namely, Catullus, who related this law about the songs of the poets: "It befits an upright poet to be chaste, but his lines need not be so. Nay, they gain in fact more

---

8 Cf. Homer, *Iliad*, bk. 20, lns. 232-235; Virgil, *Aeneid*, bk. 1, ln. 28; St. Justin Martyr, *First Apology*, c. 21 (PG 6, 362A).

9 *On the Consulship of Stilicho*, bk. 1, lns. 168 f.

salt and attractiveness, when voluptuous and immodest."[10] Indeed, this sentiment of Catullus is to be laughed at, and he should rightly be hissed and booed off the stage by every wise man.[11] Who would not laugh that the poet says that he is chaste, who thinks about lust, dwells on obscene things, writes, speaks, and sings about lascivious and immodest things? As each man is, so he speaks and writes. On account of these incitements to evils, which the poets give to their listeners and readers, Plato, the most serious philosopher, reckoned that they ought to be exiled from a good city, lest by their association they would completely infect the whole city.[12]

Up until now we have spoken about the morals, that they are vitiated among the heathen writers; but it is necessary that we proceed further to say how wrongly those men think about those things which one ought to believe, and how openly they oppose the Catholic faith. Everything that we are all held to believe regarding Christ's two natures, namely, His Divine and human natures: all those things the heathens not merely oppose, but ridicule and mock. They do not acknowledge the triune and one God, but instead they adore many gods fighting amongst themselves. They do not understand that God is the Creator of all things, because they believe that nothing can come into being from nothing, and so they teach that the world was without a beginning, and will exist

---

10 *Carmina*, poem 16, lns. 5-8.
11 Cf. Cicero, *Stoic Paradoxes*, paradox 3, n. 26: "If an actor moves a little out of time with the music or recites a verse that is one syllable too short or too long, he is hissed and booed off the stage [*exsibilatur, exploditur*]."
12 Cf. *Republic*, bk. 3 (398a); bk. 8 (568b): "'Wherefore,' said I, 'being wise as they are, the poets of tragedy will pardon us and those whose politics resemble ours for not admitting them into our polity, since they hymn the praises of tyranny.'" Cf. St. Augustine, *City of God*, bk. 2, c. 14 (PL 41, 58-60).

Last cause: Constant and incautious reading of books of heathens

without an end.[13] The majority of them do not know that God is the rewarder of the good, and punisher of the wicked, and believe that nothing is left after this life, but rather that the soul perishes along with the body. Although there are those among them who believe that the soul is immortal, they speak of rewards for the good and punishments for the wicked, which are very far removed from Christian piety. They also never thought about the fall and perdition of the human race, and its origin, and hence they are unable to understand the renewal of it made by Christ Our Savior. They not only do not believe that God descended from heaven for us, and took a human nature, and in it suffered hunger, thirst, sorrows, and various sufferings of the body, and at length underwent death on the wood of the Cross for our sins, but they think that those who teach and preach such things are foolish: "We preach Christ crucified," says Paul, "unto the Jews indeed a stumblingblock, and unto the Gentiles foolishness" (I Cor. 1, 23). Behold the whole pinnacle of the Christian religion unknown by the heathens, and profane writers, and opposed and mocked by many of them.

And hence it is very clearly proved that the constant reading of them can greatly harm Christian men, especially the incautious and the weak. Wherefore Paul, knowing very well that very much poison is in these profane writers, admonishes that we ought to be cautious about reading them: "Beware," he says, "lest any man cheat you by philosophy, and vain deceit; according to the tradition of men, according to the elements of the world" (Col. 2, 8). [Ambrosiaster], when interpreting which words in his commentaries on Paul's epistle, says: "Paul speaks here of earthly philosophy, by which those who want to be thought of as wise in this world are habitually seduced... He is absorbed in probable causes and possible explanations, believing that there is nothing as true as what is observed and understood in the

---

13 Cf. St. Thomas, I, q. 46, a. 1, arg. 3.

elements. Because what we have in front of us and see with our eyes seems attractive and desirable, it seduces those who think that spiritual reasoning is to be despised and ridiculed because they have no hope for the future. Bound to carnal logic, they attribute all power to the stars and do not think that anything heavy can possibly be taken up to heaven, or that anything light can come to the earth. Rejecting the power and providence of God, they deny that any corporeal thing can be brought into being without some admixture of different things. They know that it is possible to read in the ancient Divine tomes of the Hebrews that many things were done by Moses which the human mind does not accept, and similarly in the new books there are things done by the Lord or through the Apostles which human thought finds incredible. Paul calls this tradition or philosophy fallacious and inept, because it is not worked out according to the power of God but according to the weakness of the human mind, which restricts the power of God to the limits of its own knowledge, so that no one will ever believe that it is possible to do anything other than what carnal reason accepts. In this way they can employ individual parts of divinity in different ways of worship, so as to tie down the mind of the unskilled and prevent them from reaching up to the true God. It does not lead to Christ and not to the one God. It does not lead to Christ but away from Him in Whom the 'fulness of the Godhead' (v. 9) is found."[14]

There is yet something else adjoined to their false teaching in the books of heathens and of other profane men, namely, eloquence, which gives them great powers for harming. For those things, about which they discuss, they treat not coarsely and unrefinedly, but they polish with great skill, and adorn with great elegance of words, such that if the matters

---

14 *Commentary on Colossians* (PL 17, 428C-429B) (translated by Gerald L. Bray, in *Commentaries on Galatians-Philemon* (Downers Grove, Illinois: InterVarsity Press, 2009), p. 88).

Last cause: Constant and incautious reading of books of heathens

themselves which they treat would perhaps deter the minds of those reading, the very splendor of the oration, and the ornamentation of the words, is able to entice. And thence it happens that the poison of the teaching mixed with such great sweetness of words, can so much more easily harm the incautious, the more willingly it is drunk by them, since they consider not what hides within, but only the outward sweetness of the words. Now if someone perhaps does not know how great is the force and power of eloquence, let him read Valerius Maximus, in chapter nine of book eight,[15] where he proves by many and various examples, that its power is so great that often it can draw men's minds no matter how distant to itself, and persuade and soften hardened minds.

About which matter, although many examples could be cited, nevertheless I wish to offer only one and a very efficacious one, which Cicero relates in the *Tusculan Disputations*,[16] and after him Augustine.[17] Plato in a certain book, which is called *Phaedo*, very eloquently disputes about the immortality of the soul, and proves that it is immortal.[18] When Cleombrotus of Ambracia had read this book, not pressed by any trouble, he immediately cast himself from a wall, so that from this life, full of miseries, he might pass on to another, which he believed is much better. Regarding him there exists a Greek epigram of Callimachus, which I do not know who translated into Latin, saying the following: "Farewell, O Sun, said Cleombrotus of Ambracia, and leapt from a lofty wall into Hades. No evil had he seen worthy of death, but he had read one writing of Plato's, *Phaedo*. He should have read with no such reference."[19] Certainly just

---

15 *Facta et Dicta Memorabilia*.
16 Bk. 1, n. 84.
17 *City of God*, bk. 1, c. 22 (PL, 41, 35-36).
18 Cf. 70c ff.
19 Epigram 24 (translated by G. R. Mair, in *Callimachus: Hymns and Epigrams; Lycophron; Aratus* (Cambridge, MA: Harvard

from this example one can easily establish how powerful eloquence is for moving men's minds, which could move a man not bothered by any difficulty, such that he would voluntarily inflict death upon himself, which all men abhor by nature.

Hence Paul, knowing very well this force and power of eloquence, admonishes the faithful that they carefully take heed not to be deceived by it. Beware, he says, lest any man cheat you in loftiness of speech.[20] Paul surely had known that that loftiness of speech is very powerful for persuading to anything. Thus lest anyone allege that he was deceived through sublimity of speech by Christ Our Savior, or His Apostles: wherefore Christ Our Savior did not want that the Evangelical teaching would consist in great adornment of speech: "But we have this treasure in earthen vessels," he says elsewhere, "that the excellency may be of the power of God" (II Cor. 4, 7). Whence it is that Christ Himself, Who is the Wisdom of God, when just born was placed between two animals, and was wrapped in poor swaddling clothes.[21] God's Wisdom is put between an ox and an ass, so that He might instruct the ignorant, and teach the slow-witted. Now He Who permitted to be wrapped in poor swaddling clothes likewise also wished to be preached with humble words by His followers. And hence He took to Himself not polished orators, or skilled rhetoricians, or powerful argumentations: "But the foolish things of the world," the same Paul says, "hath God chosen, that he may confound the wise" (I Cor. 1, 27).

University Press, 1977)). The last line is taken from the commentary of Juan Luis Vives on *The City of God*. Cf. *St. Augustine, Of the Citie of God: With the Learned Comments of Io. Lod. Vives* ([London]: George Eld, 1610), p. 35.
20   Cf. Col. 2, 8 & I Cor. 2, 1.
21   Cf. Lk. 2, 7.

Last cause: Constant and incautious reading of books of heathens

How much the eloquence of heathen writers harms the Christian man, Origen clearly explains upon the occasion taken from the figure of the Old Testament in his second homily on Jeremias, where, when expounding the passage of the same Jeremias, "Babylon hath been a golden cup in the hand of the Lord, that made all the earth drunk" (51, 7), he speaks thus: "Nabuchodonosor, wishing to deceive men through the deceitful cup of Babylon, did not mix the potion he was preparing in an earthen vessel, nor in what was a little better, in an iron, copper, or pewter vessel, or what is superior to these, silver. Choosing rather a gold vessel in which he combined the potion so that whoever sees what is attractive about the gold, touched by the beauty of the radiant metal and drawn totally with the eyes by its splendor, does not consider what is inwardly hidden, and accepting the cup, drinks, ignoring that it is the cup of Nabuchodonosor. You will understand what is called the golden cup in the present text if you note that the deadly words of the most evil teachings have a certain kind of arrangement of speaking, a kind of attractive eloquence, a kind of beauty of order, and if you know how each of the poets, who are thought along with their disciples as the most well-spoken men, have formed the golden cup and injected the venom of idolatry and the venom of obscenity, the venom of those teachings which slay the soul of man, the venom with the false name of knowledge... I have often seen a golden cup, decorated with the beauty of words, and when I consider the venom of its teachings, I have perceived that it is the cup of Babylon."[22]

And Blessed Jerome in his *Commentary on Jonas the Prophet*, near the end of chapter three, when speaking about the eloquence of the heathens, says these words: "What the influence of eloquence and secular wisdom is among people

---

[22] *Homilies on Jeremias*, hom. 21, n. 7 (PG 13, 538D-539B). This translation was taken from *Homilies on Jeremiah and 1 Kings 28* (Washington, D. C.: CUA Press, 2010), pp. 267 f.

of this age is witnessed to by Demosthenes, Tullius [Cicero], Plato, Xenophon, Theophrastus, Aristotle, and other orators and philosophers who are regarded as kings among mankind, and whose precepts are regarded not as the precepts of mortal beings but are received as Divine oracles... Whence it is also said in Jeremias concerning Babylon: 'Babylon hath been a golden cup... that made all the earth drunk.' Who has not been made drunk by the eloquence of this age? Whose souls have not been dulled by the putting together of words and the splendor of their eloquence?"[23]

From these things is it now very clearly proved that one of the greatest causes whence heresies arise is the constant and incautious reading of the writings of heathens. For if those things that they teach clearly oppose the Catholic faith, and their eloquence has great force (as we said) for convincing men of those things that they teach, there is no reason why someone could rightly doubt that the constant and indiscrete reading of them can greatly harm Christians, especially if they apply themselves to them from childhood without great discretion. For then that tender age is like wax for easily receiving the impression of whatever thing: and those things which it then receives, it retains for a long time, and with difficulty lets go. For Horace said very well: "Once a fresh jar is imbued with a scent, it will long retain the fragrance."[24] With which agrees that which Solomon says: "A young man according to his way, even when he is old he will not depart from it" (Prov. 22, 6). And indeed, it has been proven in fact that many of those who were given to books of heathens from their tender years have fallen into various heresies, or have given great suspicion of heresy.

---

23 C. 3 (PL 25, 1142C-1143A & C). This translation is taken from Timothy Hegedus' thesis, *Jerome's commentary on Jonas: Translation with introduction and critical notes* (1991), *Theses and Dissertations (Comprehensive)*, pp. 53 f.
24 Horace, *Epistles*, bk 1, letter 2, lns. 69 f.

Last cause: Constant and incautious reading of books of heathens

And in order to make this opinion of mine more certain and more firm, I now wish to relate both ancient and recent things, whereby it is clearly proved that the constant reading of heathen writings was the source of many heresies. The first of all heretics, who arose after the preaching of the Gospel, was the well-known Simon the Magician, about whom there is mention in the Acts of the Apostles.[25] Epiphanius bears witness, in celebrated work which he made against all heresies,[26] that this man borrowed the fabrications of his heresies from Philistion [of Nicaea], an ancient comic poet. He relates the same thing about the Gnostic heretics, that they composed the fables of their heresies in imitation of the same poet, Philistion.[27] Concerning Valentinus the same Epiphanius relates that he was deceived by heathen poetry full of fables.[28] Finally, Tertullian refers to many of the ancient heretics, who drew their heresies from heathen philosophers, when speaking thus: "Indeed heresies are themselves instigated by philosophy. From this source came the Aeons, and I know not what infinite forms, and the trinity of man in the system of Valentinus, who was of Plato's school. From the same source came Marcion's better god, with all his tranquility; he came of the Stoics. Then, again, the opinion that the soul dies is held by the Epicureans; while the denial of the restoration of the body is taken from the aggregate school of all the philosophers; also, when matter is made equal to God, then you have the teaching of Zeno; and when any doctrine is alleged touching a god of fire, then Heraclitus comes in. The same subject-matter is discussed

---

25 Cf. Acts 8, 9-11.
26 *Panarion*, bk. 1, heresy 21, c. 3, n. 4 (PG 41, 290B).
27 *Ibid.*, heresy 26, c. 1, n. 7 (PG 41, 331C).
28 *Ibid.*, heresy 31, c. 3, n. 3 (PG 41, 478B): "They have done nothing else than to copy the pretended poetic art of the Greeks' imposture and heathen mythology, changing nothing except for their altered foreign coinage."

over and over again by the heretics and the philosophers; the same arguments are involved."[29]

But let us proceed further, and let us bring forth examples of other heretics, who came forth after Tertullian. Priscillian's heresy teaching that men are bound to the fatal stars, came down from the error of the heathen philosophers.[30] For (as [Nemesius of Emesa] relates[31]) "the Stoics, Chrysippus[32] and Philopator,[33] and many other brilliant philosophers point out nothing other than that everything happens according to fate."[34] When Jovinian says that all sins are equal, he imitated the Stoic philosophers, who teach these things.[35] However, when he says that fasting has no merit, and equates [virginity] to matrimony, he clearly shows himself to be (as Blessed Jerome reproaches him[36]) a disciple of Epicurus. The renowned Emperor Julian, who, on account of the Catholic faith having been completely rejected by him, bears the name Apostate until this day, drew the poison by which he was infected from the reading and association which he constantly had with heathen philosophers, so that he became not merely a heretic, but an apostate, and

---

29 *Prescription against Heretics*, c. 7 (PL 2, 19A-B).
30 Cf. Pope Leo I, Letter 15, c. 11 (PL 54, 685C-686A). St. Jerome says Priscillian was "an enthusiastic votary of Zoroaster and a magician before he became a bishop" (Letter 133 (To Ctesiphon), n. 4 (PL 22, 1153)).
31 St. Gregory of Nyssa's *De Fato* is cited here, which work is now known to be taken from Nemesius' *De natura hominis*.
32 Chrysippus of Soli died in ca. 206 B.C.
33 Philopator flourished ca. 140 A.D.
34 *De natura hominis graece et latine* (Halle an der Saale: Gebauer, 1802), c. 35, p. 92.
35 Cf. St. Augustine in his *On Heresies, to Quodvultdeus*, c. 82, where he says, "[Jovinian] maintained, as did the Stoic philosophers, that all sins are equal" (PL 42, 45); St. Jerome, *Against Jovinianus*, bk. 2, n. 21 (PL 23, 315B).
36 *Ibid.*

Last cause: Constant and incautious reading of books of heathens

a very fierce persecutor of Christians.[37] From the *Historia Tripartita*[38] it is evident that the skill of the rhetorical art, and then the long association with the sophist Epiphanius, greatly harmed Apollinaris of Laodicea. Whence did John Wycliffe, and however many imitated him on this point, saying that nothing happens contingently, but rather everything proceeds from an absolute necessity, such that those things which happen, could not happen otherwise, draw this heresy? Was it not from the teaching of Aristotle, and other philosophers? For all these men not knowing God's power, upon whose choice everything depends, and considering only the natural order of causes, did not attribute anything to the Divine will, but all to necessity.

Now he who more clearly shows that he was deceived by the teaching of philosophers was Peter Abelard, who said that nothing ought to be believed, which cannot be proved by

---

37   Cf. Socrates Scholasticus, *Ecclesiastical History*, bk. 3, c. 1 (PG 67, 370B-371B): "In grammar Nicocles the Lacaedemonian was his instructor; and Ecebolius the Sophist, who was at that time a Christian, taught him rhetoric: for the emperor [Constantius II] had made the provision that he should have no pagan masters, lest he should be seduced to the pagan superstitions. For Julian was a Christian at the beginning. ... [Libanius the Syrian Sophist] had retired to Nicomedia, where he opened a school. ... Julian was, however, interdicted from being his auditor, because Libanius was a pagan in religion: nevertheless he privately procured his orations, which he not only greatly admired, but also frequently and with close study perused. As he was becoming very expert in the rhetorical art, Maximus the philosopher arrived at Nicomedia... whom the emperor Valentinian afterwards caused to be executed as a practicer of magic. ... From him [Julian] received, in addition to the principles of philosophy, his own religious sentiments, and a desire to possess the empire. ... [W]hile in private he pursued his philosophical studies, in public he read the sacred writings of the Christians..."

38   Bk. 5, c. 44 (PL 69, 1023D-1024B).

natural reason. And whence does this arise except from the philosophers? For these men want to measure every teaching by the capacity of their intellect alone: and those things which do not accord with their judgment, they immediately reject: finally, they do not want to accept anything which their intellects cannot comprehend by natural reason. And whence such a great diversity among philosophers comes forth, because since no one wants to subject himself to the judgment of another, nor admit anything which does not agree with his own judgment, it was necessarily bound to happen that there would be as great a variety of teachings, as there is a variety of judgments. Now this liberty of thought, and consequent variety [of teachings], is clearly opposed to the Catholic faith, which ought to be one for all, and in which (as Paul says) one ought to be "bringing into captivity every understanding unto the obedience of Christ" (II Cor. 10, 5).

Concerning Martin Luther, who came forth in this time of ours, there is no reason why we might think that he drew the poison of his heresies from the reading of heathen writers. For when he firstly began to pour forth his heresies, either by word or by writing, he knew absolutely no Greek, little Latin, as his prior writings indicate. And he was defending his heresies not with knowledge of languages, but by certain argumentations and sophistries; even though he himself reproaches all scholastic theologians for this, calling them all sophists. Nevertheless many others wound their way into the Lutheran family, whom I do not doubt took much harm from the reading of heathen writings for easily accepting heresies. Certainly Philip Melanchthon was very well versed in the Greek and Latin languages, and very erudite in the writings which are called the humanities, and very much taken up with extensive reading of the heathen philosophers (as his writings indicate). I am still very surprised about one thing regarding him, how he could deny the freedom of choice, since he has known by experience in himself such great

Last cause: Constant and incautious reading of books of heathens

liberty of speech, so that he never fears to teach whatever he pleases, and what pleased him at one time, he afterwards he felt displeased him so much, that he did not hesitate to revoke. There are other Lutherans, yet very few, similar to Philip Melanchthon, who, from the reading the poets, and other heathen orators, accepted (like he) very much poison.

Notice how many examples we have brought forth, by which it is clearly proved that the continual and incautious reading of profane writers gave to many the occasion of many heresies. There still are many others besides all these, who, even though they were not branded as heretics, and reckoned as such by all, nevertheless gave not a small suspicion of heresy about themselves, on account of the many things which they said and wrote according to the teaching of heathen writers, to whom they were excessively given from childhood. Pomponius Laetus,[39] Domizio Calderini,[40] Antonio Urceus,[41] and some others of the same ilk who now are still alive, have a bad reputation in many men's minds, because they gave great suspicion of heresy. How great a suspicion of heresy in our time Erasmus of Rotterdam gave, a man certainly very learned in Greek and Latin, it is unnecessary to now relate, since it is very well known to the whole world. For even though he has not been condemned of heresy up until now by a suitable judge, and proclaimed a heretic, still many writers, while he was alive, branded him with this crime. And the University of Paris condemned many of his assertions by a public censure, some of which it deemed to be heretical, others suspect of heresy, and others scandalous. Erasmus when responding to which censure, although

---

39 Julius Pomponius Laetus (1446-1478), also known as Giulio Pomponio Leto, was an Italian humanist.
40 Domizio Calderini, baptized as Dominicus (1446-1478) was an Italian humanist.
41 Antonio Urceo, called Codro (Latin, Antonius Urceus Codrus; 1446-1500) was an Italian humanist.

Book 3, Chapter 8

he shows that he had a Catholic mind in many things, still in certain other things did not fully purge himself (as many think) of the suspicion which was had about him. It is evident that this evil happened to him from the fact that from his tender years he was for a long time turning over in his mind the Greek and Latin poets and orators, from whom he received a great liberty of speech, so that he would immediately pour out in public whatever he pleased.

Who does not recognize in him the liberty of Lucian [of Samosata], the deriding and mockery of all? He imbibed the mind and style of Lucian to such an extent, that he was called Atheos, that is "without God," by many men even of his own nation, just as Lucian. He certainly was a man given very good intelligence by God, and hence fortunate, if he perhaps had been content with his lot, and had attempted only those things which were equal to his strength. But after reaching manhood, which he had given nearly entirely to the poets and orators, he undertook to interpret Holy Writ, which he had learned without a teacher leading the way. And in the interpretations and annotations of them he introduced many things, which if he had omitted, he would have acted much more wisely. For often it happens that those who have their palate and tongue imbued with the bitterness of very bitter foods from excessive consumption, whatever they may then drink or eat, tastes bitter to them; and those who have stood in the sun's rays for a long time, to them whatever they may subsequently see presents itself with the color that their eyes, vitiated by dimness, carry around within them. So likewise those who have consumed a great part of life in the profane poets and orators, especially in the heathen philosophers, by very tenaciously retaining the liberty of speech which they learned from them, do not understand what Holy Writ is, but what they bring with themselves.

Finally as a confirmation of those things which we have said, I cite the testimony of Blessed Jerome, who in his commentaries on Jonas the prophet, near the end of chapter three, when discussing worldly eloquence, says these words: "Powerful, noble, and rich men have great difficulty in believing in God; then how much more so for the masters of speech! Their mind is blinded by riches, wealth, abundance; they are surrounded by vices and cannot see virtues; they judge the simplicity of the Holy Scripture not by the majesty of its meanings, but by the lowliness of its words."[42]

---

42 *Commentaria in Jonam* (PL 25, 1143C).

Chapter IX

Concerning the remedy against the aforesaid cause of heresies.

We have now manifestly proved with many reasons and many examples that the continual and incautious reading of profane writings is the clear cause of many heresies. But there is a need for us to counterattack this, and to prepare an antidote for such a powerful poison, cautiously however, so that by desiring to altogether remove this cause, we do not bring about another cause of much greater evils. For just as the continual and indiscrete reading of profane books can be the cause of heresies, so on the contrary to completely abstain from the books of heathens, could generate many heresies. Because the liberal arts, which can hardly be learned from others besides the heathen writers, are so necessary for the understanding of Sacred Scripture, that ignorance of them is able to produce many heresies, as it has proved from actual experience, that many heresies have proceeded from it. For knowledge of grammar is firstly necessary, and not a cursory, but a full and consummate knowledge, so that he may know the meaning of words, and their composition and structure. From the ignorance of which matter it is evident that many have fallen into various heresies. And lest due to a lack of examples, someone would lose trust in my words, I wish to presently cite examples, whence it may be established that what I say is true.

Helvidius, because he was ignorant of the force and power of these words: "firstborn," "before," "until," babbled against the purity of the Most Holy Virgin, saying that she was not perpetually a virgin, but after Christ was born she was known by Joseph her spouse. All the Manichaeans, speaking out of ignorance of the difference between these prepositions [in Latin], *ex* and *de*, said that God produces our souls from [*de*] His substance. Logic is often necessary in Holy Writ. Because it is that which sets down the form of definitions, divisions, and conclusions; and without knowledge of these things hardly any serious writing can be fully understood. From the ignorance, or perhaps inadvertence, of this discipline many men possessing a great name erred regarding the correct understanding of Sacred Scripture. Origen not carefully considering how many universal expressions ought to be understood in Sacred Scripture, said that all men will at length be saved, occasioned by some passages of Sacred Scripture, wrongly understood by him. "I will pour out," God says through the prophet Joel, "my spirit upon all flesh" (2, 28). And Paul [wrote]: "God hath concluded all in unbelief, that he may have mercy on all" (Rom. 11, 32). Which "all," even if there are others, was said not because God will in the end spare all men, and not perpetually condemn anyone, but by "all" He understands men of every kind, and of every age, and of every rank and dignity, both of the Gentiles and of the Jews. In which passages that word of universality, "all," (as we speak according to the manner of logic) does not distribute to the individuals of the groups, but to the groups of individuals.

Erasmus of Rotterdam, not understanding the force of the argument, and its discussion, by which Christ Our Savior tries to prove against the Jews, that no one can pluck the sheep out of His hand, by the fact that no one can snatch them out of His Father's hand, and by the fact that He and the Father are one:[1] erred saying that in those words of Christ the word, "one," can mean only the unity of minds. Which word if taken there (as Erasmus says) according to that meaning, Christ would conclude wrongly, and the argument would be worthless, as I proved in that work which I published, *Against All Heresies*, in the section on "God" [*Deus*], in the

---

1 Cf. Jn. 10, 29-30.

Remedy for the constant and incautious reading of books of heathens

sixth heresy.[2] Augustine testifies that knowledge of the history of the heathens is highly necessary for the understanding of Sacred Scripture, in book two of *On Christian Doctrine*, where he shows that some men from ignorance of these things erred in regard to Sacred Scriptures.[3] One ought to know the properties and powers of things, so that thence we can grasp the mystical meaning of Sacred Scripture, which ought to be investigated through the resemblances of these things. Yet only the natural philosophers teach the knowledge of these things, such as Aristotle, Theophrastus, Plinius, and [Pedanius] Dioscorides. Thus just as the heathen books have many harmful things, so also they have many useful

---

2 "In John [chapter] ten, the Lord says: 'The Father and I are one' (v. 30). How is an Arian going to be vanquished by this evidence, unless you tell him that the word 'one' in the Scriptures can only mean 'what is of the same substance'? Now, since the Scriptures provide innumerable passages which teach that it can be understood as referring to consent or mutual love, I fail to see how far this will help to confirm the opinions of the orthodox, or to repress the stubbornness of the heretic. However, that Christ is speaking there of the concord He has with the Father can be inferred with a high degree of likelihood, since He is not referring to His statement about being one with the Father, but to the fact that He called God His Father, and was thus in an extraordinary fashion calling Himself the Son of God" (Erasmus, *In Novum Testamentum Annotationes* (Basel: Froben, 1555), p. 803). Just before saying this quotation, Erasmus wrote: "So far we have dealt with what can be inferred from the verse. But here we are clearly dealing with the reliability of the witness, not about the substance of persons. For if this word 'one' in many other places means 'agreement' rather than 'the unity of an individual,' what is so strange in our interpreting it here in a similar way? How often do we read in either Testament 'one heart,' 'one spirit and soul,' 'one voice,' 'one mind,' when this signifies agreement and mutual love? Since this trope is so familiar in the Scriptures, what is stopping us from assuming the same meaning here?"

3 C. 28, nn. 42-43 (PL 34, 55-56).

and necessary things for the full understanding of Holy Writ. Therefore it is not good that all the books of the heathens be rejected by all Christians, since they are necessary for many, and as many as they wish can profit much from them.

Next, the brilliance of expression and the ornamentation of language, which can be taken from them, even though it is not necessary for a Christian man, still is useful for many things, especially for those who teach others by word or writing. For eloquence comes from the arrangement of those things which, in and of themselves, are neither good nor bad, but from the good or bad use of them, they become either good or bad. For just as eloquence is something bad for a heathen or heretic, because by it both of these will persuade their hearers or readers of their errors: so likewise it is something good for a Catholic teacher or preacher, because by it both become more powerful for directing the minds of the hearers or readers. Still there are some men of such a malignant nature, that they condemn everything which they cannot attain: and hence it happens that they abhor and persecute as an enemy eloquence, which is far removed from them, and which they despair to attain. "What has a jackdaw to do with a lyre, or pigs with amber or perfume?"[4]

Thus on account of these things, those who will perhaps try to reprove me, because I have not cursed eloquence (as they [have done]), I bring forth the testimony of Augustine as a witness of my opinion, who says these words: "Eloquence, indeed, is the skill of speaking, suitably explaining what we think: which should be used, when we think correctly.

---

4 The was a common Greek adage. Cf. Erasmus, *Adagia chiliades* 1.4.38 (alias n. 339; cf. *Adagiorum Chiliades iuxta locos communes digestae*, p. 439). Lucretius, *De rerum natura*, bk. 6, ln. 973-974: "Though unto us the mire be filth most foul, / To hogs that mire doth so delightsome seem." Aulus Gellius, *Attic Nights*, Preface, n. 19: "The daw knows naught of the lyre, the hog naught of marjoram ointment."

Heretics have not used it in this manner. For surely, if they had thought correct things, there would be not only nothing bad, but something true and good, which they could have eloquently explained. Therefore, you have accused eloquence in vain by the mention of these examples. For indeed, a soldier is not to go unarmed for the good of his country, just because some have used arms to harm the country: nor, for that reason, should good and learned doctors not use medical tools for the sake of health, because unskilled and wicked individuals also misuse them unto ruin. For who is unaware, that just as those things which were aimed at were useful or useless; so too, eloquence, that is, the skill and faculty of speaking, is useful or useless, depending on whether what is said is useful or useless? I do not believe that you are unaware of this."[5] And in chapter thirty-seven of the second book of his *On Christian Doctrine*, he teaches the same thing.[6] From whose words it is proved clearly enough that they are very far from the truth who expressly accuse eloquence, which, it is evident, is not bad of itself, but through the fault of those misusing it; indeed which could be useful for many things, if someone would want to use it well.

The reading of heathen books can be beneficial for another use of Christian men not to be despised, namely, so that probing their secrets, we can more easily conquer them by disputation. And in this way we will pierce them with their own sword, just as David did against the proud Goliath, killing him with his own sword.[7] For so Blessed [John] Damascene ordered to be done, when speaking thus: "But if we are able to pluck anything profitable from outside sources, there is nothing to forbid that. Let us become tried money-dealers, heaping up the true and pure gold and discarding the spuri-

---

5   *Against Cresconius the Grammarian*, bk. 1, c. 1, n. 2 (PL 43, 447-448).
6   N. 50 (PL 34, 58-59).
7   Cf. I Kings 17, 51.

ous. Let us keep the fairest sayings but let us throw to the dogs absurd gods and strange myths: for we might prevail most mightily against them through themselves."[8] For from the heathens' own opinions, which they assert about their gods, very strong arguments are taken against themselves for refuting their empty errors. For when about the renowned Jupiter, whom Virgil calls the father of the gods, and king of men,[9] they relate such rapes, adulteries, abductions, deceptions, lies, and such things which any nation well established abhors, prohibits, and punishes, we can easily gather therefrom that he was not a god, but a very disgraceful man. Next, Mercury's thefts, trickeries, and deceptions: moreover, the wicked anger of Juno against the Trojans, in addition the strifes of the fighting gods among themselves, some of whom are said to have favored the Trojans, others the Greeks, clearly show that they had nothing of true divinity, since the morals of this kind, not only Socrates, or Pythagoras, or Diogenes, but any other prudent man, and lover of virtue, would reject and abominate.

Now when a Christian and educated man when disputing against the heathen philosophers and poets, having taken up arms from them, shall have defeated them, he will bring back great glory for God's honor. It is indeed a beautiful victory, to confute the opposing side with the words of their own testimonies, and to conquer the enemy with his own arms, and to prove that the arguments of the disputer supports your rather than his opinion. For many of the renowned, illustrious, ancient writers triumphed with these arms against the heathens. Justin the Philosopher, and Christ's martyr, wrote a book in favor of the Catholic faith against the heathens, which he called, *Exhortation to the Greeks*,[10] in which from

---

8 *On the Orthodox Faith*, bk. 4, c. 17 (PG 94, 1178B).
9 Cf. *Aeneid*, bk. 8, lns. 572-573; bk. 10, lns. 18 & 112.
10 PG 6, 241-312. St. Justin Martyr's authorship is today disputed but it is verified by Eusebius of Caesarea in his *Church History*, bk.

the sayings of the heathens themselves he proves that their errors are false and baseless. Tertullian did this same thing in his *Apology Against the Heathens*.[11] Origen did the same thing in his *Apology* against Celsus.[12] Bishop Eusebius of Caesarea fights with the same arms for the Catholic faith, in the work which he made, *Preparation for the Gospel*,[13] and in another whose title is, *Demonstratio Evangelica*.[14] Bishop Cyril of Alexandria fights in the same way in the ten books whereby he confutes and refutes the blasphemies of Julian the Apostate which he had spewed out against the Gospel of Christ Our Savior.[15] In the same way Bishop Theodoret of Cyrus pleads the case for the Catholic faith in the work which he entitled, *The Cure of the Greek Maladies*.[16] Finally, Lactantius Firmianus, who in the books of *The Divine Institutes*[17] had fought for the Christian religion against the heathen with arms of this kind, at length in the book, *On the Workmanship of God*, says these words: "Then, accordingly, I will exhort you with greater clearness and truth to the learning of true philosophy. For I have determined to commit to writing as many things as I shall be able, which have reference to the condition of a happy life; and that indeed against the philosophers, since they are pernicious and weighty for the disturbing of the truth. For the force of their eloquence is incredible, and their subtlety in argument and disputation

---

4, c. 18 (PG 20, 374C), by Stephanus Gobarus who ascribes it to him in the sixth century (*Miscellany*), as well as by Photius (*Bibliotheca*, codex 232 (PG 103, 1099C)).
11 *Apologeticus adversus Gentes pro Chrisitianis* (PL 1, 257A-536A).
12 PG 11, 642-1632.
13 PG 21, 21-1408.
14 PG 22, 9-794.
15 *Against Julian* (PG 76, 510-1058).
16 PG 83, 775-1152.
17 PL 6, 111A-822A.

may easily deceive anyone; and these we will refute partly by our own weapons, but partly by weapons borrowed from their mutual wrangling, so that it may be evident that they rather introduced error than removed it."[18]

For this reason Emperor Julian the Apostate (as [Cassiodorus[19]] relates in the life of that man), when striving to spread paganism in all his dominion, and for Christianity to be driven away, firstly in fact commanded the Christians not to read the teachings of the poets or philosophers. "We were wounded," he said, "by our own arrows, according to the proverb: for armed with our writings, they undertake war against us."[20] From all these things it is clearly established that it can be very harmful if all the writers of the heathen were banished by the Church, and all Catholic men were to abstain from reading them, since they often (as we proved) are necessary for understanding Sacred Scripture. But, because on the other hand we said that they can greatly harm, especially to the incautious and the weak, it is necessary that we show some caution, whereby we can profit from the reading of heathen writers, without any harm.

Now this caution consists (as I think) in a twofold consideration, one of which is about the books themselves which are to be read; the other is about the things that are contained in the same books. And as to what pertains to the books, I do not think that they all ought to be read, and much less be given to children, but some of them I reckoned ought to be banished from the whole Christian world, such that they could not be read by anyone: because they could hardly do good, and often they are wont to do harm to those reading so easily and quickly, that they seem to contain instantaneous poison in themselves. Such are the books of some poets so obscene, so lascivious, containing in them such voluptuous words,

---

18 C. 20 (PL 7, 76A-77A).
19 Eutropius is incorrected cited here.
20 *Historia Tripartita*, bk. 6, c. 17 (PL 69, 1040D).

Remedy for the constant and incautious reading of books of heathens

that they easily move the minds of the readers, especially the tender youth, to inordinate desires and lewdness. Such is the renowned Catullus, whose censure about composing verses we cited in the immediately preceding chapter. Such are Tibullus and Propertius in every respect. Such is Ovid in his many works, the most lascivious of all the poets. And I do him no injury, by thinking him to be such, since he himself, pressed by his own conscience, reckoned the same thing about himself, when speaking thus:

> I speak unwillingly now: don't touch the tender poets!
> Disloyally I banish even my own gifts.
> Shun Callimachus: he's no enemy of love:
> and as well as Callimachus, you Philetas do harm.
> I'm certain Sappho made me sweeter on my lover,
> and Anacreon's Muse gave out no rigid rules.
> Who can have read your songs, in safety, Tibullus,
> or you, Propertius, whose work was Cynthia alone?
> Who could depart harshly from reading Gallus?
> And I'm not sure some such doesn't sound in my songs too.[21]

And if this heathen and lascivious poet thinks and argues this, Christian teachers of children ought to be ashamed, who give such books to children to be read, by whose voluptuous words, imbued with indecent ideas, their minds are moved to desiring lascivious and shameful things. And I do not reckon that anything different ought to be said about Terence, whom nearly all teachers give to children: for in his writings you will not find anything but certain love stories, and mixed with these reproofs of parents, disobediences of children, deceptions of servants, and allurements of prostitutes. Now

---

21 *Remedia Amoris*, lns. 757-766 (A. S. Kline (poetry translation), *Ovid: The Love Poems-The Amores, Ars Amatoria and Remedia Amoris*).

what else are love stories to the heart of an adolescent, than a proximate danger for debaucheries? These are truly those communications about which Menander[22] by that verse sanctified by Paul the Apostle said: "Evil communications corrupt good manners" (I Cor. 15, 33). Things themselves without words have invited and attracted the minds of children; words without things allured to themselves: thus the eloquence of these men applied to such things is nothing other than a sweet condiment added to sweet poison.

Among the many very good ordinances of the Spartans, which they decreed for ruling well their nation, one (as Plutarch relates[23]) is this, whereby they strictly forbade performances of tragedies and comedies, so that the citizens would not hear either in earnest or in jest anything opposed to their laws. For laws forbid rapes, incests, adulteries, abductions: they forbid deceptions, injuries, public enmities, broken agreements, thefts; all of which the poets are wont to attribute to their gods. For this reason they drove out the poet Archilochus, when he came to Sparta, because they heard that he had written in verses, that it is better to throw away one's arms than to die.[24] If the heathen rulers of the Spartans cared with such great diligence to drive away comedies and tragedies from their nation, it was much more just that Christian rulers, who ought to have much greater care of good morals, would completely forbid not only the performances of comedies and tragedies, but also the reading of the same, and especially that they would not be given to the tender souls of children.

---

22 Cf. the comedy, *Thais*, which is no longer extant. "This iambic trimeter is taken from a comedy of Menander" (St. Jerome, *Commentary on Titus* (PL 26, 573C)).
23 *Instituta Laconica*, n. 33, in *Moralia* (239b), translated by Frank Cole Babbitt (London: Harvard University Press, 1957), vol. 3, p. 441.
24 *Ibid.*, n. 34 (239b).

Remedy for the constant and incautious reading of books of heathens

Perhaps some advocate of these poets, desiring to defend them, will say that on account of the knowledge of the Latin language, and for teaching the quality of diction, such books ought to be given to children. But he who so speaks, is greatly mistaken. Because that quality of diction ought to be taken rather from orators, and others who wrote in prose, than from the poets who, to fully satisfy the rules of the lyrics, often use the same words otherwise than one ought. And in this way they pass over the rules of grammar, lest they forsake the rules of the lyrics. Next, if it were necessary to give the poets to children, one should have given other much better ones, who could injure morals and religion less. They have Virgil, the chief of the poets, who even though he relates many heinous deeds of the gods, still in other respects is not as pestilent as the others. They have Lucan, "more suitable for imitation," as Quintilian says, "by the orators than by the poets."[25] They have Horace, the most chaste of the poets. They have Persius and Juvenal, rebukers of vices. And we ourselves also have Christian poets, most eloquent men, Juvencus, Sedulius, Prudentius, Aratus, Lactantius, Victorinus [Afer], Paulinus [of Nola], who in the judgment of many men, in many things compete with the heathen poets, and in some things conquer them.

We also have among the more recent poets, Baptista Mantuanus, Jacopo Sannazaro,[26] Marcantonio Flaminio,[27] who recently paraphrased many of David's Psalms in heroic verse.[28] I reckon that those Christian poets in the first place ought to be given to children, from whom they could gain skill in the Latin language along with piety and religion. But

---

25 *Institutio Oratoria*, bk. 10, c. 1, nn. 90-91.
26 In Latin, Actius Sincerus Sannazarius.
27 Also known as Marcus Antonius Flaminius.
28 *M. Antonii Flaminii Carminum Libri Duo: Ejusdem Paraphrasis In Triginta Psalmos, Versibus Scripta* (Leiden: Gryphius, 1548).

I think that the rest of the heathen poets, if they ever ought to be read, ought to be read only by those who have already advanced in virtue and religion. And I think that completely the same thing ought to be said about those who wrote similar lascivious and obscene things in prose as what I have said about the lascivious poets, such as Apuleius in his book, *The Golden Ass*. Nor do I exclude from this rule and censure those books written about fictions and false loves in vernacular languages, which please the readers so much, that they prefer them to many serious and veracious writers. In which things we now see to have happened that which Paul long before had predicted would come to be: "They will indeed turn away their hearing from the truth, but will be turned unto fables" (II Tim. 4, 4). It certainly matters little in which language the book was written, if in one equally as in another those things were written which can be conducive neither for morals nor for religion.

Regarding all the rest of the heathen writers, I reckon that this distinction ought to be considered, that those especially ought to be chosen, which evidently least oppose the Christian religion and good morals. Wherefore among all the heathens I would especially prefer that Cicero be given to those who learn the Latin language. Because just as he is the greatest author of Roman eloquence, so he is very beneficial for establishing the souls of men in good morals. After Cicero I give the second place to Pliny the Younger. But before all these men I wish that to children some small works of Christian men would be given, who were very eloquent in the Latin language as were Cyprian, Lactantius, Jerome, Ambrose, and Paulinus [of Nola]. For children instructed by these men could learn those things which pertain to the Christian religion and good morals, along with the correct notion of speaking and writing. Now once the children reach adolescence, and have been grounded in the faith, and sufficiently instructed about Christian morals, then it would be

Remedy for the constant and incautious reading of books of heathens

profitable to grant them free license of going through the heathen orators and historians.

As to the philosophers, I think that it would be well done that Aristotle be imitated, whom the whole school of recent philosophers has accepted as the greatest leader. For he contains fewer things than others, which oppose the Christian religion, and teaches better than the others those things which pertain to morals and civil government. For Plato, even though he approaches nearer (as Augustine says[29]) to the Christian religion, still those things which he teaches, he discusses not as clearly and distinctly as Aristotle, but by certain figures and enigmas, which can scarcely be understood. Next, he disputes through dialogues. Which thing gives occasion for not a small difficulty, because it is often unknown which side of the two disputants he wishes to hold. For which reason I reckon that he ought not to be read by children, but only by learned men.

Concerning the mathematical writers I think that those ought to be rejected as a whole, who discourse about astrology, especially judicial.[30] For nearly all of those things are full of lies, and teach many things which ought to be very far removed from a Christian man. The other mathematicians,

---

29 "Certain partakers with us in the grace of Christ, wonder when they hear and read that Plato had conceptions concerning God, in which they recognize considerable agreement with the truth of our religion. Some have concluded from this, that when he went to Egypt he had heard the prophet Jeremias, or, while travelling in the same country, had read the prophetic Scriptures, which opinion I myself have expressed in certain of my writings" (*City of God*, bk. 8, c. 12 (PL 41, 237)).

30 "Judicial astrology—more important branch of this occult art—depended for its predictions upon the position of the planets in the 'twelve houses' at the moment of the birth of a human being. The calculations necessary to settle these positions were casting the horoscope or the diagram of the heavens (*thema coeli*) at the nativity" ("Astrology," *Catholic Encyclopedia*, vol. 2, p. 18).

who teach arithmetic, geometry, perspective, or cosmography, I think ought to be read. Because they contain many things, very beneficial for human uses, and nothing is taught in them which opposes the Catholic faith.

Christian rulers can grant this remedy against heresies, lest they arise, by commanding in all the lands subject to them, that the teachers of children give to them only the books of heathens which harm them less, and rather can be beneficial for piety and morals. The necessary discretion having been then had about the books of heathens, such that those are chosen which can harm less and profit more, another consideration of things remains to be made about the same books now selected, such that having rejected the false teachings, we would approve, and accept for our use, only those things which can be more useful to the Christian religion, or which are not contrary to it. For which choice, so that it may be done correctly, two kinds of persons can be useful, namely, teachers who teach others, and the same who listen to masters, or learn by themselves without a teacher. The first ones who ought and can be supported are the teachers and masters who explain heathen books to others. For these men as often as they find something opposing the Catholic faith in the book which they accepted to be explained, ought, as leaders of the blind, to diligently and skillfully admonish their students, so that they would keep away from it as from a very dangerous fall. About which matter there is a truly necessary Christian decree published in the [V] Lateran Council, in session eight, whose words are these: "Moreover we strictly enjoin on each and every philosopher who teaches publicly in the universities or elsewhere, that when they explain or address to their audience the principles or conclusions of philosophers, where these are known to deviate from the true faith—as in the assertion of the soul's mortality or of there being only one soul or of the eternity of the world and other topics of this kind—they are obliged to devote their every effort to clarify for their listeners the truth of the Christian religion, to teach it by convincing arguments, so far as this is possible, and to apply themselves to the full extent of their energies to refuting and disposing of the philosophers' opposing arguments, since all the solutions are available."[31]

Next, after the diligent admonitions of the teacher it is necessary that they themselves who listen to the teachers, or who by themselves read the books of the heathens without a master leading the way, that they take care and diligently attend to avoid the errors, and accept only those things which are clear and in accordance with the Christian religion, but abstain from the rest as from poison. Hence Basil [the Great] when instructing young men, how the books of the heathens ought to be read, says: "For just as bees know how to extract honey from flowers, which to men are agreeable only for their fragrance and color, even so here also those who look for something more than pleasure and enjoyment in such writers may derive profit for their souls. Now, then, altogether after the manner of bees must we use these writings, for the bees do not visit all the flowers without discrimination, nor indeed do they seek to carry away entire those upon which they light, but rather, having taken so much as is adapted to their needs, they let the rest go. So we, if wise, shall take from heathen books whatever befits us and is allied to the truth, and shall pass over the rest. And just as in culling roses we avoid the thorns, from such writings as these we will gather everything useful, and guard against the noxious."[32]

Now in order that the readers can correctly carry out this advice of Basil, they ought to do three things. The first is that when they undertake to read heathen books, they ought to undertake being firm and stable in the faith, always have it before their eyes, and resolve to believe Sacred Scripture

---

31 December 19, 1513 (Mansi 32, 842D-E).
32 *Address to Young Men on the Right Use of Greek Literature*, n. 3 (PG 31, 570C-D).

and the Catholic Church more than two thousand philosophers teaching the opposite opinion. For on account of this resolve of the mind alone, one ought to hope in God, that He will not permit them to be deceived by reading the books of the heathens. If, however, someone wavering or doubtful would undertake to read them, he will be easily drawn into their error by them.

The second thing that is necessary for them is humility, whereby one does not want to rely upon his own prudence, but acknowledges that he is a man who could be easily deceived, and if he were to read some arguments by them opposing the Catholic faith, which perhaps he himself does not know how to solve, he would not hesitate to admit his own ignorance, rather than say that Scripture is mistaken, or the Church errs. And in this way always preferring Sacred Scripture and the Church's opinion to his own judgment, although it is opposed to very strong argument taken from the reading of the heathens, he will never succumb. For (as Solomon says) "Where humility is, there also is wisdom" (Prov. 11, 2).

Finally, a third thing is necessary, that when one reads the books of heathens, that one considers more the meaning than the words; that one attend to what, rather than how something is said. For he who only has considered the embellishment of the words, and not the things themselves, will be easily deceived by the heathens, who shine with excessive brilliance of words. He who rightly carries out all these things, will easily distinguish what is true from what is false, the precious from the worthless, the holy from the profane, and in this way he will safely undertake the reading of the heathens, so that he may benefit from it, having rejected their errors, turning the truth of the Catholic faith to his own suitable use: just as of old an Israelite man could, with permission of the Law, join to himself by matrimony a woman taken from the heathens, who seemed beautiful to

Remedy for the constant and incautious reading of books of heathens

him: "If thou go out," the Mosaic Law says, "to fight against thy enemies, and the Lord thy God deliver them into thy hand, and thou lead them away captives, and seest in the number of the captives a beautiful woman, and lovest her, and wilt have her to wife, thou shalt bring her into thy house: and she shall shave her hair, and pare her nails, and shall put off the raiment, wherein she was taken: and shall remain in thy house, and mourn for her father and mother one month: and after that thou shalt go in unto her, and shalt sleep with her, and she shall be thy wife" (Deut. 21, 10-13).

I reckon that if a Christian man would want to join himself to a teaching of the heathens, it ought to be done in this manner. For Blessed Jerome in the letter which he wrote to Magnus, a Roman orator, whose beginning is, "That our friend Sebesius," interprets about the same teaching of the heathens those things which the Law of Moses commanded to do regarding a captured heathen woman, before she was taken as a wife. For when he was rebuked that he mixed together the words of heathens with ecclesiastical books, and defiled sacred with profane things, wishing to show that it is licit for him, and that he did it after the example of many saints, he cites Paul among others as an example, who cited verses of the Greek poets several times to confirm his opinion. And at length when speaking about the same thing, he says these words: "And as if this were not enough, that leader of the Christian army, that unvanquished pleader for the cause of Christ, skillfully turns a chance inscription into a proof of the faith.[33] For he had learned from the true David to wrench the sword of the enemy out of his hand and with his own blade to cut off the head of the arrogant Goliath. He had read in Deuteronomy the command given by the voice of the Lord that when a captive woman had had her head shaved, her eyebrows and all her hair cut off, and her

---

33 "For passing by, and seeing your idols, I found an altar also, on which was written: To the unknown God" (Acts 17, 23).

nails pared, she might then be taken to wife.[34] Is it surprising that I too, admiring the fairness of her form and the grace of her eloquence, desire to make that secular wisdom which is my captive and my handmaid, a matron of the true Israel? Or that shaving off and cutting away all in her that is dead whether this be idolatry, pleasure, error, or lust, I take her to myself clean and pure and beget by her servants for the Lord of Sabaoth?"[35] Jerome not merely interprets that law of Deuteronomy of secular wisdom, or of a truth born and raised among the heathen, and captured by the Christians, but also suggests that it can be interpreted from it.

Hence I considered it to be worthwhile for me to do, if when explaining each part of that law, I would adapt for this end, that it would be allowed to read the books of heathens so that thence we may learn some things in part. The ecclesiastical Doctors went out for a fight against their enemies, when they went forth to overthrow the teachings of worldly wisdom. Paul says that among the weapons with which they were equipped for the fight is "the sword of the Spirit (which is the word of God)" (Eph. 6, 17). Those holy men were armed with swords of this kind, concerning which the Royal Prophet says: "Two-edged swords in their hands to execute vengeance upon the nations, chastisements among the people" (Ps. 149, 6-7). In this war, a beautiful woman is sometimes captured: because learned and believing men when searching the books of the heathens, among their false teaching which they strive to overthrow, find some beautiful truth and becoming opinion, which pleases them in a remarkable way. And if anyone wishes to transfer this into the house of the Catholic Church, and join it to himself as a wife to a husband, it is not forbidden: yet on this condition, that firstly he shave the girl's hair, cut her nails, put off the

---

34 Cf. Deut. 21, 10-13.
35 Letter 70, n. 2 (PL 22, 665-666).

Remedy for the constant and incautious reading of books of heathens

clothing in which she had been taken, and remaining among us, mourn for her father and mother for one month.

Hair and nails are unnecessary for the life of the human body, nor for constituting its complete substance: but rather they are completely superfluous. Therefore to cut the hair of the girl, and to pare her nails, means that whatever in that beautiful truth found among the heathens, was superfluous, and completely useless, may be cut off. And because clothing more often serves for boasting and vain glory, than for a covering, whence it is that the putting off of the clothing, in which the girl had been taken, means that the truth found among the heathens, should be stripped of the swelling and covering of arrogance with which it is found clothed among the heathens, who, saying that they are wise and prudent among themselves, never knew to speak humbly: but with haughtiness and ambition for glory. Therefore this woman under another clothing ought to be joined to us who have learned that same truth from them not with that pompousness and that haughtiness as they [have]: but we ought to write and profess with sober gravity and without any disdain. Yet she when remaining with us ought to weep for her mother and father, namely, for those by whom she was born. She is said to weep, not because she weeps herself: but because she provokes those who read [that truth] in the writings of the heathens, to lament the perdition of the great men who could write such things.

For by this figure of speech we are accustomed to use in a common proverb, when saying that a letter is sad, which makes the readers sad, and that a house is sad, which provokes its inhabitants to sadness. Holy Writ often uses the same figure. For Paul says: "The Spirit himself asketh for us with unspeakable groanings" (Rom. 8, 26). He is said to "ask" and to "groan" because He Himself filled with His grace those whom He makes to ask and to groan. And Blessed Peter when speaking about Judas Iscariot in the Acts of the Apostles says among other things: "And He hath possessed a field of the reward of iniquity" (1, 18). He says that he "possessed" because he was the cause so that that field would be possessed, when the silver pieces having been cast down by him in the Temple, the priests commanded that the potter's field would be bought with that money, to be a burying place for strangers. For that Judas himself did not possess it is evident from Matthew, who relates that that field was bought after Judas had hung himself with a halter.[36] Thus nothing prevents that we, when using the same figure of speech, say that the truth found in the writings of the heathens weeps for its parents: because it provokes us, who are lamenting for those who wrote it, to weep. For by its provoking, we often admire the intelligence of those whose perdition we lament. But the Law commands that this weeping be done for a month: because those heathen writers, since they did nothing good in their lives by which they could avoid the everlasting anger of God: it is befitting that they lament that their whole lives were unproductive of good works. Who does not deservedly pity Socrates, Plato, Aristotle, Plutarch, Cicero, Seneca, and Pliny the Younger, all of whom it is evident said many excellent things regarding virtue, and wrote very many very weighty sentences? It certainly ought to be lamented that they who were endowed with such great intelligence, and wrote so many very weighty sentences for the benefit of others, did not know how to find the way, whereby avoiding hell, they could arrive at eternal glory.

It seemed good to me to unfold the image and representation written in Deuteronomy so extensively, so that under that shell of the letter I might manifest the hidden truth, which teaches us how we ought to adapt for our use the true opinions found in the books of the heathens. According to this manner, many very learned and holy men, both Greek

---

36 Cf. Mt. 27, 5-7.

and Latin, a list of whom Jerome composed in the letter cited above to Magnus the orator, profited from the reading of the heathen writers: and thence transferred many weighty opinions for the use of the Catholic faith. And not only these men, who even though learned and holy, yet wrote as men, but those who spoke by the inspiring of the Holy Ghost, whose tongue was "the pen of a scrivener that writeth swiftly" (Ps. 44, 2), converted for their use somethings from the books of the heathens as though wrongly retained by them. For Blessed Jerome testifies that there are certain things in the books of the prophets taken from the books of the heathens, and that "Solomon proposed questions to the philosophers of Tyre and answered others put to him by them."[37] But putting aside these things, about which what we say is not so clear, let us come to Paul, the marvelous herald of the Gospel, about whom it cannot be denied that he used the words of heathen poets. For in the First Epistle to the Corinthians, he cites this verse of Menander: "Evil communications corrupt good manners" (15, 33). And in the Epistle to Titus he cites the short verse of the poet Epimenides, whom he calls "a prophet" of the heathens, speaking thus: "The Cretians are always liars, evil beasts, slothful bellies" (1, 12).[38] And when disputing with the Athenians, he cites part of a non-metrical verse of Aratus, by these words: "For we are also his offspring" (Acts 17, 28).[39]

Thus imitating these men renowned for holiness and learning, let us not completely abstain from the books of the heathens: but let us read those which are sufficient, and for as long as it is allowed, not, however, all of them: but only those which cannot harm too much, and are unable to quickly poison, and from which we can take some benefit. Which

---

37 Letter 70, n. 2 (PL 22, 665).
38 *Cretica*. Cf. St. Clement of Alexandria, *Stromata*, bk. 1, c. 14 (PG 8, 758C).
39 *Phenomena*, ln. 5.

if we would read carefully (as one ought), and in this way as the true Israelites, having taken of the gold and silver from the Egyptians, as from unjust possessors, we may construct the tabernacle of theology, in which, having attained the knowledge of the true God, we may worship Him (as we are held to do), tending towards Him with faith, hope, and charity.

Exhortation of the Author to Christian Rulers. Concerning the just punishment of heretics.

These are all the antidotes which, desiring to advise the whole of Christendom, I could think up with great solicitude. Perhaps more remedies will occur to others endowed with sharper intelligence, yet I do not think that they will be better than these, which have now been expounded and fully explained by me. I have exerted myself as best as I could, and so that I may give back with usury the talent entrusted to me to God, from Whom I have received [it], I have tried to assist the Catholic Church being threatened with ruin to the extent that I could, exposing the roots of all heresies, so that when they have been removed, one may easily go out against all heresies, lest they arise any more. It remains that all you Christian rulers of the world, in whatever name of dignity or magistracy you are reckoned, very diligently take care to completely pull out these roots of heresies which we have now shown, and in this way you could easily with God being the helper protect the people committed to you from all poison of heresy. But if you wish to cast off this duty onto the bishops alone and the ecclesiastical rulers, saying that this care has been enjoined upon them alone: hear what God says through Isais the prophet about you and the about

Holy Mother Church throughout the world: "Kings shall be thy nursing fathers" (49, 23). A nursemaid nourishes an infant with milk, cherishes with sweet words, and soothes with songs. Yet, even though the nursemaid[40] presents and serves those provisions which are necessary, the guardian[41] provides and searches for those things for the boy: just like his nursemaid. If someone strikes the boy, or tries to harm him in any way, his protection is entrusted to the guardian, because he is able to protect and defend the boy more strongly. If the nursemaid were to neglect that care of the boy which he is held to have, it is incumbent upon the guardian to exhort, entreat, reprove her, and finally to render service to the boy in her place. I certainly admit that it is the proper office of bishops and of other ecclesiastical rulers, to nourish the Christian people, like common nursemaids, with the milk of God's word, and to feed them with stronger food when it shall be necessary. But it is incumbent upon emperors and kings, and all other rulers of the world, that they strive to defend the people committed to them from the public enemies of the faith as best as they can, and punish the enemies themselves who attempt to harm the people: so that, having been forced by the fear of punishments, they may learn what is best for themselves and for others. Therefore recognize, O rulers of the world, that you, as Paul says, "are the ministers of God, serving unto this purpose" (Rom. 13, 6), that those who act wrongly may "be afraid of the power" (v. 3).

O kings and rulers, you ought to do something else in addition, so that you may show yourselves to be the

---

40 The nursemaid (*nutrix*) was a wet nurse. She raised the child until about the age of seven.

41 Well-to-do Roman children spent most of their time under the direct care not of their parents but of the guardians or tutors, usually older and trusted male slaves, called often by the Greek term *pedagogue* ("child leader").

true guardians of the Church according to God's precept. That is, that in a timely manner you should succor the nursemaids' very clear negligence and sloth, by exhorting, beseeching, in all patience, as befits God's ministers, by rebuking, so that those things which they owe to the Christian people, they would diligently bestow. Finally, you should especially take care of that which, as they say, forms the stern and prow of this matter, that you allow only those to be appointed rulers of souls whom you shall have known to be able to fulfill their duty very well. Otherwise God will require [you to render an account for] the souls who perish under your care, for having entrusted, or having allowed to be entrusted, the sheep to those whom you knew were wolves.

End of the whole work, On the Just Punishment of Heretics.

Letters of Approbation

Testimony of examination and approbation of this work made by the Ordinary of Salamanca.

Since the Very Reverend Doctor Quodorniga, the Vicar and ordinary Official of this diocese of Salamanca, entrusted to my faith the censorship of this book entitled, *On the Just Punishment of Heretics*, and hence I saw, read through, and fully examined the same book, and by my testimony I declare that everything conveyed in it is pious, confirming the orthodox faith, and extirpating opposing heresies, and moreover establishing sound morals: but pulling out the opposites by the roots. All which things to this end having been certainly carried out with marvelous talent, and worked out with diligent industry. Hence whatever in it is so far from being either opposed or dissonate with the Catholic faith, or the piety of the Christian religion, or holy morals: that this book ought to be approved and accepted by all in the highest degree: which certainly holds fast, and is able to make more firm the constant and firm in faith, but it makes firm the wavering and even the erring, it leads back to the straight path, yet it is especially useful, and plainly necessary, to those for whom the inquisition of the true faith has been entrusted. Indeed, he instructs the same men, and he also indicates to them, with a singular dexterity and perspicacity, and shows as if with a finger, how their office ought to be performed according to the Divine rules. He also trains ecclesiastical rulers, as well as all taking care of souls, and moreover puts before their eyes their serious and very great burden, and then clearly teaches the manner whereby they could entirely fulfill their office. Add to these things that he gravely and wisely admonishes preachers of God's word, how they can correspond to their office of preaching committed to them (as they are bound according to sacred rules), so that they could attend to, with God's help, the salvation of souls, which they ought to especially desire. Certainly which testimony, because it is true, I have determined to confirm with the signature of my hand. Given in Salamanca on the third day of the month of June. In the year of the Lord 1547.

Master Francisco Sancho, Professor[1]
Salamanca.

Testimony of examination and approbation of this work made by the Minister General of the Franciscan Order.

To the most dear to us in Christ, the venerable Father, Friar Alfonso de Castro, of the Franciscan Order, of the regular Observance, of the province of Saint James, preacher, and most erudite reader, and highly approved Father, Brother John Calvus, Minister General and servant of the whole same Order, greetings [*salus*, or salvation] in the Author of the same salvation, the Lord Jesus Christ.

Such is the fecundity and richness of your intelligence, that devoting to continual lucubrations, studies, and compositions, you daily strive to bring to light something new. Thus since you wish that a volume, containing three books, which you entitled, *On the Just Punishment of Heretics*, to be published, and moreover you wrote, for the honor of the most high God, of the whole of Christendom, and the glory of our Franciscan Order, and the common benefit of the readers: We, who gave the aforesaid volume to the venera-

---

1 Francisco Sancho (ca. 1500–1578) was the bishop of Segorbe, a commissioner of the Holy Office and a theologian at the Council of Trent.

ble Father, Friar Andrés de Vega, the very learned praelector, to be examined, and we have ascertained that it is (as he himself related to us) in all things, and throughout, consonant and conformed to the Catholic and orthodox Doctors, being unwilling to hide any longer such a great treasure hidden until now, so that we may do the will of ourselves and you, with the merit of salutary obedience, we give you permission to hand over the memorable volume for publication. Farewell in the Lord, and pray for the same for us. Given in Trent, on the twenty-seventh day of July. In the year 1546.

To the Readers

I beseech you, fair readers, that you would not want to judge about this work merely from its title, thinking that only common and secular things are treated in it, which are often wont to be treated by others when discoursing about the same matter. For this work has many more things hidden away than it promises on the surface. Because not only lawyers, but also theologians can benefit from it in many places, as the author admonishes in the book's preface. If you make a trial of it, I do not doubt that you would approve of and extol the same work with greater praises than I. Therefore read happily, and look kindly upon our labors.

www.ingramcontent.com/pod-product-compliance
Lightning Source LLC
Chambersburg PA
CBHW051309060526
44119CB00102B/424/J